The Oxford Companion to

Children's Literature

Daniel Hahn is a writer, editor, and translator, with some fifty books to his name. With Leonie Flynn and Susan Reuben he has edited the award-winning *Ultimate Book Guide* series of reading guides for children and teenagers. Recent work includes translating a Portuguese novel and editing a two-volume collection of new children's fiction from around Europe.

Humphrey Carpenter (1946–2005) was a writer and broadcaster. He wrote many books, including *Secret Gardens*, and biographies of *J. R. R. Tolkein*, *The Inklings*, *W.H. Auden*, *Ezra Pound*, *Benjamin Britten*, and *Spike Milligan*.

Mari Prichard co-authored *The Oxford Companion to Children's Literature* and *A Thesaurus Companion* with her husband, and also *and Hosts*.

The Oxford Companion to
Children's
Literature

SECOND EDITION

DANIEL HAHN

With a Foreword by Michael Morpurgo

FIRST EDITION

HUMPHREY CARPENTER AND MARI PRICHARD

OXFORD
UNIVERSITY PRESS

OXFORD
UNIVERSITY PRESS

Great Clarendon Street, Oxford, OX2 6DP,
United Kingdom

Oxford University Press is a department of the University of Oxford.
It furthers the University's objective of excellence in research, scholarship,
and education by publishing worldwide. Oxford is a registered trade mark of
Oxford University Press in the UK and in certain other countries

© Second edition Humphrey Carpenter, Mari Prichard, and Oxford University Press 2015
© First edition Humphrey Carpenter and Mari Prichard 1984
Foreword © Michael Morpurgo 2015

The moral rights of the authors have been asserted

First published 1984
First published as an Oxford University Press paperback 1999
Second Edition published in 2015
Second Edition published in paperback 2017

Impression: 1

Published in the United States of America by Oxford University Press
198 Madison Avenue, New York, NY 10016, United States of America

British Library Cataloguing in Publication Data
Data available

Library of Congress Cataloging in Publication Data
Data available

ISBN 978-0-19-969514-0 (Hbk.)
ISBN 978-0-19-871554-2 (Pbk.)

Printed in Great Britain by
Clays Ltd, St Ives plc

DEDICATED TO THE MEMORY OF
PETER OPIE
(1918–1982)

and

To Leonie and Susan, Ultimately

Foreword

All of us fortunate enough to be readers and writers have come to it our own way, that's for sure. There is no formula for encouraging a love of literature that works universally or predictably even. I am living proof of that. I was a reluctant reader, and to some extent I confess I still am. That is to say I found as a child that it was hard for me to be able or willing to concentrate on a book, particularly if I had been told I had to read it, and if I knew that I was going to be tested on it, or have to answer questions about it afterwards. Playing out was preferable. (Still is, to some extent, which is perhaps why I remain such a confirmed procrastinator as a writer.) However, this reluctant reader somehow ended up much less reluctant, and became a story maker, and a passionate advocate for the cause of bringing books to children and children to books. The explanation for all this, if there is one, is a story in itself. So I shall tell it.

I come from a family where bookshelves lined the walls from floor to ceiling. My grandfather, who was much revered, was a great poet and academic, and wrote books of biography and art. A kindly man of formidable intellect. My stepfather was an author too—of history and travel books, mostly—also with a formidable intellect, and worked as an editor at Penguin Books. It was expected therefore that I and my siblings would take to books like ducks to water, beginning rather young with *Oliver Twist* in very small print. We were judged very much on how we coped with these great classics, how sophisticated and informed we were when discussing them. All of this made me feel rather inadequate, and bewildered too, because until then I had thought I loved stories and books.

My mother, an actress, used to read to us every night, and always the poetry and stories she loved, Rudyard Kipling's *Just So Stories*, John Masefield's *Sea Fever*, Lewis Carroll's 'Jabberwocky'. I don't think it was ever for more than a quarter of an hour or so, but they were precious moments. I know now it was she who sowed the seed. She did it because we knew even then how much she loved what she read to us. (She also knew I am sure that books and stories are the high road to knowledge and understanding, and that lives are the poorer without them.) We sensed her love of stories and words, because of how she read them, with total commitment, with passion and rhythm, and with dancing rhyme. She made stories exciting and funny, made words sing, and it was a glorious music.

But then I grew up, and soon learned, that the books—proper books they were called— which I was supposed to read for myself now, at home and at school, were long and difficult, and that I was being judged by my response to them. My first school, St Matthias in the Warwick Road, London, only confirmed that stories were now much more to do with spelling tests and grammar tests and comprehension tests, and handwriting tests, than about the deep enjoyment I had once found in them. If you failed the tests, there was detention or the ruler, or just the humiliation of failure.

So for some while I abandoned books, so far as I could. I went through the motions of English Literature at school because I had to. I had exams to pass. And I did too, just. But I rarely read for enjoyment, Robert Louis Stevenson, still my great mentor, almost the single exception. So Stevenson held my hand through this barren time. Meanwhile I played my rugby and my cricket and forgot about books almost entirely. At school I had a teacher who tried to remind me that there was something more to life than rugby, and one day gave me a book of Wordsworth's poems, his favourite poet. I can never look at daffodils without thinking of that teacher, or that book, or that poet. 'Earth has not anything to show more fair' should have been written about daffodils, not the Thames. In my view. The poems never left me. Later, at university at King's College, London, I had another wonderful teacher who

sat in his musty suit on the corner of a desk and read us 'Sir Gawain and the Green Knight'. He read it with the same passion and commitment I remembered from my mother. He meant it. As she had. And my school teacher had. Between them they had kept the spark alive.

Then a few years after this I found myself standing in front of a class of Year 6 children and trying to engage them with stories. I made sure there was a library in the classroom full of all kinds of books, fiction and nonfiction. We wrote poems together and broadcast them. We made drama together. We brought stories alive, together, for me and for them, at the same time, for many, for the first time. And I made it an absolute rule that from 3 to 3.30 every afternoon we had story time. I would sit on the corner of the desk and read them a story I loved, and loved with a passion. I knew now that this was the key, simply to pass on what you have loved yourself, and read it in such a way that they know it, read it from inside the book, not simply as a reader in class. And never, never ask questions afterwards. Let them go home with story ringing and singing in their heads.

Then one day I got it wrong. The book I had chosen was not working. Maybe I wasn't reading it with enough commitment. I don't know. Anyway, taking my wife's advice—she was a teacher too—I did not persist the next day with a story that was not resonating. Instead I did as she told me and made up one of my own. All night it took me. Then the next day, I 'screwed my courage to the sticking place'—why does that Shakespeare fellow think up the only way to say something for ever afterwards!—walked into the classroom at 3 o'clock and told them my made-up story, from the heart, looking them in the eye, meaning every word of it, because I wanted it to be as true to them as it was to me. It got around that Mr Pongo was telling his own stories. The head teacher came in and sat at the back one Friday afternoon. She liked what she heard, and said it should be published. She told me to write it out for her by Monday morning. So I did and sent it to Macmillan Education, who asked me to write five more stories, and said they would even pay me some money. Eat your heart out, Roald Dahl, I thought!

So this has been the tale of one talemaker, storyteller, writer, reader, teacher, grandfather, father, boy. All of whom now love stories, but whose grammar and punctuation still leave something to be desired.

MICHAEL MORPURGO

January 2015

Contents

Introduction

It has been more than three decades since the publication of Humphrey Carpenter and Mari Prichard's *Oxford Companion to Children's Literature*. In that time almost everything about children's literature has undergone dramatic change. If we leave aside the obvious over-hauling of the publishing world, the advent of the Internet, shifts in the role of children's writers and in particular their relationship to their readers, there's just the sheer *volume* of books today to contend with. (And with that volume comes seemingly infinite variety, too, of course.) The number of books being published for children in the English-speaking world, and almost everywhere else, has exploded, and their profile has, too. Children's writers and children's books make the news pages—yes, I'm thinking of Harry Potter, but there are others, too; children's writers become celebrities (also, regrettably, the other way around); major characters are seen as brands for massive commercial exploitation; and the quickly expanding young adult market has spawned a generation of readers for what we now call 'crossover' fiction. The English-speaking world continues to be a huge exporter of writing for children and teenagers (and a lamentably sluggish importer), with translations of English-language writing flooding bookshops around the world, even as subtitled versions of the tie-in films flood the local cinemas. The scale is staggering.

The world depicted in the last *Companion* is one in which Roald Dahl was still at the height of his productive powers; indeed, many writers who came before him, born in the late nineteenth century and the very early years of the twentieth, were still alive, and many were still working. The last year to get significant coverage in the old volume was 1982—this was the year of Dahl's *BFG*, and a new Borrowers book by Mary Norton. Needless to say, the words 'crossover', 'gruffalo', and 'quidditch' were nowhere to be found.

My own copy of *The BFG* is my single best-loved possession. It's signed by both Dahl and Quentin Blake, from when my dad took me (aged eight) to see the two of them talking at the National Theatre. It was the first time I'd seen a real writer, and the first time I became aware that there was such a thing as book publishing—until then, books either were or they weren't, but from that day I knew that there were new ones being made; there was a Dahl book that wasn't in existence yet, but was on its way, and would be finished soon and available on such-and-such a date. (This will come as no surprise to children today.) That moment—1982, with *The BFG* and my rather belated realization that new books were being produced and published every day, the canon expanding faster than anyone could track—is essentially the moment I pick up the baton from Humphrey and Mari and get to work on this *Companion*.

The starting point for this new volume is, of course, the old one, and there's a huge amount of material that has been carried over. The old *Companion* was clever, erudite, discriminating (and unashamedly opinionated)—of course I wanted to keep as much of it as I could. Only a very few entries from the old edition have been completely removed, so even those writers who seemed significant in the seventies but whose time has passed retain their place here (in 1984 the entry on G. A. Henty was 2,597 words long, compared with 425 on Dahl); but that continuity is important, I think. Every entry has been trimmed back, however, a sometimes agonizing process, given how tightly written and beautifully compact they were to begin with; but a process necessary to make space for the new.

So what's new? Well, in addition to the edited and updated versions of the old material, there are more than 900 new headwords, with additions stretching from Douglas *Adams (British writer, 50 words) to Lisbeth *Zwerger (Austrian illustrator, 46 words). The prize for

the most substantial newcomer, not surprisingly, goes to ***Harry Potter** (1,584 words). A few new entries are plugging what seemed to me to be gaps in the pre-1983 world, but most are contemporary—hence the large young-adult contingent represented. This book's centre of gravity is the UK, but the coverage of the rest of the English-speaking world has been improved considerably, with large numbers of Anglophone writers from Australia, Canada, Ireland, New Zealand, and the US in particular, as well as some of these countries' notable book titles, prizes, etc. The rest of the world has its place, too, but this is necessarily limited by the Anglocentric perspective, so writers tend to be included where they have a significant English-language presence, major international readerships, international prizes and not only domestic ones, and so on. (There is greater coverage of the non-Anglophone children's literature world in Jack Zipes's four-volume *Encyclopedia of Children's Literature*, which is highly recommended. It's also the place to find scope and depth where this book has of necessity been brief.)

Decisions for what to include in a book like this will always be based on judgements, so the book's blind spots will be my blind spots; my prejudices will be easily discerned from my choices, from how I've chosen to deploy my half-a-million words. I've sought to be both fair and representative, even while knowing that the very attempt is foolhardy; this means including books and writers I believe are exceptionally good, and whose work I believe will survive. (Yes, I'm altogether resigned to the certainty that the next editor will laugh at me in 2049.) I've also included those writers whose success has itself been undoubtedly influential, regardless of how I feel about their literary merit; even if I don't like a book, I can't pretend it doesn't exist if it has led to a whole wave of wannabe writing also about—oh, just say, for example—vampires. There are a few relatively early-career writers and illustrators included, where my confidence in their success is partly prospective as well as retrospective, but the great majority are very well established; they're acclaimed by critics and peers, or loved by readers, or—in fortunate cases—both of these at once.

Errors in the old volume have been corrected, some of these as a result of readers helpfully writing in. I do rather feel we ought to apologize to any correspondents who have been waiting twenty-eight years to see these rectified. I have doubtless added many errors of my own to this volume, but I hope this book's electronic incarnation will allow us to respond to corrections just a little more speedily this time around.

Half a million words might seem like a generous amount of space, but given the book's scope it feels barely adequate. I have a long list of fine writers and illustrators and books I admire very much but have excluded; some have as much right to be here as some of the inclusions, but haven't made it in for lack of space and reasons of balance or representation. (Frankly, I was often scrabbling around for reasons *not* to include people.) In many cases I have privileged writers whose work travels internationally, with readerships that go beyond their domestic ones—this internationalist bias will explain both inclusions and exclusions that I suspect will surprise children's books experts in their respective countries. This is not, however, a dictionary of writers and illustrators, but a companion, whose aim is not to provide comprehensive data, but to allow—to encourage—digression. 'A companion should be companionable,' as Aunt March once said in a *Little Women* film. I've always liked her. Oh, and the number of column inches of an entry is not, it should be said, a raw indicator of importance or fame, before anyone starts counting.

And while I was talking about experts . . . The scope of this book is preposterous—literature for young children and older children and teenagers from any period in history in the UK and the rest of the English-speaking world and everywhere else, too—from Canadian picture books to Irish young adult fiction to folk tales to Japanese manga; and there is a very, very large part of the terrain in which I cannot claim great expertise, so I have benefited enormously from the advice of those who can. In addition to those whose names appear further below, these people made suggestions or agreed to look at lists: Rita Auerbach, Christine Baker, Betsy Bird, Katy Derbyshire, Emma Dryden, Nikki Gamble, David Levithan, Robin Morrow, Sally-Ann Spencer, Roger Sutton, Lisa von Drasek, Jenni Woodroffe; as well as

the many, many others who responded to calls for help on Facebook and Twitter. (A special last-minute thank-you to Mark Burgess.) A lot of friends in the children's books world weighed in with help of various kinds. Emma Langley happened to be sitting next to me on a plane, so did an impromptu edit of part of the letter 'C'. Philippa Milnes-Smith (sitting next to me on a bus) made valuable introductions to experts in the US. I have talked about children's books with Joe Marriott over many, many lovely dinners over the years we've been friends, and his fingerprints will be all over this, too. Anthony McGowan gave me Grimm advice at the eleventh hour. New entries were drafted or revised by Abigail Anderson, Jon Appleton, Avgi Daferera, B. J. Epstein, Briony Everroad, Ariel Kahn, Gillian Lathey, Hannah Love, Mary Medlicott, Lawrence Schimel, Anne Siebeck, Alexandra Strick, Alan Tasker, Alex Valente, Kay Waddilove, and Laura Watkinson, on subjects in which they were particularly expert. I owe a lot of people lunch.

Cathie Tasker was immensely helpful for coverage of Australia and New Zealand, sharing her considerable knowledge and her time with great generosity. Karen Williams helped me with the difficult task of cutting down and revising some of the old material and knocking things into shape—truly I'm not sure how I would have managed this without her. And Leonie Flynn, Sophie Hallam, Ferelith Hordon, Susan Reuben, and Madelyn Travis went above and beyond, helping me with first drafts of large numbers of entries—again, my gratitude to them is immense. As well as being good and generous friends, Leonie and Susan have for over a decade been my co-editors on the *Ultimate Book Guide* series, and our conversations over that decade have informed everything I think about children's literature.

Everyone at OUP has been a pleasure and a privilege to work with, as always. My huge thanks to the whole editorial team, in particular my editor Joanna Harris who was a generous source of guidance, encouragement, expertise, and almost infinite patience over these past years. (Fortunately only 'almost', or the book would never have got finished at all.) Abi Humphries Robertson coordinated the book's production, which was an unusually complicated process for many reasons (several of them my fault), and did so efficiently and with remarkable and reassuring calm. Our copy editor Donald Watt and proofreader Penny Trumble were more than diligent in their work transforming my chaotic manuscript documents into the finished text that you are reading now. Even as I write this, four months before publication, Kirsty Doole and Hannah Paget have already begun the task of spreading the word about its imminent arrival—I'm sure it couldn't be in better hands for the next stage of its journey. Lastly, what a delight to have a David Roberts picture on the cover! I'm a big fan of David's work, and thrilled he's allowed us to use this beautiful thing on our book.

One final, and essential, thank you. When I took on this book, it was clear that I was going to have to meet Mari Prichard, who with her late husband Humphrey Carpenter researched and wrote the first edition, the book I was just about to start hacking about and scribbling all over and generally messing up. I was worried that she might not be interested, might not be keen to help. I was also worried—even more worried—that she might be *too* interested, *too* eager to help, and even jealously protective of her and Humphrey's very fine piece of work. There is a perfect middle ground, however, and Mari found it—over these three and a half years she has been helpful and generous, interested but never demanding. It has been a huge pleasure to work with her, and a privilege to have had the opportunity to reconsider and reshape the work she and Humphrey did thirty years ago for a book I so admire.

<div align="right">DANIEL HAHN</div>

Brighton, 2014

AaB *See* GREAT A, LITTLE A, BOUNCING B.

A Apple Pie A traditional alphabet jingle; *see* ABC BOOKS for its early appearances in print. It has often been published as a separate book, for example John *Harris's *History of the Apple Pie, Written by Z* (1808).

In 1886 it was made into a *picture book by Kate *Greenaway, engraved and printed by Edmund *Evans. The oblong pages of this contain a fine collection of Greenaway figures. However, John *Ruskin, Kate Greenaway's cherished friend and adviser, complained that she had drawn 'stockings down at heel, and shoes with the right foot in the left and the left in the right'. Ruskin also complained about the lettering: 'And when, ever—did you put red letters like the bills of a pantomime—in any of *my* drawings? and why do it to the public?'

Abbey Girls In stories by Elsie *Oxenham.

ABBOTT, Jacob (1803–79) New England writer, author of the *Rollo books, who founded Mount Vernon, one of the pioneer Massachusetts girls' schools, and was a Congregational minister.

His first successful book was *The Young Christian; or a familiar illustration of the principles of Christian duty* (1832). The first two Rollo books appeared in 1835, heralding a series which eventually comprised twenty-eight titles.

In all, he was the sole or joint author of nearly 200 books, many of them biographies of famous historical figures. He also wrote *books of instruction in a number of school subjects, and composed a series of 'Story Books' for the New York firm of Harper. His *Franconia stories have some distinction, but the greater number of his books, though very popular in his day, have not survived the changes of fashion, and seem workmanlike but uninspired. They had some popularity in England, but were not as successful there as in America.

ABC books Designed to teach the letters of the alphabet, were also known as Abcee, Abcie, or Absey books ('Then comes your answer like an Absey book', Shakespeare, *King John*, 1. i), or Abcedarium.

From the medieval period until the 18th cent. the teaching of letters was closely associated with *religious instruction. The alphabet was printed as part of a *primer that was chiefly a book of prayers, and the *hornbooks that were widely used for the teaching of letters included the Lord's Prayer and an invocation to the Trinity.

Shortened versions of the primer, in which a few pages of prayers followed the ABC itself, became common in the 16th cent. One of the earliest to have survived is that published in London *c.*1538 by Thomas Petyt. This prints the alphabet in the lower-case of black-letter type, and also shows a table of vowels and of syllables (ab, eb, ib, ob, ub, ba, be, bi, bo, bu, etc.) which were to be recited forwards and backwards until the child had learnt them by heart; such a table was known as a syllabary or syllabarium. Then comes a selection of prayers and graces to be said before and after meals.

Many other 16th-cent. English printers produced ABCs, with different combinations and texts of prayers. By 1545 some attempt was being made by the religious authorities to regulate these variations, just as the Prayer Book itself was regulated, and an injunction was issued against 'the diversitie of primer books that are now abroad'.

By the late 17th cent. the usual accompaniment to the alphabet in children's primers was a *catechism. A number of *Puritan writers included alphabets in their books for children. For example, John *Bunyan began his *Book for Boys and Girls* (1686) with a table of letters, vowels and consonants, and some advice on the teaching of reading: 'After these [the letters] are known, then set your Child to spelling, Thus T-o, to, T-h-e, the, . . . S-i-n, sin, . . . C-h-r-i-s-t, Christ, . . . R-i-g-h-t-e-o-u-s-n-e-s-s, Righ-te-ous-ness.'

Meanwhile the alphabet was also being taught in a fashion designed to amuse rather than to edify. The earliest known English pictorial alphabet in print appears in John Hart's *A Method or comfortable beginning for all unlearned* (1570), in which woodcuts illustrate each letter with an object. The *Orbis Sensualium Pictus* of *Comenius, published in English in 1659, included a picture-alphabet in which letters were identified with the sounds of various animals: G as the gaggling of a goose, B as the baa-ing of a lamb, etc. It appears that by this time there was also in use a jingle to help children to learn their letters; it was quoted in 1671 by the Cambridge writer John Eachard as being a familiar thing known to all his readers: 'A Apple-pasty, B bak'd it, C cut it, D divided it, E eat it, F fought for it, G got it, &c.'

In 1693 John *Locke, in *Some Thoughts Concerning Education*, argued the case for alphabet-books or toys that taught the letters by means of entertainment. In the next year, 1694, was published *A *Playbook for Children* by 'J.G.', which included such sentences as 'Ap-ples are for Chil-dren, that know the Letters', 'a Bear is a wild beast that has long hairs', and so on through the alphabet. An alphabet-rhyme beginning 'A was an Archer, and shot at a Frog' appeared in *A *Little Book for Little Children* by 'T.W.', which was printed at the beginning of the 18th cent. This rhyme made what seems to have been its first appearance in print in America in 1764 in a primer entitled *Tom Thumb's Play-Book; To teach Children their letters as soon as they can speak*. The same book also included a version of the jingle quoted by Eachard the previous century, beginning 'A Apple Pye'.

A reading-book of 1742, *The Child's New Play-Thing*, issued by Mary *Cooper, contained a version of 'A was an Archer' which could be cut out, letter by letter; on the back of this was printed 'A was an apple pie'. From this time on, light-hearted alphabet-books for children based on one or other of these rhymes began to be common. A favourite title was *The Tragical Death of A, Apple Pie*, or simply *A Apple Pie*.

The 19th cent. saw the introduction of alphabet-books in Britain and America which were based on various subjects, such as animals, birds, the farmyard, the seaside, railways, children's names, nations, kings and queens, and the Bible. The letter X frequently defeated the compilers of such alphabets. For example, in *The Child's Picture Alphabet* (c.1850), it is the only letter not accompanied by an illustration. In *Cousin Honeycomb's Alphabet of Trades* (c.1856) it is admitted that 'The letter X no trade will show, | Unless we to the brewer go; | One who ready has for sale, | Rows of XX and XXX ale.' In *The Alphabet of Common Objects* (c.1860) it is made to stand for Xerxes—scarcely common and not an object. Edward *Lear parodied this genre of alphabet-books in several alphabets (*see* NONSENSE SONGS, STORIES, BOTANY, AND ALPHABETS) of his own, while in *A *Moral Alphabet* (1899) Hilaire *Belloc wrote:

> No reasonable little Child expects
> A Grown-up Man to make a rhyme on X.

Illustrators of the 19th cent. who produced picture alphabets in *toy books included Walter *Crane (*Walter Crane's Noah's Ark ABC*, 1872; *Walter Crane's Absurd ABC*, 1874; and *Baby's Own Alphabet*, 1874) and Kate *Greenaway (an alphabet in The *English Spelling Book*, 1855 edn; and *A Apple Pie*, 1886). Among 20th-cent. alphabet books, one of the most popular is Robert Crowther's *movable picture book, *The Most Amazing Hide-and-Seek Alphabet Book* (1977), in which an animal hides behind each letter and is revealed when a tag is pulled.

In one sense, the production of illustrated alphabet books has been a surprising victim of the recent growing globalization of the children's books world; today's large Anglophone publishers of picture books depend increasingly on foreign rights sales of their books for their business model, which is problematic when in most places 'A' is not, in fact, 'for Apple' at all. Production continues steadily enough, however, with some artists bypassing traditional representational illustrations in favour of the more graphic (Marion Bataille's elegant pop-up *ABC3D*, 2008) or opting for the simply rather surreal (Mitsumasa *Anno's *Anno's Alphabet*); and alphabets of animals, from Ape to Zebra, continue to be a popular strand of the genre. A particularly witty subversion can be found in Paul *Zelinsky and Kelly Bingham's brilliant *Z Is for Moose* (2012).

Abner Brown Villain in *The *Midnight Folk* and *The *Box of Delights* by John *Masefield.

academic study of children's literature *See* CHILDREN'S LITERATURE AS ACADEMIC STUDY.

ACHEBE, Chinua (1930–2013) Nigerian novelist who made his name with *Things Fall Apart* (1958), a picture of Igbo society in the

late 19th cent., wrote several children's books. *Chike and the River* (1966, illustrated by Prue Theobalds) is about a boy who leaves his village to go and live with his uncle in the big city. *How the Leopard Got His Claws* (1972), *The Flute* (1977), and *The Drum* (1977) are based on Igbo folk tales.

Across Five Aprils (1964) A novel by Irene *Hunt.

Acts of the Romans See GESTA ROMANORUM.

ADAMS, Douglas (1952–2001) British writer best known for his 'five-part trilogy' of brilliantly imaginative comic sci-fi that begins with *The *Hitchhiker's Guide to the Galaxy*. Other books include two works of fantasy detective fiction, *Dirk Gently's Holistic Detective Agency* (1987) and *The Long, Dark Tea-Time of the Soul* (1988).

ADAMS, Richard (George) (1920–2016) British author who worked in the Ministry of Housing and Local Government, and later in the Department of the Environment, eventually holding the rank of Assistant Secretary. In 1974 he became a full-time writer.

Adams came to worldwide fame with his first novel, *Watership Down* (1972), which for several years was a 'cult' book with both children and adults. *Shardik* (1974) is an ambitious myth-like novel about a huge bear who emerges from a forest and is received by a tribe as their god, reincarnated. *The Tyger Voyage* (1976) and *The Ship's Cat* (1977) are a pair of pastiche *ballads, each lavishly illustrated, the first by Nicola *Bayley and the second by Alan Aldridge. Adams returned to the prose *animal story with *The Plague Dogs* (1977), a novel about two dogs who escape from an experimental laboratory—a book with many resemblances to *Watership Down*, but with a more obviously didactic content (especially its attack on vivisection). *The Girl in a Swing* (1980), an erotic fantasy, was Adams's first book written exclusively for adults. *The Iron Wolf* (1980) is a collection of unfamiliar folk tales, told by different narrators.

ADAMS, Revd William See CHERRY-STONES, THE.

ADAMS, William Taylor See OLIVER OPTIC.

ADAMSON, Jean and Gareth See TOPSY AND TIM.

Adventure series (from 1949) by Canadian-born American author Willard Price (1887–1983), these books follow teen zoologists Hal and Roger Hunt as they travel the world to capture wild animals for their collector father. The first in the series was *Amazon Adventure* (1949)—another thirteen would follow, including *African Adventure, Cannibal Adventure, Arctic Adventure*, etc. Price's stated aim was to stimulate his young readers' interest in the animal kingdom. Three decades after Price's death, Anthony *McGowan was commissioned to revive the series, with books that featured a new generation of the Hunt family and replaced their principal motivation, the animal collection now giving way to a new imperative: conservation. The new phase began in 2012 with *Leopard Adventure*.

Adventures of a Donkey, The A story by 'Arabella *Argus', first published by William *Darton in 1815 and often reprinted. It makes a step forward in the development of the *animal story for children in that the animal narrator is not merely an observer of human vices and virtues but is chiefly concerned to tell his own story. The hero is Jemmy, who describes himself as 'an Ass of the Eighteenth Century'. He tells of his upbringing, his first experiences at the hands of humans, and his subsequent adventures as he passes from owner to owner. There was a sequel, *Further Adventures of Jemmy Donkey* (1821).

Adventures of a Pincushion, The, designed chiefly for the use of Young Ladies A novel for children in two volumes by Mary Ann *Kilner, first published by John *Marshall *c*.1780. The pincushion is made by two girls, and begins to narrate its history. A young visitor accidentally carries the pincushion home with her; a kitten finds it and plays with it, leaving it wedged under a bookcase, where it remains for a long time. It is discovered during a house removal, is given to 'a chair-woman [*sic*], who was hired to clean the house', and passes from her to her granddaughter who takes it to school. Her friends fight over it, one of them steals it, and it is eventually dropped by a girl who is attending a tenants' dinner at a great house. It is thrown out with the crumbs, and ends its days in tatters in the back yard.

The story is a vehicle for moral observations upon the virtues and vices of the children through whose hands the pincushion passes. This moral element concerns Mrs Kilner far

more than the plight of the pincushion itself, which concludes the book by remarking calmly that its final catastrophe should teach the readers 'that no seeming security can guard from those accidents, which may in a moment reduce the prospect of affluence to a state of poverty and distress'.

The book, which was often reprinted, seems to have inspired the author's sister-in-law Dorothy Kilner to write *The *Life and Perambulation of a Mouse* (1783), and it was imitated by Mary Ann Kilner herself with *Memoirs of a Peg-Top* (*c.*1805). Later books for children in the same genre include Richard *Johnson's *Adventures of a Silver Penny*, published by Elizabeth *Newbery *c.*1787, the same publisher's undated *Adventures of a Silver Threepence* by 'Mr Truelove', the anonymous *Adventures of a Work-bag* (*c.*1815), and two of J. G. Rusher's *Banbury juvenile booklets, *The Adventures of a Halfpenny* and *The History of a Banbury Cake* (both *c.*1830).

Adventures of Billy Topsail, The (1906) A novel by Norman *Duncan, one of the best Canadian *adventure stories. Billy Topsail is the son of a fisherman at Ruddy Cove on the Newfoundland coast. He capsizes his boat and is rescued by his dog, catches an outsize giant squid, gets himself stuck while trying to climb a dangerous cliff, is trapped more than once on ice-floes, joins several crews as ship's boy, is involved in shipwrecks, and is finally put 'on the books' as a fully-fledged fisherman, after he has saved the life of a fleet-owner's son.

Adventures of Herr Baby, The (1881) A novel by Mrs *Molesworth.

Adventures of Huckleberry Finn (Tom Sawyer's Comrade), The A novel by 'Mark *Twain' (S. L. Clemens) begun in the summer of 1876 but not completed until 1884. It was published in that year by Chatto and Windus of London and early in 1885 by Charles Webster of New York.

The book is a sequel to *The *Adventures of Tom Sawyer*, at the end of which Tom and Huckleberry Finn found themselves in the possession of a large sum of money. Huck's share has been invested, and at the opening of *Huckleberry Finn* he is living in the house of the Widow Douglas, who treats him kindly, but whose civilized ways make Huck feel 'all cramped up'. He renounces the fortune, but is kidnapped by his drunkard father and taken to a cabin on an island. He escapes, and is soon

heading down the Mississippi on a raft, accompanied by Jim, a Negro slave who is running away from his owner. They hope to reach Cairo, Illinois, and then go up the Ohio River to the free States, where Jim will be out of trouble; but by accident they are borne further south, deeper into slave-owning lands. They are joined by two confidence-tricksters, who eventually sell Jim into captivity for 40 dollars. Huck is about to rescue Jim when he is joined by Tom Sawyer, who is visiting relations in the south, and (somewhat to Huck's confusion) Tom concocts an absurd rescue-plan which involves the maximum of trouble, purely for the sake of adventure. No sooner is Jim freed than Tom reveals that Miss Watson, his owner, has died, and in her will has given Jim his freedom—so that the escape-plot was entirely unnecessary. Huck is given a home by Silas Phelps and his wife, on whose plantation Jim was held captive, but, at the end of the book, confesses his intention of breaking free once more from the civilized life.

The greater part of *Huckleberry Finn* is a brilliant work, combining immense narrative excitement with a constant questioning of the moral values both of American society and its outcasts. Like *Tom Sawyer*, it was not written specifically for children, but uses the child hero as an unprejudiced observer of the world around him. The final chapters, however, adopt quite a different tone; in them, Clemens seems to be burlesquing the very adventure-story that he has been writing. Tom Sawyer's antics in these chapters have irritated readers since the book's first appearance, and have often led to it being branded as only a partial success. Certain critics, however, argue that it has dramatic unity, and that the boys' approach to the task of 'rescuing' Jim is the culmination of what has been implied throughout the novel—that Huck's motives are as selfish as anyone else's, and that the help he gives to Jim is casual and largely for the fun of it, and fails at several crucial moments.

The book's American publisher, Charles Webster, was Clemens's nephew by marriage; he was set up in business by him in 1884, with *Huckleberry Finn* as the first new book to be brought out by the firm. Unfortunately a malicious engraver tampered with one of the plates of E. W. Kemble's illustrations, adding a male sex organ to the figure of Silas Phelps in a picture showing him talking to his wife. The page had to be cut out and a substitute stuck in by hand, which delayed American

publication (originally intended to be in time for Christmas 1884) until February 1885. The book was thus published in England a few months before it appeared in the States.

When it did go on sale, reaction was largely hostile. Though Joel Chandler *Harris praised it publicly, the magazine *Life* attacked the book for its 'coarse and dreary fun', and said it was completely unsuitable for young people, while Louisa M. *Alcott declared: 'If Mr Clemens cannot think of something better to tell our pure-minded lads and lasses, he had best stop writing for them.' Many were outraged by the author's apparent condoning of Huck's habit of smoking a pipe, and of the considerable whisky-drinking which goes on in the book. The Public Library of Concord, Mass., *banned it as 'trash and only suitable for the slums'. But sales were high (51,000 copies in America by May 1885), and enthusiastic reviews soon began to appear. *Century Magazine* called it 'capital reading', and dubbed Huck 'immortal'. In England it was praised in the *Athenaeum* as consisting of 'such scrapes and experiences as make your mouth water', and, six years later, Andrew *Lang wrote in the *Illustrated London News*: 'There are defects of taste, or passages that seem to us deficient in taste, but the book remains a nearly flawless gem of romance and of humour.'

Since then, *Huckleberry Finn* has been read in millions of copies in innumerable languages. As well as being a milestone in children's fiction, it marked a significant development in the American novel. In 1938 Ernest Hemingway declared of it: 'All American writing comes from that. There was nothing before.' Yet attacks on it continue, and it is still banned from some American libraries at the instigation of such extreme *Puritan-style organizations as The Moral Majority. (*See also* BANNED BOOKS.)

Adventures of the Little Wooden Horse, The (1938) By Ursula *Moray Williams. When Uncle Peder, the toymaker, falls ill and loses everything, the Little Wooden Horse decides it is up to him to save the day. Off he trundles to make his fortune. It does not prove easy and his journey takes him across the sea to face many obstacles. On the way he loses his sight, a leg, and his wheels, but nothing daunted he carries on. His bravery and his generosity bring him friends, a fortune, and, in the end, safely home. However, unlike other related characters (*Pinocchio, say), he remains firmly a toy.

The Little Wooden Horse is the archetypal younger son who succeeds through his qualities. His adventures can be overwhelming but never terrifying; his triumphs reassuringly satisfying. Like *Gobbolino*, by the same author, *Little Wooden Horse* is a deserved classic. Indeed, the two join forces in *The Further Adventures of Gobbolino and the Little Wooden Horse* (1984).

Adventures of the Wishing-Chair *See* WISHING-CHAIR SERIES.

Adventures of Tom Sawyer, The A novel by 'Mark *Twain' (S. L. Clemens) first published in 1876. It describes the hero's boyhood in St Petersburg, a village on the Mississippi. Tom, who lives with his brother Sid and his Aunt Polly, is constantly playing truant from home and school. With two friends, Joe Harper and Huckleberry Finn ('son of the town drunkard'), he disappears to an island where they live like *pirates. The three are presumed dead, and return just in time to attend their own funeral. Tom and Huck witness a murder in a graveyard, and Tom is eventually the cause of the culprit getting his just desserts. Tom and Becky Thatcher, whom he loves, nearly die when they become lost in a network of caves. At the end of the book, Tom and Huck become rich beyond their dreams, having unearthed a treasure-chest that was among the swag of Injun Joe, the murderer.

Clemens began the book in the summer of 1874, apparently with no other plan than to write something about childhood. He put the book on one side after a few weeks, not returning to it until the following summer. It was finished by July 1875, and only then, after getting friends to read it, did he realize that he had written something that was primarily a children's book. In the preface, he wrote:

Although my book is intended mainly for the entertainment of boys and girls, I hope it will not be shunned by men and women on that account, for part of my plan has been to try pleasantly to remind adults of what they once were themselves, and of how they felt and thought and talked, and what queer enterprises they sometimes engaged in.

Clemens, needing money, hoped to get it into print at once, but his publisher Elisha Bliss of the American Publishing Company of Hartford, Connecticut (Clemens's home at this time), had too many books in hand to bring it out immediately, and to Clemens's fury it did not appear until December 1876. The first American edition had illustrations by

T. W. Williams. Meanwhile *Tom Sawyer* had already appeared in Britain, in an edition without illustrations, published with the author's authority by Chatto and Windus in June 1876.

The book was not at first a particular success. It received enthusiastic (if slightly cautious) reviews on both sides of the Atlantic, but sales took a little time to pick up. Second editions appeared in America and Britain in 1877 (the British edition now including the illustrations by Williams), and after this it was reprinted every few years in both countries, as well as achieving much popularity in Canada.

Tom Sawyer was closely based on Clemens's own childhood in Hannibal, Missouri, Aunt Polly and Sid Sawyer resembling his own mother and brother, and the hero being 'a combination of three boys I knew', one of whom was himself. Even the murder of the doctor by Injun Joe, melodramatic as it seems to modern readers, was taken from life: Clemens had witnessed the stabbing of a young Californian by a drunken comrade. McDougal's Cave, where Tom and Becky get lost, was based on a limestone cavern near Hannibal that presented just such a threat to the local children.

Tom Sawyer, like its even more brilliant sequel, *The *Adventures of Huckleberry Finn* (1884), rejects the moral code of earlier 19th-cent. children's books, Tom being utterly amoral by the standards of such writings. Such moral courage as he does display springs chiefly from self-interest: he confesses to damaging the teacher's book in order to draw his wrath away from Becky, the real culprit, and thereby win her admiration; and he only reports the truth about the murder because he can get no peace from hideous dreams until he has done it. In one scene he gains a prize in *Sunday School entirely dishonestly, by means of a financial transaction. The only 'virtues' that the book commends are ingenuity, physical endurance, and a sense of humour.

adventure stories These stories for children, especially boys, may be said to have had precursors in the medieval *romances, many of which were read by children in debased *chapbook form. The modern adventure story is descended directly from *Robinson Crusoe* (1719), which was soon being imitated, most notably in *The *Swiss Family Robinson* (1812–13). The first skilled 19th-cent. British writer to provide adventure narratives especially for children, Captain *Marryat, modelled all his stories for young people more or less

directly on this pattern, marooning a family or an individual in some remote place, and giving an account of their methods of survival.

The *Robinsonnade continued to provide the format for many books, such as The *Desert Home by Mayne *Reid (1852) and R. M. *Ballantyne's celebrated The *Coral Island (1858). But these writers and their contemporary W. H. G. *Kingston introduced another motif into the adventure story, that of the young Englishman (often a mere boy) who goes out into the wilds, mingles with 'natives' and hunters, and comes back toughened, having learnt their ways. These early adventure story writers usually included passages of simple piety in their stories, but they indulged in little moralizing. The adventure story was, therefore, a considerable step forward from the *moral tale.

The first British writers in the genre generally portrayed 'natives'—whether Native Americans (*see* 'INDIANS' OF NORTH AMERICA), Inuit, or others—with some sympathy, following the example of American author James Fenimore *Cooper in respecting the Native American's wisdom and stoic calm. They made no special virtue of being white and British. Only Ballantyne, a man notably concerned with his own heroic image outside the pages of his books, put any deliberate emphasis on toughness. A typical hero of his tales, Ruby Brand in *The Lighthouse* (1865), is described as 'noted for great depth of chest, breadth of shoulder, and development of muscle'.

Ballantyne's lead was followed by G. A. *Henty, the most prolific and widely read of the Victorian adventure story writers, who was responsible for establishing most of the clichés of the genre, and whose stories are certainly often guilty of racial and class arrogance. Yet Edgar Osborne (*see* OSBORNE COLLECTION) argued that Henty and his imitators were valuable teachers. Osborne wrote of 'the debt we owe to those boys' writers of the nineteenth century who did so much to stimulate the spirit of adventure amongst young people, many of whom went overseas and did much towards building up our present Commonwealth of nations'.

Henty's work was paralleled in America by such authors as Harry *Castlemon, who used his own experiences in the Civil War as the basis for many of his tales. Other popular American writers in the genre included Oliver *Optic, Elijah *Kellogg, J. T. *Trowbridge, Noah *Brooks, Charles C. *Coffin, and Charles A. *Stephens.

Alongside this growing tradition of comparatively respectable adventure-story writing in Britain and America, there existed a much cruder popular genre, directly descended from the sensational matter of the chapbooks. In Britain this took the form of *penny dreadfuls, many of which romanticized the exploits of notorious criminals. In America the equivalent was the *dime novels, in which *westerns predominated. Various attempts were made to counteract the influence of penny dreadfuls, the most notable result being the establishment in Britain, in the last decade of the 19th cent., of *Harmsworth's series of boys' adventure weeklies; the most celebrated of these were *Marvel (1893–1922), *Pluck (1894–1916), and *Union Jack (1894–1933). At the same period in Britain the Henty tradition was continued in books by such writers of *boys' stories as Captain F. S. *Brereton, 'Herbert *Strang', and Percy F. *Westerman, all of whom wrote stories about the First World War. They in turn were succeeded by Captain W. E. *Johns, creator of the *Biggles series (1932 onwards). In 1921–2 D. C. *Thomson & Co. of Dundee introduced the first of their 'Big Five' adventure weeklies, *Adventure, *Rover, and *Wizard, which were followed by *Skipper (1930) and *Hotspur (1933); these were known as 'tuppenny bloods', and provided a constant flow of stories, chiefly aimed at working-class readers, about such improbable heroes as *Wilson the Wonder Athlete. During the late 19th and early 20th cents., boys' adventure papers in Britain also made much use of the type of adventure story pioneered by R. L. *Stevenson in *Treasure Island (1883) and by Rider *Haggard in *King Solomon's Mines (1885), and of the *detective story and the Jules *Verne style of *science fiction tale.

For much of the 20th cent. the tendency was for the 'serious' adventure story for children to draw less on the Ballantyne–Henty tradition than on works of a rather different kind. Two seminal books are *Bevis (1882) by Richard Jefferies and *Two Little Savages (1903) by Ernest Thompson *Seton, both of which proved that small-scale and entirely plausible adventures could hold just as much excitement as more melodramatic narratives. Arthur *Ransome in the 1930s made full use of this discovery. The success of his *Swallows and Amazons and its sequels led to a fashion in Britain, from about 1935 to 1960, for 'holiday adventures', in which children (often a brother and sister) arrive at a country village or seaside resort and find themselves involved in the detection of crime, or in some kind of treasure hunt connected with local history. The *Famous Five series by Enid *Blyton (1942 onwards) shows this genre at its most banal.

By the latter half of the 20th cent. and the early years of the next, what might be considered adventure stories had diversified into a set of subgenres. The higher-octane spy story is one of these, with Anthony *Horowitz's *Alex Rider series being a particularly popular one, beginning in 2000 with *Stormbreaker*. James Bond has been reinvented for a younger readership, in a series of 'Young Bond' books begun by Charlie *Higson and, continued, from 2014, by the prolific and versatile Steve Cole (creator of the enormously popular 'Astrosaurs' series). In addition, adventure can often be blurred with *fantasy. This can either be in a new world altogether, as in the *Wind on Fire trilogy, or where ordinary children are not just separated from a safe environment (e.g. in *The *Hunger Games*) but from the world as they know it, as in *His Dark Materials. This may be because of the 'quest' element of a lot of fantasy, the strongest example being T. H. White's groundbreaking *The *Sword in the Stone*. There are however, still adventure stories in the older tradition, such as Eva Ibbotson's *Journey to the River Sea* and more recently Katherine *Rundell's *Rooftoppers*.

ÆLFRIC (*fl.* 1006) Abbot of Eynsham, Ælfric was the author of two of the earliest English *books of instruction for children, a Latin grammar and a *Colloquy*. The preface to the grammar explains that it was translated into Anglo-Saxon from a Latin original by Priscian so that it would be understood by 'you little boys of tender years', presumably pupils in the monastic schools. The *Colloquy* is a dialogue, in Anglo-Saxon with an interlinear Latin translation, between a schoolmaster and his pupils; this was a form of literature common in Europe as a device for teaching boys Latin.

AESOP Supposed author of a celebrated collection of *fables which, though not composed for children, have always been popular with them. Aesop reputedly lived in the mid-6th cent. BC, and is said by Herodotus to have been a slave on the island of Samos. Legend describes him as an ugly, deformed little man, whose audience laughed at his grotesque appearance but also at his brilliant story-telling. Though no certain historical information about him survives, it seems likely that some such person did exist, and did compose many

of the fables that bear his name, though in later centuries it became the custom to credit him with the authorship of fables that were in fact the work of others.

Each of Aesop's fables, the majority of which concern animals (especially the fox, the wolf, and the lion), points a moral or has a moral interpretation attached to it. Despite this, the fables rarely recommend high ideals of conduct, but usually demonstrate the plainer virtues of common sense, moderation, and worldly wisdom. A frequent theme is how to save one's own skin and remain on good terms with those who are in power.

The fables, of which there are several hundred, are recorded in numerous Greek manuscripts, which contain widely differing versions of the individual fables. Aesop's fables were adopted by Latin writers, and later by the French, who in the 17th cent. produced their own brilliant fabulist, *La Fontaine.

The first English collection of the fables to be printed was that of *Caxton (1484), based on a French text taken from the German of Heinrich Steinhöwel, who had made a collection of the fables earlier in that century. Caxton's book, which (like most versions of the fables) included a 'Life of Aesop', was illustrated with nearly 200 *woodcuts.

Among notable English versions of the 17th cent. are an elegantly illustrated verse text by John Ogilby (1651) and an edition by the Tory political pamphleteer Sir Roger l'Estrange (1692). L'Estrange, who was nicknamed 'Dog Towzer' by a London mob at the height of his attacks on dissenters and his attempts to prove the non-existence of a 'popish plot', set out to make a comprehensive collection of the fables. In the next century there appeared an edition by Samuel Croxall (1722) which, like l'Estrange's, was aimed largely at children (it was dedicated to the five-year-old Lord Halifax), and was also intended to correct the Tory bias of l'Estrange's 'Morals' drawn from the fables. This was also the intention of Samuel *Richardson, whose collection of the fables was printed in 1740.

In 1757 John *Newbery published his *Fables in Verse ... by Abraham Aesop*. An edition closer to the Greek than Newbery's, but nevertheless meant for children, was that of Robert Dodsley (1761); this proved very popular, and was reprinted many times. In 1818 Thomas *Bewick illustrated his own version of Croxall's text, as *The Fables of Aesop, and others*.

An 1848 edition with a text by the Revd Thomas James had pictures by *Tenniel. In 1883 Randolph *Caldecott produced an illustrated selection in which the fables were augmented with 'modern instances', cartoons demonstrating similar events in terms of Victorian society. Walter *Crane's *The Baby's Own Aesop* was printed in *colour by Edmund *Evans in 1887, with the fables in rhyme. A Macmillan edition of 1894 had the fables 'selected, told anew and their history traced' by Joseph *Jacobs, with illustrations by Richard Heighway. In 1912 the fables were illustrated by Arthur *Rackham. Since that time, notable versions have included one with *wood engravings by Boris Artzybasheff (1933); retellings by James *Reeves with illustrations by Maurice Wilson (1961), and by Michael *Morpurgo with illustrations by Emma *Chichester Clark (2004); and freer adaptations such as Vivian *French's *Aesop's Funky Fables* illustrated by Korky *Paul (1999).

Affectionate Parent's Gift, The, *and the Good Child's Reward* (1828) A book of *moral tales in verse by the English writer Henry Sharpe Horsley. Subjects include 'A Visit to Newgate' and 'A Visit to the Lunatic Asylum'.

After Bath, *or (if you prefer) The Remarkable Case of the Flying Hat* (1945) A *fantasy by the British journalist and novelist Vaughan Wilkins (1890–1959). It concerns the family of the Lord Wizard of Minchester; his wife owns a flying hat that does the shopping for her, but it disappears. The Lord Wizard goes in search of it, accompanied by two of his children's toys, McAlpin the 'Kolar bear' and an elephant named Mr Velvet, whose job in the household is to sniff sugar up his trunk and then spray it neatly on the family's portions of apple pie.

AGARD, John (1949–) Award-winning poet who moved to the UK from Guyana in 1977 with his partner, the poet Grace *Nichols. Language, culture, and identity are key themes in Agard's work. His well-known poem 'Half-Caste' distils an emotional and political charge for young readers and has featured in the British school exam anthologies since 2002. *I Din Do Nuttin and Other Poems* (1983), beautifully illustrated by Susanna Gretz, features tender reminiscences of his childhood in Guyana alongside notably astute reflections of multicultural Britain in the early 1980s. Agard's long-term collaboration with illustrator Satoshi *Kitamura has produced several picture books which address sociopolitical and environmental issues, for example, *We Animals Would Like*

a Word with You (2000), and modern satirical takes on classic tales with *Goldilocks on CCTV* (2011) and the Dante-inspired *The Young Inferno* (2008). In 2012, Agard was awarded the Queen's Gold Medal for Poetry.

Agathos, *and other Sunday stories* (1840) By Bishop Samuel Wilberforce (1805–73), one of the most popular Victorian *religious books for children. The title story is about a valiant soldier who, alone of all his troops, obeys his king's injunction to always wear his armour, and so is ready for the attack of the *dragon when it comes. All the stories in the book are simple allegories, and most conclude with a dialogue in which their meaning is explained. *Agathos* had a wide readership in America and was translated into French and German.

AGEE, Jon (1960–) American illustrator and author with a distinctly wry sense of humour. From the success of *The Incredible Painting of Felix Clousseau* (1989), about an artist whose paintings come to life and cause chaos, to *The Retired Kid* (2008), a book about how being a child can be such hard work, he has delighted and amused readers of all ages. His fascination with wordplay engendered works such as *Go Hang a Salami! I'm a Lasagna Hog! and Other Palindromes* (1991) and *Elvis Lives! and Other Anagrams* (2000). He has also written the book and lyrics for two off-Broadway children's musicals.

AHLBERG, Allan (1938–) British children's author and poet, who has written many enduringly popular picture books.

An illegitimate child in an era when this was not socially acceptable, Ahlberg was adopted and brought up in Oldbury in the Black Country. His adoptive family was poor and he grew up with, in his own words, 'no books, and not much conversation'. He has identified himself as the baby in *Peepo* (1981), one of the many books he published in collaboration with his illustrator wife Janet *Ahlberg. Ahlberg also wrote about his childhood in *The Boyhood of Burglar Bill* (2007) and more recently in a book for adults, *The Bucket: Memories of an Inattentive Childhood* (2013).

Ahlberg wanted to be a writer ever since he was a child, but he did an eclectic range of jobs first, including working as a gravedigger and plumber's mate.

His first three collaborations with Janet were *Burglar Bill*, *The Old Joke Book*, and *The Vanishment of Thomas Tull*, all in 1977. In 1978, the couple published *Each Peach Pear Plum*, a fairy-tale hide-and-seek book which has become a classic.

In 1980, the Ahlbergs had a daughter, Jessica. As a baby, she was fascinated by the Mothercare catalogue, and this inspired her parents to produce *The Baby's Catalogue*, an intricate visual depiction of the everyday things that populate a baby's world. When Jessica was two, the Ahlbergs had the idea for *The *Jolly Postman*—a book about a postman delivering letters to a number of well-known fairy-tale characters. The concept was unusual in that each double-page spread had an envelope with a real letter inside that the reader could take out. This idea was immensely complex to bring to fruition, and took three years of careful collaboration with the publisher and printer. The book was eventually published in 1986, and was an enormous critical and commercial success.

Janet died in 1994, a tragedy which stopped Allan writing for a considerable time. His way back into his work was to produce *Janet's Last Book* (1997). Originally privately published, it was a tribute to his wife, and included his selection of her sketches, roughs, and illustrations. Up until this point, Ahlberg had been published by Puffin, but after his wife's death he found it too painful to continue to work with them, so he moved to Walker Books. There he was edited by Vanessa Clarke. Their professional partnership turned into a personal one, and the two of them married.

When Jessica grew up, she became an illustrator herself. She collaborated with her father on some of his more recent titles, including *Half a Pig* (2004), *The Boy, the Wolf, the Sheep and the Lettuce* (2005), and *Goldilocks* (2012).

Ahlberg has also written poetry. Two of his most famous collections are the school poems *Please Mrs Butler* (1984) and *Heard It in the Playground* (1991).

Ahlberg has said, 'Just because a book is tiny and its readers are little doesn't mean it can't be perfect. On its own scale, it can be as good as Tolstoy or Jane Austen.'

AHLBERG, Janet (1944–94) British illustrator of children's books. Together with her author husband Allan *Ahlberg, she produced many picture books which have become widely regarded as classics.

Janet and Allan met at teacher training college in Sunderland in the 1960s and they married in 1969. Janet asked Allan to write her a story that she could illustrate, and thus began one of the most successful partnerships in the

history of children's books. The result was *The Brick Street Boys* (1975).

The Ahlbergs went on to produce many popular and acclaimed titles. *Each Peach Pear Plum* (1978), is a hide-and-seek book in which the reader has to spot fairy-tale characters hidden in the illustrations. *Peepo* (1981) uses peepholes cut in the page so that the child can spy what is coming next. It depicts a 1940s working class home with amazing intricacy, full of cosy clutter and with a father in soldier's uniform. The *Jolly Postman* (1986), about a postman delivering mail to a series of well-known fairy-tale characters, used a ground-breaking format. *Starting School* (1988) is a book intended for children doing just that, and shows the everyday life of a primary classroom, from the rows of toilets and the classroom rabbit to the book corner and the school assembly.

Janet painted scenes with immense detail, depicting all the recognizable paraphernalia of domestic life. Allan's spare text and Janet's intricate pictures work together so that the observant child can always spot many things that are happening in the story beyond the overt narrative.

Janet died of breast cancer at the age of 50, leaving a remarkable and influential legacy of now classic picture book work.

AIKEN, Joan (Delano) (1924–2004) Author, best known for a series of 'alternate history' novels. The daughter of the American poet Conrad Aiken, she was born at Rye in Sussex, her father and her Canadian mother having come to England for the sake of their children's education. In her late teens she began to have poems and stories published. In 1953 there appeared *All You've Ever Wanted*, her first collection of short stories for children, which was followed by a similar book, *More Than You Bargained For*. In the year that this was published, 1955, her husband died. She subsequently took a job as features editor of the magazine *Argosy*, where she stayed until 1960, before turning to full-time authorship. *The Kingdom and the Cave* (1960) was her first full-length children's novel, a *fantasy about a kingdom threatened by a sinister underground people. Her first distinctive book was The *Wolves of Willoughby Chase* (1962), which established her as a writer of wild humour and unrestrained imagination. It proved to be the beginning of a series of novels set in an imaginary period of English history, the reign of the late Tudor-Stuarts in the early 19th cent., the house of

Hanover having never succeeded to the English throne. The supporters of the Hanoverians, in fact, play much the part in the novels that the Jacobites did in real 18th-cent. England.

In no sense at all are Joan Aiken's books *historical novels: her treatment of the past is entirely freehand, somewhat in the manner of Leon *Garfield. Her novels can be described as gothic fantasies, with suggestions of *Dickens in their characters and incidents. *Black Hearts in Battersea* (1964) concerns the Hanoverian conspiracies against James III, and introduces the Cockney waif Dido Twite, who features in several later books. *Night Birds on Nantucket* (1966) describes a plan to assassinate the King by means of a long-distance cannon fired across the Atlantic. *The Whispering Mountain* (1968) is about the rediscovery of a legendary bardic harp in a Welsh monastery; critics have perceived in it an element of parody of those children's stories in which elaborate riddles from the past are unravelled by child heroes and heroines. In *The Cuckoo Tree* (1971) the reign of Richard IV is about to begin, and the Hanoverians plan to wreck his coronation. Later books in the series include *The Stolen Lake* (1981), *Dido and Pa* (1986), and *Midwinter Nightingale* (2004).

These novels form the first and most original strand of Joan Aiken's writing. She also produced a number of short story collections which she calls 'fairytales . . . set mainly in the present day'. They include *A Necklace of Raindrops* (1968), *A Small Pinch of Weather* (1969), *Not What You Expected* (1974), and *The Faithless Lollybird* (1977). Humour plays as large a part in these as in her novels; a typical story, the title piece in *A Small Pinch of Weather*, describes the disagreement between Miss Sophy Ross, hereditary Weather Witch of a small Scottish town, and a retired Bishop who has learnt his own methods of controlling the weather from African witch doctors. Joan Aiken has also written tales for younger children about what she calls 'extra-intelligent animals', most notably stories about the small girl Arabel and her talking raven Mortimer Jones, who cries 'Nevermore!' when he is upset; these were commissioned by BBC television's *Jackanory, and were published in *Arabel's Raven* (1972) and several later books.

Joan Aiken discussed her craft in her book *The Way to Write for Children* (1982).

AIKEN, John (1747–1822) Physician and man of letters, brother of Mrs *Barbauld, he was joint author with her of *Evenings at Home*

(1792–6). His other books included *The Calendar of Nature* (1784) (*see* NATURAL HISTORY).

AIKIN, Lucy *See* POETRY FOR CHILDREN.

AINSWORTH, (William) Harrison (1805–82) Wrote a number of *historical novels which, though not intended particularly for children, were enjoyed by them. They include *The Tower of London* (1840), *Old St Paul's* (1841), an account of the Fire of London, and *Guy Fawkes* (1841). His novel *Rookwood* (1834) helped to create the legend of *Dick Turpin.

***Aladdin,** or the Wonderful Lamp* A tale from the *Arabian Nights*, which has become popular as a children's *fairy story and even more as a *pantomime.

The story is set in China. Aladdin is the son of a tailor; his father dies, but he makes no effort to support his mother and grows ever idler. One day a Moorish magician from Africa sees him, and decides that he is the lad he needs for a magical enterprise. Declaring that he is Aladdin's long-lost uncle, he lures the boy to a hill outside the town and reveals a stone slab which guards the entrance to a series of caves which contain a hoard of riches. Opening the cave, he sends Aladdin in, instructing him to bring back a lamp which hangs inside. Aladdin fetches the lamp, and also stuffs his clothes full of the jewels that he finds in the caves. The magician means to take the lamp and abandon Aladdin, but the boy cannot hand the lamp up to him because his clothes are so full of jewels. Enraged, the magician causes the cave door to shut, with Aladdin inside. Left to his fate, Aladdin toys with a magic ring the magician gave him in order to protect himself inside the caves, and a *jinn, the Slave of the Ring, immediately appears. At Aladdin's request he releases him from the caves, and Aladdin goes home and shows his mother the lamp. She decides that it is in need of cleaning, and no sooner has she begun to polish it than another, more powerful, jinn appears, the Slave of the Lamp. He is able to carry out any request, and he has soon fetched fine food for Aladdin and his mother, served on priceless gold plates.

With the aid of the Slave, Aladdin is soon a rich man. He sees and falls in love with the Sultan's daughter, the princess Bedr-el-Budr, determines to marry her, and sends his mother to the court with costly gifts for the Sultan. The gifts are so remarkable that the Sultan agrees to the marriage, but the Vizier reminds him that the princess is already betrothed to his own son, and in the event she marries not Aladdin but this other young man. Aladdin, enraged, orders the Slave of the Lamp to fetch the princess and her husband to his house on their wedding night, lying in their marriage-bed, before they can consummate the marriage. He then turns the bridegroom out of the bed, has him shut in the privy for the night, and gets into bed with the princess, though he places a drawn sword between them and does not touch her. The same thing happens on successive nights, and eventually the marriage is declared null and void because it cannot be consummated.

Aladdin then renews his suit for the princess, who falls in love with him, and eventually, after the Slave of the Lamp has built him a magnificent palace, he is married to the princess. The magician returns from Africa to China, disguises himself as a lamp-seller crying 'New lamps for old!', and manages to obtain the magic lamp from the princess, who is unaware of its power. He then uses the lamp to remove Aladdin's palace—with the princess inside—from China to Africa, while Aladdin is out hunting. Aladdin pursues the magician and the palace to Africa, and arranges for the princess to give the magician drugged wine, after which Aladdin kills him. He then orders the Slave of the Lamp to transport the palace back to China, where he and the princess live happily for the rest of their lives—after disposing of the magician's equally vicious brother, who makes a brief appearance at the end of the original story, attempting to do mischief in revenge for the magician's death.

Aladdin was first printed in the *Mille et une nuits*, a French text of the *Arabian Nights* issued in parts between 1704 and 1717. The book was the work of the French orientalist Antoine *Galland, but the tale did not appear in any of the Arabic manuscripts of the *Nights*. (The same is true of *Ali Baba.) Galland may have had another Arabic source, and recorded meeting a Syrian storyteller not long before publishing *Aladdin*. Alternatively, it was thought that Galland might have adapted the story himself from some European source. For example, a Bohemian folk tale tells how the hero Jenik saves a dog, a cat, and a serpent from being killed; in return he is given an enchanted watch which procures him a fine palace and a princess for a bride; similarly the hero of an Albanian story acquires a wishing-stone and prospers in the usual fashion, but the stone is stolen by a rascally Jew on the

night of the wedding, and it is used to transport the palace with the princess to a distant sea-shore. Other analogues to *Aladdin* have been recorded in Italy and Greece.

Writing in the late 19th cent., Sir Richard Burton, Victorian translator of the *Nights*, alleged that Galland did after all take the tale of *Aladdin* from an oriental manuscript; he said he had found such a manuscript in the Bibliothèque Nationale in Paris, and though it was dated as late as the early 1800s it purported to be a transcript of a text dated 1703, the year before Galland's *Nuits* began to appear. Even if this dating is spurious, and the manuscript is no more than a reworking of Galland's text (which is perfectly possible), there is no reason why Galland should not have collected the story from some oral oriental source.

Aladdin first appeared in English in 1721-2, in the ninth and tenth volumes of *The Arabian Nights Entertainments*, the anonymous 'Grub Street' translation of Galland's French text of the *Nights* which was issued in parts during the first three decades of the 18th cent. This version, entitled 'The Story of Aladdin: or, The Wonderful Lamp', gave Aladdin's father's name as Mustapha, and described the Slave of the Lamp as 'a hideous Genie of gygantick Size'. A much shorter and more genteel version of the tale was printed in *The Oriental Moralist*, an abridgement of the *Nights* for children published by Elizabeth *Newbery *c*.1791. In this, Aladdin, after acquiring the lamp, 'abandoned all his youthful companions, and associated only with men of sense and character'. The Vizier's son, far from having to spend the night in the lavatory, was put by Aladdin 'into the stable on some clean straw'. Later versions for children have been similarly discreet.

Aladdin's true popularity in England did not begin until it was made into a pantomime. This first happened in 1788—one of the first occasions when a fairy story was used as the basis of a pantomime—when *Aladdin; or, The Wonderful Lamp* was performed at Covent Garden at Christmas. This set the fashion for innumerable other *Aladdins* which were staged in British theatres throughout the 19th cent.

Once it had appeared on the stage, the story began to be printed as a separate book for children. The first instance seems to have been *Aladdin, or, The Wonderful Lamp, A tale for the nursery* (1805), one of *Tabart's series of *Popular Stories*. Since then, it has been re-issued again and again in various retellings, but it is still more popular as a

pantomime than a book—only *Cinderella* is performed more often on the British pantomime stage. Modern dramatizations owe much to H. J. Byron's *Aladdin*, first performed at the Royal Strand Theatre at Easter 1861. (A schoolboy production of this version is described in the story 'Slaves of the Lamp' in *Stalky & Co.*). Byron squeezed in as many jokes about China tea as he could manage: the Vizier's son was named Pekoe, and Aladdin's mother was called Widow Twankay, a reference to a variety of green tea that was popular at the time. Widow Twankay or Twankey she has remained, just as the magician has retained the name that Byron gave him, Abanazar. A popular animated *Disney version (no longer set in China) was released in 1992.

Aladdin, Mr *See* MR ALADDIN.

Alan Breck Stewart In *Kidnapped* by R. L. *Stevenson.

ALBOROUGH, Jez (1959-) British illustrator and writer of picture books, usually featuring animals, which include the hugely popular *Hug* (2000), a twenty-eight-word book of which twenty-four words are 'hug'. It introduced Bobo, the little chimp who has gone on to feature in several other Alborough works. Other notable books include *Duck in the Truck* (1999, the first of many Duck titles), in which a duck is in a truck—*a truck that gets stuck in some yucky brown muck*; and a series featuring Bear, beginning with *Where's My Teddy* (1992).

ALCOTT, Louisa May (1832-88) Author of *Little Women*. She was the second of four daughters of Amos Bronson Alcott, a New England transcendental philosopher and experimenter in education, who at various times set up schools with radical methods. His ideas met with much opposition, and during Louisa's childhood he abandoned teaching and tried to keep his family by farming a small piece of land in Concord, Mass. The family nearly starved, and eventually Louisa's mother was left to provide almost single-handed for the household, while Alcott sat writing his journals, waiting for the world to accept his ideas.

As soon as she was old enough, Louisa helped to provide an income by running a small school, going briefly into domestic service, and taking in sewing. She was much influenced by her father's friends Henry David Thoreau and Ralph Waldo Emerson, and she formed a strongly romantic attachment to Thoreau.

Together with her sisters she performed amateur theatricals, and wrote melodramatic plays for them to act; some of these were published posthumously in 1893 as *Comic Tragedies*. In 1854 a collection of moral stories with a fairyland setting, which she had written at the age of sixteen, appeared in print under the title *Flower Fables*. By this time she had determined to try to provide full financial support for her family, who had left Boston. Remaining there, she undertook the tutoring of an invalid girl and continued to take in sewing. In 1857 her younger sister Elizabeth died of the effects of scarlet fever, caught from a destitute family whom the Alcotts had nursed; this is commemorated in the death of Beth in the second part of *Little Women*. Recovering from the shock of this bereavement, Louisa found she could get a reasonable income by writing lurid stories for *dime novel publishers and Boston newspapers; these were published pseudonymously, and had such titles as 'Pauline's Passion and Punishment' and 'The Curse of the Coventries'. She also wrote two serious novels, which were eventually published as *Moods* (1864) and *Work* (1873); the first arose from her love for Thoreau, and the second recounted her experiences in trying to earn a living.

In November 1862, during the second year of the Civil War, she volunteered for hospital service at Georgetown. Conditions were terrible, her own health broke down, and she contracted typhoid fever and pneumonia. Up to this time she had never been seriously ill; now (as she afterwards observed) she was never to be well again, largely because she was heavily dosed with the currently fashionable medicine, calomel, which caused mercury poisoning.

In 1865 she travelled to Europe as paid companion to an invalid; returning home, she took the job of editor of a Boston children's magazine, *Merry's Museum. She was also encouraged by Thomas Niles, chief editor at the Boston publishing house of Roberts Brothers, to write a book for girls, and, though this was not much to her taste, she began it in the hope that it would pay off at least some of her parents' continuing debts. The result was *Little Women*.

The first volume of *Little Women* was published late in 1868, with huge success, and a second part, best known in England as *Good Wives*, appeared early the following year. The royalties which resulted from the two volumes were soon producing enough for Louisa to wipe out all family debts.

Her next novel, *An Old-Fashioned Girl* (1870), was the story of Polly Milton, a girl struggling to support herself in Boston just as Louisa Alcott had. *Little Men* (1871) returned to the March family, and was written in order to provide money for Louisa's sister Anna, who had just been widowed and left with two children to support. It is set at Plumfield School, which is run by Jo and her husband (on the lines of Bronson Alcott's educational theories). *Eight Cousins; or, The Aunt-Hill* (1875) has as its heroine Rose, an orphan in the care of her aunts, who has to come to terms with the presence of a self-styled 'Clan' of boisterous boy-cousins; in its sequel, *Rose in Bloom* (1876), Rose is encouraged to choose one of the cousins as a husband. *A Modern Mephistopheles* (1877) harked back to Louisa Alcott's Gothic dime-novel style, and was issued by Roberts Brothers in a series in which celebrated authors published a new book anonymously, and readers were asked to guess who had written it.

By now Louisa could afford to buy for her parents the house in Concord that had been Thoreau's home until his death in 1862. Her next children's novel, *Under the Lilacs* (1877), was commissioned as a serial by the magazine *St Nicholas, and described the adventures of two small girls, a boy fugitive from a circus, and a performing poodle. *Jack and Jill* (1880), written during a period which saw the death both of Louisa's mother and of her sister May, begins with a sledge accident; the heroine has to spend a year convalescing, and her bedroom becomes the centre of her young friends' ebullient social life. Louisa Alcott also wrote many short stories for children, some of which were published under the series titles 'Aunt Jo's Scrap-Bag' and 'Lulu's Library'; the latter was named after May's small daughter Louisa or Lulu Nieriker, for whom Louisa Alcott cared after her mother's death. These stories tended to be sentimental and more obviously didactic than *Little Women*. A final March book, *Jo's Boys*, appeared in 1886, and is set at Plumfield, where Jo's husband is now President of a college.

Louisa Alcott's father died on 4 March 1888, and two days later she herself, worn out by looking after him while in constantly poor health, died in her sleep.

ALDEN, Isabella Macdonald *See* 'PANSY'.

ALDERSON, Brian W. (Wouldhave) (1930–) Historian and critic of British children's books. He worked in the book trade

from 1952 until 1963, before becoming Senior Lecturer (on Children's Literature and the Book Trade) in the School of Librarianship at the Polytechnic of North London; in 1967 he was also appointed Children's Books Editor of *The Times*, a post he held for nearly three decades. He has edited re-issues of historic children's books, including many of the *Fairy Books* of Andrew *Lang, and revised F. J. H. *Darton's *Children's Books in England* for the third edition (1982). His other work includes a translation of stories from *Grimm (1978) and an anthology of rhymes for children, *Cakes and Custard* (1974), illustrated by Helen *Oxenbury. He was awarded the 1968 *Eleanor Farjeon Award for his contribution to the world of children's literature.

ALDHELM (?640–709) Abbot of Malmesbury and Bishop of Sherborne, Aldhelm was the author of a *book of instruction for monastery schoolboys, *De Septenario*, which included a treatise on the making of Latin verse in the form of a dialogue between a pupil and his teacher. The book also contained a collection of *riddles in Latin hexameters, which the pupil was asked to solve.

Aldiborontiphoskyphorniostikos A game, issued in book form by A. K. Newman, *c*.1822, and by *Dean & Munday in 1824, in which each player had to read a section of a story featuring characters with almost unpronounceable names. It is reproduced in the *Opies' *Nursery Companion* (1980). The compiler and illustrator was R. Stennett, who is supposed to have been the illustrator of the original edition of *Dame Wiggins of Lee*.

Aldine Publishing Company Established in London in the 1880s, the company at first specialized in reprints of American *dime novels, and also produced late examples of Victorian *penny dreadfuls (*Dick Turpin*, *Spring-Heeled Jack*, and so on). They produced such 'libraries' as 'The Boy's First-Rate Pocket Library' and the 'Invention, Travel and Adventure Library'. These continued to appear until the 1930s.

ALDRICH, Thomas Bailey *See* STORY OF A BAD BOY.

ALEXANDER, Mrs Cecil Frances (1818–95) Author of several celebrated hymns for children, she was the daughter of an officer in the Marines, and later the wife of the Archbishop of Armagh. Her *Hymns for Little Children*, which contains 'All things bright and beautiful',

'Once in royal David's city', and 'There is a green hill far away', was published in 1848.

ALEXANDER, Lloyd (Chudley) (1924–2007) American writer of *fantasy, best known for his *Prydain cycle of novels. He studied at the Sorbonne, and worked as a translator of Sartre and other French authors before beginning to write children's fiction. The Prydain cycle began in 1964 with *The Book of Three*. After its conclusion, in *The High King* (1968), Alexander wrote such books as *The Marvellous Misadventures of Sebastian* (1970), the story of a wandering musician; *The First Two Lives of Lukas-Kasha* (1978), a cat story in the style of the *Arabian Nights*; the India-inspired *The Iron Ring* (1997); and the Vesper Holly series, beginning in 1987 with *The Illyrian Adventure*.

Alexander and the Terrible, Horrible, No Good, Very Bad Day (1972) A picture book by Judith *Viorst, illustrated by Ray Cruz. Alexander is grumpy today and everything just goes wrong for him, and it's annoying and not fair, and there's no dessert in his lunch bag, and he doesn't get a window seat in the car, and there are lima beans for dinner and he *hates* lima beans, and he wants to move to Australia instead. Deservedly popular for over forty years (and adapted for both screen and stage), the book offers children a reassuring conclusion: sometimes, it says, days can just be like that. Tomorrow might be better. Alexander—who is named after Viorst's real-life son—would feature in two more books: *Alexander, Who Used to Be Rich Last Sunday* (1977) and *Alexander, Who's Not (Do you hear me? I mean it!) Going to Move* (1995), both by Viorst and illustrated respectively by Cruz and by Robin Preiss Glasser 'in the style of Ray Cruz'. An omnibus edition of the three books, *Absolutely, Positively Alexander*, appeared in 1997.

ALEXIE, Sherman (1966–) Poet, filmmaker, and writer for adults and *young adults whose work is heavily influenced by his experiences as a Native American growing up on the Spokane Indian reservation. *The Absolutely True Diary of a Part-Time Indian* (2007) is based on Alexie's own life and tells of a Native American boy desperate to break away from a life he hates and fulfil his ambition to become a cartoonist.

Alex Rider The hero of a hugely successful series of action novels by Anthony *Horowitz. Alex is a fourteen-year-old recruited to work as a spy for MI6, following the death of his

uncle and guardian. He undertakes the role very reluctantly. The series begins with *Stormbreaker* (2000), in which Alex is tasked with investigating the suspicious actions of billionaire, Herod Sayle (Lebanese in the original UK edition, but changed to Egyptian for US publication). *Stormbreaker* was followed by eight further novels, in each of which Alex faces James Bond-like adventures, battling fiendish baddies in exotic locations. The series concluded in 2011 with *Scorpia Rising*, though a prequel, *Russian Roulette*, appeared two years later. Consistently pacy and action-packed, the books have also spawned graphic novel versions and an unremarkable big-screen adaptation.

Alfie In Shirley *Hughes's sequence of picture books, Alfie is a four-year-old boy whose little domestic adventures and trials have won him and his companions millions of admirers around the world. He first appeared in 1981, in *Alfie Gets in First*, a book that brilliantly splits each double-page into an inside and an outside (Alfie on one side, having locked himself in the house; Mum on the other, increasingly desperate on the doorstep); the tension between what the words say and what the pictures show is brilliantly realized. This was followed in 1982 by another storybook, *Alfie's Feet* (Alfie has new boots, and needs to learn left and right), then *Alfie Gives a Hand* (1983), *An Evening at Alfie's* (1984), and many more since. Along with his toddler sister, Annie Rose, their parents, grandmother, and their neighbours, Alfie's world is completed by a group of friends, among them pesky best friend Bernard, who celebrates his birthday in *Alfie Gives a Hand*. Hughes's detailed drawings and small-scale stories create a world for Alfie and his little dramas that children and their parents recognize as they read.

Alfie Atkins *See* BERGSTRÖM, GUNILLA.

ALGER, Horatio, Jr. (1832–99) Prolific American writer who popularized the rags-to-riches theme in US juvenile books. He was born in Massachusetts, the son of a Unitarian minister, and was educated at Harvard. His first successful story, *Ragged Dick; or, Street Life in New York with the Boot-Blacks*, was serialized during 1867 in *The Student and Schoolmate*, a *magazine edited by 'Oliver *Optic', and was published as a book the next year. He addressed poor boys in the US's fast-growing cities, and created the 'Alger hero' who raises himself to respectability and success (not necessarily riches) by hard work,

thrift, and resisting temptation; he usually then also benefits from good luck and the help of a generous adult. Alger's many other successes included *Luck and Pluck; or, John Oakley's Inheritance* (1869), *Tattered Tom; or, the Story of a Street Arab* (1871) (which was in fact the story of a girl, 'not one of the conventional kind'), *Phil the Fiddler; or, the Story of a Young Street Musician* (1872), and *Struggling Upward; or, Luke Larkin's Luck* (1890). Alger chose Edward *Stratemeyer to finish and publish his last book.

A short period as a Unitarian minister ended when he was charged with 'unnatural familiarity with boys'. He resigned and no further action was taken. When *Alger, a Biography without a Hero* was published in New York in 1928, it appeared to expose traits that included high living and womanizing. This was widely quoted until the writer of it, Herbert R. Mayes, confirmed in the 1970s that it had been a hoax, almost all fiction, intended as a parody of the debunking biographies then in vogue. A genuine biography, by Gary Scharnhorst and Jack Bales, appeared in 1985.

Ali Baba and the Forty Thieves A story found in the **Arabian Nights*. Ali Baba, a poor woodcutter, observes from a hiding-place forty robbers concealing their spoils in a cave, whose door moves at the command 'Open, Sesame!' He repeats these words and enters the cave himself, carrying off some of the vast hoard of wealth that he finds there. He tries to keep his discovery secret, but his rich brother Cassim learns of it and sets out for the cave himself. Having opened the door, Cassim prepares to carry off riches, but he is so excited that he forgets the magic words and cannot get out. He is soon discovered there by the robbers, who kill him and cut his body into four pieces.

Ali Baba returns to the cave and finds his brother's remains. He carries them home, together with more gold, and employs a shoemaker or tailor, Baba Mustapha, to sew the corpse together so as to make the death look natural. The robbers, meanwhile, find that the corpse has gone, and more gold with it. They determine to discover who it is that knows their secret. One of them goes to the town, finds Baba Mustapha, and learns from him the location of the house where he sewed up the corpse. The robber marks the door with chalk, but Ali Baba's slave Morgiana discovers this and makes similar chalk-marks on neighbouring houses. This happens a second time, but on a third occasion the robber commits

the identity of the house to memory, and he and his comrades plan to murder Ali Baba.

They acquire big oil-jars, in which they hide, and these jars are carried into the town. Their leader, posing as an oil merchant, asks Ali Baba if he may stay the night in his house, and leave his jars in the yard. During the night, the slave Morgiana comes into the yard to fill her lamp with oil from the jars and hears a robber whisper 'Is it time, master?' Realizing what the robbers' plan is, she heats a quantity of oil and pours some of it into each of the jars, so that all the robbers are scalded and choked to death. When their leader discovers what has happened he flees, but returns to the town disguised as a silk merchant. He comes to dinner with Ali Baba, intending to kill him, but is recognized by Morgiana who stabs him. She is rewarded by being given her freedom, and she marries Ali Baba's son. Ali Baba pays further visits to the cave, and he and his son prosper on the wealth they obtain from it.

The story, first printed by Antoine *Galland in his French translation of the *Nights* begun in 1704, is not in the accredited Arabic manuscripts of the *Arabian Nights*. Galland's source may have been the Syrian Maronite storyteller, Youhenna (or 'Hanna') Diab, who gave him oral versions of several of the stories. There are also European parallels including a North German story of a cave of riches in a wood, whose owner is not a robber but a monk. A tale in *Grimm, *Simeli Mountain* (also known by other, similar, titles), closely resembles the first part of *Ali Baba*, as far as the death of the brother. The quartering of the corpse, the sewing-up, and the chalking of the doors may have been derived from a story in Herodotus, in which, after the robbery of a royal treasury, a series of similar exploits are performed by the hero to recover the headless body of his brother and escape detection. A parallel to the robbers hiding in the jars and their discovery and death is found in a folk tale from Cyprus, in which an *ogre attempts to rescue his wife by arriving at court with a party of black men hidden in bales.

'Sesame', the word used in Galland's narrative for the opening of the door, is the French name for a plant found widely in the Middle East, and for the oil-producing seed taken from it. In the story it seems to be a term of no significance. Several analogues of the tale have 'Little door, open!' in place of such a word. The Grimms' version has 'Semsi mountain, open up', but it is not known whether 'Semsi' is related to 'Sesame'.

The story first appeared in English in 1722, in the 11th volume of the *Arabian Nights Entertainments*, the anonymous English translation of Galland's text that was issued in parts by several *chapbook publishers. It was printed there under the title 'The Story of Ali Baba, and the forty Thieves destroyed by a Slave'. At the beginning of the 19th cent. it became popular as a children's chapbook, versions being issued by N. Kelly of Dublin *c*.1800, by *Tabart in the series *Popular Stories* which began to appear in 1804, and by *Kendrew of York *c*.1810. *Ali Baba* has often been produced on the stage.

Alice's Adventures in Wonderland
(1865) By 'Lewis *Carroll'—C. L. Dodgson—this book revolutionized children's literature with its fantastic plot and brilliant use of *nonsense. Characters such as the White Rabbit, the Caterpillar, the Ugly Duchess, the Cheshire Cat, the Hatter and the March Hare, and the Gryphon and Mock Turtle, all of whom are encountered by Alice after her descent of a rabbit-hole and her attempt to get through a tiny door into a rose-garden, had never before been created for the amusement of children, without any moral purpose whatsoever. Harvey *Darton has observed of the story that 'it was the coming to the surface, powerfully and permanently, the first un-apologetic appearance in print, for readers who sorely needed it, of liberty of thought in children's books'.

The story was an expansion of *Alice's Adventures Under Ground*, which was begun as an extempore tale told to ten-year-old Alice Liddell and her sisters Lorina and Edith, daughters of the Dean of Christ Church, Oxford, during a boat trip on 4 July 1862. According to a fifth member of the party, a young don named Robinson Duckworth, 'When we had conducted the three children back to the Deanery, Alice said, as she bade us good-night, "Oh, Mr Dodgson, I wish you would write out Alice's adventures for me."' Duckworth alleged that Dodgson then 'sat up nearly the whole night, committing to an MS book his recollections of the drolleries with which he had enlivened the afternoon'. The truth, however, seems to be rather different. Dodgson did record in his diary that, on the morning after the boat-trip, while travelling on a train from Oxford to London, he wrote out 'headings' for the story (that is, a synopsis), but he apparently did no actual writing for the time being. Meanwhile the children wanted more; Dodgson wrote in his diary:

August 6 (Wednesday)... In the afternoon Harcourt and I took the three Liddells up to Godstow, where we had tea; we tried the game of 'the Ural Mountains' on the way, but it did not prove very successful, and I had to go on with my interminable fairy-tale of *Alice's Adventures*.

Soon after this, Dodgson had one of his periodic disagreements with Mrs Liddell, the children's mother. As a result, he did not see the three girls for some time, and it was a chance meeting with them in one of the Christ Church quadrangles on 13 November that prompted him to write down the story at last: 'Began writing the fairy-tale for Alice, which I told them July 4, going to Godstow—I hope to finish it by Christmas.'

The story was not, in fact, completed in fair copy until the New Year, while the drawings which Dodgson had decided to provide (much in the manner that he had illustrated such volumes of juvenilia as *The *Rectory Umbrella*) took even longer; in March 1863 he borrowed a book of natural history from the Deanery to help get the pictures of some of the animals right. Moreover by this time the project had ceased to be simply a gift-book for Alice. She was eventually given the finished manuscript in November 1864; but long before this Dodgson sent it to the family of George *MacDonald, with whom he was on friendly terms, asking whether it might be suitable for publication.

Mrs MacDonald read it aloud to her children with great success—her son Greville 'wished that there were sixty thousand volumes of it'—and in May 1863 she returned the manuscript to Dodgson, advising him to publish it. He received the same advice from other families to whom the story was shown, and he decided to ask the Clarendon Press (that is, the University Press at Oxford) to print it at his own expense. During the summer of 1863 Thomas Combe, one of the Printers to the University, supplied him with specimen pages. At first Dodgson intended to use his own illustrations, and he took a trial drawing on wood to a London blockmaker, asking him to improve it while cutting it. In October 1863 Combe introduced him to the London publisher Alexander Macmillan, who that year had brought out Kingsley's *The *Water-Babies*; Macmillan agreed to distribute Dodgson's book for him on commission. By January 1864 Dodgson had decided that he needed a professional illustrator. Tom Taylor, dramatist and writer for *Punch*, whom Dodgson met and photographed in the autumn of 1863, introduced him to one of his magazine's most accomplished cartoonists, John *Tenniel, who, after reading Dodgson's manuscript, agreed to illustrate the book.

Meanwhile Dodgson had decided to expand the book and slightly rewrite some of the existing story, removing private jokes and inserting two new set-pieces, 'Pig and Pepper' and 'A Mad Tea Party'. He sent part of the first chapter of the revised version to the Clarendon Press in May 1864, and the next month asked Tom Taylor's advice about a title:

I should be very glad if you could help me in fixing on a name for my fairy-tale...The heroine spends an hour underground, and meets various birds, beasts, etc. (*no* fairies), endowed with speech. The whole thing is a dream, but *that* I don't want revealed till the end. I first thought of 'Alice's Adventures Under Ground', but that was pronounced too like a lesson-book, in which instruction about mines would be administered in the form of a grill; then I took 'Alice's Golden Hour', but that I gave up, having a dark suspicion that there is already a book called 'Lily's Golden Hours'. Here are the other names I have thought of:

$$\text{Alice among the} \begin{cases} \text{elves} \\ \text{goblins} \end{cases}$$

$$\text{Alice's} \begin{cases} \text{hour} \\ \text{doings} \\ \text{adventures} \end{cases} \text{in} \begin{cases} \text{elf-land} \\ \text{wonderland} \end{cases}$$

Of all these I at present prefer 'Alice's Adventures in Wonderland'. In spite of your 'morality', I want something sensational. Perhaps you can suggest a better name than any of these.

At the same time, Dodgson was still completing the illustrations for the manuscript *Alice's Adventures Under Ground*, which was to be given to Alice Liddell. Though he drew a portrait of Alice herself on the last page—and later covered it with a photograph of her—his model for the other drawings seems to have been not her but (as one of his biographers, Anne Clark, has suggested) probably her younger sister Edith. As for Tenniel's drawings, Dodgson does not seem to have entertained the idea that he should portray any of the Liddell sisters. He sent Tenniel a photograph of Mary Hilton Badcock, a small girl of his acquaintance who had long blonde hair held back with a band. Tenniel did not use her, or any other child, as a live model—Dodgson thought him 'mistaken' in this—but his pictures of Alice do bear some resemblance to this photograph.

Dodgson had hoped that *Alice's Adventures in Wonderland*, the title he had finally chosen,

would be published in time for Christmas 1864; but by October of that year Tenniel had finished only one drawing, and the next month the artist's mother died, which caused him great distress. Macmillan agreed with Dodgson's suggestion of postponing publication until Easter 1865, but Tenniel was dilatory, and did not hand in his final drawings until June. The Clarendon Press moved fast, and had 2,000 copies ready by the end of that month; one of them, bound in white vellum, was sent to Alice Liddell. Dodgson called at Macmillan's and inscribed about twenty presentation copies—whereupon he heard from Tenniel that the artist was 'entirely dissatisfied with the printing of the pictures'. Dodgson took this criticism very seriously and decided to scrap the whole edition, even though he looked like losing nearly £500 as a result. He took pains to recover the presentation copies (eighteen were returned to him), and eventually bound copies and unbound sheets were sold to D. Appleton & Co. of New York, who would issue them as the first American edition in 1866.

The printing was now entrusted to the firm of Richard Clay, who had a new edition ready during the autumn. The book was at last published in November 1865, bearing the date 1866 on the title page, this being common practice at the time. Dodgson was delighted with the book's appearance.

Reviews were mixed. The *Athenaeum* thought it a 'stiff, over-wrought story', and *The Times* had more to say about the pictures than the text, though it called it 'an excellent piece of nonsense'. However, the *Court Circular* said: 'If there be such a thing as perfection in children's tales, we should be tempted to say that Mr Carroll had reached it.' The *Sunderland Herald* was one of the few journals to perceive the crucial fact that 'it has no moral, and . . . does not teach anything. It . . . is without any of that bitter foundation which some people imagine ought to be at the bottom of all children's books.'

Despite the largely lukewarm critical reception, sales were good, and by the end of 1866 the book was being reprinted (3,000 copies), with further reprints a year and two years later. By 1870 sales had reached 25,000. In 1898, the year of Dodgson's death, the total given for Britain alone, in an advertisement by the publisher, was 86,000 copies of the red-cloth original edition, and a further 70,000 of the green-cloth 'People's Edition'. Nevertheless the book and its author did not appear in

the popularity poll in Edward Salmon's **Juvenile Literature As It Is* (1888).

During his lifetime Dodgson retained control of all aspects of publication, and sometimes called in copies which did not come up to his very high standard of printing. These were then often presented by him to hospitals or other charitable institutions. A 'People's Edition', revised and reset, was issued by Macmillan in December 1887, and included as a postscript 'An Easter Greeting to Every Child Who Loves "Alice"', first printed privately for Dodgson to distribute to child friends and then issued by Macmillan as a separate pamphlet in 1880. Dodgson also produced a version of the story rewritten for children up to the age of five, *The *Nursery 'Alice'* (1889).

After copyright expired in 1907, innumerable publishers in England and America produced their own editions. Illustrators in the century since have included Arthur *Rackham (1907), Mabel Lucie *Attwell (1910), Willy *Pogany (1929), Mervyn *Peake (1947), Ralph Steadman (1967), Salvador Dali (1969, limited edition), Tove *Jansson (1977, first published in Sweden in 1966), Helen Oxenbury (1999, winning the *Greenaway Medal) and most recently Robert *Ingpen (2009). There is also an exceptional *pop-up adaptation by Robert *Sabuda (2003).

Despite the difficulties of translating the book into other languages, Dodgson arranged for versions in French (1869), German (1869), and Italian (1872) to be made, choosing the translators himself and paying critical attention to their work. During his lifetime, translations into Swedish (1870), Danish (1875), Dutch (c.1875), and Russian (1879) also appeared, but these were made independently of Dodgson and Macmillan and at least one of them was a piracy. To date, the book has been translated into over 150 languages (with more than 7,600 editions and reprints). Warren Weaver's *Alice in Many Tongues* (1964) is devoted to this subject, and in the US a collaborative project on the translations is working towards publication.

Dodgson took a keen interest in the first adaptation of the book for the professional stage, an operetta by Henry Savile Clarke first performed in 1886. Since then, *plays have been made of it again and again. The book was first filmed in 1903; it ran for about twelve minutes and was the longest film so far produced in Britain. Later screen adaptations include a Paramount version of 1934, a cartoon

by *Disney in 1951, and a television film by Jonathan Miller (1966) in which the creatures of Wonderland were portrayed as typical members of Victorian society.

Martin Gardner's *Annotated Alice* (1960) prints the originals of the poems and songs which Dodgson parodies in the story. These parodies, which George Eliot told Edmund *Evans she 'strongly objected' to, are almost invariably of verses that were well known to 19th-cent. child readers, and which were typical of the literary diet of Victorian nurseries. Isaac *Watts's 'How doth the little busy bee' and ''Tis the voice of the sluggard' reappear as 'How doth the little crocodile' and ''Tis the voice of the Lobster'; Mary *Howitt's '"Will you walk into my parlour?" said the spider to the fly' becomes the Lobster Quadrille; Jane *Taylor's celebrated poem 'The Star' is reborn as 'Twinkle, twinkle, little bat!'; and Robert *Southey's 'The Old Man's Comforts' becomes 'You are old, Father William'. The extreme sentimentality of attitude towards very young children sometimes shown in the 19th cent.— Dodgson himself, in other moods, frequently indulged in it—is ridiculed in the Duchess's song, 'Speak roughly to your little boy, | And beat him when he sneezes', and in the episode of the baby turning into a pig. The dry-as-dust *books of instruction given to children are mocked in the Mouse's Tale ('This is the driest thing I know') and in the nonsensical recitations of geography and scientific facts by Alice herself. The book's nose-thumbing attitude to the banal didacticism of the *moral tale, which for many years dominated English children's literature, is expressed by the Duchess's assertion that 'Everything's got a moral, if only you can find it', followed a moment later by an example of a nonsense moral: 'Take care of the sense, and the sounds will take care of themselves.'

Alice encouraged a number of children's authors to write stories of the same sort. One of the earliest imitations was *Mopsa the Fairy* (1869) by Jean *Ingelow; others include *Speaking Likenesses* (1874) by Christina *Rossetti, *Davy and the Goblins* (1884) and *The Admiral's Caravan* (1891) by the American writer Charles E. *Carryl, *Down the Snow Stairs* (1887) by Alice *Corkran and *Katawampus* (1895) by Edward Abbott *Parry (both unusual in that they combine Wonderland-type plots and characters with an old-fashioned moral purpose), *Wanted—a King* (1890) by 'Maggie Browne', *The Wallypug of Why* (1895) by G.E. *Farrow, and *David Blaize and the Blue Door*

(1919) by E. F. Benson. Most of the imitations failed to come near the standard of *Alice*, and only Carroll himself possessed the skill to copy it successfully—arguably, even to improve on it—in *Through the Looking-Glass* (1871). On the other hand two very different books, the characteristically American *Wonderful Wizard of Oz* (1900) and the equally characteristically Australian *Dot and the Kangaroo* (1899) managed to learn from Dodgson without trying to copy him. *The *Phantom Tollbooth* (1961) by Norton *Juster recaptures the *Alice* style more naturally than do most other imitations (though according to Juster, he had never read *Alice* at the time he wrote it).

Alice is not an invariable favourite with children, many of whom are frightened or puzzled by it. On the other hand its admirers have included countless well-known authors, some of whom, such as W. H. Auden, Walter *De La Mare, and Robert Graves, have written critical essays on it. A selection of these, together with Freudian, Jungian, and other interpretations of the story, is to be found in *Aspects of Alice* (1972) edited by Robert Phillips.

In tribute to the book's genesis, 'Alice's Day' is today commemorated annually in Oxford.

Alice's Adventures Under Ground The first version of *Alice's Adventures in Wonderland*. Dodgson presented the 90-page illustrated manuscript, bound in green morocco, to Alice Liddell on 16 November 1864, inscribed: 'A Christmas Gift to a Dear Child in Memory of a Summer Day'. The book was kept by her until 1928, when it was auctioned at Sotheby's and was bought by A. S. W. *Rosenbach for £15,400; he shortly afterwards resold it, with two copies of the first edition of *Alice's Adventures in Wonderland*, for almost twice the price. In 1948 it was bought by a group of Americans, including Rosenbach, and convened by the then Librarian of the Library of Congress, who presented it to the British Museum in appreciation of Britain's part in two World Wars.

In 1886 Dodgson arranged for Macmillan to issue a facsimile, with an introduction by himself. Further facsimile editions have since been printed.

Alice's Adventures Under Ground differs from *Alice's Adventures in Wonderland* chiefly in that it is much shorter, there being no 'Pig and Pepper' or 'Mad Tea Party' chapters. Instead of the Duchess there are references to a 'Marchioness', but she turns out to be the

Queen of Hearts. There are also a number of private jokes: the party of animals dries itself after the wetting in the Pool of Tears by going to 'a little cottage', a reference to an expedition on 17 June 1862 when the Liddell girls, Dodgson, and his friend Robinson Duckworth dried themselves at a riverside house after a soaking in the rain. Duckworth had a fine singing voice, and at one point Alice says: 'How nicely the Duck sang to us as we came along through the water.' Instead of the Lobster Quadrille, the Gryphon and the Mock Turtle sing a refrain: 'Salmon come up! Salmon go down!', a burlesque on 'Sally come up', which was often sung by the Liddell children.

Alice Through the Looking-Glass *See* THROUGH THE LOOKING-GLASS.

ALIKI (Aliki Liacouras Brandenberg) (1929–) American writer and illustrator, born in New Jersey to Greek parents, who studied at the Philadelphia Museum School of Art. Her first book, *The Story of William Tell* (1960) was written during a brief spell living in Switzerland with her Swiss husband. She has written and illustrated both fiction and carefully researched *non-fiction on a wide variety of subjects, including occasional collaborations with other writers, among them her husband, Franz (1932–).

ALLAN, Mabel Esther (1915–98) British author of about 130 popular novels for teenage girls, including *career novels (e.g. *Ballet for Drina*, 1957, the first in a long Drina series written as 'Jean Estoril'), *school stories, and thrillers.

ALLEN, Pamela (1934–) One of Australia and New Zealand's finest creators of picture books, who by 2013 had illustrated fifty books, many of them award winners. Her most famous books include *Who Sank the Boat?* (1982), which gained an *IBBY Honour Diploma for Illustration in 1984, and the *Mr McGee* books. (The books in this series sparked a mixed response as on one occasion Mr McGee is shown naked.) Other titles include *Mr Archimedes's Bath* (1980—her debut), *Bertie and the Bear* (1983, *CBCA award), *A Lion in the Night* (1985), and *Belinda* (1992).

Allen often uses poetic techniques, notably onomatopoeia and repetition, and her texts are known for their strong rhythm. She has a light touch, and a whimsical writing style featuring a strong point of view and humour. The characters are very expressive and her illustrations are known for their use of white space,

beautiful composition with clear typography, and lively movement. Her usual technique is watercolour with pen and ink, and her work is always fresh and original with strong themes cleverly handled.

In 2004 Allen received New Zealand's most prestigious award for children's literature, the *Margaret Mahy Medal. She has won or been shortlisted for many other awards and has been translated into French, Swedish, and Japanese. In 2005 she was made a member of the Order of New Zealand in recognition of her services to children's literature.

ALLINGHAM, William (1824–89) Anglo-Irish poet and friend of the Pre-Raphaelites, who wrote 'The Fairies', a six-stanza poem (based on a traditional Scottish verse) beginning

> Up the airy mountain,
> Down the rushy glen,
> We daren't go a-hunting
> For fear of little men.

It has been a favourite in children's anthologies since its publication in 1850; the first to include it was Coventry Patmore's *Children's Garland* (1862). In 1883 it was published as a separate book with illustrations by E. Gertrude Thomson. Allingham was commissioned to write a verse text for *In Fairy Land* (1870), a book designed to display lavish *colour pictures drawn by Richard *Doyle and printed by Edmund *Evans. Allingham's *Rhymes for the Young Folk* was published in 1887, with illustrations by Harry *Furniss, Kate *Greenaway, and others.

His wife Helen Allingham (*née* Paterson) illustrated a number of children's books, among them novels by Mrs *Ewing.

All-of-a-Kind Family (1951) The first in a series by Sydney Taylor (1904–78), who based it on her own experiences of growing up in a Jewish family in Manhattan's Lower East Side. It's a humble immigrant family of five girls: Ella, Henny, Sarah (aka Sydney herself), Charlotte, and Gertie; the girls are close and their lives are full of small-scale adventure. There were four sequels. Following Taylor's death, her husband set up the Sydney Taylor Book Award to recognize the best Jewish children's books published in the US.

All things bright and beautiful A children's hymn by Mrs C. F. *Alexander.

ALMEDINGEN E. M. (Martha Edith von Almedingen) (1898–1971) Born in St Petersburg, Almedingen came to England in 1923;

she wrote fiction for children and adults, much of it set in pre-Revolutionary Russia. She also produced non-fiction books about Russia. Many of her novels are based on her own family's history; *Anna* (1972), her last children's book, is the story of her great-grandmother's upbringing in a wealthy Russian merchant household.

ALMOND, David (1951–) British novelist, born in Newcastle in the north-east of England, the setting for most of his work. Almond came quickly to prominence with the publication of his first work for older children and teenagers, *Skellig*, in 1998, which was followed a year later by *Kit's Wilderness*, and a further series of distinctively voiced novels that include *The Fire-Eaters* (2003), set against the backdrop of the Cuban Missile Crisis; and *Clay* (2005), in which Davie meets Stephen Rose—the new kid in town—who might have strange, dark powers.

While set in a familiar, real world, Almond's novels are infused with a sense of things unexplained, with energies that lie behind everyday, solid objects, with spirits and inspirations underlying the natural world. His rich prose and sophisticated concerns have made him a critical success, with his books also appreciated by adult readers. (Indeed, like many so-called 'teen writers', Almond prefers not to describe himself as writing for any one particular age group.) He has also published books for younger children, including *My Dad's a Birdman* (2007), illustrated by Polly *Dunbar; and collaborated with artist Dave *McKean on *The Savage* (2008) and *Slog's Dad* (2010). His haunting Orpheus-inspired *A Song for Ella Gray* won him the 2015 *Guardian Children's Fiction Prize; he has also won the *Carnegie Medal and the *Whitbread Children's Book Award (twice), and in 2010 was named recipient of the prestigious international medal, the *Hans Christian Andersen Award.

A.L.O.E. ('A Lady of England') Pseudonym of **Charlotte Maria Tucker** (1821–93), who between the 1850s and 1890s wrote many *evangelical novels for children which were notably strict and didactic even by the standards of the times. The daughter of an Indian civil servant, she underwent a conversion to evangelical beliefs, and at the age of fifty-four decided to become a missionary in India, where she worked with great success for the rest of her life. Her writing made much use of allegory, for example in *The Giant Killer, or the battle which all must fight* (1856).

Her books were very widely read in her time; among them are *Wings and Stings* (1855), an animal *fable, *The Story of a Needle* (1858), *The Rambles of a Rat* (1857), and *The Crown of Success* (1863), an allegory in which four children are left under the guardianship of the old gentleman Learning, and compete to win the crown for the best-furnished head.

alphabet *See* ABC BOOKS.

ALTHEA (Althea Braithwaite) (1940–) British children's author, illustrator, and publisher, who founded her own publishing company to promote her small-format picture books for very young children. These included a popular fifteen-book series about *Desmond the Dinosaur* (1967–89)—the company was called Dinosaur Publications. Much of her prolific output was simply illustrated non-fiction books for young children (originally written for her son), including the *Talk It Over* (1973–89) and *Choices* (1997–99) series. Some of them were researched with children themselves.

ALTSHELER, Joseph A. (Alexander) (1862–1919) Popular and prolific American boys' writer, author of such books as *The Young Trailers: a story of early Kentucky* (1907), and novels about the Civil War, for example *The Guns of Bull Run* (1914).

Amazing Grace (1991) A picture book by Mary *Hoffman, beautifully illustrated by Caroline Binch. Grace is a girl who 'loves stories', until, one day, she asks to play the part of Peter Pan in her school play. She is told she can't—not only is she a girl, but she is also black. It was a groundbreaking picture book that openly challenged racism and essentialist notions of race whilst celebrating multicultural communities (*see* MULTICULTURALISM). It has become hugely successful in both the UK and the US, selling over a million and a half copies worldwide. There are a further six 'Grace' stories in the series.

Amazing Maurice and His Educated Rodents, The (2001) A novel by Terry *Pratchett, a twist on the *Pied Piper story, in which Maurice, a cat, leads a team of rats from village to village to make the villagers believe there's a rodent infestation from which flute-playing Keith (who is also in on the scam) can deliver them. While set in Pratchett's much-loved *Discworld, *The Amazing Maurice* . . . stands apart from its series predecessors in narrative terms, and is the first Discworld

novel written for younger readers. Though Pratchett had been much loved for two decades before the appearance of *The Amazing Maurice...*, it was this book that earned him his first major award, when it was named winner of the 2001 *Carnegie Medal.

Amber Spyglass, The The concluding book in the *His Dark Materials* trilogy by Philip *Pullman.

AMBRUS, Victor G. (Gyozo) (Laszlo) (1935–) Artist and creator of *picture books, who was born in Budapest. He left Hungary in 1956 and came to live in England, taking a diploma at the Royal College of Art. He began his book career before graduation, illustrating stories by Rosemary *Sutcliff, K. M. *Peyton (the *Flambards* trilogy), and many others. He produced his first picture book in 1965, *The Three Poor Tailors*, which won him the *Kate Greenaway Medal. Among his later picture books are *Brave Soldier Janosh* (1967), a version of the Hungarian story of Háry János, *The Little Cockerel* (1968), and *The Sultan's Bath* (1971). Besides these stories, which strongly reflect his Hungarian upbringing, he has produced such non-fiction books as *Horses in Battle* (1975). This again won him the Kate Greenaway Medal, awarded jointly to it and to his picture book *Mishka* (1975). He has also illustrated various retellings by James Riordan and Geraldine *McCaughrean, the 1980s reissues of the *Billy Bunter books, and his own Dracula series (from 1980). He has latterly become better known as the resident artist on Channel 4's *Time Team* TV programme.

Amelia Bedelia A harebrained maidservant who takes all instructions literally, in stories by Peggy *Parish.

Ameliaranne A resourceful small girl in stories by Constance Heward (1884–1968) (*Ameliaranne and the Green Umbrella*, 1920, and others, some by different authors).

American Library Association (ALA) Founded in 1876, this is the oldest (and largest) library association in the world. The ALA administers a number of prestigious children's book awards, including the *Caldecott Medal, the *Newbery Medal, the *Michael L. Printz Award, and the *Laura Ingalls Wilder Award. It also records examples of challenged and *banned books in the US.

American Spelling Book, The A *primer by the celebrated American lexicographer Noah Webster (1758–1843). It was his first published work, being issued in 1783 as Part I of *A Grammatical Institute of the English Language, comprising an easy, concise, and systematic method of education, designed for the use of English schools in America*. In 1787 a new edition, thoroughly revised by Webster, was issued as *The American Spelling Book*. Webster revised it again in 1804, and in 1829 it was retitled *The Elementary Spelling Book*.

It was Webster's goal to promote an American culture and spelling, and the book was just one of his efforts to achieve this. The main part of it does not differ much in content from the typical spelling-books and primers of the period, but it is preceded by an 'Analysis of Sounds in the English Language', and was influential in the establishment of standard American spelling and punctuation. Some editions carried a portrait of Webster, so crudely engraved that it made him look like a porcupine; it is said to have frightened many child readers from their lessons.

American Sunday-School Union An interdenominational organization founded in 1817 to establish *Sunday schools 'without distinction of sect, or creed, or custom'. In 1830 it deliberately set out to create an indigenous children's literature, and began to publish large numbers of stories of the type first popularized in England by Hannah *More in her *Cheap Repository Tracts. In contrast with the American Tract Society (*see* RELIGIOUS TRACT SOCIETY) it commissioned American writers to produce stories with American subjects and settings; the results were usually published anonymously, often with the statement that the book was 'Revised by the Committee of Publication'. The Union took care to make its wares attractive, and chose some of the best illustrators of the day. Its books played a large part in the lives of American children for about three decades from 1830, until the public *library movement began to provide more attractive literature for the masses.

American Tract Society *See* RELIGIOUS TRACT SOCIETY.

AMICIS, Edmondo De *See* CUORE.

Ami des enfans *See* CHILDREN'S FRIEND.

Ananse (Anansi the spider) A trickster from African and West Indian mythology. Stories about him have been collected in Ghana by Peggy *Appiah, while West Indian versions of Ananse stories appear in a *Brer Anansi* series by David P. Makhanlall (*The Best of Brer

Anansi, 1973, et al.). Sir George Dasent includ-
ed 'Ananzi' tales in the second edition of his
**Popular Tales from the Norse* (1859).

Anastasia Krupnik (1979) A novel by Lois
*Lowry. Ten-year-old Anastasia Krupnik is
bookish and funny and keeps a green note-
book in which she writes ever-changing lists of
her likes and dislikes. Her teacher doesn't ap-
preciate her, her grandmother has dementia,
and, worst of all, her mother is going to have a
baby! There are eight further books in the
series. Anastasia's younger brother Sam fea-
tures in four books of his own.

Anatole A French mouse in stories by the
American writer Eve Titus (1922–2002), with
illustrations by Paul *Galdone. The first book
in the series appeared in 1956.

ANDERSEN, Hans Christian (1805–75)
Danish writer, the author of over 150 *fairy
stories and other tales, either of his own in-
vention or based on folk themes, many of
which have become international classics of
children's literature. Andersen was born and
brought up in Odense, then the second city of
Denmark, the only son of a free-thinking shoe-
maker who loved literature but was embit-
tered by his lack of formal education and by
the fantasy that he came from a family of
prosperous, even aristocratic, origin, brought
down by misfortune. Andersen's mother was
almost illiterate and deeply superstitious; she
was fifteen years her husband's senior, and
had an older, illegitimate daughter, brought
up elsewhere. But the family seems to have
ranked among the respectable poor and An-
dersen considered his childhood happy. He
was not aware of want, a greater embarrass-
ment being the insanity of his paternal grand-
father, which contributed to his lifelong fear
that he would go mad himself.

Andersen's father doted on him, and read to
him from the **Arabian Nights*, *La Fontaine,
and Danish dramatic works; he made him *toy
theatres, and took him to the Odense play-
house. Andersen recalled in his autobiography
that, because such a visit could only seldom be
afforded, he made friends with the distributor
of the playbills, was given one every day, and
'with this I seated myself in a corner and
imagined an entire play, according to the
name of the piece and the characters in it.
That was my first, unconscious poetizing'.

He went to local schools, and often visited
the spinning-room of the asylum and work-
house where his grandmother tended the

garden; there he would trade embroidered
scraps of schoolroom information for the folk
songs and tales of the spinners.

The boy was eleven years old at the time of
his father's death; shortly afterwards he left
school and worked briefly in local factories.
However, he had a good singing voice, man-
aged to work his way into walk-on parts in the
local theatre, and began to be known among
the local bourgeoisie for his singing and dra-
matic recitations. This culminated in an inter-
view with the Crown Prince of Denmark. But
the boy was then bitterly disappointed at
being told that he should learn a trade before
embarking on any more sensational career;
and he decided, at the age of fourteen, to
take all his savings and go to Copenhagen.

He knew no one there. An Odense well-
wisher gave him an introduction to the leading
ballerina at the Royal Theatre in Copenhagen;
but when he presented it, took off his boots in
front of her, and improvised a dramatic scene
complete with singing and dancing, she
thought him mad. He managed to talk his
way into the house of the director of the
Royal Theatre's song school, and impressed
him and his dinner guests enough for them
to collect subscriptions to support him while
he was taught music. During the next three
years he had small parts at the theatre, and
submitted plays to it anonymously, without
success. Then his voice broke, and he could
no longer work.

Rescue this time came from Jonas Collin, a
senior civil servant and governor of the Royal
Theatre. Collin became Andersen's most not-
able benefactor, and the whole family grew to
be his lifelong friends; Edvard, Collin's son,
eventually came to manage much of the busi-
ness of publishing Andersen's work, including
correcting his always uncertain spelling.

Collin secured a royal grant for Andersen to
be educated at a state grammar school, but
this belated education was an unhappy expe-
rience. At seventeen he was put in a class of
twelve-year-olds; the headmaster mocked and
bullied him, and he had to go to a private tutor
before, at the age of twenty-three, passing the
university matriculation examination that was
the passport to the professional classes. He
now openly chose the career of writer, had a
play performed, and fell in love.

The first of his series of unrequited passions
was for Riborg Voigt, sister of a fellow student.
She appeared attracted to him but was already
informally engaged, and Andersen made the
strange gesture of both declaring his love for

her and renouncing her to his rival at the same time. Meeting her long afterwards led to his writing *The Sweethearts*, a tale about a superior morocco leather ball which refuses to become engaged to a spinning top; years later the ball lies rotting in the rubbish bin, while the top is honoured and respected. At Andersen's death a letter from her was found hanging in a pouch at his neck.

Andersen now had to support himself by writing; he published poetry, librettos, translations, and travel books, and became a phenomenon of some interest, though also of amusement, to sophisticated Danish society. His social awkwardness was still obvious, and he was physically ungainly, tall, with a large nose and small eyes; his emotions, both of joy and despair, were generally extreme and unrestrained, and his persistence in reading his own works aloud at every opportunity, coupled with an absurd sensitivity to criticism, incurred complaints about his vanity and egotism, though at the same time he was acknowledged to be witty and good company.

His next love was Louise, younger daughter of Jonas Collin, who as a young girl had always taken his part against family teasing. She was fond of him, but was careful not to give him any encouragement, and was soon engaged to someone else. Andersen took revenge by casting her as the haughty princess in *The *Swineherd*, and as the prince in *The *Little Mermaid*. To recover from his disappointment he travelled extensively in Germany, France, and Italy, sketching and keeping diaries, and gathering material for his novel *The Improvisatore* (1835), which effectively made his international reputation.

The small, cheap booklet that came out later the same year was in complete contrast. It was called *Eventyr fortalte for Børn*, 'Tales told for Children'. The word 'eventyr', generally rendered 'fairy stories', is in fact related to 'adventure', and has the sense of a short fantastic story for any age of reader. Andersen wrote to a friend: 'I have done a couple of stories I remember having liked when little, and that I think are not generally known. I have written them exactly as I would tell them to a child.' In fact three of the stories were based on folk tales: *The *Tinderbox*, 'Little Claus and Big Claus', and *The *Princess on the Pea*. The fourth, *Little Ida's Flowers*, was Andersen's own invention.

Critics complained at the roughness of Andersen's deliberately colloquial style, at the immorality of 'Big Claus and Little Claus' (which hints at adultery involving a church official), and at the lack of instructive content, given the intended audience of children. But more of the tales followed, generally in small batches every Christmas, and by the end of ten years both Andersen and his public were agreed in recognizing his mastery of this form of story.

Andersen wrote that 'how much could be accomplished through the fairy tale became clearer and clearer to me as I learned through the years of my own power and its limitations'; and the proportion of his tales that were wholly original increased as time passed. Ideas for these, he said, 'lay in my mind like seeds and only needed a gentle touch—the kiss of a sunbeam or drop of malice—to flower'. He frequently used his stories to revenge himself on detractors and enemies, and even his retellings of folk stories were personal: 'Most of what I have written is a reflection of myself. Every character is from life.'

Andersen's last unrequited love gave another deeper meaning to his story of the nightingale. Jenny Lind, nicknamed 'The Swedish Nightingale', gave her first performances in Denmark in 1843. Andersen had already met her, knew of her phenomenal singing voice, and noted that like him she had risen by artistry from lowly origins. Now he wrote in his diary: 'I love her.' Jenny Lind, however, much as she liked Andersen's company, did not love him. They remained friends and continued to meet socially, but from this point he seems to have accepted that he would remain single. *The Nightingale* was a celebration of Jenny Lind's voice and natural style, triumphing over the fashionable artificiality of Italian operatic convention. He wrote that her art had a more ennobling influence on him than any books or men.

He continued to write and to travel, though his love of going abroad was always warring with a terror of missing trains, losing his passport, or being burnt alive in his hotel. (He always carried a coil of rope in his luggage.) In Berlin he became a friend of the brothers *Grimm, though their first meeting was blighted by Jacob's never having heard of him. He visited England and Scotland in 1847, and met Mary *Howitt, who was one of his English translators, and Charles *Dickens. He was generally so enchanted with his reception that he sent five stories to be published in England in 1848, six weeks ahead of their Danish appearance, entitled *A Christmas*

Greeting to my English Friends and dedicated to Dickens. The friendship remained warm until Andersen overstayed his welcome in 1857, when he was invited for two weeks to Dickens's house and stayed for five, apparently oblivious of the family strain around him. He was never asked back, and Dickens stuck up a card on the dressing-room mirror of the spare room: 'Hans Andersen slept in this room for five weeks—which seemed to the family AGES!' But in general Andersen was welcome in the houses of the cultured and aristocratic all over Europe. His autobiography, *The Fairy Tale of My Life* (1855), is full of his pride in this achievement. In his last years he was given a home by the Melchiors, a banking family in Copenhagen, and he died at their summer villa, at the age of seventy, of cancer of the liver. His last fairy tales were published in 1872; the second collected edition of 156 fairy tales and longer stories appeared in 1874, the year before his death.

Selections of Hans Andersen's stories first appeared in English in 1846. Mary Howitt's *Wonderful Stories for Children* contained ten tales, and two other selections by different translators came out in the same year: Charles Boner's version, *A Danish Story-Book*, was published in February, just after the Howitt edition, and Caroline Peachey's translation, *Danish Fairy Legends and Tales*, appeared in May. Andersen's work was immediately naturalized into English children's literature, and was the second great element, after Grimm, in the revival of public enthusiasm for fairy tale and fantasy. However, another collection, published in 1847, was introduced as being distinguished by containing 'those pieces which seemed most suitable for *juvenile* reading', and translators often softened or bowdlerized Andersen's work: *The Princess on the Pea* was even modified by one of them, presumably for reasons of delicacy, to *The Princess and the Bean*. Andersen's humour, his colloquial diction, and his deliberate storyteller's gestures and roughness of style were often lost. His reputation for sentimentality is also partly the fault of his translators, though something close to the sentimental can be found in many of the tales, as well as a vein of what Naomi *Lewis called 'submissive, almost superstitious piety'.

Andersen was adamant that he was writing for all ages. He eventually dropped 'told for children' from the title of his tales, and he was furious at a proposal for a statue to depict him surrounded by children. He wrote in his autobiography: 'I had arrived at the conviction that people of different ages were equally amused by the tales. The children made themselves merry for the most part over what might be called the actors; older people, on the contrary, were interested in the deeper meaning.' His ability to humanize the inanimate, or elements of nature, or household objects, does seem appropriate for children; on the other hand his humour, the veiled autobiographical element in his stories, and his treatment of such themes as love, changes of fortune and status, grief, and death, are only fully appreciated by adults. In one of his last stories, 'The Cripple', a bedridden boy reads aloud from a book of fairy tales to his work-bowed family; the father is entranced by two of the stories, which are 'like two sun rays in the warped, cowed soul of the man'; and the book of fairy stories carries Hans, the crippled boy, 'where his legs refuse to go—out into the world beyond the cottage walls'.

Andersen's life and stories were used as the basis of a Hollywood film starring Danny Kaye, *Hans Christian Andersen* (1952), which, though a sentimental travesty of the true facts, contained several songs by Frank Loesser that became popular with children, most notably 'The Ugly Duckling'.

Andersen's influence may be seen in English fairy stories of the later 19th cent., though he was not often imitated successfully—an exception being Oscar Wilde's *The *Happy Prince* (1888).

Innumerable artists have illustrated English editions of Andersen (not to mention individual stories), ranging from the highly unsuitable Mabel Lucie *Attwell (1913) to Arthur *Rackham (1932), Rex Whistler (1935), Val *Biro (2005), Emma *Chichester Clark (1999, retold by Naomi Lewis; and 2010, retold by Martin *Waddell), and Joel *Stewart (2004, Lewis again).

Andersen Award *See* Hans Christian Andersen Award.

ANDERSON, Alexander (1775–1870) American wood engraver, son of a printer in New York City. He taught himself *copperplate engraving at the age of twelve, using rolled-out pennies as plates; eight years later he first saw *Bewick's work, and was inspired by it to become the first American to practise sophisticated wood engraving, as opposed to merely making crude *woodcuts. He subsequently produced his own version of Bewick's *History of Quadrupeds*. Among many books illustrated

by him were editions of *Aesop, John *Aikin's *Calendar of Nature*, *Berquin's *Looking-Glass for the Mind*, *Foxe's Book of Martyrs*, The *Pilgrim's Progress*, *Robinson Crusoe*, and *Sandford and Merton*. He contributed engravings to the influential American *nursery rhyme collection *Mother Goose's Melodies* (1833). He was a qualified doctor of medicine.

ANDERSON, C. W. *See* BILLY AND BLAZE.

ANDERSON, Laurie Halse (1961–) American writer best known for her unflinching *young adult fiction, most notably *Speak* (1999), in which Melinda Sordino is the victim of rape and subsequently ostracized at her school; the trauma causes her to withdraw into herself and stop speaking altogether. Anderson returned to the same school setting, and some of the same characters, for her next novel, the painful, powerful *Catalyst* (2002). Other books include *Chains* (2008), which opened Anderson's 'Seeds of America' trilogy, and introduced Isabel, a determined 13-year-old slave girl at the time of the American Revolutionary War. The trilogy continued with *Forge* (2010), and concluded with *Ashes* (2016). *Fever, 1793* (2000) is another historical novel, this time set during Philadelphia's yellow fever epidemic.

ANDERSON, M. T. (Matthew Tobin) (1968–) American writer of ambitious *young adult fiction, whose challenging, thought-provoking, sometimes satirical works include the dystopian novel (*see* DYSTOPIAN FICTION) *Feed* (2002), which tells the futuristic story of an America in which all young people are implanted with a chip—'the feed'—which connects them to a network on which they become dependent. *Feed* was followed by the vast, bold, two-part historical novel, *The Astonishing Life of Octavian Nothing, Traitor to the Nation*. The award-winning first volume, *The Pox Party* (2006), set in Revolution-period Boston, is narrated by Octavian, the son of an African princess; though a slave, Octavian is highly educated, and used as a test to determine whether his race is intellectually inferior to his white masters. The story concludes in *The Kingdom on the Waves* (2008), this volume being an epistolary novel. Anderson has also written picture books and fiction for younger readers.

And Now, Miguel (1953) A novel by Joseph *Krumgold.

ANDREWS, Jane (1833–87) Massachusetts schoolteacher who wrote a series of books in which *geography, *history, and *natural history were taught by means of stories. The best known were *The Seven Little Sisters who Live on the Round Ball that Floats in the Air* (1861), *Ten Boys who Lived on the Road from Long Ago to Now* (1885), and *The Stories Mother Nature Told Her Children* (1888).

Androcles and the Lion A *play by George Bernard Shaw (1856–1950), first produced in London in 1913. The play, which is loosely based on a *fable by the Roman writer Aulus Gellius, is charged with Shaw's usual polemic and wit. It was written because he was contemptuous of *Peter Pan*, and wanted 'to show Barrie how a play for children should be handled'; but much of it is above children's heads, and, though it sometimes receives school performances, it has not gained an important place in the repertoire of children's theatre.

And to Think that I Saw It on Mulberry Street (1937) The first children's book by Dr *Seuss, in which he first used his gift for that now-familiar rhyming, rolling anapaestic tetrameter (also the metre of the title line) to tell a *tall tale dreamed up by Marco as he walks to school and back along Mulberry Street, of all the things he saw on his way.

Andy Pandy A little clown *puppet in the BBC television programme *Watch with Mother*, from 1950 onwards. The stories were told by Maria Bird, who also wrote Andy Pandy books. Andy's friends were Teddy and the rag doll Looby Loo.

Anecdotes and Adventures of Fifteen Gentlemen The second earliest known book of *limericks, published by John *Marshall c.1821, in imitation of *The *History of Sixteen Wonderful Old Women*. Unlike the latter, some of its verses have a new rhyme-word in the last line, e.g.:

> There was a sick man of Tobago
> Lived long on rice-gruel and sago;
> But at last, to his bliss,
> The physician said this:
> 'To a roast leg of mutton you may go.'

This was the limerick that Edward *Lear recalled as having inspired his *Book of Nonsense*.

Anecdotes and Adventures was probably the work of the light verse writer Richard Scrafton Sharpe (c.1775–1852); the illustrations were by George *Cruikshank's elder brother Robert.

Angelica Princess in *The *Rose and the Ring*.

Angelina Ballerina A picture-book series by American writer Katharine Holabird (1948–) and British illustrator Helen Craig (1934–) about a little mouse who dreams of being a famous ballerina and will think of nothing else until she realizes her dream; in the first book in the series, *Angelina Ballerina* (1983), she does just that. Set in the town of Chipping Cheddar in Mouseland, the series now runs to more than twenty books (plus spin-offs, dolls, etc.). The books have been hugely popular with thirty years' worth of young (mostly girl) readers, and their stories have been successfully animated, with Judi Dench providing the voice for Angelina's teacher, Miss Lilly Mouseakova.

Angus A dog in stories by Margery *Flack.

Angus, Thongs and Full-Frontal Snogging The first volume of the 'Confessions of Georgia Nicolson', a ten-book series of comic fictional diaries by Louise *Rennison. In it, we meet fourteen-year-old Georgia, who begins her diaries with the humiliation of attending a costume party dressed as a stuffed olive, and then proceeds accidentally to shave off her own eyebrows. (Rennison claimed many of Georgia's experiences are based on her own.) She is convinced she will never get a boyfriend, and her anxiety about relationships with the opposite sex fuels much of the drama in her life, and much of the comedy in the books. Through the series we meet Robbie (the Sex God), best friend Jas, and the rest of the Georgia's world (including the titular Angus, who is Georgia's cat). With the success of Georgia's distinctive voice (her inventive slang and use of particular cultural references led to the books being published with a glossary for the benefit of non-UK readers) and Rennison's fine comic timing, these very funny books have since spawned countless pale imitations.

ANHOLT, Catherine (1958–) and **Laurence** (1959–) Multi-award-winning British husband-and-wife picture-book team, who met at art school and have been in constant professional collaboration ever since. Most famous of their joint creations is perhaps the *Chimp and Zee* series (which gave its name to the Dorset bookshop they owned for a time, 'Chimp and Zee, Bookshop by the Sea'). Their picture books for young children are often about family life, and are based on their own. The 'Anholt's Artists' series, which Laurence Anholt illustrated as well as writing, tells well-researched stories of real children who met great artists—it began with *Camille and the Sunflowers* (1994); other titles include *Degas and the Little Dancer* (1996) and *The Magical Garden of Claude Monet* (2003). Between them—in collaboration and apart—the Anholts have produced over 200 books, and have been translated into thirty languages.

Animals of Farthing Wood, The (1979) The first book in a series of the same name by Colin Dann (1943–). It tells the story of a group of animals forced to flee their homes in Farthing Wood, which is under threat of development, and undertake the perilous journey together to White Deer Park, a distant nature reserve, facing countless obstacles and adventures along their way. The group is led by Fox and Badger; it is Badger who suggests that all the animals (many of them natural predators of their travelling companions) take an oath not to harm one another as they make their journey—The Oath of Mutual Protection. There were a number of sequels, including *The Fox Cub Bold* (1983).

animal stories These were available to children from the earliest days of written literature in the form of *fables. Talking beasts featured in orally transmitted *fairy stories, and fabulous creatures as well as real animals were portrayed in *bestiaries. The beginning of English children's bookselling on a large and regular basis in the mid-18th cent. immediately led to the production of books featuring animals, one of the earliest being John *Newbery's 1752 volume *A *Pretty Book of Pictures for Little Masters and Misses*. In the same publisher's **Goody Two-Shoes* (1765) the heroine befriends and is helped by a number of creatures, while Newbery's *The Valentine's Gift* (1765) includes a character named 'old Zig-Zag' who has a horn which enables him to understand the language of beasts and birds; they tell him about the sufferings inflicted on them by mankind.

From the 1780s full-length stories for children began to appear in which an animal narrated his life history, or played the principal part. The first of such books seems to have been *The *Life and Perambulation of a Mouse* (1783) by Dorothy *Kilner, which may have been suggested by a similar narrative intended for adult readers, *The History of Pompey the Little: or, the Life and Adventures of a Lap-Dog*, published by Mary *Cooper in 1751 and ascribed to Francis Coventry, this being a picaresque tale satirizing human fashion and foibles. Several purposes can be discerned

behind children's books of this kind: to use the animal narrator or hero as an observer of, and commentator upon, human behaviour; to write a *moral tale with animals as principal characters; to persuade children not to inflict cruelty upon animals; and to describe animal behaviour as it actually is. Most stories combined two or more of these purposes. Examples include *Fabulous Histories (later known as The Robins) and The Two Farmers, both written by Mrs *Trimmer and published in 1786; *Keeper's Travels in Search of His Master (1798) by Edward Augustus Kendall; Marvellous Adventures; or, the Vicissitudes of a Cat (1802) by Mrs *Pilkington; The Adventures of Poor Puss (1809) and *Felissa, or the Life and Opinions of a Kitten of Sentiment (1811) by Mrs Ludlow. The theme of human cruelty predominated in the anonymous The Hare, or Hunting Incompatible with Humanity: written as a Stimulus to Youth towards a Proper Treatment of Animals (1799), in which a human father whose family rescues the hare from a hunt observes of the pastime of hunting: 'It has given me much pleasure, my dear children, that none of you display an inclination for this barbarous diversion; so long as you can amuse yourselves rationally, you will never have occasion to recur to it.'

Alongside this serious or semi-serious vein of animal narratives, there appeared in the early 19th cent. a number of comic *poems featuring ridiculous animal antics, most notably *Mother Hubbard (1805) and *Dame Wiggins of Lee (1823). The illustrated poem The *Butterfly's Ball (1806) inspired a number of imitations featuring different members of the animal kingdom.

The early spate of prose animal stories effectively came to an end with two books by 'Arabella Argus', The *Adventures of a Donkey (1815) and Further Adventures of Jemmy Donkey (1821). After this, no notable British work of children's fiction featuring animals appeared until 1855, when *Parables from Nature by Mrs Gatty began to be published. The next decade saw the publication of The *Dog Crusoe (1861) by R. M. *Ballantyne and The True, Pathetic History of Poor Match (1863), describing the experiences of a puppy who is owned by a family of children; it was written by 'Holme Lee' (Harriet Parr), and was the first children's book to be illustrated by Walter *Crane. The animal-as-narrator story, dormant since the days of 'Arabella *Argus', made a brief but brilliant return in 1877 with Anna Sewell's *Black Beauty, which became

one of the bestselling children's books of all time. It was imitated in Marshall Saunders's *Beautiful Joe (1894).

Richard Jefferies' *Wood Magic (1881) introduced a new kind of tale, in which a boy becomes involved in the feuds of the animals and listens to their conversations. In some respects this foreshadowed *Kipling's immensely successful *Jungle Books (1894 and 1895). The same period also saw the publication of Sir John Fortescue's Exmoor tale The *Story of a Red-Deer (1897).

Two Canadian writers pioneered yet another new type of animal story, in which creatures were presented dramatically but realistically: *Wild Animals I Have Known by Ernest Thompson *Seton appeared in 1898, and *Red Fox by Charles G. D. *Roberts in 1905. This lead was followed in America by such writers as Jack *London and Alfred Payson *Terhune.

Meanwhile the fable form had once again appeared. *Uncle Remus (1880), by Joel Chandler *Harris, was an outstanding collection from America, while in England Kenneth *Grahame, in The *Wind in the Willows (1908), and Beatrix *Potter, in many books for young children, used animals as types of human character, and as actors in a predominantly social comedy. This approach typified most British stories about animals between the two World Wars, which ranged from the *Doctor Dolittle books of Hugh *Lofting (1920 onwards) to the *Little Grey Rabbit series by Alison *Uttley (1929 onwards). During this period, Britain produced almost nothing of note in the way of realistic animal narratives, with the exception of Henry *Williamson's books, especially Tarka the Otter (1927). The pseudonymous *Moorland Mousie (1929), in the Black Beauty tradition, was the precursor of *pony stories, which began in earnest with A *Pony for Jean (1936) by Joanna Cannan.

The 1920s, 1930s, and 1940s saw the appearance of many notable Canadian and American animal stories, in which realism predominated. Roderick Haig-Brown's *Ki-Yu: A Story of Panthers (1934) was in the Seton tradition, while The *Yearling (1938) by Marjorie Kinnan Rawlings and *My Friend Flicka (1941) by Mary O'Hara used children's affection for animals to highlight difficult human relationships. Will James's *Smoky, The Cowhorse (1926) was a cowboy version of Black Beauty. Dhan Gopal Mukerji, an Indian writer living in America, produced a number of animal books of which the most

successful was *Gay-Neck, The Story of a Pigeon* (1927). Eric Knight's *Lassie Come-Home* (1940) led to the making of a series of *Lassie films about a heroic collie dog.

Mid-century American writers of animal stories include E. B. *White (with *Charlotte's Web*), Jean Craighead *George, Marguerite *Henry, and Walt *Morey. Modern Canadian books include The *Incredible Journey* (1960), a story on the Lassie model by Sheila Burnford, while in England the outstanding animal story of the period was *Watership Down* (1972) by Richard *Adams. Australia made many contributions to the genre, ranging from Dorothy *Wall's 1930s stories about Blinky Bill the Koala to Elyne Mitchell's *Silver Brumby* series of *horse stories (1958 onwards).

More recently animal stories have been seen as primarily suitable for younger children, often with an element of the fantastical, as the animals generally have voices, speaking among themselves if not to people. This is evidenced in the work of Dick *King-Smith, the talking animals of E. B. White, and popular packaged series *Animal Ark* towards the end of the 20th cent. Newer books regularly have a conservational slant, such as the realistic animal stories of scientists Nicola Davies and Gill Lewis in the UK, or in the US, Katherine *Applegate's *Newbery Medal-winning The One and Only Ivan* (2013), written from the perspective of a gorilla kept in a shopping centre zoo. Applegate is also famed for her popular *Animorph* series, in which five children are given the ability to 'morph' or transform into any animal they touch, in order to slow down an alien invasion. Picture books also commonly focus on animal stories, with Anthony Browne's *Gorilla* (1983) being an obvious example. Books for older children tend to move the animal characters into fantasy, such as the dæmons of Philip Pullman's *His Dark Materials* series or S. F. Said's *Varjak Paw* duology (2003 and 2005), or into allegory, such as Richard Kurti's *Monkey Wars* (2013).

Anna A twelve-year-old orphan in a series of popular realistic novels by Martha Sandwall-Bergström (1913–2000), set in the early 1900s. The series, which begins with *Kulla-Gulla* (1945), has been translated widely.

Annals of the Poor See DAIRYMAN'S DAUGHTER.

Anna Maria Rat in *The Tale of Samuel Whiskers* by Beatrix *Potter.

Anne of Green Gables (1908) A very popular Canadian novel by L. M. *Montgomery. An elderly brother and sister, Matthew and Marilla Cuthbert of Avonlea (a fictitious community in Prince Edward Island, Canada's smallest province), send to an orphanage for a boy to help them on their farm, Green Gables. By mistake they are sent an eleven-year-old girl, with red hair, precocious and talkative. This is Anne Shirley ('but oh, please do call me Cordelia . . . Anne is such an unromantic name'). She picks a fight with anyone who mentions the colour of her hair, causes havoc at Green Gables and in the village, but comes to be much loved. Eventually she wins a scholarship to college, but Matthew dies and she decides to give up the scholarship in order to work as a teacher, look after Marilla, and prevent the sale of Green Gables.

L. M. Montgomery wrote a number of sequels to the original book: *Anne of Avonlea* (1909), *Anne of the Island* (1915), *Anne's House of Dreams* (1917), *Rilla of Ingleside* (1921), *Anne of Windy Poplars* (1936), and *Anne of Ingleside* (1939).

Anne of Green Gables is the most popular and enduring of a host of similar *girls' stories published in the United States and Canada in the first years of the 20th cent., other examples being *Rebecca of Sunnybrook Farm* (1903) and *Pollyanna* (1913). It has been filmed (with about a dozen screen adaptations over the years), staged, and translated into many languages, and continues to find many new readers on both sides of the Atlantic. While the appeal of *Anne of Green Gables* is universally accepted, Sheila Egoff in *The Republic of Childhood* (2nd edn 1975) criticizes the sequels for their 'increasingly sentimental dishonesty'.

Anne's popularity has survived right through the 20th cent. and into the 21st. Her centenary was marked with the release of a prequel, *Before Green Gables*, written by Budge Wilson (2008).

Annie See LITTLE ORPHAN ANNIE.

ANNO, Mitsumasa (1926–) Japanese illustrator and author, famous for creating picture books with no, or almost no, words but with detailed and intricate pictures that encompass many media, from watercolour to collage. He is sometimes compared to M. C. Escher in that his work often includes subtle visual jokes. He worked as a teacher before bringing out his first book, *Fushigi na E* (US title: *Topsy Turvies*) in 1968. His later books include *ABC no*

Hon (US and British title: *Anno's Alphabet*), which was published in 1974. *Anno's Counting Book* (1975) begins with an empty landscape to which features are added one by one. Anno later turned to 'bird's-eye view' landscape books, such as *Anno's Journey* (1977) and *Anno's Britain* (1981), which include details from famous paintings and allusions to well-known children's stories. The Mitsumasa Anno Museum in Tsuwano houses a collection of his works.

annual Since the mid-19th cent. a yearly publication usually associated with a *magazine, but at first less specific in meaning. The first children's annual was a sheet printed in 1645 by the parents of Zurich, for their children to find in the city library, to celebrate the New Year; this *Neujahrsblätter*, or *Neujahrsstücke*, was made up of an engraving and some verse. In England a century later, publishers such as John *Newbery developed a trade in occasional miscellanies, suitable as presents, with such books as *Nurse Truelove's New Year Gift* (by 1753). However, S. G. *Goodrich, alias *Peter Parley, alleged that 'The first work of the annual kind, entitled the *Forget-Me-Not*, was issued by Ackermanns of London, in the winter of 1823, while I was in that city.' He recorded that this form of illustrated miscellany then became the rage.

Children's annuals soon joined in the fashion. T. Crofton *Croker claimed that his *The *Christmas Box* (1828) was first in the field. Among the others was Mrs S. C. Hall's *The *Juvenile Forget Me Not*, which ran from 1828 every year until 1837. From around 1840 this independent form of annual ran side by side with the species that was a magazine's Christmas compendium, such as *Peter Parley's Magazine* and *Annual* (1840 onwards). At first these latter productions were simply bound volumes of a year's periodical parts, perhaps embellished with extra *colour plates. In some cases, however, an annual outlived its parent magazine, by 30 years in the case of *Peter Parley's*.

An unusual case of an annual begetting a magazine, rather than the other way round, was Basil Blackwell's *Joy Street*, in the 1920s.

Annuals in the first half of the 20th cent., in Britain and America, were generally associated with *comic or cartoon characters; in more recent years, while they remain consistently popular, they have evolved from this strong association and are now spawned by a variety of popular interests (television programmes, sports, singers, etc.).

ANSTEY, F. (Thomas Anstey Guthrie) (1856–1934). Born in London, the son of a military tailor, he went to school at Surbiton in Surrey, at an establishment that was the original of 'Crichton House' in his celebrated novel *Vice Versa*, published when he was 25. He wrote many other books, including *Paleface and Redskin* (1898), a collection of short stories for children, and *Only Toys!* (1903), a full-length *fantasy, but he was never able to repeat the commercial and artistic success of *Vice Versa*. He did, however, have a long career as a humorous writer for *Punch*, and he produced one other story which was really popular with children, *The *Brass Bottle* (1900). He originally intended his pseudonym to be 'T. Anstey' (i.e. his first two names), but it was misprinted as 'F. Anstey', and he allowed this to remain.

Ant and Bee Heroes of a series of books for small children by the British writer Angela Banner (1923–2014), published from 1950. Banner wrote them in order to help teach her son to read, so they use predominantly simple recurring vocabulary. There are now thirteen in the series, the most recent (teaching shapes) being *Ant and Bee Go Shopping* (published in 2014 as part of an updated reissue of the series).

Anyhow Stories for Children (1882) A collection by Mrs W. K. Clifford (1846–1929). Chiefly moral in character, the stories have elements of almost gratuitous horror. Most striking is 'The New Mother', in which a naughty brother and sister are told by their mother that to punish them she will go away for ever, and will 'send home a new mother, with glass eyes and a wooden tail'. She carries out her threat, and the children run away from their home at the sound of the new mother's approach—they can hear her wooden tail being dragged along the floor. The story terrified Harvey *Darton in childhood: 'Getting on for fifty years after I met her first, I still cannot rid my mind of that fearful creation.' The *Anyhow Stories* were reprinted several times.

APPIAH, Peggy (1921–2006) *See* ANANSE.

APPLEGATE, K. A. (Katherine Alice) (1956–) American author whose work ranges from picture books to *young adult novels. She co-wrote the series *Everworld* (1999–2001), *Remnants* (2001–3) and *Animorphs* (1996–2001) with her husband, Michael Grant (now also a successful young adult novelist in his own right), though they were published

under her name alone. Many of the *Animorphs* books were ghost-written. The series was adapted for television. Applegate's middle-grade novel *Home of the Brave*, about a Sudanese refugee living in the United States, won the *SCBWI's Golden Kite award. She won the 2013 *Newbery Medal for *The One and Only Ivan*, about a gorilla living in a glass case in a shopping mall. Other titles include the early chapter-book series *Roscoe Riley Rules*.

Apprentices, The *See* GARFIELD'S APPRENTICES.

apps Abbreviated from 'application programs'. With the rise of digital technology and non-paper reading devices (computers, tablets, smartphones, e-readers), the first decade of the 21st cent. saw children's books publishers begin hesitantly to explore the possibilities these advances brought with them, both as delivery mechanisms for conveying (and enhancing) conventionally written stories (not merely seeking to substitute hard-copy books of plain text, but even in some cases offering viably attractive alternatives to full-colour picture books), and as a medium for exploring entirely new kinds of narrative, and for complementing and marketing existing texts. Publishers soon began to experiment with new ways in which stories can be explored beyond merely publishing books electronically, and some of the more technologically ambitious have created, alongside straightforward *e-book versions, more dynamic interactive apps for mobile devices (games associated with the books, etc.) to accompany them—especially for bestselling books or major brands. In some, the 'original' text is essentially unchanged, but surrounded by additional content; in others the very idea of an association with a monolithic print 'original' is anathema—the origins of these story apps, technically immersive and often nonlinear, cannot be separated from the interactivity and multimedia for which they were designed and which define the user's experience. With few exceptions the possibilities have mostly not yet been realized on a large commercial scale, but progress is rapid, and by the time you read this paragraph, it is almost certainly out of date. (It is worth noting, too, that the traffic is not only one-way, with entirely original apps and games frequently leading to spin-off books.)

Arabel's Raven (1972) A collection of stories by Joan *Aiken.

Arabian Nights' Entertainments, or *The One Thousand and One Nights* Arabic collection of tales of diverse origin, assembled over many centuries. Arabic versions of Indian and Persian folk tales probably formed the basis of the collection in the 8th cent., and more stories were then added from across the Arabic-speaking world.

The framing story in which the tales are set concerns Scheherazade, who is determined to delay her royal husband's plan of killing her—he has taken to murdering his wives because the first was unfaithful to him—by telling him a story every evening. She leaves each evening's tale incomplete until the next day, so that he has to spare her life in order to hear its conclusion. He is so entertained that he finally abandons his murderous plan.

The book was introduced to Europe by Antoine *Galland, whose *Mille et une nuits* was published in France between 1704 and 1717. This version was very freely based on a Syrian manuscript of the *Nights*, but three of its most famous stories came from other sources. *Aladdin* and *Ali Baba* had no written Arabic source, and *Sinbad the Sailor* came from a different group of stories. Galland's text remained standard until the mid-19th cent., parts of it even being translated back into Arabic.

Galland's text was translated into English almost as soon as it began to appear in France, a so-called 'Grub Street' English version (named because it was the work of a hackwriter) being issued by *chapbook publishers from about 1706 onwards. *Sindbad* appeared in this version in 1712, and *Aladdin* and *Ali Baba* in 1721–2.

The first English selection from the *Nights* made specially for children was *The Oriental Moralist or the Beauties of the Arabian Nights Entertainments*, published by Elizabeth *Newbery *c*.1791. This was supposedly the work of 'the Revd Mr Cooper', really the hack-writer Richard *Johnson, who alleged in his introduction that he had met with Galland's book at an inn, while travelling on the Continent, and had decided to produce an English version that 'carefully expunged every thing that could give the least offence'. He also added moral reflections, and, as he admitted, 'considerably altered the fables . . . to promote the love of virtue'. The *Nights* can still provoke censorship. In 2010 an attempt by Islamist lawyers in Egypt to have it *banned for obscenity was dismissed, on the grounds that it had been published for centuries, a previous

ruling specifically permitted it, and it had been an inspiration to countless artists.

At the end of the 18th cent. several of the individual stories from the *Nights* began to be printed as separate books for children. The favourites were, of course, *Aladdin, Ali Baba,* and *Sindbad,* but other tales sometimes appeared. Among later collections of stories from the *Nights* retold for children are *Dalziels' Illustrated Arabian Nights' Entertainments* (1863–5) (*see* DALZIEL) with pictures by *Tenniel, Millais, and others; *The Arabian Nights Entertainments* edited by Andrew *Lang (1898); and *Stories from the Arabian Nights* with a text by Laurence *Housman and illustrations by Edmund *Dulac (1907). The most celebrated English edition of the complete *Nights* is that of Sir Richard Burton, published in 1885, while preeminent among the countless contemporary editions is the 3-vol. translation by Malcolm Lyons (2008).

ARAI, Ryoji (1956–) Internationally acclaimed Japanese picture-book artist and illustrator with a distinctive, playful style. Colour is the medium through which Arai expresses his stories; his work is vibrant and spontaneous, appealing to both children and adults alike. He has won a number of awards for his work, including the Shogakukan Children's Publication Culture Award in 1997 for *Usotsuki no tsuki* (*The Lying Moon*) by Rintaro Uchida, the Special Award at the 1999 Bologna Book Fair (*see* BOLOGNA RAGAZZI AWARDS) for *Nazo nazo no tabi* (*A Journey of Riddles*) by Chihiro Ishizu, and the Kodansha Award for Picture Books in 2000 for *Mori no ehon* (*The Forest Book*) by Hiroshi Nagata. Arai was awarded the *Astrid Lindgren Memorial Award in 2005 for his contribution to children's literature.

ARDAGH, Philip (1961–) British children's writer, who first found acclaim with his Eddie Dickens trilogy (beginning with *Awful End*), which introduced children to his surreal sense of humour (all daft jokes, anarchic plotting, and knowing asides). His subsequent work, every bit as silly (in a good way), includes the 'Unlikely Exploits' series, beginning with *The Fall of Fergal* (illustrated, like Eddie Dickens, by David *Roberts), a series of *Grubtown Tales* (beginning in 2009 with *Stinking Rich and Just Plain Stinky*, which won him that year's *Roald Dahl Funny Prize*), a book written in collaboration with former Beatle Paul McCartney (*High in the Clouds*, 2005), and *The Grunts* series (beginning in 2012, illustrated by Axel *Scheffler). Besides his books, Ardagh is best

known for his implausible height and impressive beard.

Arden family In *The House of Arden* and *Harding's Luck* by E. *Nesbit.

ARDIZZONE, Edward (1900–79) Illustrator and author, born at Haiphong in China, the son of Auguste Ardizzone, an Italian by birth who had become a naturalized Frenchman and spent his working life in the Far East. In 1905 Edward and his brother and sister were brought back to Britain by their mother, English by birth, who was an amateur watercolourist and had a gift for storytelling. The family led a nomadic life, spending some time in Ipswich, where Edward explored the docks and began to take an interest in ships. He was sent to a public school in Dorset, which he hated, and then moved with his family to London, where they lived at Elgin Avenue in the Maida Vale district.

In childhood he was inspired to become an artist by a small late Victorian illustrated edition of *The *Pilgrim's Progress*. After leaving school he began to earn his living as a clerk in the City of London, but he 'doodled' secretly at his desk, and in the evenings studied life-drawing at the Westminster School of Art. He took a special interest in the London that lay around him, sketching the habitués of the ornately seedy pubs of Maida Vale and the plump prostitutes on the street corners. In 1927 he gave up office work to concentrate on art, a step that appalled his father but had the support of his mother. He made small sums out of drawing book-jackets, and then, on the advice of one of his former schoolmasters, Desmond Coke, author of *The *Bending of a Twig*, he made some illustrations to a picaresque 17th-cent. novel and showed them to various publishers as a demonstration of his talent. Interest was shown in them by Peter Llewelyn Davies, one of J. M. *Barrie's wards, who was then (as 'Peter Davies') a London publisher, and he commissioned a set of drawings for a book by Sheridan Le Fanu. At the same time—1928—Ardizzone married; no other book commissions followed the Le Fanu work for some time, but he made some money from commercial work, including a series of drawings for Johnny Walker whisky advertisements. He also began to hold one-man shows in a London gallery.

In 1936 his two children Philip and Christianna were five and six years old, and he made an illustrated book of one of the stories he had told them, *Little Tim and the Brave Sea*

Captain. This was published that year by Geoffrey Cumberlege of the Oxford University Press, who was then in charge of the New York branch and issued it there. In its first version (Ardizzone later rewrote and redrew it for a 1955 edition) it was not very striking; Ardizzone had not yet developed his distinctive style as an illustrator, the story and text were so simple as to be almost naïve, and the book's chief attraction was its big pages and the excellent reproduction of the watercolours, by the then fairly new method of offset *lithography. It was not a great commercial success, but Cumberlege accepted a second book, *Lucy Brown and Mr Grimes* (1937). This was a near disaster: the original version was set in a children's playground, and told how Mr Grimes ('very old, very ugly, and very sad') liked to say hello to little girls and boys, but was upset when they ran away. He sees Lucy Brown ('she looked so pretty that he had to go and talk to her'), and buys her an ice-cream; eventually he adopts her and leaves her all his money. Ardizzone was apparently unaware of the dangers of encouraging small girls to talk to strangers in public places; moreover in his original drawings Mr Grimes positively leers at Lucy. The book proved unacceptable to American librarians; it, too, was later revised and redrawn, and in the new version it was explained that Mr Grimes was an old family friend, already known to Lucy. *Tim and Lucy Go to Sea* (1938) brought the characters from the first two books together, with Mr Grimes buying a steam yacht and taking them both to sea.

Ardizzone's range and technique were widened by his work as an official war artist in France, North Africa, and Italy between 1939 and 1945—'A maddening war,' he wrote; 'only the dead and the dying stay still for you to draw.' After 1945 he began to be much in demand as an illustrator of other writers' books. His work included a 1946 edition of *Peacock Pie, a version of The Pilgrim's Progress* (1947), editions of *Dickens and Trollope, Eleanor *Farjeon's *The Little Bookroom* (1955), a retelling of *Peter and Wendy* by Eleanor *Graham (1962), re-issues of Graham *Greene's children's stories, and several books by James *Reeves. The *Little Tim series continued. *Tim All Alone* (1956) won the first *Kate Greenaway Medal and the final book was *Tim's Last Voyage* (1972). Ardizzone also wrote and illustrated similar books with other child heroes, such as *Nicholas and the Fast-Moving Diesel* (1947) and *Paul, the Hero of the*

Fire (1948), and illustrated a series of 'Nurse Matilda' books by his cousin Christianna *Brand.

Ardizzone was the most eminent British children's illustrator between 1945 and 1970, with a reputation as high in America as in his own country. His characteristic style, which makes great use of cross-hatching, appears casual—childlike, in the best sense of the word—but was worked out over many years, and only became fully developed after the Second World War. It is particularly suited to nostalgic scenes of Edwardian city life, with fog-bound streets and the cosy interiors of sitting-rooms. (Ardizzone also made use of the 'balloon' with speech in it.) The stories in the 'Tim' series seem almost ridiculously simple to adult readers, and in all his books Ardizzone as an author is naïve to the point of absurdity. But children are entranced by his mixing of the matter-of-fact with the exotic—for example, the alarming results of the boy Ginger's use of a bottle of hair restorer in *Tim to the Rescue* (1949).

ARDIZZONE (Adams), Sarah (1970–) British translator from the French. One of the few translators in the Anglophone world with an expertise in working with books for children, Ardizzone is responsible for bringing into English significant work by Daniel *Pennac, Timothée *De Fombelle, Barroux, Faïza Guène, among others, as well as Joann Sfar's graphic-novel adaptation of *The *Little Prince. She has twice won the *Marsh Award.

Are We there Yet? (2004) A children's picture book by Alison *Lester. Grace and her family travel Australia, discovering famous places and meeting people. It is presented in short blocks of text, not unlike a photo diary, with maps which show the family's progress. Pen-and-wash illustrations show scenes and vignettes reminiscent of photos of the landmarks. Lester shows her strength in detailing family life with small subplots in the illustrations. Strong characterization, poetic techniques, the wry humour of Grace's point of view, the appealing repetitive phrase providing pace and structure, and the bright, clear illustrations make this a very appealing book.

Are You There God? It's Me, Margaret (1970) Influential novel by American author Judy *Blume about a twelve-year-old who talks to God about her struggles with growing up, conformity, and faith. Although Margaret's

search for a religion is central to the book, it was its frank treatment of puberty, a rare subject in children's fiction at the time, that gave *Are You There God?* a devoted following among girl readers for over a generation. It is on the *American Library Association's list of most frequently *banned books of the 1990s and 2000s.

ARGUS, Arabella Pseudonymous author of a number of early 19th-cent. children's books which, though moral in outlook, have more spirit than many of their contemporaries. Her best work was *The *Adventures of a Donkey* (1815). She also wrote *The Juvenile Spectator* (1810), in which she portrayed herself as 'a very comical old woman' who observed and commented on juvenile behaviour.

ARMITAGE, Ronda (1943-) New Zealand-born, UK-based writer of picture books, best known for her collaborations with her husband, the illustrator David Armitage (1943-). *The Lighthouse Keeper's Lunch* (1977) started a much-loved series of nine books that tell humorous, heart-warming stories about Mr Grinling, the white cottage that he lives in, and the lighthouse that he looks after. Other books include *Queen of the Night* (1999), about a girl who learns how not be a afraid of the dark, and *A Quarrel of Koalas* (1992), about a mother who decides to behave as badly as her offspring.

ARMSTRONG, Richard (1903-86) British author who won the *Carnegie Medal with *Sea Change* (1948), about an apprentice on a cargo ship—the first of his many sea stories for boys (set on a variety of types of ship). Armstrong himself served in the Merchant Navy from 1920 until 1937.

ARMSTRONG, William H. *See* SOUNDER.

ARNOLD, Thomas (1795–1842) Headmaster of Rugby School from 1828 to 1842, and architect of much of the modern UK public school system; he was the father of Matthew Arnold. He features as 'the Doctor' in *Tom Brown's Schooldays* (1857).

Around the World in Eighty Days (1873) Originally *Le tour du monde en quatre-vingts jours*, an adventure novel by Jules *Verne, in which English gent Phileas Fogg takes up a £20,000 bet to see whether he can circumnavigate the globe within eighty days. Accompanied by his French valet Passepartout, Fogg spends the closing months of 1872 on a race across the continents by rail and steamer. The book has been regularly adapted for the screen, stage, and radio, and Fogg and his journey (and the book's title) have become a common cultural reference point. According to Verne's biographer Peter Costello, the book was suggested by a journey round the globe made in just that number of days in 1870 by George Francis Train, an eccentric and wealthy Bostonian, and also by an autobiographical narrative, *Round the World* (1872), by another American, William Perry Fogg, whose surname Verne gave to his own hero. Verne's novel in turn inspired others to take the trip, the record during Verne's lifetime being 54 days.

Arrietty In *The *Borrowers* by Mary *Norton.

Arrival, The (2006) Shaun *Tan's epic, wordless graphic novel which represents a meta-narrative of migration told in filmic sepia. It has won numerous awards and is one of Tan's best-known works. Generations of seemingly displaced people feature in the endpapers to begin, and end on, the stories of countless numbers who have experienced similar journeys. Unknown alphabetic forms and inspection cards become part of the reader's passage as we follow a father's separation from his family into a new and strange world. The novel is divided into seven chapters, taking the reader through different stages in the father's migratory experience: the journey and escape from a snake-like threat, the subsequent arrival and negotiation of a surreal new world of totems and alien creatures. Tan drew inspiration for the novel from photographs and anecdotal stories by people from many different countries and historical periods, including his father, who emigrated from Malaysia to Australia in the 1960s.

Artemis Fowl (2001-12) A series of comic adventure fantasies by Irish writer Eoin *Colfer. Described by Colfer himself as '*Die Hard* with fairies', the books feature twelve-year-old Artemis Fowl, a criminal mastermind; in the first book, Artemis kidnaps Captain Holly Short, an elf in the Lower Elements Police reconnaissance squad (LEPrecon) in the hope of ransoming her for fairy gold. Other popular recurring characters in the series include the kleptomaniac dwarf Mulch Diggums (remembered for his legendary flatulence), and Foaly the centaur, technical consultant to Holly and her colleagues. The series concluded in 2012 with the eighth volume, *Artemis Fowl: The Last Guardian.*

Arthur, King Supposed early British warrior and ruler, the hero, together with his knights, of innumerable stories from the early medieval period to the present age.

What seems to be the earliest recorded reference to Arthur is in the Welsh elegy *Gododdin*, ascribed to the late 6th-cent. poet Aneirin, where it is said that a certain hero's valour was 'second only to Arthur's'. In the same century the chronicler Gildas recounted the Britons' defeat of Saxon invaders at the battle of 'Mons Badonicus' (Mount Badon), which he dated at about AD 500; this victory was later credited to Arthur. The fact that a number of people born in Celtic (i.e. non-Saxon) areas of the British Isles in the late 6th and early 7th cents. were named Arthur, a name not previously recorded in Britain, suggests that some national figure called Arthur existed at that time, or shortly before.

The early 9th-cent. history of Britain by Nennius lists twelve victories won, apparently against the Saxons, by Arthur, among them 'Mons Badonis'. The *Annales Cambriae* (mid-10th cent.) records 'the battle of Badon, in which Arthur bore the cross of Our Lord Jesus Christ three days and three nights on his shoulders', and 'the Battle of Camlann, in which Arthur and Medraut [Mordred] fell'.

If a historical Arthur did exist, the details of his achievements were quickly forgotten, and he metamorphosed into a figure of legend. This is shown by the innumerable Arthurian place names (Arthur's Seat, etc.) that are found throughout Britain.

By 1100 Arthur had become the central figure of a flourishing body of Welsh tradition. The story of *Culhwch and Olwen* (possibly late 11th cent.), which is found in *The *Mabinogion*, presents him as ruler not just of Britain but apparently of Brittany, France, and Normandy too. This tradition seems to have been passed to the Anglo-Normans and the French by the Bretons, who brought the Arthurian matter across the Channel in their migration from Celtic Britain. Among Breton traditions about Arthur was the belief, also held in Cornwall, that he had not died but would return to reign again. It was said that he had survived at Avalon, an Elysian island to which his wounded body had been conveyed after his last battle. Later tradition associated this island with the town of *Glastonbury in Somerset, perhaps because its name was erroneously thought to mean 'Island of Glass'.

The figure of Arthur in English, as opposed to Celtic, tradition was first given substance by Geoffrey of Monmouth (*c.*1100–55), who wrote in Latin. The Arthurian matter in his *History of the Kings of Britain*, which he claimed to have translated from 'a very old book in the British language' but which was mostly his own invention, begins with the childhood of the magician and seer *Merlin. The boy, who was begotten on his mother by some spirit or incubus, demonstrates his powers of prophecy, is responsible for the erection of Stonehenge, and magically contrives for the King of Britain, Uther Pendragon, to seduce the wife of the Duke of Cornwall. From this union Arthur is born. After the death of his father Arthur is made king; he wins a victory against the Saxons at Bath (Geoffrey's version of 'Mons Badonis'), conquers the Scots, Picts, and Irish, rebuilds churches, and restores Britain to its former glory. He then marries Guinevere, the descendant of a Roman family, after which he sets out to conquer the whole of Europe. Arthur learns that Mordred has crowned himself King of Britain and is living adulterously with Guinevere. Arthur cancels his planned attack on Rome and returns to Britain. Guinevere, meanwhile, flees and enters a nunnery. In the conflict that ensues Mordred is killed and Arthur receives a mortal wound; he is carried off to Avalon, handing the crown to the son of the Duke of Cornwall; 'this in the year 542 after our Lord's Incarnation'.

In the year that Geoffrey of Monmouth died the Norman poet Wace completed his *Roman de Brut*, an account of British history from the time of Brutus, the country's supposed first king; this was based largely on Geoffrey's *History*. To Geoffrey's Arthurian matter he added the detail of 'the Round Table, of which the Bretons tell many a fable'; it was built, he said, at Arthur's orders to prevent the knights quarrelling over precedence. Wace's poem provided a source for the Middle English *Brut*, whose author Laȝamon added more details to the Arthurian story. These included an account of Arthur's departure for Avalon in a boat which appears mysteriously from the sea to fetch him.

At about this time there grew up the story of *Tristan or Tristram and his love for Isolde or Isolt (also Iseult), which was at first independent from the Arthurian matter but was later made part of it. The Tristan legend was taken up by several late 12th-cent. poets, most notably Chrétien de Troyes, whose poems were concerned with the 'Matter of Britain', a body of stories about Arthur's knights and their deeds apparently current in his day. Chrétien's *Lancelot* tells how the knight Lancelot du Lac sets out to rescue Guinevere from an

abductor and is smitten with love for her. Chrétien's *Perceval* introduces into the Arthurian story the quest of the *Grail, a mysterious golden vessel. This poem was not completed before Chrétien's death, and the true nature of the Grail was never explained by him. In the French poetry of Robert de Boron (12th–13th cent.) it was explained as being the chalice in which Christ celebrated the Last Supper. De Boron's *Merlin*, which explained the Round Table (established by Merlin) as a replica of the table of the Last Supper, also gave an account of Arthur winning the crown as a youth by drawing out a sword that had been fixed magically in a stone.

The 13th-cent. French prose *Lancelot* provided a full history for the knight who had first appeared in Chrétien's poetry, and gave an account of his adulterous love for Guinevere. In this narrative, Lancelot, under the influence of a potion that convinces him that he is lying with Guinevere, begets a child on the daughter of Pelles, king of the Grail Castle. This child is Galahad.

This story is continued in the *Queste del Saint Graal*, the next book in what is known as the 'Vulgate Cycle' of medieval Arthurian prose romances. In this, Galahad is brought to Arthur's court, where, like Arthur himself as a child, he draws a sword from a stone, and sits in the Siege Perilous, the seat at the Round Table that may only be occupied by the pure knight who will complete the quest for the Grail. Galahad does indeed eventually complete that quest, and he and his companions are present at a mass in the Grail Castle (Corbenic) where the sacrament is administered by Christ himself, before the Grail and the lance which accompanies it are taken up to heaven. Galahad himself dies soon afterwards in a holy ecstasy. The 'Vulgate Cycle' ends with the *Mort Artu*, in which Arthur discovers Lancelot's adultery with the queen, the regent Mordred acts treacherously in Arthur's absence, and the story moves to its usual close. In one of the final passages the knight Giflet unwillingly casts Arthur's sword Excalibur into a lake, where it is received by a hand rising from the water.

During the 13th, 14th, and 15th cents. a large number of English prose and rhymed *romances on Arthurian subjects were written. It is, however, not to these but to the work of Sir Thomas *Malory that the Arthurian legends chiefly owe their survival in modern literature and books for children. Malory's Arthurian romances, written in prose, were printed by

*Caxton in 1485. Caxton's edition of Malory was reprinted in 1498 by his successor Wynkyn de *Worde, by William Copland in 1557, and again by Thomas East, c.1585. Arthur was still a figure of some importance in Tudor times; Henry VII called his first son Arthur, so that if this prince had not died in 1502 there would have been a real King Arthur. Later in the same century, Spenser in *The *Faerie Queene* (1589 and 1596) made the character of Prince Arthur a symbol of the perfection of all virtues. But even in Malory's time there had been a perceptible vulgarization of the Arthurian material, and by Shakespeare's day the Arthurian names could apparently be used to raise a laugh. The Fool in *King Lear* refers flippantly to Merlin's prophecies, while the clown Gobbo in *The Merchant of Venice* is named Launcelot. By this time, too, chroniclers had cast serious doubts on the reliability of Geoffrey of Monmouth's *History*. The Tudor antiquary John Leland did make efforts to defend Geoffrey, but in general the intellectual climate of the Renaissance and the Reformation made learned and religious persons in England contemptuous of the Arthurian romances and the legend of the Grail. Roger *Ascham regretted that the *Morte* had been read by royal children in earlier generations: 'What toys the daily reading of such a book may work in the will of a young gentleman or a young maid . . . wise men can judge and honest men do pity.'

Malory's narrative was reprinted by William Stansby in 1634, but after that it did not appear in print again for nearly 200 years. During the 17th cent. Milton contemplated writing an Arthuriad, but abandoned this plan in favour of *Paradise Lost*. Dryden's *King Arthur* (1691), described as a 'dramatick opera' and set to music by Purcell, took as its story a version of Arthur's wars against the Saxons, but bore little resemblance to Geoffrey of Monmouth's or Malory's accounts. Meanwhile Arthur and his knights were frequently alluded to in the popular stories printed in *chapbooks, his reign being the period in which many heroes (e.g. *Tom Thumb) were supposed to have lived. In the 18th cent. no substantial version of the Arthurian stories was printed.

By the beginning of the 19th cent, educated taste had changed again to favour romance and medieval legend. In 1816 Stansby's edition of Malory was twice reprinted rather carelessly, one edition announcing that it was somewhat expurgated, 'to render the text fit for the eye of youth'. The following year the

poet Robert *Southey produced a more scholarly version, based on a copy of Caxton. Southey explained that, despite the scarcity of old copies of the *Morte*, it had been one of his favourite books in childhood, and added: 'Were it modernised and published as a book for boys it could hardly fail of regaining its popularity.'

Further scholarly editions followed Southey's, and there was a general revival of interest in Arthur. Mrs *Sherwood's story *The Cloak*, written in 1835, describes a mother telling her children tales of 'king Arthur, and the Knights of the Round Table, with the wonderful exploits of the enchanter Merlin'. In 1842 Tennyson wrote his first Arthurian poem, which he eventually called 'The Passing of Arthur', and later in the 19th cent. Swinburne, Matthew Arnold, and William *Morris composed Arthurian poetry, while in Germany, Wagner wrote two Arthurian operas, *Tristan und Isolde* (1865) and *Parsifal* (1882).

Shortly after the middle of the 19th cent. Southey's supposition that the Arthurian story could become a popular children's book began to be proved correct. *The Story of King Arthur* by 'J.T.K.' (Sir James Knowles) (1862) was arguably the first version for young readers; it was published in the hope that it would pave the way for a revival that would put the legends back 'in boys' libraries'. It was perhaps this that Kenneth *Grahame read during his childhood in the 1860s; in *The *Golden Age* (1895) he speaks of '*Arthur*—second favourite with Charlotte for his dames riding errant, and an easy first with us boys for his spear-splintering crash of tourney and hurtle against hopeless odds'. The distinction of being the first Arthurian book for children is, however, more usually accorded to *The Boys' King Arthur*, the work of the American writer Sidney *Lanier. This was published in New York in 1880 and in London the following year, with illustrations by Alfred Kappes. Lanier based his text closely on that of Malory, though he censored passages that he believed ought not to be 'given entire'. He omitted the numerous adulteries and fornications of Malory's narrative, including Lancelot's liaison with Guinevere and the extramarital begettings of Arthur and of Galahad. He also cut out the episode of Tristram and Isolde drinking the love-potion. His book proved immensely popular and was reprinted many times.

An English *King Arthur and his Knights of the Round Table*, designed for children, was produced in 1884 with a text by Henry Frith, an author of boys' adventure stories, who followed Lanier in expunging what he called 'questionable matter'. In his text (for example) Uther marries Igraine before begetting Arthur on her, rather than afterwards, as in Malory; this alteration was accepted by many subsequent redactors of the story. Frith also invented a marriage between Lancelot and Pelles' daughter, so as to legalize the conception of Galahad. He went further than Lanier in omitting all mention of the love of Tristram and Isolde.

Mary Macleod, in *The Book of King Arthur and His Noble Knights*, published in London in 1900, restored the love-potion and even alluded delicately to the nature of the relationship between Lancelot and Guinevere. The American author and illustrator Howard *Pyle produced a four-volume mock-medieval retelling of Malory, beginning with *King Arthur and His Knights* in 1903. Other versions of the legends, many of them published for school use and some based on Tennyson's Arthuriana rather than Malory's, followed in profusion, the Arthurian stories being one of the most popular subjects with publishers of children's books for many years. By the second half of the 20th cent. the tendency was once again to return to Malory's original narrative. Roger Lancelyn *Green's *King Arthur and the Knights of the Round Table* (1957) is one of the best retellings from this period; it is closer to the *Morte* than many of its predecessors, and also draws on other medieval Arthurian texts. But the most original treatment of the Arthurian material in the 20th cent. was by T. H. *White. In 1938 he published *The *Sword in the Stone*, a highly inventive and witty account of Arthur's boyhood and his relationship with the eccentric Merlin. White continued the story in subsequent books, and his Arthurian cycle was published in one volume in 1958 as *The *Once and Future King*.

Other 20th- and 21st-cent. children's writers who have tackled the Arthurian material include Rosemary *Sutcliff, Susan *Cooper, Kevin *Crossley-Holland, Catherine *Fisher, and Philip *Reeve.

Arthur, George *See* GEORGE ARTHUR.

ARTHUR, Ruth M. (Mabel) (1905–79) British author of a large number of romantic-gothic novels for teenage girls, including *Dragon Summer* (1962), *Portrait of Margarita* (1968), and *After Candlemas* (1974).

ARUNDEL, Honor (Morfydd) (1919-73) Welsh-born children's author who produced a number of popular stories for teenage girls, including *A Family Failing* (1972), an account of the dissolution of a once-happy family.

ASBJØRNSEN, Peter Christen (1812-85) and **MOE, Jørgen** (1813-82) Norwegian collectors of folk tales. They became friends while at school together, and were inspired to collect and publish traditional stories after reading the work of the brothers *Grimm. Their *Norske Folkeeventyr* ('Norwegian Folk Tales') was issued in various editions during the 1840s, and an enlarged critical edition appeared in 1852. Asbjørnsen was a professional naturalist, while Moe, who became much admired as a poet, was eventually made Bishop of Christiansand. The two also published various collections of folk tales and *fairy stories independently of each other and with different collaborators. Their stories were illustrated by a number of artists including Erik Werenskiold and Theodor Kittlesen, and these drawings have appeared in a number of English editions of the tales.

The stories that they collected are in many cases versions of folk tales found elsewhere in Europe. *The Twelve Wild Ducks* closely resembles *The Twelve Brothers* in Grimm and *The *Wild Swans* by *Andersen; *East of the Sun and West of the Moon* belongs to a large family which also includes *Beauty and the Beast; *Boots who ate a match with the Troll* is an analogue of *Jack the Giant-Killer* and *The *Valiant Little Tailor; and *Hacon Grizzlebeard* has the same origins as Andersen's *The *Swineherd. Yet the stories have a very distinctive character, and show many traces of being descended from the Norse mythology found in the *Prose* and *Poetic *Eddas. The description of Hell in *Why the Sea Is Salt*, as a place where firewood and meat have some use, is closer to the domain of Hel in the Norse cosmogony than to the Christian place of punishment. Christianity, indeed, is only half assimilated into the stories, Christ sometimes appearing in them in a manner reminiscent of Odin; *see* MASTER SMITH, THE, for example. A characteristic feature of many of the stories is the appearance of *Trolls, a generally malevolent race of beings developed from the *giants of Eddic mythology.

The majority of Asbjørnsen and Moe's tales were first translated into English by Sir George Dasent, whose *Popular Tales from the Norse* appeared in 1859, and has remained the standard English version. Many of them subsequently appeared in the *Fairy Books* of Andrew *Lang. The stories have never had the popularity in English-speaking countries that has been enjoyed by the tales of Grimm, Andersen, and *Perrault, but they sometimes appear in modern collections.

ASCHAM, Roger (1515-68) Tutor to Elizabeth I when she was in her teens, and the author of *The Scholemaster* (published posthumously in 1570), a treatise on the methods and objectives of education. He argued that children should be allured to learning rather than forced. His method of teaching Latin was that of 'double translation', by which the pupil first translates a passage from Latin to English and then turns it back into Latin, a practice favoured in the 17th cent. by John *Brinsley. *See also* ARTHUR.

ASHFORD, Daisy *See* YOUNG VISITERS, THE.

ASHLEY, Bernard (1935–) Prolific British author of everything from first readers to tough *young adult novels whose teaching career in south and east London inspired much of his writing, leading him to deal with social issues, race, and the effects of a broken society. His books include *The Trouble with Donovan Croft* (1974), a bold novel about a West Indian boy fostered by a white family, and *A Kind of Wild Justice* (1977), the grimly realistic story of a boy whose father is an alcoholic and mother a prostitute. Many of his books focus on the effects of conflict, including *Johnnie's Blitz* (1995), *Ronnie's War* (2010), *Jack and the German Spy* (2013), as well as *Little Soldier* (1999), the powerful story of a young survivor of a civil war in Africa now finding himself in London, which was shortlisted for the *Carnegie Medal and the *Guardian Children's Fiction Prize.

Aslan The great lion in the *Narnia stories of C. S. *Lewis.

Asriel, Lord Lyra's guardian in the *His Dark Materials* trilogy.

Astérix French *comic hero, a diminutive, moustachioed Gaul who lives in a village in Armorique (Brittany) which is the last holdout against the Romans. Together with such friends as the dull-witted Obélix, and with the aid of a magic potion made by the druid Getafix (Panoramix, in the French), Astérix keeps the Romans at bay. He is the creation of René Goscinny (text) and Albert Uderzo (pictures), and first appeared in the French

comic weekly *Pilote* in 1959, since when his adventures have been published in many books.

Much of the fun of the Astérix stories lies in the names, which have been skilfully adapted in the English translations by Anthea *Bell and Derek Hockridge; for example, Postaldistrix the postman, Centurion Armisurplus, Cacofonix the Bard, and the dog, Dogmatix.

Following Goscinny's death in 1977, Uderzo continued to produce the albums alone, somewhat less successfully. The job was only passed down to a new writer-artist pair in 2011—Jean-Yves Ferri and Didier Conrad produced volume 35 in the series, *Asterix and the Picts*, in 2013.

Astrid Lindgren Memorial Award

Awarded since 2003 in honour of Astrid *Lindgren, this is one of the world's most prestigious (and valuable) prizes, given annually to one or two recipients; winners can be children's writers or illustrators, or people or organizations that promote children's literature. Recipients of the prize, which is worth five million Swedish kronor, have included Maurice *Sendak and Christine *Nöstlinger (both 2003), Lygia *Bojunga (2004), Philip *Pullman and Ryoji *Arai (both 2005), Katherine *Paterson (2006), Sonya *Hartnett (2008), Kitty *Crowther (2010), Shaun *Tan (2011), Guus *Kuijer (2012), and Meg *Rosoff (2016).

Atalanta A girls' *magazine published in Britain from 1887 to 1898. One of its first editors was L. T. *Meade. It had many high-quality serials and stories, by such authors as Rider *Haggard, Mrs *Molesworth, and Robert Louis *Stevenson.

ATKINSON, M. E. (Mary Evelyn) (1899–1974) British writer of children's stories in imitation of Arthur *Ransome, beginning with a series about the Lockett family (*August Adventure*, 1936, and others).

Atlantis A lost continent supposedly submerged under the Atlantic Ocean. It is visited by the children in *The *Story of the Amulet* (1906) by E. *Nesbit.

At the Back of the North Wind A novel by George *MacDonald, first published as a serial in *Good Words for the Young*, with illustrations by Arthur *Hughes, between November 1868 and October 1869, and issued as a book by Strahan & Co., with the Hughes illustrations, in 1871.

Diamond, the young son of a coachman, sleeps in a hay loft over the stable, and one night is awoken by the voice of North Wind, who reveals herself as a beautiful woman with long hair, takes him in her arms, and carries him across London. He meets Nanny, a girl crossing-sweeper who lives with her gin-drinking old grandmother. Some days later North Wind takes Diamond to the country 'at the back of the north wind', a land which seems to lie north of the polar ice, but which is a place of lush pastures and streams, not a part of this world at all.

Meanwhile Diamond's father's employer has lost all his money—the result of North Wind sinking a ship in which he had a financial interest—and the family have to move into dingy lodgings; the father becomes a cab-driver, but falls ill, and Diamond takes over the cab, which he drives very competently. He helps to get Nanny the crossing-sweeper into hospital when she is taken ill, and does what he can to mend the ways of a neighbour, a drunken cab-driver who beats his wife. His father recovers and is taken on as coachman by Mr Raymond, a philanthropist by whom Diamond has been befriended. Diamond's family move (with their horse) to Mr Raymond's country house, and the ménage is also joined by the girl Nanny and her lame friend Jim. These two gradually come to despise Diamond because he seems to them almost half-witted, but he is in fact turning more and more (in his mind) to the North Wind and the country that lies at her back. Eventually—by the time that the narrator himself has appeared in the story, and has befriended him—Diamond is found dead; or rather, as the narrator puts it: 'They thought he was dead. I knew that he had gone to the back of the north wind.'

The story, which was MacDonald's first novel for children, is rambling, especially in the later part of the book, and is too long entirely to sustain the compelling quality of the opening chapters. But it is a remarkable piece of work, a milestone in children's fiction in that it combines the qualities of the *fairy story at its best with the expression of social and moral concerns, and usually manages to have a didactic content without overt preaching. Influences on it include *Dickens, Hans *Andersen, and perhaps Charles *Kingsley; but MacDonald's vivid style lifts it far above the level of imitation.

Though the country at the back of the north wind—an idea taken from Herodotus—is undoubtedly Purgatory (MacDonald refers obliquely to Dante when describing it), the

story, like all MacDonald's *fantasies, is a parable rather than a strict allegory. North Wind is partly a personification of the will of God; there is a passage in which she discusses the fact that she seems to be both cruel and kind. But it is also made clear that she is only the servant of a higher power; she says she merely 'obeyed orders' in sinking the ship. She is also a mother-figure; Diamond thinks that her voice is 'more like his mother's voice than anything else in the world', and he is happiest when 'nestling close to her grand bosom'. Diamond himself, like characters in other MacDonald novels, is a Christ-like child who has a sweetness of manner which leads many people to regard him as 'not quite right in the head'.

At the Back of the North Wind includes the short fairy story 'Little Daylight', told to the children in hospital by Mr Raymond, which has sometimes been reprinted separately. Among the poems Diamond recites to his baby brother is 'Where did you come from, baby dear?', which has achieved a certain independent fame, or perhaps notoriety.

ATTWELL, Mabel Lucie (1879–1964) Illustrator who was born in the Mile End district of London, the daughter of a butcher. She went to Regent Street and Heatherley's art schools, but disliked the formal training and soon left, beginning to earn money by selling fairy pictures. In 1908 she married Harold Earnshaw, a painter and illustrator, and when he lost an arm in the First World War she managed to support him and their three children. Her first notable work was the illustration of children's classics for the publisher and greetings card manufacturer Raphael *Tuck: *Mother Goose* (c.1909), **Alice's Adventures in Wonderland* (1910), **Andersen's fairy stories (1913), an abridged **Water-Babies* (1915), and *Grimm (1925). She also illustrated *Peter Pan and Wendy* (1921) (*see* PETER AND WENDY), and her drawings for that story have been used again and again.

During the 1920s and 1930s, as Brian *Alderson has written, 'Mabel Lucie Attwell children were ubiquitous.' In greetings cards, books, and a Mabel Lucie Attwell *annual (published from 1922 until ten years after her death) she exerted the same kind of influence on children's fashions and adult attitudes to children as Kate *Greenaway had in her day. Her talent was soon submerged in the endless pictures of chubby, dimpled babies and infants, including a celluloid doll modelled on her infants and called 'Diddums', with the result that her name

became synonymous in Britain with the sentimentalization of childhood.

ATWATER, Richard and Florence *See* MR POPPER'S PENGUINS.

AULNOY, Marie-Cathérine Le Jumel De Barneville De La Motte, Comtesse d' (c.1650–1705) One of the central figures in the French fashion for *fairy stories; she wrote twenty-five fairy tales, among the best-remembered being *The *Yellow Dwarf, The *White Cat,* and *The *Blue Bird.*

Mme d'Aulnoy came from a good Norman family, and married in her mid-teens a man some three times her age. The marriage was not a success. She had six children, the paternity of the last three being sometimes doubted. She and her mother apparently plotted to have the Comte d'Aulnoy executed for high treason; they failed, and the two men who actually made the accusation, presumed to be their lovers, were executed instead. After this Mme d'Aulnoy seems to have temporarily retreated to a convent or, according to other accounts, spent some time in Spain. In 1690 she published a romantic novel, *L'Histoire d'Hypolite Comte de Duglas,* which contains the first known appearance in print of a fairy story in the fashionable court style. The hero, while attempting to rescue his beloved from a nunnery, is asked to divert the company and 'Exerting all his presence of mind, he endeavoured to recollect the particulars of a *Fairy Tale* he had somewhere read.' There follows a fairly long and ornate tale of the King of Russia, whose love for a fairy keeps him on an enchanted island for three centuries, but who dies when at last he chooses to return to his mortal life.

Mme d'Aulnoy was known as an entertaining raconteur, witty, and desirable company, who preferred to write with friends talking around her. She seems soon to have become one of the central figures in the fashion for telling fairy stories as adult salon amusements. Some time before 1696 fairy tales of her composition, such as *La Belle aux cheveux d'or,* began to circulate in fashionable company, and by mid-1697 the first three volumes of her *Contes des fées* were in print, followed in 1698 by *Contes nouveaux, ou Les Fées à la mode*: eight volumes altogether, containing such stories as *Gracieuse et Percinet, L'Oiseau bleu, Le Prince Lutin, Le Rameau d'or, L'Oranger et L'abeille* and *Finette Cendron* (an amalgamation of the themes of *Perrault's stories *Hop O' My Thumb* and *Cinderella).

Mme d'Aulnoy stated a wish to be admired for the new life her retellings gave to old tales. She may have used (according to M. E. Storer in *La Mode des contes de fées*, Paris, 1928) the folklore of Normandy, where she was born and brought up; this included a vengeful dwarf, and water spirits who were placated with butter tartlets, both possible inspirations for *The Yellow Dwarf*. Along with other fairy-story writers of the time she also probably borrowed incidents from the French equivalent of *chapbooks, and from other printed sources. But full sources for most of her tales cannot be traced.

Stories by Mme d'Aulnoy first appeared in English in 1699, with more in 1707 (*The History of the Tales of the Fairies; newly done from the French*) and 1716 (in the fourth part of *The Diverting Works of the Countess D'Anois*). A large three-part collection appeared in 1721-2. By 1773 Francis *Newbery had brought out a selection of Mme d'Aulnoy's stories entitled *Mother Bunch's Fairy Tales. Published for the Amusement Of... Little Masters and Misses*, this being apparently the first English collection of the stories published explicitly for children. *Mother Bunch was presumably taken up as the nursery author for Mme d'Aulnoy's stories so as to parallel *Mother Goose's relationship with Perrault. Mme d'Aulnoy's tales became staples of the chapbook market, generally attached to Mother Bunch, and a *pantomime called *Mother Bunch and the Yellow Dwarf* was performed in 1807, with others on the same theme at intervals throughout the century. James Robinson *Planché published a translation of them in 1855, in which following 'the many liberties' he had taken 'in adapting them to the stage, made it a point of conscience... to adhere as rigidly as possible to the original text on this occasion'. Another new translation, with an introduction by Thackeray's daughter Anne Ritchie, appeared in 1892, and retellings of many of Mme d'Aulnoy's stories were included in the *Fairy Books* of Andrew *Lang. Some have also been made the basis of 20th-cent. children's *picture books.

Richness of detail, profusion of incident, and considerable length, characterize Mme d'Aulnoy's writing (together with, according to one critic, a particular interest in animals and a penchant for jam). Compared with those of Perrault her tales in their original form seem long-winded and over-elaborate, but they have succeeded in surviving in periodic retellings, both of single and collected tales.

Mme d'Aulnoy's name has been variously spelt D'Anois, d'Aunois, Dunois, Aunoy, etc.

AUNT CHARLOTTE Pseudonym sometimes used by Charlotte M. *Yonge, chiefly for a series of books of *history (1873 onwards).

AUNT EFFIE (Jane Euphemia Browne) (1811-98) Author of *Aunt Effie's Rhymes for Little Children* (1852) and *Aunt Effie's Gift for the Nursery* (1854).

AUNT FRIENDLY (Sarah S. T. Baker) (1824-1906) Author and compiler of such books as *Aunt Friendly's Nursery Keepsake* (1870).

Aunt Judy's Magazine One of the most popular mid-Victorian children's *magazines. It was founded in 1866 under the editorship of Mrs Margaret *Gatty, mother of Juliana Horatia *Ewing, and was published monthly by Bell and Daldy of Fleet Street.

Its title was taken from the family nickname for Juliana Horatia; many of her stories appeared in print in its pages, as serials, and there were also poems, articles on *natural history, a summary of readers' letters to the editor (including progress reports on fund-raising for an 'Aunt Judy Cot' in the Great Ormond Street Children's Hospital), as well as articles on the historical and religious associations of each month, and *reviews of children's books (in June 1866 the magazine praised *Alice's Adventures in Wonderland* as 'exquisitely wild'). The introduction to the first issue stated that the magazine was 'intended for the use and amusement of children'; a seriousness of purpose was discernible, but a balance was achieved between entertainment and information. Famous contributors over the years included Lewis *Carroll, whose story 'Bruno's Revenge' was commissioned for the magazine by Mrs Gatty in 1867, and proved to be the germ of *Sylvie and Bruno*. The magazine was generously illustrated with *wood engravings, and pictures were supplied by, among others, George *Cruikshank, Randolph *Caldecott, and Gordon *Browne.

Though the magazine had something of a bias towards girl readers, the young A. A. *Milne was among a number of boys who read it enthusiastically.

AUNT LOUISA (Laura B. J. Valentine) (1814-99) Author and compiler of such *toy books as *Aunt Louisa's Birthday Gift* (c.1875).

AUNT MARY Pseudonym of Mary *Hughes, for such books as *Aunt Mary's Tales* (1811) and *Aunt Mary's New-Year's Gift* (1819).

AUSTIN, Stella (d. 1893) British author of a number of books that portray children as lovable, winsome rascals. Her best known story was *Stumps* (1873), whose heroine, a four-year-old girl, is 'made up of dimples' and speaks baby talk.

Austin family In *Meet the Austins* and *The Young Unicorns* by Madeleine *L'Engle.

Australian Aboriginal writing and illustration The first appearance in print of Aboriginal legends was when they were recorded and transcribed or retold by European Australians in the 19th cent. One of the earliest was K. Langloh Parker's *Australian Legendary Tales* (1896), its first edition illustrated by the Aboriginal artist Tommy McRae. Later other non-Aboriginal authors used the legends, notably Patricia *Wrightson, who based novels on mythical creatures from Aboriginal mythology.

A number of picture books from Dick *Roughsey, Aboriginal artist and storyteller from Far North Queensland, were published in the 1970s and 1980s. The most famous was *The Rainbow Serpent* (1975), winner of the *CBCA Picture Book of the Year. Later Roughsey collaborated with Percy Trezise to keep bringing his stories to publication.

Poet Oodgeroo Noonuccal (1920–93)—till she adopted a traditional name, Kath Walker—wrote a series of short autobiographical stories which build into a longer work, called *Stradbroke Dreamtime* (1972). In 1993 this book was illustrated in a deluxe edition by Aboriginal artist Bronwyn Bancroft and gained mention as a notable book from the CBCA.

Sally Morgan wrote *My Place* (1987), a memoir for adults of growing up in 1950s Australia and discovering her Aboriginal heritage when an adult. Excerpts from this book are often used in schools. Since then Morgan has written several children's picture books, and illustrated some of them. These books are often named as notable books by the CBCA.

Australian poet, Roland Robinson (1912–92), a founder of the Jindyworobak movement, was born in Ireland, but came to Australia in 1921. He deeply respected Aboriginal culture and meticulously recorded the stories, especially those of Percy Mumbulla from the south coast of New South Wales. Robinson believed that the Aboriginal people spoke naturally in iambic pentameter, and claimed he only punctuated their stories. Three of Mumbulla's stories were later illustrated as children's picture books by Bronwyn Bancroft—*Dirrangun* (1994), *Minah* (1995), and *The Whalers* (1997).

Illustrator Arone Raymond Meeks used ochre and gouache on rag paper and paint made from clay to create *Enora and the Black Crane* (1991), which won the UNICEF Ezra Jack Keats International Award for Excellence in Children's Book Illustration. Several of his other picture books have achieved international acclaim, including *When the World Was New* (1988) and *Pheasant and Kingfisher* (1987).

Bronwyn Bancroft now writes and illustrates children's picture books. *Why I Love Australia* (2011) is a song of praise to the country's urban and regional landscapes illustrated with bright, brilliantly coloured and designed illustrations.

Aboriginal storyteller and writer Boori Monty Pryor (1950–) has created highly successful books in collaboration with both Jan *Ormerod and Meme McDonald. His most famous is *Shake a Leg* (2010). Pryor was named Australian Children's *Laureate with Alison *Lester in 2012. Other notable books include *My Mob Going to the Beach* (2004) by Sylvia Emmerton, illustrated by Jaquanna Elliot.

Australian Legendary Tales (1896) A collection of aboriginal folk tales made by Mrs Kate Langloh Parker (1855–1940). Together with her *More Australian Legendary Tales* (1898) it became the best known and most influential of the early collections of aboriginal stories.

Mrs Parker was born at Encounter Bay in Australia, the daughter of Henry Field, a pioneer squatter. While on her first husband's settler station, Bangate, on the Narran River in New South Wales, she learnt the language and began collecting the tales of the local aboriginal tribe, the Euahlayi-speaking Noongahburrahs, believing that 'we should try, while there is yet time, to gather all the information possible of a race fast dying out.' Andrew *Lang, with whom she corresponded, added an introduction to the book and to its successor, giving the tales some anthropological context and relating them to classical myth.

Mrs Parker's first book contained thirty-one stories, together with the native text of the first tale, concerning Dinewan the Emu and

Goomblegubbon the Bustard, and how Goomblegubbon tricked the emus into cutting off their own wings, and Dinewan in revenge played the trick that condemned the bustard to have only two children. The twenty-two tales of the second book include several of Byamee the 'big man', god and hero.

AVERY, Gillian (Elise) (1926–2016) British children's novelist and historian of children's fiction; she worked for some years as a newspaper reporter, and as a staff member of *Chambers Encyclopaedia* and the Oxford University Press. When she and her husband moved to Manchester, she began to write a cycle of novels mainly set in Oxford in the 1870s, drawing largely on her interest and expertise in Victorian children's fiction. The first of these, *The *Warden's Niece*, was published in 1957, and can in retrospect be seen as one of the children's books that marked the beginning of a renaissance in English juvenile fiction. Several of the characters created in it—notably the eccentric Revd Mr Copplestone and the ebullient Smith boys, sons of an Oxford professor—reappeared in further novels in the cycle: *Trespassers at Charlecote* (1958), *James Without Thomas* (1959), *The Elephant War* (1960), which centres on an attempt to save an elephant at the London Zoo from being sold to Barnum's Circus, *To Tame a Sister* (1961), *The Peacock House* (1963), and *The Italian Spring* (1964), in which Maria, heroine of *The Warden's Niece*, is taken on a visit to Italy by a bachelor cousin. During this period Gillian Avery also wrote *The Greatest Gresham* (1962), one of her most admired books; it is the story of the girl Julia Gresham, living in a London suburb in the 1890s, who longs to be great but does not know how she should go about it.

Call of the Valley (1968) takes a Victorian boy from his native Radnorshire to Manchester, in the service of a rich employer. *A Likely Lad* (1971), which won the *Guardian Children's Fiction Prize, is a sharply observed study of family rivalry and class distinction in late 19th-cent. Manchester, centring on young Willy Overs and his struggles against a well-meaning but dominating father, who has constricting plans for Willy's future.

A Likely Lad was the last of Gillian Avery's full-length *historical novels for children. In 1971 there appeared *Ellen's Birthday*, the first of six short books for younger readers set in the Victorian period. Typical of them is *Ellen and the Queen* (1972), in which the ebullient

Ellen Timms manages to get a sight of the unthinkable: Queen Victoria's legs. *Huck and her Time Machine* (1977) was an uncharacteristic book for Gillian Avery, a fantasy set in the present day.

Gillian Avery edited modern re-issues of works by 19th-cent. authors, including Mrs *Ewing. She is also the author of *Victorian People in Life and Literature* (1970); *Childhood's Pattern: a study of the heroes and heroines of children's fiction, 1770–1950* (1975); and *Behold the Child: American children and their books, 1621–1922* (1994).

AVERY, Harold (1867–1943) A writer of *school stories who was educated at Eastbourne College; his first books were *The School's Honour and other stories* (1895), *An Old Boy's Yarns* (1895), and *Frank's First Term, or Making a Man of Him* (1896). He continued to publish until two years before his death. His stories resemble those of Talbot Baines *Reed, but he lacked Reed's specifically Christian ethos, and centred his narratives on football, rowing, and other sports.

AVI (Edward Irving Wortis) (1937–) American children's writer, whose more than seventy books span the range from picture books to teen fiction. His 1990 adventure novel *The True Confessions of Charlotte Doyle*, about a teenage girl crossing the Atlantic in the 19th cent., was awarded a Newbery Honor (*see* NEWBERY MEDAL). He received the same award for *Nothing but the Truth*, which focuses on a teenage act of defiance, two years later. The first novel in the historical *Crispin* trilogy, *Crispin: The Cross of Lead*, received the Newbery Medal in 2003. Avi worked as a librarian for many years and started writing for young people when he had his own children.

A Was an Archer An alphabet rhyme (*see* ABC BOOKS) first printed *c.*1705. It has sometimes appeared as a separate book, for example under the title *The Hobby-Horse, or the High Road to Learning*, published by John *Harris in 1820, and as *An Illustrated Comic Alphabet*, drawn by Amelia Frances Howard-Gibbon in 1859, published in facsimile (from the manuscript in the *Osborne Collection) in 1966.

Away Goes Sally (1934) A novel by Elizabeth *Coatsworth.

AWDRY, Revd W. (Wilbert Vere) (1911–97) Author of the celebrated 'Railway Series' of British children's books about *Thomas the

Tank Engine and his fellow locomotives. He was born at Ampfield in Hampshire, where his father was Vicar. It was from his father that he acquired an interest in railways: the Revd Mr Awdry senior had a two-and-a-half-inch gauge railway in the garden, and used to take his son walking along the local railway track; the platelayers were his parishioners and greeted him respectfully. The family later moved to Box in Wiltshire, within 200 yards of where the Great Western Railway main line climbed a steep gradient, and Wilbert would lie in bed listening to the engines. 'It needed little imagination', he has written, 'to hear, in the sounds the train engine and banking engine made, what they were saying to each other . . . From that time there developed in my mind the idea that all steam engines had personality and could express it.'

He was sent to Dauntsey's School in Wiltshire, then went to St Peter's Hall, Oxford, before training for ordination at Wycliffe Hall, Oxford. During the 1940s he had a curacy at Kings Norton near Birmingham; he was now married with children, and it was while his three-year-old son Christopher had measles that the railway stories began to be told, being written down on scraps of paper. His wife persuaded him to offer them for publication.

There is a biography by Brian Sibley, *The Thomas the Tank Engine Man* (1995).

Awful End (2000) The first book in the Eddie Dickens trilogy by Philip *Ardagh. This first volume introduces a lunatic cast, including Mad Uncle Jack, Even Madder Aunt Maud (who lives in a cow-shaped carnival float called Marjorie), St Horrid's Home for Grateful Orphans, and a stuffed stoat called Malcolm. The series is illustrated by David *Roberts.

awful warning *See* CAUTIONARY TALE.

AYMÉ, Marcel *See* WONDERFUL FARM, THE.

Babar the Elephant Hero of a series of *picture books (and now major international brand), written and drawn by the French artist Jean *de Brunhoff (1899–1937), then by his son Laurent (1925–). The books started out as a bedtime story told by Jean's wife Cécile to their children; then Jean began to illustrate and publish them. His first Babar book was *L'Histoire de Babar, le petit éléphant* (1931), translated into English three years later as *The Story of Babar, the Little Elephant*. This tells of Babar's birth and childhood in the Great Forest; his mother is killed by a hunter and he runs away to a city, where he is adopted by a rich old lady who buys him smart clothes and gives him a home. His cousins Arthur and Celeste join him, but soon all three elephants feel drawn back to the forest, and when they return, Babar and Celeste (who are engaged to be married) are elected King and Queen of the Elephants.

The book was visually outstanding; when it first appeared, nothing of the kind had been published in Europe or America. An extra-large page size was used by Brunhoff for *lithographed drawings with plenty of colour and detail, accompanied by a hand-written text; the whole was designed with great skill, cunning use being made of white space as well as drawings. Brunhoff's apparently naïve narrative style concealed a certain wit. The book was seen by A. A. *Milne, who persuaded his publishers, Methuen, to bring out the first English edition, to which he himself wrote a brief preface which concludes: 'I salute M. de Brunhoff. I am at his feet.'

Next came *Le Roi Babar* (1933) (translated as *Babar the King*) and many more, including *Babar en Famille* (1938) (*Babar At Home*) and *Le Voyage de Babar* (1939) (*Babar's Travels*), three of them published posthumously. Jean de Brunhoff's son Laurent was twelve when his father died of tuberculosis at the age of thirty-seven, but not very long afterwards he was producing further volumes in the series, beginning with *Babar et ce coquin d'Arthur* (1946) (*Babar and that Rascal Arthur*). Later titles included three designed to teach English, German, and Spanish. Laurent also created a new series about a giraffe, Serafina. Unfortunately as the years passed the quality of the books deteriorated substantially, and by the mid-1960s Laurent was writing and drawing Babar stories with indifferent illustrations and unimaginative storylines; the hand-lettering had been abandoned in favour of a printed text, and the page size was conventionally small.

Baba Yaga The Bony-legged One, a celebrated *witch of Russian folklore, who lives in a house on chicken-legs and flies about in a mortar, using a pestle as oar and a broom to sweep away her tracks.

BABBITT, Natalie (1932–2016) American author-illustrator, who after an initial collaboration with her husband worked alone on fiction that is thoughtful and thought-provoking. *Dick Foote and the Shark* (1967) and *Phoebe's Revolt* (1968) are stories in verse. Her first novel, *The Search for Delicious* (1969), tells how a boy is sent around a kingdom conducting a survey as to what people mean by the word 'delicious', with strange and often unwelcome results. Among her later novels are *The Devil's Storybook* (1974), a collection of delightfully wicked stories portraying the Devil as a scheming practical joker who comes to Earth to play tricks on unsuspecting people bound for Heaven, and *The Eyes of the Amaryllis* (1977), which begins with a sea captain's widow waiting for a message from her long-dead husband. She is most famous, however, for *Tuck Everlasting* (1975), about a family who drink from a spring that gives eternal life. It has been filmed twice.

Babe *See* SHEEP-PIG, THE.

Babees Book *See* BOOKS OF COURTESY.

Babes in the Wood *See* CHILDREN IN THE WOOD.

baby books Books for babies and toddlers have grown into a huge market in recent decades, supported both by powerful opportunistic marketing possibilities and, less crassly, by a growing understanding of the importance of books to children's development, even that of the very youngest babies. They come in various formats for different settings—board books, waterproof books for the bath, books with clips to attach to strollers, and so on—each object designed robustly to withstand chewing, drooling, throwing, etc. Independent exploration of the book is often encouraged, with design features such as textures that are interesting to the touch (Fiona Watt and Rachel Wells's *That's Not My . . .* series—forty-one titles and counting, beginning with *That's Not My Puppy* in 1999—is a particularly popular recent example), moving parts (lift-the-flap books such as **Dear Zoo*—toddlers' fine motor skill development can also be supported by use of such things), or some kind of noise-making function. These books are often repurposed versions of things already existing as popular **picture books, some of which may be made available in three or four different formats. Many books for babies and toddlers, including picture books, teach concepts and words, and encourage understanding of narrative patterns and habits of reading and sharing books, as well as providing the obvious opportunities for adult and child to bond through the experience.

Baby-Sitters Club, The See Martin, Ann M.

Baby's Opera, The (1877) A collection of **nursery rhymes illustrated by Walter *Crane.

BACON, R. L. (Ronald Leonard) (1924–2005) New Zealand author of *The Boy and the Taniwha* (1966), a **picture book about a Māori boy's upbringing and his fear and curiosity about a demon of Māori legend; the illustrations, by the Māori artist Para Matchitt, evoke traditional carvings and cave-paintings. Bacon and Matchitt also collaborated on *Rua and the Sea People* (1968). Bacon also wrote *Again the Bugles Blow* (1973), in which a modern Māori boy witnesses the Land Wars between his people and the white settlers a century earlier.

Bad Child's Book of Beasts, The (1896) The first book of comic verse by Hilaire *Belloc, published by Alden & Co. of Oxford; the first printing sold out within four days. The illustrations were by 'B.T.B.', Belloc's Oxford friend Lord Basil Blackwood, who used his young cousin Harold Nicolson, dressed up in an Eton suit, as a model. The book—which is loosely modelled on the medieval **bestiaries—contains several notable pieces, such as 'The Yak', 'The Whale', and 'The Big Baboon'.

BADEN-POWELL, Robert Stephenson Smyth, First Baron Baden-Powell (1857–1941) Founder of the **Boy Scouts. After an education at Charterhouse, he was commissioned in the Hussars, and studied woodcraft, reconnaissance, and scouting while stationed in India. Fame came to him for his defence of Mafeking during the Boer War. His book *Aids to Scouting* (1899), which laid stress on personal initiative, careful observation, and working in small groups, was not intended for use by children, but was taken up enthusiastically by teachers, which gave Baden-Powell the idea of forming the Boy Scouts. A trial camp was held on Brownsea Island in Poole Harbour in 1907, and the next year **Scouting for Boys* began to appear in parts, leading to the formation of Boy Scout groups all over Britain. In 1909 eleven thousand Scouts gathered at a Crystal Palace rally, and Baden-Powell's sister began to establish the parallel scheme of **Girl Guides. In all he wrote some thirty books on scouting and related topics, most of them illustrated by himself.

Badger In The **Wind in the Willows* by Kenneth *Grahame.

Badjelly the Witch In a story of that name by Spike *Milligan.

Baggins, Bilbo See Bilbo Baggins.

Baggins, Frodo See Frodo Baggins.

Bagheera Panther in The **Jungle Books* by **Kipling.

BAGNOLD, Enid (1889–1981) British popular author; her books include **National Velvet* (1930), and a **family story for children, *Alice and Thomas and Jane* (1935).

Bagthorpe Saga, The A series by Helen **Cresswell about the Bagthorpe family. *Ordinary Jack* (1977) concerns the ambitions of Jack Bagthorpe, the only member of the family who has no outstanding talents—his sister Tess, for example, 'was thirteen and read Voltaire in the original for pleasure and was a Black Belt in Judo, besides talking like a dictionary'. Jack's Uncle Parker devises a scheme for him to win fame by taking up prophecy and other occult practices, but naturally everything misfires. The first of many sequels

Absolute Zero (1978) takes its title from Zero, Jack's mongrel dog. The tenth and final book in the series, *Bagthorpes Battered*, appeared in 2001.

BAILEY, Carolyn Sherwin (1875–1961) Prolific American author and compiler of children's books, who was for many years editor of the magazine *American Childhood*. She won the *Newbery Medal for a *doll story, *Miss Hickory* (1946).

BAKER, Jeannie (1950–) British-born, Australian artist and author who uses distinctive mixed-media collage to illustrate her books, which focus on family, the environment, and sustainability. *Where the Forest Meets the Sea* (1988) is about the disappearing kelp forests. *Window* (1991) uses the changing view from one boy's window to show powerfully and wordlessly the disastrous effects of urban sprawl—though a companion book *Belonging* (2004) is more hopeful about our future. *Mirror* (2010) consists of two wordless stories designed to be read simultaneously, through which we see two boys' lives, one in urban Sydney and the other in a village in Morocco.

Baldmoney A gnome in *The *Little Grey Men* by *'B.B.'

BALDWIN, James (1841–1925) American writer who was the author of popular retellings of legends for children. These include *The Story of Siegfried* (1882), illustrated by Howard *Pyle, *The Story of Roland* (1883), and *A Story of the Golden Age* (1887). His graded 'readers' for schools, such as *School Reading by Grades* (1897), were much used.

Baldwin Library of Historical Children's Literature Originally a collection of children's books assembled over nearly thirty years by Ruth M. Baldwin, an American university teacher, and eventually presented by her to the University of Florida at Gainesville, where it was formally opened in 1982. It has continued to expand and now contains over 130,000 volumes, both English and American, spanning a period from the mid-17th cent. to the present.

ballad In present-day use, a term for a narrative song, focusing on a single event or situation, economical in style, and probably orally transmitted at least through part of its history. Repetition, sometimes of a nonsense phrase, is often used, both for effect and apparently also to lighten the load on the singer's memory. Metre and stanza-length vary from ballad to ballad, though 'Ballad metre' (4, 3, 4, 3 with a rhyming scheme a, b, a, b or a, b, c, b) is common.

The folk ballad is essentially impersonal in tone, containing no judgements, whereas a minstrel ballad, such as *Chevy Chase, might praise one noble family or otherwise display a political view. The ballad form, and many of its themes, are international, and some one-third of surviving traditional English ballads have counterparts among Scandinavian and other European ballads. Opinion divides on whether ballads were originally composed by individuals or by communities collectively, for instance during great festivities. It is also argued that who composed them does not matter, since they became public property, dependent on tradition for their continued life. Surviving English ballads range widely in subject, from religious (several early carols have the characteristics of ballads) to historic, humorous, and bawdy. Before children's entertainment was differentiated from that of adults, it can be assumed that everyone enjoyed the singing of ballads, such as those of *Robin Hood. From the 16th cent. onwards, *broadside ballads, a debased form of ballad composition, printed on one large sheet of paper with the stanzas displayed in columns down the width or 'broadside', were sold cheaply all over Britain by pedlars. In these broadsides *romance material like *Guy of Warwick* appears along with new humorous, romantic, or bawdy compositions, or with expanded songs and verses telling sensational or tragic tales such as *The *Children in the Wood*. Most broadsides were illustrated by crude *woodcuts, and some also appeared, expanded, as *chapbooks. These ballads were also popular in America.

Antiquarian interest in early ballads in the second half of the 18th cent. went hand in hand with research into the origins of *nursery rhymes (Joseph *Ritson collected both), and many nursery rhymes are in fact lines from otherwise forgotten broadside ballads, such as 'Lavender's blue, diddle, diddle', which is based on a thirty-two-line broadside published some time before 1685. Ballads have also sometimes helped to date a nursery rhyme by quoting or near-quoting it.

BALLANTYNE, R. M. (Robert Michael) (1825–94) One of the most accomplished 19th-cent. writers of *adventure stories; he was the son of a Scottish newspaper proprietor, whose brother printed *Scott's novels. Ballantyne's father was

given the task of copying them for the compositor, so that nobody should know who had written them. Scott's financial ruin involved the Ballantynes as well as himself, and at the age of sixteen Robert Michael, who had already been taken away from school, was apprenticed to the Hudson's Bay Company and sent off to Canada. He spent several years in remote settlements, living a rough life and trading in furs with the 'Red Indians'. He then returned to Scotland. In 1848 he published his journal of life with the Hudson's Bay Company. The death of his father and of his sister made him deeply religious. In 1853 he produced a juvenile version of another author's book about North America, and this proved such a success that the Edinburgh publisher Nelson suggested that he write a boys' adventure story. He began work on *The *Young Fur-Traders*, at first entitled *Snowflakes and Sunbeams*, which was published in 1856.

The great success of *The Young Fur-Traders* led Ballantyne's publishers to ask for any further children's books he might have, and he next offered them something very different, a version of *The *Three Little Kittens* with illustrations by himself (1856). This was followed by further 'Kitten' books, including *The Kitten Pilgrims* (1882). Other *picture books which he wrote and drew included versions of *My Mother* and *The *Butterfly's Ball* (both 1857).

His next adventure story was **Ungava*, again based on his Canadian experiences, closely followed by *The *Coral Island*, both published in 1858; the latter is generally regarded as his finest work, and was widely influential. The same year came *Martin Rattler; or a Boy's Adventures in the Forests of Brazil* and in 1860 *The World of Ice; or Adventures in the Polar Regions*. The **Dog Crusoe* (1861) was among his best stories. After *The *Gorilla Hunters* (1861), Ballantyne abandoned his Edinburgh publishers and obtained a better deal in London, which encouraged him to write even more prolifically. He also began to research his books from life, so as to achieve greater verisimilitude. For *The Lifeboat, a Tale of our Coast* (1864) he met and talked to crews; for *The Lighthouse* (1865) he spent two weeks with the keepers at Bell Rock Lighthouse; for *Fighting the Flames* (1867) he went out with the London fire brigade. R. L. *Stevenson, in the dedicatory poem to **Treasure Island* (1883), dubbed him 'Ballantyne the brave'.

His escapades became even more outlandish. He helped to drive the London–Edinburgh express, which resulted in *The Iron Horse* (1871); tried out a new diving suit in the Thames, and wrote *Under the Waves* (1876); and wandered about the General Post Office disguised as a detective, an exploit that led to *Post Haste* (1880). For *Pirate City* (1874) he went to Algiers and dressed himself as an Arab. Only towards the end of his life did he once again base his books chiefly on his past experiences, abandoning his strange journeys in favour of home life at Harrow-on-the-Hill with his wife and children. Nevertheless he continued to write prolifically—fourteen full-length adventure stories appeared between 1884 and 1890—though his later books were thin stuff, with implausible turns of plot and predictable denouements.

His stories were among the first to portray boys enjoying real adventures by themselves, away from home and free from parental restraints. The plots are heavily action-based and Ballantyne's heroes tend to be one-dimensional, being invariably manly, broad-chested, and unhesitating when faced with any physical challenge. Modern readers are also likely to be irritated by the moments of sentimentality or piety which occur with some frequency. But the books—especially the earlier ones—are redeemed by the degree of information they offer about unusual ways of life, and they have a no-nonsense briskness which makes them still very readable.

Ballantyne's Miscellany (1863–66) A series of eighteen small *adventure stories by R. M. *Ballantyne, intended to instruct the poor and uneducated in religion, and to teach them history, geography, and science.

Ballet Shoes, *a story of three children on the stage* (1936) The first children's book by Noel *Streatfeild, and the story that created the genre of the *career novel. Pauline, Petrova, and Posy Fossil are three adopted children, brought up in London; their surname was invented because their rescuer is a fossil-hunter, Great-Uncle-Matthew ('GUM'). The three 'vow to try and put our name in history books because it's our very own'. They attend the Children's Academy of Dancing and Stage Training; Petrova and Pauline play the two children in *The *Blue Bird*, and Pauline begins a career on the professional stage which eventually leads to Hollywood and stardom. Posy, whose ballet shoes came with her when she was adopted, eventually leaves to train as a dancer in Czechoslovakia, while Petrova turns her back on the performing arts and

takes up flying. The account of the stage school and the girls' professional experience gained vividness from the author's own memory of work as an actress when she was a young woman.

Streatfeild gives a subtle and entertaining portrait of the girls' relationship with each other and with the other members of their strange household, doing this with an accomplishment that few children's writers in any country had achieved since *Little Women*, which at times *Ballet Shoes* closely resembles. Though Streatfeild went on to write further career novels, she turned increasingly to families as a source of her narrative.

Ballet Shoes, which was originally illustrated by Ruth Gervis, was an instant success—Hatchard's bookshop in Piccadilly had to ration customers to one copy each—and it has remained in print ever since, a classic of 20th-cent. children's fiction.

Baloo Bear in The *Jungle Books* by *Kipling.

Bambi A story by 'Felix *Salten', originally published in German in 1923. It recounts the life of a young forest deer from birth to full maturity, and tells of his mother's death and a forest fire as well as his courtship of the female Faline. Written in a heightened style, with much speech between the animals (and even at one point a conversation between two leaves), it was not intended specifically for children, but had soon become accepted internationally as a children's book. The first English translation appeared in 1928, by Whittaker Chambers with an enthusiastic foreword by John Galsworthy. It was animated by *Disney in 1942.

Banbury An Oxfordshire town which features much in *nursery rhymes, partly because the 18th-19th cent. Banbury printing firm of Rusher put it into their children's book rhymes. 'Ride à cock-horse to Banbury Cross' apparently predates that, and was sometimes 'Coventry Cross'.

BANCROFT, Bronwyn See AUSTRALIAN ABORIGINAL WRITING AND ILLUSTRATION.

bande dessinée See BD.

Band of Hope See TEMPERANCE STORIES.

BANG, Molly (1943-) American author and illustrator. Inspired by the work of Arthur *Rackham, Bang's early books were collections of folk tales. She is a three-time Caldecott Honor winner (*see* CALDECOTT MEDAL) for *The Grey Lady and the Strawberry Snatcher* (1981), *Ten, Nine, Eight* (1983), which was also shortlisted for the *Kate Greenaway Medal, and *When Sophie Gets Angry—Really, Really Angry . . .* (1999), which won the Charlotte Zolotow Award. The latter two books were influenced by her daughter Monika Bang-Campbell, with whom she collaborated on the *Little Rat* series. In recent years, Bang has turned to writing about science for young people.

BANKS, Lynne Reid See REID BANKS, LYNNE.

Banks family In *Mary Poppins* by P. L. Travers.

banned books Books for children, among them many classics, have been challenged or banned around the world with great frequency, to protect young children from material deemed too adult and disturbing, or to prevent access to information or stories that seem to threaten religion, ideology, or social norms.

In the English-speaking world, such challenges and bans are particularly prevalent in certain contexts in the US. The *American Library Association responded to the frequency of attempts to ban books in the US by instituting, from 1982 onwards, an active campaign against banning. It keeps records of challenged and banned books in the US, and counts as a 'challenge' an attempt to remove or restrict access to a book because of objections by an individual or a group. Challenges generally come from teachers, parents, and religious leaders, asking for books to be removed from schools, libraries, bookshops, and other locations. If the work is then removed and made unavailable, this is a ban. The Association accepts the right and responsibility of parents to restrict access by their own children to books they consider inappropriate; the campaign is against censorship by others, which 'for protection or any other reason violates the First Amendment', the country's incorporation of free speech into the constitution.

Books for children banned in various institutions or places in the US include the *Harry Potter series, Philip Pullman's *His Dark Materials* trilogy, the *What's Happening to My Body* books by Lynda Madras (1987), and works by Roald *Dahl, Shel *Silverstein, and Dr *Seuss, among others. According to the American Library Association, some of the reasons for challenging or banning these and other books are that adults object to what they perceive as violence, environmentalism,

religion, satanism, drugs, gangs, inaccuracy, or offensive language. The *Hunger Games trilogy has been deemed too violent, The Great Gilly Hopkins (1978) by Katharine *Paterson was thought to portray biological parents negatively, and Harper Lee's *To Kill a Mockingbird (1960) was challenged for racism, despite being about fighting racial inequality. One of the earliest banned books for children was Mark Twain's The *Adventures of Huckleberry Finn (1884). Reasons for challenging it have included the fact that it is written in dialect, thought to be inappropriate for children; that it is humorous in ways felt to be unsuitable for both children and women; and that it is both racist and against racism. Some new editions of the book have replaced the word 'nigger'.

The most common reasons for challenging books in the US appear to be sex and *sexuality. Over a twenty-year period, from 1990–2010, nearly 11,000 challenges were recorded in the US. Of the books challenged, over 3,000 were deemed 'sexually explicit'; more than 300 books were challenged for being 'anti-family' (which could be on the basis of parents not being heterosexual, but could also refer to a single parent or a child being raised by grandparents instead of parents); over 800 challenges were about homosexuality, including concern that children would be recruited or 'tempted' into being homosexual if they read literature featuring non-heterosexual characters; over 600 were about nudity and over 300 about sex education. In addition, more than 2000 were challenged for being 'unsuited to age group'.

Examples of books challenged or banned for how they portray sexual orientation include the picture books Heather Has Two Mommies by Lesléa Newman (1989), Daddy's Roommate by Michael Wilhoite (1991), and And Tango Makes Three by Justin Richardson and Peter Parnell (2006); all three are in the top ten most challenged books in the US because challengers argue that these works promote a 'gay agenda'. Among *young adult books, Nancy *Garden's Annie on My Mind (1982) and the Rainbow trilogy (2001) by Alex Sanchez are both in the top 50 list of most frequently challenged texts.

Books with heterosexual sexual content that have been challenged include novels by Judy *Blume, which feature masturbation and sexual intercourse, and Anne Frank's The *Diary of a Young Girl, thought inappropriate because of its depiction of developing sexuality.

Challenging and banning may lead to general censorship, whether by governments or publishers, or by authors practising self-censorship out of fear of not being able to get their works published.

BANNER, Angela Creator of *Ant and Bee.

BANNERMAN (Watson), Helen (Brodie Cowan) (1862–1946) Author and illustrator of *Little Black Sambo, born in Edinburgh, the daughter of an army chaplain. She married an army doctor, lived with him in India, and wrote Little Black Sambo in 1898, while travelling between Madras and the hill station where her two daughters were staying during the hot season. It was followed by a number of others in the same style and format: these include Little Black Mingo (1901), Little Black Quibba (1902), Little Black Quasha (1908), and Little Black Bobtail (1910). In the 1930s, Bannerman wrote Sambo and the Twins (1938). Little White Squibba was found among her papers at her death, and was published in 1966. All Bannerman's books celebrate the ingenuity of children of South Indian or Tamil origin. However, her books have been attacked because of their supposed *racism. This issue prompted a new version of her first book to be published under the title The Story of Little Babaji in 1996.

BARBAULD, Anna Laetitia (1743–1825) The author of a number of popular and influential writings for children. She was the daughter of John Aikin, DD, a Leicestershire schoolmaster who, when she was fifteen, became classical tutor at the dissenting Warrington Academy in Lancashire. Anna Laetitia was educated entirely at home; she read very widely in Classical and modern European writings. When she was thirty she published her first volume of poems; it was immediately successful, and went through four editions in the first year. In 1774 she married the Revd Rochemont Barbauld, a dissenting minister of French descent who had been educated at her father's school. They set up home at Palgrave in Suffolk, where Mr Barbauld became minister to a local chapel, and here they established a boys' boarding-school. This proved a great success, largely due to Mrs Barbauld's own efforts.

She and her husband had no children, but they adopted a nephew, Charles Rochemont Aikin. Anna Laetitia herself had learnt to read before she was three; now, finding no book suitable for teaching Charles his letters, she wrote *Lessons for Children, a series of which the first small volume was published in 1778. It set a new standard for reading-books,

and inspired Richard *Edgeworth to begin his own work in the field. In 1781 came her very successful *Hymns in Prose for Children*. She became something of a literary celebrity, and by 1785 she and her husband were able to afford to give up their school. During this period Anna Laetitia contributed to her brother John *Aikin's popular series for young people, *Evenings at Home* (1792-6). In 1802 the Barbaulds moved to Stoke Newington, where John Aikin had been his home. Mr Barbauld, who had always been unstable, eventually became entirely insane, and died in 1808. Anna Laetitia then devoted herself entirely to literary work; she prepared an edition in 50 volumes of the best English novels, and made a selection of the best passages from English prose and poetry, as well as writing more of her own verses and essays.

Her reputation has suffered from the general disparagement of the *moral tale, and in particular from an attack by Charles *Lamb, who thought 'Mrs Barbauld's stuff' too dull and instructive compared to the stories that had amused him in childhood. A century after Lamb, she was placed by E. *Nesbit among the unpleasant Book People (nasty authors) in *Wet Magic* (1913). Since the 1990s, however, her work has enjoyed a resurgence with the rise of feminist literary criticism which has also reassessed Romanticism through the writing of women. In addition, her writing for children and her pedagogic methods have now been recognized as groundbreaking. In 2009 William McCarthy published the first modern biography of Barbauld.

BARBER, Antonia *See* MOUSEHOLE CAT, THE.

BARBOUR, Ralph Henry (1870-1944) American author of *school stories, set in private academies for boys. They include *The Spirit of the School* (1907) and *Double Play, a story of school and baseball* (1909). Some of his stories were serialized in *The *Youth's Companion*.

BARING-GOULD, Sabine (1834-1924) Author of such popular hymns as 'Now the day is over' and 'Onward Christian soldiers'; he wrote the first of these for the children of a mission school in the Yorkshire village where he was curate. He collected and published folk songs, folklore, and *ghost stories, produced a *Book of Fairy Tales* (1894) and *Old English Fairy Tales* (1895), and, with Cecil Sharp, edited the long-lived *English Folk Songs for Schools* (1907).

BARKER, Cicely Mary (1895-1973) British author-illustrator of *Flower Fairies* (1923) and other books in the same series, which portray fairy children, each dressed to represent a different kind of flower.

BARNARDO, Dr Thomas John (1845-1905) British philanthropist who opened the first of his celebrated children's homes in London in 1867. He publicized his work with a number of tracts in which he related how he rescued *street Arabs, for example *A City Waif: How I Fished for and Caught Her* (c.1881). He was also the moving force behind *Our Darlings* (1882 onwards) (originally *The Children's Treasury*), a *magazine which specialized in sentimental engravings of children and stories of rescued waifs.

BARNE, Kitty (Marion Catherine) (1883-1957) British children's author; she wrote many *plays for children and two *career stories, *She Shall Have Music* (1938) and *Family Footlights* (1939)—before coming to prominence with *Visitors from London* (1940). This *Carnegie Medal winner is about a group of London children evacuated to Sussex because of the bombing. She then produced several other novels dealing with the impact of war, including *Musical Honours* (1947), in which a returned prisoner of war finds that his younger children do not remember him.

BARRETT, Angela (1955-) British illustrator whose atmospheric, detailed paintings and slightly stylized figures make her work both classic and distinctive. Known for her period illustrations, she carries out extensive research before beginning a new piece of work. Standout titles include *Beauty and the Beast* (2010), retold by Max Eilenberg, a biography of Joan of Arc (1998) by Josephine Poole, and an edition of Paul Gallico's *The *Snow Goose* (2007). Barrett won the W. H. Smith Illustration Award in 1991 for *The Hidden House* by Martin Waddell and was shortlisted for the *Kate Greenaway Medal in 1993 for *Beware, Beware!* by Susan *Hill.

BARRETT, Anne (Mainwaring) (1911-86) British children's writer best known for *Songberd's Grove* (1957), a story about Teddy boys of the 1950s, and *Midway* (1967), in which a lonely boy creates the fantasy figure of a tiger, who becomes his confidant.

BARRIE, J. M. (James Matthew) (1860-1937) Author of *Peter Pan*. He was born on 9 May 1860 at Kirriemuir, a small town north of Dundee,

the ninth child of David Barrie, a weaver, and Margaret Ogilvy, a stonemason's daughter.

The first six years of Barrie's life were unclouded. He played with a friend's *toy theatre, and acted impromptu dramas in the wash-house opposite the family home—a little brick building that he later identified as 'the original of the little house the Lost Boys built in the Never Land for Wendy'. He devoted much of his time to reading *penny dreadfuls, though when he saw a condemnation of this class of fiction in the magazine *Chatterbox he went out and buried his stock of them in a field. He loved stories about desert islands, his favourite of all being Ballantyne's The *Coral Island, undoubtedly an inspiration for the Never Land.

James's eldest brother Alexander, nearly 20 years his senior and with considerable academic ability, opened a private school in Lanarkshire. The second Barrie son, David, was sent there in 1866, but a few months later he died from falling on his head while ice-skating. His mother Margaret Ogilvy, in J. M. Barrie's words, was 'always delicate from that hour'. James himself became a substitute for David in his mother's affections; she used to talk to him about her own childhood, during which, after her own mother's death, she had been 'mistress of the house and mother to her little brother'. This was to lead Barrie to write of Wendy mothering the Lost Boys. Meanwhile in Margaret Ogilvy's memory her dead son always remained as he had been, a boy of thirteen who would never grow up—an origin of Peter Pan.

At the age of thirteen Barrie was sent to school in Dumfries, where he joined a make-believe *pirate crew of boys. He attended the town theatre and founded a school dramatic society, for which he wrote a number of plays. Some were simply lifted from dramas he had seen, but one, 'Bandelero the Bandit', was an original piece of work based on penny dreadfuls and the stories of Fenimore *Cooper, for which he and his friends had a great liking. By the time that Barrie left school he wanted to be an author, and it was only reluctantly that he embarked on a conventional university education at Edinburgh. During his student days he became painfully conscious that he was different from most other young men. He was small of stature, never growing beyond five feet two inches, and he was also uneasy about his contemporaries' interest in sex.

Barrie's first job was as a journalist on the *Nottingham Journal*. But this newspaper could not afford to go on employing him, and he decided to try to earn a living in London as a freelance writer. He moved there in 1885; among those editors who willingly bought his work was W. E. Henley of the *National Observer*, friend of Robert Louis *Stevenson (one of Barrie's idols) and patron of Kenneth *Grahame. Barrie made a particular success of semi-fictionalized articles describing life in Kirriemuir (which he called 'Thrums') and in a community of 'Auld Lichts' such as his mother had been brought up in. These writings were collected in Auld Licht Idylls (1888) and A Window in Thrums (1889), which, together with a third book about Scottish life, The Little Minister (1891), made him a fashionable and best-selling author. Robert Louis Stevenson himself now wrote to Barrie that he thought him 'a man of genius'.

During the 1890s Barrie began to write for the London stage, his first substantial play being Walker, London (1892), a comedy about an impostor. Its cast included a young actress named Mary Ansell, whom Barrie himself 'discovered', and with whom he fell in love. They were married in 1894. Years later, when the marriage came to a dramatic end, there were rumours that Barrie was impotent and that it had never been consummated, but there is some evidence that this was untrue. Certainly the Barries' marriage was profoundly unhappy. Mary took refuge in keeping dogs, of which the first was Porthos, a St Bernard named after one of the *Three Musketeers, of which Barrie himself became inordinately fond, and which provided the first germ of the dog Nana in Peter Pan. For his part, Barrie began to write a novel, Sentimental Tommy (1896), which laid bare much of his own agonized personality. The book appeared in the same year as Margaret Ogilvy, Barrie's portrait of his mother, who had died in 1895.

In 1896 Barrie and his wife visited America, chiefly to meet the Broadway theatrical producer Charles Frohman and to discuss with him a dramatization of The Little Minister; the friendship with Frohman was a large factor in the creation of Peter Pan. Back in England, Barrie wrote a sequel to Sentimental Tommy, entitled Tommy and Grizel, which describes Tommy Sandys's adult years as a fashionable writer in London, and his deeply unsatisfactory marriage to his childhood sweetheart, Grizel. Barrie himself said that the book would 'contain what ordinary biographies omit', and it was indeed very candid about what was obviously his own marriage: 'He was a boy

only...And boys cannot love. Oh, is it not cruel to ask a boy to love?...He was a boy who could not grow up.'

The Barries remained childless, and while Mary directed her motherliness towards her dogs, Barrie himself became close friends with other people's children such as the daughter of W. E Henley and the sons of the writer Maurice Hewlett. Then, while walking in Kensington Gardens with the Hewletts, Barrie made the acquaintance of two boys named George and Jack, aged five and three; they could often be found there with their nurse, who pushed their baby brother Peter in a perambulator. When Barrie's play of *The Little Minister* opened with great success in 1897, he attended a celebratory dinner party and sat next to 'the most beautiful creature that he had ever seen'; she turned out to be the boys' mother, Sylvia Llewelyn Davies.

She was married to Arthur Llewelyn Davies, a young and not very successful barrister, and she was the daughter of George du Maurier (*Punch* artist and author of *Trilby*) and the sister of the actor Gerald du Maurier. Sylvia, her husband, and her children, lived at 31 Kensington Park Gardens, where Barrie soon became a familiar figure, loved by the boys for his ability to amuse them with such tricks as eyebrow-wiggling and for the strange and whimsical stories he told them.

Of the boys, it was George, the eldest, strikingly good-looking, who at first became Barrie's favourite. He chronicled his growing friendship with the boy in *The *Little White Bird* (1902). It was in this book that the figure of Peter Pan appeared, developed initially from the idea that George's baby brother Peter, like all babies, was once a bird and could still fly; but Peter Pan soon took on a far greater significance than this small piece of whimsy, and came to occupy the central chapters of the book.

Barrie's fondness for the Llewelyn Davies boys has been interpreted as paedophilia, and certainly the physical beauty of George affected him, as is shown by his description of 'David' in *The Little White Bird*. However, in collaborating with biographer Andrew Birkin for the book, *The Lost Boys* (1979), the only surviving Llewelyn Davies brother, Nico, denied any impropriety on the part of Barrie. What is certain is that Barrie was, in his way, in love with the boys' mother, Sylvia, and looked forward to the birth of her fourth child in 1900 as if it were his own. It proved to be another boy, named Michael.

In 1900, the Barries bought a country retreat, Black Lake Cottage near Farnham in Surrey. Here, Barrie worked at his next play, *Quality Street* and began to introduce the Llewelyn Davies boys to the delights of *pirates, 'Red *Indians', and desert islands; for the games that he had played during his schooldays in Dumfries were perfectly suited to the Black Lake from which the cottage took its name.

Barrie took photographs of these exploits, and made a book out of them, *The Boy Castaways of Black Lake Island*. It was printed for him by Constable's and given a gilt-stamped binding in the exact style of *The Coral Island*, but only two copies were produced, one for Arthur Llewelyn Davies, the boys' father, and one for Barrie himself. Arthur, who reputedly did not like Barrie, instantly lost his copy. The second is now housed in Yale University library. Barrie's play *The Admirable Crichton* (1902) used the same desert-island theme, reworked for an adult audience.

From *The Boy Castaways* and *The Little White Bird* it was only the shortest of steps to *Peter Pan*. Barrie was encouraged to make that step by the success of 'The Greedy Dwarf', a *pantomime which he wrote for performance at the Llewelyn Davies's London house at Christmas 1900; the cast included Sylvia Llewelyn Davies, her brother Gerald du Maurier (the future performer of Captain Hook), Barrie himself, and Porthos the dog. Another inspiration to him was Seymour Hicks's play *Bluebell in Fairyland*, to which he took the boys a year later. This led him to consider writing a 'fairy play' of his own. On 23 November 1903 he began the first draft of what he initially called 'Anon, A Play', which was soon to become the most celebrated work of his life. After undergoing many changes and refinements (which were themselves far from final), *Peter Pan* opened on the London stage the following Christmas, to be hailed almost unanimously as the finest play ever written for children, and a classic of imaginative literature. (For the detailed history of its composition and the original and subsequent productions, *see* PETER PAN.)

A fifth son, Nicholas, was born to the Llewelyn Davieses just as Barrie was beginning to write *Peter Pan*. Michael, the fourth boy, was now of an age to interest Barrie just as much as George had done at first, and Barrie became deeply attached to him. During 1906 the boys' father was discovered to have cancer of the jaw, and he died the following year, leaving

very little money. Barrie, who was already vir-
tually in the position of father to the boys, now
became so in all but name. His own marriage
came to an end in 1909 when his wife admit-
ted infidelity with Gilbert Cannan, a young
lawyer, and after the divorce it seems that
Barrie hoped to marry Sylvia Llewelyn Davies.
But she too was discovered to have cancer,
and she died in August 1910. Her imprecisely
worded will named him among several people
who were to be guardians to the boys, and he
assumed that responsibility single-handedly at
once, somewhat to the resentment of Jack and
Peter (who was now at Eton and bitterly hated
being identified, incorrectly, with Peter Pan),
but to the delight of George, Michael, and
Nicholas.

For the rest of his life Barrie 'did his best',
and was in fact an unfailingly kind, tolerant,
and undogmatic father-substitute. Yet his
dominant role in the boys' lives, especially
and increasingly in Michael's, inevitably
struck their contemporaries as in some unde-
finable way unhealthy.

In April 1912, quite without warning to the
public, a statue of Peter Pan appeared over-
night in Kensington Gardens. The work of Sir
George Frampton, it was commissioned and
paid for by Barrie, and was erected in secrecy
to give the impression that it had come there
by magic. His career as a playwright continued
to be on the whole successful, though it was
still by *Peter Pan*, which had become an an-
nual Christmas institution in London, that he
was best known. Not until *Dear Brutus* (1917)
did he again create an enduring and brilliantly
conceived drama. Once more, it was strongly
and painfully autobiographical, its theme
being the giving of a 'second chance' to a
number of adults whose lives have gone pain-
fully wrong, among them Mr Purdie, a man
who must always be pursuing some woman
other than his wife, and the lonely Will Dearth,
whose marriage is tragically childless and
who, through the magic worked during the
play, is temporarily given a dream-child. Bar-
rie's last theatrical success, the ghost-play
Mary Rose (1920), which had a considerable
popular triumph at the time of its first produc-
tion, grew partly out of the death of Sylvia
Llewelyn Davies.

Two other bereavements were to come to
Barrie. George Llewelyn Davies, who as a boy
had inspired the book from which *Peter Pan*
grew, was killed in Flanders during 1915. Then
in 1921 Michael, who now meant more to
Barrie than had anyone else in his life, was

drowned in the Thames near Oxford in a sus-
pected homosexual suicide pact with a fellow
student. Peter committed suicide long after
Barrie's death, in 1960.

Michael's death was in effect the end of
Barrie's life; Nicholas ('Nico'), the one Lost
Boy who remained with him, could not re-
place Michael in Barrie's affections. From
1918 Barrie became involved in another of
his tantalizing and enigmatic relationships
with an attractive young woman, in this case
Lady Cynthia Asquith, who acted as his secre-
tary, though she could not type or take short-
hand. His last play *The Boy David* (1936), a
version of the Bible story of David written for
the actress Elisabeth Bergner, was by no
means unremarkable, but was the work of a
tired man. He died the year after it was
produced.

BARRY, Margaret Stuart (1927–) British
author of comic *fantasy stories, including the
Simon and the Witch series (from 1976), about
a schoolboy and a *witch, and *Maggy Gump-
tion* (1979), whose heroine is a *doll living in
an attic peopled by eccentric toys.

Bartimaeus *See* STROUD, JONATHAN.

BASE, Graeme (1958–) Australian author/
illustrator of picture books. His second book,
Animalia (1986), is still his most famous, and
there are now several companion volumes.
Animalia is an alphabet book with a short
poetic text for each spread, and detailed, com-
plex, poster-like illustrations with ornate type.
Base's texts are often poetic, his illustrations
detailed and richly coloured. Readers are
invited to look for hidden objects or animals,
a feature first developed for *The Eleventh Hour*
(1989), a mystery story, where text and pic-
tures work together to engage readers in a
search for hidden objects, secret codes, and
word puzzles. His sophisticated humour and
complex art lends itself to computer games,
*apps, and promotions where readers solve a
problem related to the illustrations. His work
continues to impress, and is often on the
*CBCA shortlist or its *Notable Books* list.

Bash Street Kids, the A group of unruly
schoolchildren in a cartoon strip in *Beano*.

Basil Brush A fox puppet in British chil-
dren's television programmes, and in books
by Peter Firmin.

Basket of Flowers, The The English title of
Das Blumenkörbchen (1823) by Christoph
Von *Schmid, which became the archetypal

*Sunday school book after its translation in 1833. It is the story of an elderly gardener and basket-maker and his pious daughter Mary, who is wrongly condemned for the supposed theft of a ring; her father dies a holy death, and eventually all is set right. It was one of the most popular *reward books throughout the 19th cent., and, astonishingly, was still in print for use in African missions in 1972.

Bastable family In *The *Story of the Treasure Seekers* and other books by E. *Nesbit.

Batchelder Award (Mildred L. Batchelder Award) Established in 1966 to honour children's books published in the United States that have been translated from other languages. Presented annually since 1968, the award has gone to books by writers including Erich *Kästner, Christine *Nöstlinger, Uri *Orlev, René *Goscinny, Alki *Zei, Janne Teller, and Cornelia *Funke, with winning translators including Anthea *Bell, Laura Watkinson, Hillel Halkin, Cathy Hirano, Edward Fenton, and Patricia *Crampton.

Batman Created by American artist Bob Kane in 1939 in *Detective Comics*, an American *comic book whose publishers wished to imitate *Superman. Batman is a millionaire, Bruce Wayne, who as a child vowed revenge on all criminals because of the murder of his parents. He stalks the city streets in bat-like cloak and mask, as an avenging vigilante. His henchman is Robin the Boy Wonder, whom he has adopted. Batman has featured in innumerable radio and television programmes, and is regularly recreated on the big screen (though these most recent developments of the franchise now serve adults more than children).

battledore An instrument like a small racket, used for playing shuttlecock. The term was also applied to the wooden or cardboard tablets which gradually superseded the *hornbook as a device for teaching children to read. Some battledores had handles and were rectangular in shape, as had been the hornbooks, while others were rounded like rackets. They lacked the true hornbook's covering of horn, but the printing was sometimes protected by a coat of varnish. However, from the mid-18th cent. most battledores were produced without handles, and were simply pieces of thin cardboard, folded twice to make a booklet of two pages with a narrow flap at the front. The invention of these was claimed by the Salisbury bookseller Benjamin

Collins, business associate of John *Newbery, who began to manufacture a *Royal Battledore* in association with Newbery in 1746. Other specimens were sold under such titles as *The British Battledore, The Infant's Battledore,* and *The New Improved Battledore.* The wording printed on them varied greatly, but the alphabet featured prominently, and, unlike the hornbooks, entertainment was usually aimed at as well as instruction; there were often illustrations. Battledores were produced until about the middle of the 19th cent.

Baudelaire, Violet, Sunny, and **Klaus** Orphans in *A *Series of Unfortunate Events.*

BAUER, Joan (1951-) American author of books for *young adults who started her career in journalism before moving on to screenwriting. Widely popular and award-winning in America, her books are influenced by her own childhood and by a belief that adversity makes you stronger. Her first novel was written when she was housebound following an accident—*Squashed* (1992), about a prize-winning vegetable (but really about more important things) was a success, and its blend of serious issues layered with humour and a positive outlook set the pattern for her subsequent works. *Rules of the Road* (1998) and its companion *Best Foot Forward* (2005) are her most autobiographical stories, clearly showing the pain of having an alcoholic parent. *Hope Was Here* (2000), which draws on her time spent waitressing while at high school, was a Newbery Honor Book (*see* NEWBERY MEDAL). In *Tell Me* (2014), twelve-year-old Anna is staying with her grandmother to avoid her troubled parents, but she makes a discovery that overshadows preparations for the town's Flower Festival.

BAUER, Jutta (1955-) Award-winning German illustrator, cartoonist, and animator perhaps best known for her *Selma* series (from 1997) about a sheep searching for happiness. Bauer was awarded the *Deutscher Jugendliteraturpreis in 2001 for the picture book *Schreimutter.* She was a runner-up in 2002 for *Opas Engel (Grandpa's Angel,* UK edition 2005) a picture book that subtly addresses Germany's Nazi past and received a Special Prize for Illustration in 2009. In 2010 she was honoured with the *Hans Christian Andersen Award for her lasting contribution to children's literature. Her picture book *The Queen of Colours* (1998; UK edition 2014) first appeared as an animated short and stars

Queen Matilda, whose commands for colour simply explode off the page. Bauer's distinctive pen-and-ink illustrations and use of colour convey great humour in simple lines but under that frivolity there is often a deeper or more poignant message about life itself.

BAUM, L. (Lyman) Frank (1856–1919) Author of the original 'Oz' stories; he was born in Chittenago, New York, the son of an oil magnate and theatre owner. He had a defective heart, was forbidden to play games, and spent much of his childhood reading; he was sent to Peekskill Military Academy, but was withdrawn after being taken ill with heart trouble. At home, he set up a small printing press and began to produce a family newspaper. He also became an actor and during the 1870s toured the state with Shakespearian companies. Eventually he began to work in the family oil business, and also to earn a living as a journalist.

In 1882 he staged a melodrama with book, music, and lyrics by himself, *The Maid of Arran*, based on a popular novel of the time. The production toured as far afield as Canada and Kansas, as well as playing in New York City. The same year Baum married Maud Gage, daughter of a prominent suffragette. Two sons were soon born, and in order to support his family Baum returned to the oil business, this time as salesman for Baum's Castorine, an axle lubricant. But his father died, the Castorine company had to be sold, and Baum and his family moved to South Dakota. In the town of Aberdeen they opened a store, Baum's Bazaar, but this closed after two years. Baum then became editor of a weekly newspaper, but this enterprise, too, only lasted for a short time. He next went to Chicago, working first as a journalist and then as a travelling salesman.

He now had four sons, and for some time had been amusing his children with stories based on *nursery rhymes. In 1897 there was published a book of these, *Mother Goose in Prose*, with illustrations by the young Maxfield *Parrish. In the same year Baum gave up his travelling salesmanship on the advice of a heart specialist and founded *The Show Window*, a periodical for window dressers (or, to use the American term, window trimmers). This led to the formation of the National Association of Window Trimmers, of which Baum became Secretary. He also wrote *The Art of Decorating Dry Goods Windows and Interiors* (1900). At about the same time he met the illustrator William Wallace Denslow, and collaborated with him on a *picture book of rhymes, *Father Goose, His Book* (1899). This became a best-seller, and was followed by two more in similar vein, *The Army Alphabet* and *The Navy Alphabet*, both illustrated by Denslow and published in 1900.

The success of *Father Goose* led Baum to buy a summer cottage on Lake Michigan which he named 'The Sign of the Goose'. It also encouraged him to make a children's novel out of a bedtime story he had told to his sons. This became *The *Wonderful Wizard of Oz* (1900), the greatest success of Baum's career. The next year Baum produced *American Fairy Tales*; *The Master Key*, a story about a boy who conjures up a *genie out of the electrical gadgetry which is his hobby; and another full-length fairy tale, *Dot and Tot of Merryland*. This was his last collaboration with Denslow as illustrator, the two having quarrelled about the artist's right to a share in the royalties of a proposed musical entitled *The Wizard of Oz*. Baum's next books were *The Life and Adventures of Santa Claus* (1902) and *The Surprising Adventures of the Magical Monarch of Mo and His People*, a revised version of a Lewis *Carroll-like story originally published in 1900 as *A New Wonderland*.

The huge success of the stage production of *The Wizard of Oz* (1902) encouraged Baum to write more Oz books. *The Marvelous Land of Oz* (1905) relates the adventures of Tip, an Oz boy who is brought up under the care of a *witch. His companions are Jack Pumpkinhead, a creature resembling the Scarecrow and the Tin Man in the first Oz book, a Saw-Horse, and a creature by the name of 'H.M. Woggle-Bug, T.E.', the first initials standing for 'Highly Magnified' and the last for 'Thoroughly Educated'. At the end of the story, Tip is given a magical sex-change and proves to be Princess Ozma, rightful ruler of Oz. This book was adapted for the stage as *The Woggle-Bug*, but without success, and Baum now began to write potboiler fiction for money: adventure stories (the 'Boy Fortune Hunters' series) which appeared under the name 'Floyd Akers', stories for young children under the pseudonym 'Laura Bancroft', and *girls' stories (the very popular 'Aunt Jane's Nieces' series) as 'Edith Van Dyne', to name but some of his aliases.

On the proceeds of the first of these potboiler novels, the Baums toured Europe and North Africa during 1906, and while in Paris Baum became interested in the possibilities of the

cinematograph. Returning to America, he made a series of short films based on Oz stories; these were hand-coloured, and trick photography was used. Baum took them on tour, introducing them to the audience himself, but with little success. More Oz books followed; *Ozma of Oz* (1907) reintroduced the character of Dorothy, heroine of the first book; next came *Dorothy and the Wizard in Oz* (1908), *The Road to Oz* (1909), and *The Emerald City of Oz* (1910). Baum also wrote another non-Oz fantasy, *Queen Zixi of Ix* (1905).

In 1911 Baum and his family moved to Hollywood, hoping that the Californian climate would improve his health; they built a house there which was named 'Ozcot'. But the same year Baum became bankrupt. His next fairy stories, *The Sea Fairies* (1911) and *Sky Island* (1912), did little to mend his fortunes, and he returned to Oz with *The Patchwork Girl of Oz* (1913), *Tik-Tok of Oz* (1914), and *The Scarecrow of Oz* (1915), thereafter producing a new Oz title every year until his death. *The Tik-Tok Man of Oz* was staged as a musical with some success, and the 'Oz Film Manufacturing Company' produced *The Patchwork Girl of Oz* and other titles, but children's movies did not have much appeal at this time, and the company closed down. Baum was ill in the final years of his life, but he continued to work hard until the very end.

The Oz series had by this time become so popular that it was continued (with permission) after Baum's death by Ruth Plumly Thompson, a young Philadelphia children's writer, who produced a book annually until 1939. Further titles in the series were then written by John R. Neill, who had illustrated all the Oz stories except the first. Since Neill's death in 1943 other Oz stories, by different authors, have occasionally appeared.

Baum's writing cannot be called distinguished. Even *The Wonderful Wizard of Oz* is no more than workmanlike in construction—the story is told considerably better in the 1939 MGM film version than in the book—and the numerous sequels are largely reworkings of the same themes over and again, though they are told with pace and humour. His work has never been universally admired, because of its stylistic flaws, and some American public libraries have been proud to announce that they do not stock his books. But he is a figure of great importance in the history of children's fiction in the United States, being the first writer to create an unforgettable full-length original American *fantasy.

BAUMANN, Hans (1914–88) German children's author. He worked briefly as a teacher in Bavaria before war service, during which he was taken prisoner in France. He became a full-time writer in the 1950s, and soon made an international reputation with his carefully researched *historical fiction. His books include (in translation) *The Caves of the Great Hunters* (1954), *Sons of the Steppe* (1957), and *The Barque of the Brothers* (1958).

BAWDEN, Nina (1925–2012) British author who began her career as an adult novelist in 1953, and published her first children's book four years later. She would eventually earn an equally high reputation in both fields, and said of her dual role: 'The things I write about for adults, I write about for children, too: emotions, motives, the difficulties of being honest with oneself, the gulf between what people say and what they really mean.'

Her early children's stories were conventional *adventure stories: *Devil by the Sea* (1957), *The Secret Passage* (1963), *On the Run* (1964), *The White Horse Gang* (1966), *The Witch's Daughter* (1966), *A Handful of Thieves* (1967), and *The Runaway Summer* (1969). But in *Squib* (1971) she produced a more striking story, about children who encounter a maltreated boy and discover that the realities of life can be 'more frightening than a hundred old witches'. *Squib* proved to be a transitional book; its successor, *Carrie's War* (1973), was a fine and original achievement, an account of wartime evacuee children in Wales, based on Nina Bawden's own evacuation there in the 1940s. *The *Peppermint Pig* appeared in 1975 and won her the Guardian Award (*see* GUARDIAN CHILDREN'S FICTION PRIZE).

Rebel on a Rock (1978) is a sequel to *Carrie's War*, and appears to revert to the adventure-story mode of Nina Bawden's early work; in fact it is an ironic inversion of the conventional children's thriller, for the intervention of the children in a political coup in a Mediterranean country produces not the usual happy ending, but disaster—as it probably would in real life. *The Robbers* (1979), illustrated by Charles *Keeping, similarly inverts expectations, for when its boy heroes begin to act out their fantasies about thieves they find themselves in deep trouble. *Kept in the Dark* (1982) is a psychological thriller, somewhat reminiscent of the plays of Harold Pinter, about the invasion of a household by a sinister young man. This was followed in 1989 by *The Outside Child*, a coming-of-age story; and in 1995 by

Granny the Pag, about the relationship between Cat and her unusual grandmother.

At her best—in *Carrie's War* and *The Peppermint Pig*—Nina Bawden portrays a child's view of the world with an almost unique skill. She accepts, for example, that children are fascinated by the horrific, as the opening passage of *The Peppermint Pig* demonstrates:

Old Granny Greengrass had her finger chopped off in the butcher's when she was buying half a leg of lamb. She had pointed to the place where she wanted her joint to be cut but then she decided she needed a bigger piece and pointed again. Unfortunately, Mr Grummett, the butcher, was already bringing his sharp chopper down . . .
'What happened afterwards? Did she spout blood?'
'No, it was a clean cut,' mother said . . .
Poll . . . said suddenly: 'If he sold it to eat, I expect it would taste like a sausage with bone in it.'
'More meaty,' Theo said. 'They put bread in sausages.'

BAXENDALE, Leo (1930–) British cartoonist and *comic strip artist, creator (for the *Thomson comics) of such characters as Minnie the Minx, the Bash Street Kids, and Little Plum.

BAYLEY, Nicola (1949–) British illustrator whose Royal College of Art final diploma portfolio was spotted by the publisher Tom Maschler, who commissioned her to illustrate *Nicola Bayley's Book of Nursery Rhymes* (1975). Her exquisitely detailed, subtly hued style uses a series of minute brushes to create the fine airbrush-like stippling which characterizes her pictures. She is famous for her depictions of cats, and her work includes *The Tyger Voyage* (1976), a prose-poem by Richard Adams, Antonia Barber's *The *Mousehole Cat* (1991), Gretchen Woelfe's *Katje, The Windmill Cat* (2002), and her own books, including *The Necessary Cat* (1998).

BAYNES, Pauline (Diana) (Mrs Fritz Gasch) (1922–2008) British illustrator. Her first book was J. R. R. *Tolkien's *Farmer Giles of Ham* (1949), for which she provided witty mock-medieval drawings. As a result of Tolkien's recommendation she was taken on by C. S. *Lewis and his publisher to illustrate the *Narnia books, beginning with *The Lion, the Witch and the Wardrobe* (1950). She is still best known for her memorable drawings for these books, though she illustrated many other authors' stories. Her later illustrations for Tolkien's work include some strikingly beautiful pictures in *The Adventures of Tom Bombadil* (1962), though the maps and other ephemera that she produced as adjuncts to *The *Lord of the Rings*, at the height of popular enthusiasm for that book, show a certain incongruity between her style and Tolkien's. She was awarded the *Kate Greenaway Medal for her illustrations to Grant Uden's *Dictionary of Chivalry* (1968).

'B. B.' (D. J. (Denys James) Watkins-Pitchford) (1905–90) British author and illustrator. His first books for children were a pair of *animal stories, *Wild Lone* (1938) and *Sky Gipsy* (1939), about a fox and a goose, and all his books reflect his naturalist's knowledge of the countryside. In 1942 he wrote *The *Little Grey Men*, a fantasy which won that year's *Carnegie Medal. *Down the Bright Stream* (1948) was a sequel. Perhaps his best book, however, was *Brendon Chase* (1944).

Watkins-Pitchford always illustrated his own books under his own name, while identifying their author merely as 'B.B.' His other fiction for children includes two comic stories, again about gnomes, *The Forest of Boland Light Railway* (1955) and *The Wizard of Boland* (1959), and a series about 'Bill Badger', who lives on a canal boat. (Watkins-Pitchford was the illustrator of a classic of canal literature, L. T. C. Rolt's *Narrow Boat*, published in 1940.) He also illustrated editions of *Prince Prigio* (1961) and *Granny's Wonderful Chair* (1963).

BD (bande dessinée) (literally: 'drawn strip') The Francophone incarnation of *comics. The origin of BD is also part of perpetually ongoing debates and controversies, though many specialists identify Swiss caricaturist Rodolphe Töppfer (1799–1846) as one of its first authors. One of the major differences between comic books and BD is that the latter have never been as casually dismissed as their Anglophone counterparts, and have been called the 'ninth art' since early criticism of the medium. Additionally, there are traditionally distinct styles of drawing in BD, rather than house styles or authors' takes, as in the US comic book industry. Initially recognized as a predominantly children-aimed publication, with characters such as *Bécassine* (early 1900s), the BD has grown in its target audience and reception. *Hergé's *Les Aventures de *Tintin* introduced travel writing and the colonial propaganda of the time to young audiences, in part because of the political context of their publication. Albert *Uderzo and René *Goscinny's *Astérix le Gaulois* employs the quasi-historical setting

of a small rebellious village in Gaul at the time of the Roman Empire's expansion, and its idiosyncratic and pun-riddled villagers. The series explores different languages, countries, cultures, and stereotypes, the historical elements blending with contemporary politics and current affairs, in 35 published volumes (*albums*) ranging from Goths, Egyptians, Romans, and Picts to more thematic volumes about theatre, the Olympics, and school tales. Other notable BD series include Pierre 'Peyo' Culifford's *Les Schtroumpfs* (*The Smurfs*), Maurice 'Morris' de Bevere's *Lucky Luke*, and the internationally acclaimed work of Jean 'Moebius' Giraud, who contributed to some of the most successful science-fiction films (and comics) in history.

Beadle's Dime Novels See DIME NOVELS.

BEAMAN, S. G. Hulme See TOYTOWN.

Beano A British *comic published by D. C. *Thomson of Dundee; it first appeared on 30 July 1938. The best-known character featured in it is *Dennis the Menace. Other *Beano* heroes include Beryl the Peril, Minnie the Minx, Roger the Dodger, and the Bash Street Kids.

Bear Called Paddington, A See PADDINGTON.

beast-epic A development of the *fable into a lengthy tale or cycle of tales concerning animals. Like the fable, the beast-epic points a moral or series of morals about human behaviour. A notable example is the *Roman de Renart*, the French medieval precursor of *Reynard the Fox*. Dryden used the beast-epic as the framework of *The Hind and the Panther* (1687), and a modern example of the genre is George Orwell's *Animal Farm* (1945).

BEATTY, Patricia (1922–91) American author of children's books, chiefly *historical novels, many of them written with her husband John (1922–75). They include *Campion Towers* (1965), in which a Massachusetts Puritan girl gets involved in the English Civil War. Another Civil War novel, *Charley Skedaddle* (by Patricia alone) was published in 1987 and won the Scott O'Dell Award.

BEAUMONT, Mme Marie Leprince de (1711–80) Writer for children who was born in Rouen. To escape an unhappy marriage she emigrated to England in about 1745, and worked for some years as a *governess. In 1756 she published her *Magasin des enfans,*

ou dialogues entre une sage gouvernante et plusieurs de ses élèves, a four-volume work inspired by Sarah Fielding's *The *Governess* (1749). It was translated into English in 1757 as *The Young Misses Magazine*. Following the then new fashion of combining instruction with entertainment, the *Magasin* takes the form of conversations between a governess, named 'Mrs Affable' in the English translation, and her pupils, who are aged from five to thirteen. Into these conversations are introduced stories, among them *Beauty and the Beast* and *The *Three Wishes*, which made their first appearance in England in this book.

Mme de Beaumont used these and other *fairy stories partly as a vehicle for moral instruction, but she wrote colloquially and with an informality that was something of an innovation when addressing children. Her other books include an *Éducation complète* (1753), and *Le Nouveau Magasin français, ou Bibliothèque instructive* (1750–5).

Beautiful Joe, an autobiography (1894) The first of a series of *animal stories by the Canadian writer Marshall *Saunders. This imitation of *Black Beauty* has as hero a dog who is maltreated by his first master, a cruel milkman, who cuts off his ears and tail. His subsequent adventures run the gamut of sentimentality and melodrama.

Beauty and the Beast A *fairy story which first appeared in English in 1757, in a translation from a French narrative (published the previous year) by Mme de *Beaumont.

A rich merchant loses his fortune and has to lead a life of poverty in the country. His two elder daughters complain about their situation, but the youngest works hard to help her father; she is known by everyone as 'Beauty'. One day her father, on a journey, gets lost in a forest and comes across a large, apparently deserted mansion. There he eats a meal, finds a good bedchamber, and goes to sleep. Next morning he plucks a rose from the garden so that he may take it back to Beauty. However a Beast, who is the owner of the house, appears and, though he has willingly allowed the merchant to eat, drink, and sleep there, he objects violently to the theft of the rose, threatening the merchant with death. But when he learns that the merchant has daughters, he says he will spare him providing one of them will come to the house willingly, and suffer on behalf of her father. The merchant returns home, and when Beauty hears what has happened, she insists on setting out

for the Beast's palace, with her father. At the palace, Beauty tells her father that he must abandon her and go home, she having been told by a fairy in a dream that her good action shall not go unrewarded. She is left alone, and finds everything splendidly prepared for her. The Beast asks her to marry him, but she refuses. She spends three months at the palace, and every evening he pays her a visit; she soon comes to look forward eagerly to this, daily discovering 'some valuable qualifications in the monster'. Eventually he agrees to let her go to visit her father, though he warns her that he will 'die with grief' if she does not return in a week. She agrees to this, but when she gets to her father's house, she is detained by her sisters, and when at last she finds herself back at his palace, she discovers him in the palace grounds, apparently dead. She manages to rouse him and declares that she will marry him. As she says these words, the Beast is transformed into 'one of the loveliest princes that eye ever beheld; who returned her thanks for having put an end to the charm, under which he had so long resembled a Beast'. Beauty is now told by the fairy that appeared to her in her dream: 'You have preferred virtue before either wit or beauty, and deserve to find a person in whom all these qualifications are united; you are going to be a great queen.' Beauty's sisters are punished by being turned into statues.

The immediate source of Mme de Beaumont's 'La Belle et la bête' was the lengthy story in Mme Gabrielle Susanne Barbot de Gallon de Villeneuve's *Contes marins* (1740), a collection of tales supposedly told by an old woman during a long sea voyage. 'Cupid and Psyche', recorded by Apuleius in *The Golden Ass* (2nd cent. AD), is the earliest known variant of the Beauty and the Beast story but there is a much larger group of folk tales in which women or men are married to various creatures or even objects that eventually turn into humans. Such stories include *Perrault's story *Riquet À La Houppe* and Straparola's *The Pig King*.

Mme de Beaumont's version of the story was immediately adopted into English folklore, and was part of the Enlightenment desire to teach children about the virtues of good behaviour through narrative. The earliest retelling of it seems to have been in *The Polite Academy,* a miscellany published by R. Baldwin in 1762. *Beauty and the Beast* was sometimes printed as a *chapbook (e.g. by Richardson of Derby, *c.*1830) and has often

been made into a melodrama or a *pantomime, for example, a stage version by J. R. *Planché, performed at Covent Garden in 1841, a memorable film by Jean Cocteau in 1946, and a popular 1991 *Disney version.

Because of Winn-Dixie (2000) A novel by Kate *DiCamillo, a Newbery Honor book (*see* NEWBERY MEDAL). It is the heart-warming story of ten-year-old Opal, who is facing a lonely summer after moving to a new home with her preacher father. Befriending a stray dog whom she names Winn-Dixie opens doors, and Opal finds herself making friends—some of them surprising. What is even better, she and her father are finally able to talk about Opal's mother who has left the family. There is a 2005 film adaptation.

BECHSTEIN, Ludwig (1801–60) A collector of German folk tales, following the example of the brothers *Grimm. His collections appeared between 1823 and 1856. A selection from them was published in English in 1854 as *The Old Story-Teller*, and another in 1872, entitled *As Pretty as Seven*. *The Rabbit Catcher* (1962) is a collection of retellings from Bechstein by Randall *Jarrell.

BECK, Ian (1947–) An established British author and illustrator, well known for his classic pen-and-ink illustrations. Beck began his career as a freelance illustrator, working mainly for mainstream consumer magazines, as well as designing and illustrating album covers. He was commissioned by Oxford University Press for his first illustrated book *Round and Round the Garden* (1983) and continued illustrating other author's children's books until his first solo project *The Teddy Robber* in 1989. A number of his subsequent picture books received international awards, such as *Home before Dark* (1997). Beck's first novel *The Secret History of Tom Trueheart, Boy Adventurer* (2006) is a playful interpretation of traditional fairy tales which proved to be a great success. This was followed by the sequels *Tom Trueheart and the Land of Dark Stories* (2008) and *Tom Trueheart and the Land of Myth and Legends* (2010).

BEDE (673–735) Early English historian and scholar who wrote a number of *books of instruction for children and young people while he was a monk at Jarrow. The first of these, *De Orthographia*, consists of several hundred Latin words arranged under letters of the alphabet. Each word is the subject of a brief

comment. Two other schoolbooks composed by Bede were intended for more advanced pupils: *De Arte Metrica* gives instruction in the writing of Latin verse, and *De Schematibus et Tropis* is an exposition of the figures of speech. Bede also composed three books of scientific writings for his pupils in Northumbrian schoolrooms: *De Natura Rerum*, an account of the physical universe, and two works concerned with time and the methods of reckoning it, *De Temporibus* and *De Temporum Ratione.*

BEDFORD, F. D. (Francis Donkin) (1864–1954) British illustrator of such books as E. V. *Lucas's Forgotten Tales of Long Ago* (1906), and editions of stories by *Dickens and George *MacDonald. His style somewhat resembled that of Arthur *Hughes.

Bedknob and Broomstick A novel by Mary *Norton, originally published in two parts as *The Magic Bedknob* (USA 1943, Britain 1945) and *Bonfires and Broomsticks* (1947). The story concerns the friendship of three children with Miss Price, an English spinster living in a country village, who at the start of the first book is learning to be a *witch. Thanks to one of her spells, the children are able to travel about in space and time. *Bedknob and Broomstick*, which was issued in one volume in 1957 and was later made into a musical film by the *Disney studios (as *Bedknobs and Broomsticks*), contains all the stock ingredients of English *fantasy writing for children, with little of the originality of the same author's The *Borrowers. Yet Mary Norton's handling of these stock themes is striking; she is less interested in the children's magical experiences than in the very real problems that would occur if magic did exist, and in Miss Price's ambiguous moral relationship with her occult art.

Bedonebyasyoudid, Mrs A fairy in *The *Water-Babies* by Charles *Kingsley.

Beechnut In the *Franconia* stories of Jacob *Abbott.

Beegu (2003) A picture book by Alexis *Deacon. Beegu is a creature from another world who finds herself on Earth, where she shouldn't be, and wants to find her way back to her parents. Her attempts to make friends with the natives are met with hostility, until she meets a group of children, who are more welcoming. A touching and hopeful story, and

Deacon's artwork is—as always—original and beautifully executed.

Bee-Man of Orn, The (1887) A comic short story by Frank *Stockton, about an old beekeeper who, granted the possibility of becoming anybody he chooses, decides to be a baby. It was reissued in 1964 with illustrations by Maurice *Sendak.

Beetle In *Stalky & Co.* by Rudyard *Kipling.

BEETON, Samuel Orchart (1831–77) British publisher who founded the *Boy's Own Magazine*. He was the husband of the celebrated cookery and domestic author (who wrote her books at his suggestion). After his death his name was used for *Beeton's Christmas Annual*, where, in 1887, *Sherlock Holmes first appeared in print.

Beginner Books A series of American *picture books for young readers, originally created by Dr *Seuss.

BEHN, Harry (1898–1973) American writer who produced several books of poems for children, illustrated by himself, beginning with *The Little Hill* (1949). He also wrote children's stories and translated Japanese *haikus* for children, in *Cricket Songs* (1964) and *More Cricket Songs* (1971).

BELL, Anthea (1936–) British translator, one of the few literary translators in the English-speaking world to specialize in books for children. Her first commissioned translation was a children's book, *Preussler's Little Water-Sprite* (1960), and she has gone on to translate dozens more, mostly from French and German, including several books by Cornelia *Funke (including the *Inkheart* trilogy), Erich *Kästner, René *Goscinny's *Le *Petit Nicolas* and new versions of stories by the brothers *Grimm. She is perhaps best known in this field, however, for being the translator (with Derek Hockridge) of all the books in the *Astérix series, which has allowed her to show off her virtuosity in rendering the books' humour and dense wordplay. She claims to have picked up the lateral thinking required for such work from her father, Adrian, the first setter of the *Times* crossword. She won the *Marsh Award in 1996 (for her translation of *A Dog's Life* by Christine *Nöstlinger), in 2003 (*Where Were You, Robert?* by Hans Magnus Enzensberger), and 2007 (*The Flowing Queen* by Kai Meyer); and the *Batchelder Award on a record four occasions (1976, 1979, 1990, and 1995). Besides her children's career, she is also one of the most renowned

translators of French- and German-language books for adults.

BELL, R. S. W. (Robert Stanley Warren) (1871–1921) British author of *school stories, published in *The *Captain*, of which he was the founder and first editor, and in other boys' papers.

BELLAIRS, John (1938–1991) American author best known for his fifteen gothic mystery novels for young adults. He received numerous awards and widespread acclaim for his three bestselling series, featuring, respectively, Lewis Barnaveldt, Anthony Monday, and Johnny Dixon. Famous titles include *The House with a Clock in Its Walls* (1973), *The Letter, the Witch, and the Ring* (1976), *The Treasure of Alpheus Winterborn* (1978), and *The Curse of the Blue Figurine* (1993). Edward *Gorey created artwork for many of his books. In 1992 a historical plaque was placed on Cronin House, the inspiration for *The House with a Clock in Its Walls*, in Bellairs' hometown of Marshall, Michigan.

Bella Swan *See* TWILIGHT.

BELLOC, (Joseph) Hilaire (Pierre René) (1870–1953) Author, poet, and militant Catholic who wrote several notable books of comic verse for children. Of mixed French and English descent, he was brought up in Sussex and educated under Cardinal Newman at the Oratory School in Birmingham. He became a scholar of Balliol College, Oxford, and, while staying on in that city after taking his degree in the hope of obtaining a college fellowship, he wrote *The *Bad Child's Book of Beasts* (1896), which came out in the same year as his first volume of serious poems. *More Beasts for Worse Children* followed in 1897, *The *Modern Traveller* in 1898, A *Moral Alphabet* in 1899, *Cautionary Tales* in 1907, and another book in the same vein, *More Peers*, in 1911. For all these, his illustrator was 'B.T.B.', initials which stood for Lord Basil Blackwood, who became a close friend of Belloc's when they were both Balliol undergraduates. In the Belloc books— and there alone, for he published scarcely any other drawings—Blackwood developed into one of the finest comic draughtsmen of all time. Both author and illustrator have, however, been accused of anti-semitism in their work.

Blackwood was killed in the First World War, and when Belloc returned to the same vein of verse in the years that followed it, Nicolas Bentley supplied the illustrations, with almost equally felicitous results. This collaboration produced *New Cautionary Tales* (1930) and *Ladies and Gentlemen* (1932).

Belloc's dark sense of humour has always been popular with young readers and he still has collections in print. They inspired a number of imitations, for example, *Wonderful England!* (1902) by Mrs Ernest Ames—which lacks any of Belloc's wit—and, much more notably, the comic verses of Harry *Graham.

BEMELMANS, Ludwig (1898–1962) Author and artist, best known for the *Madeline* series. A larger-than-life character, Bemelmans grew up in Austria and emigrated to the USA in 1914, where he worked in the hotel industry. He published his first children's book, *Hansi*, in 1934. It was, however, the picture book *Madeline*, written in 1939, that was to bring him worldwide acclaim. Telling the story of a plucky little schoolgirl living in an 'old house in Paris that was covered in vines', it was the first of a series of seven books, the last of which was published posthumously in 1999. Bemelmans was also an artist, essay writer, novelist, and humourist.

Bending of a Twig, The (1906) A novel by Desmond Coke, about the experiences of the boy Lycidas Marsh at Shrewsbury School. It sets out to parody the conventional *school story and to show the falsity of the picture of school life given in such books, but soon deteriorates into a conventional example of the genre. It was extremely popular in its day. Coke (1879–1931) was a pupil at Shrewsbury himself and later became a schoolmaster.

BENÉT, Stephen Vincent and **Rosemary** *See* BOOK OF AMERICANS, A.

Ben Gunn In *Treasure Island* by R. L. *Stevenson.

Benjamin Bunny In stories by Beatrix *Potter.

Benn, Mr *See* MR BENN.

BENNETT, John *See* MASTER SKYLARK.

BENSON, E. F. *See* DAVID BLAIZE AND THE BLUE DOOR.

BENSON, Mildred Wirt (1905–2002) American writer who for fifty-eight years worked as a journalist whilst also writing for children. From 1929 to 1947 she worked as a ghostwriter for the *Stratemeyer Syndicate, penning twenty-three of the first thirty *Nancy Drew books, using the pen name Carolyn Keene. The character Nancy

Drew was conceived by Edward Stratemeyer, and Benson wrote her stories on his basic ideas. For her work she received a flat fee of $125 and no rights. However, when Stratemeyer died he willed one-fifth of the Syndicate's royalties for each series to its contributing ghostwriters. Benson wrote many books under her own name, such as *Tale of the Witch Doll* (1939), the first of the *Penny Parker Mystery Stories*, and under pen names, such as Joan Clark, under which she wrote the *Penny Nichols Mysteries* (1936).

BERENSTAIN, Stan (1923–2005) and **Jan** (1923–2012) American artists and authors, creators of the long-running and popular series of books about *The Berenstain Bears*. Inspired to draw animals by their enthusiasm for Dr *Seuss's books, in turn they were first edited by Theodor Geisel (Dr Seuss himself), who in his real life role as an editor championed their work, starting with *The Big Honey Hunt* (1962). Dealing with everyday life that would be familiar to young children, the books enjoyed a success that led to a TV series, toys, and the continuation of the series by Mike Berenstain, their son.

BERESFORD, Elisabeth (1926–2010) British writer. Her first children's books, published from 1957, were conventional *adventure stories and thrillers. In 1964 she produced the first of a number of *Nesbit-style fantasies, *Awkward Magic*. Then in 1968 came the beginning of her *Womble stories, in which she created a race of creatures who became a national craze in Britain.

BERG, Leila (1917–2012) British children's author and editor, born of Jewish parents in Salford, Lancashire, a background reflected in her story *A Box for Benny* (1958). Already the writer of many books for children, in 1968 she conceived, edited, and wrote a large part of the *Nippers series, which for the first time put the real situations and conversations of young schoolchildren into primary school readers. She also wrote books for adults about children's rights and education, and won the *Eleanor Farjeon Award in 1974.

BERGSTRÖM, Gunilla (1942–) Swedish writer, the most read Swedish children's author after Astrid *Lindgren. Bergström was born in Gothenburg, Sweden, in 1942, and has written and illustrated more than forty picture books; her illustrations tend to be in a collage style. Most of the books are about Alfons Åberg, a young boy who lives with his single father. The texts include *God natt Alfons Åberg* (*Good night Alfons Åberg*, 1972), *Mera monster, Alfons!* (*More monsters, Alfons!*, 1992), and *Skratta lagom! sa pappa Åberg* (*Laugh just enough! said Pappa Åberg*, 2012). The Alfons Åberg books have been translated into many languages, but only a few have appeared in English, with the protagonist renamed Alfie Atkins. Bergström has also written books about siblings Bill and Bolla; Bolla is Bill's disabled younger sister. Besides these picture books, Bergström has also produced plays and screenplays, songs for children, and scenography.

BERNA, Paul *See* Hundred Million Francs, A.

Berners family In *Magnolia Buildings* by Elizabeth Stucley.

BERQUIN, Arnaud (1747–91) French author of *moral tales. He was born in Bordeaux, went to Paris, and there began to make a reputation as a writer for children. His best-known work was *L'Ami des enfans*, published in parts during 1782–3, which was translated into English as *The *Children's Friend*; another version appeared under the title *The *Looking-Glass for the Mind*. He produced an imitation for children of *Sir Charles Grandison*, and translated *Sandford and Merton* into French.

Bertie's Escapade A short story by Kenneth *Grahame, published posthumously in 1944.

BESKOW, Elsa (1874–1953) Swedish illustrator and author of more than thirty *picture books, published between 1897 and 1952. She chose simple subject-matter and worked in soft-toned watercolours. Most of her books were *fairy stories or descriptions of old-style country life.

Bessie Bunter Sister to *Billy Bunter. She occasionally appeared in stories about *Greyfriars, her brother's school, in the weekly *Magnet. In 1919 she was given her own series in the new *School Friend, and Charles *Hamilton, creator of Billy Bunter under the pseudonym 'Frank *Richards', was commissioned to write it. But his characterization of Bessie was too crude for girls' tastes, and the other girls at her school, Cliff House, were too sketchily drawn. Hamilton was replaced by other writers, all working under the pseudonym used by him in the opening numbers of *School Friend*, 'Hilda Richards'. Other Cliff House girls included Barbara Redfern, Captain

of the Fourth, the tomboy Clara Trevlyn, and the kindly Marjorie Hazeldene.

BESTALL, Alfred (1892–1986) British cartoonist and illustrator who drew and wrote the *Rupert Bear strip for the *Daily Express* from the mid-1930s until 1965.

bestiary A form of literature highly popular in medieval Europe, in which fantastic descriptions of real and imaginary animals are used to illustrate Christian dogma and morals. The pelican's supposed habit of killing its young and reviving them with its own blood after three days is used as an allegory of Christ's death and resurrection, the two horns of the antelope are equated with the Old and New Testaments, and so on.

Medieval Latin and French bestiaries were based on the Greek *Physiologus*, written in the 3rd or 4th cent. AD. This was a compilation of pseudo-science perhaps derived from *fables. Bestiaries were often lavishly illustrated. The fictitious 'natural history' contained in them found its way into folklore and thence into many books for children. For example, Francis Newbery's (*see* NEWBERY, JOHN) *Natural History of Birds* (1778) alludes to the legend that a lion is afraid of a cock, *Peter Pan* (1904) makes use of the belief that wolves flee if you look at them backwards through your legs, and a poem by J. R. R. *Tolkien in *The Adventures of Tom Bombadil* (1962) is based on the bestiaries' account of a sea-creature large enough to be mistaken for an island.

T. H. *White translated a Latin bestiary under the title *The Book of Beasts* (1954). A 17th-cent. book which much resembles the bestiaries is Topsell's *Historie of Foure-Footed Beastes* (1607); this was imitated by Thomas *Boreman in *A *Description of Three Hundred Animals* (1730). In about 1783 John *Marshall published a children's *chapbook entitled *Jack Dandy's Delight; or, The History of Birds and Beasts: in Verse and Prose*. This was recognizably descended from the bestiaries; each woodcut of an animal was accompanied by a piece of moralizing. Books with the same title were issued by other publishers. John Newbery's *Pretty Book of Pictures for Little Masters and Misses* (by 1752) also has affinities with the bestiaries.

Hilaire *Belloc produced comic examples of the genre in *The *Bad Child's Book of Beasts* (1896) and *More Beasts for Worse Children* (1897). E. *Nesbit's story 'The Book of Beasts' (in *The Book of Dragons*, 1900) describes a bestiary whose beasts come alive when the pages are turned.

BETTELHEIM, Bruno (1903–90) Viennese psychologist, resident in the USA from 1929, specializing in the treatment of emotionally disturbed children. In *The Uses of Enchantment: the Meaning and Importance of Fairy Tales* (1976) he argues that *fairy stories 'speak about his severe inner pressures in a way that the child unconsciously understands and . . . offer examples of both temporary and permanent solutions to pressing difficulties'.

Bettina (Bettina Ehrlich) (1903–85) Viennese author-illustrator resident in Britain from 1938. Her *picture books include *Poo-Tsee, the Water-Tortoise* (1943), *Of Uncles and Aunts* (1963), and *A Day in Venice* (1973).

Bevis: the story of a boy (1882) A novel by Richard Jefferies (1848–87), a sequel to his *Wood Magic*. The book is set in a landscape closely resembling that of Jefferies's own childhood home, a farm by Coate Water, near Swindon in Wiltshire. The book charts the adventures of the adolescent Bevis and his friend Mark as they navigate a punt on the Longpond near their home. Later they fit out a sailing boat for themselves, playing the role of savages, explorers, soldiers, or castaways. They have a battle with other boys, voyage across 'The New Sea', as the Longpond has now become, and set up a camp with a stockade on an island which they name 'Formosa'. Their families have no idea of their whereabouts, but they are eventually discovered by Loo, a labourer's daughter, who becomes their devoted slave before they return home triumphantly.

The book was first published in three volumes. An illustrated edition of 1891 abridged the text severely, but it was restored in full for a third edition of 1904 which had an introduction by E. V. *Lucas, who wrote: 'I know of no other boys' book which so eliminates direct adult influence. Bevis's parents are the merest shadows . . . Mark's practically do not exist.' *Bevis* was reprinted a number of times during the 20th cent.

Jefferies has also been much admired as a nature writer and in *Richard Jefferies and the Ecological Vision* (2006) Brian Morris identifies him as a pioneer environmentalist.

Bevis of Hampton, Sir One of the most popular medieval English *romances, a favourite with children for more than 400 years. The Middle English poem *Sir Beues of*

Hamtoun, based on the Anglo-Norman *Boeve de Haumtone*, dates from the 13th or early 14 cent. Bevis is the son of Guy, Earl of South-Hampton. His mother arranges for his father to be killed and marries his murderer, the Emperor of Almaine. She sells Bevis to Saracen merchants, who take him to Armenia, where he becomes chamberlain to King Ermin, whose daughter Josian falls in love with him. The plot then relates in detail Bevis's defeat of Brademond, King of Damascus, who has demanded Josian in marriage, Bevis's imprisonment by Brademond, and his subsequent escape and eventual revenge on his stepfather and mother. The giant Ascopart, initially sent to recapture Bevis after his escape is another key figure in the narrative. Ascopart becomes Bevis's page after he has defeated him and intervenes in numerous scenes to aid the protagonist. However he eventually betrays Bevis and is killed by Bevis's ally, Saber. At the end of the narrative, Bevis attacks Edgar, King of England, in revenge for depriving his family of their lands, and Edgar, on the verge of defeat, agrees that Bevis's son may marry his daughter and take the throne after him. Finally Bevis and his wife die peacefully and Bevis's son Guy founds a monastery where the monks are to sing masses for the souls of his parents.

Sir Bevis of Hampton is found in several medieval manuscripts, and the poem was printed very early in the 16th cent. by Wynkyn de *Worde and also by Richard Pynson. Only a fragment of de Worde's edition survives, but a copy of Pynson's is intact in the Bodleian Library, and, besides being adorned with the printer's *woodcuts, has a child's crude drawing in one of the margins, which suggests that the book was used by at least one young reader. The story was reprinted, both in verse and prose, many times in the 16th, 17th, and 18th cents. In 1846 a version for children by 'Ambrose Merton' (W. J. *Thoms) was printed as one of *Gammer Gurton's Story Books*, and there have been retellings by Laura Hibbard (1911), W. S. Durrant (1914), and Aylwin Sampson (1963).

Bewick, Thomas (1753–1828) The finest of all English practitioners of *wood engraving. He and his younger brother John (1760–95) illustrated a number of books that were read by children from the late 18th cent. onwards. At the age of fourteen Thomas was apprenticed to a Newcastle engraver, Ralph Beilby, and learnt to engrave on wood and metal. At

this period the art of wood engraving had sunk to a low level in England; few engravers rose much above the standard of the crude *woodcuts done for *chapbook illustrations, and *copperplates were preferred for finer work. The making of woodblocks was only a small part of Beilby's work, but Bewick quickly proved expert, using the effect of what was cut away from the block (and left white) as much as what was left behind to receive ink. He developed the use of fine metal-engraving tools to cut across the end grain of boxwood and was therefore able to produce pictures as sophisticated and delicate as could be achieved in any monochrome medium.

His work began to attract praise locally, and he was soon undertaking cuts for Thomas Saint, a Newcastle printer of chapbooks and *broadsides. Books which certainly contain some of his earliest work include *A New Invented Hornbook* (1770) and *The New Lottery Book of Birds and Beasts, for children to learn their letters by as soon as they can speak* (1771). He also completed a set of cuts for *Gay's *Fables*, which were so good that Beilby sent five to the Society of Arts, who awarded Bewick a prize of seven guineas.

When Bewick had finished his apprenticeship he came to London, working for various printers and engravers, including (according to his memoirs) 'Mr Carnan & Mr Newbury [*sic*] of St Pauls church yard'. The capital, however, did not suit him, and he returned to Newcastle, going into partnership with his old master, Beilby. For some years he was more concerned with other aspects of the firm's work than wood engraving, but he found satisfaction in teaching his art to his younger brother John, whom he had taken on as apprentice. Meanwhile he himself occasionally illustrated books, notably an edition of *A *Pretty Book of Pictures for Little Masters and Misses: or, Tommy Trip's History of Beasts and Birds*, which was published by Saint of Newcastle in 1779. He also provided cuts for Saint's 1779 edition of Gay's *Fables*, and for at least one edition of *Select Fables*, issued by Saint in 1784.

Though his engravings in these books were often modelled on the work of earlier illustrators, they invariably improved on them, both in their technique and composition, and in the portrayal of plants, animals, and birds. Bewick continued to delight in the first-hand observation of nature, and this was vital to the success of the first work of his own devising: *A General*

History of Quadrupeds on which he began work in 1785. This work was partly modelled on a book that Bewick had read in childhood, Thomas *Boreman's volume A *Description of Three Hundred Animals. Berwick's partner Beilby wrote the text for *Quadrupeds*, which was published in Newcastle in 1790, and was soon being reprinted at frequent intervals. Bewick followed it with a *History of British Birds*. This time he collaborated with Beilby on the text, but quarrelled with his old master when he found that Beilby wanted to be named as sole author. In consequence the partnership was split up; when the first volume, 'Land Birds', appeared in 1797, no author was named, though the engravings were credited to 'T. Bewick'. For the second volume, 'Water Birds' (1804), Bewick engaged the Revd Henry Cotes to help him with the text.

The *History of British Birds*, of which Bewick himself was the principal publisher, proved very successful. By 1826 'Land Birds' had reached an eighth edition and 'Water Birds' a sixth. Innumerable children turned its pages, and found it fascinating, largely because of the striking vignettes with which Bewick filled up blank spaces at the end of sections. Charlotte Brontë, in *Jane Eyre*, has her heroine reading the book and being gripped by these pictures, and Charles *Kingsley summed up the Victorian affection for Bewick in The *Water-Babies (1863), when he wrote:

If they want to describe a finished young gentleman in France, I hear, they say of him *'Il sait son Rabelais.'* But if I want to describe one in England, I say, *'He knows his Bewick.'* And I think that is the higher compliment.

After the *Birds*, the only major work undertaken by Bewick was an edition of Croxall's *Aesop, with the text revised by Bewick himself, published in 1818. In this, as perhaps in the *Birds*, he was assisted by his pupils. In his later years he continued to manage his engraving business in Newcastle, and he died there at the age of 75.

Many books besides those mentioned have had their engravings attributed to Bewick. It is often impossible to know whether the attribution is correct, for not only was his work unsigned but he had a number of apprentices who worked in his style. His brother John, who died in his mid-thirties, illustrated a number of children's books, e.g. an edition of *Berquin's *Looking-Glass for the Mind* published by Elizabeth Newbery in 1792. His work, though good for the time, did not have the distinction of his brother's.

Thomas Bewick not only raised the art of wood engraving to the highest level, but was also the first person to make the work of the illustrator as important in books for children as the text. In America, his work was imitated with great skill by Alexander *Anderson. Jenny Uglow's *Nature's Engraver: A Life of Thomas Bewick* (2006) explores his life and cultural context as well as reproducing examples of his watercolours and many of his engravings.

BFG, The (1982) A children's novel by Roald *Dahl. BFG stands for 'Big Friendly Giant', which is just what the protagonist is, as distinct from the other giants in the story, who, besides being even bigger (and bearded) are not friendly at all. Where the other giants like to eat 'human beans', the BFG spends his days mixing dreams in his laboratory and his nights stalking through town blowing them in people's windows through a massive trumpet. That is how he meets Sophie, a little girl who finds herself awake at the witching hour one night and sees him at work, and he is forced to kidnap her to stop her from telling anyone about him. Sophie and the BFG become friends, and together they hatch a plot (with some help from the Queen of England) to catch all the mean giants and trap them in a pit where they are forced to eat disgusting snozzcumbers for ever after. *The BFG* is one of Dahl's most imaginative and vivid books (helped by the Quentin *Blake illustrations that accompany it), and remains one of his best-loved. The humour, as so often in Dahl, comes from the wild and disgusting, and his language is as playful as ever. An appealing live-action *film adaptation from Steven Spielberg, starring Mark Rylance in the title role, was released in 2016.

Bianca, Miss *See* MISS BIANCA.

Bibi (1930) By the Danish author Karin Michaelis (1872–1950), *Bibi* was translated into about a dozen other European languages shortly after its publication, with an English version (1933) by Rose *Fyleman. Bibi Stensen is the daughter of a stationmaster in Jutland. Her chief delight is running away from home—simply so that she can explore Denmark. She attends a funeral, learns from a burglar how to climb sheer walls, acquires a wounded stork named Jens, and goes up a cathedral tower and rings the bell. Wherever she is and whatever she is doing, she sends a letter to her father recounting her exploits.

The book, which has several sequels, was written with something of the same purpose

as the Swedish *The *Wonderful Adventures of Nils* (1906–7) by Selma *Lagerlöf—that is, to show Danish children the rich variety of life in their country—though *Bibi* is at once more down-to-earth and more comic than *Nils*. In some respects it anticipates **Pippi Longstocking* (1945) by Astrid *Lindgren.

Bibles and **Bible stories** for children began to appear in the late 17th cent. *Youths Divine Pastime* by Nathaniel *Crouch (1691, often reprinted) contained 'forty remarkable Scripture histories, turned into ... English verse'. Another *Puritan, Benjamin *Harris, brought out a Bible 'done into verse for the benefit of weak memories' in 1698. One of the first versions of the Bible for children to have illustrations was 'The Youths Visible Bible', printed in 1675 as part of *Nolens Volens: or, You shall make Latin whether you Will or No*, by Elisha Coles. This consisted of scriptural passages arranged alphabetically by key words; each of these words was illustrated in a facing *copperplate. It seems to have been responsible for the introduction, some time later, of *hieroglyphic Bibles.

The firm of *Newbery published a number of illustrated children's Bibles. Their *Holy Bible abridged ... for the use of children* first appeared *c*.1757 and was often re-issued. A tiny 'thumb' Bible, *The Bible in Miniuture* [sic], *or a Concise History of the Old and New Testaments*, was issued by Elizabeth Newbery in 1780, in imitation of a *miniature book produced by earlier publishers. It contained a summary of the chief events of the Bible, with chapter and verse references to the original; its measurements were $1\frac{1}{2} \times 1\frac{1}{4}$ in. Newbery's also issued a *Pocket Bible for Little Masters and Misses* (1772) and children's versions of the New Testament.

The early 19th cent. saw a number of *chapbook reductions of the Bible, such as *The New Pictorial Bible* (Glasgow, 'Printed for the Booksellers', *c*.1820), a twenty-four-page version in which excerpts from the best known passages were illustrated with *woodcuts. Paraphrases of certain biblical stories also sometimes appeared as chapbooks.

Mrs Sarah *Trimmer, stern critic of children's books at the beginning of the 19th cent., objected to hieroglyphic Bibles on the grounds that they exposed 'the Sacred Volume to the ridicule and contempt of infidels'. She herself devoted much energy to presenting Bible stories in a form suitable for children.

Her *Sacred History, selected from the Scriptures; with annotations and reflections* was first published in six volumes in 1782. She also produced several sets of copperplate prints illustrating biblical stories; these were 'designed as ornaments for those apartments in which children receive the first rudiments of their education', and were accompanied by 'descriptions' printed in book-form, which recounted the various incidents in simple language.

During the 19th cent. many 'Family Bibles' were published, often containing illustrations and notes, and also 'Children's Bibles', abridgements of both Testaments, again with pictures, and including questions and explanations. One of the earliest children's writers to retell Bible stories in a plain but exciting manner was 'Felix Summerly' (Sir Henry *Cole), whose *Bible Events* appeared as part of his '*Home Treasury' in 1843.

Examples of retellings from the 20th cent. include *Stories from the Bible* (1929) by Walter *de La Mare and *City of Gold and other stories from the Old Testament* (1980) by Peter *Dickinson, which won the *Carnegie Medal.

Bibliothèque rose A series of red-bound children's books issued by the French publisher Hachette from the mid-19th cent. They were guaranteed 'safe reading' for children, and consisted chiefly of *moral tales. The 'Sophie' stories of Mme de *Ségur (see MALHEURS DE SOPHIE) were the most popular.

Bidpai, Fables of See PANCHATANTRA.

Big Ears In the *Noddy books by Enid *Blyton.

Biggles A heroic British airman, detective, and adventurer, the creation of Captain W. E. *Johns, in books published between the 1930s and 1970s.

Biggles first appeared in Johns's magazine *Popular Flying* at the beginning of the 1930s. *The Camels are Coming* (1932) was a collection of Biggles's wartime exploits, and took its title from the Sopwith Camels flown by him and his fellow pilots. Next came *The Cruise of the Condor* (1933), the first Biggles story to be set in peacetime and to involve its hero in the detection and prevention of crime.

Biggles's full name is Major James Bigglesworth, DSO, MC; during the First World War he 'commanded No. 266 Squadron in France', was 'victor of thirty-five combined combats and many others unclaimed', and 'was known ... from Belgium to the Swiss

frontier' for his exploits against 'the Hun'. Biggles's 'close friend and comrade-in-arms' is Captain Algernon Lacy, 'more often simply known as Algy'. His other associates are Flying-Officer Ginger Hebblethwaite (second only to Algy in Biggles's affections), Flight-Sergeant Smyth, an NCO 'who had been Biggles's fitter on more than one desperate enterprise in civil as well as military aviation', and such airborne pals as the monocled Lord Bertie Lissie and the American Tex O'Hara.

Biggles is the quintessential stiff-upper-lipped Englishman, a hero in the *Henty mould who dislikes civilian life. He and his author have little love for most foreign races; a typical character in an early Biggles book talks about 'Indians, niggers, and half-breeds, the scum of the earth'. Only the Germans regularly earn respect, and are regarded as worthy adversaries.

After such adventures as *Biggles Hits the Trail* (1935) and *Biggles Flies West* (1937), the intrepid airman's immediate future was conveniently settled by the outbreak of the Second World War. He was even more active in it than in the 1914–18 conflict, played a vital part in the Battle of Britain, and after the war joined the 'Air Section of Scotland Yard', spending the next quarter-century as its 'chief operational pilot' answerable to one Air Commodore Raymond. In fact the ending of the war made little difference to him, for his chief enemy in the 1950s and 1960s was one Erich von Stalhein, a 'Boche' of the old order, who could be relied on to turn up anywhere from the polar regions to the Caribbean.

By 1967 and one of the last books, *Biggles and the Dark Intruder*, the author Captain Johns was showing distinct signs of exhaustion, while Biggles himself, by then presumably well into his seventies, seemed to lack something of his old energy. But his diction had not changed ('By Jingo, laddie, you're right!'), and even the aircraft seemed curiously reminiscent of the Royal Flying Corps in 1916.

According to Peter Berresford Ellis and Piers Williams (*By Jove, Biggles!*, 1981), there are 102 Biggles books in all. Many have remained in print, despite frequent censure by those who deplore their jingoistic attitudes. Geoffrey *Trease wrote: 'It may well be that in years to come they will be read chiefly by half-incredulous research students, investigating the social values prevalent in children's fiction during the second quarter of the 20th century.'

Big Red (1945) A novel by Jim *Kjelgaard.

Big Snow, The (1948) A *picture book by Berta and Elmer *Hader awarded the 1949 *Caldecott Medal.

Big Tiger and Christian (1950) English title of a novel by Fritz *Mühlenweg.

Bigwig Rabbit in *Watership Down* by Richard *Adams.

Bilbo Baggins Hero of The *Hobbit by J. R. R. *Tolkien.

'Billabong' books A series of fifteen novels with an Australian background, immensely popular in their time, by Mary Grant *Bruce. The first, *A Little Bush Maid* (1910), introduces the Linton family: David Linton, a widower, and his children, Jim aged fifteen and twelve-year-old tomboyish Norah, who live on a large settler station in Northern Victoria. Around the family are gathered their farm workers, Hogg the Scots flower gardener and Lee Wing the Chinese vegetable gardener, always at loggerheads, Black Billy the aboriginal, and others who provide humorous scenes. Jim's schoolmates Harry and Wally come to stay, and the incidents include Norah rescuing her father's prize flock of sheep from a bush fire and riding to save the life of a bush hermit who turns out to be her father's long-lost friend. Norah manages both to have all the skills usually expected of a boy in such books, and to display the refining influence of a woman on station life.

Further 'Billabong' books, beginning with *Mates at Billabong* (1911) and ending with *Billabong Riders* (1942), took Norah to school and to London and Ireland and back, married her to Wally, sent the boys to Europe to war, and brought up a new generation. Bruce sustained the saga so successfully that the 'Billabong' books soon acquired a huge following and became something of an institution in Australian life, though editions appeared less frequently after the Second World War.

BILLINGS, Hammatt (1818–74) American illustrator whose work appears in the first edition of Harriet Beecher Stowe's *Uncle Tom's Cabin* (1852); in *A *Wonder-Book for Girls and Boys* (1851) and *Tanglewood Tales* (1853) by Nathaniel Hawthorne; and in some of the 'Little Prudy' stories of Sophie *May.

Bill's New Frock A novel by Anne *Fine.

Billy and Blaze (1936) A story of a boy and his horse, by American author-illustrator C. W. Anderson (1891–1971). It was the first of a long series of 'Blaze' books, which concluded with *Blaze Finds Forgotten*

Roads (1970). Anderson wrote other *horse and *pony stories.

Billy Bunter (William George Bunter)

Until the advent of *Harry Potter, probably the most famous schoolboy in English popular fiction. He was the creation of 'Frank *Richards' (i.e. Charles *Hamilton), who first invented him before 1900, but was rejected by the magazine editor to whom he was offered. In 1908 *Harmsworth's Amalgamated Press, for whose papers Hamilton was already writing, commissioned him to create a new fictional school for the start of their weekly magazine *Magnet*, which was first issued on 15 February that year. For the opening number Hamilton wrote the story 'The Making of Harry Wharton', in which Colonel Wharton of Wharton Lodge sends his headstrong nephew to the ancient and famous public school Greyfriars, at Friardale in Kent. At school, Harry Wharton finds himself sharing a study with Frank Nugent, a bully named Bulstrode, and 'a somewhat short junior, with a broad, pleasant face and an enormous pair of spectacles', who makes his first entrance falling over Harry Wharton's recumbent body. This is Billy Bunter, at first only a minor character in the stories; when he appears in illustrations in the early issues of *Magnet*, he is depicted as a plump but otherwise quite normal-looking schoolboy. Wharton soon becomes the leader of the 'Famous Five', of which the other members are Nugent, the ever-cheerful Bob Cherry, the sturdy Johnny Bull, and Hurree Jamset Ram Singh, Nabob of Bhanipur.

Gradually Bunter began to play a larger part in the stories, and became more and more grotesque. He acquired the nickname 'The Fat Owl of the Remove' (the Remove being the form or class to which he and the Famous Five belonged). In 1909 he built such a huge fire for his cooking operations in Study No. 1 that he set the entire building alight; in the same year he ate an entire Christmas pudding at a sitting. He soon started to engage in nefarious enterprises to raise cash for buying 'tuck', in the meanwhile always expecting a postal order that never arrived. Illustrations now showed him as almost spherical, with the face of an adult (both crafty and gross), and dressed in an enormous pair of check trousers. Artists who depicted him over the years included Hutton Mitchell, Arthur Clarke, Leonard Shields, and Charles H. Chapman, the last being generally regarded as the best.

Bunter often met his Waterloo in the form of Mr Quelch, the Remove form master—'"You will take five hundred lines, Bunter." "Oh, crikey!"' Sometimes he would persuade the Famous Five to take his part ('"I say, you fellows, I expect to see fair play"'), but usually he was in hot water, letting out his inimitable cries: '"Yarooooh! Oh crikey! Ow! Wow! Beast! Oh crumbs! Ow! Oooooooooooh!"'

Though by the 1920s he was the star of the Greyfriars stories—at one time the *Magnet* was subtitled 'Billy Bunter's Own Paper'—he never took them over entirely, and many weeks' issues were scarcely concerned with him. The cast of Greyfriars characters eventually became huge; among the best known were: Fisher T. Fish, a boy from 'Noo York'; Lord Mauleverer, the schoolboy millionaire; Skinner, the 'cad' of the Remove; Vernon-Smith, *nouveau-riche* and a 'bounder'; Coker, the Fifth Form 'funny man'; and the Chinese boy Wun Lung (George Orwell, writing in *Horizon* in 1940, said of the Greyfriars stories that 'the assumption is . . . that foreigners are comic'; to which Charles Hamilton replied: 'Foreigners *are* funny.') Also notable were the school porter William Gosling ('All boys ought to be drownded at birth'); *Ferrers Locke the detective, a relative of Dr Locke the Greyfriars headmaster, who sometimes appeared to investigate mysteries at the school; and *Bessie Bunter, Billy's sister, who occasionally turned up with her fellow pupils from Cliff House, the girls' school.

Magnet continued to publish new stories by Hamilton until its demise in 1940, though in the final years even enthusiasts felt that 'Frank Richards' was repeating himself.

In 1947 Bunter reappeared, first at 'Sparshott School' in a shilling series written by Hamilton for the publisher William Merritt. Then new stories of Bunter at Greyfriars were commissioned from Hamilton by Charles Skilton, who published them in hardback at 7s.6d. with huge success. A little later, Cassell published Billy Bunter titles. All this kept Hamilton, who was by now in his 70s, extremely busy—much to his delight. The Bunter revival was aided by the dramatization of many of the stories on BBC Television between 1952 and 1962, with Gerald Campion satisfying virtually all Greyfriars fans with his performance as Bunter. The stories also had the distinction of being banned by some schoolmasters and librarians, along with those of Enid *Blyton. This, of course, made children want to read them all the more; a cartoon by 'Giles' from

the early 1960s shows a long queue of would-be readers in a children's library, with books tucked under their arms, and one of the staff saying to another: 'Yaroo! Back come all the Fanny Hills and Lady Chatterleys—out go all the Billy Bunters.'

Billy the Kid Hero of *westerns; in real life William H. Bonney, alias Henry McCarty, alias Henry Antrim. He is said to have been born in 1859, and during his youth in Santa Fe escaped from prison after a sentence for petty thieving. He became a fugitive, murderer, and cattle-rustler, and was involved in the 1878 'cattle war' of Lincoln County, New Mexico, where his activities earned him the undeserved reputation of a champion of the oppressed. After his death he quickly became the subject of lengthy newspaper articles and *dime novels. Walter Woods's popular 1903 drama *Billy the Kid* presented him as a quixotic romantic who is driven to kill by cruel circumstances, an interpretation reinforced by Walter Burns's *Saga of Billy the Kid* (1926), which finally established the prototype in western fiction of the heroic outlaw.

biography for children *See* HISTORY AND BIOGRAPHY.

BIRCH, Reginald (1856-1943) American artist who illustrated *Little Lord Fauntleroy* (1886) and *Sara Crewe* (1887) by Frances Hodgson *Burnett, and provided many pictures for *St Nicholas. One of the most accomplished American illustrators of his day, he drew in a markedly 'English' style, resembling that of Gordon *Browne and other late Victorian line artists.

BIRD, Maria *See* ANDY PANDY.

BIRD, Richard (William Barradale-Smith) British writer of *school stories which appeared in *Captain* during the First World War.

BIRDSALL, Jeanne *See* PENDERWICKS.

Birds' Christmas Carol, The (1887) A story by Kate Douglas *Wiggin.

Birdy Jones In the 'Birdy' books by E. W. *Hildick.

BIRO, Val (Balint Stephen) (1921-2014) Illustrator and author who was born in Budapest and came to Britain before the Second World War, training at the Central School of Art. He wrote and illustrated a 'Gumdrop' series of *picture books about a vintage car, based on his own 1926 Austin Healey. The first was *Gumdrop: the Adventures of a Vintage Car* (1966). He also illustrated books by many other authors.

BISHOP, Clare Huchet (1899-1993) American author who made her name with her first book, *The Five Chinese Brothers* (1938), illustrated by Kurt *Wiese. The brothers look exactly alike, but one can swallow the sea, one has an iron neck, one can stretch his legs, one cannot be burned, and one can hold his breath indefinitely. The first is condemned to death, but each of them stands in for him in turn at the attempted execution. Clare Huchet Bishop's other books include *The Man Who Lost His Head* (1942), illustrated by Robert *McCloskey, and *Twenty and Ten* (1952), illustrated by William Pène *Du Bois.

BISHOP, Gavin (1946-) New Zealand author and illustrator of picture books whose mix of European and Māori ancestry strongly influences his work. He was an art teacher for thirty years before becoming a full-time writer. His first book, *Mrs McGinty and the Bizarre Plant* (1981), tells of a grumpy old lady whose life is turned around when she grows a large and strange plant—the book is set in a recognizable Christchurch and is a classic to many South Islanders. His clear imagery and use of colour has led to his style sometimes being compared to that of artists such as Maurice *Sendak, particularly in *Mr Fox* (1982). With books of Māori myth such as *Maui and the Sun* (1996) he started to reclaim his own background, and with *The House That Jack Built* (2012) has rewritten a traditional tale to encompass colonization and imperialism, and their effect on New Zealand. He has illustrated the work of many other New Zealand writers, including Margaret *Mahy and Joy *Cowley.

Bitem Fox in *The *Midnight Folk* by John *Masefield.

BLACK, Holly (1971-) American author of books for children and young adults. *The Spiderwick Chronicles*, a fantasy series created with and illustrated by Tony *DiTerlizzi, recounts how three children discover sprites, brownies, and other faerie creatures when they move to an old house—it begins with *The Field Guide* (2003). The books were turned into a film in 2008. For older readers the *Modern Tale of Faerie* urban fantasy series, starting with *Tithe* (2002), tells of fiercely independent Kaye, who comes between two warring faerie kingdoms. The slightly younger ghost story *Doll Bones* (2013) is about friends on the

verge of adolescence and a doll infused with the presence of a dead girl. Black is also co-author, with Cassandra *Clare, of the *Magisterium* series, starting with *The Iron Trial* (2014).

Black Arrow, The (1888) A novel by R. L. *Stevenson.

Black Beauty: *the autobiography of a horse* (1877) By Anna *Sewell, the most celebrated *animal story of the 19th cent., an account of a horse's experiences at the hands of many owners, ranging from the worthy Squire Gordon to a cruel cab-owner. The book revived the 'animal autobiography', a genre popular in the late 18th and early 19th cents. (examples from that period include *The *Life and Perambulation of a Mouse*, 1783, and *The *Adventures of a Donkey*, 1815) but which had been dormant for half a century. It was published on 24 November 1877 and at first sold slowly, but by the time of the author's death the following April sales were approaching 100,000 copies. Soon its publisher, Jarrold of Norwich, was advertising four different English editions, and also translations into French, Italian, and German, these being the first of many foreign editions. In 1935 Jarrold estimated that world sales had reached 'not less than twenty million'. *Black Beauty* was also instrumental in raising awareness of animal welfare and in abolishing the use of the bearing rein on horses in Victorian England.

Black Beauty has spawned many imitations, including the Canadian book *Beautiful Joe* (1894) by Marshall *Saunders (which has a dog as hero), *Smoky, The Cowhorse* (1926) by Will James, and *Moorland Mousie* (1929) by 'Golden Gorse', which helped to establish the *pony story as a popular genre in England.

Black Bull of Norroway, The A *fairy story collected in various forms in the British Isles during the 19th cent. The version printed in Joseph Jacobs's *More English Fairy Stories* (1894), taken from Chambers's *Popular Rhymes of Scotland*, falls distinctly into two parts. In the first, the youngest of three sisters sets out to seek her fortune, riding on the back of a black bull. It takes her on three successive nights to three castles, at each of which she receives a gift to be used in time of need. In the second part, no longer accompanied by the bull, she finds herself at the foot of a glass mountain. She is only able to climb this after serving a blacksmith for seven years, at the end of which time he makes her 'iron shoon' with which she walks up it. At the top, she

learns of 'a gallant young knight that had given in some clothes all over blood to wash, and whoever washed them was to be his wife'. The washerwoman and her daughter cannot manage it, but the girl performs the task. However, the knight is tricked into marrying the washerwoman's daughter. The heroine then uses the gifts she received at the three castles to purchase three nights in the knight's bed. Unknown to her, on the first two nights he is given a sleeping draught by the washerwoman and is unaware of the girl's presence. On the third night he is warned not to drink the potion; as a result, 'he heard, and turned to her'. The washerwoman and her daughter are put to death and the knight and the girl are married.

A different form of the story, entitled *The Glass Mountain*, was collected in Ireland and printed in *Folklore* in June 1893, while in September that year the same journal printed a Lincolnshire variant. These two narratives make more sense of the story in that the bull is a shape-changer, who is beast by day and man by night. He and the heroine are married at the beginning of the story, but by failing to keep her word to her husband the girl loses him. She only manages to reclaim him after embarking on a quest which involves climbing the glass mountain.

The story, of which no entirely satisfactory version seems to exist, is undoubtedly very old, being mentioned in *The Complaynt of Scotland* (1548) and in Sidney's *Arcadia* (1590). A glass mountain, which is ascended to break an enchantment, features in the story of *The Raven* in *Grimm, and an ivory mountain plays a somewhat similar part in Mme d'*Aulnoy's story *The *Blue Bird* (*L'Oiseau bleu*). *The Brown Bear of Norway* in Andrew *Lang's *Lilac Fairy Book* is a tale on the same model as *The Black Bull of Norroway*, and is coherent and well-shaped, but it lacks the glass mountain. The Norwegian story *East of the Sun and West of the Moon* resembles *The Black Bull* in many respects, and is perhaps the best tale of the group.

Black Hearts in Battersea A novel by Joan *Aiken, set in a similar alternative historical reality to that of *The *Wolves of Willoughby Chase*.

Blackie & Son A leading Scottish publisher of children's books from the early 19th cent. In 1809 John Blackie (1782–1874) succeeded to the Glasgow business of W. D. & A. Brownlie, and twenty years later became printer to Glasgow

University. A London office was opened in 1830. Among children's authors published by the firm were G. A. *Henty, George *MacDonald, and Angela *Brazil. Blackie's had for many years one of the most varied and interesting children's lists, ranging from *annuals and paperbound story-booklets priced at a few pence to finely illustrated editions of classics.

Black Jack (1968) A novel by Leon *Garfield. When Black Jack is hung, Tolly, in the wrong place at the wrong time, is left watching over the body. However, Black Jack is not dead, and the two find themselves unwilling partners on the run. It is the encounter with mad Belle that provides the catalyst for change. Their journey takes them through a richly populated 18th-cent. landscape, as they tumble from one situation to another before they achieve their goal: finding Tolly's uncle, the Sea Captain. One of Garfield's earliest novels, *Black Jack* is characterized by the author's love of atmosphere and action, which ensures that it never feels like a history lesson, but rather an adventure in a historical setting.

BLACKMAN, Malorie (1962–) An award-winning British screenwriter, playwright, and author of over fifty titles, including *young adult fiction, short stories, and picture books. Before she became a writer she worked in the computing industry, the influence of which is evident in some of her novels such as the technological thriller *Hacker* (1992) and *Thief!* (1995) set in a computer-dominated future. *Pig-Heart Boy* (1997), shortlisted for the *Carnegie Medal, focuses on the issue of organ transplantation and was adapted for television by the BBC. Her novel *Cloud Busting* (2004) won the Smarties Silver Award and is a moving story of friendship written entirely in verse. As a Black British author, Blackman has cited the lack of *diversity in publishing as both a barrier and an inspiration in her writing. In an attempt to address the imbalance in publishing, Blackman features black protagonists in most of her titles, although race or ethnicity is mostly incidental to the narrative. It was not until her fiftieth novel *Noughts and Crosses* (2001) that she tackled issues of racism directly. Blackman explores teenage fatherhood and homosexuality in her book *Boys Don't Cry* (2011), which was accompanied by the *MyCriBaby* *app. In 2013, she was named the UK's eighth Children's *Laureate.

Black Pig Ship in the *Captain Pugwash books by John Ryan.

Black Ships before Troy *See* SUTCLIFF, ROSEMARY.

Black Stallion In books by Walter *Farley.

Blackstick Fairy in *The *Rose and the Ring* by W. M. Thackeray.

BLACKWOOD, Freya (1975–) Australian picture-book illustrator who helped create special effects on the film sets of *Lord of the Rings*. By 2013 she had illustrated fifteen books. In this decade she has won the *CBCA Book of the Year: Early Childhood four times. *Look, a Book!* (2012) with Libby *Gleeson, which was shortlisted for the CBCA Picture Book of the Year, captures the imagination, showing joy in a desolate landscape. In 2010 she won the *Kate Greenaway Medal for her illustrations for Margaret *Wild's *Harry and Hopper* (2009), also chosen as a White Raven book in the same year—it is a touching story of a relationship between a boy and his dog. Today she is often teamed with Gleeson and in 2013 she illustrated Gleeson's *Banjo and Ruby Red*, a heart-warming story of a dog who befriends a chicken and protects it when it is injured, which uses more and brighter colours than her usual palette, and more movement in the illustrations. Her work continues to gain acclaim for depth of characterization and interpretation.

BLAKE, Quentin (Saxby) (1932–) British illustrator whose spindly, eccentric line drawings are instantly recognizable, and suited to children's and adult books alike. Blake was brought up in Kent and studied at Downing College, Cambridge. He then worked as a teacher of French. He had no artistic training up to this time, but from 1949 began to contribute cartoons to *Punch,* and attended life classes at Chelsea School of Art. In 1957 he became a freelance illustrator. He was eventually appointed Head of the Department of Illustration at the Royal College of Art.

He began to illustrate children's books in 1960 (his debut was *A Drink of Water and other stories* by John Yeoman, with whom he would collaborate again many times), and by the 1970s was in demand for books by such authors as Joan *Aiken, Russell *Hoban, Roald *Dahl, and even Dr *Seuss (*A Great Day for Up* in 1974 was one of only two books published in Geisel's lifetime to feature a Seuss text set to pictures by another illustrator). More recently he has illustrated two bestselling novels by David *Walliams.

The partnership with Dahl began with *The Enormous Crocodile* (1978) and continued until Dahl's death, but Blake would also go back and illustrate Dahl's earlier books, replacing the work of the original illustrators—Blake's spikily energetic pictures and Dahl's wildly inventive prose were a perfect match, and to most readers they are now inseparable.

A series of collaborations with Michael *Rosen culminated in their most remarkable joint work, when Blake illustrated *Michael Rosen's Sad Book* (2004). While Blake's sprightly style may have seemed a peculiar choice for a heartbreaking book about grief, the result is superb. Its success just emphasized one of the things that makes Blake's work unique—his entirely consistent, distinctive, utterly recognizable style which can nonetheless cover an enormous range, without apparently changing.

Among Blake's more than 300 illustrated books are many of his own picture-book titles, including *Patrick* (1968), *The Adventures of Lester* (1978), *Mister Magnolia* (1980), which won the *Kate Greenaway Medal, the counting-book, *Cockatoos* (1992), *Clown* (1995), an exemplary piece of visual—entirely wordless—storytelling, and *Zagazoo* (1998). They all share an apparent childlike simplicity in their pictures and a great sense of fun. Marcus *Crouch has called him 'a genuinely funny artist with humour at the very core of his being'.

Blake's distinguished career has won him the *Hans Christian Andersen Award and the *Eleanor Farjeon Award, and he was named the UK's first Children's *Laureate on the scheme's establishment in 1999. He was a keen supporter and trustee of the House of Illustration, which opened in London in 2014 with an exhibition of Blake's work.

BLAKE, Sexton *See* SEXTON BLAKE.

BLAKE, William (1757–1827) Poet, painter, and engraver, the son of a London hosier. At the age of ten he was sent to a drawing school, and was afterwards apprenticed to a copperplate engraver (*see* COPPERPLATE ENGRAVING). By the time he was twelve he had begun to write poetry. Having completed his apprenticeship and studied at the Royal Academy, he began to earn his living as an engraver, one of his principal employers being Joseph Johnson, publisher of Mrs *Barbauld and Maria *Edgeworth. At the age of twenty-five he married, and soon afterwards opened a print shop, though this was a short-lived venture. In 1787 his brother Robert died

of consumption; after nursing him for a fortnight, William had a vision of Robert's soul rising through the ceiling, 'clapping its hands for joy', and he was afterwards convinced that he was being instructed by Robert as to how he should produce his 'illuminated books'. He invented his own method, relief etching, by writing or painting text and other lines on the plate with acid-resistant medium and leaving white around the poem to be hand-coloured, or 'illuminated' like a medieval manuscript. One of the first of these books was *Songs of Innocence* (1789), a book not so much written for children as seeing the world through childlike visionary eyes. In 1794 he published those poems and a further group as *Songs of Innocence and of Experience*.

Blake undoubtedly knew the poetry of Isaac *Watts, but he departed utterly from the moralistic conventions of almost all earlier versifiers for children, and from the poetic fashions of his day. Though in this and in his later work he anticipated the Romantic movement which was to begin in earnest a few years later, his achievement was too original to be appreciated for many decades after his death. Poems such as 'The Lamb' from *Songs of Innocence* and 'The Tyger' from *Songs of Experience* were then much anthologized for children, and often given to them to learn by heart and recite. 'The Tyger' remains one of the best-known English poems.

Blake has inspired countless writers and illustrators for children. Among them the *picture book *A Visit to William Blake's Inn: Poems for Innocent and Experienced Travelers* by Nancy *Willard, illustrated by Alice and Martin *Provensen (1981); and his work also features in David Almond's *Skellig*. There is a huge body of classical, jazz, folk, pop, and contemporary music settings of his poems.

BLAND, Nick (1973–) Australian picture-book author/illustrator whose most popular books are *The Very Cranky Bear* (2008) and its sequels. In 2012 he won *CBCA Book of the Year: Early Childhood for *The Runaway Hug* (2011). *King Pig* (2013) is a hilarious cautionary tale with some similarities to the '*Emperor's New Clothes'. This pig learns to share with the sheep, but he remains selfish enough for the story to be believable. Like the work of Bruce *Whatley and Julie *Vivas, his compositions often use white space, large central characters, and clear type, and his characters are bold, bright, and expressive.

BLEGVAD, Erik (1923–2014) Illustrator who was born in Copenhagen, where he trained at the School of Arts and Crafts and subsequently worked in an advertising agency. In 1950 he married an American painter, Leonore Hochman, and they settled for some time in the United States. Later they made their home in London. Blegvad's early work as an illustrator included *Bedknob and Broomstick* (the 1957 one-volume edition) by Mary *Norton and *The Gammage Cup* (1959) by Carol *Kendall. He and his wife produced a number of their own *picture books, such as *Mr Jensen and Cat* (1965).

Blind Pew In *Treasure Island* by R. L. *Stevenson.

BLISHEN, Edward (1920–96) British author and reviewer of children's books who worked from 1946 to 1959 as a schoolmaster. He edited the *Oxford Book of Poetry for Children* (1964), was co-author with Leon *Garfield of *The *God Beneath the Sea* (1970), and compiled other story collections and works of reference for children, among them the *Junior Pears Encyclopaedia* (1961). His many autobiographical books include *Roaring Boys* (1955), a memorable account of teaching in a London secondary modern school.

BLOCK, Francesca Lia (1962–) American author of more than twenty-five books of fiction, non-fiction, short stories, and poetry. Block was born and is still based in Los Angeles, the city that is the background to her work, infusing it with a strong sense of place. Using magic realism and a style full of imagery and metaphor, art, and music, she is most famous for the six novels in her *young adult *Weetzie Bat* series (from 1989), which charts the exploits of a bleached-blonde, kooky girl (who might resemble the young Francesca), her friends, and their wild L.A. lifestyle. She is a strong champion of equal rights for all, and her books have characters from every possible background and sexuality, which has led to at least one group campaigning to have them burned.

BLOOMFIELD, Robert (1766–1823) British poet and author who worked as a poor shoemaker in London, made Aeolian harps, and was unsuccessfully engaged in the book trade. His works include a children's story, *The History of Little Davy's New Hat* (1815), and *The Fakenham Ghost* (1813), reprinted for children from his *Rural Poems* (1802).

BLOS, Joan W. (Winsor) (1928–) American children's novelist who won the *Newbery Medal for *A Gathering of Days: a New England girl's journal, 1830–32* (1979).

Blossoms of Morality, The (1789) A collection of didactic pieces by Richard *Johnson, published by Elizabeth *Newbery.

Bluebeard A story found in *Perrault's collection *Contes de ma mère L'Oye* (1697) under the title *La Barbe bleue*.

A man of some wealth has a blue beard which makes him so ugly that women avoid him, but he behaves so pleasantly to the daughter of a neighbouring family that she agrees to marry him. When Bluebeard is absent one night, his wife unlocks a door her husband has forbidden her to open and finds the corpses of Bluebeard's previous wives inside. Bluebeard returns home unexpectedly and realizing what his wife has discovered states that she too must meet her death. She manages to delay her murder to allow time for her brothers to arrive and kill Bluebeard. The wife then inherits the estate and remarries 'a very honest man, which made her forget the bad time she had spent with Bluebeard'. Perrault's 'Moralités' that end the tale point out the danger of curiosity and also add the wry comment that such a story is rarely likely to take place now, as husbands do not dare to cross their wives.

Commentators have often suggested that the story may have a historical foundation, and the resemblance has been pointed out between Bluebeard and Gilles de Rais (1404–40), a French nobleman who murdered huge numbers of children. The story has also been compared with the legend of Comorre the Cursed, a 6th-cent. Breton chieftain who murdered his wives when they became pregnant. However, the principal motifs of Perrault's story are common enough in folk tales, and seem to be quite independent from these historical traditions. The door (or box) which may not be opened without disastrous results features in many folk stories, and a story in the Grimms' collection entitled *Fitcher's Bird* resembles *Bluebeard* in many particulars. The mass murderer who keeps the bodies of his female victims in a room in his house is also the subject of *Mr Fox*, a tale printed in Joseph *Jacobs's *English Fairy Tales* (1890) and was apparently in oral circulation in England in the 18th cent. *The Robber Bridegroom* in Grimm is also a variant of the Bluebeard story.

It is interesting, however, that the 'Moralités' which conclude Perrault's story foreground the insubordination of the wife in unlocking the door rather than the guilt of the husband's murderous deeds, a focus preserved in a *c*.1850 version of the story entitled *The story of Blue Beard; or, the effects of female curiosity* (Glasgow, 'Printed for the booksellers'). Both Grimm stories and other antecedents are not, however, so judgemental of the wife and more recently, in line with feminist revisionings of fairy tales, Margaret Atwood has offered a rewriting of the Bluebeard story (*Bluebeard's Egg*, 1983) based not on Perrault but on the Grimms' *Fitcher's Bird*. *Bluebeard* has not been printed in collections for children as often as have Perrault's other stories, for obvious reasons, though it appears in certain juvenile volumes, e.g. *Bluebeard bold and bad, and other stories*, edited by 'Lady Kathleen' (*c*.1910).

Bluebell in Fairyland, *a musical dream play in two acts* By Sir Edward Seymour Hicks (1871–1949), with music by Walter Slaughter and lyrics by Aubrey Hopwood; it was apparently the first full-length original children's *play (that is, neither a *pantomime nor an adaptation of a book) to be performed on the London stage. First produced in December 1901, it was thereafter revived annually for some time; the first production was seen by J. M. *Barrie, who was encouraged by it to write *Peter Pan*. *Bluebell in Fairyland* tells how Bluebell, a London flower-girl, finds herself in the Kingdom of the Sleepy King, who lies fast asleep in a cave while his throne is occupied by a usurper. She restores him to his kingdom, wakes to find it all a dream, but is rescued from poverty by a kind old gentleman.

Blue Bird, The (*L'Oiseau bleu*) A *fairy story by Mme d'*Aulnoy, the source of the name 'Prince Charming' for a fairy-tale or *pantomime hero.

A widowed king with an only daughter, Florine, marries again. Jealous of Florine's superior beauty, the new queen does everything to favour her own daughter. When the girls are of an age to marry, Prince Charming visits the court, and the queen's daughter is presented to him. Florine is allowed only old, soiled clothes to wear, and hides in shame, but the prince sees her and falls in love with her unconcealable beauty. The queen imprisons her and condemns the prince to be a blue bird for the next seven years. Meanwhile Florine is told that the prince is to marry her stepsister.

The blue bird hears her grieving at her window, discloses his real identity, and for two years comes every night to bring her jewels and speak to her. Eventually he regains his proper shape, the stepsister is turned into a sow, and all turns out well.

The Blue Bird appeared in Mme d'Aulnoy's first collection of fairy tales, *Contes des fées* (1697), and was among the earliest to be translated into English, in 1699. It is usually counted among her most successful tales, and is generally included in collections of her work.

Blue Bird, The A *play for children by the Belgian dramatist and symbolist poet Maurice Maeterlinck (1862–1949), first published in English in 1909. A boy and girl, Tyltyl and Mytyl, son and daughter of a poor woodcutter, are visited on Christmas Eve by an old woman who asks them to search for 'the bird that is blue', telling them, 'It's for my little girl, who is very ill.' She then reveals herself as the Fairy Bérylune, and causes their cat and dog to acquire the power of speech, sending Tyltyl and Mytyl off on their quest with these as companions together with the spirits of Fire, Water, Bread, and Sugar. The children visit the Land of Memory, the Palace of Night, and other strange places, and often think that they have found the Blue Bird, but are always disappointed. Eventually the children find themselves at home in bed on Christmas morning; the old neighbour comes, and they give her their own pet bird—finding, as they do so, that it is blue.

The Blue Bird, an allegorical narrative of the search for happiness, is a work of great charm and delicacy, but it requires a very large cast and elaborate staging, and since its original productions it has rarely been performed, though a production features in Noel *Streatfeild's *Ballet Shoes* (1936). It was filmed in 1939, with Shirley *Temple as Mytyl, and a second film version of 1976 was a USA–USSR co-production. In 1977 the story of the play was used as the basis of a *picture book by Brian *Wildsmith.

Blue Fairy Book *See* FAIRY BOOKS, compiled by Andrew *Lang.

Blue Peter A television magazine programme intended for children between five and twelve-years-old, broadcast by the BBC from 1958, and edited for many years by Biddy Baxter. It has been variously once, twice- and thrice-weekly, but by 2014 was broadcasting a single weekly show. It uses a team of

presenters to introduce items about all aspects of life, and it specializes in charitable appeals, which can evoke a huge response from children. For many years it claimed to be the most popular British children's television programme, and may be seen as an inheritor of the robust but serious-minded tradition of mid-19th-cent. children's *magazines. The basic format remains unchanged even now in the 21st cent. In 2000 the programme launched the *Blue Peter Book Awards.

Blue Peter Book Awards British children's book prize associated with the BBC television programme *Blue Peter*, awarded since 2000. Originally judged by both adults and children, for most of its existence it has awarded books in three categories: Best Book to Read Aloud, Book I Couldn't Put Down, and Best Book with Facts (with an overall 'Book of the Year' chosen from the category winners). Notable winners in these three categories (or their more recent, renamed equivalents) have included *Room on the Broom, Man on the Moon* (Simon Bartram), and *Lost and Found*; The *Wind Singer, Feather Boy* (Nicky *Singer), *Mortal Engines, Montmorency* (Eleanor *Updale), *Private Peaceful*, and The Outlaw Varjak Paw* (S. F. Said); and *Terrible Tudors* (*see* HORRIBLE HISTORIES), The Ultimate Book Guide, and The Worst Children's Jobs in History* (Tony Robinson).

BLUME, Judy (1938–) Popular writer of American *young adult fiction who was born in New Jersey and educated at New York University. Blume came to fame with *Are You There, God? It's Me, Margaret* (1970), in which an eleven-year-old girl longs for the onset of puberty, and expresses her hope in the form of prayers: 'I just told my mother I wanted a bra. Please help me grow, God, You know where.' Later Blume novels include *Then Again, Maybe I Won't* (1971), about a boy who gets psychiatric help to cure nervous dyspepsia; *It's Not the End of the World* (1972), in which a girl desperately tries to keep her divorcing parents together; *Deenie* (1973), whose heroine suffers from curvature of the spine; and *Blubber* (1974), about a fat girl. *Forever* (1975), the story of an adolescent romance, is explicit in its description of sexual encounters. All these books portrayed real modern dilemmas recognizable to Blume's teenage readers, and she is today considered one of the pioneers of young adult writing. Blume also achieved critical and popular success with a comic novel for younger readers,

Tales of a Fourth Grade Nothing (1972), which has a sequel, *Superfudge* (1980).

BLYTH, Harry (1852–98) Author of Victorian boys' stories. As 'Hal Meredith' he wrote the first *Sexton Blake* tale in 1893, and contributed to several *Harmsworth papers.

BLYTON, Enid (Mary) (1897–1968) The most commercially successful British children's author of her time. She was born in London, and spent her childhood in the suburb of Beckenham. Her parents' marriage was quarrelsome, and when she was nearly thirteen her father, who made a living from various forms of business enterprise, walked out. Enid was shattered by this, and took to writing sentimental poetry as a psychological escape. In her early teens she had a poem accepted by one of Arthur *Mee's magazines. She was educated at a Beckenham girls' school, where she became head girl and captain of games.

Failing to get on with her mother after her father's departure, she left home as soon as she could. Her parents had wanted her to be a concert pianist, but she abandoned musical training and studied to be a *kindergarten teacher, learning the *Froebel and *Montessori methods. While working as a *governess to four small boys, she began to have verses, stories, and humorous pieces accepted by magazines. In 1922 appeared her first book, *Child Whispers*, a collection of poems, many of which resemble the fairy verses then being made popular by Rose *Fyleman. The next year came *Real Fairies*, with subject-matter reminiscent of the pictures of Mabel Lucie *Attwell, who was then at the height of her success. Enid Blyton also began to contribute large numbers of stories, verses, and short *plays for children to the journal *Teachers' World*, which was distributed widely through British schools. By 1924 her name was well enough known in the school world for the publishing firm of Newnes to commission *The Enid Blyton Book of Fairies*.

She was greatly attracted to her editor at Newnes, Major Hugh Pollock, a married man with a distinguished war record, whose wife had left him. She determined to marry him, and wrote in her diary 'I want him for mine.' By the time of their wedding, in August 1924, she had given up her governess work and was earning a substantial income from writing. The Pollocks lived first at a new house in Beckenham, which Enid named 'Elfin Cottage', but when it was threatened by the building of an arterial road they moved to a cottage

at Bourne End in Buckinghamshire. During the first years of her marriage Enid produced such works as *Sunny Stories for Little Folk* (1926 onwards), and retellings of *Aesop, *Uncle Remus, *Robin Hood, and other standard nursery fare; she also edited such part-works as *The Teachers' Treasury* (1926) and *Modern Teaching: practical suggestions for junior and senior schools* (1932).

The Pollocks' marriage seems to have been initially happy. Their hopes of having children were at first disappointed but finally a daughter, Gillian, was born in 1931.

In the 1930s Enid Blyton became known to innumerable children from the Enid Blyton Children's Page in *Teachers' World*. This contained a letter from her—a cosy narration of events in her domestic life—together with another supposedly from her dog, Bobs, and a story, poem, or competition. The response to the page was enormous; letters were sent in their hundreds by child readers, and any charitable appeal met with instant results. Meanwhile she produced several children's books each year. But it was not until 1937 that she wrote her first piece of full-length children's fiction. This was *Adventures of the Wishing-Chair*, which proved to be the first in a *Wishing-Chair* series, Blyton and her publishers always being quick to exploit any successful idea. Her next full-length stories were *Mr Galliano's Circus* and *The Secret Island* (both 1938); there was soon a 'Circus' series too, while *Naughty Amelia Jane* (1939), a story based on her daughter Gillian's rag doll, had many sequels as well. The first *Famous Five* story appeared in 1942 (*The *Secret Seven* came a few years later), and Enid Blyton had soon diversified into *school stories, with sets of books about 'The *Naughtiest Girl in the School' (1940 onwards), '*St Clare's' (1943 onwards), and '*Malory Towers' (1946 onwards). These were only a fraction of her output, which by the late 1940s totalled more than 30 books a year, and was keeping a whole host of London publishers busy. She usually produced between six and ten thousand words per day, working with a portable typewriter on a board across her knees.

In 1935 her second daughter Imogen was born. The marriage had now become very difficult, with Blyton's husband Hugh drinking heavily, and becoming seriously ill in consequence. During the Second World War, by which time the family was living at 'Green Hedges', a house in Beaconsfield, she and her husband were divorced and she married

Kenneth Darrell Waters, a London surgeon. The war diverted the attention of gossip-writers from these events, which contrasted with the picture of cloudless family life drawn by Blyton in her columns in *Teachers' World* and *Sunny Stories*.

Blyton in fact only became a household name during the 1950s, when she began to produce stories about *Noddy, for many years her most celebrated (and notorious) creation. It was during this period, and largely because of the Noddy books, that she began to attract considerable criticism from children's book reviewers, librarians, and educationalists, who accused her of mediocrity and alleged that she wrote in a vocabulary so limited that (as one critic put it) it was 'drained of all difficulty until it achieved a kind of aesthetic anaemia'. By the end of the 1950s her books were being deliberately excluded from *libraries in Britain and overseas. Enid Blyton invariably answered attacks by saying that she gave children what they wanted, and took no notice of critics over twelve years of age. She also pointed out that if children could not borrow her books from libraries they would buy them with their own money— which proved to be true, for sales increased dramatically; her income by the late 1950s was reportedly over £100,000 per annum. But she was privately very resentful of attacks and threatened legal action if there was any question of libel.

Her health deteriorated in the early 1960s, and she began to lose her memory; after about 1964 she produced little other than Noddy books. Her second husband died a year before her.

The official biography of Blyton by Barbara Stoney (1974), the first of several biographies in the decades after her death, makes no secret of her intense personal ambition, stubborn character, and dislike of being thwarted. Her unhappy childhood seems to have made her determined to the point of ruthlessness, and also nearly incapable of settled personal relationships. (There are certain resemblances here to Frances Hodgson *Burnett.) What all agree on, both friends and detractors, is that she had outstanding business acumen and knew how to make the very most out of what talent she had.

Objections continue to be raised against her work, and will be as long as it remains in print. When Sheila Ray examined the question in *The Blyton Phenomenon* (1982), she reported that Blyton was still and overwhelmingly the

most popular children's author in the eight-to-twelve age group in Britain (a title subsequently lost to *Harry Potter), and gave an account of some recent criticisms of the stories, including accusations of *racism and sexism, as well as regular criticism of their formulaic nature, reactionary attitudes, and lack of literary skill. While the occasional library exclusion still happens, the books for the most part do remain available today, while disapproving adults continue to try to encourage children to read something else. To no avail, of course: over the first decade of the 21st cent., Blyton was the UK's tenth bestselling author. Total sales of her books to date are estimated to have exceeded 600 million copies.

board books See BABY BOOKS.

Bobbsey Twins In stories published by the American *Stratemeyer Syndicate, under the pen name Laura Lee Hope (*Bobbsey Twins: or, Merry Days Indoors and Out*, 1904, and many other titles). There are two sets of twins: Bert and Nan, aged eight, and Freddie and Flossie, aged four. The books are jolly, cosy *family stories, described by Margery *Fisher as 'a nursery soap-opera'. The stories were revised for a new edition in 1950 and further editions continued to appear for decades thereafter.

Bobby Brewster A small boy in stories by H. E. *Todd, to whom strange and magical things happen. The Brewster books were published between the 1940s and 1970s, and have been translated into a number of languages.

Bob Cherry One of the 'Famous Five' in the *Billy Bunter stories.

Bod Character in a series of British television cartoons and *picture books by Michael and Joanne Cole.

Bodley books A very popular series of *travelogue storybooks by Horace E. *Scudder, featuring a New England family in the late 1840s and early 1850s. The first, *Doings of the Bodley Family in Town and Country* (1875), describes their move from a town out to a farm, where the children learn country ways. This was followed by *The Bodleys Telling Stories* (1877), *The Bodleys on Wheels* (1878), which describes a tour of Massachusetts, *The Bodleys Afloat* (1879), concerned with the sea, *Mr Bodley Abroad* (1880), in which the father sends letters from Europe recounting his experiences there, *The Bodley Grandchildren and their Journeys in Holland* (1882), *The English Bodley Family* (1884), and *The Viking Bodleys* (1885).

bogey (bogeyman) An imaginary being invoked by adults to frighten children into good behaviour. In the 18th and early 19th cents. bogies played a large part in nursery lore; they were often given names, such as Rawhead-and-Bloody-Bones, Tom-Poker, and Bull Beggar; these three are mentioned in the 'Letter from a Lady' which opens *Tommy Thumb's Song Book* (1744), where the reader is warned not to frighten the child by mentioning them. The story *Mr Miacca* in *English Fairy Tales* (1890) concerns a bogey-man who is in effect an *ogre, and catches small boys and cooks them. Frances *Crompton's novel *The *Gentle Heritage* (1893) ingeniously exploits children's mixed feelings (fear and fascination) about bogies. The word 'bogey' may be derived from a Welsh form *bwg*, 'ghost'; modern Welsh has *bwgan* for 'bogey'. (The word 'boggart' has the same derivation.) *Fungus the Bogeyman* (1977) by Raymond *Briggs creates an entire underworld of bogies, and documents their character and habits.

BOJUNGA NUNES, Lygia (1932–) Brazilian author, one of only four people to win both of the major international children's book awards, the *Hans Christian Andersen Award and the *Astrid Lindgren Memorial Award (the others being Maurice *Sendak, Katherine *Paterson and Christine *Nöstlinger). Her varied output includes *Os colegas* (1972, her debut, which won the prestigious Jabuti Prize; translated as *The Companions*, 1989); *O meu amigo pintor* (1987; *My Friend the Painter*, 1991); *A bolsa amarela* (2005); and *Corda bamba* (1979)—these last two, like many of her novels, explore the power of children's fantasy and imagination.

Bologna Ragazzi Awards A range of awards announced annually at the Bologna Children's Book Fair, the world's leading trade fair for children's books. Bologna Ragazzi Awards, selected by an international jury, are given in a number of (varying) categories, which include '*Opera Prima*' (for debuts), 'New Horizons' (for publishers from the Arab world, Latin America, Asia, and Africa), and 'Digital' (for children's books-inspired *apps and other innovative products using interactive media).

BOND, (Thomas) Michael (1926–) British author of the *Paddington Bear stories who worked for some years as a BBC television cameraman. His first Paddington book appeared in 1958; eight years later he became a full-time writer. He has also written a 'Thursday' series about an orphan mouse (1966 onwards), stories about Parsley the Lion and other animals with herb-names (1969 onwards), and books about the guinea pig *Olga de Polga (1971 onwards).

BOND, Ruskin (1934–) Indian author and poet of English descent who is credited with a pioneering role in the development of Indian children's literature. Bond's many children's books include *The Room on the Roof* (1956), about an orphaned sixteen-year-old Anglo-Indian boy who runs away from home—Bond himself was only seventeen when he wrote it.

Bond's books are often set in the Himalayan foothills, including *Angry River* (1972) and *The Blue Umbrella* (1974). He is admired for his short stories—collections include *The Road to the Bazaar* (1980), *When Darkness Falls* (2001), and *The Kashmiri Storyteller* (2001)—many of which are now studied in India on school curricula. He has also produced a children's biography of Nehru (1976) and *Tales and Legends of India* (1982). *Love Among the Bookshelves* (2014) is part autobiography and part anthology, as it charts his life through stories he has loved.

BONHAM, Frank (1914–88) American author of such 'realistic' novels as *Durango Street* (1965), about a black boy on parole, and *Gimme an H, Gimme an E, Gimme an L, Gimme a P* (1980), which deals with an attractive high school cheer-leader who tries to conceal her personal problems.

Bonzo A cheeky dog drawn by the British artist G(eorge) E. Studdy (1878–1948). First created in 1912, Bonzo became a very popular figure in the 1920s, appearing on postcards, in the form of toys and other products, in *annuals, and in a series of silent cartoon films made in 1924.

Book for Boys and Girls, A, or, *Country Rhimes for Children* Later entitled *Divine Emblems*, a volume of poems by John *Bunyan. The first edition (1686) also contained a short 'help to Children to learn to read English' in the form of letters, numerals, and spelling advice. The verses draw spiritual lessons from such homely (and sometimes odd) subjects

as the mole, the post-boy, the top, a pound of candles falling to the ground, stinking breath, fly-blows, and a pair of spectacles. Bunyan expressed his intentions thus: ' . . . by their Playthings I would them entice | To mount their Thoughts from what are childish Toys | To Heav'n, for that's prepar'd for Girls and Boys.' Two of the verses have tunes attached, possibly Bunyan's own.

The first edition contained 74 poems, but 25 had been removed by 1701, some, perhaps, because they seemed too coarse. The ninth edition, published by John Marshall of Gracechurch Street, 'adorned with cuts', was entitled *Divine Emblems: or, Temporal Things Spiritualised, Fitted for the Use of Boys and Girls*. Ten more editions appeared in England in the 19th cent.

Bunyan is thought to have drawn his inspiration from *Aesop, biblical parables, popular *emblem literature, and such popular *Puritan poets as *Keach, rather than from the more sophisticated contemporary court poetry. Although his verse now seems strained, it was fresh and original for its time, and a few of the poems are still printed in anthologies.

Book of Americans, A (1933) A collection of (occasionally moralistic) verses by the American poet and novelist Stephen Vincent Benét (1898–1943) and his wife Rosemary, about famous figures of American history, from Columbus to Woodrow Wilson, with illustrations by Charles Child.

Book of Discoveries, A (1910) The first of John *Masefield's children's books. Two brothers, Mac and Robin, possessed of catapults and imagination, trespass on the estate of Mr Hampden, an unusual landowner and naturalist. Rather than punish them, he turns their curiosity and love of adventure to profit by making them learn about their surroundings and the past. The book is full of Masefield's love of the English countryside, and of his enthusiasm.

Book of Knowledge, The See CHILDREN'S ENCYCLOPAEDIA.

Book of Nonsense, A by *Derry Down Derry* Celebrated collection of *limericks by Edward *Lear, first published on 10 February 1846 by Thomas McLean of 26 Haymarket, London. The first edition consists of two parts, each bound separately in card covers. Each has on the front this limerick, accompanied by Lear's illustration to it:

There was an old Derry down Derry,
Who loved to see little folks merry:
So he made them a Book,
And with laughter they shook,
At the fun of that Derry down Derry.

Each part consists of thirty-six *lithographed leaves, laid out oblong and bearing (on one side only) one of Lear's drawings with its accompanying limerick at the bottom.

A second edition of *A Book of Nonsense* was published by McLean in one volume in 1856, with the author's name again given as 'Derry Down Derry'. In 1861 *Routledge, Warne and Routledge, on commission from Lear himself, issued a third edition, for which Lear had the original lithographs replaced by new *wood engravings made from his drawings by the brothers *Dalziel, who printed the book. He also supplied forty-three new limericks with accompanying drawings. Three limericks which had appeared in the original edition were deleted: 'There was an old man of Kildare', 'There was an old sailor of Compton', and 'There was an old man of New York'. When the first printing of this edition (2,000 copies) sold out, Routledge quickly bought the copyright from Lear and re-issued it. In two years it had reached a 'fourteenth edition', and a 'twenty-seventh' by 1889, the year after Lear's death. The 1861 printing and all subsequent editions named Lear as author.

The first American edition appears to have been that brought out by Willis P. Hazard of Philadelphia in 1863, based on a Routledge printing of the same year. The book was also published during the 1860s by John Bradburn and James Miller, both of New York. It soon became as popular in America as in England, new editions appearing there almost every year.

Reviewers expressed huge enthusiasm for the limericks. The *Examiner* for 18 November 1876 wrote:

We all know what followed upon the publication of this volume. It was in vain that the serious-minded members of every family publicly sneered at these picturesque little quintains; they were invariably discovered laughing in private over what they openly mocked at. The metrical discovery was so simple, so obvious, that everyone adopted it.

Lear did not in fact make any 'metrical discovery'. His limericks were, technically speaking, more pedestrian than some of those in *Anecdotes and Adventures of Fifteen Gentlemen*, the book which had given him the idea for his own verses. For the most part he did not attempt to produce a surprising or comic

rhyme in the last line, but merely repeated the last word of the first line. But he improved upon this earlier, anonymous book almost beyond measure. For the mild drolleries of the *Anecdotes* he substituted a humour that is always grotesque and frequently violent. The Old Men and Old Ladies of his verses engage in the weirdest of pursuits, which usually earn them the censure of society; and this censure sometimes takes a horrific form.

Only occasionally does the individual escape from, or avenge himself upon, society. The Old Man with a poker, when laughed at for having painted his face red, simply 'knocked them all down with his poker'. But if persons of unconventional behaviour evade the criticism of the world at large, Lear himself fills the role of critic when he supplies, in the last line, some adjective (often unexpected) which brands the behaviour of the limerick's subject as scarcely acceptable; so the Old Man of Apulia, who feeds his sons on buns, is 'whimsical', while the Young Lady of Turkey, who weeps whenever the weather is bad, is 'capricious'. Possibly Lear acquired this trick from *The *History of Sixteen Wonderful Old Women*, the earliest known book of limericks, published by John *Harris in 1820, which has a number of verses where an adjective is introduced in this fashion in the last line, such as 'This whimsical woman of Spain' and 'This pious old woman of Leeds'.

Lear's verses have some affinity with *nursery rhymes, which are often concerned with violent happenings and eccentric conduct. But the Lear limericks are far more rational than the random—and sometimes utterly nonsensical—goings-on of the nursery rhyme world, and they almost always present the theme of the eccentric or unhappy individual in conflict with, or exiled from, normal life and society.

Among imitations of the *Book of Nonsense* is *Funny Figures* (1858), the work of Edward *Bradley, a humorist who usually wrote under the name 'Cuthbert Bede'.

Book of Nurture See BOOKS OF COURTESY.

Book of Three See ALEXANDER, LLOYD.

Books for Keeps One of the UK's leading independent children's book magazines. Launched in 1980, it won the prestigious *Eleanor Farjeon Award for outstanding contribution to the world of children's books in 1996. Now available to browse, print, or download online, *Books for Keeps* remains an invaluable resource,

published six times a year, reviewing thousands of children's books and providing up-to-date articles and news from the industry.

Books for the Bairns A series of sixty-two-page illustrated booklets containing well-known *fairy stories and folk tales and other popular matter, published from 1896 by the British editor W. T. Stead (1840–1912), initially under the imprint of his *Review of Reviews*.

books of courtesy Handbooks of instruction in the manners and customs of polite society, written for children and young people from the 15th to the 19th cents. The earliest were intended for the sons of noblemen who were being brought up in wealthy households, or at court. The 15th-cent. *Stans Puer ad Mensam* ('The Boy Standing at Table') instructs its reader not to fidget when addressing the king. This short book is in verse; the English translation of the Latin original was ascribed to John Lydgate. It was printed by *Caxton and again by Wynkyn de *Worde in the late 15th cent., and reprinted during the 16th cent. Its instructions were very simple: to keep the hands and fingernails clean, not to swear or pick the teeth, not to spill food, etc. Among other verse treatises on manners from the same period are *The Babees Book* (*c.*1475), and *The Book of Curtesye*, which was printed by Caxton *c.*1477–8.

A more substantial work is *The Boke of Nurture* (mid-15th cent.) by John Russell, who describes himself as 'Usher' (teacher) to Humphrey, Duke of Gloucester. It begins with the complaint of a lad who cannot find employment in a lord's household because he knows no domestic skills. The narrator offers to teach him, and the rest of the book consists of detailed instructions about the work of the various household officials—butler, chamberlain, etc. Much attention is paid to the carving of meat and to cookery, and there is a table of precedence to be considered when making seating arrangements. Russell's book was adapted and printed by Wynkyn de Worde as *The Boke of Keruynge* (Carving). Another *Boke of Nurture*, by Hugh Rhodes, was printed several times during the mid-16th cent. Rhodes, described as 'of the Kinges Chappell', gave instruction in domestic service, and also provided general rules of conduct.

Among the most widely read 16th-cent. treatises on manners was the *De Civilitate Morum Puerilium* of Erasmus, published with an English translation by Robert Whittington

in 1532, under the title *A lytil Booke of good maners for chyldren*. Erasmus emphasized the importance of an education in the liberal arts as a means of achieving true nobility. His book was used in English schools, and was recommended more than a century later by Charles *Hoole.

Among the many books of courtesy that appeared during the first half of the 17th cent. were *Youths Behaviour, or Decencie in Conversation* (*c.*1641), translated from the French by an eight-year-old boy, Francis Hawkins, and printed at his father's request, and *Cacoethes' Leaden Legacy: or His Schoole of ill manners* (1624), in which the reader was expected to follow the contrary practices to those recommended; e.g. 'It is good manners so soone as you are up, | To have your head in the Cupboord, and your nose in the cup.'

After the 17th cent., courtesy-books often took the form of parental advice, and began to concern themselves more with moral attitudes. *The Gentleman's Calling* (1660) described what its author believed to be the duties of the wealthy classes: generosity to the poor, not running up debts with tradesmen, the prudent management of estates, etc. Francis Osborne's two-part *Advice to a Son* (1656 and 1658) was addressed to a young man of undergraduate age, and included advice on love and marriage, foreign travel, and religion, such as 'A good Religion might be composed out of the Papist's *Charity*, the Puritan's *Words* and the Protestant's *Faith*.' Such sentiments caused the Vice Chancellor of Oxford to forbid the city's booksellers to stock Osborne's book, on the grounds that it was atheistical. As a result of this publicity the book, which was very popular with students, sold all the better.

Girls were counselled as well as boys. The author of *The Gentleman's Calling* published *The Ladies Calling* in 1673; its opening chapters were entitled 'Of Modesty', 'Of Meekness', 'Of Affability', and 'Of Piety'. In 1658 John Heydon wrote *Advice to a Daughter*, but this was no more than an attack on Osborne's *Advice to a Son*. More serious advice to girls was given in *The Lady's New-year's Gift: or, Advice to a Daughter* (1688) by William Savile, Lord Halifax. This offered many principles of conduct, albeit tempered with some cynicism. The book was addressed to Halifax's daughter Elizabeth, who became the mother of the fourth Lord *Chesterfield, author of the famous *Letters* to his own natural son and

godson, which came to be one of the most successful courtesy-books of all time.

John *Newbery included among his many publications for children a book about behaviour, *Letters on the most Common, as well as Important, Occasions in Life* (1758). It was prefaced with advice on 'Epistolary Writing', and consisted of letters written chiefly by celebrated persons (the Earl of Oxford to Alexander Pope, Anne Boleyn's last letter to Henry VIII, etc.). He also published *The Polite Lady ... a series of letters from a mother to her daughter* (1760). Two rival booksellers to Newbery, Baldwin of London and Collins of Salisbury, produced (c.1760) a book of manners modelled more closely on the old pattern, *The Polite Academy*. Other books of social instruction from this period include *The Polite Preceptor* (1776), a collection of writings on behaviour by celebrated essayists.

Early 19th-cent. books of manners include *The Prize for Youthful Obedience* (published by *Darton and Harvey in 1800), an illustrated account of the exemplary behaviour of various children, and *The Good Boy's Soliloquy* (1810), a *picture book giving examples of good and bad behaviour, with a text of rhyming couplets. Though books of courtesy for children are found later in the 19th cent., their function was gradually taken over by the *moral tale which flourished from about 1780 to 1830, and which in turn gave rise to more sophisticated didactic fiction for the young.

books of instruction Educational manuals for the use of children which have existed since the first schools were established. Among the earliest English school-books are the *De Orthographia* (c.700) of *Bede and the *Grammar* and *Colloquy* of *Ælfric (fl.1006). The *Colloquy* sets an important precedent by making some attempt to entertain the pupil as well as to instruct him. These books were aids to the teaching of Latin, which, since it was the language of the Church and of cultured reading, was the purpose of all early English institutional teaching.

By the time of Chaucer several types of school were in existence in Britain, including the song-schools, where boys were taught to sing the services of the Church and were given an elementary education with the aid of *primers and other simple books which taught the alphabet, the syllables, and a few prayers. In the grammar schools, older pupils studied Latin with the aid of such books as the *Ars Minor* of Donatus, an elementary textbook on

the parts of speech. With the rise of the universities, grammar schools also began to provide an elementary training in logic and rhetoric. These subjects, together with Latin grammar, made up the 'Trivium' or threefold curriculum that was the first stage in an education in the 'seven liberal arts', which were 'liberal' in the sense that they provided for the training of a free man (*liber*). The four remaining subjects, which were taught at universities, were known as the 'Quadrivium': arithmetic, geometry, astronomy, and music. Books were not greatly used, the usual method of teaching being for the master to read aloud from his own manuscript, and dictate notes.

The Renaissance produced not only a number of writings on children's education, such as Sir Thomas Elyot's *The Boke named the Governor* (1531) and Roger *Ascham's *The Scholemaster* (1570), but also a number of innovatory school-books. The first printed Latin grammar written in English was the work of John Stanbridge, usher at Magdalen College School in Oxford early in the 16th cent. During that century the variety of grammars in use in different schools caused much confusion. As a result, a royal proclamation of Henry VIII ordered that one book and no other should be used. This was the work known as *Lily's Grammar*, which in its earliest form had been composed for St Paul's School in London. Despite its avowed objective to consider 'the tenderness and capacity of small minds', it became a sore trial to many schoolboys in the next two and a half centuries, during which it remained in use as the only officially approved Latin grammar.

During the 17th cent. Latin was still being taught as a spoken language, to be used in conversation in class, with penalties for those who lapsed into English. To help the boys gain the fluency that this required, a number of books were printed which gave Latin renderings of schoolboys' conversations or of sayings well known to them, e.g. *Parœmiologia Anglo-Latina* (1639). The dialogue-form was much used, just as it had been in the time of Ælfric. John *Brinsley, a Nonconformist school-master and educationalist, composed a Latin grammar (1615) in which the accidence of the language was taught by questions and answers. One of his contemporaries, Charles *Hoole, was among the first to recommend the reading of English literature for his pupils' profit and amusement. Hoole also made a translation of the *Orbis Sensualium Pictus* of *Comenius, which is usually

regarded as the first instructive *picture book for children; it was plagiarized in James Greenwood's *The London Vocabulary* (third edition 1713, in print till 1828).

The English educational system of the 17th cent. was subjected to much criticism, most notably by John *Locke in his *Thoughts concerning Education* (1693). Locke objected to the usual method of learning the works of classical writers—'scraps of authors got by heart'—and proposed a much wider educational programme. Though Locke's ideas were not put into practice in the grammar schools, a new type of school grew up after the Restoration, which was able to exercise some freedom in its curriculum. These were the Nonconformist academies, at which such Dissenting writers as *Defoe and Isaac *Watts were educated. Defoe recorded that at his school, in London, the subjects taught included French, Italian, Spanish, mathematics, natural science, history, geography, logic, and politics.

It was in the mid-18th cent., at a time when English education was at a low ebb in grammar schools, public schools, and universities, that booksellers began to publish works of instruction designed to be read by children in their own homes rather than at school. One of the earliest sets of such books was also one of the most ambitious, *The *Circle of the Sciences*, first published by John *Newbery between 1745 and 1748. Soon afterwards, writers such as Anna Laetitia *Barbauld, Maria *Edgeworth and Eleanor *Fenn began to provide reading matter for young children that was based on the infant's own experience of the world. At the beginning of the 19th cent. many booksellers took this one stage further, and started to issue simple primers that were entertainingly illustrated. An innovator in this was John *Harris, whose *Paths of Learning Strewed with Flowers* (1820) explained its purpose as 'to entwine roses with instruction'. Other books published by Harris and his contemporaries taught simple arithmetic in an entertaining fashion, e.g. *Marmaduke Multiply's Merry Method of Making Minor Mathematicians* (1816–17). Such books were sometimes attacked as being too frivolous for instructional use, and they found no favour with the disciples of Mrs *Trimmer.

Far more characteristic of the first half of the 19th cent. were the plainer books of facts (often using the catechetical method) like *Mangnall's Questions*, the *Conversations* of Mrs *Marcet, the *History Books* of Mrs *Markham, *The *Child's Guide to Knowledge*, and the extensive series of works known as *Pinnock's Catechisms*. Another notable figure in the field was *Peter Parley, a pseudonym first used by an American and subsequently adopted by several English writers of instructive books. The passion for 'facts', indeed, was the dominating force in the children's book market from about 1830 to 1850, far outweighing the demand for works of the imagination, or even for *moral tales. It was satirized by *Dickens in *Hard Times* (1854) in the figure of Mr Gradgrind, and by Charles *Kingsley in *The *Water-Babies* (1863), which is an eloquent plea for the restoration of the imagination to its former place of importance.

In America the first children's book of instruction to be published was *The *New England Primer* (c.1687). During the following three-quarters of a century, American schoolbooks were for the most part reprints of popular English books, such as Hoole's translation of *Sententiae Pueriles* ('Sentences for Children'), printed in Boston in 1702; George *Fox's *Instructions for Right-Spelling*, printed in Philadelphia in 1702; Nathaniel *Crouch's *Some Excellent Verses for the Education of Youth*, printed in Boston in 1708; and James Hodder's *Hodder's Arithmetick*, printed in Boston in 1719. Not until the mid-18th cent. did American writers begin to produce their own instruction-books in any quantity. Early examples of these include John Gordon's *Mathematical Traverse Table* (Philadelphia, etc., 1758), Anthony Benezet's *The Pennsylvania Spelling-Book* (Philadelphia, 1776), and Robert Davidson's *Geography Epitomized* (Philadelphia, 1784). Jedediah Morse's *Geography Made Easy* (1784) and Noah Webster's *American Spelling Book* (1783) were very popular, and in the 19th cent. the *McGuffey Eclectic Readers had a huge influence.

The 20th cent. saw the production of immense numbers of non-fiction books for children, for use in home and school. Particular mention should be made here of two sets of publications which began to appear at the start of the century, and which were both revolutionary in their approach. In 1908 the *Children's Encyclopaedia* was founded by Arthur *Mee; it packed an enormous amount of information in palatable form into its richly illustrated pages, and played a large part in the education of several generations. In 1911 Ward Lock began to publish their *Wonder Book* series, in which Ships, Trains, Aircraft,

and many other aspects of modern life were presented highly attractively in photographs and words, setting an example that was soon followed by other publishers. (*See also* NON-FICTION FOR CHILDREN.)

books of trades Giving accounts, and often pictures, of trades, crafts, and other employments, they first appeared in the mid-18th cent. One of the earliest is *A General Description of all Trades, digested in Alphabetical Order* (1747), intended for use when instructing the young. It is not illustrated, but describes in much detail the work, qualifications, pay, hours, City companies, arms, mottoes, and social status of the various trades. The trade of Bookseller 'is esteemed a very polite and profitable one in the Shop-keeping Way'.

The Book of Trades, or Library of the Useful Arts was published in three volumes, illustrated with *copperplates, by *Tabart in 1804-5, and was praised by Mrs *Trimmer. In 1818 John *Harris issued *A Visit to the Bazaar,* a description of the Soho Bazaar in London. One of the most popular of such publications was *The Book of Trades; or, Circle of the Useful Arts* (R. Griffin and Thomas Tegg, 1837). S. G. *Goodrich, the original *Peter Parley, wrote *The Book of Trades...for the use of the young* (1855). Among a number of later examples is *The Boy's Book of Trades and the tools used in them* (1866), which includes 'Manufacture of Gas'. A number of *ABC books of the mid-19th cent. had trades as their subject.

Bookstart A national programme in the UK, run by *Booktrust, gifting free books to families with children aged 0-4 years old. Founded in 1992 by Wendy Cooling, it was the first national book-gifting programme in the world and its work is now being replicated by 'affiliates' in more than thirty other countries. The programme is premised on research that highlights the importance of reading with very young children and the impact that this has on their literacy attainment in later years. Booktrust has also initiated a number of other book-gifting programmes such as Booktime (age 4-5), Booked Up (age 11-12), and The Letterbox Club for children in foster families (age 7-13), each of these providing free books for children at crucial transition stages in their development.

Book Thief, The (2005) A novel set in Nazi Germany by Australian author, Markus *Zusak. Nine-year-old Liesel picks up a book at her brother's funeral. She can't read but her foster mother teaches her and Liesel eventually begins stealing books from the Nazi administrator's home to read to the man hiding in the basement. The narrative of death is very strong, and the writing style intense and unusual, with poetic snippets and short sentences often carrying harsh facts. This book was published to critical acclaim and was promoted to *young adult readers in America. It was made into a film in 2013.

Booktrust An independent UK charity established in 1921 (with different names in its earlier years) that aims to empower people through a positive engagement with reading, writing, and creativity. It is widely known for its book-gifting programme *Bookstart. The public campaigns raise an awareness of books and reading, as well as providing resources and tools to support children and adults alike. Booktrust organizes the largest group of high-profile literary prizes in the UK and runs a range of literary promotions, including the Children's *Laureate, Best New Illustrators Award and Children's Book Week. In 2014 Booktrust announced new Best Book Awards; the inaugural winners included Lucy *Cousins, Stephan Pastis, Jeff Kinney (*see* DIARY OF A WIMPY KID) and John Green's *The *Fault in Our Stars.*

Booktrust Teenage Prize A prize for UK-published *young adult fiction, awarded annually by *Booktrust between 2003 and 2010. Winners included *The *Graveyard Book, The *Curious Incident of the Dog in the Night-Time, The Knife of Never Letting Go* (*see* CHAOS WALKING), and books by Anthony *McGowan, Anne Cassidy and Sarah *Singleton.

Boone, Daniel *See* WESTERNS.

Bo-Peep *See* LITTLE BO-PEEP; see also INFANT AMUSEMENTS.

BOREMAN, Thomas (*fl.*1730-43) London bookseller and publisher, the first to specialize in books for the amusement and instruction of children. He anticipated the work of John *Newbery by a few years, and though his output was nothing like as large or influential as Newbery's he set a style for juvenile books which Newbery may deliberately have copied.

By 1730 Boreman had established his business in the City of London, operating on Ludgate Hill and in the Guildhall. His activities in the juvenile market began with *A *Description of Three Hundred Animals* (1730), which was followed by two further volumes; all three

books were apparently his own work. In 1740 appeared the first of his *Gigantick Histories*, a children's series which by 1743 had totalled ten volumes. There is no evidence that he published after that date.

Like Newbery, Boreman subscribed to the belief of *Locke that the instruction of children is best combined with entertainment. On the other hand, like Newbery, Boreman showed no enthusiasm for *fairy stories and tales of marvels such as were found in *chapbooks.

Boreman's books were often generously illustrated (though with rather crude *woodcuts), and were bound in boards covered with *Dutch paper. Advertised as sold 'near the two giants in Guildhall', they were published by subscription, and lists of child subscribers were a prominent feature. To judge from these lists, no more than 500 copies were printed of most of his books, though by the end of the series this number had risen somewhat and Boreman was receiving orders from the Isle of Wight, Wales, Ireland, and even America.

Boreman's books, now extremely rare, are described in Wilbur M. Stone's *Gigantick Histories of Thomas Boreman* (1933).

Borrowers, The (1952) By Mary *Norton, the story of a family of tiny people who live beneath the floors of an old country mansion and survive by 'borrowing' things from the household above them. It was Mary Norton's third book for children, being preceded by the two parts of *Bedknob and Broomstick*, and had its origin in her own short-sightedness in childhood, which led her to peer closely at the plants and creatures of hedgerows and imagine a small race of humans living among them. This private fantasy was banished when she was given spectacles and sent to boarding-school, but it recurred during the economic Depression of the 1930s, whose victims seemed to her to be in a similar situation to her tiny people.

The world of Pod, Homily, and Arrietty—whose distortions of human names emphasize their strange relationship with the 'human beans' upstairs—is entirely parasitical. Everything that the Borrowers have is taken from the big people. Their dependence on them is grotesque: once, there were other Borrower families living in the house, whose diet consisted of leavings from the meal served in the particular room whose crannies they inhabited. Those who lived in the breakfast-room ate only breakfast, those in the drawing-room ate only tea, and so on. Yet this was a Golden Age by comparison with the present time, for now all the other Borrowers have fled, driven away by the cat or other terrors, and only the 'Clocks' (Pod and his family, so-called because their front door is under the grandfather clock) remain, living an agoraphobic and almost airless existence. The gates between them and the upper world are, as Arrietty begins to realize, as much to keep themselves in as to shut predators out. Arrietty is warned of the perilous consequences of being 'seen' by a big person; when she begins to be friends with a boy who has come to stay in the house, she tries to convince herself and her parents that this fraternization is harmless. But inevitably it leads to the discovery of the Borrowers and the destruction of their whole way of life: only just escaping alive, they have to flee from the big house out into the terrors of the open air, hoping to make a new life for themselves in the fields.

Two of Mary Norton's many skills in the story are her close attention to detail—such as the 'borrowed' chessman, a knight, whose upper half makes a statue in the Borrowers' sitting-room while the lower half forms the pedestal for their dining table—and the fact that she has constructed a complicated frame around it, using Arrietty's diary, the reports of the boy to his sister, and the sister (now an old woman) telling the whole tale to Kate, a listening child. *The Borrowers* is clearly not intended as allegory, but is susceptible of many interpretations. It is partly a study of a child (Arrietty) coming to terms with the limitations of her parents' world; it seems also—if the reader looks beyond the superficial class-structure of the story—to be a parable about the parasitical dependence of the *rentier* class (the Borrowers) on those who are the means of production (the 'human beans' upstairs).

Mary Norton wrote four sequels, *The Borrowers Afield* (1955), *The Borrowers Afloat* (1959), *The Borrowers Aloft* (1961), and *The Borrowers Avenged* (1982). The first three, like the original volume, were illustrated by Diana Stanley, the last by Pauline *Baynes. In 1971 Mary Norton also published a short story about a Borrower, 'Poor Stainless'. An animation, *Arrietty*, appeared in 2010.

BOSCO, Henri (1888–1976) French author of a series of 'Pascalet' novels based on his own Provençal childhood: *L'Enfant et la rivière* (1955), *Le Renard dans l'île* (1956), and *Barboche* (1957). All have been translated into English.

BOSTON, L. M. (Lucy Maria) (1892–1990) British children's writer, best known for her *Green Knowe books who was born in Southport, Lancashire, into a family she described as 'rigidly, rabidly puritanical'. When she was eleven, her parents moved to the country for her mother's health, 'and from that moment, life was as different as for a butterfly getting out of its chrysalis'. She was sent south to a boarding school, then to a finishing school in Paris, then to Somerville College, Oxford. She cut short her university education to serve as a nurse in France during the First World War. She married an English officer, had one son, and for a time lived on the continent. But in 1935 her marriage was dissolved, and soon afterwards she returned to England, purchasing the manor house at Hemingford Grey in Huntingdonshire. It was this house which, when she was over sixty, made her become a writer, inspiring her to produce a series of books about 'Green Knowe' (written 1954–64), an English manor house in history and the present day.

After the five Green Knowe stories, Boston wrote *The Castle of Yew* (1965), a short book for younger children about a magic garden. *The *Sea Egg* (1967) is her most celebrated book outside the Green Knowe series; she imitated it in *Nothing of the Sort* (1971), which is about a girl's encounter with a dryad, and in *The Fossil Snake* (1975), the story of a fossil that comes alive. *The Guardians of the House* (1974) resembles *The Castle of Yew*. She returned to Green Knowe and concluded the series with *The Stones of Green Knowe* (1976), which tells the story of the building of the house in the 12th cent.

Boston Globe–Horn Book Awards A set of awards given annually since 1967 by the *Boston Globe* newspaper and the *Horn Book* for children's and *young adult books published in the US in three categories: fiction and poetry, non-fiction, and picture books. Since 2003, the fiction category has been won by Anne *Fine, David *Almond, Neal *Shusterman, Kate *DiCamillo, M. T. *Anderson, Sherman *Alexie, Terry *Pratchett, Rebecca *Stead, Tim *Wynne-Jones, Vaunda Micheaux Nelson, Rainbow Rowell, and Andrew *Smith. Apart from the three annual winners, each year two runners-up in each category may be named 'Honor Books', and the awards occasionally give a 'special citation', most recently (2008) for Shaun Tan's *The *Arrival*.

Bott, Violet Elizabeth See VIOLET ELIZABETH BOTT.

Bottersnikes and Gumbles (1967) A comic novel for children by the Australian author S. A. Wakefield, illustrated by Desmond Digby: an account of the strife between the amiable, easy-going Gumbles and the predatory, vicious Bottersnikes, who try to catch Gumbles in old jam tins and then enslave them. There are two sequels, *Gumbles on Guard* (1975) and *Gumbles in Summer* (1979).

BOUILLY, Jean Nicolas (1763–1842) Revolutionary French politician, who was the author of two collections of stories for children, written in a manner somewhat resembling that of Maria *Edgeworth: *Contes à ma fille* (1809) and *Contes aux enfants de France* (1824–5).

BOUTET DE MONVEL, Maurice (1850–1913) French illustrator. His books include an edition of the *fables of *La Fontaine, and *Jeanne d'Arc* (1896), with a text written by himself. The book was translated into English in 1897, and has since been re-issued in facsimile. Like Walter *Crane, Boutet de Monvel was influenced by Japanese art, and he worked in a flat, delicate style.

B.O.W.C. series See DE MILLE, JAMES.

BOWDLER, Thomas (1754–1825) of Edinburgh 'Purifier' of Shakespeare. He trained as a doctor of medicine but devoted most of his life to charitable works—he was a promoter of the Society for the Suppression of Vice. In 1818 he published *The Family Shakespeare in ten volumes; in which nothing is added to the original text, but those words and expressions are omitted which cannot with propriety be read aloud in a family.* Though this was published in Thomas Bowdler's name, it is believed that much of the editing was carried out by his sister Harriet. The excisions included all the obvious sexual innuendoes, but were not as insensitive to the texts as posterity has supposed; the Bowdlers restrained themselves from cutting *Othello* and the Falstaff scenes in *Henry IV* too heavily, realizing that despite the many references to sex they had qualities of greatness. *The Family Shakespeare* was often reprinted, and had soon introduced the term 'bowdlerize' into the language.

BOWLER, Tim (1953–) Acclaimed British author of psychological thrillers and other fiction for young adults. His first novel *Midget* (1994), set in Bowler's home town of Leigh-on-Sea, is a disturbing narrative of sibling rivalry. Bowler

has won numerous awards including the *Carnegie Medal for *River Boy* (1997), a magical tale of love and bereavement. His novel *Starseeker* (2002) was adapted for the stage in 2006. Bowler's urban thriller series *Blade* (2008–10) revolve around a fourteen-year-old boy and chronicles his journey over eight novels, touching upon contemporary and provocative themes such as knife crime and gang culture. His most recent thriller is *Night Runner* (2014).

Box of Delights, The, *or When the Wolves Were Running* (1935) A fantasy by John *Masefield, sequel to *The *Midnight Folk*. The story developed from the question in Masefield's mind: would it be possible to stop a cathedral service? Kay Harker, now some years older, becomes involved with Cole Hawlings, who has lived from pagan times and has a magic box that can take people into the past. Abner Brown, villain of the first book, wants the box so as to travel back in time and find Arnold of Todi, a necromancer who has discovered the Elixir of Life.

The Box of Delights is particularly suited to radio adaptation, and has been broadcast several times by the BBC. Though it is among the best children's *fantasy novels of its period, notable (like its predecessor) for its blend of black comedy and magic, its construction is somewhat looser and more random than *The Midnight Folk*. It is not always convincing: Masefield did not bother to give correct titles for the various ranks of Anglican clergy and the author's slight lack of confidence in his creation becomes apparent when, in the end, it turns out to be 'all a dream'—which the first book was not.

Boy: *Tales from Childhood* (1984) A volume of childhood memoirs by Roald *Dahl. In an Author's Note, Dahl says *Boy* is not an autobiography, merely a collection of vivid things that happened to him that he has never forgotten. From the Welsh childhood with his widowed mother through early memories of liquorice bootlaces (made, apparently, out of rat), The Great Mouse Plot, and holidaying with grandparents in Norway to his prep school in Weston-super-Mare, with giant Headmasters (one of whom would become Archbishop of Canterbury) and terrifying Matrons and repeated canings and a lot of confectionery (chocolate tastings that would inspire *Charlie and the Chocolate Factory*), to faked appendicitis, a car crash, dealing with the Boazers (i.e. prefects) at Repton, and his skill at fives and photography. *Boy* concludes

when the twenty-year-old Dahl is despatched to East Africa to take up his first job, with Shell. The story is taken up in a sort of sequel, *Going Solo* (1986).

Boy Hunters, The, *or Adventures in Search of a White Buffalo* (1852) By Mayne *Reid. Basil, Lucien, and François, the three sons of a French naturalist and hunter living in Louisiana, are sent to procure the skin of a white buffalo, which is wanted for a museum. After encounters with many animals, the boys are captured by 'Red *Indians' and are about to be put to death when Basil is discovered to be carrying a pouch containing the pipe of a great Indian chief. With the help of their former captors, the boys finally find and kill a white buffalo.

BOYLSTON, Helen Dore (1895–1984) American writer of *career novels for girls; she qualified as a nurse, served in a British army hospital in France at the end of the First World War, and continued in nursing until the late 1940s, reaching senior positions in several New England hospitals. Her first book, *Sue Barton, Student Nurse*, appeared in 1936, and was followed by six sequels, which took their heroine up to the rank of 'Superintendent of Nurses'. Then came four 'Carol' novels about life on the stage, beginning with *Carol Goes Backstage* (1941). The Boylston books are examples of the career novel at its most simple, to the point of banality, and are only notable as the first in the genre to be written in America.

Boy Meets Boy (2003) A novel by David *Levithan. One of the earliest teen novels in which the principal character is gay and yet neither tormented by his sexuality nor punished for it. This was groundbreaking: a joyous book, set in a town where acceptance is the norm, where the quarterback can also be the cross-dressing homecoming queen, and a story in which the traditional 'boy meets girl, boy loses girl, boy reunites with girl' is subverted. *Boy Meets Boy* is inspirational, aspirational, funny, and touching, and has been a lifeline for many teenagers.

BOYNE, John (1971–) Irish author of fiction for children and teenagers (as well as adult novels). Boyne's first book for young readers, and still his most famous, was *The Boy in the Striped Pyjamas* (2006), which tells the story of nine-year-old Bruno, whose family moves away from their Berlin home because his father has been promoted to the job of running

a concentration camp, 'Out-With', on the or-
ders of 'The Fury'. Through the camp fence
Bruno befriends a Jewish boy, which promises
some kind of redemption, but things end
badly. Though this remains his best-known
(albeit controversial) work, Boyne's subse-
quent books—for a younger readership—are
more accomplished. *Noah Barleywater Runs
Away* (2010) is a fairy tale about Noah, who
leaves home and runs off into the forest to
escape his problems, where he finds the
most amazing toyshop and learns some valu-
able lessons (there may be some *Pinocchio* in
there, too); and in *The Terrible Thing that
Happened to Barnaby Brocket* (2012), eight-
year-old Barnaby's disagreeable parents de-
cide they want to be rid of him, just because
he's different (he doesn't obey the laws of
gravity), which leads to his going on an adven-
ture around the world, meeting other people
who are different, too, and learning how im-
portant it is to be happy being himself. These
last two books feature delightful illustrations
by Oliver *Jeffers. *Stay Where You Are and
Then Leave* (2013), Boyne's fourth novel for
young readers, is the story of nine-year-old
Alfie Summerfield, whose father goes off to
fight in the First World War.

BOYNTON, Sandra (1953–) American au-
thor, illustrator, cartoonist, and songwriter.
Sandra Boynton grew up in a liberal Quaker
family in Philadelphia. Her father was a teach-
er who became a founder of Boynton Cook
Publishers, now owned by Heinemann. After
studying English at Yale University, where
Maurice *Sendak was among her lecturers,
she designed and sold irreverent greeting
cards. She was soon signed by the Chicago
company Recycled Paper Greetings, which at
one point sold up to eighty million of her cards
a year. The best known, a 1975 birthday card
that read 'Hippo Birdie Two Ewes' and was
accompanied by a cartoon drawing of each
animal, sold 10 million copies. While at
drama school in 1977, Boynton published her
first picture book, *Hippos Go Berserk!*, and she
has since gone on to write and illustrate over
fifty picture and board books featuring her
trademark whimsical cartoon animals (often
hippos) and satisfyingly silly texts. Six of Boy-
nton's books are on the *Publishers Weekly*
list of bestselling children's books of all time,
including *A to Z* (1982), *Oh My! Oh My! Oh
Dinosaurs!* (1993), and *Blue Hat, Green Hat*
(1982), which teaches children about colour,
and also about getting dressed: a turkey puts

on various items of clothing the wrong way
round. *Moo, Baa, La La La!* (1982) introduces
animal sounds, but the pigs get theirs wrong.
In *The Going to Bed Book* (1982), a crowd of
animals on an ark share their bedtime routine
below deck, and farmyard animals happily
'promenade two by two' in square-dance
style in *Barnyard Dance* (1993), with the
exception of a cat, which appears distinctly
unamused.

In 2008, Boynton was awarded the Milton
Caniff Lifetime Achievement Award by the
National Cartoonists Society. In addition to
her writing and illustrating, she is also a song-
writer, music producer, and director. She has
released four albums of children's music with
Michael Ford and has directed videos of their
music. Their 2002 book and album *Philadel-
phia Chickens* was nominated for a Grammy
Award and was on the *New York Times* best-
seller list for almost a year. Boynton lives in
Connecticut, in a converted barn with a hippo
weathervane.

**Boy's Adventures in the Wilds of Aus-
tralia, A;** *or, Herbert's Note-Book* (1854) A
*travelogue for children by William *Howitt,
the product of his two years spent in Australia
from 1852, and one of the earliest Australian
children's books. The boy Herbert and his
father, brother, cousin Harry (a 'great chemist
and natural philosopher'), and 'Mr B, the
Painter', travel around the country on horse-
back with a tarpaulin-covered cart. The book
is episodic, with much emphasis placed on
careful and accurate observation of landscape,
flora, and fauna, though there are many ad-
ventures, either experienced by Herbert's
party and their travelling companions, the rath-
er lower class Popkins family, or recounted
in the anecdotes of the people they meet.
Howitt spares his readers little when describing
native cannibalism and other unpleasant as-
pects of 'a picture of savage life which would
not, I think, enchant even a Rousseau', but
he is free of the crude contempt for natives
which appears in many other boys' stories on
the subject.

Boy Scouts A movement first founded in
Great Britain in 1908 by Lord *Baden-Powell,
who wrote *Scouting for Boys*. The Scout
movement was established in the United
States in 1910, where it was associated with
such earlier outdoor organizations as the
'Woodcraft Indians' of Ernest Thompson
*Seton.

Boys of England A weekly *magazine founded in 1866 by Edwin *Brett, one of the leading British publishers of *penny dreadfuls. It promised its first readers that it would 'enthrall you by wild and wonderful but healthy fiction', and its contents, though sensational, were less objectionable than those of many penny dreadful publications. Occasional moralizing passages helped to raise the tone, and prizes were offered for competitions in the form of rabbits, cricket sets, dogs, and volumes of *Shakespeare. It was a huge success. H. G. *Wells as a boy was one of its readers. It was in *Boys of England* that the *Jack Harkaway stories first appeared, in 1871. The magazine ceased publication after a few years and should not be confused with the *Boys of England Novelettes*, a series of stories published weekly by Brett in about 1880.

Boy's Own Magazine, The (1855–1874) A *magazine founded by Samuel Orchart *Beeton. It claimed to be an experiment in pitching its material at a higher level than was customary for boys, and included mathematical and philosophical questions among its pieces of biography, stirring *history, and miscellaneous knowledge. The later and more famous *Boy's Own Paper* owed something, including its title, to Beeton's example. A new but short-lived series, *Beeton's Boy's Own Magazine*, was edited by G. A. *Henty from 1888 to 1890.

Boy's Own Paper, The A juvenile *magazine, familiarly known as *BOP*, published from 1879 to 1967. At first issued in both weekly and monthly versions, it became monthly only from 1913. For most of the paper's lifetime there was also an *annual. The *Girl's Own Paper* was its companion magazine.

The *Boy's Own Paper* was created by the *Religious Tract Society (RTS) to compete with the cheap and sensational 'blood and thunder' magazines and novelettes then generally thought to be a corrupting influence on the young (*see* PENNY DREADFULS). The Society's prospectus for the paper announced that the editors 'understand boyhood well, enter heartily into its pursuits and pleasures. True religion, in their view, is a spirit pervading all life, in work, in play; and in this conviction, rather than any purpose of direct doctrinal teaching, this tone is given to the paper.' The format was carefully chosen on the basis of what was already successful in the market, but the text, illustrations, paper, and printing were of particularly high quality. There were also fine *colour plates each month, and extra ones in the annual. The title was derived from that of Samuel *Beeton's by then defunct *Boy's Own Magazine*, and the weekly price was perfectly competitive with the 'bloods'—one penny. The Religious Tract Society's literary superintendent, Dr James Macaulay, was the nominal first editor.

The first issue of the *Boy's Own Paper*, for Saturday 18 January 1879, opened with a *school story, 'My First Football Match, by an Old Boy'. Among other items in the first issue were an article on *natural history by the Revd J. G. Wood, called 'Out with a Jack-knife', and the first part of 'From Powder Monkey to Admiral; or, the stirring days of the British Navy' by W. H. G. *Kingston. There were also pieces on outdoor *sports and magic lanterns, puzzles and competitions, and appeals for correspondence.

The paper was so successful that within three months another came out copying it in format and title—*The Boys' World*—and further imitators followed. But the *BOP*'s circulation rose to a quarter of a million within five years, and the survey of boys' reading in Edward Salmon's *Juvenile Literature As It Is* (1888) indicated that it was far and away the most popular magazine for that sample. The RTS sometimes felt, however, that success was at the expense of some of the original ideals, and would also have liked greater prominence for 'Christian truth and influence'. Nevertheless the paper held to its fairly independent course, and stories by R. M. *Ballantyne, G. A. *Henty, Conan *Doyle, and Jules *Verne appeared in its pages.

The readership was largely middle-class, the *BOP*'s school stories being set in the new boarding schools for the sons of successful businessmen, though there were also articles aimed at office boys and other lower wage earners. For all the RTS's doubts, schoolmasters and parents generally welcomed *BOP*.

A history of the *BOP*, written by its last editor, Jack Cox, and entitled *Take a Cold Tub, Sir!*, was published in 1983 by Lutterworth Press, successors to the Religious Tract Society.

boys' stories (boys' fiction) Terms sometimes used to describe the whole field of *adventure stories, *school stories, *detective stories, and other kinds of popular fiction which proliferated in Britain from the mid-19th

to the mid-20th cents. The term is especially used with reference to the weekly *magazines, descendants of *penny dreadfuls, which were published by the *Harmsworth and *Aldine companies and a number of other firms and individuals. Hundreds of such story-papers appeared, some taking their titles from the heroes of their most popular stories, others appealing to patriotism, such as *Young Gentleman of Britain, Sons of Britannia,* and *The Young Englishman,* all of which were published by *Emmett Brothers. The notion that boys in particular prefer to read (or perhaps ought to read) books of active heroism has never really gone away, however dated it may seem, and to this day many books of adventure, spying etc. continue to be typically marketed to male readers. *See also* GENDER.

'Boy stood on the burning deck, The'
The first line of a poem by Mrs *Hemans.

BRABOURNE, Lord *See* KNATCHBULL-HUGESSEN.

BRADLEY, Edward (1827–89) Writer (under the pseudonym Cuthbert Bede) of *The Adventures of Mr Verdant Green,* a celebrated comic novel about Victorian Oxford, and author of several books for children. His *Fairy Fables* (1858) appeared in the same year as his imitation of Edward *Lear's celebrated *Book of Nonsense,* which was entitled *Funny Figures* by 'A. Funnyman'.

BRADMAN, Tony (1954–) British writer and anthologist. Bradman has written for most age ranges, from picture books and books for young readers, such as his popular *Dilly the Dinosaur* series (twenty books, from 1986), to longer novels for older readers, re-tellings, and educational reading schemes. He has edited dozens of anthologies of short fiction and poetry for children, featuring many prominent writers, but also, and most influentially, showcasing promising new talent. (Siobhan *Dowd's career as a children's writer began with an invitation from Bradman in 2003 to contribute to one of these anthologies.)

BRAITHWAITE, Althea *See* ALTHEA.

Braithwaite, Pandora *See* PANDORA BRAITHWAITE.

BRAND, Christianna (1907–88) British writer of detective stories, and author of several children's books, notably a 'Nurse Matilda' series of comic tales about a nanny, beginning with *Nurse Matilda* (1964). These were illustrated

by her cousin Edward *Ardizzone. The books had a resurgence of sorts with the release in 2005 of the film *Nanny McPhee,* which was based on the series and scripted by Emma Thompson. There was a sequel in 2010.

BRANFORD, Henrietta (1946–99) English author of books for children of all ages. Her early death from cancer led to the creation of two awards, the *Branford Boase Award for debut children's fiction and the Henrietta Branford Writing Award for writers under the age of nineteen. Her books are characterized by warmth and compassion, particularly the groundbreaking *Fire, Bed and Bone* (1997), which tells the story of the 1381 Peasants' Revolt from the point of view of an old hunting dog who experiences emotions such as love, loss, and fear in the same way as humans, and *The Fated Sky* (1996), about a Viking girl trying to escape death. For younger readers there is the wonderful series about *Dimanche Diller* (1994), complete with dastardly deeds, evil guardians, and a feisty young heroine.

Branford Boase Award A British prize awarded annually to the year's best debut novel for children or teenagers. Established by Julia *Eccleshare and Anne Marley in 2000 in memory of writer Henrietta *Branford and her editor Wendy Boase, both of whom had died the previous year, the award is unusual in that it is shared between the author and her or his editor, in recognition of the editor's role in bringing a debut author to market. The award's success in talent-spotting has been impressive, consistently recognising debut works by writers who subsequently go on to achieve great things—among them Marcus *Sedgwick, Mal *Peet, Meg *Rosoff, B.R. Collins, Frances *Hardinge, Sally Prue, Kevin *Brooks and Siobhan *Dowd.

Brass Bottle, The (1900) A novel by 'F. *Anstey', the author of *Vice Versa.* Horace Ventimore, an unsuccessful architect, buys an antique brass bottle at an auction and discovers that it contains a *genie. The genie brings Ventimore a wealthy client, showers him with costly gifts, creates an oriental palace in his lodgings (to the disgust of his landlady), and stages a magnificent banquet for his prospective in-laws—which results in his engagement being broken off. Ventimore is eventually left with no choice but to seal the genie once more into the bottle. *The Brass Bottle* is alluded to in the closing pages of

Five Children and It, and it seems probable that it, and others of Anstey's novels, helped to suggest to E. *Nesbit the possibility of writing children's stories in which magic is introduced into the modern world with near-disastrous consequences.

Brave Little Tailor, The *See* VALIANT LITTLE TAILOR, THE.

BRAY, Libba (1964–) American author of *young adult novels. Her first novel published under her own name, the Victorian gothic *A Great and Terrible Beauty* (2003), was a *New York Times* bestseller. The other titles in the Gemma Doyle trilogy are *Rebel Angels* (2005) and *The Sweet Far Thing* (2007). *Going Bovine* (2009), about a sixteen-year-old boy with mad cow disease, won the *Michael L. Printz Award. *The Diviners* (2012) is the first in a planned four-book series of supernatural mysteries set in 1920s New York. The next in the series is *Lair of Dreams* (2015).

BRAZIL, Angela (1869–1947) Popular and prolific British writer of *girls' stories with *school settings. She was born in Preston, Lancashire, the daughter of a cotton manufacturer of Irish descent, and was educated at Manchester High School and at Ellerslie College, Manchester, where she became head girl. In her schooldays, she herself experienced the type of fervent romantic friendship with other girls that she and other writers in the genre made a feature of their stories, apparently unaware of its sexual implications. Angela Brazil's biographer Gillian Freeman suggests that this helped to retard her emotionally, and to make her obsessed with schoolgirl 'crushes' for the rest of her life. After school she studied art at Heatherley's, and then, after her father's death, travelled extensively with her mother. When she was in her mid-thirties someone suggested she write a novel, and the result was *A Terrible Tomboy* (1904). Then she offered her first school story, *The Fortunes of Philippa*, to *Blackie's, who published it in 1906 and thereafter produced all her books.

The Fortunes of Philippa is the story of a ten-year-old who comes from South America to stay with English cousins and attend a boarding school. The book is narrated in the first person, and is somewhat tentative in manner. *The Third Class at Miss Kaye's* (1908) reverted to third-person narrative, and was much livelier in tone. The first characteristic Brazil novel, it puts plenty of emphasis on organized

sports, especially hockey and cricket. After this, Angela Brazil soon firmly established herself as the female equivalent of Talbot Baines *Reed, for a long period producing several books each year.

Her heroines tend to have such names as 'Ethelburga' and 'Avelyn' (who appear in *For the School Colours*, 1918). There is plenty of emphasis on romantic friendships, especially in *Bosom Friends* (1909), and *A Fourth Form Friendship* (1911). The plots are well constructed but have a mechanical air about them; Angela Brazil's method was to plan out the story before devising the characters of the girls who were to feature in it. Most of all, her books were famous—or notorious—for their slang:

> 'I say, let's play a trick on the prefects!'
> 'What a blossomy idea!'
> 'They richly deserve it!'
> 'It would be just top-hole!' . . .
> 'A very jinky notion.'

Angela Brazil claimed that she took down this sort of conversation from real schoolgirls, overheard on the school train between Coventry, where she lived, and Leamington Spa. The slang irritated many adults—perhaps because girls who read the books tended to copy it— and several headmistresses banned the Brazil novels from their schools as a result.

Angela Brazil (who pronounced her surname to rhyme with 'dazzle') continued to write until the end of her life, her last book being *The School on the Loch* (1946). Some of her stories were reprinted in paperback in the years after her death, but they seem now to have come definitively to the end of their popularity and are little read today.

Bremen Town-Musicians, The A story collected by the brothers *Grimm, now sometimes published as a stand-alone picture book. A group of ageing animals, wishing to escape being put to death by their owners, set out on the road to Bremen with the intention of finding work as musicians. On their journey they discover a band of robbers who are enjoying their spoils at a house in the forest. Bursting into the house, the animals drive out the robbers, who believe them to be ghosts. The animals settle down to sleep, the robbers send one of their number back to the house to investigate, and in the darkness he is attacked by each of the animals in turn. The robbers do not dare to return to the house, and the animals make it their home.

The story is probably derived from a *fable in which a band of animals play similar tricks on a wolf who comes to their woodland home. The Grimms themselves printed another tale which resembles it, *The Ragamuffins*, in which the host of an inn who has given shelter to a cock and a hen, a duck, and a pin and needle is rewarded in much the same fashion.

'BRENDA' (Mrs G. Castle Smith) Author of one of the best known English *street Arab tales, *Froggy's Little Brother* (1875). She also wrote *'Especially those', a story on the prayer 'for all conditions of men'* (1875), *Lotty's Visit to Grandmama* (1877), and *Victoria-Bess, The Ups and Downs of a Doll's Life* (n.d.), which was illustrated by T. *Pym.

Brendon Chase (1944) A novel by *'B.B.', illustrated by the author (D. J. Watkins-Pitchford), the story of three runaway boys who live in a forest and see themselves in terms of *Robin Hood and his outlaws.

BRENTANO, Clemens (1778-1842) German poet and author who was joint editor with Achim von Arnim of *Des Knaben Wunderhorn* ('The Boy's Wonder-horn'), a collection of more than 700 German folk songs and traditional rhymes. The collection was issued in three volumes from 1806 to 1808; the last volume contained 'Kinderlieder' (children's songs). *Des Knaben Wunderhorn* inspired the *Grimms to collect traditional *fairy stories from oral sources in Germany. Brentano himself wrote a number of original fairy stories (*Märchen*) most of which were published posthumously, though the best known, *Gockel und Hinkel*, appeared in 1838. A 1961 retelling of it by Doris Orgel has illustrations by Maurice *Sendak.

BRENT-DYER, Elinor M. (1895-1969) British author of nearly 100 *girls' stories, chiefly with *school settings. She created the '*Chalet School' series, beginning in 1925 with *The School at the Chalet*. Brent-Dyer was herself headmistress of a school in Hereford.

BRERETON, Capt. Frederick S. (Sadleir) (1872-1957) A regular officer in the British Army who wrote boys' *adventure stories with war settings. He began with the Boer War (*With Rifle and Bayonet*, 1900) before turning his attention to the First World War, producing such books as *Under Haig in Flanders* (1918). He was a cousin of G. A. *Henty, whose style he copied. His heroes are 'stocky lads who can

take a heap of hammering and come out fresh in the end', and who rarely suffer more than a flesh wound, even in the trenches of the Somme, so that they can go home intact and marry the squire's daughter.

Brer Rabbit Trickster hero of many of the *Uncle Remus stories.

BRESLIN, Theresa (1947-) Critically acclaimed Scottish author who started writing whilst working as a librarian and has, to date, written more than thirty books for children and young adults. *Whispers in the Graveyard* (1994), the story of evil awakening when an old rowan tree is felled, is a modern classic. *The Dream Master* series (1999) is about a boy whose dreams are actually real—taking him to other places and times. Her books for older readers pack a serious punch, particularly *Remembrance* (2002), about a group of friends dealing with all the conflicts and horrors of the First World War and *Divided City* (2005), which deals with sectarianism and racism in modern Glasgow.

BRETT, Edwin (1828-95) British publisher of *Boys of England* and of many *penny dreadfuls. During his lifetime he issued twenty-one boys' story-papers, such as *Young Men of Great Britain, Boys' Comic Journal*, and *Halfpenny Surprise*.

Briar-Rose *See* SLEEPING BEAUTY, THE.

Bridge to Terabithia (1977) *Newbery Medal-winning novel by Katherine *Paterson. After Leslie beats Jess in a race, the two become inseparable friends, spending much of their free time in an imaginary woodland kingdom they call Terabithia. But tragedy strikes when Leslie is killed in an accident. The book is based on a true incident: the best friend of Paterson's son died after being struck by lightning. The novel has become a classic, but has also been the subject of censorship battles. According to the American Library Association, it was ninth of the 100 books most frequently *banned from school libraries (with challenges on several different grounds) between 1990 and 2000.

BRIGGS, Katharine M. (Mary) (1898-1980) British folklorist and writer for children who was one of three daughters of an artist; after reading English at Lady Margaret Hall, Oxford, she was awarded a D.Phil. for her thesis on folklore in 17th-cent. literature. Before the Second World War she wrote a number of *historical novels and plays, but had no literary success

until the later years of her life. Her first book to have a lasting reputation was *Hobberdy Dick* (1955), the story of a hobgoblin living in a 17th-cent. English manor-house. *Kate Crackernuts* (1963) is a *fantasy about two girls, set in 17th-cent Scotland. However, it was not these but non-fiction works on folklore which finally made Briggs's name. Books such as *The Anatomy of Puck* (1959) and *Folktales of England* (1965) proved to be the preparation for her monumental *Dictionary of English Folk-Tales*, published in four volumes in 1970–1. *A Dictionary of Fairies* (1976) made some of her researches available in one-volume popular form.

BRIGGS, Raymond (Redvers) (1934–) British illustrator and author who was born in London, the son of a Co-operative Dairies milkman. He wanted to be a cartoonist, and went to Wimbledon School of Art, then to the Slade. Discovering that he had no talent for painting, he began to illustrate books while still a student. In 1963 he married the painter Jean Taprell Clark, who died ten years later.

Briggs took a decade and a half to establish his characteristic visual and verbal style. In the early 1960s he wrote and illustrated three *adventure stories of a very conventional kind, *Midnight Adventure* (1961), *The Strange House* (1961), and *Sledges to the Rescue* (1963). His first *picture book was a collection of *nursery rhymes, *Ring-a-Ring o'Roses* (1962); two others of the same type followed: *The White Land* (1963) and *Fee-Fi-Fo-Fum* (1964). In 1966 there appeared his *Mother Goose Treasury*, a huge undertaking in which he provided almost 900 pictures, about half of them in colour, illustrating almost all the known nursery rhymes. It was in this book that his talent for eccentric comedy first developed to the full; it won him the *Kate Greenaway Medal.

Briggs's first picture book containing a prose story, rather than rhymes, was *The *Elephant and the Bad Baby* (1969), with a text by Elfrida *Vipont. *Jim and the Beanstalk* (1970), for which Briggs himself wrote the text, is a witty sequel to the famous fairy story. In 1972 there appeared his *Fairy Tale Treasury*, for which the text was provided by Virginia *Haviland. *Father Christmas* (1973) was the first book of which it might be said that only Briggs could have written and drawn it. Using a *comic-strip format, which became one of Briggs's hallmarks from now on, it portrays a Santa Claus who hates wintry weather:

'Blooming snow! I hate winter! Work, work, work!' Briggs has said that the book was influenced by childhood memories of his father setting off on milk-rounds in the early morning; it is also a celebration of an old man's way of life—a spartan little brick house with outside lavatory, but good plain food, a hot-water-bottle, a cat and dog to welcome him home, and a mug of cocoa before bed. *Father Christmas* won Briggs a second Kate Greenaway Medal.

Father Christmas Goes On Holiday (1975), a rather tame sequel, was followed by something utterly unexpected and unforgettable, which brought Briggs fame among adults as well as children. This was *Fungus the Bogeyman* (1977), a modern myth in comic-strip form which most readers found deliciously horrible. *The *Snowman* (1979) is a wordless and ultimately sad story about a snowman who comes alive, but is all too mortal. *Gentleman Jim* (1980) showed Briggs moving away from a strictly child readership (as he had perhaps begun to do in *Fungus the Bogeyman*); its hero is an attendant in a gentleman's public lavatory who turns highwayman. The same 'hero' features in *When the Wind Blows* (1982), which makes no pretence of being for children: here, Briggs uses his comic-strip style to devastating effect as he shows what would be the real result, for plain, ordinary people like Jim and his wife Hilda, of nuclear war. Similarly *Ethel and Ernest* (1998), the true story of his parents's life together, though in familiar Briggs style, was not published for children. This was followed by another children's book, *Ug* (2001), about a stone-age boy attempting to invent soft trousers.

Briggs's technical accomplishments are considerable—see, for example, the highly realistic backgrounds in *Father Christmas*—but he is also master of the comic-strip style; characteristic Briggs figures have big, clumsy faces with protruding chins and button eyes. His work from *Father Christmas* onwards shows, among other things, a remarkable ability to find subjects exactly suited to his unusual talents.

BRINK, Carol Ryrie (1895–1981) American author of many children's novels, of which the best known is *Caddie Woodlawn* (1935), about a tomboy and her family living in the woods of western Wisconsin in pioneer days. It was based on the real childhood experiences of the author's grandmother, and emphasizes the delights of being 'a pioneer and an American'; Caddie's father renounces the inheritance of

an English peerage because acceptance would involve giving up US citizenship. The book won the *Newbery Medal in 1936, and has been reprinted many times. Mrs Brink's other novels include a sequel, entitled *Magical Melons* (1944); *Baby Island* (1937), a *Robinsonnade about two girls shipwrecked with a cargo of babies; and *Winter Cottage* (1968), in which a city family escapes the misery of the Depression by moving to the country.

BRINSLEY, John (*fl.* 1615) A *Puritan writer of schoolbooks and books on education. After taking his degree at Cambridge in the 1580s, Brinsley became noted for his ability at teaching Latin and Greek. He believed fervently that Latin was best taught by translating it into English, which thereby removed the 'butcherly feare' that most children felt when trying to master it. His pupils were expected to learn how to render the English translation back into polished Latin. Brinsley argued the case for this and other techniques of teaching in *Ludus Literarius: or, The Grammar Schoole* (1612). He also wrote *The Posing of the Parts* (1615), in which the pupil was taught the accidence and grammar of Latin by means of questions and answers, much like a *catechism.

Brinsley published a number of his 'grammaticall' (i.e. strictly literal) translations of Latin works, which were to be used by children in schools run according to his principles. These included the fables of *Aesop and *Pueriles Confabulatiunculae: or Children's Dialogues* (1617), which gives a vivid glimpse of the 17th-cent. schoolboy.

BRINSMEAD, H. F. (Hesba Fay) (1922–2003) Australian children's author. Her first novel, *Pastures of the Blue Crane* (1964), is about Ryl, a self-centred girl, who changes for the better when she becomes joint owner of a run-down farm. *Season of the Briar* (1965), about a group of boys working on weed-spraying in Tasmania, was followed by *Beat of the City* (1966), a study of four Melbourne teenagers. *A Sapphire for September* (1967) is about a sixteen-year-old Sydney girl who goes on a gem-hunting expedition in the Blue Mountains. *Isle of the Sea Horse* (1969) is a *Robinsonnade with a group of teenagers as castaways; *Listen to the Wind* (1970) is about the friendship between a white girl and an aboriginal boy. *Longtime Passing* (1971) and *Once There Was a Swagman* (1980) are *family stories based on the author's childhood in the Blue Mountains; the last-named title and *The Honey Forest* (1977),

which has a similar setting, are intended for younger children than were Mrs Brinsmead's earlier books.

BRISLEY, Joyce Lankester *See* MILLY-MOLLY-MANDY.

broadside A large sheet of paper printed on one side only, generally containing a *ballad or some other ephemeral material for popular consumption, usually illustrated with one or more *woodcuts or engravings. The term 'broadsheet' has often been used, but now is more strictly applied to sheets printed on both sides.

Manuscripts of ballads were probably offered for sale before the invention of printing. One of the earliest printed ballads, the *Gest of Robyn Hode*, was issued by Wynkyn de *Worde at the end of the 15th or beginning of the 16th cent.; it was in the form of a pamphlet. The true broadside ballad began to be popular a little later in the 16th cent., and was soon flourishing in the political and religious turmoil of Henry VIII's reign. The success of the broadside, which could be bought cheaply on street corners, seems to have contributed to the decline of the professional minstrel, who by Elizabeth I's reign was legally classed with vagabonds. In 1556 the newly incorporated Stationers' Company began to require registration of ballads before they could be printed.

Broadside ballads were often based on recent events, especially crimes. Their subject-matter—scandals, murders, monstrous births and strange animals, religious and political comment, bawdy tales—resembles that of certain modern popular newspapers. The titles of some of the broadsides found in one 17th-cent. collection in the Bodleian Library gives some idea of their character: *A pleasant Song of the valiant Deeds of Chivalry, atchieved by noble Knight, Sir Guy of Warwick* (*see* GUY OF WARWICK); *A Mournful Ditty of the Lady Rosamond, King Henry the seconds Concubine* (*see* FAIR ROSAMOND); *Robin Hood and the Tanner* (*see* ROBIN HOOD); *A Memorable Song on the unhappy hunting in Chevy Chase* (*see* CHEVY CHASE). Broadsides could also be religious in their subject-matter, e.g. (in the same collection) *A very Godly song intitled, the earnest petition of a Faithfull Christian ... made upon his death-bed.*

In America, where English traditional ballads often survived intact among rural communities, many broadside ballads were printed during

the Revolutionary War; e.g. *American Bravery: or Great Britain, and her copper-colored Allies defeated; Lady Washington's Lamentation for the Death of her Husband*, etc. (titles taken from the Isaiah *Thomas Collection of Ballads, American Antiquarian Society).

BROCK, C. E. (Charles Edward) (1870–1938) and **H. M. (Henry Matthew)** (1875–1960) British illustrators; C. E. Brock specialized in *Dickens, *Scott, and other classic authors, while his brother H. M. Brock illustrated many books of *fairy stories, including his own collections of *Fairy Tales* (1914) and *Nursery Tales* (1934).

BRODERIP, Frances Freeling (1830–78) Sister of Tom *Hood, Broderip wrote several children's books, including *Tiny Tadpole and other tales* (1862) and *Tales of the Toys, told by themselves* (1869), both of which were illustrated by her brother.

***Bromeliad* trilogy** See PRATCHETT, TERRY.

BROOKE, L. (Leonard) Leslie (1862–1940) Celebrated British illustrator and author of *picture books who is best remembered for *Johnny Crow's Garden* (1903) and its sequels. The son of a Liverpool business man, Brooke began to work as an artist in 1889, illustrating stories by Evelyn *Everett-Green for the publisher *Blackie. He went on to provide pictures for *The *Carved Lions* (1895) and other stories by Mrs *Molesworth. His first major success was with the illustrations to Andrew *Lang's *Nursery Rhyme Book* (1897). In about 1899 there appeared his illustrated edition of poems by Edward *Lear, *The Pelican Chorus*, and this was followed in 1900 by *The Jumblies and other nonsense verses*. Besides the *Johnny Crow* books, he produced a number of lively illustrated versions of nursery tales, beginning with *The *Three Little Pigs* and *Tom Thumb* (both 1904).

L. Leslie Brooke has been described as a 20th-cent. successor to Randolph *Caldecott, to whose work his own bears a marked resemblance.

BROOKS, Kevin (1959–) British novelist for young adults. His books are well written and hard-hitting, containing adult themes such as prostitution, drug abuse, and death. His first book, *Martyn Pig* (2002) won the *Branford Boase Award for a debut novel. It concerns a boy who accidentally kills his alcoholic father. *Candy* (2005) is about a young junkie prostitute and her relationship with a musician. *iBoy* (2010) tells the story of sixteen-year-old Tom, who, owing to a freak accident, finds himself with fragments of an iPhone embedded in his skull, with extraordinary—and thought-provoking—consequences. *Naked* (2011) takes a reader back to the summer of 1976, to London, an urgent world of up-coming bands and secrets.

Brooks's stories are often open-ended, with no neat answers. They are at least as much concerned with the internal world of the protagonists as the external events affecting them, and they have a restless, relentless energy. In *The Bunker Diary* (2013), six victims are locked in an underground bunker by a mysterious kidnapper—the book (controversially, given its exceptionally bleak ending) won the 2014 *Carnegie Medal.

BROOKS, Noah (1830–1903) American journalist and editor who wrote several books for boys describing pioneer life in America during the mid-19th cent. These include *The Boy Emigrants* (1876) and *The Boy Settlers, or, Early Times in Kansas* (1891).

BROOKS, Ron (1948–) Australian children's book illustrator who has received many awards. Some of his earliest books are classics of Australian picture-book publishing—*John Brown, Rose and the Midnight Cat* (1977) and *The Bunyip of Berkeley's Creek* (1974). *Old Pig* (1995), where Old Pig puts her affairs in order before spending the night in Granddaughter's arms, was awarded Best Book of the Year 1997 by the *New Yorker* and the *Chicago Tribune*. *Fox* (2000) was a runner-up for the *Kate Greenaway Medal in the UK and winner of several Australian awards including the *CBCA Picture Book of the Year 2001. *Drawn from the Heart* (2012) is an intelligent and poignant memoir of Brooks's life as an illustrator.

BROOKS, Walter R. See FREDDY.

BROSTER, D. K. (Dorothy Kathleen) (1877–1950) British *historical novelist. One of her most widely read books was *The Flight of the Heron* (1925), about a friendship between an English officer and a Highlander supporting Bonnie Prince Charlie in 1745. D. K. Broster was assumed by many of her readers to be a man (an impression she took no steps to correct).

BROWN, Marc (1946–) American author and illustrator who was inspired to develop his gentle, watercolour-based style by a high-school teacher. He always knew he wanted to

illustrate children's books, but along the way had many short-lived jobs, including truck driver, cook, and teacher. With over a hundred books to his name, he is most famous for the series that began with *Arthur's Nose* (1976), which told the story of Arthur, an aardvark who doesn't like his nose, and which was made into a TV series (1999). From that one book came many more chronicling Arthur's childhood experiences, through which his nose does eventually get smaller—though how is never (so far) explained. Brown has illustrated many other books, including a series about life's milestones, the *Dino Life Guides for Families* series (1992), with his wife, the artist Laurene Krasny Brown.

BROWN, Marcia (1918–2015) American writer and illustrator; she was an English teacher and then children's librarian, publishing her first *picture book in 1946. She won the *Caldecott Medal three times: for her version of *Cinderella* (1954), for *Once a Mouse* (1961), and for *Shadow* (1982), which she translated from Blaise Cendrars' French poem, *La Féticheuse*. In 1992 she also won the *Laura Ingalls Wilder Medal. Her collection of essays, *Lotus Seeds, Children, Pictures, and Books* (1986), contains lectures and essays written from 1949 ('What is a Distinguished Picture Book?') to 1984.

BROWN, Margaret Wise (1910–52) Prolific American writer of books for young children, including *The Fish with the Deep Sea Smile* (1938) and the *Noisy Book* series (1939 onwards). *See also* GOODNIGHT MOON.

BROWN, Pamela (1924–89) British children's author. Her first novel, *The *Swish of the Curtain* (1941), begun when she was fourteen, tells the story of a young people's theatre company. With her earnings from it, she trained as an actress at the Royal Academy of Dramatic Art, and worked on the professional stage as 'Mela Brown', to avoid confusion with another actress of the same name. She wrote several sequels to her first book, and other children's novels, though it is for her debut that she is still best remembered.

BROWN, Roy (Frederick) (1921–82) British children's writer of socially realistic stories with urban settings, the first being *A Saturday in Pudney* (1966). His books deal with children on the run from approved schools, teenage criminals, and backward adolescents. He himself taught in a primary school, and then until 1975 was head of a school for autistic children. His later novels include *The Siblings* (1975) (US title, *Find Debbie!*, 1976),

about the disappearance of a psychotic teenager, and *Collision Course* (1980), the story of a young man suffering a nervous breakdown.

BROWNE, Anthony (1946–) An internationally renowned British author and illustrator, best known for his sensitive portrayals of near-human chimps and gorillas. Browne's narratives often deal with the darker side of familial and social relationships, and often contain morals for the adult reader. *Gorilla* (1983), considered a modern classic and winner of a remarkable number of awards including the *Kate Greenaway Medal and the *Kurt Maschler Award, is a sad tale of a young girl whose father has no time for her.

Browne's distinctive illustrative style is a unique blend of hyperrealism and the surreal, complete with intertextual references, *trompe l'œil* effects, and visual puns. His work is richly multilayered and embedded in artistic heritage, often referencing well-known paintings. In 2000, Browne was the first British illustrator to win the *Hans Christian Andersen Award for his services to children's literature. Browne was the Children's *Laureate from 2009–11, focusing his celebrity on promoting the importance of visual literacy and creativity for children.

BROWNE, Frances (1816–79) Author of *Granny's Wonderful Chair*; she was born in Donegal and was blinded by smallpox in infancy. Nevertheless as an adult, while living in London, she earned a living as a writer, contributing to the magazine *Leisure Hour* for twenty-three years.

BROWNE, Gordon (Frederick) (1858–1932) Son of *Dickens's illustrator 'Phiz' (H. K. Browne), Gordon Browne illustrated books by Mrs *Ewing, *Henty, Andrew *Lang (*Prince Prigio*), L. T. *Meade, E. *Nesbit, and many other children's authors. He himself wrote and illustrated *Nonsense by A. Nobody* (1895), followed by *Some More Nonsense* (1896).

brownie The name in Scottish and North of England folklore for an *elf-like creature, said to come out at night and finish the housework left undone in the day, in return for a reward of milk or cream and food. Brownies were said to leave the house for ever if clothes were put out for them to wear. This happens in the *Grimm story *The Elves and the Shoemaker*. Mrs *Ewing's book *The *Brownies and Other Tales* (1870) gave rise to the notion of helpful children being referred to as Brownies, and so led to the eventual adoption of the name

Brownies for junior *Girl Guides (they were earlier known as Rosebuds). Mrs Ewing made further use of the Brownie theme in *Lob-Lie-by-the-Fire (1874). Mrs D. M. *Craik's Adventures of a Brownie (1872) was very popular. In America, Palmer *Cox wrote and illustrated Brownie stories in verse for the magazine *St Nicholas from the 1880s onwards.

Brownies and other tales, The (1870)
By Juliana Horatia *Ewing, this book takes its title from the story of two motherless brothers, who are lazy and give no help to their father. When one of them goes in search of a *brownie whom he wants to do the work of the house, he learns that he and his brother are the only real 'Brownies'. The two of them then begin to get up early in the morning, secretly, to do the housework before their father comes downstairs. The moral is that 'all children are Brownies . . . when they are useful and considerate'. The story suggested to Lord Baden-Powell the adoption of the name 'Brownies' (in 1918) for junior *Girl Guides, and the first handbook for Brownies (1920) opened with an abridged version of the tale. The use of the name 'Brown Owl' for the leader of the Brownie pack derives from the Old Owl in Mrs Ewing's story, who shows the boy what he and his brother must do.

BROWNING, Robert See PIED PIPER OF HAMELIN, THE.

BRUCE, Dorita Fairlie (1885–1970) Writer of *school stories for girls; she created books about '*Dimsie' (Dimsie Goes to School, 1921, and many others), 'Nancy' (The New Girl and Nancy, 1926, and many others), and 'Springdale School' (Captain of Springdale, 1932, and many others). Her books came in the *reward category, and were published by the Oxford University Press, in the days before it had a more discriminating policy towards children's fiction.

BRUCE, Mary Grant (1878–1958) Author of the immensely popular '*Billabong' books and other stories of Australian family and country life. Born at Sale, Gippsland, in Victoria, she knew the bush well in childhood. Her children's fiction first appeared serialized on her weekly children's page for the Leader. She went to London in 1913 and began to work for the *Harmsworth newspapers, and in 1914 she met and married a distant cousin, Major George Evans Bruce, who also wrote books, including boys' *adventure stories.

Mary Grant Bruce wrote some forty books in all, including the fifteen 'Billabong' books about the Linton family and their friends. Her other children's stories included Timothy of Bushland (1912), which used a fairy-tale form for description of nature, and The Happy Traveller (1929), about a boy escaping from an orphanage. She herself thought her collection of aboriginal legends, The Stone Axe of Burkamukk (1922), of greater consequence.

BRUCHAC, Joseph (1942–) American author, poet, storyteller, scholar, and musician of *Native American ancestry whose books for children are part of his ongoing work to keep alive the culture of his Abenaki forebears. His understanding and scholarly interest in indigenous American stories has led to many of his books being retellings of folk tales, such as The Boy Who Lived With Bears (1990), an Iroquois story, The First Strawberries (1993), a Cherokee story, and Between Earth and Sky (1996), legends of Native American sacred places. His work also tells American history through Native American eyes, with novels set during the War of American Independence, in The Arrow Over the Door (1998), and the French/Indian war, in The Winter People (2002). The Earth Under Sky Bear's Feet (1998) is a collection of Native American poetry. He also writes *young adult fiction, including the future-set Killer of Enemies (2013). Through his work with the Wordcraft Circle of Native American Writers and Storytellers, he has helped numerous Native American authors become published.

Bruin Boys A group of naughty animals whose ringleader is *Tiger Tim, first appearing in 1904.

BRUNA, Dick (1927–) Dutch artist and writer, creator of an outstandingly successful series of small *picture books for very young children. His father and grandfather ran the A. W. Bruna publishing company, and, after leaving school, Dick was set to learn the publishing and bookselling trade in Utrecht, in London (where he worked for W. H. Smith), and in Paris. However he wanted to be a graphic artist rather than remain in the book business; he studied at art school in Amsterdam, but gave it up after six months. Thereafter he began to make a living by drawing book jackets and posters. He married in 1953, and in the same year produced a simple book for children, De Appel (published in England in 1966 as The Apple). In 1955 came De kleine

koning (in England, *The Little King*, 1962), and his first two books about '*Miffy', a rather solemn-faced little rabbit to whom exciting things happen. When Bruna and his wife began to bring up children of their own, he discovered the virtue of extreme simplicity, both in drawings and text, as a way of entertaining the very young and teaching them to read. In later books he reduced the pictures to little more than geometrical outlines, filled in with solid colour, yet at the same time managing to convey subtleties of character and expression.

His great success came from 1959 onwards, when his books began to appear in the small, square format by which they are strikingly recognizable today. This square-format series included re-issues of his earlier books (first published in vertical shape), as well as new titles. Many of the new books were about Miffy (whose name in the Dutch originals is 'Nijntje'); others concerned the adventures of the small dog Snuffy ('Snuffie' in Dutch), the first of which appeared in 1969. Bruna also produced simple retellings of traditional *fairy stories. One of his most popular books is *B is for Bear*, first published in Dutch in 1967 as *B is beer*. He has also had great success with wall friezes.

By the mid-1960s Bruna books were appearing in many European and other languages including Japanese; a decade later, more than 3¼ million copies had been sold in Britain alone. Several of these have been translated by Patricia *Crampton.

BRUNHOFF, Jean and **Laurent de** *See* BABAR THE ELEPHANT.

BRYAN, Ashley (1923–) American illustrator and writer who was born and brought up in New York. Though he started young, he was not published till he was nearly forty, becoming in 1962 the first African American man to publish a children's book as both writer and illustrator; in 2009 his body of work, highly versatile in artistic style and medium, would win him the *Laura Ingalls Wilder Medal. Much of his work deals with the African American experience, for which he has been recognized as a multiple winner and multiple runner-up for the *Coretta Scott King Awards, for books such as *Beat the Story Drum, Pum-Pum* (1980), a collection of Nigerian folk tales, and *Let it Shine: Three Favorite Spirituals* (2007). An illustrated autobiography, *Ashley Bryan: Words to My Life's Song*, was published in 2009.

BUCKERIDGE, Anthony (1912–2004) British author of the *Jennings* series who taught for many years in a preparatory school before becoming a full-time writer. Besides the *Jennings* books, he wrote a 'Rex Milligan' series of *school stories.

BUCKLEY, Arabella B. (Burton) (1840–1929) Writer of books of popular *science for children including *The Fairy-Land of Science* (1879), based on lectures given to children in London. The book's chapter titles include 'Sunbeams, and the Work they do', 'A Drop of Water on its Travels', and 'The History of a Piece of Coal'. She was also the author of *Life and Her Children: glimpses of animal life from the amoeba to the insects* (1880) and *Winners in Life's Race, or the great backboned family* (1882).

BUDDEN (Halsey), Maria Elizabeth (?1780–1832) Wife of a Major in the East India Company, Budden was one of John *Harris's most prolific authors. Her best known stories were *Always Happy!!! or, Anecdotes of Felix and his Sister Serena* (1814) and *Claudine, or Humility, the basis of all the virtues* (1822). She also wrote several books of 'True Stories' from history, two volumes of moral instruction (*Nursery Morals*, 1818, and *Hints on the Sources of Happiness*, 1819), and *A Key to Knowledge; or, Things in Common Use Simply and Shortly Explained* (1814), which was still in print in 1841.

Buffalo Bill American folk hero, in reality William F. Cody (1846–1917), a rider for the Pony Express and a frontier scout during the Civil War. In 1869 he became acquainted with Edward Zane Carroll Judson (1823–86), an author of *dime novels, who began to write 'Buffalo Bill' stories about Cody's exploits under the pseudonym 'Ned Buntline'. Judson was an even more colourful character than Cody: his exploits included shooting a jealous husband and then being nearly hanged by a lynch mob. His first Buffalo Bill tale was 'Buffalo Bill, the King of Border Men', serialized in the *New York Weekly* beginning in December 1869. In 1872 Judson brought Cody and 'Texas Jack' (J. B. Omohundro) to Chicago where they appeared in a play about their exploits, *The Scouts of the Prairie*, which Judson had written in four hours. The play was utterly absurd—even Cody observed that four hours seemed a long time to take to write such a thing—but it proved a great success, and toured major American cities. Thereafter

Cody became a showman, and in 1883 opened his celebrated Wild West Show, which travelled in America and Europe. This had much influence on subsequent *westerns.

Bugs Bunny American cartoon hero who first appeared in the late 1930s in films released by Warner Brothers. He has also featured in *comic strips.

Bulbo Prince in The *Rose and the Ring by W. M. Thackeray.

Bulldog Drummond Hero of stories by 'Sapper' (Cyril McNeile, 1888–1937), published from 1920 onwards; an ex-army officer who foils the activities of international crook Carl Peterson.

bumper books A term used in Britain from about 1925 to describe mass-produced children's books, printed on cheap and lightweight but very thick paper, to make them look as large as possible. They usually contained non-copyright material for which the publishers did not have to pay royalties; they were printed in large type so as to spread the contents as thinly as possible, and they reused the same illustrations again and again.

Bumpo Prince in the *Doctor Dolittle books by Hugh *Lofting.

Bumppo, Natty In the *Leather-Stocking Tales by James Fenimore *Cooper.

Bunkle British schoolboy hero of a series of mystery novels by M(argot Mary) Pardoe (1902–96), beginning with Four Plus Bunkle (1939).

Bunter, Bessie See BESSIE BUNTER.

Bunter, Billy See BILLY BUNTER.

BUNTING, Eve (1928–) American author, born in Northern Ireland. Bunting's prolific output ranges in subject matter from retellings of Irish folk tales to stories about family and history, to picture books about homelessness and war. She won the 1976 Golden Kite Award for One More Flight, about a boy who runs away from a foster home and befriends a man who heals wounded birds, and an Edgar Award in 1993 for the mystery Coffin on a Case. Smoky Night (1994), about the race riots in Los Angeles. This also won illustrator David Diaz the *Caldecott Medal. One Candle (2002) was a Sydney Taylor Honor Award winner.

BUNYAN, John (1628–88) Celebrated *Puritan author and poet. Born at Elstow in Bedfordshire, the son of a maker and mender of

pots and kettles, he went to school and then took up his father's trade: the derogatory term 'tinker' was usually applied to him in his lifetime. He was recruited as a soldier during the Civil War, and often referred later to his belief that his life was saved by another soldier's casually exchanging duties with him at a siege. Bunyan then settled again at Elstow, married, and had four children, one of them blind. (He had two more children by his second wife.) The reading of two religious books, bought by his wife, began his gradual conversion from the swearing, dancing, bell-ringing, leader of Sunday sport in his village to a devout Nonconformist: Grace Abounding to the Chief of Sinners (1666) is his spiritual autobiography. Bunyan became a travelling preacher, and was imprisoned for a total of 12 years for preaching in public without licence; much of his writing was done in prison, including the first part of The *Pilgrim's Progress (1678). Bunyan became Pastor of Bedford, continued to travel to preach, and died in London. His book of verses for children, A *Book for Boys and Girls, later known as Divine Emblems, was published in 1686.

bunyip A mysterious and ill-defined creature of Australian legend, traditionally regarded as a man-eating swamp-dweller, but in children's books usually treated more humorously. Judith Whitlock produced a 'Bunyip' series (The Green Bunyip, 1962, and others), and Jenny *Wagner and Ron *Brooks wrote and illustrated The Bunyip of Berkeley's Creek (1973), in which a solitary bunyip emerges from the bottom of a creek in the hope of discovering what he looks like.

BURCH, Robert (1925–2007) American children's novelist; he was born in Georgia and wrote about rural life in that state during his youth, in such books as Tyler, Wilkin, and Skee (1963), Skinny (1964), and Queenie Peavy (1966).

BURDER, George (1752–1832) Founded the *Religious Tract Society and wrote *Early Piety (1776).

BURGESS, Gelett See GOOPS.

BURGESS, Melvin (1954–) An English author described as 'the godfather of YA fiction' (see YOUNG ADULT) and one of the most controversial British writers for young adults. Burgess shot to notoriety with his novel *Junk (1996) about heroin-addiction for which he won the *Carnegie Medal and the *Guardian Children's Fiction Prize in 1997. Burgess' early

works, *The Cry of the Wolf* (1990), *An Angel for May* (1992), and *The Baby and Fly Pie* (1993), were also all shortlisted for the Carnegie Medal. Burgess's appetite for the taboo and ability to whip up a media storm resurfaced in his two novels *Lady: My Life as a Bitch* (2001) and *Doing It* (2003)—later adapted as the television series *Life as We Know It* in the US. Both books deal with teenage sexuality, the first focusing on seventeen-year-old Sandra, whose sexual antics result in her turning into a dog, while *Doing It* focuses on the sexual exploits of three teenage boys. Both titles sparked intense debate and resulted in a call for parental guidance on the covers of his novels. Burgess has been accused of courting controversy for the sake of sales, but this underestimates the quality of his work, which attracts young adults and explores necessary themes whilst also opening them up to debate. His latest novel *The Hit* (2013) is a hard-hitting, hedonistic teenage fantasy.

BURGESS, Thornton W. *See* OLD MOTHER WEST WIND.

BURNETT, Frances Hodgson (1849–1924) Author of *Little Lord Fauntleroy* and *The *Secret Garden*, she was born Frances Eliza Hodgson, the child of a North of England ironmonger. Her father died when she was three, whereupon her mother took over the family business. Frances was brought up in Manchester. She went to a small private school in a neighbour's house, and soon began to entertain her schoolfellows with tales of high romance, which she wrote down in old kitchen notebooks.

By the time she was in her teens the family ironmongery business had ceased to prosper. Her mother sold it, and the family crossed the Atlantic in 1865 to Knoxville, Tennessee to join Mrs Hodgson's brother, who had emigrated to America. Here Frances made friends with the family of the local physician, Dr Burnett, whose eighteen-year-old son Swan soon fell in love with her. She began to try to make money out of writing, in order to supplement the meagre family income, and almost at her first attempt had stories accepted by a magazine editor, Mrs Sarah Josepha *Hale. In 1870, when Mrs Hodgson died, the twenty-year-old Frances was left to provide for the family. Thus she now began to write furiously, sometimes producing as many as half a dozen potboiling short stories in a month. These appeared in numerous American magazines, including the prestigious *Scribner's*. In 1873, she married Swan Burnett, now an established physician,

and her first son, Lionel, was born in 1874, her second, Vivian, in 1876.

The prospect of married life in Knoxville seemed, however, a tiresome restraint to her, so she persuaded an editor to advance enough money for her to take her family to Paris. Returning to America, Mrs Burnett published her first novel for adults, *That Lass o'Lowrie's* (1877), a Lancashire story, which was a huge success on both sides of the Atlantic and was adapted for the stage. Further novels were equally successful. The Burnetts had settled in Washington, where Frances was lionized. But the death of Lionel from tuberculosis in 1890 was shattering for her, and brought on depression. Her marriage was not happy, and eventually she and her husband established separate households and divorced in 1898.

During the 1880s Mrs Burnett wrote several novels under the influence of Henry James, including *A Fair Barbarian* (1881), an account of an American girl in England. In 1883 she began to write for the immediate audience of her own boys, and the result was *Little Lord Fauntleroy*, which started to appear as a serial in the magazine *St Nicholas* in 1885; it was in part a portrait of her son Vivian, for whom she had made the velvet suit the book made famous. Its success led her to write again for children and *Sara Crewe* appeared in 1888. In 1895 came *Two Little Pilgrims' Progress*, the story of a brother and sister who go to the World's Fair in Chicago.

By this stage of her life Mrs Burnett divided her time between America and Europe, establishing an English home in a manor house in Kent. In 1900 she married a young protégé, a ne'er-do-well actor and medical student named Stephen Townesend; the marriage ended within two years. In 1902 she dramatized *Sara Crewe* as *A Little Princess*, and subsequently rewrote the book, giving it the same title as the play. Between 1906 and 1909 she wrote a number of slight, unambitious children's books, several of which had originated in tales told to her boys. In 1909, while laying out a garden at a new home she was building on Long Island, she began *The Secret Garden* (1911), her best and most enduring work. After more Atlantic crossings she wrote another children's story which has survived the years, *The *Lost Prince* (1915). But tastes were changing, and her final adult novel, *Robin*, published in 1922 in two parts, was dismissed by the *Times Literary Supplement* as 'syrup'. She died at her Long Island home four weeks before her 75th birthday. A new biography

of Hodgson Burnett by Gretchen Gerzina appeared in 2004, and Ann Thwaite's earlier biography was reissued in 2007.

BURNFORD, Sheila See INCREDIBLE JOURNEY, THE.

BURNINGHAM, John (MackIntosh) (1936–) Much loved and admired British artist and author of over sixty picture books. He left Summerhill school at the age of seventeen. A conscientious objector, he avoided military service by joining the Friends Ambulance Unit. This was followed by forestry work, farming, slum clearance, building work in Italy, and demolition work in Israel before he returned to study at the Central School of Art in London. His first book, *Borka, the Adventures of a Goose Without Feathers* (1963), was an immediate critical success (winning him the *Kate Greenaway Medal), which was quickly followed by a commission to illustrate the original three-volume *Chitty Chitty Bang Bang* and a rich and painterly *ABC* (1964), though his most distinctive, sketchy, naïve style—using coloured pencils, cross-hatched, and with ink washes—did not develop fully until *Mr Gumpy's Outing* (1970), a deadpan story of an ill-fated punting expedition (another Greenaway winner, Burningham becoming the first double-winner in the prize's history). Equally successful were *Come Away from the Water, Shirley* (1978) and *Time to Get Out of the Bath, Shirley* (1979), in which the mother's prosaic remarks in the text contrast hilariously with Shirley's private fantasies, which are shown in the pictures. Burningham's comic inventiveness is allowed full rein in *Avocado Baby* (1982), in which a baby acquires superhuman strength through eating mashed avocado, while later works range from the utterly whimsical to the thoughtful and somewhat melancholy—notable titles include *Granpa* (1984), *Aldo* (1991), *Cloudland* (1996), and *The Magic Bed* (2003). He is married to fellow illustrator Helen *Oxenbury, with whom he has collaborated on *There's Going to Be a Baby* (2011).

BURRAGE, Edwin Harcourt (1839–1916) British writer for boys' papers who created such serials as 'Handsome Harry of the Fighting Belvedere' (which introduced the character of Ching Ching), 'Broad Arrow Jack', 'Tom Tarter at School', and 'The Island School'. He worked for the *Aldine company, *Emmett Brothers, *Harmsworth, and other publishers.

BURROUGHS, Edgar Rice (1875–1950) Creator of *Tarzan. He served in the US Cavalry against the Apache, but was discharged from the army when he was found to be under age then worked as a cattle drover, gold dredger, storekeeper, and railway detective. Eventually he decided he could improve on the average *dime novel, and wrote *Tarzan of the Apes* (1914). In the years that followed, apart from producing Tarzan sequels, he wrote *westerns, *science fiction, and other kinds of popular stories. He could compose a full-length novel in a weekend, and once did so, for a bet. He became a millionaire during his first ten years as an author.

BURTON, Hester (Wood-Hill) (1913–2000) British children's author who won the *Carnegie Medal with *Time of Trial* (1963), about an early 19th-cent. bookseller's daughter, whose father is imprisoned for publishing seditious material about social conditions. She wrote a number of other *historical novels for young people and a novel set in wartime, *In Spite of All Terror* (1968), in which an East End girl is evacuated to Oxfordshire.

BURTON, Virginia Lee (1909–68) American author-illustrator of *picture books about machines or inanimate objects endowed with personalities. *Choo Choo* (1937) is the tale of a railway engine that runs away from its daily work; *Mike Mulligan and his Steam Shovel* (1938) tells how an unexpected job is found for a machine that has become obsolete; *The Little House* (1942) follows the misfortunes of a country cottage as a big city grows up around it. A snow-plough is the heroine of *Katy and the Big Snow* (1943), which was followed by *Maybelle the Cable Car* (1952). Virginia Lee Burton, who was born in Massachusetts and worked as an artist for a Boston newspaper before her marriage, also wrote and illustrated *Calico the Wonder Horse* (1941) and *Life Story* (1962), an account of the evolution of life on earth.

BUSCH, Wilhelm See MAX UND MORITZ.

BUTLER, Dorothy (1925–2015) New Zealand author of *Cushla and her Books* (1979), an account of how the use of books from a very early age helped to bring about a startling improvement in a severely disabled child (one of Mrs Butler's own granddaughters). She also wrote *Babies Need Books* (1980), in which she argued that books should be given to babies from the very earliest months, and edited *The Magpie Said: stories and poems from New Zealand* (1980).

Butterfly's Ball and the Grasshopper's Feast, The A poem for children by William Roscoe, very popular in England in the first half of the 19th cent. It begins:

Come take up your hats, and away let us haste,
To the Butterfly's Ball, and the Grasshopper's Feast.

The following couplets (fifteen in the original version) tell how various insects and other creatures make the journey to the ball, eat and dance, and are provided with light by 'their watchman, the Glow-worm'.

The poem first appeared in print during November 1806. In that month it was published both in the *Gentleman's Magazine* and in the *Ladies Monthly Museum* (the two texts differ slightly). The *Gentleman's Magazine* attributed the authorship to William Roscoe (1753–1831), Member of Parliament for Liverpool; he was said to have written it for his ten children. It was also stated that the poem had been 'set to Music by Order of their Majesties, for the Princess Mary'. It appears that Roscoe had sent the verses to the musician Sir George Smart, who set them as a glee which was performed by the three daughters of George III during a visit to Weymouth.

On 1 January 1807 the poem was published by John *Harris, who took his text from the *Gentleman's Magazine* version—he had shares in that journal. He produced it as a book in the small squarish format (5 × 4 in.) favoured by him at the time. Each page had a *copperplate engraving after drawings by W. *Mulready, with lines of verse inscribed at the top. The various creatures were depicted either in human form, or with humans riding on their backs. The book was evidently reprinted many times in the months that followed, and in 1808 a new edition was issued, with fresh engravings and some revision and expansion of the text, which now appeared on separate pages from the illustrations. The creatures were now depicted realistically, though the new drawings had less charm than those in the first edition. The book was re-issued again and again in the years that followed; an edition published by Harris in 1841 was described as the 21st. Other publishers issued their own printings, and the poem circulated in cheap copies as a *chapbook.

The comparative levity of *The Butterfly's Ball* ensured its popularity and sparked a whole series of other texts in the same vein, of which the most successful was *The *Peacock 'At Home'*. Many other publishers joined Harris in publishing at least 30 imitations of *The Butterfly's Ball*, until popularity waned in the late 1820s.

The Butterfly's Ball continued to appear in print throughout the 19th cent., often featuring in anthologies of children's verse. It was often printed in America, appearing there as early as 1808. In 1973 it was revived, with spectacular illustrations by Alan Aldridge and a new verse text by William Plomer.

BUTTERWORTH, Hezekiah (1839–1905) American writer for children, born in Rhode Island. He was connected with *The *Youth's Companion* from 1870 to 1894, during which time his contributions greatly increased its circulation. He is now chiefly remembered for his *Zigzag Journeys* series of *travelogue storybooks.

BUTTERWORTH, Oliver *See* ENORMOUS EGG, THE.

BYARS, Betsy (1928–) American author of over sixty books for children and *young adults. She began to write in the early 1960s, but made no great impression until *The Summer of the Swans* (1970), the story of a girl protective of her damaged brother. It won her the *Newbery Medal. Byars' books are realistic, often with characters who have worries that overshadow their lives, such as Benjie in *The *Eighteenth Emergency* (1973), who lives in terror of being beaten up by the school bully; Retta in *The Night Swimmers* (1980), who is trying to run the household after the death of her mother, but is devoured by the feeling that nobody appreciates her; and Clara in *The Animal, The Vegetable, and John D Jones* (1982), who is locked in bitter rivalry with her sister Deanie for the affection of her father after his divorce. Meanwhile *The Pinballs* (1976), about three children who become friends in a foster home, is acknowledged as an early *young adult classic. With a large back catalogue, Byars' books vary greatly, from the mysteries of the *Herculeah Jones* series, starting with *The Dark Stairs* (1994), to the humour of the Blossom Family series, starting with *The Not-Just-Anybody Family* (1986), to *The Midnight Fox* (1970), a compelling and thought-provoking story of a boy's friendship with a fox. Together they confirm her as one of the best and best-loved American children's writers of her day.

Cabinet des fées *See* FAIRY STORIES.

CABOT, Meg (1967–) Prolific American author whose *The *Princess Diaries* series (2000–9) was made into a *Disney movie. Cabot's books are humorous, romantic, full of sharply accurate dialogue, and deal lightly with issues such as self-esteem and image. For Cabot's younger readers there's the *Allie Finkle's Rules for Girls* series (2008). For older ones there's a story of romancing the president's son in *All American Girl* (2002), and the *Airhead* series (2009), in which a super-brainy girl finds herself swapped into a bimbo's body. Many of her books deal with the paranormal, such as *The Mediator* series (2004), about a girl who helps ghosts move on to the afterlife, the *Missing* series (2001), about a psychic girl who can find missing children, and the *Abandon* series (2012), a dark fantasy about life and death.

Caddie Woodlawn (1935) A novel by Carol Ryrie *Brink.

CADY, Harrison (1877–1970) American illustrator, specializing in humorous animal cartoons; his work appeared in *St Nicholas, Life,* and other journals.

Calamity Jane In *westerns fiction, a tough female frontier scout who wears men's clothing and shares adventures with *Deadwood Dick. The 'real' Calamity Jane was Martha Jane Canary (*c.*1852–1903), who toured in burlesque shows.

CALDECOTT, Randolph (1846–86) Illustrator who with Walter *Crane and Kate *Greenaway formed the triumvirate of great British children's illustrators of the late Victorian period. He was born in Chester, the son of a shopkeeper, and was educated at the local grammar school, after which he was sent to work in a bank at Whitchurch in Shropshire. Hints of Cheshire and Shropshire countryside, churches, manor-houses, and farm buildings, appear in many of his drawings. When he was

about twenty-six he moved to London in order to concentrate on art, enrolling at the Slade School. He began to contribute comic drawings to the magazine *London Society* and to other periodicals, and in 1875 he scored a huge success with his illustrations to *Old Christmas*, a selection from the *Sketch Book* of Washington *Irving.

This attracted the notice of the engraver and printer Edmund *Evans, who was keen to issue a new cheap series of children's books, and in 1878 he and Caldecott began an immensely fruitful collaboration, which almost immediately secured Caldecott a permanent place in the front rank of illustrators. For each Christmas during a period of eight years, Caldecott and Evans (with *Routledge as publishers) produced two *picture books (of the type then known as *toy books) printed largely in *colour. For a text Caldecott usually chose a *nursery rhyme or a piece of 18th-cent. light verse or *nonsense. Evans allowed him to spread himself very freely, so that there were sometimes only three or four words to a page; the drawings varied from casual, almost impressionistic, monochrome sketches to whole pages of colour in which the reader's eye was constantly drawn to some new detail. The settings, like Kate Greenaway's, were usually idealized late 18th cent. Caldecott's style had resemblances to both Crane and Greenaway, but his drawings were far less rigid than Crane's and far more humorous than Greenaway's. Nothing like them had been seen before in children's books.

The first two of these Caldecott-Evans books were *John Gilpin and The *House That Jack Built (1878). They were followed by *The Babes in the Wood* (*see* CHILDREN IN THE WOOD), in which Caldecott put Evans's face on one of the villains and his own features on the dying father, and *The Mad Dog* (a comic poem by *Goldsmith), both published in 1879. Then came *Three Jovial Huntsmen* and *Sing a Song for Sixpence* (1880); *The *Queen Of Hearts* and *The Farmer's Boy* (1881); *The Milkmaid* and

Hey Diddle Diddle (1882); *A *Frog He Would A-Wooing Go* and *The Fox Jumps Over the Parson's Gate* (1883); *Come Lasses and Lads* and *Ride a Cock Horse* (1884); and, in 1885, versions of Goldsmith's *Elegy on that Glory of her Sex, Mrs Mary Blaize* and *The *Great Panjandrum*. The books were priced at one shilling.

In 1880 Caldecott married Marian Brind. In 1882 the Caldecotts moved to Kensington. Caldecott meanwhile contributed to the weekly *Graphic* and other magazines, and among the books he illustrated were three by Mrs *Ewing: an 1883 edition of **Lob Lie-By-The-Fire*, **Jackanapes* (1884), which was largely constructed around his drawings, and *Daddy Darwin's Dovecote* (1884). In 1883 he produced his own version of *Aesop (with a new translation from the Greek by his brother Alfred), which included 'Modern Instances', cartoons recasting the fables in terms of Victorian daily life. He also exhibited at the Royal Academy and elsewhere, though he made little impact as a painter.

Caldecott's health was often poor, owing to bouts of rheumatic fever. In October 1885 he travelled to America for a sketching trip, encountered a surprisingly cold winter in Florida, and was taken seriously ill, dying in February 1885 at the age of only thirty-nine. One of his final commissions was to produce illustrations for a version of **Jack and The Beanstalk* in English hexameters by Lord Tennyson's son Hallam, and this was published in 1886 with Caldecott's trial sketches.

His admirers included Beatrix *Potter's father, who bought a number of the original drawings for the Evans picture books, and Beatrix spent some time during her early years carefully copying Caldecott's work, so as to master his style. The pictures of 'dressed animals' in *A Frog He Would A-Wooing Go*, and also his portrayal of country scenes, are an undoubted influence on her own drawings. Indeed the effects of his work were far-reaching. Maurice *Sendak wrote of him: 'To me, his work heralds the beginning of the modern picture book. There is in Caldecott a juxtaposition of picture and word, a counterpoint that never happened before.'

Caldecott Medal Awarded for illustration annually since 1938. It is given by the Association for Library Service to Children, part of the *American Library Association. Named after Randolph *Caldecott, the medal recognizes 'the artist of the most distinguished American picture book for children published

in the United States during the preceding year'. Each year a number of runners-up are named 'Caldecott Honor Books'. For a full list of winners to date, *see* APPENDIX, C.

Call it Courage (1941) A novel by Armstrong *Sperry.

Call of the Wild *See* LONDON, JACK.

Callum McGregor *See* NOUGHTS AND CROSSES.

CALVINO, Italo (1923–85) Prolific Cuban-born Italian poet, writer, critic, and political activist, who also gave his name to one of the most sought-after Italian literary prizes for first-time novelists, and its Cuban counterpart for young talent. Considered one of the most influential and experimental Italian writers of the 20th cent., a good half of his production deals with folklore and speculative and popular fiction as allegorical approaches to post-war Italy and intellectual engagement. His varied work includes the mammoth collection of 200 fables/folk tales from all over the country, translated from local dialects and linguistic minorities such as Corsican, with the equally mammoth title of *Fiabe italiane raccolte dalla tradizione popolare durante gli ultimi cento anni e trascritte in lingua dai vari dialetti da Italo Calvino* (1956), which has been much read by children and widely translated.

Camelot The supposed place of King *Arthur's court. Sir Thomas *Malory identified it with Winchester, though another tradition places it at Cadbury in Somerset, where there is an ancient hill-fort.

CAMERON, Eleanor (Butler) (1912–96) American children's author. She began her career as a writer of *science fiction, with a 'Mushroom Planet' series (1954 onwards), but later moved on to realistic novels about adolescence, such as *A Room Made of Windows* (1971), *The Court of the Stone Children* (1973), and *To the Green Mountains* (1975).

CAMERON (Butt), Lucy Lyttleton (1781–1858) Sister of Mrs *Sherwood and wife of a Shropshire clergyman, Cameron was the author of a number of moral and religious tales for children, of which the best known were *The History of Margaret Whyte; or, The life and death of a good child*, written when she was seventeen, and *The Two Lambs* (1803), an allegory whose heroes, Peace and Inexperience, are saved from the jaws of a lion by a Good Shepherd. In 1828 she

revised *Janeway's *Token for Children* for 'modern ears'. Though she was overshadowed by her famous sister, many of her books became very popular and remained in print for half a century.

CAMPBELL, Rod (1945–) Scottish-born creator of interactive books for young children. His hugely popular classic *board book *Dear Zoo* (1982) established his reputation for *novelty books for the under-fives. Other titles include the *Buster* series (from 1988) about a young baby going to the zoo, having a birthday party, and other first experiences. Producing a mixture of flap books, board books, or 'touch and feel', Campbell engages young children through physical play in order to draw them into the reading process. His texts are simple, often with a repeating element or rhyme with bold, colourful illustrations.

CAMPE, Joachim Heinrich (1746–1818) German educationist, author of *Robinson der Jüngere* (1779–80) (*see* ROBINSONNADES), and *Die Entdeckung von Amerika* (1780–2), an account of the early voyages of discovery of the New World. From this were extracted and translated into English such books as *The Discovery of America, for the use of children and young persons* (1799), which would provide many children with their first introduction to the voyages of Columbus and others, and the very popular *Polar Scenes, exhibited in the voyages of Heemskirk and Barenz to the Northern Regions*, first published by John *Harris in 1821.

Camp Fire Movement An American organization (also found in Britain) akin to the *Girl Guides or Girl Scouts. Founded in 1911, it spawned such stories as Jane L. Stewart's *Camp Fire Girls at the Sea* (1914), and provided some of the subject matter for novels by the English writer Elsie *Oxenham.

Canadian Crusoes, *a tale of the Rice Lake Plains* (1852) By Catharine Parr *Traill, the first notable work of Canadian children's fiction. Hector and Catharine Maxwell, children of a Scots emigrant and his French Canadian wife, together with their cousin Louis Perron, become lost during a day's walk into the backwoods of Ontario. They manage to make a tolerable existence for themselves, living off wild fruits and creatures. They are in danger from warring Mohawks and Chippewas and rescue a Mohawk girl they name Indiana. She joins them and helps them survive and, at the end of the story, becomes Hector's wife.

CANNAN, Joanna *see* PONY FOR JEAN, A.

CANTON, William (1845–1926) British poet and writer, was well known in his day for his studies of childhood. *The Invisible Playmate* (1894) is a commemoration of his daughter by his first marriage, who died in infancy. For his daughter by his second marriage, Winifred Veda, he wrote *W.V. Her Book* (1896) and *A *Child's Book of Saints* (1898). 'W.V.', as she was always known, herself died in 1901, and that year he wrote and published *In Memory of W.V.*

Cap o' Rushes A folk story recorded by Joseph *Jacobs in *English Fairy Tales*; it is of the *Cinderella type.

Captain, The A boys' *magazine published in Britain by Newnes, from 1899 to 1924, at first under the editorship of R. S. W. *Bell. It was famous for its *school stories by P. G. *Wodehouse. More light-hearted in tone than the *Boy's Own Paper*, it was not quite as lively as its contemporary *Chums* or the *Harmsworth papers.

Captain Flint Parrot in *Treasure Island* and character in the *Swallows and Amazons* books by Arthur *Ransome.

Captain Haddock In the *Tintin* books, the hero's friend and regular companion on his adventures. A sea captain (and the owner of Marlinspike Hall), Captain Haddock is an eager tippler (Loch Lomond single malt is a favourite) and given to colourful alliterative swearing: 'Billions of blue blistering barnacles!' is typical (in the English-language translation). Tintin and Haddock first meet in *The Crab with the Golden Claws* (1941).

Captain Hook The villain in *Peter Pan.

Captain January Story by Laura E. *Richards.

Captain Nemo In *Twenty Thousand Leagues Under the Sea* by Jules *Verne.

Captain Pugwash A comic *pirate, creation of the British cartoonist and animator John Ryan (1921–2009). He first appeared briefly in the *Eagle*, then on television in the 1950s and 1970s, and in *picture books. Pugwash believes himself to be bold, bad, and fearless, but he turns to jelly at the sight of his dreadful enemy, Cut-Throat Jake. Of his crew on the *Black Pig*, only Tom the Cabin-Boy has any real nerve.

Captains Courageous, *a story of the Grand Banks* (1897) A novel by Rudyard *Kipling. Harvey Cheyne, the spoilt adolescent son of an American millionaire, is washed overboard from the ship that is taking him and his over-anxious mother to Europe. He is rescued by a crew member of the 'We're Here', a fishing boat from Gloucester, Massachusetts, and is obliged to spend the summer fishing-season on board, earning his keep, before the boat will take him back to land and restore him to his parents. The experience not only toughens him physically, but changes him into a good-natured and sharp-witted young man. His father responds by giving him a responsible position managing the sailing-ships which he owns.

The story is somewhat on the model of *Sandford and Merton,* but Kipling is less concerned to describe Harvey's development of character than to give a detailed picture of the life of the Massachusetts fishing-boats. He wrote the book towards the end of the period that he spent living in New England, and said of it: 'I wanted to see if I could catch and hold something of a rather beautiful localized American atmosphere that was already beginning to fade.' *Captains Courageous* first appeared as a serial in *McClure's,* beginning in November 1896.

Captain Underpants (from 1997) A popular series by Dav Pilkey (1966-), already classics of their kind—a kind that is all about farting, snot, toilets, wacky hilarity, and daft titles, such as *Captain Underpants and the Revolting Revenge of the Radioactive Robo-Boxers* (2013). George Beard and Harold Hutchins are the fourth-grade class clowns who accidentally turn their grouchy school principal into a character from their own comic book, *Captain Underpants.* These books, often disapproved of by adults, are much loved by boys who think they don't like reading.

Caractacus Potts An inventor in *Chitty-Chitty-Bang-Bang* by Ian Fleming.

Carbonel (1955) A series of stories by Barbara *Sleigh, first published with illustrations by Violet Drummond. When Rosemary buys an old birch broom and then a regal-looking cat, her holidays suddenly become more interesting—and exciting. For the broom is a witch's broom; the cat, Carbonel, a royal cat abducted when a kitten. Rosemary, with her new friend John, must reinstate him in his rooftop kingdom. This involves not just detective work, but the excitement of magic.

Deft storytelling and a plot in which magic takes place in the real world contribute to the novel's enduring appeal—sixty years on, it remains in print today. Carbonel reappeared in the sequels, *Kingdom of Carbonel* (1960) and *Carbonel and Calidor* (1973).

career novels appeared simultaneously in Britain and America in 1936. The first British book was *Ballet Shoes* (1936) by Noel *Streatfeild, which she followed by a number of others, with such subjects as tennis and the film industry. The year 1936 also saw the publication of *Sue Barton, Student Nurse,* by the American writer Helen Dore *Boylston, who subsequently produced more nursing stories, and the 'Carol' series about an actress.

A number of British authors followed Noel Streatfeild's lead. A teenager, Pamela *Brown, wrote a story about a theatrical group, *The *Swish of the Curtain* (1941), and afterwards produced other career books, including *To be a Ballerina* (1950) and *The Television Twins* (1952). Kitty *Barne's *She Shall Have Music* (1942) and Elfrida *Vipont's *The Lark in the Morn* (1948) and its sequel were about especially talented musical children. In 1952 Bodley Head, followed by Chatto & Windus (1954), launched mass-market series of career novels for girls, written to a formula. A selection of boys' titles was later published by Chatto and Oxford University Press, but they never enjoyed the popularity of the girls' series.

The career novel for girls has been an undervalued genre; the books should be regarded as signifiers of the growing independence of women during the 1950s and 1960s. Despite their reflection, in most cases, of the gender-based career choices operating for young girls at the time, the formulaic patterns of the novels used traditional narrative modes to engage readers and offer some radical alternatives to domesticity. While romantic endings usually prevailed, all the protagonists nevertheless opted to continue in their careers after marriage. Awareness of the wider female opportunities available in the post-war world is also evident in the choices promoted by titles such as *Anne in Electronics* (1960), *Eve at the Driving Wheel* (1957), and *Margaret Becomes a Doctor* (1957).

Carey family In stories by Ronald *Welch.

CARLE, Eric (1929-) *Picture-book artist who was born in the United States to German

parents. He spent much of his childhood in Stuttgart, then came back to the USA in 1952, and worked as a designer for newspapers and advertising. His career in children's books began with an invitation from Bill Martin, Jr. (1916–2004) to collaborate on the book that would become *Brown Bear, Brown Bear, What Do You See?* (1967), which teaches colours and animals. There were direct follow-ups to this—*Polar Bear, Polar Bear, What Do You Hear?* (1991), *Panda Bear, Panda Bear, What Do You See?* (2003), and *Baby Bear, Baby Bear, What Do You See?* (2007)—all in his distinctive style. Carle works with a collage of coloured or hand-painted tissue paper, which he sticks to the page to form primitive pictures such as a child might make. Other long-standing favourites of Carle's more than seventy books are *The Grouchy Ladybug* (1977; UK: *The Bad-Tempered Ladybird*) and *The Very Busy Spider* (1984), but the book for which he became best known was *The *Very Hungry Caterpillar* (1970), a cleverly designed counting book with holes through the pages.

In 2002, Carle and his wife Barbara founded the Eric Carle Museum of Picture Book Art in Amherst, Massachusetts. The following year his own extensive picture-book career was rewarded with the *Laura Ingalls Wilder Medal.

CARLSON, Natalie Savage (1906–97) American children's author who began her career with *The Talking Cat and other stories of French Canada* (1952), her mother's family being French Canadian. Her fiction includes *The Happy Orpheline* (1957) and *The Family Under the Bridge* (1958), both comic stories set in France.

CARNAN, Thomas *See* NEWBERY, JOHN.

Carnegie Medal An annual British award, instituted by the Library Association in 1936 to mark the centenary of the birth of Andrew Carnegie, philanthropist and benefactor of *libraries. It is awarded to the author of what is judged to be the outstanding book for children published during the previous year. Initially it was limited to English writers whose books were published in England, but from 1969 any book written in English and published first, or concurrently, in the United Kingdom has been eligible; and in 2015 eligibility expanded to include books translated into English from other languages, too. It is now administered by the Chartered Institute of Library and Information Professionals (*CILIP), and has developed to involve a highly successful, and growing, shadowing scheme, with some 5,000 school groups shadowing the judging of the 2014 award by reading shortlisted books, sharing reviews, voting, and so on. For a full list of winners to date, *see* APPENDIX, F.

CARNEY, Julia A. (1823–1908) Remembered for the poem 'Little Things', which begins

> Little drops of water,
> Little grains of sand,
> Make the mighty ocean
> And the beauteous land.

She was a schoolteacher from Boston, Massachusetts, and is said to have written the poem for a *Sunday school tract. It has sometimes been attributed to the Revd E. Cobham Brewer, but he apparently only wrote some additional verses.

Carousel (1995–) A thrice-yearly UK-based magazine guide to the world of children's books, with reviews of new titles, interviews, and other features. It has its origins in Anne Wood's quarterly *Books for Your Children* (1965–95).

Carpenter, Humphrey (1946–2005) British writer, broadcaster, and musician. Oxford-born and educated Carpenter wrote the biography of *Tolkien (1977) and then a group biography of the Inklings, an Oxford literary group whose members included Tolkien and C.S. *Lewis (1978), which won the Somerset Maugham Award. His later biographies include one of Spike *Milligan (2004); and with his wife Mari Prichard (1947–) he produced the annoyingly hard-act-to-follow first edition of this *Oxford Companion to Children's Literature* (1984). This was followed a year later by *Secret Gardens*, a study of what is now considered the first golden age of writing for children, spanning the period from *Kingsley and *Carroll to *Milne. Carpenter's own writing for children included *The Captain Hook Affair* (1979), in which children go into classic stories, and characters come back with them into the real world, and *Mr Majeika* (1984), with its sequels, delightfully funny books for young readers which tell the story of a wizard who comes into St Barty's Primary School (arriving by flying carpet) to teach Class Three. There have been adaptations for audio and television.

Carrie's War (1973) The best known of Nina *Bawden's children's books, the story of a brother and sister evacuated to wartime Wales, where they are given a home by the bullying, Bible-thumping Councillor Samuel

Evans and his timorous sister. Carrie tries to heal the breach between Mr Evans and his relations who live in a nearby farmhouse, but in doing so she precipitates disaster.

CARROLL, Lewis (Charles Lutwidge Dodgson) (1832–98) Author of **Alice's Adventures in Wonderland*, **Through the Looking-Glass*, and other classics of *nonsense for children. He was the third of eleven children of the Revd Charles Dodgson and Frances Jane Lutwidge. Charles was brought up in the Cheshire village of Daresbury where his father, a graduate of Christ Church, Oxford was curate.

Charles's mother educated the children herself when they were small, and noted that at the age of seven Charles had read *The *Pilgrim's Progress*. His other nursery books included the **Early Lessons* of Maria **Edgeworth and *The *Shepherd of Salisbury Plain* by Hannah *More.

When Charles was eleven, in 1843, his father moved to a more lucrative living, the rectory of Croft near Darlington in Yorkshire. At the age of twelve he was sent for just over a year as a boarder to the grammar school at Richmond, about ten miles from Croft. Here he was happy and hard-working. The headmaster reported to his parents that the boy had 'a very uncommon share of genius', observing his 'love of precise argument', and his ingenuity in Latin verse composition in replacing the usual forms of nouns and verbs with 'convenient forms of his own devising'. In 1846 he was sent on to Rugby, where he was unhappy at first. He was bullied, and was probably mocked for the stammer he had developed in childhood. On the other hand, he rarely came home for the holidays without a prize for Classics, Divinity, or Mathematics.

In the holidays he began to produce a series of family magazines for the amusement of his brothers and sisters. The first, begun when he was about fourteen, was called *Useful and Instructive Poetry* and consisted of humorous verses. Some of these were *limericks, while others parodied the conventions of contemporary poetry for children; one poem, in *ballad form, has the moral 'Never stew your sister'. Other magazines followed, illustrated by Charles himself in a style that was crude but often very funny. *The Rectory Magazine*, early in the series, included contributions from various members of the family, and these indicate that parodies, puns, and nonsense were made up by other Dodgson

children as well as Charles. In 1850, after leaving Rugby and while working at home for his Oxford matriculation, Charles produced another single-handed effort, *The *Rectory Umbrella*, which shows that by this time he had considerable skill as a comic writer. He also built, and wrote plays for, a marionette theatre.

He went up to Christ Church, Oxford, as a commoner, early in 1851 and won a scholarship later that same year. In 1852, while still an undergraduate, he was nominated by his father's old friend Dr Pusey to a Studentship at Christ Church. This meant that Dodgson now had £25 a year and the right to remain in residence at the college for the rest of his life, providing he proceeded in due course to Holy Orders and remained unmarried. Meanwhile he continued his undergraduate studies, achieving only a Third Class in 'Greats' (Philosophy and Ancient History) but being awarded a First in Mathematics at the end of 1854.

Early in 1855 Christ Church appointed him Sub-Librarian of the college; he also began to tutor undergraduates, eventually becoming an official Mathematical Lecturer. When not teaching he read widely, visited London theatres with friends, and began to be interested in photography, acquiring his first camera and set of chemicals in 1856. He also began to publish comic poetry and prose.

A cousin put him in touch with the novelist Frank Smedley, who in turn showed some of his verses to Edmund Yates, who was starting a penny rival to *Punch* entitled *The Comic Times*. Between August and November 1855 four pieces by Dodgson appeared in its pages, amongst them 'I never loved a dear Gazelle' (a parody of a poem by Thomas Moore) and 'She's all my fancy painted him' (an early version of 'The White Rabbit's evidence'). During 1855 Dodgson also wrote the first stanza of '*Jabberwocky'. After the *Comic Times* ceased publication at the end of 1855, he began to contribute to its successor, also edited by Yates, *The Train*, which printed an early version of his parody of Wordsworth (the verses about the 'aged, aged man', later given to the White Knight), as well as 'Hiawatha's Photographing'. Several of Dodgson's contributions to *The Train* were serious poems, such as 'Solitude'. He had previously used the pseudonym 'B.B.' (initials whose meaning he never explained), but Edmund Yates did not care for this, and when he printed 'Solitude', he gave as the poet's name one that he chose

from a list of alternatives supplied by Dodgson: 'Lewis Carroll'. This was formed by Latinizing Dodgson's two first names, reversing their order, and then translating them back into English.

In June 1855 the Dean of Christ Church, Thomas Gaisford, died. The man chosen to succeed him was Henry George Liddell, headmaster of Westminster School. Liddell was in his mid-forties. He and his wife, the former Miss Lorina Reeve, had at this time four children: Harry, Lorina Charlotte, Alice Pleasance, and Edith Mary.

The Liddell family moved into the Deanery at Christ Church early in 1856, and on 25 April Dodgson, who had been given permission to help a friend photograph Christ Church Cathedral from the Dean's garden, met the children:

The three little girls were in the garden most of the time, and we became excellent friends: we tried to group them in the foreground of the picture, but they were not patient sitters. I mark this day with a white stone.

Lorina Liddell was aged six. Dodgson had already made friends with her at a musical party at the Deanery the previous month. Alice was nearly four, and Edith two. The 'white stone' was Dodgson's indication of a memorable occasion.

The girls' brother Harry, aged eight or nine, quickly became friends with Dodgson, and this encouraged Dodgson to make frequent visits to the Deanery, armed with his camera. By the autumn of 1856 he had begun to spend time in the Deanery schoolroom with the children and their governess, Miss Prickett. He was often asked to dine at the Deanery, and sometimes received direct invitations to spend time with the children.

During the summer of 1857 Dodgson met and photographed Tennyson, whose poetry he much admired (though he sometimes parodied it). Two years later he was introduced to George *MacDonald, whose children soon became friends with him. Meanwhile at Oxford he began to publish a series of mathematical textbooks designed to help undergraduates with their studies; there were soon more than half a dozen of these in print. He also began to prepare himself for Holy Orders, a step which was required of him if he were to retain his Studentship at Christ Church. It would have been expected that eventually he would leave the college and become a parish priest, just as his father had done; but he had 'no sort of inclination' to contemplate this, and though he was ordained Deacon in 1861, thereby

satisfying the college's requirements, he never proceeded to Priest's Orders.

The volumes of Dodgson's diary for the period from April 1858 to April 1862 have disappeared, but it is clear that during this time his friendship with the Liddell children flourished. He began to have a particular interest in the second daughter, Alice, taking a number of photographs of her singularly and in groups with her sisters. The results of these photographing sessions were often remarkable; Tennyson reputedly said of Dodgson's portrait of Alice, aged about eight, dressed as a beggar girl, that it was 'the most beautiful photograph he had ever known'.

At Christmas 1861 he gave Lorina, Alice, and Edith a copy of Catherine Sinclair's *Holiday House, with an acrostic verse on their names inscribed in it. In May 1862 (in which month Alice celebrated her tenth birthday) the three girls began—as was apparently already their habit in the summers—to accompany him on boat trips on the Isis (Thames). There was one such trip on 17 June 1862, when the party also included one of Dodgson's aunts and two of his sisters, who were visiting Oxford, as well as Robinson Duckworth, a contemporary of Dodgson's from Trinity College. On this occasion, the whole party was drenched with rain—an episode which probably gave rise to 'The Pool of Tears'. Two days afterwards, in the words of Dodgson's diary, he and Duckworth:

made an expedition *up* the river to Godstow with the three Liddells: we had tea on the bank there, and did not reach Christ Church again till quarter past eight, when we took them on to my rooms to see my collection of micro-photographs, and restored them to the Deanery just before nine.

A few months later, Dodgson added these words on the opposite page: 'On which occasion I told them the fairy-tale of *Alice's Adventures Underground* which I undertook to write out for Alice.'

The result of this was the manuscript *Alice's Adventures Under Ground*, which Dodgson wrote out in fair copy, illustrated, and eventually presented to Alice Liddell as a gift for Christmas 1864, though by this time he had considerably expanded the tale, had enlisted John *Tenniel to draw new pictures, and had arranged that the London firm of Macmillan should publish it on commission from him, under the title *Alice's Adventures in Wonderland*. The book was finally published in time for Christmas 1865. However, Dodgson's close friendship with the Liddell children

did not survive until the story had appeared in print.

Dodgson's relationship with Alice Liddell has been the subject of much contemporary critical comment and speculation. In Dodgson's diary for 25 June 1863, he records a trip taken with the entire Liddell family to Nuneham but after this a page has been removed and there is no further significant reference to the family until 5 December, when Dodgson describes holding 'aloof' from them at some Christ Church theatricals. This has led some commentators to speculate that the rift was due to Mrs Liddell's realization that Dodgson wanted to marry Alice. However, Edward Wakeling, a leading Carroll scholar, refutes such speculation entirely, citing a note referring to the missing page of the diary that explains that Dodgson and the Liddells discovered speculation that the former was 'using the children as a means of paying court to [their] governess', thus the lack of contact was by mutual consent to attempt to dispel these rumours. He states categorically that 'there was no major and lasting rift with the Liddells'; and no evidence to suggest that Dodgson wished to marry Alice.

In 1867 Dodgson began to give serious consideration to what he called 'the second volume of Alice', having told Macmillan less than a year after the publication of the first book that he had 'a floating idea of writing a sort of sequel'. He delayed serious work, however, until the matter of an illustrator could be settled. Tenniel was at first unwilling to work for Dodgson again, having found him fussy over the first book, and Dodgson approached Richard *Doyle. Nothing came of this, and in April 1868, after another fruitless visit to Tenniel, Dodgson considered two other artists, Noel Paton (illustrator of The *Water-Babies) and, briefly, W. S. Gilbert, whose comic drawings (signed 'Bab') he had seen. Paton pleaded ill health, and urged that 'Tenniel is the man'. Tenniel finally gave way, and said he thought he might have the pictures ready for publication by Christmas 1869. However, Dodgson's father, who since 1854 had been Archdeacon of Richmond, now died suddenly; Dodgson recorded that this was 'the greatest blow that has ever fallen on my life', and he did not send the first chapter of the new book to Macmillan until 12 January 1869. At this stage he planned to call it Behind the Looking-Glass, and What Alice Saw There.

While he was at work on it Macmillan issued Phantasmagoria (1869), a collection of his verses, both light and serious, taking its title

from a long comic poem about a conversation with a ghost. The new Alice book progressed very slowly. According to one of Dodgson's child friends, Rosa Franklin, Dodgson had already received galley proofs for a good deal of the story before he decided 'what to make the Red Queen turn into'. The text was not finished until January 1871, and there was a lengthy correspondence between the author and Macmillan about the production of the book, Dodgson being extremely concerned about every detail of print, illustrations, title page, and even the drying of the paper after it had been manufactured. The book was finally published, under a title suggested by Dodgson's friend Liddon, Through the Looking-Glass, and What Alice Found There, in December 1871; it bore the date 1872.

Dodgson was now devoting a good deal of his energy as a parodist and satirist to local causes. The New Belfry (1872), The Vision of the Three Ts (1873), and The Blank Cheque (1874) were protests against various college and university innovations. In July 1874 the line 'For the Snark was a Boojum, you see' came spontaneously into Dodgson's head, and he began to piece together The *Hunting of the Snark, his third and final masterpiece of nonsense, which was eventually published in the spring of 1876.

Rhyme? and Reason?, a reprint of poems from Phantasmagoria with illustrations by A. B. *Frost, together with the whole of The Hunting of the Snark, was published in 1883. Apart from this he wrote a number of pamphlets, such as Twelve Months in a Curatorship (1884), a humorous account of his first year as Curator of Christ Church Common Room, and Parliamentary Elections (1884), a serious outline of a scheme for proportional representation. He also invented and published a number of games, e.g. Doublets, a word-puzzle (1879) and The Game of Logic (1886), an attempt to make formal deductive logic clear and entertaining to children. He took a close interest in Henry Savile Clark's stage adaptation of both Alice books into a children's operetta (1886). In 1889 Macmillan published The *Nursery 'Alice', Dodgson's own simplification of the first Alice book, with coloured versions of Tenniel's pictures.

For many years Dodgson had been at work on a long children's story, a patchwork of fragments which had occurred to him at different times, and which was to be serious as well as comic: *Sylvie and Bruno eventually appeared in 1889, with a continuation published in 1893. Much of Dodgson's time in

these later years was devoted to the invention of such devices as the 'Nyctograph', a contraption to enable a sleepless person to write in the dark, and the publication of such books as *Pillow-Problems thought out during sleepless nights* (1893). His last major work was *Symbolic Logic* (1896–7), an attempt to popularize formal logic and accuracy of thought. He became ill with a bronchial infection at Christmas 1897, and died a few weeks later at the Guildford house which had been his home in the vacations since the death of his father.

Biographical curiosity about Dodgson was scarcely satisfied by S. D. Collingwood's *Life and Letters of Lewis Carroll* (1898), and there have been many other studies of his life, some of which—most notably Langford Reed's *Life of Lewis Carroll* (1932)—present him as the two halves of a distinctly split personality, the humourless and sentimental C. L. Dodgson and the anarchic genius of nonsense Lewis Carroll. But as Derek Hudson remarks in his biography *Lewis Carroll* (1954, revised 1976), we perhaps do not help ourselves, or our understanding of Dodgson, by looking for two men instead of one. In *Euclid and his Modern Rivals* (1879), for example, Carrollian humour intrudes upon Dodgson's mathematics, and works such as *Phantasmagoria* demonstrate a sophisticated and rather worldly humour of the *Punch* school which conforms to neither the supposed 'Carroll' or 'Dodgson' sides of the man. More recent biographical work, such as that of Karoline Leach's *In The Shadow of the Dreamchild* (1999), examined Carroll's diaries and letters (inaccessible to many early scholars) and showed how a Carrollian 'myth' developed which presented Carroll as a shy bachelor with an endless fascination for young girls, instead of the sociable man who had close relationships with many men and grown women. While this view was by then not controversial, her inference that he had intimate, probably sexual, relationships with adult women, possibly including Mrs Liddell, was generally rejected. Despite periodic controversy, Lewis Carroll remains one of the best-known authors of children's books and *Alice's Adventures in Wonderland* in particular holds a key position in the canon of children's literature for finally setting children's books free to explore complex imaginative and comic worlds.

Carrots: *Just a Little Boy* (1876) A novel by Mrs *Molesworth.

CARRYL, Charles E. (Edward) (1841–1920) A New York stockbroker and director of railroad companies, who was inspired by the works of his near-namesake Lewis *Carroll to write *fantasies in the *Alice vein, initially for his daughter Constance, and then for readers of *St Nicholas*. The first of these was *Davy and the Goblin* (1884); then came *The Admiral's Caravan* (1891), which describes the child Dorothy's encounters with a series of wooden figures that come alive on Christmas Eve.

Carry on, Mr Bowditch (1955) A novel by Jean Lee *Latham.

Carson, Kit *See* KIT CARSON.

CARSON LEVINE, Gail (1947–) American author, most famous for her retelling of the Cinderella story, the Newbery Honor (*see* NEWBERY MEDAL) title *Ella Enchanted* (1997), which was made into a film in 2004. Fascinated by *fairy tales, Levine has written *Fairest* (2006), a version of the Snow White story set in the same world as *Ella Enchanted*, and a series of stories called *The Princess Tales* (2002). In 2005 she wrote *Fairy Dust and the Quest For the Egg* (2005), a book that was the starting point for the Disney Press *Disney Fairies* franchise, set in J. M. *Barrie's Neverland on Fairy Haven island.

CARTER, Bruce (Richard Hough) (1922–99), British author who used his pseudonym for many of his children's novels, including books of *science fiction (*The Deadly Freeze*, 1976, and others) and *historical novels such as *Peril on the Iron Road* (1953).

Carter, Nick *See* NICK CARTER.

CARTER, Peter (1929–99) British *historical novelist for children who began his writing career with *The Black Lamp* (1973), set in Lancashire during the Industrial Revolution. His later books include *The Gates of Paradise* (1974), about William *Blake, and *The Sentinels* (1980), a story of British naval anti-slavery patrols in 1840. Carter worked as a builder's labourer before becoming a mature student at Oxford University; he then was a teacher until he could write children's books full-time.

CARUS WILSON, the Revd **William** *See* WILSON, THE REVD WILLIAM CARUS.

Carved Lions, The (1895) A novel by Mrs *Molesworth, illustrated by L. Leslie *Brooke. Geraldine and her brother Haddie are fascinated by the wooden lions which stand outside a cabinet-maker's shop. When their parents go to South America, Geraldine runs away from school, comes to the shop, and falls asleep from weariness. She dreams that the

lions take her and Haddie on their backs over the sea to rejoin their parents. Waking, she learns that she will not have to go back to school, but will be looked after by kind friends until her parents return. The book is among the most popular of Mrs Molesworth's works, and has reappeared in print several times in the 20th cent.

Casson Family series A sequence of books by Hilary *McKay, following the fortunes of the artistic and unconventional Casson family—unconventional, and yet profoundly recognizable to anyone who has, or has ever had, a family of their own. We meet them first in *Saffy's Angel* (2001, winner of the *Whitbread Award), which introduces readers to—in descending age—Caddy (short for Cadmium), Indigo, Saffy (Saffron), and Rose, and describes Saffy's journey to discover her place in the family. *Saffy's Angel* was followed by *Indigo's Star* (2004), *Permanent Rose* (2005, shortlisted for the Whitbread Award); *Caddy Ever After* (2006); and *Forever Rose* (2007), as the series worked its way with humour and affection through the dramas, major and minor, in the siblings' domestic lives.

Castle Blair, *a story of youthful days* (1878) A novel by Flora L. Shaw (1852–1929). Adrienne, sent from France to live with her bachelor uncle in his Irish castle, finds it full of his brother's children, who are running wild. The book deals chiefly with their conflict with Mr Plunkett, agent for the estate. It is ahead of its time in its lifelike portrayal of the children, and its vivid picture of Irish rural life. (Shaw is also remembered for having written an essay in 1897 in *The Times*—where she was 'Colonial Editor'—suggesting the British Protectorate on the Niger river should be called 'Nigeria'.)

CASTLEMON, Harry (Charles Austin Fosdick) (1842–1915) American author who wrote some sixty *adventure Stories for boys. Many of them were based on his experiences as a boy, when he ran away from his home in Buffalo, NY, to join the navy, and fought on gunboats during the Civil War. His best known hero was Frank Nelson, whose adventures were recorded in the 'Gun-Boat' series, beginning with *Frank the Young Naturalist* and *Frank on a Gun-Boat*, both published in 1864.

Catcher in the Rye, The (1951) A novel by J. D. Salinger (1919–2010); the story of teenager Holden Caulfield and his detached, critical view of the adult world. Hugely popular with young American readers, it influenced a whole generation of American *young adult fiction written during the 1960s and 1970s, and remains a significant cultural landmark today.

catechism A series of questions and answers designed to instruct in the principles of the Christian religion. The term was apparently first used early in the 16th cent., but the practice of catechizing is much older and seems to have been widespread in medieval England.

At the Reformation the Protestant emphasis on the importance of religious instruction caused large numbers of catechisms to be composed. In 1553 there was printed, under letters patent from Edward VI, *A short Catechisme . . . for all Scholemaisters to teache*. Another catechism for schools, by Alexander Nowell, Dean of St Paul's, was first published in 1570 and remained widely in use until the end of the 17th cent. Many catechisms were composed for the use of children in *Sunday schools, e.g. *Familiar Instructions for Young Children* (n.d.), from which this is an excerpt: '*Q.* Are all children good? *A.* No; many are very naughty, and God does not love them.'

The question-and-answer form used in catechism was adopted in many secular books for the education of children; *see* BOOKS OF INSTRUCTION.

CATHERALL, Arthur (1906–80) Prolific British writer of *adventure stories; his first book, *Rod o' the Rail*, appeared in 1936. He served in the Royal Air Force in the Second World War and travelled widely for 'background' for his stories, many of which were published under pseudonyms.

Cat in the Hat, The (1957) By Dr *Seuss, one of the best loved of all American children's books. Written in lively rhyming verse—its uncommon read-aloud-ability certainly adding to its great popular success—it tells the story of two children, left alone while mother is out, being visited by the eponymous Cat, who walks on his hind legs and wears a red bow tie and a red-and-white striped hat. This Cat wants to have fun (against the advice of the sensible family goldfish), but this fun involves unleashing utter chaos on the home—things are only just tidied up in time for mother's return. In order to meet a challenge from publisher William Spaulding to produce a reading primer 'that first-graders can't put down', *The Cat in the Hat* was constructed from a list of 223 sight words supplied to Seuss by his editor. (Seuss later revealed

that he wanted a rhyming title and, going through the list, found the words 'cat' and 'hat' the only suitable rhyming pair, so that was what the book would have to be about.)

There have been adaptations in various media, keeping either the wild anarchy of the book or its riotous humour, but as yet never satisfactorily both. A sequel, *The Cat in the Hat Comes Back*, was published the year after the first book; in it the two children are visited not only by the Cat himself, but by twenty-six ever-diminishing little cats, named A-Z.

CATNACH family British printers of *chapbooks, many of which were for children. John Catnach (1769-1813) was born in Fifeshire and worked as a printer in Berwick-on-Tweed, Alnwick, and Newcastle before moving to London just before his death. His business there was taken over by his son James (1792-1841), known as 'Jemmy', who reprinted versions of many existing children's books.

Catriona (1893) A novel by R. L. *Stevenson.

Catweazle A wizard in stories by the British writer Richard Carpenter (1929-2012).

CAUSLEY, Charles (Stanley) (1917-2003) British poet who wrote several books of poems for children which reflect his knowledge of, and feeling for, his native Cornwall. They include *Figure of 8: narrative poems* (1969), *Figgie Hobbin* (1970), *The Tail of the Trinosaur* (1973), a narrative poem about a prehistoric monster which comes back to life, and *The Hill of the Fairy Calf* (1976), an Irish fairy story in verse. Causley often uses *ballad form, and refers to figures from *Cornish folklore, though sometimes he deals with more recent events in Cornish history, such as the occasion on which Parson Hawker of Morwenstow dressed up as a *mermaid to hoax his parishioners. Causley's *The Sun Dancing* (1982) is an anthology of Christian verse illustrated by Charles *Keeping.

cautionary tales Stories or poems giving warning about the dangers of foolish behaviour, which first appeared in the late 18th cent. One of the earliest collections was *Vice in its Proper Shape*, published by Elizabeth *Newbery c.1774. It contained prose accounts of 'the wonderful and melancholy transformation of several naughty masters and misses into those contemptible animals which they most resemble in disposition'. In 1801 *Darton and Harvey published three volumes of *Accidents and Remarkable Events*, a collection of gory happenings supposedly taken from real life. Other books of cautionary tales from this period include *Dangerous Sports* (1803), written by the surgeon James Parkinson, *A Present for a Little Girl* (Darton and Harvey, 1805), which contains warnings about household accidents, and *Tales Uniting Instruction With Amusement* (John *Harris, c.1810).

The use of verse for cautionary tales seems to have been the invention of Ann and Jane *Taylor, several of whose *Original Poems for Infant Minds* (1804-5) are of the 'Awful Warning' type. They were emulated by Elizabeth Turner in The *Daisy (1807) and *The Cowslip* (1811). Adelaide O'Keeffe (1776-1865) also wrote excellent examples of the genre.

A new note was introduced into the genre with the grotesqueries of *Struwwelpeter, first printed in English in 1848. This hovered halfway between real warnings and comedy; it remained for Hilaire *Belloc to parody the genre, with superbly funny results, in *Cautionary Tales for Children* (1907).

Cautionary Tales for Children, *Designed for the Admonition of Children between the ages of eight and fourteen years* (1907) The fifth in a series of comic books with verses by Hilaire *Belloc and Pictures by 'B.T.B.', Belloc's friend Lord Basil Blackwood. It parodies the 19th-cent. genre of *cautionary tales, and begins with the story of Jim, who let go of his nurse's hand at the Zoo and was eaten by a lion. The moral of this is that children should 'always keep a-hold of Nurse | For fear of finding something worse.' The book, which has supplied generations of readers with comic quotations of this sort, also includes the macabre histories of 'Matilda, who told Lies, and was Burned to Death', recalling the story of the child Mary who meets a similar fate in *Original Poems for Infant Minds* (1804-5). *Cautionary Tales* concludes with the story of 'Charles Augustus Fortescue', a child of incredible goodness, who in consequence of his rectitude 'accumulated an Immense Fortune'.

CAXTON, William (c.1420-91) Caxton introduced printing to England, and published a number of books which, though not specifically intended for children, appealed to young readers. Among these were his translation of *The *History of Troy* (1473-4), the first book to be printed in English, *Reynard the Fox* (1481), the fables of *Aesop (1484), and *Malory's *Morte Darthur* (1485).

Cay, The (1969) A novel by Theodore *Taylor about a black adult and a white child marooned on a desert island, and finding that they become mutually dependent.

CBCA The Children's Book Council of Australia, an organization with a current mission to engage the community with literature for young Australians through promotion, supporting writers and illustrators, fostering the role of library and literature professionals, providing greater equity of access to reading, and celebrating outstanding work through its annual awards.

The CBCA was formed in 1946 to promote children's books of literary merit and now administers six literary awards—CBCA Book of the Year: Older Readers, CBCA Book of the Year: Younger Readers, CBCA Book of the Year: Early Childhood, CBCA Picture Book of the Year, CBCA Eve Pownall Award for Information Books, and the Crichton Award for Children's Book Illustration. The CBCA Awards Foundation raises funding to give winners a financial reward, as well as the prestige of a win, shortlisting, or inclusion in the *Notable Books* list for that year.

Each state of Australia has its own Branch and Sub-branches, and responsibility for the organization, under the direction of the National Board, is rotated through the states. The Australian Capital Territory Branch financially supports the Lu Rees Archives, and the New South Wales Branch awards the Lady Cutler Award to a person who has given distinguished service to children's literature. The CBCA has also published *Reading Time*, a quarterly reviewing journal, since 1967.

CBI Book of the Year Awards (formerly the **Bisto Book of the Year Awards**) Presented annually by Children's Books Ireland to writers and illustrators born or resident in Ireland. There is a debut category (named after Eilís *Dillon), a 'book of the year' category, and a trio of 'merit' awards. Since the first award in 1991, multiple winners have included Kate *Thompson, Marie Louise *Fitzpatrick and Oliver *Jeffers (a total of seven times each); Siobhan Dowd and Gerard Whelan (four apiece); and P. J. *Lynch, Éilís Ní Dhuibhne and Siobhan *Parkinson (three apiece). Other notable winners over the years have included *Artemis Fowl, The *Boy in the Striped Pyjamas*, and *A Bit Lost* (Chris *Haughton).

celebrity books A phenomenon which has become prevalent in the early years of the 21st cent., whereby people who are famous in some other walk of life (or simply famous for being famous) publish books for children, with the implied assumption that this is an easy step for them or their brand managers to take. The result has been a tide of books, some apparently arbitrary or just chasing a trend (books by former glamour models about ponies, say), others more understandable: books by footballers set in youth footballing academies, and books by famous dancers about young girls who want to be famous dancers. The quality of some of these is passable, not least because the books are often ghostwritten by professional writers. When the celebrity in question writes his or her own book, the results have been mixed, but fame can still produce a bestseller from poor material, such as the pop star Madonna's 2003 debut for children, *The English Roses*. The television comic actor David *Williams is one celebrity to have diversified into children's books from elsewhere in the entertainment world and managed to do it to some critical acclaim, but such examples remain few and far between.

Celtic Fairy Tales (1892) Selected and edited by Joseph *Jacobs, this was the first drawing together of mythological, bardic, and folktale material from the different Celtic traditions of Ireland, Scotland, and Wales, in a form suitable for children. Jacobs selected tales that were 'characteristically Celtic', including the famous *Irish folk tale of Deirdre of the Sorrows and the *Welsh legend of Beddgelert.

At a time of intense political activity over the question of a separate Ireland, he wrote in his introduction that if his book 'could succeed in giving a common fund of imaginative wealth to the Celtic and Saxon children of these isles, it might do more for a true union of hearts than all your politics.'

Celtic traditional tales *See* CELTIC FAIRY TALES; *see also* CORNISH FOLK MATERIAL; IRISH FOLK TALES; SCOTTISH FOLK MATERIAL; WELSH TRADITIONAL TALES.

censorship *See* BANNED BOOKS.

CHAFFEY, M. Ella *See* YOUNGSTERS OF MURRAY HOME, THE.

Chalet School In stories by Elinor *Brent-Dyer, beginning with *The School at the Chalet* (1925). These were set in an international school in the Tyrol and centred on the

character of 'Joey' Bettany, an English girl who rises to be head of the school and then in adult life becomes a writer of girls' stories. The last book in the series, *Prefects of the Chalet School*, was published posthumously in 1970.

CHALMERS, Mary *See* HARRY.

CHAMBERS, Aidan (1934–) British educationalist, critic of children's literature, and *young adult novelist, who has worked as a teacher and was for seven years an Anglican monk. With his American wife Nancy (1936–) he founded *Signal, a review of children's literature, and the two of them shared the 1982 *Eleanor Farjeon Award. He has written his own books and plays for children and is the author of *The Reluctant Reader* (1969). In 1978 he published his debut novel for teenagers, *Breaktime*, which, though not his debut, was the book that launched his acclaimed *Dance* sequence—a series of bold and intelligent young adult novels not connected in plot but with certain stylistic and thematic congruences. *Breaktime*—which among other things features a particularly memorable and formally inventive presentation of a loss of virginity—was followed by *Dance on My Grave* (1982), a groundbreaking portrait of a gay teen relationship, and *Now I Know* (1987), which asks questions about religion and faith. *The Toll Bridge* (1992) was then followed by *Postcards from No-Man's Land* (1999), which won the *Printz Award and the *Carnegie Medal, and used two parallel stories set in the Netherlands to tackle big questions such as sexuality, euthanasia, and war. The sequence concluded with the huge and ambitious *This Is All: The Pillow Book of Cordelia Kenn* (2005). In 2012 Chambers published *Dying to Know You*, a touching story about the growing friendship between a teenage boy and his girlfriend's favourite writer. Chambers won the 2002 *Hans Christian Andersen Award.

CHAMPNEY, Lizzie (Elizabeth) Williams (1850–1922) American author for children, who wrote stories of past times, such as the Great-Grandmother's Girls series; this began with *Great-Grandmother's Girls in New Mexico, 1670–1680* (1888). She was best known for her series of *travelogue storybooks about the three Vassar girls. When she took them to England, in *Three Vassar Girls in England* (1884), she used the chance to hit back at such books as Mrs Trollope's *Domestic Manners of the Americans* (1832):

'What I find particularly galling,' continued Barbara, is the fact that the English are so supercilious. They fancy that they understand us perfectly, while they have not the remotest conception of what Americans really are.'

Changes trilogy (1968–70) By Peter *Dickinson, a series of novels about an England which has turned against machinery and the modern way of life, and has regressed to ignorance, malice towards outsiders, and a suspicion of all things mechanical. The books originally appeared in reverse order of their story. *The Weathermonger* (1968) describes the end of 'the Changes', as these events are known: two children discover that the alteration has been caused by the exhumation of *Merlin and his revulsion towards the modern world. They restore him to his long sleep, and the English people come out of their mental darkness. *Heartsease* (1969) describes the rescue by some children of an American investigator, sent to discover the cause of the Changes, who has been put in the stocks by English villagers, stoned, and left for dead. *The Devil's Children* (1970) is about a twelve-year-old girl who herself feels the revulsion towards machinery and is adopted by a band of Sikhs, who are immune to it, but need her as a 'canary' to sense danger and warn them of it. The 'Changes' trilogy is variable in quality: *The Weathermonger* has many of the improbabilities of the contemporary *adventure story (e.g. two children piloting a small boat across the Channel) and an inherently absurd plot (Merlin's state of mind is the consequence of his addiction to morphine, administered by the Welsh chemist who has accidentally dug him up). But there are many powerful passages in the book, and the two later volumes lack any such absurdities.

Chaos Walking (2008–10) A fantasy trilogy by Patrick *Ness. The opening volume, *The Knife of Never Letting Go* (2008), introduces us to Todd Hewitt, who lives in a place where there are no women, and where the thoughts of all the men can be heard all the time (this is called Noise)—and of the animals, too, as Todd's dog, Manchee, plays a memorable role. Todd meets a girl—Viola—and they go on the run. The second book, *The Ask and the Answer* (2009), introduces a second voice—Viola's—and builds the tensions of the first story into a great battle between two factions, with Todd and Viola forced into involvement on opposing sides. The series concludes with *Monsters of Men* (2010), where the

war explodes in scale and complexity, and stakes rise before a thrilling and deeply satisfying conclusion. For the final volume, new voices are added to the mix, including one of the 'Spackle' (natives of this world). Each book in the trilogy is excitingly paced with a cast of engaging characters—its popularity with teen readers is testament to this—but taken together the trilogy is also a complex study of responsibility, difference, maturity, and power, and it is one of the more ambitious and accomplished works for *young adult readers in recent years. It won the *Booktrust Teenage Prize (for vol. 1), the *Costa Book Award (vol. 2), the *Carnegie Medal (vol. 3), among many others.

chapbooks Works of popular literature sold for a few pence, often by itinerant pedlars or 'chapmen' (from Anglo-Saxon *cēap*, 'barter, business, dealing', hence 'cheap'). Chapbooks were in circulation from the 16th to the 19th cents. They often contained short versions of *romances, *ballads, and popular tales such as *Jack the Giant Killer, *Tom Thumb, and *The *Seven Champions of Christendom*, usually illustrated with a few crude *woodcuts. The term 'chapbook' was probably not used to describe this type of literature until the mid-18th cent., if not later.

The first cheap printed books for a popular market began to appear in England during the 16th cent. They often contained controversial political or religious comment, in spite of legal restrictions on such material, and were then sold by travelling chapmen. Henry Chettle in *Kind-Harts Dreame* (?1592) mentions 'prety chapmen' who are 'able to spred more pamphlets by the state forbidden than all the booksellers in London'.

The abolition of the court of Star Chamber in 1641 gave more freedom to printers, and in the years that followed there was a marked increase in cheap books. Popular storybooks now became a regular part of the chapman's wares. Among the most frequently printed titles were, besides those already mentioned, *Bevis of Hampton*, *Guy of Warwick*, *Valentine and Orson*, *Don Bellianis of Greece*, *Fortunatus*, *Dick Whittington, the story of *Bluebeard, The *Children in the Wood*, *Tom Hickathrift, *Fair Rosamond*. Other books that were abridged into chapbook form included *Robinson Crusoe*, *Don Quixote*, the fables of *Aesop, and religious works such as *Watts's *Divine Songs* and *The *Pilgrim's Progress*. Also popular were *jestbooks, tales and ballads of *Robin Hood.

Few chapbooks before the late 18th cent. were written or printed specifically for children, but evidence suggests they were widely read by the young. Many *Puritan and secular writers complained of the bad effect that they had on tender minds. John *Bunyan admitted that in his young days he had preferred 'a Ballad, a Newsbook, *George* on horseback, or *Bevis* of Southampton' to reading the Scriptures. But in the early 19th cent., Romantic-era figures such as Wordsworth, Coleridge and Lamb write nostalgically of chapbooks, seeing them in opposition to the many works of instruction and the *moral tales that proliferated in the late 18th and early 19th cents. (as, for example, Wordsworth did in *The Prelude* (v, 364–9, 1805–6 version)). Chapbooks hold a vital but complex position in the development of children's literature in this period.

By 1800 chapbooks for children were being produced in some quantity. They often contained an extended version of some *nursery rhyme, and narrated the 'tale' or 'history' of characters such as *Mother Hubbard, *Dame Trot, *Jack Sprat, *Tom The Piper's Son, and *Cock Robin; these books were in doggerel verse, usually with a woodcut on each page.

Chapbooks were generally printed on one sheet of paper, folded into a single gathering. In the 17th and early 18th cents. the usual page size was about 15 x 10 cms or $6\frac{1}{2} \times 4$in. and there were generally twenty-four pages, though chapbooks with only twelve or even eight pages were produced. At the end of the 18th cent. the preferred size, especially for children's chapbooks, had diminished to a mere 10 x 6 cms or $4 \times 2\frac{1}{2}$in. and there were usually sixteen pages. The earlier chapbooks had leather or similar bindings. The later tendency was to do away with this; for a time, rough 'sugar bag' paper was used, or (especially for the small children's chapbooks) *Dutch paper wrappers.

The limitations of space in the chapbook often meant that the text to be printed had to be severely cut. If it was still too long the printer would change to a smaller size of type midway in the book. Conversely, if, as sometimes happened, the text proved to be too short, the type-size was increased as the book progressed. The woodcuts were often very crude, and the same blocks would appear again and again in different chapbooks to illustrate quite different stories and incidents.

Until about 1750 London had little opposition as the centre of the English chapbook trade. Most printers in the capital who

produced cheap literature had their premises in or near Aldermary Churchyard. Prominent among them were William and Cluer Dicey, and John *Marshall. Later in the 18th cent. the provinces began to produce chapbooks in large numbers. Printing businesses which issued them flourished not just in such major cities as Newcastle, York, and Manchester, but also in a number of smaller towns, such as Lichfield, Alnwick, and Devonport.

Chapbooks were published in large number in Scotland and in Ireland (chiefly Dublin). The Scottish printers favoured coarsely humorous stories; the hero of one of these was himself a seller of chapbooks, 'John Cheap the Chapman'. Scots tastes also favoured pamphlets about the life of John Knox and other divines. Among works abbreviated by Scottish printers was the *Bible, reduced by one Glasgow publisher to a mere twenty-four pages, including illustrations.

In America chapbooks of the same type as those found in England were widely distributed, becoming especially popular in the late 18th and early 19th cents. Among notable publishers of them was Isaiah *Thomas of Worcester, Massachusetts. Equivalent literature was produced in European countries, examples being the German *Volksbücher* and the French *Bibliothèque bleue*.

The standard of chapbooks varied greatly from printer to printer. Many were badly written, and they were often badly printed. On the other hand, printers specializing in books for children such as *Kendrew of York, Rusher of Banbury and *Lumsden of Glasgow, produced good-quality work, with clear type and well-cut blocks for the illustrations, which were often hand-coloured.

In the last decade of the 18th cent. the style of the chapbooks was imitated by Hannah *More in her didactic series of *Cheap Repository Tracts, a set of publications chiefly designed for *Sunday schools.

Despite the variable quality of their printing, chapbooks were immensely popular with both children and adults of all social classes. For many generations, too, they gave children a wide range of reading matter which could not be found elsewhere.

Chapbooks survived into the early 20th cent. However, in the mid-19th cent. their function as popular entertainers was chiefly taken over by *penny dreadfuls in England and *dime novels in America.

CHAPMAN, C. H. *See* BILLY BUNTER.

CHAPONE, Hester (1727–1801) British author of *Letters on the Improvement of the Mind* (1773), originally composed for her niece; it became a popular classic of its age, and was often reprinted. It was an influence on Mary Wollstonecraft when she was writing *A Vindication of the Rights of Women* (1792).

chapter books Short works of (usually) fiction for new and intermediate readers, more substantial and text-heavy than *picture books but still typically illustrated throughout (unlike most older fiction) and divided up into chapters of manageable length.

Chapter of Kings, The An elementary *history book published by John *Harris in 1818. It consists of a rhyme in which one line is given to each of the Kings of England. Each line is accompanied by an illustration of a king, with his dates. The rhyme was based on one composed by the entertainer John Collins (*c*.1738–1808).

CHARLESWORTH, M. L. *See* MINISTERING CHILDREN.

Charlie and Lola A series of books by Lauren *Child about a high-spirited and quirky little girl, and narrated by her long-suffering brother. The titles are *I Will Not Ever NEVER Eat a Tomato* (2000), *I Am Not Sleepy and I Will Not Go to Bed* (2001), *I Am Too Absolutely Small for School* (2003), and *Slightly Invisible* (2010).

Each book begins, 'I have this little sister, Lola. She is small and very funny.' Lola has a highly distinctive voice—imperious and determined, with eccentric turns of phrase. Charlie is a loving and nurturing big brother with extraordinary reserves of patience. The artwork uses a collage effect, mixing painting and photography, and the typography changes all the time to suit the story.

The books have been turned into a hugely successful television series, and a number of tie-in titles have been written that are not by Lauren Child.

Charlie and the Chocolate Factory (1964) A celebrated *fantasy by Roald *Dahl, the story of young Charlie Buckett, who, when his family are starving, wins a ticket which permits him to see round the mysterious chocolate factory owned by Mr Willy Wonka and manned by the pigmy Oompa-Loompas. Charlie and his Grandpa Joe are accompanied on the tour by four other children and their parents, all variously grotesque.

(An earlier draft featured more children.) The book proved to be a world bestseller, but attracted some adverse criticism for the supposed *racism in the treatment of the Oompa-Loompas (originally portrayed as African pygmies) and for the depiction of Charlie's elderly grandparents. The central part of the book is a modern *cautionary tale, and includes verses which are a pastiche of *Struwwelpeter, as each of the other children on the tour meets with a gruesome fate. Charlie is the only child to make it to the end, and is rewarded with the chocolate factory itself.

The book was originally illustrated by Faith *Jaques in the UK and Joseph Schindelman in the US, and a subsequent edition by Michael *Foreman (1985). It was eventually reissued with pictures by Quentin *Blake, who by then had come to be identified as Dahl's regular illustrator. *Charlie and the Chocolate Factory* has been twice filmed, in 1971 (as *Willy Wonka and the Chocolate Factory*) and 2005; notable stage adaptations include a 2013 West End musical. There is a sequel, *Charlie and the Great Glass Elevator* (1972).

Charlie Brown See SNOOPY.

Charlie Chan An inscrutable Chinese *detective in books by Earl Derr Biggers (1884–1933), published in the 1920s. Film adaptations began to appear from 1926, as well as TV adaptations, countless comic books, board games, etc.

CHARLOTTE ELIZABETH (Charlotte Elizabeth Tonna) (1790–1846) English *evangelical writer of such books as *Helen Fleetwood* (1841), a novel about a factory town, and *Conformity* (1841), the story of two related families and their different characters. She was rabidly opposed to Roman Catholicism and Socialism, and tried to combat Popery in Ireland by writing for the Dublin Religious Book & Tract Depository. Among her works for children are the *moral tales contained in *Tales and Illustrations* (4th edn, 1844).

Charlotte Sometimes, a novel by Penelope *Farmer.

Charlotte's Web (1952) Classic American children's novel by E. B. *White. The pig Wilbur, runt of his litter, is saved from immediate slaughter by Fern, the farmer's daughter. But Wilbur soon learns that he will be killed in the end, for bacon. One person, though, declares that she can save him: a grey spider named Charlotte, who lives in a corner of the barn,

and who brings about what seems to be a series of miracles to keep Wilbur from the butcher's knife, writing words in her web to describe him: 'some pig', 'terrific', 'radiant', and 'humble'. The ending is triumphant and tear-jerking. Other memorable characters include Templeton, a gluttonous rat. Adaptations include a 1973 animation and a 2006 live-action film.

CHATELAIN, MME **Clara de** (1807–76) Author, composer, and friend of Victor Hugo, who wrote a number of books for children in English, including *Jocko, the Brazilian Ape* (1860), the story of a monkey who sets out from Brazil to see the world. She made in 1852 an English translation of *Andersen's fairy stories.

Chatterbox A long-lived British *magazine for children, established in 1866 by the Revd J. Erskine Clarke (founder also of *The *Children's Prize*), to provide healthy reading at a price (one halfpenny) which would compete with *penny dreadfuls. In its early years *Chatterbox* contained a mixture of serial stories, factual articles, and a moderate degree of *religious instruction. In 1901 F. J. Harvey *Darton became the editor, and managed to conduct a 'secret purge' of Erskine Clarke's regular contributors, replacing their 'blandly benevolent' writings with more adventurous material, such as John *Masefield's story *Jim Davies*, which appeared as a serial. *Chatterbox* survived until 1948.

CHAUCER, Geoffrey (?1340–1400) Author of *The Canterbury Tales*. He wrote a *Tretis of the Astrolabie* (1391), an account of the astrolabe with instructions how to use it, which is addressed to 'Littell Lowis my sone', who was probably about ten years old at the time.

CHAUNCY, Nan (Nancen) (Beryl Masterman) (1900–70) Children's author who emigrated from Britain to Australia when she was a child and settled in Tasmania, where all her books take place. Her early novels, of which the first was *They Found a Cave* (1948), were conventional *adventure stories, but by *Tiger in the Bush* (1957) she had become more interested in character than plot. This and its sequels, *Devil's Hill* (1958) and *The 'Roaring 40'* (1963), are studies in the relationships of the Lorenny family, who live in a remote corner of the Tasmanian mountains. *Tangara: 'Let Us Set Off Again'* (1960) marked (along with Patricia *Wrightson's *The Rocks of Honey*, published in the same year) the first successful attempt by any Australian children's author to combine

realism with aboriginal folk materials; in it a white girl makes contact with a young aboriginal in an earlier century, and brings her from the past to prevent a modern tragedy.

CHAUNDLER, Christine (1887–1972) British *girls'* story author of the 1920s and 1930s; her books include *The Chivalrous Fifth* (1928). She also wrote *The Children's Author: a writer's guide to the juvenile market* (1934).

Cheap Repository Tracts (1795–8) A series of pamphlets for *Sunday school pupils devised, and largely written, by Hannah *More. The aim was to provide suitable reading-matter for the children and young people of the poor, who were being taught to read, but might fall victim to the vulgarities of the *chapbooks and the seditious writings of Tom Paine and his followers, who looked favourably on the French Revolution. Hannah More decided to supply popular writings whose style would be 'somewhere between vicious papers and hymns', which would 'attack gross immorality or dishonest practice', and would bring readers 'to still higher things'. The plan was to produce three Tracts each month: a story, a *ballad or some other poem, and a suitable Sunday reading. The Tracts were to be priced extremely cheaply, at a halfpenny, a penny, or three-halfpence, and the cost would be largely borne by subscriptions from charitable gentlefolk.

Well aware that she must make the Tracts entertaining in order to keep readers' attention, Hannah More collected a set of contemporary chapbooks and deliberately copied their format, using the same sort of cheap paper, rough printing, and crude woodcuts. (Later editions of the Tracts were printed on better paper for those gentry who wished to buy them, and were made up into bound volumes.)

The series was launched at the beginning of 1795, and among the earliest titles was one that became the best known of the entire series, *The *Shepherd of Salisbury Plain*, written by Hannah More herself under the pseudonym 'Z'. Other titles by Hannah More in the series include *The History of Tom White, the Postillion* (1795), the story of a boy who throws off wicked ways and eventually becomes a prosperous farmer; a ballad entitled *Patient Joe; or the Newcastle Collier* (1795); and *Black Giles, the Poacher* (1796). She eventually wrote some 50 of the 114 Tracts that were published. Other writers for the series included two of her sisters and various members of the

'Clapham Sect', a group of Church of England Evangelicals. The *Divine Songs* of Isaac *Watts were included in the series.

Titles were deliberately fashioned to resemble the sensational content of the chapbooks, e.g. *Execution of McLean, the Gentleman Highwayman* (1797) and *History of the Plague in London* (1797). However, everything between their covers was invariably highly moral in content, and usually severely religious too. Nor was much criticism of the existing social order allowed; religion and social status quo were presented as going inseparably hand in hand, and the poor were told that 'their distresses arise nearly as much from their own bad management as from the hardships of the times.' The Tracts were written in a lively style that had a wide appeal, especially to children.

Tracts were issued in threes at monthly intervals throughout 1795, 1796, and 1797. Sales were enormous; by the summer of 1795 they had reached 700,000 and, partly as a result of large orders from America, the two million figure had been passed by the following March, so that the Tracts were paying for themselves and no longer needed to be supported by subscription. Sales were swollen by Hannah More's practice of breaking the longer stories up into serials and issuing them part by part; the Tracts were also widely used as *reward books in Sunday schools. The series did not, however, continue beyond 1798, in which year only a few new titles were published.

The success of the Tracts led to the formation in 1799 of the *Religious Tract Society, though this had no connection with Hannah More, and its members regarded her publications as insufficiently *evangelical.

CHEAR, Abraham (d. 1668) A *Puritan writer of poems for children, who appears to have been a West of England Baptist minister. He wrote some of his verses while in prison for his dissenting beliefs. His poems are printed in *A Looking-Glass for Children* (1672), one of the first books for children to use the device of narrative as a mirror to reflect positive or negative models. Chear was much admired by his fellow Dissenters, and his poems were reprinted in other collections.

Cherry-Stones, The, *or, Charlton School: a tale for youth* (1851) An early *school story, described as 'partly from the MSS. of the Rev. William Adams . . . edited by the Rev. H. C. Adams'. It is set in a small private school. Harry Mertoun gains popularity among his schoolfellows by rescuing a cricket ball from

the squire's grounds. He spies a fine cherry-tree there, and returns at night to steal fruit from it. Then his conscience troubles him, and 'what was to be done with the stones?' He buries them, but is haunted by remorse and by the stones themselves, which keep reappearing. The author, the Revd William Adams (1814–48), Fellow of Merton College, Oxford, and Vicar of St Peter-in-the-East in that city, was well known for his 'Sacred Allegories', particularly *The Shadow of the Cross* (1842). His brother, who completed and edited *The Cherry-Stones*, was a Fellow of Magdalen College, and himself went on to write a number of school stories.

Cherub series *See* MUCHAMORE, ROBERT.

Cheshire Cat In **Alice's Adventures in Wonderland*.

CHESTERFIELD, Philip Dormer Stanhope Fourth Earl of (1694–1773) Author of the celebrated *Letters* to his natural son and godson, giving advice on matters that a young man should understand much in the tradition of *books of courtesy. The letters were not intended for publication, but they were printed after Chesterfield's death, in 1774. In the same year Francis *Newbery issued a condensed version designed to be put into the hands of children, under the title *Lord Chesterfield's Maxims*. This was reprinted a number of times, and other abbreviated editions for young readers were produced by other publishers.

Cheval sans tête, Un *See* HUNDRED MILLION FRANCS, A.

Chevy Chase An early *ballad which became, according to Addison, writing in the *Spectator* in 1710, 'the favourite ballad of the common people of England'. It apparently arose from the Battle of Otterburn, fought in 1388, or a similar bout of border warfare. In the ballad story, the English Earl Percy determines to hunt, with fifteen hundred men, in Chevy Chase, the Cheviot Hills on the border between England and Scotland; this is in a spirit of bravado, since the land belongs to the Scots Earl Douglas. After a morning's hunting, Earl Douglas arrives with a force to challenge the trespassers. Battle begins; by the day's end, both Douglas and Percy are slain, and few men on either side escape alive. The ballad ends with a prayer that God 'grant henceforth that foule debate | Twixt noble men may cease.'

Chevy Chase probably dates, in its original form, from the 15th cent. Sir Philip Sidney wrote in his *Defence of Poesie* (1579–80): 'I never heard the old song of Percy and Douglas that I found not my heart moved more than with a trumpet; and yet it is sung but by some blind crowder [fiddler], with no rougher voice than rude style.' *Chevy Chase* continued to be published during the 18th cent. in *chapbook or 'penny history' form, usually with a prose version preceding the ballad, to make it more of a tale and to fill up the book. It was revived in 1843 as part of The *Home Treasury series edited by Sir Henry *Cole ('Felix Summerly').

CHICHESTER CLARK, Emma (1955–) An established British illustrator who has collaborated with authors such as Michael *Morpurgo, Roald *Dahl, and Margaret *Mahy. Chichester Clark studied at the Royal Academy of Art (1980–3) under Quentin *Blake and Michael *Foreman. In 1988, she won the Mother Goose Award for the most exciting newcomer to children's book illustration with her illustrations of *Listen to This* (1987), a collection of short stories edited by Laura Cecil. Chichester Clark has also written and illustrated over twenty of her own books, including the Melrose and Croc series (from 2005), and the Blue Kangaroo series, the first of which, *I Love You, Blue Kangaroo!* (1998) was shortlisted for the 1998 *Kate Greenaway Medal.

Chicken-licken A nursery story collected in the mid-19th cent. by J. O. *Halliwell and sometimes reprinted in story collections or as a separate book. Chicken-licken is walking in a wood when an acorn drops on her head. She believes that the sky has fallen, and warns her friends Hen-len, Cock-lock, Duck-luck, Drake-lake, Goose-loose, Gander-lander, and Turkey-lurkey. They all set off to tell the king, but they meet Fox-lox, who says he will show them the way; he takes them to his fox-hole, where he and his cubs eat them up. The story is sometimes given the title *Henny-Penny* or *Chicken Little*; the latter was used as the title of a novel by Betsy *Byars (1979), about an anxious boy.

CHILD, Lauren (1965–) An English writer and illustrator best known for her *Charlie and Lola picture books (later made into an award-winning television series) and the *Clarice Bean series of picture books and novels. Child introduced Charlie and Lola in 2000 with *I Will Not Ever NEVER Eat a Tomato*, which won the annual *Kate Greenaway

Medal in 2001. Child is known for her distinctive illustrative style, which uses both traditional and digital techniques. Her swirling multimedia collages of typography and image include magazine cuttings, textiles, photography, and digital artwork as well as traditional watercolours. Her background in graphic design, fine art, theatre, and chandelier-making can be seen in *The Princess and the Pea* (2005), where Child recreated her fairy-tale world 'off the page' in a miniature set which was then photographed by acclaimed portrait photographer Polly Borland. Other picture books include *That Pesky Rat* (2002). Child's work is hugely popular amongst children and spans a wide age range, including a Clarice Bean spin-off series for teenagers about the thirteen-year-old detective Ruby Redfort.

CHILD, Lydia Maria (1802–80) American novelist and campaigner against slavery. She edited *The *Juvenile Miscellany* and was the author of *The Girl's Own Book* (*c*.1831), a compendium of articles on conversation, manners, and amusements, which was very popular on both sides of the Atlantic.

Child and His Book, The (1891) A pioneer study of the history of books for children, by Mrs E. M. *Field, published in 1891 by Wells Gardner, *Darton & Co. The book surveys the subject from before the Norman conquest until 1826, stopping at this date because the appearance at this time of *The *Child's Guide to Knowledge* marked (says Mrs Field) 'a new departure and awakened a new interest in this sphere of work, and because the subsequent period, the modern era, as we may call it, is at once too full and too familiar for profitable discussion.' Mrs Field paid particular attention to *books of instruction and to the history of English education.

child authors Many children have written books which were subsequently published. One of the earliest was Francis Hawkins, the eight-year-old author of *Youths Behaviour* (*c*.1641), a *book of courtesy based on a French original. Mary Shelley, daughter of William *Godwin and Mary *Wollstonecraft and the author of *Frankenstein*, wrote, at the age of eleven, *Mounseer Nongtonpaw; or, The Discoveries of John Bull in a Trip to Paris*, a comic squib which was published by her father in 1808, with illustrations by *Mulready.

A number of British professional children's authors began their careers when still very young themselves; they include Mrs *Hemans

and Mrs *Ewing, and in the 20th cent. Pamela *Whitlock. American authors who made an early start include S. E. *Hinton, Ruth *Nichols, and John *Steptoe. The most famous child novel of all time is *The *Young Visiters* (1919) by Daisy Ashford. Probably the most commercially successful case of juvenile authorship was the invention of *Superman by two teenagers, Jerry Siegel and Joe Shuster.

Child Life (1871) An anthology of poems for children by John Greenleaf *Whittier. The selection was made on the principle of 'combining simplicity with a certain degree of literary excellence. As well as including poems by celebrated names such as Tennyson and *Southey, Whittier printed such pieces as *The *Owl and the Pussy-Cat* and George *MacDonald's 'The Baby' ('Where did you come from, baby dear?') from *At the Back of the North Wind*. He also published a companion volume, *Child Life in Prose* (*c*.1872).

Children in the Wood, The A *broadside ballad, subsequently a *chapbook and *pantomime subject, with the alternative title *The Babes in the Wood*. The ballad was registered in 1595. In the *ballad story the babes, a three-year-old boy and a younger girl, are the children of a wealthy Norfolk gentleman. He and his wife fall sick and die at the same time, leaving the children in the care of an uncle until they come of age to receive their substantial inheritance. If the children should die first, the uncle inherits; so he soon falls to plotting and hires two ruffians to murder the orphans. Believing they are going to visit London, the children set off in the company of the ruffians. They chatter so charmingly on the way that one man is tempted to relent. In the ensuing quarrel the harder-hearted one is killed, and the other then leads the children into a wood and deserts them. They wander, first feeding on blackberries, finally dying in one another's arms. Retribution falls on the uncle and the remaining ruffian, and the ballad ends with a warning to all guardians of orphans to be just, 'Lest God with such like Misery, | Your wicked Minds requite.'

The broadside ballad, registered as *The Children in the Wood, or The Norfolk Gentleman's Last Will and Testament*, was immensely popular during the 17th and 18th cents. in Britain and in America and passed into oral tradition. The story was adapted for printing as a chapbook from about 1700 and many different prose versions exist, some greatly extending the tale and giving the main characters

Italianate names, perhaps deriving from an early play that may have inspired the ballad. The title *The Babes in the Wood* was common by the late 18th cent.

The story became a pantomime subject when pantomime fashion veered from classical to chapbook themes at the beginning of the 19th cent. On the stage *Robin Hood and his men were introduced to effect the obligatory happy ending, and some prose versions since then have also allowed the children to be found asleep in the wood and rescued. Sarah *Trimmer, among others, found the tragic version unfit for children, but it has continued to be published. An 1879 revival of the original ballad was made in the form of a *picture book by Randolph *Caldecott; another, published in 1972, was illustrated by Edward *Ardizzone.

Children of the New Forest, The (1847)

The last children's book to be completed by Captain *Marryat, and the first enduring British *historical novel for children. Edward, Humphrey, Alice, and Edith Beverley are left orphaned at their family home in the New Forest after their father's death fighting on the Royalist side in the Civil War. To avoid detection by the Roundheads they are sheltered by an old forester, Jacob Armitage, who passes them off as his grandchildren and educates them in the ways of the forest. After the death of Jacob, Edward fights on the side of Charles II in the Battle of Worcester. At the Restoration, the children come into their inheritance again, and Edward marries Patience, daughter of a moderate Cromwellian, whom he has rescued from a fire.

The character of Jacob has the same degree of piety as does *Masterman Ready in Marryat's story of that name, but the book's didactic content is easily outweighed by its excitement. As Marryat's biographer Oliver Warner observes, 'there are few people who, given *The Children of the New Forest* when young, cannot return to it with pleasure.'

Children's Book Council of Australia

See CBCA.

Children's Book Week

An annual celebration of books for children and young people, now held in many countries, with activities in libraries, school libraries, bookshops, and elsewhere to encourage reading—with the emphasis on the joy of reading. The US week began in 1919, so that it is that country's longest-running national literacy

initiative. The British Book Week began in the 1930s and is now run by *Booktrust.

Children's Crusade

A religious movement begun in 1212, in which thousands of European children set out to regain the Holy Land from the Muslims by love rather than force. It ended in disaster, with many of the children who joined it being sold into slavery. Historical fiction on the subject includes *The Children's Crusade* by Henry *Treece (1958) and B. R. Collins's *young adult novel, *The Broken Road* (2012).

Children's Encyclopaedia, The

Edited by Arthur *Mee and published by *Harmsworth's Amalgamated Press from 1908.

Mee was struck by the number of questions his seven-year-old daughter Marjorie asked her mother, and he proposed the publication of a work that would provide answers. *The Children's Encyclopaedia* was first issued in 50 fortnightly parts at 7d. each, between 17 March 1908 and 1 February 1910. It was not a conventional encyclopaedia with entries arranged alphabetically, but was divided into fourteen sections; material from several of these sections was included in each issue, not arranged according to any particular system. When the whole work was in print an index was issued to accompany it.

The sections each had the heading 'The Child's Book of . . .', for example, 'The Child's Book of Golden Deeds' and 'The Child's Book of Its Own Life'; other subjects included 'the Earth', 'Bible Stories', 'Wonder' (answers to miscellaneous questions), 'Nature', 'All Countries', 'Poetry', and 'Things to Make and Things to Do'.

The Children's Encyclopaedia was full of detailed information on every kind of subject, lavishly illustrated with photographs or halftone drawings. A typical issue might include a feature on how paper is made and books are printed, answers to such questions as 'Why don't trains come off the railway lines?', gardening hints, the story of the Civil War and the execution of Charles I, the tale of Moses in the bulrushes, and instructions in making a model chapel out of cardboard. Story material included excerpts from *Aesop; among books serialized was *Don Quixote*. There were also lessons in grammar, handwriting, and arithmetic.

Sheer information predominated over anything that could be called polemic, but there was an undertone of patriotism ('In our own happy country the love of little children is stronger than in almost every other land',

reads a typical article), and of *temperance campaigning. For example an article on microbes turns aside from its theme to attack alcohol and public houses; Mee was an ardent campaigner against drink and tried to introduce Prohibition to Britain.

The Children's Encyclopaedia was not an instant success, but circulation gradually built up and well before the conclusion of the original part-issue it was also being published in volume form. At the end of the part-issue in 1910 a serial re-issue was begun in monthly parts under various titles, including (from 1911 to 1914) *The Children's Magazine*; it then became *My Magazine*, in which form it appeared monthly until 1933.

By 1946 twenty-six editions of the *Encyclopaedia* had been published in Britain, at first in twelve volumes and then in ten. An authorized American edition was produced by the Grolier Society, as *The Book of Knowledge*, and became even more successful than the British version; by 1946 more than fifty million volumes of it had been sold. There were also various American pirate editions. The *Encyclopaedia* was also translated into French (as *Qui? Pourquoi? Comment?*), Italian, Spanish, Portuguese, Arabic, and Chinese. It continued in print in Britain until the 1950s.

Children's Friend, The The title given to many English translations of Arnaud *Berquin's *L'Ami des enfans*. The first of these began to appear in parts in 1783, just after the part-issue of the original French work had been concluded. *The Children's Friend* is a collection of *moral tales, such as that of Little Annabella, who loses her mother in a crowd in consequence of having rashly stopped to look at a dog cart. As well as being widely read in English, *L'Ami des enfans* was used in its original language to teach French to English children.

Children's Friend, The An *evangelical penny monthly published in Britain from 1824 to 1882. Its founder was the Revd William Carus *Wilson, portrayed as 'Mr Brocklehurst' in *Jane Eyre*. It featured *Janeway-like accounts of the pious deaths of young children, and gave warnings of hell-fire to those who were naughty.

Children's Garland from the Best Poets, The (1862) One of the first *poetry anthologies for children, compiled by the poet Coventry Patmore (1823–96) with the help of his first wife Emily. The Patmores'

aim was to include 'nearly all the genuine poetry in our language fitted to please children'. This criterion led them to exclude 'nearly all verse written expressly for children, and most of the poetry written about children for grown people'. Nothing by *Watts or the *Taylors was put in the book, which opened with *Blake's 'Piping down the valleys wild' from *Songs of Innocence*, and included Milton's 'Song on May Morning', songs from *Shakespeare, many of Wordsworth's shorter poems, Keats's 'La Belle Dame Sans Merci', Tennyson's 'The Charge of the Light Brigade', Poe's 'The Raven', Matthew Arnold's 'The Forsaken Merman', and an abbreviated version of Coleridge's 'The Rime of the Ancient Mariner'. Patmore explained that 'in a very few instances, I have ventured to substitute a word or a phrase, when that of the author has made the piece in which it occurs unfit for children's reading.' New editions appeared in 1873 (with illustrations) and 1883.

Children's Hour The daily early evening radio programme for children transmitted by the British Broadcasting Corporation from 1922 to 1964. One of its first 'discoveries' (in 1928) was S. G. Hulme Beaman's *Toytown; other books to be helped to fame during the 1930s as a result of broadcast adaptations included Barbara Euphan Todd's *Worzel Gummidge stories. Books already enjoying success were broadcast, too, among them the *Swallows and Amazons series of Arthur *Ransome. During the early 1950s the popularity of Children's Hour was unabated; dramatizations included *Winnie-the-Pooh (with Norman Shelley as Pooh), the *Jennings stories of Anthony *Buckeridge, *Norman and Henry Bones, the Boy Detectives* by Anthony C. Wilson, a country series by Ralph Whitlock entitled *Cowleaze Farm*, 'Polly and Oliver' stories by David Scott *Daniell, and original plays by L. du Garde *Peach.

Children's Laureate *See* LAUREATE.

children's literature as academic study In the past few decades, children's literature has become a field of academic study in its own right. Academics write analyses of childrens' literature for both general and academic readership, and there are also undergraduate courses and postgraduate programmes in the subject. Much of this work started in the 1960s in Scandinavia and the English-speaking countries, but now research

and teaching in the field is being done all over the world.

Initially, some of the texts on this subject primarily explored different works or the history of children's literature, discussing what sorts of texts were published where and when, and why different topics or styles come into vogue at different times, and they also looked at what it means to write for children, and how this changes depending on the age of the intended audience. Indeed, a large number of books and articles on children's literature are still interested in such questions. Examples are Barbara E. Travers and John F. Travers' *Children's Literature: A Developmental Perspective*, and *Children's Literature: Approaches and Territories*, edited by Janet Maybin and Nicola J. Watson.

Other academic texts focus on specific genres and how they can be best understood. For instance, Jack *Zipes takes on fairy tales in his book, *Fairy Tales and the Art of Subversion*. Meanwhile, both Perry Nodelman's *Words and Pictures* and Maria Nikolajeva and Carole Scott's *How Picturebooks Work* help explain the connections between images and words, and how *picture books can be read and understood.

Still other works study particular authors, illustrators, and texts from a certain country or culture. An example here is *Dr. Seuss: An American Icon* by Philip Nel, in which he analyses the many contributions Theodor *Seuss Geisel made to the fields of both children's literature and art. The Casebook series published by Palgrave Macmillan includes a number of such books, each dedicated to an important children's author, such as Melvin *Burgess or Roald *Dahl.

Some academic works are more theoretical and/or philosophical, or connect the subject to other fields, such as psychology, linguistics, neuroscience, or multiculturalism. There are now works specifically about subjects like *translation, too: texts such as Riitta Oittinen's *Translating for Children*, Gillian Lathey's *The Role of Translators in Children's Literature: Invisible Storytellers*, or Emer O'Sullivan's *Comparative Children's Literature*, as well as edited collections, such as Jan Van Coillie and Walter P. Verschueren's *Children's Literature in Translation: Challenges and Strategies*. Many such books approach the translation of children's literature from a variety of angles. Some of the texts serve as case studies, analysing how a specific text/author/genre has been translated from one language to another (or

even several others). Another recent area of study is *gender and *sexuality in children's literature, with works such as *Are the Kids All Right?: The Representation of LGBTQ Characters in Children's and Young Adult Lit* by B. J. Epstein or Kathryn James' *Death, Gender and Sexuality in Contemporary Adolescent Literature*.

Alongside the proliferation of academic texts on books for children and young adults, some universities are also now beginning to teach children's literature as a degree subject of its own (at both undergraduate and postgraduate level), rather than simply including it as one component of a larger course.

Children's Newspaper, The Published weekly by *Harmsworth's Amalgamated Press from 22 March 1919 to 1 May 1965. It was edited by Arthur *Mee from its inception until his death in 1943.

Its forerunner was *The Little Paper*, published in the monthly serial re-issue of Mee's *Children's Encyclopaedia* (eventually known as *My Magazine*) from 1910. The *Children's Newspaper* proper was a twelve-page journal (later expanded to sixteen pages) which at first cost three-halfpence. Its news items resembled the contents of the *Children's Encyclopaedia*, in that they emphasized the achievements of heroic and ingenious individuals, with headlines like 'A NOBODY BECOMES A SOMEBODY: Wonderful Wireless Man of U.S.A.'. There were photo-pages (with subjects such as 'Painting the Forth Bridge' and 'Springtime in the Countryside'), a serial story, 'Picture-News and Time Map' (a map of the world with time differences and insets putting news stories in their geographical places), and 'The Editor's Table', a miscellany of anecdotes, jokes, and verses. The paper's political line during the 1930s was uncertain; for example, the issue for 11 January 1936 contains a doggerel verse attacking the Nazis for persecuting the Jews, but an editorial by Mee just over a month later includes this passage: 'The Germans are entitled to their own form of government, and if they like to make a hero of Herr Hitler have we a right to question their obedience?'

The paper's circulation was considerable from its earliest years, but it may be suspected that this popularity was the result of parental approval rather than of a great appetite for news among child readers.

Children's Prize, The Later *The Prize for Boys and Girls*, and finally *The Prize* (1863–

1931) A children's *magazine begun by the Revd J. Erskine Clarke, who had behind him the experience of five years publishing a 'little serial' and who went on to found *Chatterbox in 1866. The Children's Prize was at first firmly religious in tone, but not ponderously, and it mixed fact, fiction, verse, and occasional humour. It boasted a high and up-to-date standard of illustration. Nevertheless it was the periodical alighted on by *Ruskin when he chose in the February 1875 issue of Fors Clavigera to condemn, for its class consciousness, poor writing, small print, and general inappropriateness, 'the literature which cheap printing enables the pious to make Christmas presents of for a penny'.

Children's Rights Workshop A British radical group which came into existence in the 1970s to promote non-*sexist, non-*racist children's books. It set up the *Other Award, and the journal Children's Book Bulletin.

Child's Book of Saints, A (1898) By William *Canton, written for his daughter 'W.V.' (Winifred Veda) and published in the USA as W. V.'s Golden Legend. Illustrated by T. H. Robinson, brother of Charles and W. Heath *Robinson, it was one of the first modern books of *religious instruction to have literary quality.

Child's Companion, The A *magazine founded by the *Religious Tract Society in 1824. It contained stories, verses, information, and a serial, all related to religion, *Sunday school, or missionary activities. It survived under different titles, with its piety becoming less conspicuous, until 1932.

Child's Garden of Verses, A A collection of poems by Robert Louis *Stevenson, first published in 1885. The verses are both a description of childhood as seen by an adult, from the outside, and an attempt by Stevenson to re-create the sensations of his own childhood as he had felt them. The book is dedicated to Alison Cunningham, his nurse from his earliest days at his Edinburgh home. Many of the poems were written while he was ill in bed with suspected tuberculosis, and perhaps because of this they often look back to his frequent illnesses in childhood: 'When I was sick and lay a-bed, | I had two pillows at my head . . .'. Others record his fear of the dark as a child; yet bedtime leads to 'The pleasant land of counterpane', or (in another poem) 'The Land of Nod'. Not many of the poems are outstandingly memorable in themselves,

but, read as a sequence, the book is the most notable collection of serious poems to be written for children since *Original Poems, for Infant Minds (1804–5) by Ann and Jane *Taylor.

Stevenson began to write children's verses while at Braemar in Scotland during the summer of 1881, at the same period as he was working on *Treasure Island. He was inspired by Kate *Greenaway's Birthday Book for Children (1880), whose verses (by Mrs Sale Barker) he thought he could equal. He wrote about 14 poems at this time; by March 1883 there were about 48, which he proposed to publish in a small illustrated book, perhaps to be called Nursery Verses. He later chose the title Penny Whistles and, under this name, a collection of the poems was set up in type and proofs were printed in the autumn of 1883. Only two copies survive. Of these forty-eight poems, nine were not reprinted in A Child's Garden of Verses when it was eventually published in March 1885, now containing 64 poems.

The first edition was printed on high-quality paper but had no illustrations. In this form it was re-issued in July 1885 and again in 1888. In 1896, two years after Stevenson's death, an edition appeared with illustrations by Charles *Robinson—a beautifully produced book, published by John Lane, The Bodley Head. This might claim to be the definitive edition (it was re-issued in 1976 by the Scolar Press), but there have been other illustrated versions, including one of 1927 by Kate Elizabeth Olver, and one of 1966 by Brian *Wildsmith.

A Child's Garden of Verses inspired Walter *de la Mare to write *Songs of Childhood (1902).

Child's Guide to Knowledge, The (1825) By 'A Lady' (Fanny Umphelby, 1788–1852); a collection of questions and answers about subjects of general knowledge, on the model of *Mangnall's Questions and *Pinnock's Catechisms. It was originally published under the title 262 Questions and Answers. The questions were mainly about the physical world, e.g. the nature and manufacture of foodstuffs, clothes, etc. The Child's Guide was reprinted many times in the fifty years following its publication. Later editions had new matter added by the author's nephew Robert Ward.

Child's History of England, A By Charles *Dickens, first published in his magazine Household Words at intervals during 1851–3, and printed in book form in three volumes in 1852, 1853, and 1854. The idea originated in Dickens's desire to provide a *history book for

his own eldest son. His approach to history was vigorous and highly prejudiced. Henry VIII is described as 'a blot of blood and grease upon the History of England', and James I is referred to as 'His Sowship'. Queen Victoria 'is very good, and much beloved'.

Chimp and Zee See ANHOLT, LAURENCE.

CHIPPERFIELD, Joseph E. (Eugene) (1912–76) Prolific British writer of *animal stories who first made his name with *Storm of Dancerwood* (1948, revised 1967), the story of the friendship between an alsatian dog and a blind vixen. His many other books include *Ghost Horse: Stallion of the Oregon Trail* (1959) and *Banner, the Pacing White Stallion* (1972).

Chitty-Chitty-Bang-Bang: the magical car A series of stories for children by Ian Fleming (1908–64). *Chitty-Chitty-Bang-Bang* was first published in 1964 in three volumes, illustrated by John *Burningham. An omnibus edition appeared in 1971.

Chitty-Chitty-Bang-Bang is a 'twelve cylinder, eight litre, supercharged Paragon Panther', a remarkable motor car which can fly and turn itself into a hovercraft. Its owner is Commander Caractacus Potts, an inventor who has created sweets that whistle; he and his children Jeremy and Jemima make amazing journeys in the car and outwit the crook Joe the Monster.

A highly successful film of 1967 based on the stories had a screenplay by Roald *Dahl and songs by Richard and Robert Sherman, and a stage musical adaptation (with a book by Jeremy Sams) opened in the West End in 2002. There are recent sequels by Frank *Cottrell Boyce.

Chocolate War, The (1974) A novel by Robert *Cormier, set in a private Catholic boys' day-school in America. Brother Leon, left in charge of the school while the headmaster is away sick, plans a fund-raising effort in which the boys will sell 20,000 boxes of chocolates in the neighbourhood. He obtains the unofficial backing of the school's Mafia-like secret society, the Vigils, led by adolescent mobster Archie Costello. But neither Brother Leon nor the Vigils have reckoned with the obstinacy of a junior, Jerry Renault, who simply refuses to sell the chocolates. For a time Renault is a school hero; then an outcast, ripe for destruction. Four decades after publication, *The Chocolate War* remains one of the most powerful of all *young adult novels.

CHORPENNING, Charlotte (Lee Barrows) (1872–1955) Head of Children's Theatre at the Goodman Theatre, Art Institute of Chicago, from 1931 to 1952. She wrote nearly thirty *plays for children, largely adaptations of classic stories.

Chrestomanci (1977–2006) A series of seven books by Diana Wynne *Jones. Their intricate plotting, humour, and adventure are among Jones's best. With shades of *Doctor Who* and written long before *Harry Potter, they are set in the Twelve Related Worlds—a place where interrelated dimensions overlap and where magic exists. Each book stands alone, telling stories centred on a powerful wizard, the Chrestomanci. The series comprises: *Charmed Life* (1977), *The Magicians of Caprona* (1980), *Witch Week* (1982), *The Lives of Christopher Chant* (1988), *Conrad's Fate* (2005), *The Pinhoe Egg* (2006), and *Mixed Magics: Four Tales of Chrestomanci* (2000), though the ideal reading order is a highly contested issue.

CHRÉTIEN DE TROYES (late 12th cent.) French poet; see ARTHUR.

CHRISMAN, Arthur Bowie (1889–1953) American writer; his *Shen of the Sea* (1925), a set of stories inspired by Chinese folklore, won the *Newbery Medal.

Christie's Old Organ, or 'Home, Sweet Home' (1875) By Mrs O. F. *Walton, one of the most popular British *evangelical stories of its day. Old Treffy, a forlorn barrel-organist whose favourite tune is 'Home, Sweet Home', is befriended by a ragged orphan, Christie, who takes over the instrument when Treffy becomes too ill to play. Learning that he has only a month to live, Treffy, who knows nothing of religion, becomes fearful. Christie enlists the help of a chapel minister, ensures that his dying friend becomes convinced of salvation, and, after Treffy has died a holy death, himself becomes a Scripture-reader at the mission room.

Christmas Books A series of stories by Charles *Dickens. The first of them, *A Christmas Carol*, was written during 1843. It appeared in print that Christmas, and was so successful that he followed it up the next Christmas with *The Chimes*. In 1845 came *The Cricket on the Hearth*, subtitled 'A Fairy Tale of Home', in which a household spirit helps to arrange the lives of two poor families. The last two stories in the series were *The*

Battle of Life (1846) and *The Haunted Man* (1848).

Christmas Box, The A children's *annual, published in 1828 and 1829, edited by T. Crofton *Croker. The book has some claim to be the first annual for children in England. *The Christmas Box* contained an eclectic mix of stories, verses, plays, and articles, among them a brief history of the Napoleonic wars and the first publication of Scott's poem 'The Bonnets of Bonny Dundee', which is parodied in chapter 9 of *Through the Looking-Glass*. Contributory authors such as Maria *Edgeworth and Mary *Howtit, alongside the humorist and practical joker Theodore Hook, illustrate *The Christmas Box's* unusual mix of the comic and the moral, which prompted F. J. H. Darton to call it 'ahead of its time'. 'The History of Asim and Asgard', in the first volume, was probably the first appearance in an English children's book of a Norwegian folk tale.

Christmas Carol, A *See* CHRISTMAS BOOKS.

Christmas-Tree Land (1884) A story by Mrs *Molesworth.

CHRISTOPHER, John (C. S. Youd) (1922–2012) British author of *science fiction and *fantasy novels for adults and children. *The White Mountains* (1967) is the first volume in the *'Tripods'* tetralogy. The next John Christopher book for children was *The Lotus Caves* (1969), in which two boys escape from the boredom of life on a Moon research station and discover the Plant, an extra-intelligent growth which has created a domain in which humans can live a lotus-eating existence and never grow old. *The *Guardians* was published in 1970, followed by *The Prince in Waiting* (1970), *Beyond the Burning Lands* (1971), and *The Sword of the Spirits* (1972), which form a second trilogy, this time about an England which has reverted to a primitive, violent way of life. *Dom and Va* (1973) is a grim reconstruction of life among human tribes half a million years ago. *Wild Jack* (1974), set once again in a future England, concerns a modern *Robin Hood; *Empty World* (1977) is a *Robinsonnade about a teenager who is the lone survivor of a plague.

Christopher Robin In books by A. A. *Milne.

chromolithography *See* COLOUR; LITHOGRAPHY.

Chronicles of Narnia *See* NARNIA.

Chronicles of Pantouflia *See* PRINCE PRIGIO.

CHUKOVSKY, Kornei (N. I. Korneichuk) (1882–1970) Soviet children's author and defender of imaginative children's literature. His book *Malen'kie Deti* (1925, revised several times), which was translated into English as *From Two to Five* (1963), is a polemic against those in Russia who would deny children access to *nonsense, *fantasy, and *nursery rhymes. Chukovsky translated many English-language children's classics into Russian, including *Doctor Dolittle. Among his own children's books, which are written in vigorous comic verse, is *Krokodil*, a long narrative poem about a crocodile; *Tarakanishche* ('The Cockroach') (1924), a *fable in which the entire animal kingdom is terrified of a cockroach—until a sparrow gobbles it up; and *Moidodyr* ('The Washstand'), in which an animated washstand moralizes about little boys and cleanliness.

Chums A British boys' *magazine founded in 1892, with Sir Max Pemberton as first editor. Like the *Boy's Own Paper, which it competed with but never equalled in popularity, it was middle class, respectable, and approved by parents. It was full of *adventure, informative articles, and patriotism. In 1894 it ran *Treasure Island (the second time that *Stevenson's book had been serialized) 'with new and original illustrations'. It changed from weekly to monthly in 1932, published its annual only from 1934, and that ceased in 1941.

CHURCH, A. J. (Alfred John) (1829–1912) A grammar school headmaster who became Professor of Latin at University College, London, and wrote many versions of classical stories adapted for children. *Stories from Homer* was published in 1876, and *The Children's Odyssey* and *The Children's Iliad* in 1907. He also produced retellings of Virgil and other ancient writers, and wrote a number of children's *historical novels, mostly set in classical times.

CHURCH, Frederick Stuart (1842–1924) American illustrator, best remembered for his comic animal drawings which appeared in *Harper's Young People.

CHURCH, Richard (Thomas) (1893–1972) British poet and novelist who wrote seven children's books, including *The Cave* (1950), in which five boys are lost in a limestone cavern, and *Dog Toby: a frontier tale* (1950), the

story of a group of children and their dogs who live on either side of a national frontier but are unaware of its significance.

Church Mice, the Heroes of a series of adventures in *picture books by the British author-illustrator Graham Oakley (1929–), published from 1972 to 2000. The leaders of the mice are Arthur and Humphrey, and the stories also feature Sampson, the church cat, who has taken a vow never to eat the mice.

CIARDI, John (Anthony) (1916–86) American poet who produced a large number of books of verse for children, beginning with *The Reason for the Pelican* (1959). His children's poems are mostly comic, and some resemble the verses of Edward *Lear.

CILIP The UK's Chartered Institute of Library and Information Professionals, established in 2002 (through a merger of the Library Association and the Institute of Information Scientists) to support and advocate for the work of its members. CILIP is now the body that awards both the *Carnegie Medal and the *Kate Greenaway Medal, two high-profile book awards judged by a panel of professional librarians.

Cinderella The most popular of all *fairy stories. It first appeared in print in the format best known today in 1697 as one of the *Contes de ma mère l'Oye* of *Perrault, under the title *Cendrillon, ou la petite pantoufle de verre*.

Although there are many hundreds of variants of the Cinderella story, Perrault's version is the one most widely known to Anglo-American audiences. A gentleman with a good and virtuous daughter remarries a proud and haughty woman who has two daughters of the same nasty temperament. In the household the girl is made to perform menial tasks and to sit in the chimney corner when she has completed her work. This earns her the name Cendrillon / Cinderella. The King's son gives a ball, to which Cinderella's stepsisters are invited. Cinderella is distraught she cannot also attend the ball. When the stepsisters have left, Cinderella's godmother appears to facilitate the transformation of a pumpkin into 'a beautiful coach all gilded', six mice into horses, and six lizards into footmen. Finally she transforms Cinderella's rags into a beautiful dress and gives her 'a pair of slippers made of glass, the prettiest in the world.' Cinderella climbs into the coach and is warned that she must not stay at the ball beyond midnight, as at that instant her coach, horses, and servants will resume

their former shapes. At the ball the King's son falls in love with Cinderella and begs her to return to a second ball the next evening. Cinderella attends this ball also, but in her haste to leave by midnight loses one of her glass slippers. A few days later the prince announces that he will marry whoever is the owner of the foot for which the glass slipper was made. Despite searching the kingdom no owner is found. At Cinderella's house her stepsisters try to squeeze their feet into the slipper to no avail. Finally Cinderella asks to try and to the astonishment of all, the slipper fits perfectly. Cinderella's Godmother then reappears and 'having touched Cinderella's clothes with her wand, made them more magnificent than they had ever been before'. The sisters throw themselves at Cinderella's feet to beg forgiveness, which she readily gives. She is then taken to the prince, who marries her; she provides lodgings for the sisters in the palace, and on the day of her own wedding they are married to two *grands Seigneurs* of the court.

The earliest written appearance of a story resembling *Cinderella* was in the 9th cent. AD, in a Chinese collection of tales and folklore, the *Yu Yang Ts Tsu*, whose author said he had collected the story orally from a family servant. In this version, a girl named Yeh-hsien is brought up by a stepmother who ill-treats her and kills the fish who has befriended her. At this point a man comes down from the sky and tells the girl that the fish's bones will make her wishes come true. With the help of the bones, Yeh-hsien obtains fine clothes and golden shoes in which she goes to a festival. There she loses one shoe, which is found and sold to a king, who is intrigued by its smallness, and who eventually traces her. She appears before him wearing the shoes, 'beautiful as a heavenly being'; he makes her his chief wife, and the stepmother and her unpleasant daughter are killed by 'flying stones'.

The first European book to include a Cinderella-type tale was the *Pentamerone* (1634) of Basile. In this is found (Day 1, tale 6) the story of Zezolla, daughter of a widowed prince, whose stepmother treats her in the usual fashion. Zezolla's degradation to a menial at the kitchen grate earns her the nickname *La gatta cennerentola*, 'the Cat among the Cinders'. However, Zezolla acquires a magic date tree which has the power to dress her in magnificent clothes. She goes to a feast and is seen by a king, who fails to discover who she is. On a third feast day she lets slip a shoe, which is found and taken to him. After many attempts

to find the foot that it fits, Zezolla is at last traced; she is crowned queen, and her stepsisters depart from the court in a torment of jealousy.

In the early 19th cent., the Grimm brothers found a group of Cinderella tales in Hesse, from which they constructed their own version, *Aschenputtel*. In this, the source of the magic clothes is a hazel tree, planted by Aschenputtel on the grave of her own mother. When the stepsisters are trying to fit the shoe to their feet, one of them cuts off one of her own toes and the other slices off part of a heel in order to squeeze it on. Equally severe punishment is meted out at the end of the tale, where the stepsisters, rather than receiving forgiveness, have their eyes pecked out by doves and 'so they were punished for their wickedness and malice with blindness for the rest of their lives'.

These are only some of the best-known Cinderella variants; innumerable other tales based on the same motifs have been recorded. There are also variants of the Cinderella story where the perpetrator of the tyranny against the heroine is the father rather than the stepmother, often because of his sexual desire for his daughter. Perrault features one such story named *Peau d'asne* (Donkey Skin), which he published in 1694 shortly before his *Cendrillon* appeared in print. Joseph Jacobs's *Cat-Skin* (in *English Fairy Tales*, 1890) is another version in a similar vein.

Perrault's story was first published in English in 1729, in *Histories, or Tales of Past Times*. In the late 18th cent, it began to appear separately as a *chapbook, one of the earliest examples being *Cinderilla; or, the Little Glass Slipper*, a verse retelling with woodcuts on each page, published as a *miniature book by T. Evans of London c.1785. During the 19th cent. Perrault's 'Cendrillon' story became a favourite with producers of *pantomimes. More than ninety stage productions of the story were performed in Britain during the 19th cent., the first being at Drury Lane in 1804. The rise of the pantomime dame encouraged producers to give the parts of the 'Ugly Sisters', as they came to be known, to male actors. This in turn has affected their characterization in modern storybook versions, where they are often portrayed as grotesque to the point of absurdity. Yet most modern retellings retain Perrault's ending, in which the sisters, horrid as they may be, are allowed to join the *beau monde* at court and to live as happily ever after as Cinderella and her Prince Charming.

Circle of the Sciences, The A series of *books of instruction published by John *Newbery. The books were first issued between 1745 and 1748, and were frequently reprinted by Newbery and his successors. Subjects covered were Grammar, Rhetoric, Poetry, Geography, Chronology, Arithmetic, and Logic (including Metaphysics and Ontology). The books were lengthy treatises, usually composed in the question-and-answer format, but otherwise making few concessions to young readers.

CLA Book of the Year for Children Awarded annually by the Canadian Library Association for the best book by a Canadian citizen or permanent resident of Canada. Past winners include Brian *Doyle (a record four times); Kit *Pearson, and Kenneth *Oppel (three apiece); Jean *Little, Tim *Wynne-Jones, and Anne Laurel Carter (twice each); Sheila Burnford (for The *Incredible Journey*), Mordecai *Richler, and Christopher Paul *Curtis.

CLAPP, Patricia (1912–2003) American author of two notable *historical novels for young readers: *Constance: a story of early Plymouth* (1968) and *I'm Deborah Sampson: a soldier in the War of the Revolution* (1977). Both are the stories of adolescent girls, the first a fourteen-year-old who has come over on the *Mayflower*, the second a New Englander in the late 18th cent. (a real historical figure) who disguises herself as a man and fights in the Revolution. Patricia Clapp also wrote a number of *plays for children.

CLARE, Cassandra (1973–) Emerging from the online *Harry Potter *fan fiction world, American author Clare writes dark *young adult fantasy pitched perfectly for teens who want tortured heroes and love triangles, with angst and action more important than style. *City of Bones* (2007), first in the six-part *Mortal Instruments* series, is about Clary Frey, whose ordinary life in Manhattan is destroyed when she stumbles upon a group of tattooed Shadowhunters killing what she finds out is a demon. *Clockwork Angel* (2010), book one of *Infernal Devices*, goes back to Victorian London and the Shadowhunters' work there. A movie of *City of Bones* was released in 2013.

Clarice Bean Character in a series written and illustrated by Lauren *Child; the series combines both picture books and novels that feature Clarice Bean and her canny cast of friends. The first three picture books begin

with *Clarice Bean, That's Me* (1999), followed by *My Uncle Is a Hunkle, Says Clarice Bean* (2001; *Clarice Bean, Guess Who's Babysitting?* in the US) and *What Planet Are You From, Clarice Bean?* (2001). *Utterly Me, Clarice Bean* (2002) is Child's first novel that introduces Clarice Bean to an older audience, followed by *Clarice Bean Spells Trouble* (2004) and *Clarice Bean, Don't Look Now* (2006). These Clarice Bean novels also became the basis of Child's spin-off Ruby Redfort series in 2011.

Clarissa An eight-volume epistolary novel by *Richardson published in 1747–8. Clarissa, a young lady of good fortune, is wooed by the unscrupulous Lovelace. She is eventually won over and allows herself to be abducted, but afterwards dies of shame; Lovelace is killed in a duel by her cousin. A one-volume abridgement of *Clarissa*, intended for children, was issued by Francis *Newbery (nephew) in 1768 or 1769, and was reprinted several times. Other abridgements followed, and the book continued to be read by children during the 19th cent.

CLARK, Ann Nolan (1896–1995) American author of lyrical books about and for Native American children, who worked for forty years in the US Bureau of Indian Affairs. She 'quickly realized that there were no textbooks which Indian children could relate to', and wrote a book in free verse about their way of life, *In My Mother's House* (1941). She subsequently produced many readers for them, and wrote such novels about the lives of indigenous people in Latin America as *Secret of the Andes* (1952), which beat *Charlotte's Web* to the the *Newbery Medal, and *Santiago* (1955).

CLARK, Catherine Anthony (1892–1977) One of the first Canadian authors of *fantasy for children. Her six novels are set in the wilds of British Columbia, and usually describe the adventures of a boy and girl who become involved in a magical quest; they include *The Golden Pine Cone* (1950), *The Silver Man* (1958), and *The Hunter and the Medicine Man* (1966).

CLARK, Samuel (1810–75) Partner in the publishing house of *Darton and Clark. Clark, a Quaker, wrote many *books of instruction for children, especially in *geography. They include *The Book of the United Kingdom, written by Uncle John* (1841), *Reuben Ramble's Travels in the Western Counties of England* (1845), and *The Child's Treasury of Knowledge and Amusement* (c.1845). He modelled his style on the *Peter Parley books, and

sometimes used the Parley pseudonym; he also wrote as 'the Revd T. Wilson'.

CLARKE, J. Erskine Founder of *The *Children's Prize* and *Chatterbox*.

CLARKE, Mary Cowden *See* SHAKESPEARE.

CLARKE, Pauline (1921–2013) British children's author, best known for *The *Twelve and the Genii* (1962) (in the United States, *The Return of the Twelve*), which won her the *Carnegie Medal. She also wrote *historical novels, *adventure stories, and books for young children as 'Helen Clare'.

CLARKE, Rebecca Sophia *See* SOPHIE MAY.

CLEARY, Beverly (1916–) American children's novelist, perhaps best known as the creator of Ramona Quimby and her world. One of the best-loved children's writers of the 20th cent., Cleary published her first book, *Henry Huggins*, in 1950; this celebrated the lives of ordinary children in suburban Portland (where Cleary grew up), as they attempt various money-making schemes, which inevitably lead to trouble. The books are characterized by their gentle humour and satisfyingly simple plots. Five further books followed about Henry, his sister Beezus, and friends. One of the most memorable characters was eight-year-old Ramona, a neighbourhood child who often gets in Henry's way, about whom Cleary went on to write eight charming novels—for a slightly younger audience—most recently *Ramona's World* (1999).

Another skilfully drawn character is twelve-year-old Leigh Botts, who enters into a correspondence with his favourite author, Boyd Henshaw, and in so doing reveals information about the difficulties in his own life. The author encourages Leigh to keep a diary in which he can address and become reconciled to his insecurities, and move on from them. Funny and moving, *Dear Mr Henshaw* won the *Newbery Medal in 1984 and was followed, several years later, by an appealing but not especially necessary sequel, *Strider* (1991), about Leigh's new friendships and the challenges of looking after a dog rescued from a beach.

Amongst Cleary's other work, *The Mouse and the Motorcycle* (1965) describes the adventures of a mouse, Ralph, who learns to ride a toy motorcycle; and *Fifteen* (1956) was a groundbreaking book about adolescent romance, written before *young adult fiction

became a recognised genre, and before explicit books such as Judy Blume's *Forever*.

CLEAVER, Hylton (Reginald) (1891–1961) Prolific British writer of *school stories who was educated at St Paul's School, London, and had his first story accepted by *Captain* when he was twenty-two. Most of his stories were about Harley or Greyminster Schools; his first novel was *Roscoe Makes Good* (1921). For many years he was a sports writer for the London *Evening Standard*; he also wrote plays and some adult fiction.

CLEAVER, Vera (1919–93) and **Bill** (1920–81) Husband-and-wife American writers for young people. Vera was born in Virgil, South Dakota, and grew up in Florida, where she and her husband later made their home.

The Cleavers' books are chiefly set in the rural South of America, and are in the 'Southern Gothic' tradition of such writers as Carson McCullers and Flannery O'Connor. *Ellen Grae* (1967), their first novel, takes place in the small town of Thicket, Florida, peopled by eccentric and lethargic townsfolk whose lives are virtually stagnant. Ellen, lodging with the McGruders while her parents get a divorce, takes mental refuge in the telling of tall stories, but finds that real life is more horrific than anything in her fantasies. *Lady Ellen Grae* (1968) is an unremarkable sequel, but in *Grover* (1970), again set in Thicket and including Ellen Grae in its cast, the Cleavers produced another striking book. At first, Grover has something of Tom Sawyer and Huckleberry Finn in him; he likes to slip away from his responsibilities and go fishing in his boat, or get into comic scrapes with his friends. Then his mother, dying of cancer and unable to face the pain, shoots herself, and Grover has to cope with his father's grief and refusal to accept help.

All the Cleavers' work is founded on a reconsideration of the traditional plots, attitudes, and heroes and heroines (especially heroines) of American 'realistic' children's fiction. The central character in a typical Cleaver book is usually an adolescent girl whose family is having to adjust to new circumstances—most notably Mary Call Luther in *Where the Lilies Bloom* (1969), the Cleavers' most widely read novel, which is about a family trying to make a living collecting medicinal plants in the mountains of North Carolina. Mary Call, in this book and its sequel *Trial Valley* (1977), keeps the family together after her father's death, but does it through real strength of character, not simply through *Pollyanna-ish cheeriness. Delpha in *Delpha Green and Company* (1972), the daughter of a failed restaurant-owner turned preacher, behaves in exactly the manner made famous by Pollyanna and the heroines of *Rebecca of Sunny-Brook Farm*, *Anne of Green Gables*, and a host of similar books, but eventually she learns that she must 'do away with the always-cheerfulness'.

Dust of the Earth (1975) presents a family notably lacking in the loving warmth that was traditional in American juvenile fiction. The Cleavers' harshest book, *The Mimosa Tree* (1970), echoes 19th-cent. *evangelical novels about waifs in big cities (e.g. *The *Lamplighter*), but the Cleavers make something very different of their material. Marvella Profitt comes to Chicago with her blind, helpless father and her younger brothers and sisters. They have been forced out of their backwoods farm and have no money; the promised Government assistance does not materialize, and Marvella and one of her brothers turn to petty crime to keep the family alive. Retribution does not come upon them (as it undoubtedly would have done in 19th-cent. stories); they simply decide for themselves, after a time, that this way of life is morally unacceptable and go back to the country.

The Cleavers' other books include *The Whys and Wherefores of Littabelle Lee* (1973), *Queen of Hearts* (1978), and *A Little Destiny* (1979), all of which are about adolescent girls rising to the challenge of apparently impossible family situations. Their fiction is widely recognized as rising far above the level of most early American writing for teenagers.

CLEMENS, S. L. *See* TWAIN, MARK.

CLEMENT, Rod (1961–) Australian political cartoonist and picture-book author/illustrator, known for the strong compositions of his illustrations with extensive use of white space in his books. His work is humorous and offers a fresh view of the world. His most popular book is *Edward the Emu* (1988), written by Sheena Knowles. *Counting on Frank* (1990), an Honour Book for *CBCA Picture Book of the Year 1991, is about a boy who loves to calculate and count—he knows how many humpback whales would fit in his house and how long it would take to fill his bathroom with water.

Clever Polly and the Stupid Wolf
(1955) By Catherine *Storr, this is a lively

collection of stories featuring Polly, a recognizably true-to-life little girl, and her encounters with a very stupid wolf. Their continued appeal lies not just in the characterization of the two main characters but in the narrative style, which lends itself to being read aloud. The reassuring everyday setting combined with references to familiar wolf-based *fairy tales adds to the attraction. Further stories about Polly and the wolf appeared in *The Adventures of Polly and the Wolf* (1957) and *Last Stories of Polly and the Wolf* (1990).

CLEWES, Dorothy (Mary) (1907–2003) Prolific British children's author of books for all age-groups, ranging from a *Henry Hare* series for the youngest (1950 onwards) to problem fiction such as *Missing from Home* (1975), which is about a broken marriage.

Cliff House The girls' school attended by *Bessie Bunter. It featured in *School Friend* (1919–29), and in other papers for girls published by *Harmsworth's Amalgamated Press.

CLIFFORD, Martin A pseudonym of Charles *Hamilton, used for his *Tom Merry Stories.

CLIFFORD, Mrs W. K. *See* ANYHOW STORIES.

CLIFTON, Lucille (1936–2010) African-American poet who produced verse *picture books about a black child named Everett Anderson, beginning with *Some of the Days of Everett Anderson* (1970), illustrated by Evaline *Ness. She also wrote prose stories for children.

Cloudy with a Chance of Meatballs
(1978) A picture book by American author Judi Barrett, illustrated by Ron Barrett. A man tells his grandchildren a story about a town called Chewandswallow, where food falls from the sky at mealtimes. But when the weather pattern changes, the precipitation grows to dangerous proportions and the townspeople must flee to a place where their food is dispensed by more conventional means. There are two sequels, *Pickles to Pittsburgh* (2000) and *Planet of the Pies* (2013). *Cloudy with a Chance of Meatballs* was voted one of the Top 100 Picture Books of all time in a 2012 *School Library Journal* poll and was adapted for a 2009 feature film.

Clown (1995) A completely wordless picture book by Quentin *Blake, in which a pile of toys is thrown into the rubbish, but the toy clown leaps out again and goes off on an adventure across the big city in search of someone who can help him save his friends. An expert piece of storytelling—even by Blake's particularly high standards—full of wit and movement, and one of the finest examples of what narrative pictures can do.

COATSWORTH, Elizabeth (Jane) (1893–1986) American author of some ninety books for children published between 1927 and 1975. She first attracted widespread notice with *The Cat Who Went to Heaven* (1930), the story of an oriental artist commissioned to paint the Buddha for a temple, whose cat works its way into the picture and so achieves eternal bliss; the book won the *Newbery Medal. It was the product of a year's journeying in the East. Coatsworth's travels are also reflected in such books as *Troll Weather* (1967) and *The Wanderers* (1972), which are respectively about Norway and Ireland. But her principal territory in fiction is America, especially Maine, where from 1932 she made her home with her naturalist husband Henry Beston (himself the author of several children's books). *Away Goes Sally* (1934) is the first of a series of five 'Sally' books, *family stories set in the years following the American Revolution; it tells how Sally's aunt and uncle move up to Maine from Massachusetts by putting a house on sledge-runners, so that the aunt need never leave her own fireside. Other books by Elizabeth Coatsworth include *Here I Stay* (1938), a novel for older readers about Margaret Winslow, a girl who insists on remaining on her father's Maine farm after his death, despite the fact that everyone else is moving West. She also wrote an 'Incredible Tale' series about New England, of which the first book was *The Enchanted* (1951), and several books of *poetry for children.

Cobwebs to Catch Flies: *or, Dialogues in Short Sentences, Adapted to Children from the Age of Three to Eight Years* A book to aid the teaching of reading by Eleanor *Fenn, first published by John *Marshall *c.*1783. The first volume consists of sentences with, at first, no word longer than three letters, gradually increasing to six letters. Each dialogue is on a feature of daily life: 'The Cat', 'The Morning', 'The Window', etc. The second volume introduces more elaborate topics, and gradually takes the reader up to four-syllable words. Each chapter has a *woodcut headpiece. Besides being reprinted by Marshall a number of times, the book was pirated by other publishers and continued to appear in print throughout the 19th cent.

Cockatoos (1992) A counting book by Quentin *Blake. Professor Dupont has ten cockatoos, who decide to play a trick on him and hide themselves—hilariously—around the house, leaving the reader to find them in the pictures and count up: one cockatoo in the dining-room, two cockatoos in the kitchen, three cockatoos in the bedroom, and so on.

Cocker's Arithmetic A *book of instruction which first appeared in 1678 and was ascribed to Edward Cocker (1631–75), schoolmaster and arithmetician; it was published after his death under the editorship of his friend John Hawkins. The book remained very popular throughout the 18th cent., and eventually more than 100 editions were printed in the British Isles. Cocker was also celebrated as a writing master, and his name appeared on the title page of nearly thirty *copybooks.

COCKETT, Mary (1915–97) Prolific British author of stories for young children, including a *Jonathan and Felicity* series (1954 onwards), which resembles *Janet and John*, and a set of *Joppy Stories* (1972).

Cock Robin Subject of a *nursery rhyme which was often printed as a separate miniature *chapbook from the late 18th to the mid-19th cent., usually under the title *The Death and Burial of Cock Robin*. It has been suggested that the rhyme refers to the downfall of Robert Walpole's ministry in 1742, and it certainly first appeared in print at this period, the first four verses being included in *Tommy Thumb's Pretty Song Book* (1744) and the entire rhyme being published c.1770. On the other hand, certain features of its language have been taken to suggest that it may be much older, and some commentators believe that it may have had its origin in a myth, possibly the death of the *Norse god Balder.

COFFIN, Charles Carleton (1823–96) New England writer and war correspondent in the American Civil War who wrote a number of books for children in which American *history was vividly recounted. These include *The Boys of '76* (1876), set in 1776 during the Revolutionary War, and *The Boys of '61* (1881), a record of his own observations and experiences during the Civil War. He wrote in the style of a popular journalist, often using the present tense to bring his narrative alive, and not troubling to disguise his pro-Union feelings.

COKE, Desmond *See* BENDING OF A TWIG, THE.

COLE, Babette (1950–2017) An award-winning English illustrator, author, and picture-book creator, best known for her *Princess Smartypants* series (the first of which was published in 1986) and *Prince Cinders* (1987)—a rebellious and subversive take on traditional fairy tales. Cole is also well known for her irreverent take on 'issues' such as sex, divorce, death, and puberty but always in a way that is distinctively fun and zany—and completely her own. One of her most successful books, *Mummy Laid an Egg!* (1994), features a double-page spread full of imaginative illustrations of couples enjoying themselves in a variety of positions. Cole won the *Kurt Maschler Award for *Drop Dead!* (1996)—a controversial take on growing up and getting old.

COLE, Sir Henry (1808–82) Editor of *The *Home Treasury* series of books under the pseudonym 'Felix Summerly'. Cole began in the 1840s to write a series of handbooks on celebrated buildings in London, based largely on materials in the Public Record Office, where he worked for many years. For these he used the nom de plume 'Felix Summerly'. At the same time, the wants of his eight children encouraged him to initiate the *Home Treasury* series, which was notable for its revival of a number of *fairy stories that had fallen into disrepute in the earlier part of the 19th cent. He also produced the first English Christmas card, issued in 1846 at 'Summerly's Home Treasury Office'. It pictured a large family eating and drinking merrily. The designer was J. C. Horsley, who illustrated some of the *Home Treasury* books. Cole also helped to initiate the National Course of Art Instruction, which was taken by, among others, Kate *Greenaway.

Cole Hawlings In *The *Box of Delights* by John *Masefield.

COLERIDGE, Sara (1802–52) Daughter of Samuel Taylor Coleridge and wife of Henry Nelson Coleridge (her cousin), Sara wrote *Pretty Lessons in Verse, for Good Children* (1834). The book was partly modelled on the verses of Ann and Jane *Taylor, though Mrs Coleridge deplored the 'pictures of mental depravity, bodily torture, and . . . adult sorrow' which she found in some of the Taylors' work, and intended that her own volume should contain 'nothing but what is bright and joyous'. Her verses were vigorous and unaffected, if a little

banal at times. The best known poem in it is that beginning 'January brings the snow | Makes our feet and fingers glow.' Mrs Coleridge was also the author of *Phantasmion* (1837), a lengthy *fairy story.

Cole's Funny Picture Book A celebrated Australian miscellany of amusement, humour, good advice, and puzzles, in words and pictures, compiled for family entertainment and first published on Christmas Eve 1879. The originator was Edward William Cole (1832–1918) of Cole's Book Arcade in Melbourne, an enterprising and eccentric entrepreneur whose deeds included advertising for a wife on the front page of a newspaper—and getting one. The book is said to have sold a thousand copies on the day of publication, and it would be reissued regularly for more than a century afterwards. Cole also produced a *Funny Picture Book No. 2* and *No. 3*.

COLFER, Eoin (1965–) Internationally acclaimed Irish author, who was first inspired to write by the Viking stories he was told in primary school. His books are quirky, funny and intelligent—and though his name is most famous for the *Artemis Fowl* (1999) series, featuring the best non-heroic hero ever (he's a genius criminal mastermind—and thirteen-years-old), all Colfer's books are worth reading, from those for younger readers, such as *The Legend of Spud Murphy* (2004), to *Benny and Omar* (1998) set in Tunisia. In 2009 he completed a follow-up to Douglas Adams's *The *Hitchhiker's Guide to the Galaxy* series, *And Another Thing . . .* and in 2013 launched a new series with *W.A.R.P.*, about an FBI witness relocation programme which relocates people to Victorian London and one of the teen agents who ends up back in time, being chased by a super-villain.

Collection of Pretty Poems For the Amusement of Children Three Feet High, by Tommy Tagg, Esq., A (?1756) Published by John *Newbery; an anthology of some sixty pieces of verse, mostly anonymous, each set below a detailed illustrative *woodcut. They are on such topics as 'The Vanity of Ambition', 'The Grasshopper', 'A Printer composing the Lilliputian Magazine', 'How to Laugh', 'Repentance', 'A Stingy Beau', and 'The Road to Riches'.

COLLINS, Suzanne American author of *The *Hunger Games*.

Collins' Magazine for Boys and Girls *See* YOUNG ELIZABETHAN.

COLLODI, Carlo (Carlo Lorenzini) (1826–90) Author of *Pinocchio*. He was born in Florence and became a journalist by profession; 'Collodi' was the name of his mother's home town. He took part in the struggle for Italian independence, and founded a satirical magazine, *Il lampione*. He was also a theatrical censor. In 1875 he decided to write for children, because 'grownups are too hard to satisfy.' He translated *Perrault's tales, then wrote an original story, *Giannettino* (1876), the first of a series of books in which instruction in various subjects was conveyed by means of amusing tales. *Pinocchio* began to appear as a serial in 1881 and was published as a book two years later. Lorenzini's publisher is said to have made a fortune out of it, but Lorenzini himself died too early to witness its international success.

colour in children's books Experiments in printing more than one colour on a page took place early in the development of each of the printing techniques. Gutenberg and his associates printed in two colours from woodblocks, and by the 17th cent. *copperplates were sometimes carefully inked by brush in different colours each time they were used. By the beginning of the 19th cent. coloured aquatints, commonly of views such as a watercolourist might paint, were being printed for the adult market; *Blake had invented his own idiosyncratic method of colour printing; and the possibilities of multi-coloured printing from engraved wood blocks were recognized, though the number of separate colour blocks then thought necessary, in some cases 30 for a single page, made this, too, a luxury process. Until almost the middle of the 19th cent. only one way of achieving coloured books was generally cheap enough for the children's market: the application of colour by hand.

Hand-colouring was commercial because for the most part it was done by cheap labour, often children, using production-line methods, sometimes with stencils to speed their work further. But even hand-coloured illustrations did not appear in commercial children's books until the early 19th cent. The first publisher to produce them regularly with notably pleasing results was John *Harris; he and his contemporaries generally printed the outlines for colouring from copper or other metal engravings, though some cheaper and cruder

books of the time contained hand-coloured *woodcuts.

At its best hand-colouring could produce delightful results, the water-colours having a delicacy scarcely equalled by later and more sophisticated processes. But by the mid-19th cent. hand-colouring was competing with imported cheap lithographed books, and was near the end of its surprisingly long commercial life.

The expression 'Penny Plain, Twopence Coloured' has given rise to the belief that hand-coloured children's books of the early 19th cent. were very cheap. The phrase, which is in fact the title of an essay on *toy theatres by R. L. *Stevenson, is misleading; for example, the early juvenile publications of John Harris cost 'One Shilling plain, and Eighteen-pence coloured'. The high price of coloured books at this period meant that many purchasers chose the plain version, took it home, and coloured it themselves.

The first colour-printing method cheap enough to rival hand-colouring was *lithography, which became increasingly efficient during the first quarter of the 19th cent. The name 'chromolithography' was coined for the French patent application in 1837, and by the 1840s it was the obvious process for cheap, mass-produced colour books for children. Many of those first seen on the English market came from printers in Germany, where the process was invented; *Struwwelpeter was among the earliest. By the 1860s English printers were turning out chromolithographed toy books in large numbers.

Meanwhile colour-printing from wood blocks also made progress. George Baxter's wood block process was used for the frontispiece to *Caroline Mordaunt* (1835) by Mrs *Sherwood, published by *Darton (see GOVERNESS); this and another book by Mrs Sherwood which Darton brought out the same year (*Social Tales for the Young*) are the first known instances of printed colouring in English children's books. From 1845 the same publisher's *Peter Parley's Annual* (see PETER PARLEY'S MAGAZINE) had plates in colour. From around 1845 colour printed from *wood engravings became commoner; Sir Henry Cole's *Home Treasury* series was available coloured, as were some of Joseph Cundall's *Gammer Gurton's Story Books.

In the 1860s Edmund *Evans's outstanding work in colour printing from wood brought good-quality colour printing into children's books at all prices, and the strangely prolonged supremacy of monochrome came to an end. For a while in the 1860s hand-colouring, lithography, and wood engraving competed on near equal terms (as far as cost was concerned) in children's book illustration, but hand-colouring soon dropped out, lithography was generally eschewed by the best artists, and wood engraving in its turn had a life-span longer than might have been expected.

The final innovation of the 19th cent. was the introduction of coloured half-tone photomechanically produced blocks. The earliest children's books using this process colour work, such as those illustrated by Arthur *Rackham, were luxuries, gift books probably only to be looked at under adult supervision. Their plates were subtle and sumptuous, and the process required that they be printed on coated, shiny paper, more expensive than, and obtrusively different from, the rougher paper generally used for text. (Beatrix *Potter's books were printed entirely on coated paper, text included.) However, by the beginning of the 20th cent. most of the techniques for producing modern colour-illustrated children's books had been mastered.

In the 1930s offset-lithography became the most popular and economical method of reproducing colour in *picture books, early examples being, in France, Jean de Brunhoff's *Babar stories (1931 onwards) and the *Père Castor series (1932 onwards), and, in Britain, Kathleen Hale's *Orlando the Marmalade Cat* (1939).

Colour printing today is mostly done by CMYK 'colour separation', with digital scans to split the image into three colours; the three separated images can then be printed in combinations of cyan, magenta, and yellow (and black) inks, an unsurpassable technique that will doubtless itself be surpassed in due course, too.

COLUM, Padraic (1881–1972) Irish poet, playwright, and man of letters, born in Longford, the son of the master of the town workhouse. In 1914 he emigrated to the United States, and while there wrote a number of children's books. These include *The King of Ireland's Son* (1916), a collection of *Irish folk tales woven into one narrative, *The Adventures of Odysseus and the Tale of Troy* (1918), *The Children of Odin: a book of Northern myths* (1920), *The Golden Fleece and the Heroes Who Lived before Achilles* (1921) (all these were illustrated by Willy *Pogány), and *The Island of the Mighty* (1924), retellings of stories from *The *Mabinogion*. He also wrote original fiction for children, including *The Peep-Show Man* (1925).

Columbus, voyages of See CAMPE.

COLWELL, Eileen H. (1904–2002) Pioneer British children's librarian who studied at University College, London, worked in Bolton, and in 1926 moved to Hendon in North London. There was no *library service for children there, so she established one, and it subsequently became famous. In 1937 she helped to found the Association of Children's Librarians, and was its first secretary. She edited many collections of stories for children, and also wrote a book on *storytelling (1980).

Come Hither, *a collection of rhymes and poems for the young of all ages* An anthology compiled, with an introductory story and notes, by Walter *de la Mare, first published in 1923, with *wood engravings by Alec Buckels. An expanded edition, without illustrations, appeared in 1928; a third, with wood engravings by Diana Bloomfield, in 1960.

Come Hither is remarkable first of all for the range of poems it includes: anonymous medieval verse and children's *games-rhymes jostle with pieces by Robert Frost, Thomas Hardy, and Edward Thomas and other modern poets. (De la Mare admitted that he had included one or two 'bits of rhymes' of his own in the book, over the word 'Anon.') The introduction, a typical de la Mare short story, describes how a boy named Simon discovers an old house, Thrae, whose master, Nahum Taroone, is away from home; his aunt (or possibly mother) Miss Taroone welcomes Simon and allows him the freedom of Nahum's room, which is in a tower; here he discovers many books, of which his favourite is a volume of poetry entitled *Theotherworldie.* From this he copies the poems that he has particularly come to love. Theresa Whistler, de la Mare's biographer, points out that 'Thrae' is an anagram of Earth, and 'Nahum Taroone' (phonetically) of 'human nature'. The notes that conclude *Come Hither* were originally meant to be brief and to the point, but (in Whistler's words) 'turned into a whole extra anthology, a kind of ruminating discursive conglomerate'. Among the first readers of *Come Hither* was W. H. Auden, then a schoolboy starting to write poetry: 'It taught me at the start that poetry does not have to be great or even serious to be good.'

COMENIUS, John Amos (Komenský, Jan Amos) (1592–1670) Educational reformer and author of an innovatory book for children. He was born in Moravia and became a Protestant pastor, but had to flee his home during a religious persecution. He worked as a teacher in Poland, visited England in the hope of establishing a college on his 'pansophist' system of education, and lived for a time in Sweden. He wrote many textbooks and works on education. His *Orbis Sensualium Pictus* (1658) was the outcome of his being asked to reorganize a grammar school in Hungary; on his arrival, he found the pupils so ignorant that he began to devise this *picture book which even the most unlettered child could read and learn from.

Comenius believed that universal education would produce a Utopian society. He argued that a pupil must observe a thing with his senses before he can grasp it by means of words; hence his belief in the importance of pictures in books. His *Janua Linguarum Reserata* (The Gate of Tongues Unlocked) (1631) was widely approved as a great advance in the method of teaching languages.

comics The overall Anglophone term for the medium that includes *graphic novels, comic books, *BD, *fumetti,* *manga, *historietas,* and more. They have been defined by the shorthand 'sequential art' (Will Eisner and Scott McCloud), and have predecessors in cave drawings, Greek vases, and the Bayeux Tapestry. Though the critical debate is still ongoing, one of the origins of the medium is identified in 18th-cent. England, with William Hogarth's sets of engravings telling a satirical story, among them 'A Rake's Progress'. In the first half of the 19th cent., a Swiss schoolmaster, Rodolphe Töpffer, made comic illustrated novels for his pupils, with fanciful happenings and grotesque figures that anticipated modern technique. Another precursor of the modern comics medium was Wilhelm Busch's *Max und Moritz* (1865).

The first British comic to appear regularly was *Ally Sloper's Half Holiday* (1884 onwards), which was published in London by the *Dalziel Brothers; it featured the adventures of a gin-drinking and disreputable proletarian loafer, and was aimed at office boys and the like. In 1890 *Harmsworth launched *Comic Cuts* and *Chips,* which were intended to catch the *penny dreadful Market; like other early comics, they contained many one-picture jokes, as well as comic strips. *Chips* featured Wearie Willie and Tired Timmie, a pair of tramps. *Chips* and *Comic Cuts* survived until 1953.

After the arrival of the first Harmsworth comics many British imitators appeared. The

first to be unequivocally for children was *Rainbow (1914 onwards), which was in full colour and featured *Tiger Tim and the Bruin Boys; it lasted until the 1950s, as did *Tiger Tim's Weekly* (1920 onwards). At the same time national newspapers began long-running comic strips within their adult newspapers, such as *Rupert Bear. The 1920s saw the arrival of *Film Fun*, containing the supposed adventures of film stars such as Laurel and Hardy. Shortly before the Second World War the Dundee firm of D. C. *Thomson launched *Dandy* and *Beano*, which brought a new roughness of humour into the comic, and featured such outrageous characters as Desperate Dan, Dennis the Menace, Roger the Dodger, Beryl the Peril, Minnie the Minx, and Pansy Potter. Harmsworth's Amalgamated Press responded with *Radio Fun*, a tougher and cruder version of *Film Fun*, and with *Knockout*, a very Thomson-like production. More titles began after the war and in the 1950s, including *The Tiger* with Roy of the Rovers.

In 1950 Hulton Press, publishers of *Picture Post*, entered the comic field with *Eagle*, which was soon joined by several companion papers. The 1960s saw the death of many long-established British comics, and such as survived were in many cases produced by the giant International Publishing Corporation, which absorbed the Amalgamated Press and numerous other concerns. Thomson's, however, remained independent, producing *Beano*-like comics, such as *Beezer*, as well as romantic picture-strip publications. There are also comics based on television serials and film adaptations, with the incredibly popular IDW Publishing *My Little Pony: Friendship is Magic* reaching some of the highest peaks in sales of licensed comics during 2013. A new weekly comic, *The Phoenix*, was launched in Britain in 2011 by David Fickling, funded by subscription and mixing humour, adventure, and text stories. From its second year it became available worldwide as an iPad *app.

Comics in Britain have generally been regarded as either for children or for adults. In America there is on the whole no such sharp division. Moreover, American comic art has traditionally been disseminated not in the form of the British 'comic' (a separate weekly illustrated tabloid) but in syndicated newspaper strips and comic books, either in single-issue 'floppies' or trades, both paperback and hardcover. Some identify the first true American comic strip in 'Little Bears and Tigers', which ran in the *San Francisco Examiner* from 1892. The first celebrated character to feature in a strip was The Yellow Kid, who initially appeared in the *New York World* in 1896. The *Katzenjammer Kids*, direct descendants of *Max und Moritz*, were first created in the *New York Journal* in 1897; their strip is the oldest still in existence. 'Krazy Kat', for many years regarded as the highest achievement of US comic strip art, was the creation of George Herriman, and ran from 1910. Krazy Kat, Ignatz Mouse, and the 'policeman' Offisa Pupp form a triangle of unrequited love, set against a surrealistic background. Other celebrated American strips of the early and mid-20th cent., include *'Little Orphan Annie' (1924 onwards), 'Buck Rogers' (from 1929 as a comic strip), 'Dick Tracy' (1931 onwards), 'Flash Gordon' and *Li'l Abner* (both 1934 onwards), and 'Peanuts' (1950 onwards), which includes the dog *Snoopy. It has been argued that American comic books are descendants of the *dime novels, which led to the creation of the *Superhero genre, with characters such as *Superman (1938 onwards) and *Batman (1939 onwards). Various screen cartoon figures also feature in comic books, e.g. *Bugs Bunny, *Tom and Jerry, *Transformers, Adventure Time*, and other popular TV animated series.

Comics as a medium have expanded their serialized, printed form to include webcomics, digital distribution, motion comics, original graphic novels (i.e. not tied to any existing narrative or series), biographies, autobiographies and memoirs, silent comics, abstract comics, and multiple adaptations of other media.

Notable and distinguished creators in different incarnations of the medium include *Hergé, creator of the *Tintin BD series, Raymond *Briggs in such books as *Fungus the Bogeyman*, Neil *Gaiman and his extremely popular *Sandman* series, Osamu Tezuka, creator of *Astro Boy* and multiple other manga series, and many, many more. Current wide interest in the form is reflected in the books about it, such as George Perry and Alan Aldridge, *The Penguin Book of Comics* (1971), Maurice Horn (ed.), *The World Encyclopaedia of Comics* (1976), and Randy Duncan and Matt Smith, *The Power of Comics: History, Form and Culture* (2009).

In the past, there has been much criticism of comics, especially during the *horror comic vogue of the 1950s; but they now attract less hostility than do television or action video

games, and have become study subjects in academic institutions, highly valued by fans and collectors, who pay large sums for rare back issues, and the basis for mainstream media, from TV to cinema.

CONNOR, Ralph (Revd **Charles William Gordon**) (1860–1937) Canadian author of books about pioneer life, sometimes set in Glengarry County, Ontario. Two of them, *The Man from Glengarry* (1901) and *Glengarry Schooldays* (1902), were very popular with children, though they are spoiled for modern readers by the saccharine portrayal of the central characters.

Contes de ma mère l'Oye A collection of *fairy stories by *Perrault, in which were first set down *Bluebeard, *Cinderella, *Diamonds and Toads, *Hop o' my Thumb, *Little Red Riding-Hood, *Puss in Boots, *Riquet à la houppe, and The *Sleeping Beauty. The book, originally published in 1697 as *Histoires ou contes du temps passé*, was translated into English by Robert Samber as *Histories, or Tales of Past Times* (1729). This translation was responsible for the introduction of these stories to England, and eventually for the adoption of the name *Mother Goose into the English language.

There are two views as to what were Perrault's sources for the stories. According to the first, he took them from popular tradition; according to the second, he acquired them from earlier literary versions in French and Italian. The first was the view accepted by Perrault's contemporaries, and it is still widely held today. Yet there is no trace of any of the stories before 1697 in the *livres de colportage*, the French *chapbooks, in which most popular tales that were in circulation appeared sooner or later. Perrault's fairy stories were only printed in these books after his collection of them had been published. Moreover, he needed to look no further than certain literary works of the 16th and 17th cents. to find versions of four of his tales. The anonymous French *romance *Perceforest* (Paris, 1528), the *Piacevoli Notti* ('Delightful Nights') of Gianfrancesco Straparola (Venice, 1550–3), and the *Cunto de li Cunti* (Tale of Tales), a collection of fairy stories in the Neapolitan dialect by Giambattista Basile, generally known as the *Pentamerone and published in 1634–6, contain between them stories which closely resemble *The Sleeping Beauty, Puss In Boots, Diamonds and Toads*, and *Cinderella*. (The individual articles on these stories

provide a detailed discussion of their sources.) It is not improbable that Perrault knew *Perceforest* and the *Piacevoli Notti*. Though the *Pentamerone* was not accessible to him, it was well known in Italy, and stories from it may have been told to him by an Italian in his circle of friends in Paris. A source for a fifth tale, *Riquet à la houppe*, may have been a novel published a year before Perrault's *Contes* appeared.

Against the view of Perrault's sources being chiefly literary is the fact that nothing closely resembling three of his tales, *Little Red Riding Hood, Hop o' my Thumb*, and *Bluebeard*, can be found in literature earlier than the appearance of his book, while stories much like *Bluebeard* seem to have been in oral circulation in Europe before Perrault's time. Nor can there be any doubt that the basic motifs of his tales are all found in early literature and mythology, and may therefore be regarded as a part of popular tradition.

Moreover his vocabulary, while it includes many literary or poetic words, is also largely of the kind that 17th-cent. dictionaries classed as 'populaire' or 'de bas usage'. While the inclusion of such words may itself have been a literary or poetic device, designed to give an appearance of simplicity, it might also be taken as an indication that the stories were collected at least partly from oral tradition, and that they may have been told to Perrault or his children.

It has often been stated that Perrault's stories first appeared in print in the pages of a periodical, *Recueil de pièces curieuses et nouvelles*, published by Moetjens of The Hague between 1694 and 1701, but it is now generally accepted that this was a piracy of the Paris printings of the tales. Claude Barbin published the first edition of the book in January 1697, under the title *Histoires ou contes du temps passé, avec des Moralitez*, but the book, which had been reprinted twice in Holland and once in France by the end of that year, soon came to be known as *Contes de ma mère l'Oye*. These words appeared on a plaque in the frontispiece, an engraving by Clouzier based on a coloured illustration in the manuscript of the book which had been written out for its dedicatee, 'Mademoiselle', niece to Louis XIV. The book was presented as the work of 'P. Darmancour', this being Perrault's youngest son, Pierre Perrault Darmancour (*see* PERRAULT for a discussion of whether the boy was involved with the book's composition).

The *Contes* were probably set down by Perrault with children chiefly in mind, though with the expectation that adults would enjoy them too. There are elements in the stories which aim at an adult readership, such as the ending of *Hop o' my Thumb*, which satirizes the preoccupation of the court at Versailles with extramarital love-affairs, and also the awakening of the Sleeping Beauty, which reads like a fashionable romance rather than a folk tale.

The stories were soon being handed down by word of mouth, in the form in which Perrault told them, all over the world, so that when 19th-cent. folklorists began to collect folk tales and classify them scientifically, they used the Perrault form of each story as the 'basic type' around which to arrange their classification.

In 1888 Andrew *Lang published an edition of the original French text, with an introduction and notes. Countless modern English translations of Perrault have since appeared; some of these include three stories by him which were published separately in his lifetime and did not appear in the 1697 first edition: *Peau d'asne* ('Donkey Skin'), *Les Souhaits ridicules* (a version of The *Three Wishes*), and *Griseldis* (The Patience of Griselda), which is a tale from Boccaccio.

Conversations See MRS MARCET.

COOK, Captain James (1728–79) Circumnavigator and explorer, a popular subject for children's books in the late 18th and 19th cents. The 1796 abridged *Captain Cook's Third and Last Voyage, to the Pacific Ocean* was used as the basis of some of the later children's versions, e.g. one published by John *Marshall in 1800. In 1890 W. H. G. *Kingston produced his own account of Cook's life.

COOLIDGE, Susan (Sarah Chauncy Woolsey) (1845–1905) Author of *What Katy Did*. She was born in Cleveland, Ohio; she was a notably tall child, quick-witted, and impatient, like her heroine Katy Carr. Her younger sisters Jane, Elizabeth, and Theodora provided the models for Katy's sisters Clover, Elsie, and Joanna (known as Johnny), while her brother William and an orphaned cousin Theodorus became Phil and Dorry in the stories of the Carr family. Sarah spent much of her childhood in New Haven, Conn.; her father's family was closely connected with Yale University.

During the Civil War Sarah worked as a nurse, and then began to write prolifically.

Her first children's book, *The New-Year's Bargain* (1871), is a collection of stories told to two children, Thekla and Max, by each of the twelve months of the year, who are introduced to them by Father Time. It was published with much success by Roberts Brothers of Boston, whose chief editor Thomas Niles had already guided Louisa M. *Alcott to success with *Little Women*; it may have been at his suggestion that Sarah Woolsey wrote *What Katy Did* (1872). *What Katy Did At School* appeared in 1873. 'Susan Coolidge' (a penname adopted in imitation of 'Margaret Coolidge', a pseudonym used by her sister) next produced a number of collections of short stories, many of which first appeared in the magazine *St Nicholas*. Later full-length novels include *Eyebright* (1879) and *A Guernsey Lily* (1880), suggested by a visit to the Channel Islands. She returned to the exploits of the Carr family with *What Katy Did Next* (1886), which describes a tour of Europe, *Clover* (1888), and *In the High Valley* (1890). Besides writing children's books, Woolsey edited the correspondence of Fanny Burney and Jane Austen, as well as publishing several volumes of her own verse.

COOLING, Wendy See BOOKSTART.

COOMBS, Patricia See DORRIE.

COONEY, Barbara (1917–2000) American picture-book author and illustrator of more than 100 books. Her mother was an artist, and she encouraged Cooney's interest in painting and drawing. Cooney went on to study art history at Smith College and began working as an illustrator in 1940. Though born in Brooklyn, New York, she spent much of her life in her beloved state of Maine, where several of her works are set. She was twice awarded the *Caldecott Medal, for her adaptation of *Chanticleer and the Fox* and for *Ox-Cart Man* by Donald Hall. *Miss Rumphius*, the book Cooney felt was closest to her heart, won the National Book Award (shared with William *Steig) in 1983.

COOPER, Helen (1963–) British illustrator and author of many much-loved picture books; her artwork, jewel-like in its clarity, has won her the *Kate Greenaway Medal for both *The Baby Who Wouldn't Go To Bed* (1996) and *Pumpkin Soup* (1998) and was shortlisted for *The Bear Under the Stairs* (1993), the latter two about the richness of a

child's imaginative life. *Pumpkin Soup* spawned two sequels, *Delicious* (2003) and *A Pipkin of Pepper* (2006), to continue the story of Cat, Duck, and Squirrel.

COOPER, James Fenimore (1789–1851) Author of the celebrated **Leather-Stocking Tales*; he was brought up in a prosperous family at Cooperstown, NY, a settlement established by his father. After being dismissed from Yale, Cooper went to sea for three years, then married and settled down to the life of a country gentleman, only being impelled into authorship when he declared to his wife that he could write a better novel than the one they were reading together. The result was *Precaution* (1820), a conventional novel of English society, which was followed by *The Spy* (1821), set during the American Revolution. This was very successful. Next came *The Pioneers* (1823), the first of the *Leather-Stocking* books. *The Last of the Mohicans* appeared in 1826 and *The Prairie* (1827) was written while he was in Europe. Much of Cooper's later life was devoted to controversy: he quarrelled with his neighbours about property rights and with his fellow countrymen about his disillusionment with America. The last *Leather-Stocking* novels to appear were *The Pathfinder* (1840) and *The Deerslayer* (1841). Others of his many books were read by children, including *Mark's Reef* (1847), a **Robinsonnade* originally called *The Crater*. Cooper, who has been called the American Walter **Scott, had no first-hand knowledge of the frontier life he described, but wrote with exceptional vividness and was influential in his portrait of Native Americans ('*Indians') as stoic and sagacious.

COOPER, Mary (d. 1761) London printer and publisher from *c.*1742 to 1761 who issued three innovatory books for children: *The Child's New Play-Thing* (*see* ABC BOOKS) and the first two collections of **nursery rhymes, under the titles **Tom Thumb's Song Book* and *Tom Thumb's Pretty Song Book*. Mrs Cooper was the widow of Thomas Cooper, one of the most prolific pamphlet publishers of his time. She took over the business when he died and continued to run it until her own death.

COOPER, Susan (1935–) British author who worked as a journalist on the *Sunday Times* before becoming a full-time writer and moving to America. Between 1965 and 1977 she published the influential and hugely popular *The *Dark Is Rising* sequence, starting with *Over Sea, Under Stone* (1965), which weaves Arthurian legend, British myth, and original fantasy into a stunning whole—the series remains one of the cornerstones of children's **fantasy-writing in English. The success of the series has perhaps eclipsed Cooper's other writing for children, which is of a consistently high standard and richly imagined. Books include *Dawn of Fear* (1970), set in London during the Second World War, *King of Shadows* (1999) a time-travel story featuring Shakespeare (an American boy visiting London finds himself mysteriously transported back to the old Globe), *Victory* (2006), in which Admiral Nelson links two children living hundreds of years apart, and *Ghost Hawk* (2013), the mysterious and moving story of a Native American boy and his encounter with European settlers.

copperplate engraving The most popular medium for fine book illustration in the 17th and 18th cents. The line is cut into a smooth metal plate, generally copper until the 19th cent., but sometimes another metal such as steel or zinc, and the waste or 'burr' is scratched up by the graver or burin, then removed. (Another technique, dry-point, leaves the burr to contribute to the finished impression.) Ink is then pressed on to the whole plate, into all the lines and other excisions, but is afterwards wiped off the smooth unengraved surface so that only the excised parts print, a process generically known as 'intaglio'. From an early stage, intaglio impressions were also made by etching, the excision of the design by acid after scratching it through an acid-resisting film on the metal plate. Engraving and etching were often combined, so that it becomes hard to distinguish between an engraving in which (for speed) the first outlines were etched, and an etching that has been given some final touches with a graver.

The advantages of copperplate over **woodcuts were that the artist or engraver's own line actually became the line on paper; copper could take finer, more detailed work; and the depth of ink transferred from the crevices of the plate produced a very black, even slightly embossed effect. However copperplate has the disadvantage of all intaglio, as opposed to relief (and, later, lithographic) methods: that it is not compatible with printing from type, which again is inked on the surface like a woodcut. Copperplates could therefore only appear on the same page as type if the paper went through two separate printings; and most

commonly they were used for separate illustrations, pasted or bound into a book.

Copperplate illustrations needed finer, costlier paper than woodcuts and the metal tended not to stand up to long print runs, and so their use in children's books was on the whole limited to frontispieces or ornamented title-pages, and sometimes a few additional plates, such as in John *Newbery's *Tom Telescope* (1761). Copperplates had a brief vogue in juvenile books in the first decade of the 19th cent., following the success of *The *Butterfly's Ball* (1807), in which John *Harris commissioned engravings after *Mulready. Harris, however, soon turned to *wood engraving as a more suitable medium for the hand-coloured pictures in his later books. At about the same time steel began to be used as a more durable alternative to copper as the main metal for plates, but the increasing sophistication of wood engraving, following the high standard set by *Bewick, soon largely eclipsed the popularity of both copper and steel.

As with wood engraving, the artist's and the engraver's functions were usually separate (Hogarth was a notable exception), and William *Blake earned his living reproducing other men's work on copperplate. George *Cruikshank began his professional life mainly as an etcher, working on his own plates; his illustrations for *Grimm and much of his other well known work is etched, either on copper or steel, but he also drew on wood for engraving.

Cops and Robbers (1978) A picture book by Janet *Ahlberg and Allan *Ahlberg. 'Ho Ho for the robbers / The cops and the robbers Ho Ho!'—this satisfying chant is the refrain that punctuates the action as Granny Swag and the robbers of London town threaten to ruin Christmas. However, they have not reckoned on the 'upstanding Constable Pugh', who, it seems can do anything, including crosswords. The combination of Janet Ahlberg's distinctive illustrations, which follow the storytelling style of the comic, with Allan's jaunty verse made this an immediate success when it first appeared. Its continuing appeal to children and parents has ensured its status as a modern classic.

copybooks Volumes containing instruction in, and examples of, the art of elegant handwriting. They began to appear in England in the late 16th cent., when an effort was being made by a number of writing masters to revive calligraphy, which had declined following the introduction of printing. The first engraved

English copybook was *A booke containing divers sorts of hands* (1570). A notable 17th-cent. example was *The Writing Schoolemaster* by John Davies of Hereford (? *c.*1610). Edward Cocker, the supposed author of *Cocker's Arithmetic*, was responsible for nearly 30 copybooks which appeared in the second half of the 17th cent. In the 18th and 19th cents. it became a common practice to leave blanks in the books for the pupils to fill in.

Coraline (2002) One the darkest, and most original products of Neil *Gaiman's literary mind. The book tells the story of young Coraline and her parents' move into a new house, and her discovery of a distorted, specular Other World on the other side of a door— and its horrific dwellers, controlled by the even more terrifying, buttons-for-eyes, witchlike Other Mother. The significant *horror tone marks its difference from Lewis Carroll's *Through the Looking Glass*, though that is definitely an influence. *Coraline* won the Hugo Award for Best Novella (2003), the Nebula Award for Best Novella (2003), and the Bram Stoker Award for Best Work for Young Readers (2002). It was adapted into a stop-motion animated film in 2009, directed by Henry Selick. The story also features a dimension-hopping, not entirely helpful Black Cat.

Coral Island, The, *A Tale of the Pacific Ocean* (published 1858, though on general sale from Dec. 1857) A novel by R. M. *Ballantyne. The first edition was illustrated by the author. Young Ralph Rover is shipwrecked on a South Sea island with two companions, Jack Martin and Peterkin Gay. After discovering the delights of coconuts, bread-fruit, and oysters, they are nearly killed by a shark and witness a fight between two factions of cannibals. Ralph is captured by a *pirate, Bloody Bill, and after being forced to spend some time on the seas with him, witnesses Bill's death and sails the pirate schooner single-handed back to the island. With Jack and Peterkin he then makes a voyage to another island, where the boys are imprisoned by natives, only being freed through the intervention of missionaries.

Ballantyne took many of the incidents from *The Island Home; or the Young Cast-Aways* (1851) by the American writer James F. Bowman. *The Coral Island* quickly became one of the most popular 19th-cent. *adventure stories, and was translated into most European languages during the 50 years following publication. Among its most devoted boy-readers were the young Robert Louis

*Stevenson and J. M. *Barrie, and it played a large part in the creation of both **Treasure Island* and **Peter Pan*. It also inspired William Golding (1911–93) to write **Lord of the Flies* (1954). In Ballantyne's sequel, *The Gorilla Hunters* (1861), Ralph Rover, Peterkin Gay, and Jack Martin, now grown men, sail to Africa to search for the little-known gorilla—which had featured in Paul *Du Chaillu's book *Explorations and Adventures in Equatorial Africa*, published a few months before *The Gorilla Hunters*.

Coram Boy (2000) Historical novel by Jamila *Gavin and winner of the *Costa Children's Book Award. Fact meets fiction in the violent and corrupt city of London in the 18th cent. *Coram Boy* is a fast-paced thriller centred on the lives of two boys: Toby, the son of an African slave, and Aaron, an illegitimate son of a wealthy family. Their lives are inextricably bound together by the Foundling Hospital, a home for orphans established in 1741 by Thomas Coram. *Coram Boy* has also been adapted for stage in the US and UK, receiving many awards.

Corduroy (1968) A picture book by American artist Don Freeman (1908–78). Corduroy is a teddy bear in the toy department of a large store. At night he goes off in search of his lost button. In the morning, a little girl—Lisa—comes to the store and buys him (with the money from her own piggy bank) and takes him away. Finally Corduroy has a home, and a friend. Originally turned down by several publishers, Freeman's sweet story, simply told with bright, appealing pictures, has been more than vindicated by a popularity that is huge and enduring.

COREN, Alan (1938–2007) Editor from 1978 of the British humorous magazine *Punch*, Coren wrote an 'Arthur' series of comic *westerns and *detective stories for children.

Coretta Scott King Award Named in honour of Martin Luther King's wife, a political activist and civil rights leader in her own right, the Coretta Scott King Award has been made annually since 1970 for outstanding portrayals of African-American experience by African-American authors. Since 1974, illustrators have also been recognized. The first author award was won by Lillie Patterson for *Martin Luther King, Jr.: Man of Peace*, and the most recent author winner is Rita Williams-Garcia for *P.S. Be Eleven* (2014). Illustrator George Ford won the 1974 award for *Ray Charles* by Sharon Bell Mathis. Bryan Collier was the 2014 illustrator winner for *Knock Knock: My Dad's Dream for Me*. Each year a number of runners-up are named 'Coretta Scott King Honor Books' for each category.

CORKRAN, Alice (1852–1916) British author who wrote *Down the Snow Stairs* (1887), a *fantasy partly derived from Lewis *Carroll, but with a strong moral content.

CORMIER, Robert (1925–2000) American novelist who made his name as a writer for older children with *The *Chocolate War* (1974). This was followed by **I Am the Cheese* (1977), *After the First Death* (1979), which begins with a busload of small children being hijacked by terrorists, and *Eight Plus One Stories* (1980), a collection of short stories about childhood and adolescence.

Cormier, a Massachusetts journalist, was one of the outstanding American writers to appear on the *young adult list during the 1970s. His theme is the destruction of innocent and altruistic people by a harsh world: Jerry Renault in *The Chocolate War* learns that he does *not* dare (in T. S. Eliot's words) to 'disturb the universe'; the boy in *I Am the Cheese* has his mind destroyed by his interrogators; and Kate, heroine of *After the First Death*, is shot dead at the end of the story. 'There are no taboos,' Cormier said in an interview shortly before his death. His books, in consequence, are uncompromising and sometimes make for uncomfortable reading, but his narrative skill is such that it is very difficult to put them down.

CORNER, Julia (1798–1875) English author of *plays for children. Her series of *Little Plays for Little People* were published by *Dean & Son, beginning in 1854. They were all adaptations of *fairy stories and were in rhyming couplets. Corner was inspired in this work by watching children act charades. In a preface, she wrote: 'I am aware that some persons object to juvenile amusements that bear any affinity to theatricals but... if proper subjects be selected, and care taken that they convey some useful or moral lesson, I am convinced ...that such performances would be calculated to do good rather than harm.'

Cornish folk material Such material available for children's reading was scant when Joseph *Jacobs assembled *Celtic Fairy Tales* in 1892. Enys Tregarthen brought out *The Piskey Purse, Legends and Tales of North Cornwall* (her home) in 1905; it contained a few stories of the 'small

people', 'little Brown Piskey-Men' among them, and she followed this with *North Cornwall Fairies and Legends* (1906). In 1940, some years after her death, stories collected from her were published in America as *Piskey Folk*. The 20th-cent. Cornish poet Charles *Causley made much use of his county's folklore in his writing for children.

Costa Children's Book Award A category of the Costa Book Awards, and one of the most significant children's books prizes in the UK. Originally the Whitbreads, the awards were renamed the Costas in 2006 following a new sponsorship agreement. The prize (an award of £5,000—formerly £3,000) has been given annually since 1972 for a children's book (for readers of seven years and upwards) by an author of British or Irish nationality, or who is resident in the UK or Ireland. For a full list of winners, *see* APPENDIX, G.

COTTIN, Sophie *See* ELIZABETH, OR THE EXILES OF SIBERIA.

COTTON, John *See* MILK FOR BABES.

COTTON, Nathaniel (1705–88) Physician and poet who wrote *Visions in Verse, for the Entertainment and Instruction of Younger Minds* (1751), a collection of odes on different aspects of human life. The verse is unremarkable, but the book was much admired and was reprinted a number of times.

Cotton-tail Rabbit in stories by Beatrix *Potter.

COTTRELL BOYCE, Frank (1959–) British writer who had a long and successful career as a screenwriter before publishing *Millions*, which was adapted from his own script. This outstanding book, which is a comedy with a love of the absurd, and with moments of genuine pathos, won the *Carnegie Medal. Its depiction of Liverpool is a tribute to the city which the author admitted he sometimes painted too bleakly in his scripts for television.

The Unforgotten Coat (2012) is a short, powerful novel, about the friendship between two brothers, who are refugees from Mongolia now resident in Liverpool, and Julie, the girl who is tasked to befriend them. There are stories within the story as the boys recreate impulses of their old life through photographs (which illustrate the book), and in an adult Julie addressing the friendship left behind in her youth. The novel was commissioned by The Reader Organization of Liverpool, distributed widely free of charge, and won the 2013

*Guardian Children's Fiction Prize. It contains elements of fantasy rooted in reality which have inspired Cottrell Boyce's other novels. These include *Framed* (2005)—about the life-changing imposition of a valuable art collection on a small community, which extends Cottrell Boyce's exploration of children's concepts of wealth and poverty—and *Cosmic* (2008), a comedy set partly in space, which shines a light on our place in the universe.

His most recent work has been three continuations of Ian Fleming's classic stories, beginning with *Chitty Chitty Bang Bang Flies Again* (2011) (*see also* CHITTY-CHITTY-BANG-BANG), commissioned by the Fleming Estate. He has said that one of the appeals of the project was the chance to create credible but sympathetic adult characters in a children's story. The books were generally warmly received and the time-travel plot praised, though they have less depth of characterization than Cottrell's Boyce own works.

counting-out rhymes Verses used in children's games (*see* GAMES-RHYMES) when one of the players must be chosen for a special role, usually chaser or catcher. A rhyme is repeated by one of the players, who points at each of the others in turn; the child on whom the last number or syllable falls is the one chosen. The best known of such rhymes is 'Eeny, meeny, miney, mo', or 'Eena, meena, mina, mo'.

Count Olaf The villain in *A *Series of Unfortunate Events*.

courtesy-books *See* BOOKS OF COURTESY.

COUSINS, Lucy (1964–) British author-illustrator most famous for the *Maisy series. Cousins grew up in Kent and did a BA in graphic design before completing a postgraduate degree at the Royal College of Art. Soon after leaving college, she published her first title about Maisy and her friends. The vibrantly coloured Maisy books now come in every shape and size, from tell-the-time books and flap books, to books with squeaks and rattles. Cousins has also written and illustrated other titles, including *Jazzy in the Jungle* (2002), about a baby lemur, *Hooray for Fish* (2005), which explores a fantastical underwater world, and *Noah's Ark* (1993).

COVILLE, Bruce (1950–) American author of children's books whose childhood desire to write was sidetracked by a diverse career including gravedigging, toy-making, and teaching.

Coville's first book was published in 1977. *The Magic Shop* series (1982) is typical of his light, funny, and fast-paced style, as is the *My Teacher Is an Alien* (1989) series, this time about a class who must thwart their not-quite-human teacher. *Into the Land of the Unicorns* (1994) is the first in a series in which a girl must save the unicorns' country from invasion. He is also continuing Paula *Danziger's *Amber Brown* series, with *Amber Brown Is Tickled Pink* (2012).

Cowardly Lion In *The *Wonderful Wizard of Oz* and other books by L. Frank *Baum.

cowboys Cattle hands, especially in the West of the United States. They began to feature regularly in *dime novels during the 1880s, one of the earliest such books to include the word 'Cowboy' in its title being *Lone Star, the Cowboy Captain* (1882) by Prentiss Ingraham, a hack-writer who specialized in stories about *Buffalo Bill. Formerly, during the period of the Revolutionary War in America, the word 'cowboy' had been used for members of pro-British guerrilla bands.

Unlike other types of *western hero (the outlaw, the gambler, the gunfighter, the trapper and man of the mountains), no historical person was used in popular fiction as the 'typical' cowboy. A wholly fictional character, the nameless hero of Owen Wister's novel *The Virginian* (1902), became the first well known representative of the group. *See also* 'INDIANS' OF NORTH AMERICA

The cowboy-turned-writer Will James (1892–1942) wrote a number of children's books, including *Smoky, the Cowhorse*.

COWELL, Cressida (1966–) British artist and author whose childhood alternated between school in London and holidays on a remote Scottish island, where—with no TV or contact with the outside world—her imagination conjured magic from the rocky, cave-ridden island involving Vikings, together with the dragons who eventually became heroes of the hugely successful and captivating *How to Train Your Dragon* (2003). The series continues with a projected eleven titles, a set of films, a TV series, and an arena show. Cowell illustrated these books herself, while her delightful series of picture books about Emily are drawn by Neal Layton, starting with *That Rabbit Belongs to Emily Brown* (2007).

COWLEY, Joy (1936–) New Zealand author of picture books and novels for children and adults. She began to write as a teenager, editing the children's page of her local paper, the *Manawatu Daily Times*, though it was when

her son had difficulty in learning to read that she started to write children's stories in order to help him. This resulted in her working on the Story Box reading programme, which aimed to make learning to read fun. Since then she has written over 600 books and travelled the world promoting *multiculturalism in children's literature. Her award-winning books include *The Silent One* (1980), which tells of the friendship between a deaf Pacific Islander boy and a turtle, *Bow Down Shadrach* (1990), which starts a trilogy about family life and an attempt to save the old family horse, and *Hunter* (2004), in which the lives of a Māori boy in 1805 and a city girl in 2005 somehow overlap. She has won eight *New Zealand Post Children's Book Awards including Book of the Year twice, and in 1992 was awarded the *Margaret Mahy Medal.

Cow Who Fell in the Canal, The (1957) A story by Phyllis *Krasilovsky.

COX, Palmer (1840–1924) Canadian author-illustrator, born in Quebec. At the age of forty he began to illustrate stories for the magazine *St Nicholas*, and also contributed his own poems, with illustrations. Looking for a theme for a series, he hit upon *brownies, remembering Scottish fairy tales heard in childhood. The stories that resulted were told in rhyming couplets, and were vigorously illustrated. They were afterwards published in book form. The first of the thirteen books, *The Brownies: Their Book* (1887), sold over a million copies in Cox's lifetime. Later adventures were in effect *travelogue storybooks, taking the Brownies to such places as Flodden Field, Killarney, Mount Vesuvius, and the Philippines, and the length and breadth of the United States. *Palmer Cox's Brownies* (1895), a three-act stage entertainment, ran for nearly five years. The books' continuing popularity some generations later is indicated by the fact that the small hero of Eleanor *Estes's *Rufus M* (1943) climbs through a coal cellar to get one from the local library.

CRAIK (Mulock), Dinah Maria Mulock (1818–87) Author of one of the most popular adult novels of the 19th cent., *John Halifax, Gentleman* (1856), as well as a number of children's books, including *The *Fairy Book* (1863), *The Adventures of a Brownie* (1872; *see* BROWNIE), and *The *Little Lame Prince* (1875). She was married to G. L. Craik, a partner in the publishing house of Macmillan, and was a friend of George *MacDonald.

CRAMPTON, Patricia (1925–2016) Transla- from Swedish and German, one of the few British translators to make her name particu- larly for her work on children's literature, which ran to some two hundred books (though her first job, when she was straight out of Oxford, was as translator at the Nurem- berg Trials). She was responsible for translat- ing a number of Astrid *Lindgren's books into English, including *Ronia, the Robber's Daugh- ter* (1983) and *Karlsson on the Roof* (1975), and she produced the first rhyming translation of Dick Bruna's *Miffy* stories (having been told it couldn't be done). She won the *Marsh award in 1999 with her translation of Gudrun *Pausewang's *The Final Journey*; the *Batchelder Award in 1984 and 1987; and the 1991 *Eleanor Farjeon Award for her overall contribution to children's literature.

CRANCH, Christopher Pearse (1813–92) American poet, painter, and humorist who wrote and illustrated two children's novels: *The Last of the Huggermuggers* (1855), a *Gul- liver-like story in which a young shipwrecked sailor discovers an island inhabited by two *giants, the last of their race, and *Kobboltozo* (1856), a sequel about an evil dwarf on the same island. They are of interest as being among the few original *fairy stories to be written in 19th-cent. America, but they had no lasting life, perhaps on account of a certain self-consciousness of style.

Crane, Walter (1845–1915) Artist, one of the most popular English illustrators of chil- dren's books in the late 19th cent., and one of the early exponents of the *coloured picture book. Born in Liverpool, the son of a portrait painter, he was apprenticed to a London *wood engraving firm, and studied fine art at the same time. In 1863, he was introduced to Edmund *Evans the colour printer, for whom he did covers for 'yellow back' cheap novels, and then, from about 1865, children's *picture books, in the series of *toy books Evans was producing for the publishers *Warne and *Routledge. In all he designed some 50 of these books, generally with traditional or *fairy story texts, sometimes with words by his sister Lucy or himself. At first they were priced at 'Sixpence; or mounted on Linen, One Shilling'; then from 1874 they were published in the larger format of Routledge's shilling series, with considerably more ambi- tious pictures and with Crane's name now a selling point. These series were immensely

successful, and they were still being issued in bound collections twenty-five years after their first appearance.

Crane took the work of making children's books entirely seriously, identifying their spe- cial appeal to artists of his generation: 'They are attractive to designers of an imaginative tendency, for in a sober and matter-of-fact age they afford perhaps the only outlet for unrestrained flights of fancy open to the mod- ern illustrator, who likes to revolt against the despotism of facts.'

From about 1869 onwards Crane's toy books show increasing mastery of the possi- bilities of colour printing, and in books such as *The Fairy Ship* (1870) there also appears the influence of Japanese prints. Also characteris- tic of Crane was his filling of the whole frame of a picture, his clear line and his bold use of black, his care for detail of decoration, dress, and furniture, and his concern that text should be integrated with illustration. He frequently calligraphed a text, or a part of it.

Toy books were by no means Crane's only enterprise for children. Among other commis- sions, he illustrated a number of Mrs *Moles- worth's books. He worked with Edmund Evans to produce a lavish and innovative com- bination of colour and music printing, *The Baby's Opera* (1877), which was a popular success despite its high price. *The Baby's Bou- quet* (1879) and *The Baby's Own Aesop* (1887) followed and they were published together as *Triplets* in 1899. Private books which Crane illustrated for his own family were the origin of three more titles: *Slateandpencilvania* (1885), *Little Queen Anne* (1886), and *Pothooks and Perseverance* (1886), published together as *The Romance of the Three Rs* (1886). Crane also collaborated in two experimental reading *primers, *The Golden Primer* (with J. M. D. Meiklejohn), and *The Walter Crane Reader* (with Nellie Dale), followed by *The Dale Readers Book II*. Lewis *Carroll wrote in 1878 to ask him to illustrate his short story *Bruno's Revenge*, but the project came to nothing.

Crane's work for adults spanned the whole range from oil painting to wallpaper design (he was commissioned to base a nursery wall- paper on his children's work), and he became a leading figure in the late 19th-cent. move- ment to rehabilitate good design and crafts- manship. He was associated with William *Morris and his socialist theories, contributed political cartoons to socialist periodicals, and illustrated *The Child's Socialist Reader* (1907) by A. A. Watts, a pioneer of British Socialism.

Crane lectured on art and wrote on aesthetics, and in 1898 he became Principal of the Royal College of Art and Design.

According to a tribute at his death by a friend (C. R. Ashbee), Crane remained a naïve, childlike character, choosing to live in a fairy-tale world rather than in humdrum reality, alongside his wife who called herself 'Mistress Crane' and who once received astonished guests 'dressed as a sort of sunflower'.

CREECH, Sharon (1945–) American author, the first American to win the *Carnegie Medal, for *Ruby Holler* (2002), a story of orphaned twins adopted by an eccentric elderly couple and how meeting the right people can change any life; and the first person to win both that and the *Newbery Medal, the latter for *Walk Two Moons* (1994). Growing up in a large, sociable family, Creech was a teacher before turning full-time to writing, and though her first books were published while living in England, she only found fame once she returned to America. Humane and thoughtful, her stories are often overshadowed by death, while their themes of independence, growing-up, and trust are always softened by gentle humour. Other important works include *The Wanderer* (2000), in which a sea voyage leads to two young people understanding more about their place in the world, the superb *Love That Dog* (2001), written in poetry about a boy who hates poetry, and *Chasing Redbird* (1997), about thirteen-year-old Zinny and her attempts to come to terms with grief, guilt, and loss.

CRESSWELL, Helen (1934–2005) British children's writer. Her early books fall into two types: poetic *fantasies, such as *Where the Wind Blows* (1966), the story of a girl who follows the wild geese to the world's end, and broadly comic stories (on the lines of Richmal Crompton's *William series) about a small boy named Jumbo, beginning with *Jumbo Spencer* (1963). These two strands of Helen Cresswell's writing came together in her first book to receive wide praise, *The *Piemakers* (1967), a distinctive blend of comedy and fantasy. *The Signposters* (1967), about a family who travel England measuring distances and painting signs, was in the same vein, while *The Night-Watchmen* (1969) introduced a more sinister element into what was now identifiable as the Cresswell type of comic novel. *The Outlanders* (1970) is a fantasy about a family in search of a mysterious radiant child; *The Beachcombers* (1972) returns to the *Piemakers* style, while

The Bongleweed (1973) is a black comedy reminiscent of John *Wyndham's *The Day of the Triffids*.

In 1973 she was commissioned to write a series of stories for BBC Television's *Jackanory*, and the result was *Lizzie Dripping* (1973), whose heroine, a dreamy adolescent, has a private fantasy-figure in the form of a *witch who lives in a churchyard. Several other books in this series were published in 1973 and 1974. *The Winter of the Birds* (1975), one of Cresswell's most ambitious novels, is an ironic and complex book about eccentricity and heroism. Her most notable achievement is generally thought to be The *Bagthorpe Saga, of which the first book, *Ordinary Jack*, appeared in 1977. This was widely welcomed as that rare thing in children's literature of the time: a sophisticated comic novel. Bagthorpe would run to ten books, written between 1977 and 2001, during which time Cresswell wrote dozens of other novels for children (including *Moondial* (1987), a time-slip story, and *The Return of the Psammead* (1982, a sequel to the books by E. *Nesbit), as well as TV adaptations of her own work and those of other authors (*The *Demon Headmaster*, *Five Children and It*, *Famous Five*, etc.). In 2000 she was joint winner of the British Academy of Film and Television Arts (BAFTA) Children's Writer Award.

She was equally at home with high humour and mystery, slapstick and menace. She wrote over a hundred children's books for a variety of publishers and said of them, 'Whatever the outward settings of my stories, the adventures they chart are essentially inner ones.' She also said, 'Over and over, in book after book, I assert this sense of the thinness of so-called reality compared with the richness of life lived in the light of the imagination.'

CREWS, Donald (1938–) American author and illustrator of innovative picture books that celebrate family and machines. From art school he was drafted into the army and it was while stationed in Germany that he started work on what would be his first published book, *We Read: A-Z* (1967), which moved away from the traditional images for an A-Z book and offered abstract ideas instead. *Freight Train* (1978) was his first major success, using simple images and language to convey what colours are and how they combine and change. The same train appears in *Shortcut* (1992), which shows the dangers of railway lines and speeding trains. His blocky,

very graphic style is shown best in *Truck* (1980), which simply follows a delivery truck on a cross-country journey.

Cricket in Times Square, The (1960) A novel by George *Selden.

cries of London Phrases which were called out in the streets by itinerant sellers of food and other commodities, and by people offering their trades. The cries became a stock subject for illustrated books from the 17th to the 19th cents., many of which were for children.

London cries are mentioned in the 15th-cent. poem 'London Lickpenny', which has been ascribed to John Lydgate. Printed collections of cries began to appear in the late 17th cent. They consisted of engravings of the various street-sellers with their cries printed beneath, and often a descriptive verse for each one. By the late 18th cent. several publishers of *miniature books for children were producing their own versions; Francis (nephew) and Elizabeth *Newbery published many editions of *The Cries of London, as they are daily exhibited in the Streets*. In 1820 John *Harris issued *Sam Syntax's Description of the Cries of London*. The printers *Kendrew of York and Rusher of Banbury adapted the cries under the titles *The Cries of York* and *The Cries of Banbury and London*.

Cries of London were often printed in America, and there were soon being produced, in the early 19th cent., *Cries of Philadelphia* and *Cries of New York*.

Crockett, Davy *See* DAVY CROCKETT.

CROCKETT, S. R. (Samuel Rutherford) (1860–1914) British author of *historical novels, among them *The Black Douglas* (1899), set in 15th-cent. Scotland. He was also the author of *The Surprising Adventures of Sir Toady Lion*, published in 1897 with illustrations by Gordon *Browne. One of a series of whimsical stories about childhood, it has as heroes two small boys, one of whom calls himself 'Napoleon' and the other 'Sir Toady Lion', this being 'his own first effort at the name of his favourite hero Richard Coeur-de-Lion'. The book receives qualified praise from E. *Nesbit's Oswald Bastable: 'It is the only decent book I have ever read by *Toady Lion*'s author. The others are mere piffle. But many people like them.'

CROKER, T. (Thomas) Crofton (1798–1854) Irish antiquary who published the pioneer *Fairy Legends and Traditions of the South of Ireland* in three volumes in 1825–8 (*see* IRISH FOLK TALES). The book was much admired by *Scott, and stories from it were translated into German by the brothers *Grimm. Though not originally designed for children, it was read by many, especially in the one-volume editions (with illustrations) which were later made of it. Croker also edited *The *Christmas Box* (1828 and 1829), probably the first English children's *annual.

CROMPTON, Frances E. (Eliza) (1866–1952) British author, chiefly remembered for *The *Gentle Heritage* (1893). Her other books include *Friday's Child* (1889) and *Master Bartelmy* (1892).

CROMPTON, Richmal (Richmal Crompton Lamburn) (1890–1969), author of the *William books. She was the daughter of a clergyman and schoolmaster, and was brought up in Lancashire; after studying at London University and becoming Classics Mistress at Bromley High School she contracted poliomyelitis in 1923 and was severely crippled. She gave up her job, but had already begun to write the *William* books, which proved a huge and lasting success. She also wrote a large number of popular novels for adults.

CROSS, Gillian (1945–) British children's author well-known for her six novels (and one novella) in the *Demon Headmaster* sequence (1982–2002), which has been successfully adapted for television. The premise of this engaging series is a school where the children are exceptionally compliant, being under the spell of the eponymous Demon Headmaster.

The Demon Headmaster aside, Cross rarely returns to the same characters or setting—from the beginning of her career, her books ranged widely in setting and theme. Her work embraced high concepts before the term became fashionable in description of *young adult literature—the Lost Trilogy, comprising *The Dark Ground* (2004), *The Black Room* (2005), and *The Nightmare Game* (2006), is cleverly plotted science fiction in which characters find themselves in an alien world, dwarfed in comparison to their surroundings.

Cross's books are page-turners, but their literary value has also been recognized. After several shortlistings, Cross won the *Carnegie

Medal for *Wolf* (1990), her outstanding novel about Cassy, whose estranged father is a member of the IRA—a thriller imbued with genuine terror, but also heartfelt characterization. Her next novel, *The Great Elephant Chase* (1992), won the Nestlé Smarties Book Prize and the *Whitbread Children's Book Award. Set in the USA in the 1840s, it tells the story of two children's race across a wild landscape with a fugitive elephant, pursued by its unscrupulous owners. She continues to produce some of the most satisfying children's books available. Her recent novel, *After Tomorrow* (2013), is a story of survival in a Britain of the near future, where society has broken down and violence is commonplace.

CROSSAN, Sarah (1978–) Irish novelist, based in the UK, best known for her novels in free verse (see VERSE NOVELS): *The Weight of Water* (2012), an unsentimental but moving story of an immigrant girl and her mother settling in Britain, which won Crossan a *CBI Eilís Dillon Award; and *One* (2015), the story of conjoined twins faced with a difficult choice, which won her the 2016 *Carnegie Medal. Prose novels include the Carnegie-nominated *Apple and Rain* (2014), in which Apple's reunion with her mother, after a long absence, is not as straight-forward as she had hoped.

CROSSLEY-HOLLAND, Kevin (1941–) British author, poet, translator and editor, who first became known to children for his retellings of Anglo-Saxon legends. These include *Beowulf* (1982), illustrated by Charles *Keeping, and *British Folk Tales* (1987; reissued in 2001 with illustrations by Emma *Chichester Clark as *The Magic Lands: Folk Tales of Britain and Ireland*). Other collections—not specifically aimed at children—include *The Penguin Book of Norse Myths* (1980). Crossley-Holland went on to publish highly accomplished children's fiction, from the *Carnegie winning *Storm* (1985), a short and atmospheric *chapter-book for younger readers illustrated by Alan Marks, to two excellent *historical series for older children or *young adults: his mediaeval Arthur trilogy (2000–2003), beginning with *The Seeing Stone*, which marks a high point in contemporary children's *Arthurian writing (the first volume winning Crossley-Holland the *Tir na n-Og Award and the *Guardian Children's Fiction Prize); and a Viking saga, which began in 2012 with *Bracelet of Bones*.

crossover books A term used for books seen as spanning the sometimes spurious division between *young adult fiction and adult fiction. Notable examples include *The *Curious Incident of the Dog in the Night-Time*, *His Dark Materials*, and latterly *The *Fault in Our Stars*. To capitalize on what was seen as a great opportunity to market children's fiction to a huge potential adult market, the *Harry Potter series was famously made available by British publishers Bloomsbury with a choice of 'children's' or 'adult' covers. (Naturally, while the phenomenon is discussed as something of a novelty, the idea that books might be shared by readers of different generations in a family has nothing new about it at all.)

One of the explanations for the recent rise in adults reading books that have been published principally for young readers is the appeal of writing that is strong on narrative, when this was sometimes out of fashion in literary fiction for adults. Crossover fiction can be welcomed as an interesting stretching of the boundaries of what is being read by all kinds of readers, but it is often plagued by tiresome controversy about whether certain works *should* be read by one group or another, and thus whether the crossover phenomenon is an example of adult society being irretrievably dumbed down.

CROUCH, Marcus (1913–96) British critic of children's books and librarian. His books include *Treasure Seekers and Borrowers* (1962) and *The Nesbit Tradition* (1972), and he wrote many reviews for *Junior Bookshelf* and other journals.

CROUCH, Nathaniel (?1632–?1725) English miscellaneous writer, editor, and publisher, the author of various books for children and adults which were mostly rewritings of the works of others. He used the pseudonym 'R. B.' or 'Richard Burton'; after his death this became 'Robert Burton'. He was well known for his series of shilling history books, which Dr Johnson noted were 'very proper to allure backward readers'.

Crouch's *The Young Man's Calling* (1678) was for the most part a pirating of Samuel Crossman's *Youth's Monitor* (1664), to which Crouch added various semi-historical stories intended to excite and amuse; these were illustrated with engravings. His other works include *Delightful Fables in Prose and Verse* (1691), *Winter-Evening Entertainments* (*c.*1725), which consisted of *riddles and other amusements, illustrated with *woodcuts, and *Choice Emblems, Divine and Moral, Antient and Modern* (1684) (*see* EMBLEM BOOKS).

Though Crouch was contemporary with, and sympathetic to, the *Puritan writers for children, he was more interested in the commercial possibilities of such books than the spiritual benefit they imparted to the reader.

CROWTHER, Kitty (1970–) An award-winning Belgian illustrator and author of children's books, working mainly in French and occasionally in Dutch. She has created over thirty-five books of her own as well as illustrating the books of others such as Bart *Moeyaert and Toon Tellegen. Crowther made her debut in 1994 with *Mon Royaume* (My Kingdom), followed by a wordless picture book *Va faire un tour* (Go for a Walk) in 1995. The jury of the Gouden Griffel awarded her a 'Vlag en Wimpel' in 1997 for the illustrated book *Mon ami Jim* (Jack and Jim), a book which celebrates *diversity and the friendship between a seagull and a blackbird. Further recognition followed in 2003 and 2005, when she received the Silver Pencil for *In het pikkedonker* (In the pitch dark) and *Kleine Dood en het meisje* (Little Death and the Girl). Her work is extremely emotive, drawing on themes such as family conflict, difference, death, and loneliness but her illustrations, using traditional mediums of pencil and ink, are intimately engaging and dreamlike, offering the reader both hope and submission into dark alternate realities. In 2010 she received the *Astrid Lindgren Memorial Award.

CROWTHER, Robert *See* NOVELTY BOOKS.

Cruella de Vil In *The *One Hundred and One Dalmatians* by Dodie *Smith.

CRUIKSHANK, George (1792–1878) Generally regarded as the most brilliant English book illustrator of his period, he was the son of Isaac Cruikshank, an artist and caricaturist. He began to make money from his pictures when in his early teens; many of his early published drawings were topical cartoons. In 1823 he illustrated the first English translation of the *Grimms' fairy tales. He was *Dickens's first illustrator, providing pictures for *Sketches by Boz* (1836–7) and *Oliver Twist* (1838). He had a huge success with *The Bottle* (1847), a series of drawings showing the degradation of a family through drink. As a result of this he himself became a total abstainer.

In 1853 he began to publish *fairy stories with illustrations, rewriting them in the process, often adding a teetotal moral. In his version of *Hop o' my Thumb* (1853), Hop's father is a Count who loses his money through drink;

at the end of the story he becomes a reformed character, is appointed prime minister, and introduces Prohibition. A similar theme of the dangers of drink runs through his versions of *Jack and the Beanstalk* (1854), *Cinderella* (1854), and *Puss in Boots* (1864). These four tales were published in one volume as *George Cruikshank's Fairy Library* (1870). The rewriting of them infuriated Dickens, who attacked Cruikshank in an article in *Household Words* (1 Oct. 1859). Cruikshank wrote an equally spirited reply in the form of a letter supposedly from Hop o' my Thumb.

CRUTCHER, Chris (1946–) American author, family therapist, and child protection expert. In 2000, he was awarded the Margaret A. Edwards Award lifetime achievement award for his writing for teenagers. Much of his work has been challenged or *banned for its frank depiction of sex, drug use, homosexuality, AIDS, racism, and rape. Titles include *Running Loose* (1983), *Chinese Handcuffs* (1989), *Athletic Shorts: Six Short Stories* (1991), *Staying Fat for Sarah Byrnes* (1993), *Whale Talk* (2001), and *Period 8* (2013). 'A Brief Moment in the Life of Angus Bethune' from *Athletic Shorts* was made into a 1995 film.

Cuckoo Clock, The (1877) The best known novel by Mrs *Molesworth, first published by Macmillan, with illustrations by Walter *Crane. Griselda comes to an old house inhabited by two aunts. She is lonely and hopes for a playmate. Becoming intrigued by the cuckoo clock in the room where she does her lessons, she eventually discovers that the cuckoo can fly out and talk to her and has the power to take her on strange adventures. Eventually the cuckoo leads her to a playmate, a little boy named Phil, and, happy in his companionship, she bids farewell to the magic bird.

The book is generally regarded as a classic; it has often been reprinted, and is still in print today.

Cue for Treason (1940) A historical novel by Geoffrey *Trease. Peter Brownrigg is on the run, pursued by the vengeful Sir Phillip. A chance meeting with a troupe of travelling players leads him to London and the Globe Theatre. As an actor under the aegis of Shakespeare he should be safe. But there is treason afoot and Sir Phillip is involved. It is up to Peter, together with Kit, an heiress in disguise, to foil the plot to kill the queen. In this novel Trease moves away from the more radical

stance of his earlier novels without ignoring some of the problems of the age. The result is a lively adventure that sets the tone for his later work.

CUMMING, Primrose (1915–2004) British author of *pony and *horse Stories, beginning with *Doney* (1934).

CUMMINS, Maria Susanna (1827–66) Massachusetts author of *The *Lamplighter*, and contributor to the *Atlantic Monthly*.

CUNDALL, Joseph (1818–95) London publisher specializing in high-quality children's books, most notably *The *Home Treasury* series of 'Felix Summerly'. He employed many of the best artists of his day as illustrators.

Cuore (1878) By Edmondo de Amicis (1846–1908), one of the two internationally celebrated 19th-cent. Italian children's books (the other being *Pinocchio*). *Cuore* ('Heart') is the fictional diary of a boy's third year in a Turin municipal school. It was written in order to foster juvenile appreciation of Italy's newfound national unity, for which its author had fought. The book is often highly emotional, even sentimental, but it gives a vivid picture of Italian urban life at the time. *Cuore* was translated into English as *Heart* (1895), and again four years later as *Enrico's Schooldays*. It has appeared in more than twenty-five languages.

Curdie Hero of *The *Princess and the Goblin* and *The *Princess and Curdie* by George *MacDonald.

Curious George (from 1941) A young monkey whose curiosity is always getting him into hilarious trouble, in a series of children's books by illustrator Hans Augusto *Rey and his writer wife, Margret Rey, two refugees from war-torn Paris who carried the original *Curious George* manuscript with them, based on a character who had appeared in a previous book. The books have been continuously in print ever since. After Hans's death Margret continued the series with a variety of other illustrators. The longevity of the series has been secured through the addition of a TV series, an animated film, and various spin-off books.

Curious Incident of the Dog in the Night-time, The (2003) *Crossover Book by Mark Haddon (2003). Taking as its title a quotation from Conan Doyle's *Sherlock Holmes story 'Silver Blaze' (1892), this novel is, in the words of its narrator, 'a murder mystery'. Except there are no human bodies. Told

by fifteen-year-old Christopher, a boy who is different, it follows his attempt to find out who killed his neighbour's dog. His investigation finds him overcoming very real personal difficulties. Though it is never stated, it is widely accepted that it is about a boy with Asperger's Syndrome. Winning the Whitbread Book of the Year Award 2003 (*see* WHITBREAD CHILDREN'S BOOK AWARD), the *Guardian Children's Fiction Prize 2003, and the *Booktrust Teenage Book Award 2003, the novel was published simultaneously on both an adult and a children's fiction list, an early example of the modern crossover novel. An exceptionally good, award-winning dramatization premiered at London's National Theatre in 2012.

CURTIS, Christopher Paul (1953–) African-American author of books for children, who took a year off working in a car factory to produce his debut, *The Watsons Go to Birmingham—1963* (1995), a heartfelt and funny tale of a family heading into the racist south of America at a dark and violent time. *Bud, Not Buddy* (1999) once again shows the author's light touch in recreating the past, giving an amazingly authentic voice to an orphan searching for his father during the Depression—it won Curtis the *Coretta Scott King Award and the *Newbery Medal. *Elijah of Buxton* (2007) is about the first child born in Buxton, Canada, a settlement founded by runaway slaves.

CUSTER, George Armstrong (1839–76) American folk hero. He distinguished himself in the Civil War, fought a long campaign against the Sioux, and died in an attack by '*Indians' led by Sitting Bull. Custer seems to have been a flamboyant and inhumane character, but he quickly became a national hero. Once made respectable, he was an especial favourite with boys' writers of fiction and biography. Frederick Whittaker, whose dime biography *The Dashing Dragoon; or, the Story of Gen. Geo. A. Custer* appeared in 1882, told his youthful readers to study hard, because this was how Custer had got into West Point; not to fight (Custer 'never had a single fight in all his boy life'); and not to smoke and drink. In Elbridge S. Brooks's *Master of the Strong Hearts* (1898), sixteen-year-old Jack Huntingdon of New York City goes west to find adventure, and serves under Custer. Edward L. Sabin's *On the Plains with Custer* (1913) has a similar boy hero, Ned Fletcher, who escapes from captivity by the Indians, becomes a bugler boy with Custer, and participates in his campaigns.

Dab Dab Duck in the *Doctor Dolittle books by Hugh *Lofting.

Daddy Darwin's Dovecote (1884) A story by Mrs *Ewing.

Daddy Long-Legs (1912) A popular novel by the American writer Jean Webster. Jerusha ('Judy') Abbott, an inmate of an orphanage, is selected to be sent to college with her fees paid by one of the trustees, who wishes to remain anonymous. Judy calls him 'Daddy Long-Legs'. The greater part of the book consists of letters to him.

Jean Webster (1876–1916) was the daughter of Mark *Twain's business partner Charles L. Webster. *Daddy Long-Legs* has been staged, filmed (including a 1955 version with Fred Astaire and Leslie Caron), and produced as a British musical comedy, *Love from Judy* (1953).

dæmons In *His Dark Materials*, by Philip Pullman, these are animal-like companions associated with each human character, taking a form which offers some clue as to that character's nature. (Children have dæmons that can change their form, but the process of growing up 'settles' them for good.) People and their dæmons must remain close together; when the General Oblation Board performs an 'intercision', separating person and dæmon by means of a kind of guillotine, the process is distressing and painful. Dæmons that play particularly significant roles in the story are those attached to Lyra (Pantalaimon, a pine marten), Lord Asriel (Stelmaria, a snow leopard), and Mrs Coulter (an unnamed golden monkey).

DAHL, Roald (1916–90) British author who was born in Llandaff, South Wales, of Norwegian parents. He went to Repton School, and then worked for the Shell Oil Company in London and Africa before serving in the RAF in the Second World War as a fighter pilot. His schooldays and early career in Air Force service would form the basis of his two volumes of memoirs for child readers, *Boy* (1984) and

Going Solo (1986). Dahl's wartime experiences led him to write his first children's book, *The Gremlins* (1943), a *fantasy about the race of tiny people who, in Air Force slang, were blamed for all the technical troubles that pilots experience; the story was serialized in *Cosmopolitan Magazine* and the film rights were bought by *Disney, though filming never took place. (A 1984 film, *Gremlins*, had other origins though it took some inspiration from Dahl's idea.) Later in life he would write the screenplay for Ian Fleming's *Chitty-Chitty-Bang-Bang*.

After the war, Dahl began to make a reputation as a writer of highly idiosyncratic short stories, in such collections as *Kiss Kiss* (1960); he won the Mystery Writers of America Edgar Allan Poe Award twice for individual tales and once for a TV adaptation of one of his stories. In 1953 he married the actress Patricia Neal; they had three children, to whom he began to tell bedtime stories. *James and the Giant Peach* (1961), the first of these to reach print, is a comic fantasy about a small boy who travels the world inside a huge peach, in company with several giant insects. Like most of Dahl's children's books, it first appeared in print in the US. His next novel, *Charlie and the Chocolate Factory* (1964), became a worldwide bestseller. *Charlie and the Great Glass Elevator* (1972) is a sequel.

Dahl's other children's books include *The Magic Finger* (1966), first illustrated by William Pène *Du Bois; *Fantastic Mr Fox* (1970), the story of a fox's wily struggles against three farmers; *Danny, the Champion of the World* (1975), a somewhat more realist story about a motherless boy's adoration of his father, who takes him poaching; *The Wonderful Story of Henry Sugar and six more* (1977), a collection of miscellaneous pieces for older children; *The Enormous Crocodile* (1977), a picture book; *The *Twits* (1980), the story of an ugly and unpleasant husband and wife; *George's Marvellous Medicine* (1981), a grotesque story about a boy who doses his horrible grandmother with

a medicine which does dreadful things to her; and *Revolting Rhymes* (1982), gruesomely comic versions of traditional *fairy tales. Later novel-length fiction includes *The *B.F. G.* (1982), the story of a kindly, vegetarian giant who, with the aid of Sophie and the Queen of England, pens up the child-eating giants for ever; *The *Witches* (1983), about a boy who finds himself staying at the hotel where the national witches' association is holding its AGM; and *Matilda* (1988), about a precociously intelligent schoolgirl. Quentin *Blake illustrated all Dahl's books from *The Enormous Crocodile* onwards, and subsequently went back to produce illustrations for the earlier work, too; the two men's work has become very closely entwined in reader's minds.

Dahl's stories have raised objections from some adult readers, who find them a mixture of the glutinous and the cruel, but more than fifty years since his debut they continue to have an enormous and enthusiastic following among children themselves. His energy, imaginative inventiveness in character and language, and consummate storytelling skill have kept him on bestseller charts to this day, and his books are still regularly cited on lists of favourites, and regularly adapted for stage and screen.

In 2005 the Buckinghamshire house in which he spent his later years was opened to the public as the *Roald Dahl Museum and Story Centre. Donald Sturrock's *Storyteller* (2010) is a good authorized biography.

Dairyman's Daughter, The A tract written by the Revd Leigh Richmond (1772–1827), which subsequently became one of the most frequently issued *evangelical stories in England. This 'Authentic and Interesting Narrative', as the title-page describes it, is the story of Betsy, elder of two daughters of an old dairyman. Her younger sister leads an intemperate life, but thanks to Betsy she repents on her deathbed, while Betsy herself supports her old parents in their declining years, falls ill with consumption, and dies a pious death. The tale was first published in the *Christian Guardian* in 1810 and was afterwards collected in *Annals of the Poor* (1814) along with other tracts by the same author.

Daisy, The, or, *cautionary stories, in verse. Adapted to the ideas of children from four to eight years old* By Elizabeth Turner (d. 1846), published by John *Harris in 1807. The verses, illustrated by headpiece engravings or *woodcuts, give simple examples of good and bad

behaviour and its rewards and punishments. The poems are *cautionary tales in the mode of Ann and Jane *Taylor, but the only child to come to serious harm is 'Miss Helen', who, as a result of running too quickly, falls down a well and is drowned. The volume was very popular, as was the author's second similar work entitled *The Cowslip* (1811). Turner also published *The Pink* (1835) and *The Crocus* (1844). *The Daisy* was parodied, for the amusement of adult readers, in *The New Child's Guide to Knowledge* (1911) by Laurence *Housman, which was dedicated ironically to Turner.

Daisy Chain, The, or, *Aspirations, a family chronicle* (1856) A novel by Charlotte M. *Yonge. It describes the life of the May family of Market Stoneborough, a quiet old English town. Dr May is the local medical man, and his family of eleven children lead the happiest of lives until, in a carriage accident, their mother is killed, their father has his arm severely injured, and the eldest daughter Margaret is invalided. The central character is Ethel, whose personality resembles that of Miss Yonge herself. She learns Latin and Greek from her brother Norman's books, until she is persuaded to concentrate on more ladylike pursuits, and she is the prime mover in a plan to establish a church and *Sunday school in the poor district of Cocksmoor. Her eldest brother Richard eventually becomes the incumbent of the new church. The 'Daisy Chain' of the title is Dr May's pet name for his family.

The book provides a vivid account of mid-19th-cent. family life, and played an important part in the development of the *family story. Miss Yonge followed it with a sequel, *The Trial; or, more links of the Daisy Chain* (1864).

Daleks Robot-like creatures in *Doctor Who*.

DALY, Maureen See SEVENTEENTH SUMMER.

DALY, Niki (1946–) South African author and illustrator of picture books who started to write books as showcases for his paintings. His books have strong African themes and use bright, luminous watercolours to celebrate the multicultural nature of his homeland. *Not So Fast, Songololo* (1985) is simply the story of a boy going shopping with his grandmother, but along the way the reader lives and breathes the township's sights and smells. In *Jamela's Dress* (1999) a girl can't resist showing off the fabric for her mother's new dress, but accidentally ruins it—though with a little luck all turns out well. Jamela returns in several more

books, including *Song for Jamela* (2009), which involves a TV talent show. *Pretty Salma* (2006) retells the story of **Little Red Riding Hood* in an African setting.

DALZIEL Brothers The leading English *wood engraving firm of the Victorian period; they made blocks for innumerable illustrated books of merit during the period 1855–75. George Dalziel (1815–1902) came to London from his native Newcastle to be pupil to an established engraver, then set up in business by himself, and was joined by his brothers Edward (1817–1905), John (1822–69), and Thomas (1823–1906). During the 1840s the brothers undertook engravings for *The *Home Treasury* series of fairy stories, worked for George *Cruikshank, and collaborated with several of the Pre-Raphaelites. In the 1860s they cut new blocks for *Lear's enlarged *Book of Nonsense*, and engraved *Tenniel's illustrations to *Alice's Adventures in Wonderland*, in connection with which they engaged in 'a great deal of correspondence, always of the most agreeable nature, ... with the Rev. Mr Dodgson'. From 1857 they printed and sometimes published books themselves, under the imprint The Camden Press. In 1863–5 they issued their own edition of the *Arabian Nights*. In 1884 the Dalziels began to publish the first British *comic, *Ally Sloper's Half-Holiday*.

The Dalziel Brothers were noted for the fidelity with which they reproduced artists' drawings; but when they retired at the end of the 19th cent. they observed, in their autobiography, that the new processes of making line and half-tone blocks by photo-mechanical methods were an improvement on the old techniques—a judgement with which not everyone would now concur.

Dame Trot A character of children's *chapbook literature. *Old Dame Trot, and Her Comical Cat* was apparently first published in 1803, but the dame and her cat were known at least a hundred years earlier. The story, which is in verse, consists of episodes very like those in the rhyme of *Mother Hubbard, which was not published until 1805 and may have been influenced by it.

A different version, with more wit, and not so obviously resembling the Mother Hubbard verses, was printed by John *Harris in 1819, with the claim that it was taken from 'the Original in the Hubbardonian Library'.

Dame Wiggins of Lee, and her Seven Wonderful Cats A comic poem first published by *Dean and Munday, jointly with A. K. Newman, in 1823. Dame Wiggins keeps 'seven fine cats', who go to school, and earn the gratitude of a farmer by nursing a sick lamb. The title-page claimed that the poem was 'written principally by a lady of ninety', and it was later alleged that this was a Mrs Pearson who kept a toyshop in Fleet Street; though credit for putting the poem into shape was given to the light versifier Richard Scrafton Sharpe, who was probably the author of *Anecdotes and Adventures of Fifteen Gentlemen*. Dame Wiggins is merely doggerel in the *Mother Hubbard tradition, but it proved very popular, and was much admired by John *Ruskin in his childhood. He later wrote of its 'meritorious rhythmic cadence', and in 1885 he had it reissued, with additional verses by himself and extra illustrations by his protégée Kate *Greenaway. The original poem and illustrations are reproduced in Iona and Peter *Opie's *Nursery Companion* (1980).

DANA, Richard Henry *See* TWO YEARS BEFORE THE MAST.

Dan Dare Spaceman in stories in **Eagle*.

Dandy A British *comic published by D. C. *Thomson of Dundee; it first appeared on 4 December 1937. Its chief hero is Desperate Dan, a gigantic stubble-chinned American *cowboy-type who lives with his Aunt Aggie and eats Cow Pie (with the horns left in).

DANIELL, David Scott (Albert Scott Daniell) (1906–65) British children's author, who for some years was best known for his 'Polly and Oliver' stories about a drummer-boy in the Napoleonic wars and his girl cousin. Daniell also wrote a large number of non-fiction books about aircraft, ships, and other aspects of modern life.

Danish fairy and folk tales Collected in Svend Grundtvig's *Danske Folkeeventyr* (1876 and subsequent volumes); selected *fairy tales from this work, for children, were published in Jane Mulley's *Fairy Tales from Afar* (1900).

DANN, Colin *See* ANIMALS OF FARTHING WOOD, THE.

Danny, the Champion of the World *See* DAHL, ROALD.

DANZIGER, Paula (1944–2004) American writer. As colourful a character as any in her novels, Danziger drew on her experiences of a dysfunctional family and many years teaching

to become one of the first to write about real life for pre-teens. There is no fluffy fantasy here, just honest—and very funny—looks at weight, divorce, friends, and problem parents, all written without a hint of sermonizing. Hugely popular in her native America, she also had a book slot on the 1990s UK TV show *Live and Kicking*. Her debut, *The Cat Ate My Gymsuit* (1974), had a wonderfully fresh voice and tells of Marcy, who thinks she's fat and worthless, but finally finds something that makes her realize she matters. It was followed by other classics such as *The Divorce Express* (1982) which deals with (obviously) divorce, but also how change isn't always for the worse; *Make Like a Tree and Leave* (1992); and the long-running *Amber Brown* series for younger readers, starting with *Amber Brown Is Not a Crayon* (1993), in which messy-haired, straight-talking Amber has to deal with her best friend moving away.

Darbishire Schoolboy in the **Jennings* books by Anthony Buckeridge.

Dark Is Rising, The An influential sequence of five *fantasy novels by Susan *Cooper, describing a cosmic struggle between Dark and Light set in the modern world. *Over Sea, Under Stone* (1965) describes how three children on holiday in Cornwall discover a *Grail. In the second volume, *The Dark Is Rising* (1973), Will Stanton, aged eleven, learns that he is the last of the Old Ones and has a quest to find the Signs of the Light which will defeat the Dark. *Greenwitch* (1974) begins with the theft of the Grail by the forces of the Dark, and concerns the making of a leaf image of a woman which acquires supernatural powers. The sequence concludes with *The Grey King* (1975), which won the *Newbery Medal, and *Silver on the Tree* (1977), both set in Wales; these novels are based, more specifically than are the earlier books, on the legends of King *Arthur. *The Dark Is Rising* has been compared to the works of J. R. R. *Tolkien and C. S. *Lewis, and has generally been received with enthusiasm by critics and fantasy-lovers alike.

DARLEY, F. O. C (Felix Octavius Carr) (1822–88) Leading American illustrator of the mid-19th cent. He was a friend of Washington *Irving and illustrated editions of several of his books, as well as works by Longfellow and Harriet Beecher *Stowe.

Darling family In **Peter Pan* by J. M. *Barrie.

DARTON, F. J. (Frederick Joseph) Harvey (1878–1936) Historian of children's literature; he was a member of the celebrated publishing family of *Darton. For some years he edited the magazine **Chatterbox*, which was published by the family firm. His own literary output was considerable and included a life of Mrs *Sherwood, several works of literary history, books about the English countryside, and editions of such 'forgotten' classics as *The *Seven Champions of Christendom*. His *Children's Books in England: five centuries of social life* (1932) was the first scholarly work on this subject, and is still generally regarded as the finest, though its value was not properly recognized until many years after its author's death. It was revised and expanded by Brian *Alderson for a new edition published in 1982.

DARTON family A Quaker family who were publishers of children's books for almost 150 years. William Darton senior (1755–1819) went into business in London *c.*1785, together with members of the Harvey family. He was the publisher of, among others, Ann and Jane *Taylor. His son William (1779–1854) published with his father and separately. There were, at various times, a number of different imprints: Darton & Harvey, Harvey & Darton, Darton & Clark, Darton & Co., etc. In the late 19th cent. the family continued to be involved with publishing, in the firm of Wells Gardner, Darton & Co. Their connection with it ceased in 1928, when the business was sold, though the imprint continued to be used for about 30 years more. *See also* DARTON, F. J. HARVEY.

DASENT, Sir George Webbe *See* POPULAR TALES FROM THE NORSE.

DAUGHERTY, James (Henry) (1889–1974) American illustrator and author who won the *Newbery Medal for *Daniel Boone* (1939).

D'AULAIRE, Edgar Parin (1898–1986) and **Ingri** (1904–80) Author-illustrators resident in America who produced many *picture books between 1931 and 1972. He was born in Germany, she in Norway. They won the *Caldecott Medal with *Abraham Lincoln* (1939).The classic collection *D'Aulaire's Book of Greek Myths* (1962) remains in print over half a century after its first publication.

D'AULNOY, Mme *See* AULNOY.

David Blaize and the Blue Door (1919) A *fantasy by E. F. Benson, illustrated by H. J. *Ford. David Blaize, a small boy, discovers a door under his pillow and, going through,

finds himself in a land peopled by Wonderland-like creatures. The book is one of the more genuinely imaginative fantasies written under the influence of Lewis *Carroll. Edward Frederick Benson (1867–1940), son of Archbishop Benson, was a British popular novelist, well known for his 'Dodo' and 'Lucia' stories. He wrote two other 'David' books, *David Blaize* (1916), a conventional *school story, and *David of King's* (1924), set at Cambridge.

DAVIES, Andrew (Wynford) (1936–) British screenwriter, playwright, and novelist who has written a number of children's books including *Conrad's War* (1978) and the 'Marmalade Atkins' series about an impossibly naughty girl.

DAVIS, David (William Eric Davis) (1908–96) Introduced and edited the BBC's *Children's Hour for many years until its demise in 1964. His wife, Barbara *Sleigh, was a successful children's author.

DAVISON, Frank Dalby Australian author of *animal stories, among them *Man-Shy* (1931), the story of a heifer. He also wrote *Children of the Dark People* (1936).

Davy and the Goblins (1884) A *fantasy by Charles E. *Carryl.

Davy Crockett American folk hero, in reality Colonel David Crockett (1786–1836), a notorious braggart who died a hero's death in the defence of the Alamo. His supposed autobiography, *A Narrative of the Life of David Crockett* (1834), appeared in many editions, and even before his death his legendary exploits began to be featured in other popular literature.

From the 1870s Crockett began to be the subject of *dime novels, e.g. *The Texan Trailer; or, Davy Crockett's Last Bear-Hunt* (1871) by Charles E. LaSalle. In 1956 the Walt *Disney organization sparked off a huge Davy Crockett revival with their film *Davy Crockett, King of the Wild Frontier*. This caused Crockett-style imitation coon-skin hats (with the tail hanging down the wearer's back) to become fashionable among boys, and the *ballad written specially for the film ('Born on a mountain-top in Tennessee . . .') was adapted into many comic versions by children all round the world.

DAWLISH, Peter (James Lennox Kerr) (1899–1963) Popular British writer of boating stories for boys. The series began with *Dauntless Finds Her Crew* (1947) and ended with *Dauntless Goes Home* (1960).

DAY, Thomas (1748–89) English writer, author of *Sandford and Merton*. Day lived most of his life according to the principles of philanthropy, austere simplicity, and manual labour that he recommended in *Sandford and Merton*. A disciple of *Rousseau, whom he met in Paris, Day tried to find the ideal wife by taking two twelve-year-old girls from orphanages and educating them according to his version of the precepts in *Émile*. Neither girl proved acceptable, and he eventually married a well-educated heiress who admired his writing. Besides *Sandford and Merton* (1783–9) and *The *History of Little Jack* (1788), he wrote political tracts and some poetry.

DAY LEWIS, C. *See* LEWIS, C. DAY.

Day of the Triffids, The *See* WYNDHAM, JOHN.

DEACON, Alexis (1978–) An English picture-book creator, illustrator, and author whose odd and brilliant first picture book *Slow Loris* (2002) was shortlisted for the *Blue Peter Book Awards shortly after his graduation from Brighton University. This was quickly followed by *Beegu* (2004). Deacon's ethereal illustrative style is reminiscent of classic English book illustrations whilst having a distinctly contemporary, often alien, feel. His characteristically muted palette, with moments of bright colour, contributes to this otherworldly feel, which is further achieved by small drawings being enlarged, rearranged, recopied, and coloured, and by his use of linseed oil to create hazy and dreamlike worlds—as, for example, in *While You Are Sleeping* (2007). The stunning *Croc and Bird* (2012) is another highlight. Deacon has also illustrated for other authors, including *Jitterbug Jam* (2004) by Barbara Jean Hicks, which features a cast of eerie, yet appealing, monsters, and Oscar *Wilde's *The Selfish Giant* (2013). He is himself the author of *A Place to Call Home* (2012) and *Cheese Belongs To You* (2013), both illustrated by Viviane *Schwarz.

Deadwood Dick The first masked rider of *western fiction, hero of *dime novels and other sensational works of fiction. Stories about him appeared as early as 1877, when Edward L. Wheeler began to write a series of tales for the Beadle's Half-Dime Novel series. The first, *Deadwood Dick, the Prince of the Road*, has Dick proposing to *Calamity Jane.

She turns him down, and their relationship continues its vicissitudes in more than 30 sequels. The tales are bloodthirsty, and Deadwood Dick and his lady live 'lives branded with commingled shame and honour'. They are both killed (not for the first time) in *Deadwood Dick's Dust; or, the Chained Hand* (October 1885), and Wheeler seems himself to have died at about this time. However, the publishers Beadle and Adams were not prepared to let a good thing vanish, and in January 1886 the Half-Dime Novel series saw the appearance of *Deadwood Dick, Jr.; or, the Sign of the Crimson Crescent*, published under Wheeler's name. Deadwood Dick Jr. afterwards appeared as a *detective in the *Aldine 'Life and Adventure Library' series.

Dealings with the Fairies (1868) The first collection of *fairy stories by George *MacDonald, illustrated by Arthur *Hughes. It contained *The *Light Princess, The *Giant's Heart*, 'The Shadows', 'Cross Purposes', and *The *Golden Key*.

DE AMICIS, Edmondo *See* CUORE.

DEAN family Publishers of children's books in London from the late 18th cent. Thomas Dean was in business before 1800; the firm later became Dean and Munday, and as such it published a number of attractive illustrated books, such as *A *Gaping, Wide-Mouthed, Waddling Frog* (*c*.1822). Dean's became specialists in *toy books and *movable picture books. For many decades of the 20th cent. (and into the 21st) it published Enid *Blyton.

DE ANGELI, Marguerite (Lofft) (1889–1987) American author-illustrator who won the *Newbery Medal for *The Door in the Wall* (1949), a *historical novel set in medieval England.

Dear Nobody (1991) A novel by Berlie *Doherty which won the *Carnegie Medal. It tells the story of the relationship between Chris and Helen, and what happens when Helen finds out she is pregnant. It is narrated from two perspectives: one is in the first person by Chris, as he looks back on the previous months, and we get right to the heart of his feelings about his impending fatherhood; the other is in the form of letters addressed to Helen to 'Dear Nobody', her unborn child, and we learn of her fear of the future and her sense of isolation. But *Dear Nobody* is, above all, a love story. It deals not only with romantic love, but familial love, too. It is striking in its achievements as an excellent novel, not merely an 'issues' book about pregnancy. The characters are subtly drawn, their backgrounds fleshed out, and their changing relationship authentically described.

DEARY, Terry *See* HORRIBLE HISTORIES.

Dear Zoo (1982) A picture book by Rod *Campbell. With its repeating text and flaps to lift, *Dear Zoo* has been a favourite with toddlers for over three decades. Each page introduces an animal sent by the zoo as a potential pet, but each one has something wrong with it (too fierce, too big, too grumpy, etc.); finally the nice zoo people send a puppy. 'He was perfect! So I kept him.'

Deborah Dent and Her Donkey A comic poem with illustrations, in the manner of *Dame Wiggins of Lee*, published by *Dean and Munday with A. K. Newman in 1823. Dame Deborah Dent keeps not one but five donkeys, whose attributes represent the five senses, and the poem describes their adventures. It achieved some popularity, and *c*.1850 Dean and Munday's successors issued a new version, *Dame Deborah and Her Comical Donkeys*.

DE BRUNHOFF, Jean (1899–1937) and **Laurent** (1925–) Father and son creators of the *Babar* books. Jean de Brunhoff was born in Paris and studied at the École Alsacienne. The books that made his name started out as a bedtime story told by Jean's wife Cécile (née Sabouraud, 1903–2003) to their children; then at the boys' request Jean began to illustrate and publish them. Some years following Jean's early death from tuberculosis, Jean and Cécile's eldest son Laurent, also a painter, continued the series, illustrating the books in his father's style (latterly in collaboration with his wife, Phyllis Rose). Though he has also created characters of his own, Laurent remains most noted for continuing the series first conceived and developed by his parents.

DE CHATELAIN, Mme *See* CHATELAIN.

Deerslayer, The *See* LEATHER-STOCKING TALES.

DEFOE, Daniel (?1660–1731) Author of *Robinson Crusoe*, he was the son of a London butcher, James Foe. He changed his name to Defoe when he was in his forties. He was brought up a Nonconformist and sent to a dissenting school, but instead of becoming a minister he went into business as a hosiery merchant and seems to have travelled widely

in Europe; he became bankrupt in 1692. After being involved in Monmouth's rebellion against James II he began to write political tracts, and in 1701 published *The True-born Englishman*, which defended the Dutchness of William III on the grounds that the English are a mongrel race. In 1702 his *Shortest Way with the Dissenters*, a satirical pamphlet ironically calling for the total suppression of religious nonconformity, got him into trouble with Parliament, and he was imprisoned and pilloried. While in Newgate Prison he began to publish *The Review*, a periodical on current affairs, which paved the way for the *Tatler* and *Spectator*.

In 1719 he published *Robinson Crusoe*. He had already shown himself a master of the fictitious narrative in several short pieces, including a ghost story and an imaginary account of an earthquake; a contemporary commented on his journalism that he was 'truly a master . . . of forging a story and imposing it on the world for truth'. *Robinson Crusoe* was presented as fact rather than fiction—it was based on the real experiences of a shipwrecked Scotsman, Alexander Selkirk—and its huge success encouraged Defoe to continue in the same vein. He published *Moll Flanders* and *Colonel Jack* in 1722 and *Roxana* in 1724. His *Journal of the Plague Year* appeared in 1722. By 1725, when he was in his mid-60s, he had become fairly prosperous and was living with his wife and children in Stoke Newington. He died 'of a lethargy' in 1731.

Defoe composed nothing intended specifically for young readers, but many of his works, particularly *Robinson Crusoe*, still remain popular with young readers and **Family Instructor* (1715 and 1718) shows an intimate understanding of the difficulties of family life and the characters of children. *See also* ROBINSONNADES.

DE FOMBELLE, Timothée (1973-) French novelist and playwright, whose books include two acclaimed and award-winning duologies for children and young adults, both translated into English by Sarah *Ardizzone. The first, *Tobie Lolness* (2006–7; English translations *Toby Alone* (2008) and *Toby and the Secrets of the Tree* (2010), the former winning the 2009 *Marsh Award) is an eco-fable about a microscopically small thirteen-year-old boy whose family life in a great oak tree is under threat. Meanwhile *Vango* (2010–11; English translations *Between Sky and Earth* (2013) and *A Prince without a Kingdom* (2014)) is a thrilling adventure story set in Europe in the 1930s, about a nineteen-year-old on the run, and his quest for identity and truth.

DEGEN, Bruce (1945-) American author and illustrator who worked as a teacher, a set designer for opera, a printmaker, and in advertising before making his mark with witty, colourful illustrations for picture books. His collaboration with Joanna Cole (1944-) on *The Magic School Bus* (1986–2006) series blends science with humorous storytelling. It features Ms Valerie Frizzle, her class, and the class pet lizard, who board an anthropomorphic bus for field trips to places such as the solar system, inside the human body, or the past to find out about famous scientists. In the original story, *The Magic School Bus at the Waterworks* (1986), the class discover that even a boring trip can be fun. The series has been greatly expanded through chapter books, first readers, computer games, and DVDs.

DE GENLIS, Mme *See* GENLIS.

DE GOLDI, Kate (1959-) A New Zealand author of children's and *young adult books. Both her children's and young adult books are known for their rich, playful language, friendly humour, and strong characterization. Family is a key theme in her work, particularly family secrets or suppressed issues which come to the surface over the course of the narratives. Her young adult novels *The Sanctuary* (1996), *Love, Charlie Mike* (1997), and *Closed, Stranger* (2004) may be considered *crossover books, as is the coming-of-age novel *The 10 PM Question* (2008), which made her known to international audiences. The novel and its German translation won several book awards. De Goldi also successfully self-published several picture books with illustrator Jacqui Colley, the best known being *Clubs*, which was selected as Book of the Year at the *New Zealand Post Children's Book Awards 2005. In 2012, she published her first illustrated junior fiction book, *The ACB with Honora Lee*. Among other awards, De Goldi won the prestigious *Margaret Mahy Medal in 2011.

DE GRAFT-HANSON, J. O. (1932–2002) Ghanaian author of a series of 'Papa Ewusi' stories, published in the 1970s, in which a small boy encounters creatures from Ghanaian folklore.

DE JONG, Meindert (1906–91) Children's novelist who was born in the Netherlands. When he was eight his family emigrated to America, settling in Grand Rapids, Michigan. During the Second World War he was an official war historian with the USAF in China, which was later to lead to his book *The House*

of *Sixty Fathers* (1956), about a Chinese boy fleeing from the Japanese.

De Jong's fiction, apart from this one excursion to the Far East, is set either in his native Friesland or in American Mid-Western farm country. His early books (*The Big Goose and the Little White Duck*, 1938, was the first) were largely *animal stories. He had been writing for many years before he produced his first novel of real distinction. This was *Shadrach* (1953), illustrated by Maurice *Sendak: a very simple story about a little boy who has been promised a rabbit, is given it, worries about its thinness, loses it, and finds it again, fat and healthy. *Shadrach* is a perfectly crafted book, outstanding for its author's ability to see the world through the little boy's eyes. The year after it appeared, De Jong won the *Newbery Medal with *The Wheel on the School* (1954), in which Dutch schoolchildren plan to entice storks to nest on the roof of their school by placing a wheel there.

De Jong continued to write animal stories, including *Hurry Home, Candy* (1953), *Along Came a Dog* (1958), and *The Last Little Cat* (1961). His next really striking piece of work was *The Singing Hill* (1962); set in rural America, it describes the relationships between a small boy, isolated when the older children in the family leave home, his grandfather, and an old horse. *Far Out the Long Canal* (1964), perhaps De Jong's finest achievement, returns to a Dutch setting, and is the story of Moonta, a boy who (because of sickness) has not learnt to skate. Suddenly his village is in the grip of the sharpest frost in years, and his chance has come.

De Jong's later books include *Journey from Peppermint Street* (1968), which won him the first *National Book Award in 1969. De Jong was also the winner of the 1962 *Hans Christian Andersen Award.

DE LA MARE, Walter (John) (1873–1956) Poet, essayist, and writer of fiction. In 1902, three years after his marriage to Elfrida Ingpen (which produced four children), he had his first book of poems, *Songs of Childhood*, published under a pseudonym. Two years later came a novel, *Henry Brocken*, and in 1910 another novel, *The Return*, and also *The *Three Mulla-Mulgars* (later reissued as *The Three Royal Monkeys*). His adult collection *The Listeners and other poems* (1912) included his most famous poem, which begins ' "Is there anybody there?" said the Traveller, | Knocking on the moonlit door.' His next collection of

verse, *Peacock Pie* (1913), was an immediate and lasting success. *Memoirs of a Midget* (1921) became his most admired novel, while *Come Hither* (1923) is generally regarded as the most imaginative poetry anthology for children of its period. This was followed by many other books, including *Told Again* (1927), a volume of retellings of traditional *fairy stories (reprinted in 1959 as *Tales Told Again*), and *Stories from the Bible* (1929). De la Mare's *Collected Stories for Children* appeared in 1947.

De la Mare was not affected by literary movements, and his writing, both in verse and prose, largely defies classification. His short stories for children are a unique blend of traditional materials with highly idiosyncratic invention. David Cecil has written of them: 'Incident and character alike are fanciful and mysterious, the emotional tone heightened and lyrical...The houses are secret and irregular, full of dark nooks and twisting staircases...The children are queer children ...the bachelors and old maids are solitary, eccentric, often a trifle crazy.' De la Mare's verse has had a profound effect on later writers of poetry for children.

DELTA, Penelope (1874–1941) Pioneering Greek children's writer, the first to take an interest in the field and to attempt to provide Greek children with good books that entertained them, had a moral content, inspired in them a love for their country, and taught them their nation's history. Her books, which include *A Tale Without a Name* (translated by Mika Provata-Carlone, 2013) and *Secrets of the Swamp* (translated by Ruth Bobick, 2012), include novels, fairy tales, and short stories, and many have become classics. The majority of her books can be described as historical fiction. She was inspired by the Byzantine era, the Macedonian Struggle, and other major political and military events of her time. Her simple, easy style, her clear descriptions, and the fact that she wrote in demotic Greek resulted in her books' strong popular appeal.

DE MELLO BREYNER ANDRESEN, Sophia (1919–2004) Portuguese poet and writer, the author of several much-loved works for children, beginning in 1958 with *A Menina do Mar* ('The Sea-Girl'), about a boy who becomes friends with a girl from the sea, and *A Fada Oriana* ('Oriana, the Fairy'), in which a fairy neglects the forest she is supposed to watch over. Other notable books include *O Cavaleiro da Dinamarca* (1964, 'The Danish Knight') and *O Rapaz de Bronze* (1966,

'The Bronze Boy'). While her children's books have not received the international acclaim they deserve, she continues to be held in great affection by readers young and old in her native Portugal.

DE MILLE, James (1833–80) Canadian author who wrote prolifically for both children and adults. His greatest success was his 'B.O. W.C.' (Brethren of the White Cross) series. The series began with *A Book for Boys* (1869), and continued with *The Boys of the Grand Pré School* (1870), *Picked Up Adrift* (1872), and *Treasure of the Sea* (1873).

Demon Headmaster, The (from 1982) A timelessly funny six-book series by Gillian *Cross about a headmaster who has hypnotized his entire school into becoming so perfect that the kids there even work through break times. Everyone, staff, pupils, and parents, all think the headmaster is wonderful, but newcomer Dinah suspects something sinister is at work. Which of course it is. The unnamed villain is ousted by Dinah and her friends, though he turns up again in different guises in the sequels, and the children have to outwit their teacher in a series of exciting and inventive scenarios. The books have also been made into a TV series.

DE MORGAN, Mary Augusta (1850–1907) Sister of the Pre-Raphaelite artist and writer William De Morgan, Mary published several collections of short original *fairy stories, of which the best known were *On a Pincushion and other fairy tales* (1877), *The Necklace of Princess Fiorimonde and other stories* (1880), and *The Windfairies and other tales* (1900). Her stories are entertaining and not unmemorable, but lack the visionary power of her contemporary, George *MacDonald.

DENNIS, C. J. (Clarence James) (1876–1938) Popular Australian poet, best known for his *Songs of a Sentimental Bloke* (1915) and *The Moods of Ginger Mick* (1916). He also wrote *A Book for Kids* (1921), a collection of verse and stories with characteristically Australian subjects, illustrated by himself. His Edward *Lear-like narrative poem *The Glugs of Gosh* was published as a *picture book in 1974.

DENNISON, Muriel *See* SUSANNAH OF THE MOUNTIES.

Dennis the Dachshund In the *Toytown* stories of S. G. Hulme Beaman.

Dennis the Menace In the British comic *Beano*, a tousle-headed troublemaking boy. In the month that he first appeared in print, March 1951, a comic strip of the same name started to be syndicated in the US. The American Dennis is somewhat milder and younger than his British counterpart. Both UK and US Dennises are still making mischief more than sixty years later. In 2014 Steven Butler published the first volume of the UK Dennis's 'diary'.

DENSLOW, W. W. *See* WONDERFUL WIZARD OF OZ, THE.

DENTON, Terry (1950–) Australian illustrator of over thirty books, who also writes picture books and occasionally creates puzzle and other books. His first book, *Felix and Alexander* (1985), won the *CBCA Picture Book of the Year in 1986. His work for younger readers is usually humorous, lively line illustration, but his picture books are richly coloured and often poignant, sometimes pen-and-wash, sometimes acrylic. Denton helped to develop the television programme, *Lift-Off*, in 1990 and worked on it for another two years. He has collaborated with Australian authors Paul *Jennings and Ted *Greenwood on the *Spooner or Later* books (from 1999), with Andy Griffiths on several series including *13-Storey Treehouse*, and with many others. A frequent award-winner in all categories, Denton has a flair for understanding children, their fears, and their humour.

DEPAOLA, Tomie (1934–) An American author and artist who has written and/or illustrated over 250 titles. DePaola is particularly well known for his *Strega Nona* series about an Italian 'grandma witch' and the adventures of her neighbours. The first title in the series, *Strega Nona*, received a Caldecott Honor in 1976 (*see* CALDECOTT MEDAL). DePaola was born in Connecticut to an Irish-Italian family, and he has written several autobiographical picture books, among them *26 Fairmount Avenue* and *Nana Upstairs & Nana Downstairs*. Other series include the *Bill and Pete* stories, about a crocodile and his trusty avian toothbrush, and the *Barker Twins* series. DePaola studied fine art at the Pratt Institute, and later taught art in California and New England, before retiring to focus on his children's books.

DE REGNIERS, Beatrice Schenk (1914–2000) American author of books for young children, including *A Little House of Your Own* (1954) and *May I Bring a Friend?* (1964).

DE ROO, Anne (Louise) (1931–2007) New
Zealand children's author who wrote *adven-
ture stories such as *The Gold Dog* (1969), *Boy
and the Sea Beast* (1971), and 'novels of char-
acter' such as *Cinnamon and Nutmeg* (1972).

DE SAINT-EXUPÉRY, Antoine *See* LITTLE
PRINCE, THE.

***Description of Three Hundred Ani-
mals, A*** A work of *natural history for chil-
dren, ascribed to Thomas *Boreman. The first
edition was published by him in 1730, and was
followed by a supplementary volume 'particu-
larly for the entertainment of youth' in 1736,
and another in 1739. Later editions include
several issued by the *Newbery family from
1774 onwards. The book was based largely
on Topsell's *Historie of Four-Footed Beastes*,
and includes a number of fabulous creatures,
such as the Cockatrice, a serpent which walks
half-upright and is said to be born from an egg
laid by a cock. The *Description*, which continued
to appear in various forms during the 19th cent.,
was one of Thomas *Bewick's earliest readings,
though he called it 'a wretched composition'.

Desert Home, The, *or the Adventures of a
Lost Family in the Wilderness* (1852) The first
novel by Mayne *Reid to be written specially
for boys. It is modelled on *The *Swiss Family
Robinson*. A party of traders discovers, in
an oasis settlement in the Mexican desert, a
home established by the Rolfe family from
England, whose father narrates their experi-
ences. Crossing the desert they were attacked
by '*Indians' and having survived this they
decided to remain where they were and live
by trapping beavers. At the end of the book the
Rolfes return to civilization with the traders.
The story has sometimes been published
under the title *The English Family Robinson*.

Desmond the Dinosaur In stories by
*Althea.

Desperate Dan Character in *Dandy.

DESSEN, Sarah (1970–) American author of
books for young adults whose debut, *That
Summer* (1996), was published while she was
working as a waitress. Inspired by her own
schooldays, Dessen's books chart the lives of
girls, their friends, and families with poign-
ancy, truth, and a sharp eye (and ear) for all
the minutiae of everyday life. They are well
written and never overly sentimental. Some of
her best books are *This Lullaby* (2002), *The
Truth About Forever* (2004), and *The Moon
and More* (2013).

detective stories These began to play a
large part in children's cheap popular reading
matter towards the end of the 19th cent. The
genre's origins may be traced back to narra-
tives of criminal deeds in *chapbooks, pica-
resque stories about such characters as *Dick
Turpin, and Gothic novels, while James Feni-
more *Cooper describes 'detection' by means
of tracking footprints in wild country in his
Leather-Stocking Tales. The first true detec-
tive story is generally held to be Edgar Allan
Poe's *Murders in the Rue Morgue* (1841). Poe's
story made a great impression in France,
where the exploits of a real pioneer detective
Eugène Vidocq (1775–1857) were already well
known, and subsequently the *roman policier*
became a very popular form of French fiction.

Meanwhile in Poe's native country of Amer-
ica detection began to be the theme of the
*dime novel during the 1870s. One of the
earliest American detective stories was *The
Detective's Ward; or, the Fortunes of a Bowery
Girl*, a New York melodrama by 'Agile Penne',
serialized in the *Saturday Journal* (one of the
cheap periodicals issued by Beadle and
Adams, leading dime novel publishers) from
10 June to 22 July 1871. Further stories of this
sort appeared during the remainder of the
1870s, and even established *western heroes
began to turn detective, e.g. in *Deadwood Dick
as Detective; a Story of the Great Carbonate
Region*, one of the Beadle's Half-Dime Novel
series, written by Edward L. Wheeler, creator
of the *Deadwood Dick stories, and published
in 1879. Meanwhile the term 'sleuth-hound'
or 'sleuth' (apparently from the Old Norse
'sloð', 'tracker'), began to be used; a detective
in Munroe's Dime Novels was named 'Old
Sleuth', and in 1882 the weekly *Boys of New
York* published the story *Young Sleuth, the
Detective, in Chicago*. Soon, established au-
thors of western tales, such as Prentiss Ingra-
ham, chronicler of the deeds of *Buffalo Bill,
were turning their hands to crime fiction, and
by the late 1880s detective stories were at least
equal in number to westerns in the lists of
popular publishing houses. Typical titles
from this period, published in 'Beadle's Boy's
Library of Sport, Story and Adventure', are
Howard M. Boynton's *Kid Keen in New York;
or, the Western Wonder on an Eastern Case*,
and Percy Preston's *The Café Detective; or, Roy
Kennedy's Big Score*, both issued in 1890. For a
time the fashion was for specialist detectives,
e.g. the 'Post Office Detective', the 'Revenue
Detective', and the 'Hotel Detective'. No real
attempt was made to create a popular

detective with a distinctive personality until the first appearance of *Nick Carter in 1886.

In England, the first of Conan *Doyle's 'Sherlock Holmes' stories, A Study in Scarlet, was published in Beeton's Christmas Annual for 1887 (see BEETON, SAMUEL ORCHART) and the next year it appeared as a book. Doyle's second Holmes tale, The Sign of Four, was published in the American periodical Lippincott's Magazine in 1889, and in July 1891 *Strand Magazine began to publish Holmes short stories. (Various written-for-children spin-offs have appeared in recent years, including Andrew Lane's Young Sherlock Holmes series, beginning in 2010 with Death Cloud.) At the other end of the intellectual scale, *Sexton Blake made what was probably his first appearance in *Marvel in 1893. The next year the same paper saw the first appearance of *Nelson Lee, the detective who becomes a schoolmaster.

The popularity of these figures led to the creation of many more, in the pages of the *Harmsworth juvenile papers and their imitators. The first girl sleuth to be featured in magazines in Britain seems to have been 'Sylvia Silence', who appeared in the Harmsworth Schoolgirls' Weekly in 1922. The 'Valerie Drew' stories and other magazines were popular during the 1930s, and similar characters continued to be created after the Second World War.

The success of *Emil and the Detectives (1929) led to many imitations in which groups of children outwit hardened criminals. These range in quality from C. Day *Lewis's The Otterbury Incident (1948), a work of some imagination, to the formulaic and predictable *Famous Five books by Enid *Blyton. In the US, Phyllis A. Whitney (1903–2008) wrote large numbers of Blyton-style child-detective books between 1949 and the late 1970s.

Despite the rise of the television thriller, which glorifies the toughness of the police and criminals, the traditional detective story for young readers in the 1960s and 1970s continued to flourish. America produced the *Linda Craig, *Hardy Boys, and *Nancy Drew series of books, as well as the (then) internationally successful Three Investigators series, created by Robert Arthur Jr.; in Sweden the parody 'Ture Sventon' stories by Åke Holmberg, and the 'Masterdetective Blomkvist' stories by Astrid *Lindgren (in English, 'Bill Bergson') have been popular. Eleanor *Updale's Montmorency books are a rare example of children's books with adult protagonists, but for the most part the successful detective stories in the children's market remain those in which the protagonists' age corresponds reasonably closely to the age of their readers. (Another exception, of course, is the dedicated investigative reporter *Tintin, though admittedly his age is rather hard to pin down with any precision.)

Many recent or contemporary children's writers specialize in detective/mystery stories and sustain their characters for extensive series—Joan Lowery Nixon is a notable recent mystery writer in the US, for example, or latterly Caroline Lawrence in the UK with her Roman and western series; and British writer Tanya *Landman, best known as the author of first-rate *young adult novels, has also written a series of mysteries for young readers (younger than usually served by this genre)—the Poppy Fields mysteries—including one set at a literary *festival. In addition, there are also plenty of versatile novelists whose varied bodies of works include superior examples of what might be characterised as detective stories among them—Philip Pullman's The *Ruby in the Smoke is a fine representative of the genre.

DE TREVIÑO, Elizabeth Borton (1904–2001) American author who won the *Newbery Medal for I, Juan de Pareja (1965), about a boy who is slave to the painter Velázquez.

Deutscher Jugendliteraturpreis The German youth literature prize, awarded annually since 1956. With awards in five categories (three more than when it was launched), including one selected by a youth jury, the prize makes no stipulation for a book's language of origin, so has been won by many non-German authors, which brings it unusual international attention. Winners include John *Green, Patrick *Ness, Suzanne *Collins, Graham Gardner, Margaret *Wild, Philip *Ardagh, Bart *Moeyaert, Shaun *Tan, Grégoire Solotareff, Markus *Zusak, Guus *Kuijer, Ted van Lieshout, Peter *Sís, etc. Since 1991 there has in addition been a lifetime achievement award for a German writer, illustrator, or translator, won to date by, among others, Mirjam Pressler, Klaus Ensikat, Wolf *Erlbruch, Harry Rowohlt, Rotraut Susanne Berner, Jutta *Bauer, and Andreas Steinhöfel.

DHONDY, Farrukh (1944–) Indian-born author for teenagers and adults who has lived most of his life in the UK. He has produced several collections of short stories, some about his Indian childhood, others describing young

Asian immigrants in Britain. Collections include *East End at Your Feet* (1976) and *Come to Mecca* (1978), which deal with the lives of young people in a diverse city, never shying away from its racial problems, which he handles with unusual honesty (especially unusual for the time at which these books were written). In 1978 too he published his first *young adult novel, *The Siege of Babylon*.

Diamonds and Toads A *fairy story by *Perrault, first printed in 1697 in the *Contes de ma mère L'Oye* as *Les Fées*.

A beautiful, sweet-tempered girl is rewarded for her kindness to a fairy by being granted the gift that, whenever she speaks, flowers and precious stones drop out of her mouth. Her disagreeable mother, seeing this, decides that the girl's unpleasant sister should meet the fairy in the hope that she will be rewarded in the same way. The elder girl, however, does not recognize the fairy and is rude to her. As a result she finds that, whenever she opens her mouth, she lets fall a stream of toads and snakes. The younger girl marries a prince, but the elder is turned out of her home and dies.

Numerous parallels to the story exist, one of the closest being the tale of 'The Two Cakes' in the *Pentamerone* (Day 4, tale 7). The story first appeared in English in 1729 in *Histories, or Tales of Past Times*, as *The Fairy*. It later became known as *Diamonds and Toads*, or *Toads and Diamonds*. F. *Anstey, author of *Vice Versa*, turned the tale into a squib against *evangelical books for the young in *The Good Little Girl* (1890).

Diary of a Killer Cat A series for young readers by Anne *Fine.

Diary of a Wimpy Kid (2007) In 2004 designer and computer programmer Jeff Kinney (1971–) started *Wimpy Kid* as an online cartoon that he added to daily. It was an instant success, eventually gaining over twenty million hits. The cartoons were published in book form in 2007 and have since gained international acclaim and many, many sequels. The series follows the life of middle-school weakling Greg Heffley and his friends and family. Written in diary form, the books are light on words, very funny, and heavily illustrated with cartoons, lists, and notes. Spin-offs include video games, a Cheese Touch board game, a series of films, film tie-in books, and the *Diary of a Wimpy Kid Do-it-yourself Book* (2008).

Diary of a Wombat (2002) A picture book by Jackie *French, illustrated by Bruce *Whatley, which has many sequels. Just as the title suggests, the books offer a wombat's view of the world: this is Mothball's diary. The strengths of the writing lie in the very believable point of view, droll humour, and naïve, yet rhythmic, language. The illustrations have a sketchy acrylic style, giving the impression of watercolour. The design features strong composition using white space and a simulated hand-lettered typeface. The books have achieved popularity in Australia and America.

Diary of a Young Girl, The By Anne Frank, a young Jewish girl living in Amsterdam during the Second World War, who went into hiding with her own and another family to escape from Nazi persecution. Anne's diary, written in Dutch from her thirteenth birthday onwards with stoicism, insight, and considerable literary merit, details her day-to-day life in hiding—its challenges, irritations, and fears. It is written in the form of letters to a number of imaginary friends, then to one only—Dear Kitty.

Anne did not survive—the last diary entry is on 1 August 1944, after which the family's hiding place was betrayed, and they were arrested by the Gestapo and deported to concentration camps. Anne later died of typhus at Bergen-Belsen. After the war her diary was discovered, and was first transcribed into German by her father, the only surviving member of the immediate family, for friends and relatives in Switzerland. An edited version that excluded Anne's references to her growing sexual awareness was published in Dutch in 1947 and a fuller English-language edition, translated by Barbara Mooyaart-Doubleday, in 1952. A play based on the book won the Pulitzer Prize in 1955. A full text was subsequently published, but there have been attempts to ban this version (*see* BANNED BOOKS) because of its sexual content, while allowing children the original version (six attempts in US schools and counties since 1990). Susan Massotty's 1995 translation, based on the unexpurgated text, is now the most complete English-language version.

The Diary of a Young Girl remains one of the most important documents about the Holocaust, and the first thing that many children read on the subject.

DIAZ, Abby Morton (1821–1904) American author, best known for *William Henry's Letters to His Grandmother* (1870), a boy's accounts of his life at boarding school. Her other books include *The Cats' Arabian Nights* (1881).

DICAMILLO, Kate (1964–) An internationally bestselling American writer of children's fiction whose books often feature animals and magic. Her first novel, *Because of Winn-Dixie* (2000), introduces India Opal Buloni, a lonely ten-year-old girl and her new-found friend, a dog called Winn-Dixie (this was released as a feature film in 2005 by Twentieth Century Fox). Her third novel *The *Tale of Despereaux: Being the Story of a Mouse, a Princess, Some Soup, and a Spool of Thread* (2003) won the *Newbery Medal and was also released as a film in 2008. *The Miraculous Journey of Edward Tulane* (2006) about a cold-hearted china rabbit won the *Boston Globe–Horn Book Award for Fiction in 2006. *The Magician's Elephant* (2009), a magical tale of the young Peter Augustus Duchene, is beautifully illustrated by artist Yoko Tanaka. DiCamillo is also known for the *Mercy Watson* series, illustrated by Chris Van Dusen, and the award-winning *Bink and Gollie* series, co-authored with Alison McGhee and illustrated by Tony Fucile. The hilarious *Flora and Ulysses* (2013, richly and imaginatively illustrated by K. G. Campbell) won DiCamillo her second 2014 *Newbery Medal, a decade after her first.

DICEY, William and **Cluer** *See* CHAPBOOKS.

Dicey's Song See HOMECOMING.

Dick Barton, Special Agent Hero of a BBC radio serial first broadcast in October 1946. The serial was not initially intended for-children, but was quickly adopted by a juvenile audience all over Britain and was a runaway success. There was a good deal of public criticism that young people should be allowed to listen to such sensational stuff, and in 1951 the serial was taken off the air; its principal writers, Edward J. Mason and Geoffrey Webb, were transferred to the BBC's new serial about country life, *The Archers*.

DICKENS, Charles (1812–70) Celebrated author whose novels in his own time defied definition by reader age; he also wrote several books especially for children: *A *Child's History of England* (1851–3), *A *Holiday Romance* (1868), and a *Life of Our Lord*, composed solely for the use of his own family and not published until 1934. His *Christmas Books* (1843–8), which included *A Christmas Carol*, were read in many nurseries, while abridgements and retellings for children have been made of many of his novels. The novels themselves, even in their original form, were read by children as soon as they were published; in 1888

Dickens easily won a poll (in *Juvenile Literature As It Is*) of boys' favourite authors, and his works remained a staple of childhood and adolescent reading in the 20th cent. Many are memorable for their depictions of childhood.

Dickens, who admired and knew Hans Christian *Andersen, was a champion of the cause of *fairy stories against the nursery moralists; he complained when his old illustrator George *Cruikshank bowdlerized several well-known fairy tales.

Dickens, Eddie *See* AWFUL END.

DICKINSON, Peter (1927–2015) British children's novelist and poet. He was born in Zambia and worked for many years on the editorial staff of *Punch* magazine before turning to writing in his early forties, subsequently producing a steady output of children's books and adult thrillers, and winning major awards for both. His children's fiction began with the *dystopian *Changes trilogy, starting with *The Weathermonger* (1968) (which was subsequently made into a TV series), and he continued to use the past, the future, or his own created worlds to express his ideas about society, in books including *The Dancing Bear* (1972), which describes the journey of a young slave in the Dark Ages, *The Gift* (1973), in which a boy with the 'gift' of perceiving pictures in others' minds discovers a plan for a murder, and *The Blue Hawk* (1976), about a boy priest caught up in a political upheaval.

With *Tulku* and then *City of Gold* (1980), a collection of stories from the Old Testament, which was illustrated by Michael *Foreman, Dickinson became the first author to win two *Carnegie Medals, and remains only one of two to win a pair consecutively (the other being Patrick *Ness).

More recently, in *The Ropemaker* (2001), a girl with no magic finds she has to protect her family from the empire's sorcerers, while the prehistoric epic *The Kin* (1998) is a sophisticated four-part novel telling one story from four points of view and along the way exploring the origins of language, the development of skills, and the organization of society.

Dick Turpin Foremost hero of the highwayman stories that became a staple of *penny dreadfuls and other popular juvenile literature from the mid-19th cent. The historical Richard Turpin lived from 1706 to 1739; he was a butcher's apprentice who began as a livestock thief, smuggler, and housebreaker, specializing in torturing the occupants of isolated

farmhouses into giving up their valuables. After working around London he finally travelled to York, where he was hanged for horse-stealing. He was celebrated in his time, but most of the details of the legend, his horse Black Bess, his gallantry and style, and the feat of riding from London to York without a break, were invented by Harrison *Ainsworth in his novel *Rookwood* (1834), or by Ainsworth's countless successors.

In the 1860s Turpin was the hero of Edward Viles's *Black Bess, or the Knight of the Road*, a weekly penny dreadful which ran for nearly five years. Turpin, like Robin Hood, was a prime example of popular literature romanticizing a criminal, a practice which the Establishment feared and condemned. Indeed, the *Robin Hood legends did provide a model for the Turpin stories' portrayal of justified robbery, with the gross Lord Mayor of London occupying something of the role of the Sheriff of Nottingham.

Other historical highwaymen whose exploits fuelled the 19th-cent. thirst for this kind of fiction included *Jack Sheppard, Claude Duval (1643–70), and Jack Rann (d. 1774). But most of the incidents and people in such tales as *Captain Midnight, Gentleman Jack, May Turpin,* and *Starlight Nell* were the creations of their anonymous authors.

Dick Whittington In reality Richard Whittington (d. 1423), wealthy mercer, three times Mayor of London, in 1397, 1406, and 1419. He married Alice Fitzwarren, daughter of a West Country land-owner, made large loans to Henry IV and Henry V, and was a benefactor of the City of London, financing among other works an almshouse for the poor and the rebuilding of Newgate gaol. The nursery legend of Dick Whittington, the poor orphan whose cat made his fortune, seems to have made its first appearance in a play, now lost, which was licensed in 1605, or possibly in a *ballad of earlier date. A ballad on the subject which came out in the same year is thought to have been created by Richard *Johnson, so he is sometimes credited with originating the legend. The story rapidly became a favourite subject for other ballads and *chapbooks.

According to the 17th-cent. ballad, Whittington is born of poor parents and goes to London to work as a kitchen scullion in the household of a merchant. He is so beaten by the cook-maid that he runs away, but as he escapes he hears London's bells suggesting the words 'Turn again Whittington ... Lord Mayor of London.' He returns and acquiesces in apprentice life. He has a cat which he sends as a 'venture' on a merchant ship. The cat proves to be worth 'many a fair thousand pound' to a rat- and mice-infested foreign land, and Whittington receives enough money to become a merchant. He rises in the City, is made Lord Mayor, and lends his king money for wars in France, but then burns the bonds, taking no repayment. The ballad then gives a fairly accurate list of the benefactions of the real Richard Whittington and exhorts all citizens to feed the poor. The first verse has already pointed the moral of hope for low-born apprentices.

Prose chapbook versions add more details; among them that young Dick had often heard that the streets of London were paved with gold, 'and his intention was to get a hatful of it'; that he bought his cat because his own garret was overrun with mice; and that he was befriended by his master's daughter, Mistress Alice Fitzwarren, whom he later married.

There seems to be no historical evidence associating the original Whittington with a cat, and despite much speculation, when or by whom the London merchant and the wondrous cat were joined together remains a mystery.

In the 19th cent. *Dick Whittington* continued to be exploited as a tract to encourage virtue in young readers; *A New Year's Address to Sunday School Girls and Boys* (1881) saw in it the lessons of 'Stop and Think', 'Listen', and 'Seek and Use our one Talent'. There were also attempts in print to find the 'Real' Whittington, by the Revd Samuel Lysons (1860) and Walter Besant and James Rice (1881). The story of Whittington has long been, and remains, one of the most popular *pantomimes. Cynthia *Harnett explored the Whittington legend in *Ring Out, Bow Bells!* (1953).

Dido Twite In novels by Joan *Aiken.

DIEKMANN, Miep (1925–) Dutch children's novelist, whose stories are set in the East Indies; they include an *adventure story entitled *De Boten van Brakkeput* (1956) (English, *The Haunted Island*, 1959) and *Gewoon een Strattje* (1959) (*Just a Street*, 1963), a story of backstreet life.

DILLON, Eilís (1920–94) Irish writer who produced a large number of children's books. She set many of them on islands off the west coast of Ireland, e.g. *The Coriander* (1963), about an ancient feud between the inhabitants

of Inishgillan and Inishthorav. A few of her books are in Gaelic. There is a *CBI award in her name.

DILLON, Leo (1933–2012) and **Diane** (1933–) American husband and wife illustrators, whose work was almost always a collaborative effort, influenced by Leo's Trinidadian heritage and their respective East and West coast American ones. They met at art school, marrying soon after and initially focusing on covers and interior work for science fiction books. Their children's picture-book work led to their winning the *Caldecott Medal in consecutive years, for *Why Mosquitoes Buzz in People's Ears* (1975) by Verna Aardema (1911–2000) and *Ashanti To Zulu: African Traditions* (1976) by Margaret Musgrove (1943–). *Rap a Tap Tap: Here's Bojangles, Think of That* (2002) was also written by them, and it tells the life story of the African-American tap dancer, Bill 'Bojangles' Robinson. Their work for older readers included the original covers for Garth Nix's *Old Kingdom* trilogy (*see* SABRIEL).

dime novels Works of popular sensational American fiction, published in series and sold for a dime (ten cents). The true dime novel began to appear regularly in 1860, when Irwin Beadle & Co. of New York inaugurated their series 'Beadle's Dime Novels' with *Malaeska; the Indian Wife of the White Hunter*, a story by the popular novelist Ann St Stephens.

Cheap sensational paper-covered literature had been published by a number of American firms for more than thirty years before that date. Originally this 'yellow-covered' or 'yellow-back' literature, as it was known from the colour of its paper wrappers, was derived almost entirely from British popular fiction of the time, and consisted of revamped Gothic novels, and imitations of *Scott, *Dickens, and Harrison *Ainsworth—much as did the English *penny dreadfuls of the same period. A little later *sea stories (imitative of *Marryat and others) became the fashion in America; then, by the mid-19th cent., tales of pioneer life on America's own frontiers began to appear in large numbers.

In 1858 Erastus Beadle (1821–94), Robert Adams (1837–66), and Erastus's brother Irwin Beadle (1828–82) moved to New York City from Buffalo, NY, where they had published a children's *magazine, *The Youth's Casket*. Irwin, who was a printer, advertised a *Dime Song-Book* from his New York premises, and this was followed in 1859 by a *Dime Cook Book* and other non-fiction titles of this sort. The Beadle's Dime Novel series began in June

1860, and was advertised as 'Books for the Million! A Dollar Book for a dime!! 128 pages complete, only Ten Cents!!!' By the end of that year thirteen titles had been published, and the firm's name had been changed to Beadle and Adams. A few months later, in February 1861, Erastus Beadle established an English branch of the firm in London and the series began to appear there as Beadle's American Library, price sixpence each book.

In 1863 Irwin Beadle left the firm and set up in partnership with one of his clerks, George Munro; as Irwin P. Beadle & Co., and then as George Munro & Co., this rival firm began to produce its own Ten Cent Novels. Many other competitors soon appeared on the scene, and by the 1870s many sorts of cheap fiction were available. Sales of dime books were increased by the Civil War; the novels were widely distributed to troops on both sides and were said to be 'the soldier's solace and comfort in camp and campaign'.

Besides the original Dime Novel series, Beadle's issued books under such titles as New Dime Novels, Pocket Novels, Beadle's Dime Library, and (from 1881) The Boy's Library of Sport, Story and Adventure—though in fact boys had formed a very large part of the readership from the start. Most Beadle novels were of about 100 pages and had plain or coloured wrappers, usually with an illustration on the front. There were also quarto and octavo broadsheets (e.g. The Boy's Library) of sixteen or thirty-two pages. The dime novels contained about 80,000 words; there was also a Half-Dime Library selling at five cents and containing about half that number of words.

Dime novels were largely the work of hacks. One of the more notable of such authors was Edward Sylvester Ellis (1840–1916), a New Jersey schoolmaster who at the age of twenty had a manuscript accepted by Beadle's. This was *Seth Jones; or, the Captives of the Frontier* (1860). The great success of this led Beadle's to give Ellis a contract for four novels a year. He later wrote for other publishers and used many pseudonyms. Among others who wrote this form of fiction for cash was the young Louisa M. *Alcott; the fees were sometimes large enough (they ranged from about $75 to $700 per title) to attract famous names such as Mayne *Reid.

Until the early 1880s frontier and pioneer life was the favourite subject for dime novels; the War of American Independence was sometimes used as a setting, and '*Indians' (Native Americans) appeared again and again. Many of

the stories featured such folk heroes as *Buffalo Bill and *Davy Crockett. In general each dime novel was complete in itself, though there were many 'companion stories' containing further adventures of the same characters, and Beadle's did print serials in their *Saturday Journal* (1870–82) and *Banner Weekly* (1882–97).

From the early 1880s *detective fiction began to take over as the principal subject, eventually overshadowing even *westerns. A favourite character in the Beadle's Half-Dime Library (launched in 1877) was *Deadwood Dick. In its earliest years the firm of Beadle insisted on high standards from its authors, and had prohibited 'common-place stories, or serials, of the character of those published in the "Blood-and-thunder" newspapers'; there was also a ban on 'characters that carry an immoral taint'. These standards were soon abandoned in the face of competition, with the consequence that dime novels soon came to contain much that shocked parents. Many children were forbidden to read them, and had to take refuge in hay-lofts or (in one recorded case) a dog-kennel to peruse these thrilling adventures. Clergy preached against dime novels, and even newspapers expressed uneasiness about them, but nothing could keep them out of the hands of young Americans, and of many older readers too.

During the 1890s many new 'libraries' of boys' stories were inaugurated, featuring such new-style heroes as *Nick Carter, and the older firms such as Beadle's began to lose their hold on the market. In 1898 Beadle and Adams was sold to another firm, and its remaining stock was disposed of, though the Beadle imprint continued to appear for a few years more.

Though the dime novels came to be almost universally condemned in America, they provided millions of readers with entertainment; moreover, in the words of John T. McIntyre (foreword to *The House of Beadle and Adams* by Albert Johannsen, 1950): 'This type of story ... was the first absolutely American thing; it has rooted itself deeply and, as can be seen, persists in various forms today.'

DIMMOCK, (Frederick) Hayden (1895–1955) Editor of the British boys' magazine *The Scout* from about 1915 to 1954. He originated Bob-a-Job Week.

Dimsie Heroine of *school stories for girls by Dorita Fairlie *Bruce, beginning in 1921 with *Dimsie Goes to School* (originally published as *The Senior Prefect*) and ending with *Dimsie Carries On* (1942). 'Dimsie' Maitland is the archetypal jolly English schoolgirl. The Dimsie books were second in popularity with British girls during the 1930s only to the stories of Angela *Brazil.

Dinah Cat in *Alice's Adventures in Wonderland* and *Through the Looking-Glass* by Lewis *Carroll.

Dirty Bertie (2002) The original *Dirty Bertie* was a picture book both written and illustrated by David *Roberts. The huge success of the boy who liked nothing better than to dig around in rubbish, get filthy, fart loudly, and pick his nose (often at the same time) led to a series of chapter books, illustrated by David Roberts but now written by Alan MacDonald (1948–). The books have titles such as *Pants!, Yuck!,* and *Pong!* and are perfect for boys discovering the joys of reading through ever-popular scatological themes.

disabled characters in children's books Disability in historical children's literature was often associated with weakness, sickness, isolation, and personal tragedy. Forms of physical disability were frequently aligned with unfavourable personality traits or used as a form of 'shorthand' to suggest evil. Many texts had religious undertones, with disability sometimes symbolizing a punishment for some form of wrongdoing, sometimes only significant as the precursor to a cure, and often a reason to depict the disability as a reason for pity, piety, or martyrdom.

The International Year of Disabled Persons (1981) saw librarians encouraged to make use of a list of books that proved disabled characters could be portrayed in a positive, fully three-dimensional, and convincing manner—including titles such as Rosemary Sutcliff's *The *Eagle of the Ninth.* Awareness of the need for such books grew and the proportion of children's books featuring disabled characters has since risen. Nevertheless, the overall number remains extremely low. It is also worth noting that it does not necessarily follow that all such books depict disability both positively and accurately. Few titles succeed in achieving both these criteria whilst also achieving a high quality of narrative and/or illustration and with suitable appeal for the intended audience.

Books featuring disability often fall into the category of 'issue' books. While such books can have a valuable role to play in terms of helping audiences to understand disability, there is a risk that such books are considered

'niche' publications. Equally, there is a danger that a character's personality can appear to be defined solely by his or her disability. There is clearly, therefore, also a need for books which simply include disabled people without comment, presenting fully rounded personalities who just happen to be disabled.

In 1999, the picture book *Susan Laughs* by Jeanne *Willis succeeded in making a particular mark with its delightfully positive message about equality, and Michael *Foreman's approach in *Seal Surfer* (1997) was particularly subtle. In 2003, The *Curious Incident of the Dog in the Night-Time* by Mark Haddon led the way in mainstream *young adult fiction by bringing a condition generally identified as Asperger's Syndrome to the fore. More recently, *Wonder* (2012) by R. J. Palacio generated mass interest (and a reaction known as the 'wonder effect') with its account of a student with a facial deformity in a high school community, and a universal message about kindness to others. Also particularly noteworthy is *Whisper* (2012) by Chrissie Keighery, which succeeds in accurately portraying deafness and its spectrum of emotions and experiences, all within an absorbing mainstream read.

However many gaps remain. Books featuring disabled parents are particularly few and far between, and there are still many forms of disability which are scarce in books, for example learning disability, and complex and multiple forms of disability.

Discworld (1983–) A fantasy series by Terry *Pratchett, set on the eponymous circular, flat world which rests on the shoulders of four elephants, travelling through the universe while standing on the back of space-turtle Great A'Tuin. It includes over forty books, starting with *The Colour of Magic* (1983), with themes explored falling mostly under the fantasy and comedy banners, though there are also marked satirical and parody elements that deal with historical and current events. Five books in the series are overtly aimed at a younger audience: *The *Amazing Maurice and His Educated Rodents* (2001, winner of the *Carnegie Medal), *The Wee Free Men* (2003), *A Hat Full of Sky* (2004), *Wintersmith* (2006), and *I Shall Wear Midnight* (2010), the last winning the Andre Norton Award, and the last four all featuring trainee witch Tiffany Aching. Other recurring and best-received characters include: Death, with his white horse Binky, all caps dialogue lines and fascination with life; sadistic, multidimensional

Luggage; and orange-furred, banana- and knowledge-loving Librarian, whose vocabulary is mostly limited to 'ook'.

DISNEY, Walt (Walter Elias) (1901–66) The leading American maker of cartoon films who began work with a team of animators in the 1920s, initially producing films which mixed cartoon drawings with live human figures; the first of these was *Alice's Wonderland* (1923). The character *Mickey Mouse was born in 1928, and made Disney's name. Next came the Silly Symphony series of short cartoons (1929 onwards), which introduced *Donald Duck. Mickey Mouse films also spawned the characters of Pluto and Goofy.

The Silly Symphonies were often based on well known folk tales; the greatest success of the series was The *Three Little Pigs* (1933), made famous by a song featured in it, 'Who's Afraid of the Big, Bad Wolf?' In 1937 Disney released his first full-length film, again using traditional material; this was *Snow White and the Seven Dwarfs. It was followed by (among others) *Fantasia and *Pinocchio (both 1940), *Dumbo* (1941), *Bambi* (1943), *Cinderella* (1950), Alice in Wonderland (see ALICE'S ADVENTURES IN WONDERLAND) (1951), *Peter Pan* (1953), The *Sleeping Beauty* (1958), The *Sword in the Stone* (1963), *Mary Poppins* (1964), two *Winnie-the-Pooh* films (1966 and 1968), and The *Jungle Book* (1967). During the later part of Disney's life his studio also began to make fully live-action adventure films, beginning with *Treasure Island* (1950). After Disney's death, the company continued to produce animated films, including a version of *Robin Hood* (1973) that portrayed all the characters as animals. Subsequent Disney adaptations include The Rescuers (1977), The Little Mermaid (1989), Beauty and the Beast (1991), and Aladdin (1992), all based on pre-existing stories (q.v.).

Disney drew heavily on children's literature for his films, and also sometimes enriched it; his Snow White, still as popular in the 1980s as it was in the 1930s, is a magnificent visualization of *Grimm, and his Mary Poppins improved substantially on the book. The Silly Symphonies are a fine achievement by any standard. But too often he debased writers' and artists' work; The Sword in the Stone was only one of many examples of vulgarization and tasteless handling of the original, and it is regrettable that many children now think of Winnie-the-Pooh as the Disney animators depicted him rather than as drawn by E. H.

*Shepard. Disney himself made no bones about his intentions: 'Be commercial. What is art, anyway? It's what people like. So give them what they like. There's nothing wrong with being commercial.'

DITERLIZZI, Tony (1969-) American author and illustrator of fantasy literature featuring space adventures and imaginary creatures. DiTerlizzi is best known for *The Spiderwick Chronicles* (2003–4), about three children who unearth a field guide to fairies, trolls, and goblins. He created the series with Holly *Black, along with the follow-up books *Beyond the Spiderwick Chronicles* and other associated titles. Among his other works are the picture books *The Spider and the Fly* (2002), which won a Caldecott Honor Award (*see* CALDECOTT MEDAL), and *G is for One Gzonk!* (2006), the chapter book *Kenny and the Dragon* (2008), a homage to Kenneth *Grahame's *The Reluctant Dragon*, and the middle-grade space fairy-tale trilogy beginning with *The Search for WondLa* (2010), which is being made into a feature film.

diversity In children's literature, a multifaceted and complex topic that resists a simple single definition. It can refer to diversity in format and form, encompassing visual, oral, electronic, or live performance, as well as diversity in language, content, and style. However, its most usual meaning in discussion of children's literature is diversity of the social, ethnic, and economic groups represented in books. This represents a political shift from the previously predominant ideal of multiculturalism (a term still widely used; *see* MULTICULTURAL) to a broader term that includes class, ethnicity, language, religion, *disability, age, *sexuality, culture, geography, family structures, and *gender.

Dives Pragmaticus A book for the instruction and entertainment of children published in 1563. Its full title is *A booke in Englysh metre, of the great Marchaunt man called Dives Pragmaticus, very preaty for children to rede: wherby they may the better, and more readyer, rede and wryte wares and Implementes, in this world contayned*. Its author was Thomas Newbery, probably brother to Ralph Newbery, 'Master of the Printing House' to Elizabeth I.

The book, which is in verse, begins with a preface in which Dives Pragmaticus (i.e., 'a rich man skilled in business') describes

himself and lists those who buy merchandise from him:

Al Brewers, Bakers, Butchers and Cokes,
Al Printers, Stationers, and sellers of bokes:
Al Poulters, and Pedders, that ryde day and nyght,
Al Farmours and owners, that in money delyght
 (etc.)

The body of the book is taken up with 'The Names of All Kynd of Wares', a verse catalogue of types of merchandise.

Inventories of this kind were sometimes used to form the basis of a simple Latin-English dictionary, though in the case of Newbery's book the purpose seems to have been simply to instruct children in the names of trades, professions, and wares.

Divine Emblems: *or Temporal Things Spiritualised* The later title of John *Bunyan's book of poems for children, *A *Book for Boys and Girls*.

Divine Songs, *Attempted in Easie Language for the Use of Children* A book of hymns and 'Moral Songs' for children by Isaac *Watts, published in 1715 with later additions. His preface 'to all concerned in the education of children' defends the use of verse against *Puritan charges of frivolity with the arguments that 'Verse was at first designed for the Service of God, tho' it hath been wretchedly abused since', and that rhyme and metre would make the duty of learning truth easier and more delightful. To the original Songs, Watts added in later editions a 'Cradle Hymn' and five more Moral Songs.

Though the Puritan stress on the innate wickedness of children lay behind the *Divine Songs*, and the fear of early death and of hell were still prime tools of education, Watts gave more emphasis to praise and thankfulness as suitable religious emotions for a child, and displayed a gentleness new for his time.

The book was immediately successful. Some twenty editions were published in Watts's lifetime, and an American edition had appeared by 1719. In the following hundred years millions of copies were put into circulation, phrases from the songs such as 'improve the shining hour' became household expressions, samplers were embroidered with texts from the book, and it was used as a standard *reward book for *Sunday school children. Lewis *Carroll parodied two of the *Divine Songs* in *Alice's Adventures in Wonderland* (1865); 'How doth the little busy bee' becomes 'How doth the little crocodile', and ''Tis the

voice of the sluggard' becomes "Tis the voice of the lobster'—jokes which depended on the originals still being widely known in nurseries, as they still were in the 1860s. But by the end of the 19th cent., *Divine Songs* had been over-used; it seemed dated in its combination of Calvinism and sentiment, and no popular edition was printed after 1901.

Thomas *Bewick was among those who contributed to the many illustrated editions of *Divine Songs*, and in its heyday the book was often published with tunes. A critical edition, with facsimiles of early versions, edited by J. H. P. Pafford, was published in 1971.

DIXON, Bob The author of *Catching Them Young: Sex, Race and Class in Children's Fiction* (1977); *see* RACISM.

DIXON, Franklin W. *See* HARDY BOYS, THE.

Doasyouwouldbedoneby, Mrs *See* MRS DOASYOUWOULDBEDONEBY.

Doctor Dolittle stories A series written and illustrated by Hugh *Lofting. The first of the twelve books is *The Story of Doctor Dolittle, being the history of his peculiar life at home, and astonishing adventures in foreign parts,* published in New York in 1920 and in England in 1922. *The Story of Doctor Dolittle* introduces 'John Dolittle, M.D.', physician in the country town of Puddleby-on-the-Marsh, whose patients desert him because his house is full of animals. In consequence he grows poor, but, at the suggestion of his parrot Polynesia, he becomes an animal-doctor. 'Give the silly people up,' the parrot tells him, 'if they haven't brains enough to see you're the best doctor in the world.' Polynesia begins to teach him the language of animals, and he soon has a vast clientele of sick creatures clamouring for attention. When a plea for help comes from a plague-ridden country of monkeys in deepest Africa, Dr Dolittle borrows a ship to make the journey. In gratitude for his work as a healer the monkeys present him with a Pushmi-pullyu, a remarkable two-headed animal which the Doctor takes back to England.

The book's instant success encouraged Lofting to write *The Voyages of Doctor Dolittle* (1922), which was equally popular and won him the *Newbery Medal. This book is much longer than the first, and it contains no 'writing down' to children. Several memorable human characters make an appearance, including Matthew Mugg the cat's-meat man, and there are such imaginative inventions as a floating island which deflates when it is punctured, and a huge sea snail with a transparent shell which can be used as a submarine.

This maturing and improvement of both narrative and pictures continued through four more books. (Lofting is almost unique in children's literature in being the author of a series that almost consistently improves rather than deteriorates as it goes on.) *Dr Dolittle's Post Office* (1923), *Dr Dolittle's Circus* (1924), *Dr Dolittle's Zoo* (1925), and *Dr Dolittle's Caravan* (1926) saw him at his peak, producing comic narratives beneath which lay seriousness of purpose springing largely from his experiences in the trenches during the First World War. Dolittle is the champion of his animals against all forms of human cruelty towards them—zoos, bullfights, fox hunting, and so on—and these abuses are often attacked specifically; but there is also despair about human nature, and a fear and hatred of war which sometimes comes to the surface.

Dr Dolittle's Garden (1927) came out in the year in which Lofting's first wife died, and is disorganized and scrappy. *Dr Dolittle in the Moon* (1928) was intended to be the last in the series, of which Lofting was now tired. But the other children's books that he wrote in the years which followed were not a great success, and he restored his old hero to earth in 1933 with *Doctor Dolittle's Return*, which has much of the old excitement. The last book in the series, *Dr Dolittle and the Secret Lake*, was not published until just after Lofting's death, in 1948. Two further posthumous titles, *Dr Dolittle and the Green Canary* (1950) and *Dr Dolittle's Puddleby Adventures* (1952), are collections of stories first published in the *New York Herald Tribune*.

The Dolittle books are unlike anything else in children's fiction, being distinguished by an oddly deadpan style of narrative, dialogue, and illustration that is sometimes, but not always, a mask for irony. They scarcely deserve to be classed as *animal stories, being principally a vehicle for Lofting's plea for pacifism and tolerance of the unconventional. In the 1970s they were attacked for *racism, on account of their crude portrayal (in the first two books) of a black man, Prince Bumpo. This was certainly a misjudgement on Lofting's part, the result of the first book's debt to Belloc and other humorists of that vein, and is not characteristic of the series as a whole.

The Dolittle stories are not set in any particular period—they wander about between

the early 19th and early 20th cents., to judge from references to Darwin, the Crimean War, and other historical people and events. A film based on them, *Doctor Doolittle*, was released in 1967, with Rex Harrison in the title role, and with songs by Leslie Bricusse.

Doctor Who A *science fiction television series for children and adults, first broadcast by the BBC in 1963. The Doctor and his companions travel through time and space in their capsule Tardis, which from the outside appears to be a police telephone box. Their most celebrated enemies are the robot-like Daleks. Many *Doctor Who* paperbacks have been published, a number of them written by Terrance Dicks, who was script editor to the programme for many years. In 2005, after a hiatus of 16 years, the Doctor returned to television screens, where the series today remains as popular as ever with viewers both young and old, while new books continue to appear (by a range of writers, many of them children's authors).

DODD, Lynley *See* HAIRY MACLARY.

DODDRIDGE, Philip (1702–51) Nonconformist preacher who wrote a volume of *poems for children, *The Principles of the Christian Religion: Expressed in plain and easy Verse* (1751). The style resembles that of Isaac *Watts.

DODERER, Klaus (1925–) Professor of Children's Literature at Johann Wolfgang Goethe University in Frankfurt am Main, first director of the *Institut Für Jugendbuchforschung, and editor of the *Lexikon Der Kinder- und Jugend-Literatur*.

DODGE, Mary (Elizabeth) Mapes (1831–1905) Children's writer and editor. Her best known book is *Hans Brinker* (1865). In 1870 she became juvenile editor of *Hearth and Home*, and three years later was appointed editor of *St Nicholas*, the leading high-quality children's periodical of its day, which owed much of its success to her.

DODGSON, C. L. *See* CARROLL, LEWIS.

Dog Crusoe, The, *A Tale of the Western Prairies* (1861) A novel by R. M. *Ballantyne. A young hunter, Dick Varley, rescues a Newfoundland puppy from being cooked alive by a Native American squaw, and brings it up, naming it Crusoe. In their subsequent adventures together in the North American wilds, Crusoe more than once saves Dick's life, as well as rescuing a drowning child and

discovering a party of white men who have been captured by Native Americans (*see* 'INDIANS' OF NORTH AMERICA).

Dogger (1977) A much-loved picture book by Shirley *Hughes. It's the heartstring-tugging story of a boy called Dave who accidentally leaves his toy dog—Dogger—behind at the park. The next day Dogger shows up for sale on a stall at the school summer fair, and it takes a bit of luck and an act of generosity from Dave's big sister Bella to get Dogger back where he belongs. *Dogger* won Hughes her first *Kate Greenaway Medal.

Dogmatix In the English translations of the *Astérix books, a dog (as the name suggests) belonging to *Obelix. A brave and loyal friend, he originally met the Gauls in *Asterix and the Banquet*, and stayed. In the original French he is Idéfix.

Dog So Small, A (1962) A novel by Philippa *Pearce. Ben Blewitt longs for a dog as a companion. His grandfather promises him one on his birthday; but when the day comes the present is not a real dog but a picture of a chihuahua. Ben at first despises the picture, but gradually the dog in it becomes the centre of his fantasy world—'a dog so small you could see it only with your eyes shut'. At first the fantasy seems to enrich his life, but its influence soon proves to be destructive.

DOHERTY, Berlie (1943–) Novelist and picture-book writer. She has won the *Carnegie Medal twice, first for *Granny Was a Buffer Girl* (1986), about several generations of a Sheffield family, from the 1930s to the 1980s, and later for *Dear Nobody*. Doherty's novels for older children and young adults also include *Jeannie of White Peak Farm* (1984), about the first love of a teenage girl who lives on an isolated farm; *Street Child* (1993), a story based on an orphan boy in London who inspired Dr Barnado to set up his children's homes; *Holly Starcross* (2001), about a girl long estranged from her father, who comes back into contact with him; and *The Company of Ghosts* (2013) about a sixteen-year-old stranded on a Scottish island who begins to sense she is not alone there. Doherty has also written a number of picture books, including *Willa and Old Miss Annie* (1994) and *Jinnie Ghost* (2005), as well as some poetry collections and radio plays.

Doing It *See* BURGESS, MELVIN.

Dolittle, Doctor *See* DOCTOR DOLITTLE STORIES.

doll stories A genre that developed out of such books about the fortunes of inanimate objects as *The *Adventures of a Pincushion* by Mary Ann Kilner (*c*.1780). Examples include Mary Mister's *The Adventures of a Doll* (1816), **Memoirs of a London Doll* (1846) by Richard Henry Horne, Mrs *Gatty's *Aunt Sally's Life* (1862), and *Victoria-Bess: the Ups and Downs of a Doll's Life* by '*Brenda' (*c*.1880). The American writer Rachel Field, in **Hitty* (1929), used a doll as the basis of a *historical novel. Rumer *Godden, a very accomplished writer of doll stories, used the genre to portray human conflict and crisis. Naomi *Lewis edited a collection of doll stories, *The Silent Playmate* (1979). Among later examples of the genre is *Maggy Gumption* (1979) by Margaret Stuart *Barry.

Dolor, Prince *See* PRINCE DOLOR.

Donald Duck A *Disney cartoon character who first appeared in a Silly Symphony film, *The Little Wise Hen* (1934).

DONALDSON, Julia (1948–) British author of some of the most successful picture books of modern times, hugely popular with both parents and children for their distinctive bouncing rhymes which make them perfect for reading aloud. Donaldson had been writing songs for children for many years (for television and stage) when she was first approached by a publisher to ask whether one of these songs might be made into a picture book—*A Squash and a Squeeze* was published in 1993, and it introduced Donaldson not only to the picture-book market but also to the illustrator who would become her most regular collaborator, Axel *Scheffler. Since that date, Donaldson and Scheffler have collaborated on more than a dozen books (and counting), perhaps the most celebrated being *The *Gruffalo* and **Room on the Broom*. Other collaborations—most of them award-winning and all spectacularly bestselling—include *Tiddler* (2007), the brilliantly told story of a small fish given to telling tall tales; *The Snail and the Whale* (2003), about a snail who wants to see the world, and is given a lift by a humpback whale, eventually saving the whale's life; *The Smartest Giant in Town* (2003), about a scruffy giant who buys himself a smart set of clothes which he ends up giving away to animals in need, which won the *Red House Children's Book Award; *Monkey Puzzle* (2000—North American title: *Where's My Mom?*), about a baby monkey's search for its mother; and *The Highway Rat* (2011, based on Alfred Noyes's poem, 'The Highwayman'); among others.

Outside the work with Scheffler, Donaldson has also written (mostly) rhyming picture books for illustration by David *Roberts (*Tyrannosaurus Drip*, 2007; *The Troll*, 2009; *Jack and the Flumflum Tree*, 2011); Lydia Monks (*What the Ladybird Heard*, 2011, and several more); Emily *Gravett (*Cave Baby*, 2010); Joel *Stewart (*The Magic Paintbrush*, 2004); Charlotte *Voake (*The Further Adventures of the Owl and the Pussycat*, 2013, after Edward *Lear); Anna Currey (*One Ted Falls out of Bed*, 2004; *Rosie's Hat*, 2006); Nick Sharratt (*Chocolate Mousse for Greedy Goose*, 2005, among others); and, recently, for one of her very best books, *The Paper Dolls* (2012), a superb new illustrator, Rebecca Cobb. Donaldson is also the author of a work of short fiction for children, *The Giants and the Joneses* (2004), the *Princess Mirror-Belle* series (from 2005), also illustrated by Lydia Monks, and a *young adult novel, *Running on the Cracks* (2009).

Performance and music are important to Donaldson's work and the way she presents it to children (she still writes songs). In 2011 she was named the UK's seventh Children's *Laureate, using her two-year tenure particularly to encourage performance of plays and poetry for children.

***Don Bellianis of Greece* (*Don Belianis of Greece*)** A popular *romance which was among the favourite reading of 17th- and 18th-cent. schoolboys in England. Its first appearance in print in English seems to have been in 1598, in a translation from the Italian. The story apparently originated in Spain. Don Bellianis is the son of the Emperor of Greece. When he is only 15 he subdues a lion and kills a giant. His later adventures include a fight with the giant king of Cyprus and a voyage to an enchanted island. *Don Bellianis* often appeared during the 18th cent. as a *chapbook, usually under the subtitle or alternative title *The Honour of Chivalry*. It was mentioned by Steele in the *Tatler* in 1709 as being among the favourite books of his eight-year-old godson.

Dong with a Luminous Nose, The A poem by Edward *Lear, first published in **Laughable Lyrics* (1877). Lear's biographers have identified the Dong's sad wanderings with the author's own lonely and restless life.

DONNELLY, Jennifer (1963–) Weaving real-life crimes into her stories, American author Donnelly infuses her books with a

passionate plea for her readers to make their own choices in life and not be just swept along on a tide controlled by others. Her most famous book, published in 2004, is the *Carnegie Medal-winning *A Gathering Light* (originally *A Northern Light* in the US), a novel that weaves a real-life murder into a story of survival that encompasses race, class, poverty, prejudice, and the power of words. *Revolution* (2011) tells two intertwined stories, one of a modern grief-stricken girl and the other of a girl caught up in the French Revolution. *Tea Rose* (2003) and its sequels are set in the Whitechapel of Jack the Ripper.

DONOVAN, John (1928–92) American author of *young adult novels, best known for *I'll Get There, It Better Be Worth the Trip* (1969), one of the first books for young readers to deal with homosexuality. Donovan has also served as Executive Director of the Children's Book Council, New York.

Don Quixote The English title of Spain's most celebrated work of fiction, *Don Quijote de la Mancha*, the work of Miguel de Cervantes Saavedra (1547–1616). Since the appearance of the first part in 1605 it has been widely read and enjoyed by children, especially in abbreviated versions. Among abridgements which have appeared in English was one issued by Francis *Newbery in 1778 as *The Life and Exploits of the Ingenious Gentleman Don Quixote*. Further editions were published by Elizabeth Newbery and John *Harris. Later illustrated versions for children include those with pictures by A. B. Houghton engraved by the *Dalziel Brothers (1866), and by Walter *Crane (1900). A children's abridged version by Martin Jenkins was published in 2009, illustrated by Chris *Riddell.

Don't Let the Pigeon Drive the Bus! (2003) A picture book by Mo *Willems. When a bus driver goes on a break, he asks readers not to let the Pigeon drive his bus. The bird has other ideas, though. It appeals to readers for permission, at first politely and then, with increasing desperation, using every trick in the book, including bribery, a guilt trip, and a full-blown tantrum. With childlike cartoons and muted flat colour, Willems's hilarious debut picture book won multiple honours and spawned several sequels.

DORÉ, (Paul) Gustave (1832–83) French painter and sculptor, notable for the grotesque fanstasy he brought to illustrating English children's books, including an 1866 edition of Baron *Munchausen, *Fairy Tales Told Again* (anon., ?1879), and E. H. *Knatchbull-

Hugessen's *Higgledy-Piggledy* (1875). But his hugely well-known illustrations for books such as *Don Quixote* would also have been seen by many children in his time and since.

Dormouse In *Alice's Adventures in Wonderland* by Lewis *Carroll.

Dorothy In *The *Wonderful Wizard of Oz* by L. Frank *Baum.

Dorrie A little *witch in stories by the American author-illustrator Patricia Coombs, beginning with *Dorrie and the Wizard's Spell* (1974). Dorrie's 'hat is always crooked and her socks never match'; her mother is 'the Big Witch'.

DORSET Mrs *See* Peacock 'At Home', The.

Dot and the Kangaroo A classic Australian *fantasy by Ethel C. Pedley. It was published posthumously, in London in 1899 and in Sydney in 1906. Dot is a small girl lost in the bush, well aware that her parents' search might find her too late. Looking up from her tears she sees a kangaroo which 'evidently understood that Dot was in trouble'. The Kangaroo confides: ' "I knew what was the matter with you at once . . . for I feel just the same myself. I have been miserable, just like you, ever since I lost my baby kangaroo. You must also have lost something . . . " ' The Kangaroo (who doesn't think, but always jumps to conclusions, in ten foot leaps) begins a long quest for Dot's home, with Dot spending much of the time in her pouch, 'the cosiest, softest little bag imaginable'. *Dot and the Kangaroo* owes much to Lewis *Carroll, but its preaching against human brutality and folly is entirely serious. It has been reissued many times, adapted for the stage, and filmed.

DOUCE, Francis *See* Gammer Gurton's Garland.

Dougal In *The *Magic Roundabout*.

DOUGLAS, Amanda (Minnie) (1837–1916) American author of the 'Kathie' stories, beginning with *Kathie's Three Wishes* (1871). Kathie is a good and earnest little girl who spreads comfort wherever she goes, with her bright face and loving ways. Amanda Douglas also wrote *A Little Girl in Old New York* (1896), and similar volumes about other American cities.

DOWD, J. (James) H. British artist who published several books of somewhat sentimental pencil-sketches of children, beginning with *Important People* (1930). The books were very popular with children themselves.

DOWD, Siobhan (1960–2007) British writer of insightful fiction for young adults and human rights activist. Dowd worked extensively with the writers' organization International PEN and co-founded English PEN's readers and writers programme, taking authors into prisons and schools in socially deprived areas. Her first published story for children was commissioned by author Tony *Bradman for his collection of short stories about racism, *Skin Deep* (2004). Following a remarkable debut, A *Swift Pure Cry*, Dowd published *The London Eye Mystery* (2007), about a boy with Asperger's syndrome, which won numerous awards. At the time of her death from breast cancer, she had written two more novels which were published posthumously, *Bog Child* (2008), which won the *Carnegie Medal and *Solace of the Road* (2009). Dowd had begun to sketch out ideas for another children's novel before her death, about a young boy coming to terms with his mother's terminal illness. Children's publisher Walker Books arranged for Patrick *Ness to write the story in her memory and for Jim *Kay to illustrate it. A *Monster Calls* (2011) subsequently won both the Carnegie Medal and the companion *Kate Greenaway Medal in 2012, a double award unique in more than fifty years. The Siobhan Dowd Trust is a charity established in her name to bring books and reading to young people in the UK.

Down the Snow Stairs (1887) A *fantasy by Alice *Corkran.

Down with Skool! *See* MOLESWORTH.

Dowsabel A *witch in stories by Lorna *Wood.

DOYLE, Sir Arthur Conan (1859–1930) Creator of *Sherlock Holmes. He was born in Edinburgh and educated at Stonyhurst School (his family were Roman Catholic), then at Edinburgh University. After studying medicine he practised as a doctor in Southsea from 1882 to 1890. In 1887 appeared the first Holmes novel, *A Study in Scarlet*; soon Holmes stories became a regular feature of *The *Strand Magazine*. Among Doyle's many other books are a number of *historical novels, such as *Micah Clarke* (1889), which is set during Monmouth's rebellion, and *The White Company* (1891) and *Sir Nigel* (1906), describing the chivalrous exploits of a company of medieval knights errant. Doyle also wrote several *science fiction stories: *The *Lost World* (1912), a *Verne-like tale in which 'Professor Challenger' discovers an Amazon plateau inhabited by prehistoric beasts, and *The Poison Belt* (1913). He was knighted in 1902. In 1920 he wrote an article in the *Strand* accompanying photographs that apparently proved the existence of *fairies.

DOYLE, Brian (1935–) Acclaimed Canadian author of books for children and young adults. As a child he lived in the city of Ottawa and in a remote cabin, and both settings appear in his stories. His childhood was less than idyllic, and the early death of his sister, who had Down's syndrome, and the effect it had on his family shades his work, as does his father's alcoholism, but though they deal with difficult issues, his books never moralize. He worked as a journalist and a teacher before his first book, *Hey, Dad!* (1978), was published, followed by his first teen book, *Up to Low* (1982). That book's protagonist, Tommy, appears in *Angel Square* (1987), about a place in urban Ottawa where racism is rife. *Spud Sweetgrass* (1992) and *Spud in Winter* (1995) were a departure from his usual style, being comic mysteries.

DOYLE, Malachy (1954–) Irish author who began his career in advertising in England, and then gave it all up to raise a family and work in schools specializing in Special Education Needs in Wales. At the age of forty, he brought his experiences to writing for children. Doyle's writing covers a wide age range, including picture books and novels for young adults. His picture book *Hungry! Hungry! Hungry!* (2000), illustrated by Paul Hess, won the White Ravens Award 2002. *The Dancing Tiger* (2005), illustrated by Steve Johnson, won the Nestlé Children's Silver Book Award. His first teenage novel, *Georgie* (2001), about a mentally ill teenager orphaned by his mother's murder won the *Tir na n-Og Award. Many of his books are inspired by Welsh and Irish folklore, including *Sleepy Pendoodle* (2002), *Antonio on the Other Side of the World*, *Getting Smaller* (2003), and *Tales from Old Ireland* (2008).

DOYLE, Richard (1824–83) One of the most popular illustrators of the Victorian period, Doyle was the son of a painter and caricaturist. He became a regular contributor to *Punch* when he was only nineteen, and drew the cover picture which was used for more than a century, but left the staff in 1850 because, as a Roman Catholic, he objected to the magazine's attacks on the papacy. One of his first

commissions after going freelance was to illustrate Ruskin's *King of the Golden River* (1851). Other children's books to which he contributed include *Fairy Tales of all Nations* (1849) and a retelling by J. R. *Planché of The *Sleeping Beauty* (1865). Some of his most attractive drawings are found in *In Fairyland* (1870), a series of pictures with a verse-text by William *Allingham.

DOYLE, Roddy (1958–) Irish author most famous for his books for adults, including the Man Booker Prize winner *Paddy Clarke Ha Ha Ha* (2003), who also writes for children and young adults. His scatological classic, *The Giggler Treatment* (2000), is hilarious reading (especially popular with boys) and has three sequels all about Rover the dog and the Gigglers—magical creatures who exact revenge on adults who are mean to children. *Wilderness* (2007) is for older children and is about an adventure holiday in Finland that goes horribly wrong. His most accomplished work for young readers to date is the charming, tender *Greyhound of a Girl* (2011), about a girl, her mother, her dying grandmother, and the ghost of *her* mother on a wild road trip. And while Doyle's main body of work is for adults, it too is often enjoyed by older teens.

dragons These creatures feature in early English poems, mythology, and story. In 1898 Kenneth *Grahame published the short story 'The Reluctant Dragon' in his book *Dream Days*, and the next year E. *Nesbit published *A Book of Dragons*. Among other dragon anthologies are *A Book of Dragons* by Ruth Manning-Saunders (1964) and *The Hamish Hamilton Book of Dragons* (1970) by Roger *Lancelyn Green. Dragons play important parts in J. R. R. *Tolkien's stories *The *Hobbit* and *Farmer Giles of Ham* (1949), Rosemary *Manning's *Green Smoke* (1957), and Ursula Le Guin's *Earthsea series. Cressida Cowell's Viking hero has a dragon friend in *How to Train Your Dragon*, Chris d'Lacey's dragons appear in his *Last Dragon Chronicles*, a sequence that starts with *The Fire Within* (2001), while dragons are at the heart of Christopher Paolini's *Inheritance series, starting with *Eragon*, and many different species appear in the *Harry Potter series.

DRAGT, Tonke (1930–) Dutch writer, best known for her classic *De brief voor de koning*, an adventure story about an aspiring knight (1962; translated as *The Letter for the King*, by Laura Watkinson, 2013). Its sequel, *The Secrets of the Wild Wood*, appeared in English in 2015. Her other titles include *De zevensprong* (1966; *The Song of Seven*, 2016), which became a popular television series, and *Torenhoog en mijlenbreed* (1969, 'Sky High and Miles Wide'), set in space in the distant future. Fantasy and science fiction are frequent elements of her work. During the Second World War, Dragt was imprisoned in a Japanese camp in the Dutch East Indies, where she wrote her first stories. Dragt created the illustrations for her own books, and also for books by Paul Biegel, E. *Nesbit, and Alan Garner's *Elidor*.

Dream Days *See* GOLDEN AGE, THE.

Dromkeen Medal An Australian award, initiated in 1982. It is presented annually by the governors of the Courtney Oldmeadow Children's Literature Foundation to an Australian citizen who has significantly contributed to the appreciation and development of children's literature. The Oldmeadow family were Melbourne booksellers who initially bought the Dromkeen homestead on the outskirts of the city as storage for their book stock. They then made it into a museum to house picture-book art. In 1985 Scholastic Australia bought the property and the collection to guarantee its continued existence and promote its importance to children's literature. The State Library of Victoria became custodians of the collection in 2013 to provide continued access and use of this collection. Recipients of the Foundation's Dromkeen Medal include Lu Rees, Maurice *Saxby, Patricia *Wrightson, Robert *Ingpen, Jennifer Rowe (*see* RODDA, EMILY), Graeme *Base, Ann James, Shaun *Tan and Libby *Gleeson.

DRUMMOND, V. H. (Violet Hilda) (1911–2000) British author-illustrator of *picture books, notably *Miss Anna Truly* (1945), *The Flying Postman* (1948), and her *Little Laura* series (1960 onwards), which is characterized by an arch style of narrative, e.g.: 'It is feared that this unfortunate turn of events may make Laura weep.'

DUANE, Diane (1952–) American author of *young adult and adult fantasy, and science fiction, who worked as a psychiatric nurse before becoming assistant to the author David Gerrold (1944–), who encouraged her to write. Her nine-volume *Young Wizards* series begins with *So You Want to be a Wizard?* (1983) and tells of a bullied girl, Nita, who

finds escape into an alternate dimension through a book on wizardry she discovers in the library—the subsequent books follow her epic adventures. Duane's *Star Trek* tie-in novels, particularly *Spock's World* (1988), are hugely popular and she co-wrote the *Net Force Explorers* (1998) series with Tom Clancy (1947–2013).

DU BOIS, William Pène (1916–1993) American author-illustrator who has created a number of eccentric children's books of startling originality and humour. He is best known for *The *Twenty-One Balloons* (1947), but there are many others. Typical is *The Alligator Case* (1965), involving ninety circus performers dressed in alligator skins—and one real alligator. Du Bois also illustrated many books by other writers.

DUBOSARSKY, Ursula (1961–) Australian picture-book, junior fiction, and occasionally *young adult author, who has received many prizes for her work, including a record five New South Wales Premier's Literary Awards. She won the 2011 *CBCA Eve Pownall Award for Information Books for *The Return of the Word Spy* (2010). The *Word Spy* books celebrate language—words and grammar—in a light-hearted way, with puzzles, puns, alphabets, etymology, and more.

Dubosarsky's first book, *Maisie and the Pinny Gig* (1989), was quickly followed by *Zizzy Zing* (1990), and by 2013 she had written forty-four books and contributed to ten anthologies. Her varied, award-winning novels include *The White Guinea Pig* (1994), *First Book of Samuel* (1995), *Theodora's Gift* (2005), and *The Red Shoe* (2006). *The Golden Day* (2011) is a beautifully written mystery about the disappearance of a teacher and was an *IBBY Honour Book in 2014. Her lively and entertaining picture books include *The Terrible Plop* (2009) and *Too Many Elephants in This House* (2012).

Dubosarsky's books often feature family life in a contemporary, realistic setting with the protagonists negotiating their way through a confusing and sometimes dangerous or surreal world. Although her style has occasionally been described as energetic, it is sophisticated, yet direct, which allows her occasionally to choose topics and themes not usually addressed in children's fiction.

From 2006 Dubosarsky worked at the *NSW School Magazine* for several years and completed a doctoral thesis on the work of Rumer *Godden and Mary *Norton. She was twice

nominated for the *Astrid Lindgren Memorial Award, and Sonya *Hartnett, a former winner, described Dubosarsky as the 'most graceful, most original writer for young people in Australia'.

DU CHAILLU, Paul (Belloni) (1835–1903) Explorer who carried out an expedition into the African interior in 1856. He subsequently wrote *Explorations and Adventures in Equatorial Africa* (1861), which at once provided material for *The *Gorilla Hunters* (1861) by *Ballantyne and was quarried by later *adventure story writers. Du Chaillu's accounts of pygmies, gorillas, and other wonders were at first received sceptically, but his discoveries were confirmed by later travellers. He himself wrote popular books about his adventures, of which editions were produced for children; they include *Stories of the Gorilla Country* (1867), *Lost in the Jungle* (1869), and *The Country of the Dwarfs* (1871).

Duchess A dog in *The Pie and the Patty-Pan* by Beatrix *Potter.

Duchess, The (Ugly) In *Alice's Adventures in Wonderland*.

DUDER, Tessa (1940–) New Zealand writer and editor. A former champion swimmer, she used her own experiences for her most successful books, the 'Alex' quartet, about a teenage girl who wants to be an Olympic swimmer. The first book, *Alex* (1987) (US title: *In Lane Three, Alex Archer*) was followed by *Alex in Winter* (1989), *Alessandra—Alex in Rome* (1991), and *Songs for Alex* (1992). She won *Esther Glen awards for the first three volumes, among countless other prizes. Other books include *Jellybean* (1985, updated edition 2010), about a girl whose cellist mother doesn't have time for her, and she herself becomes increasingly interested in music (Duder has also herself been a musician). *The Tiggie Tompson Show* (1999) is the first in a *young adult trilogy. She has also written a life of Margaret *Mahy (2005) and edited an illustrated collection of Mahy's verse, *The Word Witch* (2009).

DUFFY, Carol Ann (1955–) Scottish-born poet and playwright who was the first woman appointed as Britain's Poet Laureate in 2009. Her poetry for adults is studied at UK schools and universities and is known for its sometimes satirical wit and accessible narrative style. Duffy has also widely published poetry, anthologies, and picture books for children, often subverting gender roles and exploring

mythical and historical characters. Her picture book *Queen Munch and Queen Nibble* (2002), illustrated by Lydia Monks, is a bright, celebratory story of the blossoming relationship between two very different queens from neighbouring realms. She is a keen fan of *fairy tale, myth, and magic, and her other picture books include *The Lost Happy Endings* (2006), illustrated by Jane *Ray, about the theft of happy endings, and *The Princess' Blankets* (2008), a tale of a princess who can never get warm. Her collaboration with paper-cut artist Rob Ryan was shortlisted for the *Kate Greenaway Medal in 2012.

DUGGAN, Maurice (Noel) (1922–75) New Zealand author of short stories for adults who also wrote two children's books, *Falter Tom and the Water Boy* (1957) and *The Fabulous McFanes and other children's stories* (1974). The first is a delicate, unusual novella about an old sailor who is taken beneath the waves by a mer-boy.

DULAC, Edmund (1882–1953) Artist and stage designer, born in Toulouse, who was the illustrator of the *Arabian Nights* (1907) and collections of *fairy stories by Hans Christian *Anderson and others. His often very opulent, painterly work rivalled that of Arthur *Rackham in popularity, and was largely confined to expensive de luxe editions.

DUMAS, Alexandre (1802–70) Known as 'Dumas the elder' or 'Dumas père', he was the author of two of the most popular *historical novels of the 19th cent., *Le Comte de Monte-Cristo* (1844–5) and *Les Trois Mousquetaires* (1844; *The *Three Musketeers*). He also wrote a *fairy story, *Les Aventures d'un casse-noisette* (1845), based on a tale by E. T. A. *Hoffmann.

Dumbledore, Professor Albus Headmaster of *Hogwarts in the *Harry Potter series.

Dumbo A film by Walt *Disney, released in 1941; the story of a baby elephant whose ears are so big that he can use them to fly.

DUNBAR, Joyce (1944–) Author of over eighty books for children. The daughter of a steelworker, she grew up in an industrial town in Lincolnshire. She taught English for twenty years, and published her first children's book at the age of thirty-five. Dunbar likes to address life's big questions in her stories, and Philippa *Pearce once said that she has a 'passionate authenticity of imagination'. Her *Mouse and Mole* series was turned into an animation featuring the voices of Richard Briers, Alan Bennett, and Imelda Staunton. In 1998, Dunbar published *Tell Me Something Happy Before I Go to Sleep*, illustrated by Debi *Gliori, a comforting bedtime story that helps to allay night-time fears. She is the mother of author-illustrator Polly *Dunbar.

DUNBAR, Polly (1980–) An author-illustrator and puppet maker. She has collaborated with authors such as Margaret *Mahy (*Down the Back of the Chair*, 2006) and David *Almond (*My Dad's a Birdman*, 2007), and her mother Joyce *Dunbar (*Shoe Baby*, 2005), as well as writing many of her own books. *Shoe Baby* became the first production of Long Nose Puppets, a puppet company she set up with Katherine Morton. Dunbar achieved critical acclaim in 2007 with her picture book, *Penguin*, which won numerous awards. Her *Tilly and Friends* series, featuring a little girl and her animal companions, has been adapted as a television series for CBeebies.

DUNCAN, Lois (1934–2016) American author, famous through the success of the film version of her book, *I Know What You Did Last Summer* (1973), but her suspense-driven writing deserves to be read—especially as her books are far scarier than any film made from them. Tightly plotted and written *young adult novels such as *Killing Mr Griffin* (1978), *Stranger with My Face* (1981), and *Gallows Hill* (1995) are excellent examples. *A Gift of Magic* (1960) and *The Third Eye* (1984) explore her belief in the reality of ESP. Sadly, real life inspired *Who Killed My Daughter?* (1981), as it tells of her search for the truth behind the murder of her eighteen-year-old daughter, Kaitlyn.

DUNCAN, Norman (1871–1916) Canadian novelist who wrote three *adventure stories for boys, *The *Adventures of Billy Topsail* (1906), *Billy Topsail and Company* (1910), and *Billy Topsail, M.D.* (1916). He also wrote adult novels.

DUNNE, J. W. (John William) (1875–1949) Aeronautics engineer, author of two books for children in which fantasy is blended with *science: *The Jumping Lions of Borneo* (1937) and *An Experiment with St George* (1939), a sequel to the story of St *George and the dragon.

DURACK, Mary (1913–94) Australian author, one of the earliest writers who tried to make children aware of the lives of Aborigines. *The Way of the Whirlwind* (1941) is her best-remembered book.

Durango Street (1965) A novel by Frank *Bonham.

Dursley family In the *Harry Potter series. Following the death of his parents when he is just a baby, Harry Potter is raised by Vernon and Petunia Dursley (Petunia is his maternal aunt), at 4 Privet Drive. The Dursleys lavish affection on their slow-witted son Dudley, while forcing Harry to sleep in a cupboard under the stairs. Things change when Harry discovers his magical powers (unlike the magical Harry, the Dursleys are *muggles), but the boy still comes home to stay with the family in the summer break between school years (and between books in the series). The Potter books frequently begin and/or end in the Dursleys' world.

Dust *See* HIS DARK MATERIALS.

Dutch paper A floral paper used to cover children's books in the 18th and early 19th cents. Both expensive and cheaper versions had patterns of flowers, leaves, and fruit, with the addition of gold leaf in the higher-cost paper. Although at least one English manufacturer, B. Moore of Newgate Street, London, was producing the paper in the mid-18th cent., it was often imported from Germany and Italy, frequently via Holland—hence its name, though 'Dutch' may also be a corruption of 'Deutsch'. Its earliest use for a children's book seems to have been in 1740, for the first of Thomas *Boreman's series of *Gigantick Histories. This example was followed by John *Newbery for many of his juvenile books, and other publishers followed suit. The paper was often pasted on to thin cardboard to make a binding, but a thick version of it was also used by itself for a paper wrapper.

DUVOISIN, Roger (Antoine) (1904–80) Swiss-born illustrator-author who created many *picture books, including a 'Happy Lion' series (1954 onwards) with texts by his wife Louise Fatio, and stories about a silly goose named Petunia (1950 onwards) for which he wrote the words. From 1936 he was a prolific illustrator of books by other authors.

dwarfs Entering children's literature from the *Norse and Germanic tradition, dwarfs are found in such works of mythology as the *Eddas, the *Volsungasaga*, and the *Nibelungenlied*. Traditional *fairy stories making notable use of them include The *Yellow Dwarf, *Snow-White and Rose-Red, and *Snow White and the Seven Dwarfs. J. R. R. *Tolkien wrote much about them in The *Hobbit and The *Lord of the Rings.

dystopian fiction In children's literature, serving to articulate society's greatest fears for young readers and offer them a glimpse of imagined futuristic possibilities. A subgenre of *science fiction or speculative fiction, it depicts a narrative environment in which society has all but broken down and extreme forms of governmental, societal, or environmental disorder have taken over. The genre grew in popularity from the early 1950s when fear of the Cold War was increasingly represented in novels such as Andre *Norton's Star Man's Son: 2250 AD (1952) and Madeleine L'Engle's A *Wrinkle in Time (1962). Post-apocalyptic visions of the future remained popular well into the 1980s, for example Gudrun *Pausewang's Die Letzen Kinder von Schewenborn (1983; translated as The Last Children, 1988) and Louise *Lawrence's Children of the Dust (1985). While picture books such as David *Wiesner's Tuesday (1991), Shaun *Tan's The Viewer (1997) or Margaret *Wild's Woolvs in the Sitee (2006) are successful, even playful examples of it, the genre is most popular, unsurprisingly, in the teenage and *young adult fiction market. Educational theorists attribute this to teenagers' growing ability to think about abstract ideas such as government, power, and freedom (see also PIAGET, JEAN). Dystopian fiction can, therefore, communicate with young readers about current issues and their fears for their environment, and allow them a space to reflect upon their society and its future. Having waned in popularity in the 1990s (with Lois Lowry's The *Giver a very significant exception), dystopian fiction made a significant comeback in the new millennium, reflecting concerns such as consumerism, global warming, plastic surgery, conflict, the speed of technological change, reality television, and popular titles included M. T. *Anderson's Feed (2002), Jan *Mark's Useful Idiots (2003), Scott *Westerfeld's Uglies (2005), Malorie Blackman's *Noughts and Crosses (2001–8), Suzanne Collins's The Hunger Games (2008–10), and Patrick Ness's *Chaos Walking trilogy (2008–10), among many others. The massive success of the Collins in particular further increased mass appetites for the genre, and it was followed by several other blockbuster series, including James Dashner's The Maze Runner (from 2009) and Veronica Roth's Divergent (from 2011), the first book in each series being made into films in 2014.

Each Peach Pear Plum (1978) A classic rhyming picture book by Janet *Ahlberg and Allen *Ahlberg, which incorporates *nursery-rhyme and *fairy-tale characters into a cumulative rhyme. With each spread the simple text steps from one setting to the next (Mother Hubbard's house, Jack and Jill's hill, Robin Hood's forest, etc.), building pleasingly for the reader to a communal, festive ending. Meanwhile Janet Ahlberg's delightful country-side pictures are full of details to be discovered. It won the *Kate Greenaway Medal.

EAGER, Edward (1911–64) American writer of *fantasy in imitation of E. *Nesbit. His series of magic books begins with *Half Magic (1954).

Eagle A British *comic first published on 14 April 1950 by Hulton Press. It was the brain-child of the Revd Marcus Morris, vicar of an Anglican parish church at Birkdale in Lanca-shire, and of Frank Hampson, a cartoonist. Morris originally intended to produce a spe-cifically Christian illustrated paper for boys, but under Hampson's influence the scope of the project was widened, so that *Eagle* came to be in effect a modern version of the *Boy's Own Paper*. The leading strip was 'Dan Dare, Pilot of the Future', a *science fiction serial in which the chief villain was the Mekon of Venus, a humanoid with a giant bulbous green head. *Eagle* also featured 'The Adventures of P.C. 49' (based on a radio serial), 'Harris Tweed, Extra Special Agent' (a humorous strip), short stories, lessons in sports, hobby instructions, and con-tributions by the Revd Chad Varah, who later founded the Samaritans organization. Hulton also produced companion papers for girls and young children, *Girl*, *Robin*, and *Swift*.

Eagle was taken over by Odhams Press in 1960, whereupon Morris and Hampson left. It survived until 1969. 'Dan Dare' continued for a time in *Lion*, another comic, and in the 1970s he also featured in certain *annuals. Then in March 1982 *Eagle* was revived by IPC, though in a very different form, containing photostories

of a conventionally sensational type. Only 'Dan Dare' remained as a link with the original comic.

Eagle of the Ninth, The (1954) The first *historical novel for children by Rosemary *Sutcliff to achieve lasting success, and the opening story in her cycle about the Roman occupation of Britain. Marcus, invalided out of the Roman army in Britain after his first and only battle as a centurion, sets himself the task of discovering what happened to an entire legion, the Ninth, which some years before had marched beyond Hadrian's Wall to deal with an uprising and was never heard of again. Lost with the legion was its standard, a silver Eagle; moreover the legion, which was sus-pected of cowardice and desertion, numbered among its commanders Marcus's father. To-gether with a Briton, the former slave Esca, Marcus penetrates deep into hostile country, and discovers much that he did not want to know before the Eagle is finally found.

The book, besides showing a mastery of the historical period, resembles *Kidnapped and the thrillers of John Buchan in its account of Marcus and Esca's flight from the Celtic tribes-men beyond the wall. Moreover their mis-sion—to recover an object whose possession by the enemy may cause untold harm—and the description of their quest bear a striking, though obviously coincidental, resemblance to The *Lord of the Rings*.

The novel was serialized on *Children's Hour, and proved one of that programme's most popular items of all time. A film adapta-tion, *The Eagle*, opened in 2011 to mixed re-ception, both from critics and from the book's many devoted fans. Other titles in the se-quence of stories include *The Silver Branch* (1957), *The *Lantern Bearers* (which won the *Carnegie Medal) and *Sword at Sunset* (1963).

Early Lessons A series of storybooks by Maria *Edgeworth, first published by Joseph Johnson in 1801. They were innovatory in

their combination of simple reading-matter with practical information.

Harry and Lucy was based on a child's reading-book, *Practical Education*, published by Miss Edgeworth's father in 1780; it is a simple narrative of three days in the life of a brother and sister. By means of observation and asking questions, the two children learn about the world around them. Besides being intended to offer simple reading matter (the book includes a glossary of harder words), the story is also designed to emphasize the importance of a child developing a rational and inquiring mind.

Rosamond is more concerned with moral development. In the first and most celebrated of its chapters, 'The Purple Jar' (originally published in *The *Parent's Assistant*, 1796), the seven-year-old heroine covets a purple jar that stands in a chemist's window. Her mother tells her that she can afford to buy Rosamond either the jar or a pair of shoes which she needs badly. Rosamond chooses the jar, but when it is brought home she finds that it is merely a plain glass vessel containing purple liquid, and is an utter disappointment. Her shoes soon wear out, and she repents of her choice: 'I hope I shall be wiser another time.' Other stories also contain an overt moral message. For example, in 'Day of Misfortunes' Rosamond gets up late, has to dress in a hurry, and finds that everything is going wrong. However, she soon forgets her troubles when she saves the life of a robin that she finds half-starved and frozen. Her mother remarks: 'I am very much pleased to see that you can command your temper, and that you can use your understanding to govern yourself.'

Frank was intended to be the first book used by young readers of the series, and was aimed at four- to six-year-olds. It describes the adventures of a boy of six, and, like *Harry and Lucy*, concentrates on providing facts about the physical world, such as the different characteristics of a potato and a horse-chestnut, and how to make a kite. A final volume in the original *Early Lessons* series contained other stories that had first appeared in *The Parent's Assistant*.

Early Lessons was reprinted in various forms, and 20 years later Maria Edgeworth began to produce continuations of the three principal books. *Rosamond: a sequel* (1821), *Frank: a sequel* (1822), and *Harry and Lucy concluded* (1825) were intended for older children; as Miss Edgeworth wrote in a preface to one of them, her aim yet again was 'to exercise

the powers of attention, observation, reasoning, and invention . . . [and] to excite a thirst for knowledge'. By this time, Mrs *Trimmer had stated her objections to the 'want of religious instruction' in *Early Lessons*, and to the suggestion that 'the child . . . makes discoveries by his own unassisted reason'.

E. *Nesbit uses the names Harry and Lucy (undoubtedly with intended irony) for the quarrelsome brother and sister in her short story 'The Twopenny Spell', in *Oswald Bastable and Others* (1905).

Early Piety; *or, Memoirs of Children Eminently Serious* (1776) By George *Burder (1752–1832), founder of the *Religious Tract Society. It was modelled on the *Token for Children* by James *Janeway, and consists of 'The Entertaining History of Master Billy and Miss Betsey Goodchild', in which those children hear or tell such tales of piety as the story 'of a very good girl that died happy before she was seven years old'. The book was widely distributed in *Sunday schools during the first half of the 19th cent.

Earp, Wyatt *See* WYATT EARP.

Earthsea Setting of five novels and other stories by Ursula *Le Guin. *A Wizard of Earthsea* (1967) introduces Ged, a young sorcerer's apprentice living on one of the many islands in Earthsea who has an unquenchable thirst for knowledge of magical powers. While studying at a college of sorcery, he unintentionally brings into the world a spirit from the dead which is bent on his destruction. *The Tombs of Atuan* (1969) introduces Arha, priestess of the Dark Ones, whose personality has been perverted by her cult; Ged helps her to escape and to become herself again. *The Farthest Shore* (1972) takes Ged on a quest to the land of the dead to restore the balance between life and death, which has been upset by evil forces. *Tehanu*, published in 1990, was subtitled 'The Last Book of Earthsea'; this was followed in 2001 by *The Other Wind*.

Though the Earthsea books were written during the popular obsession with invented mythologies which followed the 'campus cult' of *The *Lord of the Rings*, they are no mere Tolkien imitations. Le Guin has a brisk confidence in her own invented world, and performs the rare feat of managing to be funny while writing this kind of fiction.

The British critic and author David *Rees has observed that the three first novels all 'deal with the fundamental problems of

adolescence—discovering qualities and limitations; acquiring skills; and with the questions: who am I? what is my place in the world? can I function adequately and maturely?'

Earthy Mangold Scarecrow in the *Worzel Gummidge stories by Barbara Euphan *Todd.

East A boy in *Tom Brown's Schooldays by Arthur *Hughes.

EASTMAN, P. D. See SEUSS, DR.

East of the Sun and West of the Moon

A Norwegian *fairy story collected by *Asbjørnsen and Moe, and first published in English in *Fairy Tales of All Nations (1849). A girl is carried off by a white bear. She is brought to a fine palace, where every night a man lies down beside her in bed, though she never sees his face. Eventually, goaded by her mother, she lights a candle to look at him, and finds that he is a handsome prince. She drops three spots of tallow on his shirt, thereby waking him. He tells her that he is enchanted into a bear by day and must now, because she has seen his face, leave her forever and marry a princess 'with a nose three ells long', who lives in a castle that is East of the Sun and West of the Moon. The girl, by great exertions, follows him to this castle, bearing a number of precious objects. With these she bribes her way into the prince's chamber at night, but the long-nosed princess has given him a sleeping potion. On the night before his wedding to Long-Nose she rejects the potion, and when the girl manages to wash the spots of tallow off his shirt she is revealed as his true love. Long-Nose and her mother burst with rage, and the prince marries the girl.

The story is one of a group of similar tales that includes the legend of Cupid and Psyche, The *Black Bull of Norroway, and *Beauty and the Beast.

Eat Your Peas (2000) A picture book with words by Kes Gray and illustrations by Nick *Sharratt which introduces a little girl called Daisy, who would go on to star in several further books. In Eat Your Peas her increasingly desperate mother tries to persuade her to, please, eat her peas, offering her a selection of rewards that gets bigger and more surreal on every page. As so often in children's books, the child proves more than capable of outsmarting the parent; Daisy is spared the peas, and she and mum end the book eating ice cream instead. Other Daisy picture books by Gray and Sharratt include You Do (2003),

Yuk! (2004), and 006 and a Bit (2006). She has also featured in several storybooks.

e-books (electronic books) Texts primarily read on screen through various portable e-book readers, computers, smartphones, or other electronic devices. Whilst experimentation began in the first half of the 20th cent., it was not until the rise of personal computers that e-books were made available to the wider public. CD-ROMs provided early examples of e-books, but are now much less used, as the internet provides fast and accessible downloading of digital content. As new types of digital reading arise, such as *apps and direct online content, e-books are more commonly defined as digital equivalents of printed books which provide a similar linear reading experience; however, they can also contain multimedia and hyperlinked content, in a similar way to apps, such as film, animation, read-aloud, sound effects, and other enhanced features. The growth in opportunity to create new literary experiences, such as the Read/Write potential of online collaborative sharing, has led educationalists and publishers alike to think about how children can encounter text and interact digitally.

ECCLESHARE, Julia (1951–) Children's books critic, and since 1998 the children's books editor of The Guardian. Her own publications include a guide to the *Harry Potter novels (2002), The Rough Guide to Books for Teenagers (2002, with Nicholas Tucker), Beatrix Potter to Harry Potter: Portraits of Children's Writers (2002), and 1001 Children's Books You Must Read Before You Grow Up (2009). A former book editor, Eccleshare is also permanent chair of the judging panels for the *Branford Boase Award (which she co-founded) and the *Guardian Children's Fiction Prize. In 2000 she was herself awarded the *Eleanor Farjeon Award for her contribution to children's literature.

Edda The name given to the two chief ancient collections of *Norse myths. The Poetic or Elder Edda, a collection of cosmogonical, mythological, and heroic poems, survives in a manuscript of the 13th cent., though much of it is considerably more ancient in origin. The Prose or Younger Edda, a manual for poets by the 13th-cent. writer Snorri Sturluson, contains a narrative of the adventures of the gods. The first English retelling of the Eddic stories for children was in *Heroes of Asgard (1857) by the *Keary sisters.

EDGAR, J. G. (John George) (1834–64) Author of many works of *history and biography as well as *historical novels. His books include *The Heroes of England: stories of the lives of England's Warriors by Land and Sea* (1858), which begins with a life of the Black Prince and deals with great soldiers and naval leaders up to Sir Henry Havelock, hero of the Indian Mutiny, and *Footprints of Famous Men, designed as Incitements to Intellectual Industry* (1854), whose subjects include George Washington, Robert *Southey, Joshua Reynolds, Christopher Wren, James Watt, and Adam Smith. Much of his work first appeared as articles in boys' *magazines.

Edge Chronicles, The (1998) An epic series from collaborators Paul *Stewart (writer) and Chris *Riddell (illustrator), which combines complex world-building, a cast of thousands, and more battles and quests than any reader could wish for. The book that started the hugely successful series is *Beyond the Deepwoods* (1998), the first of the *Twig Trilogy*, about a boy called Twig who lives with the Woodtrolls, but is searching for where he truly belongs. With three trilogies complete and a single volume rounding it up to ten and seemingly there to sew the *Chronicles* up, the collaborators soon gave in, and *The Cade Saga: The Nameless One* (2014) introduces another branch to the series.

EDGEWORTH, Maria (1767–1849) Author who has been described as 'the first English classic writer for children'. She was noted for her children's stories, and for her writings on education, which were collaborations with her father Richard Lovell *Edgeworth (1744–1817).

Maria was born in Oxfordshire in January 1767, third child of Richard Lovell Edgeworth and Anna Maria Edgeworth. Maria's mother died when she was five years old and during his life her father remarried a further three times, eventually fathering twenty-two children. After periods at school in Derby and London, Maria eventually moved with her father to the family's estate at Edgeworthstown, County Longford, Ireland, where she helped look after her step-siblings and run the estate. She was home-tutored in law, science, and literature by her father.

Maria had begun to write stories for family entertainment during her childhood, and she now developed the habit of jotting them down on a slate, trying them on the children, and

writing them out properly on paper if they met with approval. In 1791 she and her father began to plan a series which would include a general essay on education and a number of stories for early readers. The first result was *The *Parent's Assistant* (1796), a collection of *moral tales by Maria, of which the best known is 'The Purple Jar', the story of Rosamond, who prefers a gaudy jar to a new pair of shoes. The collection, which went into several editions, also included several *plays for children. As Maria's step-siblings grew up, she turned her attention to stories for older children, which appeared in *Moral Tales* (1801). In 1801 there was also published *Early Lessons*, a series of storybooks in large print and a small-page format, intended for children learning to read. In addition she published a plea for educational reform in 1795 entitled *Letters for Literary Ladies*. Meanwhile in 1798 she and her father published their essay on the upbringing of children, under the title *Practical Education*. Its 25 chapters were each concerned with one aspect of a child's environment and education.

In 1800 Edgeworth began to make a name for herself as an adult novelist with *Castle Rackrent*, which was followed by *Belinda* (1801) and other works of fiction. During a visit to Paris in 1802–3 she regretfully refused a proposal of marriage from a Swedish inventor. Her father remained her guide for the rest of his life, often contributing prefaces to her storybooks. Her books, especially those for children, remained popular throughout the 19th cent. (there are several references to her in the writings of E. *Nesbit), and some of her stories for young readers occasionally appeared in print in 20th-cent. collections.

Maria Edgeworth's stories were vividly written. She had a good ear for natural dialogue, and above all made flesh-and-blood characters out of many of the children she portrayed. E. V. *Lucas calls her the earliest real 'novelist for the nursery'. However, the prevalence of didactic intent in her stories led many critics of children's literature to dismiss Edgeworth's work in line with other examples of the moral tale as 'limp' and lacking 'vital spark', and thus having no lasting influence on children's literature after the fashion for didacticism had died away. However, recent scholarship and a reassessment of Romantic era writing by women have resurrected the work of Edgeworth and others, and emphasized the way in which such works can be read as forming part of a radical and progressive

ideology that challenges the social construction of the child, particularly the female child. An important collected edition of Maria Edgeworth's works (the first since the 19th cent.) was completed in 2003 under the general editorship of Marilyn Butler.

EDGEWORTH, R. L. (Richard Lovell) (1744–1817) Irish writer, educationalist, and inventor, father of children's writer Maria *Edgeworth.

R. L. Edgeworth was an Anglo-Irishman descended from a family notable for fast living and debts. He married the daughter of an impoverished Gloucestershire landowner, and lived for some years in England. By the 1760s he had made the friendship of Thomas *Day, the author of *Sandford and Merton*. The two men were greatly struck by the ideas of *Rousseau, and Edgeworth set about bringing up his eldest child Richard according to the principles set out in *Émile*. The experiment was successful as far as it went, though he soon abandoned it because of distractions.

In 1773 his first wife died and Edgeworth married again. Abandoning his discipleship of Rousseau, he became determined to find some other way of educating his younger children. He examined various *ABC books and *primers, but was satisfied only with *Lessons for Children* by Mrs *Barbauld, which began to appear in 1778. With the aid of this, two of his children learnt to read in six weeks. Edgeworth decided that Mrs Barbauld's pioneering work should be built on, and that children must be provided with clearly written stories based on their own experience of the world. He and his second wife Honora composed a simple tale about two children, Harry and Lucy, getting up in the morning, making their beds, having breakfast, and asking their parents questions about the world around them. This was published, ostensibly as part of a series, under the title *Practical Education* (1780). Honora also began to make notes of children's reaction to different forms of experimental teaching. In 1779 she died of consumption, having instructed her husband to marry her younger sister so as to provide a mother for his family. This he did, and soon afterwards moved his household to Edgeworthstown, the family estate in County Longford, Ireland.

In 1785 he was one of the founder members of the Royal Irish Academy, which still exists; membership is considered to be the highest mark of academic achievement in Ireland. The next years were spent engaged with agriculture and invention (Edgeworth invented an early form of the caterpillar tractor) and with a collaboration with his daughter Maria on a new book also entitled *Practical Education*, which was concerned with the education of children. This was published in 1798. He became a guiding light in the life of his (now famous) daughter and contributed to her work. He was elected a member of the Board of Commissioners to inquire into Irish education in 1806, and died in 1817.

***Editha's Burglar** See* SARA CREWE.

EDMONDS, Walter D. (Dumaux) (1903–98) American author who won the *Newbery Medal with his first children's book, *The Matchlock Gun* (1941), a story about Dutch settlers in America (all his fiction is about pioneer days). He was given a *National Book Award for *Bert Breen's Barn* (1975).

education *See* BOOKS OF INSTRUCTION.

Edward Cullen *See* TWILIGHT.

EDWARDS, Dorothy (1914–82) British writer for children who was associated for many years with the BBC's *Listen with Mother*. It was for that programme that she wrote stories about *My Naughty Little Sister*; the first volume of these was published in 1952, and there were many sequels.

EDWARDS, Monica (Le Doux) (1912–98) British author who began to publish *pony stories in 1947, her first book being *Wish for a Pony*. From this conventional start she developed her popular and well-regarded 'Romney Marsh' series, recounting the adventures of Tamzin, Rissa, Roger, and Meryon. Later titles include *The Nightbird* (1955), *No Going Back* (1960), and *A Wind is Blowing* (1969). In 1947 she also began a series about the Thornton family, the first volume being *No Mistaking Corker*. The Thorntons move from Hampshire to Punchbowl Farm in Surrey, named after the Devil's Punchbowl, and later books deal with the family life of Andrea, Dion, Lindsey, and Peter. They include *Spirit of Punchbowl Farm* (1952), *The Wanderer* (1953), and *The Wild One* (1967).

Eeyore In *Winnie the Pooh* and *The *House at Pooh Corner* by A. A. *Milne.

EGGLESTON, Edward (1837–1902) American author who was born in Indiana and became a Methodist minister and writer and editor of *Sunday school magazines. He is now chiefly remembered for *The Hoosier Schoolmaster* (1871), based on the experiences of his brother as a teacher in backwoods

Indiana, and *The *Hoosier Schoolboy* (1883), a study of the same kind of school seen from the point of view of the pupils.

EGNER, Thorbjørn (1912–90) Norwegian author-illustrator. His books include *Karius og Baktus* ('Karius and Baktus') (1949), a very popular story which warns children to clean their teeth—it describes the merry life of a couple of bacteria who live in a boy's teeth, and whose only fear is of the toothbrush.

EGOFF, Sheila *See* OSBORNE COLLECTION.

Egyptian folk tales These have been collected for children in, among others, Roger Lancelyn *Green's *Tales of Ancient Egypt* (1967) and Helen Mitchnik's *Egyptian and Sudanese Folk-tales* (1978).

EHRLICH, Bettina *See* BETTINA.

Eighteenth Emergency, The (1973) A humorous school story by Betsy *Byars about bullying and being bullied, notable for the skill with which it captures the concerns and anxieties of its young protagonist, making it as attractive and relevant today as when it first appeared. When twelve-year-old Benjie (also known as Mouse) provokes the school bully, Marv Hammerman, he knows there is no escape. Mouse can think of strategies to handle sudden shark appearances, strangulation by boa constrictor, and fifteen other crises, but he hasn't accounted for the eighteenth emergency: being targeted by Marv Hammerman. Byars adopts a light touch to address the theme of bullying and despite its serious subject matter, the novel is warm-hearted and funny.

EKWENSI, Cyprian (Odiatu) (1921–2007) Nigerian novelist, and a senior official in his country's Ministry of Information before the Biafran war, Ekwensi wrote a number of books read widely by African children. His most attractive and original children's book is *An African Night's Entertainment* (1962), an *Arabian Nights*-style story about a rich man who snatches a girl away from her childhood sweet heart and marries her himself, with disastrous consequences.

Eleanor Farjeon Award Given annually since 1966 (following *Farjeon's death the previous year) by the UK's Children's Book Circle (CBC) to an individual or organization that has made a significant contribution to the children's books world. It has been awarded to writers and illustrators (Quentin *Blake,

Philip *Pullman, Jacqueline *Wilson, Naomi *Lewis, Aidan *Chambers), to translators (Patricia *Crampton), to critics and publishers (Julia *Eccleshare, Kaye *Webb), and to other individuals (Wendy *Cooling, Margaret *Meek) and organizations (*Seven Stories, The *Federation of Children's Book Groups). Candidates are nominated and voted for by CBC members.

Elements of Morality (1790) A collection of *moral tales freely translated by Mary *Wollstonecraft from *Das moralische Elementarbuch* (1785) by C. G. *Salzmann.

Elephant and the Bad Baby, The (1969) A picture book illustrated by Raymond *Briggs, with a text by Elfrida *Vipont, this story of a baby who wouldn't say 'please' has become a read-aloud classic. The baby is riding on the back of an elephant, and they run through the town—*rumpeta rumpeta rumpeta*—with more and more people chasing after them, until the bad baby finally does say 'Please!' and the elephant carries him back home. (With the butcher, the baker, the grocer, etc. all still in pursuit.)

elf A species of supernatural being found in the Norse *Eddas*. In modern European literature 'elf' is rarely more than a synonym for *fairy, but J. R. R. *Tolkien in *The *Lord of the Rings* presents them quite differently, as somewhat godlike immortals, possessed of superhuman powers of craft and art.

Elidor (1965) The third novel by Alan *Garner. Four children, exploring derelict backstreets in modern Manchester, find themselves transported into the land of Elidor, which is dying because three of its four Treasures have been captured by the forces of evil. The book originated as a half-hour radio play, broadcast by the BBC in 1962. It draws on the *Grail legends and their accompanying Waste Land motif, as well as on Platonic philosophy—to name only a few of the strands identified by Garner, and by Neil Philip in his study of Garner's writings, *A Fine Anger* (1981). More was packed into it, indeed, than could be carried by the narrative, yet the story is always intensely exciting, while the realistic dialogue shows a big advance on Garner's first two books.

For the name 'Elidor', *see* WELSH TRADITIONAL TALES.

ELIOT, T. S. *See* OLD POSSUM'S BOOK OF PRACTICAL CATS.

Elizabeth, or, The Exiles of Siberia A story by the French novelist Sophie Cottin (1770–1807),

first published in 1806 and translated into English three years later. Elizabeth is the daughter of a Polish patriot exiled to Siberia by the Tsar. She manages the arduous journey from Siberia to St Petersburg, where she successfully implores the Tsar for her father's freedom. The story was frequently reprinted, and was a favourite tale with young ladies in the early 19th cent.

Ella Enchanted (1997) A *young adult novel by Gail *Carson Levine, which takes a handful of traditional fairy-tale tropes and spins them on their head. Ella is blessed at her christening with the gift of obedience—obedience to everyone. As she grows up, she is handed the fate of many fairy-tale heroines in that her mother dies, her father remarries, and her step-family is really *not* very nice. But Ella is strong-willed enough to fight the gift and win her freedom, and save the prince too. Further explorations of fairy tales can be found in *The Two Princesses of Bamarre* (2001), *Fairest* (2006), and *Ever* (2008).

Ellen Montgomery Heroine of *The *Wide, Wide World*, by Susan Bogert *Warner.

ELLIN, E. M. (Elizabeth Muriel) (1904–82) New Zealand author of two children's novels, *The Children of Clearwater Bay* (1969) and *The Greenstone Axe* (1975), both set in pioneer days.

ELLIOTT (Belson), Mary (?1794–1870) English author of a large number of *moral tales. One of the earliest and best known was *The Orphan Boy* (1812), a story ('founded on fact') of a nameless infant discovered on a coach near Bristol, brought up by the landlady of an inn, and eventually identified as the nephew of a wealthy man. The book was mentioned in *The *Fairchild Family* as being enjoyed by the children. Among Mrs Elliott's numerous other works, all of which were published by William *Darton, was *The Adventures of Thomas Two-Shoes* (1818), a sequel to *Goody Two-Shoes*. She wrote several books of poems, including *Simple Truths in Verse* (1812) and *The Rose* (1824). Marjorie Moon published a checklist of her work in 1987.

ELLIS, Deborah (1960–) Canadian author and peace activist. Ellis writes novels and nonfiction about the effects of poverty and conflict on children from around the world. She won the *Governor General's Literary Award for Juvenile Fiction for her first book, *Looking for X* (1999), set in a poor section of Toronto.

She is best known for her *Breadwinner* series, about the experiences of Parvana, an Afghan girl living under the Taliban, and her best friend Shauzia. *The Breadwinner* (2000) won the Women's International League for Peace and Freedom's Jane Addams Children's Book Award. There are three sequels.

ELLIS, Edward Sylvester *See* DIME NOVEL

Elmer (1989) By David *McKee, a glorious celebration of elephants, humour, and the joys of being different, which has been a nursery companion to countless children, selling close to five million copies in forty languages. With simple but expressive illustrations, McKee's first *Elmer* book shows multicoloured Elmer being teased by his grey friends. One day he decides that he's fed up with being different, so he tries to fit in by painting himself grey—but none of his friends recognize him . . . until it rains and the paint washes off. He learns then that his friends really do love him for what he is, fun-loving, brightly coloured, and just himself. There are many sequels that continue to enthral, amuse, and celebrate *diversity.

Eloise (1955) First in a series of books written by Kay Thompson (1909–98), and illustrated by Hilary Knight (1926–). A dog who looks like a cat, a British nanny, and a raisin-eating turtle are the friends of a girl who lives in the Plaza Hotel in New York, a girl whose mischievous adventures are amusing and timeless. The original four books were written by Thompson, but they were so popular that not only have films and television versions been made, but the series has been continued by other writers, though none captures the charm of the originals.

Elsie Dinsmore (1867) A novel by the prolific American children's writer Martha Farquharson (1828–1909). Elsie, whose mother is dead and whose father is absent in Europe, is being brought up by relatives who show her only limited affection. When her father appears, he too has little love for her at first, but Elsie eventually wins his heart through her piety and meekness. The book proved so popular that it was eventually followed by more than twenty-five further 'Elsie' titles. Her books were almost as successful in the UK as in America. Modern readers, besides finding Elsie a prig, have observed that there are disconcerting sexual overtones to her relationship with her father, who is always 'stooping to press a kiss on the little upturned face'. Elsie marries a man of her father's age.

elves See ELF.

Elzevir Block In *Moonfleet* by J. Meade *Falkner.

emblem books Sets of pictures chosen for their symbolic meaning, combined with a text that explains the symbolism and points a moral, often religious. Such books were derived from the *Emblemata* of a 16th-cent. Milanese writer, Andrea Alciati. Emblem books were sometimes produced for children, for example, in England J. H. Wynne's *Choice Emblems...for the Improvement and Pastime of Youth* (1772), and in America *Instructive and Entertaining Emblems* by 'Miss Thoughtful' (1795). A typical emblem, from the latter, is a young stork carrying its aged parent on its back, as storks were believed to do; this is presented as an example of filial duty and affection.

John *Bunyan's collection of poems written largely in the emblematic tradition, *A *Book for Boys and Girls* (1686), was republished with illustrations in 1724 as *Divine Emblems*, and afterwards known by this title. The genre was parodied by Robert Louis *Stevenson and his stepson Lloyd Osbourne in the privately printed *Moral Emblems* (1882), a small collection of ridiculous verses with absurdly crude woodcuts made by Stevenson himself.

Emil and the Detectives (*Emil und die Detektive*) (1929) A novel by Erich *Kästner, illustrated by Walter *Trier. Emil Tischbein, ten-year-old son of a poor widow, is sent from Neustadt to Berlin, where he is to spend the holidays with relatives. In his pocket is a sum of money, hard-earned by his mother and intended for his grandparents; on the train it is stolen. Rather than call the police, Emil decides to chase the suspect himself, and when the train arrives in Berlin he soon acquires the assistance of a whole tribe of schoolchildren. The thief is caught, his guilt is proved, and he is discovered to be a bank-robber for whom the police have been searching. Emil becomes famous and is given a reward; his grandmother announces the moral of the story, which is 'Always send money by postal order!'

The first English edition (1931, a translation by Margaret L. Goldsmith) had an introduction by Walter *de la Mare. The book was an instant success both in Germany and other European countries, and there have been many imitations, such as Enid *Blyton's long-running series about The *Famous Five. (Eileen *Colwell remarked of the *Emil* genre at its worst: 'What chance has a gang of desperate criminals against three small children?') One of the few books of this type to match up to Kästner's story is Paul Berna's *A Hundred Million Francs* (*Le Cheval sans tête*, 1955). *Emil and the Detectives* was adapted for the stage by Carl Miller, premiering at London's National Theatre in 2013.

Émile A treatise on education by *Rousseau, first published in 1762. The book argues that humanity is by nature good, but is corrupted by social conventions: 'There is no original sin in the human heart; the how and why of the entrance of every vice can be traced.' Rousseau describes an imaginary pupil, Émile, who is to have the perfect upbringing and education from Jean-Jacques, his tutor, whose ideas will protect the Natural Man in him from the destructive forces of society.

Like *Locke, whom he much admired, Rousseau argues that in infancy children should not be swaddled or cosseted, but should be allowed plenty of fresh air to toughen them. However he disagrees with Locke's assertion that children acquire a moral sense through an adult reasoning with them. Instead he believes that the child should be taught to do the right thing by means of sheer adult authority: 'Let him only know that he is weak and you are strong...Thus you will make him patient, equable, calm, resigned, even when he does not get all he wants, for it is in man's nature to bear patiently with the nature of things.'

Rousseau declares that the study of languages and history is entirely useless to young children, who have no idea of the real significance of the words and concepts involved. He regards even the *Fables* of *La Fontaine as too subtle for young minds. Almost the only book he recommends for children is *Robinson Crusoe*, from which they may learn 'the exercise of the natural arts'. Education is to be conducted on the principle of whetting the child's curiosity and no more. At puberty Émile is to be taught *history, but he will not be given *religious instruction until he is capable of reasoning the truth of religion for himself.

The final section of *Émile* is concerned with the hero's female counterpart, whom Rousseau calls 'Sophy'. He believes that 'the man should be strong and active; the woman should be weak and passive'. Female education should encourage gentleness and the learning of domestic skills. The book ends with the marriage of Émile and Sophy.

Émile was condemned by the French parliament for its supposed hostility to church

and state, but it was very widely read in France, and two English translations appeared within a few months of its publication in Paris, both entitled *Emilius and Sophia*. The book's stamp may be seen on certain late 18th-cent. English writings for children, notably *Sandford and Merton* by Thomas *Day.

EMMETT Brothers British publishers of boys' story-papers during the latter half of the 19th cent. The five brothers, of whom one, George, had taken part in the Charge of the Light Brigade, wrote many of the stories themselves. They were in close rivalry with Edwin *Brett, but never equalled his success.

Emperor's New Clothes, The A story by Hans Christian *Andersen, first published in 1836 and translated into English in 1846. An emperor who is obsessed with beautiful clothes is visited by two swindlers, who tell him that they are weavers and can make the finest cloth ever seen. He commissions them to make a suit of clothes, and they begin work—with an empty loom, telling him that the material has 'the strange quality of being invisible to anyone who is unfit for his office or unforgivably stupid'. The emperor, his courtiers, and all the townspeople are unwilling to admit that they cannot see anything, and the emperor actually parades naked in his 'new clothes' before a little child observes: 'He doesn't have anything on!' The story is based on traditional materials—tales of similar deception are found in many countries—but Andersen added a satirical edge of his own.

Enchanted Castle, The (1907) A novel by E. *Nesbit. Gerald, Jimmy, and Kathleen discover a magnificent castle which they decide to pretend is enchanted. In a maze in the garden they find Mabel, the niece of the castle's housekeeper. When she shows them a secret room in the castle, the enchantment becomes real. The book is more complex in structure than anything Nesbit had previously written for children. The critic Julia Briggs has pointed out that it attempts a 'sustained examination of childhood fears', and 'swings unsettlingly between the everyday world and the world of childish nightmare'. It is perhaps too ambitious to be entirely successful, but it reaches a fine pitch of grotesque comedy when the Ugli-Wuglies, a group of scarecrow-like human figures that the children have manufactured out of household objects, actually come alive, thanks to a casual wish.

Enchanted Doll, The (1849) A story by Mark *Lemon.

ENDE, Michael (1929–95) German writer of *fantasy. He came to fame with *Die unendliche Geschichte* (*The Never-Ending Story*, 1979), in which a child enters a fantasy world by reading about it. *Momo*, another fantasy novel, was published in 1973.

Endless Steppe, The (1968) A memoir of growing up during the Second World War, by Esther Hautzig (1930–2009). Esther and her family live a comfortable life in the city of Vilnius, in Poland (now in Lithuania), until 1941, when they are arrested by Russian soldiers and deported to a forced labour camp in Siberia. The book tells of their years in exile, the privations they endure, and Esther's resilience and resourcefulness in the face of hardship. It won the inaugural award from the Association of Jewish Libraries, later the Sydney Taylor Book Award.

English Fairy Tales A collection by Joseph *Jacobs, illustrated by John D. Batten, published in 1890. Besides such well known tales as *Jack and the Beanstalk*, *Jack the Giant Killer*, *Tom Thumb*, and *Dick Whittington*, it included British variants of celebrated European stories, such as *Cap o' Rushes* (a version of *Cinderella*), *Mr Fox* (see BLUEBEARD), *Kate Crackernuts* (see TWELVE DANCING PRINCESSES, THE), and *The Well of the World's End* (see FROG PRINCE, THE). Jacobs gave the sources of all his stories, many of which were taken from the publications of J. O. *Halliwell, but felt free to rewrite them whenever he thought it desirable. In 1894 he issued *More English Fairy Tales*. The two books (reissued in 1979, slightly abridged, in one volume) are still sometimes used today to provide the texts for modern *picture-book versions of traditional stories.

English Schoolmaster, The A *primer by Edmund or Edward Coote, headmaster of the grammar school at Bury St Edmunds. First published in 1596, it was remarkable for its time in the care that it takes to teach the pupil to read and spell by easy and methodical steps. It begins with a syllabary or syllabarium (*see* ABC BOOKS); then come many pages of simple lessons by which the child may learn to read common words. There are also instructions to the schoolmaster as to how the book should be used, which are printed in small type in the margin. Many chapters conclude with reading exercises designed to

appeal to schoolboys. The second part of the book deals with more complicated rules, which are set out in dialogue form. There is also a *catechism, prayers, metrical psalms, some simple instruction in arithmetic and *history, and a short spelling dictionary.

The English Schoolmaster became immensely popular, and was still being reprinted at the beginning of the 18th cent.

English Spelling Book, The A famous *primer first published in 1801. By 1819 a publisher of it was claiming that it had reached its '241st edition', and it was still in print 70 years later. Its author was the Revd William Mavor (1758–1837), who before taking holy orders was writing-master to the children of the Duke of Marlborough. He was the author of some 40 textbooks for children and other writings.

The English Spelling Book begins with an illustrated alphabet (*see* ABC BOOKS), followed by a syllabary, tables of simple words, and reading exercises. The book also includes lessons in *natural history; a selection of *fables and poems; various *moral tales and observations; outlines of *geography, *history, arithmetic, and astronomy; rules of English spelling, punctuation, and grammar; tables of Latin and French words and phrases in common English use; and a *catechism. An edition published by *Routledge in 1885 had illustrations by Kate *Greenaway.

Enormous Egg, The (1956) A novel by the American author Oliver Butterworth (1915–90). A hen belonging to the Twitchell family lays an enormous egg from which there hatches a triceratops. The story deals with young Nate Twitchell's determination to keep the animal as a pet, and was largely a satire on modern life in the USA.

ENRIGHT, Elizabeth (1909–68) American author-illustrator of seventeen children's books. They include *Thimble Summer* (1938), a *Newbery Medal winner about a girl on a Wisconsin farm during a time of drought and the Depression; *The Sea is All Around* (1940), in which the orphan Mab Kendall comes to live with an aunt on an island off the Atlantic coast; and a series of books about the Melendy children, beginning with *The *Saturdays* (1941). Though her books resemble many other *family stories published in America between the two World Wars, they are full of vitality.

Eragon *See* INHERITANCE SERIES.

ERASMUS *See* BOOKS OF COURTESY; PARŒ-MIOLOGIA ANGLO-LATINA.

ERDRICH, Louise (1954–) American author with part *Native American heritage. Erdrich has a tribal affiliation to the Turtle Mountain Band of Chippewa Indians in North Dakota, where she grew up, and her books often feature Native American characters and settings. Her Birchbark series chronicles the life of Omakayas and her Ojibwa community, beginning in the mid-1800s. The books are often said to offer an alternative perspective to Laura Ingalls Wilder's *Little House* books. *The Birchbark House* (1999) was a National Book Award finalist, while the fourth book in the series, *Chickadee* (2012), won the Scott O'Dell Award for Historical Fiction. Erdrich's other works include the picture books *Grandmother's Pigeon* (1996) and *The Range Eternal* (2002).

Eric, or, Little by Little, *a tale of Roslyn School* (1858) A celebrated *school story by F. W. *Farrar. Eric Williams, aged twelve, is sent to school in the Isle of Roslyn. At first he attends as a day pupil and lives at home. When his parents sail for India, he becomes a boarder and begins to get regularly into trouble, not because of any real viciousness of character but because he is too weak-minded to stand out against the general trend of schoolboy behaviour. He overhears indecent words, and does not speak out against this evil. Soon he is on trial for another crime—supposedly having written a rude remark about a master on a noticeboard—in an episode reminiscent of *Juvenile Trials* (1771) by Richard *Johnson. The real perpetrator of this offence is discovered and expelled, but Eric is now sliding fast: he takes to smoking (which he really detests, but thinks 'manly') and drinking in a low public house. His drunkenness eventually earns him a sentence of expulsion from the school, though this is commuted into a flogging. However, nothing can now go right for Eric and he runs away to sea, where he is grossly ill-treated by the captain; he returns home mortally ill. However, his seagoing experience has cleansed him morally; his name has now been cleared from suspicion of a theft of money at school, and he dies a holy death with his schoolfellows at his bedside.

The original of 'Roslyn', or at least of its physical setting, was King William's College on the Isle of Man, where Farrar himself was at school; but, as well as drawing on his own

boyhood memories, the book reflects his experiences as a schoolmaster at Marlborough and at Harrow. He explained to a friend that several of the boys in it were based on Harrovians, one of whom 'brutalised himself by drink, was expelled, and went to sea'. *Eric* was an immediate success on its publication in the autumn of 1858, and was reprinted again and again during the remainder of the 19th cent. However, *Kipling mocks the story extensively in his story based on his own school days, *Stalky & Co.*

The book's natural span of life seems to have come to an end with a reprint of 1911, after which it did not appear again until Hamish Hamilton reissued it in 1971 as a historical curiosity, with an introduction by John Rowe *Townsend. *Eric* is, in fact, a throwback to the *moral tale of the late 18th and early 19th cents. Harvey *Darton has described it as 'a kind of immovable moral jelly-fish left behind by the tide'.

ERLBRUCH, Wolf (1948–) One of Germany's most important and successful authors and illustrators of children's books. He has won numerous awards including the *Deutscher Jugendliteraturpreis (1993, 2003) and the *Hans Christian Andersen Award. Erlbruch asks existential questions in many of his works, such as 'Why am I here?' in *The Big Question* (2005) or 'How do we get here?' in *The Miracle of the Bears* (2006), and explores the nature of death in his best book to date, *Death, Duck and the Tulip* (2007; tr. 2008). *The *Story of the Little Mole Who Knew It Was None of His Business* (1989; tr. 1994), written by Werner Holzwarth and illustrated by Erlbruch, is a sweet-smelling tale of revenge and asks some different fundamental questions in order to explore the varieties of animal excrement. Erlbruch's drawings are often soft and delicate, with an exquisite colour palette, combining humour and sentimentality to address difficult topics.

ESTES, Eleanor (Ruth) (1906–88) American children's author who began her writing career with the books by which she is still best known, her three novels about The *Moffats. She won the *Newbery Medal for *Ginger Pye* (1951), a story about a boy's search for his lost dog. Her later books include *Pinky Pye* (1958), which is a sequel to *Ginger Pye*, and *The Alley* (1964), a *detective story. She was born in West Haven, Connecticut, was Children's Librarian in New Haven before her marriage (in

1932), and then worked for some years in the New York Public Library.

Esther Glen Award The longest-running and most renowned prize for New Zealand children's literature. It is a laureateship which has been awarded since 1945 by the Library and Information Association of New Zealand Aotearoa 'for the most distinguished contribution to New Zealand literature for junior fiction', although there is not always an annual recipient. It is named in memory of Alice Esther Glen (1881–1940) who was New Zealand's first notable author of children's books. Past recipients include Kate *De Goldi, Maurice *Gee (twice), Tessa *Duder (three times), and Margaret *Mahy (six times).

ESTORIL, Jean *See* ALLAN, MABEL ESTHER.

ETS, Marie Hall (1893–1984) American illustrator and author of a number of *picture books for very young children; she won the *Caldecott Medal with *Nine Days to Christmas* (1959), a story set in Mexico about a Christmas toy which becomes a new star in the sky.

EUWER WOLFF, Virginia (1937–) An American novelist and former English teacher. Her six *young adult novels feature sympathetic characters who are outsiders academically, socially, or racially. She is best known for her trilogy beginning with *Make Lemonade* (1993), in which fourteen-year-old LaVaughn tries to earn enough money to go to college by babysitting for a seventeen-year-old's two children. A lyrical depiction of inner-city poverty, the chaos and challenges of the characters' lives and the urban setting are balanced by the elegant form of the books, which are written in short chapters of free verse. In the sequel to *Make Lemonade*, *True Believer* (2001), LaVaughn is a year older. Written in the same form, *True Believer* won the National Book Award and was a *Michael L. Printz Award Honor Book. *This Full House* (2009) completes the trilogy. Wolff's 1991 novel, *The Mozart Season*, won the 2011 Phoenix Award, given by the Children's Literature Association for the best English-language book that did not win a major award when it was first published. Wolff's two other books for young people are *Bat 6* (1998) and *Probably Still Nick Swansen* (1988).

evangelical writings for children have their beginnings in such *Puritan books of the 17th cent. as *Janeway's famous *Token for Children*, a set of accounts of juvenile

deathbeds, which was imitated by a number of 18th-cent. writers, e.g. George Burder in *Early Piety* (1776) and Leigh Richmond in *The *Dairyman's Daughter* (c.1810). Burder and Richmond were both closely associated with the *Religious Tract Society, which during the 19th cent. published many evangelical stories for children. One of the first notable authors of juvenile fiction to use the term 'evangelical' of herself was Mrs *Sherwood, whose many stories, including *The *Fairchild Family* (1818 onwards), gave fervent expression to the doctrines of human sinfulness and salvation through faith in Jesus. Her sister Mrs *Cameron's books were just as fervent and nearly as popular. A later evangelical story which had much success in Britain was *Ministering Children* (1854), while America produced such books as *The *Wide, Wide World* (1850), *The *Lamplighter* (1854), *Elsie Dinsmore* (1867), and the works of '*Pansy'. These all sold hugely; as Gillian *Avery has observed (in *Childhood's Pattern*, 1975): 'Time and again evangelical writers hit the jackpot, and were able to bask comfortably in the winning thought, as few best-selling writers are able to do, that they had won souls as well.'

From the 1860s stories of pious children triumphing over the horrors of slum life became fashionable in Britain, perhaps as a result of the new interest in urban poverty created by Henry Mayhew's survey *London Labour and the London Poor*, which was completed in 1862. Books like *Jessica's First Prayer* (1867) and *Christie's Old Organ* (1875) exploited this interest, and were reprinted again and again.

The themes and motifs of evangelical stories generally included some of the following: the pious early deaths of children; the importance of Sunday observance and of a belief in salvation; fear and hatred of Roman Catholicism; and children showing drunkards and sinners the error of their ways and converting them. The poor were not encouraged to rise in the world, and the only comfort regularly offered to them in these books was 'the comfort of religion'. On the other hand there can be no doubt that such books did help to make the reading public more aware of the plight of the poor, especially poor children, and many of their authors were active in improving social conditions; Hesba *Stretton, for example, was one of the founders of the London Society for the Prevention of Cruelty to Children. Moreover many young readers were moved to tears by such stories, and read them again and again.

EVANS, Edmund (1826–1905) The most celebrated Victorian printer of children's books in *colour; his patronage and methods of reproducing the work of Walter *Crane, Kate *Greenaway, and Randolph *Caldecott played a large part in creating their reputation. He was born and went to school in London, and was apprenticed to a *wood engraver, after which he started in business as an engraver on his own. He equipped himself with hand-presses, and from the first was adept at suggesting subjects to artists and publishers so as to generate engraving work for himself. He quickly developed a trade in colour work, especially in the cheap bright paper book-covers for the new station bookstall customers. (These books were known as 'yellowbacks' from the glossy tinted paper often used for their covers.) Colour printing from woodblocks was being done by other firms, but was comparatively uncommon, and Evans developed a mastery of it that soon made it a favourite of artists and publishers.

Evans's technique was only a refinement of what other printers were doing. His peculiarities were that he used wood-blocks exclusively, was particularly careful in his mixing of colours, and (most important of all) took great pains to school his artists in the possibilities and limitations of the medium, working closely with them throughout. He generally either had the artist draw the 'key block' directly on the wood or would photograph a monochrome sketch on to the wood himself, and then engrave and print proofs from it. Then he would engrave the blocks to be printed in as few colours as necessary. Evans used oil colours, as far as possible mixed by hand in exact reproduction of the artist's choice. When Kate Greenaway wanted her *Mother Goose or the Old Nursery Rhymes* (1881) printed on rough paper, he achieved the effect by soaking each sheet in water after printing, to restore its texture without damaging the colour.

Evans initially worked for the adult market; then in 1863 he met the eighteen-year-old Walter Crane, started to employ him on yellowback covers and, around 1865, began to collaborate with him on children's *picture books. Among the first were a *Railroad Alpha bet* and a *Farmyard Alphabet* published in *Routledge's series of *toy books (some fifty more followed). Evans also produced toy books for Frederick *Warne. (The first appears to have been *Aunt Louisa's Sunday Picture

Book, 1867 or earlier.) They began priced at sixpence each, and the number of colours—in other words, the number of times the sheets were passed through the presses—had to be severely curtailed for economy; in his more expensive books, Evans used ten or more colours.

Evans later printed more ambitious children's books in colour: his blocks for Richard *Doyle's In Fairyland* (1870) were remarkably large for wood engraving, and the book required from eight to twelve colours. He was also prepared to take commissioning and publishing risks himself, the best known case being his first book with Kate Greenaway, *Under the Window* (1877). At around the same time Evans invited the already well known Caldecott to turn his hand to coloured children's books, with equally notable results.

Evans was a first-rate engraver and a pious man. He was married with three daughters and two sons, who carried on his business after his retirement in 1892. Although he was well aware of the three-colour process of photo-mechanical colour reproduction, which was developed towards the end of his life, he felt that it had not been sufficiently perfected to compete with his woodblock method during the period in which he was working. But he knew that process work would soon become the main commercial method, and from 1902 his firm would be the printers of Beatrix *Potter's work, in three-colour halftone.

Evenings at Home (1792–6) A collection in six volumes of stories, poems, and dialogues for 'the instruction and amusement of young persons', mostly written by John *Aikin, with contributions by his sister Anna Laetitia *Barbauld. One of the more notable pieces is 'Trial of a Complaint made against sundry persons for breaking the windows of Dorothy Careful, Widow, and Dealer in Gingerbread', a story of detection set in a school, and modelled on *Juvenile Trials* by Richard *Johnson. The series was reprinted many times, often in one volume. Mrs *Molesworth named it as one of the handful of books which, in her childhood, was possessed by almost every family and read avidly.

EVERETT-GREEN, Evelyn (1856–1932) Prolific British writer of *girls' stories and other types of children's fiction. She was educated at Bedford College, London, and at the Royal Academy of Music, before working as a nurse. Her first stories were published in the 1880s, and many of them appeared as *reward books issued by the *Religious Tract Society and the *Society for Promoting Christian Knowledge. Titles include *Dorothy's Vocation* (1890), *Golden Gwendolyn* (1893), and *Adventurous Anne* (1916).

EWING, Juliana Horatia (Gatty) (1841–85) Late Victorian children's writer who was the daughter of a Yorkshire clergyman and the granddaughter of the naval chaplain in whose arms Nelson died; to this, she owed her second Christian name. Her mother Margaret *Gatty wrote works of *natural history (most notably *Parables from Nature*) and children's stories of domestic life, in order to supplement the family income; her *Aunt Judy's Tales* (1859) and *Aunt Judy's Letters* (1862) took their title from the family nickname for Juliana Horatia, who was already known in the family circle as a storyteller. In 1866 Mrs Gatty's publishers engaged her to found *Aunt Judy's Magazine*, to which Juliana Horatia immediately became a frequent contributor, most of her stories making their first appearance in its pages. Her mother soon willingly relinquished the role of author to her daughter, and in 1862 Juliana Horatia's first collection of tales was published. By the time she wrote *Mrs Overtheway's Remembrances* (1869) she had become a fluent and competent narrator of the events of daily life as seen by a child.

In 1867 she married Major Alexander ('Rex') Ewing. The Ewings went to Canada shortly after their marriage, and lived in Fredericton, New Brunswick, for more than two years; several of Mrs Ewing's short stories have a Canadian setting. She and her husband later made their home at Aldershot and elsewhere in England.

In 1870 Mrs Ewing produced *The *Brownies and Other Tales*, a collection of stories with illustrations by *Cruikshank, which was eventually responsible for the name *Brownie being given to junior *Girl Guides. It was followed by *A Flat Iron for a Farthing* (1872), the childhood reminiscences of the only son of a widowed father, and *Lob Lie-by-the-Fire* (1874). While at Aldershot Mrs Ewing also wrote *Six to Sixteen* (1875), a novel about an orphan girl growing up, which became a favourite of the young *Kipling, and *Jan of the Windmill* (1876), the story of a foundling, brought up by a West Country miller and his wife, who eventually becomes a famous painter. *A Great Emergency* (1877) is the story of a family which craves adventure. In 1879 the

Zulu war prompted her to write **Jackanapes*. It was published as a book in 1883, with illustrations by *Caldecott. *Daddy Darwin's Dovecote* (1884), an attempt to recapture the author's Yorkshire childhood, is the story of a workhouse boy who is taken in by a grumbling old pigeon-racer and smallholder, whose dovecote and farm he eventually inherits. *The Story of a Short Life* (1885) returned to the army setting of *Jackanapes*. Worn out by frequent house-moves and a neglected illness, probably cancer of the spine, Mrs Ewing herself died at the age of only forty-four.

Her books are vivid and energetic, and she had more skill as a stylist than her contemporary Mrs *Molesworth, though the diction of her narratives is so sophisticated that at times she seems to be writing a novel about childhood for an adult readership, rather than a book for children. Realistic and rarely oversentimental in her portrayal of children, she excelled at evoking different ways of life, especially rural and army households. Her *fairy stories, of which there are a number scattered through her writings, have a clear moral purpose but also a vivid imagination; for example, 'The Land of Lost Toys' (in *The Brownies*) describes a young girl put on trial by her broken and neglected toys and threatened with punishments that exactly correspond to her own treatment of her playthings.

She was an unqualified success with children in her lifetime and for long after; among her many admirers were *Kipling and E. *Nesbit, who thought her own work inferior to Mrs Ewing's. Yet none of her books has become a classic. John Rowe *Townsend judges of her novels that 'none of them seems... to have the vitality that will carry a book on through changing times and tastes'.

Mrs Ewing's life and work is the subject of a 1961 monograph by Gillian *Avery.

EYRE, Frank (1910–88) Critic of 20th-cent. children's literature; he was children's books editor at the Oxford University Press and played a large part in improving the standard of juvenile fiction published under the Oxford imprint. He subsequently went to Australia, where he exercised a large influence over that country's children's books, becoming President of the Federal Australian Children's Book Council. His *Twentieth Century Children's Books* (1952) was revised as *British Children's Books in the Twentieth Century* (1971).

fable A fictitious narrative; the term is used especially of stories in which animals or inanimate objects are the protagonists. There is a meaning hidden beneath the surface of the tale, and the intention is usually to make some comment, often satirical, on human conduct. The tradition of the fable in Western culture began in effect with *Aesop (6th cent. BC). In India the *Panchatantra*, which was in existence by the 6th cent. BC, included many fables that gradually found their way into European literature and folklore.

In the 17th cent. *La Fontaine composed fables which soon became almost as well known as those of Aesop. Other fabulists whose work was known to children in the 18th and 19th cents. include *Gay and *Godwin, and, in Russia, *Krylov. In America Joel Chandler *Harris collected Negro fables and retold them as the *Uncle Remus* stories (1880 onwards).

Before the publication of fiction intended specially for children began to be common in Europe, fables played an especially large part in children's reading-matter.

Fables Ancient and Modern, *Adapted for the Use of Children from Three to Eight Years of Age, by Edward Baldwin, Esq.* Really the work of William *Godwin, and published by him and his wife, under the imprint 'Thomas Hodgkins', in 1805. Godwin extends fables to make the moral clearer and provides happy endings where possible. The first edition had plates probably engraved by *Blake after *Mulready. The book had reached ten editions by 1824. It was also issued by the Godwins in French.

Fabulous Histories. *Designed for the Instruction of Children, respecting the Treatment of Animals* Later known as *The History of the Robins*, or *The Robins*, a story by Mrs Sarah *Trimmer, first published in 1786. Originally composed for the author's children, the book promotes kindness to animals, 'over whom the Supreme Governor hath given [human beings] dominion'. In accordance with her general censure of non-realistic fiction, Mrs Trimmer emphasizes that her use of talking animals is not realistic, but that children should read her work as 'a series of Fables, intended to convey moral instruction applicable to themselves'. In the story four robins, Robin, Dicky, Flapsy, and Pecksy, are reared by their parents in a gentleman's orchard. The two children of the house, Miss Harriet and Master Frederick Benson, show exemplary benevolence to them, feeding them on crumbs. But members both of the Redbreast and of the Benson families can be naughty or thoughtless, and earn rebuke. The eldest robin is jealous and belligerent; Master Frederick is impulsive and careless, though good-hearted. Other characters join the story, including a mother so immoderately devoted to her exotic pets that her own children suffer, and a boy whose barbarously cruel behaviour to animals leads to his becoming a school bully and eventually to his being killed by a fall from a badly-treated horse. The Redbreast family, meanwhile, grows tame and friendly, cared for by the family of the good Mrs Benson, who always 'consulted the welfare of inferior creatures, and neither spoiled them by indulgence, or injured them by tyranny'.

The book continued to be popular, though increasingly abridged, throughout the following century, and even into the beginning of the 20th cent.

face-rhymes *See* INFANT AMUSEMENTS.

Faerie Queene, The (published in 1589 and 1596) By the English poet Edmund Spenser (?1552–99) and 'retold' for children, in prose, by a number of authors in the late 19th and early 20th cents. Versions include *Stories from the Faerie Queene* (1897) by Mary Macleod and *The Faery Queen and her Knights* (1910) by A. J. *Church.

Fairchild Family, The An immensely popular series of *evangelical children's books by

Mrs *Sherwood, intended, in the words of the title page, 'to show the importance and effects of a religious education'. The first part, written while the author was living in India and published in 1818, introduces Mr and Mrs Fairchild, who live in a house in the English countryside, and their children Lucy, Emily, and Henry. The story draws on Calvinist doctrine to emphasize the 'human depravity' (original sin) of the children and thus their need for redemption. Mr Fairchild and his wife take every opportunity presented by domestic life to draw religious lessons for the children in order both to prepare their souls for Heaven and to act in a godly manner in this world. Thus Mr Fairchild, in an (in)famous scene, takes them to see the body of a man who has killed his brother in a quarrel hanging on a gibbet. Likewise, when Henry steals an apple his father locks him in an attic room from breakfast-time till evening, without food, explaining: 'It is better . . . that he should be punished in this world . . . than grow up to be a liar and a thief, and go to hell when he dies.'

According to the *Dictionary of National Biography*, 'most children of the English middle-class born in the first quarter of the nineteenth century may be said to have been brought up on *The Fairchild Family*'. By 1848 the first volume had reached its 17th edition. In 1842 a second part appeared, in which there was some softening of the Calvinism of the first book, and more emphasis was put on the love of God and the power of divine grace. A third part, written jointly by Mrs Sherwood and her daughter Sophia, appeared in 1847. One-volume editions of all three parts, or sometimes Parts I and II, continued to appear until after the First World War, though later printings were usually abridgements which omitted the most extreme religious exhortations and excised the passage describing the visit to the gibbet. The work of Nancy M. Cutt and Patricia Demers provides further discussion of Mrs Sherwood and evangelical fiction for children.

fairies Now chiefly associated with stories for children, but the word *fairy* apparently has its origin in the *Fata* or Fates of classical times, who controlled the destinies of all men. Katharine *Briggs, in her *Dictionary of Fairies*, suggests that the word *fairy*, which the *Oxford English Dictionary* does not record as appearing before the 14th cent., was originally the combination *fay-erie*, meaning 'the state of enchantment'. In fact, though the form *faerie* or *faery* may have existed in Middle English, its first recorded use is by Spenser, who in *The Faerie Queene* employed it as an archaism and may even have invented it.

Fairy traditions flourished in folk tales, and in the late 16th and early 17th cents. there was a brief English literary fashion for fairy writings. It was largely initiated by *A Midsummer Night's Dream*, in which *Shakespeare characterized the fairies as small in stature, a detail which he probably took from his native folklore and which had scarcely appeared before in literature. This caught the imagination of early 17th-cent. poets such as William Browne, Robert Herrick, and Michael Drayton, whose *Nimphidia* (1627) describes the doings at the fairy court: the knight Pigwiggen, whose horse is an earwig, sends a bracelet of emmets' eyes to his love, Queen Mab. This tradition of diminutive fairies has influenced characterization in many modern writings, for example Tinker Bell in **Peter Pan*. Small with wings became the common fairy image (when not used in the sense of *fairy stories). A 1920s vogue for fairies is associated with the faked Cottingley fairy photographs, but also with children's books such as Cicely Mary *Barker's *Flower Fairies* (1923) and a series of fairy books (1923–8) by Marion St John Webb, illustrated by Margaret Tennant.

In contrast, the *fées* of the cult for *fairy stories in France at the end of the 17th cent. were full-sized people with formidable characters. The Fairy Godmother of *Perrault's most celebrated story, **Cinderella*, may exercise an entirely benevolent influence over the heroine (her status as Godmother recalls the ancient belief in the presence of the heathen Fates or fays at a child's name-giving), but in the same author's **Sleeping Beauty* the wicked fairy attempts to bring about the death of the princess, and in Mme d'*Aulnoy's tale *The *Yellow Dwarf*, the part played by the Desart Fairy is far from attractive.

Fair Rosamond A *ballad which was among those widely read by children up to the 18th cent. It tells how Rosamond Clifford, daughter of Walter de Clifford and mistress of Henry II, was poisoned in her 'Bower' at Woodstock by Queen Eleanor. The legend, first recorded in Higden's *Polychronicon* (mid-14th cent.), was turned into a ballad in the late 16th cent. by the popular versifier Thomas Deloney. The ballad was printed several times as a *broadside, and the story was also published more than once in prose, as a *chapbook. In *The *Enchanted Castle* (1907) by E. *Nesbit, the

child Mabel is 'playing at Fair Rosamond' just before she is first discovered by Gerald, Jimmy, and Kathleen.

fairy *See* FAIRIES.

Fairy Book, The A collection of traditional *fairy stories published in 1863 and described as 'rendered anew by the author of *John Halifax, Gentleman'*—that is, Mrs D. M. *Craik. The stories were taken largely from *Perrault, Mme d'*Aulnoy, and *Grimm. The book, one of the best collections of its period, was reprinted in 1922 and again in 1979.

Fairy Books A series of anthologies of *fairy stories, beginning with *The Blue Fairy Book*, which were compiled for children by Andrew *Lang between 1889 and 1910. They put both well known and obscure tales (some of them recently collected and never before printed) into a form that was accessible and attractive. The books became classics in their own right, and endured long in print with comparatively little alteration.

The books were published by Longmans, for whom Lang was literary adviser, and at first Lang had no intention of there being a series. However, the books met with such popularity that the series finally stretched to twelve fairy books of different colours, and spawned other types of anthologies by Lang, such as *The True Story Book* (1893), not to mention imitations issued by other publishers.

For each of the books Lang himself selected the tales, commissioned necessary translations or adaptations, and wrote a preface. But only twice, in the first two books, did he retell a story himself. For the rest, a number of friends and relatives were enlisted—though increasingly the work was done by Lang's wife, Leonora Blanche Lang, *née* Alleyne. Nevertheless, when the series got under way, Lang himself was often popularly supposed not merely to have adapted the tales but to have actually made them up.

The first of the series, *The Blue Fairy Book* (1889), contained thirty-seven tales, among them almost all the 'classic' fairy stories—the best known tales from *Perrault, Mme d'*Aulnoy, the *Arabian Nights*, and *Grimm. Lang also included *Dick Whittington* and *Jack the Giant Killer* from English tradition, and selected from the *Cabinet des fées*, Chambers's *Popular Traditions of Scotland*, and *Asbjørnsen and Moe's collection of Norwegian stories. Rather oddly, he also commissioned an abridgement of the voyage to Lilliput from

Gulliver's Travels to be done for the book. He himself made an adaptation from Greek mythology, the story of Perseus and the Gorgon; but he gave it the title 'The Terrible Head'. *The Red Fairy Book* (1890) added *Russian fairy tales to more from French, German, *Norwegian, and English sources; *Jack and the Beanstalk* appears here, and Lang made an abridgement ('The Story of Sigurd') from William *Morris's translation of the *Volsungasaga. The Green Fairy Book* followed in 1892, *Yellow* in 1894, then *Pink* (1897), *Grey* (1900), *Violet* (1901), *Crimson* (1903), *Brown* (1904), *Orange* (1906), *Olive* (1907), and *Lilac* (1910). From his early use of exclusively European sources, Lang moved on to include stories from Africa (via French versions) and Japan (via a German translation). He introduced numerous Russian and other Eastern European stories to the nursery, and by the time he assembled the *Brown*, *Orange*, and *Olive* books he was drawing on Native American, Persian, Brazilian, Berber, Turkish, Sudanese, and American sources, as well as several collections of *Indian fairy tales. Among other inclusions were the English tales of *The *Three Bears* and *The *Three Little Pigs* (in the *Green Fairy Book*), the old *chapbook story of *Fortunatus* (in the *Grey*), and several stories by Hans Christian *Andersen (in the *Pink*).

The Fairy Books were exceptionally generously illustrated, though none matched for sheer quantity the 138 illustrations, many set in the text, of *The Blue Fairy Book*. The first two books had pictures by H. J. *Ford with collaborators Jacomb Hood (for the *Blue*) and Lancelot Speed (for the *Red*), but thereafter Ford alone supplied the pictures, which were usually highly successful. From the *Violet* onwards, *colour plates were included.

In 1975 there appeared a new edition of *The Blue Fairy Book*, with a text 'refurbished' by Brian *Alderson, who deleted some stories and provided extensive notes; this volume was illustrated by John *Lawrence. Further Alderson editions followed: *Red* in 1976 (illustrated by Faith *Jaques), *Yellow* in 1980 (ill. Erik *Blegvad) and others.

Fairy Caravan, The Written and illustrated by Beatrix *Potter; published in America in 1929, but not issued publicly in Britain until 1952. The book was commissioned by the McKay company of Philadelphia, Beatrix Potter's American publishers, who wanted something specially for her readers in the United States. Though it was some years since she

had produced a book, she put together a lengthy volume—far longer than her best known stories—which used as its starting-point 'The Tale of Tuppenny', written in 1903 but never published. *The Fairy Caravan* is nominally set in 'the Land of Green Ginger', though after the opening chapter the scenery is clearly that of Beatrix Potter's beloved Lake District. Tuppenny, a dilapidated guinea-pig, has a bottle of hair-restorer poured over him, whereupon his hair starts growing at an alarming speed, so that he takes on a monstrous appearance. He runs away and joins a troupe of performing animals.

Fairy Spectator, The, *or The Invisible Monitor* (1789) A work by 'Mrs Teachwell' (Eleanor *Fenn) on the lines of Sarah Fielding's *The *Governess*. One of the pupils at Mrs Teachwell's academy dreams of a dragonfly which changes into a fairy who proclaims herself the child's guardian. Mrs Teachwell herself then makes up a story about Miss Child, a motherless girl who grows 'proud, selfish, peevish, and vain'; a fairy appears to her, telling her: 'I am the guardian of your mind; I know all your thoughts.' She gives Miss Child two enchanted looking-glasses, one to show her as she really is and one as she might and should be. As a result Miss Child mends her ways. She is then given a choice of three magical objects: a purse which will always be full of money, a bonnet which will convey her anywhere, and a ring to make her invisible (cf. *Fortunatus*). However, being now of an entirely prudent nature, Miss Child rejects the gifts because they have their moral dangers. She is rewarded by being made into a fairy and appointed guardian to Mrs Teachwell's girls. She gives one of them a magic rose as an aid to good conduct: it pricks the recipient whenever she errs, or even merely thinks wicked thoughts.

The book is notable as being a rare excursion by one of the 'monstrous regiment' of writers of *moral tales into the realm of *fairy stories, though of course the fairy element is made to serve a strictly moral purpose.

fairy stories (fairy tales) Short narratives, set in the distant past, of events that would be impossible in the real world. Traditional fairy tales are a subset of folk tales which also include *fables and legends. They are 'wonder tales', characterized by magical happenings and may include *fairies, but do not need them. The heroes and heroines are usually mortal human beings, though with no psychological complexity. Such creatures as *giants, *dwarfs,

*witches, and *ogres frequently play a part, as well as talking animals. The term *contes des fées* was adopted as a description of such stories in France at the end of the 17th cent., and the English translations of the French *contes* of this period introduced the expressions 'fairy tale' and 'fairy story' into the English language.

Traditional fairy stories were oral literature, passed on by storytellers, but there were also written versions well before the modern systematic collection of oral tales. Oral and literary continually mingle, and many tales now owe their best-known form to particular writers or collectors. But the genre still has characteristics of oral transmission. Stories deal with real human experience in an unmanageable and unjust world, and the hope of transformation and happy ending. They feel familiar, and have crossed borders freely; examples from the same family of fairy tales are found across many cultures. Repetitions and other features still suggest telling, and single elements can be taken out, used elsewhere, and still be 'fairy tale'.

Tales resembling some of the fairy stories that are known in English today appear in several early oriental story collections, such as the Indian *Panchatantra* (which was in existence by the 6th cent. AD) and the *Katha Sarit Sdgara* ('Ocean of Streams of Story'), the *Book of Sindibad* (which probably originated in Persia at the beginning of the 9th cent.), and the *Arabian Nights*. The earliest recorded analogue of *Cinderella* is found in a Chinese book of folk tales of the mid-9th cent. Several of these collections use a frame story to provide a reason for a whole series of tales being told one after another. This type of book eventually began to appear in Europe. One of the earlier examples was Chaucer's *Canterbury Tales* (*c*.1387), which included a fairy story told by the Wife of Bath. In Italy in the mid-16th cent., there appeared the *Piacevoli notti*, which was followed in 1634 by the *Pentamerone* of Giambattista Basile; this included versions of *Cinderella*, *Snow White*, and several other celebrated fairy stories.

Such books were not designed for children (their narratives were often violent or bawdy). *Chapbooks, which were widely read by children, did include such tales as *Tom Thumb* (first printed in 1621), as well as versions of many medieval *romances which contained marvels and magical happenings. But the true fairy tales circulated in England only in oral form. There was something of a fashion for fairies among late 16th- and early 17th-cent. English writers, but the results of this, such as *The *Faerie Queene, A Midsummer Night's*

Dream, and Drayton's *Nimphidia*, moved far beyond popular fairy stories. Moreover, magical wonders and marvels which often co-existed with Catholic belief were deplored by the *Puritan writers who, later in the 17th cent., were among the first authors to provide books for children in England and America.

When at last the fairy story was partly rehabilitated in England as respectable reading matter, it was because of the extraordinary fashion for it which sprang up briefly in French aristocratic and cultured society towards the end of the 17th cent. France had its stock of fairy and other folk tales in oral circulation, and these had sometimes been retold for a sophisticated audience—for instance, Jean d'Arras' 14th-cent. retelling of the story of Mélusine, the water sprite (*see* UNDINE). By the 17th cent., such tales were generally thought appropriate chiefly for children, but at the same time, fairy tales, along with classical mythology, were also being used to provide themes for court entertainments, and as verbal embellishments for flattery and intrigue. In other words, the imagery of fairyland was prevalent in polite French company before the fashion for retelling its stories began in earnest.

The immediate setting for this new fashion was a French reading public sated with the long—sometimes ten-volume—novels of the previously favoured literary genre. Salons, usually of intellectual or would-be intellectual ladies and their male guests, now wanted something that could be read and discussed, encouraging the now favoured art of conversation, all in one session. Mme de Maintenon, first the governess of Louis XIV's children, then his mistress, later his wife, possibly also contributed to a general sense that stories fit for children were suitable for adults.

Mme d'*Aulnoy, in 1690, was the first writer of this fashion to publish a fairy story, slipping it into a novel, though there is no evidence that she was in any other sense an originator of the cult. The following year *Perrault had his *Griselidis* (a verse tale in the manner of *La Fontaine) read to the Académie française, and in November 1693 he published in the journal *Le Mercure galant* another verse story, this time much more of a fairy tale, *Les Souhaits ridicules* (a version of The *Three Wishes*). The following year he published this and *Peau d'asne* together. In the next year, 1695, Perrault's niece Mlle l'Héritier, who was the centre of a particularly illustrious circle of women,

published her *Œuvres meslées*, containing her own fairy tales. Some six months later *The *Sleeping Beauty (La Belle au bois dormant)*, the first prose fairy tale by Perrault, appeared in *Le Mercure galant*. In May 1696 a novel by Mlle Bernard was printed, with two fairy stories woven into it, one of them a version of *Riquet à la houppe*, a tale which Perrault included in his own famous collection of eight tales, *Histoires ou contes du temps passé* (*see* CONTES DE MA MÈRE L'OYE), which went to the publishers later the same year. Mme d'Aulnoy's tales were already in oral circulation; they were in print the following year. The vogue reached its height in 1697 and 1698, with new stories being published by Mme d'Aulnoy, Mlle de la Force, and Mme de Murat, and with a few men, such as the Chevalier de Mailly, joining them in print. In 1697 a Paris theatre showed a burlesque *Fées, ou Contes de ma mère l'Oye*. By 1699 volumes of fairy tales in the fashionable style were beginning to be published in the provinces, and the Abbé de Villiers was impelled to complain about the cult in a series of *Entretiens sur les contes de fées*, castigating most of them as empty trifles lapped up by women. The fashion was, in fact, already beginning to wane. A few new titles appeared, from authors such as Mme Durand and Mme d'Auneuil; then in 1704 the French text of the *Arabian Nights* was published, and taste changed. When the products of the fashion for fairy stories were gathered together in *Le Cabinet des fées* (from 1785), they extended to forty-one volumes, with Perrault's tales occupying the first half of Volume One.

Apart from Perrault's, the stories from this French fashion are almost all characterized by their literary and artificial style, their length, and their overabundance of incident and description. The Abbé de Villiers complained that most of the authors had forgotten that the tales were originally for children, who would now be bored by their style and length. The majority of the stories were intended merely as literary trifles, bagatelles, holidays from reason, which their authors often left unsigned or only initialled. They did not pretend to be original; several writers confessed to borrowing from servants, from the venerable romances of the *Bibliothèque bleue* (the French equivalent of chapbooks), and from the French translation of the *Piacevoli notti*. The Abbé de Villiers allowed two partial exemptions from his criticism, choosing, in fact, the only authors who outlasted the fashion: in

Mme d'Aulnoy he found some things to admire, and he also approved the simple style of Perrault, who (he recognized) scarcely belonged to the cult.

Perrault's *Contes* reached an English readership in 1729, as *Histories, or Tales of Past Times*. Fairy stories by other French writers were occasionally included in English collections, and some years later a French exile to England, Mme de *Beaumont, published her versions of *Beauty and the Beast* and *The Three Wishes* (1756). Meanwhile, during the first three decades of the 18th cent., there was published, volume by volume, an English translation of *Galland's French text of the *Arabian Nights*.

For a time, those fairy stories which appeared in English did so in a form which suggests that they were regarded as a means of instruction as well as amusement. Perrault's tales were often printed in a bilingual English-French edition for use as a schoolbook—it was in this form that they reached America, in 1695—while Mme de Beaumont printed her fairy stories as part of her *Magasin des enfans*, a series of dialogues between a governess and her pupils.

However, in about 1768 the firm of *Newbery reissued Perrault's *Contes* with the English text unencumbered by French, and at about that time the individual tales from the book began to appear as popular chapbooks, which took them to a very wide child readership. In the late 18th cent., the writers of *pantomimes for the London theatres began to turn to fairy stories for their subject matter, and in the early 1800s a number of recently established publishers for children began to issue books of fairy tales, a notable example being *Tabart, whose *Popular Tales*, appearing over several years in the early 19th cent., included many of the French stories. Native English tales such as *Jack and the Beanstalk* were now regarded as acceptable to a genteel readership, and began to appear in print. During the mid-19th cent., other tales circulating orally in the British Isles were collected by such people as J. O. *Halliwell and Robert Chambers (*Popular Rhymes of Scotland*, 1842 and 1870).

Though the 18th cent. was the period in which fairy stories as we know them first gained a firm footing in English culture, it also saw the growth of a movement of opposition to them which was even stronger than that launched earlier by the Puritans. The concern among educated people to bring up their own children (and, by the end of the century,

the children of the poor) in the Christian religion and to avoid ignorant superstition led to a widespread hostility towards tales of the supernatural. Educationalists of both the *Locke and *Rousseau schools were wary of them, and the growing popularity of *moral tales by such writers as Mrs *Barbauld and Maria *Edgeworth, as well as their numerous imitators, led to the belief that fairy stories could be entirely dispensed with as nursery reading. Such few as did appear in the books of didactic writers, e.g. in *The *Governess* (c.1749) and *The *Fairy Spectator* (1789), were made to serve a strictly moral purpose. Mrs *Trimmer, in *The *Guardian of Education* (1802–6), could afford to speak condescendingly of a new edition of *Cinderella* and other fairy tales as 'tales, which were in fashion half a century ago'. When Perrault's tales were reissued in about 1803, Mrs Trimmer admitted that she had enjoyed them in her own childhood, but declared that 'we do not wish to have such sensations awakened in the hearts of our grandchildren, by the same means; for the terrific images, which tales of this nature present to the imagination, usually make deep impressions, and injure the tender minds of children, by exciting unreasonable and groundless fears. Neither do the generality of tales of this kind supply any moral instruction level to the infantine capacity.'

Despite attacks of this kind, and the belief that fairy stories were now out of fashion, publishers continued to reissue collections of them with such regularity that it is evident there was still an audience for them. A few years later, in 1823, the number and variety of fairy tales available to English children was greatly increased by the appearance of the first translation of the work of the brothers *Grimm. In 1825–8 came *Croker's Irish fairy tales. During the 1840s the stories of Hans Christian *Andersen began to appear in English, while the *Home Treasury series of Sir Henry *Cole ('Felix Summerly') gave the stamp of respectability to many of the older-established tales. The collection *Fairy Tales of All Nations* (1849) introduced stories from all over the world to English readers; in 1857 appeared *Heroes of Asgard*, a retelling by the *Keary sisters of Norse myths for children, and in 1859 Sir George Dasent produced his translation of Norwegian folk tales, entitled *Popular Tales from the Norse*. In 1890 came *English Fairy Tales*, to be followed by other British collections by the same editor, Joseph *Jacobs. By the end of the century, translations were

available of collections of *Danish, *Indian, and *Russian tales. Andrew *Lang based his series of *Fairy Books* (from 1889) on these and other printed sources, as well as tales in manuscript, obscure books, and even the oral tradition. This renaissance of the traditional fairy story was related to a new wave of imaginative writing. See, as further guides to fairy tale, *The Oxford Companion to Fairy Tales* (2000) by Jack *Zipes, and *Once Upon a Time* (2014) by Marina Warner. For an account of the growth of the 'modern fairy story', *see* FANTASY.

The battle between the opponents and defenders of fairy stories was repeated in 20th-cent. Russia, where the fairy story found an eloquent champion in K. *Chukovsky. In America, the psychologist Bruno *Bettelheim argued that fairy stories contribute to the emotional health of the child. Modern interpretations of fairy tales in literature and film are numerous and often reflect contemporary movements and concerns. For example, the re-evaluation of the role of the 'damsel in distress' in works such as Angela Carter's *The Bloody Chamber* (1979) and Robert Munsch's *The *Paper Bag Princess* (1980) reflects the contemporary feminist movement, while Jon *Scieszka's *The Stinky Cheeseman and Other Fairly Stupid Tales* (1992) takes advantage of familiar fairy-tale tropes to construct parodically humorous postmodern stories.

Fairy Tales of All Nations (1849) A collection of translations by 'Anthony R. Montalba' (whose surname was really Whitehill), made from tales in Hebrew, Russian, Sanskrit, Icelandic, and other languages. It was illustrated by Richard *Doyle, and was later reissued as *The Doyle Fairy Book* (1890).

FALCONER, Ian See OLIVIA.

FALKNER, J. (John) Meade (1858–1932) British author of *Moonfleet* (1898), bibliophile, and scholar. His two other novels, *The Lost Stradivarius* (1895) and *The Nebuly Coat* (1903) are both mystery stories.

Family From One End Street, The, *and some of their adventures* (1937) Written and illustrated by Eve *Garnett, describing the life of the Ruggles family, who live in a poor district of the English Midland town of 'Otwell', at no. 1, One End Street. Mrs Ruggles is a washerwoman and her husband is a dustman. The eldest daughter, the fat and plain Lily Rose, does her best to help her mother, but not always successfully; her equally plain younger

sister Kate wins a scholarship to the local grammar school.

The Family From One End Street won the *Carnegie Medal, and was much praised when it first appeared, because it was the first 20th-cent. British children's book to try to describe in detail the character of working-class life. (E. *Nesbit had touched on this theme in *Harding's Luck*, 1909, but only briefly.) Further reflection convinced some of the book's original admirers that they were wrong, and that the author's attitude to the Ruggles family is deeply patronizing. Frank *Eyre wrote in 1971: 'We praised too highly *The Family From One End Street* because it was all we could find of that sort to praise'.

Family Instructor, The A book of religious and moral instruction by *Defoe, published in parts in 1715 and 1718. It takes the form of dialogues between parents and children, masters and servants, and husbands and wives. The style is vivid and entirely naturalistic. The father is presented as part worldly, part religious—much like Defoe himself—and his own children frequently make him feel that he has erred. The book was very popular; it had reached an eighth edition by 1720, and was reprinted later in the 18th cent.

family stories These novels of family life for young readers, have their origin in those *moral tales of the late 18th and early 19th cents. which used the events of an ordinary home life to make didactic points about good and bad behaviour. Charlotte M. *Yonge's lengthy novel *The *Daisy Chain* (1856) was influential, and probably gave Louisa *Alcott a model for *Little Women* (1868), the first classic of the genre.

Little Women encouraged many American writers to try their hand at family stories, one of the first and best results being *What Katy Did* (1872) by Susan *Coolidge; *Five Little Peppers and How they Grew* (1881) by Harriet *Lothrop was another popular example. Meanwhile some American writers, such as Horace E. *Scudder in his *Bodley series of *travelogue storybooks, used the family story to impart educational information.

In England during the late 19th cent. many authors were writing family stories, Mrs *Ewing and Mrs *Molesworth being perhaps the most distinguished. No masterpiece appeared, however, until E. *Nesbit produced *The *Story of the Treasure Seekers* in 1899. Her work had been to some extent anticipated in Australia, where

Ethel M. *Turner had published *Seven Little Australians* in 1894.

Notable 20th-cent. British family stories included novels by Noel *Streatfeild, Eve Garnett's *The *Family from One End Street* (1937), and Helen *Cresswell's comic *Bagthorpe Saga* (1977–2001). In America the genre continued to flourish, in the hands of such writers as Elizabeth *Enright, Eleanor *Estes, and Madeleine *L'Engle. Australia made many contributions to it, including novels by H. F. *Brinsmead, Nan *Chauncy, Reginald *Ottley, Joan *Phipson, and Eleanor *Spence. Though this is perhaps not much discussed as a meaningfully distinct genre today, there are still many writers who write on a realist and domestic scale and take as their subject the web of relationships between a family group—Hilary *McKay's witty, sympathetic, and insightful books are exemplary of this type.

Famous Five, The Heroes of a series by Enid *Blyton, begun in 1942 with *Five on a Treasure Island*. The five are four children, siblings Julian, Dick, and Anne, and their cousin 'George' (Georgina), and her dog Timmy. Their holidays together invariably land them in the middle of smugglers, thieves, and other villains, whose deeds they unmask. Originally intended to consist of six books, the series eventually totalled twenty-one, the last being *Five Are Together Again* (1963). By that time, six million copies had been sold in hardback; the stories were also published in several European countries, filmed, and staged. The character of 'George' was based by Enid Blyton on herself as a child. They remain in print today, though their popularity is not what it was. From 2010, titles from the series began to be reissued with some updating to make them more appealing to 21st-cent. children.

Another 'Famous Five', who preceded the invention of Enid Blyton's (and probably suggested the name), are the five boys who share a school study in the *Billy Bunter stories of 'Frank *Richards'.

Famous Tommy Thumb's Little Story-Book, The An English children's book published in about 1760 by S. Crowder and Benjamin Collins. It contained the story of *Tom Thumb*, a number of *fables, and nine *nursery rhymes, including the first printings of 'This pig went to market' and 'Little Boy Blue'. It seems to have been the first collection of nursery rhymes to appear in America, being printed by John Mein of Boston in 1768 and by John Boyle of Boston in 1771.

FANELLI, Sara (1969–) A designer and illustrator who was born in Italy but studied in London and is still based there; her work has been very influential because of its unique graphic style and innovative approach to working with paper. In *The Onion's Great Escape* (2012) the reader has to answer questions so as to help physically free the onion from the rest of the book—it sounds strange, but the reality is marvellous. Equally hard to describe is her take on *Pinocchio* (2003), for though the book is traditionally constructed, the illustrations are vibrantly fresh and make readers look at the old story anew. Fanelli's work has been exhibited all over the world and in 2006 she was commissioned by London's Tate Modern to design the entrances to their newly updated permanent exhibitions.

fan fiction (fanfiction; fanfic; FF; fic) Stories written for fun, not profit, using the work of other writers as a launch pad. Stories, characters, and people from sources as diverse as manga, TV, books, movies, boy bands, and cartoons have all been transformed by fan writers. Though the term is relatively new, the idea—to take a story you have loved and want to continue it, or to explore the 'what ifs' of the story taking a different direction—is not new: fans of Jane Austen wrote about her characters, Sherlock Holmes pastiches emerged in the early 1900s, and Jean Rhys wondered about Mrs Rochester and so wrote *The Wide Sargasso Sea*. Fan fiction as we know it now emerged in the wake of *Star Trek* in the 1960s, and zines (bound collections of stories) followed. From an obscure hobby spread mostly by word of mouth, the Internet transformed the genre, leading to an explosion of stories, millions of them written by young adults. Fanlore.org is a Wiki for all things fandom. Fan fiction is now even starring in its own published fiction: *Fangirl* (2013) by Rainbow Rowell (1973–) centres on a girl whose life revolves around her obsession with the fictional 'Simon Snow' series.

Fantasia (1940) An animated film by Walt *Disney, which provides a visual interpretation of a musical score consisting of such classical pieces as *The Nutcracker Suite* by Tchaikovsky (*see* NUTCRACKER) and Dukas's *The *Sorcerer's Apprentice*. A 'sequel' of sorts, *Fantasia 2000*, was released in 1999.

Fantastic Beasts and Where to Find Them *See* HARRY POTTER.

Fantastic Mr Fox (1970) A novel for young readers by Roald *Dahl.

fantasy A term used (in the context of children's literature) to describe works of fiction, written by a specific author (i.e. not traditional) and usually novel-length, which involve the supernatural or some other unreal element. This however proves to be a nebulous and wide-ranging term, encompassing as it can many books that would otherwise be viewed as '*animal stories' but feature a talking animal, or 'toy stories', where inanimate objects are given conscious characters. Fantasy is closely related to the traditional *fairy story, and the birth of fantasy-writing in Britain coincided with the 19th-cent. revival of interest in, and admiration for, the orally transmitted fairy tale. The first example of the genre is generally thought to be F. E. Paget's The *Hope of the Katzekopfs (1844); Ruskin's The *King of the Golden River came out in 1851, and Thackeray's The *Rose and the Ring was written two years later. Then in 1863 came Charles *Kingsley's novel The *Water-Babies, which contained an eloquent defence of works of the imagination and an attack on *Peter Parley and other writers of the same school (satirized by Kingsley as 'Cousin Cramchild' and 'Aunt Agitate'), who believed that children should only be given books of facts.

Two years after The Water-Babies came *Alice's Adventures in Wonderland (1865), which was at once revolutionary (in that it showed the limitless possibilities of fantasy) and inimitable. A number of writers attempted to follow Carroll's lead; they included Jean *Ingelow, Christina *Rossetti, Charles E. *Carryl, Alice *Corkran, Edward Abbott *Parry, G. E. *Farrow, and E. F. Benson (in *David Blaize and the Blue Door). Few of them came near the achievement of Alice. Meanwhile George *MacDonald took a very different approach to fantasy writing, following somewhat in the footsteps of Hans Christian *Andersen. In short stories like The *Light Princess (1864), and in his later full-length books, beginning with *At the Back of the North Wind (1871), he produced tales in which a brilliant imagination was subtly blended with a didactic purpose. The only other writer of the late Victorian period to come near his achievement was Oscar Wilde, in his collection The *Happy Prince (1888).

'F. Anstey', in *Vice Versa (1882), used fantasy for humorous ends, and his work (especially The *Brass Bottle, 1900) was one of the inspirations of E. *Nesbit's fantasy novels, of which the first was *Five Children and It (1902). This and its sequels established a

pattern that was to be used by many later children's writers: the intrusion of magic into the real, modern world, with alarming but usually comic consequences. At the same time that Nesbit was writing, J. M. *Barrie created an enduring nursery myth in *Peter Pan (1904). Outstanding pre-1914 fantasies from European countries include *Pinocchio (1883) by 'Carlo Collodi' and The *Wonderful Adventures of Nils (1906–7) by Selma *Lagerlöf.

Australia's contributions to the genre have included Ethel C. Pedley's *Dot and the Kangaroo (1899), Norman Lindsay's The *Magic Pudding (1918), and, in more recent years, a number of novels by Patricia *Wrightson which make use of Aboriginal legends. Fantasy was slower to take root in the United States than in Britain. Frank *Stockton, in the 1870s, was among the first American writers to try his hand at it. Davy and the Goblins (1884) and The Admiral's Caravan (1891) by Charles E. *Carryl are conscious imitations of Alice. More original, though crude in its execution, is Frank Baum's enduring The *Wonderful Wizard of Oz (1900).

Fantasy-writing flourished in England between the two World Wars, and was indeed the dominant form in children's fiction there at that period, this being a time when realism seemed to elude many British children's authors and when changing social conditions made the realistic juvenile novel particularly difficult to attempt. The *Doctor Dolittle Stories of Hugh *Lofting (1920 onwards) had humour but also a quiet melancholy; The *Midnight Folk (1927) and The *Box of Delights (1935) by John *Masefield were full of vigour; *Mary Poppins (1934) by P. L. *Travers introduced an immortal character to the nursery; J. B. S. Haldane's *My Friend Mr Leakey (1937) made fresh use of magic; and The *Sword in the Stone (1938) by T. H. *White included a superb set of scenes where the boy Wart is transformed into different animals. Yet during this period only The *Hobbit (1937) by J. R. R. *Tolkien combined a rich imagination with a completely disciplined narrative.

The 1940s saw the emergence of several more British fantasies, two of which, The *Wind on the Moon (1944) by Eric Linklater and *After Bath (1945) by Vaughan Wilkins, showed how easily the genre could get out of hand. In contrast, C. S. *Lewis's series of *Narnia novels (1950 onwards) were perfectly disciplined works by an outstanding imaginative writer, working in the tradition not only of Nesbit but of MacDonald as well.

Lewis's place as the leading British fantasy writer in the 1950s was taken over in the next decade by Alan *Garner, whose novel *The *Weirdstone of Brisingamen* (1960), though flawed and immature, was as important in its way as *Five Children and It* had been, for it suggested the format for a new kind of fantasy, in which present-day children encounter primeval magical forces and experience frightening (rather than comic) adventures. Garner himself further explored the possibilities of this in *Elidor* (1965). His lead was soon followed by other writers, including Susan *Cooper, in her sequence *The *Dark Is Rising* (1965 onwards), Peter *Dickinson, in his *Changes* trilogy (1968–70), and Penelope *Lively, in a series of novels beginning with *Astercote* (1970). It may be argued, however, that the outstanding British children's fantasy of this period was *Tom's Midnight Garden* (1958) by Philippa *Pearce, a *time-slip story which owed nothing to Garner, and might have been written at any time from the Edwardian age onwards.

Among modern European fantasies, *Pippi Longstocking* (1945) by Astrid *Lindgren has been hugely successful, and the *Mrs Pepperpot stories by Alf Prøysen, first published in Norway, have been read very widely. Germany's Michael *Ende and Ottfried *Preussler have produced distinctive books, while the *Moomin stories of the Finnish author Tove Jansson are among the most popular fantasies of all time.

During the 1960s, America began to produce fantasies written somewhat under the influence of Tolkien and C. S. Lewis, examples being the *Prydain cycle by Lloyd *Alexander (1964–8), stories by Madeleine *L'Engle (most notably A *Wrinkle in Time, 1962), and the *Earthsea trilogy by Ursula *Le Guin (1967–72). Meanwhile a more essentially American brand of fantasy, owing something to Baum and 'Oz', had found occasional exponents, such as Carl Sandburg in *Rootabaga Stories* (1922) and Robert *McCloskey in *Homer Price* (1943). After 1945 this vein of fantastic humour was further mined by William Pène *Du Bois, in the *Twenty-One Balloons* (1947) and other stories, and by Sid *Fleischman, in a number of comic novels. There was an increase in talking animal stories such as those by E. B. *White, in *Stuart Little* (1945) and *Charlotte's Web* (1952), a type still used today in novels such as K. A. Applegate's *The One and Only Ivan* (2011). Toy stories developed from Blyton's fairy tale-esque toys to

books such as Russell *Hoban's deeply philosophical *The *Mouse and His Child* (1967). By the late twentieth century, it was time for a new set of landmarks to take the place of Tolkien and Lewis as reference points for the genre—*Harry Potter, *His Dark Materials* and *Twilight were significant among these. While never entirely eclipsing their predecessors—and drawing much on the influence of, for example, Tolkien, Lewis, Diana Wynne *Jones, and others—these helped to define the territory for another generation of writers. Other significant (if only variably influential) examples from recent years include William Nicholson's *Wind on Fire* trilogy, Eoin Colfer's *Artemis Fowl* series, Rick Riordan's *Percy Jackson* books and many of Eva *Ibbotson's novels, such as *The Secret of Platform 13* (1994). Certain types of fantasy have grown in ambition and popularity as a result of the explosion of *young adult publishing—*dystopian fiction is one example in a regularly changing landscape.

FARADAY, Michael (1791–1867) Outstanding British chemist and physicist who gave lectures for children in London each Christmas for many years. Two courses of these were afterwards published as books, 'edited by William Crookes'; judging by the very informal style of the books, they are probably verbatim transcripts of the original lectures. The two volumes are *The Chemical History of a Candle* (1861), in which this household object is used as the starting-point for a vivid account of combustion, gases, electricity, and much more, and *On the Various Forces of Nature and their relations to each other* (1863). Walter *de la Mare wrote of the first: 'If every writer of learning and imagination made it his happy privilege to write but one book for the young on his own beloved subject, and put his *whole mind* to it, just as Faraday wrote his *History of a Candle*—what joy there would be for children yet unborn.'

Far-Distant Oxus, The (1937) A novel written in imitation of the *Swallows and Amazons* stories by Arthur *Ransome. It was the work of two British schoolgirls, Katharine Hull (1921–77) and Pamela *Whitlock, who were aged fifteen and sixteen when the book was written. They sent the manuscript to Ransome, who recommended it to his publisher Jonathan Cape. Pamela Whitlock illustrated it in the Ransome manner, and Cape duly published it. Ransome's plain style is ably

imitated, perhaps even improved upon. The same authors wrote two sequels, and after the Second World War they also collaborated on a *fantasy novel, *Crowns* (1947).

FARJEON, Eleanor (1881–1965) Influential children's poet and author, born in London, the daughter of the novelist B. L. Farjeon. She received virtually no formal education, but, with her brothers, was encouraged to write stories and poems. Her first success was *Nursery Rhymes of London Town* (1916), which gave fanciful explanations of the origins of London district and street names. *Martin Pippin in the Apple Orchard* (1921) is a collection of stories in which a wandering Sussex minstrel achieves the release of an imprisoned girl by storytelling to her captors. It was originally regarded as an adult book. She also produced about thirty books of verse for children. Her other writings include several *plays for children (notably *The Glass Slipper*, 1944) and twelve novels for adults. She was one of the most prolific British children's writers of her day. Her work reflects her admiration for, and friendship with, Edward Thomas and Walter *de la Mare. Her poetry includes 'A Morning Song', which became the hymn 'Morning has Broken'. Of her stories, the best description is her own, written in the introduction to *The Little Bookroom* (1955), a selection of her short stories: 'Seven maids with seven brooms, sweeping for half-a-hundred years, have never managed to clear my mind of its dust of vanished temples and flowers and kings, the curls of ladies, the sighing of poets, the laughter of lads and girls.' Many of her tales draw on her love of Sussex, where she lived in a cottage during the First World War. *The Little Bookroom* won her the *Carnegie Medal and she received the first *Hans Christian Andersen Award in 1956. The award that bears her name (*see* ELEANOR FARJEON AWARD) was established shortly after her death.

FARLEY, Walter (Lorimer) (1915–89) American author who wrote a *Black Stallion* series about a horse from Arabia (1941 onwards).

FARMER, Nancy (1941–) American author best known for her fantasy and science fiction. The *Sea of Trolls* trilogy (2004–9) blends history, humour, and mythology in a quest fantasy featuring Vikings, trolls, and mermaids.

Farmer's 2002 novel *The House of the Scorpion*, set in the 22nd cent. and with a plot involving cloning and drug barons, won the National Book Award and was a Newbery Honor Award winner (*see* NEWBERY MEDAL). A sequel, *The Lord of Opium*, was published in 2013. She won two other Newbery Honor Awards, for *The Ear, the Eye and the Arm* (1994) and *A Girl Named Disaster* (1996), both set in Africa, where Farmer lived for many years.

FARMER, Penelope (1939–) British children's author of *fantasy novels, of which the best known are *A Castle of Bone* (1972), an allegory about a boy discovering his own nature through time-changes; and *Charlotte Sometimes* (1969), the third of her books about the Makepeace sisters, a clever and original *timeslip and identity-swap story. (The two Makepeace books that precede it are *The Summer Birds* (1962) and *Emma in Winter* (1966).)

Farmer Giles of Ham (1949) An amusing medieval story by J. R. R. *Tolkien, about a farmer and a dragon called Chrysophylax.

FARNOL, Jeffery (1878–1952) British author of historical romantic novels, including *The Amateur Gentleman* (1913) and *Beltane the Smith* (1915).

FARQUHARSON, Martha *See* ELSIE DINSMORE.

FARRAR, F. W. (Frederick William) (1831–1903) Author of *Eric, or, Little by Little*, he was born in India, the son of a missionary, and was educated chiefly at King William's College, Isle of Man, the original of 'Roslyn' in *Eric*.

Farrar distinguished himself academically as an undergraduate at London and at Cambridge, where he became a Fellow of Trinity College. He was ordained, and taught for many years at Harrow School, where he became a housemaster and where he wrote *Eric*. This was followed by a novel based on his Cambridge days, *Julian Home: a tale of college life* (1859). His second book for children, *St Winifred's, or, the World of School*, appeared in 1862, published anonymously. He wrote one other novel, *The Three Homes: a tale for fathers*, and was also the author of a very large number of works on theology, Greek grammar, philology, education, and other subjects. In 1871 he became headmaster of Marlborough College. After four years at Marlborough, he became a Canon of Westminster and

Rector of St Margaret's Church, which serves the Houses of Parliament. His liberal religious views delayed further preferment for a long time (like Charles *Kingsley, he refused to accept the doctrine of eternal punishment for the wicked), but in 1895 he was appointed Dean of Canterbury, where he remained for the rest of his life. His marriage in 1860 produced ten children. He is chiefly remembered for *Eric* (and even this is scarcely ever read now), but in his time, through his sermons and other writings, he exerted, in the words of the *Dictionary of National Biography*, 'a vast popular influence upon the religious feeling and culture of the middle classes'.

FARROW, G. E. (George Edward) (1862–?1920) British writer, one of the few authors to make his name by imitating the *nonsense of Lewis *Carroll. His best known book was *The *Wallypug of Why* (1895).

Fat Controller In *Thomas, the Tank Engine* and other railway stories by W. V. *Awdry.

Father Christmas (Santa Claus) Father Christmas owes his origins to the Dutch cult of St Nicholas, patron saint of children.

It is said that his bringing gifts to children was first transferred from his own saint's day to the night of Christmas Eve by the English in New York in the early 19th cent., who knew of him from the many Dutch residents in that city. It appears that a particular New Yorker may have in fact been responsible for the change: Clement Clarke *Moore, whose poem *A *Visit from St Nicholas* (also known as *The Night Before Christmas*) appeared in print in 1823, and was the first piece of literature to describe Father Christmas/Santa Claus in the way he is generally known by children today.

*Dickens's *A Christmas Carol* (1843) portrays the Ghost of Christmas Present as a genial bearded giant in a robe bordered with fur. So, when the notion of St Nicholas as a sleigh-driving, chimney-descending present-giver first arrived in England (presumably in the pages of Clement Clarke Moore's poem), it could be attached to an existing image and name.

Father Christmas or Santa Claus is the subject of several notable children's books besides Moore's poem. *The Life and Adventures of Santa Claus* (1902) by L. Frank *Baum invents a history for him which deprives him of his sainthood and instead makes him a mortal child brought up by *elves. *The Father* *Christmas Letters* by J. R. R. *Tolkien (published posthumously in 1976 but written and drawn for the author's children, Christmas by Christmas, from the 1920s) describe the trials of domestic life in Father Christmas's home at the North Pole. Raymond *Briggs's *Father Christmas* (1973) presents its subject as an old grumbler who hates going out in the snow: 'Blooming Christmas here again! ...Blow the blooming snow...Blooming chimneys!'

Father Fox's Pennyrhymes (1971) A collection of verses by Clyde *Watson.

Fatherless Fanny; or, A Young Lady's First Entrance into Life, being the memoirs of a little mendicant (1811) An anonymous novel about a girl abandoned at a ladies' boarding school. No money is sent to pay her fees, and so she becomes a charity pupil. She is adopted by Lord Ellincourt, and is thereby introduced into society. The book was popular with girls for about two generations, and was often reprinted. Its opening chapters seem to have been the inspiration for *Sara Crewe* (1887) by Frances Hodgson *Burnett.

Fattypuffs and Thinifers The English title of *Patapoufs et Filifers* (1930) by the celebrated French biographer, novelist, and essayist André Maurois. It was first translated into English in 1941. The brothers Edmund and Terry, one of whom is fat and the other thin, discover two countries beneath the surface of the earth. One is occupied by the Thinifers, who, besides being excessively thin, obey a rule of life which means 'going without lunch and working six days a week'; the other, the land of the Fattypuffs, is occupied by an obese and lazy population whose only interests are eating and sleeping. The two nations are perpetually in conflict; the Thinifers invade the land of the Fattypuffs, but contact leads to greater understanding, and the races unite under one government.

Maurois (1885–1967) wrote one other children's book, *Le Pays de trente-six mille volontés* (1930). It is possible that *Fattypuffs and Thinifers* is an oblique comment on Anglo–Gallic relations—though the book has a wider moral significance, as well as being very funny. The 1968 edition has illustrations by Fritz *Wegner.

FAUCHER, Paul *See* PÈRE CASTOR.

FAULKNOR, (Chauncey) Cliff (Clifford Vernon) (1913–2009) Canadian author of novels about 19th-cent. *Indians, including

the trilogy *The White Calf* (1965), *The White Peril* (1966), and *The Smoke Horse* (1968).

Fault in Our Stars, The (2012) A *young adult novel by John *Green, which had massive success as a *crossover title. Green's tearjerking story makes something original of the currently popular 'child with cancer' young adult trope (most of it far more sentimental and manipulative than this). It is the story of two remarkable teenagers—Hazel Grace Lancaster and Augustus Waters—who fall in love, and quickly, because both of them are terminally ill and want to enjoy their lives while they can. Following huge commercial success, the novel—which, while not Green's best, is strongly voiced and emotionally substantial—was made into a weepy movie in 2014.

Fauntleroy, Little Lord *See* LITTLE LORD FAUNTLEROY.

FAUSTINO, Paul *see* PEET, MAL.

Feats on the Fjord (1841) A story by Harriet *Martineau.

Federation of Children's Book Groups A network established in the late 1960s to connect a number of children's book groups around the UK. Today the Federation runs the national Red House Book Awards, an increasingly high-profile prize awarded annually since 1980 in three age categories, with the winners (uniquely for a national prize) being chosen entirely by children. Among other valuable initiatives the Federation hosts an annual national conference every spring and promotes National Non-Fiction Month for children in November.

FEELINGS, Tom (1933–2003) African-American author, illustrator, and political activist who started his career as a cartoonist, creating the groundbreaking comic strip *Tommy Traveler in the World of Negro History* for an influential Harlem newspaper in 1958, telling of a black boy's dream adventures in American history—the strips were collected into a book in 1991. From the 1960s he concentrated on children's books, illustrating his own work and that of others, including Julius *Lester's *To Be a Slave* (1968), both *Moja Means One: Swahili Counting Book* (1971) and *Jambo Means Hello: A Swahili Alphabet Book* (1974), which were written by his wife, Muriel Feelings (1938–2011), and *The Middle Passage: White Ships / Black Cargo* (1995), a wordless evocation of a slave's journey into captivity in the West.

Fe, fi, fo, fum *See* JACK THE GIANT KILLER.

FEIFFER, Jules *See* PHANTOM TOLLBOOTH, THE.

Felissa, or the Life and Opinions of a Kitten of Sentiment An *animal story published in 1811 by John *Harris, the author being a Mrs Elizabeth Ludlow. Felissa, a Persian Blue descended from *Puss in Boots, is brought up in the castle of the Earl of Glamorgan, and is then given to the Earl's granddaughter Louisa. Her mistress accidentally sticks a pin into Felissa while dressing her in baby clothes, whereupon Felissa scratches her and is thrown out of the house. She lives for a time in a country rectory, where the boys of the household maltreat her. Running away, she encounters 'the most charitable lady living' (who despite her reputation proves to be spiteful and mean); then she meets a poet whose behaviour does not live up to the ideals promulgated in his verse; eventually she is rescued from drowning by a girl, Fanny Morgan, has kittens of her own, and is delighted to witness the marriage of Fanny and one of her earlier benefactors. Though the book's plot is similar to many other animal stories of the period, it has particular charm and wit. Harris reissued it in 1822.

Felix Summerly *See* COLE, SIR HENRY.

Felix the Cat American cartoon character, one of the first to become famous. He was created by the animator Pat Sullivan in about 1921.

Fénelon, François de Salignac de la Mothe- (1651–1715) Theologian and educationalist who wrote *Les Aventures de Télémaque* (1699) while he was tutor to the young Duke of Burgundy. It was a free adaptation of *Homer, in which the experiences of Telemachus in search of his father Ulysses became a vehicle for Fénelon's political and moral ideas. The book was translated into English in the year of its publication, as *The Adventures of Telemachus the Son of Ulysses*, and became the standard version of Homer for children for at least the next hundred years. In 1707 there appeared an English version of Fénelon's *De l'Éducation des filles* ('Instructions for the Education of a Daughter'), and his *Twenty Seven Moral Tales and Fables* (1729) also had some popularity.

FENN (Frere), Eleanor (Ellenor), Lady (1743–1813) A prolific author of *books of

instruction and other works for children. She was the wife of the Norfolk antiquary Sir John Fenn, the first editor of the *Paston Letters*, and though she had no children of her own she was active in the *Sunday school movement, and was well known in Norfolk as a philanthropist. She wrote under such pseudonyms as 'Mrs Teachwell', 'Mrs Lovechild' and 'Solomon Lovechild'. Her many books, most of which were first published by John *Marshall, include *Cobwebs to Catch Flies* (c.1783), *The Juvenile Tatler* (c.1783), *The *Fairy Spectator* (1789), *Fables, by Mrs Teachwell* (1785), and *Rational Sports* (c.1785), a set of instructive dialogues, as well as several grammars and works on *natural history.

FENN, George Manville (1831–1909) One of the most prolific British writers of boys' *adventure stories during the 1880s and 1890s; titles by him include *Devon Boys: a tale of the North Shore* (1887) and *Nat the Naturalist, or, a boy's adventures in the Eastern seas* (1899). Though his books had vitality, they were never as successful as those of his friend and contemporary G. A. *Henty, whose biography he wrote in 1907.

Ferdinand the bull In *The *Story of Ferdinand* (1936) by Munro *Leaf.

Ferrers Locke A *detective in the 'Frank *Richards' and 'Martin *Clifford' *school stories of Charles *Hamilton.

festivals As a mass of popular literature festivals have sprung up recently (most ubiquitously in the UK but elsewhere in the world, too), their programmes have typically come to incorporate extensive and often imaginative programming for children, families, and schools. In addition to children's components of broader literature festivals (Hay, Edinburgh, Cheltenham, and Oxford, for example), there are now others dedicated only to writers and illustrators for children, such as the Bath Children's Literature Festival, the Pop Up festivals and the touring Children's Bookshow. This has mirrored a greater expectation in the past decade for children's writers and illustrators to contribute to the marketing of their book in essentially performative ways—a treadmill of school visits and public events, which are increasingly expected to be high-energy and interactive.

FIELD, Mrs E. M. (1856–1940) Author of *The *Child and His Book*, Mrs Field also wrote a number of stories for children, such as *Bryda*

(1889), a tale of the Indian mutiny, and *Master Magnus; or the prince, the princess, and the dragon* (1895). She was born Louise Frances Story.

FIELD, Eugene (1850–95) Children's poet whose best-known poem is 'Wynken, Blynken, and Nod'. His collections include *A Little Book of Western Verse* (1889).

FIELD, Rachel *See* HITTY.

FIELDING, Sarah (1710–68) Author of *The *Governess* (1749), she was the sister of Henry Fielding. She made her name with *The Adventures of David Simple in Search of a Faithful Friend* (1744), and wrote several other novels.

Fifteen (1956) A novel by Beverly *Cleary, one of the first successful pieces of *young adult fiction; it is the story of Jane, her first boyfriend, and her first dating. For many years it was very popular in America, and in Britain, where it was first published in 1962.

Fifth Form at St Dominic's, The The most celebrated of the *school stories of Talbot Baines *Reed, written for the *Boy's Own Paper* and serialized in it during 1881 and 1882. It was published as a book in 1887, by the *Religious Tract Society, with illustrations by Gordon *Browne, and much reprinted.

Horace Wraysford and Oliver Greenfield are among the unofficial leaders of the Fifth, at St Dominic's public school, in the form's constant warfare against the older boys of the Sixth. Oliver's younger brother Stephen, a new boy at the school, is victimized by the bully Loman, and through him becomes involved with a dishonest publican, Cripps. The story reaches a climax when Oliver is suspected of having stolen an examination paper from the headmaster's study, so helping himself to win a valuable scholarship. It eventually transpires that the paper was stolen by Loman, who hoped to win the scholarship money so as to pay a debt to Cripps.

The moral code of the book and some of its incidents recall the 'Muscular Christianity' of *Tom Brown's Schooldays. Though St Dominic's is an idealized school (the author had no personal experience of public school life), and the book lacks a little of the verisimilitude of *Tom Brown's Schooldays*, *Eric, or, Little by Little*, and *Stalky & Co.*, the story is more elaborately plotted than in any of those books, and is told with great vigour and conviction. It inaugurated the British fashion for school stories, which lasted from its publication until the Second World War.

Fighting Fantasy (from 1982) In the pre-digital gaming world, Ian Livingstone and Steve Jackson changed lives with these innovative role-play gamebooks. Using their own enthusiasms, the founders of the Games Workshop chain—who also were the first to import Dungeons and Dragons to the UK—wrote a modestly published first book, *The Warlock of Firetop Mountain*. Within two months it had been reprinted eleven times, and three decades later there are now over sixty volumes, along with action figures, board games, role-playing game systems, magazines, and *apps. Mystifying to the uninitiated, the books were unlike any others in that you read each one non-sequentially, spinning dice or making decisions that would take you back and forth though the adventure—basically a computer game in a book.

Finding Violet Park (2007) Accomplished debut novel by Jenny *Valentine which won her the *Guardian Children's Fiction Prize. Lucas meets Violet Park in a cab office, but it is an unusual meeting because Violet is dead; it is the urn with her ashes that has been left there. Intrigued, Lucas, desperately clinging on to the idealized memory of his absent father, embarks on a search for Violet herself. On the way Lucas makes surprising discoveries, faces betrayal, finds new friends, and achieves a new maturity. It was published in the US as *Me, the Missing and the Dead*.

FINE, Anne (1947–) British writer, almost unique amongst children's authors in that consistent critical acclaim for her work is matched by popularity with young readers.

Her first books, now published together as *On the Summerhouse Steps* (1978, 1979, reissued in one volume 2006) were light, sunny reads, but with her fourth, *Round Behind the Ice House* (1981)—a story of the erosion of the close bond between twin boy and girl siblings—Fine mastered the art of delivering a well-crafted, literary work in a convincing, accessible voice which instantly engaged the reader. This style has enabled her to tackle a plethora of thorny issues—such as philosophy in *On Planet Fruitcake* (2013), the ways girls and boys are treated differently in *Bill's New Frock* (1989), and compassion in world farming in *The Chicken Gave It to Me* (1992), all books for young readers—in irresistibly entertaining stories.

Fine has acknowledged that there is an educative aspect to her work: a short story 'Fight the Good Fight' was written to assure her own daughters that she was firmly on their side in the anti-smoking argument. (So spare are Fine's novels that ventures into short-story writing are rare, but *Very Different*, 1999, valuably brings together some of her most entertaining explorations of philosophical ideas.)

Fine continues to produce satisfying, thought-provoking, and entertaining stories for younger readers, when other authors are focused on *young adult fiction. Her mischievous, hilarious series of six books about Tuffy the Killer Cat (1994–), who wreaks havoc on the lives of his ever-loving family, are international bestsellers.

It is her work for older readers which has garnered her many awards—including *Carnegie Medals for both *Goggle-Eyes* (1989) and *Flour Babies* (1992, which also won the *Whitbread Children's Book Award) and another Whitbread for *The *Tulip Touch* (1996). *Madame Doubtfire* (1987) was adapted into a popular Hollywood film (as *Mrs. Doubtfire*, 1993). *Up on Cloud Nine* (2002), about Ian's friendship with Stolly, the school 'fantasist' (now lying in a hospital bed), was 'highly commended' for the 2002 Carnegie Medal (an honour she received on a record three occasions).

Fine sometimes returns to familiar territory but explores it in different ways. In *The Tulip Touch* (1996), the narrator, Natalie, confronts the question 'Are people born evil?' Edward, in the masterful *Blood Family* (2013), has survived years of cruelty at the hands of his mother's boyfriend. At seven, he is rescued and taken into care, but the legacy of his past remains. Or was there inherent badness inside him all along? The novel is told from different viewpoints, including Edward's foster parents, care workers, and Edward himself. *The Devil Walks* (2009) is a companion novel: another story of a child imprisoned by a disturbed parent and corrosive past, but its Gothic setting removes it from reality and makes for an altogether lighter, if possibly lesser, read.

Providing readers with a balanced series of arguments is a hallmark of Fine's work for children (unlike her adult fiction, which tends to side only with the narrator). *Step by Wicked Step* (1995) presents an array of stepfamily stories, casting children and parents variously as hero and villain, while *Goggle-Eyes* firmly cheered on the child's side until she came round to the interloper's point of view.

finger-rhymes *See* INFANT AMUSEMENTS.

FINLEY, Martha Farquharson *See* ELSIE DINSMORE.

Finn Family Moomintroll *See* MOOMIN.

Firebird, The A *Russian folk tale collected by A. N. Afanasyev in his volumes of Russian folklore (1855–64). A firebird's feather is found, and when the Tsar sees it he wants to obtain the bird itself. The hero, Ivan, has to fetch the bird, then to bring a magical bride to the king, then to rescue her wedding-gown from the bottom of the sea. The story forms the second half of the celebrated Russian verse-novel *The *Little Hunchbacked Horse*, and was made into a ballet with music by Stravinsky (1910).

First Going to School; *or the story of Tom Brown and his Sisters* By 'M. Pelham' (i.e. Dorothy *Kilner), this book was published by *Tabart in 1804, and is of interest as being among the earliest *school stories. Young Tom Brown, who is delighted at the prospect of going away to boarding school, writes a series of letters to his sisters and his father when he gets there. He describes the pranks of the naughtier boys and the punishments they receive; an old sow is dressed up in one of the ushers' clothes, and her piglets, in the boys' nightcaps and shirts, are put into the beds. The result is floggings, and even the expulsion of a boy who refuses to repent. Tom reports that despite all this he will return home for the holidays 'with a very good character' from his master.

FIRTH, Barbara (1928–2013) An English illustrator best known for her long collaboration with author Martin *Waddell. Firth began her career in the fashion industry but also worked freelance producing illustrations for several non-fiction children's titles. In the 1980s, Firth began to illustrate fiction for Walker Books, for example, David Lloyd's *Great Escapes*, a series of animal stories. Her career subsequently blossomed and, while she illustrated for a number of different authors, Firth's partnership with Waddell became the most significant. The first book in their *Little Bear* series, *Can't You Sleep, Little Bear?* (1987), won the Smarties Book Prize and the *Kate Greenaway Medal in 1988. Waddell and Firth later collaborated on another award-winning title, *The Park in the Dark* (1989), which won the *Kurt Maschler award in 1989.

FISHER, Catherine (1957–) Welsh author and poet, whose work is woven through with the myths and legends of Britain, particularly Wales. Strangely undervalued in the UK, her work is complex, beautifully written, and superbly characterized. Science fiction, fantasy, myth, and contemporary suspense often all mix in her stories, as she challenges preconceptions of what fantasy means. Perhaps the best example of Fisher's work to date is *Corbenic* (2002), a rich and dark contemporary Grail story. *The Relic Master* series (1998) and *The Snow-Walker Trilogy* (1993) deserve to be considered classics of their kind, and *The Oracle Trilogy* (2003), which blends Greek and Egyptian cultures and myths, was an international success. In 2012 she began a new series with the dark and haunting *Obsidian Mirror*.

FISHER, Dorothy (Frances) Canfield (1879–1958) American author, remembered chiefly for *Understood Betsy* (1917), about a neurotic city-bred girl staying with country relatives in Vermont.

FISHER, Margery (1913–92) British critic of children's books. She wrote *Intent Upon Reading* (1961), a critical survey of what had been published for British children between 1930 and 1960. In May 1962 she began to publish *Growing Point*, a periodical containing reviews (mostly written by herself) of new children's books. Her other writings include *Matters of Fact* (1972), a companion volume to *Intent Upon Reading* covering non-fiction, and *Who's Who in Children's Books: a treasury of the familiar characters of childhood* (1975).

FISK, Nicholas (David Higginbottom) (1923–2016) British children's author whose books are predominantly science fiction; they include *Grinny* (1973), a sinister tale in which an apparently friendly visiting old lady turns out to be part of a malevolent alien invasion; and the futuristic *A Rag, a Bone and a Hank of Hair* (1980), in which, following a nuclear holocaust, new people are manufactured out of ones long dead: the Reborn. Fisk also edited *The Puffin Book of Science Fiction* (1993).

FITZGERALD, John D. *See* GREAT BRAIN, THE.

FITZHUGH, Louise (1928–74) American children's author-illustrator, best known for *Harriet the Spy. Her other books include *Nobody's Family is Going to Change* (1974), about a prosperous New York black family whose children do not want to follow parental plans for their future.

FITZPATRICK, Marie-Louise (1962–) Irish author and illustrator who was born and still lives in Dublin. From childhood her dream had been to illustrate children's books, and after working in graphic design, illustrating stories for magazines, and teaching she finally made her mark with *Izzy and Skunk* (2010), a story about a little girl, her worries, and how she learns to cope even without her favourite toy. Her clear, expressive style developed further with the thoughtful, imaginative *There* (2009), in which a girl ponders what the future might hold, and *The New Kid* (2014), which proves that imagination is the best defence against bullies. Fitzpatrick made a shift into writing novels with the ghost story, *Timecatchers* (2010), and then to *young adult with *Dark Warning* (2012), which is set in Georgian Dublin. She has won the *CBI Book of the Year Award on three occasions (and several in other categories).

FITZPATRICK, Sir Percy *See* JOCK OF THE BUSHVELD.

Five Children and It (1902) A novel by E. *Nesbit. Robert, Anthea, Jane, Cyril, and their baby brother 'the Lamb' are left to stay in the country while their parents are away. They discover the Psammead, a sand-fairy with the power of granting them wishes; but it does so reluctantly, for it is a cantankerous, self-pitying creature, owing some of its characteristics to the cuckoo in Mrs *Molesworth's story *The *Cuckoo Clock*, and to the raven in another of her books, *The *Tapestry Room*. Each of the children's daily wishes, which are unmade at sunset, brings unforeseen trouble, whether being 'beautiful as the day' (which proves to be 'perfectly beastly'), having a gravel pit full of gold, or encountering '*Indians'. Several of the wishes are accidental, irredeemably out of the children's mouths before they can think of something more sensible (much as in the folk tale *The *Three Wishes*).

Five Children and It was the first of E. Nesbit's *fantasies (it was followed by two sequels, *The *Phoenix and the Carpet* and *The *Story of the Amulet*); it displays all the powers of portraying lively, bantering children that marked her earlier, realistic, children's stories.

Parts of *Five Children and It* first appeared in the *Strand Magazine*. The original illustrations by H. R. *Millar include a portrayal of the Psammead of which the author herself strongly approved. The book was dedicated to E. Nesbit's own 'Lamb', her infant son John. It established a formula for children's fantasy-writing which has been followed by many authors in England and elsewhere. There have been several worthy sequels by other hands—perhaps the best is *Five Children on the Western Front* by Kate Saunders (2014).

Five Chinese Brothers, The (1938) By Clare Huchet *Bishop.

Five Little Peppers and How They Grew, The (1881) A *family story by Harriet M. *Lothrop, about the poor and fatherless Pepper children; the story largely concerns the youngest, Phronsie.

Fiver Rabbit in *Watership Down* by Richard *Adams.

FLACK, Marjorie (1897–1958) American author-illustrator of *picture books, best known for her series of comic stories about Angus, a Scottie dog (1930 onwards). Her other books include *The Story about Ping* (1933).

Flambards (1967) The first novel in a series by K. M. *Peyton. Christina, a twelve-year-old orphan heiress, is summoned to live at Flambards, an Essex country house, by her Uncle Russell. Christina becomes involved in a complicated relationship with Will, who hates hunting; with her uncle, who dominates the household with his drunken rages and passion for horsemanship and kennels; with the elder son, Mark, who is coming more and more to resemble his father; and with Dick, a groom, who teaches her to ride and falls in love with her. The second volume, *The Edge of the Cloud* (1969), which won the *Carnegie Medal, begins with Christina's elopement with Will. In the third book, *Flambards in Summer* (1969), Will has been killed in the First World War, and Christina returns to Flambards. The story is continued in *Flambards Divided* (1981).

Flambards and its sequels established K. M. Peyton as one of Britain's leading authors for older children or teen readers. Its popularity was increased when it was filmed, some years after publication, by Yorkshire Television.

FLANAGAN, John (1944–) After successfully working in the worlds of advertising and TV, this Australian author turned his hand to writing books in order to try and engage his own young son in reading. His first book, *Ruins of Gorlan* (2004), was deliberately given a slightly built, apparently 'weaker' hero, in order to show that muscle isn't everything—and luckily the idea engaged not just his son but readers all over the world, as it

became the beginning of the internationally successful *Ranger's Apprentice* series. Comprising thirteen books so far, the series also has a spin-off called *The Brotherband Chronicles* (2011).

Flashman Bully in **Tom Brown's Schooldays* by Thomas *Hughes, and in novels by George MacDonald Fraser.

Flat Iron for a Farthing, A (1872) A story by Mrs *Ewing.

Flat Stanley (1964) By American writer and editor Jeff Brown (1926–2003), first in a series for younger readers, originally illustrated by Tomi *Ungerer and later by Scott Nash, Jon Mitchell, and others. It is the story of Stanley Lampchop, who is squashed flat in his sleep by a falling bulletin board; his new 2D shape allows him to fly like a kite and be posted across the country in an envelope. Having originally devised the first book as a bedtime story for his sons, Brown himself wrote five sequels, and since his death there have also been spin-off series penned by other writers.

FLEISCHMAN, (Albert) Sid (Sidney) (1920–2010) American comic novelist for children. His books owe a little to Mark *Twain; for example, *Chancy and the Grand Rascal* (1966) is a *Huckleberry-Finn-like story of an orphan setting out to reunite his scattered siblings, and taking up with a long-lost uncle who is a professional trickster. Many of Sid Fleischman's other books are **Tall Tales* in the *Munchausen tradition; his 'McBroom' series concerns the impossible adventures of a happy-go-lucky family. For example, in *McBroom's Wonderful One-Acre Farm* (published under that title in Britain in 1972) the family acquires land so fertile that plants spring up the moment seed is sown. Fleischman is also a deft hand at the wisecrack:

'Mr Jackson, you're meaner 'n a barrel of rattlesnakes.'

'I come by it naturally,' he answered. 'Runs in the family. There's so many of us Jacksons in hell, ma'am, our feet are sticking out of the windows.'

(from *Me and the Man on the Moon-Eyed Horse*, 1977.)

FLEMING, Ian *See* CHITTY-CHITTY-BANG-BANG.

Flight of the Doves, The (1967) A thriller for children by Walter *Macken.

Flook A *comic strip published in the London *Daily Mail* from 1949. Drawn by the jazz musician Wally Fawkes, and written at various times by Humphrey Lyttelton, George Melly, Barry Norman, and Barry Took (and once, briefly, by Sir Compton Mackenzie). Though intended initially for children, it soon acquired a satirical tone.

Flopsy Bunnies In stories by Beatrix *Potter.

Flour Babies (1992) A novel by Anne *Fine. Simon Martin and his classmates in 4C are horrified to learn that they must each look after a bag of flour as if it were their baby. However, the experiment leads to some surprises—not least an opportunity for Simon to reflect on his own home experience. Fine won her second *Carnegie Medal for this thought-provoking, yet humorous treatment of a serious situation faced by many young people.

Flower Fairies A series of books by Cicely Mary *Barker.

Folk Tales from Asia for Children Everywhere A series published from 1975 by UNESCO and the Tokyo Book Development Centre. The stories, from countries all over Asia, were selected by an editorial board representing five nations, and retold and illustrated by writers and artists from the country of origin. The aim was to create 'a sense of common identity among readers of many lands'.

FOLLEN, Eliza Lee (Cabot) (1787–1860) American author who wrote several books of *poetry for children, including *Little Songs* (1833). She was a prominent abolitionist, and slavery features in several of her poems.

She is sometimes erroneously named as the author of **Three Little Kittens*.

FORBES, Esther *See* JOHNNY TREMAIN.

FORD, H. J. (Henry Justice) (1860–1941) Illustrator of Andrew *Lang's many **Fairy Books*. Ford, a notable cricketer, was a friend of J. M. *Barrie and designed *Peter Pan's original costume.

FORDE, Catherine (1961–) Glasgow-based Scottish playwright and author of *young adult novels whose career has always revolved around her love of literature and words, including being a lexicographer. Her breakthrough novel was *Fat Boy Swim* (2003), the story of a boy who feels useless and how an unlikely friendship changes his life. Books such as *Sugarcoated* (2008) and *Fifteen Minute Bob* (2010) speak clearly to teenagers, being

fast-paced, emotionally engaging, and clearly rooted in the realities of the modern world.

FOREMAN, Michael (1938–) One of the best-known and most prolific contemporary British illustrators with over 250 titles to his name, over seventy of those featuring his own text as well as illustration. As a child he was almost killed by an incendiary bomb, and that brush with death led him to a lifetime of pacifism and a body of work that illuminates the preciousness of life and the future in a pencil-and-watercolour style that is subtle, realistic, and expressive. His debut, *The General* (1961, with Janet Charters), was published when he was still at college, and it was reissued in a 50th anniversary edition in 2010. His work has won many awards, and he is acknowledged as being influential in changing the perception of picture books as being solely for a very young audience. Early thought-provoking books such as *War and Peas* (1974) and *Dinosaurs and All That Rubbish* (1972) continue to be relevant and deservedly popular. *Seal Surfer* (1997) is a beautiful story about the passing of time, through the tale of a boy befriending a young seal who later saves his life, which also contains a subtle message about *disability. In 2005 he published a collection of his own re-tellings of *Classic Fairy Tales*.

Foreman's own wartime experiences fill *War Boy* (1989), one of the most important books for younger readers about what war is like, which won Foreman one of his two *Kate Greenaway Medals. *War Game* (1993) is the heartbreaking story of four WW1 recruits and their time in the trenches, including the Christmas game of football in no man's land—Foreman dedicated it to his four uncles who died in the war. The preoccupation with war remains significant in his more recent work, including, for instance, *The Tale of Ali Pasha* (2013), in which an old man shares his memories of Gallipoli and the tortoise he befriended there.

Besides illustrating his own texts, Foreman collaborates frequently with other writers, including Terry Jones (on several occasions) and Peter *Dickinson, and illustrated a 1985 *Puffin Books edition of *Charlie and the Chocolate Factory*. His first collaboration with Michael *Morpurgo on *Arthur, High King of Britain* (1994) led to a particularly successful creative partnership, which would include *Billy The Kid* (2000), in which a Chelsea pensioner tells his life story, *The Mozart Question* (2007), which also reflects on the Holocaust, and many of Morpurgo's subsequent novels.

FOREST, Antonia (Patricia Rubinstein) (1915–2003) British author of *girls' stories about the Marlow family, their schooldays, and their doings in the holidays. The novels, which began with *Autumn Term* (1948), are distinguished by relatively naturalistic and witty narrative and dialogue.

FORESTER, C. S. (Cecil Scott) (1899–1966) Creator of 'Captain Horatio Hornblower, RN', Forester studied medicine but became a professional writer and bridge-player. Hornblower first appeared in print in 1937 in *The Happy Return*; Forester dreamed him up after buying three volumes of a naval magazine from the Napoleonic period in an antiquarian bookshop. Forester's own experience on the water was, at that time, confined to river-trips in a dinghy (about which he wrote books), but he sailed briefly with the Royal Navy during the Second World War to gain material for his documentary novel *The Ship* (1943). He produced many Hornblower novels, including *Mr Midshipman Hornblower* (1950), and they have been read avidly by children. There have also been several Hornblower adaptations for both the big and the small screen. Forester's one book specifically written with children in mind was *Poo-Poo and the Dragons* (1942).

Forever (1975) A *young adult novel by Judy *Blume portraying a teenage girl's first sexual relationship. Kath meets Michael at a party and gradually falls in love with him. She loses her virginity to him, a scene which is described in considerable detail. When the book was published, it garnered, on the one hand, strong criticism from those who felt that young people should not be given such graphic descriptions of sexual intercourse, and on the other hand, high praise from those who felt the book was an invaluable educational tool, as well as an excellent story. Nearly forty years after it was published, it is regarded as the first important novel about sex for teenagers.

FORTESCUE, Sir John See STORY OF A RED-DEER, THE.

Fortunatus A medieval European *romance which became a popular *chapbook in England. It was mentioned by Wordsworth in *The Prelude* (v. 364–9, 1805–6 version) as among the stories that had delighted him when he was a boy.

In the chapbook version Fortunatus leaves his native Cyprus in search of a livelihood and comes eventually to a wood, where he falls asleep and wakes to find the lady Fortune

standing over him. She offers him a choice of gifts. He asks for riches, and is given a purse from which at any time he can draw ten pieces of gold; it will remain effective for his lifetime and the lifetime of his children, but not thereafter. With the aid of the purse he acquires a retinue of servants and travels the world, eventually marrying and begetting two sons, Ampedio and Andolocia. Journeying east, he is shown by the Soldan a hat that can convey the wearer instantly from one part of the globe to another. Fortunatus immediately claps it on his head and wishes himself on board his own ship, thus acquiring the hat for himself. With its aid he makes many more journeys, but eventually grows old and, before dying, hands over purse and hat to his sons. The younger, Andolocia, goes to England with the purse, and falls in love with the king's daughter, who tricks him into handing the purse over; she also manages to acquire the hat. Andolocia gets hat and purse back, but is imprisoned and finally murdered on account of the purse, while the hat is destroyed by his brother on his deathbed.

Thomas Dekker based a comedy, *Old Fortunatus* (1600), on the story. *The History of Fortunatus* was among the most popular items of cheap literature from the late 17th to the 19th cents., and versions have been published in the 20th cent. The story appears in the *Grey Fairy Book* (1900) of Andrew *Lang.

FOSDICK, Charles Austin *See* CASTLEMON, HARRY.

Fossil family In **Ballet Shoes* by Noel *Streatfeild.

FOUQUÉ, La Motte *See* LA MOTTE FOUQUÉ.

Four Feathers, The (1902) An adventure novel by A. E. W. *Mason.

Four to Fourteen A handlist of recommended books for children, published in Britain by the National Book League. The editor of the 1950 edition (revised 1956) was Kathleen *Lines.

Four Winds Farm (1887) A novel by Mrs *Molesworth.

FOX, George (1624–91) Founder of the Society of Friends who wrote, with a fellow *Quaker, Ellis Hookes, a *Primmer* [i.e. *primer] *and catechism for children* which was first published in 1670 and reissued in 1673 with corrections and additions as *Instructions for Right Spelling*. It was so popular that by 1769 it had been reprinted at least twelve times in England; it was also the first English spelling-book to be published in America, an edition appearing in Philadelphia in 1702. The book consists of an alphabet, a list of words broken up into separate syllables, a series of sentences summarizing or commenting on biblical stories, a set of proverbs, a series of examples of hard words and homophones, etc., a table of weights and measures, a perpetual calendar, and a *catechism. This is unusual in that the child asks the questions and the teacher answers. The catechism defends the Quakers against their accusers, and in turn castigates the ministers of the various churches as 'Deceivers and False Prophets'.

Fox was also the joint author of a *Battle-door for Teachers & Professors to learn Singular & Plural* (1660), the title being a pun on *battledore. This extraordinary book attempts to justify the Quaker use of the second person singular, 'thou', by citing other languages which make the distinction between singular and plural forms of address.

FOX, Mem (1946–) Australian author of children's picture books who originally taught literacy studies in Adelaide, and is now a literacy consultant in Australia and the US. *Reading Magic* (2001) is a passionate encouragement for the love of reading in early childhood.

Her first book, **Possum Magic* (1983), also started the career of illustrator Julie *Vivas. By 2013 it had sold three million copies. Fox's poetic approach to writing a picture-book text often features repeating patterns and phrases, strong rhythm, predictability and appealing, often animal, characters. Many of Fox's books, such as *Wilfrid Gordon McDonald Partridge* (1984), *Hattie and the Fox* (1986), and *Hunwick's Egg* (2005) have captured the popular imagination. Most of her books are sold in Australia and internationally. *Where is the Green Sheep?* (2004) won the *CBCA Early Childhood Book of the Year. This book has a poetic text about all the different kinds of sheep. And where is the green sheep? 'There she is . . . fast asleep.'

Fox has received many honours and much acclaim for her numerous children's books. In 1990 she was awarded the *Dromkeen Medal and in 1993 a medal of the Order of Australia for services to the cultural life of Australia.

FOX, Paula (1923–) American novelist, born in New York City. Her first children's book was *Maurice's Room* (1966) about an eight-year-old dedicated to his collection of

junk. *A Likely Place* (1967) is the story of a few days in the life of Lewis, whose fussy parents leave him in the care of an eccentric babysitter who lets him wander where he wants.

These early books set out the key themes of Paula Fox's work for children. She writes about isolated children—generally boys—who have difficulty in relating to other people, but who begin to make real contact with others after going through some out-of-the-ordinary experience. *How Many Miles to Babylon?* (1967) begins with James, a young black boy, failing to understand or be understood by the three aunts with whom he lives in a Manhattan tenement. He is kidnapped by three young thugs who want to use him as a stooge in their dog-stealing racket, and by the time James escapes, he has somehow been changed, and can begin to communicate with the aunts and with his mother. Gus in *The Stone-Faced Boy* (1968) is the middle child in a large family; none of his siblings cares much about him, so he takes refuge in blankness of facial expression and as far as possible blankness of emotion. Then an outlandish cigar-smoking great-aunt arrives, and at the same time one of Gus's sisters loses a dog, which goes out into the snow and is caught in a trap. In the middle of the night Gus reluctantly agrees to rescue it, and by the time he returns he has done private battle with his innermost fears and uncertainties, and has become a person to be reckoned with in the family. *Portrait of Ivan* (1969) has the same theme and structure.

In *Blowfish Live in the Sea* (1970), generally regarded as Paula Fox's most exciting handling of her theme, the 'non-communicator' is Ben, an eighteen-year-old dropout from high school, whose mother has remarried and whose father is a drifter. The story is told by Ben's half-sister Carrie, the only person who can get through to him; it concerns Ben's decision to leave home and try to make a new life with his father.

Paula Fox won the *Newbery Medal with *The Slave Dancer* (1973), which is a less characteristic work, a *historical novel about a New Orleans boy press-ganged onto a slave ship in 1840. She returned to her usual subject matter in *A Place Apart* (1980), which is about thirteen-year-old Victoria Finch, who moves (after the death of her father) from Boston to a small New England town.

Fox has also written books for younger children; they include *Hungry Fred* (1969), about a boy so hungry that he even eats the furniture, and *The Little Swineherd and other tales* (1978), a collection of folk tales with a frame story about a duck and a goose. There are also adult novels, and two volumes of memoirs, the first, *Borrowed Finery* (2001), about rejection at birth by her mother, rescue by her Cuban grandmother, and an itinerant and turbulent childhood in which she was passed between relatives and strangers in Cuba and the US. She won the *Hans Christian Andersen Award in 1978.

Foxe's Book of Martyrs The popular title of *Actes and Monuments of these latter perilous times touching matters of the Church* by John Foxe (1516–87). The original book, composed in Latin and first published in English in 1563, is of enormous length, being a history of the Church from the earliest times, with special emphasis on martyrdom, particularly the Protestant martyrs who died during Mary's reign. Its purpose is to indict 'the persecutors of God's truth, commonly called papists'.

Its vivid, readable style, especially in the dialogues between the martyrs and those who persecuted them, made it attractive to young readers from the start, despite (or perhaps because of) the horrific accounts of the executions. It was recommended as reading for children by Thomas White, author of *A *Little Book for Little Children* which appeared in 1660. Abridgements began to appear a few years after the original publication, sometimes with illustrations. In 1826 there appeared *A Book of Martyrs, for the Young*, the work of Isaac *Taylor, father of Ann and Jane *Taylor.

Fox in Socks (1965) An enduring tongue-twisting tale by Dr *Seuss. It begins with a fox (in socks) and a box, and a Knox. Knox in box. Fox in socks. They are then joined by chicks and bricks and blocks and clocks (with ticks and tocks). As the fox tries to teach the Knox his ever trickier tongue-twisters, the mayhem grows. Eventually the Knox loses patience and shoves the fox into the bottle where the tweetle beetles are having their paddle battle in a puddle (on a noodle-eating poodle)—a conclusion that is Seuss at his silliest and most sublime.

FOXTON, Thomas (*c*.1695–1740) Author of *Moral Songs Composed for the Use of Children* (1728), a book of verse in imitation of Isaac *Watts.

Frances A small badger in a series of stories by Russell *Hoban.

Franconia A rural community in New England, scene of a series of books by Jacob *Abbott, published between 1850 and 1854: *Wallace, Beechnut, Caroline, Madeline, Agnes, Stuyvesant, Mary Bell, Mary Erskine, Adolphus,* and *Ellen Linn.* The most notable character is Antoine Bianchinette, a French boy of precocious sagacity who arrives in Franconia and is nicknamed 'Beechnut'. The stories lack any great excitement, but give a good picture of rural life at the time.

FRANK, Anne *See* DIARY OF A YOUNG GIRL, THE.

Freddy A pig in stories by the American writer Walter R. Brooks (1886–1958), illustrated by Kurt *Wiese. Freddy the pig first appeared in 1927; then new Freddy books were published throughout the 1930s, 1940s, and 1950s, the last being *Freddy and the Dragon* (1958).

FREEDMAN, Russell (1929–) US author of biographies of prominent Americans and others from history (the Wright brothers, Martha Graham, FDR, Crazy Horse, Confucius), and other *non-fiction (though he prefers the term 'factual') books for children. Notable among his nearly fifty well-researched, illustrated books is *Lincoln: a Photobiography* (1987), which won him a *Newbery Medal, an exceptionally rare accolade for a factual work. His many other awards include a *Boston Globe-Horn Book Award (for a life of Eleanor Roosevelt), as well as the 1998 *Laura Ingalls Wilder Medal.

FREEMAN, Don *See* CORDUROY.

FRENCH, Jackie (1953–) One of Australia's most highly regarded children's authors, writing picture books, junior fiction and *young adult and information books. Her career as a children's novelist began with junior fiction, and gradually extended into other age ranges. Her writing reflects her interest in nature, conservation, and the environment. She chooses an issue, and presents it in an appealing, flowing style with a natural warmth. French's work spans humour, science fiction, historical fiction, and fantasy, often with challenging themes such as war, refugees, or poverty.

French was established as a novelist for younger readers before she began writing picture books. For many of these books, she is teamed with illustrator Bruce *Whatley. Their most famous picture book is *Diary of a Wombat,* and its sequels. French's picture books feature a strong pace and humour, and are often sparked by a quirky fact or unusual point of view. The sad story of the 2011 Brisbane floods was told in *Flood* (2012), which was an Honour Book for the *CBCA Picture Book of the Year in 2012. It is now joined by *Fire* (2014).

The success of *Hitler's Daughter* (1999), which won the 2000 CBCA Book of the Year: Younger Readers, ensured that she would be able to explore strong themes in her future work. In *Hitler's Daughter,* set in the Second World War, Heidi believes she is the secret daughter of Hitler, and her story is juxtaposed with the lives of the storyteller and her listeners as they wait for the bus in present-day Australia. *Refuge* (2013) is an evocative story about several child refugees, from different times, who play together on a sandy beach. The similarities between the refugees are poignant.

French is dyslexic and calls herself 'a passionate worker for literacy, the right of all children to be able to read, and the power of books'. She is the winner of many literary and children's choice awards, and was declared the Australian Children's *Laureate for 2014–15.

FRENCH, Vivian (1945–) British author and storyteller who, since 1990, has published over two hundred books. Prolific in both output and imagination, she produces picture books, first readers, and sophisticated stories for older readers. She is most famous for *The Tiara Club* (2006), a series about a school for princesses which led to a variety of offshoots, such as *The Tiara Club at Ruby Mansions* (2007) series and *The Tiara Club at Diamond Turrets* (2009). *Draglins* (2007), a more boy-friendly series, is about young dragons, and *Stargirl Academy* (2013) is about a magical school in the clouds. Her series for older readers, *Tales From the Five Kingdoms,* starts with the brilliant *Robe of Bones* (2007).

FREUD, Clement *See* GRIMBLE.

Friar and the Boy, The A popular *ballad, which often appeared in *chapbooks read by young people from the 16th to the 19th cents. Several historians of, or commentators on, children's literature have deplored it as being in bad taste, but it is a typical example of chapbook humour.

A boy who gives food to an old man is rewarded with three magic gifts: a bow that never misses its mark, a pipe which causes all

who hear it to dance, and the power of making his stepmother break wind with a huge noise whenever she glares at him. The stepmother, to be revenged for the embarrassment the boy causes her through this, persuades a visiting friar to beat him, but the boy plays his pipe and the friar is made to dance about in a thorn bush until his clothes are torn off. The friar has the boy summoned before the ecclesiastical authorities, but the court breaks up in disarray when the boy plays the pipe.

The frere and the boye was printed by Wynkyn de *Worde *c.*1512 and reappeared in print again and again during the next 300 years. Later editions often carried the subtitle *The Young Piper's Pleasant Pastime.* Eventually, a second part of the story was added, in which the boy acquires further magical gifts by which he can cause havoc, including the power to make horns appear on cuckolds' heads.

One printing of the ballad (1628) bore the comment on the title-page: 'Very delectable, though unpleasant to all Step-mothers.'

Friar Bacon A popular English *chapbook that was in circulation from the 16th to the 19th cents. It was loosely based on the figure of Roger Bacon (1214–92), whose scientific writings caused him to be regarded as a necromancer. The chapbook describes how Friar Bacon, with the aid of a fellow conjurer, Friar Bungay, makes a head of brass, and with the aid of the Devil gives it the power of speech. After waiting day and night for several weeks for the head to say something, the two friars hand over the responsibility of observing it to Bacon's servant, Miles, and they both then fall asleep. The head speaks two words: 'Time is', and then, a little later, says: 'Time was'. Miles thinks Bacon would be furious if he were woken to hear such trivial things. Finally the head says: 'Time is past', and falls down and breaks. Bacon awakes, discovers what has happened, and curses the servant.

Friar Tuck *See* ROBIN HOOD.

Frisby, Mrs In *Mrs Frisby and the Rats of NIMH* by Robert C. *O'Brien.

FRITZ, Jean (1915–) American author who made her name with a series of biographies for children which include *And Then What Happened, Paul Revere?* (1973) and *What's The Big Idea, Ben Franklin?* (1976). She also wrote children's fiction, including *Brady* (1960), the story of a runaway slave.

Frodo Baggins Hero of *The *Lord of the Rings* by J. R. R. *Tolkien.

FROEBEL, Friedrich (Wilhelm August) (1782–1852) German educationalist, founder of the *kindergarten movement.

Frog *See* VELTHUIJS, MAX.

Frog and Toad In books by Arnold *Lobel.

Froggy's Little Brother (1875) By '*Brenda' (Mrs G. Castle Smith), this was one of the most popular English *Street Arab tales. Froggy and Benny are two orphaned children living in a garret; Benny dies, and Froggy is taken to an orphanage where he acquires another 'brother', an abandoned child. The moral, underlined by the author at the end, is that the poor 'show us how to be truly and greatly generous in their willingness to share the last crumb of comfort'.

Frog he would a-wooing go, A A popular song adopted as a *nursery rhyme. It is descended from a *ballad known in the 16th cent., and recorded under the title 'The Marriage of the Frogge and the Movse' in Thomas Ravenscroft's *Melismata* (1611). It had become a nursery song by the 1780s, though early in the 19th cent. it was also popularized by comedians. It has sometimes been printed as a separate juvenile book, e.g. an 1883 version illustrated by Randolph *Caldecott.

Frog Prince, The A *fairy story first set down by the brothers *Grimm, but known before the 19th cent.

A princess drops a golden ball, her favourite toy, into a spring, and a frog appears, offering to fetch it out for her if she will agree to love him and let him live with her. She agrees, but when he retrieves the ball, she goes off home with it, ignoring his plea that she should take him with her. However, the frog persists and the king, hearing what his daughter has promised, makes her keep her word. The frog is allowed to eat off her plate, and even to sleep in her chamber. But the princess only takes him upstairs very reluctantly, and when he demands to get into her bed, she flings him against the wall, intending to kill him. However, he turns into a beautiful prince, who explains that he was given the shape of a frog by a wicked witch; only the princess could rescue him, and he is now 'her dear companion and husband'.

This form of the story was found in Hesse, where the Grimms also discovered another

version in which the princess has two elder sisters who refuse to help the frog; she, however, cooperates, and he sleeps on her pillow for three nights before changing spontaneously into a prince without violent intervention.

The Grimms called the tale 'one of the oldest in Germany'. A version of it, *The Well of the World's End*, was collected in Scotland in the 19th cent., and may have been known there as early as the 16th cent. This begins with a girl— not a princess—setting out on the apparently impossible errand of fetching water from a well in a sieve. The frog appears and tells her what to do (stop up the sieve with moss and clay); in return for this advice she has to welcome him into her home and bed. Finally he asks her to chop off his head with an axe, which brings about his change into a human being. This story was printed by Robert Chambers in his *Popular Rhymes of Scotland* (1842). J. O. *Halliwell, in *Popular Rhymes and Nursery Tales* (1849), filled out Chambers's version, and Halliwell's form of the story was further embroidered by Joseph Jacobs in *English Fairy Tales* (1890).

FROISSART, Jean (?1337–c.1410) French chronicler of 14th-cent. English history who provided the material for many children's *historical novels written from the mid-19th cent. onwards. In 1879 was published Sidney *Lanier's *The Boy's Froissart*.

From the Mixed-Up Files of Mrs Basil E. Frankweiler (1967) *Newbery Medal-winning novel by E. L. *Konigsburg. It is the story of Claudia and Jamie, who run away from home and move instead into the Metropolitan Museum of Art in Manhattan. The Mrs Frankweiler of the title, the book's narrator, is a rich, elderly eccentric, who has sold the museum a Renaissance statue which the children believe is by Michelangelo.

FROST, A. B. (Arthur Burdett) (1851–1928) American illustrator and cartoonist. His work in children's books included illustrations to an edition of *Uncle Remus* (1895), and to poems in *Rhyme? and Reason?* (1883) by Lewis *Carroll.

FULLER, Roy (Broadbent) (1912–91) British poet whose work for children included the novels *Savage Gold* (1946), *With My Little Eye* (1948), and *Catspaw* (1966), a *fantasy which is a parable about the Cold War. *Seen Grandpa Lately?* (1972) and *Poor Roy* (1977) are books of poetry for children.

FULLER, S. and **J.** (*fl.* 1810) Of 'The Temple of Fancy', Rathbone Place, London, S. and J. Fuller issued a small series of books which featured paper dolls with movable heads (*see* MOVABLE PICTURE BOOKS). The series seems to have begun with *The History of Little Fanny, exemplified in a series of figures* (1810). In this story in verse, Fanny runs away from home when she is not allowed to wear her new winter clothes; she has adventures as a beggar and an errand-girl and eventually, repentant, is restored to her family. The book contains seven hand-coloured paper-doll figures, a movable head which can be fitted to each of these in turn, and four head-pieces. Others in the series (which totalled at least eleven titles) include *The History and Adventures of Little Henry* (1810), a similar story featuring a boy, *Ellen, or the Naughty Girl Reclaimed* (1811), *Phoebe, the Cottage Maid* (1811), a version of *Cinderella* (1814), and *Frederick, or the effects of disobedience* (1816), which includes an adventure at the Battle of Waterloo.

Fungus the Bogeyman (1977) A *picture book by Raymond *Briggs, displaying the lifestyle and habits of *bogeys as Briggs conceives them. They live underground, love putrefaction, and deplore the clean habits of surface-dwelling humans. The book aroused cries of delighted disgust from critics, and briefly became a cult with adults and children. Fungus reappeared in 1982 in a *pop-up book (or in this case 'Plop-Up') by Briggs.

FUNKE, Cornelia (1958–) German author who spent time as a social worker and illustrator before turning to writing full-time. Her action-packed fantasy stories have led her to being tagged 'the J. K. Rowling of Germany'. *The *Thief Lord* (2000), was the first of her books to be translated and is about two orphaned children on the run in atmospheric Venice, and it was an immediate success. *Inkheart* (2003) starts a series about how stories can come to life, while *dragons are the stars of *Dragon Rider* (2004). A new series, beginning with *Reckless* (2010), is about a mirror-world. She also writes picture books and the *Ghosthunters* (2006) series for younger readers. She currently lives in America.

FURNISS, Harry (1854–1925) Illustrator, the son of an English civil engineer practising in Ireland. He came to London when he was nineteen and soon made a reputation as a cartoonist, eventually joining the staff of *Punch* as a Parliamentary artist. His association with Lewis

*Carroll began in 1889 when he illustrated *Sylvie and Bruno*. Other children's books with pictures by him include *The *Wallypug of Why* and **Wanted: a King*. A brisk, impatient man, Furniss wrote (in *Confessions of a Caricaturist*, 1901) a scathing but not unadmiring account of Carroll, whom he described as 'a wit, a gentleman, a bore and an egotist', adding: 'I was wilful and erratic, bordering on insanity. We therefore got on splendidly.'

FYLEMAN, Rose (Amy) (1877–1957) Children's poet, author, and playwright who produced many books, but is now remembered only for the poem 'Fairies', which appeared on the first page of her *Fairies and Chimneys* (1918). She contributed to *Punch*, and thereby made the acquaintance of A. A. *Milne; it was at her suggestion that he wrote his first children's verses, which he contributed to *The Merry-go-Round*, the children's magazine she was editing.

GÁG, Wanda (Hazel) (1893–1946) Author-illustrator of *picture books, who was born in Minnesota, the eldest child of Eastern European parents, and spoke no English until she went to school. She went to art school in Minneapolis and New York, and then began to exhibit *wood engravings, etchings, and lithographs. She was eventually approached by a publisher to see whether she was interested in juvenile books. She immediately took three picture books from her 'Rejection Box', where they had lain for some time, and these were accepted for publication.

The first, *Millions of Cats*, appeared in 1928 and was an instant success. It told the story of an old man who went to find a cat for his wife and came back with

> Hundreds of cats,
> Thousands of cats,
> Millions and billions and trillions of cats.

Like Wanda Gág's other picture books, *Millions of Cats* had a hand-lettered text and illustrations which reflected her Eastern European ancestry and her experience as a wood engraver. The book was widely praised. A year later (1929) came *The Funny Thing*, an eccentric story of an old man who weans a dragon from a diet of children's dolls. *Gone Is Gone, or the story of a man who wanted to do housework* (1935) was a folk tale about a peasant couple who exchange roles, remembered from Wanda Gág's childhood. She spent much of her adult life sharing a New Jersey farm with her sisters and brother; in her late thirties she married and moved to New York City. Her last original picture book was *Nothing At All* (1941), the story of an invisible dog.

GAIDAR, Arkady (1904–41) Soviet children's novelist. His best known book is *Timur i ego Komanda* ('Timur and his Team') (1940), the story of a group of boys helping the families of soldiers who have gone to the front. The story was filmed, and its popularity led to the formation of 'Timurite'

children's groups throughout the USSR, emulating the deeds in the book.

GAIMAN, Neil (1960–) US-based British novelist, born in Portchester in the south of England, who established himself as a novelist with *Good Omens* (1990), co-written with Terry *Pratchett, after a career as a freelance journalist and writer of short fiction. He then rose to worldwide stardom with his groundbreaking comics series *The Sandman* (1989–96; prequel/sequel series *The Sandman: Overture* launched in 2013) and was confirmed in it with his novel *American Gods* (2001). The overarching themes of his production, in all mediums and formats, from radio to screenplay to novels to comics, are those of the uncanny, of familiar, yet strange occurrences and objects, and of the underlying magic of everyday happenings. His dark humour, fantastical themes, and numerous literary allusions, present throughout his work, have gained him followers and fans by the millions, spanning the written, printed, digital, visual, and academic worlds, and the nickname 'Scary Trousers'. He has published several picture books for younger children, collaborating with artist Dave *McKean on *The Day I Swapped My Dad for Two Goldfish* (1997), *The Wolves in the Walls* (2003), and *Crazy Hair* (2009). With both McKean and Chris *Riddell, he has published parallel editions of the illustrated teen books *Coraline* (2002) and *The *Graveyard Book* (2008). Similarly, two versions were released of *Fortunately, The Milk . . .* (2013), with Riddell and Skottie Young respectively on illustrations. His picture book *Chu's Day* (2013), illustrated by Adam Rex, was bought by more oblivious adults who complained about the simplicity than the intended audience of parents of young children. Gaiman has won the *Newbery Medal, the *Carnegie Medal, Nebula Awards, Hugo Awards, Bram Stoker Awards, and Locus Awards, most of them multiple times. He is a fan of cats.

GAINE, Hugh (1726–1807) New York printer of children's books. He sold juvenile books at the sign of the 'Bible and Crown', though after Independence he dropped the words 'and Crown'. His books resembled John *Newbery's, from whom they were sometimes pirated.

Galahad, Sir In the legends of King *Arthur, the knight marked out by his purity as the one who will achieve the Quest of the Holy *Grail.

GALDONE, Paul (1907–86) Illustrator, born in Budapest, who came to the United States at the age of fourteen. Most of his *picture books are based on folk tales, *fables, or well-known rhymes. Examples are The *House that Jack Built (1962), The *Three Little Pigs (1971), and The History of Mother Twaddle (1975). He also illustrated the *Anatole series by Eve *Titus.

GALLAND, Antoine (1646–1715) French orientalist, the first European translator of the Thousand and One Nights (see ARABIAN NIGHTS' ENTERTAINMENT), under the title Les Mille et Une Nuits. His versions appeared in twelve volumes between 1704 and 1717. His translations, with some stories added from other sources, became the basis for translations into many other languages. His were free translations, often expurgated, and adapted to the French taste for fairy stories created by his contemporary and friend Charles *Perrault, the father of the *fairy tale, with which Galland's Nights have much in common. He worked and travelled in the Middle East, and his translations from Arabic, Turkish, and Persian included an unpublished translation of the Qur'an.

GALLICO, Paul (William) (1897–1976) American author whose first work of fiction was The *Snow Goose (1941); later stories include The Small Miracle (1952), and Flowers for Mrs Harris (1958). All his novels have been read by children; he also produced books specifically for them, including Snowflake (1952), The Day the Guinea-Pig Talked (1963), and Manxmouse (1968).

games-rhymes Verses or chants accompanying games played spontaneously by groups of children in school playgrounds, streets, or other places where they are not being supervised closely by an adult. The rhymes, and the games themselves, are passed on with variations and innovations from one generation to the next. Rhymes are used, for example, to announce the start of a game, to determine which player is to take on the role of chaser or catcher ('Eeny, meeny, miney, mo') (see COUNTING-OUT RHYMES), to taunt the chaser, to announce the occupation of safe territory, and to scare the players before the catcher jumps at them. There are an immense number in existence, and they are always subject to local variation. There are rhymes for every kind of game: seeking, racing, fighting, daring, guessing, pretending. Rhymes and their accompanying games are adapted or devised to fit new circumstances or fashions; many have been based on television programmes.

Children's games in Britain were first examined seriously by Joseph Strutt in Glig-Gamena Angel Deod, or, The Sports and Pastimes of the People of England (1801), though he gave little space to them, and quoted no rhymes. In 1894 and 1898 Alice Bertha Gomme published a two-volume study, The Traditional Games of England, Scotland, and Ireland, which dealt solely with children's games, arranging them in alphabetical order of name and quoting many rhymes. Lady Gomme, wife of a pioneer folklorist, conducted her survey in the belief that children's games were chiefly of interest as survivals of primitive folk customs. Meanwhile in America, William Wells Newell published Games and Songs of American Children (1883, augmented 1903). Newell's book included the tunes of many games-rhymes. He believed, as did Lady Gomme, that the games were a dying custom, and that the rhymes would disappear.

Collectors of the 20th cent. took a very different view. Surveys such as Paul G. Brewster's American Nonsinging Games (1953) and, most notably, Iona and Peter *Opie's Children's Games in Street and Playground (1969) recognize that as old games die, new ones develop. 'There is no town or city known to us', write the Opies, 'where street games do not flourish ...During twenty years' inquiry, we have not met a child who was unable to tell us something interesting.'

Gammage Cup, The (1959) A *fantasy by Carol *Kendall.

Gammer Gurton's Garland An early collection of *nursery rhymes made by Joseph *Ritson, and published in 1783 or 1784 (see GARLAND). The book was divided into two parts, the first consisting of songs and the

second of rhymes, and seventy-nine pieces were included. A revised edition was published in about 1799. In 1810, after Ritson's death, a much enlarged version was issued, probably at the instigation of Francis Douce (1757-1834), a bibliophile and former Keeper of Manuscripts at the British Museum. Douce apparently bought a parcel of Ritson's books at the sale of his effects in 1803, and subsequently added to Ritson's collection of rhymes, writing new discoveries into his own copy of *Gammer Gurton's Garland*. This book and others of Ritson's form the nucleus of the Douce Collection in the Bodleian Library.

The first edition and the reprint of *c*.1799 were the size of a small juvenile book, though there were no *woodcuts to illustrate the rhymes. In contrast, the 1810 edition, though still subtitled 'for the amusement of all little good children', was the size of a pamphlet, and had the appearance of being intended for antiquarians or folklorists.

Gammer Gurton's Story Books A series issued *c*.1845 by Joseph *Cundall. It consisted of a number of old *chapbook tales and *ballads, edited for children by the antiquary W. J. *Thoms under the pseudonym 'Ambrose Merton', or 'Amb Mer'. Titles included *Bevis of Hampton*, *Guy of Warwick*, *Robin Hood*, *Tom Hickathrift*, and *Fair Rosamond*. The series was also issued in an omnibus volume, *The Old Story Books of England* (1845).

Gandalf Wizard in *The *Hobbit* and *The *Lord of The Rings* by J. R. R. *Tolkien.

GANTOS, Jack (1951–) American author who grew up in Florida, the Caribbean, and Norvelt, Pennsylvania. He began writing while still in primary school, but his ambition to become a writer was derailed when he became involved in drug smuggling as a teenager and spent a year in jail. The events of his colourful life are detailed in his autobiography, *Hole in My Life* (2002), which was named a Michael L. Printz Honor Book (*see* MICHAEL L. PRINTZ AWARD). Following his release from prison, Gantos began writing again. His first book, about an incorrigible red cat, *Rotten Ralph* (1976), was written while he was an MA student and illustrated by Nicole Rubel. Its success led to further books and a television series. Gantos' other books feature unusual events and well-drawn characters. The Jack Henry stories, written as diary entries, are based on episodes from his childhood. The Joey Pigza books are about a boy with ADHD. *Joey Pigza Swallowed the Key* (1998) was a National Book Award Finalist and *Joey Pigza Loses Control* (2000) was a Newbery Honor book (*see* NEWBERY MEDAL). Other books about Joey Pigza are *What Would Joey Do?* (2002) and *I Am Not Joey Pigza* (2007). Gantos has promised a fifth and final book about Joey. The semi-autobiographical *Dead End in Norvelt* (2011) is narrated by a character named Jack Gantos. A funny and sweet mystery, the book won the Newbery Medal and the Scott O'Dell Award for Historical Fiction. The sequel, *From Norvelt to Nowhere*, was published in 2013.

gaping wide-mouthed waddling frog, A An accumulative rhyme first printed in *The *Top Book of All*, *c*.1760, and sometimes issued as a separate book, e.g. by *Dean and Munday, with A. K. Newman & Co., *c*.1822, and in a version illustrated by Walter *Crane in 1872.

GARD, Joyce (Joyce Reeves) (1911–93) British author of *historical novels and other stories for children, including *Woorroo* (1961), *The Dragon of the Hill* (1963), and *The Mermaid's Daughter* (1969).

GARDAM, Jane (Mary) (1928–) British novelist, whose first book, *A Few Fair Days* (1971), was a collection of linked stories based on her own childhood. It is very accomplished, but also restrained. By contrast, Gardam's first full-length novel, *A Long Way from Verona* (1971), is exuberant from the first sentence: 'I ought to tell you at the beginning that I am not quite normal having had a violent experience at the age of nine.' The book describes a few months in the life of adolescent schoolgirl Jessica Vye, daughter of a left-wing schoolmaster-turned-clergyman, and a pupil at a girls' school on the north-east coast at Teesside. Jessica's 'violent experience' is being told by a professional literary man that she is 'a writer beyond all possible doubt'—an opinion not at first shared by her teachers. The book, like Jessica herself, is wild and often outrageous, and has many of the qualities of a masterpiece.

Equally accomplished is Jane Gardam's next novel, *The Summer after the Funeral* (1973), an account of what happens to the beautiful and statuesque Athene Price. Athene, too, has had a 'violent experience'—she has come to believe, half-seriously, that she is a reincarnation of Emily Brontë. Similarly Marigold Green, the heroine of *Bilgewater* (1976), is absorbed in

literature—in this case Hardy and Joyce—as she battles through her own stormy adolescence.

These three novels established Jane Gardam as a late-arriving, but leading writer in what might be called the 'second golden age' of English children's literature. Her books attracted considerable admiration—Auberon Waugh called her 'head and shoulders above the normal run'—and the only aspect of her work to attract adverse criticism has been the élitism of her frequent literary references, though it has to be accepted that these are integral to her plots. She brought to children's books, or at least to books for older children and teenagers, a merciless observation which produces such characters as Primrose Clark, the gin-drinking lesbian in *The Summer after the Funeral*, to whom Athene is driven to say: 'You are the ghastliest woman I have ever met in my whole life.'

After *Bilgewater*, Jane Gardam turned largely to adult fiction, but returned to writing for children with *The Hollow Land* (1981), another set of linked stories, this time set in the Cumbrian fells and concerning a holidaying London family and their relations with the 'locals'. In the 1980s and 1990s she also published a few shorter books for younger children, but has to date continued to focus mostly on her adult fiction.

GARDEN, Nancy (1938–2014) American author of over thirty books, although best known for her novel *Annie on My Mind* (1982). Telling the story of how Annie and Liza meet and fall in love, it was one of the first *young adult novels to portray lesbians positively and to this day remains among the most frequently challenged books at schools and libraries in the US. She is also the author of *Hear Us Out!: Lesbian and Gay Stories of Struggle, Progress, and Hope, 1950 to the Present* (2007). She was the recipient of the Robert B. Downs Intellectual Freedom Award in 2000 and the Margaret A. Edwards Award from the American Library Association in 2003 (*see also* BANNED BOOKS; SEXUALITY).

GARDNER, Sally (1953–) An award-winning English author and illustrator who has sold over two million books and whose work has been translated into over twenty-two languages. After a career as a set and costume designer, she started writing and illustrating picture books before her first novel for older readers *I, Coriander* (2005) won the Nestlé Children's Book Prize Gold Award in 2005.

Gardner has continued to write and illustrate books for younger audiences, including her well-known *Magical Children* series and, more recently, the popular *Wings & Co* series, but it is her work for young adults that has received most acclaim. In 2013, her exceptional novel *Maggot Moon* (2012), a modern dystopian fable set in the 1950s whose protagonist is fifteen-year-old dyslexic Standish Treadwell, won both the *Costa Children's Book Award and the *Carnegie Medal. Gardner is herself dyslexic and is a strong public role model, speaking out on dyslexia. Her disturbing novel *The Double Shadow* (2011) also received great critical acclaim and was long-listed for the Carnegie Medal in 2013. Her novel *Tinder* (2013), featuring stunning drawings by David *Roberts, is inspired by the classic Hans Christian *Andersen fairy tale, *The *Tinder Box*, and is set during the Thirty Years War.

GARFIELD, Leon (1921–96) British author of eccentric novels for young readers, chiefly set in the 18th cent. He was born and educated in Brighton. His training in art was interrupted by the Second World War, during which he served in the Medical Corps in England, Belgium, and Germany, experiences he drew on frequently for his writing.

His first published book, *Jack Holborn* (1964), was submitted to the publisher Constable as an adult novel, but an editor, Grace Hogarth, saw a children's story in it, and persuaded him to cut and alter it with this in mind. In fact, like all Garfield's fiction, it cannot be classified as exclusively 'juvenile' or 'adult'. He said: 'Really, what I try to write is that old-fashioned thing the family novel, accessible to the twelve-year-old and readable by his elders.' Even so, it is striking that in a later book, *The Strange Affair of Adelaide Harris*, an attempted rape plays a crucial part in the plot, and there is some blunt conversation about sex between two schoolboys. On the other hand the typical Garfield story has an exuberance of plot that is closer to boys' adventure stories than to conventional adult novels, and children or adolescents always play the leading parts in his novels.

Jack Holborn shows Garfield at his most typical from the opening sentences:

My story must begin when I boarded the *Charming Molly* at Bristol. Before that there's little to tell. My name is Jack, surnamed 'Holborn' after the Parish where I was found: for I had neither father nor mother who'd care enough to leave me a name of their own.

A wild and gory tale, it has touches of *Treasure Island*, though it is marred by a convoluted and sometimes even incomprehensible plot.

Garfield's second book, *Devil-in-the-Fog* (1966), showed comparatively little development from *Jack Holborn*. Again, a search for identity was the theme, the hero in this case being a boy brought up by a group of strolling players and then claimed as the long-lost heir to a dying nobleman. Garfield has said of this recurrent motif in his books: 'I use the quest for identity . . . because I have a passion for secrets and mystery. And the secret and mystery of another individual seems to me the only mystery one can unravel endlessly—and still be uncertain.'

The climax of Garfield's first period as a writer came with his third book, *Smith* (1967), a *Dickens-like story of a young London pickpocket , and the macabre *Black Jack* (1968). Like his first two novels, and a number of his later books, they were illustrated with great skill and sensitivity by Antony *Maitland.

After *Black Jack*, Garfield's work moved in a number of different directions at once. He wrote *Mr Corbett's Ghost*, published in America in 1968 and in the UK (with two other short stories) the following year; this is the tale of an apprentice who procures the death of his hated master, and lives to regret it. The short novel *The Ghost Downstairs* (1972) is an ingenious variation on the Faust theme. The Garfield book to attract most attention during this period was *The *God Beneath the Sea* (1970), a retelling of Greek mythology written in collaboration with Edward *Blishen, which won the *Carnegie Medal; a sequel, *The Golden Shadow*, appeared in 1973. Perhaps his most remarkable achievement in these years was *The Strange Affair of Adelaide Harris* (1971), a fast-moving farce set in Regency Brighton, which begins when two schoolboys at a private academy decide to imitate the ancient Spartans and (just for an experiment) expose the baby sister of one of them on a hillside.

Meanwhile Garfield continued to produce full length 'serious' novels with historical settings—if any of his work can be regarded as entirely serious, for his writing is invariably exuberant and flamboyant. *The Drummer Boy* (1969) is set on a nameless, timeless battlefield; *The Sound of Coaches* (1974) is about the adopted son of a coachman trying to discover who his father really was; *The Prisoners of September* (1975) is set during the September Massacre in France in 1792; and *The Pleasure Garden* (1976) is a blackly comic story about the Mulberry Garden in London, where courting couples are spied on by ragged children for purposes of blackmail. These books were admired and praised, but were not regarded as equalling the achievement of *Smith* and *Black Jack*, while *The Confidence Man* (1978), the story of a group of 18th-cent. Protestants, attracted unfavourable criticism for its convoluted plot. Only with *John Diamond* (1980, published in the US as *Footsteps*), the story of a boy who sets out to right the wrongs committed by his swindler father, did Garfield attract the same degree of enthusiasm as he had with *Smith* and *Black Jack*; this book won the *Whitbread Children's Book Award for its year.

The best of Garfield's full-length novels are outstanding. But if he achieves lasting fame, it may not be for these but for *Garfield's Apprentices*, a cycle of twelve short books published between 1976 and 1978, in which the lives of London apprentices during the late 18th cent. are used as vehicles for Garfield's chief preoccupations: the search for personal identity and the ambiguous nature of good and evil. In this series, style and subject matter are perfectly blended to produce a narrative that is at times almost visionary. He also wrote two volumes of *Shakespeare stories (1985 and 1994).

Garfield's Apprentices A cycle of twelve short, linked novels by Leon *Garfield, about London apprentices in the 18th cent. The series begins with *The Lamplighter's Funeral* (1976), which tells how an old lamplighter acquires as an apprentice a strange wraith-like youth, who, with his light, illuminates the darkest corners of the city and exposes the horrors that lie there. *Mirror, Mirror* (1976) is the story of a country lad, apprenticed to a mirror-frame carver, who is tormented by his master's daughter. The remaining titles in the series, published between 1976 and 1978, are *Moss and Blister, The Cloak, The Valentine, Labour in Vain, The Fool, Rosy Starling, The Dumb Cake, Tom Titmarsh's Devil, The Filthy Beast*, and *The Enemy*. London poverty and social injustice, and, on a more symbolic level, the themes of light and darkness and personal identity, appear again and again in the cycle. The series is illustrated by Antony *Maitland and Faith *Jaques. All twelve stories were reissued in one volume in 1982, without illustrations, as *The Apprentices*.

garland A term used from the 17th to the 19th cents. to denote the gathering into one volume, usually a *chapbook, of a number of

poems or *ballads. *Robin Hood's Garland*, a collection of verse narratives about the outlaw, was a popular chapbook title, and the term 'garland' was also used by Joseph *Ritson when he published *Gammer Gurton's Garland*.

GARNER, Alan (1934-) The most widely discussed British children's writer of the 1960s and 1970s; he was born in Congleton, Cheshire, into a working-class family whose history and craftsmanship he was eventually to celebrate in *The *Stone Book* (1976) and its companion volumes. He spent his childhood in the family's native village, Alderley Edge, whose landscape features again and again in his fiction. He was severely ill during childhood, ('for the first ten years of my life . . . I did very little but lie in bed') and he has spoken of 'the loneliness of an only child who was paralysed . . . I think perhaps part of the reason for writing was to make myself live the life that in some way I was prevented from living as a child.' He won a coveted place at Manchester Grammar School—one of the most intellectually demanding schools in Britain—and in consequence began to suffer a severance of the roots that bound him to his family. He found that he 'shrivelled away' from his family, and his adolescence was spent in learning to reject their values.

Despite his history of illness, Garner enjoyed a remarkable athletic career as a schoolboy. At the age of eighteen he was said by his school to be 'the fastest schoolboy sprinter in Great Britain', and the experience of intense physical effort is described frequently in his writings. He went into the Royal Artillery for National Service, then to Magdalen College, Oxford, to read Classics. He has said of his classical education: 'I was fortunate in that my training was not in English [Literature] . . . I was trained in the schools of Latin and Greek.' The result was that Greek drama became his literary yardstick. In a notable interview (with Aidan *Chambers, published in *Signal* and reprinted in *The Signal Approach to Children's Books*, edited by Nancy Chambers, 1980), Garner also mentions his childhood love of *Dandy and *Beano, and remarks of his own work: 'When I'm really flying, it's Aeschylus writing "Desperate Dan".'

Neil Philip, whose book *A Fine Anger* (1981) is a study of Garner and his work, observes that during his early years Garner was 'possessed by the urge to excel'. As a consequence of reading William Golding's *Lord of the Flies*, which was published in his twenty-first year,

he determined to be a writer. Finding Oxford's attitude to the classics too rarefied, he left the university without taking his degree and returned to Cheshire. There, in the late summer of 1956 when he was twenty-two, he began his first book, *The *Weirdstone of Brisingamen*, eventually published four years later. In 1956 he also married for the first time; he and his wife had three children. He was later divorced, and married again in 1972.

The Weirdstone of Brisingamen and its sequel *The Moon of Gomrath* (1963) would come to be dismissed by some critics as little more than apprentice works, foreshadowing greater stuff to come. And while Garner himself regards them in this light—he has spoken of *The Weirdstone* as 'technically . . . inept' and 'one of the worst books published in the last twenty years'—both novels are written with an energy and conviction almost unique for their period and genre. The fact that they have remained in print testifies to their appeal to readers, and they also helped to inspire a number of new children's writers in Britain, such as Penelope *Lively and Susan *Cooper, to make their own attempts at a blend of the mythical and the realistic.

Garner's next novel, *Elidor* (1965), was again concerned with the intrusion of myth into the modern world, but this time it was the contemporary setting of the story—decaying urban Manchester and its suburbs—which chiefly held Garner's attention. There is a chilling moment when the children, running away from a supernatural horror, discover that their cries for help are being deliberately ignored by the neighbours. Garner has said of this that it was a turning-point in his work, 'the moment of realising that it is a very savage world'.

Elidor, though startling, is an uneven, flawed book; the Elidor myth itself is too lightly sketched in, and the ending seems uncertain. Garner's next novel, *The *Owl Service* (1967), seems by contrast a perfectly structured piece of work, in which myth and reality exactly fit together. This complex novel won Garner the *Carnegie Medal and the *Guardian Children's Fiction Prize.

Garner's *Red Shift* (1973) is an even more difficult work. Again the structure is tripartite, but this time there are three independent stories, operating at different periods of time. *Red Shift* was almost universally attacked for incomprehensibility (the *Times Literary Supplement* called it 'probably the most difficult book ever to be published on a children's list').

On the other hand Aidan *Chambers praised the 'terrible accuracy' with which Garner represented the dialogue of present-day adolescents.

Alongside his major work Garner has produced a number of other books and plays. *Holly from the Bongs* (first published in 1966, with music by Garner's fellow novelist William *Mayne) is a nativity play written for his local school. It was later recast as an opera with music by Gordon Crosse, and in this form was performed in Manchester in 1974 and filmed by the BBC. *The Old Man of Mow* (1967) is an unusual *picture book with text by Garner and photographs by Roger Hill, the story of two boys searching the Cheshire landscape for the Old Man of the title, unaware till the end that he is a curiously-shaped rock. In *The Hamish Hamilton Book of Goblins* (1969), which Garner edited, he brings his sharp ear for language to his retellings of traditional tales. *The Guizer: a Book of Fools* (1975) collects stories about fools and tricksters, some of which Garner rewrites in Cheshire speech. He has also had radio and television plays performed, including dramatizations of *The Owl Service* (Granada Television, 1969) and *Red Shift* (BBC Television, 1978), both of which add to the novels rather than simply 'adapting' them.

Garner is a slow writer. He says of this: 'I have to stay with books until they are ready. I have to cook up a head of pressure inside me until the books appear to burst out because it's better to have them out than in.' *Red Shift* was six years in the writing, and after its publication three more passed before another major work by Garner appeared in print. When it came, it was a story of less than a hundred pages, in large type: *The Stone Book* (1976). Yet it was Garner's greatest achievement so far.

Garner explains that *The *Stone Book Quartet* was not at first meant to be a quartet—only the first book was initially envisaged—and that the idea grew from 'an educational project' discussed with his editor at Collins (Linda Davis), in which it was suggested that Garner would write something for reluctant readers. The eventual outcome was what Garner calls 'the only work which I would permanently want to hold on to'. The four books (of which the remaining three were published in 1977 and 1978) portray members of Garner's own family in their Cheshire village at four points in time, from the mid-19th to the mid-20th cents. They are prose-poems in which the Cheshire speech comes singing and alive from the page, and in which the theme of craftsmanship inspires Garner to create a 'myth' as rich as—and far more striking than—anything in his earlier fiction. Brian *Alderson wrote of them that they 'seem to lie beyond any making'. Garner recognizes that *The Stone Book Quartet* remakes the bonds between himself and his family which he severed in adolescence and brings to an end the tension between him and his origins which can be perceived in virtually all his earlier writing.

Garner's later novels, *Strandloper* (1996) and *Thursbitch* (2003), are for adults. He concluded the *Weirdstone* trilogy in 2012 with *Boneland*.

GARNETT, Eve (1900–91) British author and illustrator. During the Depression of the 1930s she observed working-class social conditions, which gave her the idea for her first and most celebrated book, *The *Family from One End Street* (1937). She subsequently wrote and illustrated two sequels, and also produced two collections of short stories, *In and Out and Roundabout* (1948) and *Lost and Found* (1974).

GATES, Eleanor *See* POOR LITTLE RICH GIRL.

GATTY, Margaret (Scott) (1809–73) British children's writer and editor who was the mother of the celebrated children's novelist Mrs *Ewing. She founded *Aunt Judy's Magazine* in 1866; her books include *Parables from Nature* (1855 onwards).

GAVIN, Jamila (1941–) Anglo-Indian British author who spent her early childhood in India before settling in the UK. After a career in television and radio at the BBC, Gavin began writing after her children were born. This was, in part, to address the lack of *diversity in children's books at the time, which she felt failed to reflect the multi-ethnic and multicultural realities of the UK. Since her first book, *The Magic Orange Tree and Other Stories* (1979), Gavin has written over thirty children's books. *The Surya Trilogy* (1992–97) follows the epic story of a brother and sister across two generations of an Indian Sikh family in the time of Partition. For younger readers, Gavin wrote the well-known *Grandpa Chatterji* series about intergenerational and cross-cultural relationships, which was adapted for television in 1997. She has also written *Tales from India* (2011), a collection of Hindu stories about creation. In 2000, Gavin won the *Whitbread Children's Book Award for *Coram Boy*.

Gawain, Sir A knight of King *Arthur, who plays a part in most of the Arthurian romances. The most remarkable of these is the 14th-cent. alliterative poem *Sir Gawain and the Green Knight*, in which Gawain comes almost unscathed through a long adventure offering many temptations. This poem has several times been modernized or retold for children. Among 20th-cent. versions is a retelling for children in prose by M. R. Ridley (1934), and a verse translation by J. R. R. *Tolkien (1975). By contrast, in *Malory's *Morte Darthur* Gawain is the bitter enemy of Lancelot, who has killed his three brothers; he helps to worsen relations between Lancelot and Arthur, and is killed in Arthur's conflict with Mordred.

GAY, John (1685–1732) Author of *The Beggar's Opera* (1728) who wrote a book of *fables in verse, first published in 1727 as *Fables by Mr Gay*. The fifty fables were all original, and reflected Gay's disappointments at court and his failure to achieve social advancement.

The *Fables* were elegantly illustrated, and soon became part of the diet of English middle-class children. One of them, 'The Hare and many Friends', was sometimes printed as a separate juvenile book. It is referred to by Jane Austen in *Northanger Abbey* as having been learnt in childhood by Catherine Morland.

Gay-Neck, the story of a pigeon (1927) Children's novel by Dhan Ghopal Mukerji. Chitra-griva ('gaily-painted neck') is a domesticated Calcutta pigeon, the pet of the narrator, who trains him as a carrier. He is taken up into the Himalayas, where he becomes lost and has many adventures. In the second part of the book he is used as a carrier for the Indian Army in France during the First World War. The book won the *Newbery Medal. D. G. Mukerji (1890–1936) also wrote eight other books of *animal stories.

GEE, Maurice (1931–) New Zealand writer of mainly *young adult novels. His fantasy and science fiction includes *Under the Mountain* (1979), in which slug-like creatures threaten to destroy the world; the 'O' trilogy: *The Halfmen of O* (1982), *The Priests of Ferris* (1984), and *Motherstone* (1985); and the 'Salt' trilogy: *Salt* (2007), *Gool* (2008), and *The Limping Man* (2010). Other works include *The Champion* (1989), about an African American in 1940s New Zealand, and *The Fat Man* (1995), which, along with *Motherstone*, won

the *Esther Glen Award for the most distinguished contribution to New Zealand literature for young people. In 2002 Gee was awarded the *Margaret Mahy Medal for his lifetime contribution to children's literature.

Gem, The One of the *Harmsworth weekly boys' papers, published by Amalgamated Press. It was founded early in 1907, and initially contained *adventure stories, alternating with *Tom Merry tales by 'Martin Clifford' (Charles *Hamilton). By the end of the first year, Tom Merry (amalgamated with the *St Jim's stories) had taken over entirely, and stories of the exploits of him and his schoolfellows appeared weekly in the paper until its closure at the outbreak of the Second World War.

gender The issue of gender in children's literature has two major, often related aspects: first, the writing and marketing of books for specific genders, and secondly, gender roles and the portrayal of gender in works for young readers.

Once children's literature became accepted as a field, authors and publishers began considering whether boys and girls needed different types of books. Particularly starting in the Victorian and Edwardian eras in the UK, adults thought that since boys and girls were preparing for different futures, they required different literary texts. Books for girls generally had little adventure in them, and were religious or domestic-based works, meant to encourage girls to dedicate themselves to church and home. Louisa May Alcott's *Little Women* (published in two volumes in 1868–9) and *Wives and Daughters* by Elizabeth Gaskell (serialized in 1864–66) are two examples. Books for boys, meanwhile, were meant to encourage them to be adventurous, brave, patriotic, and good providers. Works by Rudyard *Kipling, Jules *Verne, Sir Walter *Scott, and James *Fenimore Cooper were popular.

Even today, although it is recognized that boys and girls should have the same opportunities and options, books are frequently still gender-specific. Texts marketed for female readers still focus on relationships and the home, such as those by Judy *Blume or Jacqueline *Wilson, while texts marketed for boys tend to feature more adventures, as well as dinosaurs, zombies, motor vehicles, and other such items. Anthony Horowitz's *Alex Rider* series (starting in 2000) is typical. In addition, non-literary works such as Conn and Hal Igguldenˈs *The Dangerous Book for Boys* (2006) emphasize gender roles. The

marketing of books for particular audiences is made even more blatant than during earlier eras, as the books tend to be colour-coded (pink for girls, blue for boys) and carefully designed (light, flowered, and featuring people for girls, while the covers of boys' books are more likely to show animals, monsters, rockets, and places).

It is true that more books in recent decades feature active girls, perhaps starting with Beverly Cleary's *Ramona books (published from 1955), and also including Louise Fitzhugh's *Harriet the Spy (1964), works by Katherine *Paterson and Cynthia *Voigt, and, more recently, by Philip *Pullman, Cornelia *Funke, *Avi, and Suzanne *Collins. Nonetheless, even many of these works still emphasize relationships and romance, such as Collins' *Hunger Games series (2008–10) with its love triangle.

There are rare books that subvert gender roles by playing on readers' assumptions of their protagonists' genders—the classic example being The *Turbulent Term of Tyke Tiler (1977); a more recent example is Hayley Long's What's Up with Jody Barton? (2012).

The newest issue related to gender to develop in children's literature is the depiction of intersex, transvestite, transgender, and genderqueer characters (*see also* SEXUALITY). My Princess Boy, which is by Cheryl Kildavos (2011), is a picture book about a boy who likes pink and enjoys wearing tiaras and other princess clothes. While there is no indication that this boy is transgender, in that he seems to identify as a boy and, of course, the title suggests he is and will remain a boy, the book is positive, because he is accepted for who he is and how he likes to dress. Marcus Ewert's 10,000 Dresses (2008) is another picture book, this one explicitly transgender. The main character, Bailey, dreams about beautiful dresses and longs to make them and wear them. However, Bailey's family is not understanding or supportive, because Bailey was declared male at birth. Although Bailey faces some problems, she is still a confident person who believes in herself and who looks elsewhere for support. Some readers might find the ending upsetting, in that there is no resolution with Bailey's family—the only person to be accepting of her is a young friend who lives nearby.

Three of the most remarked-upon *young adult novels on this topic are Luna by Julie Ann Peters (2004), Ellen *Wittlinger's Parrotfish (2007), and Cris Beam's I Am J (2011). Luna is about a transwoman, Liam, who was declared male at birth and wants to be affirmed female and become known as Luna. The novel is told from the point of view of Regan, Luna's younger sister, and Liam/Luna comes across as self-involved and selfish. Wittlinger's book is about Grady, who is declared female, but is male, and it is told from his perspective; while the text sounds didactic at times, it does at least show a broader perspective on trans issues. Beam's I Am J features more diversity than many books for younger readers—J has one Jewish parent and one Puerto Rican Catholic one— and J also has more facets to his life than just his gender. Other recent texts include Beautiful Music for Ugly Children by Kristin Cronin-Mills (2013) and Alex as Well by Alyssa Brugman (2014); the latter is one of the few books to feature an intersex character.

genie A word originally used, with the spelling *génie*, by French translators of the *Arabian Nights, to represent Jinnee, a variation of *jinn. It is also used in English versions of stories from that book, especially the tale of *Aladdin. The *Brass Bottle (1900) by 'F. *Anstey' brings a genie into the modern world, with alarming consequences, as does The Third Class Genie (1975) by Robert *Leeson.

GENLIS, Stéphanie Félicité Ducrest de Saint-Aubin, Comtesse de (1746–1830) French author of works on education and books for children which became popular in England. She acted as governess to the children of the Duc de Chartres, and was his mistress. Her volume of letters on education, which largely followed the ideas of *Rousseau, appeared in English as Adelaide and Theodore (1783); it attacked *fairy stories as containing 'ridiculous ideas' and lacking any 'moral tendency'. Her *moral tales were translated into English as *Tales of The Castle (1785). She also wrote a number of didactic *plays for children, published in English as *Theatre of Education (1781).

Gentle Heritage, The (1893) A novel by Frances E. *Crompton. The Scrope children fear a neighbour, who they suppose is a *bogey because of his black eyeshade. He proves to be a blind man, whose gentleness makes a deep impression on them. The book has occasionally been reprinted.

geography and travel books for children began to appear in Britain as soon as

juvenile publishing became a serious enterprise. In 1737 the London booksellers Edward Littleton and John Hawkins published *The Geography of Children; or, a short and easy method of teaching or learning geography*, translated from a French work by Abbé Nicolas Lenglet du Fresnoy; versions of this remained in print until the early 19th cent. Thomas *Boreman's series of *Gigantick Histories* (1740 onwards) described the 'curiosities' of London, and John *Newbery included Geography in his *Circle of The Sciences* (1745 onwards). In America, Jedediah Morse's *Geography Made Easy* (1784) was the most enduring of the early books on the subject.

Exploration proved a popular topic; accounts of the voyages of Captain *Cook were produced for juvenile readers, and J. H. *Campe's *Discovery of America* and *Polar Scenes* were favourites. Many writers of *moral tales turned their hands to travel stories, e.g. Mrs *Hofland, whose books include *The Young Northern Traveller* (1813), 'being a series of letters from Frederic to Charles, during a tour through the north of Europe', and *Alfred Campbell, the Young Pilgrim* (1825), 'containing travels in Egypt and the Holy Land'. Isaac *Taylor wrote a series of *Scenes . . . for the amusement and instruction of little tarry-at-home travellers*, describing Asia, America, and other lands; these were published between 1818 and 1830. Books of this kind, together with the informative 'Tales' about many countries of the world written by the original *Peter Parley (S. G. *Goodrich), led to the development particularly in America of the *travelogue storybook, which flourished especially during the 1870s and 1880s. Jane *Andrews's *Seven Little Sisters who live on the Round Ball that Floats in the Air* (1861) was another popular American geography book. In England, the publisher Samuel *Clark, partner in the firm of *Darton and Clark, was one of the most prolific writers about English topography for children; his books include *The Book of the United Kingdom, written by Uncle John for his Youthful Friends* (1841) and *The Boy's Book of His Own Country* (?1862). Clark modelled his style on the 'Peter Parley' books, and even wrote a counterfeit Parley, *Tales about Canada, by Peter Parley* (1839).

The modern British children's author Geoffrey *Trease revived the genre of the fictionalized geography book with his *Young Traveller* series, which took its readers to India and Pakistan, England and Wales, and Greece, and was published between 1949 and 1956.

Non-fiction writing for children about the wider world continues to be left mostly to large-format, comprehensively illustrated books, which are wide-ranging and published in considerable numbers and in just about every imaginable presentational style (while suffering, like so much non-fiction, from variable quality and certain unfortunate, and unmerited, associations with curriculum materials). In recent years, a drive to boost children's understanding of the world has increasingly been connected with ideas of *multiculturalism and the celebration of a range of the world's cultures; alongside this, a larger number of books have also begun to introduce ideas of ecology and global citizenship.

Geography Made Easy (1784) By Jedediah Morse, this was one of the earliest, and for long the most popular, of American *geography books. The greater part of it consisted of a description of America; this contained such remarkable statements as that the inhabitants of Connecticut are 'characterised for being intemperately fond of law suits and little petty arbitrations'. As to other lands, it is recorded that in the Friendly Islands the chieftains 'have women sit beside them all night, and beat on different parts of their body until they go to sleep'; and that in China 'the fatter a man is they think him the handsomer'.

George, St Patron saint of England. Very little is known of the historical St George, though it is now generally accepted that he did exist and was probably a soldier martyred in the 4th-cent. persecution of Christians. St George was said to have appeared and helped the crusaders at the battle of Antioch in 1089, and later to have been seen by Richard I, the Lionheart. He became a favourite saint of English warriors, and a focus for growing nationalism and the cult of chivalry. The Order of the Garter was founded under his patronage, *c*.1347, and he replaced St Edward the Confessor as patron saint of England.

The legends associated with St George seem to be of diverse origin. His fight with a *dragon and rescue of a captive maiden may derive from the legend of Perseus and Andromeda. Elements of the story of Alexander the Great, including the magnificent horse, are also among the ingredients. A full narrative of these legends appeared in the 13th-cent. *Golden Legend* by Jacobus a Voragine; *Caxton printed his own *Golden Legend*, based on this, which was immensely popular, and in *broadside ballad form, and in *The *Seven*

Champions of Christendom (1596-7) by Richard *Johnson, the story reached an even wider audience. It supplied characters for the *mummers' play, and was popular reading among children throughout the 17th, 18th, and 19th cents.

Kenneth *Grahame's story *The Reluctant Dragon* (1898) has St George agreeing to let a dragon off with a flesh-wound because the creature wishes to do no one any harm. *An Experiment with St George* (1939) by J. W. *Dunne is a sequel to the traditional story of the saint and the dragon.

GEORGE, Jean Craighead (1919-2012) American author of *animal stories and novels about nature, some of them written with her husband John L. George. They include *Julie of the Wolves* (1972), which won the *Newbery Medal, and *My Side of the Mountain* (1959), a *Robinsonnade about a boy who runs away from his New York home and lives for a year in a tree-house in the Catskills.

George Arthur In *Tom Brown's Schooldays*.

George's Marvellous Medicine (1981) A novel for young readers by Roald *Dahl.

GERAS, Adèle (1944-) With a father in the colonial service, as a child Geras lived in many places around the world before returning home to England. After Oxford University she taught, acted, and sang before turning to writing full-time in 1976, beginning a career of books that cross genres and ages. A writer of great subtlety and style, her best work includes *Troy* (2000) (about the women involved in that famous siege), *Ithaka* (2005) (about those Odysseus left behind), and *Dido* (2009) (a love triangle turning about Aeneas). *Happy Ever After* (aka *The Egerton Hall Trilogy*) (1990) collects three classic, brilliantly reimagined fairy stories.

GERSTEIN, Mordicai (1935-) American author, illustrator, and director of animated films. Gerstein's first published children's illustrations were for his collaboration with Elizabeth Levy on the mystery *Something Queer is Going On* (1971), which became a successful series. As author-illustrator of nearly forty books, his work covers the full age range and a diverse range of topics. He won the *Caldecott Medal in 2004 for *The Man Who Walked Between the Towers* and the Sydney Taylor Book Award in 2005

for *Sholom's Treasure: How Sholom Aleichem Became a Writer*, by Erica Silverman.

GERVAY, Susanne (1951-) Australian children's novelist, now beginning to write picture books. She is most famous for *I Am Jack* (2000), a junior novel on the theme of bullying which nevertheless remains light-hearted and has insight and humour. It has been made into a play from the 14th to the 18th for Young People. Gervay is a tireless worker for the children's book community and received the Lady Cutler Award for Services to Children's Literature in 2007.

Gesta Romanorum (Acts of the Romans) A collection of tales that was popular with readers of all ages from the 14th to the 18th cents. The book is a synthesis of legends, romances, and saints' lives, presented as if it were history. Each tale is set in the time of a Roman emperor. The *Gesta* was compiled from many sources, and was written first in Latin and later translated into English. The earliest version to be printed in England (c.1510-15) was that of Wynkyn de *Worde. The *Gesta* was afterwards reissued many times, and its stories appear in many other works of literature. Among tales found in it are those of King Lear and his daughters, the casket scene in *The Merchant of Venice*, and *Androcles and The Lion*. Each story has an allegorical exposition or 'moral' attached to it.

Getafix In the *Astérix books, the elderly white-bearded druid who brews the magic potion that the Gauls take to give them the superhuman strength needed to fight Julius Caesar's soldiers. In the original French, he goes by the name of Panoramix.

Ghost of Thomas Kempe, The (1973) A comic novel by Penelope *Lively, which won its author the *Carnegie Medal. The meddlesome ghost of a 17th-cent. sorcerer returns to haunt his former home in an Oxfordshire village, and decides that James, a boy now living there, shall be his apprentice.

ghost stories While conventional ghost stories—that is, scary stories of hauntings by the spirits of the dead—are hardly a new form, there are few examples of what can properly be considered ghost stories for children and teenagers before the middle of the 20th cent. This is not to say that children and teenagers were not reading these stories, merely that they were reading adult fiction of this type,

including popular writers such as M. R. James (1862–1936), Sheridan Le Fanu (1814–73), and Edgar Allan Poe (1809–49) (just as, more recently, Susan *Hill's terrifying *The Woman in Black* (1983) has been much read by teens, though not written explicitly for them). Wilde's 'The Canterville Ghost' (1887) and Henry James's *The Turn of the Screw* (1898) have both been popular with young readers, too. A small number of early ghost stories were written specifically for children, however: for instance, one features in William *Howitt's *The Boy's Country-book* (1839), and in America examples appeared in Joel Chandler *Harris's *Nights with Uncle Remus* (1883); and famously, of course, the ghosts of Christmas Past, Present, and Yet to Come, and Jacob Marley are central to *Dickens's *A Christmas Carol* (*see* CHRISTMAS BOOKS); but until the 1950s examples were rather few and far between.

There was a particular flurry of activity in the 1960s, 1970s, and early 1980s in the UK, with some of the best children's writers of the period beginning to take an interest in ghosts, writing or collecting stories on the subject: they include Leon *Garfield (*Mr Corbett's Ghost and other stories,* 1969); Ruth *Manning-Sanders (*A Book of Ghosts and Goblins,* 1968, and *A Book of Spooks and Spectres,* 1969); William *Mayne (*Ghosts, Spooks, Spectres,* 1967, edited by Mayne himself under the name 'Charles Molin', and *Ghosts: an anthology,* 1971); Philippa *Pearce (*The Shadow-Cage and other tales of the supernatural,* 1977); and there are major novels by K. M. *Peyton (*A Pattern of Roses,* 1973, and *Marion's Angels,* 1979); Gene *Kemp (*The Clock Tower Ghost,* 1981); Robert *Westall (*The *Watch House,* 1977); and Joan *Robinson (*When Marnie Was There,* 1967). Many of these were influenced by adult ghost writing, Gothic fiction, and adult horror. More recent children's *horror has used ghosts; and they are a common device in a number of *timeslip novels.

While ghost stories proper—those stories of hauntings intended to chill the reader—continue to be written today (Berlie *Doherty's 2013 novel *The Company of Ghosts,* say, or many stories by Chris *Priestley), ghosts also feature in quite different kinds of book, including light or comic fantasy—see, for example, the work of Eva *Ibbotson, Chris *Riddell's *Goth Girl and the Ghost of a Mouse* (2013) or Penelope *Lively's *The *Ghost of Thomas Kempe* (1973). Ghosts can be drawn as

altogether benevolent presences, too, as in *The *Graveyard Book* (2008), Susan *Cooper's *Ghost Hawk* (2013), Geraldine *McCaughrean's *The Positively Last Performance* (2013), or Roddy Doyle's *Greyhound of a Girl* (2011), all four of these highly inventive modern uses of ghost characters.

Giant Jam Sandwich, The (1972) A classic picture book by John Vernon *Lord, with verses by Janet Burroway, telling the story of the summer in Itching Down when '*four million wasps* flew into town'. To deal with this nuisance, the inhabitants decide to make a giant jam sandwich to use as bait from a loaf of bread the size of a mountain, with butter and jam by the spadeful. When the wasps descend on the jammy bread, helicopters drop a second slice on top, trapping them. The readable verses and in particular Lord's richly coloured ink and crayon illustrations have kept this book popular for over four decades.

giants Recorded in many mythologies as having been the first race of people to inhabit the earth. Most *fairy stories give giants an evil and brutish character, much like the *ogres of French tales; but there is also a tradition of giants being benevolent. One such is Brân the Blessed of *Celtic tradition, while such English hill-figures as the Cerne Abbas Giant, carved in the chalk, seem to indicate a belief in them as god-like and protective beings. Modern fairy tales which show some originality in the treatment of giants include *The Last of the Huggermuggers* (1855) by Christopher Pearce *Cranch, *The Selfish Giant* by Oscar *Wilde (which was published in *The *Happy Prince,* 1888), *Jim and the Beanstalk* (1970) by Raymond *Briggs, and *The BFG* (1982) by Roald *Dahl. Anthologies of giant stories have been edited by Ruth *Manning-Sanders and William *Mayne.

Giant's Heart, The A short story by George *MacDonald, first published in 1863 in the *Illustrated London News* (as 'Tell us a Story'), and often reprinted in collections of his tales. Two children wander into Giantland and find themselves in the house of a giant who eats little children. They learn that the giant's heart is not in his body but is guarded by an eagle on the top of a mountain. With the aid of a tribe of spiders, they obtain the heart, and squeeze a drop of spider-juice upon it, which causes it to shrink, and gives the giant dreadful pain. He promises never to eat children again, but as

his heart is being returned to him he rushes at them with a yell of vengeance—whereupon the boy plunges his knife into the heart and kills the giant.

GIBBONS, Alan (1953–) English author, teacher, poet, educational consultant, and passionate advocate of books and reading. His gritty, realistic, and gripping *young adult books include: the *Legendeer* trilogy, starting with *The Shadow of the Minotaur* (2000), in which mythology and computer games collide; *An Act of Love* (2011), about friendship, extremism, and war; and the deeply unsettling horror series *Hell's Underground* (2007). A brilliant speaker in schools, he is also familiar from TV and radio because of his Campaign for the Book (founded in defence of public and school libraries) and No SATisfaction (authors against 'SATs' testing).

GIBBS, (Cecilia) May (1877–1969) Australian author-illustrator who wrote a number of stories about 'gumnut babies' (small children who supposedly grow on gumnut trees), the best known being her *Snugglepot and Cuddlepie* series (1918 onwards). She drew a newspaper *comic strip, 'Bib and Bub', which ran for over forty years from 1925.

GIBERNE, Agnes (1845–1939) British author of sentimental novels for children, many of which were published by the *Religious Tract Society. The first was *Willie and Lucy at the Sea-side, for very little children* (1868); among those that followed was *Five Little Birdies* (n.d.), the story of a family of orphan children.

Gigantick Histories (1740–3) A series of *miniature books by the pioneer children's publisher and bookseller Thomas *Boreman. The first to be issued was *The Gigantick History of the two famous Giants, and other Curiosities in Guildhall, London* (1740) a book of 112 pages, including two *woodcuts. It was reprinted later the same year, and again in 1741. Boreman, who probably wrote the text himself, had his shop at the Guildhall; the two giants of the title are Gog and Magog, huge figures which stood there. Their history takes up virtually the entire book. A second *Gigantick History*, containing more information about the Guildhall, was published in 1740 and reprinted the following year.

Next, Boreman issued two volumes describing *Curiosities in the Tower of London* (1741). The first of these books contained woodcuts

and descriptions of animals to be seen in the Tower zoo—Boreman had already published, and probably written, *A *Description of Three Hundred Animals* (1730)—while the second included a *ballad, 'The Wolf in Sheeps Cloathing', describing an attempt to steal the Crown Jewels in the reign of Charles II. Other books followed, in the same format: *The History and Description Of the famous Cathedral Of St Paul's, London* (1741), *The History Of St Paul's, Volume the Second, to which is added, an Account of the Monument of The Fire of London* (1741), and *Westminster Abbey . . . by the Author of the Gigantick Histories*, which was published in three volumes in 1743.

In 1742 Boreman published *The History Of Cajanus The Swedish Giant*, an account of Daniel Cajanus, who was born in Finland in 1709 and visited England, where he was displayed by a showman because of his huge size.

Boreman's books seem to have helped to set the style for those of John *Newbery, which began to appear in 1744. The four-volume series *The Curiosities of London and Westminster Described*, published by Newbery's successors from about 1770, was probably suggested by Boreman's publications.

Giglio In *The *Rose and The Ring* by Thackeray.

Giles Gingerbread, *A Little Boy who Lived upon Learning, The Renowned History of* (1764) A small illustrated storybook published, and possibly written, by John *Newbery. The story begins with young Giles being rebuked by his father for trying to jump on to the back of Sir Toby Thompson's coach instead of using the door. 'A poor Man, or a poor Boy may get a coach, if he will endeavour to deserve it. Merit and Industry may entitle a man to any Thing.' The gaffer proceeds to tell the now obedient Giles how Sir Toby himself, by being attentive at school, honest, and industrious, rose from poor errand-boy to partner, and then heir to his benefactor's business. Giles Gingerbread now desires to read, 'that he might become as great a Man as Sir Toby Thompson', and the rest of the book is taken up with lessons in letters (cut out of gingerbread, so that at one point Giles eats up his words), in religion, in morality, and sense.

Gingerbread Man, The A children's folk tale common in English-speaking countries in the 19th cent. A piece of gingerbread is baked in the shape of a man, with currants for eyes. It escapes from the kitchen and runs away from

the house and down the road, being pursued by all whom it passes. Each time it meets someone it boasts of those from whom it has already got away, adding 'And I can outrun you too-o-o!' At last it meets a fox, who pretends to be deaf and lures the Gingerbread Man very close so as to hear what it says— and then eats it up. This is the essence of the story as recorded, under the title *Johnny Cake*, in **English Fairy Stories* (1890). In most other versions the Gingerbread Man meets his end while being carried across a stream by the fox.

Girl Guides British name for the female equivalent of **Boy Scouts. The Girl Guide movement was set up by Lord *Baden-Powell with his sister Agnes, and was well established by 1914. After the First World War the name *Brownies was used for the junior branch; this was taken from *The *Brownies and Other Tales* (1870) by Mrs *Ewing. In America, the Girl Scouts were founded in 1912 in Savannah, Georgia, by Mrs Juliette Gordon Low (1860–1927). The first British author to write Girl Guide novels was Dorothea *Moore.

Girl of the Limberlost, A (1909) A popular *girls' story by the American novelist Gene Stratton *Porter, set in the Limberlost Swamp in Indiana. Elnora Comstock, daughter of an unloving widowed mother, manages to pay for her own high school education by selling moths which she has collected in the swamp. The book is an unusual mixture of detailed *natural history and melodrama.

Girl Scouts *See* GIRL GUIDES.

Girls' Friend One of the most popular *Harmsworth juvenile papers, published between 1899 and 1931. It contained stories for working girls, with titles like 'Only a Barmaid', 'Madge o' the Mill', and 'Only a Laundry Girl'. Its companion papers were *Girls' Reader* (1908–15) and *Girls' Home* (1910–15), and its opposite number was *Boys' Friend* (1895–1927), which in turn had its companions.

Girl's Own Paper, The Companion magazine to *The *Boy's Own Paper*. It first appeared almost exactly a year after the *BOP*, in January 1880, and its format and price were the same. The initial number included a serial story of elopement and reconciliation, an account of the girlhood of Queen Victoria (complete with full-page portrait, suitable for framing), a brief history of ladies' fashion, competitions, and articles on sewing and cooking. There was much encouragement of

duteous behaviour and home-making skills. But whereas the age limit for entrants in *BOP* competitions was sixteen, for girls it was twenty-five; the *Girl's Own Paper* was thus never as clearly a juvenile publication as its partner, and its contents increasingly reflected this. It survived until 1965, by which time it had the title *Heiress*.

Selections from the *GOP*'s advice column ('Answers to Correspondents') have been published in *Oh, No Dear! Advice to Girls a Century Ago* (1982), edited by Roy Hindle, and *Great Grandmama's Weekly: A Celebration of the Girls' Own Paper, 1880–1901* (1988), edited by Wendy Forrester.

girls' stories These stories were pioneered in America, early writers in the genre there being Elizabeth Stuart Phelps Ward, whose **Gypsy Breynton* books appeared in 1866-7, and 'Sophie *May', who was writing her 'Little Prudy' series during the 1860s. Two juvenile classics, **Little Women* (1868) and **What Katy Did* (1872), were chiefly concerned with girls, and a few decades later there was a fashion for stories about bright, energetic, jolly girls with a passion for setting the world to rights. Kate Douglas Wiggin's **Rebecca of Sunnybrook Farm* (1903), Jean Webster's **Daddy Long-Legs* (1912), and Eleanor Hodgman Porter's **Pollyanna* (1913) were among the most popular of these. Gene Stratton Porter's *A *Girl of the Limberlost* (1909) and Eleanor Gates's **Poor Little Rich Girl* (1912) were two other American successes from this period. Australia began to produce some striking girls' books at about the same time, the best examples before 1914 being Louise Mack's **Teens* (1897) and the early **Billabong* books by Mary Grant *Bruce.

In Britain the girls' story began to establish itself as a popular genre in the 1880s, with the arrival of L. T. *Meade and Evelyn *Everett-Green (Meade virtually created the girls' *school story, set in boarding establishments for young ladies). Though they and other girls' authors of the period were writing at a time when female emancipation was a burning topic, they gave no real support to it and implied that higher education and other such activities of the 'modern girl' or 'new woman' were really just an unusual prelude to married domesticity.

*The *Girl's Own Paper*, founded in 1880, attempted to generate the same excited devotion in its readers as did *The *Boy's Own Paper*, but seemed uncertain whether to aim at girls

or young women, and included many articles on housekeeping and advice to servants. Hutchinson's *Girls' Realm,* established in the 1890s, set out to be more progressive, but by the time it ceased publication in 1914 had become thoroughly conformist, and was publishing stories attacking the suffragettes and praising domestic bliss.

In 1904 there first appeared on a title page the name of the British author Angela *Brazil. As Mary Cadogan and Patricia Craig wrote in *You're a Brick, Angela!* (1976), the definitive study of the British girls' story, 'The era of the young lady had at last come to an end ... Angela Brazil's girls [were] "a rosy, racy, healthy, hearty, well-grown set of twentieth-century schoolgirls."' Hockey sticks and bosom friendships dominated the Brazil novels, and the dialogue was characterized chiefly by slang: '"Did you have jolly hols?" "Absolutely ripping, thanks."'

During the same period, *Harmsworth's were publishing three papers for a young working-class female readership: *Girls' Friend* (1899–1931), *Girls' Reader* (1908–15), and *Girls' Home* (1910–15). Other publishers followed the Harmsworth lead, and brought out their own papers for factory and shop girls, in which *Cinderella*-type rags-to-riches stories and romantic novelettes predominated.

The formation of the *Girl Guides shortly before the First World War produced a sub-genre of girls' stories of its own, beginning with Dorothea *Moore's *Terry the Girl Guide* (1912). Akin to this was the American *Camp Fire Movement.

The British girls' school story reached its peak (in quantity, though not quality) between the two World Wars. Dorita Fairlie *Bruce created her '*Dimsie', 'Nancy', and 'Springdale' books, and Elinor *Brent-Dyer produced the long-lived '*Chalet School' series. Cadogan and Craig wrote of these books: 'The tendency ... is always to gravitate towards the average: no one is seriously intellectual or completely stupid: no one is ruthless or unreformably *bad.'*

In contrast, certain British girls' books and magazines had a different aim. Between the wars, Harmsworth's Amalgamated Press began to publish a fresh series of girls' papers, most notably *The *School Friend* (1919–40, latterly as *Schoolgirl),* in whose pages *Bessie Bunter appeared. These papers also featured such heroines as the girl pilots 'Kit and Joan Fortune, the intrepid Flying Sisters', and rags-to-riches stories by Horace Phillips, such as *Only A Scholarship Girl.*

Two new types of British girls' story were born in the 1930s, the *pony story and the *career novel; there was also a fashion for girl *detectives. The Second World War had little immediate effect on girls' fiction, apart from producing the character of 'Worrals of the WAAF', created by W. E. *Johns, the *Biggles author; she made her first appearance in the *Girl's Own Paper* in 1940. Enid *Blyton followed with two school series somewhat in the Brazil mould, *Malory Towers* and *St Clare's,* both of them unremarkable in everything but their huge and enduring popularity.

The 1950s saw the beginning of a general improvement in British children's fiction, leading to a decline in the number of books written specifically for girls. Writers such as Nina *Bawden, Jane *Gardam, and Penelope *Lively were, in the words of Cadogan and Craig, presenting 'heroines who are complex, unaccountable, capable of irony, judgement, self-realization'.

In America the *Stratemeyer Syndicate published books for girls including the hugely successful *Nancy Drew girl detective series (from 1930), but for much of the 20th cent. the *family story was a far more popular genre there. However, such novels by Judy *Blume as *Are You There, God? It's Me, Margaret* (1970) and *Forever* (1975) were targeted firmly at a female readership, and paved the way for a movement of writing for older children and younger teens that dealt with what were seen as specifically girl-centred concerns—a direct corollary of the 'chick lit' phenomenon in the adult market, though often written to a higher standard. Writers like Meg *Cabot, Sarah *Dessen, Ann Brashares, and Maureen *Johnson in the US (at least in some of their books), and Louise *Rennison, Joanna Nadin, and Cathy Cassidy in the UK continue this trend (arguably so does Jacqueline *Wilson, who tends to write female protagonists for an overwhelmingly female readership); the result is a flood of books for children and teenagers with pink and pastel covers (and glitter for the young ones), presumably to the delight of marketing departments everywhere; but many of these writers are producing more interesting books than their packaging suggests, and they are often done a disservice by pigeonholing them reductively for readers of one gender to the exclusion of the other (*see also* GENDER).

Giver, The (1993) The award-winning *dystopian novel by Lois *Lowry. Jonas is twelve, growing up in an apparently utopian society that has embraced 'sameness' and obliterated

deep emotion. Coming of age, Jonas is chosen to take on the role of Receiver of Memory, in other words to hold all memory of what went before. But the memories change how he perceives his ultra-controlled world and put him in touch with The Giver, the previous Keeper, under whose tutelage he finds happiness and, eventually, freedom. Personal freedom remained the subject of the sequels, *Gathering Blue* (2000), *Messenger* (2004), and *Son* (2012). A flashy, superficial film adaptation came out in 2014.

Giving Tree, The (1964) A picture book by American author and illustrator Shel *Silverstein. Accompanied by childlike black-and-white drawings, it tells the story of the relationship between a boy and the female tree who offers shade and a branch for a swing; then, as the boy grows up, apples to sell, branches to build a house, and her trunk to build a boat, until finally only a stump is left. A multimillion seller, it has nevertheless been criticized by many for what they see as its message of equating good mothering with martyrdom.

Glass Mountain, The *See* BLACK BULL OF NORROWAY, THE.

Glastonbury A Somerset town long associated with King *Arthur. When the antiquary John Leland visited Glastonbury during the 1530s, he saw in the Abbey a tomb of black marble, where bones supposed to be Arthur's had been reinterred. Another account of the tomb records its inscription as: 'Hic jacet Arturus, rex quondam, rexque futurus' ('Here lies Arthur, once the king, and the future king'). This suggested the titles of both T. H. *White's cycle of Arthurian novels, *The *Once and Future King* and Philip *Reeve's *Here Lies Arthur*.

GLEESON, Libby (1950–) Once best known for her books for younger readers, Gleeson is now acknowledged as an award-winning picture-book author and is writing and teaching in this category. Her writing is highly-regarded—in 2011 she received a Special Award from New South Wales Premier's Literary Awards and in 2013 she won the Australian Prime Minister's Literary Award for Children's Fiction for her older-readers novel, *Red* (2012), a vivid, layered, and gripping mystery about a girl who has lost her memory after a cyclone.

A tireless advocate for writers, she became a member of the Order of Australia (AM), 'for service to literature as an author and as an advocate for the development of literacy

and learning in schools, as a mentor to young writers, and through a range of executive roles with professional literary organisations'. Gleeson was awarded the Lady Cutler Award in 1997 and the *Dromkeen Medal in 2011.

Clancy and Millie and the Very Fine House (2009), a heart-warming story about making friends when you move to a new house, won the Patricia Wrightson Prize for Children's Literature and was the 2010 CBCA Book of the Year: Early Childhood.

Banjo and Ruby Red (2013) shows a warm relationship between the dog Banjo and Ruby, one of the chickens he herds into the pen each night.

In writing, Gleeson often focuses on social issues, emotions, and problems associated with growing up, usually in the context of family life. Her work has consistently received good reviews and many of her books have won awards. Her most famous picture book is *The Great Bear* (1999), shortlisted for the *CBCA Picture book of the Year in 2000 and winner of the *Bologna Ragazzi Award in the Fictions for Infants category in 2000, the only time this award has been given to an Australian title. This is the story of a dancing bear, set free, and the story resonates with powerful emotion and themes of freedom.

GLEITZMAN, Morris (1953–) Australian novelist, born in England, who emigrated to Australia in 1969. His books range from laugh-out-loud humour to searingly painful subjects such as teenage cancer and the Holocaust. The opening of his novel *Bumface* is surely one of the funniest in children's literature. *Two Weeks with the Queen* (1990) is about a boy, Colin Mudford, whose younger brother Luke has terminal leukaemia. Colin decides that if only he can meet the Queen, she can put him in touch with the best cancer doctor in the world, who will be able to save his brother. In *Blabber Mouth* (1993), eleven-year-old Rowena Batts has trouble making friends at school, because of having a highly embarrassing father. Inspired by his own Jewish background, Gleitzman has also written a series of four books about the Holocaust: *Once* (2006), *Then* (2009), *Now* (2010), and *After* (2012) (*see* ONCE).

GLIORI, Debi (1959–) award-winning British writer and illustrator of (mostly) picture books, including *The Trouble with Dragons* (2008), *The Scariest Thing of All* (2011), *Dragon Loves Penguin* (2013), and *What's the*

Time, Mr Wolf? (2012), which is inspired by the playground game and draws on classic *nursery rhymes for its cast of characters. Perhaps Gliori's best known picture book is the delightful *No Matter What* (1999), a reassuring story of a little fox who worries that his mother will not love him forever.

Gobbolino *See* WILLIAMS, URSULA MORAY.

Goblin Market *and other poems* (1862) By Christina *Rossetti, with frontispiece and title page by her brother Dante Gabriel Rossetti. It takes its title from the first poem in the book, the story of two sisters, Laura and Lizzie, who hear the tempting cry of fruit-selling *goblins as they come down the lane. Laura succumbs, buys the fruit and eats it, but only longs for more; and now she cannot hear the goblins' cry or get more of their wares. She pines away and is near death. Lizzie, against all her inclinations, seeks out the goblins and allows them to press their fruits upon her, though she will not open her mouth to taste them. The juices run down her skin, and she hurries home to her sister. Laura licks the juices off her, and is purged of her longing, recovering her health.

Christina Rossetti herself denied that the poem was an allegory. In recent times, however, the poem has been variously interpreted as an expression of feminist politics, a Christian allegory, a critique of Victorian marriage, and of a burgeoning commercial culture; nevertheless its fantastic imagery and fast-paced rhythm have also been enjoyed by children. An edition of 1933 has illustrations by Arthur *Rackham.

goblins Mythical beings in *fairy stories, generally regarded as malevolent towards humans. The word *gobelyn* or *goblyn* is recorded in English from the 14th cent., and has been thought to be derived from a Greek word describing the wicked spirits invoked by rogues. By Shakespeare's day, if not before, *goblin* seems to have meant unequivocally a malevolent spirit ('Be thou a spirit of health or goblin damn'd', *Hamlet* i. iv), and though *hob-goblin* was sometimes used for a better-natured class of *fairy, this was not always so; *Bunyan, in his most famous hymn, couples 'hobgoblin' with 'foul fiend'. In 1862 Christina *Rossetti, in *Goblin Market* describes goblins who take the shapes of various animals, and who press seductive and dangerous fruit on human purchasers. In 1871 George *MacDonald gave goblins an important role in *The *Princess and the Goblin*, perhaps drawing on

the tradition of the earth-dwelling Dark Elves of the Icelandic *Eddas, and describing them as subterranean creatures who mine for precious metals, and who have distorted human features. This portrayal of goblins was imitated to some extent by J. R. R. *Tolkien in *The *Hobbit* (1937), though in his later work *The *Lord of The Rings* he coined the word 'Orcs' for such creatures.

See also *The Hamish Hamilton Book of Goblins* (1969), edited by Alan *Garner.

God Beneath the Sea, The (1970) A retelling of Greek mythology by Leon *Garfield and Edward *Blishen, illustrated by Charles *Keeping; a winner of the *Carnegie Medal. The book deals chiefly with the birth and conflicts of the gods. It has been severely criticized for its lush language, but has had many child admirers. A sequel, *The Golden Shadow* (1973), centres on the dealings of the gods with men.

GODDEN, (Margaret) Rumer (1907–98) British novelist who wrote a number of children's books whose protagonists are *dolls, beginning with *The Dolls' House* (1947), which as Frank *Eyre has observed 'brilliantly succeeds in depicting adult situations and conflicts'. Another of her doll stories is *Impunity Jane* (1954), in which a doll gets into the hands of a gang of boys.

GODWIN, William (1756–1836) and his second wife **Mary Jane** (1766–1841) Publishers of many early 19th-cent. children's books. William Godwin also wrote and edited a number of juvenile works, either pseudonymously or anonymously.

Godwin was the son of a Dissenting minister, and was for a time himself a Nonconformist preacher, but by the time he was 30 he had begun to earn a living (usually meagre) as a writer in London. His *Political Justice* (1793) established him as a radical philosopher; he also wrote the remarkable novel *Caleb Williams* (1794), half thriller and half polemic against the tyranny of the rich. In 1796 he began to live with Mary *Wollstonecraft, whose *Original Stories from Real Life* had appeared in 1788, and who had tried to drown herself after the break-up of her relationship with Gilbert Imlay, by whom she had a daughter. She and Godwin both disapproved of marriage, but when she became pregnant by him she agreed to be his wife; she died shortly after the birth of the child, Mary, who eventually eloped with Shelley and wrote *Frankenstein*.

Godwin was left with his own daughter and with Fanny, the child of the Imlay–Wollstonecraft affair. After several attempts to find a second wife he married, in 1801, Mrs Mary Jane Clairmont. She had two children of her own, and another was shortly born to her and Godwin. He now had five children to support, and was often short of money. In 1804 he seems, though the evidence is rather thin, to have begun work for the children's publisher *Tabart as the editor of the series *Popular Stories, which included tales from the *Arabian Nights and *Perrault and one of the earliest printed versions of *Jack and The Beanstalk. It may, on the other hand, have been Mrs Godwin who undertook the work. Perhaps this venture suggested to the Godwins the idea of setting up in the juvenile book business. In 1805 they opened a shop in Hanway Street, Soho, which they named 'The Juvenile Library'. Here they began to publish children's books, at first under the name of their manager, Thomas Hodgkins, Godwin's own reputation being unsuitable for a children's publisher.

Their first publication was *Fables Ancient and Modern* (1805) by 'Edward Baldwin', a pseudonym for Godwin himself. In the same year they also issued a comic poem based on the nursery rhyme The *Queen of Hearts; this was probably the work of Charles *Lamb, who had been introduced to Godwin by Coleridge in 1800. Lamb disliked Mrs Godwin, but nevertheless was glad enough to accept commissions from her, the first—and best—result being *Tales from Shakespear (1807). Other Lamb books followed; meanwhile 'Edward Baldwin' contributed a *History of England, for the use of schools and young persons* (1806), while 'Theophilus Marcliffe' (another disguise for Godwin himself) wrote The *Looking-Glass* (1805), which was an account of the early life of the artist William *Mulready, and a *Life of Lady Jane Grey* (1806). Other pseudonymous Godwin books published by the firm included The *Pantheon* (1806), *Dramas for Children*, a collection of stories published in 1809, histories of Greece and Rome, and a 'New Guide to the English Tongue', issued in various forms as a part of other school-books. Godwin's ten-year-old daughter Mary contributed a humorous poem based on some verses by Dibdin, *Mounseer Nongtongpaw,* which was published by the Juvenile Library in 1808.

The publishing business did well enough at first for the Godwins to move in 1807 to a larger shop, 41 Skinner Street, Holborn. The name of 'M. J. Godwin' now appeared on title pages. Mrs Godwin continued to print books by the Lambs, and in 1814 she issued the first English version of The *Swiss Family Robinson,* translated from the German probably by Godwin himself.

By this time the firm was less prosperous; printing and binding costs were considerable and booksellers were tardy in paying for what they bought. In 1822 Godwin became bankrupt. His unhappy marriage and his constant need to borrow money from his friends destroyed most of his self-respect. Mrs Godwin continued to publish children's books from an address in the Strand during the 1820s, but Godwin himself seems to have had little to do with the business. His last major work was a *History of the Commonwealth of England,* published in four volumes between 1824 and 1828.

Goggle-eyes (1989) A novel by Anne *Fine which won her the *Carnegie Medal and the *Guardian Chidren's Fiction Prize. When Helen runs out of the classroom, Kitty is sent to help her; sitting in the lost property cupboard, Kitty tells the story of Goggle-eyes, her name for the man taking the place of her father. The process is a journey not just for Kitty but for the reader as well. *Goggle-eyes* explores a situation familiar to many young people—a parental divorce followed by the arrival of a step-parent. Though the background reflects its 1980s setting, Fine's intelligent and humorous treatment ensures its continued relevance and accessibility.

Going Solo See Boy.

Golden Age, The (1895) By Kenneth *Grahame, a book of short stories with autobiographical overtones, describing the daily amusements and experiences of five brothers and sisters living in a large house in the country.

In a prologue, the narrator looks back to his childhood and condemns the adults (the 'Olympians') who ruled over it as 'hopeless and incapable creatures', unable to understand or participate in childish pleasures, and who also get little fun out of their own way of life. The children are perpetually contrasted with these adults. Among the most memorable stories in the book are 'A White-washed Uncle', in which a visiting relative proves to dislike the Olympians as much as do the children, and 'The Finding of the Princess', in which the narrator (as a small boy) wanders into the garden of a great house and surprises

two lovers, whom he assumes to be a fairy-tale Princess and her Prince. The book ends with Edward, the eldest, leaving home to go to boarding school. A second volume containing similar pieces, *Dream Days*, appeared in 1898.

Both books were received rapturously by the critics and the public, and together they made Kenneth Grahame's reputation, so much so that when *The *Wind in the Willows* appeared in 1908, it was felt at first to be a disappointment by comparison with them. However, they are little known now to modern readers. The illustrations by E. H. *Shepard, first issued in 1928, certainly attract child readers, but the books were intended for adult readers, and they present not a child's-eye view of the world but an adult's perception and interpretation of that view. They seem to have contributed to a shift in attitudes towards children, and so paved the way for the great children's writers of the Edwardian period.

Golden Compass, The US title for the first book in the *His Dark Materials* trilogy.

Golden Goose, The A *fairy story collected by the *Grimms. Three sons set off into the forest, in turn. The elder two refuse refreshment to an old man, but the youngest, Dummling, shares food and drink with him, and is rewarded by finding a goose with feathers of pure gold. He stays the night at an inn, and when the host's daughters try to steal a feather from the goose, they stick fast to it. Next day he sets off again, and they are obliged to run after him, still stuck to the goose. Other characters also find themselves stuck fast to the girls. The procession arrives in a city, where a king has offered his daughter's hand to the first person who can make her laugh— which she never does. The princess catches sight of the procession and roars with laughter. Dummling claims her hand, but is obliged to get the old man from the forest to help him perform three apparently impossible tasks before he finally gains it and can live happily with the princess.

Golden Key, The A short story by George *MacDonald, first published in *Dealings with the Fairies* (1867). A small boy (Mossy) finds a golden key at the end of the rainbow, and sets off in search of the lock to which it belongs. Meanwhile a girl (Tangle), neglected by the servants who are bringing her up, is drawn out of her house by the fairies and led by a strange creature, a fish which flies through the air, to the house of a beautiful lady who says

that her name is Grandmother. Here the boy and girl meet, and Grandmother sends them both off to look for the keyhole. On their quest they age very fast, and years pass in what seems days. Mossy at last discovers the key-hole, and, after passing through death into eternal life, they ascend into 'the country whence the shadows fall'.

The story, which is MacDonald's greatest flight of the imagination, is susceptible of many interpretations; but MacDonald was not an allegorist, and it is doubtful whether he intended it to have any specific 'meaning'. It has sometimes been reprinted as a separate book; an edition of 1967 has illustrations by Maurice *Sendak and an afterword by W. H. Auden.

Golden Snitch In the *Harry Potter books, the small, winged golden ball both teams are attempting to capture during a game of *quidditch.

Goldilocks and the Three Bears *See* THREE BEARS, THE.

GOLDING, William *See* LORD OF THE FLIES.

GOLDSMITH, Oliver (?1730–74) Poet, play-wright, and essayist, friend of Johnson and Swift and their circles, and dubbed by Horace Walpole 'an inspired idiot'. From 1760 he was associated with the publisher John *Newbery and his successors, and was one of the writers employed to contribute to Newbery's children's books. Goldsmith's finances were always in disarray; Newbery rescued him by offering regular payment and accommodation with one of his relatives. Later he took him into his own country house at Islington, paid for his keep, and managed all his money. In return, Goldsmith began by writing articles for Newbery's periodical the *Public Ledger*; later he contributed to *The Art of Poetry on a New Plan* and other educational books, wrote *The *History of England* in a series of letters from a nobleman to his son (1764), and was responsible for much of the text of Newbery's edition of *Plutarch's Lives* (1762–3). There are arguments in favour of his having written or partly written *Goody Two-Shoes* (1765). Touches characteristic of him are often seen in *Mother Goose's Melody*.

Goldsmith's 'Elegy on that Glory of her Sex, Mrs Mary Blaize' was issued as a children's illustrated book by John *Harris in 1808, and his 'Elegy on the Death of a Mad Dog' by T. Hodgson in 1810. Both poems were made

into *picture books by Randolph *Caldecott, in 1885 and 1879 respectively.

golliwog A type of doll invented by the artist Florence K. *Upton, in a picture book published in 1895, which proved to be the first of a 'golliwogg' series. Later golliwog stories include the 'Rufty Tufty' tales by Ruth Ainsworth. The derogatory nature of the word has since come to be recognized, and its use—and the dolls and stories associated with it—are today generally held to be unacceptable.

Gollum In *The *Hobbit* and *The *Lord of the Rings* by J. R. R. *Tolkien.

good manners *See* BOOKS OF COURTESY.

Good Master, The (1935) A novel by Kate *Seredy.

Goodnight Moon (1947) A classic picture book for the youngest children, with a simple rhyming text by Margaret Wise *Brown and bold pictures by Clement Hurd (1908–88), alternating between colour and black-and-white. A gentle bedtime story, it takes the child through a series of goodnights: goodnight moon, goodnight light and the red balloon, goodnight kittens, goodnight mittens. The colour illustrations begin brightly, dimming as the book progresses, as the little rabbit snuggles into bed and is lulled to sleep. *Goodnight Moon* has become one of the most ubiquitous of all picture books in the US, and achieved some popularity elsewhere, too. Recent parodies include 2011's *Goodnight iPad*.

Goodnight, Mr Tom (1981) Taking the unpromising ideas of maternal child abuse and the Second World War, Michelle *Magorian somehow conjured up one of children's literature's most moving and readable accounts of friendship. It can appeal to both children and adults, though it is usually the adults who are most unsettled by the subject matter. A young evacuee, William, ends up in a village called Little Weirwold and in the care of a grumpy loner, Mr Thomas Oakley. The boy believes himself to be full of sin, the old man sees a youngster covered in bruises, and from that starting point the story unfolds. Uplifting, sad, funny, joyful, this is a modern classic.

GOODRICH, Samuel Griswold (1793–1860) American author and publisher, the original *Peter Parley. He developed a new style of *book of instruction which was notable for its simplicity, readability, and attractive presentation; the information was set out in chatty style, and the books were generously illustrated. They were immensely successful in America and were soon being pirated and imitated in Britain, where other writers and publishers appropriated the name 'Peter Parley' for themselves.

Goodrich wrote in his autobiography:

Do not children love truth? If so, was it necessary to feed them on fiction? Could not History, Natural History, Geography, Biography, become the elements of juvenile works, in place of fairies and giants, and mere monsters of the imagination?

In 1826, he established himself in Boston as a publisher and author, and the next year began a project of 'making an improvement in books for the young', beginning with *The *Tales of Peter Parley about America*. The book's narrator, supposedly 'a kind-hearted old man', described as 'gray and lame' (Goodrich himself had walked with a stick since a riding accident in 1821), may have acquired his name from Hannah More's tract *Parley the Porter*, though according to Goodrich's daughter it was derived from the French verb *parler*.

After a few months the book began to be in demand all over America, and from then on until his death Goodrich turned out 'Parley' books on the history of Greece and Rome, on trades, animals, biblical geography, astronomy, mythology, and a host of other subjects. By 1856 he could claim the authorship or editorship of 116 Peter Parley titles, and a total sale of seven million copies of all his works in America alone. He worked for up to 14 hours a day, sometimes employing other writers, including Nathaniel *Hawthorne and Hawthorne's sister Elizabeth, to provide material for him. A periodical edited by him, *Parley's Magazine,* began to appear in 1833, and he later founded another *magazine, called *Merry's Museum*. He had no connection, however, with the British *Peter Parley's Magazine*.

By this time imitations of the Parley books and piracies of the real thing were being produced in England, notably by the publisher Thomas Tegg. When Goodrich was in London in 1832 he called on Tegg and, instead of picking a quarrel, signed a contract with him to provide new Parley books for Tegg himself, in return for proper payment. (Goodrich, always a businessman, took several of the Parley imitations home with him and published the two he liked best.) But Tegg failed to keep the terms of the contract—though he later handed £400 to Goodrich—and he and others

continued to issue unauthorized Parley books in Britain. Goodrich was especially incensed when British versions portrayed Parley as a loyal British sailor, for the real Peter Parley had served as a militiaman in the 1812 war between Britain and America.

In 1850 Goodrich was appointed US Consul at Paris; while there he continued to produce Parley books and issued several children's volumes on the same lines in French. Ten years later, after returning to America, he died of a heart attack, having made his name, or at least his pseudonym, known to innumerable children on both sides of the Atlantic.

The Peter Parley books were not, however, universally admired. In England, Sir Henry *Cole deplored the fact that they had displaced fairy stories and other imaginative writings; as a result he initiated his 'Felix Summerly' *Home Treasury series, which reprinted such tales. This, in turn, roused the resentment of Goodrich, who in his autobiography denounced Cole's books, as well as *Halliwell's work in collecting nursery rhymes and folk tales.

Good Words for the Young A *magazine for children which ran as a monthly from 1868 until 1877 (by which time its title had changed to *Good Things for the Young of All Ages*). The first editor was Norman Macleod, who already edited the adult *Good Words*. He was a friend of George *MacDonald, who contributed *At the Back of the North Wind* as a serial in the magazine's first year, illustrated by Arthur *Hughes. MacDonald himself briefly took over as editor in the second year of publication, and his *Ranald Bannerman's Boyhood* was also serialized in the magazine. Among the other eminent writers who contributed was Charles *Kingsley, with his series 'Madam How and Lady Why'. *Good Words for the Young* was ambitious; it was sixty-four pages long and its standard of illustration was impressive. It was notable, too, for its particularly broad-minded Christian stance.

Goody Two-Shoes A children's story, one of the most successful publications of John *Newbery, published in 1765 under the full title *The History of Little Goody Two-Shoes; Otherwise called, Mrs Margery Two-Shoes. With the Means by which she acquired her Learning and Wisdom, and in consequence thereof her Estate*. The book was illustrated with one fine engraved frontispiece, and numerous crude *woodcuts.

The title-page displays the humour characteristic of Newbery's productions: 'See the Original Manuscript in the Vatican at Rome, and the Cuts by Michael Angelo.' The introduction contains political sentiments close to those of Oliver *Goldsmith's *The Deserted Village*, thus providing some evidence in support of Goldsmith's authorship of *Goody*. The heroine's father, Meanwell, is a tenant farmer harassed off his land by a tyrannical squire: 'Ah my dear Reader, we brag of Liberty, and boast of our Laws; but the Blessings of the one, and the Protection of the other, seldom fall to the Lot of the Poor; and especially when a rich Man is their Adversary.' The 'editor' inveighs against the contemporary practice of combining traditional small tenant farms into large units. The introduction is admitted, however, to be 'for Children of six feet high', and hints at a mystery of authorship: 'Why, do you suppose this is written by Mr Newbery, Sir? This may come from another Hand.'

At the start of the story proper, the heroine Margery and her brother Tommy are orphaned, their father being seized with a fever. Their mother dies soon after. Ignored by relatives and in a ragged state—Margery has only one shoe—the children are befriended by a charitable gentleman, who offers to take Tommy to London and make a sailor of him, and orders new shoes for Tommy's sister. Margery, now staying with a local clergyman, is inconsolable at the loss of her brother until her new shoes arrive. She then repeatedly cries out 'See, two shoes', and earns her nickname. But the squire now forces her to leave the clergyman's home. Left to herself, she decides to learn to read by borrowing books from children coming back from school, and reading till they return. Margery is soon more knowledgeable than the parish children, and becomes an itinerant tutor to them; she eventually succeeds Mrs Williams on her retirement from the local 'College for instructing in the Science of ABC'. There, Mrs Margery is a model of enlightened teaching, kindness to animals, and patience in adversity. Finally she marries a wealthy widower, Sir Charles Jones, and 'is made a Lady'. Her brother Tommy comes back from sea after making his fortune. Margery buys up the estate of the tyrannical squire, returns it to separate tenancies, and leads a life of unparalleled generosity. After her death the poor weep at her monument.

Goody Two-Shoes was almost certainly written at a time when Goldsmith was working regularly for John Newbery. Commentators such as Washington *Irving and Charlotte

M. *Yonge have seen Goldsmith's stamp in the book's humour and pathos, as well as in its political flavour. William *Godwin is said to have repeatedly declared Goldsmith to be the author, and the Misses *Bewick, daughters of the engraver, passed on their father's similar belief. On the other hand Newbery's and Goldsmith's accounts, specific about Goldsmith's part in other books, do not mention *Goody*, and other authorities support the tradition in the family of Giles Jones, another of Newbery's writers, that he was the author, which might explain Margery's becoming 'Lady Jones'. Giles's brother Griffith is another candidate, as is John *Newbery himself.

Goody Two-Shoes was an immediate success. It was printed in America by 1775; Isaiah *Thomas published it in 1787; *chapbook printers copied and abridged it, sometimes reducing its original 156 pages to a mere eight. In about 1830 it was available in the form of twelve woodcuts, with one-line captions, on a *broadsheet. It was also imitated, for instance by John *Marshall & Co., with their *Little Goody Goosecap*. A book about Goody's brother, *The Adventures of Thomas Two-Shoes* (1818), was written by Mary *Elliott.

A writer in the *Athenaeum* in 1871 said of *Goody* that 'for fifty years her history was the delight of every child in England that could read.' The book was reprinted regularly until 1850, but was afterwards only reissued periodically. There were only a few 20th-cent. printings, several of them in America, including one edited by Wilbur Macey Stone for the American Antiquarian Society in 1940.

Goofy A dog in *Disney cartoons.

Goops The creation of the American author-illustrator Gellett F(rank) Burgess (1866–1951). They first appeared in his San Francisco literary magazine *The Lark*, where they were used to satirize intellectual attitudes. Burgess remodelled them for a long series of juvenile books, beginning with *Goops and How To Be Them* (1900). In these, the Goops were balloon-headed children representing different kinds of naughtiness. For instance, in *Goop Tales Alphabetically Told* (1904), there is a different Goop for each letter of the alphabet: Abednego, so called 'Because to bed he would not go', Bawlfred, 'because he bawls when he is hurt', Cawlomar, 'because he always calls his Ma and tells on his brothers and sisters', and so on.

Goosebumps *See* STINE, R. L.

GOREY, Edward (1925–2000) Artist, illustrator, cartoonist, set and costume designer, and author of some of the quirkiest, drollest, and most enduringly loved images to come out of 20th-cent. America. Darkly edged, surreal, and deeply ironic, his Gothic pen-and-ink, cross-hatched illustrations were cult favourites long before his animated credits for the US TV series *Mystery!* in 1980 made him more widely known. *The Insect God* (1963) is about the awful fate of beribboned Millicent and *The Gashlycrumb Tinies* (1963) is a macabre alphabet that starts with 'A is for Amy who fell down the stairs' and gets no more cheerful than that. Whether without words at all or with his favourite rhyming couplets, Gorey's books have no set age of audience—just everyone who relishes the amusements of a good, grim story.

Gorilla (1983) A picture book by Anthony *Browne which won both the *Kurt Maschler Award and the *Kate Greenaway Medal and has become a classic. It is the sensitive story of a lonely little girl and the imaginative adventure she enjoys in the company of a friendly gorilla, which leads to a satisfying conclusion. The magic realism of the story is enhanced and supported by Browne's thought-provoking artwork, which challenges the reader while encouraging exploration.

Gorilla Hunters, The *See* CORAL ISLAND, THE.

GORKY, Maxim (Alexei Maximovich Peshkov) (1868–1936) Russian novelist and dramatist. he first volume of his autobiography, *Detstvo* ('Childhood') (1913), has often been enjoyed by children, and he wrote some stories especially for them, for example *The Little Sparrow*, which in 1979 was produced as an English-language *picture book by a Russian state publisher. Gorky was active in promoting the use of children's books in the USSR after the Revolution.

Gormenghast (1946–59) A convoluted, exacting, memorable, and darkly Gothic modern literary classic that is fantasy of the highest order. Illustrator Mervyn *Peake invokes an utterly believable world peopled by grotesques and oddities, a world in which his hero, Titus, yearns for personal freedom rather than the duty and tradition into which he is born. *Titus Groan* (1946), *Gormenghast*, (1950), and *Titus Alone* (1959) are all set in the acutely realized Castle Gormenghast.

Pcakc had planned others in the series, but died before he could complete them.

GOSCINNY, René (1926–77) One half of the Uderzo-Goscinny empire that created the phenomenal *Astérix series. Born in Paris to a family of Jewish immigrants from Poland, Goscinny spent his childhood in Argentina and later went to New York in 1945. He worked as an illustrator and began writing for the series 'Lucky Luke' by Maurice de Bevere (aka Morris) as well as a number of children's books. In 1951, Goscinny returned to Paris where he met his lifelong collaborator Albert *Uderzo. Goscinny and Uderzo along with Jean-Michel Charlier and Jean Hebrad founded the publishing and advertising agency Édifrance/Édipresse, launching the comic magazine *Pilote* which first introduced Astérix in 1959. Goscinny is also well known for writing the Le *Petit Nicolas* series illustrated by Jean-Jacques *Sempé. In 1956, Goscinny began a collaboration with *Tintin* magazine and his early creation 'Oumpah-pah le Peau-Rouge', with Uderzo, was eventually adapted for serial publication from 1958–62. Another popular series, 'Iznogoud', with Jean Tabary, was first published in *Record* in 1962 and later in *Pilote*. Goscinny died in Paris aged just 51. In 1996 the René Goscinny Award for young comic writers was launched at the Angoulême International Comics Festival.

Gotham A village near Nottingham, England, proverbial for the stupidity of its inhabitants. A *nursery rhyme tells of the 'three wise men of Gotham' who 'went to sea in a bowl'. A collection of stories about the villagers' foolish behaviour, *Merry Tales of the Mad Men of Gotham*, was apparently first printed in the 16th cent. and became a popular *chapbook. This collection, ascribed to 'A. B. Doctor of Physick' (possibly the Tudor physician and writer Andrew Boorde), contained some 20 anecdotes of absurd goings-on in Gotham, some of which were borrowed from other *jest-books. Similar stories are told of other 'silly villages'; for example, the inhabitants of one Oxfordshire village are said to have put manure around the base of their church tower to make it grow higher. Many of the children's tales of Isaac Bashevis *Singer feature the stupidities of the people of Chelm, a 'silly village' from Yiddish tradition.

GOUDGE, Elizabeth (de Beauchamp) (1900–84) British popular novelist who wrote a number of children's books, including *Ilenrietta's Ilouse* (1942) and *The *Little White Horse* (1946), which won the *Carnegie Medal.

governess Literally and originally 'a woman who governs', governess was being used by the 16th cent. to mean 'a woman who has the charge of a young person', 'a female tutor'. During the 18th cent. it was sometimes applied to the teacher or proprietor of a school, apparently because (as one writer put it) 'the word *mistress* has a vulgar sound with it'. Mrs Teachum in Sarah Fielding's *The *Governess* (1749) is a clergyman's widow turned school owner. As the 19th cent. advanced, the term came to be applied almost exclusively to the women who resided in upper- or upper-middle-class households and had responsibility for teaching all the younger children and often the older girls too, the boys being sent away to school when they began to grow up. Such governesses were usually from genteel but poorly-off families; as the *Spectator* put it in 1882, 'governessing was the only occupation for "ladies" without means'. Their plight as half-servant, half-gentry, frequently featured in novels, most notably Charlotte Brontë's *Jane Eyre* (1847). *Caroline Mordaunt; or, The Governess* (1835) by Mrs *Sherwood is the story of a governess who is constantly being dismissed for impertinence or other faults of character.

A number of 19th-cent. children's authors worked as governesses at various times in their life, but the only 20th-cent. one to have done so seems to be Enid *Blyton.

Governesses in 20th-cent. children's fiction have not generally been treated kindly by their authors; Sylvia Daisy Pouncer in *The *Midnight Folk* (1927) by John *Masefield spends her evenings as a *witch, and the governess in *Mistress Masham's Repose* (1947) by T. H. *White teams up with the odious Vicar. Miss Slighcarp in *The *Wolves of Willoughby Chase* is even worse.

Governess, The, *or, little female academy* A book for the moral instruction and entertainment of girls. The earliest known edition is dated 1749, and describes itself as being 'By the Author of David Simple'. This was Sarah *Fielding.

Mrs Teachum, a clergyman's widow, establishes a small school for girls, whose nine pupils narrate their life histories and read or tell stories to each other. Among these are a tale about two *giants, and a so-called *fairy story, 'The Princess Hebe'. The moral of each tale is heavily underlined. *The Governess* is,

however, partly redeemed for modern readers by the characterization of the schoolgirls, especially Jenny Peace, the eldest, who patiently resolves the quarrels of the others.

The Governess was reprinted many times until 1804, and was included by Charlotte *Yonge in her *Storehouse of Stories* (1870). It was imitated by Mme de *Beaumont in her *Magasin des enfans* (1756), which contained *Beauty and The Beast*. A later imitation is *Mrs Leicester's School* (1809) by the *Lambs. Sternly moral as Sarah Fielding's book now seems to be, it was nevertheless attacked as frivolous by Mrs *Trimmer, and in 1820 it was reissued in a bowdlerized version under the same title by Mrs *Sherwood, who inserted a great deal of austerely devotional matter into the text. Mrs Sherwood also substituted various *moral tales for those in the original book.

M. F. Thwaite, in *From Primer to Pleasure* (2nd ed., 1972), points out that *The Governess* is 'the first continuous piece of fiction written for children...as significant in its way as Newbery's *Little Pretty Pocket Book* issued five years earlier'. Critics such as Mitzi Myers have seen *The Governess* as critical to a Georgian tradition of female educators that challenges patriarchy and inscribes 'maternal and pedagogical power'.

Governor General's Literary Awards
The major national book awards of Canada, first given in 1936. Since 1987 they have included two children's books categories, one for text and one for illustration, in each of English and French (a single English-language 'juvenile' award was given from 1949 to 1958). Past winners of the awards, which are managed by the Canada Council for the Arts, include Tim *Wynne-Jones (twice), Iain Lawrence, Jon *Klassen, Kenneth *Oppel, Stéphane Jorisch (four times), Isabelle Arsenault (three times), Janice Nadeau (three times), Deborah *Ellis, and Marie-Louise *Gay (twice); and in the first wave of 'juvenile' category winners, Kerry *Wood (twice), Farley *Mowat, and John F. *Hayes (twice).

GRAHAM, Bob (1942–) Australian picture book author/illustrator, who won the *CBCA Picture Book of the Year in 1988 for *Crusher is Coming!* (1987), about Pete who wants to impress the tough footy hero. Which means no stuffed toys, no fairy cakes, and no little sister... but it turns out that Crusher surprises him and likes them all, too. Graham won this award again in 1991 for *Greetings from Sandy Beach* (1990), the story of a camping holiday

on which the family shares the beach with a busload of schoolkids and the Disciples of Death, the bikie gang who were 'okay when you got to know them'. He won this award again in 1993 for *Rose Meets Mr Wintergarten* (1992), the story of how Rose befriends the scary Mr Wintergarten when her ball goes over his fence; and in 2012 for *A Bus Called Heaven* (2011), which begins with a decrepit bus that captures Stella's imagination and becomes the focus for the community. In 2002 he won the CBCA Book of the Year: Early Childhood with *Let's Get a Pup!* (2001), in which Kate chooses a lively puppy, but even the puppy wished for Rosy. She is old and comfortable, so they go back to get her the very next day. He won this award again in 2009 with *How to Heal a Broken Wing* (2008). In *Silver Buttons* (2013), Graham captures an ordinary moment framed by a child taking his first step, and contrasts it with large and small events happening around the world. As we expect from Graham, the smallest details add depth and meaning to the strong themes of the book, and it seems that a single moment can make a difference.

Graham's books are timeless, with an emotional and moral resonance. He believes his characters are 'decent' people. His soft watercolours exude a warmth and understanding of sometimes scruffy, yet lovable characters in simple urban or farmyard settings. Small touches, such as a child's painting on the fridge, typify his settings, underlining the warmth of family relationships. The deep, lucid, yet humorous texts possess a gentle naivety, and the narrative voice ensures a strong emotional response from readers. Graham chooses themes which are deeply personal but sometimes allegories for world events.

GRAHAM, Eleanor (1896–1984) Editor of many children's books and author of four children's novels, Graham worked as a children's bookseller and publisher before being asked by Allen Lane to found *Puffin Books, of which she was in charge until 1961.

GRAHAM, Harry (1874–1936) Writer of comic verse. He was educated at Eton and Sandhurst, was commissioned in the Coldstream Guards, served in the Boer War, and wrote *Ballads of the Boer War* (1902) in the style of *Kipling. His real fame began with *Ruthless Rhymes for Heartless Homes*, first published in 1899 under the pseudonym 'Col. D. Streamer'. The verses in this and many later

volumes by Graham are somewhat in the style of *Belloc, but much more gruesome, for example:

> Father heard his Children scream,
> So he threw them in the stream,
> Saying, as he drowned the third,
> 'Children should be seen, *not* heard!'

The rhymes, and variations on them, soon passed into oral tradition in the UK and the United States. Graham, who served in the First World War, contributed to the scripts of many West End plays and the librettos of operettas, including *White Horse Inn* and *The Maid of the Mountains*.

GRAHAME, Kenneth (1859–1932) Author of *The *Wind in The Willows* who was born in Edinburgh on 8 March 1859, the third child of James Cunningham Grahame, a lawyer with an aristocratic background and an increasing problem with alcohol. The family moved from Edinburgh to Argyllshire shortly after Kenneth's birth, where, four years later, the children's mother died of scarlet fever, not long after giving birth to a fourth child. The father decided he could not manage to look after the children, and he sent them south to their maternal grandmother, Mrs Ingles, who lived at The Mount, Cookham Dean, a village near the Thames in Berkshire. She was authoritarian and cold; her character and house contributed much to Kenneth's book *The *Golden Age*.

Despite a brief spell back under the care of their father, James Cunningham's drinking ensured the children lived predominantly with their grandmother, first in Cookham Dean, then in Cranbourne. Kenneth's father finally moved to France and had no further contact with his children. In 1868, when he was nine, Kenneth was sent as a boarder to St Edward's School in Oxford. Here at last he found some sort of stability, and he did well in academic work and games. He also began to explore the upper reaches of the Thames in a canoe. Oxford itself fascinated him, and he looked forward to happy days there as an undergraduate. But the family could not afford to send him to the University. Instead a clerkship was obtained for him in the Bank of England. After spending two years in an uncle's office in Westminster he began work there in 1879. The failure to enter Oxford University was one of the biggest disappointments of his life.

And yet, life at the bank was not particularly uncongenial to him; the 'Old Lady of Threadneedle Street' was in those days a colourful institution which tolerated and even encouraged eccentricity, and he did well at his work

and soon began to be promoted to positions of responsibility. Moreover, out of office hours he took pleasure in exploring London, particularly the restaurants of Soho, which appealed to his love of a southern, Mediterranean culture. One evening in one of these eating places he encountered Frederick James Furnivall, founder of the Early English Text Society, a man notable for his Johnsonian manner and Rabelaisian wit. Furnivall was a member of the Christian Socialist movement with which Charles *Kingsley and Thomas *Hughes were closely associated. He introduced Grahame to the works of *Malory, *Hakluyt, *Ruskin, and William *Morris; moreover, he encouraged him to write.

After early attempts at poetry, Grahame decided that his forte was the essay, somewhat in the style of Robert Louis *Stevenson. In 1887 he began to have short pieces accepted by London magazines. A regular theme of them was escape from the burden of everyday working life. He espoused so-called 'paganism', professing delight in the rural deity Pan—a fashionable notion among writers of this period. His feeling for the English countryside was close to (and perhaps partly influenced by) the writings of Richard Jefferies, author of *Wood Magic* and *Bevis*.

In 1893 a collection of his essays was published under the title *Pagan Papers*. By this time he had been taken up by W. E. Henley, then editing the *National Observer*. Henley was a friend of R. L. Stevenson and one of the originals for Long John Silver in *Treasure Island*; he made Grahame a regular contributor to his paper, and tried to persuade him to give up the Bank for full-time writing, but without success. Grahame was internally under great strain; while one side of him was drawn to a Bohemian wayfaring life, another (which went towards the creation of Mole in *The Wind in the Willows*) remained timorous and conventional, glad to remain in the safe shelter of regular salaried employment. In fact he was very successful at the Bank; he was appointed Acting Secretary and then in 1898 became Secretary, one of the youngest men to be appointed to this post.

Pagan Papers went virtually unnoticed by the critics, but it did contain six stories about a family of parentless children in a country house (stories based on Grahame's own childhood at Cookham Dean) which attracted the attention of some readers. In 1895 these stories reappeared, with the addition of others about the same children, under the title *The*

Golden Age. The book was an immediate and huge success, and at once made Grahame's literary reputation. The sequel *Dream Days* (1898) was even more enthusiastically received. Grahame thus became established as a writer about childhood, though not as a writer for children.

About a year before *Dream Days* was published Grahame met Elspeth Thomson, three years his junior, the daughter of an Edinburgh inventor. A dominating woman with a strong streak of mawkish sentimentality, she seems to have taken the initiative in their courtship. They were married in July 1899, and spent their honeymoon mostly at Fowey in Cornwall, at the invitation of Grahame's friend Arthur *Quiller-Couch. The Fowey River seems to have contributed almost as much to *The Wind in the Willows* as the Thames; moreover at Fowey Grahame met Edward Atkinson, a bachelor with a passion for boating. He went towards the making of the Water Rat, as did Furnivall.

On 12 May 1900 a son was born to the Grahames. He was christened Alastair, and soon became known as Mouse. He was blind in one eye and only poorly sighted in the other, but his mother pinned all her hopes on him, convincing herself that he had no handicap and was intellectually brilliant. Meanwhile Kenneth's relationship with his wife was far from easy; according to Peter Green's biography of him, he was 'shattered and repelled' by adult sexuality, and as a result 'retreated even further than before into his safe, private world—a world, this time, not of children but of animals'.

After the publication of *Dream Days* he virtually gave up writing for eight years. Then he began to tell bedtime stories to Alastair. He recorded that on the night of his fourth birthday (12 May 1904) the boy 'had a bad crying fit . . . and I had to tell him stories about moles, giraffes & water-rats.' This was the beginning of *The Wind in the Willows*. The story grew during a period of four years, first purely as an amusement for 'Mouse', then with a hope of publication. During this period Grahame began to live once again by the Thames, taking a lease on a house in his old childhood haunt of Cookham Dean. The book finally appeared in print in the autumn of 1908.

Shortly before it was published, Grahame resigned from the Secretaryship of the Bank of England. Officially this was because of poor health, but there is some evidence to suggest that he was forced to take early retirement, possibly because a new Governor of the Bank thought him incapable.

The Grahames' son Alastair was a difficult child. Having been pampered and protected from the world during his childhood, he was sent off to school at Rugby, where he was so miserable that he had to be removed after six weeks. Eton was tried next; the boy stayed there for one year, after which he was removed and sent to a private tutor. In 1918 he went up to Christ Church, Oxford, vicariously fulfilling one of his father's dreams, but he was deeply miserable there, being handicapped by his bad eyesight, and perhaps the excessive expectations of his parents. After two years as an undergraduate he wandered one night on to the railway lines north of the city and apparently lay down on the rails; his decapitated body was found the next morning. The coroner's jury included several senior members of Christ Church, which may be why a verdict of accidental death was passed, much to the relief of the Grahames.

Grahame spent much of the remaining part of his life in what Peter Green has described as 'a paralysing indolence'. He wrote virtually nothing (though he did edit *The Cambridge Book of Poetry for Children*, which appeared in 1916). After Alastair's death, Kenneth and Elspeth's life became hermit-like and eccentric. The couple moved back to the Thames, to Pangbourne, and it was here that Grahame died suddenly, of a brain haemorrhage, early in the morning of 6 July 1932. The epitaph on his headstone in St Cross Churchyard, Oxford, was written by his first cousin Anthony *Hope, author of *The Prisoner of Zenda*:

'To the beautiful memory of Kenneth Grahame, husband of Elspeth and father of Alastair, who passed the River on the 6th July 1932, leaving childhood and literature through him the more blest for all time.'

The most up-to-date biography of Grahame is Alison Prince's book *An Innocent in the Wild Wood* (2009).

Grail, Holy In the legends of King *Arthur, a sacred and mysterious cup or vessel. A 'graal' is mentioned without explanation in the *Perceval* of the 12th-cent. French poet Chrétien de Troyes; this is its first appearance in the Arthurian stories. Later writers identify it with the cup with which Christ instituted the sacrament of Communion at the Last Supper, though apparently the Grail legends owe as much to Celtic pagan mythology as to Christianity.

The Grail was supposedly brought to England by Joseph of Arimathea. The quest for it forms a major part of the Arthurian cycle in the writings of *Malory and others. Only *Galahad of all Arthur's knights is found pure enough, with his companions Percival (Perceval) and Bors, to be granted the vision of Christ holding the Grail, and to receive it from his hands. They convey it to Sarras, where Galahad, at his own request, dies. The Grail is then carried up to heaven and is never seen again.

A Grail features in Susan *Cooper's modern fantasy sequence for children, *The *Dark Is Rising* (1965–77).

GRAMATKY, Hardie (1907–79) American author-illustrator, best known for his 'Little Toot' stories about a tug-boat (*Little Toot,* 1939, and others).

grammar books *See* LILY'S GRAMMAR; *see also* PRIMER.

GRANDVILLE, J.-J. (J.I.I. Gérard) (1803–46). French illustrator. His illustrations for the *Fables* of *La Fontaine, in an edition of 1838, have become famous, and he also provided pictures for an 1840 French printing of *Robinson Crusoe. Un Autre Monde* (1844), an extraordinary collection of *nonsense drawings loosely linked by a text, has been postulated as a source for *Tenniel's illustrations to *Alice's Adventures in Wonderland* (1865), and perhaps even for parts of Lewis *Carroll's text; it includes a drawing of a battle between playing cards, and another of a weeping golden calf which resembles the Mock Turtle. Certainly Grandville has had an influence on many later artists, from *Doré to *Disney.

Grange Hill A British television series about a comprehensive school, first broadcast by the BBC in 1978, and originally scripted by Phil Redmond; novels based on the series were written by Robert *Leeson. It ended in 2008.

Granny's Wonderful Chair *and its Tales of Fairy Times* (1856) A collection of *fairy stories by Frances *Browne set within a 'frame' tale. The girl Snowflower lives in a cottage with her grandmother, who goes away on a journey, leaving her chair as company for the girl. Every night it tells Snowflower a story, and, when she wishes to travel, it takes her anywhere that she wants to go. It brings her to the court of the discontented King Winwealth, to whom it narrates a series of tales, several of which emphasize the good results of virtue and the punishment of greed. Snowflower is rewarded by the king, and this arouses the jealousy of Queen Wantall and Princess Greedalind. They meet their deserts, and Snowflower's grandmother returns to her.

The book, which contains some of the best original short fairy tales of its period (most written in the *Grimm tradition), went through a number of editions in the late 19th cent. Even so, Frances Hodgson *Burnett, who had loved it in her childhood, believed it to be 'lost', and rewrote part of it from memory in the magazine *St Nicholas* in 1887. The book was then 'rediscovered', and Mrs Burnett contributed an introduction to an edition of 1904.

graphic novels for *young adult readers. The term is now conventionally used to describe longer (often book-length), more complex *comics. In the best examples, these utilize the relationship between image and text to create a layered and involving reading experience. Graphic novels for young adult readers are a vibrant and rapidly expanding phenomenon. Despite their diversity, they have key thematic preoccupations, as exemplified by the following seminal examples.

Multimedia artist Dave *McKean collaborated with Neil *Gaiman on the *Sandman* comics series, and picture books such as *The Day I Swapped my Dad for Two Goldfish* (2004) and *Wolves in the Walls* (2003). In his subtle visual treatment of David Almond's *The Savage* (2009), the charged interaction of image and text movingly articulates the rage and grief of Blue, the young protagonist, dealing with the death of his father. The novel charts Blue's own creative and ultimately therapeutic journey as the writing brings to life the titular savage. The ability of aesthetic engagement to heal grief is also at the heart of Brian Selznick's *The *Invention of Hugo Cabret* (2007). Selznick utilizes the visual language of silent film, especially the work of Georges Méliès, alternating between wordless pencil-drawn sequences and sections of conventional prose narrative.

Selznick's use of intertextual references to other media in both form and content is utilized by Bryan Talbot in *The Tale of One Bad Rat,* as a means of exploring dark and difficult subject matter. The experiences of a runaway girl who has been abused by her father are mediated through her recollection of Beatrix *Potter tales. The emotional space this distancing affords her ultimately enables both growth and healing.

The pleasures and perils of first love are movingly depicted in Craig Thompson's auto-biographical novel *Blankets* (2003). Growing up in a fundamentalist Christian community which sees his artistic abilities as a threat, Thompson tenderly charts his discovery of love and his burgeoning sexuality at Church camp. Thompson frames his recollections through a carefully constructed novelistic structure with a bravura use of visual imagery that develops alongside his protagonist. A different kind of conflict lies at the heart of another adolescent love story, *Skim* (2008), by Canadian cousins Mariko and Jillian Tamaki. Ostensibly the diary of a lesbian teenage Wiccan who has an affair with her teacher, this novel sets the visual depiction of her experiences against her verbal self-constructions in her diary, challenging the reader to read between the lines.

This engagement with non-normative forms of identity and culture finds its fullest expression in one of the key thematic strands of young adult comics, the representation of the cultural other. Marjane Satrapi's autobiography *Persepolis* (English trn. Blake Ferris and Mattias Ripa, published in two vols, 2003–4) depicts the childhood of the daughter of radical parents under the rise of the Ayatollahs in Iran. The visual element of this book amplifies the cultural journey of the protagonist, while the style of the work synthesizes the iconographic traditions of East and West, as Satrapi's parents engineer her escape to Paris. French cartoonist Joann Sfar's *The Rabbi's Cat* (English trn. Alexis Siegel and Anjali Singh, 2005) begins in Morocco and similarly ends in Paris. His spirited heroine must enter the modern world and leave her village far behind. She is both helped and hindered by her cat, which after an unfortunate incident with the family parrot is able to talk, and demands a bar mitzvah from her rabbinic father.

Like much graphic work for young adults, these examples all provide an insider's perspective on selves and communities on the brink of major change, of young characters fusing complex cultures, coming to terms with trauma and tragedy in works celebrating the transformative power of verbal and visual narrative.

While younger children tend to be served by other kinds of *comics, some children's books have been given graphic-style novel treatments. There is a bumper assortment of graphic re-imaginings in *The Graphic Canon of Children's Literature* (2014).

GRAVES, Robert (Ranke) (1895–1985) English poet and prolific man of letters who wrote a number of children's books. *The Penny Fiddle* (1960), *Ann at Highwood Hall* (1964), and *The Poor Boy who Followed his Star* (1968) are collections of poems. *The Big Green Book* (1962), illustrated by Maurice *Sendak, is a comic story about a boy who finds a book of spells; another story by Graves, *Two Wise Children,* appeared in 1966.

GRAVETT, Emily (1972–) English picture-book creator who burst onto the scene with her debut book *Wolves (2005), which she created whilst on her BA Illustration course at Brighton University. *Wolves* went on to win the *Kate Greenaway Medal in 2005 and a Boston Globe–Horn Book Honor in 2007 (*see* BOSTON GLOBE–HORN BOOK AWARDS). This marked the beginning of an illustrious career, with several highly acclaimed picture books quickly following suit. Just two years later, Gravett was awarded a second Kate Greenaway Medal for *Little Mouse's Big Book of Fears* (2007). Gravett's success as a picture-book artist lies in her quirky, confident storytelling and individual style. Her picture books for younger children are expressively soft in line and colour—*see* ORANGE PEAR APPLE BEAR (2006). Her books for older children, on the other hand, are full of postmodern and metafictive devices, with spectacular displays of colour, collage, fold-out maps, flaps, magic, and real rat's urine, pushing the boundaries of what a picture book can be to create multi-faceted reading experiences for both adult and child. Other exceptional titles include *The Odd Egg* (2008) and *Matilda's Cat* (2012), and range from the simplest for the youngest children (*Monkey and Me*, 2007) to the more complex for older ones (*Meerkat Mail*, 2006). They are all, without exception, full of irresistibly characterized animals.

Graveyard Book, The (2008) An enchanting novel by Neil *Gaiman, which follows the tale of Nobody 'Bod' Owens, a child raised by the inhabitants of a graveyard, including the Owens ghosts, vampiresque Silas, and wolfish Miss Lupescu. The structure is reminiscent of Rudyard Kipling's *The *Jungle Book* (1894), with each chapter narrating a different episode in Bod's life, and with the uniting narrative thread of tracking the reason for the murder of his parents, when he was a toddler, by the man Jack and the society of Jacks of All Trades. Published in parallel black-and-white illustrated editions, with Dave *McKean for the 'adult' version and Chris *Riddell for the 'young', it was the first book to win both the

*Newbery Medal (2009) and the *Carnegie Medal (2010), among many other awards.

GRAY, Elizabeth Janet (Elizabeth Gray Vining) (1902–99) American novelist who won the *Newbery Medal with *Adam of the Road* (1942), a novel set in Chaucerian England.

GRAY, Keith (1972–) An English writer of *young adult novels. His first novel *Creepers* (1996) was published when he was just twenty-four and shortlisted for the 1997 *Guardian Children's Fiction Prize. He went on to write several more award-winning books, mainly featuring young teenage boys: *Happy* (1998), *Warehouse* (2002), and *Malarkey* (2003) are all well-written, action-packed, gritty young adult reads. In 2005 he published *The Fearful*, about the legacy of an ancient legend in a small town, and followed this in 2008 with his best book to date, the excellent *Ostrich Boys*. Gray has also edited two anthologies for teenagers, *Losing It* (2010), about virginity, and *Next* (2011), about the afterlife. Gray is also a reviewer and a regular judge on book prize panels. In 2008 he was the first ever Virtual Writer in Residence for Scottish Book Trust, producing online creative writing videos to encourage young writers.

GRAY, Nicholas (Stuart) (1922–81) British actor, director, and playwright, Gray wrote a number of *plays for children based on *fairy stories, and several original *fantasy novels including *The Apple-Stone* (1965), the story of a group of children who find a stone that can bring inanimate objects to life.

Great A, little a, bouncing B, *The cat's in the cupboard and she can't see me* A *nursery rhyme first printed in *Tommy Thumb's Pretty Song Book* (1744). The sign 'AaB' was used by at least one 18th-cent. London children's bookseller, Thomas Bailey of Bishopsgate, and probably also by John *Marshall, for his shop was described as the 'Great A, and bouncing B Toy Factory'. There was also a shop in Shoe Lane in 1787 known as the 'Bouncing B', where histories of *Tom Thumb could be bought.

Great Brain, The (1967) The first of a series of stories by John D. Fitzgerald (1906–88), describing childhood in Adenville, Utah, at the turn of the century. The 'great brain' of the title is the narrator's brother Tom, always alert to exploit every situation for his own benefit.

Great Emergency, A (1877) A story by Mrs *Ewing.

Great Panjandrum, The A piece of *nonsense current in the late 18th and 19th centuries. It is said to have been made up by the actor and playwright Samuel Foote (1720–77), in order to test the memory of the old actor Charles Macklin, who claimed he could learn anything at a glance. Foote challenged him to commit this to memory on the spot:

> So she went into the garden to cut a cabbage-leaf, to make an apple-pie; and at the same time a great she-bear, coming up the street, pops its head into the shop. 'What! no soap?' So he died, and she very imprudently married the barber; and there were present the Picninnies, and the Joblillies, and the Garyalies, and the great Panjandrum himself, with the little round button at top, and they all fell to playing the game of catch as catch can, till the gun powder ran out at the heels of their boots.

This was apparently the first use of the word 'Panjandrum'. The piece is also credited to another 18th-cent. actor, James Quin, and an Irish variation has been recorded. It was first printed by Maria *Edgeworth in *Harry and Lucy Concluded* (1825) (*see* EARLY LESSONS), where it is credited to Foote. In 1885 it was used as the basis of a *picture book by Randolph *Caldecott, who portrayed the Panjandrum as a schoolmaster with cap and gown.

Great Piratical Rumbustification, The + The Librarian and the Robbers (1978) A pair of stories—published together—by Margaret *Mahy. When the retired pirate captain, Orpheus Clinker, arrives to babysit for the Terrapin family, the result is a Piratical Rumbustification with surprises and fireworks for all. Where there are pirates in the first story, there are robbers in the second. Here, it is Miss Laburnum, the beautiful librarian, who is the heroine and though kidnapped by the Robbers, she never loses her presence of mind. These lively tales exemplify Mahy's wit, humour, imagination, and love of language, their spirit captured in the illustrations by Quentin *Blake.

Great Uncle Bulgaria One of the *Wombles.

GREDER, Armin (1942–) Swiss-born illustrator who lived and worked in Australia for thirty years. From 1992 he illustrated seven books for Libby *Gleeson. They also wrote *Making Picture Books* (2003). *The Great Bear* (1999) was shortlisted for the 1999 Best

Designed Children's Book and won the *Bologna Ragazzi Award in 2000. They won the 2002 *CBCA Picture Book of the Year for *An Ordinary Day* (2001) and APA Best Designed Children's Picture Book for that year. Greder was Australia's nomination for the prestigious *Hans Christian Andersen Medal in 2004 for his body of work. In 2007 he wrote and illustrated the haunting *The Island* (2007), which was shortlisted for the CBCA Picture Book of the Year for 2008. John *Marsden considers it 'one of my ten favourite picture books of all time'. It was followed in 2010 by *The City*.

Greek myths and legends *See* HOMERIC LEGENDS.

GREEN, Evelyn Everett *See* EVERETT-GREEN.

GREEN, John (1977–) American author of *young adult fiction. Green grew up in Florida and went to a boarding school in Alabama. Bullied at school, Green was a Religious Studies major at university and planned to become an Episcopal priest, but a period working in a hospital for seriously ill children led him to become an author instead. Green's novels deal unsentimentally with big issues—philosophy, love, life, and death—and feature witty, intelligent teen characters. They are typically approachable, warm, and life-affirming.

Some autobiographical material is woven into his novels: the protagonist of his 2005 debut, *Looking for Alaska*, for instance, leaves Florida for an Alabama boarding school. With echoes of John Knowles's *A *Separate Peace*, *Looking for Alaska* won the *Michael L. Printz Award, marking Green out as a major new voice in teenage fiction. His second novel, *An Abundance of Katherines* (2006), was a runner-up for the Printz Award, and the third, *Paper Towns* (2008), debuted at number five on the New York Times bestseller list and won the Edgar Award for best young adult novel. The film rights were sold and Green was contracted to write the screenplay. Green collaborated with David *Levithan on *Will Grayson, Will Grayson* (2011), a runner-up for the *American Library Association's Stonewall Award for LGBT literature for young people. Green's 2012 novel, *The *Fault in Our Stars*, about the romance between two teenage cancer patients, reached number one on the New York Times Bestseller list, was *Time Magazine*'s number one novel of 2012, and was released as a feature film in 2014. He has contributed stories to several anthologies,

and with Maureen *Johnson and Lauren Myracle wrote *Let it Snow: Three Holiday Romances* (2008).

In addition to his writing, Green develops creative projects using technology. He maintains a video blog channel with his brother Hank, and the two host an annual conference for people who make online videos. The brothers launched an educational internet video series called Crash Course, on subjects including history, literature, biology, and chemistry. In 2014 Green and his wife, Sarah Urist Green, announced that they would produce an Internet series on art with PBS.

GREEN, Roger (Gilbert) Lancelyn (1918–87) British author and historian of children's literature. His books include biographies of Andrew *Lang (1946) and C. S. *Lewis (with Walter Hooper, 1974), monographs on J. M. *Barrie, Lewis *Carroll, and Rudyard *Kipling, and *Fifty Years of Peter Pan* (1954), based partly on his own experiences as a professional actor in that play. *Tellers of Tales* (1946), a study of children's writers, has been reprinted and revised. He wrote several original children's stories and produced anthologies, such as *The Hamish Hamilton Book of Dragons* (1970), and retellings of traditional tales, for example *King Arthur and his Knights of the Round Table* (1953), *The Adventures of Robin Hood* (1956), and *Heroes of Greece and Troy* (1960).

GREENAWAY, Kate (1846–1901) English artist, writer of verses, and illustrator of children's books whose vision of sunlit and flower-surrounded children clothed in imaginary 18th-cent. costume inspired not only devoted readers and countless imitators, but also a persistent fashion in children's dress.

Kate Greenaway was born in Hoxton, London, the second of the four children of John Greenaway, an engraver of substantial reputation but, at least during Kate's childhood, of uncertain income. Shortly after Kate was born, John Greenaway sent his family away in order that he might concentrate on an important commission. For Kate the experience was crucial. With her mother and the other children she stayed with relatives at Rolleston, a village in Nottinghamshire, to which she made regular return visits later in childhood. Rolleston was not only her first experience of the countryside; she felt it to be her real home, a country of the mind that she could always reimagine when London or adult life weighed heavy: 'I suppose I went to it very young before

I could really remember and that is why I have such a wild delight in cowslips and apple blossoms.'

Rolleston was set in comparatively prosperous farmland, and she saw it at its best, in summer. Later she remembered its countryside, the farm events, the somewhat archaic dress of villagers, the precise colours of flowers and clothes, and used these memories throughout her life to inform her paintings, though she also feasted her eyes on the street life of London. Each return from Rolleston to the capital gave her a sense of loss:

I live in a London street, then I long and long
To be the whole day the sweet Flowers among

she was later to write, in characteristically awkward but heartfelt verse.

In childhood she read the poems of Ann and Jane *Taylor and *chapbook versions of *fairy stories, loving The *Sleeping Beauty, *Cinderella, and *Beauty and The Beast best; and she enjoyed illustrated editions of *Shakespeare.

She was shy, small, short-sighted, and plain—and very much aware of her gracelessness. She was educated partly at home and, somewhat unsuccessfully, at a series of dame schools; more important was her drawing and the special bond she developed with her father through her interest in his work. At the age of twelve she started to attend formal art classes (she enrolled in the National Course of Art Instruction, instituted by Sir Henry *Cole), and went on to study in the Female School of Art in South Kensington and at the Slade School. But she never developed much understanding of the anatomy of the human figure; the limbs in her drawings are often mere appendages to her clothes, and several of the figures she drew appear to have two right feet.

She first exhibited publicly at the age of twenty-two, and her early paid work included the design of anonymous coloured Christmas cards and valentines, as well as book illustration, among other things for Frederick Warne's *toy books; but on the whole the books in which her first published drawings appeared were crudely printed and unremarkable. On some occasions her black and white book illustrations were engraved by her father. Her early cards and exhibited drawings already show children dressed in part-remembered, part-invented late 18th-cent. frocks, coats, and bonnets. She was her own needlewoman (her mother kept a dress shop for a time), and made the garments worn by her

models; she generally drew from the life and was good at amusing the children who modelled for her. Before long she had created the beginnings of the fashion for 'Kate Greenaway' children's clothes.

For some ten years she made a moderate living doing a mixture of hack-work and serious painting. Then, around 1877–8, Edmund *Evans the *colour printer, who was a friend of Kate Greenaway's father and knew her work, took a remarkable chance with some of her drawings and the verses she had composed to accompany them. He wrote of it:

John Greenaway brought his daughter . . . to show me the drawings she had made for a book: miscellaneous odd drawings with nonsense verses written to them. I bought them at once for I thought they would make a telling child's book: we settled the title Under the Window, from the first line of one of the verses.

Because he used the comparatively costly procedure of engraving four or five colour blocks as well as the outline, Evans had to price *Under the Window at six shillings, a far cry from the sixpenny and shilling toy books that then dominated the market. Nevertheless (according to his memoirs) he decided on his own account to print 20,000 copies for his first edition, which appeared in time for Christmas 1879. He later reminisced that 'the edition sold out before I could reprint another edition; in the meantime copies were sold at a premium.' Eventually his reprintings reached 70,000 copies, with some 30,000 more for the French and German markets.

Kate Greenaway's relationship with Edmund Evans continued to be happy; she thereafter allowed almost no one else to print her *picture books, and she quickly reached a mutually acceptable profit-sharing agreement with the printer. More successful collaborations followed, among them The Birthday Book for Children (1880), with verses by Mrs Sale Barker; Mother Goose or the Old Nursery Rhymes (1881); Little Ann, a selection of Ann and Jane Taylor's verse (1883); The Language of Flowers (1884); Kate Greenaway's Painting Book (1884); *Marigold Garden (1885), the second book with Kate Greenaway's own verses; *A Apple Pie (1886); an edition of The *Pied Piper of Hamelin (1888); and Kate Greenaway's Book of Games (1889). She also produced almanacks every year from 1883 to 1897 (with the exception of 1896), and illustrated books as diverse as an 1885 edition of The *English Spelling Book (from which the capital letter pages were later more successfully

published as *Kate Greenaway's Alphabet*), John Ruskin's *Fors Clavigera, Letters to the Workmen and Labourers of Great Britain* (1883) and his **Dame Wiggins of Lee* (1885), and Bret Harte's *Queen of the Pirate Isle* (1887). The work of book illustration as such, however, never greatly appealed to her, and she generally avoided it. Her picture books, and the almanacks or calendars which she produced between 1889 and 1898, were almost all hugely successful. A penalty of that success was that, much to her annoyance, her style was widely imitated, and Edmund Evans considered that the sheer volume of poor substitutes for her work available in the shops substantially diminished her sales by the 1890s. One of her last commissions was to illustrate *The April Baby's Book of Tunes* (1900), by Elizabeth von Arnim (1866–1941), the author of **Elizabeth and Her German Garden* (1898).

John Ruskin was an admirer of her work from the start, largely because he could find again and again in her drawings an image of innocent and classic childhood beauty which recalled to him Rose La Touche, with whom he had fallen in love when she was nine years old. After *Under the Window* was published, he wrote to Kate Greenaway and began to treat her as his protégée, intending to promote her success and help mould her talent. For the first two years they communicated only by letter, and when Ruskin, now addressing her as 'Kate', eventually invited her to his Cumberland home, she went for a month's visit, was entirely charmed by Ruskin, and thereafter lived chiefly for the excitement which she experienced from his attention, languishing whenever she felt neglected by him.

Ruskin publicly praised her work in glowing terms that his contemporaries found embarrassing (notably in an 1883 Oxford lecture), but he attempted to fend her off when she seemed to be too dependent on his advice. When she made plain how much she loved and needed him he sent her flirtatious letters adorned with kisses, but he would sometimes peremptorily put off visits from her, and would make clear that she was only one of a string of female admirers. In his attempts to make her a greater artist he often ignored her need to earn a living (in her later years she also supported her parents), and she came to realize that her only sure way of catching Ruskin's attention was by drawing the 'girlies' he delighted in. And whereas her genius was for inventing and drawing clothes and accessories, Ruskin would have had these done away with in pictures meant for his eyes:

As we've got so far as taking off hats [he wrote to her], I trust we may in time get to take off just a little more—say mittens—and then—perhaps—even shoes! and—(for fairies) even . . . stockings—and then—.

Kate Greenaway never married; in later years her parents lived with her in the house she had built at Frognal, in Hampstead. Towards the end of her life reviewers began to complain that she was merely repeating herself. Needing money, she took up oil-painting because canvases fetched higher prices than water-colours in the galleries; but she died (at the age of 55) before she had learnt enough of the technique to profit by it.

Her most celebrated books continue to reappear regularly in print. During the 20th cent. she has been the subject of three biographies; the first by M. H. Speilmann and G. S. Layard (1905) is largely a work of piety, but the second, by Rodney Engen (1981), gives a full account of her relationship with Ruskin. Her most recent biographer is Ina Taylor, who published *The Art of Kate Greenaway: A Nostalgic Portrait* in 1991.

Kate Greenaway was well aware that the vision of the world she celebrated in her pictures was too partial, too sunlit for all tastes. But to a friend she wrote: 'What do you think, is it not a beautiful world? . . . Have I got a defective faculty that few things are ugly to me?'

Greenaway Medal *See* Kate Greenaway Medal.

GREENE, Bette (1934–) American children's author who wrote *Summer of My German Soldier* (1973), about an Arkansas girl who harbours an escaped German prisoner-of-war.

GREENE, Graham (1904–91) Celebrated British novelist who wrote his first *picture book for children, *The Little Train*, in 1946, and published it anonymously. Its success led Greene to write *The Little Fire Engine* (1950), *The Little Horse Bus* (1952), and *The Little Steam Roller* (1953). Originally illustrated by Dorothy Craigie, these books were all later reissued with pictures by Edward *Ardizzone.

Green Eggs and Ham (1960) A picture book by Dr *Seuss, in which a grumpy, nameless Seuss creature is pestered by Sam-I-Am to try the eponymous dish, which he claims not to like under any circumstances. Not in a box, not with a fox. Not in the rain, not on a train. With bouncing rhymes and an unstoppable momentum, this is more of the usual Seuss silliness and, as such, impossible to resist.

GREENFIELD, Eloise (1929–) American author of picture books, novels, poetry, and non-fiction that warmly portrays the African-American experience. Notable titles include *Sister* (1974), which was the *New York Times* Outstanding Book of the Year, and *Paul Robeson* (1975), winner of the Jane Addams Children's Book Award. *Africa Dream* (1976) won the *Coretta Scott King Award and Greenfield has also been a Coretta Scott King Honor Award winner for books including *The Great Migration: Journey to the North* (2011), *Night on Neighborhood Street* (1991), *Nathaniel Talking* (1989), and more. She is the recipient of a Virginia Hamilton Literary Award.

Greengage Summer, The See GODDEN, RUMER.

Green Knowe The house at the centre of six novels by Lucy M. *Boston; in real life the Manor, Hemmingford Grey in Cambridgeshire. Dating from 1130, and reputedly one of the oldest continuously inhabited houses in Britain, it was bought by Lucy Boston in 1937 and is still owned by her family.

The first book in the sequence, *The Children of Green Knowe* (1954) set the scene for all the subsequent novels based on the house. Toseland—or Tolly (the character modelled on Boston's son Peter, who provided the atmospheric illustrations to the book and its sequels)—is unable to join his father and stepmother in Burma for Christmas, so finds himself sent to Green Knowe, the home of his great-grandmother, Mrs Oldknow. There, through the stories she tells him, he meets the children from the past who once lived in the house. This imaginative and seamless movement between past and present is at the heart of the next two titles in the series: *The Chimneys of Green Knowe* (1958), in which Tolly's adventures in the 18th cent. are linked to the financial worries of Mrs Oldknow, as she meets blind Susan and Jacob and finds the jewels stolen and lost in the fire that destroyed the 'modern' wing; and *The River of Green Knowe* (1959), in which three children from very different backgrounds find themselves at Green Knowe for the summer—like Tolly, they slip between the present and the past to experience the memories of the landscape.

A Stranger at Green Knowe (1961—winner of the *Carnegie Medal) departs from this pattern. It reintroduces Ping, a Chinese orphan from book three. Hanno, the gorilla from London Zoo, has escaped and arrives at Green Knowe, where Ping is once again spending the summer. Over three intense days, an unlikely friendship springs up. The house and its gardens return as the focus of *An Enemy of Green Knowe* (1964), in which Tolly and Ping unite to protect Green Knowe from the witch, Melanie Powers. Again the action hinges on the past history of the house and its inhabitants.

The Stones of Green Knowe (1976), which concludes the series, is the most historical. The action is seen through the eyes of Roger, the son of the Norman knight who built Green Knowe. Once again past and present merge as Roger moves backwards and forwards in time to see where his home came from and what it would become.

Highly acclaimed when they first appeared, the Green Knowe novels are deservedly regarded as classics for the strength of their writing and their imaginative content.

Green Mountain Boys See THOMPSON, DANIEL P.

Green Smoke (1957) The first of a four-book series of *dragon stories by Rosemary *Manning.

GREENWOOD, Ted (Edward Alister) (1930–99) Australian illustrator and author who produced such unconventional *picture books as *V.I.P., Very Important Plant* (1971) and *Terry's Brrmmm GT* (1974). He aims at paring drawings and story to a minimum, leaving the reader to work things out. He also illustrated *Sly Old Wardrobe* (1968) and *The Glass Room* (1970), both by Ivan *Southall.

GREY, Mini (1965–) Author-illustrator, born in a Mini in a car park in South Wales. Her picture books have received much critical acclaim and received many awards. She began her career in theatre design, and then went on to become a primary school teacher, but her ambition was to get a book published. This she achieved in 2002 with her first picture book, *Egg Drop*, about an egg that dreams of being able to fly. *Biscuit Bear* (2004), about the precarious life of a bear made out of cookie dough, won the Nestlé Smarties Gold Prize in 2004. *The Adventures of the Dish and the Spoon* (2006), about a dish and a spoon who run off together and set sail for America, won the *Kate Greenaway Medal in 2007. Grey has written three books about Traction Man, an action hero who patrols the house saving toys and household objects: *Traction Man is Here*, which was shortlisted for the Kate Greenaway Medal and the *Blue Peter Book Award in 2006, *Traction Man Meets Turbodog* (2008),

and *Traction Man and the Beach Odyssey* (2011). In 2008 Grey was chosen as one of *Booktrust's 'Best New Illustrators'.

Greyfriars A fictional school in the writings of 'Frank Richards' (Charles *Hamilton). It is supposedly at Friardale in Kent, on the site of a monastery, and was founded by Edward VI. Its most famous pupil is *Billy Bunter.

GREY OWL (Archibald Stansfeld Belaney) (1888–1938) Canadian author. Born in England, he spent some years as a trapper and hunter in Ontario, then became repelled by cruelty and killing and turned to conservation, setting up his own beaver sanctuary. His only children's book, *The Adventures of Sajo and Her Beaver People* (1935), describes a year in the life of two beaver kittens who are rescued by an '*Indian'. Belaney took the name Grey Owl when he was adopted as a blood brother by the Ojibwa tribe in 1910.

GRIFFITH and FARRAN London publishers of children's books, successors to the *Newbery family and John *Harris. William Darling Griffith (1805–77) was in partnership with Robert Farran from 1856; their successors continued the firm under various imprints (including Griffith, Farran, Okeden and Welsh) until about 1911. Frances *Browne and Jean *Ingelow were among the firm's authors, and it was at their suggestion that G. A. *Henty began to write boys' *adventure stories.

Grimble + Grimble at Christmas (1974) Two short novels by Clement Freud (1924–2009), illustrated by Quentin *Blake, and published together. Genuinely hilarious and totally unique, these two stories introduce us to the eccentric world of Grimble (his real and only name), a boy of 'about 10' (his parents are a bit vague about dates). In the first book Grimble is left to fend for himself with an oven full of sandwiches while his parents are in Peru; in the second he sets about various peculiar schemes to raise money for Christmas.

GRIMM, Jacob Ludwig Carl (1785–1863) and his brother **Wilhelm Carl** (1786–1859) Philologists, collectors, and editors of the *Kinder- und Hausmärchen* ('Nursery and Household Tales'), now most commonly known in the English-speaking world as 'Grimm's Fairy Tales'. This gathering of over 200 tales and children's legends includes *The *Frog Prince*, *Rapunzel*, *Hansel and Gretel*, *The *Valiant Little Tailor*, *The *Bremen Town-Musicians*, *Snow White and The Seven Dwarfs*, *Rumpelstiltskin*, *The *Golden Goose*, *Hans in Luck*, *The *Twelve Dancing Princesses*, and *Snow-White and Rose-Red*.

The brothers were born in Hanau, near Frankfurt, in the then independent German state of Hesse. Their father, a lawyer, was town clerk of Hanau; he died when Jacob, the eldest of his six surviving children, was eleven, and the family was left in some privation. Jacob and Wilhelm studied law at Marburg University, and there they began to be absorbed both by the new discipline of the historical study of law and by German folk poetry, which had already been the object of the Romantic movement's enthusiasm. In 1805 two of the Grimms' friends, Achim von Arnim and Clemens *Brentano, published *Des Knaben Wunderhorn*, their collection of German folk songs, together with an appeal for the gathering of popular tales from the people while they were still remembered. The Grimms began collecting such tales the following year.

Jacob was employed briefly as a clerk in the Hessian War Office, until the Napoleonic invasion of 1806 disrupted the state and then put Napoleon's brother Jerome Bonaparte on the throne as King of Westphalia. In 1808 Jacob became private librarian to Jerome; in the same year his mother died, leaving him responsible for the family. Wilhelm, meanwhile, suffered from poor health, including a heart condition, which made regular employment impossible, but the brothers worked together on folk tales, treating their collection as material for an eventual history of German literature. However, their friend von Arnim argued that they should immediately publish the fairy tales they had gathered so far; and the first volume of the *Kinder- und Hausmärchen* appeared by Christmas 1812, dedicated to Frau Elisabeth von Arnim 'for the little Johannes Freimund'—her son.

In 1813 Hesse was liberated from the French, and Jacob entered the service of the restored Elector of Hesse, to become a somewhat unwilling civil servant, present at the Congress of Vienna and on missions to Paris. The following year Wilhelm started work in the Elector's library. The two laboured there together until 1829. The second volume of the *Kinder- und Hausmärchen* appeared in 1814. A second edition of both volumes, considerably revised and with frontispiece drawings by their brother Ludwig, was issued in 1819, and a volume of notes, commentary, and some new material came out in 1822.

The *Kinder- und Hausmärchen* made the Grimms famous, both in Germany and abroad, though they remained sensitive to the criticism that the study of *fairy stories was too trivial a pursuit for serious scholars. They moved on to the collecting of local legends, their *Deutsche Sagen* (1816–18); Jacob increasingly devoted himself to Germanic philology, the first volume of his *Deutsche Grammatik* appearing in 1819 and marking the beginning of the scientific historical study of the Germanic languages.

From 1829 to 1837 the brothers taught at Göttingen University, but they were among a group of professors who refused to acquiesce in the Elector of Hanover's quashing of the state's liberal constitution. Consequently they were dismissed and exiled. They then took up the suggestion that they should begin work on a new German Dictionary, which might give them some financial and political independence. This was, however, a huge task, and when Wilhelm died, the dictionary had only reached the letter D. Four years later, at Jacob's death, work had progressed as far as F. The dictionary was not finished until more than a hundred years later.

The relationship between the two brothers was remarkably close from childhood; they shared rooms as children and students, and lived in the same house and worked in adjacent studies in later life. They were never willingly parted. Although the work on folk tales became increasingly Wilhelm's province and that on grammar Jacob's, they continued to work together and publish jointly. Jacob characterized himself as quiet and single-minded. He remained a bachelor. Wilhelm, though delicate in health, was more convivial. He married in 1825 Dorothea (Dortchen) Wild, who had been a childhood neighbour and was a contributor of some of the tales in the *Kinder- und Hausmärchen*. They had three children.

The brothers Grimm began collecting folk tales at a time when this was not in itself an unusual activity. Their sources were largely close friends and neighbours. Wilhelm's future wife, Dortchen, for example, told them *Hansel and Gretel* and many more. They visited villages and spinning rooms, and instructed friends how to collect for them. The most notable source of all was Dorothea Viehmann, a tailor's wife in a nearby village who sold eggs. Friends of the Grimms, knowing her talent, persuaded her to call with her eggs at the Grimms' house. She was given good coffee, and in return eventually told twenty tales that were new to them, including *The Goose-Girl* as well as several variants of others.

The published volumes each contained a few tales from written sources, but it was oral collection that the brothers believed to be crucial. They insisted on the importance of the tales as part of the nation's literary history, many of them being closely related to the great myths and heroic legends of Germanic culture; *Little Briar-Rose*, for example, they regarded as a folk reincarnation of the enchanted sleep of Brynhild in the *Volsungasaga*.

The Grimms' work quickly became international; they translated a selection of *Croker's Irish fairy tales into German, corresponded with Sir Walter *Scott on Scottish balladry, and worked on Slav and Scandinavian folk literature. In turn their work inspired collectors and folklorists all over the world.

The Grimms were somewhat ambiguous in their attitude to their general, non-scholarly readers, and in particular to an audience of children. The first edition of the *Kinder- und Hausmärchen* was unillustrated, and had all the scholars' apparatus of a long introduction and notes; but one of its dedicatees was a child, and though it was criticized as too coarse and unsuitable for the young it was immediately read by children of the Grimms' friends. The brothers, moreover, frequently gave copies as presents to children. When they saw a copy of the first English translation, published in 1823 with children in mind, edited by Edgar Taylor and illustrated by George *Cruikshank, they at once emulated it with a selection of some fifty of the most popular tales, in a cheaper illustrated edition designed to reach the nurseries. In all, seven editions of the *Kinder- und Hausmärchen* were published in the Grimms' lifetime. After the brothers' death more tales and variants were culled from their manuscripts, and their main work was freshly edited in the light of later scholarship.

The tales have been translated into well over 100 languages. Taylor's 1823 English translation of the Grimms' work as *German Popular Stories* and the second volume published in 1826 effectively revolutionized the conventional English attitude to fairy tales, and rehabilitated *fantasy as generally acceptable reading-matter for the young, although controversy over the suitability of particular incidents continues to the present day. The Cruikshank illustrations, which the Grimms themselves admired, remain inextricably associated with the tales.

In 1839 Taylor published a new selection, called *Gammer Grethel or German Fairy Tales and Popular Stories*, using some of Ludwig Grimm's illustrations as well as Cruikshank's. Numerous English-language editions and all manner of selections, retellings, and expurgated versions have followed. Notable illustrators have included Richard *Doyle, Arthur *Rackham, and Maurice *Sendak. The first full and almost entirely unbowdlerized translation into English, containing the first English version of the notes, was that of Margaret Hunt (1884) with an introduction by Andrew *Lang. Among modern translations which attempt to convey the exact character of the originals is that by David Luke, in *Selected Tales* (Penguin Classics, 1982). Philip Pullman's 2012 reworking of these stories in *Grimm Tales for Young and Old* emphasizes the importance and currency of the brothers' legacy. *See also* ZIPES, JACK.

The Grimms have been widely revered as the virtual founders of the modern scientific study of folklore. It has always been known that they polished the tales for publication, but the impression has usually been given by their biographers and critics that they revered the actual words of the teller, however apparently unsophisticated, inconsistent, or nonsensical. The Grimms themselves encouraged this belief. However, a study of their work by John M. Ellis, entitled *One Fairy Story Too Many* (1983), argues that this view of them is entirely mistaken. Ellis alleges that 'far from diligently seeking out folk sources', most of their sources were 'middle-class, literate' people, many of them young, 'far from the preferred type of the old peasant woman'. Indeed, many stories were not of German origin at all, not least because many of the Grimms' sources were Huguenots whose first language was French, and who knew their Perrault well. Ellis also points out that the manuscript copies of their source material that the Grimms sent Brentano in 1810 show 'an *enormous* discrepancy' between what they had collected and the texts they published. These alterations, and changes that the Grimms made in subsequent editions, give the impression that they were trying to substitute for the arbitrary events and often chaotic ethics of the true folk tale a 'more rational and less dangerous' world, in which events had causes and effects of a kind acceptable to educated readers. Whatever objections may be offered to Ellis's case, it must be observed that, if his interpretation of their role is correct, the Grimms were doing no more than Perrault seems to have done with his original

material. If they were, indeed, retellers rather than true collectors, their work resembles that of virtually all pre-20th-cent. folklorists, for whom accuracy of transmission was less important than the achievement of an acceptable literary content and style. Important 21st-cent. scholarship on the Grimms has been undertaken by Jack Zipes and Maria Tatar. Donald R Hettinga published a scholarly biography of the brothers, *The Brother's Grimm: Two Lives, One Legacy* in 2001.

GRIPE, Maria (1923–2007) Swedish children's author of realistic, reflective novels about childhood. These include a *Josephine* trilogy (1961–2), and an 'Elvis' series about the imaginative life of a small boy (*Elvis Karlsson*, 1972, and others). Many of her books have appeared in English.

GROBLER, Piet (1959–) An internationally renowned South African-born illustrator and picture-book creator now living in the UK. He has received numerous awards including a Silver Medal in the Japanese Noma Concours for Picture Book Illustration in 1997 and 2003; he was a nominee for the South African *IBBY honour list in 2001 and 2005–6; and he received the Golden Apple award at the Biennial of Illustrations Bratislava in 2009. His illustrative style is full of colour and offbeat quirkiness which enhance and give life to the texts he illustrates. Grobler has illustrated for fellow South African authors Beverley *Naidoo and Dianne *Hofmeyr, giving full flavour to their African tales. Altogether he has illustrated over eighty children's books by other writers, as well as a number of his own books, including *Please Frog, Just One Sip!* (2002) and *Little Bird's ABC* (2005).

Growing Point *See* FISHER, MARGERY.

Gruelle, Johnny *See* RAGGEDY ANN.

Gruffalo, The (1999) A picture book in rhyming verse by Julia *Donaldson, with illustrations by Axel *Scheffler, which quickly became a huge bestseller, the current sales tally sitting at over five million copies in over fifty languages. The story carries a message that brains will defeat brawn. A mouse (so it begins) takes a walk in a deep, dark wood, and one by one he encounters a fox, an owl, and a snake, all potential predators, but scares them away by telling them he's on his way to meet a 'Gruffalo', a monster whose favourite food is 'roasted fox'/'owl ice-cream'/'scrambled snake'. It turns out that this Gruffalo does in fact exist,

and when he in turn threatens to eat the mouse, the mouse devises a clever way to trick him, too. It won a *Blue Peter Book Award, and has been adapted for screen and stage (and merchandise of all sorts). A sequel, *The Gruffalo's Child*, was published in 2004. The Gruffalo himself makes a cameo appearance in a number of other Donaldson-Scheffler books.

Gruffanuff In *The *Rose and The Ring* by *Thackeray.

GRUNDTVIG, Svend *See* DANISH FAIRY AND FOLK TALES.

Guardian Children's Fiction Prize (formerly **Guardian Award**) Presented by the *Guardian* newspaper, annually since 1967, for the outstanding work of children's fiction by a British or Commonwealth author published during the previous year. In contrast with most awards, previous winners are not eligible to win the prize a second time. For a list of winners, *see* APPENDIX, H.

Guardian of Education, The A periodical published from 1802 to 1806, at first monthly, then quarterly, by Mrs Sarah *Trimmer; it contained the first serious attempt to *review the whole range of books being published for children, and to survey the history of the genre to date. The advertisement for the first issue announced the intention 'to caution Young Mothers, and others of the Female Sex who are engaged in the important Business of Education against the Attempts which are making to banish Christianity from the Nursery and the School . . . to assist Parents and Governesses in their Choice of Books for the instruction and Amusement of Children and Youth, as far as the Principles of Religion and Good Morals are concerned'.

Mrs Trimmer's standpoint was that of the Established Church. She also believed that there was a conspiracy against Christianity with its source in France, in the philosophy of Voltaire and *Rousseau and the ideals of the French Revolution, abetted by the fashion in England for the French language, French *romances, and education in accomplishments rather than in religion. Thus Mrs Trimmer objected to **Early Lessons* by Maria *Edgeworth for its Rousseauist belief in learning by discovery; to **Sandford and Merton* because 'there is a great danger of sowing the seeds of democracy and republicanism in the youthful breast'; and to *John Gilpin as being regrettable for putting 'an honest, industrious tradesman' into a ridiculous situation. She recommended taking a pair of scissors to the socially critical parts of **Goody Two-Shoes.* Although she admitted that *fairy stories had delighted her as a child, she felt that few of them were justified by a good moral; most, she said, were pure fancy, 'and not infrequently at the hazard of inflaming the imagination and the passions of youth'. On the other hand many of Mrs Trimmer's criticisms have not dated. She confessed to being diverted by **Mother Hubbard* both as child and adult, and she was concerned that illustrations for an edition of **Bluebeard* were unnecessarily lurid for an already horrific story.

In addition to book reviews Mrs Trimmer included in *The Guardian of Education* a continuing essay on Christian education and its history, more evidence for her French conspiracy theory, and extracts from sermons. Eventually the burden of keeping up with children's book publication and reviewing it became too great. She hoped to continue the periodical as an occasional publication, but it was never revived after 1806.

Guardians, The (1970) By John *Christopher. After his father is killed in a freak accident, Rob Randall finds himself on the run. To escape from the controlled, conformist world of the Conurb, the only life he has known, he must go over the Fence to the County. Here he finds an idyllic society of privilege. But this harmony comes at a price, a price some find too high. In this early example of the *dystopian novel for a younger audience, Christopher explores themes more often found in adult novels of the time. The author was already known for his **Tripods* trilogy.

Gub Gub A pig in the *Doctor Dolittle books by Hugh *Lofting.

Guess How Much I Love You (1994) A picture book by Sam McBratney, illustrated by Anita Jeram. Little Nutbrown Hare is anxious—how much does Big Nutbrown Hare love him? Together they explore an expanding number of scenarios until the final assurance: 'right up to the moon—AND BACK'. Unusual in featuring a male adult while addressing a fundamental concern for the youngest, this was an immediate success, a success that also owed much to Jeram's illustrations. Shortlisted for the *Kurt Maschler Award 1994 and selected to feature as an *American Library Association Notable Book 1996, this massive bestseller has been translated into fifty-three languages, sold tens of millions of copies, and

been published and republished in a variety of formats (it has also been adapted for the screen and prompted sequels, merchandise, etc.).

GUGGENMOS, Josef (1922–2003) German poet and writer for children, whose very simple lyric verses have been compared to *Blake's. His *picture books include *From Sunrise to Sunset* (1972).

GUILLOT, René (1900–69) French children's author of over fifty novels. He specialized in *adventure stories such as *Les Compagnons de la fortune* (1950) (English, *Companions of Fortune*, 1952).

Guinevere *See* ARTHUR.

Gulliver's Travels An adult satire by Jonathan Swift (1667–1745) which, usually abridged for the purpose, has also become a classic of children's literature, read as a traveller's tale. Originally published in 1726 as *Travels into several Remote Nations of the World. By Lemuel Gulliver, first a surgeon, and then a captain of several ships*, it purported to be a factual account of four voyages: to *Lilliput, a kingdom of beings no more than six inches tall; to Brobdingnag, a land of *giants; to the flying island of Laputa with its absurd scientists and inventors; and to the country of the Houyhnhnms, admirably rational horses. Much of the satire was of contemporary politics and behaviour, though portrayed in a manner that gave it lasting relevance: high heels and low heels in Lilliput represented Whigs and Tories; courtiers absurdly leaping and creeping for the prizes of coloured silks referred to the Orders of the Garter, Bath, and Thistle; wars of religion were seen in Lilliputian terms as conflict between those who opened eggs at the big end and those who believed exclusively in the little end. The fact that the book may be read with little awareness of satire derives from Swift's care to make details realistic.

Swift believed that the book would 'wonderfully mend the world', but his previous experience of persecution as a result of his published satire made him take pains to conceal the authorship of *Gulliver*. He negotiated the sale of the book through a third party, and had the manuscript dropped at night on a London publisher's doorstep after he had returned to Ireland.

The first edition was furnished with imaginary maps and a frontispiece portrait of Lemuel Gulliver. Early readers are known to have looked for Lilliput in their own atlases. Nevertheless Swift's authorship was widely recognized, and keys and counterattacks to the satire followed quickly on publication.

The first printing of *Gulliver* sold out in a week, and the book was almost immediately translated into French and Dutch, serialized in journals, and published in abridged form. Three weeks after the book appeared Swift's friends John *Gay and Alexander Pope wrote to him (17 November 1726): 'From the highest to the lowest it is universally read, from the Cabinet-council to the Nursery.' It was early felt that certain parts of the book were too 'immodest and indecent' even for adult readers, such as Gulliver's accounts of excreting while on Lilliput, or (almost universally offensive) the details of the bodily functions and sexual behaviour of the foul and degenerate Yahoos. These were, and are, regularly omitted, in the spirit of an 1867 edition which was 'carefully edited by a clergyman' so that 'it may, with confidence, be submitted even to the perusal of children'.

Versions of *Gulliver*, with the story reduced to bare outlines, began to appear as *chapbooks in the late 18th cent. One of the first editions specifically for children was that published by *Tabart in 1805, with three coloured *copperplates. In children's retellings or abridgements, the voyage to Lilliput often appears alone, or only with that to Brobdingnag. The Lilliput adventure, retold by the poet May Kendall, was included by Andrew *Lang in the original editions of his *Blue Fairy Book* (1889). Film versions of the story include one by Paramount in the 1930s. Among the many illustrators of *Gulliver* have been Arthur *Rackham, Willy *Pogány, Rex Whistler, and David Jones. Chris *Riddell has illustrated a recent children's version by Martin Jenkins (*Jonathan Swift's Gulliver*, 2004).

Gumble's Yard (1961) The first children's novel by John Rowe *Townsend, set in 'The Jungle', a district of poor housing in the city of Cobchester. A family of children realize that they may be 'taken into care' by the local authority when Walt, father of two of the children, and Doris, the woman he lives with, both walk out on them at the same time. They discover an attic over a row of disused cottages on a canal wharf and make a home for themselves there, doing their best to earn money and be independent. But Gumble's Yard, their new home, is also a hiding-place used by a gang of crooks, and the story turns into a thriller before the question of the children's

future is resolved. *Gumble's Yard* was one of the first British children's books to try to deal with the subject of 20th-cent. urban poverty.

Gumdrop A vintage car, hero of stories by Val *Biro.

GUNN, Jeannie (Mrs Aeneas) *See* LITTLE BLACK PRINCESS, THE.

GUTHRIE, T. A. *See* ANSTEY, F.

GUY (Cuthbert), Rosa (1922–2012) An influential African-American author, playwright, and civil rights activist. Born in Trinidad, Guy moved permanently to New York when she was ten years old. Her celebrated trilogy *The Friends* (1973), *Ruby* (1976), and *Edith Jackson* (1978) features three young women negotiating their friendships amidst the tough realities of 1970s Harlem. It was notable for its exploration of lesbian relationships, which was rare at the time in *young adult fiction. Guy also adapted and translated Birago Diop's *Maman-Caïman* (1961; English trans., *Mother Crocodile*, 1981), for which her illustrator John *Steptoe won the *Coretta Scott King Award in 1983. Her novel *My Love, My Love, or The Peasant Girl*, a Caribbean retelling of Hans Christian *Andersen's *The Little Mermaid*, was adapted into the hit Broadway play *Once on This Island* in 1985 and nominated for eight Tony awards.

Guy of Warwick A popular medieval *romance. Guy, the son of the steward to the Earl of Warwick, loves Felice, the Earl's daughter. She will only accept him if he demonstrates his bravery. He leaves England and performs many exploits overseas, eventually returning home and marrying Felice. His later adventures include killing a *dragon in Northumberland and fighting the giant Collebrand, who has been brought to England by the Danish invaders. He is made Earl of Warwick, but spends the latter part of his life as a poor pilgrim, to atone for his sins. He accepts food and drink sent daily to him and other pilgrims by his wife, but she does not recognize him until his death.

Guy of Warwick, which appears in several medieval manuscripts, was first printed by Wynkyn de *Worde *c.*1500. Various versions were published in prose and verse during the following 400 years. The *broadside and *chapbook retellings drastically reduce the length of the story for reasons of space (the original poem was some 11,000 lines in length), but they add the episode of Guy killing the Dun Cow of Dunsmore Heath.

Versions specifically for children include a miniature edition published by C. Sheppard (*c.*1780), a version (1808) based on Dugdale's *Antiquities of Warwickshire*, and a retelling by G. H. Gerould (1912).

Gypsy Breynton (1866) One of a series of *girls' stories which were among the earliest writings of the American novelist Elizabeth Stuart Phelps Ward (1844–1911), who was best known for *The Gates Ajar* (1868), which is on the subject of life after death. *Gypsy Breynton* has as its heroine a twelve-year-old girl of tomboyish character but much charm. It was followed by three sequels. All the books were published under the author's maiden name of Elizabeth Stuart Phelps.

H

HABBERTON, John *See* HELEN'S BABIES.

HACK (Barton), Maria (1777–1844) English children's author, sister of Bernard Barton, the poet and friend of Charles *Lamb. She was well known for her *Winter Evenings; or, Tales of Travellers* (four volumes, 1818–20), a collection of travellers' stories; *English Stories*, a set of historical 'Events and Characters' published between 1820 and 1825; and *Harry Beaufoy; or, the Pupil of Nature* (1821), in which a mother instructs her son in natural phenomena and encourages him to deduce from them the existence of God.

HADATH, (John Edward) Gunby (c.1880–1954) Prolific writer of *school stories who was for many years Senior Classics Master at Guildford Grammar School. His best known books were about the *Stalky-like schoolboy 'Sparrow', e.g. *Sparrow in Search of Expulsion* (1939).

HADDON, Mark *See* CURIOUS INCIDENT OF THE DOG IN THE NIGHT-TIME, THE.

HADER, Berta (Hoerner) (1890–1976) **and Elmer (Stanley)** (1889–1973) American author-illustrators of *picture books, best known for *The Big Snow* (1948), about wild animals enduring a severe winter.

Hag Dowsabel A *witch in stories by Lorna *Wood.

HAGGARD, Henry Rider (1856–1925) English author, born in Norfolk. At the age of nineteen he went to South Africa as secretary to Sir Henry Bulwer, governor of Natal. Soon after his return to England in 1879 he married a Norfolk heiress. He began to read for the bar, but decided he wanted to be a writer. After publishing two unsuccessful novels he wrote *King Solomon's Mines* (1885), which was an instant best-seller. He immediately wrote a sequel, *Allan Quatermain* (1887), but before it appeared he had also written and published *She* (1887), an exotic fantasy about a 2,000-year-old queen, Ayesha, who has been preserved from death. It was a sensational success.

Haggard's early fame led him to become something of a public figure; he researched into conditions in rural England and was a member of several government commissions. His public service earned him a knighthood in 1912. But his private life was shattered by the death of his only son (the eldest child) in 1912, and he damaged his literary reputation in 1887 by an intemperate attack on the quality of modern fiction—which led to Haggard himself being accused of bad writing and even plagiarism. He wrote many other novels, including *The World's Desire* (1890), a collaboration with Andrew *Lang, and *Eric Brighteyes* (1891), a story based on Icelandic sagas. Haggard worked out several of his plots with the help of his friend *Kipling, but never again repeated the success of *King Solomon's Mines* and *She*.

HAIG-BROWN, Roderick (Langmere) (1908–76) Born in Sussex Haig-Brown emigrated to Canada at the age of eighteen and worked as a logger, trapper, fisherman, and guide. He is best remembered for *Ki-yu: a story of panthers* (1934). His other children's books include *Silver: the life of an Atlantic salmon* (1931), *Starbuck Valley Winter* (1943), an account of a teenager's experiences as a trapper, and *The Whale People* (1962), a *historical novel set on Canada's west coast.

Hairy Maclary (1983–2012) A series of children's picture books by New Zealand author-illustrator Lynley Dodd (1941–). The best-known is *Hairy Maclary from Donaldson's Dairy* (1983), which is now a popular stage play. Fast-paced alliterative rhyme, strong rhythm, and imaginative character names speed the stories of these lovable, scruffy domestic pets as they go about making mischief. Very lively illustrations and a clever portrayal of the larrikin animals in their setting add an edge of unexpected realism to the stories.

Hakluyt's Voyages A collection of accounts of the voyages of English explorers by Richard Hakluyt (?1552-1616), published in 1589 as *The Principall Navigations, Voiages and Discoveries of the English Nation*. His works have provided several children's writers with inspiration; for example, *The *Three Mulla Mulgars* (1910) by Walter *de la Mare is heavily indebted to Samuel Purchas's 17th-cent. version of Hakluyt.

HALDANE, J. B. S. *See* MY FRIEND MR LEAKEY.

HALE, Edward Everett (1822-1909) American author, a Boston Unitarian clergyman now principally remembered for *The Man Without a Country* (1865). This is the patriotic story of Philip Nolan who 'cried out, in a fit of frenzy, "Damn the United States! I wish I may never hear of the United States again!"'—and who is sentenced as a result to wander forever at sea and be denied any news of his country. Hale's other works include a *Family Flight* series of *travelogue storybooks for children, written with his sister Susan.

HALE, Kathleen (1898-2000) Creator of *Orlando the Marmalade Cat; she was born in Scotland, studied art, and exhibited her paintings before beginning to write and draw the Orlando stories for her two sons. Her other books for children include *Henrietta, the Faithful Hen* (1943) and *Henrietta's Magic Egg* (1973).

HALE, Lucretia P. (Peabody) (1820-1900) Author of *The *Peterkin Papers* and sister of Edward Everett *Hale.

HALE, Mrs Sara Josepha (1788-1879) Of Boston, Mass., Mrs Hale was the author of *Mary had a little lamb. She edited the *Boston Ladies' Magazine* from 1828 to 1837, and from 1834 to 1836 was in charge of *The *Juvenile Miscellany*. She later edited *Godey's Lady's Book*. Mrs Hale was the first editor to print stories by Frances Hodgson *Burnett.

Half Magic (1954) The first in Edward *Eager's sequence of seven novels featuring four children, Jane, Mark, Katharine, and Martha. When Jane picks up a strange coin off the ground, the children quickly discover it can grant wishes. Unfortunately it will only grant half of any wish, which results in a number of humorous situations until the solution is found. However, magic is tricky and though each child gets a wish, not everything is quite as expected and adult intervention is necessary at the end.

More than a little is owed to E. *Nesbit, whose work the author admired, and the humour arises from the juxtaposition of magic in the hands of a set of siblings with the contemporary world. Subsequent adventures in the series continue the theme.

HALL, Mrs S. C. (Anna Maria Hall) (1800-81) Victorian miscellaneous author, wife of the London editor Samuel Carter Hall. She wrote a number of children's books, chiefly *moral tales such as *Grandmamma's Pockets* (1849). She was also the editor of one of the first British *annuals for children, *The *Juvenile Forget Me Not* (1828-37).

HALLIWELL (Halliwell-Phillips), James Orchard (1820-89) Antiquary and collector of *nursery rhymes and nursery tales. He made a reputation for scholarship at a remarkably early age, becoming a Fellow of the Royal Society before he was nineteen, though he left Cambridge without a degree. One of his earliest publications was *The *Nursery Rhymes of England* (1842), compiled for the Percy Society. The volume was an immediate and lasting success, and, together with Halliwell's *Popular Rhymes and Nursery Tales* (1849), it formed the basis of many subsequent nursery rhyme collections. Halliwell's books were the first scholarly study of the English rhymes, and the first to cite early sources and establish the antiquity of many rhymes. Halliwell claimed to be presenting a selection from a thousand or more rhymes that he had collected 'principally from oral tradition', but he is known to have used rather more printed sources than he admitted.

HAMILTON, Charles (Harold St John) (1876-1961) British writer of *boys' stories; an astonishingly prolific author who, during a career spanning more than seventy years, created *Billy Bunter, *Tom Merry, and a whole host of other heroes whose adventures were followed by boys of generation after generation. The best known of his many pseudonyms was 'Frank *Richards'.

Hamilton was born in the Ealing district of West London, the son of a journalist and one-time bookseller and stationer. His father died when he was seven and the family thereafter frequently moved house. Charles attended various church day-schools in the Ealing district, and apparently also a private preparatory school; he claimed that he had never been to a state school. The writer and broadcaster John Arlott visited him towards the end of his life,

and asked him if he had been to a public school:

He was very evasive on this point. He would not say that he had, but he more or less dared me ever to say that he had not. I came away with the impression that, like so many of his boyish admirers, he had never been to a public school, but he wished that he had. And perhaps indeed, in his heart and mind, after all those years of writing, he really believed that he had.

Certainly Hamilton acquired a good knowledge of Latin and French, and a thorough all-round education; he once published a Latin version of 'Waltzing Matilda'.

He wrote prolifically during his schooldays, and in his late teens began to have stories accepted by publishers of boys' *magazines. He also made a little money as a songwriter and illustrator. In about 1895 he started to contribute to the growing empire of *Harmsworth juvenile papers. In 1906 he created *St Jim's, the first of his fictional schools, in the pages of *Pluck, and the next year began to write stories about the schoolboy Tom Merry in the new Harmsworth weekly *Gem. A few months later these two sets of stories were combined, and the adventures of Tom Merry at St Jim's ran in *Pluck* (with breaks and re-runs) up to the Second World War. Hamilton's pseudonym for these stories was 'Martin Clifford', which was concocted by him from R. M. *Ballantyne's *Martin Rattler* and Bulwer-Lytton's *Paul Clifford*. Next, Percy Griffith, the young and voluble editor of *Gem*, announced to Hamilton that he was starting another boys' weekly for Harmsworth's Amalgamated Press, to be called *Magnet*; he asked Hamilton to provide the stories that would fill it each week. Hamilton had the impression that Griffith doubted that one man could possibly produce so much 'copy' week after week—*Gem* was continuing as usual—and he himself felt that 'it was rather a big thing.' But he agreed, and wrote the first story of Harry Wharton, Billy Bunter, and Greyfriars for the opening issue of *Magnet* early in 1908, this time using the pseudonym 'Frank Richards'. The choice of name was made carefully. As he wrote in *The Autobiography of Frank Richards* (1952), a book which mostly refers to its subject in the third person:

The chief thing was to select a name totally different from those under which he had hitherto written: so that when he used the name, he would feel like a different person, and in consequence write from a somewhat different angle. I have been told—by men who do not write—that this is all fanciful...This only means that they don't understand.

Hamilton usually managed the huge output now required of him quite easily, producing the week's *Gem* and *Magnet* stories (and often fiction for other boys' papers as well) in no more than ordinary working hours, often less. It was roughly the equivalent of writing an average-length novel (about 70,000 words) each week. He wrote straight on to his typewriter, which for year after year was the same Remington machine, and rarely made alterations or corrections before sending the typescript off to the editorial office. For the rest of the time he enjoyed himself, spending money as fast as he earned it, travelling widely in Europe and losing considerable sums at the roulette tables of Nice and Monte Carlo. He was an inveterate gambler—something that the 'Frank Richards' who wrote the Greyfriars stories with their conventional morality could never have approved of.

In 1915 he was asked to create yet another school story series, this time for the Harmsworth paper *Boys' Friend*. The school *Rookwood and the authorial pseudonym 'Owen Conquest' were the results, though neither was so close to Hamilton's heart as were 'Frank Richards' and Greyfriars. Another invention was *Bessie Bunter, who after a number of appearances in the *Magnet* was given her own series in *School Friend* when it began publication in 1919. For this Hamilton wrote as 'Hilda Richards'. But his manner seems to have been too crude for girls' tastes; at all events, after what he described as 'some spots of bother', he was taken off the paper, and the Bessie Bunter stories were continued by other writers. The Amalgamated Press was also in the habit of replacing the genuine 'Frank Richards', 'Martin Clifford', and 'Owen Conquest' with other writers using the same names when Hamilton was ill or had failed to send in copy, or simply when acceptable substitutes were found. This never ceased to annoy him. Meanwhile the real identity of 'Frank Richards' and the others was a closely guarded secret. Few readers, if any, suspected that all these celebrated school stories were the work of the same writer, and much effort was spent in laying false trails. Hamilton himself wrote a series about the boyhood of 'Frank Richards & Co.' at Cedar Creek, a backwoods school in Canada (a country he had never visited), and there were sometimes stories in the Harmsworth papers about Frank Richards, Martin Clifford, and Owen Conquest meeting each other.

By the 1920s Hamilton was producing about a million and a half words of fiction every year. He began to suffer from eye strain and had to use a heavily inked typewriter ribbon in order to read what he was writing. But he carried on as successfully as ever, and created yet another identity for himself as 'Ralph Redway', author of stories about the 'Rio Kid' in *Boys' Friend*. He also wrote, under his own name, a 'Ken King of the Islands' *adventure series in *Modern Boy*. Apart from all this, he produced other stories for other papers under other pseudonyms; no one has yet managed to trace and identify all his work, and by his own estimate he was the inventor of nearly 50 fictional schools.

Though he earned about £2,500 a year—a substantial income for that era—he spent it fast, and the closure of *Gem* and *Magnet* at the outbreak of the Second World War put him into awkward financial straits. But he found new markets for his work, and after the war was over a Billy Bunter revival quickly began. This was initiated by the publisher Charles Skilton, for whom Hamilton wrote new Bunter stories which appeared in hardback. 'Tom Merry' books were soon appearing too; other publishers commissioned fresh tales, and by 1950 Hamilton, in his mid-70s, was as busy as ever. He was aggressive towards critics, and threatened legal action on at least one occasion when he thought his books were about to be attacked in print. He was at work until the end of his long life, which came on Christmas Eve, 1961. Since his death he has become the subject of an enthusiastic following which almost amounts to a cult, and his fans have produced a number of books about him and his stories.

Hamilton was the most prolific author of juvenile fiction of all time, producing something like 7,000 stories of different lengths, with a total (according to the *Guinness Book of Records*) of more than 72 million words. In these circumstances it is remarkable that his work sustained any level of quality. In fact, as E. S. Turner has pointed out in *Boys Will Be Boys* (1975), 'a sub-editor surgically disposed could have cut out every other sentence without impairing continuity'. Yet Hamilton's plots were usually crafted skillfully, and the repetition was the essence of the style and had an almost hypnotic effect on devotees.

HAMILTON, Virginia (Esther) (1936–2002) African-American writer, born in Yellow Springs, Ohio. Her maternal grandfather Levi

Perry was an escaped slave who settled in Ohio, and she grew up among a 'large, extended and complex' Perry clan.

Her fiction is reflective, idiosyncratic, and entirely concerned with the imaginative development of its black heroes and heroines. *Zeely* (1967) describes a girl's private fantasies about another girl, tall and beautiful, who keeps hogs on a farm. *The House of Dies Drear* (1968), a Gothic *adventure story, is set in the house of a murdered abolitionist. *The Planet of Junior Brown* (1971), even less conventional than its predecessors, describes a 'solar system' of homeless boys spread around a big city, and the friendship of one of them with a janitor who keeps a model of the real solar system in a basement. **M.C. Higgins, the Great* (1974), which won the *Newbery Medal, the *National Book Award, and the *Boston Globe–Horn Book* Award (the first book to gain all three), is about the life of a boy who surveys the world from the top of a forty-foot steel pole on a mountainside. Later work included *Arilla Sun Down* (1976), and a *science fiction trilogy, *Justice and her Brothers* (1978), *Dustland* (1980), and *The Gathering* (1980).

Hamilton observed that 'as a writer, my concerns begin at some point on the far side of reality . . . What I am compelled to write can best be described as some essence of dreams, lies, myths, and disasters befallen a clan of my blood relatives.'

hand-colouring *See* COLOUR.

HANDLER, Daniel *See* SNICKET, LEMONY.

handwriting *See* COPYBOOKS.

***Hans Brinker,** or the Silver Skates* (1865) A novel, set in Holland, by Mary Mapes *Dodge, who later became editor of the magazine **St Nicholas*. Hans Brinker and his sister Gretel are the children of a poor labourer who has lost his wits in a fall from scaffolding. They learn that a pair of silver skates will be given as a prize for a skating-match on the frozen canal. Gretel eventually wins the prize, but the story is chiefly taken up with Hans's successful attempt to get a great doctor to cure his father.

Hans Brinker contains the celebrated tale of the 'Hero of Harlaam', the lad who, seeing a hole in the wall of a dyke, thrust a finger into it, thus preventing the waters' escape. The story so captivated American readers that the Dutch finally erected a statue to commemorate this fictitious hero and event.

Hans Christian Andersen Award
Awarded biennially since 1956, by the *International Board on Books for Young People, to an author whose works have made an outstanding contribution to children's literature. Since 1966 an illustrator's award has also been given. For a list of winners to date, *see* APPENDIX, B.

Hansel and Gretel A *fairy story first printed by the brothers *Grimm.

A brother and sister, Hansel and Gretel, are abandoned in the forest by their parents, who cannot afford to feed them. Thanks to Hansel's foresight, the children find their way home, but the parents make a second attempt, and this time Hansel and Gretel are well and truly lost. After wandering about, they are near dying of starvation when they find a cottage which is 'made of bread and cakes, and the window-panes were of clear sugar'. They start to eat pieces of the house and are then invited in by the owner, who is kind to them, but in the morning she reveals she is a witch who wishes to eat Hansel. She locks him up in a cage and begins to fatten him with food, making Gretel work for her the while. When the witch finally lights the oven to cook Hansel, Gretel manages to push the woman inside and she is baked alive. Gretel releases Hansel from his cage, and the two of them return to their parents' house, laden with pearls and jewels which they have found at the witch's house.

The opening of the story closely resembles Perrault's *Hop o' my Thumb, and also Mme d'*Aulnoy's *Finette Cendron*. A house built of food, which is the most distinctive feature of *Hansel and Gretel*, is found in a 14th-cent. poem in a British Library manuscript, which describes an abbey far out to sea, west of Spain, which is made of pasties, cakes, puddings, and meat.

Hansel and Gretel was made into a children's opera by Humperdinck, first performed in 1893.

Hans in Luck A story collected by the *Grimms. Hans is rewarded for seven years' apprenticeship with a big lump of gold. He sets off home with it, and on the way exchanges the gold for a horse, the horse for a cow, the cow for a pig, the pig for a goose, and the goose for a grindstone. All the time, he considers himself the luckiest person alive, and when the grindstone falls into a well, he thanks God for lightening his heavy burden.

Happy Families (from 1980) A popular series of books for children just ready to read,

written by Allan *Ahlberg and illustrated by a wide variety of different artists, including Andre Amstutz, Fritz *Wegner, Colin *McNaughton, and Faith *Jaques. Based on the familiar old card game of the same name, they began with *Master Bun the Baker's Boy* (1980) and continue through various titles such as *Mr Creep the Crook* (1988) to *Mr Tick the Teacher* (1999), each book telling an engaging, warm-hearted story.

Happy Lion A series by Roger *Duvoisin.

Happy Prince and other tales, The By Oscar Wilde (1854–1900), first published in 1888 with illustrations by Walter *Crane and Jacob Hood. The stories show a marked influence of Hans Christian *Andersen and an almost uniformly bitter outlook on life. That which gives the book its title tells how the statue of a prince who was a pleasure-seeker looks down from its pedestal on human poverty and misery. With the aid of a swallow, the statue brings some relief to those who are in misery, but both it and the bird perish as a result. The best known of the other stories in the book, 'The Selfish Giant', tells how a giant prohibits children from playing in his garden, with the result that the weather in it is permanently wintry; eventually the children creep back, the spring comes, and the Giant helps an infant who proves, in the story's almost mystical ending, to be the Christ-child. Wilde said of the book that it was 'an attempt to mirror modern life in a form remote from reality...not for children, but for childlike people from eighteen to eighty'; however, he did read the stories to his own children. In 1891 he published a second volume of *fairy stories, *A House of Pomegranates*, which made no pretence of being for children; this contained 'The Young King', 'The Birthday of the Infanta', 'The Fisherman and his Soul', and 'The Star-Child'. *The Happy Prince* is frequently reprinted, and some editions include stories from *A House of Pomegranates*.

Harding's Luck (1909) A novel by E. *Nesbit, companion-piece to *The *House of Arden*. Dickie Harding, a poor lame boy, lives in a London slum. He accidentally makes a magic pattern with his favourite possessions and through it (and the agency of the Mouldiwarp, from *The House of Arden*) he is taken back in time to the early 17th cent., where he discovers that he is the son of Sir Richard Arden, and that his cousins are Elfrida and Edred from the earlier book, time-travellers

from the 20th cent. like himself. Dickie completes Elfrida and Edred's mission by finding the Arden treasure, but it then appears that in the 20th cent. he, and not their father, is the rightful Lord Arden. Dickie decides to renounce his 20th-cent. life and go back permanently into the past, where, as the 17th-cent. Richard Arden, he has a fine life; by doing this, he leaves Elfrida and Edred's father in possession of both the title and the fortune.

HARDINGE, Frances (1973–) English author whose childhood in rural Kent fostered a love of the dark, the mysterious, and the arcane. Always recognizable from her trademark black hat, she writes stories that astound, amaze, amuse, and confuse (though then resolve). With beautiful prose and characters that are remarkably defined, she spins and twists reality to make stories. *Fly By Night* (2005)—which was only published because a friend happened to show it to her own publisher—is about how Mosca and her goose, via encounters with spies, radicals, highwaymen, and high adventure, become heroes of the revolution. Their adventures continue in *Twilight Robbery* (2011). *Verdigris Deep* (2007) teaches you never to steal coins from a well and *A Face Like Glass* (2013) is about a society based on lies. In 2015 she became only the second *Costa Children's Book Award winner to take the overall 'Book of the Year' prize, with her rich and original Victorian Gothic mystery, *The Lie Tree*.

HARDY, Thomas *See* OUR EXPLOITS AT WEST POLEY.

Hardy Boys, The Frank and Joe Hardy, teenage brothers, heroes of a series of mystery novels from the *Stratemeyer Syndicate. The first volume of the first series—*The Tower Treasure*—was published in 1927 (with a revised edition in 1959). Versions and spin-off series continue to be published today, and continue to sell in large numbers. The name of the author, 'Franklin W. Dixon', is a pen name shared by the various ghostwriters who have contributed to the series over the decades.

HARGREAVES, Roger (1935–88) British author-illustrator who worked as creative director of a London advertising agency before beginning to produce the first *Mr Men* books in the early 1970s. After that he also wrote and illustrated a set of stories about 'Timbuctoo' animals—*Neigh, Oink, Snap, Puff, Roar*, etc., all published in 1979—and a 'Little Miss' series, very similar to the *Mr Men*, which first appeared in 1981.

harlequinade A type of *picture book, also known as a 'turn up', occasionally published during the 18th and 19th cents. Folded parts of a page were lifted to disclose a new picture that fitted neatly on to the remaining part of the first one. The books took their name from the fact that some of them retold the stories of London *pantomimes, in which Harlequin invariably appeared. Examples include *Harlequin Cherokee, or the Indian Chiefs in London* (1779) and *Mother Shipton* (1800), which was reproduced in facsimile in 1980 by the Friends of the Osborne and Lillian H. Smith Collections in Toronto (*see* OSBORNE COLLECTION).

HARMSWORTH, Alfred (Charles William) Viscount Northcliffe (1865–1922) Newspaper proprietor who was responsible for the foundation of large numbers of popular weekly papers for boys and girls. He became a newspaper reporter and a freelance writer in order to help support his family after his father's health broke down. Harmsworth founded his own publishing company, which eventually became the Amalgamated Press, when he was only twenty-two. He specialized in popular educators, such as the magazine *Answers*. These were so successful that in 1894 he was able to afford to buy the then almost defunct London *Evening News*. Two years later he founded the *Daily Mail*. He was created a baronet in 1903 (the year he set up the *Daily Mirror*) and a peer in 1905, and reached the height of his ambition when in 1908 he became chief proprietor of *The Times*.

Meanwhile he was producing large numbers of weeklies for young people. *Comic Cuts* and *Chips*, two of the pioneer British *comics, came off his presses for the first time in 1890. Then in 1892 appeared the first Harmsworth paper containing boys' stories, *Halfpenny Wonder*. Like the companion papers which shortly joined it, *Marvel* (1893), *Union Jack* (1894), *Pluck* (1894), and *Boys' Friend* (1895), these were intended to catch the *penny dreadful market with stories that were exciting but nevertheless 'healthy'. After this there came Harmsworth's famous *school story magazines, *Gem* (1907) and *Magnet* (1908), the latter being the vehicle for *Billy Bunter. The year 1908 also saw the appearance of the first parts of The *Children's Encyclopaedia*, edited by Arthur *Mee. Among many *girls' story magazines produced by Amalgamated Press during this period, the most successful were *Girls' Friend* (1899) and *School Friend* (1919).

In 1912 Amalgamated Press claimed that their boys' papers encouraged 'physical strength... patriotism... interest in travel and exploration, and... pride in our empire'. In 1925 they claimed that 'there is no paper with which the firm has ever been associated that, whatever its other defects, could not at any time have been placed in the hands of the most puritanical man, woman or child without raising a blush or causing the faintest thrill of distaste.' On the other hand the Harmsworth story papers consisted chiefly of what parents and teachers dismissed as 'trash', and their contribution to children's lives was in the nature of crude entertainment and excitement rather than 'quality' fiction. This, of course, was the reason for their success.

HARNETT, Cynthia (Mary) (1893–1981) British writer of *historical novels for children. She studied to be an artist at the Chelsea School of Arts. During the 1930s she began to collaborate with her writer-artist cousin G. Vernon Stokes on *picture books about life in the country (*Junk, the Puppy*, 1937, and others). Her first historical novel for children, *The Great House* (1949), is the story of an architect in the early 18th cent. She won the *Carnegie Medal with *The *Wool-Pack* (1951). *Ring Out, Bow Bells!* (1953) was the story of the real *Dick Whittington. Her later books include *Stars of Fortune* (1956), about George Washington's English forebears, and *The Load of Unicorn* (1959), a tale of the rivalry between the printers of *Caxton's day and the scriveners or professional handwriters. Her last novel was *The Writing on the Hearth* (1971), set after Agincourt and dealing with a boy who wants to become an Oxford scholar.

Cynthia Harnett illustrated her own novels (except the last) with drawings designed to inform the readers about details of daily life in the period in which the story is set. The stories themselves are also designed to inform, and each book was the product of extensive research, but the narrative is rarely weighted down with detail, and the books continue to reward any readers with much enjoyment today.

Harold and the Purple Crayon (1955) A classic American picture book by Crockett *Johnson. It's the story of little Harold, who decides to go for a walk in the middle of the night, and takes his purple crayon with him, to draw his adventures as he goes. It's dark, so he draws himself a moon; there's no path to walk on, so he draws himself one of those, and so on. With its spare text and the simplicity of its pictures—each picture is a simple image of Harold with the thick purple lines he is drawing—this is an ingenious celebration of imagination and story.

Harper's Young People An American children's *magazine published from November 1879 to October 1899; it was weekly until November 1897, then a monthly. It resembled *St Nicholas and rivalled it in popularity. Contributors included Charles Carleton *Coffin and Howard *Pyle, whose *Robin Hood stories appeared in it. In 1891 the magazine instituted an Order of the Round Table for its readers, and in 1895 changed its title to *Harper's Round Table*.

Harriet and the Matches, *The Dreadful Story About* A poem in *Struwwelpeter*.

Harriet the Spy (1964) A novel by Louise *Fitzhugh, generally regarded as one of the funniest children's books of its period. Precocious eleven-year-old Harriet M. Welsch wants to be a famous writer when she grows up; meanwhile she observes her schoolmates and writes down a private record of them in her notebook—which then accidentally falls into their hands. In the early 1980s it was occasionally *banned or challenged in schools. *The Long Secret* (1965) is a sequel.

HARRIS, Aurand (1916–96) American author of *plays for children, largely adaptations of classic stories, beginning with *Pinocchio and the Fire-Eater* (1940). He worked as a drama teacher in schools and colleges throughout the USA.

HARRIS, Benjamin (*fl.* 1673–1716) Compiler of America's celebrated *New England Primer. He was a London bookseller during the reign of Charles II. He composed verses attacking the Papacy and the Jesuits, and was more than once in trouble for his extreme dissenting views. In 1683 he published *The *Protestant Tutor*, an extreme anti-Catholic *primer for children.

Upon the accession of the Catholic James II to the English throne, Harris was among those who felt that England was no place in which to live, and late in 1686 he travelled to Boston. There he produced a new primer developed from his *Protestant Tutor*, which he called *The New England Primer*. Its success in New England was so great that when Harris returned to London in 1695 he continued to publish it. The book became popular in Britain, and remained in print there even into the 19th cent.

HARRIS, Christie (Lucy) (1907–2002) Canadian children's author. She produced retellings of '*'Indian' legends (*Once Upon a Totem*, 1963, and others); realistic novels about adolescence and young adulthood, such as *You Have to Draw the Line Somewhere* (1964); and *historical novels (*Cariboo Trail*, 1957, and others).

HARRIS, Joel Chandler (1848–1908) Author of the **Uncle Remus* stories who was born in Georgia and worked as a printer's devil before being employed as a journalist on several Southern newspapers. By 1876, when he began many years on the staff of the *Atlanta Constitution*, he had made a reputation as a newspaper humorist. After reading an article on 'Folklore of the Southern Plantation', he began to write the 'Uncle Remus' tales, which started to appear in the *Constitution* in 1879. He was soon encouraged to print them in book form, and *Uncle Remus: His Songs and His Sayings* was published in 1880, to be followed by many sequels.

Harris used to insist that he was the mere redactor of the stories, not their author; but in fact he worked with much skill on what was often not more than a bare outline of a folk story, enriching it with the speech characteristic of Georgia's black population (language which he had studied closely), and using his own considerable talents as a storyteller. These can be seen in other books he wrote for children, which include *Little Mr Thimblefinger and His Queer Country* (1894), a collection of stories linked by a frame tale about children visiting a land where animals can talk, *Wally Wanderoon and his Story-Telling Machine* (1903), partly a satire on the modern scientific influence on the old art of storytelling, *A Little Union Scout* (1904), an *adventure story set during the Civil War, and *The Bishop and the Boogerman* (1909), a comic novel for children.

HARRIS, John (1756–1846) London bookseller, publisher of children's books, and successor to the family of *Newbery; he produced a series of juvenile publications that were notable for their visual charm and elegance and for their emphasis on pure entertainment rather than instruction.

Harris was apprenticed at an early age to a London bookseller, Thomas Evans. He then worked briefly for John Murray, and finally joined the firm of Newbery. From about 1797 he was Elizabeth Newbery's manager, and in

1801 he took over the firm in his own name. At first he did little to alter the Newbery list, but in 1804 he began to publish new titles. Initially these were in the usual Newbery style, but in 1805 he issued *The Comic Adventures of Old Mother Hubbard and Her Dog* (*see* MOTHER HUBBARD). Unlike the books that were typical of the Newberys, this was intended purely for amusement and contained no didactic element whatsoever. It also had *copperplate illustrations on every page; Newbery and his successors had generally used *woodcuts, and had not often been generous with the amount of illustration. The book was in a small, almost square format (5 × 4 in.) which Harris continued to favour for some years.

The success of this book was very great, and Harris produced two more about Mother Hubbard, which were followed by *Whimsical Incidents* (1805), a poem in the same style, and *Original Ditties for the Nursery* (*c*. 1805), a book of *nursery rhymes which included the first appearances of 'Little Polly Flinders' and *Tweedledum and Tweedledee. In 1806 came, among other books, several featuring *Dame Trot, and an edition of **John Gilpin*, a poem which Harris realized had potential for children; in these, the illustrations were hand-coloured (*see* COLOUR).

In 1807 appeared *The *Butterfly's Ball*, an instant success which was reprinted again and again. It was followed by the even more successful *Peacock 'at Home'* (1807) and a number of other imitations, such as *The Council of Dogs, The Fishes' Grand Gala*, and *The Mermaid 'At Home'*. Harris also published two books of *cautionary tales in verse, *The *Daisy* (1807) and its successor *The Cowslip* (1811), both by Elizabeth Turner.

Harris did not turn his back on the profits to be made from conventionally sober books for young people. Many of Mrs *Trimmer's works were published by him, along with the books of other equally 'safe' authors. But the *books of instruction issued by him in the series 'Harris's Cabinet of Amusement and Instruction' (inaugurated in 1807) were designed to entertain as well as to teach, and they were sometimes attacked for this. A writer in the *London Magazine* for November 1820 dismissed Harris's book of *tongue-twisters, *Peter Piper's Practical Principles of Plain and Perfect Pronunciation* (1813), as 'degrading trash'. The same writer also deplored the 'gaudy glare' of Harris's coloured books. on the grounds that they spoilt children's taste for the natural colours of the real world. However, such

books in the 'Cabinet' as *Marmaduke Multiply's Merry Method of Making Minor Mathematicians* (1816–17) and The *Paths of Learning Strewed with Flowers* (1820) proved very popular with parents, and Harris also made a speciality of gaily illustrated *ABC books such as The History of an Apple Pie (1820), Nursery Novelties for Little Masters and Misses* (1819), and The Hobby-Horse (1820), which contained *A was an Archer.

By 1809 Harris's catalogue contained 419 items, all of which were for children or those teaching them. His books, sold from premises at the corner of St Paul's Churchyard formerly occupied by Newbery's successors and renamed 'The Juvenile Library' by Harris, were not cheap. Most late 18th-cent. children's books had cost only a few pence, but Harris's early juvenile publications were priced at 'One Shilling plain, and Eighteen-pence coloured', while later only the coloured eighteenpenny versions were available. As Marjorie Moon observes in her checklist of Harris's publications (1976), his customers undoubtedly came chiefly from the affluent classes.

In 1819 the firm became 'J. Harris and Son', and in the five years that followed many of the original 'Cabinet' books were reissued with new engravings and in a larger page-format, while new titles were also added, such as The *History of Sixteen Wonderful Old Women* (1820), apparently the first book of *limericks. Harris's were now firmly established as the most high-class publishers of popular children's books. Their output was imitated by other booksellers such as *Tabart, the *Godwins, and John *Marshall; the latter matched Harris's *Paths of Learning Strewed with Flowers* with his own *Path of Learning Strewed with Roses* (1821) and tried to rival Harris's limerick-book with his own *Anecdotes and Adventures of Fifteen Gentlemen* (c.1821), while another firm, *Dean and Munday, issued books that were very close to Harris's and consistently priced more cheaply, at one shilling. D. Carvalho of Finsbury Square was yet another imitator with his shilling books.

The Harris books from the period 1819–24 show the firm at its zenith. During this time the shaded monochrome copperplates of Harris's early books were replaced by sharply-drawn *wood engravings especially designed to take hand-colouring. When the professional colourists had completed their work, the result was often remarkable. In 1824 John Harris junior took over the proprietorship from his father, and showed himself to be a rather less imaginative publisher, so that the output of new juvenile titles began to diminish. In 1843 the firm of Harris was absorbed by Grant and Griffith (*see* GRIFFITH AND FARRAN), and John Harris died three years later, in his ninety-first year, a rich man.

HARRIS, Mary K. (Kathleen) (1905–66) British author of *school stories for girls, ranging from *Gretel at St Bride's* (1941), set in the conventional boarding school of girls' fiction, to *Jessica on Her Own* (1966), which takes place in a secondary modern school.

HARRIS, Rosemary (Jeanne) (1923–) British novelist. She won the *Carnegie Medal with her first children's book, *The Moon in the Cloud* (1968), the first volume in a trilogy set in Old Testament times, which treats biblical history with a good deal of licence. Her other books include *The Seal-Singing* (1971), set on a remote Scottish island. She has also made retellings of Eastern and Western legends for young readers.

Harry A cat in five small *picture books by American author-illustrator Mary Chalmers (1927–), beginning with *Throw a Kiss, Harry* (1958).

Harry, the Dirty Dog (1956) By Gene Zion (1913–75), illustrated by Margaret Bloy Graham (1920–2015), Zion's wife at the time. Harry hates baths so much that he buries the scrubbing brush in the garden and runs away. A day spent playing in the dirt turns the white dog with black spots into a black dog with white spots. His family doesn't recognize him despite repeated attempts to prove his identity, so Harry must take drastic measures in order to be welcomed back home. The endearing cartoon canine also appears in *No Roses for Harry* (1958), *Harry and the Lady Next Door* (1960), and *Harry by the Sea* (1965).

Harry and Lucy A volume in the series *Early Lessons* (1801) by Maria *Edgeworth.

Harry and the Bucketful of Dinosaurs *See* WHYBROW, IAN.

Harry Potter (1997–2007) A seven-book fantasy series by J. K. (Joanne) Rowling (1965–), which has a credible claim to be the most successful children's book series of all time. Formally conventional, but well plotted and richly imagined, it has been criticized in some quarters for derivative content and lacklustre prose, while also credited with turning millions of children on to the pleasures of

reading—though the books' enthusiastic readers and champions massively, vastly outnumber their handful of critics.

The principal setting for the series is *Hogwarts School of Witchcraft and Wizardry, reached from the *muggle (that is to say, non-magic) world by the Hogwarts Express from platform nine-and-three-quarters at London's Kings Cross Station. Each of the seven books corresponds to the events of one year of Harry Potter's school career. He is enrolled aged eleven at the start of book one, upon discovering that he is a wizard (despite being brought up by his unpleasant muggle relatives, the *Dursleys, following his parents' death). Hogwarts, under the benign directorship of Professor Albus Dumbledore, has much of the traditional English boarding school about it, except that this school's syllabus includes subjects like Defence Against the Dark Arts, Herbology, the History of Magic and Transfiguration. The staff include Professor Minerva McGonagall, head of Gryffindor (the house to which Harry is assigned upon arrival by the magical Sorting Hat); the sinister Professor Severus Snape, who teaches Potions and is head of Slytherin; and Rubeus Hagrid, a giant who is the school's Grounds Keeper and who teaches Care of Magical Creatures. For team sports, the pupils play *Quidditch, a high-speed game on flying broomsticks for which Harry finds he has considerable natural aptitude.

In the first book in the series, *Harry Potter and the Philosopher's Stone* (. . . *and the Sorcerer's Stone* in the US), Harry and his new friends Ron Weasley (cheerful, loyal, and brave) and Hermione Granger (brainy and a little bossy) learn of the existence of the Philosopher's Stone—from which is it possible to extract an elixir of life—which they believe Professor Snape is attempting to steal. They eventually discover that the real culprit is Professor Quirrell, under orders from (and sometimes possessed by) the evil Lord Voldemort, the series's main antagonist. It was Voldemort who years before had killed Harry's parents—and failed to kill Harry (leaving him only with a lightning scar on his forehead and great renown in the wizarding community); and now the evil lord is back and gathering his strength in order to take over the world. It is this struggle—Harry and the forces of good versus Voldemort and evil—that will underpin the principal drama of the whole series. Book one also introduces objects such as the Invisibility Cloak, and the Mirror of Erised, which shows the viewer whatever he or she most desires.

In *Harry Potter and the Chamber of Secrets* (1998)—year two of Harry's time at Hogwarts—Ron's sister Ginny finds an old notebook, which turns out to be the diary of a schoolboy: Tom Marvolo Riddle. The diary contains a manifestation of Riddle himself, who eventually reveals that his name is an anagram of 'I Am Lord Voldemort'—the schoolboy Tom would grow up to be Voldemort himself. The Chamber of Secrets is opened, and a basilisk let loose. Book two also includes a colony of giant spiders and a house-elf called Dobby.

Harry Potter and the Prisoner of Azkaban (1999) introduces the Dementors—guards at the wizard prison of Azkaban, from which one 'Sirius Black' has just escaped, and among Rowling's darkest creations. But it turns out that Black was framed; he was a friend of Harry's parents, and is Harry's godfather. Other key participants in book three are Lupin (a werewolf), Harry's nasty schoolmate Draco Malfoy, and Buckbeak, Hagrid's hippogriff. After the summer break, it is announced that the Triwizard Tournament is to be held at Hogwarts, and this great competition is the centrepiece of book four, *Harry Potter and the Goblet of Fire* (2000). Harry is one of four students chosen to compete in a challenge to complete a number of dangerous tasks, during which his friend Cedric is killed. The appearance in the sky of the Dark Mark confirms Voldemort's return.

In *Harry Potter and the Order of the Phoenix* (2003) Harry is taken to Sirius's home, the headquarters of the Order of the Phoenix, an organization led by Dumbledore that is dedicated to fighting Voldemort's supporters, the Death Eaters. Meanwhile Harry and his school-friends set up a student group to learn defensive skills, Dumbledore's Army. (This book was the most violent of the ever-darkening series up to that point, attracting some criticism as a result.) Preparations for the great battle continue in book six, *Harry Potter and the Half-Blood Prince* (2005), which sees Harry learn much about Voldemort's past using a Pensieve—a device for seeing other people's memories. The book introduces the concept of 'horcruxes', objects which are receptacles for part of a person's soul—to kill this person entirely, all their horcruxes must be destroyed, too. To create a horcrux, one must commit a murder. Voldemort has eight horcruxes. One of the eight is

within him; one was Tom Riddle's Diary—now already destroyed; and one is Harry himself. The climax of the book comes with Dumbledore being killed by Snape.

The series concludes with a definitive confrontation between Harry and Voldemort, in *Harry Potter and the Deathly Hallows*. This is the only book mostly set outside Hogwarts. It concerns the hunt by Harry and co. for the remaining horcruxes, and their parallel search for the three sacred 'Deathly Hallows'. Many major characters lose their lives when Voldemort and his Death Eaters attack Hogwarts, among them Severus Snape, now revealed to have been on Harry's side all along. The evil Lord Voldemort is killed in a final duel. An epilogue, set nineteen years later, shows Harry and his friends back at Kings Cross, with their own children about to board the Hogwarts Express. It concludes with the words: 'All was well.'

After a modest start—this was Rowling's debut, written in a time of some financial hardship and published with unremarkable expectations—success came quickly for the first book, thanks to many awards and enthusiastic word of mouth. By the time the seventh and final volume appeared a decade later, public anticipation was enough to make it the fastest-selling book of all time (some fifteen million copies sold in the first twenty-four hours), with queues around the block outside bookshops hosting special midnight openings with Harry Potter parties. The scale of the book production led to calls from environmental groups including Greenpeace to boycott publishers who did not use recycled paper specifically for their Potter printing.

The books' persistent dominance of the top spots on the *New York Times* bestseller list led in 2000 to the paper instituting a distinct list for children's books just to clear some space for adult fiction. (Four years later, the children's list itself would be split, differentiating between series books and stand-alones, again to allow non-Potters a chance to compete.) From quite early in the series's history, however, many of its readers were adults; Rowling's UK publisher, Bloomsbury, capitalized on this *crossover interest by releasing the series in adult-friendly jacket designs in parallel with the children's editions.

Despite its ubiquity, the series has occasionally been challenged by conservative Christian groups in an attempt to get them *banned, following accusations that they promote witchcraft, but despite the efforts of the small number of protestors, the books have sold an estimated 450 million copies around the world, and been translated (officially) into at least sixty-seven languages, so are somewhat hard to avoid.

One of the most widely visible products of the Harry Potter franchise was the eight-film series (the seventh and final volume was split into two films), which began in 2001 and concluded in 2011, with Daniel Radcliffe in the title role and a host of famous (mainly British) acting talent among the adult cast. Unusually, Rowling retained a measure of creative control throughout. The films, from a number of different directors, were of variable brilliance, but all managed to capture much of the flavour of the stories, and commercially they combined to comprise the highest-grossing film series in history. Other popular Potter spin-offs include theme parks, video games, and a fake trolley embedded in the wall at London's Kings Cross station for tourists to photograph themselves pretending to board the Hogwarts Express.

The Potter stories are in a long tradition of magic books for children (predecessors including Diana Wynne *Jones, Ursula *Le Guin, and many other creators of this kind of *fantasy), and also draw on a typical coming-of-age developmental structure and the old genre of boarding *school stories (which had for a time come to seem rather outdated for diverse modern global readerships). In turn, the books' global success led to countless inferior magic books being churned out in their wake.

J. K. Rowling has also written a number of short books associated with Harry's world: *Fantastic Beasts and Where to Find Them* (2001; itself spawning a projected five-movie series, whose first launched in 2016), *Quidditch through the Ages* (2001), and *The Tales of Beedle the Bard* (2008), the sales for all of these benefiting charities that Rowling supports. After a long development period, 2012 saw the full public launch of 'Pottermore', an official website with unpublished material, downloadable e-books, etc. Jim *Kay was selected to produce the first fully illustrated editions of the series, with book one appearing in 2015. Characters from Harry Potter's world returned in 2016 in a spectacular London stage show, *Harry Potter and the Cursed Child* (co-written by Jack Thorne, in collaboration with Rowling), set nineteen years after the end of the main series.

Harry Wharton Schoolboy hero of many of the *Greyfriars stories of 'Frank *Richards' (Charles *Hamilton).

HART (Smedley), Elizabeth Anna (1822–c. 1890) Victorian author and poet, distant cousin of Lewis *Carroll, who wrote more than twenty books for children, most of them published anonymously. They include *Poems Written for a Child* (1868), which anticipates something of the imagination of Walter *de la Mare and A. A. *Milne, and *The Runaway* (1872), a story about a runaway from school.

HARTNETT, Sonya (1968–) Australian *young adult novelist. In 1996 the dark issues in *Sleeping Dogs* (1995), which won the *CBCA Honour Book for Older Readers, generated discussion locally and elsewhere. The book features violence, abuse, incest, and a brutal ending. In 2005 she won the CBCA Book of the Year: Younger Readers with *The Silver Donkey* (2004) and the CBCA Book of the Year: Older Readers in 2008 for *The Ghost's Child* (2007), also an *IBBY Honour Book in 2009. Then Hartnett wrote her first picture books, *The Boy and the Toy* (2010) and *Come Down, Cat!* (2011), both illustrated by Lucia Masciullo. *The Midnight Zoo* (2010) won the CBCA Book of the Year: Older Readers and was shortlisted for the *Carnegie Medal in 2012. *The Midnight Zoo* is the story of two gypsy boys fleeing through a war-ravaged countryside, carrying their infant sister. They stumble into a zoo, in a story where historical truth blurs with fantasy, and the cages become a symbol for freedom.

Many of Hartnett's books have been published to much acclaim in the UK and in North America. In 1996, she won the IBBY Prize for writing for young adults for *Wilful Blue* (1994), a mystery where four young artists are commissioned to decorate a retreat with murals, but during the summer Guy becomes more maudlin and dies mysteriously. For *Thursday's Child* (2000) she won the annual *Guardian Children's Fiction Prize. In 2008 Hartnett was the first Australian to receive the prestigious (and richest) *Astrid Lindgren Memorial Award from the Swedish Arts Council for her career contribution to 'children's and young adult literature in the broadest sense'.

Hartnett is a critically acclaimed author whose books do not always follow a conventional linear narrative—they are poetic, with mood dominating over plot. Fantasy and a harsh social realism often collide to place the characters in genuine danger, so they are forced to look within for strength.

Hathi Elephant in *The *Jungle Books* by Rudyard *Kipling.

Hattifatteners In the *Moomin books by Tove Jansson.

HAUFF, Wilhelm (1802–27) A German writer who made some reputation as a novelist before his early death and brought out several collections of *fairy stories, a number of which were translated into English from the 1840s onwards. His tales often resemble the *Arabian Nights. Hauff treated traditional folk tales as the starting point for his own compositions. His story *Dwarf Long-Nose*, translated by Doris Orgel, was reprinted in 1960 with illustrations by Maurice *Sendak.

HAUGHTON, Chris (1978–) An Irish picture-book creator and illustrator, known for his bold design and distinctive colour palette. His first picture book *A Bit Lost* (*Little Owl Lost* in the United States) was first published in Korea in 2009, and has been translated into nineteen languages, winning nine awards in seven countries, including the Dutch Picture Book of the Year. Haughton received *Booktrust's Best New Illustrators Award in 2011. His second picture book *Oh No, George!* (2012) is a story that will be familiar to anyone who has ever owned a mischief-making dog; it won the Junior Magazine Picturebook of the Year Award. His third book *Shh! We Have a Plan* (2014) was shortlisted for the Association of Illustrators Awards and uses a stunning palette of blues which emphasizes the explosion of colours late on in the book. Haughton devised his own font for all of his books and works by drawing by hand or using collage, scanning, and then blocking in colour on the computer.

Haunted House (1979) By Jan *Pieńkowski, a humorous *pop-up book which helped to lead the revival of that genre in Britain. 'Let yourself in,' says the notice. At once the reader must explore the house, opening doors to find something disgusting, shivering as eyes blink or spiders creep, and jumping with shock as monsters burst from the pages. In collaboration with the paper engineer, Tor Lokvig, and with the support of publisher, Waldo 'Wally' Hunt, Pieńkowski created a pop-up book that contained not just one, but several mechanisms on each page, each working to deliver a surprise with humour. *Haunted House* was truly innovative, inspiring both readers and other artists. It won Pieńkowski the 1979 *Kate Greenaway Medal.

Haunting, The (1982) A novel by Margaret *Mahy. Barney is being haunted. He hears a voice telling him 'Barnaby is dead,' but he is very much alive. That this refers to his great-uncle makes it no less frightening. Whose

voice is it? What are the secrets behind the respectable facade of his family? Why will no one talk about the boy in the photograph? With this, her first novel for older children, Mahy, well known for her lively picture books and short stories, creates a haunting story which cleverly balances the warmth of family relationships with a chilling sense of foreboding. *The Haunting* was awarded the 1982 *Carnegie Medal.

HAUTZIG, Esther (1930–2009) Autobiographer and writer of children's fiction and non-fiction, resident in America; best known for *The *Endless Steppe* (1968), an account of how she and her parents were transported from their home in Poland to Siberia by the Russians in 1941.

HAVILAND, Virginia (1911–88) American critic and historian of children's literature, who became the first Head of the Children's Book Section of the Library of Congress in 1963. Her books include *Children's Literature: views and reviews* (1974) and *Yankee Doodle's Literary Sampler of Prose, Poetry and Pictures* (1974), an anthology of excerpts from historic pre-1900 American children's books, which she edited with her assistant and successor Margaret N. Coughlan. She compiled *The Fairy Tale Treasury* (1972), illustrated by Raymond *Briggs.

HAWKINS, Anthony Hope See HOPE, ANTHONY.

HAWTHORNE, Nathaniel (1804–64) American man of letters who wrote two celebrated books retelling myths for children. He was born in Salem, Mass., and was descended from a judge in the celebrated witchcraft trials in that town. His father, a sea captain, died when he was four, and Nathaniel spent a mostly solitary childhood. He soon decided to become a writer, and after a college education he published an unsuccessful novel. This drew him to the attention of S. G. *Goodrich, the energetic Boston writer and publisher who was at that time founding an *annual for family readership, *The Token*, in which he published some of Hawthorne's stories, for which the writer received little remuneration. Hawthorne later referred to Goodrich as 'a dealer in slip-slop on many subjects'; in fact he did a great deal of hack-work for him, compiling (with his sister Elizabeth) *Peter Parley's Universal History* (1837). He also wrote such books as *Grandfather's Chair: a history for youth* (1841) and *Biographical Stories for Children* (1842). Following the publication in 1850 of his highly successful novel *The Scarlet Letter*, Hawthorne took advantage of his new-found fame by writing *A *Wonder-Book for Boys and Girls* (1851) and *Tanglewood Tales* (1853), both intended as moneymakers.

Hawthorne's short story *The Snow-Image*, first published in 1851 in a collection of the same title, remained popular with children for many years. It is an allegory about two girls who build a child of snow which comes to life, but melts away when the girls' father intervenes.

HAYES, John F. (Francis) (1904–80) Canadian author of *historical novels for children, all set in pre-20th-cent. Canada and notable for their well-researched backgrounds and fast-moving plots. They include *Buckskin Colonist* (1947), *A Land Divided* (1951), and *The Nation Builders* (1968).

HAYWOOD, Carolyn (1898–1990) American author-illustrator best known for books about children named 'Betsy' and 'Eddie', the first in each series being, respectively, *'B' is for Betsy* (1939) and *Little Eddie* (1947).

HAZARD, Paul (1878–1944) French writer on children's literature who taught at the Sorbonne and other French academic institutions, and was one of his country's most highly regarded specialists in European literature. His close association with the United States began in 1932 when he made the first of several visits to Columbia University. His influential *Les Livres, les enfants et les hommes*, a short historical survey of juvenile literature in Europe and America, characterized by its dogmatic pronouncements about what children require in their reading-matter, was published in America in 1944 as *Books, Children and Men*.

Hazel Rabbit in *Watership Down* by Richard *Adams.

Headless Horseman See LEGEND OF SLEEPY HOLLOW, THE.

Heard It in the Playground (1989) By Allan *Ahlberg, his second collection of poems celebrating life in a primary school. It followed the success of *Please Mrs Butler* (1984). The verses are characterized by Ahlberg's sense of humour and keen ear for the language of children. Characters from the earlier collection make a reappearance; this combines with familiar school rituals and situations to enhance the immediate appeal

of the poems. *Heard It in the Playground* was awarded the Signal Poetry Award.

HEARN, Julie (1958–) After being a journalist and having a short spell teaching, English author Julie Hearn has produced a small body of critically acclaimed, sophisticated, and thought-provoking fiction. A Master's degree in Women's Studies gave her the inspiration for her first novel, *Follow Me Down* (2003), about a 'monster' in a Victorian fairground. Since then she has tackled witchcraft in *The Merrybegot* (2005), the slave trade in *Hazel* (2007), and the complex subject of madness in 2009's deeply moving *Rowan the Strange*. *Wreckers* (2013) takes her writing into a postapocalyptic future.

HEARN, Lian *see* RUBINSTEIN, GILLIAN.

HEDDERWICK, Mairi *see* KATIE MORAG.

Heffalumps are mentioned in both of A. A. Milne's *Winnie-the-Pooh books, though they never appear (except as threatening figures in Piglet's and Pooh's imagination) and all attempts to trap one prove fruitless. According to the *Shepard illustration, they are elephant-like in appearance, though as any reader of Milne knows, heffalumps do not really exist. The *Disney corporation wilfully missed the point when they created further Pooh stories (in TV series and animated films) in which friendly heffalumps recur as featured characters.

Heidi (1881) A novel by Johanna *Spyri, set in the Swiss Alps. A five-year-old orphan girl known as Heidi (her real name is Adelheid) is taken up a mountain by her cousin Dete to live with her grandfather. The old man is misanthropic and a religious sceptic; he led a wild youth, and the local people regard the death of his son and daughter-in-law (Heidi's parents) as God's vengeance on him. Nevertheless he welcomes Heidi kindly to his bare but hospitable hut and she is soon delightedly sharing his frugal life, spending all her days in summer roaming the mountain-slopes with young Peter the goatherd. In the winter she goes down the mountain every afternoon to sit with and talk to Peter's old blind grandmother, whose bleak life is greatly cheered by her.

When she is eight years old Heidi is virtually kidnapped from the mountain by Dete, who carries her off to Frankfurt to act as a companion to the crippled child of a rich family, Clara Sesemann. Heidi becomes sad and unwell; her rough country ways and her ignorance of etiquette and city life soon reduce the Sesemann household to chaos and the governess-house-keeper, Fraulein Rottenmeier, to a nervous wreck. Clara's father eventually arranges for Heidi to return to the mountains for which she is pining. She can now read, and when she repeats aloud to her grandfather the biblical story of the Prodigal Son he is moved to resume his religious beliefs. Clara Sesemann comes to the mountains, and thanks to Heidi and Peter she learns to walk. The Sesemanns become the benefactors of Peter's grandmother.

The book was first published as *Heidis Lehr- und Wanderjahre*, and came out in England in 1884 in two volumes, as *Heidi's Early Experiences* and *Heidi's Further Experiences*. It has been filmed more than once (the first version, in 1937, starred Shirley *Temple) and televised, and maintains a firm place as a favourite and a classic of international children's literature. Two sequels, *Heidi Grows Up* and *Heidi's Children* (1958), have been written by Charles Tritten. In 2010 a Swiss academic discovered a possible source for *Heidi*, a novel written in 1830 by the German author Hermann Adam von Kamp entitled *Adelaide: The Girl from the Alps*.

HEINLEIN, Robert (Anson) (1907–88) American author of *science fiction for children and adults. His first children's book was *Rocket Ship Galileo* (1947), about a group of boys who fly to the moon in a home-made rocket. Among his later stories is *Red Planet* (1949), which describes the adventures of a schoolboy with a ball-like creature that is in fact a young Martian.

Heir of Redclyffe, The (1853) By Charlotte M. *Yonge, one of the most popular novels of the mid-19th cent., much read by children and teenagers. Jo, in *Little Women, is found by her sister Meg eating apples and crying over it. The story concerns Sir Guy Morville, a generous young heir to an estate, whose character is blackened by his mean-spirited cousin Philip, and who is on his deathbed before the whole truth about his nobility of character is discovered. The book was based on an idea by Miss Yonge's friend Marianne Dyson, and was written under the critical eye of John Keble.

Helen's Babies (1876) A popular novel by the American author John Habberton (1842–1921). It purports to be an account of a vacation spent by a young uncle in charge of his sister's children, but was really based on the

escapades of Habberton's own small sons. It has humour of a fairly obvious kind and, though the manuscript was rejected by several publishers, it became a best-seller. Habberton, who was a professional journalist and editor, wrote a sequel, *Other People's Children* (1877), and a mass of other popular fiction in the hope of repeating this success.

HEMANS (Browne), Mrs Felicia Dorothea (1793–1835) One of the most popular British poets of her day, who had her first volume of verse published in 1808, when she was fourteen; this book was reissued in 1836 as *Early Blossoms, a collection of poems written between eight and fifteen years of age.* Her *Hymns on the Works of Nature for the Use of Children* was published in America in 1827, and was reissued in England in 1833, where it afterwards acquired the title *Hymns for Childhood.* Mrs Hemans's poems were often learnt for recitation by 19th-cent. children. They include 'The boy stood on the burning deck' ('Casabianca') and 'The stately homes of England'.

HEMYNG, S. (Samuel) Bracebridge (1841–1901) Late Victorian author of *penny dreadfuls, Hemyng was a London barrister. His first *Jack Harkaway story appeared in 1871; he also wrote a *Dick Lightheart* series and other works for boys.

HENKES, Kevin (1960–) American author and illustrator. Several of his picture books feature mouse characters, including *Julius, the Baby of the World* (1990), *Lilly's Purple Plastic Purse* (2006), and *Lilly's Big Day* (2006), all starring the indomitable Lilly; the Caldecott Honor Book (*see* CALDECOTT MEDAL) *Owen* (1993); and three I Can Read books about Penny. *Penny and Her Marble* (2012) was a Geisel Honor Book. Henkes won the Caldecott Medal for *Kitten's First Full Moon* (2004) and has won Newbery Honor Awards (*see* NEWBERY MEDAL) for his novels *Olive's Ocean* (2003) and *The Year of Billy Miller* (2013).

Henny-Penny *See* CHICKEN-LICKEN.

HENRY, Marguerite (1902–97) American writer of children's novels about horses. She won the *Newbery Medal for *King of the Wind* (1948), the story of an Arabian stallion and the boy who looks after him.

Henry Huggins A boy in stories by Beverly *Cleary. Henry lives in Portland, Oregon, on Klickitat Street, and is eight years old at the time of the first book, *Henry Huggins* (1950).

His adventures are always comic and involve minor domestic crises; recurring characters include his dog Ribsy and a pair of sisters called Beezus and *Ramona, about whom Beverly Cleary has written another set of books.

Henry Milner *The History of* (1822–37) A three-volume novel by Mrs *Sherwood.

Henry Reed An American boy, hero of stories by Keith Robertson (1914–91). He first appeared in *Henry Reed, Inc.* (1958), and there were five sequels, four illustrated by Robert *McCloskey. Henry spends his New Jersey summers trying to earn money with various business schemes, including a babysitting service and a town think tank. He is aided by a tomboyish girl called Midge, and chaos ensues.

HENSON, Jim *See* SESAME STREET.

HENTY, G. A. (George Alfred) (1832–1902) British writer of the most popular and enduring of the late 19th-cent. *adventure stories for boys. He was born at Trumpington, near Cambridge, the son of a stockbroker and mineowner. He spent much of his childhood ill in bed, and so read a great deal, especially in *natural history, and developed an interest in poetry. These hobbies made him vulnerable to teasing by other boys when he went to Westminster School at the age of fourteen, so he learnt boxing to defend himself and developed the strength and pugnacity which characterized him as an adult. He then went to Cambridge University to read Classics, and while there rowed and took training from professionals in boxing and wrestling. He left Cambridge when the Crimean War broke out, after volunteering for army service.

From there Henty wrote vivid letters home describing conditions, and his father approached a daily newspaper suggesting that his son would make a good correspondent for them. He remained in the army for the next five years, Henty also established his skills as a journalist. In 1858 he married Elizabeth Finucane, and they quickly had a family of four children. But in 1865 Henty's wife died, and this seems to have prompted his decision to take up full-time journalism and to become a roving correspondent. In 1866 he covered the Austro-Italian War.

Henty was an exceptionally intelligent and well-informed correspondent, and after covering the Abyssinia expedition of 1867–8 he published a collection of his despatches. In 1867 he also brought out the first of his several adult

novels, none of which achieved much success. In 1870-1 he reported on the Franco-Prussian War. On his return the publishers *Griffith and Farran approached him with an offer for a story mainly for juvenile readers, based on his experience. Their cash overcame his reluctance.

The result was two books. The first to appear was *Out on the Pampas; or, the Young Settlers* (1871), a story originally written for Henty's own children in 1868. The central family, the children of which are named after his own offspring, emigrate to farm in Argentina.

The book actually envisaged by Griffith and Farran came out a year later. It was *The Young Franc-Tireurs*, in which the two sons of an English soldier living in France become guerrilla fighters on the French side and so witness the principal events of the Franco-Prussian War. That its author had been correspondent of the *Standard* for that war was emphasized as one of the book's selling points. Henty's introduction vouchsafed that 'Many of the occurrences in this tale are related almost in the words in which they were described to me by those who took part in them, and nearly every fact and circumstance actually occurred according to my own knowledge.'

The success of the book surprised him; but he continued as a special correspondent, in Russia, Africa, Spain, India, and the Balkans. However, after the Turkish-Serbian war in 1876 he came home exhausted, and from then on remained in England. In 1880 he published another children's book, *The Young Buglers: a Tale of the Peninsular War*. By the following year, when *The Cornet of Horse: a Tale of Marlborough's Wars* came out, his formula, his policy, and his methods were finally established. For *historical novels he would order some ten books from the London Library, and would write or dictate his story with the most useful of these open in front of him. He sometimes quoted from them verbatim, and set great store by his seriousness of purpose and his accuracy. An introduction to each book, beginning 'Dear Lads', became his custom.

Henty's writing gathered esteem—'he understands boys' tastes better than any man living,' wrote *The Times*—and he gained in speed of composition. By 1886 he was generally producing four books a year, and reckoned he could write one in twenty days; in all, he published some eighty boys' stories or collections of shorter pieces, as well as eleven adult novels. In addition he edited the new boys' paper *Union Jack, Beeton's *Boys' Own Magazine*, and collaborated on an *annual, *Camps and Quarters*. He was in fact the dominant figure in English boys' fiction from 1880 until his death; it is estimated that some 25 million copies of his books had been sold by 1914. They were read all over the English-speaking world, were much pirated in America until the production of authorized editions in 1891, and came to be credited with being most English boys' main source of historical knowledge.

Harvey *Darton commented on the formulaic nature of Henty's stories, stating that 'if you have read only two or three of the seventy-odd books he wrote for boys you know most of the rest'. This formula was in part held in common with the other boys' adventure writers of the time, part his own. Most of his books have as hero a boy of fifteen or sixteen (or sometimes a pair of brothers), in unusually fine physical condition, endowed with manly skills, a good heart, and a hot head. Then a great historical movement, an insurrection, or a war engulfs the lad. What begins as boyish enthusiasm for a fight ends with maturity and an adult attitude to warfare, brought on by real danger and the responsibilities of leadership. Somewhere early in the story the hero generally saves the life of the girl he eventually marries, and at the conclusion the protagonists return from their adventures and settle happily at home, within easy reach of each other for frequent visits and reminiscing. Characteristic of Henty is his stress on the financial and social advantages of an adventurous youth; most of his heroes make their fortunes, earn comfortable and secure places amid the gentry, and need go no more to the wars.

Much of the Henty ethos can also be seen echoed in the original aims of the *Boy Scout movement, and some of the jingoism and enthusiasm to serve in the army that marked the beginning of the First World War is sometimes laid at his door. Yet his attitude to war was always serious, his heroes learn that mindless enthusiasm for fighting is immature, and they are always sickened by indiscriminate slaughter.

Henty has however been criticized for perpetuating racial and class stereotypes and British imperialism in his novels. Certainly Henty's portrayal of black characters is invariably negative and condescending (e.g. *A Roving Commission*, 1890: 'negroes are like children ... not

given to work unless they are obliged to . . . they are merry fellows.') but in other novels the qualities of indigenous peoples are praised.

Allied to this was his explicit support for the British Empire at a time when imperialism was a comparatively new and controversial issue in British politics. Henty's imperialism appears not only in books dealing with British successes, such as *With Clive in India*, but also in his treatment of the Roman Empire, in *Beric the Briton* (1893). Here again, however, Henty was not as simplistic as he is sometimes held to be. There is, for example, much criticism in *Beric* of unjust and unwise imperial administration, and earlier in the book Beric voices the sentiments of the subject people: 'In their eyes we are but savages, but wild men, who may be useful for tilling the ground for them, but who, if troublesome, should be hunted down and slain like wild beasts.'

Henty has also been criticized for his inadequate portrayal of women and his perfunctory treatment of his heroes' romances. Certainly most of his works have male protagonists and yet in those books where women or girls have opportunities for heroism, he allows them reasonably full rein. Maud, in *Out on the Pampas*, saves her brother by shooting an Indian dead with perfect aim, and one story written specially for girls, *A Soldier's Daughter* (1906), contains a heroine who is 'as good a shot as there is in the regiment both with rifle and revolver'.

Sales of Henty titles fell off after the First World War. But by then the books, with their characteristic gilding and pictures embossed on front cover and spine, their maps and full-page illustrations, were a staple of school and public libraries. In America his work is reissued by conservative publishers for the homeschool market, attracted by the steadfast morals of Henty's heroes. Henty's work is studied by Guy Arnold in his book *Held Fast For England* (1979). The Brown collection held at the University of Worcester contains an archive of work by and about Henty and boys' adventure stories.

Henty had many imitators, among them his biographer G. M. Fenn, who wrote many novels in his mould; and Captain F. S. *Brereton, a cousin of Henty's, author of a number of books in the Henty style about heroism in the First World War.

Here Lies Arthur (2007) A powerful reimagining of the *Arthur legend by Philip *Reeve. When Gwyna meets Myrddin, her life has been destroyed by Arthur's war band. However, Myrddin needs her to help him create the myth of Arthur, the Once and Future King. So Gwyna becomes Gwyn for a time and learns that history is not necessarily what happens but rather the story people want to hear, and an identity is a thing that can be created. Set against the bleak landscape of the time between the fall of Roman Britain and the establishment of Saxon England, it was awarded the 2008 *Carnegie Medal.

Hereward the Wake *See* KINGSLEY.

HERGÉ (1907–83) Pseudonym of Georges Rémi, who created the pseudonym by vocalizing (in French) his initials in reverse order—R-G. Brussels-born Hergé is best known as the creator of the *Tintin* series, which would be a huge commercial success far beyond the borders of his native Belgium.

Hermione Granger The *Hogwarts school swot, and one of Harry's two best friends, in the *Harry Potter books.

Heroes, The, *or, Greek Fairy Tales for my children* (1856) By Charles *Kingsley. The book was written because Kingsley considered Nathaniel *Hawthorne's retelling of the myths in *A *Wonder-Book for Girls and Boys* and *Tanglewood Tales* to be 'distressingly vulgar'. He chose three stories, 'Perseus', 'The Argonauts', and 'Theseus', narrating them without any of Hawthorne's prettification; for example, he accepted, unlike Hawthorne, Theseus' desertion of Ariadne. The book contained eight illustrations by Kingsley himself and was dedicated to his children Rose, Maurice, and Mary. It has appeared in print very often since its first publication.

Heroes of Asgard, The (1857) The first English retelling for children of the Icelandic mythology found in the *Eddas. It was the work of the novelist Annie *Keary and her sister Eliza. In its first edition the story is set in a frame narrative in which a Victorian family listen to an uncle telling the Icelandic tales during the Christmas holidays. This framework was omitted in later editions.

The book contains stories chosen 'only with a design to make the subject interesting to children'. It begins with an account of the Aesir (the gods or 'heroes' of the title) and how they built their citadel of Asgard. Later chapters include an account of Thor's adventures in Jotunheim (the land of the giants), the death of Baldur, and the Ragnarok or Twilight

of the Gods. *Heroes of Asgard* was often reissued, sometimes in abridgements, and still appears in print from time to time.

Herr Baby, *The Adventures of* (1881) A novel by Mrs *Molesworth.

HESSE, Karen (1952–) American author known mainly for her historical novels, including *Witness* (2001), about the effect of the arrival of the Ku Klux Klan on the inhabitants of a small town, and *Aleutian Sparrow* (2003), which tells of a family evacuated from the Aleutian Islands during World War II. Hesse won the *Newbery Medal and the Scott O'Dell Award for *Out of the Dust* (1997), set during the Depression and written in free verse. *Letters from Rifka* (1992), based on the life of her aunt, was the winner of the National Jewish Book Award and the Children's Literature Association's Phoenix Award. In 2002 Hesse won a 'Genius Award' from the MacArthur Foundation.

HEWARD, Constance (1884–1968) Creator of *Ameliaranne.

HEWINS, Caroline M. (1846–1926) Pioneer American children's librarian, born in Roxbury, Mass., in a house full of books. She was educated at the Girls' High and Normal School in Boston; the Principal was writing a book, and one day he sent her to the Boston Athenaeum to do some research for him. The scholarly atmosphere of its library impressed her so much that she persuaded her parents to let her work there after graduation. In 1875 she became librarian of the Young Men's Institute at Hartford, Conn. Arriving there, she discovered that local children were mostly reading only four authors: Horatio *Alger, 'Oliver *Optic', 'Harry *Castlemon', and Martha Finley, author of *Elsie Dinsmore*. Miss Hewins protested publicly about this state of affairs, stocked her library's shelves with better children's books, and made the Young Men's Institute Library into a service supplying literature to local schools. In 1893 it was renamed the Hartford Public Library.

Meanwhile in 1882 Miss Hewins wrote a pamphlet for the *Publishers' Weekly* entitled *Books for the Young, a guide for parents and children*; this gave suggestions for teaching 'the Right Use of Books', for example: 'Give children something that they are growing up to, not away from.' It also contained a list of recommended books. The next year she began to contribute a monthly column, 'Literature for the Young', to the *Library Journal*; this

consisted of a list of new children's books, with quotations from such *reviews of them as had appeared in newspapers and journals and also 'Notes and Suggestions', a miscellany of comments on children's reading-matter and how to select, provide, and organize it. Jennie D. Linquist observes in her essay on Miss Hewins (in *The Hewins Lectures*, ed. Siri Andrews, 1963): 'The articles Miss Hewins wrote for these magazines cover practically everything on which our library service for children is built. There are discussions on working with children in the library, in schools and clubs; on the qualities to be expected in children's librarians; on book reviewing; on the making of lists; and on the possibilities inherent in good reading. And Miss Hewins was building on all this without any pattern to follow.'

In 1926 was published *A Mid-Century Child and Her Books*, Miss Hewins's autobiography, of which the greater part is devoted to an invaluable account of her childhood reading-matter. It concludes with 'Peter Piper's Alphabet', a version of *Peter Piper's Practical Principles of Plain and Perfect Pronunciation*; Miss Hewins used to recite this as her party piece at the opening of the annual holiday exhibition in the children's room of the New York Public Library.

HEYER, Georgette (1902–74) British author of more than fifty *historical novels and *detective stories, written for adults but often read by younger readers, too. Her first, *The Black Moth* (1921), was begun when she was seventeen.

HIAASEN, Carl (1953–) American novelist, born and still living in Florida, the setting for all his work. His background as an investigative journalist and columnist for the *Miami Herald* newspaper is reflected in the moral dilemmas and environmental themes that recur in his novels, which are mystery adventures shot through with wit and humour. His first *young adult book, *Hoot* (2002), was a *New York Times* bestseller and Newbery Honor Book (*see* NEWBERY MEDAL) and was also made into a film. His other novels for this readership are *Flush* (2005), *Scat* (2009), and *Chomp* (2012).

Hiawatha, *The Song of* (1855) A narrative poem by Henry Wadsworth Longfellow (1807–82), first published by Ticknor and Fields of Boston and David Bogue of London. Hiawatha, a godlike American '*Indian', fights

his father the West Wind, defends the life of the Corn Spirit, and performs other superhuman feats before marrying Minnehaha at a great wedding feast. He finally departs for the Isles of the Blest to rule the kingdom of the Northwest Wind. The poem is in style and metre imitated from the Finnish mythological verse-narrative *Kalevala*. Illustrated editions have been published since 1856, and there have sometimes been retellings of the story in prose, e.g. Alice M. Chesterton, *Stories from 'Hiawatha'* (1910). *Hiawatha* lends itself easily to parody, one of the most successful comic imitations being 'Hiawatha's Photographing' by Lewis *Carroll, published in his *Phantasmagoria* (1869).

Many of Longfellow's other narrative poems have been popular with children, including 'Excelsior' and 'Paul Revere's Ride'.

hieroglyphic Bibles Intended largely for children, such Bibles were printed in some numbers during the 18th and early 19th cent. They presented selected passages from the *Bible with most nouns replaced by pictures. At the bottom of each page was a key in which the words were set out in full. The most popular of such productions was T. Hodgson's *Curious Hieroglyphick Bible . . . for the Amusement of Youth* (1783).

highwaymen *See* DICK TURPIN.

HIGSON, Charlie (1958–) British author, comedian, singer, producer, director, and actor. The multi-skilled Higson started his career as a decorator before turning to writing for Harry Enfield and Paul Whitehouse. His work on BBC2's *The Fast Show* (1994–2000) brought him wider recognition. In 2004, and with the estate of Ian Fleming's blessing, he took on the task of writing about James Bond's years at Eton, producing the first of five novels, *Silverfin* (2005)—a franchise later assumed by Steve Cole. Moving away from Bond, he started a horror series based on zombies, starting with *The Enemy* (2009).

HILDICK, E. W. (Edmund Wallace) (1925–2001) British children's author who taught at a Yorkshire secondary modern school before becoming a full-time writer. Realizing the need in post-war Britain for books written for, and about, working-class children, he began with a 'Jim Starling' series set in the Cement Street Secondary Modern School—*Jim Starling* (1957) was the first of seven. Then came the 'Lemon Kelly' books (*Meet Lemon Kelly*, 1963, and others) about a gang

of boys in a south of England new town. A third and similar series describes the adventures of a children's gang, 'The Questers'. Hildick also wrote books about Birdy Jones, a pop star who whistles rather than sings; several adventures set in America; and comic thrillers about 'The McGurk Organisation', a team of junior *detectives. He has written several books on the work of an author, including *Children and Fiction* (1970).

HILL, Eric (1927–2014) Creator of the Spot the Dog books. Born in North London, he began his career as a cartoonist and graphic designer, before creating his first story about Spot the Dog for his two-year-old son, Christopher, in 1978. This became *Where's Spot?* (1980), a simple lift-the-flap book in which the reader has to try and find the naughty puppy. Beneath the flaps, there is a crocodile under the bed and a hippo in the grand piano . . . but there is no sign of Spot until a helpful tortoise points the way. The book became a huge hit for its simple and appealing concept, and Hill followed it with many sequels, including sound books, pop-up books, and more. Spot has been animated for BBC children's television by David *McKee's King Rollo Productions.

HILL, Rowland (1744–1833) First chairman of the *Religious Tract Society and a popular evangelical preacher in London; he wrote *Divine Hymns, attempted in Easy Language; for the use of Children* (1790), an imitation of the *Divine Songs* of *Watts.

HILL, Susan (1942–) English author of fiction and non-fiction, most renowned for her work for adults, chiefly, in recent years, the Simon Serraillier crime series. Though she has written picture books for the very young, she has a greater teen readership, for her adult fiction: *The Woman in Black* (1983) is a terrifying ghost story that has also been made into a long-running play (and, more recently, a 2012 film); *I'm the King of the Castle* (1970) contains a most disturbing case of bullying; and *Strange Meeting* (1971) is a deeply moving story set during the First World War.

Hill, The (1905) A *school story by H. A. Vachell (1861–1955). Subtitled 'A Romance of Friendship', it describes how young John Verney, an explorer's nephew, comes to Harrow School as a new boy and immediately develops 'a wild and unreasonable yearning' for the friendship of an older boy, Henry Desmond, known as 'Caesar'. In turn, John

attracts the affections of the young Lord Esmé Kinloch, a 'frail delicate child' who is known as Fluff. The book has gained some fame (or notoriety) because of its portrayal of a romance between schoolboys, though it seems probable that the author, an Old Harrovian popular novelist who was married with two children, would have been shocked at the thought that the word 'homosexuality' might be attached to it.

HINES, Barry *See* KESTREL FOR A KNAVE, A.

HINTON, S. E. (Susan Eloise) (1950–) American author of *young adult novels who published her first book when she was seventeen. *The *Outsiders* (1967) changed the way stories were written for young adults and remains powerful and controversial, admired and reviled in equal measure. Less known but more accomplished was her third book (based on an earlier short story), *Rumble Fish* (1975), a dramatic story about tough Rusty-James and his brother Motorcyle Boy. Hinton's other stories of teen peer-pressure, violence, and gangs include *That Was Then, This Is Now* (1971) and *Tex* (1979). All four have been filmed, with actors Matt Dillon and Emilio Estevez recurring in three and all four of them, respectively. Hinton is also the author of a picture book, *Big David, Little David* (1995), and a storybook for young children, *The Puppy Sister* (1995), inspired by a real family pet.

His Dark Materials (1995–2000) A fantasy trilogy by Philip *Pullman, one of the most ambitious, in scale and imagination, in recent years. Though Pullman had written several excellent children's books before these, this was the series that brought him to the widest public attention with a well-deserved reputation as a remarkable, bold, and sophisticated storyteller.

The books tell a coming-of-age story, set across a number of parallel universes. The opening volume, *Northern Lights* (1995; US: *The Golden Compass*, 1996), introduces Lyra Belacqua, who lives with her *dæmon in Jordan College, Oxford, in a world that is rather like ours, but ruled by the Magisterium (an organization with similarities to the Catholic church). Lyra discovers the existence of the mysterious 'Dust'—an attempt to understand this will run through the trilogy. Lyra's guardian, Lord Asriel, puts her in the care of Mrs Coulter, who turns out to be behind the recent spate of missing children. Other significant characters introduced in the first book include

Lee Scoresby, a balloonist, and Iorek Byrnison, one of a band of armoured bears. The 'golden compass' of the book's American title refers to the 'alethiometer', a truth-telling device that can answer any question, which is given to Lyra by Lord Asriel. In the second book, *The Subtle Knife*, Lyra travels to Cittàgazze, where she meets Will Parry (a boy from our world), who is on a quest to find his father. The subtle knife of the title is a tool—carried by Will—that can cut open portals between worlds. In the sprawling and brilliant concluding volume, *The Amber Spyglass*, new elements and characters are introduced before a resolving culmination which includes a great battle and the death of The Authority, a pitiful God figure. Over the course of their adventures, Lyra and Will have fallen in love, but they understand that they must be parted and the portals between their worlds closed for good.

The books are intellectually complex and engaged, exploring ideas of philosophy and theology, encouraging their readers to ask serious questions about authority and in particular about organized religion (Pullman has spoken out against the use of books for children—in particular the *Narnia series—as a vehicle for proselytizing one's religious beliefs). Inevitably this has led to controversy and calls for them to be *banned; but neither the criticisms nor the complexity has prevented the trilogy from being embraced by huge numbers of enthusiastic readers, as well as celebrated with awards from very many prize juries, including both the *Carnegie Medal and the *Guardian Children's Fiction Prize for the first volume. Perhaps most notably, in 2001 *The Amber Spyglass* became the first book in the 'children's' category to win the Whitbread Book of the Year (*see* WHITBREAD CHILDREN'S BOOK AWARD). At the time of writing, this has never yet been repeated.

In 2007 a visually slick and flashy, if mostly uninspired film adaptation of the first volume by Chris Weitz was released (starring Dakota Blue Richards as Lyra, and Daniel Craig and Nicole Kidman as the adult leads), though any plans to complete the trilogy have apparently since been shelved. A two-part theatrical adaptation by Nicholas Wright at the National Theatre in London in 2003 met with greater critical success.

Pullman has published two small companion volumes from the world of the trilogy: *Lyra's Oxford* (2003), containing a story ('Lyra and the Birds') set two years after the end of the trilogy, and *Once Upon a Time in*

the North (2008), containing a story about the meeting between Lee Scoresby and Iorek Byrnison, with both books featuring engravings by John *Lawrence.

Histoires, ou contes du temps passé
See CONTES DE MA MÈRE L'OYE.

historical novels Their popularity with children began as soon as the works of the man who virtually invented the genre, Sir Walter *Scott, started to appear in print. The first was *Waverley* (1814). In a poll of 1888, published in Edward Salmon's *Juvenile Literature As It Is*, Scott was named as third favourite boys' author, with *Ivanhoe* as fourth favourite novel. And from the 1840s Alexandre *Dumas's *The Three Musketeers* (1844) and other novels were translated and published in illustrated editions for a wide readership.

Scott's huge popularity encouraged a number of British writers of *moral tales for children to set their stories in past times. Among them was Mrs *Hofland, whose *Adelaide; or, the intrepid daughter: a tale, including historical anecdotes of Henry the Great and the massacre of St Bartholomew* (1822) interwove 'the imaginary history of a young person . . . with the important and interesting detail of historical facts'. This was, however, very tame by comparison with Scott. Harriet *Martineau made a better showing in *The Settlers at Home* and *The Peasant and the Prince* (both 1841), but the historical novel for children only came of age with Captain *Marryat's story *The *Children of the New Forest* (1847).

Charlotte M. *Yonge set many of her novels in the past, the first of these, *The *Little Duke* (1854), being one of the most successful. Charles *Kingsley's *Westward Ho!* (1855) and *Hereward the Wake* (1866), although not children's books, were extremely popular with young readers, as were *The Cloister and the Hearth* (1859) by Charles Reade and R. D. Blackmore's celebrated *Lorna Doone* (1869). Among American writers whose historical romances were popular with readers in their own country was Daniel Pierce *Thompson, author of *The Green Mountain Boys* (1839). Later in the 19th cent. many *dime novels were set in the early days of the American frontier or during the American War of Independence.

In the second half of the 19th cent. writers of *adventure stories, having begun to exhaust the obvious geographical sources of excitement (gorilla-hunting in Africa, whaling in the polar regions, and so on), started to turn to history, while the growth of *magazines and the demand for *reward books created an expanding market for stories of the past. R. M. *Ballantyne's *Erling the Bold* (1869) and *The Norsemen in the West* (1872), both Viking tales, paved the way for a whole series of historical stories from G. A. *Henty, beginning with *The Cornet of Horse: a Tale of Marlborough's Wars* (1881). In 1886 there appeared *Kidnapped* by R. L. *Stevenson, arguably the masterpiece of 19th-cent. children's historical fiction, though the same author's more conventional *The Black Arrow* (1888) was just as popular when it was first published. Alfred J. *Church, adaptor of *Homeric Legends for children, was also a popular writer of historical stories; his books include *With the King at Oxford: a Tale of the Great Rebellion* (1886). Among the children's novels of Mark *Twain was *The *Prince and The Pauper* (1882), and the same author wrote *A Connecticut Yankee at the Court of King Arthur* (1889). Howard *Pyle, the well known American illustrator of *Robin Hood* and the legends of King *Arthur, produced three original historical novels, two set in Europe and one in his own country.

By 1900 the historical novel had become a staple of children's literary diet. E. *Nesbit satirized the genre, especially its mock-archaic speech, in the Chapter 'A Castle and No Dinner' in *Five Children and It* (1902). The 20th cent. saw a further flowering of historical fiction for children, with numerous novels of the highest quality being produced on both sides of the Atlantic. American books of distinction in this genre, set in their own country's earlier days (just as writers in Australia and Canada were producing many books about their own countries' pioneer days), include Rachel Field's *Hitty* (1929), Elizabeth *Coatsworth's *Away Goes Sally* (1934), the 'Little House' series by Laura Ingalls *Wilder (1932 onwards), Carol Ryrie *Brink's *Caddie Woodlawn* (1935), and *Johnny Tremain* (1943) by Esther Forbes. Many post-1945 American writers dealt with the experiences of slaves before abolition, for example Ann *Petry in *Tituba of Salem Village* (1964) and Virginia *Hamilton in *The House of Dies Drear* (1968).

In England, Geoffrey *Trease attempted in the 1930s to produce a new kind of historical fiction, written from a radical standpoint; this approach was continued by authors such as Peter *Carter and Robert *Leeson. During the 1950s Rosemary *Sutcliff, Cynthia *Harnett, and Henry *Treece began to raise historical fiction to new heights. In Britain since about 1955, in the hands of (to name but a few) Joan *Aiken, Gillian *Avery, Leon *Garfield, Jane

*Gardam, John Rowe *Townsend, Jill *Paton Walsh, Robert *Westall, and Barbara *Willard, the term 'historical novel' has ceased to have much significance, and the past has been used not as a 'costume drama' but as a means of investigating timeless human character.

The fashion for narratives set in the past has never abated, of course, though particular historical periods move vaguely in and out of popularity. Aspects of 20th-cent. history have been consistently popular in the UK, with many well-loved books being set during the two World Wars. Judith Kerr's *When Hitler Stole Pink Rabbit*, Michelle Magorian's *Goodnight Mr Tom*, and Nina Bawden's *Carrie's War* are enduringly strong examples. Writers like Michael *Morpurgo return to wartime settings with reliable frequency. The centenary of the start of the First World War in 2014 led to a renewed interest in stories of that time, which made it a particularly strong year for historical publishing. However, older historical periods are still popular but with a wider range of protagonists, with authors such as Terry *Deary, Mary Hooper, and Celia *Rees writing almost exclusively in the genre. Some authors take on a period and stay in it for prolonged series (Caroline Lawrence's *Roman Mysteries*, for instance, running to seventeen novels over nine years). As with many genres, there is also a blur with *fantasy as that genre has itself become more popular—Mary *Hoffman's *Stravaganza* series combines both, with its setting in an alternative Renaissance Italy. Many quality American children's novelists are tackling historical settings, and the US market has also seen lives in historical settings dramatized to great popular success in multi-author series such as *Dear America* (from 1996) and *American Girl* (from 1986; issued with accompanying dolls from the period in question).

Historie of Foure-footed Beastes, The

(1607) A manual of zoology and popular belief about animals compiled by Edward Topsell (?1572–1625), a London clergyman. His book, which was based on the work of a 16th-cent. Swiss naturalist, has much of the credulity of the *bestiaries. The beasts it catalogues include: the Satyr, the Sphinx, and the Unicorn, of which Topsell writes: 'They keep for the most parts in the desarts, and live solitary on the tops of Mountaines.' The book is vividly illustrated with big *woodcuts which would have appealed to any child reader. Thomas *Boreman based his *Description of Three Hundred Animals* (1730) largely on it.

Histories, or tales of past times

The title given to 18th-cent. English translations of *Perrault's celebrated collection of *fairy stories, which introduced *Cinderella, The *Sleeping Beauty, *Little Red Riding-hood, *Puss in Boots, *Bluebeard, and other stories to English readers.

Perrault's *Histoires, ou contes du temps passé*, more widely known by its later title *Contes de ma mère l'Oye*, was first published in France in 1697. The first translation into English seems to have been that dated 1729 and published by J. Pote and R. Montagu of London. The only known copy of this edition is in Harvard University Library.

The translator was named on the title-page as 'R.S. Gent', and the dedication, to the Countess of Granville, was signed 'Robert Samber'. The illustrations in the book were copied from those in the French edition, except that in the frontispiece, which depicts an old peasant woman telling a story to some well-dressed children, the words which appear on a plaque behind her, CONTES DE MA MERE LOYE, were changed to read MOTHER GOOSE'S TALES. This is the earliest known use in the English language of the name *Mother Goose.

Samber's translation was reprinted a number of times. Montagu and Pote issued a second edition in 1737 and a third in 1741. They also began to print a bilingual version. This was given the title *Mother Goose's Tales &c. in French and English*, and was described as 'very proper to be read by young Children at Boarding Schools, that are to learn the *French* tongue, as well as in private Families'. Other bilingual editions, using Samber's translation, were published in 1764 by S. van den Berg, and also by J. Melvil, both of London.

Another version of Perrault published by B. Collins and allegedly 'Englished' by G. M. Gent survives in a sixth edition, dated 1772. The same text then runs to a seventh edition, printed by Carnan and Newbery in 1777 and an eighth in 1780. Collins issued an eleventh edition in 1799 and a twelfth in 1802. Although no first edition of this text survives, research by M. J. P. Weedon from an advertisement in the *Salisbury Journal* for 1 August 1763 suggests a date of the same year. Surviving versions of this text are, in fact, almost a verbatim copy of Samber's edition, which suggests a thinly disguised piracy of that translation, issued at a price that would undercut Montagu and Pote's version; the *Salisbury Journal* advertisement of 1763 gives the price as 'only Nine-Pence',

and emphasizes that this makes it 'the cheapest as well as most entertaining Story Book ever yet published'.

John *Harris, who carried on Elizabeth Newbery's business, continued to bring out further dated and undated editions of the book into the early 19th cent.; by 1821 he had adopted a new title, *The Celebrated Fairy Tales of Mother Goose*. In the late 18th cent. the individual stories from the books began to appear as juvenile *chapbooks, and these continued to be popular throughout the 19th cent., while the entire collection of the tales sometimes appeared in chapbook form too, e.g. *Fairy Tales of Past Times, from Mother Goose*, published by *Lumsden of Glasgow in 1814. In 1872 Perrault's tales were superbly, though often frighteningly, illustrated by Gustave *Doré in a volume published in London, Paris, and New York, entitled *Fairy Tales Told Again*.

history and biography for children began to be written in some quantity in the mid-18th cent. In 1761 John *Newbery published *A New History of England, from the invasion of Julius Caesar to the present time*, and three years later he issued *An *History of England*, in a series of letters from a nobleman to his son, which was the work of Oliver *Goldsmith. The hack writer Richard *Johnson compiled a number of history books dealing with Rome, Greece, France, and North and South America, which were published by Newbery's successors and were 'designed for the use of young ladies and gentlemen'. Mrs Sarah *Trimmer originated the publication of a series of *copperplate prints of biblical and secular history, ancient and modern, which were 'designed as ornaments for those apartments in which children receive the first rudiments of their education'. Schoolroom histories like that written by Goldsmith were parodied by a teenage Jane Austen in her *The History of England* (written 1791, though not published till the twentieth century); much as twentieth-century classroom history would spawn the satirical *1066 and All That*.

In the early 19th cent. most juvenile booksellers in London were producing accounts of English history. William *Godwin wrote his own (*The History of England, for the use of schools and young persons*, 1806), while John *Marshall published the anonymous *Abridgement of English History, from the Conquest to the present reign* (c.1800). Rather later, William *Darton issued *The British Sovereigns, from

William the Conqueror to William IV (c.1830), while John *Harris produced *The British Story Briefly Told, from early times to the present period* (1832). Besides issuing conventional history books, some publishers chose to present the material in the form of verse. In 1815 Darton published *Historical Questions on the Kings of England, in verse* by Louisa Brown, and three years later came Harris's *The *Chapter of Kings*, based on a rhyme by the entertainer John Collins. The same period saw the first appearance of *Pinnock's Catechisms*, a series which included such titles as *A Catechism of Ancient History, A Catechism of Roman History*, and *A Catechism of the History of America*, all first published by about 1820. (Similar catechisms were published during the 18th cent., but do not seem to have been as successful as their 19th-cent. counterparts; an example is *The History of Greece by way of question and answer*, printed for John Newbery, Mary *Cooper, and others in 1761.)

'Mrs *Markham' (Elizabeth Penrose) began to produce her celebrated history books during the 1820s, and the equally popular *Little Arthur's History of England* appeared in 1835. During the same period the original '*Peter Parley' (S. G. *Goodrich) wrote many books which dealt with history in an informal style; his *Tales of Peter Parley about America* (1827), which opened the series, was one of the first books of American history written in that country for a child readership. Other notable American history writers for young readers include Thomas Wentworth Higginson, whose *Young Folks' History of the United States* appeared in 1875, George Makepeace Towle, who wrote a 'Young Folks' Heroes of History' series during the 1870s and 1880s, and Nathaniel *Hawthorne, whose books included *Grandfather's Chair: a history for youth* (1841) and *Biographical Stories for Children* (1842). The books of Charles Carleton *Coffin provided American children with vivid accounts of the War of American Indepence and the Civil War.

By the mid-19th cent. innumerable histories for children were being produced in England. Notable writers who contributed to the genre included *Dickens, whose *Child's History of England* appeared in 1851-4, and Charlotte M. *Yonge, who wrote the 'Aunt Charlotte's Stories' series of history books.

Among biographical works read by children between the 16th and 18th cents. was *Foxe's Book of Martyrs*. Secular biography for children may be said to have its beginning with

John Newbery's edition of *Plutarch's Lives* (1762–3, in seven volumes), while in 1801 *Tabart published *The Juvenile Plutarch, containing accounts of the lives of children, and of the infancy of illustrious men, who have been remarkable for their early progress in knowledge*. Other early 19th-cent. collections of biography for children include the anonymous *British Heroism; or biographical memoirs of some of those renowned commanders, who have extended the glory of the British nation to the remotest parts of the world*, published by J. Wallis of London in 1800, Mary *Pilkington's *Memoirs of Celebrated Female Characters* (1804), and *Biography of Eminent Persons, alphabetically arranged*, also anonymous, published jointly by Darton and John Harris in 1814, with engravings after Alfred Mills. As the 19th cent. advanced, biographies of the famous became a staple of many children's *magazines; a typical writer of such material was J. C. *Edgar.

American writers who produced biographies for young readers in the 20th cent. include Laura *Richards (lives of Florence Nightingale, 1909, Elizabeth Fry, 1916, and Abigail Adams, 1917), Albert Bigelow *Paine, whose *Boys' Life of Mark Twain* appeared in 1916, Cornelia *Meigs, who wrote a study of Louisa M. *Alcott (*Invincible Louisa*, 1933), and Jean *Fritz (several books during the 1970s). In Britain Geoffrey *Trease produced children's lives of writers and musicians, among them a biography of D. H. Lawrence (1973).

Notable general history books for children that have appeared since 1900 include *Our Island Story* (*c.*1910), *The Story of Mankind* (1921) by Hendrik *Van Loon, *Boys and Girls of History* (1926) by Eileen and Rhoda *Power, and *Mighty Men* (1924–5) by Eleanor *Farjeon. Geoffrey Trease's history books include a review of the 20th cent., *This Is Your Century* (1965). R. J. *Unstead had almost sole command of history writing for the young for decades following his *Looking at History* (1953). The stand-out commercial success of the children's non-fiction history world in recent years has been the comic *Horrible Histories* series, while in the US writers like Russell *Freedman have made a specialization of high-quality illustrated biographies for young readers (*see also* HISTORICAL NOVELS).

History of an Apple Pie *See* A APPLE PIE.

History of British Birds *See* BEWICK.

History of England, An, *In a series of letters from a Nobleman to his Son* (1764) By Oliver *Goldsmith, published in two volumes by John *Newbery. The book was at first anonymous, but Goldsmith is known to have been paid for it by Newbery. The *History* covers the subject from the earliest times to the year before publication, and it takes the form of sixty-eight letters, most of them purporting to be from the nobleman to his undergraduate son, and a number of chronological tables.

The book was criticized for being more demanding than the question and factual answer form of textbook then in vogue; Goldsmith replied in a preface to later editions that he was not writing for children, but was treating schoolboys as the men they were soon to be and deliberately exercising their judgement. 'Children', says the first letter, 'can never be too soon treated as men . . . those who are incapable of teaching young minds to reason pretend that it is impossible.' Despite such controversy the book was successful, and continued to be published in numerous new versions and editions until the second half of the 19th cent., often being abridged or 'improved' with 'Questions for Examination' added. In 1819 it was translated into Bengali for the Calcutta School-Book Society; *English History for Woolwich and Army Candidates* (1874) was based on it.

History of Little Jack, The (1788) A story by Thomas *Day, author of *Sandford and Merton*. A baby, abandoned on a moor in winter, is found by a crippled old soldier and suckled by a goat. The child grows up as naturally as an animal, with no care for clothes, and learns the qualities and accomplishments of each of his foster parents—'his papa the man, and his mama the goat'. After his foster father's death he leads a wandering and informative life, including a spell fending for himself perfectly alone on an island off the coast of Africa. He finally returns to England and becomes foreman, and by industry and honesty finally the sole owner, of a great ironworks, ending up a wealthy, respected, and philanthropic magnate. The story first appeared in 1788 in a collection called *The Children's Miscellany*, and was published separately later the same year. It has often been considered a more effective work than *Sandford and Merton*.

History of Pompey the Little *See* ANIMAL STORIES.

History of Sixteen Wonderful Old Women, The The earliest known book of *limericks, published by J. *Harris & Son in 1820, with no author named. The first rhyme in the book is:

> There was an old woman named Towl,
> Who went out to sea with her owl;
> But the owl was seasick
> And screamed for physic,
> Which sadly annoyed Mistress Towl.

The other fifteen verses are on the same model. Each is illustrated with a plain or coloured engraving.

The book, which is reproduced in Iona and Peter *Opie's *Nursery Companion* (1980), was reprinted several times by Harris's, and was soon followed by an imitation, *Anecdotes and Adventures of Fifteen Gentlemen* (c. 1821) which inspired *Lear to write his *Book of Nonsense* (1846).

History of Troy, The The first book to be printed in English, by *Caxton in 1473-4. Its full title was *Recuyell* [i.e. French 'recueil'] *of the Historyes of Troye*. It was based on a French text by Raoul Lefevre, which was itself drawn from earlier French and Latin narratives. The book proved very popular with readers of all ages, and was reprinted by Wynkyn de *Worde and many others; by the early 18th cent. it had passed through some fifteen editions. The title usually given to it in the reprints was *The Destruction of Troy*. It was reissued by William *Morris at the Kelmscott Press in 1892.

Hitchhiker's Guide to the Galaxy, The (1979–92) A humorous science fiction series by Douglas *Adams. The series comprises *The Hitchhiker's Guide to the Galaxy* (1979), *The Restaurant at the End of the Universe* (1980), *Life, the Universe and Everything* (1982), *So Long, and Thanks for All the Fish* (1984), and *Mostly Harmless* (1992). The series was described as a 'trilogy' after the publication of the third title. It was subsequently styled a 'trilogy in five parts'.

The stories were first conceived as a radio comedy, broadcast on BBC Radio 4 in 1978. Adams adapted the first four episodes to form the opening novel: *The Hitchhiker's Guide to the Galaxy*, published in 1979. This begins just as the Earth is about to be destroyed by Vogons. Earthling Arthur Dent is rescued by visiting alien Ford Prefect and they escape on a Vogon ship. They meet Ford's cousin, Zaphod Beeblebox, who has two heads and has stolen a spaceship called the Heart of

Gold. They subsequently discover the answer to Life, the Universe, and Everything (42)—although this proves to be an anticlimax, because no one knows the question.

In *The Restaurant at the End of the Universe* (1980), Zaphod, along with depressed robot, Marvin the Paranoid Android, visit the editorial offices of the Hitchhiker's Guide to the Galaxy. Zaphod is made to enter a torture device called the Total Perspective Vortex, which allows you to see how infinitely small you are in comparison with the universe. In *Life, the Universe and Everything* (1982), Ford and Arthur have to help prevent galactic war. *So Long, and Thanks for All the Fish* (1984) sees Arthur return to Earth, which is surprising, as it had been destroyed. It turns out to be a replacement Earth, provided by dolphins in their Save the Humans campaign. Finally, in *Mostly Harmless*, Arthur becomes the official sandwich-maker for a small village on the planet Lamuella.

A sixth title in the series, *And Another Thing . . .* (2009), has been written by Eoin *Colfer. The stories have also been adapted in numerous other formats, including a 1981 BBC television series, a 2005 film starring Martin Freeman as Arthur Dent and Mos Def as Ford Prefect, as well as video games, comic books, and plays.

Hitty, *Her First Hundred Years* (1929) A novel by the American author Rachel Field. Hitty, a wooden doll in rural New England in the early 19th cent., suffers many uncomfortable adventures while with her first owner, including being left in an empty church and carried off by a crow. During the following decades she goes whaling, is worshipped as a heathen idol, enters New York society and encounters Charles *Dickens on one of his American visits, and at the conclusion of the book finds herself in a New York antique shop, where she awaits further adventures.

The book, which has illustrations by Dorothy P. Lathrop, revived an old tradition in children's literature, of which early examples include Mary Ann *Kilner's *Adventures of a Pincushion* and *Memoirs of a Peg-Top*, both published in the 1780s. Rachel Lyman Field (1894–1942) wrote about a dozen children's novels, illustrating some of them herself, though *Hitty* is her only book to have achieved a lasting reputation. She was also the author of children's *plays and of several books of children's verse, and edited a collection of Mme d'*Aulnoy's stories (1928). *Hitty* was written

after she and the book's illustrator had discovered a wooden doll in a New York City antique shop. The doll was present when the book received the *Newbery Medal in 1930.

HOBAN, Lillian (1925–98) American author and illustrator of picture books. Hoban's first published illustrations were for *Herman the Loser* (1961), written by her husband Russell *Hoban. She went on illustrate another twenty-five of Russell's books, including five of the six about Frances the Badger (1960–70) (the first was illustrated by Garth *Williams) and *The *Mouse and His Child* (1967). Illustrator of over seventy books in all, Hoban is probably best known for the Frances books and for her own I Can Read series about a chimpanzee named Arthur and his little sister Violet.

HOBAN, Russell (Conwell) (1925–2011) American writer, born in Lansdale, Pennsylvania. He studied at the Philadelphia Museum School of Industrial Art, and after war service in the US Army worked as a film storyboard artist, a television art director, and a freelance illustrator. In 1944 he married Lillian Aberman (who, as Lillian *Hoban, later illustrated many of his books). Eventually, in 1965, he gave up working as an artist and became an advertising copywriter; four years later he moved to London, devoting himself to writing full-time.

Hoban's first book was a piece of non-fiction for children: *What Does It Do and How Does It Work?* (1959). He then began to write a series of *picture books, many of them about a young badger named Frances and her parents, beginning with *Bedtime for Frances* (1960); they are not *animal stories but portraits of the behaviour of a typical human child, done with wit and shrewd observation. In the Frances stories, Hoban kept his eccentric sense of humour on a fairly tight rein, but it burst out in such stories as *What Happened When Jack and Daisy Tried to Fool the Tooth Fairies* (1966) and *How Tom Beat Captain Najork and His Hired Sportsmen* (1974). The latter, which is illustrated by Quentin *Blake, is about a boy who lives with an aunt (Miss Fidget Wonkham-Strong) so inflexible that she wears an iron hat; to punish him for his habitual 'fooling around' she sends for the fearsome Captain Najork. The Captain and his 'hired sportsmen' are supposedly able to beat anybody at the crazy games to which they challenge Tom; but all his 'fooling around' has given Tom plenty of practice at such games, and he beats them roundly—and in

consequence manages to replace his aunt with a nicer one.

Hoban's peak as a children's writer came with *The *Mouse and his Child* (1967), an ambitious and highly imaginative novel, somewhat reminiscent of the fantasies of E. B. *White, which can scarcely be said to remain within the confines of a 'children's book' (it contains, for example, a parody of the later plays of Samuel Beckett). Thereafter Hoban turned largely away from children's fiction, producing such adult novels as *The Lion of Boaz-Jachin and Jachin-Boaz* (1973) and *Riddley Walker* (1980), the latter being an account of a post-holocaust society in a Britain of the future, written in futuristic language. However, he never abandoned children's fiction altogether; and two books were published posthumously: *Soonchild* (2012), a slim but rich and thoughtful fantasy novel illustrated by Alexis *Deacon, and a final picture book, *Rosie's Magic Horse*, (2012), illustrated by Quentin Blake.

Hobbit, The, *or There and Back Again* (1937) By J. R. R. *Tolkien, the outstanding British work of *fantasy for children to appear between the two World Wars, and the first of a series of books which eventually brought Tolkien world-wide fame and created a cult following.

'In a hole in the ground there lived a hobbit.' Tolkien scribbled these opening words of the book one day in the late 1920s or early 1930s, without having any idea what they meant. The story that developed from them, first told to the author's children at their Oxford home, has certain resemblances to other classics of juvenile fiction. Bilbo Baggins, the home-loving hobbit (hobbits are 'small people, smaller than dwarves . . . but very much larger than lilliputians' says the first edition), recalls the half-timid, half-heroic Mole of *The *Wind in the Willows*, while his underground house has a strong resemblance to Badger's home in the same book. The *dwarfs or 'dwarves' (as Tolkien spelt the plural, accidentally at first but later on purpose), whose arrival so disrupts Bilbo's life, are close to those who, descended from Germanic mythology, appear in some of *Grimm's fairy tales. And the wizard Gandalf, who tricks Bilbo into accompanying the dwarves on their quest to reclaim ancestral treasure from a *dragon, bears a certain, though obviously quite coincidental, resemblance to the figure of *Merlin as portrayed by T. H. *White in *The *Sword in the Stone,

published a year after *The Hobbit*. The *goblins or 'orcs', as Tolkien chose to call them in later books, who lurk beneath the Misty Mountains and nearly put an end to the dwarves' quest, are much like those in George *MacDonald's novel *The *Princess and the Goblin* (1871), a childhood favourite of Tolkien's. The notion of hobbits themselves was later traced by Tolkien himself in part to *The Marvellous Land of Snergs*, a children's book by E. A. Wyke-Smith, published in 1927; Snergs are 'a race of people only slightly taller than the average table but broad in the shoulders and of great strength.' The origins of the word 'hobbit' puzzled Tolkien himself. It appeared in his mind without conscious invention; he later suspected that it might have been suggested by Sinclair Lewis's novel *Babbit*, whose hero's character is not entirely unlike that of Bilbo Baggins, and he was also interested in the allegation, made by a reader of *The Hobbit*, that the word 'hobbit' appeared in a collection of fairy stories dating from around the turn of the century. Since Tolkien's death it has been pointed out that the story in question was probably 'The Hobyahs', in Joseph *Jacobs, *More English Fairy Tales*, 1894. The creatures in this story are not entirely un-hobbit-like, in that they are small and live underground, but their character is that of evil goblins.

Yet though *The Hobbit* has many of its roots in existing English writings for children, its innovations are far more striking than its borrowings. Tolkien's approach was close to that of *science fiction (a genre in which he took a great interest) in that he remodelled the known world for the purposes of his story. Though the setting of *The Hobbit* is left somewhat indefinite in place and time—we are told that the story takes place 'long ago in the quiet of the world'—the sequel, *The *Lord of the Rings*, makes it clear that both stories are part of the history of Middle-Earth, which is Earth at an earlier age of its existence. For the purposes of *The Lord of the Rings*, Tolkien made that world concrete in every detail—he drew maps, worked out its natural history and geology, and knew what was possible within it and what was not—but in *The Hobbit* he seems to have felt free to people his landscape with anything and anyone that took his fancy as story-teller. So it is that Bilbo and the dwarves have a brush with a party of *trolls not unlike those found in the Norwegian tales of *Asbjørnson and Moe (but Cockney-speaking), are given shelter at Rivendell, a kind of earthly paradise inhabited largely by *elves

whose behaviour resembles that of the *fairies in *A Midsummer Night's Dream* (the elves in *The Lord of the Rings* are very different in character), cross the Misty Mountains and are given shelter by Beorn, a shape-changer who is half-man, half-bear, become entangled in the webs of giant spiders, and are finally brought face to face with Smaug, a dragon closely related to Fafnir in the *Volsungasaga*.

It has become a commonplace of Tolkien criticism to say that, in doing all this, the author of *The Hobbit* drew heavily on his professional expertise as a scholar in Anglo-Saxon and Old Norse. What is not so often noticed is the story's imaginative debt to many of the tales in the *Fairy Books* of Andrew *Lang, which were among Tolkien's first reading-matter in childhood, and also the extent to which *The Hobbit* is a product of its time, a reflection of England after the First World War.

Tolkien fought in the war, as a signalling officer in the trenches of the Somme during 1916, and two of his close friends were killed in that battle. He consciously intended that the hobbits should be an imaginative representation of the English and their response to war. 'I've always been impressed,' he once said, 'that we are here, surviving, because of the indomitable courage of quite small people against impossible odds.' On another occasion he told an interviewer: 'The Hobbits are just rustic English people, made small in size because it reflects the generally small reach of their imagination—not the small reach of their courage or latent power.' His later story *The Lord of the Rings* is a conscious working-out of this theme. *The Hobbit*, too, is a study of personal heroism; or, rather, it is a demonstration of the weakness and dubious motivation of conventional heroics.

The book was almost complete by the winter of 1932, when it was read by Tolkien's friend and Oxford colleague C. S. *Lewis. For some reason Tolkien did not finish it then; he had never tried to get a work of prose fiction published, and was more concerned to devote himself to *The Silmarillion*, a body of connected myths and legends about 'Middle-Earth' at which he had been working since about 1917. The existence of the unfinished *Hobbit* did, however, become known to a few people, and it was occasionally lent to them in typescript. It eventually came to the notice of the London publishers Allen and Unwin, who persuaded Tolkien to finish it, and published it in the early autumn of 1937. Tolkien illustrated the book himself, initially with black-and-

white pen drawings in a flat style not unlike that of Hugh *Lofting and Arthur *Ransome; coloured plates were added for the first American edition, published by Houghton Mifflin of Boston early in 1938, and these have also appeared in a number of later British editions.

The book was widely praised in its early days (admirers from the beginning included Richard *Hughes and Naomi *Mitchison) and sold well enough for a second British impression to be required within a few months, but by the early 1950s it had passed somewhat out of sight. Interest in it was renewed to some extent by the publication of *The Lord of the Rings* in 1954 and 1955, but not until that book was the object of a 'campus cult' in America in 1965 did *The Hobbit* become an international best-seller (it has been translated into more than forty languages), assured of a permanent place as a classic of children's fiction. *The Hobbit* has been televised in America in the form of an animated film (1977), using a visual style that could scarcely be further from, or less appropriate to, Tolkien's own intentions. A more appropriate trilogy of live-action films directed by Peter Jackson was released in 2012–14.

HOCKING, Silas (Kitto) (1850–1935) British author of *street Arab stories, who was one of the last survivors of the old-style writers of *evangelical books for children. A typical sample of his work may be found in *'Chips', 'Joe', and 'Mike'* (1890), which contains three stories of boy-waifs (first published separately during the previous decade). Like other writers in this genre, Hocking was not concerned to alleviate poverty but to lead the poor to religion; as one of his characters expresses it, 'We shall all be well-off in the "better land."'

HODGES, C. (Cyril) Walter (1909–2004) Leading illustrator of the 1950s and 1960s. Books illustrated by him include *A *Swarm in May* (1955), *The *Silver Sword* (1956), and the early novels of Rosemary *Sutcliff. His line drawings are in the tradition of 19th-cent. book illustration. He wrote a number of *historical novels and books of *history for children, including *Columbus Sails* (1939), his first, and *The Namesake: A Story of King Alfred* (1964). He won the *Kate Greenaway Medal in 1964 for *Shakespeare's Theatre*, a first for a work of non-fiction (and still almost unique today).

HOFFMAN, Mary (1945–) A prolific British author of over 100 titles, Hoffman's work frequently reflects her political and social stance on issues such as conservation, equality, and *diversity. Her widely celebrated picture-book series *Amazing Grace* (1991) is illustrated by Caroline Binch. Other successful collaborations include *The Colour of Home* with Karin Littlewood, an emotional story of a young Somalian refugee, and *The Great Big Book of Feelings* and *The Great Big Book of Families* with Ros Asquith. Hoffman has also written a number of titles for older readers, most notably her *Stravaganza* series, set in the fictional country of Talia, inspired by 16th-cent. Italy.

HOFFMANN, E. T. A. (Ernst Theodor Amadeus) (1776–1822) German author and musician who wrote a number of *fairy stories, including *Der Sandman* ('The Sandman') (1816), which provided the plot for Delibes' ballet *Coppélia*, and *Nüsseknacker und der Mäusekönig* (Nutcracker and the Mouse King') (1816) (*see* NUTCRACKER). Hoffmann's colourful character and some of his stories provided Offenbach with the inspiration of his opera *Les Contes d'Hoffmann* (1881).

HOFFMANN, Heinrich *See* STRUWWELPETER.

HOFLAND (Wreaks), Mrs Barbara (1770–1844) British author who began to write *moral tales for children after the death of her first husband, in order to support her young son. Her best known book was *The Son of a Genius* (1812), the story of a boy whose artist father is arrested for debt; the lad sells his own pictures and raises money to procure his father's release. Mrs Hofland's other books included *The Young Crusoe* (1828), several *historical novels, books of *geography, and stories with such titles as *Integrity* (1823), *Self-denial* (1827), and *Fortitude* (1835). Her writings were extremely widely read in her day, and *The Son of a Genius* was published in many translations.

HOFMEYR, Dianne (1947–) South African author and illustrator, resident in England, who taught art for two decades before becoming a full time writer. Her collaboration with illustrator Jude Daly (1951–) led to several picture books, including *The Stone* (1998), a Persian version of the story of the Magi, and *The Star-Bearer* (2001), an ancient Egyptian creation myth. More recently she has collaborated with Jane *Ray on *Zeraffa Giraffa* (2014), about a giraffe sent as a present to the king of France. She also writes lyrical novels for older children, with strong African settings. These include *Blue Train to the Moon* (1993); *The Waterbearer* (2001), a complex adventure

involving shipwreck, slavery, and survival across Africa; and the Ancient Egyptian adventure, *Eye of the Moon* (2007), and its sequel, *Eye of the Sun* (2008).

HOGROGIAN, Nonny (1932–) American illustrator, born in New York City. She worked in the production department of a publishing house before establishing herself as an artist. She won the *Caldecott Medal twice, for *Always Room for One More* (in 1966) and *One Fine Day* (in 1972).

Hogwarts The 'School of Witchcraft and Wizardry' that is the principal setting for most of the *Harry Potter books. The school's precise location is not specified, but can be reached by a special train from Kings Cross Station's elusive platform nine and three quarters. Pupils typically attend the school for seven years (aged 11–18), receiving instruction in areas such as Defence Against the Dark Arts, Potions, and Care of Magical Creatures. Hogwarts pupils are divided into four houses, as allocated by the Sorting Hat: Gryffindor, Hufflepuff, Slitherin, and Ravenclaw. The headmaster is Professor Albus Dumbledore. Standards at Hogwarts are kept generally high despite a significant rate of staff turnover, constant peril, and not infrequent violent death.

HOLABIRD, Katherine *See* ANGELINA BALLERINA.

Hole Book, The (1908) A *picture book by the American artist-author Peter Sheaf *Newell. The story is told in verse:

> Tom Potts was fooling with a gun
> (Such follies should not be),
> When—bang! the pesky thing went off
> Most unexpectedly!

The subsequent pictures trace the damage that the bullet does, with a hole through the centre of each page. Newell also produced *The Slant Book* (1910), whose sloping pages show the progress downhill of a runaway perambulator and its occupant, and *The Rocket Book* (1912), in which a rocket fired in the basement shoots up through a block of apartments, causing astonishment on each floor.

Holes (1997) A novel by Louis *Sachar. Stanley Yelnats is sentenced to Camp Green Lake detention centre for stealing a pair of trainers, where his punishment will be to dig holes in the ground. That sentence sums up the plot of *Holes*, but only scratches the surface of what it is about, because this is a story that you have

to pay close attention to, as everything that happens happens for a reason (yes, including the onions). Appalling adults, unlikely friendships, escape, capture, and a lot of digging—in Sachar's hands these become a recipe for sublime entertainment. *Stanley Yelnats' Survival Guide to Camp Green Lake* (2003) is a hilarious sidebar; and a sequel of sorts, *Small Steps*, came out in 2007. *Holes* was adapted as a film by Walt Disney Pictures in 2003.

HOLIDAY, Henry (1839–1927) Noted Victorian mural painter and worker in stained glass. He illustrated *The *Hunting of The Snark* (1876) by Lewis *Carroll; this was reprinted, together with Holiday's illustrations, in Carroll's *Rhyme? and Reason?* (1883).

Holiday House An almost revolutionary novel for children by Catherine *Sinclair, first published by William Whyte & Co. of Edinburgh in 1839. The preface bluntly attacks the notion of the ideal child, which the *moral tale had disseminated since the 1780s, and criticizes the contemporary fashion for books of 'facts'.

Miss Sinclair writes:

The minds of young people are now manufactured like webs of linen, all alike, and nothing left to nature . . . They are carefully prompted what to say, and what to think . . . All play of imagination is now carefully discouraged, and books written for young persons are generally a mere record of dry facts, unenlivened by any appeal to the heart, or any excitement to the fancy . . . In these pages the author has endeavoured to paint that species of noisy, frolicsome, mischievous children which is now almost extinct, wishing to preserve a sort of fabulous remembrance of days long past.

The book describes the adventures of Laura, Harry, and Frank Graham, who, when their mother dies and their father goes abroad, are left in the charge of their amiable Uncle David and grandmother Lady Harriet. Their father has also provided, to look after them in the nursery, the fierce Mrs Crabtree, who despite her strong arm cannot keep Laura and Harry in order. They break their toys, get into scrapes, and derive endless fun from mocking Mrs Crabtree. As to moral teaching, their uncle gives them only one piece of what he calls important advice: 'Never crack nuts with your teeth.'

In a memorable chapter, Laura and Harry take advantage of their uncle and grandmother's absence to invite all their friends to tea. Mrs Crabtree, infuriated, refuses to provide any food for the party other than the children's usual ration of two dry biscuits

and two cups of milk. The greedy young guests, becoming rebellious, juggle with the plates and break them. Mrs Crabtree chases the ringleaders out of the house and the party ends miserably, but when Uncle David returns he readily forgives Laura and Harry, and provides a real tea-party for their friends.

Subsequently Harry sets the house on fire and Laura cuts all her hair off; they are met not with reproofs but with a shilling reward for helping to put the fire out. Mrs Crabtree observes bitterly 'that Major Graham [the uncle] was a hopeless case, as he always took part with the children, and liked nothing so much for old and young as "a ploy".' Laura and Harry are taken off to Holiday House, a country mansion belonging to friends of the family, where the children cause havoc in the household. One day, their Uncle David tells the children a 'Nonsensical Story about Giants and Fairies'. In fact this story has a marked moral (the virtues and rewards of industry), and *Holiday House* changes its character markedly in the later chapters. Frank, the children's better-behaved elder brother, becomes a sailor, is wounded in action, and comes home to die a holy death, piously exhorting Harry and Laura (in the manner of the time) to reform and become sober and dutiful.

Miss Sinclair later tried to remedy this sad ending by publishing a sequel, *The Mysterious Marriage, or Sir Edward Graham* (1854). But even Frank's death and the religious-cum-moral observations of Lady Harriet cannot outweigh the book's high spirits.

Holiday House was frequently reprinted in its original form during the 19th cent. In 1908 there appeared a version abridged by Olive Allen, which excluded the moral and religious passages and the sad ending.

At Christmas 1861 Lewis *Carroll gave a copy of the book to Lorina, Alice, and Edith Liddell.

Holiday Romance, A A children's book in four parts by Charles *Dickens, written for the American magazine *Our Young Folks*, and published there early in 1868, appearing simultaneously in an English periodical, *All the Year Round*.

The four stories are supposedly the work of children. The 'Introductory Romance' is narrated by 'William Tinkling, Esq.', aged eight. He tells about his 'marriage' to seven-year-old Nettie Ashford. His friend, nine-year-old 'Lieut. Col. Robin Redforth', is similarly wedded to Alice Rainbird, and the two bridegrooms then

try to rescue their 'wives' from the dame-school at which they are captive. The plan fails, but the 'wives' promise to be constant until they are 90. Alice Rainbird then tells the story of 'The Magic Fishbone', which is given by a fairy godmother to the Princess Alicia, who uses it to save her father's fortunes. Robin Redforth's tale is the story of 'Captain Boldheart', who launches a naval expedition against his sworn enemy, the Latin grammar master. Finally Nettie Ashford tells a tale about a country where children are in charge of grown-ups, and treat them with severity.

The stories have sometimes been reprinted, both singly and in one volume. An edition of *The Magic Fishbone* illustrated by F. D. *Bedford and published by *Warne was very popular during the first half of the 20th cent.

HOLLAND, Isabelle (1920–2002) American novelist; her best known book for young readers is *The Man Without a Face* (1972), about unhappy 14-year-old Charles and the intense friendship he forms with mysterious former teacher Justin McLeod.

Holly Short See ARTEMIS FOWL.

HOLM, Anne See I AM DAVID.

HOLMAN, Felice (1919–) American children's author; her novels include *The Escape of the Giant Hogstalk* (1974), a comic *fantasy, and *Slake's Limbo* (1974), about a boy who lives for 121 days in a cave beneath Grand Central Station in New York.

Holmes, Sherlock See SHERLOCK HOLMES.

Homecoming (1981) By Cynthia *Voigt, the first novel in a sequence of seven about the redoubtable Tillerman family. Abandoned by their mother, Dicey has to get herself and her three siblings to their only known relative, Great Aunt Cilla. The journey requires determination and ingenuity. To discover their great-aunt is dead is a shock, and they are not wanted by her daughter. Dicey realizes their only hope is to travel on to find their grandmother. It is another journey into the unknown, but what will be their welcome? The second in the series, *Dicey's Song* (1982), won the *Newbery Medal.

HOME-GALL, Edward Reginald (?1896–1974) British writer of *boys' stories; like his father W. B. Home-Gall he wrote a great deal for the *Harmsworth papers. Later he contributed to *Thomson story-papers, and other magazines. He is thought to have been the most prolific writer of boys' stories after

Charles *Hamilton; he used various pseudonyms and created (among much else) a 'Bluey Wilkinson' series about a speedway driver.

HOMER, Winslow (1836–1910) Popular American illustrator, best known for his work in *Harper's Weekly*; he contributed regularly to the *Riverside Magazine*.

Homeric legends These were first made available in English for children in a translation of Fénelon's *Adventures of Telemachus* (1699). In 1806 William *Godwin tried to make Greek mythology attractive to children in *The *Pantheon*, and two years later came Charles *Lamb's *Adventures of Ulysses*. Nathaniel *Hawthorne produced two volumes of retellings of the legends, *A *Wonder-Book for Boys and Girls* (1851) and *Tanglewood Tales* (1853), which in turn inspired Charles Kingsley to write *The *Heroes* (1856). The next notable contribution was made by Alfred J. Church, beginning with his *Stories from Homer* (1876), which was reissued in various versions. Andrew *Lang collaborated on translations of the *Odyssey* (1879) and the *Iliad* (1883), which became standard versions in English schools. Lang's *Tales of Troy and Greece* (1907) was immensely popular. In America, the Irish writer Padraic *Colum and the Hungarian illustrator Willy *Pogány produced *The Adventures of Odysseus and the Tale of Troy* (1918) and *The Golden Fleece and the Heroes who lived before Achilles* (1921). As the 20th cent. drew to a close, the stories continued to have their appeal to children's writers—these more recent offerings include Rosemary *Sutcliff's *Black Ships Before Troy* (1993) and *The Wanderings of Odysseus* (1995), and Adele Geras's *Troy* (2000), which tells the familiar story from the viewpoint of the women involved.

Homer Price (1943) A book by the American author-illustrator Robert *McCloskey, which consists of a series of comic daydreams of a small American boy living in a Middle Western town. In these daydreams Homer adopts a skunk, and with its help captures a robber gang; he gets involved with an automatic doughnut machine that is the counterpart of the broom in *The *Sorcerer's Apprentice*; and helps a local spinster to win the world championship for string saving. Homer has an Uncle Telemachus and an Uncle Ulysses. Beneath the apparent *nonsense lies some sharp satire of small-town life.

Home Treasury, The A series of children's books initiated in 1843 by Sir Henry *Cole under the pseudonym 'Felix Summerly'. The series was announced in a prospectus which explained the purpose as 'to cultivate the Affections, Fancy, Imagination, and Taste of Children'. The crucial word here was 'Imagination', for Cole proposed to reissue a number of *fairy stories and other fanciful writings which had been largely suppressed in the earlier part of the 19th cent., following attacks by such writers as Mrs *Trimmer, and which in recent years had been swamped almost out of existence by the factually-minded books published under the name of *Peter Parley.

The first *Home Treasury* books appeared in 1843; they included versions of *Beauty and the Beast*, *Little Red Riding Hood*, *Chevy Chase*, and *Reynard the Fox*, as well as *Traditional Nursery Songs* (a collection of *nursery rhymes), a reprint of Peacock's *Sir Hornbook*, and *Bible Events* (first series). The next year came *Puck's Reports to Oberon* (a collection of four original fairy stories), *Jack and the Beanstalk*, and more *Bible Events*. Later titles included *Cinderella* (?1844), *Jack the Giant Killer* (1845), and *Dick Whittington* (1847). There was also a *primer, a collection of *fables, and a book on painting. The *Home Treasury* also produced a 'Colour Box for Little Painters' and various toys.

The publisher was at first Joseph *Cundall, later Chapman and Hall. The books were handsomely illustrated, Cole commissioning pictures from such respected contemporary artists as William *Mulready. They were sold plain or coloured, in distinctive patterned covers. The stories were sensibly presented—Cole cut out the moralizing from Mme de *Beaumont's original text of *Beauty and the Beast*—and the series played a large part in making fairy stories and fanciful tales once again an accepted part of nursery literature. It was imitated by a number of other publishers, and Cundall himself imitated it with his *Gammer Gurton's Story Books* (*c.* 1845).

Homily In *The *Borrowers* by Mary *Norton.

HONEY, Elizabeth (1947–) Australian author, illustrator, and poet who grew up on a farm in the bush near Wonthaggi, Victoria. Her first book, a delightful mix of pictures, notes, and cartoons, *45 & 47 Stella Street and Everything That Happened* (1995), was an immediate success, and she has continued Henni's adventures in two other stories, one, *To*

The Boy in Berlin (2007) (written with Heike Brandt), told entirely in emails. Her picture books are just as quirky: *Ten Blue Wrens and What a Lot of Wattle!* (2012) is her all-Australian counting book that even features 'trillions of stars' and fireworks over Sydney Harbour Bridge, and *Not a Nibble!* (1996) is about a fishing holiday that lands something far better than just a fish.

Honk: the Story of a Moose (1935) By Phil Stong with pictures by Kurt *Wiese, an outstanding picture book telling the comic tale of two Minnesota boys of Finnish descent, who discover a hungry moose that has wandered into a livery stable to eat hay during a hard winter. At first they and the adults try to drive it out, but it eventually becomes their pet, and even a kind of mascot to the whole community. The book exactly captures the turn of speech and rueful humour of a predominantly Scandinavian-immigrant township.

Phil Stong (1899–1957), born in rural Iowa, was a successful adult novelist who also produced children's books, many of them *animal stories; all had illustrations by Wiese.

Hood, Robin *See* ROBIN HOOD.

HOOD, Tom (1835–74) British humorist, son of the author and poet Thomas Hood. He wrote several books for children, including *Fairy Realm* (1865), a collection of *Perrault's fairy stories retold in verse and illustrated by Gustave *Doré, and *Petsetilla's Posy* (1870). He also collaborated with his sister Mrs F. F. *Broderip.

Hook, Captain In *Peter Pan* by J. M. *Barrie.

HOOLE, Charles (1610–67) Author and translator of a number of 17th-cent. *books of instruction. He was a Yorkshire schoolmaster who came to London and made a reputation as a teacher in private schools. He published an adaptation of *Lily's Latin Grammar, as well as translations into English of *Pueriles Confabulatiunculae and the *Orbis Sensualium Pictus of *Comenius, and a version of *Aesop's fables in English and Latin. His own writings include *A New Discovery of the Old Art of Teaching School* (1660), in the first part of which he discusses how to 'teach little Children to read English with delight and profit'. He recommends that those pupils who do not have an aptitude for Latin and Greek should be encouraged to read more English books: 'By this means they will gain such a habit and delight in reading, as to make it their chief recreation, when liberty is afforded them.'

Hoosier School-Boy, The (1883) One of the first American *school stories, the work of Edward *Eggleston. 'Hoosier' is a name of disputed origin applied to the residents of Indiana.

The Hoosier School-Boy is set in 1850 in the village of Greenbank. Thirteen-year-old Jack Dudley, who has been living in the Indian Reserve, comes as a new pupil to the village school, which is ruled over by Mr Ball, the tyrannical old teacher. Jack is marked as victim by the school bully 'Pewee' Rose and by Rose's friend Will Riley. Jack gives as good as he gets, and also defends another new boy, the small but clever Christopher Columbus Risdale ('Lummy'). When three boys put gunpowder in the school stove, Jack and Lummy are whipped for not betraying the culprits' names, and as a result Lummy falls ill with a fever. Mr Ball has at last gone too far, and is removed from his job.

HOPE, Anthony (Sir Anthony Hope Hawkins) (1863–1933). British popular novelist who was a first cousin of Kenneth *Grahame. At Marlborough and Balliol he had a brilliant academic and sporting career; he was called to the bar, and began to write for magazines. His novel *The Prisoner of Zenda* (1894), the story of an Englishman who saves the throne of Ruritania by impersonating its young king, was an immediate success, and was followed by a sequel, *Rupert of Hentzau* (1898). He wrote many more novels, and was knighted during the First World War for services to the Ministry of Information.

HOPE, Ascott R. (Ascott Robert Hope-Moncrieff) (1846–1927) British author of more than 100 books for boys. His first success was *Oudendale: a Story of Schoolboy Life* (1865). Charlie Campion, a pupil at Oudendale College, shows 'pluckiness' in standing up to bullies, but gets into bad company; he drinks and smokes, and causes grave anxiety to Dr Eden the headmaster. He is rescued by the good effects of Confirmation—whereupon he falls off a cliff and dies a holy death. Hope-Moncrieff also wrote *adventure and *historical stories, and edited the *Blake's Guides* to Britain.

HOPE, Laura Lee *See* BOBBSEY TWINS.

Hope of the Katzekopfs, The (1844) Sometimes given the title *The Self-Willed Prince*; a novel by F. E. *Paget, who used the pseudonym 'William Churne of Staffordshire'. This person is supposed to be a 16th-cent. teller of fairy lore, who now wonders whether 'a race that has been glutted with Peter Parley and Penny Magazines, and such like stories of (so called) useful knowledge, will condescend to read a Fable and its moral, or to interest themselves with the grotesque nonsense, the palpable, fantastic absurdities, the utter impossibilities of a Tale of Enchantment.' The spoilt and selfish only child of King Katzekopf and Queen Ninnilinda enslaves himself to the sprite Selbst, but finally frees himself.

The book has been judged to be the first full-length children's *fantasy written in English, preceding *The *King of the Golden River* and *The *Rose and the Ring* by several years. It contains the 17th-cent. poem 'Farewell, rewards and Fairies', and it was here that Rudyard *Kipling first read it; he afterwards made use of it in *Puck of Pook's Hill* and *Rewards and Fairies*.

HOPKINS, Lee Bennett (1938–) American poet, anthologist, and educator. A staunch advocate of integrating poetry into the curriculum and children's lives, he has been recognized by Guinness World Records as 'the world's most prolific anthologist of poetry for children'. His books for educators include the seminal *Pass the Poetry, Please!: Bringing Poetry into the Minds and Hearts of Children* (1972) and *Pauses: Autobiographical Reflections on 101 Creators of Children's Books* (1995). He is the author of the autobiographical novels *Mama* (1977) and *Mama and Her Boys* (1981), about a single mother and her two sons. His autobiographical poetry collection, *Been to Yesterdays: Poems of a Life* (1995), won the Christopher Award and was also a Golden Kite Honor Book.

Hop o' my Thumb A *fairy story found in the *Contes de ma mère l'Oye* (1697) of *Perrault, under the title *Le Petit Poucet.*

A poor faggot-maker and his wife have seven boys, the youngest of whom is so small that he is known as 'petit Poucet', 'little Thumb'. The parents find that they cannot manage to feed their children and decide to abandon them in a wood, but Hop o' my Thumb leads his brothers back home. When poverty strikes again, the parents make another attempt, and this time the children are utterly lost. They come to the house of an *ogre, whose wife tries to conceal them from her husband; but he finds them and determines to eat them up next morning. While the ogre sleeps, Hop gets up and replaces his brothers' caps with the golden crowns on the heads of the ogre's seven sleeping daughters, who are all ogresses. The ogre wakes in the night and decides to kill Hop and his brothers at once, but because of the change of headgear he slits the throats of his daughters instead. By the time he discovers his mistake, the boys have escaped, and the ogre sets out to pursue them, using his 'boots of seven leagues'. When the giant rests and falls asleep, Hop steals the seven-league boots and goes in them to the ogre's house, where he tricks the ogre's wife into handing over all the gold and silver in the place. Hop then takes these riches back to his parents' house, where he is joyfully received.

Perrault adds that not all authors agree on this ending; some say that Hop went to court in the seven-league boots, where he made himself useful to the King as a messenger.

The first part of the story, in which the parents try to abandon the children, has many parallels, a close one being 'Ninillo and Nennella' in the *Pentamerone* (Day 5, tale 8). An exchange of clothing which leads to the slaying of the wrong children occurs in a collection of myths by the 2nd-cent. Latin writer Hyginus, and there is a parallel to the ogre's slaying of his daughters in *Grimm's story *Sweetheart Roland*, where, after killing her daughter, the witch puts on her 'many leagued boots, in which she went an hour's walk at every step'.

Perrault's story was first published in English in 1729 in *Histories, or Tales of Past Times.*

HORÁČEK, Petr (1967–) Award-winning Czech illustrator and artist, Horáček was born in Prague and studied at the Academy of Fine Art. In 1994, he moved permanently to the UK and began illustrating and writing picture books soon after his first child was born. Horáček won the Books for Children Newcomer Award in 2001 for his two novelty books *Strawberries Are Red* and *What Is Black and White?*, which explore colour and form in innovative ways and are illustrative of his graphic style and rich palette. Horáček uses a mix of acrylic, watercolour, collage, and wax crayons in his work, often with a simple but unusual twist in narrative. Imaginative play with an imaginary friend is celebrated in the

charming *Elephant* (2009; US title: *My Elephant*). His book *Puffin Peter* (2012) was shortlisted for the *Kate Greenaway Medal in 2012.

Hornblower A British naval officer in the novels of C. S. *Forester.

hornbook A form of *ABC book common in England from the 16th to the 18th cents. The alphabet, with other matter that the child was to learn, was printed on a piece of paper which was then mounted on a tablet of wood with a projecting handle. In order to protect the lettering, a thin sheet of translucent horn was fixed over the paper by means of a narrow edging-strips of brass held in place by small nails. The whole usually measured some $3\frac{1}{2} \times 2\frac{1}{2}$ in., excluding the handle.

Tablets of various kinds had been used to teach children the alphabet from the time of the earliest civilizations, e.g. the Roman *tabella*, on which wax was smeared and then scored with a stylus. A manuscript *c.*1400 in the British Library (Harl. MS 3954) mentions schoolchildren being taught by 'a bok...naylyd on a brede [breadth] of tre [tree, i.e. wood]'. The true hornbook was common in Shakespeare's time, being referred to in *Love's Labour's Lost*, v. i: 'Yes, yes, he teaches boys the Horn-book.'

The wording printed on hornbooks scarcely varied during the centuries. According to the usual pattern, in the top left-hand corner was a cross, followed by a capital A and then the entire alphabet in lower-case, ending with the ampersand, &. The five vowels followed, and then the alphabet was repeated in capitals. Beneath this, the vowels were printed again at the head of a 'syllabary' or table of syllables. Then followed the invocation to the Trinity, after which the Lord's Prayer was printed.

Black-letter hornbooks were manufactured until the early 17th cent., after which Roman type became common. The true hornbook eventually gave way to the *battledore.

The hornbook was often known as the 'Criss-cross-row' or 'Chris-cross', which was either a reference to the 'Christ's cross' at the top of it, or to a device which had preceded it, in which the letters of the alphabet were strung crosswise on a wire. See further A. W. *Tuer's *History of the Horn-book* (1896).

Horn Book Magazine A bimonthly review of children's literature, published in Boston, Massachusetts, founded in 1924 and still running today. The founder and first editor was Bertha E. Mahony (later Bertha Mahony Miller), and the magazine grew out of lists of recommended books which she and her assistant Elinor Whitney had issued at their Bookshop for Boys and Girls in Boston.

Mahony announced her intention, at the magazine's outset, as 'to blow the horn for fine books for boys and girls' (the magazine's title refers both to this notion and to *hornbooks), and *Horn Book Magazine* was, from its inception, the leading periodical of its kind in the United States. It awards the annual *Boston Globe–Horn Book Award.

HORNE, Richard Henry (1803–84) Victorian miscellaneous author and friend of Elizabeth Barrett Browning; he wrote *Memoirs of a London Doll* (1846) and *The Good-Natured Bear* (1846). In 1864, while visiting Australia with William *Howitt, he changed his middle name to Hengist.

Horner, Jack *See* JACK HORNER.

HORNUNG, E. W. (Ernest William) (1866–1921) British author of stories about 'Raffles, the Amateur Cracksman', which began to appear in 1899. Hornung married Arthur Conan *Doyle's sister in 1893, and Raffles, a gentleman thief and modern *Robin Hood, is something of a foil to *Sherlock Holmes.

HOROWITZ, Anthony (1955–) Prolific and hugely successful English author of books and television screenplays. He started storytelling while at school, and knew from the age of eight that he wanted to be a writer. His first book, *Enter Frederick K. Bower* (1978), was a humorous novel for children. Although he has written for adults, he is still most famous for his work for young adults and children. His much loved *Alex Rider* series, beginning with *Stormbreaker* (2000), started a wave of action-packed books specifically targeted for boys, and they have been made into graphic novels and a film. Other important series are *Groosham Grange* (1988), *The Power of Five* (2005), and *The Diamond Brothers*, starting with *The Falcon's Malteser* (1986).

Horrible Histories (from 1993) What British author Terry Deary (1946–) began as a fun way to introduce kids to history has become a massive industry with around sixty titles (the first was *The Awesome Egyptians*) with total sales of twenty-five million in forty countries, a hugely successful CBBC television series, a stage show, and a variety of merchandising. The books—written by Deary and illustrated by Martin Brown—fulfil their mission statement of 'history with all the nasty bits left in'

and include all the gore, torture, misery, mud, hilarity, mad inventions, and daftness that any child could wish for. They are sometimes commented on for occasional historical inaccuracies, but the fact that children read them insatiably may be as good an answer to that criticism as any.

Horrid Henry The protagonist of the series created by Francesca *Simon and illustrated by Tony *Ross. Horrid Henry is a fine comic anti-hero and a modern day *William, following in the long-standing tradition of 'the naughty child' in children's literature and comics. The first title, *Horrid Henry*, was published in 1994 and was followed by a further twenty-four books, as well as numerous collections, activity books, and joke books. Horrid Henry was also adapted for the screen and is a popular animated television series, nominated for BAFTA's Best Animation both in 2009 and 2010. Extremely popular worldwide, Horrid Henry is published in twenty-five languages. In 2008 *Horrid Henry and the Abominable Snowman* won the Galaxy Children's Book of the Year Award.

horror An umbrella term for book genres containing the stuff of nightmares, spooky stories, and thrilling tales, for readers who enjoy being scared silly. Much like *science fiction and *fantasy, the genre does not really have a defined outline, and elements of it can be found in a variety of books, including those belonging to the two mentioned. The more traditional strain of horror, featuring supernatural creatures, magic, a touch of gore, corpses, and stormy nights, finds its roots in works within the Gothic such as Bram Stoker's *Dracula* (1897) or Mary Shelley's *Frankenstein* (1818). In keeping with the canonical element but with a younger audience as target, one finds series such as R. L. Stine's *Goosebumps* (1992–7), the long-running multi-authored *Point Horror* (1986–), or the work of Darren *Shan. Then there is Chris *Priestley's equally terrifying but far more sophisticated *Tales of Terror* series (influenced by classic Victorian/Edwardian ghost stories), Charlie *Higson's post-apocalyptic zombie series, and some of the work of Holly *Black, Cliff McNish, and countless others. There are multiple adaptations and reworkings of texts intended for an older audience, e.g. H. P. Lovecraft, popular *ghost stories, or even the *Grimm fairy-tales, while popular horror authors for adults, such as Stephen King, are themselves widely read and circulated among younger readers. In a later incarnation, horror moves from direct manifestations of external fear, such as *vampires or zombies, to a more internal, psychological strand, as is the case in Patrick Ness's *A *Monster Calls*, in which the monster may or may not be real, but its presence still very much felt and chilling. At the same time, several tropes or settings originating in the genre have evolved into something with a quite different appeal to an audience than simply wanting to be scared, as Stephenie Meyer's *Twilight* vampires demonstrate.

Many books and authors usually classified under fantasy can easily be partially considered horror; Neil Gaiman's *Coraline* is a perfect example with its dark, twisted, and unsettling plot and other horror-like features. But there are no hard and fast rules. Gaiman's *The *Graveyard Book* holds true to the genre's traditional supernatural settings and characters but is tonally quite different, and while Roald Dahl's *The *Witches* contains elements of horror and surreal fantasy, it cannot sensibly be placed anywhere within the genre.

It is worthy of note, too, that despite the lack of a significant corpus of horror books for younger children, they are very frequently employed as protagonists in horror fiction and media for older readers. Henry James's ghostly *The Turn of the Screw* (1898) is perhaps the most famous example of all.

horror comics The term applied in Britain to certain *comics, imported from the United States between about 1950 and 1955, which contained horrific stories explicitly picturing sadistic and necrophilic practices. The comics were first brought into Britain to be sold to American servicemen stationed there, but soon went on sale to the general public, and were read by many children. A national outcry resulted in the passing of the Children and Young Persons (Harmful Publications) Act in 1955, which prevented their sale to children. The most notorious example, often cited in discussions of them, shows a midnight baseball game being played with pieces of a murdered man. Horror comics are discussed in detail in Frederic Wertham's *Seduction of the Innocent* (1955). *See also* HORROR.

Horse and his Boy, The (1954) The fifth of the *Narnia novels by C. S. *Lewis.

horse stories These have been written by many authors since Anna Sewell produced *Black Beauty* in 1877. American practitioners in the genre include C. W. Anderson, author of

Billy and Blaze (1936) and many sequels, Walter *Farley, creator of a 'Black Stallion' series (1941 onwards), and Marguerite *Henry (*King of the Wind*, 1948, and other books). In Britain *pony stories were on the whole more popular than stories about horses, but Enid Bagnold's *National Velvet* (1930) was a bestseller, and the Australian author Elyne Mitchell had huge success with her *Silver Brumby* series (1958 onwards).

HORSLEY, Henry Sharpe Author of *The *Affectionate Parent's Gift.*

Hotspur One of the D. C. *Thomson 'tuppeny blood' adventure papers for boys, published between 1933 and 1981. A companion to *Rover, *Wizard, Adventure,* and *Skipper,* it had a similar mixture of material, but contained more *school stories than the others. These were set in less pretentious academies than *Greyfriars and the other 'Frank *Richards' creations; the *Hotspur* schools were tough places, full of boisterous and outrageous boys and masters.

HOUGH, Charlotte (1924–2008) British author-illustrator of idiosyncratic and humorous books in prose and verse, such as *Wonky Donky* (1975).

HOUGH, Emerson (1857–1923) American author; his *The Story of the Cowboy* (1897) was a favourite book of Theodore Roosevelt. Hough wrote a series of boys' books chronicling the adventures of *The Young Alaskans,* the first of which appeared in 1908.

HOULSTON, F. (Frances) (*fl.* 1807–40) Printer and bookseller of Wellington, Shropshire; she published stories by Mrs *Sherwood, and thanks to the success of these and other *evangelical books she and her son opened a London office to which they eventually moved their entire business.

House at Pooh Corner, The (1928) By A. A. *Milne, sequel to *Winnie-the-Pooh.* Three out of the ten stories concern Tigger, who makes his first appearance in this book. Other memorable episodes include the building of a house for Eeyore and the invention of the game of Poohsticks. The book's concluding chapter, 'In which Christopher Robin and Pooh come to an Enchanted Place, and we leave them there', has become famous for its symbolic farewell to childhood. In fact Christopher Milne, the author's son and the original of Christopher Robin, did not leave home for

boarding school until 1930, two years after the book was published.

House in Norham Gardens, The (1974) A novel by Penelope *Lively. Clare Mayfield, aged fourteen, lives with two octogenarian great-aunts in a Victorian gothic mansion in North Oxford. The book's plot concerns her discovery in the attic of a New Guinean painted shield brought back to England by her anthropologist great-grandfather, and her feeling that the tribe from which he took it has for long wanted it back—and is coming to fetch it. The novel is also (in fact predominantly) an amusing, if somewhat idealized and cosy, account of the relationship between Clare and the great-aunts.

House of Arden, The (1908) A novel by E. *Nesbit. Edred and Elfrida Arden live with their aunt, who is obliged to keep a seaside lodging-house because her fiancé and the children's father, who were partners, were captured by brigands on the way from South America and are now presumed dead. On an outing to the nearby ruined castle that was the ancestral home of the House of Arden, Edred discovers that he must be the nearest living relative to the late Lord Arden. He begins a quest for the lost treasure of the Ardens by uttering a spell which conjures up the Mouldiwarp, the family's heraldic mole brought to life and speech. The Mouldiwarp has at least some of the character, and bad temper, of the Psammead in the same author's *Five Children and It,* and speaks with a rustic accent. With its help the children make journeys into the past to search for the treasure. They never find it, but their father and his partner magically return home. On their time-travels, Edred and Elfrida meet in the 17th cent. their cousin Richard, who despite the period in which he is living, knows all about the 20th cent. Edred and Elfrida discover that he, too, is a time-traveller; his story is told in the sequel or companion-piece to *The House of Arden, *Harding's Luck* (1909).

House that Jack Built, The A *nursery rhyme based on the principle of accumulation—one more rhyme is added in each verse. It first appeared in print in the mid-18th cent., in one of John *Newbery's children's books, but is probably much older. Various attempts have been made to prove that it is descended from 'Had Gadyo', a similarly accumulative Hebrew chant, which begins: 'A Kid, a Kid, that my Father bought with two

pieces of money'. In 1862 there was published an eccentric pamphlet by Henry George, arguing that the rhyme is really a historical allegory in which Jack represents John Bull, the rat that ate the malt is William the Conqueror, the cat that killed the rat is Henry II, and so on in similar vein.

The House that Jack Built was a popular *chapbook for children in the late 18th and early 19th cents. John *Harris produced a version of it in 1820 that was longer than usual, had elegant illustrations (plain or coloured), and remained in print for more than fifty years. An outstanding interpretation by Randolph *Caldecott appeared in 1878. The rhyme is still popular as the subject of juvenile *picture books.

The combination of political contextualization for *The House that Jack Built* and its place in the burgeoning children's book industry of the early 1800s led to a frequent use of this text as a vehicle for political satire. As Marcus Wood demonstrates in *Radical Satire and Print Culture*, the radical William Hone drew on a tradition of the appropriation of nursery verses for satiric ends initiated by John Newbery when he wrote *The Political House That Jack Built* in 1819. It was printed as a critique of perceived political oppression culminating in the Peterloo Riots, and Wood explores the importance of the nursery rhyme form to produce a satire that 'incorporates primitive taunts and a style of illustration associated with the rude humour and didacticism of children's books'. The growing children's book industry of this period, led by Harris, made this mode ripe for appropriation, and the Cruikshank-Hone collaboration produced a devastatingly effective text that was the model for later satires based on nursery verses and published by radicals such as Thomas Dolby and John Fairburn. Wood states that as a result 'nursery rhyme parody became part of the currency of popular satire'.

HOUSMAN, Laurence (1865–1959) Younger brother of poet A. E. Housman; he illustrated an edition of *Goblin Market* by Christina *Rossetti. The following year came the first of several volumes of short original *fairy stories written by him, *A Farm in Fairyland*, though these were apparently intended chiefly for an adult readership. In 1907 his retelling of stories from the *Arabian Nights* was published with illustrations by Edmund *Dulac, and in 1930 the firm of Blackwell published several short fairy stories by him. He was a friend of E. *Nesbit, and gave her the initial suggestion for the plot of *The *Phoenix and the Carpet*. His sister Clemence Annie Housman (1861–1955) was the author of a children's novel, *The Were-Wolf* (1896).

HOUSTON, James A. (Archibald) (1921–2005) Canadian author-illustrator of books about the Inuit, beginning with *Tikta'liktat: an Eskimo legend* (1965), a *Robinsonnade about a boy isolated on a barren island. Houston worked for some years as a government administrator in West Baffin in the Arctic; he also wrote stories about the Canadian '*Indians'.

HOWARD, E. G. G. (Edward George Granville) (?1793–1841) The author of *Rattlin, the Reefer*, a narrative of life at sea; it was published in 1836 with the statement that it was 'edited' by Captain *Marryat, who was a friend of the author.

HOWE, James (1946–) Prolific and versatile American author, whose works span picture books to *young adult novels. He is best known for the Bunnicula series (the first volume of which, *Bunnicula: A Rabbit-Tale of Mystery* (1979) was co-written with his first wife, Deborah Howe) which narrate the adventures of a vampire bunny rabbit (that sucks the juice from vegetables) from the point of view of the family dog, Harold. The Horris and Morris (and Dolores) picture-book series uses humour and wordplay to tackle concerns such as gender inclusion/exclusion and food intolerances. He is also the author of two series of early readers, Pinky and Rex, and Houndsley and Catina. His middle-grade novel *The Misfits* (2001) inspired a national anti-bullying initiative in the US called No Name-Calling Week.

HOWELLS, William Dean (1837–1920) Distinguished American writer and critic who wrote two books about childhood: *A Boy's Town* (1890), which was serialized in *Harper's Young People*, and *The Flight of Pony Baker* (1902). Their setting is Hamilton, Ohio, where Howells spent his boyhood—the same town that was later to inspire Robert *McCloskey's comic fantasies.

How I Live Now (2004) A *young adult novel by Meg *Rosoff. Winner of both the *Guardian Children's Fiction Prize 2004 and a *Michael L. Printz Award, Rosoff's bold debut novel is set in a Britain at war and under siege; the story is told by Daisy, a troubled teenager, and her voice, brash yet vulnerable, permeates the mood of the whole book.

When the war breaks out, Daisy and her cousins find themselves facing an uncertain future, one in which they have to rely on themselves and each other. The drama of the story is combined with a subtle exploration of teenage concerns to create a powerful novel with timeless appeal.

HOWITT (Botham), Mary (1799–1888) and her husband **William** (1792–1879) Prolific miscellaneous British authors, both born into Quaker families, who wrote a number of children's books. They married in 1821 and soon settled in Nottingham. They travelled extensively, and eventually settled on the Continent, spending the summers in Austria and the winters in Rome.

Together and separately the Howitts wrote about 180 books. Their first published work was a volume of poems, and Mary afterwards became popular as a children's poet. Volumes of her verse include *Tales in Verse: for the young* (1836) and *Hymns and Fire-side Verses* (1839). Her *Sketches of Natural History* (1834) contained her best known poem, '"Will you walk into my parlour?" said the Spider to the Fly' (parodied in *Alice's Adventures in Wonderland*). In 1836 she published *Tales in Prose: for the young*, a collection of short stories and anecdotes; her later books include a novel rather in the manner of the *moral tale, entitled *Sowing and Reaping; or what will come of it?* (1841); a story set in Heidelberg, *Which is the Wiser: or people abroad* (1842); and *The Children's Year* (1847), which she described as 'an exact chronicle . . . of the voluntary occupations and pleasures . . . of my two youngest children'. In it she notes that the children's favourite books were *Masterman Ready* and other stories by *Marryat, *The *Pilgrim's Progress*, *The *Swiss Family Robinson*, and *Bewick's works of natural history.

William Howitt's books included *The Boy's Country-book* (1839), a vivid narrative describing a childhood in Derbyshire, the county of the author's birth, and *A *Boy's Adventures in the Wilds of Australia* (1854).

The Howitts had no objection to *fairy stories and tales of the supernatural; there is a *ghost story in *The Boy's Country-book*, and in *The Children's Year* Mary speaks approvingly of *Bluebeard*, which she calls 'pleasantly dismal'. While in Heidelberg she learnt Swedish and Danish, and soon began to translate the stories of Hans Christian *Andersen, publishing a collection of them in 1846 under the title *Wonderful Stories for Children*.

Howl's Moving Castle (1986) By Diana Wynne *Jones, whose magic touch is at its best here. Sophie lives in a land governed by fairy tales, not physics, so, being the eldest of three, she is destined to come to nothing. She is set to making hats, and it turns out that her hats bestow good things on their wearers, but this talent is spotted by the Witch of the Waste, who thinks she is a rival, and she magics Sophie into an old woman. Sophie sets out to reverse the spell by seeking out the wizard Howl. With virtually every person she meets under some sort of spell, it takes Sophie a while—and many adventures—to sort everything out. Laugh-out-loud funny, serious, and beautifully written, this is fantasy for readers of all ages. There are two sequels, *Castle in the Air* (1990) and *House of Many Ways* (2008), and an exceptional animation (2004) by Studio Ghibli.

How the Grinch Stole Christmas! (1957) A picture-book fable by Dr *Seuss, in which the grumpy Grinch (who hates Christmas—some aspects of the character may be based on Seuss himself) decides to spoil things for all the chirpy *Whos* (who love it), which he attempts to do by stealing all their presents and decorations. When Christmas comes anyway, he learns a valuable lesson, that it's about more than just material things. Among many other commercial exploitations, the 2000 movie adaptation grossed approximately $345 million.

How the Whale Became, and other stories (1963) A collection of original Creation myths by Ted *Hughes. Like its precursor, Kipling's *The *Just So Stories*, it has become a classic of children's literature. However, though humorous, the stories are not cosy, but display elements of the harsh realism that is a feature of Hughes' work. They are funny, magical, tragic, and perceptive, as the animal characters reflect human behaviour in their quest to establish their identities. The original Faber edition was illustrated by George Adamson. Hughes wrote two further collections of stories on the theme of Creation, *Tales of the Early World* (1988) and *The Dreamfighter* (1995). *How the Whale Became* was adapted into an opera in 2013.

How to Heal a Broken Wing (2008) A picture book by Bob *Graham, the story of a bird found on a pavement, which is rescued and nursed back to health by a little boy. Startling visuals show the harsh aggression of a busy

city emphasized by clever perspectives, so we share in the bird's vulnerability. Although Bob Graham is an accomplished wordsmith, he has chosen to show the story unfolding through vignettes in an almost textless graphic novel approach (like that of Jan *Ormerod's *Sunshine*). We see the bird on the pavement surrounded by rushing human legs and later the healing process in vignettes. Beautiful double-page spreads celebrate the high moments—the rescue and release. Reminders of freedom and flight pervade the images, and the passing of time is also clear. It is a wistful and uplifting tale to make a reader's heart soar when Will opens his hands and the bird returns to the sky.

How to Train Your Dragon (2003) A series of books, an animation for TV, a film—what a wonderful career for a slightly shy, very clever Viking called Hiccup who was born in Cressida *Cowell's imagination when she was staying as a child on a remote Scottish island. Of course Hiccup doesn't stay shy and retiring: his ability to speak Dragonese (the language of the dragons) and his cleverness lead him to become a warrior chieftain, a fearsome sword-fighter, and all-round hero. The books are perfect for confident readers who want action, adventure, humour, great illustrations, and a lot of very funny jokes.

Hubbard, Mother *See* MOTHER HUBBARD.

Huckleberry Finn *See* ADVENTURES OF HUCKLEBERRY FINN, THE.

Hug (2000) A picture book for very young children by illustrator Jez *Alborough. With its economical text (the entire book is twenty-nine words long, of which twenty-five are 'HUG') it introduces the little chimp, Bobo, who sees how every other animal has someone to hug—but where's his mother when he needs her? Bobo has gone on to feature in two other Alborough books, *Tall* (2003) and *Yes* (2006).

HUGHES, Arthur (1823–1915) English illustrator. He was born in London and studied at the Royal Academy Schools, where he became associated with the original Pre-Raphaelite Brotherhood. Books illustrated by him include: an 1869 edition of *Tom Brown's Schooldays*; two books by Christina *Rossetti, *Sing-Song* (1872) and *Speaking Likenesses* (1874); and George *MacDonald's novels *At the Back of the North Wind* and *The *Princess and the Goblin* (both 1871). His illustrations were generally engraved in wood by the Brothers *Dalziel.

HUGHES (Robson), Mary (*fl.* 1820) Friend of Maria *Edgeworth; she wrote a number of *moral tales, including two volumes of *Aunt Mary's Tales* (*c.* 1811). In her story *The Ornaments Discovered* (1815) the orphan Fanny learns that 'amiable manners and a well-regulated mind, are the only true valuable ornaments.' *The Alchemist* (1818) describes the 'alchemical' change that Louisa Grandville undergoes when she develops from being 'careless and giddy' to a state of prudence. *The Orphan Girl* (1819) was also popular. Mrs Hughes and her husband emigrated to America, where she ran a girls' school in Philadelphia.

HUGHES, Monica (1925–2003) British-born author, resident of Edmonton, Alberta. Though she published several realistic novels, she is chiefly known for her *science fiction for children, including *Beyond the Dark River* (1979) and the Isis trilogy: *Guardian of Isis* (1980), *Keeper of the Isis Light* (1981), and *The Isis Pedlar* (1982).

HUGHES, Richard (Arthur Warren) (1900–76) British novelist. In addition to his fiction for adults, Hughes produced several collections of short stories for children, beginning with *The Spider's Palace* (1931). His hallmark in these was a zany, nonsensical humour and totally unpredictable plot construction. His children's stories were collected in *The Wonder-Dog* (1977).

HUGHES, Shirley (1927–) British illustrator and author who was born in Lancashire and studied at the Ruskin School of Art in Oxford. She began to work as an illustrator in the 1950s (William *Mayne's first two novels were among her earliest commissions), and became one of the busiest in England. She has written and illustrated a number of her own *picture books, including her debut *Lucy and Tom's Day* (1960), which has several sequels. She specializes in drawings of chubby children, with realistic backgrounds. Among her most enduring work is *Dogger* (which won the *Kate Greenaway Medal, and then, thirty years later, the 'Greenaway of Greenaways') and the series of picture books featuring young *Alfie, who was created in 1981 and is still being written into new stories more than three decades later.

Hughes's best work extracts humour from entirely credible situations; for example, her picture book *Alfie Gets in First* (1981) describes a small boy accidentally locking his mother

and sister out of the house while he is inside. *Here Comes Charlie Moon* (1980), a full-length children's novel written and illustrated by her, is about a boy staying with an aunt who runs a seaside joke shop. It was followed by *Charlie Moon and the Big Bonanza Bust-Up* (1982). In 2003 she won her second Greenaway for her **Cinderella*-inspired *Ella's Big Chance*. She also moved into the world of fiction for older children in 2012, with the novel *Hero on a Bicycle*.

Hughes was awarded the 2004 *Eleanor Farjeon Award. Her daughter, Clara Vulliamy, is also an illustrator, and the two have collaborated on the Dixie O'Day series (from 2013), with mother writing and daughter illustrating.

HUGHES, Ted (1930–98) British poet Laureate who wrote many books for children. These include a *fantasy novel, *The *Iron Man* (1968), and **How the Whale Became, and other stories*. Hughes was also the author of a number of *plays for children, which were published in such collections as *The Coming of the King* (1970).

Several volumes of his verse are intended for children. The earliest of these, *Meet My Folks* (1961), is a set of comic family portraits; next came *The Earth-Owl and other Moon-People* (1963), poems describing strange imaginary animals and plants. *Nessie the Mannerless Monster* (1964) is a comic *picture book, illustrated by Gerald Rose, written in half-rhyming verse reminiscent of William McGonagall. *Season Songs* (1975) consists of poems related to the seasons (for example, the killing of *Cock Robin is presented as the death of summer). *Moon-Whales and other poems* (USA, 1976, published in Britain two years later as *Moon-Bells and other poems*) is chiefly on the subject of animals. In 1982 there appeared *The *Rattle-Bag*, an anthology of poetry for the young edited by Hughes and Seamus Heaney, still popular today.

HUGHES, Thomas (1822–96) Author of **Tom Brown's Schooldays*. He was born at Uffington in the Vale of the White Horse in Berkshire, the son of a country gentleman and literary dilettante. After a few years at a small private school, he and his elder brother George were sent in 1834 to Rugby, then under the headmastership of Thomas *Arnold.

Dr Arnold had already been at Rugby for five years, but the school was still very rough, and most of the bullying and other abuses described in *Tom Brown's Schooldays* were witnessed or experienced by Hughes. But he enjoyed himself, and, though he was idle in school and was not very good in academic work, he eventually became captain of football and of cricket.

Hughes went to Oriel College as a commoner, and, while an undergraduate, was shaken out of his natural idleness by his engagement to Frances Ford (a clergyman's daughter), which gave him a new sense of purpose, and by experiences on a trip to Scotland which made him politically radical. After leaving Oxford he read for the bar at Lincoln's Inn, and while there came under the influence of F. D. Maurice, chaplain to the Inn. Hughes soon became one of Maurice's Christian Socialists, which led him to meet Charles *Kingsley. He taught in a night school in the London slums, helped to set up the Co-operative shop movement, and was instrumental in establishing the Working Men's College in London. Meanwhile he began to practise as a barrister and, after his marriage, set up a joint home in Wimbledon with his friend and colleague in chambers J. M. Ludlow. Here, in 1856–7, he wrote *Tom Brown's Schooldays*. After publication of this book, he worked on a novel about the scenes of his childhood, *The Scouring of the White Horse* (1858), but neither this nor the insipid *Tom Brown at Oxford* (1861) came anywhere near the popular success of his first work.

In 1865 Hughes became a radical Member of Parliament, first for Lambeth and then for Frome. He paid several visits to America, and in 1879 began a project of establishing a model community there for young Englishmen of the 'Tom Brown' type, who were to lead the outdoor life and keep themselves by farming the land. For this purpose an estate was bought on the Cumberland Plateau in eastern Tennessee, and Hughes named it 'Rugby'. The colony began well, but the original project failed. However Rugby, Tennessee, survived as a more conventional township, and Hughes's own mother spent the last years of her life there, with one of his brothers.

In 1882 Hughes became a County Court judge, and settled in Chester, in the northwest of England, where he spent most of the remainder of his life.

HULL, Katharine *See* FAR-DISTANT OXUS, THE.

HULME BEAMAN, S. G. *See* TOYTOWN.

Human Boy, The A series of short stories by the British novelist Eden Phillpotts (1862–1960), first published in Jerome K. Jerome's

magazine *The Idler* before being issued as a book in 1899. The stories are set in a small private school, Merivale. They are narrated in the first person by a boy at the school, and their humorous treatment and tolerance of such schoolboy foibles as smoking in some ways anticipates Kipling's *Stalky & Co.*, which was published in the year that *The Human Boy* appeared in book form. Phillpotts wrote four further *Human Boy* books.

Humpty Dumpty A figure of *nursery rhyme. The rhyme itself, which is a *riddle with the solution 'Egg', is not found in early riddle-books, possibly because it was too well known to deserve inclusion. It first appeared in print, in several slightly different versions, during the first half of the 19th cent.

A similar egg-riddle is found in many European countries, where the name given to the egg is, for instance, 'Hillerin-Lillerin' (Finland), 'Lille-Trille' (Denmark), and 'Hümpelken-Pümpelken' (parts of Germany). During the 19th cent. girls in America were recorded playing a game called 'Humpty Dumpty' which involved throwing themselves backwards and then trying to regain their balance. Lina Eckenstein, in her *Comparative Studies in Nursery Rhymes* (1906), suggests that the game may be older than the various Humpty Dumpty rhymes, 'for these rhymes describe "Humpty Dumpty" as sitting on a wall, or a bank, or a ledge, which for an actual egg are impossible situations. They are intelligible on the assumption . . . that the rhyme describes beings who are personating eggs.' Humpty Dumpty toys have occasionally been made, and these usually have arms and legs. This variation on the true egg-shape is probably derived from *Tenniel's illustration of Lewis *Carroll's Humpty Dumpty in *Through the Looking-Glass* (1871).

Hunca Munca Mouse in *The Tale of Two Bad Mice* by Beatrix *Potter.

Hundred Merry Tales, A Popular 16th-cent. English *jest-book. In *Much Ado About Nothing* (II. i) Beatrice says that Benedick teased her that she 'had my good wit out of the Hundred Merry Tales'. The book was first printed under the title *A C. Mery Talys* by John Rastell in 1526, and was reissued several times in that century. W. C. Hazlitt, who published a facsimile of Rastell's text in 1887, suggested that it might have been compiled by the Tudor writer and entertainer John Heywood, possibly at the instigation of Sir Thomas More.

The book's form may have been suggested by another hundred-tale work, Boccaccio's *Decameron*, though it is also reminiscent of the *Gesta Romanorum*. It consists of short comic anecdotes. Many of them are mildly bawdy. Among the stories is a tale of 'The Three Wise Men of Gotham' (*see* GOTHAM). Most of the tales have short 'morals' attached to them. The book was imitated in *Tales and Quick Answers*, first printed *c*.1535.

Hundred Million Francs, A English translation (1957) of *Le Cheval sans tête* (1955) by Paul Berna. Set in the Rue des Petits-Pauvres near the railway in a working-class district of Paris, the story takes its French title from the headless wooden horse on tricycle wheels, which is the favourite plaything of Gaby and his gang. They become involved in the detection of an unusual crime.

Berna (1908–94) has also written a number of other children's novels, some of them featuring the same characters, for example *Le Commissaire Sinet et le mulet de l'autoroute sud* (1967) (English, *The Mule on the Motorway*, 1967).

Hunger Games, The (2008–10) A trilogy by Suzanne Collins (1962–), set in a post-apocalyptic, *dystopian world, some years in the future, in a country now called Panem. In the first book we are introduced to the concept of the 'Hunger Games', a brutal tradition in which each of the nation's twelve districts is required to send two 'tributes' to the Capitol, and the twenty-four are thrown into a vast arena to battle it out until twenty-three of them are dead. Book one introduces Katniss Everdeen, chosen as one of the tributes from District 12. She is taken away from her mother, her sister Prim, her friend Gale, and she and Peeta Mellark, the other tribute, are whisked off to the Capitol to fight for their lives. In the second book, *Catching Fire* (2009), the 75th anniversary of the Games sees Katniss and Peeta playing again, against other previous victors, as rebellion brews in the districts following Katniss's rule-breaking win. In the trilogy's finale, *Mockingjay* (2010), the conflicts have descended into outright war, and Katniss is forced to evaluate whether she wants to be the symbol for an increasingly brutal rebellion that puts those she loves in danger.

Even while it is fantasy, *The Hunger Games* can be read at least in part as social commentary, too, dealing as it does with downtrodden, starving populations, authoritarian regimes, an extreme kind of reality television, and so

on. The film adaptations of the first two books were released in 2012 and 2013 to great commercial success, with the completion of the series promised.

HUNT, Helen *See* JACKSON, HELEN HUNT.

HUNT, Irene (1907–2001) American *historical novelist for children. Her first book, *Across Five Aprils* (1964) is about a family caught between the two sides in the Civil War. She won the *Newbery Medal for her second book, *Up a Road Slowly* (1966), the story of the growing-up of an orphan girl and her relationship with her eccentric aunt and uncle. Her later novels include *No Promises in the Wind* (1970), about two children roaming the United States during the Depression of the 1930s.

HUNTER, Kristin (1931–2008) American novelist whose books dealt with complex issues of race and gender. Her first and best known work is *God Bless the Child* (1964), about an inner-city girl desperate to make a better life for herself and her grandmother, who finds, however, that society, through inequality and prejudice, seems determined to make her fail. *The Soul Brothers and Sister Lou* (1968) is set in an urban world of poverty, hostile police, and feuding gangs and tells of an African-American girl discovering herself through music.

HUNTER, Mollie (1922–2012) Scottish author of historical novels for children. Subtle and beautifully crafted, her stories often deal with children who are outsiders, such as Coll in *The Stronghold* (1974), who is a boy, crippled in a raid, who plans to defend his Orkney village from the invading Romans, or Bridie in *The Sound of Chariots* (1972), a story about a girl whose father has been killed in the First World War that is really about grief and death. Many of her books are reworkings of themes from Scottish and Irish folklore, particularly the supernatural creatures such as kelpies, as in *A Stranger Came Ashore* (1975) or mermaids, as in *The Mermaid Summer* (1988).

HUNTER, Norman (George Lorimer) (1899–1995) British author, creator of *Professor Branestawm, who worked for some years as an advertising copywriter and a professional conjurer. Besides the 'Branestawm' books he wrote humorous tales of 'Incrediblania'. From 1949 until 1970 he lived in South Africa and produced no fiction, but Branestawm and other Hunter creations returned to the printed page when he came back to England, and he continued to publish new Branestawm books well into his eighties.

Hunting of the Snark, The, *An Agony, in Eight Fits* A *nonsense poem by Lewis *Carroll (C. L. Dodgson), first published in 1876.

On 18 July 1874 Dodgson was out for a walk when the line 'For the Snark *was* a Boojum, you see' came unbidden into his head, and he set to work to consider what it might be part of. By late November of that year he had written three cantos, or 'Fits', describing the strange voyage of the Bellman and his crew, the Boots, the maker of Bonnets and Hoods, the Barrister, the Broker, the Billiard-Marker, the Banker, the Beaver, the Baker, and the Butcher, and their attempt to track down a Snark. He engaged Henry *Holiday, a celebrated painter and designer of stained-glass windows, to provide illustrations.

Holiday made a drawing of the Bellman landing the Banker on shore 'By a finger entwined in his hair', and in October 1875 Dodgson had 'a sudden idea . . . of publishing the Snark poem this Christmas' with this picture as frontispiece and no other illustrations. He wrote more verses for the poem, and by 6 November judged it to be complete, with a total of 88 stanzas. But a few days later he decided to wait until the following Easter, when Holiday would have seven pictures ready. In the event there were nine, and Dodgson expanded the poem to include the episodes of the Beaver's Lesson and the Barrister's Dream. It was published at the end of March 1876 in an edition of 10,000 copies. The dedicatory poem 'to a dear child' contained an acrostic on the name of its addressee, Dodgson's then reigning favourite among his child-friends, Gertrude Chataway; her name is also found in the first words of each stanza of this poem: Girt, Rude, Chat, Away.

Though it did not have the towering success of the two *Alice* books, the poem quickly became an established part of the humour and mythology of English-speaking children. From the beginning many attempts have been made to prove that it has some secondary meaning. Contemporaries sometimes alleged (on very slim grounds) that it was a satire on the Tichborne case (1871–4) in which an illiterate Australian butcher claimed to be the son of an English aristocrat. Others have alleged it to be a parable about the search for material wealth, or a satire on the quest for social advancement, or a burlesque account of an

unsound business venture. In *The Annotated Snark* (1962), Martin Gardner interprets it as 'a poem about being and non-being...a poem of existential agony'. Dodgson himself, when asked about the meaning of the poem, simply replied 'I don't know!' Elsewhere he wrote:

I'm very much afraid I didn't mean anything but nonsense! Still, you know, words mean more than we mean to express when we use them...So, whatever good meanings are in the book, I'm very glad to accept as the meaning of the book. The best I've seen is by a lady (she published it in a letter to a newspaper)—that the whole book is an allegory on the search after happiness.

The poem has been translated into French, Italian, Swedish, Danish, and German, rendered into Latin elegaics and Virgilian hexameters. Illustrators who have provided alternatives to Holiday's pictures include Mervyn *Peake (1941), Ralph Steadman (1975), and Chris *Riddell (2016).

Huon of Bordeaux A French medieval *romance. Huon kills a son of Charlemagne in a duel, and is punished by being sent to Babylon to bring back the hair and teeth of the daughter of the Amir. Oberon, king of the *fairies, takes pity on him, and with his help Huon not only performs the task successfully but also woos and marries Esclaramonde, the Amir's daughter. Oberon names Huon as his successor on the fairy throne. Possibly *Shakespeare took the figure of Oberon from the romance, which was published in English *c.*1534, probably by Wynkyn de *Worde. Huon appears in the first story in *Kipling's book *Rewards and Fairies* (1910).

HUTCHINS, Pat (1942-) British illustrator whose debut, *Rosie's Walk* (1968), the story of a hen's perambulation around a farm, has become a classic. She won the *Kate Greenaway Medal for *The Wind Blew* (1974), a cumulative story, while other attractive and witty picture books for young children include *The Surprise Party* (1970) and *Titch* (1971).

Hymns for the Amusement of Children By Christopher *Smart, first published by T. Carnan, stepson and successor to *Newbery, in 1771. The hymns are without the eccentric brilliance of Smart's more famous works, but are filled with expressions of forgiveness of one's enemies and with a hope of eternal life to come. The penultimate hymn encourages children to give pennies to poor men in prison; Smart wrote the book while himself imprisoned for debt. The *Hymns*, which first appeared without an author's name, were reprinted several times by Carnan, who possibly hoped that they would rival the *Divine Songs* of *Watts.

Hymns in Prose for Children (1781) A collection of short devotional pieces by Anna Laetitia *Barbauld. In her introduction, the author praises Isaac Watts's *Divine Songs*, but asks 'whether poetry *ought* to be lowered to the capacities of children, or whether they should not rather be kept from reading verse, till they are able to relish good verse'. Her prose hymns are, she says, 'intended to be committed to memory, and recited'. Their style often resembles that of the psalms:

Come, let us go forth into the fields, let us see how the flowers spring, let us listen to the warbling of the birds, and sport ourselves upon the new grass.

The book also contains longer pieces of prose. Mrs Barbauld was chiefly concerned to associate the natural world with the power of God. The *Hymns* were immensely popular, continuing to appear in print, sometimes illustrated, until the early 20th cent. They were translated into French, German, Spanish, Italian, and Hungarian.

I Am David A novel by the Danish writer Anne Holm (1922–98), about a twelve-year-old boy escaping from the concentration camp where he has lived his whole life, and journeying across Europe to Denmark. It was published in Danish as *David* (1963); the English translation, by L. W. Kingsland, appeared in 1965. (It has also been published under the title *North to Freedom*.) Other books by Holm include *Peter*, a time-travel novel (1966, with the English translation by Kingsland appearing two years later), and *The Sky Grew Red* (1991), set at the time of the Napoleonic Wars (published in an English translation by Patricia *Crampton).

I Am the Cheese (1977) A *young adult novel by Robert *Cormier. Groundbreaking, tragic, and difficult, this psychological thriller is about a troubled young man, Adam, who is in an institution where he is interrogated relentlessly in order to recover suppressed memories. Intertwined with recordings of those sessions are two other stories: one, a quest-style bike ride and the other, an account of his ordinary life, family secrets, and his girlfriend. This is not a book designed to reassure its readers; it's a book to make them think. Cormier believed absolutely that young adults need not be coddled by their reading matter; rather, they should be challenged and pushed out of their comfort zones. This book, with its complex narrative and undeniably shocking ending, had a huge influence not only on its readers but on the whole of young adult fiction.

IBBOTSON, Eva (1925–2010) Children's novelist, most famous for *Journey to the River Sea*. She was born in Vienna into a non-practising Jewish family. Her mother Anna Gmeyner was a successful playwright and novelist, her father Berthold P. Wiesner, an eminent fertility doctor.

Ibbotson had, in her words, a 'very cosmopolitan, sophisticated and quite interesting, but also very unhappy childhood, always on some train and wishing to have a home'. Her family were forced to flee the Nazis and Ibbotson came to England. She was sent to a boarding school, which appeared in a fictionalized form in her novel *The Dragonfly Pool* (2008). Ibbotson's unhappy childhood fuelled a need to write stories with happy outcomes. Her son Toby said, 'It was more than that she wanted to write happy stories; she couldn't do anything else.'

She met her husband Alan Ibbotson while they were both studying at Cambridge, and married him in 1947. Ibbotson's writing career began with television drama, before she moved on to children's books. Many of her works are humorous, with supernatural or fantastic elements such as ghosts and witches. *Which Witch?* (1979) concerns a wizard named Arriman the Awful and his quest to find a wife. It was shortlisted for the *Carnegie Medal. *The Secret of Platform 13* (1994) features a platform at Kings Cross station that leads to another world—a concept that later appeared in J. K. Rowling's *Harry Potter series.

Following the death of her husband, Ibbotson wrote a more serious novel, which became her most acclaimed work. *Journey to the River Sea* (2001) won the Nestlé Smarties Book Prize, was shortlisted for the Carnegie Medal, and brought Ibbotson a new level of recognition.

The Star of Kazan (2004) gave Ibbotson her third Carnegie Medal shortlisting. Set in Vienna and Germany, it tells of Annika, abandoned as a baby, who becomes a servant to a Viennese family. One day, a rich lady announces that she is her mother, and takes her home to her German estate, but all is not as it seems. Ibbotson's final novel, *The Abominables*, was published posthumously in 2012.

Although Ibbotson's work is much read and loved, she is not the household name she deserves to be. She ranks alongside such talents as Joan *Aiken, Nina *Bawden, and Philippa *Pearce as one of Britain's great children's writers of the last fifty years.

IBBY *See* INTERNATIONAL BOARD ON BOOKS FOR YOUNG PEOPLE.

I Capture the Castle (1948) A novel by Dodie *Smith, written for adults but beloved by teen readers. Beginning with one of the most famous opening lines in modern literature, this is the delightful story of Cassandra, who lives in a crumbling castle with her eccentric, poverty-stricken family, and how her life is turned upside down with the arrival of American neighbours and their two sons. Cassandra and her sister Rose observe, flirt, become engaged, fall in love (all with the wrong man), and slowly, through the story, grow up. As Cassandra matures, so does the narrative, becoming more nuanced as she painfully learns about what she really wants out of life. Smith left the ending refreshingly open, and many a reader has spent time speculating as to exactly how the story might continue.

Illustrated Mum, The See WILSON, JACQUELINE.

Important People See DOWD, J. H.

Incrediblania *See* HUNTER, NORMAN.

Incredible Journey, The (1961) By Sheila Burnford (1918–84), the story of two dogs and a cat who make a long trek through the wilds of Canada back to their home. The author was born in Scotland in 1918 and made her home in Ontario. She wrote one other children's book, *Mr Noah and the Second Flood* (1973), an ecological parable. *The Incredible Journey* was filmed in 1963, and the film remade (as *Homeward Bound*) in 1993.

Indian fairy and folk tales These were first published in English by Mary Frere (1845–1911), daughter of the Governor of Bombay, under the title *Old Deccan Days; or, Hindoo Fairy Legends* (1868); the stories were taken down from her native *ayah*. Among later notable collections is *Wide-Awake Stories, a collection of tales told by little children . . . in the Panjab and Kashmir* (1884), the work of Flora Annie Steel (1847–1929), wife of an Indian civil servant and a pioneer of native female education in India. This book was reissued in 1894 as *Tales of the Punjab*. In 1892 Joseph *Jacobs published *Indian Fairy Tales*, basing it on Miss Frere's and Miss Steel's books, and on ancient sources, such as *The Fables of Bidpai* (*see* PANCHATANTRA; ARABIAN NIGHTS; FAIRY TALES). Later collections include: Mulk Raj Anand's *Indian Fairy Tales* (1946), J. E. B. Gray's *Indian Tales and Legends* (1961), Marcus *Crouch's *The Ivory City and other stories from India and Pakistan* (1980), and Ruskin *Bond's *Tales and Legends of India* (1982); and more recently an illustrated edition of retellings by Jamila Gavin, illustrated by Amanda Hall, *Tales from India: Stories of Creation and the Cosmos* (2011).

Indian in the Cupboard, The (1980) Stories about little people have engaged readers since Gulliver went to Lilliput. In this hugely successful series by Lynne Reid *Banks a boy, Omri, has a cupboard and a magical key—the result is that his toy Indian comes to life as Little Bull (US: Little Bear), a proud and fearless Iroquois warrior from the 18th cent. But having responsibility for a miniature human is less than easy, especially after Omri lets his friend Patrick into the secret. There are sequels: *The Return of the Indian* (1985), *The Secret of the Indian* (1989), *The Mystery of the Cupboard* (1992), and *The Key to the Indian* (1998). The original book was made into a film in 1986.

'Indians' of North America The native Americans were known to colonists as 'Indians', or sometimes 'Red Indians', from the times of the earliest European settlements. The term is controversial today, but for centuries their appearances in literature saw them referred to by that name (most notably in *westerns). These early portrayals of the 'Indian' have almost always been stereotypical.

Native Americans began to figure prominently in American art and literature during the period between the War of 1812 and the Civil War, when they were generally portrayed as examples of the Noble Savage. An impression of the Indian passing away before the onslaught of civilization was vividly given in James Fenimore *Cooper's *The Last of the Mohicans* (1826), one of the *Leather-Stocking Tales*. During this period, too, a number of researchers collected information about Native American history and culture; the writings of the ethnologist H. R. Schoolcraft served as a source for Longfellow's *Hiawatha* (1855).

Even during this time there was no doubt that the fate of the Native Americans was regarded as less important than the destiny of the United States; moreover by the 1850s the reading public had begun to tire of the Noble Savage, as can be seen by the parodies of *Hiawatha* that began to appear almost as soon as it was published. The westerns that became popular after the Civil War, largely through the medium of the *dime novel, tended to depict the Native American much

more crudely, as 'a person of little culture and less language' (Robert F. Berkhofer, *The White Man's Indian*, 1978). Their speech was restricted to little more than 'How!' and 'Ug!', while tribal differences were almost entirely ignored.

Thanks to Fenimore Cooper, *Hiawatha*, and westerns, Native Americans had become stock figures in English juvenile literature by the end of the 19th cent., as is shown by their appearance in such works as *Five Children and It* (1902) and *Peter Pan* (1904). However two writers of this period, one on each side of the Atlantic, treated them more seriously; in England, Andrew *Lang included a number of Native American stories in his *Fairy Books* (1889 onwards), while in Canada the naturalist Ernest Thompson *Seton wrote about Native American woodcraft in *Two Little Savages* (1903).

By the mid-20th cent, Native Americans had begun to receive more sympathetic treatment from some children's authors, such as Cliff *Faulknor, Scott *O'Dell, and William O. *Steele in America, and Christie *Harris in Canada, and Ann Nolan *Clark wrote books specially for Native American children. More recently, Native American authors have begun to be published in English. (*See* NATIVE AMERICAN WRITING.)

infant amusements Games with which an adult entertains a baby or small child, often accompanied by verses, many of which have become well-known *nursery rhymes. They include the following categories: (1) *Finger rhymes.* The simplest of these merely give names to each of the fingers, usually beginning with 'Tom Thumbkin' and ending with 'Little Dick' (the names of the intervening fingers vary greatly). A more elaborate finger rhyme, 'Dance, Thumbkin, dance', calls for the waggling of each finger in turn. (2) *Toe rhymes.* Again, a rhyme is used to identify each toe in turn, the most widely known being 'This little piggy went to market.' (3) *Face rhymes.* These are recited while touching each part of the face in turn, e.g. 'Brow bender, Eye peeper', etc. (4) *Nose rhymes,* e.g. 'My mother and your mother', in which the adult pretends to chop the child's nose off. (5) *Knee songs,* sung while the child is bounced on the knee, e.g. 'This is the way the ladies ride' and 'To market, to market'. (6) *Bo-peep,* in which the child's head is covered for an instant and then uncovered; rhymes are not commonly associated with this game, though one is

recorded: 'Bo-peep, Little Bo-peep, | Now's the time for hide and seek.' (7) *Tickling rhymes,* which are a prelude to the tickling of the child's palms, armpits, or knees, e.g. 'Round and round the garden' and 'If you are a gentleman'. (8) *Jumping rhymes,* recited while the adult jumps the child up and down, e.g. 'American jump'. (9) *Hand rhymes,* which encourage children to clap their hands rhythmically, such as 'Pat-a-cake, pat-a-cake, baker's man' and 'Pease porridge hot' (or 'Pease pudding hot'), or which stimulate them to guess in which of the adult's hands some small object is concealed ('Handy dandy, riddledy ro'). (10) *Foot or leg rhymes,* recited while the foot is patted ('Shoe a little horse'), or the child's shoe is put on ('Cobbler, cobbler, mend my shoe'), or its leg is moved to and fro ('Leg over leg, | As the dog went to Dover'). (11) *Hand tricks,* in which some sleight of hand is performed with the fingers, e.g. 'Here is the church, and here is the steeple', 'Here are the lady's knives and forks', and 'Two little dicky birds'. These tricks are also performed by older children to amuse themselves or each other.

Some of these verses, together with some *games-rhymes used by older children, appeared in the earliest collections of nursery rhymes. James Orchard *Halliwell included many in his *Nursery Rhymes of England* (1842) and devoted a section of his *Popular Rhymes and Nursery Tales* (1849) to a description of some of the games that accompany them. The majority of rhymes in current use have been collected in The *Oxford Dictionary Of Nursery Rhymes*.

Infant Amusements is also the title of an 1867 book by W. H. G. *Kingston, whose frontispiece was Kate *Greenaway's first published book illustration.

INGALLS WILDER, Laura *See* WILDER, LAURA INGALLS.

INGELOW, Jean (1820–97) Victorian poet who wrote a number of children's stories, the best known being *Mopsa The Fairy* (1869). Others include *Stories told to a Child* (1866) and *The Little Wonder-Horn* (1872), a series of tales afterwards reprinted in six booklets contained in a box, the whole being entitled *The Little Wonder Box* (1887).

Ingoldsby Legends, The, or *Mirth and Marvels* (1840) A book of gruesomely comic stories in verse and prose, in the manner of medieval legends and folk tales, supposedly

compiled by Thomas Ingoldsby, a country gen-
tleman, from his 'family memoranda'. It was in
fact the work of R. H. Barham (1788-1845), a
clergyman who was born at Tappington Ever-
ard in Kent, a setting he used for many of the
stories. The book was enjoyed by many Victo-
rian children; in *The *Phoenix and The Carpet*
(1904) by E. *Nesbit, Anthea and her brothers
and sisters consult it as a source-book for
magic. There are editions with illustrations by
*Tenniel (1864) and *Rackham (1898).

INGPEN, Robert (1936-) Australian illustra-
tor who received the biennial *Hans Christian
Andersen Award in 1986 for his 'lasting con-
tribution' to children's book illustration. He
has written or illustrated over 100 children's
books, and designed the *Dromkeen Medal,
which he received in 1989. Some of his most
famous books include the *Voyage of the Pop-
pykettle* (1980) and its sequels about the Hairy
Peruvians, sailing across the Pacific in a tea-
pot, and *The Idle Bear* (1986), in which the
owner of the teddy grows up. He has also
illustrated many classic children's stories. His
illustrations are highly rendered, detailed, re-
alistic, have effective use of light and shadow,
and earthy tones, and evoke a strong emotion-
al reaction in the reader. He often combines
pencil and watercolour. Although he is known
as a scientific and historical illustrator, his own
writing and illustration are often fantasy.

Inheritance series (2001-11) By Christo-
pher *Paolini, an epic fantasy series consisting
of *Eragon* (2001), *Eldest* (2005), *Brisingr*
(2008), and *Inheritance* (2011). Paolini started
what would become *Eragon* when he was fif-
teen years old. His family had the book pri-
vately published and Paolini embarked on a
tour to spread the word about the book. A
chance led to the book being discovered by
a major publisher and the books have since
become a worldwide success. The fast-paced
series tells of a boy, Eragon, who raises a drag-
on from a hatchling and whose adventures
encompass destiny, magic, and power. Criti-
cized for being derivative of other dragon-
centred fantasies, Paolini's books remain
hugely popular with children.

Inkheart (2003-8) A fantasy trilogy by
Cornelia *Funke, translated into English by
Anthea *Bell, which comprises *Inkheart*
(2003), *Inkspell* (2006), and *Inkdeath* (2008).
The series is all about the power of story—
especially when it is told by someone with
the magical power literally to bring that story

to life. Meggie only knows that her father,
who works as a bookbinder, won't read to
her, but it is only when she is much older
that she realizes why—and that a villain he
accidentally conjured from a story is hunting
them to use her father's power for his own
ends. Peopled with characters from Meggie's
books and people from her own world, this is
an epic, complex trilogy. A largely disappoint-
ing film version of *Inkheart* was released in
2008.

INKPEN, Mick (1952-) British author-illus-
trator. With warm, comforting storylines that
are fully complemented by his gentle, realistic
illustrative style, Inkpen's work is the nursery
companion to millions of children. The mas-
sively successful long-running *Kipper* series,
about a small dog, and *Wibbly Pig* (from 1995),
about a small pig whose adventures echo
those of any toddler, such as the first title,
Wibbly Pig Makes a Tent, are just some of the
more visible works from a man responsible
for a multitude of much-loved picture books.
Enchanting stories such as *The Blue Balloon*
(1989), *Threadbear* (1991), and *Penguin Small*
(1992) are others perfect for reading aloud.
He is a long-time collaborator with Nick
Butterworth (1946-).

**Institut für Jugendbuchforschung
(Institute for Research on Juvenile Books)**
Attached to Johann Wolfgang Goethe University
in Frankfurt am Main. Founded in 1963, under
the direction of Klaus *Doderer, it published the
Lexikon Der Kinder- Und Jugendliteratur.

instruction, books of *See* BOOKS OF
INSTRUCTION.

**International Board on Books for
Young People (IBBY)** An organization
based in Basle, Switzerland, with over seventy
national sections around the world. It admin-
isters the *Hans Christian Andersen Awards
and publishes an Honour List of books. IBBY
is particularly concerned to encourage the
growth of children's literature in developing
countries; its journal *Bookbird*, published
quarterly, contains articles on children's
books and reading promotion projects around
the world.

In the Night Kitchen (1970) A *picture
book by Maurice *Sendak. The boy Mickey,
woken by a noise in the night, falls through
the dark into a Night Kitchen where three
identical fat bakers mix him into their batter.
He escapes, flies into the air in a plane made

of dough, fetches the bakers a cup of milk from a giant milk bottle, and returns to his own bed.

The story grew from Sendak's childhood fascination with an advertisement for a New York bakery: 'We Bake While You Sleep!' He says: 'This seemed to me the most sadistic thing in the world, because all I wanted to do was stay up and watch.' The bakers are all three drawn in the likeness of the film comedian Oliver Hardy, and the background of skyscrapers made out of kitchen canisters and jars reflects Sendak's boyhood love of the towers of Manhattan, seen from his Brooklyn home. There are also a number of private references in the pictures—for instance, a cream packet in one illustration is labelled with addresses at which the Sendak family lived in Maurice's childhood.

When the book appeared, some librarians complained about Mickey's nudity in many pictures (he loses his pyjamas during his fall); a few painted nappies onto their copies. Sendak himself regarded the book as his tribute to popular American art of the 1930s.

Invention of Hugo Cabret, The (2007) A book of pictures and words by Brian *Selznick. Selznick himself describes it as 'not exactly a novel, and it's not quite a picture book, and it's not really a graphic novel, or a flip book, or a movie, but a combination of all these things'. There are nearly 300 beautifully detailed pencil drawings, each filling a double page, and the story is told sometimes in images, sometimes in words. Twelve-year-old orphan Hugo lives in the walls of a Paris train station and is obsessed with repairing an old automaton, because he believes that if he can do so, it will write a secret message. The story celebrates the history of cinematography—in particular the early filmmaker George Méliès, and the book itself has a highly cinematic feel. It won the *Caldecott Medal in 2008 and Martin Scorsese made a film of it, which was released in 2011.

Invisible Playmate, The (1894) An account of a child and her early death, by William *Canton.

Irish folk and fairy tales First collected systematically, and published in English, by T. Crofton *Croker in 1825, though Irish stories had occasionally appeared in *chapbooks and in other printed forms. In the 1860s a large number of tales were published by Patrick Kennedy, a Dublin bookseller who was reported to believe in *fairies and whose informants were from English-speaking

County Wexford. Towards the end of the 19th cent., much more was collected from the Gaelic speakers of the West and North. There were also bardic tales, stories of heroes such as Cuchulain and Finn, written down in volumes such as the 11th- or 12th-cent. vellum *Book of the Dun Cow*.

The Irish literary revival in the 1890s and 1900s brought with it Lady Gregory's English versions of some of these: *Cuchulain of Muirthemne* (1902) and *Gods and Fighting Men* (1904). W. B. Yeats made two important early anthologies of all types of Irish material: *Fairy and Folk Tales of the Irish Peasantry* (1888) and *Irish Fairy Tales* (1892), which had an appendix on the classification of Irish fairies.

The Cuchulain tales were handsomely adapted for children by Eleanor Hull (1909), and the following year T. W. Rolleston's *The High Deeds of Finn* appeared as a companion volume. Rolleston edited a compendium of *Myths and Legends of the Celtic Race* in 1911. Padraic *Colum, working with the illustrator Willy Pogány in America, published *The King of Ireland's Son* in 1916, and Ella Young, an Irish American who had learnt the professional storyteller's art during her youth in County Antrim, produced much-praised versions of Irish stories, beginning with *Celtic Wonder Tales* in 1923. Arthur *Rackham illustrated James Stephens's *Irish Fairy Tales* (1920) and Stephens wove them into his novel *The Crock of Gold* (1912). Among the many recent writers to cite Irish folk and *fairy stories stories as an inspiration are novelists as diverse as Malachy *Doyle, Eoin *Colfer and Tomie *DePaola.

Iron Man, The (1968) A powerful modern fairy tale by the poet, Ted *Hughes, it has remained in print since its first appearance in 1968 and is regarded as a classic of post-war children's literature. Originally published with illustrations by George Adamson, it has been reimagined by others, most recently, Laura Carlin. The 1985 edition, with illustrations by Andrew Davidson, won the *Kurt Maschler Award for the author and the artist. In 1993, Hughes published a sequel, *The Iron Woman*. The American edition appeared with the title *The Iron Giant* (the name also used for the 1999 film) to avoid confusion with the *Marvel Comic* super hero, Iron Man.

The Iron Man appears one day, striding out of the sea. Initially destroyed by a fall, he rebuilds himself and sets out to find food—scrap iron. The country folk are terrified, until the boy Hogarth, suggests a solution that enables

humans and the Iron Man to live in harmony. When the world is threatened by an alien, it is the Iron Man who must come to its rescue.

IRVING, Washington (1783–1859) Born in New York City, Irving had already established a reputation as an author when he wrote his *Sketch Book of Geoffrey Crayon, Gent.* (1819–20), a miscellany published in parts and consisting of sketches of British life, together with various European folk tales retold with American settings. These included *Rip van Winkle, which appeared in the first number and was an instant success, and The *Legend of Sleepy Hollow*, another tale that became a classic. Irving was later appointed a diplomatic attaché in Spain, which led to the writing of his *Alhambra* (1832), in which sketches of Spanish life were interspersed with Moorish tales (some traditional, some invented by Irving) on the same pattern as the *Sketch Book*. Selections from this have sometimes been published for children.

In 1875 an extract from the *Sketch Book* describing Christmas festivities in the traditional English manner was published under the title *Old Christmas*; it was Randolph *Caldecott's brilliant illustrations for this book that brought him to the attention of the printer Edmund *Evans and so began his career as a children's artist.

It's Like This, Cat (1963) A novel by Emily Cheney *Neville.

Ivanhoe See SCOTT.

I Want My Hat Back (2011) An irresistibly funny picture book by Jon *Klassen. Klassen had illustrated other writers' work before, but this was his self-penned debut. A bear has lost his hat, and following a string of encounters with other animals (who deny all knowledge), he finally tracks it down. The hat quest ends somewhat controversially in picture-book terms, with severe off-screen violence perpetrated upon the rabbit who took it. The apparent simplicity of the sparse text and the witty, subtle illustrations conceal a superb sense of style and timing, and an uncommon confidence and sophistication (and subversiveness) in the storytelling, which introduce Klassen as one of the most promising picture-book artists at work today. In 2015 it was adapted for the stage by London's National Theatre. There are two extremely good companion books: *This Is Not My Hat* (2012), which became the first book to win both the *Caldecott Medal and the *Kate Greenaway Medal, and *We Found a Hat* (2016).

Jabberwocky A *nonsense poem by Lewis *Carroll (C. L. Dodgson). The first verse, beginning ''Twas brillig, and the slithy toves', was written in 1855 and copied into Dodgson's comic scrapbook *Mischmasch* under the heading 'Stanza of Anglo-Saxon Poetry', with a set of notes explaining the various nonsense-words. The remaining six stanzas were (according to Dodgson's nephew and biographer) written in 1867, and Roger Lancelyn *Green has pointed out that they are almost certainly a burlesque of 'The Shepherd of the Giant Mountains', a translation of a German poem by *La Motte Fouqué made by Dodgson's cousin, the poet Menella Smedley. The complete text of *Jabberwocky* appeared in *Through the Looking-Glass* (1871). It has occasionally been illustrated as a stand-alone work by such artists as Joel *Stewart (2003).

Jackanapes (1879) A story by Mrs *Ewing about a boy whose father is killed at the battle of Waterloo, and who grows up to die himself on some unspecified battlefield, saving the life of a friend. It was inspired by the death of the French Prince Imperial during the Zulu War in 1879. It originally appeared that year in *Aunt Judy's Magazine*, with illustrations by Randolph *Caldecott, which were included when it was published in book form by the *Society for Promoting Christian Knowledge in 1883.

Jack and Jill Characters in a *nursery rhyme. The first verse made its initial appearance in print in the second half of the 18th cent., but the rhyming of 'water' with 'after' suggests that it may be more than a century older than this. 'Jack and Jill' was a phrase used for some centuries with the general sense of 'lad and lass'.

In the early 19th cent. fourteen more verses were added, describing a whole series of misadventures of Jack and Jill (falling off a swing, being butted by a goat, etc.), and the recriminations of Dame Gill, presumably their mother or grandmother. This fifteen-verse version was often published as a juvenile *chapbook under

the title *Jack and Jill, and Old Dame Gill*. Its second verse, in which Jack's injured head is plastered with vinegar and brown paper, has become a standard part of the nursery rhyme.

Jack and the Beanstalk A *fairy story apparently known in Britain at least since the first half of the 18th cent.

In 1734 there was published an edition of *Round about our Coal-Fire: or Christmas Entertainments*, a satirical book of anonymous authorship exposing the worthlessness of folk tales and superstitious beliefs. This edition included a chapter entitled 'Enchantment demonstrated in the Story of Jack Spriggins and the Enchanted Bean'. The chapter tells how a lazy wretch of a lad is brought up by his grandmother, a *witch. One day she drops a magic bean which the cat then discovers in the fireplace. When Jack plants it in the ground, the bean sends out a stalk which grows rapidly. He climbs up the stalk, which continues to grow, and towns appear on its leaves. At one of these towns Jack stops to refresh himself at an inn. Immediately the landlord of the inn turns into a beautiful Lady. It transpires that the woman is really Jack's grandmother's cat. Jack then declares himself married to the lady. Next day Jack, now renamed Prince John, pays a call on Giant Gogmagog, whom he kills effortlessly with a mere flick of a magic ring, whereupon he is saluted as 'Monarch of the Universe'.

This burlesque, which its author declared to be the kind of thing that proceeds from 'the Maggots in a Madman's Brain', was founded on a folk tale then in circulation. However, it was not until the beginning of the 19th cent. that the story appeared in print in a form other than parody.

The series *Popular Stories, published from 1804 onwards by *Tabart, includes *The History of Jack and the Bean-Stalk, Printed from the Original Manuscript, Never Before Published*, of which the earliest surviving copy is dated 1807. The Tabart version of the story—which

has been followed in all later substantial re-tellings—is set 'in the days of King Alfred'. Jack is the spoilt only child of a widow who, when she is reduced to poverty through his laziness, sends him to market to sell her cow. He returns not with money but with a handful of beans, which his mother promptly throws into the garden. When Jack wakes up next morning, he finds that they have taken root. 'The stalks were of an immense thickness, and had so entwined, that they formed a ladder nearly like a chain in appearance.' Jack sets out and climbs to the top, where he is accosted by an old woman who explains that she is a *fairy, and tells Jack that nearby lives a *giant, who long ago deceived and killed Jack's father and seized all his possessions. Jack has now been appointed to punish the giant for all his wickedness. Jack goes to the giant's house and steals his hen, which can lay golden eggs. He then descends the beanstalk and gives the hen to his mother. For some time the two of them live happily on the proceeds of the golden eggs, but eventually Jack sets off again up the beanstalk. This time he manages to steal the giant's money-bags and bring them home. On a third journey he takes a magic harp, but it can speak, and it calls out to the giant, who gives chase. Jack manages to climb down the beanstalk and, reaching the bottom just as the giant has begun to climb after him, fells it with a hatchet, so that the giant tumbles down and is killed by the fall.

In the year that this narrative was printed, 1807, there also appeared a metrical version of the same story, *The History of Mother Twaddle, and the Marvellous Atchievements of Her Son Jack*, by 'B.A.T.', published by John *Harris. This version differs from Tabart's in several details, and appears to derive from some other source than that behind Tabart's publication.

A beanstalk reaching into the heavens recalls both Jacob's Ladder in the Old Testament and the world-tree Yggdrasill, which stretches up into heaven and sends its roots down to hell, in the prose *Edda*. A story collected by the brothers *Grimm, 'The Flail from Heaven', resembles the English tale in that a seed sown by a countryman grows swiftly into a great tree which reaches the sky.

Tabart's *Jack and the Beanstalk* was reprinted word for word in his *Popular Fairy Tales* (1818), and was closely copied in a number of *chapbooks. The story became popular as a *pantomime, the first stage version apparently being *Jack and the Beanstalk; or, Harlequin and the Ogre* by Charles Dibdin the younger, performed at Drury Lane at Christmas 1819. Modern retellings often follow that of Joseph *Jacobs in *English Fairy Tales* (1890), in which the fairy is omitted and Jack proceeds straight to the giant's house without knowing what is in store for him.

In a short story by Walter *de la Mare, 'Dick and the Beanstalk' (published in *Collected Stories for Children*, 1947), a farmer's son discovers Jack's mother's ruined cottage, many years later, and begins his own adventure by climbing up the withered beanstalk that still stands beside it. *Jim and the Beanstalk* (1970) by Raymond *Briggs is a more broadly comic sequel.

Jackanory A children's television programme inaugurated by the BBC in 1965. In it, children's books were read 'straight to the camera', usually by well known actors, with comparatively little visual illustration—something that was previously thought impossible, but which was proved by the programme's first editor, Joy Whitby, to be triumphantly successful. Under her successor, Anna Home, the programme commissioned new stories from such writers as Helen *Cresswell and Joan *Aiken, and led to the creation of characters such as *Littlenose. The programme concluded in 1996 with Alan Bennett's reading of *The *House at Pooh Corner*, since which time there have been occasional one-off revivals and spin-off series.

Jack Dandy's Delight See BESTIARY.

Jack Harkaway Hero of many stories by S. Bracebridge *Hemyng. The first, *Jack Harkaway's Schooldays*, came out in 1871 as a serial in *Boys of England*, one of the magazines owned by the erstwhile publisher of *penny dreadfuls, Edwin *Brett. Shortly afterwards Harkaway appeared in America, pirated in *The Boys' and Girls' Weekly*, and Hemyng was attracted by a magazine contract to go there to write. Brett continued to publish new Harkaway titles, and the hero's adventures subsequently took him to sea, to Oxford, gold-prospecting, among *pirates, 'Out West among the Indians', and to other lively settings for excitement. Altogether there were eighteen titles, the later ones having the original Jack's identical son and then grandson as protagonist. He was last seen fighting Boers in 1899.

Jack Harkaway was quintessentially English, every schoolboy's idea of the popular, stylish, fearless, and lucky hero. He was expert in

every sort of fight, and he was the perpetrator of countless pranks, practical jokes, and more or less brutal punishments of sneaks and other offenders against the moral code of his kind. (The books are a useful source for 19th-cent. schoolboy and other subcultural custom and slang.) Scenes of torture and violent death were part of the Harkaway books' stock in trade, and the narrative was conducted in a breathy, short-paragraphed, sensational style.

Harkaway stories carefully avoid any charge of corrupting youth. The heroes drink, but not enough to impair their fitness, and they always do the right thing by their parents, their careers, and their sweethearts. The original Jack's girl is Emily, whom he marries at the end of the third book, after several rescues from enemies, romantic scenes, and a brief distraction in the form of a Jewish moneylender's beautiful daughter.

Hemyng wrote other similar stories for boys, including a 'Scapegrace' series about Dick Light-heart, and also more ambitious books, such as *Eton School Days*. But none was as successful as the Harkaway series. There was, briefly, a *Jack Harkaway's Journal for Boys* (1893).

Jack Horner Hero of a *nursery rhyme and of a *ballad often printed in *chapbooks. The ballad does not appear before 1763, when it was printed as a chapbook under the title *The History of Jack Horner, containing the Witty Pranks he played from his Youth to his Riper Years*. However it appears the nursery rhyme was well known long before this date. The ballad includes elements of *The *Friar and The Boy* and *Tom Thumb* and details the adventures of Jack, a boy of thirteen inches high. Jack is given a set of bagpipes by a hermit which have the power to make all who hear them dance about uncontrollably and also a coat that confers invisibility. With the aid of these gifts he exposes the adultery of an innkeeper's wife, making her dance half-naked in the street with her Quaker lover, to whose bottom is firmly stuck a chamber pot. Finally, with the aid of the pipes, Jack overcomes and kills a giant, and marries a knight's daughter, thereby becoming a squire.

Jack Sheppard Hero of *penny dreadfuls, a celebrated London thief and highwayman, born in 1702, who after many escapes from prison was hanged at the age of twenty-two. Daniel *Defoe wrote tracts about him; he also appeared in plays and *ballads, and was the subject of a novel by Harrison *Ainsworth (1839).

JACKSON, Helen Hunt (1830–85) American author who was inspired by *Uncle Tom's Cabin* to write an equivalent book to draw attention to the experiences of Native Americans. *Ramona* (1884) told the story of a mixed-race orphan girl in Southern California. It was hugely successful and, like her book *A Century of Dishonour* (1881), also influential. Her children's books include *Nelly's Silver Mine* (1878), the story of a sister and brother whose family moves to Colorado mining country.

Jack Sprat A character of *nursery rhyme, best known for the rhyme beginning 'Jack Sprat could eat no fat'. 'Jack Sprat' was often used at that time as the name for a *dwarf or other diminutive person. Another Jack Sprat verse concerns the hero's cat, which had only one ear; this was originally obscene; *see* Tom Tit's Song Book. In the mid-19th cent. the two rhymes were combined to make a *chapbook, usually entitled *The Life of Jack Sprat, His Wife, and His Cat*.

Jack the Giant Killer Hero of an English folk tale alternatively known as *The History of Jack and the Giants*. Jack is the only son of a Cornish farmer, and is endowed with wit, cheek, and ingenuity. A *giant is terrorizing Cornwall from a cave on St Michael's Mount. Jack, on learning that the giant's treasure will be his reward, undertakes to destroy him. Jack spends a night digging a pit outside the giant's cave. Having disguised the pit, he wakes the giant with a blast on his horn, sees him fall, cursing, into the trap, and finishes him off with his pickaxe.

This deed wins Jack both treasure and the title 'The Giant Killer'. He then continues in the same style, slaying the giant Blunderboar (releasing three fair ladies by the same deed) and managing to outwit a Welsh giant who has offered him false hospitality.

Jack now meets King *Arthur's son, who has set out in search of a certain enchanted lady, but has been left penniless after gallantly paying off a dead man's debts. For free lodging, Jack proposes a visit to his fearsome uncle, a three-headed giant living nearby. He goes on ahead and announces the only thing that will frighten the giant, the imminent arrival of the king's son with a thousand men. While the giant hides from the imaginary force, Jack and Arthur's son feast and help themselves to treasure. The giant, in gratitude for his safety, gives Jack a coat conferring invisibility,

a cap of knowledge, a never-failing sword, and shoes of swiftness.

When Arthur's son reaches the goal of his quest, the beautiful lady possessed by evil spirits, Jack uses his gifts to help dispose of the enchantments. Arthur's son marries the lady, and Jack for his services becomes a knight of the Round Table.

In Part Two of the story Jack, with the king's permission, sets out to rid the country of all giants and monsters, and after dispatching three and releasing their captives he meets Thunderdel, a huge giant with two heads. After some sport this giant, too, is decapitated, and Jack's last enterprise is to release a duke's daughter from the enchantments of the giant Galigantus. He marries her and lives the rest of his life happily on the fine estate now presented to him by the king.

Stories of giants were undoubtedly part of medieval English folk entertainment, and separate incidents in *Jack the Giant Killer* have counterparts in Norse Myths, and in the mythology and folk tales of several other languages. (See, for example, *The *Valiant Little Tailor*.*) One of the incidents in the Arthurian legends is the killing of a giant on St Michael's Mount. However, *Jack the Giant Killer* itself is not now thought to be much older than the earliest known printed version, a copy dated 1711, which was transcribed by J. O. *Halliwell but later lost. The likelihood is that a number of classic giant-incidents were put together in this form in the late 17th cent. The story was hugely popular as a *chapbook, and was read avidly by Dr Johnson, James Boswell, William Cowper, and Henry Fielding.

The giant's challenge, 'Fe, fi, fo, fum,' which now leads its own life as a *nursery rhyme, appears in numerous variants and seems to have been a standard ingredient of giant stories.

JACOBS, Joseph (1854–1916) Folklorist who was born in Sydney, Australia, and was educated there and at London University and King's College, Cambridge. He was a notable Jewish historian. For a time he edited the British journal *Folk-Lore*. His *English Fairy Tales* (1890), together with *More English Fairy Tales* (1894), was among the outstanding children's books of its period; Jacobs made it his business to narrate the stories in the manner in which a nurse would tell them to children, though the book also includes notes for those interested in the origins of the stories. His other works include two volumes of *Celtic

Fairy Tales (1892 and 1894), *Indian Fairy Tales* (1892), an edition of *Aesop, and a *Book of Wonder Voyages* (1896). His achievement as a folklorist and storyteller compares with that of his contemporary Andrew *Lang.

JACQUES, Brian (1939–2011) Liverpool-born author of fantasy books who took to writing in order to engage children at a home for the blind, but whose books became international bestsellers. Most famous for the twenty-two books in the *Redwall* (1986) series, in which all the characters are animals who battle for supremacy, the good (mice, badgers, voles, hares, moles, and squirrels) versus the evil (rats, weasels, ferrets, snakes, and stoats), he also produced the *Castaways of the Flying Dutchman* trilogy (2001–6).

JACQUES, Robin (1920–95) British illustrator, who provided pictures for stories by, among others, Joan *Aiken (*Black Hearts in Battersea*, 1964), Ruth *Manning-Sanders (*A Book of Giants*, 1964 and others in the same series), and Lynne Reid *Banks (*The Indian in the Cupboard*, 1980), and cover designs for many of C. S. *Forester's *Hornblower* series.

Jadis The White Witch in the *Narnia series.

James and the Giant Peach (1961) The debut children's novel by Roald *Dahl, about seven-year-old orphan James Henry Trotter (whose parents were eaten by an escaped rhinoceros), who lives with his nasty Aunt Sponge and Aunt Spiker. A mysterious old man appears with a paper bag of tiny, magical, green, glowing, squirmy things and before you know it James finds himself inside the stone of a giant, overgrown, juicy peach with seven giant, overgrown insects flying over the Atlantic, borne aloft by 502 seagulls. On their adventures, James and his friends—an old grasshopper violinist, a nervous earthworm, a mouthy centipede obsessed with his forty-two boots, and so on—encounter sharks and hail-hurling Cloud-Men, have an unfortunate collision with a rainbow, and finally come to rest impaled on the top of the Empire State Building.

JAMES, Jesse *See* Jesse James.

JAMES, Will *See* Smoky the Cowhorse.

Jammy Grammy Lammy F'Huppa F'Huppa Berlin Stereo Eo Eo Lebb C'Yepp Nermonica Le Straypek De Grespin De Crespin De Spespin De Vespin De Whoop De Loop De Brunkle Merry Christmas Lenoir *See* Polly.

Jane A female equivalent of Richmal Crompton's *William*, in a series of novels by the Australian-born British author 'Evadne Price' (Helen Zenna Smith, 1888–1985). The first was *Just Jane* (1928), and there were nine others.

Janet and John A series of graded readers for small children produced from 1949 by the London firm of James Nisbet. Described by the publishers as 'true to the best in the life of modern children', they present, in limited vocabulary, incidents in the daily life of a brother and sister; some volumes also include fairy and folk tales. In 1968 the *Janet and John* series was found to be in use in 81 per cent of British primary schools, though it was later displaced by *Ladybird Books and other reading schemes. It has often been held up to ridicule for its overwhelmingly middle-class stories and pictures and its stilted diction. Having fallen out of fashion, the series was revived in 2001, with a new series of refreshed and updated books.

JANEWAY, James (?1636–74) Nonconformist preacher, the author of *A *Token for Children* (1672), who was the son of a Hertfordshire curate. He was educated at Oxford, but it is not known whether he was ordained. He was among those officially silenced by the Act of Uniformity in 1662, which required clergymen and schoolmasters to accept the Book of Common Prayer. He became an unauthorized and sometimes persecuted preacher in London.

Janeway believed, as did his co-religionists, in a doctrine of original sin that damned all children as 'brands of hell' until they were converted and saved, and the *Token for Children* was intended as an instrument of that conversion. Apart from *The *Pilgrim's Progress* it had the most lasting success of any *Puritan book for children.

The popularity of Janeway's book led to the publication of other 'Tokens', including a *Token for Mariners* (1708) and a *Token for Youth* (1709). Both of these were ascribed to 'J. J.', but do not appear to be the work of Janeway.

Jan of the Windmill (1876) A novel by Mrs *Ewing.

JANOSCH (Horst Eckert) (1931–) Popular German author and illustrator. His more than 150 books for young readers, several of which have been published in English translations by Anthea *Bell, include *Oh, wie schön ist Panama* (1978; *The Trip to Panama*, 1978), winner of the *Deutscher Jugendliteraturpreis, *Post für den Tiger* (1981; *A Letter for Tiger*, 1981), and *The Big Janosch Book of Fun and Verse* (1980).

JANSSON, Tove *See* MOOMIN.

JAQUES, Faith (Heather) (1923–97) British illustrator of books by, among others, Allan *Ahlberg (*Happy Families*), Roald *Dahl (*Charlie and the Chocolate Factory*, English edition, 1967) and Nina *Bawden (*Carrie's War*, 1973). Her work has close resemblances to Victorian *wood engravings. She produced *picture books, but believed that 'illustrating a really good text' is the harder task.

JARRELL, Randall (1914–65) American poet and critic who wrote a number of children's stories. They include *The Bat-Poet* (1964), a satire on people's response to poetry, *The Animal Family* (1965), and *Fly by Night* (1966), all illustrated by Maurice *Sendak.

JARVIS McGRAW, Eloise (1915–2000) American writer whose work included three Newbery Honor Books (*see* NEWBERY MEDAL). Two of her most enduring books are set in ancient Egypt: *Mara, Daughter of the Nile* (1953) is the well-plotted story of a slave girl employed to spy for the queen; *The Golden Goblet* (1961) follows the exciting adventures of Ranofer, an orphan, who overcomes adversity and bad luck to win himself the chance for a happy future. In 1996, she published *The Moorchild*, about a half-elfish girl sent away to live in a human village. She also wrote three books in the long-running *Wizard of Oz series, beginning with the fortieth, *Merry Go Round in Oz* (1963).

JEFFERIES, Richard *See* BEVIS; WOOD MAGIC.

JEFFERS, Oliver (1977–) Internationally acclaimed artist and picture-book creator from Belfast, Northern Ireland, now living and working in New York. *How to Catch a Star* was his debut in 2004, and this was swiftly followed by the multi-award-winning *Lost and Found* (2005). Jeffers combines elements of illustration, painting, collage, and mixed media to produce entirely absorbing narrative worlds. His homage to the book in *The Incredible Book-Eating Boy* (2006) won the Irish Book Awards Children's Book of the Year, and his heart-rending tale of loss and love in *The Heart and the Bottle* (2010) was also distributed as an *app. Jeffers was named one of

the top ten 'rising talents in the field of illustration' by *Booktrust in 2008. His many highly original collaborations with other writers include *The Day the Crayons Quit* (2013; with Drew Daywalt), *Imaginary Fred* (2015; with Eoin *Colfer) and *A Child of Books* (2016; with Sam Winston). *Once upon an Alphabet* (2014) is not really an alphabet book.

Jemima Puddle-Duck In *The Tale of Jemima Puddle-Duck* by Beatrix *Potter.

Jennings A schoolboy in the *school stories of Anthony *Buckeridge. Jennings is a pupil at Linbury Court Preparatory School; his closest ally is Darbishire, an owlish bespectacled boy with a store of vague knowledge; his chief foe is the irritable schoolmaster Mr Wilkins (Old Wilkie). Another master, Mr Carter, tries to keep the peace. The first Jennings stories were broadcast in *Children's Hour in 1948, and began to appear in book form with *Jennings Goes to School* (1950). Since then they have been translated into many languages. Buckeridge wrote in the tradition of P. G. *Wodehouse, and though he invariably used stock characters, he was a slick farceur with a command of verbal wit.

JENNINGS, Paul (1943–) British-born Australian author, teacher, speech pathologist, and lecturer who had the distinction of being the first writer to sell a million copies in Australia. His first novel was *Unreal! Eight Surprising Stories* (1989), a book of short stories with a twist—a style that has continued though his writing career—which led to his becoming a full-time writer in 1989. He has since written over 100 stories, and has been voted 'favourite author' over forty times by children in Australia. His work for younger children includes the *Rascal* series (2004), about a naughty young dragon. His frequent collaborations with Morris Gleitzman are just as successful, particularly the *Wicked!* series (1997) and the *Deadly!* series (2000).

Jeremy (1919) First of a series of books by the English novelist Sir Hugh Walpole (1884–1941), illustrated by E. H. *Shepard. It consists of incidents in the life of eight-year-old Jeremy Cole, son of a provincial clergyman. The series, which was extremely popular in its day, continued with *Jeremy and Hamlet* (1923) (Hamlet being Jeremy's dog). Among Walpole's other fiction was *Mr Perrin and Mr Traill* (1911), set in the masters' common-room of a boys' school.

Jeremy Fisher In *The Tale of Jeremy Fisher* by Beatrix *Potter.

Jesse James (1847–82) American outlaw who, with his brother Frank, had a long career of robbery and murder. He was finally killed by one of his own gang. After his death, *dime novelists and other popular writers accorded him the kind of treatment given to *western folk heroes, making him out to be a modern *Robin Hood, and as such he has appeared in many sensational stories read by children.

Jessica's First Prayer (1867) By 'Hesba *Stretton', an immensely popular story published by the *Religious Tract Society. It describes the religious education of a London waif, who at first has to hide at the back of a chapel because she is too ragged to be allowed in. Before the end of the story she has brought about the repentance of Daniel, the chapel-attendant who tried to turn her out. The book is said to have been translated into every European and many African and Asiatic languages. There was a sequel, *Jessica's Mother* (1867).

jest books Collections of short comic anecdotes or sayings, which were often printed in the form of *chapbooks from the 16th to the 19th cent. Among the earliest is *A *Hundred Merry Tales* (1526). Many jest books contain accounts of the supposed adventures of celebrated wits or comic persons, for example *Merry Tales of Skelton* (John Skelton the poet), *The Jests of Scoggin, Merry Conceited Jests of George Peele*, and so on. In these the hero is usually shown scoring off those he encounters. By contrast, *Merry Tales of the Mad Men of Gotham* (*see* GOTHAM) is a compendium of various forms of foolish behaviour. A third group of jest books contains collections of witty remarks, jokes, and puns. (*See also* JOKE BOOKS.) The books were usually the work of hack writers, and are an ancestor of modern *comics.

In 1739 the dramatist John Mottley published, under the pseudonym 'Elijah Jenkins', *Joe Miller's Jests, or the Wit's Vade Mecum*. This took its title from one Joseph or Josias Miller (1684–1738), a comic actor in the Drury Lane company who was a reputed wit. Miller featured as the hero of a few anecdotes in the book, but it owed nothing to him, and was made up by Mottley from the usual jest-book material. *Joe Miller's Jests* was reprinted many times in England and America during the 18th and 19th cents., and numerous imitations were also published. 'Joe Miller' eventually became a popular term for a stale joke.

Jim Hawkins In *Treasure Island* by R. L. *Stevenson.

Jim Starling Hero of a series of books by E. W *Hildick.

JINKS, Catherine (1963–) Australian novelist with forty-three books published to date, including children's, young adult, and adult novels. She has won the *CBCA Book of the Year three times, the *IBBY Australia Ena Noel Encouragement Award, the Aurealis Award, and the Davitt Award for Crime Fiction. Her writing features very distinctive characters, from the inimitable Pagan, a page from 12th-cent. Europe, to the boglers who hunt bogles in a version of England in the 1870s. Her books are meticulously researched and Jinks crafts distinct voices, using the slang and language of her unique setting, and creates a strong narrative voice for each series or adult novel. She explains that she chooses topics that are 'full of high-concept, internationally appealing ideas because it's hard to make a living unless you can sell your books overseas'. Jinks writes across genres—humour, historical novels, fantasy, and picture books—but says she believes creating worlds, whether fantastic or historical, is always the same skill. Her plots always feature a great idea, often with a surprising twist and a lot of action.

She was awarded the CBCA Book of the Year: Older Readers in 1996 for *Pagan's Vows* (1995) and again in 1998 for *Eye to Eye* (1997). In 2001 her picture book *You'll Wake the Baby!* (2000) won the CBCA Book of the Year: Early Childhood. More recently, her *The City of Orphans* trilogy, beginning with *A Very Unusual Pursuit* (2013), is peopled by feisty characters in a time when science and superstition combine to fight the evil bogles lurking under Victorian London.

jinn A spirit that is said, in Muslim demonology, to have the power of appearing in human or animal form and of exercising influence over men. The word is also spelt *djin*. Jinns play a large part in the *Arabian Nights*, most notably in the story of *Aladdin*. *See also* GENIE.

Jock of the Bushveld (1907) A popular *animal story by Sir Percy Fitzpatrick (1862–1931), South African politician and author; the tale of a dog and his master in the South African goldfields.

Joe Miller *See* JEST BOOKS.

John Gilpin A *ballad by William Cowper (1731–1800). Gilpin, a London linen-draper, sets off to celebrate his wedding anniversary at an inn outside London, but his horse bolts, carries him past his destination where

his wife is waiting, and takes him all the way to Ware where its owner lives. No sooner has he arrived than the horse takes fright at a braying ass and carries him all the way home again.

The poem was based on the real adventures of a linen-draper named Beyer. He first published the verses anonymously in the *Public Advertiser* for 14 November 1782; they were an immediate success, were performed in theatres and public halls, and were circulated as a *chapbook. Cowper included *John Gilpin* in a volume of his poems published in 1785. The first children's edition was printed by John *Harris in 1806, and other publishers soon followed suit. An edition of 1828 published by Charles Tilt had illustrations by George *Cruikshank. In 1878 Randolph *Caldecott began his series of *toy books with *John Gilpin*, and the poem has often appeared in children's anthologies.

Johnny Crow's Garden (1903) The first of a series of *picture books written and drawn by L. Leslie *Brooke. The text consists of comic doggerel, which begins

> Johnny Crow
> Would dig and sow
> Till he made a little Garden.
> And the Lion
> Had a green and yellow Tie on
> In Johnny Crow's Garden.
> And the Rat
> Wore a feather in his Hat
> But the Bear –
> Had nothing to wear
> in Johnny Crow's Garden.

Further books in the series were *Johnny Crow's Party* (1907) and *Johnny Crow's New Garden* (1935), in which the lion, despite the passing of the years, had 'the very same tie on'. They are among the best publications of their period for small children.

Johnny Head-in-Air In *Struwwelpeter*.

Johnny Town-Mouse In *The Tale of Johnny Town-Mouse* by Beatrix *Potter.

Johnny Tremain (1943) A *historical novel for children by the American writer Esther Forbes (1891–1967). Johnny Tremain, a silversmith's apprentice in Boston during the War of American Independence, is injured and forced to look for other work. He becomes a rider for the *Boston Observer*, is one of the participants in the Tea Party, and is closely involved in the War of Independence. The book is constantly enlivened by the author's great understanding

of the period he describes, but it is far more than just a 'costume drama', being closely concerned with the development of Johnny's character in adversity.

Esther Forbes wrote the book after finishing her *Paul Revere and the World He Lived In* (1942); she was also the author of historical novels for adults. Her only other children's book was *America's Paul Revere* (1946). *Johnny Tremain* won the *Newbery Medal in 1944.

JOHNS, Captain W. E. (William Earle) (1893–1968) British popular author, creator of *Biggles, who was born and educated in Hertford. After serving as an infantryman at the beginning of the First World War, in 1916 he joined the then new Royal Flying Corps. He was shot down over Mannheim by the famous German air ace Ernst Udet, was wounded, taken prisoner, and sentenced to death. He escaped, but was recaptured and spent the rest of the war in a prison camp. He remained in the Air Force until 1930, when he became a reservist with the rank of Captain. He then worked as a newspaper air correspondent, and also founded the magazine *Popular Flying*, in the pages of which the Biggles stories first appeared.

Johns also wrote about the adventures of a commando named 'Gimlet' (*Gimlet Goes Again*, 1944, and other titles), and about a female Biggles, 'Worrals of the WAAF', who first appeared in print in 1941. These characters are said to have been invented at the instigation of the British government, who believed that they would help with the armed forces' recruiting drive during the Second World War. Johns also wrote some run-of-the-mill *science fiction, with titles such as *Return to Mars* (1955). For many years the sales of his children's books were reputedly higher than those of any other British 20th-cent. children's author except Enid *Blyton, and he remains popular, despite the contempt in which his work is generally held by critics. *By Jove, Biggles!*, a biography by Peter Berresford Ellis and Piers Williams, was published in 1981.

JOHNSON, Crockett (David Johnson Leisk) (1906–75) American cartoonist. He wrote and drew the comic strip *Barnaby* and children's *picture books, such as *Harold and the Purple Crayon* (1955). He was married to Ruth *Krauss, with whom he collaborated.

JOHNSON, Maureen (1973–) American writer of *young adult fiction, author of several

stand-alone novels and series since her debut, *The Key to the Golden Firebird* (2004). They include *13 Little Blue Envelopes* (2005) and its sequel *The Last Little Blue Envelope* (2011), in which Ginny travels round Europe following instructions from her late aunt; the Shades of London series of paranormal thrillers (beginning with *The Name of the Star*, 2011); and the Bane Chronicles series written with Cassandra *Clare and Sarah Rees Brennan (Johnson's first being *The Runaway Queen*, 2013). She has also collaborated with John *Green and Lauren Myracle on the bestselling *Let It Snow: Three Holiday Romances* (2008).

JOHNSON, Owen (McMahon) (1878–1952) American author who wrote a number of *school stories, including *The Varmint* (1910), *Stover at Yale* (1911), and *The Tennessee Shad* (1911).

JOHNSON, Richard (?1573–?1659) Author of *The *Seven Champions Of Christendom* and probably of the first prose version of the story of *Tom Thumb. Little is known of him except that he was an apprentice, and later freeman, of London, who produced various pieces of popular literature, including *ballads, pamphlets, a *jest book, and prose tales in the manner of the *romances.

JOHNSON, Richard (*fl.* 1770–93) Hack writer and compiler of children's books for the *Newbery family and other publishers. On the evidence of his Day-books (now in the possession of the Company of Stationers) he was responsible for the text of such works as *Juvenile Trials for Robbing Orchards, Telling Fibs, and other Heinous Offences* (1771); *The *Looking-Glass for the Mind* (1787), which was based on *Berquin's *L'Ami des enfans; The Blossoms of Morality* (1789), another book of the same kind; and a sequel to *The *Children in the Wood* entitled *The Hermit of the Forest, and the Wandering Infants* (1787). Johnson did not hesitate to plagiarize; his Day-book records that he 'wrote' a *chapbook version of *Sandford and Merton, and his *Juvenile Rambles through the Paths of Nature* (1786) was lifted from a work by Mrs *Trimmer. Under the pseudonym 'the Revd. Mr Cooper', he produced the first English text of the *Arabian Nights for children, *The Oriental Moralist* (*c.*1791). He also wrote or edited a number of *history books for the Newberys.

JOHNSTON, Annie Fellows (1863–1931) American author of children's stories who began her literary career as a contributor to

the *Youth's Companion. She made her name with The *Little Colonel (1895), which led to many sequels.

joke books Printed collections of stand-alone jokes, which have existed at least since the 4th cent. BC, though the oldest surviving example is the Philogelos ('Lover of Laughter'), from the 3rd or 4th cent. AD. Joke books intended specifically for a child audience are principally a late 20th-cent. phenomenon, sometimes deriving from magazine or comic publications (such as the *Beano in the UK). Popular examples in the UK included The Crack-a-Joke Book (a charity collection, edited by Jane Nissen and published in 1978, becoming the 1,000th *Puffin Book; reissued 1992); and The Old Joke Book (1976) and The Ha Ha Bonk Book (1982) by Janet *Ahlberg and Allan *Ahlberg. (The title of the last came from the sound of a man laughing his head off.) Though the Internet has now appeared as the great new joke-sharing forum, joke books for children still occasionally appear, especially for younger children and in association with known brands or comic authors (*Horrid Henry, *Dirty Bertie, Jeremy *Strong, etc.). See also JEST BOOKS.

JOLE, William (fl.c.1660–1710) Author of The Father's Blessing Penn'd for the Instruction of his Children, a collection of 'Godly and Delightful Verses, Riddles, Fables, Jests, Stories, Proverbs, Rules of Behaviour, And other useful Matters to allure Children to Read' (1674, often reprinted). The book, most of which is in rhymed couplets, included a verse alphabet; it was more cheerful than the usual *Puritan books of the period, and contained much that was simply intended to amuse.

Jolly Postman or Other People's Letters, The (1986) A postmodern picture-book classic by Janet *Ahlberg and Allan *Ahlberg. This much-loved intertextual tale follows a very jolly postman on his round as he delivers post to characters from well-known fairy tales. The delightful narrative verse takes the reader into the houses of the various recipients, who include Hansel and Gretel's Wicked Witch, Jack and the Beanstalk's giant, and Cinderella. The pages are interspersed with an envelope device carrying the designated delivery for the child reader to remove and read. The collection of post is exquisite in detail and includes an apology from Goldilocks to the Three Bears, a commemorative book celebrating Cinderella's marriage, and a solicitor's letter from Little Red Riding Hood to the Big Bad Wolf. The Ahlbergs won two major awards for The Jolly Postman: the 1986 *Kurt Maschler Award and the 1987 Children's Book Award. Following its success, the Ahlbergs produced two sequels, The Jolly Christmas Postman (1991), for which Janet Ahlberg won her second *Kate Greenaway Medal, and The Jolly Pocket Postman (1995), published after Janet's death in 1994.

Jo March In *Little Women by Louisa M. *Alcott.

JONES, Diana Wynne (1934–2011) An influential and much-revered British writer of original and quirky *fantasy stories. Born in London, she moved around a lot as a child because of the war; she went on to study English at Oxford, where she attended lectures by both *Tolkien and C.S. *Lewis.

Her first children's book was Wilkins' Tooth (1973); for the next four decades, she would go on to average at least one book a year. All her writing is fantasy of a very unconventional kind; as Marcus *Crouch has put it, she 'breaks all the usual rules [of the genre] . . . secure in her own virtuosity'. Each of her novels takes a standard ingredient of fantasy writing (*witches, mythological figures appearing in modern times, enchanted animals, etc.), but handles the material quite unexpectedly. For example, Charmed Life (1977) begins: 'Cat Chant admired his elder sister Gwendolen. She was a witch. He admired her and he clung to her.' This book, which won the *Guardian Children's Fiction Prize, launched Jones's seven-volume *Chrestomanci series, which features a complex universe of parallel worlds and magic.

Diana Wynne Jones's stories rarely take place in anything that could be called a 'real' world; The Magicians of Caprona (1980), another Chrestomanci story, is set in an Italy which is half Renaissance and half 20th-cent., while Eight Days of Luke (1975) introduces into a contemporary setting characters who recognizably belong in *Norse myth. The Dalemark Quartet (1975–93) is set in a pre-industrial parallel universe; in The Homeward Bounders (1981) a boy becomes part of a universe-wide game of chance. *Howl's Moving Castle (1986), one of Jones's undoubted masterpieces, is set in Ingary, a magical land where all things are possible; this work introduced Jones's work to a global audience when it was made into an animated film by Studio Ghibli in 2004.

While some of Jones's work is solidly aimed at children, there are also adult novels and some that might today be considered *young adult. Among these are *Archer's Goon* (1984), in which a Goon arrives at the Sykes house and claims the 2,000 words Quentin owed someone called Archer, and arguably also *Howl's Moving Castle* and the rich and complex *Fire and Hemlock* (1984). Jones also wrote non-fiction, most famously *The Tough Guide to Fantasyland* (1996), which parodies the clichés of much fantasy fiction and is presented in the form of a travel guide; (*The*) *Dark Lord of Derkholm* (1998) is a parody of the genre in novel form, and a good companion piece.

JONES, T. Llew (Thomas Llewelyn) (1915–2009) Welsh author, translator, and poet who was one of the most acclaimed and popular writers of books in Welsh for children. Though he started as a poet, he is best known for his mystery and adventure books for younger readers, often involving historical characters such as the Welsh pirate, Bartholomew Roberts in *Barti Ddu o Gasnewy' Bach* (1973), or the highwayman hero Twm Siôn Cati in *Anturiaethau Twm Siôn Cati: Y Ffordd Beryglus* (1963). Other important books include *Tân ar y Comin* (1975) about the Romany gypsies in Wales, and *Lleuad yn Olau* (1989) a collection of Welsh folk tales. In 2012, a school was named in his honour: Ysgol Gynradd Gymunedol T Llew Jones.

JORDAN, June (1936–2002) Caribbean-American author, poet, and activist, best known for *His Own Where* (1971), the story of two black teenagers who make a home for themselves in a deserted building near a cemetery. *Who Look at Me?* (1969) is a book of poems for children.

Josh (1971) A novel by Ivan *Southall.

***Journey to the Centre of the Earth, A* (*Voyage au centre de la Terre*)** (1864) A novel by Jules *Verne. The discovery of a manuscript describing how a journey to the centre of the earth might be made inspires Axel's uncle to attempt just that. It is an enterprise fraught with dangers as the small party travel into the unknown. Earth tremors, an underground sea, mammoths—they find much to amaze them, but the biggest surprise is where they resurface. The book was suggested to Verne by the experiences of a French geographer who had explored European volcanoes, together with memories of a tour

Verne himself had made of Scandinavia. This is one of Verne's earliest novels exemplifying the genre he invented, the *Roman de la science*, in which scientific discoveries provide a realistic basis for extraordinary adventure. Though the science is no longer current, the plot remains lively and compelling.

Journey to the River Sea (2001) By Eva *Ibbotson, this is a heart-warming adventure novel set in the Amazon. The story tells the tale of orphaned Maia, who along with corseted governess Miss Minton, is sent to live with long-lost relatives in the beautifully depicted city of Manaus in Brazil. Maia relishes the sights and sounds of the Amazon, but her new family is not at all what she expected. The Carters live their life behind closed doors, importing soggy biscuits from England, and it is not until Maia finds Finn that her adventures in the Amazon truly begin. The book was highly acclaimed, winning the Nestlé Gold Award and being named a finalist for many of the major British children's literary awards, including the *Whitbread Children's Book Award, the *Guardian Children's Fiction Prize, and the *Carnegie Medal.

JOYCE, Jeremiah *See* SCIENTIFIC DIALOGUES.

Joy Street An *annual published by Basil Blackwell of Oxford during the 1920s and 1930s. It has been described by Marcus *Crouch as 'a meeting-place for literally all the best [British] writing for children' at that time. *Number One Joy Street, A Medley of Prose & Verse for Boys and Girls* was published in 1923, and included contributions from Walter *de la Mare, Eleanor *Farjeon, Hilaire *Belloc ('Maria, Who Made Faces'), Laurence *Housman, Edith Sitwell (three poems), Rose *Fyleman, and others. The standard of production and design was very high, and there were tipped-in colour plates. Further *Joy Street* books appeared in the years that followed. A monthly *magazine grew out of *Joy Street*, edited by Fyleman and entitled *The Merry-Go-Round*; in its pages appeared A. A. *Milne's first published children's poem, 'The Dormouse and the Doctor'.

Judy Moody (2000) A series by American author Megan McDonald (1959–) and perfectly captured by illustrator Peter *Reynolds, which is popular and flawlessly pitched for young independent readers. The first book, *Judy Moody*, takes a moody Judy to her first day at school—a day she doesn't enjoy until

she gets to make a collage all about herself, which makes her forget to be in a mood at all! Judy is a brilliant creation, and her success is partly due to the fact that she is just like her readers and her adventures deal with many of the things to which that they will easily relate. A spin-off series follows her younger brother *Stink* (2005).

Julie of the Wolves (1972) A novel by Jean Craighead *George.

Jungle Books, The Two volumes of short stories by Rudyard *Kipling. Most of the stories are set in India, and all concern animals; the majority are about the boy Mowgli and his relationship with the creatures of the Jungle. Each story is followed by a poem.

The Jungle Book (1894) opens with the story 'Mowgli's Brothers', in which a human baby is given shelter by a family of wolves after Shere Khan the tiger has attacked and driven off his parents. The Mother Wolf suckles him and gives him the name 'Mowgli'. Despite the tiger's attempts to claim Mowgli as his lawful prey, the Seeonee Wolf Pack, to which Mowgli's foster-family belongs, accepts him as a cub member, and he grows up among the wolves. Two other creatures who are accepted into the wolves' councils, Baloo 'the sleepy brown bear' and Bagheera the Black Panther, help undertake Mowgli's education. When Mowgli is aged about eleven, Shere Khan returns to hunt down the boy, but Mowgli attacks Shere Khan with a burning branch, drives him away from the Pack, and then leaves the wolves himself to return to his own people, mankind. The remaining stories include 'Tiger! Tiger!', a story that tells of the destruction of Shere Khan by Mowgli, 'Rikki-Tikki-Tavi' (one of Kipling's best known stories), in which a mongoose heroically fights the cobras who are trying to kill the family in whose bungalow he lives, and 'Toomai of the Elephants', the story of a small boy who is allowed to see the mysterious dance that both wild and captive elephants sometimes perform together at night.

The Second Jungle Book (1895) begins with 'How Fear Came', a story of Mowgli and his friends in time of drought. The stories that follow it include 'Letting in the Jungle', which recounts Mowgli's revenge on the man-village, when Buldeo the hunter and his fellows try to torture and kill his parents; 'The King's Ankus', in which Mowgli is brought by Kaa the python to an underground chamber beneath a ruined city, and encounters a terrible White Cobra who guards precious treasure; and 'Red Dog', the most exciting of the Mowgli stories, which recounts how the boy, with the aid of Kaa, brings about the destruction of a pack of the dreadful *dhole*, the red hunting dogs whom all other animals fear. The final tale, 'The Spring Running', brings Mowgli to manhood, whereupon he learns that he must leave Baloo, Bagheera, Kaa, and his other old friends for human society.

The Mowgli stories were begun by Kipling during the winter of 1892, when he was living with his newly-married American wife Carrie at Bliss Cottage, Brattleboro, Vermont. According to his later recollections, he first wrote the story 'In the Rukh' (published in *Many Inventions* in 1893), in which Mowgli appears as a grown man working for the Indian Forestry Department; there is an allusion in it to Mowgli's childhood among wolves. This, said Kipling, then inspired him to write tales about that childhood; he believed the idea owed its genesis partly to a reference in Rider *Haggard's *Nada the Lily* (1892) to a man running with a wolf pack, and to a story, 'King Lion' by James Greenwood, which he had read in childhood in The *Boy's Own Magazine* for 1864; this is the tale of a hunter who finds a lion who, like himself, is a Freemason, and introduces him to leonine society.

The first *Jungle Book* story to be published was 'Mowgli's Brothers', which appeared in *St Nicholas* in January 1894. *The Jungle Book* itself was published in May that year, with illustrations by Rudyard Kipling's father, John Lockwood Kipling, who provided friezes for chapter-heads, and with line and half-tone drawings by W. H. Drake and P. Frenzeny. The book was an instant success throughout the English-speaking world, and reprints have been frequent since the first year. *The Second Jungle Book* first appeared in October 1895, with John Lockwood Kipling as sole illustrator. The stories featuring Mowgli were published in one volume in 1933 as *All the Mowgli Stories*.

Though the tales are nominally set in Central India, they were probably based on Kipling's memories of the State of Mewar in the north of the sub-continent, which he visited in 1887. It seems doubtful whether he had been into the jungle; probably his description of the terrain was based on jungle photographs that he was shown by friends. The belief that wolves have sometimes suckled children is, of course, very ancient, featuring in the legend of Romulus and Remus, and it

was still widely held in India in Kipling's day. His own father wrote in 1891, in *Beast and Man in India*, that the notion was 'here universally believed and supported by a cloud of testimony'.

It is possible to find in the *Jungle Books* evidence of the colonialist mindset which sometimes caused Kipling to be reviled during the 20th cent. But the invention and excitement of the stories continue to prove popular with both children and adults. Recent scholarship has interrogated ideas of imperialism and identity in *The Jungle Books* (see, for example, Sue Walsh's 2010 monograph *Kipling's Children's Literature: Language, Identity and Constructions of Childhood*) and counterpointed the author's unease with the power of colonialism against his often jingoistic tone (see Rooney and Nagai eds., *Kipling and Beyond*, 2010).

The speed with which *The Jungle Books* became part of nursery lore is indicated by Oswald Bastable's remark in the first chapter of *The *Wouldbegoods*, first published only six years after the first *Jungle Book* had appeared: 'Let's play jungle book, and I shall be Mowgli.' One result of the books was the formation of the Wolf Cub division of the *Boy Scouts— *Baden-Powell and Kipling were friends. The stories also undoubtedly inspired Edgar Rice *Burroughs to write his *Tarzan tales (1914 onwards). Walt *Disney's animated film *The Jungle Book*, which appeared in 1967, was very different in both story and tone, but inventive on its own terms and containing many enduring songs (in 2016, Disney would re-make this in turn as a live-action film); and more recently some of the book's themes and structure provided the inspiration for Neil Gaiman's *The *Graveyard Book* (2008).

Junior Bookshelf An independent British critical *review of children's literature. Founded in November 1936, it contained articles about and by celebrated children's authors as well as short notices of new books. It ran to sixty volumes, concluding in 1996.

Junk (1996) (US title: *Smack*) A controversial *young adult novel by award-winning British author Melvin *Burgess. Winner of both the *Carnegie Medal and the *Guardian Children's Fiction Prize in 1997, *Junk* hit the headlines with its frank and honest portrayal of teenagers addicted to heroin. The novel is told in the first person from different narrative viewpoints, largely centring on two main teenage characters, Gemma and Tar, who leave home and move to Bristol where they fall into drugs, robbery, and prostitution. The novel was criticized for its descriptive accounts of heroin use and its unashamed moral relativism. However, Burgess was also acclaimed for bringing current and relevant issues into young adult fiction. The novel was hugely successful, translated into twenty-eight different languages and adapted for TV and the stage.

JUSTER, Norton (1929–) American author, most famous for *The *Phantom Tollbooth* (1961). Juster began to write for children during a stint in the US Navy, but despite the success of *The Phantom Tollbooth*, his primary profession throughout his working life was architecture. Other works include *The Dot and the Line: A Romance in Lower Mathematics* (1963), which was made into an Oscar-winning animated film; *The Hello, Goodbye Window* (2005), which won the *Caldecott Medal for Chris *Raschka's illustrations; its sequel, *Sourpuss and Sweetie Pie* (2008); *The Odious Ogre* (2010), which he created with *Tollbooth* illustrator Jules Feiffer; and, more recently, *Neville* (2011).

Just So Stories for Little Children (1902) By Rudyard *Kipling, a set of tales interspersed with poems and illustrated by the author. The greater number of them give far-fetched humorous explanations of the chief physical characteristics of certain animals: 'How the Camel got his Hump', 'How the Rhinoceros got his Skin', 'How the Leopard got his Spots', and so on. Two other stories, 'How the First Letter was Written' and 'How the Alphabet was Made', are about a father and daughter from a prehistoric British tribe.

The book had its genesis in tales told to Kipling's eldest child Josephine at 'Naulakha', the house built for his family in Brattleboro, Vermont, in 1893. The stories were also told, a few years later, to Kipling's younger children Elsie and John, and to cousins who included Angela Thirkell the novelist; she wrote: '*The Just So Stories* are a poor thing in print compared with the fun of hearing them told in Cousin Ruddy's deep unhesitating voice.'

In January 1898 the whole Kipling family visited South Africa; this led to the writing of 'The Elephant's Child', with its reiterated references to 'the great grey-green, greasy Limpopo River'. Shortly after their arrival in the United States, Josephine died of pneumonia. The two stories of Taffy and her father Tegumai are in part about her, as are the poem which follows 'How the Leopard got his Spots' and the verses printed after 'How the Alphabet was Made', of which this is the final stanza:

For far—oh, very far behind,
So far she cannot call to him,
Comes Tegumai alone to find
The daughter that was all to him.

More stories were written during a holiday in Scotland, while Kipling was recuperating from the shock of Josephine's death, and the book was put together in time for publication in October 1902. 'The Tabu Tale', an extra story, was not completed until later; it was included in an American edition of 1903 and was added to the 1938 'Sussex' edition of Kipling's works, but it is still usually absent from separate printings of the *Just So Stories*.

Coloured plates by Joseph M. Gleeson were added to an edition of the *Just So Stories* published in America in 1912 and in Britain in 1913, but they did not come up to the achievement of Kipling's own witty black-and-white drawings, which, together with their extensive and ridiculous captions, are one of the chief delights of the book. They incorporate various hidden jokes and are often signed with the device of Noah's Ark inside a letter A; this stands for 'Ark A', which when said aloud sounds like 'R. K.', Kipling's initials.

Kipling probably got the idea of writing comic *fables explaining animals' distinguishing characteristics from the *Uncle Remus stories of Joel Chandler *Harris (1880), which include 'Why Mr Possum has no Hair on his Tail'. Much of the fun in Kipling's book lies in the parodying of the style of such traditional oriental books as the *Jataka Tales* and the *Arabian Nights*. Only one existing folk tale was used by Kipling, that of the Crab, which was taken from W. W. Skeat's *Malay Magic* (1900); Andrew *Lang's *Myth, Ritual and Religion* (1887) supplied the names of the three gods in the Kangaroo story. Other stories were apparently suggested by phrases in the Old Testament, such as Jeremiah 13: 23: 'Can the Ethiopian change his skin, or the leopard his spots?' 'The Butterfly that Stamped' grew out of Browning's poem 'Solomon and Balkis'.

The book, which has supplied generations of readers with great delight and unforgettable phrases (of which 'O Best Beloved' is the most widely remembered), was attacked in 1957 by the Revd Marcus Morris, editor of *Eagle*, in a manner recalling the early 19th-cent. objections to *fairy stories. He suggested that, because it gave a fantastic account of animals' characteristics, it 'could do damage to the child's outlook in the scientific age'.

Just William *See* William.

Juvenile Forget Me Not, The A children's *annual published in London from 1828 until 1837, under the editorship of Mrs S. C. *Hall. It was genteel and adult-looking, and was finely printed by Charles Whittingham at the Chiswick Press.

Juvenile Literature As It Is (1888) By Edward Salmon, a book intended 'to give all charged with the mental and moral welfare of the rising generation an idea of the books written for girls and boys'. It opens with a poll of children's tastes in reading-matter. The favourite authors of 790 boys were, in descending order, Charles *Dickens (223), W. H. G. *Kingston (179), Walter *Scott (128), Jules *Verne (114), Captain *Marryat (102), R. M. *Ballantyne (67), Harrison *Ainsworth (61), *Shakespeare (44), and Mayne *Reid (33). Lewis *Carroll did not feature. The same boys' favourite books were (from a much longer list) *Robinson Crusoe* (43), The *Swiss Family Robinson* (24), The Pickwick Papers (22), *Ivanhoe* (20), The Boy's Own Annual (17), the *Bible (15), and *Tom Brown's Schooldays* (15), as well as many others, including *Vice Versa* (12) and *Mr Midshipman Easy* (7). The boys' favourite *magazine was, by a huge majority, The *Boy's Own Paper (404 votes).

The girls' answers to the same poll differed in that Kingsley and Charlotte M. *Yonge came in third and fourth in the list of authors, with Andersen, *Grimm, and Louisa M. *Alcott making a reasonable showing; *Westward Ho!* won the girls' book choice, with The *Wide, Wide World* second. The *Girl's Own Paper easily topped the magazine poll, followed not by another girls' magazine, but by The Boy's Own Paper once again.

Salmon, who wrote *reviews for several London journals, surveys the *adventure story, the *historical novel, the *school story, and other genres of children's books, always with a moral tone not unlike that of Mrs *Trimmer. He does not admire the *Alice* books ('there is nothing extraordinarily original about either'), and judges Grimm and Andersen largely on their moral content.

Juvenile Magazine, The A periodical for children published in monthly parts during 1788 by John *Marshall. It was apparently only the second such venture by an English publisher (the first being John Newbery's *Lilliputian Magazine). Marshall's *magazine was designed as 'an instructive and entertaining

miscellany for youth of both sexes', and it contained improving stories, verse, simple geography and other lessons, items in French, puzzles, and *plays. The editor was Lucy Peacock, an author of *moral tales and a bookseller in Oxford Street. She accepted contributions from readers. And readers were also encouraged to ask advice on such topics as mastering an unruly passion. Mary Ann *Kilner contributed some of the verses anonymously.

Juvenile Miscellany, The An early American children's *magazine, published in Boston from 1826 to 1836, edited until 1834 by Lydia Maria *Child. The American critic Alice M. Jordan (in *From Rollo to Tom Sawyer*, 1948) writes that it was 'our first real magazine for children...noticeable in the space given American history and biography, and no less, in the countless allusions to the American landscape so different from the English background of books hitherto available to children'.

'Mary's Lamb' (i.e. *Mary had a little lamb*) appeared in print for the first time in the issue for September–October 1830. Its author, Sara Josepha *Hale, assumed the editorship of the magazine after Lydia Maria Child was forced to resign because of her outspoken espousal of the cause of the 'Africans' (black slaves) and her liberal attitude towards the '*Indians' (Native Americans), which proved too much for Boston society; she bade 'a reluctant and most affectionate farewell to my little readers'.

Kaa Python in *The *Jungle Books* by *Kipling.

KALER, James Otis *See* OTIS, JAMES.

KAMM, Josephine (Mary) (1905–1989) British author of popular novels for teenage girls, with titles such as *Student Almoner* (1955), *First Job* (1969), and *Young Mother* (1965). The latter is the story of an unmarried girl who becomes pregnant.

Kanga and Roo In **Winnie the Pooh* and *The *House at Pooh Corner* by A. A. *Milne.

Karlsson on the Roof (first vol. 1955; English trans. by Marianne Turner, 1958) A series of books by Astrid *Lindgren. Smidge (Midge) is delighted when Karlsson flies in through the window. Karlsson, small, chubby with a propeller on his back, is the ideal companion, especially if you cannot have a dog. He is, after all the World's Best . . . well, at everything, and especially the World's Best Karlsson. However, his enthusiasms, like those of all young children, do not always end well. With his anarchic attitude, Karlsson is the imaginative companion who can provide vicarious enjoyment of forbidden activities. The ambiguity over his imaginary status only serves to confirm his attraction. He returns in *Karlsson Flies Again* (1962/1977) and *The World's Best Karlsson* (1968/1980).

KÄSTNER, Erich (1899–1974) Author of **Emil and The Detectives*, Kästner was a left-wing German writer associated with Brecht and his circle. In 1933 his work was *banned by the Nazis and his books were publicly burnt, but he continued to live in Germany. His other writings for children include *Emil und die drei Zwillinge* ('Emil and the Three Twins') (1934) and *Die Konferenz der Tiere* ('The Animals' Conference') (1949). Anthea *Bell embarked on a series of retranslations of his work, from 2014.

Katawampus, its Treatment and Cure (1895) A *fantasy by Edward Abbott *Parry. 'Pater', distraught at the behaviour of his children, meets Krab the Cave-Man, who specializes in curing 'Katawampus', this being the disease of crying for what you cannot obtain. Krab takes the children off to Caveland to effect the cure.

Kate Crackernuts An English folk tale recorded by Joseph *Jacobs; also the title of a *fantasy by K. M. *Briggs. *See* TWELVE DANCING PRINCESSES, THE.

Kate Greenaway Medal Established by the Library Association of Great Britain for the most distinguished work in the illustration of a children's book during the preceding year. Named after illustrator Kate *Greenaway, it has been awarded annually since 1955. For a list of previous winners, *see* APPENDIX, E.

Katie Morag The feisty heroine of Scottish author/illustrator Mairi Hedderwick's (1939–) well-loved eponymous series. The endpapers introduce the fictional Isle of Struay, with the shop and post office where Katie Morag lives with her ever-extending family. Beautifully detailed illustrations and the grey-wash colour palette evoke an idyllic island life in which Katie is reassuringly moored. The first in the series, *Katie Morag Delivers the Mail* (1984), introduces a delicious cast of characters, including baby Liam and tractor-loving Grannie Island, who is celebrated for challenging conventional stereotypes. Hedderwick notably uses the page to shape each illustration to draw the reader into Katie Morag's adventures. *Katie Morag and the Dancing Class* (2007) was a nominee for the 2008 *Kate Greenaway Medal.

Katniss Everdeen A sixteen-year-old girl who lives with her mother and sister in District 12, where she and her friend Gale hunt illegally, beyond the fence, in order to put food on her family's table. In the first book of *The *Hunger Games*, Katniss is chosen as one of her district's tributes to fight in the Games, and the series follows her struggles to survive in the face of the massive destructive power of the Capitol.

Katy Carr In *What Katy Did* and other books by Susan *Coolidge.

Katzenjammer Kids, The America's oldest *comic strip, created in 1897 by Rudolph Dirks, initially for the *New York Journal*. It portrays the terrible twins Hans and Fritz in their endless battle against authority.

KAY, Jim (1974–) British illustrator who came to particular prominence for his deep and hauntingly black illustrations for *A *Monster Calls*, for which he won the 2012 *Kate Greenaway Medal. In 2013 publishers Bloomsbury announced that Kay would be producing the first fully illustrated editions of the *Harry Potter series; the first volume appeared in 2015.

KAYE, M. M. (Mary Margaret) (1908–2004) British author and illustrator whose childhood in India deeply affected the themes of her books. Married to a soldier, she lived in Kenya, Zanzibar, Egypt, Cyprus, and Germany before settling in England. Most famous for her adult novel, *The Far Pavilions* (1978), which was made into a TV series in 1984, she also wrote a series of detective stories, starting with *Death Walked in Kashmir* (1953), and books for children, many using the name Mollie Kaye. *The Ordinary Princess* (1980), which she also illustrated, is a delightfully grounded story of a tomboy princess who runs away rather than be forced into marriage and whose adventures in the real world in turn gift her with true love.

Kay Harker Hero of *The *Midnight Folk* and *The *Box of Delights* by John *Masefield.

KEACH, Benjamin (1640–1704) Baptist minister and author of several *Puritan books for children. His *Instructions for Children, or the Child and Youth's Delight* (1664) has a frontispiece illustrating the text 'Childhood and Youth are Vanity', with the flames of hell about to devour some children playing cards and dancing round a maypole. The book contains a section 'teaching an Easie Way to Spell and Read True English'; a series of *catechisms in the form of dialogues between a father and a three-year-old, a ten-year-old, and a grown-up son in turn. It concludes with a short moral dialogue in verse dramatizing the death of a sinful young man. *Instructions for Children* was eventually reprinted by the popular publisher J. Marshall of Gracechurch Street, London (the ninth edition), which indicates that Keach had a wide and non-sectarian reading public. His *War with the Devil, or the Young Man's Conflict with the powers of Darkness* (1676) is a verse dialogue between Youth, Conscience, the Devil, Truth, and others, 'Discovering the Corruption and Vanity of Youth, the Horrible Nature of Sin, and Deplorable Condition of Fallen Man'. The style, often colloquial, aiming not to be clever but to save souls, has been compared with, and suggested as a context for, the writings of John *Bunyan.

KEARY, Annie (1825–79) Minor Victorian novelist who wrote several books for children. These include *The Rival Kings* (1857), the story of two warring gangs of children, and *Father Phim* (1879), about an English girl recuperating from smallpox. She and her sister Eliza wrote *The *Heroes of Asgard* (1857), the first English version for children of *Norse myths.

KEATS, Ezra Jack (1916–83) One of America's most celebrated picture-book artists, best known for his *Caldecott Award-winning book *The Snowy Day* (1962). Born Jacob Ezra Katz to a Polish-Jewish immigrant family, Keats grew up in urban New York, where his books found their inspiration. *The Snowy Day* was notable for featuring a young African-American protagonist in the early 1960s, when racial tensions were rife and representations of ethnic diversity were scarce. The book received both commendation and criticism, some arguing that it did not truly represent African-American cultural identity. However, it is largely celebrated for its simplicity in telling the story of a young boy enjoying a snowy day, regardless of race. Indeed, Keats's style has more to do with the book's success than its sociopolitical significance. His colour palette and unique illustrative graphic style ensure his picture books are still celebrated and enjoyed today. The Ezra Jack Keats Foundation, set up before his death, funds literacy projects and arts programmes across the United States.

KEENE, Carolyn Author of the *Nancy Drew series of mystery novels.

Keeper's Travels in Search of his Master (1798) An *animal story by Edward Augustus *Kendall. Keeper, a dog, loses his master at a market and sets out in search of him. The story chronicles his adventures along the way. The book includes a number of authorial asides and moral observations, but Kendall portrays Keeper as a real dog and no talking animal, whose adventures are credible as well as striking.

KEEPING, Charles (William James)
(1924–88) British artist and author-illustrator
of *picture books, who was born in the Lam-
beth district of London. As a small boy he
spent much of his time looking through holes
in the fence at the back of the family house:

Everything seemed to happen in front of this fence.
It was like looking at things on a stage. You saw
people walk through the yard. They would lead a
horse through the yard. There would be a dog in the
yard. [. . .] I used to look through the cracks in the
fence, so I was always looking at this isolated situa-
tion or image moving across.

The memory of this dominates his picture
books, while the stories, such as they are (for
there is very little 'plot', usually just a series of
tableaux), are drawn from, or influenced by,
his memories of Lambeth in childhood.

In 1952 Keeping married Renate Meyer,
herself an artist, who produced several re-
markable children's books in a style not unlike
Keeping's. Keeping's regular work as an illus-
trator began in about 1956, commissioned by
the Oxford University Press, who published all
his work from then on. He illustrated stories by
Rosemary *Sutcliff, Henry *Treece, and many
others, but was never entirely content to pro-
vide conventional visual material for novels—
he argued that it is a fallacy to suppose that a
particular incident in the story can be success-
fully 'illustrated'; he believed instead that an
artist should capture mood and emotion. He
did this with great success in *Elidor* (1965) by
Alan *Garner; later he illustrated novels with
urban settings by Bernard *Ashley.

His own picture books began to appear in
the mid-1960s. The first was *Black Dolly* (1966)
(published in the United States as *Molly o' the
Moors*). Next came *Charley, Charlotte and the
Golden Canary* (1967), which won the *Kate
Greenaway Medal. This showed Keeping's
idiosyncratic brilliance with colour and the al-
most *Blake-like visionary character of his
imagination. Later books include *The Garden
Shed* (1971), *The Spider's Web* (1972), *Richard*
(1973), *Railway Passage* (1974), *Cockney Ding-
Dong* (1975), *Wasteground Circus* (1976), *Inter-
City* (1977), *Miss Emily and the Bird of Make-
Believe* (1979), and *Willie's Fire-Engine* (1980).

Keeping was widely regarded as the most
brilliant and original British artist of his gen-
eration to be working regularly for a child
audience, but the sophistication of his pictures
and his frequent rejection of conventional nar-
rative attracted criticism from those who be-
lieved his books to be above the heads of most
children and sometimes sinister, even morbid.

This morbidity is evident in one of his black-
and-white picture books for older children,
The Highwayman (1981), an illustrated ver-
sion of a melodramatic poem by Alfred
*Noyes which includes a gory picture of the
suicide of the highwayman's sweetheart. On
the other hand *The Highwayman* shows an
attempt by Keeping to get back to plain story-
telling and more comprehensible drawings. It
won Keeping the Kate Greenaway Medal for a
second time. It was followed by more black-
and-white work for older children, including
an edition of *Beowulf* (1982), adapted by
Kevin *Crossley-Holland.

KEITH, Harold (Verne) (1903–98) Ameri-
can author who won the *Newbery Medal with
Rifles for Watie (1957), a story of a Union spy
behind Confederate lines in the Civil War.

KELLEHER, Victor (1939–) Australian chil-
dren's novelist, the recipient of many awards
and commendations. He has written mostly
science fiction novels for older readers, but
also books for younger readers. He is celebrat-
ed for his careful plotting, deep characteriza-
tion, and fresh ideas. His books have been
shortlisted for or have won the *CBCA Book
of the Year: Older Readers nine times. The first
book to win CBCA Book of the Year was *Mas-
ter of the Grove* (1982) in 1983 and the latest
was *Fire Dancer* (1996) in 1997. His most pop-
ular book is *Taronga* (1986), a dystopian novel
in which Ben, a telepath, faces the wild ani-
mals of Sydney's Taronga Zoo, which seem to
have been unaffected by the Last Days. This
novel was an honour book for CBCA Book of
the Year: Older Readers in 1987.

KELLOGG, Elija (1813–1901) New England
Congregational minister who wrote twenty-
nine books for boys, beginning with *Good Old
Times; or, Grandfather's Struggles for a Home-
stead* (1878), an account of his great-grandfa-
ther's pioneer life in Maine in the early 18th
cent. His other stories include *Lion Ben of Elm
Island* (1868), *The Sophomores of Radcliffe*
(1871), and *A Strong Arm and a Mother's Bless-
ing* (1880). His stories are set during the years
after the War of American Independence.

KELLY, Eric (Philbrook) (1884–1960)
American author who won the *Newbery
Medal with *The Trumpeter of Krakow* (1928),
set in Poland during the 15th cent.

KEMP, Gene (1926–2015) British children's
author who began her writing career with a
series of 'Tamworth Pig' books for young

children, of which the first was published in 1972. *The *Turbulent Term of Tyke Tiler* (1977), a smart, energetic *school story, won her the *Carnegie Medal. Several more stories set in 'Cricklepit School' would follow. In 1981 she published *The Clock Tower Ghost*, about a struggle between a girl and a ghost to take possession of Addlesbury Tower.

Kemp's writing is brisk and unpretentious, and is characterized by its cheerful acceptance of the lawlessness of present-day schoolchildren. For instance, in one story in *Dog Days and Cat Naps* (1981), the entire Class M 13 resolves to be on good behaviour for nine days so that the school trip (cancelled because one of them has been found with a knife) shall be reinstated. The rules they set themselves include 'No groping or snogging in public', and a ban on shoplifting: 'Tom Lightfinger, a crazed look in his eyes, was found walking round the supermarket with hands sellotaped together to stop him shoplifting. "It's hard to stop doing something you've been at since you were three," he moaned.'

KENDALL, Carol (1917–2012) American author, creator of the Minnipins, a peaceful race of small people. They are described in *The Gammage Cup* (1959), illustrated by Erik *Blegvad (British title, *The Minnipins*, 1960).

KENDALL, Edward Augustus (1776–1842) English author best known for *Keeper's Travels In Search of His Master* (1798). He also wrote *The Crested Wren* (1799), *The Swallow: a fiction interspersed with poetry* (1800), and *Burford Cottage and its Robin-Red-Breast* (1835), a long novel narrated by a robin, who reports human conversations about *natural history and other improving topics, as well as relating his own adventures.

KENDREW family York printers of *chapbooks for children during the 19th cent. James Kendrew began printing in York c.1803, employing his daughters to hand-colour illustrations. He was succeeded in 1841 by his son John, who in 1848 sold the firm to William Allerston, whose nephew J. H. Carr took it over in 1874. Kendrew publications were usually of a higher standard than those of many provincial printers, and the firm's juvenile books were distributed all over England.

KENT, Jack (1920–1985) American author and illustrator of children's picture books. After dropping out of school at the age of fifteen, he began his career as a commercial artist. In 1950 he gained widespread recognition

with his comic strip *King Aroo*, which was syndicated for the fifteen years that followed. His first children's book, *Just Only John*, was inspired by his young son and was published in 1968. He is known for the much-loved *There's No Such Thing as a Dragon* (1975), about a boy whose mother won't believe that there is a rapidly growing dragon in the house (despite Billy's insistence and the evidence of her own eyes). He wrote over forty other titles, and illustrated more than twenty titles by other authors.

KER, John Bellenden (1765–1842) Botanist and man of fashion who devoted much energy to attempting to prove that English popular phrases and *nursery rhymes are, without exception, really written in a language that he called 'Low-Saxon'. Ker argued that this language, a hypothetical early form of Dutch (which was in fact his own invention), was a parent of modern English. He wrote out the rhymes in it and then 'translated' them back into English, revealing as he did so that they meant something entirely different.

Ker's project might be thought to be meant as a joke—he was known as a wit—had he not devoted a total of four volumes to it, under the title *An Essay on the Archaeology of our Popular Phrases and Nursery Rhymes* (1834–42).

KERR, (Anne) Judith (1923–) German-born, British writer and illustrator, the much-loved creator of the classic picture books *The *Tiger Who Came to Tea* and the enduring *Mog* series. Kerr's father was a famous drama critic, poet, and broadcaster of Jewish origin, which led to the family fleeing Berlin just before Hitler's election to power in 1933. The family escaped to Switzerland, and then to Paris, before finally settling in London during the war. Kerr won a scholarship to the Central School of Arts and Crafts in 1945, worked as an artist, and then as a BBC television scriptwriter before publishing her first picture book. Her novel *When Hitler Stole Pink Rabbit*, the first in the *Out of the Hitler Time* trilogy, is a moving, semi-autobiographical account of her experiences as a young refugee.

The *Seven Stories collection now houses Kerr's archives, the most significant collection of artwork by a single illustrator, spanning over seventy years, including childhood paintings, drawings, and finished artwork for most of her published books. While Kerr's early work can now seem slightly dated to some audiences (Sophie's daddy comes home to expect dinner on the table in *The Tiger Who Came to Tea*), children will continue to delight

in the warm illustrations and humour which are so characteristic of her work. Kerr has continued to publish into her nineties. Recent books include *The Great Granny Gang* (2012) and *The Crocodile Under the Bed* (2014). In 2013 she produced *Creatures*, a beautiful illustrated celebration of her life and work.

KERR, M. E. *See* MEAKER, MARIJANE.

Kes *See* KESTREL FOR A KNAVE, A.

Kestrel for a Knave, A (1968) A novel by Barry Hines (1939–2016). Widely studied at school, filmed by Ken Loach as *Kes* (1969), and beloved by many, this is the story of one day in the life of Billy, a boy from a broken home who has no hope, no money, and no prospects. He lives in a grim reality, his only love being that for the kestrel he raised from a chick. The novel is told with flashbacks, and the vile misery of Billy's day at home and school is interspersed with lyrical, exquisitely written passages about the natural world. It is heartbreaking, funny, and appallingly harsh. Hines indulges in no sentiment here, and reality was never going to hand Billy an easy time.

Kewpies Cherubic children, the creation of American artist Rose O'Neill (1875–1944). The Kewpies first appeared in *Ladies' Home Journal* in 1909.

Kid for Two Farthings, A (1953) A novel by Wolf Mankowitz (1924–98). Though not specifically a children's book, it has been enjoyed by many young readers.

Kidnapped, *being memoirs of the adventures of David Balfour in the year 1751: how he was kidnapped and cast away; his sufferings in a desert isle; his journey in the wild Highlands; his acquaintance with Alan Breck Stewart and other notorious Highland Jacobites; with all that he suffered at the hands of his uncle Ebenezer Balfour of Shaws, falsely so-called: written by himself, and now set forth by Robert Louis Stevenson* A novel by R. L. *Stevenson first published serially in *Young Folks* from May to July 1886, and issued as a book by Cassell the same year.

David Balfour, who is in his late teens, leaves his home in the Forest of Ettrick (in the Scottish Lowlands) after the death of his father, carrying a letter recommending him to his uncle Ebenezer. Ebenezer, a miser living in a tumbledown mansion, receives him with suspicion and hostility, and tries to bring about his death by sending him up the stair of a ruined tower in the darkness. This having failed, he

contrives that a sea captain, Hoseason, shall kidnap David and carry him off to sea, with the intention of selling him into slavery in America. The vessel—the brig *Covenant*—collides with a rowing boat in which the Jacobite loyalist and spy Alan Breck Stewart is travelling, being on his way to a ship that is to take him to France and his master, Charles Edward, the Young Pretender. Alan Breck is taken on board the *Covenant* in return for a bribe, and David, though he is no Jacobite, throws in his lot with Breck when he hears Hoseason and his shipmates plotting against them. Alan Breck and David manage to hold the ship's roundhouse against an attack by the sailors, but then the *Covenant* is wrecked on the rocks. David survives and he makes his way through the Highlands, and encounters Alan Breck again just as the Jacobite is witness to the murder of 'Red Fox', the merciless Colin Campbell, king's agent and scourge of the Jacobites. David himself becomes implicated in the murder, and he and Alan have a long and exhausting flight before David is able to return to his home territory, expose his uncle's criminal intentions, and inherit the estate that is his by right—whereupon he arranges for Alan to have safe passage to France.

The first edition of the book was preceded by a small private printing, made to secure copyright. Illustrations were first added to the story in an edition of 1887, for which the artist was W. Hole, and N. C. *Wyeth provided suitably dramatic pictures for an American edition of 1913.

The book is one of the most brilliant of all *adventure stories. It owes its inspiration to Stevenson's fascination with Scottish history, his admiration for *Scott, and his experience as a young man when he toured by boat the lighthouses for whose structure his father, a distinguished civil engineer, was responsible. The murder of Campbell was a real historical event, and Alan Breck a real person, who was suspected of it.

Like *Treasure Island*, *Kidnapped* is largely an exercise in moral ambiguity, David being constantly inclined to sit in judgement on Alan Breck's politics and his activities, but finding himself drawn closer and closer to this unscrupulous yet heroic man. The book, which is by turns drily comic, sardonic, and horrific, has only one major flaw, its lack of a definite ending, Stevenson finding it impossible to conclude it satisfactorily, and in effect breaking it off with David's return. He continued it in *Catriona* (1893), which describes David's unsuccessful attempt to secure the acquittal of

James Stewart of the Glens, who is put on trial for Campbell's murder, Alan Breck's escape to the continent, and David's love for Catriona, daughter of the rebel James More.

Kidnapped provided much of the inspiration for John Buchan's *The Thirty-Nine Steps* (1915), and so for a whole generation of thrillers which aped that book.

KILNER, Dorothy (1755–1836) and her sister-in-law **Mary Ann** (1753–1831) English authors of a number of popular stories for children, several of which were innovatory in giving the narrator's part to *animals and inanimate objects. Dorothy used the pseudonym 'Mary Pelham' and wrote a number of purely didactic works for children, such as *Dialogues and Letters on Morality* (?1783) and *The First Principles of Religion* (c.1787), but was chiefly noted for her fiction, which probably began life as stories told to her brother's children. Her *Life and Perambulation of A Mouse* was published by John *Marshall in 1783 and *The *Village School* appeared c.1795. Among her other books are *The Holiday Present; containing anecdotes of Mr & Mrs Jennet and their little family* (c.1780), *The Rotchfords; or the friendly counsellor* (1786), which was a book designed 'to inculcate the benevolent religion of Christianity', *The Rational Brutes; or, talking animals* (1799), in which animals complain of their cruel treatment by humans, and *First Going To School; or, The Story of Tom Brown and His Sisters* (1804).

Her brother's wife, Mary Ann Kilner (*née* Maze), was an equally popular author, writing under the pseudonym 'S.S.' Her most successful books were *The *Adventures of a Pincushion* (c.1780), the extended *moral tales *Jemima Placid* and *William Sedley* (both c.1783), and *Memoirs of a Peg-Top* (c.1783).

Kim (1901) A novel by Rudyard *Kipling. Kimball O'Hara, son of a sergeant in an Irish regiment serving in India who married a nursemaid, is brought up by a poor half-caste woman after the death of his parents. He lives in Lahore, speaks English haltingly but is fluent in the vernacular. One day there comes to Lahore a lama from Tibet, a man of pious serenity who is in search of a certain River, into which (he says) there fell an arrow shot by the Buddha himself. Kim overhears him expounding the nature of his quest and offers himself as a *chela* (disciple) to the old lama. With Kim guiding him and begging on his behalf, the lama sets off. Kim, too, has a quest: he is in search of a Red Bull on a green

field—this being, though he does not at first know it, his father's regimental emblem. Kim and the lama have not gone far on their journey when they stumble across Kim's father's regiment, and Kim's quest comes to an abrupt and apparently untimely end, for he is virtually taken into captivity by the white men, who identify him as one of their own kind and send him away to a boarding school. The lama, however, insists on paying for Kim's education, in the hope that the boy will one day be able to rejoin him on his search for the River, and Kim keeps in touch with the old man, often escaping from white society to plunge himself again into the Indian world of bazaar intrigue. Eventually Kim shows himself so capable a pupil that he is taken from school before time, and is put to work spying for the Secret Service. He meets Hurree Babu, an exotic character in the pay of the Secret Service. Kim, the lama, and the Babu tramp their way up into the Himalayas, the old man still searching for his River, while Kim and the Babu are attempting to track down and forestall two Russian espionage agents. After a violent encounter with the Russians, Kim wins high honour in the Service for his skill in making off with their documents, while the lama, at the last, discovers his River where he least expects to find it. Kim, too, has accomplished a spiritual quest: he has learnt who and what he is.

The novel, generally considered to be Kipling's finest book, was planned and written in various stages during the 1890s. The original idea came from the story told to Kipling of an Englishman, discovered among the Pathans, who had been stolen as a baby and could only speak his captors' language.

Kim was serialized on both sides of the Atlantic before its appearance in book form. Its initial reception was mixed, for Kipling was beginning to be unpopular with liberal critics for his imperialism. It is still sometimes condemned because of its unquestioning acceptance of the supremacy of the white man in the India it portrays. Though not written for children, *Kim*, with its brilliant mixture of spy story with spiritual quest, attracted and excited many young readers from the beginning.

KIMENYE, Barbara (1929–2012) Contemporary East African author who wrote a very popular 'Moses' series, an African equivalent of Richmal Crompton's *William books. The stories, which appeared from the mid-1960s, are set in an Educational Institute for the Sons

of African Gentlemen (in reality a shabby moneymaking enterprise catering for rejects from reputable schools).

kindergarten The name given by Friedrich *Froebel to an infants' school established by him at Bad Blankenburg in 1837, and afterwards used round the world for similar institutions. Froebel believed that early childhood is a time for learning through play, and he called his model school a 'child garden' because he wanted the children to develop naturally like plants in a garden. Among pioneers of the kindergarten movement in America was Kate Douglas *Wiggin, author of *Rebecca of Sunnybrook Farm*.

Kinder- und Hausmärchen See GRIMM.

KING, (David) Clive (1924–) British children's writer, best known for *Stig of The Dump* (1963), illustrated by Edward *Ardizzone. His other books include *The Twenty-Two Letters* (1966), which is set in an early Mediterranean civilization; *Me and My Million* (1976), about a boy who is given a bag containing a stolen painting worth a million pounds; *The Night the Water Came* (1973); and *Ninny's Boat* (1980).

KING, Stephen Michael (1963–) Australian picture-book author-illustrator, known for his loose pen-and-wash illustrations. His illustrations are lively, whimsical, and joyous, and show a deep appreciation of the world, especially family life, and his texts often feature onomatopoeia, lyrical prose, and deep themes, simply expressed. His work appears frequently on the *CBCA shortlist and notable books lists, and his most popular work might be *The Pocket Dogs* (1999), in which Mr Pockets carries two small dogs in his coat, which was shortlisted for CBCA Picture Book of the Year in 2001. In 1999, *Henry and Amy* (1998), a book about differences, was shortlisted for CBCA Picture Book of the Year Award. He has illustrated most of Glenda *Millard's *Kingdom of Silk* series.

King Arthur and his Knights, The Story of (1903) The first of four volumes written and illustrated by Howard *Pyle, retelling *Malory's stories of *Arthur. Pyle states: 'I believe that King Arthur was the most honorable, gentle Knight who ever lived in all the world.' He glosses over the violence and other unseemly incidents which litter Malory's tale, and his text consequently seems insipid to those well acquainted with other Arthuriana, as well as being irritating because of its mock-medieval style. The illustrations, however, are striking.

King of the Golden River, The or *the Black Brothers, a legend of Stiria* (1851) A *fantasy by John *Ruskin. An extraordinarily fertile valley is farmed by three brothers. Two, Schwartz and Hans, are mean, ugly, and hard. The third, Gluck, is the opposite, but is bullied by them and condemned to menial work. Left alone one day, he is visited by an 'extraordinary little gentleman'. Gluck gives the little man shelter, but the two brothers return and attempt to turn him out. He promises to come back at midnight. At midnight a storm tears the roof off the house (but not off Gluck's room) and devastates the valley. A visiting-card left on the table reads 'South West Wind Esquire'. When no further wind brings rain to the valley, it becomes a desert.

The brothers now turn their hand to dishonest goldsmithing, but out of the melting down of Gluck's mug comes a golden *dwarf; this is the King of the Golden River, the river which cascades down near the brothers' valley. Since Gluck had wished that this river were really gold, the king tells him on what conditions this could happen, and warns of the penalty of failure—being turned into a black stone. Hans and Schwartz each prove their black nature and fail, but Gluck's selflessness wins him the gold in the form of a new river running in his valley and again making it fertile.

The book first appeared, illustrated by Richard *Doyle, in December 1850. The author's name was not given; the introduction explained that the story had been written in 1841 'at the request of a very young lady, and solely for her amusement, without any idea of publication'. The young lady was Euphemia Chalmers Gray (Effie), twelve years old at the time. Ruskin was then in his early twenties; it was long before he established his reputations as author, artistic sage, and social reformer. Seven years later Effie became Ruskin's wife, but she eventually left him for his friend the artist John Millais.

The King of the Golden River is one of the earliest English examples of a fantasy written specifically for a child, though Ruskin regarded it as uninventive, 'a fairly good imitation of Grimm and Dickens, mixed with some true Alpine feeling of my own'.

The book proved an immediate success, and went through three editions during its first year of publication. Arthur *Rackham illustrated the fine 1932 edition.

King Rollo Hero of a series of small *picture books by David *McKee. King Rollo is a king,

attended by a magician. The stories (1979 onwards) were made into television cartoon films.

KINGSLEY, Charles (1819–75) English novelist, author of The *Water-Babies. He was the son of a clergyman who had taken Holy Orders simply to have a profession, his guardians having mishandled his inheritance. Charles was born in a Devonshire village where his father was parish priest. He went up to Cambridge in 1838, where he led a dissipated life, from which he was rescued by his decision to become a committed Christian—he had previously been troubled by religious doubt—and by his feelings for Fanny Grenfell, daughter of a prosperous family, with whom he fell in love. He managed to get a First in Classics and a Second in Mathematics, and in 1844, after Fanny's family reluctantly consented, he was married to her.

Not long before his marriage Kingsley was ordained into the Church of England, and became curate and then rector of Eversley, a village a few miles south of Reading, remaining there (with various excursions) for the rest of his life. Eschewing both the Oxford Movement and the *Evangelicals, he adopted a theology preached by F. D. Maurice, who argued that man was made in the image of God, and could live up to that image if he chose. Kingsley and others of Maurice's circle involved themselves with improving social conditions in an energetic fashion, which led to their acquiring the nickname 'Muscular Christians': Kingsley hated this tag, preferring to call himself a 'Militant Christian'. With a group that included Thomas *Hughes, author of *Tom Brown's Schooldays, Kingsley helped to publish a periodical, Politics for the People, which commented on social and economic ills. He himself wrote for it under the name 'Parson Lot'. Meanwhile in his own parish he did his best to provide education for the poor and to concern himself with their welfare. His first two novels, Yeast (1848) and Alton Locke (1850), were concerned with poverty and social evils. He gradually came to believe that change should be brought about not through revolutionary activities but by arousing the ruling classes to their duties. Hypatia (1853), a *historical novel set in the 5th cent., was partly an attack on fanaticism.

These books established his literary reputation. He turned for a time to poetry, and then began to write on *natural history, at which he was expert. Glaucus; or the Wonders of the Shore (1855) arose from a holiday with his children at Torbay. Its anthropomorphic description of some of the marine creatures foreshadowed The Water-Babies. Glaucus was ostensibly addressed to adults, but became popular with Victorian children.

In the same year Kingsley published Westward Ho!, a novel of adventure set in Elizabethan times. In 1856 came his first book explicitly for children, a retelling of Greek myths written for his own family, under the title The *Heroes.

In 1860 Kingsley accepted the Regius Professorship of Modern History at Cambridge. While at Cambridge, Kingsley also acted as history tutor to the Prince of Wales, the future Edward VII, with whom he became friendly. It was during this period that he began work on The Water-Babies, which was sparked off by a promise to provide something for his youngest child, but was also motivated by his reading a government report on child employment that noted the increased use of 'climbing boys' in the chimney-sweeping trade. The book was published in 1863.

In 1864 he became involved in a battle of words with John Henry Newman, having stated in a review that truthfulness and Catholicism did not go hand in hand, and that Newman 'informs us that it need not'. Kingsley's last major novel was Hereward the Wake (1865), the story of the 11th-cent. outlaw; and his last children's book was Madam How and Lady Why, an account of the principles of geology, in 1870.

KING-SMITH, Dick (Ronald Gordon King-Smith) (1922–2011) Acclaimed author of many humorous animal books. He grew up in the West Country, where his family ran several paper mills, and he was educated at Marlborough College. He was a soldier in the Second World War, serving with the Grenadier Guards in Italy.

King-Smith started his career as a farmer, but gave it up because of a self-confessed lack of business sense and a desire to keep the animals he liked best rather than the ones that would make him the most profit. He went on to train as a teacher and began teaching primary school children at the age of fifty-three. He was a natural communicator but struggled with teaching maths because he couldn't do long division. So after eight years, he moved onto his third, and by far most successful career: writing for children. His first book, The Fox Busters (1978), is about what happens when a group of formidable hens

turn against a fox. It was followed by several more animal stories before he wrote what became, perhaps, his most famous book, The *Sheep-Pig*.

King-Smith's output became prolific: for many years he produced seven or eight books per year. He also starred in three television series between 1983 and 1989, along with his dog Dodo and various other animals. They were *Rub-a-Dub-Tub*, *Pob's Programme*, and *Tumbledown Farm*.

King-Smith won many awards for his work. *The Sheep-Pig* won the *Guardian Children's Fiction prize in 1984; *Harriet the Hare* won the Children's Book Award in 1995; and in 1999, *The Crowstarver*, about a boy with learning difficulties, received the Special Educational Needs Award. King-Smith was children's author of the year in the 1991 British Book Awards and in 2009 he was appointed OBE for his services to children's literature.

King Solomon's Mines (1885) The first *adventure story for boys by H. Rider *Haggard. The book is narrated by 'Allan Quatermain, of Durban, Natal, Gentleman', who meets two Englishmen, Sir Henry Curtis and Captain John Good. They are searching for Curtis's younger brother, who went to seek his fortune in South Africa and was last heard of when he set out to look for the legendary King Solomon's Mines, supposed to contain the treasure of the Old Testament potentate. Quatermain has a crude map of the route to the mines made by an earlier explorer, who died on the journey, and he joins the search. The three travel across the desert, and undergo many perils, including being imprisoned in the treasure chamber of the mines by the tribal *witch Gagool. Quatermain, Curtis, and Good manage to escape via a hidden tunnel; they find Sir Henry's brother and reach Quatermain's home in Natal. Though they have had to leave the bulk of the treasure behind, they are rich, for Quatermain has put a handful of priceless gems into his pocket.

The book was written in a deliberate attempt to equal the success of R. L. Stevenson's *Treasure Island* (1883). The story was intended for a juvenile readership—it is dedicated to 'all the big and little boys who read it'—but it immediately became popular with adults, largely due to posters displayed all over London by the publishers, Cassell, which described it as 'THE MOST AMAZING STORY EVER WRITTEN'. In the first twelve months 31,000 copies were sold in Britain; thirteen American editions

appeared in the first year alone. The adventures of Quartermain et al. were parodied by *Belloc in *The *Modern Traveller* (1898).

KINGSTON, William Henry Giles (1814–80) Prolific British writer of *adventure stories who spent much of his childhood in Portugal. After settling in England he produced several books on the subject of emigration and then, from 1850, began to write stories for boys. The best known were *Peter The Whaler* (1851) and *The *Three Midshipmen* (1873) and its sequels. Kingston also produced a new translation of *The *Swiss Family Robinson* (1879) and edited a number of *annuals and periodicals for boys, including the first *Union Jack* (founded, shortly before his death). Two of his books had Canadian settings: *The Trapper's Son* (1873), a story of the Canadian West, and *Snow-Shoes and Canoes* (1876), set among fur traders in the Hudson's Bay territory.

KINNEY, Jeff See DIARY OF A WIMPY KID.

KIPLING, (Joseph) Rudyard (1865–1936) English author and poet. His father, John Lockwood Kipling, studied art and sculpture in London. Kipling *père* met his future wife, Alice MacDonald, in Staffordshire and they became engaged by the waters of the Rudyard Reservoir near Stoke-on-Trent. Immediately after their marriage in 1865 the couple left for India, where Lockwood Kipling had been appointed first Principal of the new Art School in Bombay. Here Rudyard Kipling, the elder of the Kiplings' two children, was born, and here he spent his first six years, speaking Hindi as a second language and living in a bungalow much like that described in 'Rikki-Tikki-Tavi' in *The *Jungle Books*.

In 1871 the Kiplings sent Rudyard and his sister Alice to England so that their health should not be endangered by the Indian climate, this being a common practice among English families stationed there. The two children were taken as boarders by a family in Southsea, the Holloways, who proved totally inadequate as substitute parents. Alice was indulged, but Rudyard was treated with an inhumanity practised in the name of *evangelical fervour. He described his years with the Holloways in the story 'Baa, Baa Black Sheep' (in *Wee Willie Winkie and other child stories*, 1898). He was eventually rescued from this hell, and was sent in 1878 to school at the United Services College at Westward Ho! in Devon, an establishment recently founded to prepare boys for the armed forces. His

experiences there closely resemble the goings-on in *Stalky & Co.* Though at first unhappy (there was plenty of bullying), he soon came to enjoy the tough atmosphere and to make firm friendships.

At school, Kipling wrote verse and became editor of the school magazine. It was decided that he lacked the academic ability to get into Oxford, so his father, who was now working in Lahore, obtained him a job on the *Lahore Gazette*. Kipling returned to India and began work as a journalist shortly before his 17th birthday.

The job was demanding, consisting largely of drudgery, but these years provided material for virtually all his early books. In 1886 he published a volume of verse, *Departmental Ditties*, which was praised in England by Andrew *Lang, and he also wrote the stories that were eventually collected as *Plain Tales from the Hills* (1888). This and *Wee Willie Winkie*, which appeared the same year, included a number of stories about children which Kipling modelled on the tales of Mrs *Ewing. Other volumes published in 1888 brought the total number of his stories in print to something over 70.

In 1889 he returned to England. His stories had made him celebrated there, and he was welcomed into the literary world. The next year appeared his first novel, *The Light that Failed*. He met and became engaged to Caroline ('Carrie') Balestier, an American, and after their marriage in 1892 the two set out for a trip around the world, but the bank which held Kipling's savings failed, and they returned to Carrie's hometown, Brattleboro, in Vermont. Here their first child Josephine was born, and Kipling wrote the two *Jungle Books* and *Captains Courageous*, into which he put something of his feelings about America—both his affection and his irritation. In 1896 he and his family returned to England and, while living for a short time near Torquay, Kipling began to write *Stalky & Co.* (1899). The next year the Kiplings moved to Rottingdean and Kipling worked at the *Just So Stories*, which he had begun in America for the amusement of his daughter Josephine (who now had a brother and sister). The family returned to America for a visit in 1899, but shortly after they had arrived in New York Josephine died of pneumonia. Her death and her father's feelings eventually led to the writing of one of his finest short stories, 'They', about a remote country house filled with the laughter of unseen children. Meanwhile *Kim*, begun in 1892, was finally completed in 1900.

In 1902 Kipling bought a house in Sussex, which inspired *Puck of Pook's Hill* (1906) and *Rewards and Fairies* (1910). After this he virtually gave up writing for children, the sole notable exception being *A History of England* (1911) in collaboration with C. R. L. Fletcher (Kipling's contribution was the verses which punctuate the narrative). He helped *Baden-Powell with the *Boy Scout movement, putting together some of his uncollected children's stories in *Land and Sea Tales for Scouts and Guides* (1923), including *The Gift*, one of his best.

Kipling's later years were darkened by the death of his only son in the First World War, and by the pain of an undiagnosed duodenal ulcer. He also came to be widely denigrated for the 'jingoism' of his views. His children's writings, however, survived countless changes of popular taste. Rosemary *Sutcliff, whose own books owe much to Kipling, wrote of him:

By no means every child will like Kipling...But every child should have a chance, by having one or other of the books put into his hands at the right moment, to discover whether he [does] or not. Because the child who has never run with Mowgli's wolf pack, or stood with Parnesius and Pertinax to defend the Northern Wall, [...] has missed something that he will not get from any other writer.

Kipper (1991–) By Mick *Inkpen. In books that are charming without being overly sentimental, Kipper is a curious, optimistic, and warm-hearted puppy whose adventures have grown to be one of the best loved series for pre-school children in the world. Translated into over twenty languages, the stories are universally recognizable, taking our hero through many simple but engaging adventures. In the first book, *Kipper* (1991), he decides he no longer wants to sleep in his smelly old basket, so he tries out how other animals sleep, but of course ends up happily curled back up in his own basket with his own toys and blanket. *Kipper* was made into an animated TV series in 1997.

KITAMURA, Satoshi (1956–) Japanese picture-book author and illustrator. His work had been rejected by more than twenty publishers when, in 1981, Klaus Flugge of Andersen Press asked him to illustrate *Angry Arthur* by Hiawyn Oram. It won him the Mother Goose Award for the most exciting newcomer to British illustration. Since then he has published more than sixty books, many of which he has written himself. Among his best work is

Once Upon an Ordinary Schoolday (2004), with words by Colin *McNaughton, a beautiful celebration of creativity and imagination, the colour seeping into Kitamura's grey illustrations slowly as a class of ordinary children listen to a piece of music and are changed by it. In 2010, *Millie's Marvellous Hat* was shortlisted for the *Kate Greenaway Medal for children's book illustration. Kitamura draws with a Japanese glass pen that produces occasional little blobs, making his line extremely distinctive. His stories tend to be quirky and fantastical, exploring the power of the imagination. They often feature animal characters.

Kit Carson American folk hero, in reality Christopher Carson (1809–68) frontiersman, trapper, and guide. During the 1840s he accompanied John Charles Frémont on several exploring expeditions in the Rockies, and had his character and exploits described by Frémont in published accounts of the trips. By 1848 Carson had begun to feature in magazine articles and 'yellowback' novels. A typical book about him was *Kit Carson; the Rocky Mountain Guide* (1861), written by Edward Sylvester Ellis for Beadle's Dime Biographical Library. He was subsequently used as the hero of many *westerns, such as *The Fighting Trapper; or, Kit Carson to the Rescue*, again written by Ellis and published by Beadle's in 1874, and in the 20th cent. he continued to feature in fiction about the Wild West. It is said that towards the end of his life Carson was shown a typical *dime novel about his exploits, with an illustration depicting him slaying seven Indians with one hand while he clasped a fainting maiden with the other; when asked if this was a true incident, he replied modestly: 'That there may have happened, but I ain't got no recollection of it.'

Kite Rider, The (2001) By Geraldine *McCaughrean. Subtitled *One Boy's Haunted Journey to the Top of the Sky*, this story is set in an ancient China steeped in superstition and myth. McCaughrean weaves ghosts, heartbreak, sacrifice, poverty, and adventure together, adding her own literary magic to create a timeless story of heroism. In a world where the spirits of the dead inhabit the clouds, where divination is a daily necessity, and where tradition binds the poor, Haoyou witnesses his father's death. In order to save his family Haoyou risks his own life, inadvertently finding fame, money, and freedom—but he also finds danger and a plot involving Kublai Khan himself.

Kit Haverard Heroine of novels by Elfrida *Vipont.

Kit's Wilderness (1999) A *young adult novel by David *Almond. Kit moves to the Northumberland town where his grandfather lives, and there he meets a strange boy called John Askew; Askew plays a game called Death. With the delicate, dark beauty that characterizes so much of Almond's work, *Kit's Wilderness* explores things beneath the surface, full of menace, and the spirits of the past, but this is a wilderness that is full of things that are precious, too. It won the 2001 *Michael L. Printz award.

Ki-yu: a story of panthers (1934) By the Canadian writer Roderick *Haig-Brown, this book is set on Vancouver Island and begins with a battle of wits between Blackstreak, a cruel old panther, and the hunter David Milton. After Blackstreak's death the she-panther Nass gives birth to his cub, Ki-yu. Blackstreak had been 'a killer, a waster of meat', but Ki-yu is a noble savage. Ki-yu becomes the foe of David Milton, but finally falls prey not to the human hunter but to a pack of wolves.

The book, which was originally published in America and was issued in England under the title *Panther*, records many killings in detail; the author defended this in a preface: 'Nothing in nature, so long as it is honestly observed and honestly described, can harm the mind of a child.'

KJELGAARD, Jim (James) Arthur (1910–59) American writer of *animal stories, including a series of books beginning with *Big Red* (1945), about an Irish red setter.

KLASSEN, Jon (1981–) Canadian author and illustrator. An animator for films including *Kung Fu Panda* and *Coraline*, he was recognized as a major new talent when he won the Canadian *Governor General's Literary Award for his debut as a children's book illustrator, Carolyn Stutson's *Cats' Night Out* (2010). He continued to garner further accolades for his illustration of other authors' texts and became an award-winning author-illustrator in his own right. *I Want My Hat Back* (2011), with its laconic humour, satisfying shapes, and clean design, was the *New York Times* Best Illustrated Book of the Year. The follow-up, *This Is Not My Hat* (2012), won the *Caldecott Medal and that same year *Extra Yarn*, with text by Mac Barnett, was a Caldecott Honor Book (see CALDECOTT MEDAL). Klassen was shortlisted for the 2014 *Kate Greenaway Medal

for both *This Is Not My Hat* and *The Dark*, written by Lemony *Snicket, winning with the former.

KLEIN, Norma (1938–89) American author. Her first book, *Mom, the Wolf Man, and Me* (1972), is about an eleven-year-old girl whose mother acquires a boyfriend who owns a wolfhound.

KLEIN, Robin (1936–) Australian writer who had a prolific career in the 1980s and 90s during which she won the Australian Children's Book of the Year Award for *Came Back to Show You I Could Fly* (1990), the story of the friendship between a naïve young boy and a beautiful older girl who suffered from drug addiction, and the Junior Book of the Year for *Thing* (1982), the story of a girl and her pet dinosaur. Klein's stories regularly champion the underdog, depict the fallibilities of adults (parents and teachers especially), and deal with the effects of divorce on children's lives. One of her best-known books is *Hating Alison Ashley* (1984), narrated by Erica, who is fiercely jealous of the new girl Alison's apparent wealth and sophistication. An unlikely friendship develops between them over the course of the novel, which is howlingly funny from start to finish.

Knaben Wunderhorn, Des See BRENTANO.

KNATCHBULL-HUGESSEN, Edward Hugessen First Baron Brabourne (1829–93) A great-nephew of Jane Austen and for a time a junior minister in Gladstone's government, he published between 1869 and 1886 a number of volumes of his short original *fairy stories, the first being *Stories for my Children* (1869). This opens with the tale 'Puss Cat Mew', which was a childhood favourite of J. R. R. *Tolkien; it includes an *ogre who catches his prey by disguising himself as a tree, and may have partly inspired the invention of the Ents, tree-creatures in Tolkien's The *Lord of The Rings*. Knatchbull-Hugessen claimed to model himself on Hans Christian *Andersen but his stories, though not without their attractions, have little of Andersen's skill, and are often long-winded, macabre, and sadistic.

Knife of Never Letting Go, The See CHAOS WALKING.

KNIGHT, Eric *See* LASSIE.

KNOWLES, John *See* SEPARATE PEACE, A.

KNOX, Thomas W. (Wallace) (1835–96) American writer of *travelogue storybooks, including the *Boy Travellers* series, published from 1879 onwards.

Knuffle Bunny *See* WILLEMS, MO.

KOERTGE, Ron (1940–) American poet and author of *young adult fiction. Many of his books feature unlikely relationships and witty dialogue. Three of his novels have been *American Library Association Best Books for Young Adults: *Stoner & Spaz* (2004), about Ben, a film buff with cerebral palsy, and Colleen, a tattooed druggie; *Strays* (2007), in which Ted, who talks to animals, finds friendship in a foster-family after the death of his parents; and *The Brimstone Journals* (2001), a novel in free verse told from multiple points of view. *Shakespeare Bats Cleanup* (2003) is also written in verse. There are sequels to *Stoner & Spaz* and *Shakespeare Bats Cleanup*, both well received.

KONIGSBURG, E. L. (Elaine Lobl) (1930–2013) American novelist for children, and author and illustrator of *picture books, who was for some time a teacher of chemistry. She attracted immediate attention with her first two novels, both published in 1967, which were respectively runner-up for, and winner of, that year's *Newbery Medal (a 'double' never before achieved). *Jennifer, Hecate, Macbeth, William McKinley, and Me, Elizabeth*, the runner-up (it was published in England with its title somewhat abbreviated), is about the friendship between two girls at the William McKinley Elementary School: Jennifer, who claims to be a *witch, and Elizabeth, the narrator, who becomes her apprentice in witchcraft. The Newbery winner was *From the Mixed-Up Files of Mrs Basil E. Frankweiler*.

Konigsburg's next book, *About the B'nai Bagels* (1969), was generally regarded as a disappointment, its portrayal of a Jewish family headed by a 'typical' Yiddisher-momma being attacked in some quarters as shallow. *(george)*, Mrs Konigsburg's curiously-titled fourth novel, which appeared in 1970, is about Ben, a child prodigy at chemistry who believes that his body is inhabited by George, an outspoken little man. Ben is nearly classified as schizophrenic, but it is George's shrewdness which leads him to uncover a drug-making racket in the school laboratory.

(george) is E. L. Konigsburg's most typical book, exemplifying her strengths and weaknesses. She is not especially concerned with narrative, so that crises in the story—Ben's confrontation with the aggressive stepmother

who first brands him as schizoid, and the discovery of the high-school kids making the drug LSD in the lab—are played down almost disconcertingly. Moreover at the end of the book the question of Ben's sanity is left tantalizingly open. On the other hand the portraits of Ben/George, his kindergarten-expellee brother Howard, and the sympathetic chemistry teacher Mr Berkowitz have a roundness and credibility achieved by few other 'realist' children's writers of the period.

Konigsburg's later books include two *historical novels, *A Proud Taste for Scarlet and Miniver* (1973) and *The Second Mrs Giaconda* (1975); the clever and mysterious *Father's Arcane Daughter* (1976, later reissued as *My Father's Daughter* and televised as *Caroline?* in 1990); and *Throwing Shadows* (1979), a collection of short stories supposedly narrated by children.

KORINETZ, Yuri (Iosifovich) (1923–89) Russian children's novelist. His books include *There, Far Beyond the River* (1967, English translation 1973), the story of a friendship between a Moscow boy and his adventurer uncle who takes him to the far north of Russia; and *The River and the Forest* (1974, English translation 1978), about a boy's journey through the wilds of Siberia.

KRASILOVSKY, Phyllis (1926–2014) American author of *picture books, including *The Cow Who Fell in the Canal* (1957), illustrated by Peter *Spier. Her first story, *The Man Who Didn't Wash His Dishes* (1950), was written for a small boy dying of cancer.

KRAUSS, Ruth (1911–93) American author, best known for *A Hole Is to Dig: a First Book of First Definitions* (1952), illustrated by Maurice *Sendak. Her books convey a child's viewpoint in a manner highly entertaining to adults. She was married to Crockett *Johnson.

KREIDOLF, Ernst (1863–1956) Swiss-born illustrator of *picture books such as *Die Blumenmärchen* (*Flower Fairy Tales*) (1898). His work had some resemblance to that of Walter *Crane and was influenced by art nouveau.

KRUMGOLD, Joseph (Quincy) (1908–80) American author who won the *Newbery Medal twice, with … *and Now Miguel* (1953), about a Mexican boy, and *Onion John* (1959), in which a hobo-cum-wizard finds that the local people want to build him a 'respectable' home. Krumgold was also a film producer.

KRÜSS, James (1926–97) Prolific German poet and author of stories, including *Henrietta Bimmelbahn* (1958) (*Henrietta Chuffertrain*, 1960) and *Mein Urgrossvater und ich* (1961) (*My Great-Grandfather and I*, 1964).

KRYLOV, Ivan Andreyevich (1769–1844) Russian writer of *fables. His first collection was published in 1809, satirizing the Russia of his day.

KUIJER, Guus (1942–) Dutch writer best known in the English-speaking world for *Het boek van alle dingen* (2004; translated into English as *The Book of Everything* by John Nieuwenhuizen, 2006), and turned into a successful stage play by Australian playwright Richard Tulloch. Kuijer's *Polleke* and *Madelief* books have also been very successful in the Netherlands. He won the *Astrid Lindgren Memorial Award in 2012.

Kurt Maschler Award Founded by (and named after) the British publisher of *Emil and the Detectives* (hence the trophy's nickname: 'The Emil'). Awarded between 1982 and 1999, it recognized a book whose text and illustrations were exceptionally complementary and well-integrated. Winners included Allan *Ahlberg and Janet *Ahlberg (*The *Jolly Postman*), Michael *Foreman, John *Burningham, Ted *Hughes (The *Iron Man*), Babette *Cole, Raymond *Briggs, and Barbara *Firth, as well as Helen *Oxenbury and Anthony *Browne for their respective versions of *Alice's Adventures in Wonderland.

Ladybird books British series originally published from Loughborough in Leicestershire. What began as a bookshop there, in 1867, expanded into printing and then, as Wills and Hepworth, they published their first children's books around 1915, with a ladybird as their logo. British children of the 1940s were able to read small-format hardback Ladybird books of nursery rhymes, animals stories, and *The Adventures of Wonk,* a koala. The Ladybird Key Words Reading Scheme, a set of graded readers, first appeared in 1964, with texts by William Murray (1912-1995) and pictures by Martin Aitchison (1919-2016) and Harry Wingfield (1910-2002). They featured the daily experiences of Peter and Jane, two middle-class children. The books had a visual and verbal style closely resembling that of the **Janet and John* series (first published fifteen years earlier). They proved very successful commercially, and in consequence Ladybird started to produce children's books of every kind in the same small format as the readers, ranging from *fairy stories to non-fiction, including L. du Garde *Peach's long *Adventures from History* series.

Later there were complaints of *racism and sexism in the Ladybird stories. Murray and his illustrators responded in 1974 by remodelling certain drawings and episodes, so that there was less stereotyping of sex roles, and black children played some part in the stories.

In 1968 Leila *Berg's series **Nippers* was launched by Macmillan, in an attempt to counteract Ladybird with stories that were more true to the lives of working-class children. But Ladybird's commercial supremacy remained unchallenged. Indeed, after decades of change (both to the firm—now a part of Penguin—and to the books themselves), the Ladybird brand remains strong.

LA FARGE, John (1835-1910) American illustrator whose drawings appeared in the **Riverside Magazine,* and included illustrations to *The *Pied Piper of Hamelin.*

LA FONTAINE, Jean de (1621-95) French poet, remembered chiefly for his *fables, published between 1668 and 1694.

The first six books of *Fables choisies mises en vers* appeared in the spring of 1668, and contained 125 fables; nearly 100 more were added in the edition of 1678, and another two dozen in 1693 when La Fontaine was an old man. He based them largely on *Aesop (his first collection begins with the traditional biography of Aesop himself), but also used Phaedrus, a Latin verse translation of Greek fables (by Laurentius Abstemius), and more than a dozen of the fables found in the **Panchatantra.* James Michie writes in his English translation of La Fontaine's fables (1979): 'There was hardly a fabulist, or collector of fables or adapter of fables or translator of fables, ancient or more or less modern, Italian or French, whom La Fontaine did not plunder . . . He also invented quite a few fables of his own.'

La Fontaine wrote more elegantly and wittily than any of his fabulist predecessors. His fables were first translated into English in 1734; the most notable illustrated English editions are those with pictures by J. J. *Grandville and Gustave *Doré. Among versions for children is a series of picture books by Brian *Wildsmith, based on individual fables and published during the 1960s.

LAGERLÖF, Selma (1858-1940) Swedish author who was a teacher before she submitted a piece of writing to a competition, which led to her first novel, *Gösta Berling's Saga,* being published in 1891. In 1906-7 the two volumes of her outstanding children's tale *The *Wonderful Adventures of Nils* (*Nils Holgerssons underbara resa genom Sverige*) appeared. Hugely popular, she was translated into thirty-four languages and travelled widely, including trips to Jerusalem, which inspired *Jerusalem* (1901), and to Italy, which led to *The Miracles of the Anti-Christ* (1897). In 1909 she became the first woman to be awarded the Nobel Prize for Literature.

LAIRD, Elizabeth (1943-) British author, born in New Zealand, Laird has lived and worked in many countries around the world,

particularly in the Middle East. She was a teacher before she became a writer and collector of folk tales. Her work never shies away from contentious subjects, though in her books the story is always as important as the message. Her back catalogue is consistently good, but to choose a few: *Lost Riders* (2008) is about the real-life trade in Arab boys forced to become camel jockeys; *A Little Piece of Ground* (2003) looks at the Arab–Israeli conflict from an Arab perspective; *The Garbage King* (2003) shows what slavery and poverty are doing to children in Addis Ababa; and *Jake's Tower* (2001) takes a cool look at domestic violence.

LAMB, Charles (1775–1834) and **Mary (Anne)** (1764–1847) Charles Lamb and his sister Mary wrote a number of books for children, of which the most celebrated was their adaptation of *Shakespeare for young readers.

Charles went to school at Christ's Hospital, then took a clerkship at East India House in London where he remained for the next thirty years. His family was poor, the chief income being Charles's wages and what Mary could earn by needlework; the strain on her helped to upset the balance of her mind, and in 1796 she stabbed her mother to death. The inquest judged her to be a lunatic and for a time she was confined in an asylum.

Despite the tragedy the Lambs eventually resumed something like a normal existence. In 1799 Mary was released, and she returned home to live with Charles.

Poems by Charles began to appear in print in 1796; he also wrote a tragic story, *Rosamund Gray* (1798), and two plays. In 1805 his version of *The *Queen of Hearts* was published by his friends the *Godwins. In 1807 came his first collaboration with Mary, *Tales From Shakespear*. This was a commission from the Godwins and the greater part of the work was done by Mary, Charles specializing in the tragedies. Charles followed the *Tales* with another children's book, *Adventures of Ulysses* (1808), which was based on Chapman's translation of the *Odyssey*; this, too, was published by the Godwins. In 1809 came another collaboration with Mary, *Mrs Leicester's School*, and the two combined forces again in *Poetry for Children* (1809). Charles was the author of *Prince Dorus* (1811); he may have been responsible for a *Book Explaining the Ranks and Dignities of British Society* published for children by *Tabart in 1805, and possibly also for a verse rendering of *Beauty and the Beast* (Godwin, 1811). After this period he became well known for his writings for adult readers, most notably his essays, published under the pseudonym 'Elia'. He never married, but in the 1820s he and Mary adopted an orphan girl, Emma Isola.

The Lambs wrote during the period when the *moral tale was the dominant form in literature for children, and they did not entirely escape its influence. But the *Tales from Shakespear* were to some extent a revolt against didacticism, an attempt to free the nursery from the grip of what Charles, writing to Coleridge in 1802, called 'Mrs B[arbauld]'s & Mrs Trimmer's nonsense'.

LAMBURN, Richmal Crompton *See* WILLIAM.

Lamonic Bibber *See* MR GUM.

LA MOTTE FOUQUÉ, Friedrich Heinrich Karl, Baron de (1777–1843) Author of *Undine. He was a German nobleman of French extraction, a soldier by profession, who became well known as a writer of pseudo-medieval romances. He published a quarterly magazine for Romantic literature in which *Undine* appeared in 1811. Among his other works was *Sintram and his Companions* (1814), the tale of a knight's adventures. It was a favourite childhood book of Charlotte M. *Yonge and Louisa M. *Alcott.

Lamplighter, The (1854) A novel by the American author Maria Susanna *Cummins. Gerty, a Boston waif, is ejected from her boarding house after she has attacked its proprietor for scalding her kitten to death. She is befriended by 'True' (Trueman) Flint, an ageing lamplighter. The book is very long and was not intended for children, but it was widely read by them; Rebecca Randall in *Rebecca of Sunnybrook Farm* (1903) names it among stories that she knows well, and its popularity (in Britain as well as America) was not far behind that of *The *Wide, Wide World*. It is one of the *evangelical stories mocked by *Kingsley in *The *Water-Babies*, under the name of 'the Pumplighter'.

LANAGAN, Margo (1960–) Australian author of short stories and fiction for older teens and adults whose books, though striking in their originality, are still undervalued in much of the English-speaking world. Her five volumes of short stories are all superb, with prose that is scalpel-like in its precision, and with a style and ideas that challenge the most competent reader. *Black Juice* (2004) is the collection that made her name worldwide.

Death, sex, and abuse are all faced head-on in her work, but never pandered to, though controversy is something that has followed her since the publication of *Tender Morsels* (2008), which has a dismayingly grim opening before the heroine escapes into a world of her own creation. In *Sea-Hearts* (2012, also called *The Brides of Rollrock Island*) Lanagan continues to spin her own worlds out of fairy stories, turning their themes of transformation and cruelty into something that speaks directly to readers today.

Lancelot, Sir (Launcelot, Sir) A knight of the Round Table, who plays a prominent part in the legends of King *Arthur. Lancelot du Lac first appears in the 12th-cent. French poetry of *Chrétien de Troyes, as the lover of Arthur's queen, Guinevere. In the medieval Arthurian romances he takes part in the Quest of the Holy *Grail, but is hindered by his worldliness from seeing more than a glimpse of the mysteries. However, he is the father, by a union with the daughter of the king of the Grail Castle, of *Galahad, who is destined to complete the Grail Quest.

The Arthurian narratives of *Malory tell how Lancelot is adored by Elaine, the Maid of Astolat, who dies for the love of him. His adulterous liaison with Guinevere is eventually proved to Arthur, and the queen is condemned to death. Lancelot rescues her from the stake and carries her off to his castle of Joyous Gard, and thence to Brittany. Arthur and Gawain pursue the lovers there, but Arthur is swiftly called back to Britain by news of Mordred's treachery. After the mortal wounding of Arthur in his fight against Mordred, Lancelot goes in search of Guinevere, who has entered a nunnery at Amesbury. They have a last meeting, he becomes a monk himself, returning to Amesbury only after she has just died, and soon afterwards dies himself.

Lancelot is the hero of one of the Arthurian novels of T. H. *White, *The Ill-Made Knight* (1940), later incorporated into *The *Once and Future King* (1958).

LANDELLS, Ebenezer *See* TOY-MAKING BOOKS.

LANDMAN, Tanya (1963–) British writer, best known for her strongly characterised, gripping *young adult fiction with a historical setting. Novels include *Apache* (2007), about a girl warrior in the American west in the late 19th century; and *Hell and High Water* (2016), a thrilling coming-of-age adventure about a mixed-race boy in the mid-18th century. She won the 2015 *Carnegie Medal with the superb *Buffalo Soldier* (2014), in which a recently freed African-American slave joins the US army.

Land of Green Ginger, The (1937) A *fantasy by Noel Langley. The story is a sequel to *Aladdin, and tells how Aladdin's son goes on a quest to release a magician from a spell. The author (1911–80) was a South African-born playwright and novelist who also wrote screenplays, including the 1939 MGM adaptation of *The *Wonderful Wizard of Oz*, starring Judy Garland, of which he was one of three authors.

'The Land of Green Ginger' is the setting of Beatrix *Potter's story *The *Fairy Caravan* (1929).

LANDY, Derek *See* SKULDUGGERY PLEASANT.

LANG, Andrew (1844–1912) Folklorist and man of letters, editor of *The Blue Fairy Book* and its successors, Lang was the eldest son of a lawyer and was born and brought up in Selkirk, in the Scottish border country. As a boy he heard fairy tales and legends of the area from his nurse and other local people; he read Scottish history in *chapbooks and 'every fairy-tale I could lay my hands on'. His next devotion was to the works of Fenimore *Cooper and Mayne *Reid, and he also read avidly in Dasent's *Popular Tales From the Norse*. He was educated at a local school and at Edinburgh Academy, hating Greek until he discovered Homer. As a consequence he chose a university education in Classics, first at St Andrew's, briefly at Glasgow, then finally at Oxford, as an undergraduate at Balliol College, and he became a Fellow of Merton.

Already a regular reviewer for a literary journal, he decided to leave Oxford and become a professional writer. In 1875 he married Leonora Blanche (Nora) Alleyne (1851–1933) and moved to a house in Kensington where he lived for the rest of his life. There were no children, and little is known of his personal life, but friends thought the two admirably suited, and Mrs Lang collaborated with her husband, making a substantial contribution to his books for the young as translator and writer.

Lang's interests were astonishingly diverse and his output huge. A contemporary wrote: 'His leaders in the *Daily News* read like fairy tales written by an erudite Puck. No other such combination of poet, scholar and journalist has been known in Fleet Street.' Meanwhile he published poetry and collaborated on prose

translations of the *Odyssey* and the *Iliad* ('Butcher and Lang' and 'Lang, Leaf, and Myers'), which were to have a lasting reputation as both schoolboy cribs and versions with unusual literary flair. Lang's most important contribution to scholarship at the time, however, came out of his studies in anthropology, and particularly in mythology and folklore. He was able, from his wide reading of folk tales and the classics, to argue conclusively that folk stories are not the debased relics of higher literary mythologies, but the foundation of them. With this, and with his observation that the relationship between tales told by widely separated races cannot be explained philologically, he effectively reversed prevailing opinion and made a distinguished contribution to the scholarship of his time.

Lang is best remembered for the *Fairy Book* series that began with *The Blue Fairy Book* in 1889 and ended with *The Lilac Fairy Book* in 1910. Before this, however, he had published both folk-tale translations for children and modern fairy stories of his own. *The Princess Nobody* (1884) was his response to a publisher's request to write a new text to accompany Richard *Doyle's pictures for *In Fairyland* (1869). Lang worked ingeniously round the pictures, reweaving together motifs from traditional and literary fairy tales. Many years later he declared: 'Nobody can write a *new* fairy tale; you can only mix up and dress the old stories and put characters into new dresses.'

The Gold of Fairnilee (1888) is a longer story, dealing with the fairy lore and history of the Scottish border country in which Lang was brought up; its fairies are the shadowy, rarely benevolent creatures of peasant belief, and the story was not directed at children. But *Prince Prigio*, which came out just before *The Blue Fairy Book*, was a children's entertainment. Together with its sequel *Prince Ricardo of Pantouflia* (1893) it was reissued as *Chronicles of Pantouflia* in *My Own Fairy Book* (1896), and further (though less successful) Pantouflian adventures appeared in *Tales of a Fairy Court* (1907).

In 1893, Lang published *The True Story Book*; the whole series of twenty-five annual Lang story books came to include more true stories, a *Book of Dreams and Ghosts*, *animal stories, *romances, an edition of the *Arabian Nights* (1898), books of heroes, saints, princes, and princesses, and *The Strange Story Book*, the last of the series, which was published the year after his death.

Lang's other enterprises for children included *The Nursery Rhyme Book* (1897), illustrated by L. Leslie *Brooke, and *The Blue Poetry Book* (1891). He wrote introductions to reissues of some of Charles *Lamb's children's books—*Beauty and the Beast*, *Tales From Shakespear*, and *Adventures of Ulysses*—and to Kate Langloh Parker's *Australian Legendary Tales* (1896). He himself composed some of the material for *The True Story Book* and *The Red True Story Book*, and he wrote a short biography of Joan of Arc for children (1906). His *Tales of Troy and Greece* (1907) became a children's classic; in it his retelling of *Homeric legends was supplemented from his knowledge of other ancient sources and of the latest archaeological discoveries. The Homeric world continued to fascinate him. One of his novels, a collaboration with Rider *Haggard, was *The World's Desire* (1890), the story of Odysseus' last wandering after all his family and people have been wiped out by plague.

In his capacities as publisher's reader and reviewer Lang 'discovered', or helped to fame, many of the writers of his time: among them Haggard, who became his close friend, R. L. Stevenson, Rudyard *Kipling, Arthur Conan *Doyle, Walter *de la Mare, and 'F. *Anstey', the author of *Vice Versa*. He was also an early champion of E. *Nesbit. But his taste in literature, wide as it was, still favoured the past, and adventure, romance, and fantasy. He was unsympathetic to fiction that roused painful emotion, preferring 'merry endings and prosperous heroes'.

George S. Gordon, in his *Dictionary of National Biography* essay on Lang, wrote that he was 'not an affable person, and it was his pleasure to conceal his astonishing powers of work under the air of a dilettante'. On the other hand, Lang's friends loved him for his kindness and gaiety (with its underlying melancholy), for his passion for fishing, cricket, and cats, and for his generosity.

For all his huge output and great success, Lang never accumulated any wealth, and up to the end he wrote in order to make a living. He died suddenly on a visit to Scotland, and was buried at St Andrew's—which university established an annual lecture in his name (*see* TOLKIEN, J. R. R.).

LANGLEY, Noel *See* LAND OF GREEN GINGER, THE.

LANGTON, Jane (Gillson) (1922–) American author of *fantasy in the *Nesbit tradition. Her books include *The Diamond in the Window* (1962), *The Swing in the Summerhouse* (1967), *The Astonishing Stereoscope* (1971),

and *The Fledgling* (1980), the first books in her 'Hall Family Chronicles', as well as a number of picture books and adult mystery novels.

LANIER, Sidney (1842–81) American author, poet, and musician, editor of *The Boy's Froissart* (1879), *The Boy's King Arthur* (1880), *The Boy's Mabinogion* (1881), and *The Boy's Percy* (1882) (the last was a version of **Percy's Reliques*).

Lantern Bearers, The (1959) The third of Rosemary **Sutcliff's stories of Roman and Dark Ages Britain; winner of a **Carnegie Medal. It takes up the fortunes of the family from which came the heroes of *The *Eagle of the Ninth* (1954) and *The Silver Branch* (1957), whose emblem is a dolphin. Aquila, a cavalry officer, deserts when the last of the legions leaves Britain, putting the country at the mercy of Saxon invaders.

Larry the Lamb In the **Toytown* stories.

LARSSON, Carl (1853–1919) Swedish artist; his paintings of family life and domestic interiors were published in **picture-book form as *Ett Hem* ('Our Home') (1907).

Lassie A collie dog of abnormal intelligence, courage, and initiative, heroine of many films. She was the invention of the British-born author Eric Knight (1897–1943), who was known as a novelist and cartoonist. His *Lassie Come-Home* (1940) is the story of a collie sold by her owner to the Duke of Rudling, who takes her to the north coast of Scotland. She escapes, making the 400-mile journey back to Yorkshire. The book was filmed in 1943 with a male collie named Pal playing the title role and Elizabeth Taylor co-starring. Subsequent Lassie films included *The Sun Comes Up*, which had an original screenplay by Marjorie Kinnan Rawlings, author of *The *Yearling*. Lassie's popularity soon equalled that of his/her predecessor **Rin-Tin-Tin, and he/she lived in conditions appropriate for a star, with air-conditioned kennels and a resident hairdresser and chiropodist.

Last Battle, The (1956) The seventh and final **Narnia novel by C. S. **Lewis.

Last of the Huggermuggers, The (1855) A novel by C. P. **Cranch.

Last of the Mohicans See LEATHER-STOCKING TALES.

LATHAM, Jean Lee (1902–95) American playwright and novelist for children and adults who won the **Newbery Medal with *Carry on,* *Mr Bowditch,* (1955), the true story of Nathaniel Bowditch who discovered a new method of navigating by the stars.

Latin grammar *See* LILY'S GRAMMAR.

LATTIMORE, Eleanor (Frances) (1904–86) American author of many stories set in China, beginning with *Little Pear* (1931).

Laughable Lyrics, A fourth book of nonsense poems, songs, botany, music, etc. Written and illustrated by Edward **Lear and published by Robert John Bush of London in time for Christmas 1876, with the date 1877 on the title page. It contained, amongst other works, *The *Dong with a Luminous Nose*, 'The Two Old Bachelors', *The *Yonghy-Bonghy-Bò*, 'The Pobble Who Has No Toes', 'Mr and Mrs Discobbolos', and 'The Quangle Wangle's Hat'.

Launcelot, Sir *See* LANCELOT, SIR.

Laura Ingalls In the 'Little House' books by Laura Ingalls **Wilder.

Laura Ingalls Wilder Award Instituted in 1954 and given by the Children's Services Division of the **American Library Association. Originally it was given every five years (till 1980), then this was reduced to three years, and it is now awarded every second year. It is awarded to an author or illustrator, in recognition of his or her entire body of work. Laura Ingalls **Wilder won the first award; subsequent winners include E. B. **White (1970), Beverley **Cleary (1975), Dr **Seuss (1980), Maurice **Sendak (1983), Eric **Carle (2003), Tomie **DePaola (2011), and Katherine **Paterson (2013).

Laureate Many countries in the English-speaking world (and others now, too) have laureateship schemes, which vary in their details but mostly involve a distinguished creator of children's books being appointed for a fixed term, usually two years, to act as a high-profile spokesperson for children's literature and related subjects (literacy, reading for pleasure, etc.) on a national platform. Schemes include Ireland's Laureate na nÓg (since 2010; incumbents to date: Siobhán **Parkinson, Niamh **Sharkey, Eoin **Colfer, and P.J. **Lynch); the National Ambassador for Young People's Literature in the US (since 2008; incumbents to date: Jon Scieszka, Katherine **Paterson, Walter Dean **Myers, Kate **DiCamillo, and Gene Luen Yang); and the Australian Children's Laureate (since 2012; incumbents to date: Boori Monty Pryor, Alison **Lester, Jackie **French, and Leigh Hobbs). The UK's Children's Laureate, run by **Booktrust, is the longest-running of these.

Based on an idea by Ted *Hughes and Michael *Morpurgo, it was established in 1999. Incumbents to date:

1999–2001	Quentin *Blake
2001–3	Anne *Fine
2003–5	Michael Morpurgo
2005–7	Jacqueline *Wilson
2007–9	Michael *Rosen
2009–11	Anthony *Browne
2011–13	Julia *Donaldson
2013–15	Malorie *Blackman.
2015–17	Chris *Riddell.

Lavender's Blue: *A Book of Nursery Rhymes* (1954) A wide-ranging collection compiled by Kathleen Lines which remains popular more than six decades after its first publication. It is mostly the book's illustrations by Harold Jones that mark it out. The artist was given a Special Commendation by the judging committee of the 1955 *Carnegie Medal for these, which led to the establishment of the *Kate Greenaway Medal, first awarded in 1956.

LAWRENCE, John (1933–) British artist who became noted in the 1970s for his *wood engravings illustrating such books as a reissue of Richard Adams's *Watership Down* (1977). He has produced his own *picture books, including *Rabbit and Pork: Rhyming Talk* (1975). His wood engravings have also graced work by Philip *Pullman (*Lyra's Oxford* in the *His Dark Materials* series), Martin *Waddell, and many others. In 2009 he published a richly illustrated edition of *Treasure Island*.

LAWSON, Robert (1892–1957) American author-illustrator. His first success came with his pictures for *The *Story of Ferdinand* (1936) by Munro *Leaf. *They Were Strong and Good* (1940) won him the *Caldecott Medal, and he was awarded the *Newbery Medal for *Rabbit Hill* (1944). He illustrated *Mr Popper's Penguins* (1938) by Richard Atwater.

LEAF, Munro (1905–76) American author-illustrator. He wrote many books for younger children which he illustrated himself, though he is best known for *The *Story of Ferdinand* (1936) and *Wee Gillis* (1938), both of which have pictures by Robert *Lawson.

LEAR, Edward (1812–88) Creator of *A *Book of Nonsense* and many celebrated poems for children. He was born in London, the twentieth child of Jeremiah Lear, a stockbroker.

Edward Lear's childhood was not happy. His mother had little energy to devote to him and his father paid small attention to the children; moreover in 1816 Jeremiah Lear suffered a financial crisis and the family had to reduce its standard of living. Edward leant heavily on the affection of his sister Ann, twenty-two years his senior, who became his substitute mother and his earliest teacher, giving him his first drawing lessons. But despite her kindness he looked back on his childhood with horror and with painful memories of insecurity and misery.

From an early age he became subject to attacks of depression, and by the time he was six had begun to suffer epileptic fits. He called his malady 'the demon' and did his best to keep it a secret even from close friends.

He began to write poetry in adolescence, sometimes for the amusement of a family in Sussex, where one of his married sisters lived. His verses were often comic, and sometimes parodied conventional poetic attitudes.

In his late teens Lear began to make his living by selling drawings of birds. He was allowed by the Zoological Society in London to produce a book of pictures of parrots in their new Gardens, and his *Illustrations of the Family of Psittacidae, or Parrots* was published in a limited edition by 1832. In that year he was asked by Lord Stanley, heir to the Earl of Derby, to come to Knowsley Hall near Liverpool to make a set of drawings of the creatures in the private menagerie there. Lear entered the Knowsley household virtually as a servant, but his sense of humour soon made him welcome above stairs. He began to amuse the children of the household with comic drawings and rhymes. After a friend showed him *Anecdotes and Adventures of Fifteen Gentlemen*, one of the two collections of *limericks then in existence, he began to copy this verse form, and the results met with (in his own words) 'uproarious delight and welcome'.

In 1837, having completed more than 100 pictures at Knowsley (he was also making drawings elsewhere during this period), Lear found his eyesight worsening. Lord Stanley arranged for him to visit Italy for the sake of his health, and also so that he could take up landscape painting, which would be less demanding than the close observation of animals and birds. In Rome he made friends among painters and was generally happy.

He continued to spend much of his time in Italy but made occasional visits to England, and during one of these, in February 1846,

he published his *A Book of Nonsense*, pairing the humour of his drawings and his verse. There is no evidence as to why he chose this moment to make the limericks public; probably the motive was partly financial—he lived on what he could make from his paintings and books—and perhaps he was also encouraged to do it by friends whose children he had amused. The book made no great impact at first, and Lear's attention was chiefly taken up with his work on *Illustrated Excursions in Italy* (1846) and other books of landscape pictures. It would not be true, however, to suggest that he considered his verses of less value than his paintings. In later years when other collections of this nonsense had made his name better known, he was delighted to find that he had a wide reputation as an entertainer of children.

In the summer of 1847 he visited Calabria, which along with other Mediterranean excursions provided material for further books of landscape drawings. Lear, however, was not satisfied with his technical skill, and enrolled at the Royal Academy Schools in London in the hope of improving it. During this period he got to know Holman Hunt, who became a close friend and a great supporter; another friend made at this time was Tennyson. He did not, however, achieve any celebrity for himself as an artist, and was obliged to make what living he could by turning out watercolours. Dependent on this income, on occasional commissions for oil-paintings, and on what little he could make out of his books of landscapes, he struggled on from week to week, living in rented rooms either in London or somewhere in the Mediterranean. He was often ill with asthma, and continued to suffer from depression—'the Morbids', as he called it. His health discouraged him from wintering in England, yet he could find no permanent home overseas. He also began a restless and unhappy relationship with Franklin Lushington, a young man to whom he was deeply attached but who scarcely returned his affection.

Lushington was appointed to a judicial post in the Ionian Islands, and in 1855 Lear joined him in Corfu. One of Lear's biographers, Vivien Noakes, writes: 'If Lushington had loved and encouraged him, theirs might have developed into a full homosexual relationship. As it was, Lear probably only partly realized his homosexuality, though in the deeper layers of his mind there was conflict as he fought to suppress it, a conflict which contributed to his constant state of restlessness and depression.'

His time in Corfu was largely unhappy. He wrote in his diary: 'Fanatical-frantic caring overmuch for those who care little for us is a miserable folly.'

Since the publication of *A Book of Nonsense* Lear had continued to write limericks, and in the autumn of 1861 he put together an enlarged edition of the book. It was offered to the firm of *Routledge, but they would only distribute it for Lear, leaving him to underwrite the expenses of publication himself. The edition, which appeared in time for Christmas that year, sold out, and Routledge then offered to buy the copyright. Lear, short of money as ever, sold it for £125. The book was immediately reprinted, and was reissued again and again during Lear's lifetime.

In 1866 Lear contemplated marrying, simply for companionship, and proposed to Augusta Bethell, daughter of his friend Lord Westbury. She rejected him, and he was never to have a family of his own. But he had many contacts with children, in whose company he delighted. Many of his nonsense stories and longer poems were presented to the children of friends—the most famous of all of them, *The *Owl and the Pussy-Cat*, was composed at Christmas 1867 for the sick daughter of his friend John Addington Symonds, in Cannes—and children themselves usually responded warmly to him.

Lear's later nonsense—the longer poems and the stories—was largely composed between 1865 and 1869; his *Nonsense Songs, Stories, Botany and Alphabets* was published in 1870. Though Lear never mentioned Lewis *Carroll in his letters or diaries it is possible that he read *Alice's Adventures in Wonderland* as soon as it appeared in 1865, and conceivable that Carroll's use of nonsense helped to inspire him to write more elaborate pieces than the limericks. More probably, however, he worked independently of any such influence. (Lear's poem 'The Cummerbund', though, does seem to be partly on the model of *Jabberwocky*.)

Students of Lear's work have discerned three phases of development in his nonsense writings. In the first, which includes the limericks, the nonsense is happy and inconsequential, though it sometimes has sinister undertones. In the second phase, coinciding with his years of travelling in the Mediterranean, the theme of wandering is prominent; there are either happy endings, as in 'The Owl and the Pussy-Cat' and 'The Daddy Long-Legs and the Fly', or sad but nonsensical ones, as in

'The History of the Seven Families of the Lake Pipple-Popple'. In the third and final phase humorous detachment vanishes and melancholy becomes overt, in songs like 'The Pelican Chorus' and most notably The *Dong with a Luminous Nose.

Lear was a keen amateur musician and set some of his own poems to music; his settings of 'The Pelican Chorus' and 'The *Yonghy-Bonghy-Bò' were printed alongside those poems when they were first published. More notably he was a brilliant illustrator of his own rhymes. The drawings, indeed, play an equal part to the verses. Their comedy largely springs, especially in the pictures illustrating the limericks, from the distortion of human figures, often into shapes resembling birds.

By 1870, having saved a certain amount of money, Lear was able to afford to have a house built in San Remo. He acquired a cat called Foss, to whom he was devoted, and completed *More Nonsense (1872). In 1873 he travelled to India, spending some time there at the invitation of the Viceroy, his friend Lord Northbrook. He was delighted to find that Indian children knew 'The Owl and the Pussy-Cat'. His last nonsense book, *Laughable Lyrics, was published in 1876.

In San Remo he briefly had the companionship of Hubert Congreve, a young man whom he hoped to teach to paint. But Congreve soon left Italy, and Lear, who was in love with him, came near a mental breakdown. He contracted pleurisy and bronchitis, and though he continued to work at a long-treasured project, a set of illustrations to Tennyson's poems, he became very weak, eventually dying on 29 January 1888, not long after his cat.

During the 19th cent. a number of imitations of his nonsense verse were written and published, for example Edward *Bradley's Funny Figures (1858). A number of modern children's poets show his influence in their work, but arguably his only true heir has been Spike *Milligan.

Leather-Stocking Tales A series of five novels by James Fenimore *Cooper, set on the American frontier between 1740 and 1804. The central character is the scout and hunter Natty Bumppo, whose leather stockings give the series its name. He has a close friendship with the '*Indian' (Native American) chief Chingachgook. The most celebrated book in the series, The Last of the Mohicans (1826), is set during the war of 1757 against the French and Indians; Chingachgook and his son Uncas are the sole survivors of the Mohican tribal leaders, and during the book Uncas is killed. The other titles are The Pioneers (1823), The Prairie (1827), The Pathfinder (1840), and The Deerslayer (1841). The books have sometimes been published in abridged versions for children.

LE CAIN, Errol (1941–89) British animator and book illustrator. As a child he did animation with an 8 mm camera, then worked for film and television, including a 1976 Christmas Day broadcast of The *Snow Queen performed by actors in front of his backdrops. He won the *Kate Greenaway Medal in 1984 for Hiawatha's Childhood and was commended for four others.

LEE, Dennis (Beynon) (1939–) Canadian poet who has produced several books of comic verse for children, most notably Alligator Pie (1974), which won the Canadian Library Association's Book of the Year award.

LEE, Harper See To Kill a Mockingbird.

LEE, M. and **C. Mary and Catherine** (fl. 1870–92) British authors of *historical novels, including Rosamond Fane (1870), set in the Civil War, Joachim's Spectacles (1886), and The Oak Staircase (1892), a story of the time of James II. Mary and Catherine were probably sisters, but nothing further is known about them.

LEESON, Robert (Arthur) (1928–2013) British children's author and radical critic of children's books who was for some years Literary Editor of the British daily Communist newspaper, the Morning Star.

His first children's books were *historical novels, Beyond the Dragon Prow (1973) and a trilogy, 'Maroon Boy (1974), Bess (1975), and The White Horse (1977). These books are in general written from the viewpoint of 'the people'; the Civil War of the 17th cent. is portrayed largely in terms of class struggle and the trilogy deals with such issues as slavery and women's rights. Leeson also wrote several books with contemporary settings, including The Third Class Genie (1975), It's My Life (1980), and Harold and Bella, Jammy and Me (1980). His chief success, however, was as the author of a series of paperbacks based on the *Grange Hill television series.

Leeson's pamphlet Children's Books and Class Society (1977) expresses the belief that children's literature in the 1970s was undergoing a profound change as a result of the

advent of writers with working-class backgrounds and left-wing political views. In fact his own books do not appear to differ fundamentally from those of many British children's writers from the 1960s onwards. For example, *Harold and Bella, Jammy and Me*, arguably Leeson's most accomplished book, is strikingly traditional in its references to the game of Pooh Sticks, King *Arthur, and *Robinson Crusoe*. He also published (in 1985) *Reading and Righting: the past, present and future of fiction for the young*.

LE FEUVRE, Amy (1861–1929) Writer of *evangelical stories for children, many of which were published by the *Religious Tract Society. She specialized in the portrayal of curly-headed children whose winsome ways melt the hearts of their elders and bring them to see the light of religion.

Legend of Sleepy Hollow, The A short story by Washington *Irving, first published in his *Sketch Book* (1820) and often reprinted for children. Ichabod Crane, a Yankee schoolmaster in Sleepy Hollow on the Hudson, loves Katrina Van Tassel, a farmer's daughter, and is the victim of pranks by the friends of his rival for her love.

LE GUIN, Ursula K. (Kroeber) (1929–) American novelist, born in Berkeley, California, best known to children for her highly accomplished and influential *Earthsea series, beginning with *The Wizard of Earthsea* (1967). She has also written both realist and *fantasy fiction for *young adult readers (including the three connected novels that make up the 'Annals of the Western Shore', 2004–2007), and several speculative (*see* SCIENCE FICTION) and fantasy novels for adults, including *The Left Hand of Darkness* (1969).

Leila; or, The Island (1833) A popular English *Robinsonnade, the pious story of a child shipwrecked with her father, nurse, and pet spaniel. It was written by Ann Fraser Tytler, sister of the Scottish historian Patrick Fraser Tytler. There were also two 'Leila' sequels: *Leila in England* (1842) and *Leila at Home* (1852).

LEMON, Mark (1809–70) The first editor of *Punch* who wrote several *fairy stories. *The Enchanted Doll* (1849), illustrated by Richard *Doyle, is set in London in 'olden times' and dedicated to *Dickens's daughters Mary and Kate.

Lemon Kelly In books by E. W. *Hildick.

L'ENGLE, Madeleine (1918–2007) American novelist whose first book to make an impression was *Meet the Austins* (1960), a *family story very much in the old tradition. Teenager Vicky Austin, the novel's narrator, is a member of a noisy, aggressively happy family, in which religion plays a large part. The story deals chiefly with the arrival of orphan Maggy, a spoilt and selfish child who has to be assimilated into the lovingness of the Austins. *Meet the Austins* has two sequels, *The Moon by Night* (1963) and *The Young Unicorns* (1968).

Madeleine L'Engle's reputation derives, however, from *A *Wrinkle in Time* (1962), in which explicit Christianity largely gives place to a more generalized good-against-evil mythology. This in turn has a number of sequels, published over the following twenty-seven years and now called the 'Time Quintet'.

L'Engle is an uneven author, but rises to fine heights of invention, as with 'Mrs Whatsit' and her two Fate-like companions in *A Wrinkle in Time*, which won the *Newbery Medal and retains a devoted following to this day.

LENSKI, Lois (Lenore) (1893–1974) Prolific American children's author-illustrator who won the *Newbery Medal for *Strawberry Girl* (1945), which like many of her stories explores American farming life.

LEPRINCE DE BEAUMONT, Mme *See* BEAUMONT, MME MARIE LEPRINCE DE.

Les Malheurs de Sophie See MALHEURS DE SOPHIE, LES.

Lessons for Children A series of books for young children by Anna Laetitia *Barbauld. The first, *Lessons for children, from two to three years old*, was published in 1778, and three further books followed soon after, the final volume being *for children from three to four years old*. The books, addressed to the author's adopted son Charles, were written because Mrs Barbauld found that 'amidst the multitude of books professedly written for children there is not one adapted to the comprehension of a child from two to three years old.' She also complained of 'the want of *good paper, a clear and large type*, and *large spaces*'. The first volume consisted of short sentences, related to each other to make up simple stories about a child's day. The same principle was followed in the later books, with the sentences

gradually increasing in length and complexity until quite elaborate *moral tales were being narrated.

Lessons for Children was translated into French, revised, and reissued at various intervals until the 1860s. Some editions had illustrations. The books were admired and imitated by Maria *Edgeworth and her father, and received qualified praise from Mrs *Trimmer. The tone is gentle and affectionate, and the books give a touching impression of a happy Georgian country childhood. Charles *Lamb execrated the name of Barbauld, though it is hard to see why.

LESTER, Alison (1952–) Australian picture-book illustrator and author. Of her early illustrated books, the most famous were Robin *Klein's famous *Thing* series, which won the *CBCA Picture Book of the Year in 1983 for *Thing* (1982). The *Thing* books were for younger readers and featured Emily and her pet stegosaurus with simple, stylized illustrations. The first book she wrote and illustrated, *Clive Eats Alligators* (1985), the story of each child being special in some way, won CBCA Picture Book of the Year in 1986. Her books are consistently shortlisted for CBCA awards and have won many honours. Lester writes simply and very rhythmically, capturing the point of view of her child protagonists very effectively. Her illustration technique is often pen-and-wash, or watercolour, lively and cartoony, yet with whimsical characters and often very detailed backgrounds, focussing on family life. Her plots are imaginative, initially seeming strange perhaps because of the unusual titles, but all her books are universal. *The Magic Beach* (1990), where you can find all your favourite things, has captured the public imagination, selling over 150,000 copies. In 2005 she again won the CBCA Picture Book of the Year Award for *Are We There Yet?* In 2012–13, she shared the position of Australian Children's *Laureate with Boori Monty Pryor and she became an Ambassador for the Indigenous Literacy Foundation in 2013.

LESTER, Julius (1939–) Writer, folk musician, and academic whose work features African-American themes. His first children's book, *To Be a Slave* (1968), was a Newbery Honor Book (*see* NEWBERY MEDAL). Many of his books are retellings of folk tales: he has produced four collections of Uncle Remus stories with illustrator Jerry *Pinkney, and his retelling of *John Henry*, also illustrated by Pinkney, was a 1995 Newbery Honor Book. His novel about the largest slave auction in American history, *Day of Tears: A Novel in Dialogue* (2005), won the *Coretta Scott King Award.

LEVITHAN, David (1972–) American children's book editor and author who wrote his first novel to create the book he would have liked to have read as a teen: *Boy Meets Boy* (2003) managed to subvert every stereotype that existed about gay characters in *young adult books—it is an utterly joyous story. His books deal with the highs and lows of first love of all kinds and with the complexities of growing up, and his characters are often so well realized you might expect to bump into them in the street. With *Nick and Norah's Infinite Playlist* (2006) he started an ongoing collaboration with Rachel Cohn (1968–) and in *Will Grayson, Will Grayson* (2010) with John *Green. More recent is *Every Day* (2012), whose narrator wakes up every day in a different body, and has come to terms with this, more or less, but then one day falls in love . . . *Two Boys Kissing* (2013) is a school-based drama, but it is also a many-voiced reflection on how life has changed for gay men and women.

LEWIN, Betsy (1937–) American author and illustrator who designed greetings cards before turning her hand to writing stories for children's magazines—and it was one of these that was spotted by a publisher who asked that it be expanded into a full-length book. She uses two distinct styles, one consising of watercolour washes over pen-and-ink drawings, the other more naturalistic. The former style was used in her most popular book, *Click, Clack, Moo: Cows That Type* (2000), written by Doreen Cronin (1966–), a farm-based story in which the cows negotiate hard for what they want; this influences the ducks, who get their own story in *Giggle, Giggle, Quack* (2002); and this style was also used in the Halloween story, *Click, Clack, Boo* (2013). Her more realistic style is used in her collaborations about the natural world with husband Ted Lewin (1935–), such as *Puffling Patrol* (2012), about the annual puffin rescue on the Icelandic island of Heimaey.

LEWIS, C. (Cecil) Day (1904–72) British poet who wrote two stories for children: *Dick Willoughby* (1933), a *historical novel set in the 16th cent., and *The *Otterbury Incident* (1948, illustrated by Edward *Ardizzone), a thriller-cum-*school story based on the French film *Nous les gosses*. *The Otterbury Incident* has a

good deal of vigour, and is regarded by some critics as a minor classic.

LEWIS, C. S. (Clive Staples) (1898–1963) Author of the *Narnia books for children. He was born in Belfast and educated at University College, Oxford, where he took a triple First. In 1925 he became a Fellow of Magdalen College, Oxford, remaining there until 1954 when he accepted a professorship from Cambridge. He was brought up a member of the (Protestant) Church of Ireland, but became an atheist in adolescence; however by 1931 he had returned to belief in Christianity, largely due to the influence of his friend and Oxford colleague J. R. R. *Tolkien. Lewis's conversion was immediately productive in literary terms: *The Pilgrim's Regress* (1933) is a witty (though bigoted) defence of the Christian religion, modelled on *The *Pilgrim's Progress*.

The Screwtape Letters (1942) ingeniously shows Christianity from the devil's point of view. From this it was only a short step to the first of the Narnia books, *The Lion, the Witch and the Wardrobe* (1950), which, though intended largely for sheer entertainment, had (like its six successors) a firm purpose: to re-imagine Christianity in terms of a children's *fairy story.

Lewis had no immediate child audience for his books. He was a bachelor until he was nearly sixty, though for many years he shared a house (somewhat inexplicably) with Mrs Janie Moore, a woman many years his senior. That he ever wrote for children was probably due largely to the example of Tolkien, of whose stories Lewis was a great admirer—the fact that Tolkien's *The *Lord of the Rings* was ever completed was largely the result of his encouragement. Lewis laid great store by male companionship, and his own circle of friends, known as the Inklings, met regularly in his college rooms to talk and listen to each other's work read aloud. Much surprise was caused when in 1956 Lewis married Joy Davidman, an American divorcée who only a few years afterwards died of cancer.

Lewis's children's books are too individual to have encouraged much imitation, but their influence can be seen in the stories of Susan *Cooper, and Lewis's blend of Christianity with *fantasy may have provided a model for some of the novels of Madeleine *L'Engle.

LEWIS, Hilda *See* SHIP THAT FLEW, THE.

LEWIS, Naomi (1911–2009) British critic, anthologist and translator of children's fiction,

and historian of children's literature. Her books include *A Peculiar Music* (1971), which is a selection for children of poems by Emily Brontë, and *The Silent Playmate: a collection of doll stories* (1979). She wrote introductions to many reissues of children's classics, and published many translations of the work of Hans Christian *Andersen.

LEWITT, Jan (1907–91) and **HIM, George** (1900–82) Polish-born artists who illustrated a number of children's books, including the first of Diana Ross's *Little Red Engine stories.

Lexikon der Kinder- und Jugendliteratur ('Encyclopedia of Children's and Young People's Literature') Published from 1975 under the auspices of the *Institut Für Jugendbuchforschung.

libraries for children in Britain were first found in schools, where in some cases they existed during the 16th cent. In 1660 Charles *Hoole, in his *New Discovery of the Old Art of Teaching School*, recommended more than 250 books for the school library. In the 1830s the *Religious Tract Society and the *Society for Promoting Christian Knowledge began to offer grants to national and parochial schools for establishing libraries. *Sunday schools also made books available for home reading—most churches and chapels had a Sunday school library—and reading rooms attached to Working Men's Institutes and similar organizations sometimes allowed young people to use their facilities.

The establishment of civic-owned public libraries began in Britain and America in the mid-19th cent. A few British towns had facilities for children from the start, with juvenile reading rooms being opened in Westminster (1857), Cambridge (1872), and Nottingham, where the Library for Boys and Girls in Shakespeare Street, the first separately housed children's lending library in Britain, was inaugurated in 1882. But these were exceptions, and America soon overtook Britain. Caroline M. *Hewins began pioneer work in Hartford, Conn., in the 1870s, and in 1885 the first children's library was established in New York City. By 1900 children's rooms had been set up in many of the major American city libraries, and *story telling sessions were being held. A quarter of a century later the New York Public Library, in which Anne Carroll *Moore set up the juvenile collections, had 315,000 volumes in its children's rooms and a yearly circulation of four million. In Canada

by the 1930s the Toronto Public Libraries were providing outstanding services for young people, thanks to pioneer work by Lillian H. *Smith.

By this time British supporters of library work for children were drawing much of their inspiration from across the Atlantic. John Ballinger, a Cardiff librarian, encouraged colleagues to emulate American achievements, but in 1903 observed gloomily that 'until our financial resources are improved, we can only hope to follow humbly in the footsteps of such magnificent institutions as the Carnegie libraries of Pittsburgh'. By 1932 the position had improved sufficiently for W. C. Berwick Sayers, Chief Librarian of Croydon, to write *A Manual of Children's Libraries*, which discussed books and their selection, recommended the practice of storytelling, and gave hints about exhibitions and publicity. In 1937 Eileen H. *Colwell founded the Association of Children's Librarians, and at the same time the Schools Library Section of the Library Association (later the Schools Library Association) was established.

From the beginning, children's librarians tried to offer guidance to children in search of reading matter. (It is no coincidence that the most prestigious children's literature awards in the US and UK are run by those countries' respective professional library associations, the *American Library Association and *CILIP.) This has sometimes led to the censorship of poor-quality books; in America, for example, some librarians in the early 20th cent. were proud to announce that they did not stock the 'Oz' books of L. Frank *Baum, on the grounds that they were badly written, and in Britain Enid *Blyton has suffered a similar fate (*see also* BANNED BOOKS). In New Zealand Dorothy Neal *White, children's librarian in Dunedin, began in 1937 to organize the steady withdrawal from her shelves of books by writers judged second-rate, e.g. Percy *Westerman, Elinor *Brent-Dyer, and Gunby *Hadath. To her surprise, as the quality of the library's stock improved, so the number of books borrowed by readers increased.

As late as 1951 the Library Association reported that many children's public libraries were ill-equipped, poorly stocked, and badly staffed, and that thousands of British schools had no effective library. Not until the 1960s did the situation begin to improve dramatically in Britain. According to Thomas Kelly (*A History of Public Libraries in Great Britain*, 1977) a factor in this was 'the enormous improvement in the quality of [British] children's books'. By 1964 Lancashire County Council, for example,

was providing 96 full time and part-time children's public libraries, 125 centres where books were available, 11 mobile libraries, 265 secondary school libraries, and 754 primary school libraries. This entire system had been built up since the Second World War.

In recent years, however, funding cuts have left the future of library provision under threat in many countries. A lack of political will and a lack of political obligation (in the UK, for instance, there is still no statutory requirement for publicly funded schools to have a library at all) have meant that both local and national governments have seen underused library services as an easy target for savings, with many closures and reductions in service. Increased spending on digital resources has taken their place (so the argument goes), and the expertise of trained library staff replaced by volunteers. Many high-profile children's writers, especially in the UK, have become campaigners for improved public libraries and school libraries, often citing the impact libraries had on them in their own childhoods.

Life and Perambulation of a Mouse, The

By Dorothy *Kilner, first published in 1783, apparently the first story written for children in English in which *animals are given distinct personalities, as opposed to the traditional *fable, in which the different species of creatures represent types of behaviour but are not presented as individual 'people'.

The narrator is visiting a country house where the company are to pass the time by relating their life-histories. She encounters a mouse who asks that his history be related instead of hers. His name is Nimble; he and his brothers were sent out into the world by their mother with the warning: 'Never (whatever the temptation may be) appear often in the same place.' They do not heed her words; one of them is caught and killed by a servant, while another is eaten by a cat. Nimble himself gets trapped in a jar where he almost starves to death. The narrator rescues him and promises to keep and feed him.

Much of the book is taken up with conversations overheard by Nimble and his brothers, in which adults lecture children on cruelty to animals, selfishness, and other vices.

The story was often reprinted, and is included in Charlotte M. *Yonge's *Storehouse of Stories* (1870).

Lighthouse Keeper's Lunch, The (1977)

A *picture book by Ronda and David *Armitage.

Light Princess, The A *fairy story by George *MacDonald, first published in his novel *Adela Cathcart* (1864) and reprinted in *Dealings with the Fairies* (1867), where it was illustrated by Arthur *Hughes. At the christening of a princess, her witch-aunt, spiteful at not having been invited, drops a potion into the font which causes the baby to become weightless. As a child the princess is blown from place to place about the palace, and is also incurably light-hearted—the whole story is, in fact, a pun on the word 'gravity'. A prince meets and falls in love with her, but she does not care specially for him and only tolerates his company because he goes swimming with her; she feels far more at home in the water than on land. The witch, seeing this, causes the princess's lake to drain dry; it can only be refilled by a human being sacrificing himself to plug the hole through which the water is leaking away, and allowing himself to be drowned as the water rises again. The prince offers himself, and not until the waters have covered him does the princess feel any love for him. She manages to save him, and cries for the first time in her life, whereupon the spell is broken, so that she acquires both kinds of 'gravity'. The story, which was partly suggested by E. T. A. *Hoffmann's *Princess Brambilla*, is among the most popular of Mac-Donald's short tales.

Li'l Abner American *comic strip, created by 'Al Capp' (Alfred G. Caplin) in 1934. It was filmed and made into a Broadway musical.

Lilliput Imaginary country with inhabitants no more than six inches high, the creation of Jonathan Swift. 'The Voyage to Lilliput' makes up the first part of *Gulliver's Travels* (1726), and in it Swift progressively ridicules the political life of the diminutive people as a means of satirizing in detail recent English politics. Swift also coined the adjective 'Lilliputian', and within a year it had been taken up by other writers, soon becoming a synonym for petty, diminutive, or what was appropriate to children. Among users of the word was John *Newbery in his *Lilliputian Magazine*.

Gulliver's Lilliputians feature in *Mistress Masham's Repose* (1947) by T. H. *White, which in turn was the stimulus for Andrew Dalton's *Malplaquet* trilogy (2005–9).

Lilliputian Magazine, The A publication by John *Newbery, probably the first *magazine for children in English. The first number was advertised in February 1751, price 3*d.*,

and number 3 was advertised in August 1752, though perhaps only the first two numbers actually appeared before the venture was brought to an end for lack of subscribers. The only known copies are a combination of three issues in book form, which was reprinted several times in the thirty years or so following 1752. The magazine's contents included verses, songs, biblical material, and stories. There were several *woodcut illustrations.

Lily's Grammar The Latin grammar-book used by English schoolboys from the 16th until the end of the 18th cent. William Lily (?1468–1522) was the first High Master of the school that John Colet founded at St Paul's Cathedral in London. In about 1510 Colet wrote a brief Latin grammar (in English), to which were prefixed certain prayers and precepts. He sent it to Lily for the use of the boys in the school. When it was eventually published in 1527, the book also included a set of rules (again in English) for the writing of Latin; these were attributed to Lily. To this book were then added, in 1542, an accidence and syntax in Latin. The whole was reissued in 1549 as *A Short Introduction of Grammar*, with the second part entitled *Brevissima Institutio*.

From this time on, *Lily's Grammar* (as it came to be known) remained the only authorized text for use in grammar schools, being prescribed by an edict of Henry VIII; consequently it was often referred to as the 'Royal Grammar'. Emendations were incorporated into several editions during the 17th cent., but many schoolmasters remained dissatisfied with the book, and a number of them (such as Charles *Hoole in 1653) published their own attempts to improve it. Eventually, in the mid-18th cent., a new version by John Ward was adopted. In 1758 a revision of this became *The Eton Latin Grammar*, which was finally superseded by *Public School Latin Primer*.

limerick A verse-form first used extensively in print in *The *History of Sixteen Wonderful Old Women* (1820) and *Anecdotes and Adventures of Fifteen Gentlemen* (*c.*1821). The second book suggested to Edward *Lear the idea for his *Book of Nonsense* (1846). According to the *Oxford English Dictionary*, the word 'limerick' derives from a custom of singing extemporized nonsense verses followed by the chorus: 'Will you come up to Limerick?' This explanation, which has been repeated by most other dictionaries and encyclopaedias, seems to have been based on an article in *Notes and Queries* in 1898, apparently the first year in

which the term 'limerick' was applied in print to such verses, though by this time it seems to have been in common use orally. Research in Ireland has failed to find any tradition connecting the verses with the town of Limerick, and it has been suggested that the word may be a corruption of 'Learic'.

Linda Craig Heroine of a series of American mystery novels under the pen-name Ann Sheldon, beginning with *The Palomino Mystery* (1962).

LINDGREN, Astrid (1907–2002) Author of *Pippi Longstocking* who was born in Vimmerby, Sweden. Her first children's book was *Britt-Mari lättar sitt hjarta* ('Britt-Mari finds herself') (1944). She established her reputation with *Pippi Longstocking* (Swedish title: *Pippi Langstrump*, 1945), and between 1945 and 1970 she wrote well over fifty more books, including 'Pippi' sequels, *picture books, and *plays and film scripts. After the 'Pippi' stories her most famous works include *Karlsson-on-the-Roof and *Ronia, the Robber's Daughter.

Though Astrid Lindgren's most distinguished work is in *fantasy, she has also written books in other genres, for example a 'Kati' series (1950 onwards) about a girl's adventures around the world, and stories about 'Blomkvist', a boy *detective (1946 onwards, translated into English as 'Bill Bergson'). Most of her books have appeared in a large number of languages.

LINDSAY, Norman *See* MAGIC PUDDING, THE.

LINES, Kathleen (Mary) 20th-cent. British critic of children's books who edited *Four to Fourteen, and compiled *Lavender's Blue: A Book of Nursery Rhymes* (1954).

LINGARD, Joan (1932–) British novelist whose early years living in Northern Ireland led to her writing *The Twelfth Day of July* (1972), set in Belfast during the Troubles, about the conflict between Catholics and Protestants, the political strife given a human face through the story of a teenage boy and girl who want to be together. The book has grown into a quintet—known as the 'Kevin and Sadie' series—winning many awards, and has never been out of print. The 'Maggie Quartet'—*The Clearance* (1974), *The Resettling* (1975), *The Pilgrimage* (1976), and *The Reunion* (1977)—features another resilient, independent-minded teen. Her many other consistently fine novels for children and young adults

include *Tug of War* (1989), the story of a pair of Latvian twins parted by the Second World War (Lingard's husband is Latvian); and the *Elfie and Joe* mystery series set in late Victorian London, which starts with *The Eleventh Orphan* (2008).

LINKLATER, Eric (1899–1974) Scottish author whose bibliography includes novels, biographies, autobiography, travelogues, plays, and short stories, as well as books for children. Born in Orkney of Scandinavian stock, he identified strongly as Orcadian, though he lived in many places over the course of his life. His writing career began after a spell as assistant editor of the *Times of India*, and by 1929 his work was popular on both sides of the Atlantic. His books for children started with *The *Wind on the Moon*, a picaresque fantasy about two girls whose adventures include rescuing their father from a tyrant. He wrote two other books for children: *The Pirates in the Deep Green Sea* (1949) and *Karina with Love* (1958).

Lion, the Witch and the Wardrobe, The (1950) The first of the *Narnia novels by C. S. *Lewis.

LIONNI, Leo (1910–99) Illustrator and author who was born in the Netherlands, grew up in Italy, and moved to America in 1939. Unconventional and visually intriguing, in what was at the time a highly unusual style of coloured collage, his books include *Little Blue and Little Yellow* (1959), his debut (originally conceived as a story to entertain his grandchildren), in which the characters in a story about rejection are simply blobs of colour; *Inch by Inch* (1960), about a clever inchworm; and *Frederick* (1967) about a dreamer mouse who collects colours and words to feed his friends' spirits in the dark days of winter. These last two titles were Caldecott Honor Books (*see* CALDECOTT MEDAL), as were *Swimmy* (1963) and *Alexander and the Wind-Up Mouse* (1969).

LIPPINCOTT, Joseph Wharton (1887–1976) American author of fifteen *animal stories for children, of which one of the best known is *Wilderness Champion* (1944). Lippincott was a publisher by profession; his family firm issued many children's books, including American editions of Arthur *Ransome's stories.

Listen With Mother A BBC radio programme for children under five, broadcast on weekdays from 1950 until 1982 and consisting

of *nursery rhymes and a story. For many years it was a regular feature of British middle-class family life, and the announcement which preceded the story, 'Are you sitting comfortably? Then I'll begin', became a household catchphrase.

lithography Originally a method of printing from a prepared stone, later a metal plate. From the mid-19th cent., it came into widespread use for reproducing *colour illustrations.

Edward *Lear was proud of the fact that his illustrated book of parrots (1832) 'was the first book of its kind drawn on stone in England of so large a size'.

Lithography in colour (chromolithography) was an early development, a different stone being prepared for each colour. Chromolithography was not, however, initially successful as a medium for good-quality children's book illustrations in England. Mid-Victorian colour lithography is generally condemned for being crude, garish, and oily, and few English artists approved of it—although Walter *Crane's *Flora's Feast, a masque of flowers* (1888) uses the medium with astonishing delicacy. The best coloured books for children used other processes (chiefly *wood engraving) until continental offset-lithographed books, notably French ones like Jean de Brunhoff's *Babar stories (1931 onwards), influenced fashion again in favour of the medium. In England, Kathleen Hale's *Orlando, The Marmalade Cat* (1939) and its sequels were among notable examples of the early use of offset lithography.

LITTLE, Jean (1932–) Canadian author. She has been partially sighted since birth, and many of her books feature protagonists who are resilient despite challenging circumstances. Her first novel, *Mine for Keeps* (1962), is about a girl with cerebral palsy. In *From Anna* (1972), a visually impaired girl moves from Germany to Canada just before the Second World War; its sequel, *Listen for the Singing*, won the *Governor General's Literary Award for Children's Literature in 1977. *Mama's Going to Buy You a Mockingbird*, about a boy coming to terms with his father's terminal illness, was the 1985 winner of the Canadian Library Association's Children's Book Award.

Little Arthur's History of England By 'M.C.', a popular children's *history book first published in 1835. Later editions identified it as the work of Lady Maria Callcott (1785–1842), the wife of artist Sir Augustus Callcott.

She had no children of her own, but explained in her introductory remarks: 'This little History was written for a real Arthur, and I have endeavoured to *write* it nearly as I would *tell* it to an intelligent child.' The book was couched in simple language.

A 'Century Edition' was published in 1936, since when the book has often been reprinted. Modern editions bring the story up to the present time; Lady Callcott's style has been retained, but her text has been somewhat modified in the light of 20th-cent. opinion.

Little Bear In readers by Else Holmelund *Minarik.

Little Black Princess, The (1905) By the Australian writer Jeannie Gunn (1870–1961), also known as Mrs Aeneas Gunn, this book was based on real events at a Northern Territory cattle station. Bett-Bett, the young niece of an Aborigine king, finds herself left behind after an attack by a hostile tribe. She is more or less adopted by 'the Missus' of the homestead (the author), but at the end she becomes homesick for her 'palace', the bush, and leaves for the freedom of the 'walkabout'.

The account of Bett-Bett's pranks and of the other Aborigines' customs, stories, and generally un-white behaviour is given humorously, but with great sympathy and acceptance of the fact that white practices seem equally irrational to Aborigines. Essentially, however, Bett-Bett stands for all childhood, black or white, and the book had lasting popularity. It was originally illustrated with photographs of the Aborigines and their artefacts.

Little Black Sambo, *The Story of* (1899) One of the most famous of all children's *picture books, written and illustrated by Helen *Bannerman and first published by Grant Richards of London. Little Black Sambo is 'a little black boy'; his mother is Black Mumbo and his father Black Jumbo. They give him a Red Coat, Blue Trousers, a Green Umbrella, and Purple Shoes. Going into the jungle he meets a series of tigers who threaten to eat him; he bribes them not to, giving them his clothes, shoes, and umbrella. The tigers then dispute as to who looks the most magnificent in Little Black Sambo's things and, while Little Black Sambo reclaims his possessions, they chase each other round a tree so fast that they become a pool of butter which is used by Black Mumbo to cook pancakes.

The combination of simple text and brightly coloured, almost crude drawings proved irresistible to children from the book's first appearance, but in the later 20th cent. *Little Black Sambo* came under fire for *racism, which led to its withdrawal from recommended reading lists for children. A new version of the book was published in 1996 under the title *The Story of Little Bubuji*, with illustrations by Fred Marcellino, and in 2003 Christopher Bing produced more racially sensitive illustrations for the original text. These have not, however, silenced all criticism.

Little Book for Little Children, A By 'T.W.', the first known book for children to contain traditional *nursery rhymes. Published very early in the 18th cent. (it has been variously dated at 1702 and 1712), it was designed to 'set down, in a plain and pleasant Way, Directions for Spelling, and other remarkable Matters'. It was illustrated with *woodcuts. It is one of the earliest English books to indicate an intention of entertaining children. The only known copy is in the British Library.

Another book of the same title was first published in 1660. This was the work of a *Puritan writer, Thomas White; it was printed as part of his *Manual for Parents*, and consisted of 'examples both ancient and modern of children eminent in holiness'. It was recommended to children by *Janeway in his *Token for Children*, which was probably modelled on it.

Little Bo-Peep A *nursery rhyme character. The rhyme was not recorded before the 19th cent., but 'Bo-peep' has long been the name of a game played by small children (*see* INFANT AMUSEMENTS), and the rhyming of 'sheep' with 'bo-peep' is found in an Elizabethan *ballad.

Little Briar-Rose *See* SLEEPING BEAUTY, THE.

Little Bush Maid, A (1910) The first of Mary Grant *Bruce's series of *Billabong books.

Little Colonel, The (1895) A novel by Annie Fellows *Johnston; the story of Lloyd Sherman, a small American girl living in the South after the Civil War. She is the granddaughter of Colonel Lloyd, an ex-Confederate soldier. At first the grandfather is outraged by Lloyd, rebuking her for playing with black children. But she soon wins him over and he comes to tolerate her black playmates.

Sarah Elbert observes in her introduction to a Garland reprint of *The Little Colonel* (1976) that the book shows the attitude of moderates to the South after the Civil War and portrays the New Woman (in the form of the unrestrainable Lloyd) doing her best to conquer the 'Negro Problem'. It was followed by many sequels, and in 1935 was filmed with Shirley *Temple in the title role.

Little drops of water, *Little grains of sand* The first two lines of the poem 'Little Things' by Julia A. *Carney.

Little Duke, The, *or, Richard the Fearless* (1854) The first children's *historical novel by Charlotte M. *Yonge, set in 10th-cent. Normandy. When his father is killed by the Duke of Flanders, the boy Richard becomes the Duke of Normandy; he is carried off by King Louis of France but manages to escape, and later holds the king's son Lothaire as hostage. The book is chiefly concerned with Richard's moral strength. Though at King Louis' court Lothaire treats him cruelly Richard later tames Lothaire with kindness and eventually pardons his father's murderer, Arnulf of Flanders.

Little Engine that Could, The (1945) A *picture book by 'Watty Piper' (a pen name for the publisher, Arnold Munk), illustrated by Lois *Lenski. It is the story of a small railway engine that helps another, and chugs, as it pants up the slope, 'I think I can—I think I can.'

Little Folks A British *magazine for small children which ran from 1871 until 1932. It included letters and poetry by readers among its written contributions of stories, puzzles, and riddles. Kate *Greenaway and Arthur *Rackham were among the artists who worked for it. In its later years the magazine supported a Little Folks Home 'for London's sick slum children'.

Little Grey Men, The (1942) A *fantasy written and illustrated by '*B.B.' (D. J. Watkins-Pitchford): the story of three gnomes named Sneezewort, Bald money, and Dodder, who live in Warwickshire and go in search of a missing brother. It won the *Carnegie Medal. While not precisely a children's book—the subtitle is 'A story for the young in heart'—it has something of the scope of *The* *Wind in the Willows*.

Little Grey Rabbit A character created by Alison *Uttley who, with other animals,

features in more than thirty British children's books, most of them illustrated by Margaret Tempest. The first, *The Squirrel, the Hare, and the Little Grey Rabbit*, was published in 1929. The books are somewhat reminiscent of those of Beatrix *Potter, but the stories, which quickly became very popular, are more muted in style and lack Beatrix Potter's sense of ironic comedy. Their chief strength derives from Alison Uttley's expertise in country lore. The series continued until her death in 1976, the last book being *Hare and the Rainbow* (1975).

Little Henry and His Bearer A story by Mrs *Sherwood, written during her years in India and first published in England in 1814. Henry, the orphan son of an East India Company officer, is brought up by a philanthropist who leaves him entirely to the care of a Hindu bearer, Boosy; the Hindu treats the boy with great affection. At the age of five Henry learns the Christian religion from a clergyman's daughter, who teaches him the doctrine of original sin. Henry begins to convert Boosy to Christianity, but is taken ill and dies with pious words upon his lips. Mrs Sherwood concludes the book by telling her readers: 'Little children in India, remember Henry L——, and *go and do likewise.*' The story was immensely popular in *evangelical circles; it had reached its thirtieth edition by 1840 and was translated into French, German, Hindustani, Sinhalese, and Chinese, remaining in print throughout the 19th cent.

Little House on the Prairie *See* WILDER, LAURA INGALLS.

Little Hunchback Horse, The Title of the English prose translation (by Ireene Wicker, 1946) of *Konyok Gorbunok* (1834), a 19th-cent. verse classic of Russian children's literature by Pyotr Ershov (1815–69); the story is sometimes referred to as *The Little Humpbacked Horse*.

A peasant whose grain is being mysteriously stolen at night sets each of his three sons to watch in turn. The third and stupidest, Ivan, sees the thief, a beautiful white horse; he agrees not to tell his father and is rewarded by being given three horses. Two of these are superb and are bought by the Tsar, Ivan becoming their groom at the palace; the third, Konyok Gorbunok, the Little Hunchback Horse, is three feet high with ears three feet long. He can talk (though only Ivan can hear him), and he becomes Ivan's friend and adviser. Ivan is soon the subject of jealousies and

intrigues at the palace, and when he finds a firebird's feather the Tsar sets him the task of fetching the bird itself. The remainder of the story is in fact a version of the traditional tale of *The *Firebird*, with Ivan being sent to fetch a mysterious princess and then to recover her ring and treasure chest from the bottom of the sea, which he accomplishes with the aid of the Tremendous Whale Fish.

Little Jack Horner *See* JACK HORNER.

Little John *See* ROBIN HOOD.

Little Lame Prince and his Travelling Cloak, The (1875) A novel by Mrs D. M. *Craik. Prince Dolor, lame from birth, is sent away by the Regent of his father's kingdom to a wilderness tower, where he lives a lonely life until a fairy godmother gives him a magic cloak. This acts like a magic carpet and takes him around the world. Eventually he becomes King and, when he tires of reigning, abdicates and disappears on the cloak's back. The book was one of the most popular *fantasies of the late Victorian period.

Little Lord Fauntleroy The first children's novel by Frances Hodgson *Burnett, published as a serial in **St Nicholas* from November 1885, and as a book by Scribner's of New York and *Warne of London in 1886, with illustrations by Reginald *Birch.

Seven-year-old Cedric Errol is brought up in New York City. Though he has long golden ringlets, wears a velvet knickerbocker suit, and calls his mother 'Dearest', he is no 'cissy', and his friends include a bootblack and a grocery-store keeper, Mr Hobbs. Suddenly he learns that he is the grandson of an English earl who disinherited his son (Cedric's father) because he married an American. The father has died and Cedric now becomes Lord Fauntleroy. His grandfather summons him to England, and he and 'Dearest' cross the Atlantic. At Dorincourt Castle the earl refuses to meet 'Dearest', and arranges for her to live some distance away. Cedric is allowed to see her now and then, but is given a room in the castle and is expected to spend most of his time with his grandfather. The old man is gouty and bad-tempered and has long been a tyrannical landlord, but Cedric's natural generosity and concern for the poor persuades him to begin to improve conditions on his estate. He gradually becomes very attached to the boy, and is horrified when he learns that Cedric is apparently not Lord Fauntleroy after all. An elder brother of Cedric's father

married, before his death, another American woman, who arrives at the castle with her supposed son as claimant to the title. In New York the bootblack and Mr Hobbs the grocer see a report of this in the newspapers, and discover that the rival Lord Fauntleroy is in fact an impostor. They sail to England, unmask the fraud, and see Cedric restored to his title.

The book originated in speculations by Mrs Burnett's younger son Vivian, who spent most of his childhood in America, about the character of the English aristocracy, and it was read to him while his mother was writing it. The character of Cedric was largely modelled on him—both Burnett boys called their mother 'Dearest'—and the Fauntleroy style of dress was that in which she had clothed them when they were Cedric's age.

Little Lord Fauntleroy earned wide praise on its publication; enthusiastic reviewers included Louisa M. *Alcott, and among its English admirers was Gladstone. Within twelve months 43,000 copies were in print in America and the book eventually made Mrs Burnett 100,000 dollars. The true Fauntleroy 'craze', however, did not begin until two years after publication, when Mrs Burnett adapted the book for the stage, and productions opened in New York and London. 'All over America,' writes Ann *Thwaite in her 1974 biography of Mrs Burnett, 'reluctant small boys were forced by their mothers into black velvet suits with lace collars'.

Among those dressed in Fauntleroy outfits in Britain were the infant Compton Mackenzie and A. A. *Milne. The book's potential for the cinema was soon exploited, notably in a 1921 version starring Mary Pickford, who doubled as Cedric and 'Dearest'.

Little Lord Fauntleroy does not deserve the ridicule it usually receives; Cedric, apart from his clothes and hair (which really have nothing to do with the story), is a likeable, resilient character, marked out chiefly by his philanthropy, egalitarianism, and pride at being American. However even in Mrs Burnett's own lifetime the book became (as Harvey *Darton has put it) an albatross that hung about her neck, obscuring the fact that she was the author of—among much else—excellent children's books such as *Sara Crewe* and (most of all) The *Secret Garden*. Her son Vivian was similarly burdened with the Fauntleroy tag, as was even the book's illustrator, Birch, who came to wish that he had never had any part in it.

Little Lower than the Angels, A (1987) A historical novel by Geraldine *McCaughrean, which takes its readers back—vividly, with atmosphere and excitement—to a medieval world of apprentices and travelling players, as young Gabriel runs away to join the performing troupe led by God (played by Master Garvey), and goes on the road with them and their Mysteries. As McCaughrean's debut novel, the book's language and storytelling would set a high standard that she would continue to match again and again, winning her the first of her several Whitbread Awards (*see* COSTA CHILDREN'S BOOK AWARD) and launching the career of one of the great children's writers of our times. The title comes from Psalm 8 in the *King James Bible*.

Little Man and the Little Maid, The *See* THERE WAS A LITTLE MAN.

Little Match Girl, The A story by Hans Christian *Andersen, published in 1848. A poverty-stricken little girl, walking barefoot through the snow, tries to warm herself for a few minutes by striking the matches that she hopes to sell. Each match brings her a vision, the last being of her dead grandmother, to whom she calls out: 'Take me with you!' The grandmother 'lifted the little girl in her arms and flew with her to where there is neither cold nor hunger nor fear: up to God'. Next morning the match girl's body is found frozen in the snow.

Little Meg's Children (1868) A story by Hesba *Stretton; the tale of a poor girl who after the death of her mother becomes head of the family. It was one of the most popular British *evangelical novels.

Little Mermaid, The A *fairy story by Hans Christian *Andersen. When she is fifteen years old, the youngest daughter of the mer-king rescues a young prince from shipwreck and falls in love with him. Hoping that he will return her love if she adopts human form, she visits the sea-witch and begs that her fishtail be changed into legs. The wish is granted, but at a terrible price: the legs will always be horribly painful to walk upon and the witch cuts out the mermaid's tongue in payment, so that she becomes dumb. She is also told that if the prince marries another she will immediately perish. The mermaid, now in human form, is found on the shore by the prince, who takes her to his palace and treats her with great affection, but he eventually marries another. The mermaid's body is dissolved into

foam, though her spirit does not perish as the witch had foretold: it becomes one of the 'daughters of air', who will gain immortality if they can perform good deeds or discover truly good children among human families.

Andersen published the story in 1836, and it was translated into English in 1846. The motif of a mermaid rescuing a human being from shipwreck appears in the *Pentamerone* and elsewhere in folk literature, while the detail of the mermaid gaining immortality if the prince marries her resembles *Undine* by *La Motte Fouqué, which was published in 1811 and to which *The Little Mermaid* corresponds in many points. Both stories seem to be descended from the French tale of the water-sprite Melusine, who marries a human knight. But *The Little Mermaid* is chiefly the product of Hans Andersen's own unhappiness in love.

Little Miss Muffet A *nursery rhyme character who was frightened by 'a big spider'. The rhyme has been ascribed to the physician and entomologist Thomas Muffet (also Moufet or Moffett) (1553–1604). However the nursery rhyme does not seem to have been printed before 1805, and it appears later than that date with other names attached, e.g., 'Little Miss Mopsey | Sat in the shopsey'. Lina Eckenstein, in *Comparative Studies in Nursery Rhymes* (1906), suggests that the rhyme may be related to the Cushion Dance that was associated with the May Day festival 'which at one time was the occasion for mating and marriage'.

Little Nicholas *See* PETIT NICOLAS, LE.

Littlenose A small boy in the Neanderthal age, hero of a series of stories by the British writer-illustrator John Grant. They were first told in *Jackanory*, and published in *Littlenose* (1968) and other books.

Little Orphan Annie An American *comic strip created in 1924, taking its title from a poem by James Whitcomb *Riley. It featured the adventures of a small heroine, fending for herself against the world. The strip, for many years written and drawn by Harold Gray (d. 1968), has been made into a stage and film musical, *Annie*.

Little Pear (1931) A story by Eleanor *Lattimore.

Little Pretty Pocket-Book, A, *Intended for the Instruction and Amusement of Little Master Tommy and Pretty Miss Polly* (c.1744) The first children's book published by John *Newbery. It was advertised in June 1744,

though no copy before the tenth edition (1760) survives.

The book is notable for preaching a mixture of 'Instruction with Delight', and its introduction, addressed 'to the Parents, Guardians, and Nurses in Great Britain and Ireland', admits to the influence of 'the Great Mr Locke'. Like *Locke's writings on education, it praises an active, outdoor, and uncosseted upbringing for children. There follow 'Two Letters from Jack the Giant-Killer', one to Master Tommy and one to Miss Polly, in suitably simple style, introducing the book and its accompanying ball and pincushion, 'The Use of which will infallibly make Tommy a good Boy, and Polly a good Girl'.

The first part of the book has the alphabet, 'The great A play, the little a play', etc., instead of page numbers, and is a miscellany of illustrated verses about games and pastimes (including cricket, base-ball, fives, birds-nesting, and Newbery's own newly-published educational game, Squares), each with a short moral or Rule of Life. This dissolves into *nursery rhymes, alphabet *nonsense verses, and four *fables, each with explanations from Jack the Giant-Killer. The next short section is a straightforward encouragement to duty and virtue. The book ends with some ornate verses on the seasons, some proverbs, and the customary advertisement for Newbery's other books.

There are comparatively good grounds for believing that John Newbery himself wrote and compiled the *Little Pretty Pocket Book*, since it was published before he had much time to make the acquaintance of the London writers he later employed. The book was a success: a second issue came out in 1747, and it was reprinted for at least twenty-three years after that date. There was an American printing by Isaiah *Thomas in 1787, and the book was also pirated by other booksellers. The 1767 edition has been reprinted in facsimile, introduced by M. F. Thwaite (1966).

Little Prince, The Written and illustrated by Antoine de Saint-Exupéry, and published in French as *Le Petit Prince* (1943). The first English translation—of many—was by Katherine Woods. An aviator, stranded in the Sahara Desert, encounters the Little Prince, a child who has descended to earth from the asteroid where he is ruler and sole inhabitant. The book is an allegorical-symbolical exploration of the human condition; it has proved very popular internationally since its first appearance. There is a stunning illustrated biography, *The Pilot and the Prince* (2014), by Peter *Sís.

Saint-Exupéry (1900–44) was a commercial pilot during the 1930s and wrote several books based on his experiences. During the Second World War he served with Free French forces in Morocco, and disappeared on a reconnaissance flight over the Mediterranean.

Little Princess, A See SARA CREWE.

Little Princess series (from 1986) A picture-book series written and illustrated by Tony *Ross, about a strong-willed child princess—aged about three—and her experiences of life, designed to parallel those of the books' young audience. The series began with *I Want My Potty* (about toilet training), and subsequent titles have included *I Want to Be* (1993; growing up), *I Want My Dinner!* (1995; good manners), *I Don't Want to Go to Hospital!* (2000; fear of hospital), *I Want My Dummy!* (2001; giving up dummies), *I Don't Want to Go to Bed!* (2003; bedtime), *I Want to Go Home!* (2006; moving house), *I Want My Light on!* (2007; fear of the dark), and many more, with Ross's style for illustrating the princess evolving along the way. The character has also graduated to books for slightly older readers, making her debut as 'the Not So Little Princess' in 2014.

Little Prudy See SOPHIE MAY.

Little Red Engine, The A series written by Diana *Ross, beginning with *The Little Red Engine Gets a Name* (1942), illustrated by *Lewitt and Him, in which the engine pulls a royal train and earns the name 'Royal Red'. Between 1946 and 1971 eight more titles were published, illustrated by Leslie Wood.

The books began as tales for Diana Ross's nephew John Scott, who lived above a railway cutting on a branch line.

Little Red Riding-Hood A story first recorded by *Perrault in his *Contes de ma mère l'Oye* (1697) as *Le Petit Chaperon rouge*. In Perrault's narrative, a pretty village girl, who bears her nickname on account of the red *chaperon* (hood) that she wears, is sent by her mother to take food to her sick grandmother, who lives in another village. As she is going through a wood, Little Red Riding-Hood meets a wolf who asks where she is going; when she tells him, the wolf runs ahead and eats up Red Riding Hood's grandmother. Pretending to be the old lady, the wolf lies in bed, and upon arriving at the house, Red Riding Hood is astonished at her grandmother's appearance and comments on the size of her

arms and legs and so forth. The dialogue between them concludes: '... "Grandmother, what great eyes you have!" "That's to see the better, my child." "Grandmother, what great teeth you have!" "That's for to eat you." And upon saying these words, this naughty Wolf threw himself upon Little Red Riding-Hood, and ate her.' Here, in Perrault's *Contes*, the story comes abruptly to an end. The moral which Perrault drew from the story is simply that young girls should be careful to whom they listen, for there are wolves of all sorts in wait for 'les jeunes Demoiselles'. Perrault's narrative, as well as this *moralité*, certainly emphasizes the story's sexual overtones.

No version of this story was recorded before Perrault's, though the resemblance has been noted between the concluding dialogue and a passage in the *Edda* in which Thor disguises himself as the bride-to-be of the giant Thrym in order to slaughter him ('The Lay of Thrym'). A clue to the story's origins may perhaps be found in the manuscript of Perrault's *Contes*, which is dated 1695 (*see* PERRAULT). Here, alongside the concluding dialogue between the wolf and the child, there is written in the margin an instruction to the storyteller to 'say these words [the wolf's] in a big voice to frighten the child as if the wolf were going to eat him'. The story is, in other words, a game which is meant to end with the storyteller pouncing on the listener. Andrew *Lang emphasized this in his edition of the *Contes* (1888): 'As it stands, the tale is merely meant to waken a child's terror and pity, and probably the narrator ends it by making a pounce, in the character of Wolf.'

A version of the story in *Grimm's collection, entitled *Little Red Cap*, continues the tale beyond the devouring of the child. The wolf, replete, falls fast asleep and snores so loudly that he alerts a huntsman who is passing and who comes into the cottage, suspects the worst, and snips open the wolf's stomach with a pair of scissors. Both Little Red Riding Hood and her Grandmother exit alive. The heroine then fills the wolf's stomach with stones so that when he tries to flee, he instead falls down dead. It is impossible to say whether this ending predates or postdates Perrault's version. Conceivably Perrault knew it, but omitted it as too absurd, or possibly it was invented by some later storyteller to meet children's demands that the Perrault story should end happily.

Little Red Riding Hood first appeared in English in *Histories, or Tales of Past Times*

(1729). Shortly afterwards the story began to be anthologized, appearing in a *primer of 1744 published by Benjamin *Collins, entitled *A Pretty Book for Children,* and also in The *Top Book of All* (1760). In 1803 it was made into a 'Dramatic Farce' by Charles Dibdin the younger, who presented it at Sadler's Wells under the title *Red Riding Hood; or, The Wolf Robber.*

Sir Henry *Cole's retelling (1843) in his *Home Treasury* series, which sets the story in the New Forest of England, prints the Perrault conclusion, but remarks that 'it is a grievous one, which most children dislike', and offers an alternative end in which Red Riding Hood's father and some faggot-makers hear her screams, rush in just in time, and kill the wolf. Madame Clara de *Chatelain's *Merry Tales for Little Folk* (1868) provided an ending in which the wolf is about to spring when he is stung by a wasp; a bird then warns a huntsman, who kills the wolf with an arrow. Some such happy ending appears in most of the 20th-cent. retellings of the tale. On the other hand many 19th-cent. versions retain Perrault's grim ending, e.g. *Tabart's and *Harris's *The history of Little Red Riding-Hood, in verse* (1808) and Dinah Maria *Craik's version in *The *Fairy Book* (1863), both of which follow Perrault exactly. A number of *chapbook versions conclude with the killing of the wolf *after* he has eaten Little Red Riding Hood, who is not rescued. The most gruesome ending of all is that found in a 19th-cent. Breton version recorded by Andrew *Lang in the notes to his *Perrault,* in which 'the wolf puts the grandmother in the pot, and her blood in bottles, and makes the unconscious child eat and drink her ancestress! The cock or the robin redbreast warns her in vain, and she is swallowed'.

Little Savage, The (1848–9) A children's novel by Captain *Marryat, completed after his death by his son Frank. It is the story of Frank Henniker, brought up on a remote island by a wicked old seaman, Edward Jackson, who eventually dies, leaving Frank the contented master of the place. He is finally taken to England by the widow of a missionary.

Littlest One A small boy in poems by the British writer Marion St John Webb, published in *The Littlest One* (1914) and later volumes. The verses anticipate many of the characteristics of the children's poems of A. A. *Milne.

Little Tim A series of eleven picture books by Edward *Ardizzone, beginning with *Little Tim*

and the Brave Sea Captain (1936). In this first book, Little Tim is desperate to be a sailor, but he is much too young. Undaunted, he stows away on a ship. He is discovered and put to work, and storms and shipwreck ensue. In each of the subsequent books, Little Tim has another sailing adventure. All the pictures are rendered in Ardizzone's instantly recognizable style, with ink line and delicate washes, mixing colour and black-and-white illustration.

Tim All Alone (1956) was the inaugural winner of the *Kate Greenaway Medal. The series has been made into an audio collection voiced by Stephen Fry.

Little Toot A tug-boat in stories by Hardie *Gramatky. His adventures take him across the United States and to Europe.

Little White Bird, The (1902) A novel by J. M. *Barrie which contains the first sketches for *Peter Pan. The narrator is 'a gentle, whimsical, lonely old bachelor', whose ambition is to have a son. He meets a penniless young couple whose own son David becomes a substitute in his affections. He explains to David that 'all children in our part of London were once birds in the Kensington Gardens; and that the reason there are bars on nursery windows and a tall fender by the fire is because very little people sometimes forget that they no longer have wings, and try to fly away through the window or up the chimney'. The central chapters of the book tell the story of one such child, Peter Pan, who 'escaped from being a human when he was seven days old . . . and flew back to the Kensington Gardens'.

The Peter Pan chapters of *The *Little White Bird* were reissued in 1906 as *Peter Pan in Kensington Gardens,* with colour plates by Arthur *Rackham; this was the book that first made Rackham's work famous. It should not be confused with *Peter and Wendy (1911), Barrie's novelization of the play *Peter Pan.*

Little White Horse, The (1946) A *Carnegie Medal-winning novel by Elizabeth Goudge (1900–84), which tells the story of orphaned Maria Merryweather and her new life in the West Country with her uncle and guardian at the mysterious Moonacre Manor, complete with magical beasts, eccentric people, lost love, and self-sacrifice. Red-headed Maria is a fantastic heroine, strong and good, with a moral compass that never fails. Deeply descriptive—and no longer an easy read—it repays the diligent reader with a story that can resonate through a whole lifetime. Once J. K.

*Rowling had publicly declared this to be her favourite childhood book, it returned from relative obscurity to its rightful place as an acknowledged classic. It was adapted into a film called *The Secret of Moonacre* (2008).

Little Wideawake (1875 until 1892) A *magazine for young children edited for the publishers *Routledge by Mrs Sale Barker, whose verses Kate *Greenaway illustrated for her *Birthday Book*. Among poems and stories about nature, pets, toys, and family life were some in large print for children to read for themselves. The magazine was founded in the same year as the American periodical *Wide Awake*, but was not related to it other than in the title, which was the family nickname for the editor's son.

Little Women, or *Meg, Jo, Beth and Amy* (1868) A novel by Louisa M. *Alcott, an outstanding achievement of 19th-cent. American literature, and the first children's novel written in the US to have become an enduring classic.

The book describes a few months in the lives of the March sisters. Sixteen-year-old Meg is the belle of the family; Beth, who is thirteen, is very quiet and shy; twelve-year-old Amy (who draws well), regards herself as 'a most important person'. It is the character of fifteen-year-old Jo, however, which really marks the book. She is tall, thin, coltish, and unfeminine:

'I hate to think I've got to grow up, and be Miss March, and wear long gowns, and look as prim as a China-aster! It's bad enough to be a girl, anyway, when I like boys' games and work and manners!'

The girls' mother, Marmee, runs a very happy home, but there is no money to spare, Mr March having been impoverished some years earlier as a result of helping a friend. He himself is now away from home as an army chaplain in the Civil War.

The girls are befriended by Theodore Laurence, known as 'Laurie', the grandson of a rich old gentleman next door. Meg and Jo go out to work to help support the family; Jo also organizes splendid melodramas which the four sisters perform for their friends. Old Mr Laurence gives Beth her own piano; Laurie's tutor, John Brooke, falls in love with Meg; and Beth nearly dies from an attack of scarlet fever. Jo has a short story accepted and printed by a newspaper, and hopes to begin a career as a writer. At the end of the book the girls are reunited with their father just as Beth recovers and Meg becomes engaged to John.

The book was begun at the suggestion of a publisher's editor, Thomas Niles of Roberts Brothers in Boston, Mass. Louisa Alcott wrote in her journal:

May, 1868. Father saw Mr Niles about a fairy book. Mr N. wants a *girls'* story, and I begin 'Little Women'. Marmee, Anna, and May [her mother and surviving sisters] all approve of my plan. So I plod away, though I don't enjoy this sort of thing. Never liked girls or knew many, except my sisters; but our queer plays and experiences may prove interesting.

August 26th. Proofs of whole book came. It reads better than I expected. Not a bit sensational, but simple and true, for we really lived most of it; and if it succeeds that will be the reason of it.

Little Women was published by Roberts Brothers a few weeks later, with illustrations by May Alcott. Within a short time the first printing had sold out, and Niles encouraged Louisa Alcott to produce a sequel that could be published in the spring. She began to write it at the beginning of November, noting that 'I can do a chapter a day'. As to the plot: 'Girls write to ask who the little women marry, as if that was the only end and aim of a woman's life. I *won't* marry Jo to Laurie to please any one.' The completed manuscript of the second part reached the publisher on 1 January 1869, and was quickly printed.

Little Women is outstanding for its portrayal of the tensions and delights of family life. There is a special interest for historians of children's literature in its account of the March sisters' reading-matter, which includes *Ivanhoe* (*see* SCOTT, SIR WALTER), *The *Heir of Redclyffe*, the stories of Maria *Edgeworth, and *Undine*. The book also makes frequent reference to *The *Pilgrim's Progress*, the sisters' attempts to make themselves better girls being compared to the journey of Bunyan's Christian. The model for the story was probably *The *Daisy Chain* (1856) by Charlotte M. *Yonge. In its turn, *Little Women* inspired a whole genre of *family stories, especially in America. There have been many film adaptations of *Little Women*, notably in 1933 (with Katharine Hepburn as Jo), 1949 (with the sisters played by June Allyson, Margaret O'Brien, Janet Leigh, and Elizabeth Taylor), and 1994 (Winona Ryder, Trini Alvarado, Kirsten Dunst, and Claire Danes).

In writing *Little Women*, Alcott found all the material at hand in recollections of her own childhood. Amy, Jo, Beth, and Meg are portraits of the four Alcott sisters, May, Louisa, Elizabeth, and Anna. 'Marmee', the March

children's mother, was copied from Mrs Alcott, while the failure of Bronson Alcott to provide for his family was recast by Louisa as the March father's having lost all his money 'in trying to help an unfortunate friend'. Laurie was partly suggested by a childhood friend and partly by a young Pole, Ladislas Wisniewski, with whom Louisa had a mild flirtation during her European trip of 1865.

Little Wooden Horse, *Adventures of the* (1938) A story by Ursula Moray *Williams.

LIVELY (Greer), Penelope (Margaret) (1933–) British novelist who was born in Cairo and spent much of her childhood in Egypt before her university education at St Anne's College, Oxford.

She began to write when her children were growing up, and from the first showed herself to be preoccupied with the relationship between history and the present. *Astercote* (1970) begins with a village being destroyed by the Black Death. *The Whispering Knights* (1971) has the same kind of plot, and suffers from similar faults; it reads, as John Rowe *Townsend has said, 'almost like a parody of early Garner'. Other books published around this time are *The Wild Hunt of Hagworthy* (1971) and *The Driftway* (1972). Though these early books have weaknesses which are apparent to the adult reader, they proved very popular with children.

Next came a pair of far more accomplished novels, *The *Ghost of Thomas Kempe* (1973) and *The *House in Norham Gardens* (1974), two very different treatments of their author's perennial preoccupation, the effect of the past on the present. She herself has said of this theme in her novels: 'Children need to sense that we live in a permanent world that reaches away behind and ahead of us... and that—above all—people evolve during their own lives.'

The Ghost of Thomas Kempe won Lively the *Carnegie Medal. She followed it and *The House in Norham Gardens* with two other past-and-present novels: *Going Back* (1975) and *A Stitch in Time* (1976). *Boy Without a Name* (1975) was the first of a number of short novels with historical settings that she has written for younger readers. Her least characteristic novel is *The Voyage of QV 66* (1978), a *fantasy in which the human population of Earth has been evacuated. *The Revenge of Samuel Stokes* (1981) returns to its author's past-and-present motif. Besides

writing prolifically for children, Lively has produced several novels for adults (including a Booker prize winner); these, too, tend to be concerned with the same theme.

Lizzie Dripping Heroine of stories by Helen *Cresswell.

Load of Unicorn, The (1959) A novel by Cynthia *Harnett.

LOBEL, Anita (1934–) Polish-born American author and illustrator of titles including the alphabet book *Alison's Zinnia* (1990), *Lena's Sleep Sheep* (2013), and two picture books about Nini the cat. Lobel collaborated with her husband, Arnold *Lobel, on *A Treeful of Pigs* (1979), *The Rose in My Garden* (1984), and others. Their *On Market Street* (1981) was a Caldecott Honor Book (*see* CALDECOTT MEDAL). Lobel's memoir of her childhood in wartime Poland, *No Pretty Pictures* (1998), was a National Book Award finalist and a Sydney Taylor Honor Award winner.

LOBEL, Arnold (1933–87) American illustrator and author whose books for small children display an idiosyncratic sense of humour and an outstanding ability to create comic characters with just a few words and pictures. These include *Frog and Toad are Friends* (1970), the first in a delightful set of easy-read stories about the friendship between the cheerful, extrovert Frog and the melancholic, self-absorbed Toad. His illustrations to other writers' work include a version of Sarah Catherine Martin's original *Mother Hubbard poem (1968), as well as work by Charlotte *Zolotow, Edward *Lear, and others. He won the *Caldecott Medal in 1981 for his *Fables*. He was married to Anita *Lobel.

Lob Lie-by-the-Fire, *or the Luck of Lingborough, and other tales* (1874) By Juliana Horatia *Ewing, with illustrations by *Cruikshank, this book takes its title from a short story in which a gipsy child is adopted and reared by two spinsters, owners of Lingborough Hall; they name him John Broom. He is brought up on tales of Lob, a *brownie-like creature 'who worked at night that others might be idle by day'. John, a wild, though good-natured child, runs away to sea before returning to Lingborough, where at first he hides, only coming out at night to perform Lob-like good deeds. He is finally discovered and welcomed back delightedly. The book,

which was reissued in 1883 with new illustrations by Randolph *Caldecott, was one of Mrs Ewing's most successful.

LOCKE, Elsie (Violet) (1912–2001) New Zealand author who wrote several children's novels set at various periods of her country's history, for example, *The Runaway Settlers* (1965). She also produced non-fiction for children, including several books of New Zealand history.

LOCKE, John (1632–1704) Philosopher and educationalist who influenced a number of 18th-cent. writers and publishers for children with his belief that instruction is best combined with entertainment and that the child learns quickest when it is enjoying itself. Locke was educated at Oxford and subsequently taught in that university before leaving England for Holland because of his supposed complicity in the plots of his patron, Shaftesbury. He returned in 1689 when William of Orange came to the throne, and held a government post. In 1690 there appeared his *Essay concerning Human Understanding*, which in effect founded the empirical school of English philosophy. In 1693 he published *Some Thoughts Concerning Education*, which, despite the modesty of its title, was a treatise on every aspect of the upbringing of children. Locke's chief points were:

1. Children should not be coddled, but should be allowed to develop robust health and run about in the fresh air.
2. They should learn self-discipline at an early age. Corporal punishment should only be used in extreme circumstances, but the child should be praised when it does well and made to feel ashamed if it errs. The parents must themselves set an example of good behaviour at all times.
3. Children should as far as possible be allowed to choose their own occupations: 'The fittest Time for Children to learn any Thing, is, when their Minds are in tune, and well disposed to it.'
4. Children should, at an early age, be given the rudiments of *religious instruction, but they should not be told tales about 'Sprites and Goblins' until they are old enough not to be frightened by them.
5. As soon as they can talk, children should begin to learn to read, but they should regard this as an amusement rather than a task. Locke advocates educational toys with letters inscribed on them to help children to learn.
6. After the child can read it should be given 'some easy pleasant Book suited to his Capacity . . . wherein the entertainment, that he finds, might draw him on . . . and yet not such as should fill his head with perfectly useless trumpery, or lay the principles of Vice and Folly.' Locke suggests *Aesop as the book best suited to this purpose.
7. He suggests that a tutor or 'Governor' be employed by families to teach their children.
8. He gives advice on the teaching of writing and drawing, and suggests that Latin be taught not by grammatical rules but by Latin conversations and by translation. The child should also learn 'Geography, Astronomy, Chronology, Anatomy, besides some parts of History'. He recommends that some manual trade or skill be learnt by young people, e.g. gardening, woodworking, or metalwork. He concludes the book by pointing out that, despite all his suggestions, there can be scarcely two children who should be brought up by exactly the same method.

Some Thoughts Concerning Education was reprinted again and again during the 18th cent. It seems to have had immediate effect, for what appears to have been the first native English alphabet-book designed to amuse as well as instruct, *A *Play-Book for Children*, was published in the year after the first edition of Locke's treatise appeared, 1694. Locke's attitudes may also be seen reflected in some of the children's publications of John *Newbery (e.g. his *Little Lottery-Book for Children*, which resembles Locke's lottery-ball for teaching the alphabet) and other London booksellers of the mid-18th cent. See further Samuel F. Pickering, *John Locke and Children's Books in Eighteenth Century England* (University of Tennessee Press, 1982).

Locke never married or had children. His ideas were based on his observation of families he had known or lived with and on his relations with his own father, who, though stern in Locke's infancy, had relaxed as the son grew older, and 'lived perfectly with him as a friend'. The father once begged the son's pardon for having struck him in boyhood.

LOCKHART, E. (Emily Jenkins) (1967–) American author of novels for teenagers whose books all feature strong female characters and can be seen as antidotes to the superficiality of much modern girl-centric fiction.

The Boyfriend List: 15 Guys, 11 Shrink Appoint-ments, 4 Ceramic Frogs And Me, Ruby Oliver (2005) introduced Ruby Oliver, with her sharp-as-tacks voice and her compulsion to make lists, and led to three equally hilarious sequels. The multi-award-winning *The Disreputable History of Frankie Landau-Banks* (2008) tells the tale of an independent girl who really won't take no for an answer. In 2014 she published *We Were Liars*, her most accomplished and most gripping work to date. Jenkins also writes for young children and adults under her own name.

Lockhart, Sally *See* RUBY IN THE SMOKE.

LOFTING, Hugh (John) (1886–1947) Author and illustrator of the *Doctor Dolittle books. He kept many pet animals as a child, and had a private zoo in his mother's linen cupboard. In 1916 he joined the Irish Guards (his mother was of Irish descent) and soon went to Flanders.

In the trenches he watched the sufferings of the regimental horses, which were destroyed if they became injured. He afterwards wrote of this:

If we made the animals take the same chances we did ourselves, why did we not give them similar attention when wounded? But obviously to develop horse-surgery as good as that of our Casualty Clearing Station would necessitate a knowledge of horse language . . .

From this notion the Doctor Dolittle books were born. They first appeared on paper in the form of letters to his children, Elizabeth and Colin. *The Story of Doctor Dolittle* was published in 1922 and was a great success, Lofting being compared in stature to Lewis *Carroll.

He wrote a number of children's books beside the Dolittle series. *The Story of Mrs Tubbs* (1923) and *Tommy, Tilly, and Mrs Tubbs* (1936) are *picture books for small children describing the misfortunes of a very old lady, who is helped by animal and child friends. *Porridge Poetry* (1924) is a book of comic verse for children, somewhat in the style of *Lear, *Belloc, and Carroll. *Noisy Nora* (1929) is a prose *cautionary tale about a child who is a noisy eater. *The Twilight of Magic* (1930) is a *fantasy about two children and a magic seashell. *Gub Gub's Book* (1932) grew out of the Dolittle stories, and is a comic 'Encyclopaedia of food' supposedly written by the Doctor's pig-friend, an insatiable eater. Lofting also wrote one book for adults, *Victory for the Slain* (1942), an anti-war poem.

Lofting's writings are deeply influenced by his experiences in the First World War, and his overtly comic manner scarcely conceals an underlying melancholy and even despair. He is also concerned to champion the eccentric individual against the masses; Edward *Blishen wrote of him, in a 1968 monograph: 'No one else has set out [in children's fiction] . . . to create a hero, and a notion of heroism, that is radical, pacifist, and profoundly opposed to common ideas of conventional respectability.'

LONDON, Jack (1876–1916) American short story writer and novelist. Two of his most popular books, *The Call of the Wild* (1903) and *White Fang* (1906), both of which have dogs as their central figures, have been favourites with older children.

London Bridge Subject of a celebrated *nursery rhyme that is possibly of great antiquity, and has parallels elsewhere in Europe. The rhyme, which refers to the bridge being 'broken down', suggests various ways in which it may be repaired—'With wood and clay . . . bricks and mortar . . . iron and steel . . . silver and gold'—but none of these is judged to be effective. Finally it is determined that a man shall be set to 'watch all night'. The rhyme is often accompanied by a game in which two children form a bridge with their arms and the others pass underneath as quickly as possible, before the 'bridge' collapses on them.

The implication of the rhyme is that the bridge cannot be made to stand up by ordinary physical means and that a human being must be set to watch it ceaselessly, to ward off the supernatural influences which are responsible for pulling it down. This seems to reflect the ancient superstition, which was still current in Germany in the 19th cent., that if a bridge proved difficult to build it would remain secure if a live person were walled up in the foundations, so as to act as 'watchman'. Legend has it that the bridge at Rosporden in Brittany would not stand until a four-year-old boy was immured in it.

London cries *See* CRIES OF LONDON.

Lone Piners A group of young people in books by Malcolm *Saville.

LONGFELLOW, H. W. *See* HIAWATHA.

Long John Silver In *Treasure Island.*

Looking-Glass for Children, A *See* CHEAR.

Looking-Glass for the Mind, The A collection of *moral tales, freely translated by Richard *Johnson from Arnaud *Berquin's *L'Ami des enfans*; it was first published in 1787 by Elizabeth *Newbery. A second edition of 1792 included *wood engravings by John *Bewick, brother of Thomas. By 1800, 20,000 copies had been sold, and editions continued to appear during the first half of the 19th cent.

LORD, John Vernon (1939-) A distinguished British illustrator and author, and Professor Emeritus at the University of Brighton, where he has taught illustration for over fifty years. His best known work is probably *The *Giant Jam Sandwich*, published in 1970, now a modern classic still in print over forty years later. He describes the role of the narrative illustrator whose main function is to heighten, represent, and interpret the meaning of the text for the pleasure of the reader. His exquisite and complex illustrations to classics such as *Aesop's Fables*, Edward *Lear's *Nonsense Verse*, and Lewis Carroll's *Alice in Wonderland* and *The *Hunting of the Snark* have now become treasured collectors' items. His distinctive illustrative style involves intricate pen-and-ink drawings, creating texture with fine cross-hatching or parallel lines built up with a ruler. His work is often geometric, with an emphasis on vertical and diagonal grid structures. As well as illustrating others' work, John Vernon Lord is the author-illustrator of many picture books of his own.

Lord of the Flies (1954) A novel by the British author William Golding (1911–93). Suggested by *Coral Island*, it gives a horrifying picture of what might happen if boys really were stranded on a desert island. *Lord of the Flies* was the book which made Alan *Garner want to become a writer.

Lord of the Rings, The (1954–5) A hugely influential, epic, high-fantasy novel by J. R. R. *Tolkien that was conceived as a sequel to *The *Hobbit* (1937), but grew far beyond that book both in size and scope as it gained in seriousness of purpose and depth of background as Tolkien was writing. First published in three volumes, it was only collected into a single volume in 1968. *The Fellowship of the Ring* (1954) begins the story of Frodo the Hobbit, the One Ring of Sauron, and the battle between good and evil that will settle the fate of the whole of Middle-Earth and all its denizens—humans, elves, dwarves, and all. In *The Two Towers* (1954) the fellowship

between races that had been formed in order to destroy the Ring is broken, and Frodo and Sam continue alone, while *The Return of the King* (1955) brings to a close the stories of all the main characters, with sacrifice, battles, and endings both happy and sad.

Tolkien did not intend *The Lord of the Rings* to be read by children, but despite that it is best read early, as in spirit it remains in many ways a children's book—Tolkien's friend and colleague, C. S. *Lewis observed that in it Tolkien had successfully revived medieval Romance, a genre whose appeal has always been to all ages. Companion books include *The Silmarillion* (published posthumously, 1977), the history of the First Age of Middle-Earth, and *The History of Middle-Earth*, starting with *The Book of Lost Tales* (1983), both of which were completed by Tolkien's son, Christopher.

Of the many adaptations in many media, the film cycle directed by Peter Jackson (2001-3) is worth singling out, a great popular and prize-winning success, visually powerful and rich in special-effects technology, albeit not universally loved by the book's more die-hard fans.

Lord Randal A *ballad which, in different forms, has been known to many generations of children. A young man (Lord Randal or Rendal) tells his mother that he 'fain would lie down', for he is mortally sick after eating a dish of poisoned food (in most texts, boiled eels) that was prepared for him by his sweetheart. Versions of the ballad, dating back at least to the 16th cent., have been found throughout Europe.

Lord Snooty and his Pals A comic strip in *Beano*.

LORENZINI, Carlo *See* COLLODI.

Lost and Found (2005) A touching picture book by Oliver *Jeffers about a lost penguin who just needs a friend, and finds one. Its captivating yet simple storyline and Jeffers's now familiar illustrations make it one of his best-known works. In 2006, it won the Nestlé Smarties Book Prize Gold Award, the *Blue Peter Book of the Year, and was shortlisted for the *Kate Greenaway Medal. Adapted for both film and stage, it won Best Animated Film at the 2009 BAFTA British Academy Children's Awards.

Lost Prince, The The last children's book by Frances Hodgson *Burnett, published in 1915. Marco Loristan and his father are exiles from

the mid-European country of Samavia. Like many of their fellow-countrymen they preserve the tradition that somewhere there lives a Lost Prince, descendant of the true kings of Samavia, who will one day reveal himself, claim the throne, and end the bloodshed caused by wars between the rival factions of usurpers.

The book contains some of Mrs Burnett's best character drawing, but the excitement is diminished by her inability to keep from the reader, even in the very first pages, the fact that Marco and his father are themselves the 'missing' royal family. Her chief concern in writing the story is to show how Marco's royal bearing and authority are immediately noticeable to all who encounter him, even if he is not aware of them himself. The book was reissued by Heinemann in 1966 with an abridged text.

Lost World, The (1912) A classic adventure story by Sir Arthur Conan *Doyle, frequently filmed and adapted for radio, which tells of an expedition led by Professor Challenger to find a plateau in South America where rumour says that prehistoric creatures still survive. Conan Doyle took the idea that dinosaurs had survived into the present from Jules Verne's *Journey to the Centre of the Earth*. He had been reading about the exploration of a remote part of Bolivia, and set his story there, adding in ape-men at war with a tribe of humans, a villain who betrays the expedition, hair-raising escapes, death-defying heroics, and eventual escape back to London, all of it adding up to a rip-roaring read that refuses to age.

LOTHROP (Stone), Harriet M. (Mulford) Harriet(1844–1924) Wife of the American children's publisher Daniel Lothrop of Boston, Harriet wrote many juvenile books, among them, *The *Five Little Peppers and How They Grew* (1881).

Lovechild, Mrs (Louisa; Solomon) Pseudonyms of Lady Eleanor *Fenn.

Love You Forever See MUNSCH, ROBERT.

LOWRY, Lois (1937–) American author of more than thirty books for children, who never shies away from difficult or controversial subjects, and who emphasizes the importance of friends and family in dealing with life. Set in a future dystopia, *The *Giver* (1993), with its message of challenging authority, provokes strong reactions and has been a *banned book, yet also a class reader. There are three

loose sequels in *Gathering Blue* (2000), *Messenger* (2004), and *Son* (2012). *Number the Stars* (1989) is set in Denmark during the German occupation and centres on efforts to rescue Danish Jews from deportation and death.

LUBEGA, Bonnie (1929–) Ugandan author and journalist; he has written several popular children's books, including *The Great Animal Land* (1971), about the East Africa National Parks.

LUCAS, David (1966–) An English picture-book creator known for his distinctive illustrative style and magical storytelling. His debut picture book, *Halibut Jackson* (2003), was highlighted as one of the top ten children's books in 2004 by Child Magazine and Publisher's Weekly. Lucas attributes his influences to medieval and folk art and, in particular, to an appreciation of pattern, which is evident in much of his work. His narratives also reflect his interest in *fairy tales and oral folk tradition, as many of his picture books feature modern allegorical tales such as *The Robot and the Bluebird* (2003), with many also focusing on food, e.g., *Nutmeg* (2005), *Cake Girl* (2009), and *Grendel: A Cautionary Tale about Chocolate* (2013). His brother, John Lucas (1978–), is a *young adult novelist.

LUCAS, E. V. (Edward Verrall) (1868–1938) Prolific and wide-ranging British author, journalist, and contributor to *Punch*. He edited a number of books for children, including *A Book of Verses for Children* (1897), *Old Fashioned Tales* (1905), and *Forgotten Tales of Long Ago* (1906). He also wrote introductions to reissues of children's classics, such as the 1932 edition of *Bevis* by Richard Jefferies, and from him came the suggestion that E. H. *Shepard illustrate the children's writings of A. A. *Milne.

lullaby A song or chant designed to soothe babies or young children to sleep. A Roman lullaby, 'lalla, lalla, lalla', is quoted in the *Oxford Dictionary of Nursery Rhymes*. In one of the Coventry Corpus Christi Plays (probably mid-15th cent.) there is recorded the refrain which has since become known as part of the 'Coventry Carol':

> Lully, lulla, thow litell tine child,
> By by, lully lullay, thow litell tyne child,
> By by, lully lullay!

The words 'by by' or 'bye bye', which provide the second element of 'lullaby', are also part of the repertory of lulling sounds, and hence

a child's name for sleep. 'Lullaby' had become a common word by Shakespeare's day.

Many medieval verses associated with the birth of Christ take the form of a lullaby, e.g. 'Lullay, my liking, my dere son, my sweting'. On the other hand most lullabies known to modern children and found in collections of *nursery rhymes are probably no more than a few centuries old. The most celebrated of them, 'Hush-a-bye, baby, on the tree top', is said to have been composed by an immigrant to America in the 17th cent. who observed the Native American habit of hanging birch-bark cradles from the branches of trees. This rhyme appeared in one of the earliest nursery rhyme collections, *Mother Goose's Melody*. Among the rhymes collected by Joseph *Ritson in *Gammer Gurton's Garland* (1783 or 1784) were 'Bye, O my baby' and 'Bye, baby bunting'.

LUMSDEN, J., and Son (*fl.* 1790–1840) Glasgow publishers of juvenile *chapbooks.

LURIE, Alison (1926–) Academic and novelist who was born in Chicago. Besides her many acclaimed adult novels, Lurie has written significant studies of children's literature, in particular *Don't Tell the Grown-Ups* (1990), subtitled 'Subversive Children's Literature'; and *Boys and Girls Forever* (2003), whose essays look particularly at the extent to which writers for children are people still dealing in some way with their own childhoods, her study spanning Louisa May *Alcott to Salman Rushdie. She has also compiled several collections of *fairy tales and myths (many in her own retellings), and with Justin G. Schiller co-edited the 73-volume *Garland Library of Classics of Children's Literature 1621–1932*.

LYNCH, Patricia (Nora) (1898–1972) Irish author who wrote nearly fifty books for children, published between 1925 and 1967. One of the best known is *The Turf-Cutter's Donkey* (1934), in which two poor children find themselves involved with leprechauns and all sorts of magical happenings. In this and many other books, Patricia Lynch uses magic without restraint or rules, sometimes to the detriment of the story.

LYNCH, P. J. (Patrick James) (1962–) Acclaimed Irish illustrator and author, who achieved huge international success with *The Christmas Miracle of Jonathan Toomey* (1995), written by Susan Wojciechowski, which tells the story of a gloomy woodcutter who gradually recovers his ability to find joy in life, and which was subsequently made into a film. He has twice been a winner of the *Kate Greenaway Medal, and his work is realistic and full of emotion—something that gels perfectly with his favourite subject: *fairy tales. Hans Christian *Andersen's *The Snow Queen* and *The Steadfast Tin Soldier* (1986), as well as *East o' the Sun and West o' the Moon* (1992), are perfect examples of his work. He also creates posters for Opera Ireland and the Abbey Theatre and has designed four sets of Christmas stamps for An Post (the Irish postal service). In 2016 he was named Ireland's fourth *Laureate na nÓg.

Lyra Belacqua *See* His Dark Materials.

Mabinogion, The A group of Welsh tales, known by this title since the first translation into English, by Lady Charlotte Guest, of the medieval Welsh manuscript *The Red Book of Hergest*.

The prose tellings collected in the *Red Book* and in other existing 14th- and 15th-cent. manuscripts perhaps date in composition from the 11th cent. onwards; but they had an earlier oral history and much of their material derives from ancient mythology. The best known part of the collection is the tale of the hero Pryderi, son of Pwyll, Prince of Dyfed. Other separate tales in the collection include some in which King *Arthur appears. There are also three Arthurian tales fairly closely related to French romances of the same period. Other stories in *The Mabinogion*, again different in kind, are those of Lludd and Llefelys, the Dream of Maxen (the historical Roman Emperor Maximus), and the Dream of Rhonabwy.

Lady Charlotte Guest's translation became a classic. Partly because of the interest aroused by Tennyson's use of it for *The Idylls of the King*, it was reissued in 1877 in a more popular edition, with less scholarly apparatus, and shortly afterwards versions more explicitly for children began to appear. Sidney *Lanier produced *The Boy's Mabinogion* (1881) as a companion book to his *Boy's Froissart* and *King Arthur*. In his introduction he judged the tales 'not so rich as the Arabian Nights, though they are more vigorous, and their fascination is of a more manful quality'. He also made some odd and unfavourable comparisons between Celtic literary exaggeration—an example being the warrior whose red beard covered the twenty-eight rafters of Arthur's hall—and English restraint and liking for law and order.

Towards the end of the 19th cent. modernized texts of the *Mabinogion* also became available for Welsh readers and versions for children followed, among them a penny booklet of *The Dream of Rhonabwy* published in 1901 by O. M. Edwards. Notable among the many 20th-cent. English retellings of parts of *The Mabinogion* and associated stories were Padriac *Colum's *The Island of the Mighty* (1924), Kenneth Morris's *The Book of the Three Dragons* (1930), and Robert *Nye's *Taliesin* (1967). Alan *Garner used the *Mabinogion* tale of Lleu Llaw Gyffes as the basis of *The *Owl Service* (1967) and Lloyd *Alexander was inspired by his reading of the Welsh stories to write his *Prydain Cycle* (1964–8).

MACAULAY, David (1946–) American author and illustrator of books for children. He is best known for his witty graphic non-fiction books, which have been translated into several languages. After moving with his family from Lancashire, UK, to New Jersey at the age of eleven, Macaulay started to draw seriously. He studied architecture at Rhode Island School of Design and later worked as a teacher. In 1973 his first book *Cathedral*, a guide to the construction of a fictional cathedral, received a Caldecott Honor (*see* CALDECOTT MEDAL). He went on to receive the same honour for *Castle* (1977), and the Caldecott Medal for *Black and White* (1990). He is perhaps best known for the bestselling *The Way Things Work* (1988) and its updated version *The New Way Things Work* (1998). Several of his books have been made into television series.

McBRATNEY, Sam *See* GUESS HOW MUCH I LOVE YOU.

McBroom family In stories by Sid *Fleischman.

McCAFFREY, Anne (1926–2011) American-born Irish author of science fiction and fantasy. She wrote for both the *young adult and the adult markets and won both the Hugo and the Nebula Awards for her hugely popular and influential novels and short stories. Her most important work was the invention of the fictional world of Pern in the *Dragonriders of Pern* series, which starts with *Dragonflight* (1968). This began a complex sequence of overlapping stories set on Pern and its surrounding

worlds; those series include *Harper Hall*, starting with *Dragonsong* (1968); *Renegades of Pern*, starting with *Moreta: Dragonlady of Pern* (1983); and *New Adventures of Pern* (with Todd McCaffrey (1956–), starting with *Dragon's Kin* (2003).

McCAUGHREAN, Geraldine (1951–) One of the most prolific and consistent British children's authors currently working, with over 160 books to her name. She is also one of the most admired, and has won an unprecedented three *Whitbread Children's Book Awards, as well as the *Carnegie Medal and the *Guardian Children's Fiction Prize, amongst others.

It is impossible to generalize about McCaughrean's work, and she has frequently said that she doesn't like repeating herself, so is always on the lookout for new subjects. If there is a common feature, it could be that her books regularly place children at the heart of a community or culture at a point of crisis, and force them to avert danger or improve their lot by their own ingenuity, rather than depending on the adults around them.

Her earliest publications were retellings of the *Arabian Nights* for Oxford University Press (1982), her primary publisher ever since. She has published many collections of myths, legends, and traditional tales, usually packaged as lavish gift books illustrated by renowned artists such as Emma *Chichester Clark (*The Orchard Book of Greek Myths*, 1989). She has written widely for educational publishers and contributed to popular series.

Many of her finest works are set in earlier times, such as her debut novel, *A *Little Lower than the Angels* (1987). Amongst her most ambitious is *Not the End of the World* (2004), which retold the biblical Flood story, focusing on the women and children who voyaged with Noah. Sharp, original characterization makes this book as exciting to read as McCaughrean's customary moments of danger and excitement.

Stop the Train! (2001) is a romp set in late 19th-cent. America, when the coming of the railways offers prosperity for struggling communities. But Cissy's family face ruin when they refuse to sell land to the railroad company— and the firm retaliates by refusing to stop the train, thereby cutting off their livelihood. Rarely for McCaughrean, it was followed by a sequel, *Pull Out All the Stops!* (2010). On the subject of sequels, McCaughrean won a competition to write a follow-up to J. M. *Barrie's classic, and *Peter Pan in Scarlet* was published

to much publicity in 2006. It's an inventive continuation but perhaps less satisfying than the novels in which she reveals herself to be a true original, providing stories that nobody else could create.

Smile! (2004) is a profoundly important and engaging short novel for 7–9 year olds. A light plane crashes in a desert wilderness but its occupant, a young photographer, survives, along with his Polaroid camera. He is rescued by people with whom he shares no language, but he begins to understand them when he allows them to choose subjects for the Polaroid's nine last pictures. In capturing what is important to these people, McCaughrean offers the reader an exploration of the differences and similarities between vastly different cultures.

If not always historical in setting, her books often have exotic locations, such as *The *Kite Rider* (2001). Another notable book is the wildly entertaining *Gold Dust* (1994), set in Brazil, in a town where the citizens literally strike gold beneath their very footsteps. Unsurprisingly, the town is quickly inundated with travellers seeking their own fortune. The tensions, jealousies, and competitiveness of such a situation are evoked with genuine verve and humour, typical of all McCaughrean's fine work.

McCLOSKEY, (John) Robert (1914–2003) American author-illustrator best known for *Homer Price* (1943), whose setting reflects his own childhood in Hamilton, Ohio. More about the same scene can be found in his *Centerburg Tales* (1951). McCloskey's other books include *Make Way for Ducklings* (1941), which won the *Caldecott Medal, and *Blueberries for Sal* (1948), about a small girl who goes blueberry-picking with her mother and gets mixed up with a bear family. McCloskey married Margaret Durand, daughter of Ruth *Sawyer, one of whose books he illustrated (*Journey Cake, Ho!*, 1953). He was also illustrator for Keith Robertson's *Henry Reed stories.

McCLUNG, Nellie (1873–1951) Canadian author of sentimental novels about life in Manitoba, among them *Sowing Seeds in Danny* (1908), in which twelve-year-old Pearlie (somewhat in the mould of *Pollyanna) goes into domestic service to repay her father's debts, and charms all hearts.

McCORD, David (Thompson Watson) (1897–1997) American poet; among his books of poems for children were *Far and Few* (1952),

The Star in the Pail (1975), and *One at a Time* (1977).

McCORMICK, Patricia (1956-) American author. Two of her five hard-hitting, realistic *young adult novels have been National Book Award finalists: *Never Fall Down* (2012), about an eleven-year-old slave labourer under the Khmer Rouge, and *Sold* (2006), about a girl sold into sexual slavery in India. *Sold* was made into a film (2014). Other titles are *Purple Heart* (2009), *My Brother's Keeper* (2005), and *Cut* (2003), McCormick's critically acclaimed debut about self-harm, which is on the *American Library Association's list of the 100 most challenged books 2000-9. In 2014 she published *Malala: The Girl Who Stood up for Education and Changed the World*, co-written with Malala Yousafzai.

McCULLOCH, Derek (1897-1967) Broadcaster and writer, known as 'Uncle Mac'. After losing a leg, an eye, and a lung in the First World War he joined the BBC as an announcer, and from 1933 to 1950 was in charge of the BBC's *Children's Hour. He also wrote several children's books, including *Cornish Adventure*, one of the first *Puffin fiction titles in 1941.

MacDONALD, George (1824-1905) Outstanding author of original *fairy stories and *fantasies, who was born at Huntly in Aberdeenshire, where his family, who were Congregationalists, farmed and ran a bleaching business. George was taught in a local school, then at King's College, Aberdeen, to which he won a bursary. He began to write poetry and started to turn away from the Calvinism in which he had been brought up, refusing to believe that only the elect would be saved and feeling that God's mercy was infinite.

He took his MA in 1845 and went to London, initially as a tutor to a Congregationalist family; while there he met Louisa Powell, daughter of a leather merchant, with whom in 1851 he began a long and happy marriage. He hated tutoring and gave it up in 1848, entering a Congregationalist theological college at Highbury and beginning to train for the ministry. He soon began to serve as minister of a church at Arundel in Sussex and was ordained; but he found himself being criticized by his congregation for his slack doctrine—he suggested in a sermon that the heathen might possibly find salvation. In 1853 he resigned and moved to Manchester, attracted there by the presence of his friend

A. J. Scott, principal of Owens College, who held similar religious views to his own. While in Manchester he lectured on mathematics, science, and English literature, continued preaching, and helped to found a ladies' college. In 1855 he published his first book, a long dramatic poem on the subject of married love and misunderstanding entitled *Within and Without;* its admirers included Tennyson, Lady Byron, and Charles *Kingsley. In 1857 he published a collection of poems. MacDonald's health was bad, however, and he and his family made a home for a time at Hastings on the south coast, where the air was thought to be good for his lungs, and there he began to write 'a kind of fairy tale . . . in the hope that it will pay me better than the more evidently serious work'. This was *Phantastes*, completed in two months; it was published in October 1858, MacDonald having sold the copyright for £50.

After three years in Hastings the MacDonalds moved to London, and he became Professor of English Literature at Bedford College, which gave him a small but regular income. During this period he was struggling hard to write something as successful as *Phantastes*, but it was not until 1863 that he completed *David Elginbrod*, a long, didactic, and gothically romantic novel about a young man who has a career not dissimilar to MacDonald's own. It proved extremely popular.

Over the years eleven children were born to MacDonald and his wife, and in the early 1860s he began to discover a gift for telling fairy tales to his family. Several of these stories, including *The *Light Princess* and *The *Giant's Heart*, were published by MacDonald within the framework of a loosely knit novel, *Adela Cathcart* (1864), and were reprinted in *Dealings with the Fairies* (1867), a collection of tales which also included *The *Golden Key* and had illustrations by Arthur *Hughes, who thereafter became a close friend, contributing pictures to other MacDonald books.

During this period MacDonald made friends with John *Ruskin and also with Lewis *Carroll (C. L. Dodgson), whose company was greatly enjoyed by the MacDonald children; in 1863 Dodgson submitted the manuscript *Alice's Adventures under Ground* to the family to see whether they thought it worthy of publication—which they emphatically did. MacDonald was also on close terms with F. D. Maurice, pioneer of popular education and Christian Socialism and a major influence on Kingsley. MacDonald's

friendship with Maurice led him to become a communicating member of Maurice's Church of England congregation at St Peter's, Vere Street, in London.

In 1868 the London publisher Alexander Strahan started a children's periodical, *Good Words For The Young*; the first issue included the initial instalment of a serial by MacDonald, *At The Back of The North Wind*, which Strahan published as a book in 1871. In 1869 MacDonald became editor of the magazine for a short time at a salary of £600 a year. During 1870 and 1871 *The *Princess and The Goblin* appeared as a serial in its pages; it was printed as a book in 1872.

MacDonald changed his home yet again in 1867, moving to 'The Retreat' in Hammersmith (later acquired by William *Morris and renamed 'Kelmscott House'). Here he and his family began to perform plays as annual entertainments for the poor tenants of Octavia Hill; these were often adaptations of traditional fairy stories made by Mrs MacDonald. Ruskin, Arthur Hughes, and Burne Jones were among those who would come to help with the performances.

The 1870s and early 1880s saw an immense output of MacDonald's writing. He had to labour very hard to provide money for his huge family and its various dependants, and sometimes had two or more stories running as serials at the same time. His novels during this period can be broadly divided into 'Scottish' and 'English'. Several were for children: *Ranald Bannerman's Boyhood* (1871), *Gutta Percha Willie* (1873), and *The Wise Woman* (1875)—none of these is remarkable; but in *The *Princess and Curdie* (first printed as a serial in 1877) MacDonald produced another outstanding children's book. *Sir Gibbie* (1879), the story of a *street Arab who rises in the world, has often been read by children.

In 1872-3 he made a lecture tour of America, where his books were being pirated and widely read, and where he was almost as popular an author as *Dickens.

In 1875 the MacDonald family established a home in Italy, at Bordighera, but from 1879 to 1887 they came to England each summer for MacDonald to lecture, and to perform plays as a family troupe.

The Diary of an Old Soul (1880), a poem with a stanza for each day of the year, was largely inspired by the death from tuberculosis of two of the MacDonald children, Mary and Maurice. His daughter Lilia later contracted the same disease while nursing a sick friend

and died in 1891. MacDonald's later writings reflect his grief at these losses, and also his increasing bitterness towards humanity. His last children's book, *A Rough Shaking* (1891), is a nightmarish account of the ill-treatment of a boy who has lost his mother in an earthquake, while his last fantasy novel, *Lilith* (1895), is full of disturbing symbolism. During the last years of his life he became prematurely senile and withdrew into total silence.

MacDonald once declared: 'I do not write for children, but for the childlike, whether of five, or fifty, or seventy-five.' His use of the fairy story for didactic purpose resembles that of Hans Christian *Andersen. 'The best thing you can do for your fellow,' he wrote, 'next to rousing his conscience, is—not to give him things to think about, but to wake things up that are in him; or say, to make him think things for himself.' Opinions of his work vary greatly. His admirers have included G. K. Chesterton and C. S. *Lewis, who traced the origin of his own religious conversion to a reading of *Phantastes* in adolescence. On the other hand many later readers have been disturbed by the ornate sexual symbolism in *Phantastes, Lilith*, and many other stories, and by the inflicting of pain which appears, for example, in *The Giant's Heart*, while the bitter ending of *The Princess and Curdie* is bound to raise doubts about MacDonald's world view. Nevertheless the quality of his writing and the energy of his imagination keep his best books alive and still very attractive to children. Modern criticism includes a biography of MacDonald by Rolland Hein in 1993 and a critique of the author's works for children edited by Roderick McGillis in 1992.

McDONALD, Megan *See* JUDY MOODY.

McELDERRY, Margaret K. (1913-2011) American editor and publisher. As children's books editor at Harcourt Brace, McElderry published classics by authors including, Lucy M. *Boston, Susan *Cooper, Elizabeth *Enright, Margaret *Mahy, Mary *Norton, and many more. She was the first editor to have books win the *Newbery Medal and the *Caldecott Medal in the same year: in 1952, Eleanor Estes won the Newbery for *Ginger Pye*, while *Finders Keepers* by William Lipkind, illustrated by Nicolas Mordvinoff, won the Caldecott. In 1972 McElderry moved to Atheneum, where she became the first children's editor to found her own imprint, now part of Simon & Schuster. She retired at eighty-six, but contributed to the imprint into her nineties.

MacGIBBON, Jean (1913–2002) British author of such *young adult novels as *After the Raft Race* (1976) and books for reluctant readers, for example *Hal* (1974), about a West Indian girl living in Britain.

McGOUGH, Roger (1937–) One of Britain's best-loved poets and performers for both adults and children. Described as the 'patron saint of poetry' by Carol Ann *Duffy, McGough is also a prolific writer, lyricist, broadcaster, children's author, and playwright. McGough shot onto the Mersey scene in the 1960s as one of the leading members of the Liverpool Poets, a group of young poets influenced by Beat poetry and the popular music of that time. He first reached a mass audience in the Penguin Modern Poets collection *The Mersey Sound* (1967) and with his group the Scaffold, whose song *Lily the Pink* reached number one in 1968. His work for children reflects this early philosophy and rejects perceived standards of what poetry should be; his poems are unpretentious, down-to-earth, full of humour, wit, and wordplay.

He has published more than fifty poetry anthologies and presents the BBC Radio 4 programme *Poetry Please*. He has won the Signal Award for best children's poetry book for *Sky in the Pie* (1984) and *Bad, Bad Cats* (1999) and was the recipient of the Cholmondeley Award in 1999. Amongst McGough's many collaborations with illustrators, his and Chris *Riddell's *Until I Met Dudley* (1997) brings together two inventive minds introducing children into the fascinating world of technology and 'how everyday things really work', as explained by Dudley, the techno-wizard dog. His recent collection of rare beasts, *An Imaginary Menagerie* (2011), features poems and drawings by McGough about animals both real and imaginary which epitomize his slightly zany take on life, with poems such as 'Badgers and Goodgers', 'Anaconda', and 'Lobster'. This collection is pure McGough—witty, wicked, and delighting in wordplay, with touches of mocking social commentary.

McGOWAN, Anthony (1965–) British author for children and teenagers. McGowan's books range from the young, comic, and scatological through series adventure (he was commissioned to revive the Willard Price *Adventure* series, writing four titles, beginning with *Leopard Adventure*, 2012), right up to a kind of teen noir, *Hello Darkness* (2013).

Versatile though he is, it is his ambitious work for *young adult readers that is exceptional. These smart, gripping, and often darkly funny books include *Hellbent*, which begins with a teenager being sent to hell; *Henry Tumour* (2006; US: *Jack Tumor*), a grimly hilarious book about a schoolboy with a talking brain tumour, which won him the 2006 *Booktrust Teenage Prize; *The Knife that Killed Me* (2008), a fast-paced and sometimes shocking story of teenage life that doesn't shy away from tough topical issues such as knife crime; and *Brock* (2013), a slim, potent story about Nicky, whose life is changed when he witnesses a badger being killed. Nicky and his brother Kenny return for a second story in *Pike* (2015).

MacGREGOR, Ellen (1906–54) American author of comic *science fiction stories about Miss Lavinia Pickerell, a New England spinster, beginning with *Miss Pickerell Goes to Mars* (1951).

McGuffey Eclectic Readers The most widely distributed American schoolbooks for at least seventy-five years from their first appearance in 1836. They consisted of a *primer and six reading-books, graded in order of difficulty; many children never progressed beyond the third. They owe their name to William Holmes McGuffey (1800–73), a Calvinist schoolmaster employed to compile the *Readers* by a Cincinnati publishing firm, Truman and Smith. The first two *Readers* appeared in 1836, and the *Third* and *Fourth* the next year, together with the *Primer*. McGuffey was by this time President of Cincinnati College; his publishers described him as 'formerly professor at Oxford', without mentioning that this was Oxford, Ohio.

Although the *Readers* went through many changes over the years, the format remained much the same. Short passages of prose or verse, some specially written but many selected from the works of celebrated writers, were illustrated by *wood engravings and accompanied by questions to test the pupil's comprehension and to point morals. Many British authors were represented, including *Shakespeare, *Dickens ('The Death of Little Nell'), Maria *Edgeworth, and Mrs *Hemans ('The boy stood on the burning deck'). American writers whose work could be found in their pages included Lyman Beecher, Sara Josepha *Hale (author of *Mary had a little lamb*), Washington *Irving, Nathaniel *Hawthorne, and John Greenleaf *Whittier. Prose excerpts were often rewritten freely to suit the

publisher's taste. The *Second Reader* included the celebrated (and apocryphal) story of George Washington and the hatchet ('I can't tell a lie, father; you know I can't tell a lie').

The success of the *Readers* was not due so much to their contents—there were many competitors of equal quality—as to business acumen. Winthrop B. Smith (1808–85) of the publishers Truman and Smith conceived them and promoted them skilfully. He is supposed to have become a millionaire from the proceeds of the books; W. H. McGuffey, on the other hand, received no regular royalties after he had been paid 1,000 dollars, though the publishers did send him an annual Christmas gift of smoked hams.

The *Readers* have had much criticism aimed at them; they were crudely didactic and moralistic and endorsed the values of white Protestant middle-class society, for example advocating *temperance but studiously avoiding any discussion of slavery; however, they introduced American children to a wide range of literary material. They continued in use well into the 20th cent. Stanley W. Lindberg, in *The Annotated McGuffey* (1976), observes that they 'served as a major force in shaping the present consciousness of what we now call Middle America'.

MACHADO, Ana Maria (1941–) Brazilian writer of picture books and fiction, the author of over a hundred books for children and adults, which have been translated into eighteen languages and sold close to twenty million copies. She won the 2000 *Hans Christian Andersen Medal. Notable books in her prolific and varied output include the multi-award-winning *Bisa Bia, Bisa Bel* (1982; English translation: *Me in the Middle*, 2002) about the relationship—via a photograph—between Isabel and her great-grandmother; *Era uma vez um tirano* (1982; Once There Was a Tyrant), published during Brazil's dictatorship, the story of a happy country suddenly in thrall to a tyrant, and only the children can stop him; and *História meio ao contrário* (1979; Story Half Backwards), an almost-fairy tale about a king who wants to kill the dragon which, he believes, eats the sun, causing it to get dark every night—the story ends with the prince and the princess falling in love and getting married . . . but not to each other.

Machine Gunners, The (1975) By Robert *Westall, an exceptional novel about growing up in wartime. Set during the Second World War, this is the story of Chas McGill, owner of

the second best collection of war memorabilia in town—but with ambitions to own the best. When he finds a downed German bomber, he knows his wish is going to come true—and maybe he can not only get one up on his rival, Boddser Brown, but help win the war too. This was Westall's first novel, and a remarkable way to start a literary career: funny, exciting, realistic, poignant and gripping to the last page.

MacINTYRE, Elisabeth (1916–2004) Australian author-illustrator of such *picture books as *Katherine* (1946) (US title, *Susan, Who Lives in Australia*), a comic verse tale. She also wrote *young adult fiction, for example *It Looks Different from Here* (1977), about illegitimacy and abortion.

McINTYRE, Sarah (1975–) American illustrator-author of children's books and comics, whose picture books include *Vern and Lettuce* (2010 – originally a weekly comic strip), *There's a Shark in the Bath* (2014) and *Dinosaur Police* (2015). She has collaborated with Philip *Reeve on a series of successful illustrated novels, which have won the duo many awards. She is a dynamic and effective campaigner for the recognition of illustrators' work, using the hashtag #picturesmeanbusiness.

MACK, Louise (1874–1935) Author of *Teens* and other stories of Australian girls' school life. She was born in Hobart, Tasmania, the daughter of a Wesleyan minister, and later lived in Adelaide and Sydney, where she was a contemporary of Ethel *Turner at Sydney High School. She went to London and travelled in Europe, where she was war correspondent for the London *Daily Mail* at the capture of Antwerp in 1914.

She wrote in all fifteen novels, most of them romances or 'light' literature; these have been outlived by her school series, *Teens* (1897), *Girls Together* (1898), and *Teens Triumphant* (1933). She was breaking new ground in that the books have very little connection with English *school stories; both day-school and family life are portrayed, and the centre of the first two books is the relationship between the teenagers Lennie and Mabel, two very natural and unheroic girls. *Teens Triumphant* followed the fortunes of Lennie trying to make a living in the London literary world and realizing that she must, for her spiritual health, return to Australia.

Louise Mack's younger sister Amy wrote, among other things, *Bushland Stories for*

Children and *Birdland Stories* (both 1910) and *Scribbling Sue and other stories* (1913).

McKAY, Hilary (1959-) British author of fiction for middle-grade readers, in particular an exceptionally gifted writer about families, which are consistently drawn with remarkable wit and warmth. Her first novel *The Exiles* (1991) won the *Guardian Children's Fiction Prize, and was followed by *The Exiles At Home* (1993) and *The Exiles in Love* (1996). McKay subsequently wrote a further four series: the *Casson Family* series, *Paradise House*, the *Dog Friday* trilogy (the Porridge Hall books), and *Pudding Bag School*; as well as many stand-alone titles, including a sequel to Frances Hodgson Burnett's *A *Little Princess* called *Wishing for Tomorrow* (2009). Her series for younger readers include *Lulu* and the *Charlie* series. In 2013 she published *Binny for Short*, the first in another family-centred series populated with typically endearing McKay characters.

McKEAN, Dave (1963-) English illustrator, photographer, comic book artist, graphic designer, filmmaker, and musician. He is best known for his ongoing collaborations with Neil *Gaiman, including the picture books *The Day I Swapped My Dad for Two Goldfish* (1996) and *The Wolves in the Wall* (2003), as well as all the covers to *The Sandman* (1989-96) graphic novels. In 2013 he provided black-and-white illustrations for *Phoenix*, S. F. Said's terrific story about Lucky and his attempt to save the universe, which are as good as anything McKean has done in any children's book work. He has created artwork for countless CDs and created the Mythical Creatures stamps for the Royal Mail. However, in all these diverse media his style remains unique and instantly recognizable, whether with his simple pen-and-ink or his computer-enhanced multimedia work. (*See also* GRAPHIC NOVELS.)

McKEE, David (John) (1935-) British illustrator-author, whose creations include one of the most popular characters in the picture book world, the patchwork elephant called *Elmer, and one of the most enduring stand-alone picture books, *Not Now, Bernard*.

McKee became a cartoonist while at art college, and published his first picture book, *Two Can Toucan*, in 1964. He worked extensively in children's television both on animations of characters of his own (*see* *Mr Benn and *King Rollo) and others. Elmer made his first appearance in 1968, and continues to reappear regularly in new books and merchandise today. (McKee's artwork for Elmer evolved as the series progressed, and he would later return to redraw the early books.) Like the first Elmer book, many of McKee's stand-alone picture books champion tolerance and openness, promoting strongly moral messages with sometimes explicitly political content. These fable-like stories include *Tusk Tusk* (1978), which describes a battle between the white elephants and the black elephants; *Two Monsters* (1985), in which a red monster and a blue monster live on opposite sides of a mountain and get into a quarrel; and *The Conquerors* (2004), in which a General and his army invade a nearby country, but they are made so welcome there that it is they who are ultimately conquered. In *Elmer and the Hippos* (2003), the elephants aren't happy when a herd of hippos move into their territory. McKee has occasionally illustrated work by other writers, including Forrest Wilson's *Supergran* series (which first appeared in 1978) and some of Michael Bond's *Paddington Bear books. In 1987 he won the *Deutscher Jugendliteraturpreis.

MACKEN, Walter (1915-67) Irish novelist and actor who wrote *The Flight of the Doves* (1967), the story of two children fleeing across Ireland to escape a cruel stepfather.

McKINLEY, Robin (1952-) American author of feminist *fairy-tale retellings and fantasy. McKinley's female heroes are strong, smart, and resourceful, and her books often challenge traditional fairy tales' emphasis on conventional notions of beauty and femininity. In *Beauty: a Retelling of the Story of Beauty and the Beast* (1978), the eponymous heroine's nickname is ironic rather than descriptive, while in *Deerskin* (1993), beauty leads to death and rape. McKinley's other works include *The Outlaws of Sherwood* (1988), which focuses on the story of Maid Marian, and two novels set in the imaginary land of Damar, *The Blue Sword* (1982), a Newbery Honor Book (*see* NEWBERY MEDAL) and *The Hero and the Crown* (1984), which won the Newbery Medal.

McKISSACK, Patricia (1944-) and **Fred (Fredrick)** (1939-2013) American writers, also husband and wife, who over thirty years collaborated on more than a hundred books about the African-American experience. Patricia had previously been an editor, and Fred ran a construction firm, but both quit in order to write—they were aware of how hard it was for black children to see themselves in books,

and were driven to rectify the situation. For the most part Patricia did the writing and Fred the research (and so was not always credited as a co-author even on collaborations). They won *Coretta Scott King Awards with *Christmas in the Big House, Christmas in the Quarters* (1994) and *A Long Hard Journey: The Story of the Pullman Porter* (1989), and had five other Honor Books for that award: *Sojourner Truth: Ain't I a Woman?* (1992—also a *Boston Globe-Horn Book Award winner), *Black Diamond: The Story of the Negro Baseball Leagues* (1994), *Rebels Against Slavery: American Slave Revolts* (1996), *Black Hands, White Sails: The Story of African-American Whalers* (1999), *Days of Jubilee: The End of Slavery in the United States* (2003). Patricia McKissack has also written fiction independently—her *The Dark-Thirty* (1992) was a Newbery Honor book (*see* NEWBERY MEDAL) and another Coretta Scott King Award winner.

MacLACHLAN, Patricia (1938–) American author best known for her series about the Witting family. In the first book, the *Newbery Medal-winning *Sarah, Plain and Tall* (1986), a mail-order bride from coastal Maine embarks on a new life on the Midwest prairie. MacLachlan writes spare, touching prose; many of her books focus on absence, whether through bereavement or displacement. They include *What You Know First* (1994), illustrated by Barry *Moser, about a young girl who gathers mementos of her beloved prairie before moving away, and *Edward's Eyes* (2007), in which the narrator's younger brother is killed in an accident.

McLEAN, Allan Campbell (1922–89) British author of *historical novels set on the Isle of Skye, beginning with *The Hill of the Red Fox* (1955). His work is distinguished by a concern for social justice.

MacLEOD, Doug (1959–) Australian author of picture books and comic children's novels who has also worked as a television writer and presenter. Known for the humour in his books, MacLeod now writes mostly for young adults. *The Life of a Teenage Body-Snatcher* (2010) was an Honour Book for *CBCA Book of the Year: Older Readers in 2012, shortlisted for the Victorian Premier's Literary Awards, and highly commended for the Prime Minister's Literary Awards in the same year. *The Shiny Guys* (2012) was shortlisted for the 2013 CBCA Book of the Year: Older Readers. His best-known picture book is *Sister Madge's Book of Nuns* (1986), a collection of naughty, rollicking verse about nuns, illustrated by Craig Smith. Also illustrated by Smith is *The Windy Farm* (2012): read it as a book about sustainability, be entertained by the flying pigs, or enjoy family life on this wacky farm. It is a humorous *cautionary tale. In 2008 The Australian Writers' Guild presented him with the Fred Parsons Award for Contribution to Australian Comedy on television.

McNAUGHTON, Colin (1951–) British illustrator and writer who has produced over seventy titles since 1976, ranging from picture books to early readers to books of verse. McNaughton has explained that he finds text and illustrations are inseparable—in a reversal of convention, sometimes a poem is inspired by an illustration. He sees his work as a performance in which he is director and designer as well as writer. He has recorded his poetry for audio and won the British Book Design Award twice—for the picture book, *Jolly Roger* (1989), and for *Making Friends with Frankenstein* (1993). He won the *Kurt Maschler Award in 1991 for *Have You Seen Who's Just Moved in Next Door to Us?*

In his picture books, animal characters often represent the behaviour of small children. In the Preston Pig stories, roles from the Red Riding Hood story are reversed, and the pig is cleverer than the wolf. The first book in the series of six, *Oops!*, won the 1996 Nestlé Book Prize. McNaughton introduces pertinent concepts simply and entertainingly—such as the process of making predictions in *Suddenly!* (1994). Another popular series begins with *Cushie Butterfield (She's a Little Cow)* (2004), which explores the familiar 'I don't want to go to school' syndrome.

In 2003 McNaughton published the superb *Once Upon an Ordinary Schoolday*, illustrated by Satoshi *Kitamura. His most notable collaborations, however, are with Allan *Ahlberg; together, they produced the sixteen Red Nose Readers (from 1985), a highly regarded series of graded storybooks. He also illustrated some of Ahlberg's *Happy Families*.

McNaughton has received praise for his substantial, generously illustrated poetry collections, such as *There's an Awful Lot of Weirdos in Our Neighbourhood* (1987). These are exuberant collection of verse of differing lengths and often revise familiar rhymes, with fresh and witty puns, combined with a considerable amount of playground humour.

McNEILL, Janet (1907-94) British children's author of stories about the schoolboy 'Specs

McCann' (1955 onwards), and such novels as *The Battle of St George Without* (1966), about an abandoned church threatened by a boys' gang.

M'Turk In **Stalky & Co.* by *Kipling.

Madame Doubtfire (1987) A novel by Anne *Fine which offers a typically honest, yet comic portrayal of the effects of divorce on children. Miranda Hilliard limits the amount of time her husband, out-of-work actor Daniel, from whom she is separated, is allowed to see their children, but when she advertises for a nanny it is Daniel, disguised as a woman, who gets the job. He runs the house immaculately and bonds with his children, and when his deception is finally discovered, it leads to a fairer visitation arrangement. Fine's story was filmed as *Mrs Doubtfire*, with Robin Williams in the title role, in 1993; the film was a poor imitation of the novel, though its success did lead to the book becoming a bestseller. (At the time of writing, a movie sequel is threatened.)

Madeline Heroine of a series of *picture books (with verse texts) by Ludwig *Bemelmans, published between 1938 and 1961. *Madeline* (1938) introduces Madeline and her fellow pupils in a girls' convent school in Paris—'Twelve little girls in two straight lines'. Madeline is both the bravest and the naughtiest, a perpetual anxiety to Miss Clavel the teacher. Later books in the series include *Madeline's Rescue* (1953), which won the *Caldecott Medal.

Mad Hatter In **Alice's Adventures in Wonderland* by Lewis *Carroll.

Mad Tea Party In **Alice's Adventures in Wonderland* by Lewis *Carroll.

Magasin des enfans See BEAUMONT, MME MARIE LEPRINCE DE.

magazines Children's magazines were at first collections of prose, verse, and illustrations, little distinguished from the many miscellanies that were published as single ventures, except perhaps by the inclusion of a serial story or *play printed in instalments. While the children's *annual existed in a rudimentary form in 17th-cent. Switzerland, no magazines for children seem to have appeared anywhere in Europe before the mid-18th cent. In London Mary *Cooper advertised a *Penny Medley; or Weekly Entertainer* in 1746; this was probably a series of separate titles rather than a magazine proper. John *Newbery published the **Lilliputian Magazine* in 1751. Mme De *Beaumont's *Magasin des enfans* (1756) had some affinity with magazines, though it was a collected edition from the first and never a true periodical.

The first weekly journal for children was issued in Germany; a number of such periodicals appeared during the 1770s, including C. F. Weisse's *Der Kinderfreund* (1775 to 1782), which inspired Arnaud *Berquin's *L'Ami des enfans*, a collection of *moral tales published in monthly parts in 1782–3.

The first English children's periodical known for certain to have been a monthly was John *Marshall's short-lived **Juvenile Magazine* (1788); Marshall later made two further attempts to launch a periodical, but his *Children's Magazine* only appeared for a few months during 1799 to 1800 and his *Picture Magazine* had an equally brief existence (1800 to 1801). Elizabeth Newbery brought out *The Young Gentleman's and Young Lady's Magazine* (1799 to 1800), which included the novelty of notices of recently published children's books.

As the *Sunday school movement gathered strength in Britain it created a need for periodicals with a religious bias; consequently for the first time a market and means of distribution existed that could sustain a weekly or monthly children's magazine. *The Youth's Magazine*, an *evangelical journal which published many of Jane *Taylor's verses, was founded in 1805. The *Religious Tract Society started *The *Child's Companion* in 1824. A more fiercely puritanical magazine, founded in 1826 by The Revd William Carus *Wilson, was *The *Children's Friend* (a title later used by another magazine).

As the middle of the 19th cent. approached, secular periodicals began to flourish. The English **Peter Parley's Magazine*, taking its title and style from the celebrated American author, began publication in 1839, spawning an annual at the end of its first year. The ubiquitous and cheap weekly serials known as *penny dreadfuls inspired the godly and caring to produce magazines that would compete vigorously with them, would cost as little, and would offer as much action and illustration, but of a healthier sort. Samuel Orchart *Beeton established *The *Boy's Own Magazine* in 1855, and J. Erskine Clarke set up *The *Children's Prize* (1863) and **Chatterbox* (1866) with these aims. The most successful of this type of high-intentioned but lively

magazine—indeed of all 19th-cent. British children's periodicals—was The *Boy's Own Paper*, launched in 1879; its companion The *Girl's Own Paper* first appeared a year later. Among the competitors of the 'BOP' was *Chums* (founded 1892).

The penny dreadful publishers themselves saw that there were gains to be made by publishing ostensibly 'healthy' magazines, and Edwin *Brett's paper The *Boys of England* began as a penny weekly in 1866. The first *Jack Harkaway story appeared in it. In the last decade of the 19th cent. Alfred *Harmsworth (later Lord Northcliffe) launched his campaign 'No More Penny Dreadfuls' by issuing the even cheaper *Marvel, and his *Union Jack and *Pluck established a new pattern for a boy's magazine of huge circulation. *Captain, founded in 1899 and published by Newnes, was also very popular.

One of the first British magazines specifically for girls was Charlotte M. *Yonge's The *Monthly Packet, founded in 1851; many of Miss Yonge's stories first appeared in print in its pages, and its declared intention was to train young ladies to be 'more steadfast and dutiful daughters of our beloved Catholic Church of England'. The popular *Aunt Judy's Magazine (founded 1866) was the creation of Margaret *Gatty, whose daughter Mrs *Ewing contributed many stories to its pages. Another periodical of the same character was *Good Words for The Young (1868 to 1877), with which George *MacDonald was closely associated.

Smaller children were catered for in *Little Folks (founded 1871) and *Little Wideawake. Mention should also be made of the type of magazine which catered for the entire family, adults and children; of these, The *Strand Magazine was among the longest lived and most notable.

The earliest juvenile periodical in America was the short-lived Children's Magazine, of which three numbers only were printed at Hartford, Conn., in 1789; it contained *moral tales, sentimental verses, and instructive articles. In 1802 two magazines began to be published from Philadelphia: the Juvenile Magazine, or Miscellaneous Repository of Useful Information and the Juvenile Olio. Among the many Sunday school magazines in America was the Teacher's Offering, later the Youth's Friend and Scholar's Magazine, which was published from Philadelphia for forty-one years, beginning in 1823; 1826 saw the beginning of The *Juvenile Miscellany. The longest-

lived of all United States children's periodicals was The *Youth's Companion, published from Boston between 1827 and 1929. The two papers, *Parley's Magazine and *Merry's Museum, associated with the original '*Peter Parley' (S. G. *Goodrich) were among the most successful instructive and morally didactic journals for young people. Many other American magazines were founded from the 1840s onwards, a high proportion of them in Boston. In 1865 *Our Young Folks began to appear, heralding a new era in which entertainment, especially fiction, was to predominate over teaching. Four years later came the short-lived but remarkable *Riverside Magazine for Young People (1867–70), and in 1873 was founded *St Nicholas, which in the first 30 years of its existence published many notable works of children's fiction. Among its competitors were *Harper's Young People and *Wide Awake.

The early 20th cent. in England was notable for the proliferation of the Harmsworth boys' and girls' story papers. New titles which were introduced by Harmsworth's Amalgamated Press before the First World War included *Gem (1907) and *Magnet (1908), two *school story magazines which featured the creations of 'Frank *Richards', most notably *Billy Bunter. The same publishers catered for readers of *girls' stories with such papers as *Girls' Friend and *School Friend, and published The *Children's Encyclopaedia and its associated magazines and The *Children's Newspaper; both Encyclopaedia and Newspaper were under the editorship of Arthur *Mee. After 1918, a rival to the supremacy of Amalgamated Press appeared in the shape of D. C. *Thomson & Co. of Dundee, who first launched their 'Big Five' adventure papers, Adventure, *Rover, *Wizard, Skipper, and *Hotspur, and then, shortly before the Second World War, began to produce two outstandingly popular *comics, *Dandy and *Beano.

A post-1945 British magazine with more literary content was *Young Elizabethan, founded in 1948 as Collins' Magazine for Boys and Girls and renamed just before the coronation of Elizabeth II, after which it ran until 1973. In India the Hindustan Times group's monthly children's magazine Nandan has been published in Hindi since 1964, with a mix of traditional and modern stories, poems, and factual material. The US monthly literary magazine Cricket was founded in 1973, by Marianne Carus, with the aim of commissioning the best authors and illustrators. Since

then it has built up a family of magazines for specific ages and to cover non-fiction, science, and the arts. While some popular magazines for children still exist today, they are not typically characterized by a fervent interest in quality literary writing.

Maggie McKinley Heroine of novels by Joan *Lingard, adapted for television.

Magic City, The (1910) A novel by E. *Nesbit. Philip Haldane's half-sister marries a man who lives in a large mansion and has a daughter, Lucy. Philip amuses himself in his new home by building a city of toy blocks, ornaments, and other household objects, despite the objections of the nurse who looks after him and Lucy. At night he finds that his city has grown to the height and size of a real town and he goes into it, Lucy following him. He has many adventures, including slaying a clockwork dragon, and has to contend against the nurse, who is 'Pretenderette' to the throne of the magic city (a jibe at the Suffragettes, whose views E. Nesbit did not share).

The plot was developed by Nesbit from her short story 'The Town in the Library in the Town in the Library' in *Nine Unlikely Tales* (1901). She built a Magic City for the Children's Welfare Exhibition at Olympia in 1912.

Magic Fishbone, The See HOLIDAY ROMANCE, A.

Magician's Nephew, The (1955) The sixth of the *Narnia novels by C. S. *Lewis to be published, though its story is chronologically the first in Narnia history.

Magic Pudding, The (1918) An outstanding comic book for children, written and illustrated by the Australian artist and novelist Norman Lindsay (1879–1969). Bunyip Bluegum, a koala bear, sets off to see the world. He takes up with Bill Barnacle, a sailor, and his companion Sam Sawnoff, 'the penguin bold', who are journeying through Australia in company with a steak and kidney pudding that can walk and talk, delights to be eaten, and is 'a cut-an'-come-again Puddin'' that magically makes itself whole whenever a slice has been removed.

Much of the comedy in the book derives from the characters' diction. Often this is elegant to the point of absurdity; after a quarrel, one character remarks: 'Rather than allow this happy occasion to be marred by unseemly recriminations, let us, while admitting that our admirable friend, Sam, may have unwittingly disturbed the composure of our admirable friend, Bill, at the expense of our admirable Puddin's gravy, let us, I say, by the simple act of extending the hand of friendship, dispel in an instant these gathering clouds of disruption.'

The Magic Pudding was written during the First World War to take Lindsay's mind off the death of friends on the Western Front. It sprang from an argument with a friend who said that children liked *fairy stories best of all; Lindsay replied: 'Not on your life!... The belly rules the infant mind.' Its immediate source was the episode in *Through The Looking Glass* where the leg of mutton introduces itself to Alice, who is then told: 'It isn't etiquette to cut any one you've been introduced to.' Lindsay thought that this unfairly deprived Alice (and the book's readers) of a meal. An aggressive and self-critical person, Lindsay was 'not at all proud of having produced this little bundle of piffle', but *The Magic Pudding* was an immediate success.

Lindsay wrote one other children's book, *The Flyaway Highway* (1936), but this was far less successful.

Magic Roundabout, The A series of television puppet films created for French television by Serge Danot, under the title *Le Manège enchanté*. The very popular English versions (1965 onwards) have commentaries by Eric Thompson, who has also written *Magic Roundabout* books. The occupants of the Roundabout, in Thompson's rendering, include Dougal (a dog), Brian (a snail), Dylan (a guitar-playing rabbit), and Florence (a little girl).

Magic Tree House, The (1992–) A series of fantasy time-travelling stories by Mary Pope Osborne (1949–). Beginning with *The Valley of the Dinosaurs*, each instalment follows the adventures of Jack and Annie, as they travel by means of a magic tree house from their Pennsylvania home in time and space. A link throughout the series is the quest to free *Morgan le Fey, who then provides further missions for the children to accomplish. Now numbering fifty-one titles, the series is aimed at emerging readers. Since 2000 Osborne and others have produced companion factual guides to the subjects dealt with in the stories.

Magnet, The A *school story magazine published weekly by *Harmsworth's from 1908 to 1940. It featured *Greyfriars stories by 'Frank *Richards' (Charles *Hamilton), in which the most notable character was *Billy Bunter.

Magnolia Buildings (1960) A children's book by the British novelist Elizabeth Stucley, which earned critical approval when it was published

for its portrayal of contemporary working-class life, though later it was attacked for condescension. It is a chronicle of the Berners family, who live in a block of old-fashioned flats. Stucley (1906–74) wrote several other children's books and four novels for adults; she was a headmistress and a social worker.

MAGORIAN, Michelle (1947–) English actress and children's author, best known for her first novel *Goodnight Mister Tom* (1981), which won the *Guardian Children's Fiction Prize and is now regarded as a modern classic. *Goodnight Mister Tom* was followed by *Back Home* (1984), another story about a child evacuated during the Second World War. Both novels have been adapted for the stage and screen. *A Little Love Song* (1991), again set in wartime Britain, features a young woman becoming independent and finding first love. Magorian has written four more novels—*Cuckoo in the Nest* (1994), *A Spoonful of Jam* (1998), *Impossible!* (2014) and *Just Henry* (2008), which won the *Costa Children's Book Award, as well as collections of poetry, short stories, and two picture books.

MAGUIRE, Gregory (1954–) American author and co-director of the educational charity Children's Literature New England. Many of Maguire's books are reworkings of *fairy tales for a *crossover readership, including *Confessions of an Ugly Stepsister* (1999) and *Mirror, Mirror* (2003), and, for younger readers, *Leaping Beauty and Other Animal Fairy Tales* (2004). *Wicked* (1995), a prequel to L. Frank Baum's *The *Wizard of Oz* (1904), was written for an adult readership and was adapted into a long-running musical. Among Maguire's other books are the *Hamlet Chronicles* (1993–2005), *Missing Sisters* (1994), and *What-the-Dickens: The Story of a Rogue Tooth Fairy* (2007).

MAHY, Margaret (1936–2012) New Zealand's most distinguished and versatile writer. The author of over two hundred flamboyant, extravagant, and richly inventive books, she was awarded the 2006 *Hans Christian Andersen Medal. She won the *Carnegie Medal twice, for The *Haunting* (1982) and *The Changeover* (1984).

Her journey to publication could have emerged from a Mahy story—an American editor read her work which often featured in the *New Zealand School Journal*, and asked to see everything she had written. Trunkloads of texts made their way across the Atlantic, and in 1969 five picture books were published

simultaneously, each different in style, with different illustrators, including *The Lion in the Meadow*, which is still in print today.

Many of her picture books are classics, such as *The Boy Who Was Followed Home* (1977), *The Great White Man-Eating Shark* (1989), and *Jam* (1985, which has been read as a feminist text). *Down the Back of the Chair* (2010) was a late, long text, told in playful rhyme, and a sensitive depiction of a family facing financial ruin, which has already proven to be an important part of the Mahy canon.

Many of the short stories she wrote for the *Journal* were collected in the early 1970s in the *First, Second* and *Third Margaret Mahy Story Books* (which also contained poems). Her finest story collections were *Leaf Magic* (1976), *The Chewing-Gum Rescue* (1982), and, for older readers, *The Door in the Air* (1988), which included the moving tale 'The Wind Beneath the Stars', originally a picture-book text.

Pirates were a common subject, as, for example, in the long short story *The *Great Piratical Rumbustification* (1982, teamed with *The Librarian and the Robbers*—another interest, as Mahy was for many years a highly respected children's librarian), the picture book, *The Man Whose Mother Was a Pirate* (1972), and the hilarious middle-grade novel, *The Pirate's Mixed-Up Voyage* (1983), a brilliant swashbuckling comedy with a memorable but cautionary school song.

In mid-career, Mahy began to write outstanding novels for older readers, set in New Zealand (whereas her earlier stories had vivid but non-specific locations, which often felt European, and reflected her own childhood reading—Mahy was the pioneer of an indigenous New Zealand literature).

The Catalogue of the Universe (1985) is a marvellously entertaining story of the friendship between serious Tycho and confident Angela May, which permitted Mahy to explore many of her own wide-ranging interests, which she once summarized as an endeavour to understand 'what on earth we are doing here'. *Memory* (1987), a more solemn novel than Mahy's other work, and wholly realistic in setting, tells the moving story of a wayward young man's friendship with an old woman suffering from dementia. Through meeting Sophie by chance, Jonny confronts his own recollections of his sister's death, for which he has felt partly to blame.

Ghosts and the supernatural occur frequently in Mahy's stories, as in the delightfully playful later *Dangerous Spaces* (1991).

The wonderful Flora is partial to a haunting, but meets her match in Anthea, her orphaned cousin, who comes to stay. Both girls find dreams and reality clash in a potentially nightmarish way. *See also* MARGARET MAHY MEDAL.

Maid Marian *See* ROBIN HOOD.

Maisy A mouse in books (from 1990) by Lucy *Cousins. According to Cousins, Maisy drew herself, emerging from a doodle almost fully formed. The small mouse became the hero of a series of books for very young children, which has now grown to many titles and a variety of formats. Illustrated in a simple, two-dimensional style that perfectly reflects the warm, uncomplicated stories, Cousins has created a Mouse whose days are full of the everyday adventures of her target audience, with a variety of stories, such as the first titles, *Maisy Goes Swimming* (1990) and *Maisy Goes to Bed* (1990), and *Maisy Goes to the Library* (2007). Stories are available from board books to lift-the-flap and were turned into a TV series in 1999.

MAITLAND, Antony (Jasper) (1935–) British artist who began his career as a children's illustrator with *Mrs Cockle's Cat* (1961), a *picture book with text by Philippa *Pearce, which won him the *Kate Greenaway Medal. He subsequently illustrated many of Leon *Garfield's novels, and has produced his own illustrated stories, including *James and the Roman Silver* (1965).

Make-Believe, *a children's play in a prologue and three acts* By A. A. *Milne, *Make-Believe* was first produced at the Lyric Theatre, Hammersmith, on 24 December 1918. In the prologue a girl named Rosemary tells her friends the Hubbard children that she will write a play for Christmas. She decides that it is to be called 'Make-Believe', and writes down the title, but she cannot think what to write, so the Hubbards' butler James tells her: 'Why not make-believe as it's written already?'

Make Way for Ducklings (1941) A picture book written and illustrated by Robert *McCloskey (1914–2003). Mr. and Mrs. Mallard look all over Boston for a safe place to raise their ducklings. They love the little island in the middle of the Public Garden's pond but think the park is too busy. A little while after their eight ducklings hatch, however, they return to the park with the support of Boston's policemen, who help them cross the busy roads safely. The book was awarded the *Caldecott Medal in 1942 and has never been out of print. In 1987 Nancy Schön's sculpture of the ducks was installed in Boston Public Garden.

Malheurs de Sophie, Les (1864) A collection of tales by the Comtesse de *Ségur, about a small girl whose wilful behaviour leads her into trouble. The stories, which resemble *Rosamond* by Maria *Edgeworth (*see* EARLY LESSONS), describe how Sophie burns herself with builder's lime, kills her mother's goldfish through ignorance and stupidity, and so on. *Les Malheurs de Sophie* has been translated into many languages from the original French. In England it has appeared as *Sophie* or as *The Misfortunes of Sophie*.

MALORY, Sir Thomas (d. 1471) Author of the most substantial and imaginative medieval writings about King *Arthur, Malory was born early in the 15th cent., succeeded to his father's Warwickshire estate, and was Member of Parliament for that county. By 1451 he was in trouble with the law, being accused of theft, rape, and plotting to murder the Duke of Buckingham. He was imprisoned several times for these and other offences. However, he escaped from jail three times, but he did spend some years in prison. It has often been remarked that a man who lived such a life was an unlikely person to devote his attention to Arthurian romances of high moral character. In fact Malory's Arthuriana, while it reproduces idealistic passages from its models, is chiefly characterized by a constant interest in new adventures and exploits.

Malory's Arthurian narratives, written in prose, were printed by *Caxton in 1485, under the title of the final book, *Le Morte Darthur*. Caxton explained that Malory had taken them 'oute of certeyn bookes of Frennshe', and the French *romances were certainly the chief sources, though Malory also drew on the 14th-cent. English alliterative *Morte Arthure*. His method was to disentangle from his complicated source-books a series of self-contained stories. He was not attracted by the atmosphere of *courtoisie* that pervaded the French Arthurian tradition, nor by the deeper theological implications of the French *Grail material. He wrote vigorously and economically, and most authors of children's books of Arthuriana in the 19th and 20th cents. have drawn chiefly on his work.

Malory Towers A series of books by Enid *Blyton about a girls' boarding school, starting

with *First Term at Malory Towers* (1946) and ending with *Last Term at Malory Towers* (1951). Each book deals with a successive school year, and they form an archetype for the British boarding school story. Darrell Rivers is the heroine. She is loyal and plucky, clever and sporty, with a hot temper being her only downfall. Her fellow classmates each have their own distinctive characteristics. The girls have midnight feasts, play tricks on the teachers, take part in thrilling lacrosse matches, and a new girl always shakes up the order of things in an exciting way. In the pre-*Harry Potter days, they were at the root of many a childhood fantasy of going to boarding school. Blyton's *St Clare's series followed a very similar pattern.

MALOT, Hector *See* SANS FAMILLE.

manga (literally 'involuntary drawings') The Japanese incarnation of the *comics medium. It follows a very different path from that of its Western counterparts such as the comic book and the *BD, and precursors of its modern version are found in Japanese art from different eras. It is argued, however, that the *manga* itself was born during the period of British influence in Japan, and found its figurehead in Osamu Tezuka (1928–89). Inspired by Walt Disney and Hanna and Barbera's publications and animation work, he established the foundations for *shōnen manga*, comics for boys, and even created the first *shōjo manga*, its counterpart for girls, which led to the creation of what is known in English as *Astro Boy* (鉄腕アトム, 'Tetsuwan Atom'; 1952–68), which made Tezuka a popular author outside his native Japan, where *manga* forms a good third of the comic book market. Arguably all subsections of *manga*, the *gekiga* (劇画), are publications with a more 'mature' readership in mind, while *kodomomuke manga* (子供向け漫画) are aimed overtly at children, with Fujiko F. Fujio's *Doraemon* (1969–96) being one of the most notable and popular examples of the latter. The medium also spans multiple genres, from the giant fighting robots of *mecha* to the magic-fuelled protagonists of *magical girls* (魔法少女, *mahō shōjo*), via the same-sex relationships of *yaoi* ('Boy's Love') and *yuri* ('Girls' Love') *manga*. The current longest-running series, started in 1976, is Osamu Akimoto's police comedy *Kochikame*, with its impressive 189 volumes.

Mangnall's Questions The abbreviated title of *Historical and Miscellaneous Questions*

for the Use of Young People, a popular English *book of instruction for children by Richmal Mangnall, first published in 1800. The author (d. 1820) was a schoolmistress in Yorkshire; she sold the copyright of the *Questions* for 100 guineas to Longmans, who thereafter issued edition after edition of the book.

The *Questions* begin with several chapters of *history and the biographies of leading historical figures. From the fifth edition (1806) a section was added on astronomy. There were also questions on general knowledge and an 'Abstract of the Heathen Mythology'. Miss Mangnall explained that the book was intended 'to awaken a spirit of laudable curiosity in young minds'.

Mangnall's Questions was reprinted, with various revisions and additions by different hands, for some seventy years after its original publication. Its form was copied in *Pinnock's Catechisms and The *Child's Guide to Knowledge. Angelica, in The *Rose and The Ring, was said to be able to 'answer any one of Mangnall's Questions'.

Man in the Moon Frequently referred to in stories and verses for children. According to one *nursery rhyme he was banished to the moon 'For stealing the thorns from another man's gap'. This is based on the traditional picture of the Man as carrying a bush of thorns and a lantern (referred to in *A Midsummer Night's Dream*, V. i, 'This man with lantern, dog, and bush of thorn, | Presenteth moonshine'). The best-known rhyme about the Man tells how he 'Came down too soon | And asked his way to Norwich'. There are two poems about the Man in J. R. R. *Tolkien's *The Adventures of Tom Bombadil* (1962). Simon Bartram has written several picture books about a man who lives on the moon, whose name is Bob. The first of these books—*The Man on the Moon*, 2004—won the *Blue Peter Book Award.

MANKOWITZ, Wolf *See* KID FOR TWO FARTHINGS, A.

manners, books of *See* BOOKS OF COURTESY.

MANNING, Rosemary (1911–88) British novelist who wrote a series of books about a child named Sue and her friend 'R. Dragon', beginning with *Green Smoke* (1957).

MANNING-SANDERS, Ruth (1888–1988) British author who specialized in retellings of folk tales of many nations. She compiled *A Book of Dragons* (1964) and also wrote several original

stories for children, including *Circus Boy* (1960).

MANT, Alicia Catherine (?1788–1869) A clergyman's daughter who married a Bath rector and wrote *moral tales such as *The Canary Bird* (1817, an imitation of *Fabulous Histories* by Mrs *Trimmer) and *The Cottage in the Chalk-Pit* (1822), a novel describing the developing characters of a family of children.

Mantlemass Overall title of a series of *historical novels by Barbara *Willard, beginning with *The Lark and the Laurel* (1970). They follow the fortunes of two families from the 15th to the 17th cent. Margaret *Meek wrote that 'the characters . . . are not cast in the heroic mould of Rosemary Sutcliff's heroes. Instead their very frailty makes them human, rounded.'

Man Without a Country, The *See* HALE, EDWARD EVERETT.

Man Without a Face, The (1972) A novel by Isabelle *Holland.

Māori stories Stories from Māori mythology, which underpin much of the Māori world view and the Māori's system of beliefs and rituals, began to be collected and recorded on the page by European settlers in the 19th cent. Following the Treaty of Waitangi in 1840, Sir George Grey (1812–98; from 1845 the Governor of New Zealand) persuaded some Māori chiefs to write down some of their orally transmitted legends; his collection *Nga Mahi a nga Tupuna* (1854; 'The Deeds of the Ancestors'), translated (by Grey himself, after some study of the language) and published in 1855 as *Polynesian Mythology, and Ancient Traditional History of the New Zealand Race*, artificially fixed many stories which had previously varied naturally over time and locality. In 1854 Edward Shortland (1812–93), an Englishman who had spent most of his life in New Zealand, published *Traditions and Superstitions of the New Zealanders*, and in 1882 *Maori Religion and Mythology*, a culmination of his own many years of interest and study.

Many of the tales that comprise the mythology are origin/creation stories (the universe, gods, and people) or stories of migration and settlement; these are now beginning to be represented in picture books and storybooks for today's children, sometimes by writers and illustrators of Māori origin, though these writers and the culture from which their work derives remain under-represented in most mainstream publishing. Gavin *Bishop is a popular and notable exception; among the many books dealing with the myths of his own Māori ancestry is *Maui and the Sun*, 1996, which retells one of the legends about that mythology's well-known trickster hero. Notable collections of stories from the mythology include A. W. Reed's *Favourite Māori Legends* (1965, revised by Ross Calman, 2013), which collects over thirty of the most popular of these tales; and Michael *Foreman has illustrated a collection by soprano Kiri te Kanawa, *Land of the Long White Cloud: Maori Myths, Tales and Legends* (1989).

Non-Māori writers to have dealt with the traditions and experience of the Māori include R. L. *Bacon and Joy *Cowley.

MARCET, Mrs Jane (1769–1858) Author of young persons' *books of instruction in *science and other subjects. The daughter of a rich Swiss merchant in London, she married Alexander Marcet, a Swiss-born physician and lecturer on chemistry. In 1806 she published *Conversations on Chemistry, intended more especially for the Female Sex*, which had much success, running to sixteen editions in England and selling some 160,000 copies in America during the following fifty years. Until its publication simple scientific text-books of this kind were almost unknown.

Mrs Marcet's most famous publication was *Conversations on Political Economy* (1816), which was highly praised by Macaulay and others. It was followed by *Conversations on Natural Philosophy* (1819), an exposition of the first elements of science for very young children. Further 'Conversations', on Vegetable Physiology (1829), Government (1836), the History of England (1842), and Language (1844), were produced by Mrs Marcet, who also wrote other books, including stories.

The conversational form that she employed is similar to that in Mrs *Markham's history books. Mrs Marcet did not hesitate to discuss her subject in considerable detail.

MARCHANT, Bessie (1862–1941) British writer of *girls' stories from the 1890s to the 1940s. She allowed her heroines to experience more exciting adventures and show more intrepidness than was common in girls' fiction when she began to write. Her novels had such titles as *Held at Ransom* (1900) and *Three Girls on a Ranch* (1901).

MARCHANT, John (*fl.* 1750) English author of anti-papistical tracts who wrote two unusual

books of verse for children: *Puerilia: or, Amusements for the Young* (1751) and *Lusus Juveniles: or, Youth's Recreation* (1753). The first book begins with poems for 'Little Misses' and 'Young Masters', describing activities enjoyed by children of either sex, then comes a set of 'Songs' that include verses for each month of the year.

Marchant's second volume includes such unlikely pieces as 'Decoy-Ducks: or, the Pleasures of a Brothel', which warns young men against consorting with prostitutes.

March family In *Little Women* by Louisa M. *Alcott.

March Hare In *Alice's Adventures in Wonderland* by Lewis *Carroll.

Margaret Mahy Medal A New Zealand literary prize, officially called the Storylines Margaret Mahy Medal and Lecture Award. It is presented to a person who has made a significant contribution to children's literature, publishing, or literacy. It has been presented annually since 1991 by a charitable trust and is named after its first recipient, librarian and author Margaret *Mahy. Winners to date include Lynley *Dodd (1999), Maurice *Gee (2002), Pamela *Allen (2004), and Kate *De Goldi (2011).

Marianne Dreams (1958) A fantasy novel by Catherine *Storr. Marianne is ill. Confined to bed, she amuses herself drawing with a pencil she finds in an old workbox. Her pictures invade her dreams. Marianne is in a strange claustrophobic world, shut in a house with Mark, also bedridden. In this dream world, he is dependent on what Marianne draws. Outside, there are the standing stones. Surely no threat, until Marianne, in a temper, angry with Mark, gives them eyes. The stones come alive. Critically acclaimed when first published, it retains its powerful atmosphere, and the portrayal of the two children is fresh and believable. A sequel, *Marianne and Mark* (1960), further explored their relationship.

Marigold Garden (1885) A *picture book by Kate *Greenaway, engraved and printed by Edmund *Evans and, like *Under The Window*, having her own verses as its text. It is generally judged to be the most accomplished of her books. The verses display her characteristic mixture of nursery rhyme echoes, gentle humour, and nonsense, with idealized childhood and country scenes as subjects.

MARK, Jan (Janet) (Marjorie) (1943–2006) British children's author who won a Guardian/ Penguin award for unpublished manuscripts for children with *Thunder and Lightnings* (1976), which then went on to win the first of her two *Carnegie Medals (her second was for *Handles*, 1983).

Mark's novels tended to have contemporary settings—often based in places she had lived, such as Kent, Norfolk, and later Oxford, and her own experiences—and were concerned more with evolving relationships than complex plots or high concepts. The delightful *Trouble Halfway* (1985) tells the story of the extremely conservative Amy, who is forced to take a road trip with her lorry-driving stepfather Richard, and whose suspicions of him gradually thaw.

Obsession as a means of keeping change at bay is a common tactic of Mark's characters— from Victor in *Thunder and Lightnings* onwards. *The Lady with Iron Bones* (2000) is a much overlooked story about two girls whose friendship is forged by an obsession with a statue, to which they accord fictitious powers, as a foil against their difficult domestic circumstances.

They Do Things Differently There (1994) was a frame novel about two teenage girls who invent an alternate reality to alleviate the dullness of life in a modern new town. Behind the one-liners was a story in which tension was generated by the threat of the loss of a friendship.

These books were the mainstay of her long career, which was governed by multi-book contracts from a variety of publishers who respected Mark for her reliable delivery of high-quality work. Only once did she write without commission: an adult novel, *Zeno Was Here* (1987), an examination of the creative mind and a celebration of poetry, which revealed interests she was perhaps inhibited from pursuing owing to the demands of fulfilling contracted work.

The books she wrote for publisher David Fickling—*The Eclipse of the Century* (1999) and *Useful Idiots* (2004)—revealed Mark at her most inventive and ambitious. They were not books specifically for children. They developed ideas in early books, such as the political fantasy novels, *The Ennead* (1978), *Divide and Rule* (1979), and *Aquarius* (1982).

Of all her writing, Mark most enjoyed producing short stories. She was widely anthologized and collected, and her best collections include *Nothing To Be Afraid Of* (1980, which was Highly Commended for the Carnegie Medal), *Feet* (1983), and *Enough Is Too Much Already*

(1988), which ingeniously comprised stories told almost entirely in dialogue.

MARKHAM, Mrs (Elizabeth Penrose) (1780–1837) English author of a celebrated series of *history books for children. She was the daughter of Edmund Cartwright, inventor of the power loom. After her marriage to a clergyman, from which three sons were born, she began to write history books, taking her pseudonym from a village where she had spent much of her childhood. In the 'Advertisement' to her first book, *A History of England from the first Invasion by the Romans to the end of the Reign of George III* (1823), she stated that it had originally been written for her own children. The book was notable for its 'Conversations' at the end of each chapter, of which this is an example (from the chapter describing the reigns of William the Conqueror and his successor):

Richard. I shall be very glad, mamma, when you come to a good king. It is very disagreeable to hear about bad people.

Mrs Markham. It is one of the great drawbacks to the pleasure of reading history, that it is such a painful record of human crimes.

When a new edition, enlarged and illustrated, of Mrs Markham's *History of England* was brought out by John Murray in 1826 it became a great success, and for the next four decades it was the most popular textbook of English history in schools and nurseries. In 1828 Mrs Markham published a two-volume *History of France*, which was almost as successful. She also wrote histories of Malta and Poland entirely in the form of conversations (*Historical Conversations for Young Persons*, 1836), a book of sermons for children, and a number of stories. Many editions of her history books were published in America.

After her death her publishers issued a *History of Germany* (1853) 'on the plan of Mrs Markham's Histories', but this contained no conversations. Other publishers issued pamphlets of questions based on the Mrs Markham books, designed to test the young reader's knowledge. Her unpopularity with children is attested by disparaging references to her in the novels of E. *Nesbit.

1926 saw the publication of *Mrs Markham's New History of England* by Hilaire *Belloc, which parodied the original book and poked rather bitter fun at contemporary society.

MARKOOSIE (1942–) The first Canadian Inuit author to be published in English. *Harpoon of the Hunter* (1970) was first serialized in the Inuit newsletter *Inuttituut* and then translated into English by the author. It is a bleak, plainly written story about the tracking down of a rabid polar bear which has attacked a settlement.

Marlow family In books by Antonia *Forest.

Marmaduke Multiply's Merry Method of Making Minor Mathematicians A *book of instruction in four parts first issued by John *Harris in 1816–17. It consists entirely of mnemonic rhymes designed to teach the multiplication table, accompanied by amusing illustrations, plain or coloured; e.g.: 'Twice 4 are 8. Your bonnet is not straight...Twice 11 are 22. We'll drink to the Hero of Waterloo.' The book proved very popular, and was often reprinted.

MARRYAT, Captain Frederick (1792–1848) Author of some of the best 19th-cent. *adventure stories. He was born in London, the son of a successful man of business and Member of Parliament. When he was thirteen, inspired by Nelson's victory at Trafalgar, he went to sea on the frigate *Impérieuse* and was plunged into a rough life below decks. His ship was at times involved in almost daily fights with the French and other enemies.

Marryat was given command of his own ship when still in his twenties. He performed many acts of bravery, rescuing a number of comrades who had fallen overboard, and on one occasion nearly drowned while doing so. In 1818, the year before his marriage, he was given a gold medal by the Royal Humane Society. He also won distinction for his work in signalling.

In 1829 he published a novel, *The Naval Officer, or Scenes and Adventures in the Life of Frank Mildmay*. This was a great success. The next year he resigned from the navy, published a second novel, *The King's Own*, and settled down to full-time writing. *Jacob Faithful* appeared in 1834. Among a large output, those of his earlier books which appealed to young readers were *Peter Simple (1834) and *Mr Midshipman Easy (1836). After the first flush of success as a novelist had passed, he began to write specifically for children (he had a number of his own), producing *Masterman Ready in 1841, The *Settlers in Canada in 1844, and The *Children of The New Forest in 1847. His only artistic failure in juvenile books was *The Mission, or Scenes in Africa* (1846). His last children's book, *The *Little*

Savage (1848-9), was completed after his death by his son Frank.

Opinions of his work have varied greatly. Edgar Allan Poe called it 'mediocre', but it was much admired by *Dickens. In the 20th cent. Virginia Woolf has judged him 'a sound craftsman, not marvellously but sufficiently endowed at his work'. In the history of children's literature he is notable as the first writer of adventure stories to draw chiefly upon real personal experiences, although his debt to *Robinson Crusoe* and The *Swiss Family Robinson* is considerable.

His imitators during his own lifetime include E. G. G. *Howard and Michael *Scott.

MARSDEN, John (1950-) Influential Australian writer for young adults, whose career came out of his work as a teacher. In *Tomorrow, When the War Began* a group of teens come back from a camping trip only to find that their country has been invaded and they need to hide to survive. The seven books in the series follow the friends through all the heartbreak and anguish of war. There is a follow-up trilogy, *The Ellie Chronicles* (2004), describing what happened when the war was over. Marsden also wrote the dark and shocking picture book, *The Rabbits* (2003), which was illustrated by Shaun *Tan. Since opening a school at his home outside of Melbourne he has cut back on his writing, but made the school a huge success.

MARSHAK, Samuel Yakovlevich (1887-1964) Leading Soviet children's poet of his generation. From 1923 he wrote children's books in verse. His stories include *The Ice-Cream Man* (translated into English in 1943), the story of a fat man who eats so much ice cream that he turns into a snowman. He also wrote conventionally patriotic poetry and was an editor with the state children's publishing house.

MARSHALL, Alan (1902-84) Australian author, best known for *I Can Jump Puddles* (1955), about his experience of being crippled with polio as a child. His other books include *People of the Dreamtime* (1952), a collection of aboriginal tales.

MARSHALL, Emma (1830-99) British author of over 200 children's books—a prolific output which resulted from the need to support her husband and family after the failure of the bank in which he was a principal shareholder. Her first book was *The Happy Days at Fernbank, a story for little girls* (1861). Her

work resembles that of Charlotte M. *Yonge, and reflects her own married life in West of England cathedral towns. She specialized in *historical novels, such as *Under Salisbury Spire* (1890) and *Penshurst Castle* (1894), which are respectively about George Herbert and Sir Philip Sidney.

MARSHALL, H. E. (Henrietta Elizabeth) (1876-1941) One of the most popular British writers of *history books for children during the early 20th cent. She was best known for *Our Island Story* (c.1910); her other works include *Scotland's Story* (1906), *Our Empire Story* (1908), *The Child's English Literature* (1909), and *Kings and Things: first stories from English History* (1937).

MARSHALL, James (Edward) (1942-92) Prolific American author-illustrator of books for very young children. They include *George and Martha* (1972), the first of a series about a pair of hippos (named after characters in Edward Albee's *Who's Afraid of Virginia Woolf?*), and (in collaboration with Harry Allard) books about the Stupids, a supposedly typical modern American family (1974 onwards).

MARSHALL, John (*fl.* 1783-1828) London printer and bookseller, publisher of numerous children's books. By 1783 he had established a business at 4 Aldermary Churchyard, in the heart of the *chapbook manufacturing district, though it is not known whether he was related to the John Marshall who was producing chapbooks in large numbers in London between 1695 and 1726 at the sign of the Bible in Gracechurch Street. Marshall remained in business until 1828; premises were also opened by him at Queen Street, Cheapside, and at 140 Fleet Street.

Marshall's output of children's books was very large (Harvey *Darton notes 'about seventy' between 1780 and 1790), and his authors included the *Kilners and Eleanor *Fenn. He was one of the printers who produced the *Cheap Repository Tracts* for Hannah *More in the last decade of the 18th cent. Miss More eventually quarrelled with Marshall, whom she regarded as shifty and motivated only by commercial principles; she complained that her friend Mrs *Trimmer had received poor treatment from him.

Marsh Award for Children's Literature in Translation An award presented (usually biennially) to the translator of a children's book in the UK, established in the mid-1990s to encourage publishers to acquire

more children's books from other languages. It has been won, to date, by Anthea *Bell (three times), Sarah *Ardizzone (twice), Patricia *Crampton, Betsy Rosenberg, Martin Cleaver, Howard Curtis, and Margaret Jull Costa.

MARTIN, Ann M. (Matthews) (1955-) American author whose background as a children's book editor led her to becoming a full-time writer. She is famous for the long-running *Baby-Sitters Club* series, which began with *Kristy's Great Idea* (1986), in which a club to help parents find babysitters is formed by four friends: Kristy Thomas (president), Claudia Kishi (vice president), Mary Anne Spier (secretary), and Stacey McGill (treasurer). Martin wrote the first thirty-five in the series, the many other books all being ghostwritten. To date the series has sold over 176 million books. In 2010 she added a prequel to the series, *The Summer Before*. She has also written many stand-alone novels, including *Rain Reign* (2014; UK title: *How to Find a Lost Dog*, 2016), about a girl with Asperger's syndrome who is obsessed with homonyms and whose dog goes missing one stormy night; a pair of epistolary novels written with Paula *Danziger (*P.S. Longer Letter Later*, 1998; and *Snail Mail No More*, 2000); and other series, including *The Doll People* (from 2000, with Laura Godwin, illustrated by Brian *Selznick).

MARTIN Jr., Bill See CARLE, ERIC.

MARTIN, J. P. See UNCLE.

MARTIN, Patricia Miles (1899–1986) Prolific American author of children's stories, some of them under the pseudonym 'Miska Miles'. Her books include *Mississippi Possum* (1965), *Apricot ABC* (1969), and *Annie and the Old One* (1971).

MARTIN, William (1801-67) British hack writer and editor of children's books and magazines. After working for some years as a draper, he began to earn money by writing for magazines. In 1840 he edited the first issue of *Peter Parley's Annual: a Christmas and New Year's present for young people*, which continued to appear until the 1890s. Besides writing a number of English imitations of the American *Peter Parley books and editing *Peter Parley's Magazine* from 1858 until his death, he was the author of *The Hatchups of Me and My School-Fellows* (1858), a collection of tales supposedly 'hatched up' by schoolboys after lights out in a dormitory.

MARTINEAU, Harriet (1802-76) Daughter of a Norwich manufacturer, Martineau came to fame when she was thirty by writing a series of stories illustrating political economy. She was the author of several children's books, the four best known appearing quarterly in 1841 under the series title 'The Playfellow'.

The first of these, *The Settlers at Home*, is a dramatic story of a flood which surrounds the home of a group of Dutch Protestant settlers in Lincolnshire during the Civil War. *The Peasant and the Prince* consists of two historical narratives set before and during the French Revolution. *Feats on the Fjord* describes the life of a Norwegian family, in a story including *pirates, a secret cave, and superstitions about water-sprites. It remained in print for many generations; an 1899 edition has illustrations by Arthur *Rackham. The last of the 'Playfellow' books, *The Crofton Boys*, tells how eight-year-old Hugh Proctor longs to join his elder brother at Mr Tooke's boarding school at Crofton, but finds when he gets there that school life is tough. In a playground scrap he falls from a wall and is so badly injured that one of his feet has to be amputated; but he refuses to reveal the name of the schoolfellow whose fault it was and is greatly admired for his bravery. The book is one of the earliest children's novels to make the rigours of school life its subject.

Harriet Martineau's style is brisk and the books are not overburdened with didacticism, but they are rather melancholy in subject-matter.

Martin Pippin in the Apple Orchard (1921) A set of linked tales by Eleanor *Farjeon.

Marvel One of the *Harmsworth British adventure papers for boys, first published in 1893 and thereafter issued weekly for nearly thirty years. Its opening issue declared: 'No more penny dreadfuls! These healthy stories of mystery adventure, etc., will kill them.' In fact the stories featured in *Marvel*, though they avoided the crudities found in many true *penny dreadfuls, were just as sensational. Especially popular were (from 1904) tales of 'Jack, Sam, and Pete' by S. Clarke Hook, Jack being an English roving lad, Sam an American hunter, and Pete an iron-fisted Negro with a raucous laugh. Together they roamed the world, clearing up international crises in every quarter. For a time *Marvel* also carried stories about *Sexton Blake and *Nelson Lee. By the 1920s it had become a sporting-story paper, and in 1922 it was merged with *Sport and Adventure*, which in turn was then absorbed into a new series of *Pluck*.

Mary had a little lamb A *nursery rhyme first published in 1830. A number of people have claimed to be its author or the original Mary, but it seems beyond doubt that the rhyme was composed by Sarah Josepha *Hale of Boston, Mass. The incident it describes was apparently only 'partly true'. The rhyme appeared above Mrs Hale's initials in *The *Juvenile Miscellany* for September 1830, and later that year it was printed in Mrs Hale's *Poems For Our Children*.

Mary Plain A bear in stories for small children by Gwynedd *Rae.

Mary Poppins A collection of stories by P. L. *Travers, first published in 1934 with illustrations by Mary Shepard, daughter of E. H. *Shepard. The Banks family acquire as nursemaid Mary Poppins, who refuses to give references, dictates her own terms for the job, and possesses certain surprising talents: she can slide *up* the banisters, walk into a picture drawn by her friend Bert, understand the speech of dogs, and, with the aid of a compass, travel round the world in a matter of seconds. Jane and Michael, the two elder Banks children, have the time of their life with her, and are desolate when one day the wind blows her away again as abruptly as it brought her into their lives. There were five books in the series altogether, the last one published in 1982, forty-eight years after the first. However, the continuing fame of *Mary Poppins* is largely the result of the 1964 *Disney film of the stories, with Julie Andrews in the title role.

MASEFIELD, John (1878–1967) English poet, author of novels and plays and of five books for children, including two classics, *The *Midnight Folk* (1927) and *The *Box of Delights* (1935). His mother died when he was young, and the children were put in the charge of a *governess whom they hated and tormented (Masefield himself once stabbed her with a fork) and who inspired the character of Sylvia Daisy Pouncer in *The Midnight Folk*. A little later the children's grandfather died, and they moved to his rambling 17th-cent. house, full of romance and secret passages.

Jack (as Masefield was known) wrote poetry as a boy, loved *adventure stories (especially those of Mayne *Reid) and every kind of thrilling literature, and had a facility for retelling it to entertain his younger brothers. His guardians, however, thought that writing would be an unsuitable occupation, and that the sea would toughen him up. He was sent for merchant ship training to the school-ship HMS *Conway* on the Mersey. Aged seventeen, he became a vagrant in America, sleeping rough and doing odd jobs on farms. Two years later, weak from malaria and undiagnosed tuberculosis, he worked his passage home as a steerage steward.

In London he found a job as a clerk, and gradually recovered his health, re-establishing relations with his family. Then in 1902 his *Salt-Water Ballads* was published, including his now celebrated poem 'Sea Fever'.

Ballads and Poems (1910) contains the much anthologized 'Cargoes', beginning 'Quinquireme of Nineveh'—which brought him many complaints that Nineveh was inland. In the same year appeared his first two children's books, *A *Book of Discoveries*, and *Martin Hyde, the duke's messenger*, a *historical novel about the Monmouth rebellion. The following year he published another, *Jim Davies*, about a boy pressed into the service of smugglers in early 19th-cent. Devon. Margery *Fisher, in her Bodley Head monograph on Masefield (1963), judges these books to have been remarkably vigorous for their time, with 'none of the fussiness, the jewelled period language . . . which the historical novel was suffering then'. Both these books have survived, as have others of his novels, adventure stories not written specially for children but read by them: *Captain Margaret* (1908), *Lost Endeavour* (1910), *Sard Harker* (1924), and *Odtaa* (1926).

After the First World War his work became immensely popular. Among his poems published then were *Reynard the Fox* (1919), a verse narrative about a hunt seen through the eyes of the prey which has excited many schoolchildren, and *King Cole* (1921), which has been called 'a fairy-tale for grown ups'. In this period, too, he wrote the children's classic *The Midnight Folk* (1927), using a family already established in *Sard Harker* and *Odtaa*. Two further novels by Masefield, *Dead Ned* (1938) and *Live and Kicking Ned* (1939), though not primarily for children, have been read by them; *Puffin editions of them (1974 and 1975) have illustrations by Antony *Maitland.

In 1930 he was proposed for Poet Laureate by the Labour Prime Minister, Ramsay MacDonald; the verses that he dutifully produced for royal occasions were generally thought banal, but he could turn out public poems that were heartfelt, such as one written in his eighties as a result of the assassination of President Kennedy.

His importance to children's literature rests not only on his two classic *fantasy novels and the much-anthologized poetry, but also on his promotion of simple but fine narrative and of the arts of verse-speaking and *storytelling. In 1961 the first John Masefield Story-Telling Festival was held, with his blessing, at Boys and Girls House in Toronto. His life is fully recorded in Constance Babington Smith's *John Masefield* (1978).

MASON, A. E. W. (Alfred Edward Wood-ley) (1865–1948) British popular novelist, whose adventure tales include *The Four Feathers* (1902). A friend of J. M. *Barrie, he appears in *Peter Pan* as one of the pirates, 'Alf Mason, long known and feared on the Spanish Main'.

Masquerade (1979) A *picture book by the British painter Kit Williams, which is in fact a treasure hunt; the clues are contained in the pictures and the treasure was a golden hare, made by Williams himself and actually buried. The book became a world bestseller, but the clues were not unravelled until 1982 when the hare was dug up by a reader at Ampthill Park in Bedfordshire.

Masterman Ready; or, the Wreck of the Pacific (1841–2) The first of Captain *Marryat's novels to be written specially for children. Asking his own family what sort of story they would like, he was told that they wanted a continuation of The *Swiss Family Robinson. He decided 'to write another in the same style'.

His story begins with the voyage of the Sea-grave family to Australia. The vessel is severely damaged in a storm, the Captain is injured, and soon the Seagraves find themselves abandoned on board with only Masterman Ready, a weather-beaten old seaman, to help them steer to safety. The ship runs aground and the family make their home on an island in the accepted manner of *Robinsonnades. Towards the end of the book their stockade is attacked by natives. Tommy, the thoughtless six-year-old of the family, causes the water supply to run out, and Masterman Ready is wounded while trying to replenish it. The Captain of the *Pacific*, recovered from his injury, arrives in the nick of time to save the family; but Ready dies, murmuring 'Poor little Tommy; don't let him know that he was the cause of my death.'

Volume I of the first edition, which was illustrated, took the story as far as the establishment of a home on the island. The second and third volumes appeared the next year. A second edition was printed in 1851, but the book did not become widely popular until the 1870s, when boys' *adventure stories were thoroughly fashionable.

In the novel Marryat abandoned the picaresque style of *Peter Simple* and *Mr Midshipman Easy* for a more moral and pious manner.

Master Skylark: A story of Shakespeare's time (1896) A popular *historical novel by the American author and illustrator John Bennett (1865–1956). A Stratford singing-boy is kidnapped and taken off to London, where he meets Shakespeare and is taken to sing before the queen. The book was originally illustrated by Reginald *Birch.

Master Smith, The A Norwegian folk tale collected by *Asbjørnsen and Moe and published in English in 1859 in *Popular Tales From The Norse*. A boastful blacksmith is put in his place when Christ and St Peter visit him and show that after all he is not the best blacksmith in the world. Nevertheless Christ grants him three wishes; he chooses to have the power to make anyone who sits in his pear-tree, his chair, or his purse stay there until he releases them. He uses this power to trap the Devil who has come to claim him. As a result, he is locked out of Hell, the Devil having come to fear him so much.

MATHER, Cotton (1663–1728) American *Puritan minister and writer. His works include tracts promoting 'family-religion', *catechisms, and other material for the young. In 1699 he published *A Family Well-ordered, or An essay to render parents and children happy in one another*, and in 1700 a supplement to *Janeway's *Token* entitled *A Token for the Children of New-England, or, Some examples of children, in whom the fear of God was remarkably budding, before they dyed, in several parts of New-England*.

MATHIS, Sharon Bell (1937–) African-American teacher, librarian, poet, and author of books for children and *young adults, including *Sidewalk Story* (1971), about a girl whose best friend is evicted when her impoverished mother chooses to buy food for her children rather than pay the rent, and *Teacup Full of Roses* (1972), a grittily urban story of sibling affection and rivalry. In 1973 she penned a child's biography of the singer Ray Charles, which won the *Coretta Scott King Award. *The Hundred Penny Box* (1975,

illustrated by Leo and Diane *Dillon) is about a boy and his great-great aunt. *Red Dog, Blue Fly* (1991) is a collection of poems about American football.

Matilda (1988) Written by Roald *Dahl and illustrated by Quentin *Blake, the story of a preternaturally clever, Dickens-reading five-year-old girl (with very horrible parents) starting out at Crunchem Hall Primary School, an establishment terrorized by Miss Trunchbull, a fearsome bully of a headmistress. The saving grace for Matilda is her form teacher, Miss Honey, who admires her brains and encourages her intellect and her imagination. When Matilda learns that Miss Honey has also been a victim of Miss Trunchbull's evil ways—and, what's more, that Miss Trunchbull is her teacher's aunt—she finds a way to take revenge, using some strange psychokinetic powers she has discovered she has. The whole story is delivered with Dahl's usual relish, and as with so many of his books, the horrible adults get a satisfyingly nasty comeuppance.

A good film adaptation was released in 1996, but has now been largely eclipsed by a triumphantly successful stage production—a glorious musical adaptation by Dennis Kelly and Tim Minchin, which opened first at the Royal Shakespeare Company in Stratford in 2010 to great critical acclaim, subsequently transferring to sell-out runs in London and on Broadway.

Matthew Mugg The cats'-meat-man, in the *Doctor Dolittle books by Hugh *Lofting.

Mauleverer, Lord In the *Billy Bunter stories by 'Frank *Richards'.

MAUROIS, André See FATTYPUFFS AND THINIFERS.

Maus: A Survivor's Tale (1986) By Art Spiegelman (1948–), a metafictive autobiographical *graphic novel in which Art interviews his father, Polish-Jewish Holocaust survivor Vladek, about his life and experiences in the war for a project called *Maus*. The author's strained relationship with his father is central to the book, as is his mother's suicide. Spiegelman portrays Jews as mice, Germans as cats, and Poles as pigs. A sequel was published in 1991. *Maus* won a Pulitzer Prize, the first graphic novel to do so. Before its publication as a book, it was serialized in *Raw*, a magazine published by Spiegelman and his wife, Francoise Mouly. Though this graphic novel was not written specifically for a young audience, *Maus* has become many people's first introduction to the form.

MAVOR, William See ENGLISH SPELLING BOOK, THE.

Max und Moritz, Eine Bubengeschichte in sieben Streichen (1865) ('Max and Moritz, a Boys' Story in Seven Pranks') A comic verse narrative written and illustrated by the German poet and artist Wilhelm Busch (1832–1908). Max and Moritz are two young pranksters who play tricks on the village people. They cause the Widow Bolte's chickens to strangle themselves to death. Next they trick the tailor, Meister Böck, into falling into the river, fill schoolmaster Herr Lämpel's tobacco pipe with gunpowder, and stuff Uncle Fritz's bed with mayflies which bite him in the middle of the night. But trouble eventually overtakes them, and they come to a very nasty end when a labourer, whose flour sacks they have slit open, bundles them into bags and gives them to the miller, who unwittingly grinds them into little pieces which are then eaten by the ducks. The story is illustrated with grotesque line drawings which are generally recognized as a precursor of modern comic strips and cartoon films. (The American *Katzenjammer Kids* are directly descended from Busch's book.) After *Max und Moritz*, Busch's best known book was *Plisch und Plum* (1882).

MAY, Karl (1842–1912) German author who wrote a number of *westerns set in America, which were the most popular *adventure stories in Germany in the late 19th and early 20th cents. During his early years May was often in trouble with the authorities for fraud, petty theft, and forgery; he began to write pulp fiction and invented 'autobiographies'. But with the appearance of such novels as *Im fernen Westen* ('In the Far West') (1880), *Helden des Westens* ('Western Heroes') (1890), and *Winnetou*, a novel about an '*Indian' (Native American) which appeared in several volumes between 1893 and 1910, he achieved a certain literary status.

MAY, Sophie (Rebecca Sophia Clarke) (1833–1906) American author of *girls' stories, including her very popular sets of stories about 'Little Prudy' (1863 onwards), 'Dotty Dimple', 'Flaxxie Frizzle', and 'Flyaway'. She also wrote a 'Quinnebasset' series for older girls. Her books have very little plot, but the child characters are presented naturally and with liveliness, and family relationships and a sense of place are well

conveyed. There is plenty of moral teaching, but it is handled with a light touch.

MAYER, Mercer (1943–) American author and illustrator of over 300 books. His first published work, *A Boy, a Dog and a Frog* (1967), has charming black-and-white illustrations and is an early example of the wordless picture book. His most successful creation is the cartoonish Little Critter, a hamster-like animal who first appeared in *Just for You* (1975) and has since starred in dozens of titles that treat everyday experiences with good humour. His younger sister has her own series. Other highlights among Mayer's output include *There's a Nightmare in My Closet* (1968) and the Little Monster books (1977–98).

May family In *The *Daisy Chain* by Charlotte M. *Yonge.

MAYHEW, James (1964–) A talented English illustrator and author of children's books, often to be found touring schools and festivals demonstrating his skill at drawing upside down. His first published work, *Katie's Picture Show* (1989), developed into a long-running series about a girl who explores famous paintings by climbing inside them. *Katie and the Mona Lisa* (1998) was successfully adapted for a musical stage production in 2013. In 1994 he received the New York Times Award for one of the ten best illustrated books of the year for *The Boy and the Cloth of Dreams* (1994), written by Jenny Koralek. Other books include the *Ella Bella Ballerina* series (first published in 2007), *BOY* (2004), and *Bubble and Squeak* (2013), with illustrations by Clara Vulliamy. Mayhew is also known for his multimedia concerts for children, which incorporate live orchestral music, narration, and live illustration.

MAYNE, William (1928–2010) Critically acclaimed and unconventional British children's author. He was a pupil and choirboy at Canterbury Cathedral Choir School. By the age of sixteen he had already written a novel, and he soon decided on a literary career. His first published children's book appeared in 1953, and thereafter new Mayne titles were produced at a rate that many found astonishing considering their high quality.

Mayne's first two books gave little indication of what was to come. *Follow the Footprints* (1953) and *The World Upside Down* (1954) are conventional *adventure stories. Yet both are treasure hunts, as in one sense or another are the majority of Mayne's major

books, and it is possible to observe in them many of Mayne's characteristics in embryo.

Mayne went back to his own schooldays for setting and subject matter for his next book, and produced *A *Swarm In May* (1955); the book and its first sequel, *Choristers' Cake* (1956), were immediately recognized as a new departure in English children's fiction. Hard on their heels Mayne brought out *The Member for the Marsh* (1956), the story of a schoolboy's fear and awe of a marsh that he has to cross each morning on his way to the bus. The *Times Literary Supplement* called him 'a master—*the* master in contemporary English writing for children—of setting'. The same review continued: 'He also expects his readers to think speedily. If it is a scramble to follow his quick wit at times, the book can always be read again; and the second reading often gives more pleasure than the first.'

Most of the books produced in the following decade are treasure hunts in one form or another, though the 'treasure' takes widely differing forms. In *A Grass Rope* (1957), which won Mayne the *Carnegie Medal, it is a unicorn, supposedly immured beneath the Yorkshire fells. In *Underground Alley* (1958) it is a forgotten street lying underneath a Welsh town, and in *The Thumbstick* (1959) it is an old stave which can save a family's farm from falling into the hands of a religious sect.

The importance of the geographical settings in these books suggested to some commentators on Mayne's work that his real 'heroes' were the places themselves. Others pointed out that Mayne is not really concerned to describe places but to see them through the eyes of his child characters.

There are no real heroes in Mayne's books and no villains. Sometimes there is even very little story. Most of his novels begin very slowly, with the characters gradually revealing themselves through the dialogue. (Mayne's style of dialogue was in itself idiosyncratic and oblique.) Mayne's avoidance of the conventionalities of plot and character is even more striking in a series of short novels for younger children that he began to write in 1960. None of these has much 'story', though some are more eventful than others: in *No More School* (1965) village schoolchildren keep their school open themselves when their teacher is taken ill. But *The Fishing Party* (1960) simply describes children catching, cooking, and eating crayfish. Some of these books were admired when they were first published for the charm of their style, but others came under attack as

'lacking in any point or purpose' (as a reviewer wrote of *Water Boatman*, 1964). Moreover by the mid-1960s, while Mayne's longer novels were generally being praised for their sober maturity, there was also criticism of his mannered style and lack of obvious excitement: the *Times Literary Supplement* wrote of *Pig in the Middle*: 'It is simple to the point of lacking interest...One smells here too much of the labour of creation, too little spontaneity.'

At this point in his career, Mayne visibly changed course, perhaps in reaction to his critics. Like several other English children's writers of this time, he began to abandon strict realism. *Earthfasts* (1966) is a *fantasy about an 18th-cent. drummer boy who disappears underground, playing his drum, and then emerges two centuries later, unaware that time has passed. Next came *The Battlefield* (1967), in which the forces of nature revenge themselves on humanity, and *Over the Hills and Far Away* (1968), in which a girl from post-Roman Britain, accused of being a *witch and threatened with death, changes place with a 20th-cent. girl who looks like her. In 1970 Mayne began to write books which investigate human relationships (particularly within families), without either the 'treasure hunt' device of his earlier novels or any element of the supernatural. Mayne's most ambitious book from this period is *A Game of Dark* (1971), in which a boy, mentally ill as a result of his difficult relationship with his dying father, finds himself slipping into a fantasy world in which he is the would-be slayer of a terrible *dragon.

Mayne spent most of his writing life in a cottage in the Yorkshire dales, where he also composed music—he wrote the score for the first version of Alan *Garner's *Holly from the Bongs* (1966). His 1982 entry in *Who's Who* stated that he had up to that date published 'about sixty-six' books for children. Near the end of his life Mayne served a prison sentence for sexual abuse of a number of young girls, which led to his work being dropped from many reading lists and pulled from many library shelves. His books remain, however, among the most accomplished writing for children in recent decades, though their challenges mean that they are sometimes more acclaimed critically than widely read by child readers.

M.C. Higgins, the Great (1974) By Virginia *Hamilton. Thirteen-year-old M. C. (Mayo Cornelius) lives on a mountain named after his grandmother, a former slave. When the family's home and rural way of life are threatened by the environmental destruction caused by strip-mining, M. C. comes into conflict with his father's superstitious views and must reconcile his heritage with his own beliefs and find a way to look to the future. With complex characters and poetic language, this *Bildungsroman* won the 1975 *Newbery Medal and the National Book Award.

MEADE, L. T. (Elizabeth ('Lillie') Thomasina Meade) (1854–1914) Hugely prolific author of *girls' stories; beginning at the age of seventeen she wrote more than 300 books. Her most famous story was *A *World of Girls* (1886). She was born in Cork, the daughter of a clergyman; after her marriage in 1879 to Toulmin Smith, she settled in London. For six years she edited the magazine *Atalanta*.

MEADER, Stephen W. (Warren) (1892–1977) American writer of boys' *adventure stories published from the 1920s to the 1960s; most are set in pioneer days.

MEAKER, Marijane (M. E. Kerr) (1927–) American author of *young adult novels that tackle subjects such as *racism, class, and *sexuality. Her first book, *Dinky Hocker Shoots Smack!* (1972), about a girl whose mother works with drug addicts, was among *School Library Journal*'s hundred most significant books for children and young adults of the 20th cent. Among Kerr's other titles are *If I Love You, Am I Trapped Forever?* (1973), *Gentlehands* (1978), about a teenaged boy who discovers his grandfather's Nazi past, and *Deliver Us from Evie* (1994) and *'Hello', I Lied* (1998), both featuring gay characters. Meaker won a lifetime achievement award for young adult literature from the *American Library Association.

MEANS, Florence Crannell (1891–1980) One of the first American authors to write for the *young adult market, in books such as *A Candle in the Mist* (1931), about pioneer life in the 1870s. Many of her novels were about Native Americans (*see* 'INDIANS' OF NORTH AMERICA) and other ethnic minorities in the USA.

Meddlesome Matty A poem in *Original Poems, for Infant Minds* by Ann and Jane *Taylor and others.

MEE, Arthur (Henry) (1875–1943) Editor of *The *Children's Encyclopaedia*. He was the son of

a Nottinghamshire railway fireman who brought him up according to Baptist and Radical principles. While contributing a daily column to the *St James's Gazette*, one of London's evening papers, he became noted for the vast range of knowledge displayed in his writings. This was the result not of wide reading but of the fact that he collected huge numbers of press cuttings and filed them methodically by subject. His work came to the attention of Alfred *Harmsworth (later Lord Northcliffe), who began to employ him on the *Daily Mail*, and in 1905 decided that he should compile *The Harmsworth Self-Educator*, which was issued in fortnightly parts with great success. It was succeeded by *The Harmsworth History of the World*, and then in 1908 by *The Children's Encyclopaedia*.

His other notable venture was *The *Children's Newspaper*, and his last great labour was *The King's England*, a topographical series which occupied the final twelve years of his life.

Lord Northcliffe once described Mee as 'a narrow-minded Nonconformist'. He certainly retained many of the prejudices of his upbringing, and during the First World War he launched a campaign to establish Prohibition in Britain. (Another Harmsworth employee remarked: 'Who is going to rob the working-man of his beer? Not Mee!') But in manner he was quiet and unassuming, leaving others to amass huge fortunes from his work, and it is difficult not to admire the relentless energy with which he wrote and edited so many millions of words. He once admitted privately: 'I know nothing about children!' Certainly his writings show no special understanding of them; but, as his biographer has observed, 'he was always a child himself'.

MEEK, Margaret (Meek Spencer, Margaret) (1925–) British specialist in literacy and children's literature, and an internationally influential expert who is Emeritus Reader in Education at the Institute of Education, University of London. Her influential publications include *Learning to Read* (1982), *How Texts Teach What Readers Learn* (1987), *On Being Literate* (1990), *The Cool Web* (1977), and *Coming of Age in Children's Literature* (2003), and her work remains essential reading for anyone concerned with children's reading and writing. In 1970 she received the *Eleanor Farjeon Award for services to children's literature.

Meg and Mog (1972) The first of a long series of *picture books about a *witch called Meg and her cat Mog, and their friend Owl.

The artist is Jan *Pieńkowski and the text is by Helen Nicoll. Three decades after the first book was published, the series was adapted for television animation.

MEGGENDORFER, Lothar (1847–1925) German creator of *movable picture books, such as *Comic Actors* (English edition, 1891). One of his most lavish productions, *The City Park*, was reissued in 1982.

MEIGS, Cornelia (Lynde) (1884–1973) American author who wrote some thirty books for children. Many were *historical novels, including *Master Simon's Garden* (1916), set in Massachusetts in *Puritan days, and *The Willow Whistle* (1931), a story of frontier life in the Midwest. Meigs also wrote a children's biography of Louisa M. *Alcott (1933), which won the *Newbery Medal. She was editor and part author of *A Critical History of Children's Literature* (1953, revised 1969).

Melendy children In *The *Saturdays* stories by Elizabeth *Enright.

MELTZER, Milton (1915–2009) American author, mainly of information books for young people, who was strongly influenced by his upbringing in an immigrant area of Worcester, Massachusetts. He worked as a journalist and as a public relations executive, but his hobby of historical research finally became a career when in 1956 he co-authored *A Pictorial History of the Negro in America* with Langston Hughes (1902–67). His books often told of the dispossessed and those who struggled for freedom or simply to live, including *Brother Can You Spare a Dime?* (1969) about the Great Depression; *Ten Queens* (1998), which told the stories of women who ruled in their own right; *All Times, All Peoples* (1980), a history of slavery; *The Jewish Americans, A History in Their Own Words* (1982); and *Rescue: the Story of how Gentiles Saved Jews in the Holocaust* (1988).

Mélusine *See* Little Mermaid, The; Undine.

Memoirs of a London Doll, *written by herself; edited by Mrs Fairstar* (1846) Really the work of Richard Henry *Horne. Maria Poppet, a *doll made by a poor toymaker in Holborn, is acquired by a series of families of different social standing, and observes such features of London life as *Punch and Judy and the Lord Mayor's Show. Towards the end of the book she is taken to 'The New Grand Christmas Pantomime' at Drury Lane (*see* Pantomime), complete with Harlequinade.

She is dropped on the stage, found by Colum bine, and given to the daughter of the actress's patron.

MEREDITH, Louisa Anne (1812–95) Australian artist, writer, and children's poet who was born in Birmingham, England, and settled in Tasmania. She then went on to publish works on Australian subjects; *Some of My Bush Friends in Tasmania* came out in 1860 and, probably a little later (and more specifically for children), there appeared *Loved and Lost, The True Story of a Short Life, Told in Gossip Verse*. In 1878 she brought out *Grandmamma's Verse Book for Young Australians*, much of which reappeared as *Waratah Rhymes for Young Australia* (1892). She is credited with being the first writer to put Australian experiences into verse for children.

Merlin Magician and soothsayer in the legends of King *Arthur. According to medieval tradition, first recorded in the writings of Geoffrey of Monmouth, Merlin or Merlyn was born of a union between a spirit or incubus (according to some accounts, the Devil himself) and a nun. He first appears in the Arthurian story when his services as a seer are used by the British king Vortigern.

T. H. *White, in *The *Sword in The Stone* (1938), portrays Merlin as a seer and magician whose absent-mindedness is caused by his living backwards in time rather than forwards; thus he knows all about the future but cannot easily remember the past. Merlin appears in Susan *Cooper's sequence *The *Dark Is Rising* (1965–77) as 'Merriman', while in Peter *Dickinson's *The Weathermonger* he comes back to life in the modern world and causes the population of England to turn against machinery—an idea perhaps developed from C. S. *Lewis's *That Hideous Strength* (1945).

mermaids In early use (from the 14th cent.), the term 'mermaid' sometimes referred to the Sirens of classical mythology. Hans Christian *Andersen's celebrated story *The *Little Mermaid* (1836) was partly derived from the French story of Mélusine the water-sprite (*see* UNDINE). Notable among modern children's books which feature mermaids and similar sea creatures are *Wet Magic* (1913) by E. *Nesbit and *The *Sea Egg* (1967) by Lucy M. *Boston. Others are *The *Mermaid and the Simpleton* (1949) by Barbara Leonie *Picard and *A Book of Mermaids* (1967) by Ruth *Manning-Sanders. One act of *Peter Pan* is set in 'The Mermaids' Lagoon'.

MERRIAM, Eve (1916–92) American poet and author who wrote books which explore the breaking-up of traditional sex roles, e.g. *Mommies at Work* (1961). Her collections of poems for children include *I Am a Man: Ode to Martin Luther King, Jr.* (1971).

Merrifield family In *The Stokesley Secret* by Charlotte M. *Yonge.

Merry Adventures of Robin Hood, The (1883) Written and illustrated by Howard *Pyle, the most popular and lavishly illustrated late 19th-cent. American version of the *Robin Hood stories. Pyle's Robin dwells 'in merry England in the time of old . . . within the depths of Sherwood Forest . . . living upon the King's venison, washed down with draughts of ale of October brewing'. The dialogue is mock-medieval in style, and the book is most notable for its full-page illustrations in Pyle's version of the Pre-Raphaelite style.

Merry's Museum A *magazine founded in 1841 by S. G. *Goodrich. Its principal feature was the serialization of stories by '*Peter Parley'—Goodrich himself—many of which describe Uncle Robert Merry taking a group of children on some improbable educational journey, such as a tour of Europe by balloon; such stories are described by Frank L. Mott in his *History of American Magazines* (1938):

Thomas would look down and see Greece: 'Ah, there is Greece!' he would exclaim. Then Uncle Robert would say, 'Harriet, what can you tell us about Greece?' And Harriet would be ready with an extraordinary flow of information which would last until someone spied Turkey and thus changed the subject if not the conversation.

Goodrich's association with *Merry's Museum* ended in 1854. The magazine continued under new management and in 1866 Louisa M. *Alcott was appointed editor; the magazine finally came to an end six years later.

MEYER, Stephenie American author of *Twilight.

MEYNELL, Laurence (1899–1989) Prolific British author of popular fiction who produced a large number of children's books, many as 'A. Stephen Tring'. These included a 'Penny' series for girls, beginning with *Penny Dreadful* (1949). He is now chiefly remembered for *The Old Gang* (1947), a *school story set unconventionally in a day school. Meynell made further efforts to be up to date in *Barry's Exciting Year* (1951), which describes a working-class boy's efforts to pass the eleven-plus

examination. He also wrote *career novels, under his own name (for boys) and as 'Valerie Baxter' (for girls).

Michael L. Printz Award Given by the *American Library Association for the year's best teen book. The first winner, in 2000, was *Monster* by Walter Dean Myers. Subsequent winners have included David *Almond, An Na, Aidan *Chambers, Meg *Rosoff, John *Green, Libba *Bray, Paolo Bacigalupi, Nick Lake, and Marcus *Sedgwick. The prize takes its name from a Kansas librarian who died in 1996. Each year a number of runners-up are named 'Michael L. Printz Honor Books'.

Mickey Mouse A cartoon character invented by Walt *Disney and his artists. He first appeared in *Plane Crazy* (1928), a silent film, though this was less well known than *Steamboat Willie* (1928), the first cartoon film to have a soundtrack. Mickey was drawn for many years by Ub Iwerks, Disney's chief animator. In the 1930s Mickey began to become a national craze in America, featuring in *comic strips and in merchandise. Among many Mickey Mouse films is *Gulliver Mickey* (1934), a version of *Gulliver's Travels*, and he appeared as the Sorcerer's Apprentice in that section of *Fantasia* (1940).

Midnight Folk, The (1927) A *fantasy for children by John *Masefield; it shares some characters with Masefield's adult adventures *Sard Harker* (1924) and *Odtaa* (1926), and with his later children's story *The *Box of Delights* (1935). Kay Harker, an orphan brought up by a bad-tempered *governess, learns of the legend of treasure lost or hidden by his great-grandfather, a West India merchant sea-captain. At night Kay is introduced by Nibbins the cat to the 'midnight folk', some of whom are animals and others his own old toys from the days before the governess. With these friends Kay has nightly adventures in search of the treasure. Pitted against the Midnight Folk are seven *witches, among whom is Sylvia Daisy Pouncer, the governess herself. The book, which is breathless in pace, frequently slips into characteristic Masefield verse.

Midshipman Easy, Mr *See* Mr Midshipman Easy.

Midway (1967) A novel by Anne *Barrett.

Miffy (from 1955) A small rabbit whose story is told in a series of stylized, short board books (and now picture books, puzzle books, sticker books, etc.) written and illustrated by

Dutch artist Dick *Bruna, whose primary colours with thick graphic lines delineating simple shapes have been copied and admired ever since. Two translators have brought the rhyming stories to an English audience: Patricia *Crampton, starting in 1963 with the earlier titles, and Tony Mitton (1951–) with a modern version in 2014. Miffy has been filmed for television and a wide range of merchandise is available. She also serves as a 'celebrity character spokesperson' for Unicef.

Mighty Mouse Hero of American cartoon films and *annuals. When the film series began in 1942 it was intended as a parody of *Superman.

Mike *See* Wodehouse P. G.

Mike Mulligan and His Steam Shovel *See* Burton, Virginia Lee.

Mildred Hubble Heroine of the *Worst Witch* stories by Jill Murphy.

MILES, Miska Pseudonym of Patricia Miles *Martin.

Milk for Babes A *catechism composed for children in 1641. Its author was John Cotton (1584–1652), a minister noted for his *Puritan views. His catechism was first printed in Cambridge, Mass., between 1641 and 1645, and again in London in 1646, under the title *Milk for Babes, Drawn out of the breasts of both Testaments, Chiefly, for the spiritual nourishment of Boston babes in either England: but may be of like use for any children*. After 1690 the catechism began to make its appearance in many editions of *The *New England Primer*.

The chief characteristic of *Milk for Babes* was its brevity: it had a mere 64 questions, most of them requiring only short answers, compared with the 107 of the Shorter Catechism. It was also markedly Nonconformist in character; e.g. the sacraments were described as 'a sign and seal' rather than (as in the Shorter Catechism) an actual means of salvation.

MILLAR, H. R. (1869–1940) British artist associated with *The *Strand Magazine*, for which he illustrated stories by E. *Nesbit. The first of her books to contain pictures by him was *Five Children and It* (1902); he was thereafter her favourite illustrator. He also illustrated *The Golden Fairy Book* (*c.*1895, an anonymous imitation of the Andrew Lang *Fairy Books*), Sir Arthur *Quiller-Couch's *Fairy Tales, Far and Near* (1895), and *Puck of Pook's Hill* (1906) by *Kipling.

MILLARD, Glenda (1952–) Australian children's novelist and picture-book author. She left school at the age of fifteen and did not begin to write until she was forty-five. Her books are often beautiful, with a poetic style, slightly magical plots, and whimsical characters. Her style achieves notice in prestigious awards such as the various Premier's Literary Awards, including the Queensland Premier's Literary Award for Best Young Adult book, which she received in 2009 for *A Small Free Kiss in the Dark*, a story of wartime survival. Perhaps her most famous books are the *Kingdom of Silk* series, beginning with *The Naming of Tishkin Silk* (2003). In a magic-realist world the large extended Silk family face poignant problems of everyday life and solve them with love. *Perry Angel's Suitcase* (2008) was shortlisted for the *CBCA Book of the Year: Younger Readers award in 2009—Perry is a fragile foster child who learns trust and love with the Silk family. Her picture-book texts are often in poetry, and *Lightning Jack* (2012), written in ballad form and illustrated by Patricia *Mullins, was shortlisted for the 2013 CBCA Picture Book of the Year—Sam Tully musters a wild black stallion, and in this fantasy, he races alongside Phar Lap in the Melbourne Cup. Millard's books have been published internationally and often win awards.

MILLIGAN, Spike (1918–2002) British comedian and humorous writer who came to fame in the *Goon Show* radio series in the 1950s and wrote a number of anarchic books for children. These include *Silly Verse for Kids* (1963), *The Bald Twit Lion* (1970), *Badjelly the Witch* (1973), and *Goblins* (1978, with W. Heath *Robinson's illustrations).

Millions (2004) Based on Frank Cottrell *Boyce's own screenplay for the film of the same name, this fantastic first novel was an immediate success, winning the *Carnegie Medal as well as an army of enthusiastic fans. Set in the near future, with England just about to replace sterling with the euro, it is the story of two brothers, Damian and Anthony, who find a million pounds. Sounds great, but being rich turns out to be far less fun than they imagined. A book to make readers laugh and cry, for while the brothers' predicament is funny (hmm, buy pizza or solve world poverty?) the recent death of their mother and the effect that has had on Damian in particular add many layers to the story.

Millions of Cats See GÁG, WANDA.

Milly-Molly-Mandy The creation of the British writer and illustrator Joyce Lankester Brisley (1896–1978). Milly-Molly-Mandy (really Millicent Margaret Amanda) is a little girl who lives in a 'nice white cottage' with her 'Father and Mother and Grandpa and Grandma and Uncle and Aunty'; her acquaintances include 'Little-friend-Susan'. The first book in the series was *Milly-Molly-Mandy Stories* (1928), and the last was published in 1967. The stories are very simple but have gentle humour, largely arising from the repetition of key phrases.

MILNE, A. A. (Alan Alexander) (1882–1956) Humorist, playwright, and the author of four children's classics, the verse collections **When We Were Very Young* (1924) and **Now We Are Six* (1927), and two books of stories, **Winnie-the-Pooh* (1926) and *The *House at Pooh Corner* (1928).

The son of a headmaster, he had two older brothers, and was aware as a child that he was the fairy-tale youngest son who would do best, and the 'headmaster's Benjamin'. For much of his childhood he wore long curls in the *Little Lord Fauntleroy fashion. With the second of his brothers, Ken, sixteen months his senior, he 'shared equally all belief, all knowledge, all ambition, all hope and all fear', whereas Barry, the eldest brother, stood apart, 'secure in his position as the bad boy of the family'. Ken and Alan shared a remarkable freedom, being allowed to go for long walks by themselves when they were only eight and six years old; much of Alan's highly-developed memory for the adventures and affections of his own childhood can be attributed to his sharing them, and (later) the adult recollections of them, with his brother.

On leaving Westminster School, he decided to go up to Cambridge to read mathematics at Trinity College, chiefly so that he could fulfil his real ambition—to be editor of the university magazine *Granta*, a student periodical which thought of itself as the Cambridge *Punch*. He began to write light verse and humorous prose on his own, achieved the desired editorship, and was noticed by one of the staff of *Punch* itself, in London. But in consequence his degree was poor; he disappointed his father by seeming unsuited to teaching or the Civil Service, and he decided to go to London, live on the small remains of the money set aside for his education, and write.

His first accepted piece was a burlesque of **Sherlock Holmes*. This gave him hopes of

swiftly becoming editor of *Punch*, but in his first year he made only £20 and spent all his patrimony. He moved to cheaper lodgings and gradually began to acquire regular work writing sketches and verses for *Punch* and other papers. Then, entirely unexpectedly, *Punch* invited him to become Assistant Editor at the age of twenty-four.

The job was in fact comparatively menial, apart from the writing of his own contributions, for the then Editor, Owen Seaman ('a strange, unlucky man', who has sometimes been suggested as a model for Eeyore in the Pooh stories), was particularly active in the office. But Milne now had an assured income, and was 'very young, very light-hearted, confident of myself, confident of the future'. In 1913, he married Dorothy ('Daphne') de Sélincourt, Owen Seaman's god-daughter. Because she laughed at his jokes—'she had my contributions to *Punch* by heart before she met me'— he henceforward dubbed her his 'collaborator'.

The routine of the weekly article for *Punch* began to pall after a time and by way of escape Milne started to write plays, encouraged by J. M. *Barrie whom he admired hugely. But war broke out: Milne became a signalling officer and was an instructor in England until 1916. Persuaded by his wife, he wrote a children's *play for a battalion entertainment at his camp. He then expanded it into a book, *Once Upon a Time*. A humorous and elaborate tale in the manner of Thackeray's *The *Rose and The Ring* and Lang's **Prince Prigio*, it was first published in 1917 and then revived with new illustrations by Charles *Robinson in 1925. 'Few people have read it,' wrote Milne in 1939, 'and nobody knows whether it is meant for children or for grown-ups. I don't know myself. But it was the greatest fun to do . . . It made the war seem very far away.'

Encouraged by this he wrote another play, *Wurzel-Flummery*, about a legacy which is given on condition that all the legatees adopt the same ridiculous name. Before it could be performed he was posted to France. He was eventually returned to England with trench fever, and ended the war writing patriotic propaganda for the Intelligence service.

Though Milne expected to return to *Punch* after demobilization, Owen Seaman had found an older and more congenial Assistant Editor in his absence, and he resigned. He wrote more plays, among them one for children, **Make Believe*, tried a *detective story, and became, briefly, a dramatic critic. In 1920, the Milnes' only child, a son, was born. 'We

had intended to call it *Rosemary*,' he wrote, 'but decided later that *Billy* would be more suitable. However, as you can't be christened William—at least, we didn't see why anybody should—we had to think of two other names. One of us thought of Robin, the other of Christopher, names wasted on him who called himself Billy Moon as soon as he could talk, and has been Moon to his family and friends ever since. ['Moon' was a childish attempt to say 'Milne'.] I mention this because it explains why the publicity which came to be attached to "Christopher Robin" never seemed to affect us personally.'

When the boy was about three, Milne 'wasted a morning' writing the poem 'Vespers'—

> Hush, hush, whisper who dares,
> Christopher Robin is saying his prayers.

—and gave it as a present to his wife, saying she could keep any money it might bring in. 'It turned out to be the most expensive present I had ever given her.' It also proved to be a particular torment for his shy schoolboy-teased son in later years, though a careful reading of it, as Milne was at pains to point out, reveals not a sentimental but a fairly cynical portrayal of childish egotism.

A few months later Milne was asked by Rose *Fyleman, who contributed fairy verses to *Punch*, to let her have something for a new children's *magazine she was editing, entitled *The Merry-Go-Round* (an offshoot of the annual **Joy Street*). At first he refused, then wrote for her 'The Dormouse and the Doctor', whereupon she asked for more. And so, on a rain-blighted holiday in Wales, he escaped from the crowd of fellow guests to the summerhouse, and for eleven days wrote a set of children's verses, one each day, because 'to write a few would be fun—until I was tired of it', and because 'there on the other side of the lawn was a child with whom I had lived for three years . . . and here within me were unforgettable memories of my own childhood'. He added more verses when he got home, enough for a book, and allowed some to be published in advance in *Punch*; so it was that E. H. *Shepard, a *Punch* regular, became accepted as the best person to illustrate the book. *When We Were Very Young* in fact sold half a million copies in the first ten years following publication in 1924. Milne wrote: 'I think such merit as attaches to the verses . . . was won by taking pains . . . Whatever else they lack, the verses are technically good . . . *When We Were Very Young* is the work of a light

verse writer taking his job seriously even though he is taking it into the nursery.'

A few individual fairy stories by Milne appeared in periodicals at about this time. Then the first of the storybooks, *Winnie-the-Pooh*, came out in 1926, with *The House at Pooh Corner* following in 1928. In between there was another collection of verses, *Now We Are Six* (1927). Milne wrote of the Pooh books:

The animals in the stories came for the most part from the nursery. My collaborator [his wife] had already given them individual voices, their owner by constant affection had given them the twist in their features which denoted character, and Shepard drew them, as one might say, from the living model. They were what they are for anyone to see; I described rather than invented them. Only Rabbit and Owl were my own unaided work.

The setting for the stories, 'the Forest', was also drawn from life: it was the countryside surrounding Cotchford, an extended Queen Anne farmhouse between Tunbridge Wells and East Grinstead. Milne produced no more children's books after 1928 (though a children's play, *The Ugly Duckling*, came out in 1941); he hated repeating himself, and as soon as one form ceased to amuse and challenge him he moved on to another. During the 1920s and early 1930s he wrote a number of successful plays; they were witty and whimsical and appealed to audiences nurtured on the work of J. M. Barrie. Always a champion of *The *Wind in The Willows*, in 1928 he turned Grahame's book into a children's play, *Toad of Toad Hall*. He was the author of two novels, *Two People* (1931) and *Chloe Marr* (1946), and of many essays and introductions, collections of which appeared in book form. But no new work after *The House at Pooh Corner* made much mark; public taste for his adult writing waned, and his last play, in 1938, was a failure. He resented the fact that his children's books had come to dominate his reputation, and were sometimes used as a critical stick to beat his adult work. He died at Cotchford at the age of seventy-three.

Good-looking, socially acceptable, and confident, Milne had nevertheless a measure of the extreme shyness that afflicted both his father and his son, enough to make him if not anti-social then at any rate what his son called 'a private person', his 'heart . . . firmly buttoned up'. He smoked, and could not bear to be without a pipe; he played golf. His son's portrait of him in his autobiographical *The Enchanted Places* suggests a man isolated

in adulthood as, when a boy with Ken, he never was. Daphne, Milne's wife, for all her 'collaboration', never shared his recreations; domestic life left him in some senses excluded, relegated Eeyore-like to a 'gloomy place' of the house for his own quarters and kept at a distance from his son during the boy's early years by the existence of a beloved nanny. Milne was moreover not especially good at being companionable with a young child and so, in Christopher's opinion, 'it was precisely because he was not able to play with his small son that his longings sought and found satisfaction in another direction. He wrote about them instead.'

As a boy Christopher Robin Milne did look just as E. H. Shepard drew him, with eccentrically long hair and girlish clothes, perhaps because his mother had really wanted a girl. He was small, very shy, adored his nanny, and was for the most part protected from the consequences of fame; though he read the books often, 'the stories more than the poems', and at the age of seven he sang some of the verses for a gramophone record. Later, at school, he was more vulnerable and came especially to curse 'Vespers' for the opportunities it provided for teasing him. Later still, as a young man, he grew to resent more seriously the empty fame of being 'Christopher Robin' and the unfounded assumption that the proceeds of the books relieved him of earning a living. After a career creating, with his wife, a successful independent bookshop in Dartmouth, he wrote *The Enchanted Places* partly in belated reply to all the unanswered requests for information over the years, and partly so that his own feelings about 'Christopher Robin' might be understood.

MINARIK, Else Holmelund (1920–2012) Children's writer who was born in Denmark and emigrated to the United States in childhood. She is best known for her *Little Bear* series of readers (1957 onwards), illustrated by Maurice *Sendak.

miniature books These have been produced since the earliest days of printing. They were originally intended for the practical purpose of reducing to a convenient, portable size such works as the *Bible*, prayer books, and classics of literature. Later they became fashionable for their own sake and were regarded as a technical challenge. The smallest known miniature book is $\frac{3}{16}$ in square.

Children's miniature books were produced from the mid-18th cent., among the earliest

being Thomas *Boreman's set of *Gigantick Histories* (1740–3). In about 1800 John *Marshall published *The Infant's Library*, a set of 16 illustrated books, each measuring $2\frac{1}{4} \times 1\frac{3}{4}$ in., showing daily objects, children's games, etc.; they were sold in a special varnished box which formed a miniature bookcase. Alfred Mills (1776–1833), a *wood engraver, made a speciality of designing miniature *books of instruction which were published jointly by *Darton and John *Harris, e.g. *Natural History of Forty-Eight Quadrupeds* (1815), which was about $2\frac{1}{2} \times 2\frac{1}{4}$ in.

Ministering Children: *a tale dedicated to childhood* (1854) A celebrated English *evangelical novel by Maria Louisa Charlesworth (1819–80), a clergyman's daughter. Designed to teach children 'the exercise of those kindly feelings which have the Poor for their object', it is largely concerned with the good works of the Cliffords, the family of a country squire. The Cliffords' charity is, however, of a strictly limited sort; there is no suggestion that more radical measures of poor relief might be considered; and the carrying of soups and other gifts to the poor always takes second place to the preaching and practice of religion. Gillian *Avery has remarked (in *Nineteenth-Century Children*, 1965) that the book suggests 'that God has created a world where the poor exist to train the consciences and charitable instincts of those better off, the latter being rewarded with an emotional thrill after every kind action'.

The same author also wrote *Ministering Children, a sequel* (1867), *Oliver of the Mill* (1876), and *The Old Looking-Glass; or, Mrs Dorothy Cope's Recollections of Service* (1878).

Minnipins A race of small people in stories by Carol *Kendall.

Minnow on the Say (1955) There can be few books that more perfectly evoke the joys of childhood past than this marvellous adventure story by Philippa *Pearce. The Minnow is an old canoe that David finds stranded on the banks of the river Say at the end of his garden. The rightful owner is Adam, and the boys become friends and share in an adventure to find Adam's family's long-lost treasure, a treasure that will rescue them from financial ruin. Steeped in the joys of a long, hot summer, this is a treasure hunt, a historical mystery, and the story of friendship. Pearce never patronizes her readership, making this a book that can be read and reread for a lifetime.

Miss Bianca A mouse in stories by Margery *Sharp.

Miss Pickerell Spinster space-traveller in stories by Ellen *McGregor.

Mister Magnolia (1980) A rhyming picture book by Quentin *Blake. Mr Magnolia is very jolly, in spite of the fact that he has—as the refrain reminds us—only one boot. He does, however, have all manner of other things that do at least rhyme with 'boot' (an old trumpet that goes rooty-toot, two lovely sisters who play on the flute, etc.) and he does, in a triumphant ending, get a beautiful new (unmatching) boot to make up the pair. Though this is never made explicit, *Mister Magnolia* can be read as a counting book, with the pages progressing—one old trumpet, two lovely sisters, through green parakeets who are learning to hoot (four of them), and mice marching past as he takes the salute (nine).

Mistress Masham's Repose A novel by T. H. *White, first published in 1947. The book was suggested by *Gulliver's Travels*. It tells how ten-year-old Maria visits an island on a lake, where she discovers a colony of the tiny people of *Lilliput, which has been flourishing on the island for three centuries. These Lilliputians are descendants of captives brought to England by a sea-captain, who had learned of their existence from Gulliver himself. Maria is befriended by them, but their presence on the island is soon discovered by her odious *governess and the vicar, Mr Hater. These two determine to capture the Lilliputians and sell them at a great price. Much of the book's charm derives from White's portrayal of the Lilliputians as having maintained the manners and dress of the 18th cent., when they were first brought to England.

Misunderstood (1869) A novel by the British author Florence Montgomery (1843–1923), not originally intended for children but read widely by them. Humphrey Duncombe, the sturdy son of a widowed Member of Parliament, is neglected by his father in favour of his delicate younger brother Miles, and is allowed to run wild. The two boys fall off a rotten branch into a pond; Miles escapes with a wetting, but Humphrey is fatally injured, and as he dies his father is stricken with remorse at not having loved him enough. Like Catherine Sinclair's *Holiday House* thirty years earlier, the book gave its approval to high-spirited and unruly behaviour in

children. It was very popular and probably helped to relax late Victorian attitudes to children's conduct.

MITCHELL, Elyne *See* SILVER BRUMBY.

MITCHISON, Naomi (Margaret) (1897-1999) British author, daughter of the physicist J. S. Haldane and sister of J. B. S. Haldane, author of *My Friend Mr Leakey*. Upon leaving St Anne's College, Oxford, she began to write *historical novels, beginning with *The Conquered* (1923), set during the Roman conquest of Gaul. Her subsequent long literary career included many books for children ranging in settings from the West Highlands (e.g. *The Big House*, 1950, a *Nesbit-like fantasy) to Botswana, where she spent much time in her later years and became adoptive mother to a chief (*The Family at Ditlabeng*, 1969, and *Sunrise Tomorrow*, 1973). She was involved with left-wing politics between the two World Wars, and in 1932 edited for Gollancz *An Outline for Boys and Girls and Their Parents*, a critical survey of modern knowledge and opinion from a 'left' point of view.

MLYNOWSKI, Sarah (1977-) Canadian author of books for adults and young adults, whose work as an editor of romance fiction led her to writing the chick-lit bestseller, *Milkrun* (2001). She moved into books for teen readers with the fast-paced, witty *Bras and Broomsticks* (2005), the first in the *Magic in Manhattan: All About Rachel* series. She brings her quick-fire dialogue and dizzying adventures to younger readers too with the *Whatever After* series, which turns fairy stories upside down and inside out, starting with the *Snow White story, *Fairest of All* (2012), and most recently the *Snow Queen-based *Cold as Ice* (2014).

Modern Traveller, The (1898) One of the set of comic verse books by Hilaire *Belloc with pictures by Lord Basil Blackwood ('B.T. B.'); unlike the others in the series it was scarcely intended for children, but Belloc enthusiasts regard it as the finest of the set and many young readers have enjoyed it. The narrator, a worldly-wise and unscrupulous adventurer, describes to a journalist his experiences on an expedition into the jungle, accompanied by Commander Henry Sin, an archetypal Bohemian and cad, and Mr William Blood, a speculating businessman. Sin is eventually eaten by cannibals, and as for Blood,

> It seems they sold him by the slice.
> Well, every man has got his price.

Like all the Belloc verse books, *The Modern Traveller* is in large part a parody—in this case of the late 19th-cent. *adventure story in general and of *King Solomon's Mines* (1885) in particular.

MOEYAERT, Bart (1964) Flemish writer and poet, a number of whose books have been published in English translation: *Dani Bennoni, lang zal hij leven* (2004; translated as *Dani Bennoni: Long May He Live*, by Wanda Boeke, 2008); *Het is de liefde die we niet begrijpen* (1999; translated as *It's Love We Don't Understand*, by Wanda Boeke, 2001); *Blote handen* (1995; translated as *Bare Hands*, by David Colmer, 1998); and *Broere* (2000; translated as *Brothers*, by Wanda Boeke, 2005). Moeyaert himself also translates into Dutch; his translations include Christine *Nöstlinger's *Der neue Pinocchio* from the German, and Shaun *Tan's *Rules of Summer* and *The Lost Thing* from the English.

Moffats, The A family in three novels by Eleanor *Estes, *The Moffats* (1941), *The Middle Moffat* (1942), and *Rufus M* (1943). The family lives in the small Connecticut town of Cranbury. There are four children, Sylvia ('sweet sixteen'), Joey ('the oldest son'), Jane ('the middle Moffat'), and five-year-old Rufus M. The books are set in the period just before and during the First World War. John Rowe *Townsend has described the Moffat saga as 'outstanding among family stories'.

Mog, the Forgetful Cat (1970) A picture book by Judith *Kerr, the first in a series, and one of Kerr's most enduringly popular. Mog, based on one of Kerr's own family pets, is a forgetful grey cat, 'nice but not very clever', who lives with the Thomas family. The book shows us the trouble she causes, and her own existential crises, and ends with her heroically (albeit accidentally) catching a burglar in the Thomas's house. The dozen titles in the *Mog* series conclude with *Goodbye, Mog* (2002), in which Kerr puts her old cat to sleep at last.

MOGRIDGE, George (1787-1854) Prolific British writer of moral and religious works for children and adults who often used pseudonyms, including 'Old Humphrey', '*Peter Parley', and 'Ephraim Holding'. His work was largely *evangelical in character.

Mole In *The *Wind in The Willows* by Kenneth *Grahame.

Mole, Adrian *See* SECRET DIARY OF ADRIAN MOLE, THE.

Molesworth Schoolboy (or 'skoolboy') autobiographer, the creation of British prep-school master turned humorist Geoffrey Willans with illustrations by Ronald *Searle. He made his appearance in *Down With Skool!* (1953) and *How to be Topp* (1954), *Whizz for Atomms* (1956), and *Back in the Jug Agane* (1959). This is how he introduces himself in the second book:

This is me e.g. nigel molesworth the curse of st custard's which is the skool i am at. It is uterly wet and weedy as i shall (i hope) make clear but of course that is the same with all skools...

The only good things about skool are the BOYS wizz who are noble brave fearless etc. although you have various swots, bulies, cissies, milksops greedy guts and oiks with whom i am forced to mingle hem-hem ...

MOLESWORTH, Mary Louisa (Stewart) (1839–1921) One of the most prolific late 19th-cent. English children's authors. She was the daughter of a businessman and spent most of her childhood in Manchester. Her favourite books in her youth included *Evenings At Home* by John Aikin and his sister Mrs *Barbauld, and *Jemima Placid* by Mary Ann *Kilner, and some of the sedateness and didacticism of these works can be found in her own writings. In 1861 she married Major Richard Molesworth, who had served in the Crimea and had received a head-wound which left him with 'a very violent temper'. Mrs Molesworth began to write three-volume novels for adults, in which a perennial theme was the incompatibility of hero and heroine—a reflection of the unhappiness of her marriage. For her writings she at first used the pseudonym of 'Ennis Graham', not putting her own on a title page until 1877. Her adult novels made no impact, and Sir Noel Paton, illustrator of *The *Water-Babies*, suggested that she should write for children.

In 1875 Macmillan published *Tell me a Story*, a collection of tales by her including a short *fairy story, 'The Reel Fairies', which was based on her childhood memories of inventing fairy characters from cotton-reels in her mother's sewing-box. The book was illustrated by Walter *Crane, who provided pictures for many of her subsequent works. In 1876 came her first children's novel, *Carrots*. This was followed in 1877 by *The *Cuckoo Clock*, the most enduring of her books. Next came *The *Tapestry Room* (1879), another *fantasy, this time set in northern France, where Mrs Molesworth made her home for a time after her marriage broke up and she was legally separated from her husband.

Other notable books by her from this period are *A Christmas Child* (1880), *The Adventures of Herr Baby* (1881), and *Hoodie* (1882), a portrait of her daughter Juliet. Her popularity increased fast, and her admirers included Swinburne, who thought her scarcely inferior to George Eliot. In 1883 she settled in London, and became something of a literary lion.

In all she published almost exactly 100 books. Among her later works of fantasy are *Christmas Tree Land* (1884), *Four Winds Farm* (1887), and *The Ruby Ring* (1904). But her strength really lay in the realistic portrayal of children's lives—'save in an occasional flight to fairyland,' she wrote in 1894, 'children's stories should be *real*'—and one of the best examples of this is *The *Carved Lions* (1895).

Her books are directly descended from the *moral tale, though she was usually only subtly didactic, and her books contain some delightful elements of fantasy.

Opinions about her work vary. Her 20th-cent. admirers have included Roger Lancelyn *Green, author of a monograph about her, and Gillian *Avery, who writes: 'Mrs Molesworth remembers vividly how it feels to be a child, how, even in the secure nursery world that she describes, there are worries and troubles that seem so enormous that they blot out all the sun.' But many modern readers find Mrs Molesworth's habit of making small children talk in baby language irritating almost beyond endurance. Jane Cooper published a comprehensive biography of Mrs Molesworth in 2002.

Molly Whuppie A folk tale recorded in *English Fairy Stories* (1890). The first part is virtually identical to *Hop o' *my Thumb*, Molly, the youngest of three sisters, taking the place of Hop and a *giant replacing the *ogre. After the giant has been tricked into slaughtering his own children, Molly returns three times to his house to steal his sword, his purse, and his ring. The story is sometimes printed in modern collections.

Mom, the Wolf Man, and Me (1972) A novel by Norma *Klein.

MONCRIEFF, Ascott R. Hope- See HOPE, ASCOTT R.

MONJO, F. N. (Ferdinand Nicolas, III) (1924–78) American *historical novelist for children, known chiefly for *The Drinking Gourd* (1970), about runaway slaves, *Poor Richard in France* (1973), a portrait of Benjamin Franklin, and *Indian Summer* (1968), his first book, which has been attacked for its presentation

of '*Indians' (Native Americans) as cowardly and brutal.

Monster (1999) An atmospheric, emotional and thought-provoking *young adult novel by Walter Dean *Myers, which tells the story of sixteen-year-old Steve Harmon, who is in prison, accused of murdering a Harlem shopkeeper. Steve tells his own story, all the while trying to work out the sense of what is happening by transposing the events of his trial into a screenplay. Is he innocent or guilty? With so much confused and confusing testimony, where is the truth? Dealing with peer pressure and morality, and told in a challenging and innovative format that mixes diary entries, script, and black-and-white photographs, *Monster* won the inaugural *Michael L. Printz Award in 2000.

Monster Calls, A (2010) Written by Patrick *Ness, who develops an idea that came to Siobhan *Dowd during the final stages of the cancer that led to her death in 2007. The book focuses on thirteen-year-old Conor's struggle with his mother's terminal illness, and the arrival of a terrifying, storytelling monster. Written with honesty and bravery and strikingly illustrated by Jim *Kay, the story shows the monster enabling Conor to deal with the world and people around him and ultimately gain some closure when the time comes to say goodbye. *A Monster Calls* was awarded the *Carnegie Medal for the writing and *Kate Greenaway Medal for the illustrations, the first book to win both, among countless other awards. A beautiful and harrowing film version (from Ness's own screenplay) was released in 2016.

MONTEIRO LOBATO, José Bento Renato (1882–1948) The most influential of Brazil's early children's writers. With the publication in 1920 of *A Menina do Narizinho Arrebitado* ('The Girl with the Snub Nose') he introduced the Sítio do Picapau Amarelo—Yellow Woodpecker Farm—which would be the setting for his famous series of children's novels launched the following year, about a girl and boy and their toys. Significant recurring characters include Emília (a rag doll), the Visconde de Sabugosa (a corncob puppet), the Marquês de Rabicó (a pig), and Dona Benta (the farm's owner, and grandmother to the children). The series has been regularly adapted for television in the decades since its completion. It was controversial during his lifetime for some of the political views he expressed, and more recently following accusations of racism in his portrayal of black characters. Monteiro Lobato was also a translator into Portuguese of many children's books, including tales by Hans Christian *Andersen and the *Grimms, Lewis Carroll's *Alice books, *Black Beauty and *Pollyanna.

MONTESSORI, Maria (1870–1952) Italian educationalist, who evolved a system of learning which she described in her *Montessori Method* (1912). Her educational philosophy, which encourages children to develop through freedom of movement, choice and exploration within a prepared environment, underpins the work of Montessori schools all over the world today.

MONTGOMERY, Florence *See* MISUNDERSTOOD.

MONTGOMERY, L. M. (Lucy Maud) (1874–1942) Canadian writer, author of *Anne of Green Gables* (1908), who was born in Clifton, Prince Edward Island. Her mother died when she was two, and she was sent to live with her maternal grandparents in their farmhouse. In character she seems to have much resembled her heroine Anne.

She became a teacher, but gave it up to look after her widowed grandmother, while trying to have her writing published. *Anne of Green Gables*, her first novel, was written in 1905, but was at first rejected. When it finally appeared in 1908, it became an immediate success. In 1911 she married Ewen Macdonald, a Presbyterian minister, and moved to Ontario. They had three children, including one stillborn. *Anne of Green Gables* was followed by several sequels and by the popular Emily series, beginning with *Emily of New Moon* (1923), and by many other novels and short stories. She returned to writing about Anne after a long gap.

Montgomery's writing was a relief from her husband's religious melancholy and her own periodic depression. In 2008 her granddaughter revealed a note or diary entry that indicated that Montgomery may have taken her own life in 1942, though her death was recorded as from natural causes.

Her popularity and the many translations of her work continue to bring visitors to Prince Edward Island (especially from Japan where she is exceptionally popular), the setting of her books.

MONTGOMERY, Rutherford (George) (1894–1985) Prolific American author of *adventure stories, *animal stories, and *science fiction, published from 1932 onwards. His

books include a 'Yankee Flier' series set during the Second World War.

Montmorency *See* UPDALE, ELEANOR.

Moomin family The creation of the Finnish writer and illustrator Tove Jansson (1914–2001), who wrote in Swedish. She first recorded their exploits in *Comet in Moominland* (1946, published in England in 1951). The Moomins live in Moomin Valley in Moominland, a place where 'everyone did what they liked and seldom worried about tomorrow' and where 'very often unexpected and disturbing things used to happen, but nobody ever had time to be bored, and that is always a good thing'. A Moomin is, in the words of one commentator on the books, 'a sort of cuddly hippo who walks on two legs'. Moomintroll, the chief protagonist in most of the books, is the son of Moominpappa and Moominmamma, who are characterized respectively by a top hat and a handbag. Moomintroll loves the Snork Maiden, who appears to be of the same species as himself except that she has hair on her head. His friends are Sniff, a small creature resembling a kangaroo, and Snufkin, a little man with a feather in his hat who plays the mouth organ. Other members of the household include the Hemulen, a male creature who wears a cloak or dress and is the 'leading Moomin philatelist', and the Muskrat, an irascible philosopher who sleeps all day in a hammock in the Moomins' garden.

Moomin adventures are entirely unpredictable, deadpan in their humour and wayward in plot; a typical book in the series, *Finn Family Moomintroll* (published in Finland in 1948 as *Trollkarlens Hat*), features such things as a magic top-hat, which can turn whoever or whatever puts it on into something quite different, and an encounter with the terrifying Hattifatteners, tube-like creatures who can neither speak nor hear. With their quiet, reflective air that neatly counterbalances the richness of the *fantasy and the humour, the Moomin books have proved global and enduring in their appeal.

By 1971 eleven titles had been published; between 1954 and 1968 a Moomin *comic strip appeared in the London *Evening News*. Latterly there have been countless other publications and adaptations, in addition to a large merchandising industry and even a Moomins theme park, Moomin World.

Moonfleet (1898) An *adventure story on the model of *Treasure Island*, by J. Meade

*Falkner. The fifteen-year-old narrator, John Trenchard, tells of his involvement with smugglers in the Dorset village of Moonfleet. The book is notable for the character of the innkeeper Elzevir Block.

Moon of Gomrath, The *See* WEIRDSTONE OF BRISINGAMEN, THE.

MOORE, Anne Carroll (1871–1961) After working as children's librarian of the Pratt Institute in Brooklyn, she was asked in 1906 to organize the new children's department of the New York Public Library. She was the author of several children's books, including *Nicholas, A Manhattan Christmas Story* (1924), which is an expansion of Clement Clarke *Moore's poem *A *Visit from St Nicholas*, and (from 1918) a regular reviewer. She was the first chairman of the Children's Librarians' section of the American Library Association.

MOORE, Clement Clarke (1779–1863) Author of *A *Visit from St Nicholas* (also known as *The Night Before Christmas*). He was the son of a Bishop of New York, and himself a notable Hebrew scholar. *A Visit from St Nicholas* first appeared in print in 1823 and played a very large part in establishing the modern image of *Father Christmas or Santa Claus.

MOORE, Dorothea (1880–1933) British author of *Girl Guide novels, beginning with *Terry the Girl Guide* (1912).

MOORHEAD, Diana (1940–) New Zealand author of *fantasies for children, including *The Green and the White* (1974), about the young king of a country where the ruler is chosen by lot.

Moorland Mousie (1929) The first *pony story, written by a pseudonymous author, 'Golden Gorse', whose identity is not known. It closely resembles *Black Beauty*, and is the first-person narrative of an Exmoor pony, born wild but eventually caught by farmers and taken to the house of Colonel Coke, whose ten-year-old daughter Patience treats him kindly. The author wrote several other books about riding for young people, including a sequel, *Older Mousie* (1932).

Moppet and Mittens Kittens in stories by Beatrix *Potter.

Mopsa the Fairy (1869) A *fantasy by Jean *Ingelow. A boy, Jack, discovers a nest of fairies in an old thorn tree and is taken off to fairyland on the back of an albatross. On the way he visits a country where the inhabitants

are clockwork and frees the Fairy Queen from an enchantment. He becomes specially attached to a small girl fairy, Mopsa, who is eventually transformed into the Fairy Queen herself. The story has the quality of a dream; characters change their size or their nature almost without explanation. It is one of the more successful children's books written under the influence of *Alice's Adventures in Wonderland.*

Moral Alphabet, A (1899) By Hilaire *Belloc, with pictures by 'B.T.B.' (Lord Basil Blackwood). It consists of a set of comic rhymes arranged alphabetically by subject-matter, each having an absurd moral.

moral tales Didactic fictions, either short or novel-length, which were first written for children in the mid-18th cent., and which by 1800 were the predominant genre in children's books in England. Their subject-matter was usually domestic or rural and, though *animals and inanimate objects were sometimes the heroes and narrators, anything fanciful was as far as possible avoided by the authors. The movement which popularized them was largely a reaction against *fairy stories and *chapbooks.

One of the earliest English moral tales is *Goody Two-Shoes, published by John *Newbery in 1765. In this and in other stories of the same kind from this first period the moral is quite simple; as Newbery's *Giles Gingerbread (1764) puts it, 'Merit and Industry may entitle a man to any Thing.' Giles Gingerbread becomes a rich man through his own efforts, and the heroine of *Primrose Prettyface (c.1783) is raised to the position of Lady of the Manor through being a good little girl.

Other works from this period which were influential are Sarah Fielding's The *Governess (1749) and the Magasin des enfans (1756) of Mme de *Beaumont. Both these books made some use of fairy stories but treated them warily, and Sarah Fielding warned her readers not to take the idea of *giants or magic seriously. In subsequent decades this anti-fairy story feeling grew much stronger among writers for children. Two factors seem to have been responsible: a concern to teach children the 'true religion' of Christianity, and therefore not to bring them up in superstitious beliefs (*Locke had advised parents not to let their children hear tales about 'Sprites and Goblins' until they were old enough to disbelieve them); and also the notion that children were frightened or puzzled by tales of the supernatural. As Dorothy *Kilner expressed it in her Histories of More Children than One (c.1795), young readers could easily understand 'incidents relating to a child, a plumcake, or a rattle'; she believed they preferred these to 'the prejudicial nonsense of Witches, Fairies, Fortune-Tellers, Love and Marriage', which she said were 'unintelligible, [and] consequently less interesting to the infant reader'.

Many of Maria *Edgeworth's stories show the moral tale at its best. In 'The Basket-Woman', for example, from her *Parent's Assistant (first issued in 1796), a boy and his sister are rewarded for their industry and honesty by a rich benefactor.

In the hands of Maria Edgeworth and her imitators the moral tale acquired a higher purpose than it had had before. The simple lessons about self-improvement of earlier stories were replaced by a higher ideal, the educating of a child to be rational and well-informed. Rosamond, Frank, Harry, and Lucy in Miss Edgeworth's Early Lessons (1801) learn to control their emotions through force of reason; they also discover scientific principles by observing the objects and activities of daily life. Occasionally the influence of *Rousseau, filtered through Thomas Day's *Sandford and Merton (1783-9), may be discerned. A not infrequent theme is the condemnation of novel-reading; the novel, indeed, takes the place of the fairy story in this phase as the enemy of moral writers. For example, A Tale of Warning, or The Victims of Indolence (1810) by Miss M. Woodland is the story of Agatha, who is so devoted to light romantic novels that she neglects her child and it dies. A later writer, Charlotte Elizabeth Browne (b. 1790), who wrote as '*Charlotte Elizabeth', extended the attack to include *Shakespeare and poetry.

By the end of the 18th cent. moral stories were being produced in large numbers, especially from the London publishing house of John *Marshall. Alongside the work of native authors there appeared books of French or German origin, such as *Berquin's L'Ami des enfans (1782-3), which was translated and adapted variously as The *Children's Friend and The *Looking-Glass for The Mind, Mme de *Genlis' collection *Tales of The Castle (1785), and C. G. *Salzmann's Moralische Elementarbuch (1785), which Mary *Wollstonecraft translated as Elements of Morality (1790).

Didacticism became more and more overt, and the moral tale, formulaic. Anne Thackeray Ritchie, writing an introduction to an 1897 edition of Maria Edgeworth's stories, described

the typical moral tale as featuring 'widows living in flowery cottages, with assiduous devoted little sons, who work in the garden and earn money to make up the rent. There are also village children busily employed and good little orphans whose parents generally die in the opening pages.' Some writers centred their tales on *animals, who recounted their life-histories, but in such books (e.g. Dorothy Kilner's The *Life and Perambulation of A Mouse, 1783) the animal was really only an observer of human foibles in general and of the vices and virtues of children in particular. Most moral tales consisted of little more than the relation of the daily events of a family's life, emphasizing the children's sins of omission and commission and their subsequent punishments and repentance.

Punishment, in fact, plays a comparatively small part in the moral tale. Unlike the wretched children in some of the verse *cautionary tales which began to appear in the first decade of the 19th cent., most heroes and heroines survive unscathed. They come to see the error of their ways quite spontaneously, or at least discover that their behaviour has unfortunate consequences which would have been better avoided. Occasionally a real disaster happens in consequence of a child's error; one of the schoolboys falls down a well and drowns as a result of another's stupid prank in The *Village School by Dorothy Kilner (c.1795), but for the most part the only consequences of misdeeds are a bruised limb or an awakened conscience. Children in moral tales quickly acknowledge their own faults by weeping, blushing, and other appropriate gestures. When Jane, the protagonist of Mary Elliott's The Little Meddler, lets out her pet rabbit and it is killed by a dog, the reader is told she 'spoke not, but her grief was more keen than her brother's; for, conscious that her conduct had caused the evil, she could not hold up her head'.

Adults play a large, even a predominant, part in moral tales. They are almost always present, guiding and admonishing the children, and drawing every possible lesson from what has occurred. To a modern reader the propriety of their behaviour sometimes seems questionable, to say the least. In Dorothy Kilner's Histories of More Children than One little John Strictum, who cannot read the word 'thought' in his book, is tied to a tree with a rope, without food for most of the day 'till he would be good and spell the word'.

The modern reader must wonder that these tales, with their often woodenly-named characters (such as 'Jeffery Squander', 'John Active', and 'Jack Careless', a typical trio from Mary Ann Kilner's William Sedley, c.1783), could have had any appeal to children. That they did please young readers is evident from the number of editions that were printed of many of them, and also from the fact that many of the surviving copies show evidence of having been well-thumbed (and sometimes ornamented) by children. E. V. *Lucas, writing in the early 20th cent., pointed out that 'the children of those days . . . expected didacticism . . . [they] were still the immature young of man; they had not been discovered as personalities, temperaments, individuals'. Furthermore many of the writers of moral tales, while apparently incapable of, or uninterested in, constructing an exciting story, showed a fair understanding of the character of children and an ability to portray them as flesh-and-blood individuals.

The movement which created the moral tale reached its zenith with Mrs *Trimmer, who in her *Guardian of Education (1802–5) scrutinized every example currently being published, as well as many already in print, and censured anything that seemed to her even faintly improper. In the period in which she was publishing her *reviews and the years immediately following, the moral tale became even more strait-laced. It also took on a more strongly religious colouring, largely as a result of the growth of the *Sunday school movement and the strengthening *evangelical element in the Church of England. The aim of writers was now to produce a godly, rather than a rational, child. There was also, if less explicitly, a fear that the English social order might be upset by something resembling the French Revolution, and authors of this period show a strong concern to maintain the status quo. The most notable practitioners of the moral tale who wrote in this vein were, besides Mrs Trimmer herself, Hannah *More, author of innumerable *Cheap Repository Tracts, and Mrs *Sherwood, whose *Fairchild Family (1818 onwards) shines with evangelical fervour and does not hesitate to describe the pains of hell which await the unrepentant sinner.

With these writers the moral tale reached its zenith, and soon afterwards it began to decline. Publishers such as John *Harris had, during these years, been issuing books of unapologetic levity, while the verses of Ann and Jane *Taylor had shown that a moral message could be presented with a much lighter touch than that of the Trimmers and Sherwoods.

A powerful counterblast against the moralists was delivered in 1839 by Catherine *Sinclair in her *Holiday House*, which, though certainly not without its moral and religious element, portrayed children as irresponsible ragamuffins who create chaos if left to their own devices for five minutes; what is more, it condoned such behaviour and mocked the stern Mrs Crabtree who tries to keep them under control. Meanwhile the appearance in 1823 of the first English translation of *Grimm's fairy tales gave more ammunition to those who believed that the imagination should not be suppressed in writings for children. Sir Walter *Scott wrote to Edgar Taylor, who had produced the Grimm translation, that fairy stories were 'better adapted to awaken the imagination and soften the heart of children than the "good boy" stories which have been in later years composed for them'.

The moral tale did not die; it continued in various guises. The evangelical and *temperance stories of the mid-19th cent. are its obvious descendants, while the writings of Harriet *Martineau and Charlotte M. *Yonge on the one hand and *Tom Brown's Schooldays on the other show it beginning to be transmuted into something subtler, which might be called the 'novel of character' for children. This genre may be seen more fully fledged in the works of such English writers as Mrs *Ewing and Mrs *Molesworth, and—even more—in the hands of Louisa M. *Alcott in America. Moral education remained a major element in English-language children's literature into the early 20th cent., and even since it has occasionally come to the fore again—as, for example, in some *young adult fiction of the 1970s; but it was never again to play quite such a crudely prominent part in it.

MORDVINOFF, Nicolas (1911–73) Illustrator using the pseudonym 'Nicolas', who fled the Russian Revolution with his parents when he was a small boy. He eventually settled in the USA, where in 1950 he began his collaboration on *picture books with the author William Lipkind (1904–74). As 'Will and Nicolas' they produced nearly 20 titles, including *Finders Keepers* (1951), a modern *fable, which won the *Caldecott Medal.

MORE, Hannah (1745–1833) Prolific British writer of tracts for the religious and moral education of the working classes. She was the fourth of five daughters of a High Church schoolmaster and received part of her education at a school in Bristol established by her elder sisters and subsequently run by all five More girls. Hannah was regarded as the genius of the family; she read omnivorously in European literature, began to write elegant (if dull) verse, and composed *plays for children in the family school. *A Search After Happiness*, a pastoral dialogue for girls, intended as a substitute for the dramas of loose moral content which were sometimes performed in schools, was written when she was still in her teens and was a great success when it was published in 1773. Her *Sacred Dramas* (1782), a set of verse plays on biblical stories, remained in print until the mid-19th cent., though even in Miss More's own lifetime they were satirized for their dullness.

When she was twenty-two she became engaged to a wealthy landowner, but he postponed the wedding three times and eventually the engagement was broken off. The ex-fiancé, however, insisted on settling a substantial annuity on her, and this gave her financial independence to concentrate on the literary and philanthropic work which came to occupy her life.

For a time she concentrated on drama, became friends with Garrick, and had a historical tragedy, *Percy*, produced with much success at Covent Garden in 1777. But she afterwards came to believe that the principles on which dramatic tragedy was founded were in opposition to Christianity. She turned her back on London literary life and came under the influence of the *evangelical movement in the Church of England. Partly thanks to her friendship with the anti-slavery campaigner William Wilberforce, she began to take an interest in moral and religious reforms. Her *Thoughts on the Importance of the Manners of the Great to General Society* (1788), which was among the most widely read books of its day, attacked the hypocrisies and profanities she had encountered in the houses of the rich. In *Strictures on the Modern System of Female Education* (1799) she criticized the contemporary fashion for children's dances or 'Baby Balls'. In 1792 she began to write pamphlets designed as a counterblast to such revolutionary works as Tom Paine's *Rights of Man*.

Among the abuses she attacked was the neglect of religious education, and in 1789 she and her sisters began to establish a network of *Sunday schools in the neighbourhood of Cheddar in Somerset, where they had a country cottage. This led, in 1794, to the inauguration of her scheme of *Cheap Repository Tracts, a series of pamphlets suitable for the many working-class children and

young people who were learning to read in the Sunday schools. She herself wrote about half of the 114 tracts which appeared during 1795-8: the best known was The *Shepherd of Salisbury Plain* (1795). In 1808 she published the immensely successful two-volume story *Coelebs in Search of a Wife*, in which the hero, a young man of good family, records his comments and those of his friends on current social customs as he tours England in the hope of finding 'a deserving companion for life'. In her later years Miss More wrote further political-religious tracts, this time in opposition to the radical writings of William Cobbett, who dubbed her 'The Old Bishop in Petticoats'. She retired to Clifton, near Bristol, in 1828 and at her death left £30,000, chiefly in charitable legacies.

Though not strictly a writer for children, Hannah More was responsible for creating a literary genre, in the Tracts, which was as influential on young people as had been the *chapbooks on whose format she modelled the series. She actually disapproved of the widespread publication of juvenile books; in *Coelebs*, a father speaks approvingly of his small daughter who, on her eighth birthday, resolves to give up 'all my little story books'; he declares: 'The mass of children's books...protracts the imbecility of childhood. They arrest the understanding instead of advancing it.'

More Beasts for Worse Children (1897)

A sequel to The *Bad Child's Book Of Beasts*, by Hilaire *Belloc, with illustrations by 'B.T.B.'—Lord Basil Blackwood. It includes 'The Bison', whose matted coat 'is sewn on with needle and thread'; 'The Frozen Mammoth'; and 'The Microbe', who has 'seven tufted tails with lots | Of lovely pink and purple spots'.

More Nonsense, Pictures, Rhymes, Botany, Etc.

Written and illustrated by Edward *Lear and published by Robert John Bush of London late in 1871, though it is dated 1872. The book contained a number of pages of 'Nonsense Botany', 100 *limericks, and, in a section headed 'Twenty-Six Nonsense Rhymes and Pictures', an alphabet beginning 'The Absolutely Abstemious Ass'.

MOREY, Walt (Walter Nelson) (1907–92)

American author of *animal stories in the Jack *London tradition, including *Gentle Ben* (1965), the story of a captive bear.

Morgan le Fay

Sister to King *Arthur, an enchantress and seducer. In Geoffrey of Monmouth's writings and *Malory's *Morte Darthur* she is also one of those who tend the mortally wounded Arthur after his last battle.

MORPURGO, Michael (1943–)

English author who was Children's *Laureate from 2003 to 2005 in acknowledgment of his position as one of the most popular and critically acclaimed of all contemporary children's writers. (With his friend Ted *Hughes he had also been one of the driving forces of the laureateship's establishment.)

From a career in teaching Morpurgo moved to full-time writing, and his body of more than fifty novels is now a vital part of children's reading lives. Never shying away from dealing with harsh realities, he makes difficult emotional and moral issues accessible to even young readers, exploring recurrent themes such as the countryside, animals, the misery of warfare, friendship, and survival against the odds. *The Wreck of the Zanzibar* (1995) is set amidst the hardship of living on a small island, as is *Why the Whales Came* (1985); *Kensuke's Kingdom* (1999) is about a shipwrecked boy and the stranger who keeps him alive.

Moved further into the limelight with the success in 2007 of the play version of *War Horse* (1982)—a production which would run for years in the West End, on Broadway, and around the world—Morpurgo has continued to produce humane, human, challenging, and endearing books for all ages. *Private Peaceful* (2003), his stand-out book for older readers, continued his exploration of the effects of war, as did *Shadow* (2010) about a bomb sniffer dog in Afghanistan and *A Medal for Leroy* (2012), which included the story of Walter Tull, the only black officer to serve in the British army in the First World War. Michael Morpurgo and his wife Clare founded the charity Farms for City Children, where children from deprived areas leave their city homes to experience life on a working farm.

MORRIS, Jackie (1961–)

Author-illustrator and artist whose key themes are animals, nature, folk tales, and myths. Morris's first picture book was *Jo's Storm*, written by Caroline Pitcher. She has collaborated with Pitcher on other books, including *Mariana and the Merchild*, about an old lady who finds a sea-child hidden in a crab shell. Titles that she has both written and richly illustrated include *The Snow Leopard* (2007), *Tell Me a Dragon* (2009), and *The Ice Bear* (2010). She has a deep love of the countryside and gains much inspiration from the landscape around her rural Welsh cottage.

MORRIS, William (1834–96) Pre-Raphaelite poet, author, and artist, who wrote several original stories in the style of medieval *romances which were read by children and young people; they include *The House of the Wolfings* (1889), *The Roots of the Mountains* (1890), *The Well at the World's End* (1896), and *The Sundering Flood* (1898). His associates included the artist Walter *Crane, and his stories have had an effect on a number of 20th-cent. writers of *fantasy, including J. R. R. *Tolkien.

Mortal Engines (2001–6) A sequence of four novels by Philip *Reeve, after the title of the first. They are set in a post-apocalyptic future, in which the world as we know it is very different. In a changed landscape, cities have become Traction Cities, able to move from place to place, obeying the laws of Municipal Darwinism and preying on each other. In *Mortal Engines* (2001), which was Reeve's fiction debut, the reader is introduced to Tom Natsworthy, Hester Shaw, and the terrifying, yet compelling, Stalker Shrike. Their adventures and relationships continue in the sequels, *Predator's Gold* (2003) and *Infernal Devices* (2005), before being brought to a conclusion both bittersweet and satisfying in *A Darkling Plain* (2006). Taking inspiration from steam punk, the author explores powerful themes of identity, loyalty, betrayal, love, and redemption throughout this innovative quartet. *Mortal Engines* won a Nestlé Smarties Book Award and was shortlisted for the *Whitbread Children's Book Award; *A Darkling Plain* won the *Guardian Children's Fiction Prize. A big-screen adaptation of the series by Christian Rivers and Peter Jackson was announced in 2016.

A series of three books act as prequels to the Mortal Engines quartet: *Fever Crumb* (2009), *Web of Air* (2010), and *Scrivener's Moon* (2011).

Morte Darthur See MALORY.

MORTIMER, Mrs F. L. (Favell Lee) (1802–78) Having experienced a religious conversion at the age of twenty-five she immediately devoted herself to educational work. In 1841 she married Thomas Mortimer, minister of a London chapel. Her most popular work was *Peep of Day* (1836), and she also wrote the very popular *Reading Without Tears* (1857) and *Latin Without Tears* (1877).

MOSS, Elaine (1924–) British librarian and critic who contributed greatly to the quality of children's books in her time. She wrote reviews, surveys, guides to categories of children's books, and some storybooks of her own. In 1977 she received the *Eleanor Farjeon Award for outstanding services to children's books, and in 1985 published *Part of the Pattern: a Personal History through the World of Children's Books*.

Mother Bunch A figure of *chapbook literature, also credited with the authorship of *fairy stories. The original Mother Bunch was a London ale-wife of the 16th cent., referred to in works by Thomas Nash and Thomas Dekker. In the 17th cent. the name was attached to *jest books, e.g. *Pasquil's Jests, mixed with Mother Bunch's Merriments* (1604). A popular chapbook found from the late 17th cent. onwards was *Mother Bunch's Closet Newly Broke Open*, which portrayed Mother Bunch as a wise countrywoman giving advice of a superstitious kind to maidens and young men on how to get husbands. From the late 18th cent. onwards the name Mother Bunch was often given as the supposed author of the fairy tales of Mme d'*Aulnoy, presumably in emulation of *Mother Goose's supposed authorship of the tales of *Perrault.

Mother Goose Nursery character who features in the title of innumerable books of *nursery rhymes, 'Mother Goose rhyme' being the alternative term for a nursery rhyme in America.

The expression 'Conte de ma Mère Oye'—'Mother Goose tale'—for a folk or old wives' tale seems to have been current in France by the mid-17th cent. It has been suggested that this came about because perhaps at that time 'the stock figure for a teller of tales was the old peasant woman who watched over the village geese' (Jacques Barchilon). On the other hand Mother Goose as a traditional figure of folklore, associated with tales and superstitions, has a counterpart in the German Fru Gosen, and may perhaps be compared with *Mother Hubbard. When *Perrault's *Histoires, ou Contes du temps passé* were published in France in 1697, the frontispiece showed an old woman telling tales by firelight to three children. A plaque on the wall reads 'Contes de Ma Mère L'Oye'. The earliest known publication of Perrault's fairy tales in English, the *Histories, or Tales of Past Times* of 1729, translated the plaque to read 'Mother Goose's Tales', thus introducing the name Mother Goose into the English language.

By 1768 John *Newbery's son Francis and his stepson Thomas Carnan were issuing a version of the Perrault fairy stories under the title *Mother Goose's Tales*. This appears to

have suggested the idea of reusing 'Mother Goose' in the title of another children's book, thus making her a figure to credit with nursery authorship along with such others as *Tom Thumb and Nurse Lovechild. The result was the nursery rhyme collection *Mother Goose's Melody. It has been suggested that this book, and Mother Goose's Tales, were first published by John Newbery himself, and that he himself was responsible for the decision to associate Mother Goose with nursery rhymes; but though he may have had some hand in the Melody there can be no certainty about it, and he does not seem to have had anything to do with the Tales.

Around 1825 Munroe and Francis of Boston published *Mother Goose's Quarto and then in 1833 their *Mother Goose's Melodies. This large collection was the first to be distributed widely outside the publishers' own state and is probably responsible, along with its imitations, for the lasting marriage of Mother Goose and the nursery rhyme in America.

American affection for Mother Goose seems to have given rise to a strange piece of invented history. One John Fleet Eliot had a letter published pseudonymously in the Boston Transcript of 14 January 1860, stating that Mother Goose was in fact a Boston lady of a family named Goose or Vergoose who came from England in the mid-17th cent. When her daughter Elizabeth married the printer and publisher Thomas Fleet (John Fleet Eliot's great-grandfather) and produced a grandson for her, she poured out for his benefit 'in the most melodious strains, the songs and ditties which she had learned in her younger days, greatly to the annoyance of the whole neighbourhood—to Fleet in particular, who was a man fond of quiet'. Thomas Fleet's only remedy for this nuisance was (supposedly) to collect and print the rhymes under the comic title 'Mother Goose's Melodies', in 1719, thus predating any English book of that title. John Fleet Eliot's story was soon taken up and printed as fact in reference books and introductions to new Mother Goose books.

The existence of Mother Goose as a nursery figure by the end of the 18th cent. led to her introduction into *pantomime. In 1806 there was performed at the Theatre Royal, Covent Garden, Harlequin and Mother Goose; or, the Golden Egg, in which Grimaldi played the Clown. The association of her with the *fable of The Goose that laid the Golden Eggs was taken up by *chapbook publishers, and shortly afterwards there began to appear such titles as

Old Mother Goose or, The Golden Egg. Mother Goose has continued to feature in the title of nursery rhyme books all the way into the 21st cent.

Frank L. *Baum, author of The *Wonderful Wizard of Oz, scored his first success as a children's writer with a collection of original rhymes entitled Father Goose, His Book (1899).

Mother Goose Rhymes See NURSERY RHYMES.

Mother Goose's Melodies, the only Pure Edition A collection of *nursery rhymes published by Munroe and Francis of Boston, Mass., in 1833, with many subsequent editions. The book was based on the same material as their *Mother Goose's Quarto, but reselected and with individual rhymes from many other sources.

The publishers commissioned new engravings from various artists, such as Abel Bowen and Nathaniel Dearborn of Boston and Alexander *Anderson of New York. This was in contrast to the more usual practice among children's book publishers of mainly using stock *woodcuts or simply copying the illustrations of earlier books. The cover engraving of Mother Goose's Melodies shows a goose in gown and frilled cap, surrounded by listening goslings, though the introduction is illustrated with the customary *Punch-like old woman.

Perhaps 100,000 copies were printed, though only a handful survive; the book was so successful that it inspired many piracies and imitations, and it is generally granted the credit for *Mother Goose becoming the favourite 'sponsor' of nursery rhymes in America.

Mother Goose's Melody: or, Sonnets for the Cradle A book of *nursery rhymes published by John *Newbery or by one of his successors. It is a small volume in two parts, the first consisting of fifty-one nursery rhymes, described as 'the most celebrated Songs and Lullabies of the Old British Nurses, calculated to amuse Children and excite them to Sleep'. Many of these are the first appearances in print of continuing favourites, e.g. 'Hush-a-by baby', 'Dong dong bell', 'High diddle diddle', 'Jack and Gill', and 'Se [sic] saw, Margery Daw'. The rhymes are equipped with a preface, with editorial remarks in a mock scholarly style which have sometimes been interpreted as satire on the editing of ballads in *Percy's Reliques of Ancient English Poetry, published in 1765. The second part of the book consists of 'Songs and Lullabies by Shakespeare'.

Mother Goose's Melody seems to be a classic case of a children's book being 'read to pieces', so that whole editions have disappeared without a trace. The earliest surviving dated copy of the book is one published by Francis Power, John Newbery's grandson, in 1791. Thomas Carnan, Newbery's stepson, registered the book for copyright and advertised it as newly published in the *London Chronicle* in 1780; this is the earliest certain date that the book can be given. Earlier datings rest mainly on uncertain evidence that Oliver *Goldsmith took a hand in the enterprise while he was working for John Newbery from 1762 to 1767. Goldsmith is known to have been fond of the company of children and of entertaining them with the game and rhyme now known as 'Two little dickie birds', which is printed in *Mother Goose's Melody* in its earlier form of 'There were two blackbirds'. Also Goldsmith is known to have been annoyed by *Percy's Reliques*, which may account for any mockery of it in the preface to the nursery rhymes. The *Opies therefore suggest 1765 or 1766 as the most likely date of publication.

Against this, however, is the fact that John Newbery was fairly consistent in advertising his wares, and since no notice of *Mother Goose's Melody* before 1780 has yet been found it is more usually argued that Newbery himself did not publish the book, but that it belongs instead to the output of his successors in the family firm, most probably Carnan. In fact Carnan's 1780 advertisement declares that it is 'Now first published from the papers of that very great writer of very little books, the late Mr John Newbery'; and while this may be no more than an attempt to associate the book with Newbery's by then prestigious name, it might be a true statement.

Mother Goose's Melody was rapidly pirated in England and America. Isaiah *Thomas's 'Second Worcester Edition' of 1794 (the first was perhaps in 1785) is almost identical with the Newbery family's. From this collection followed the others that set the fashion for *Mother Goose books in America.

Mother Goose's Quarto, *or Melodies Complete* A collection of *nursery rhymes published by Munroe and Francis of Boston, Mass., c.1825, and based on Isaiah *Thomas's edition of *Mother Goose's Melody* and on Tabart's *Songs for The Nursery*. It survives in only one known copy. Its version of 'See saw sacradown' preserves Thomas's emendation of 'London' to 'Boston', but adds: 'Boston

town's chang'd into a city, | But I've no time to change my ditty.' Boston officially became a city in 1822.

Mother Goose's Tales *See* Histories, or Tales of Past Times.

Mother Hubbard A *nursery rhyme character. The verses beginning 'Old Mother Hubbard | Went to the cupboard, | To fetch her poor dog a bone' were first published in *The Comic Adventures of Old Mother Hubbard and Her Dog*, issued by John *Harris in 1805. The dedication ascribed 'these Notable Sketches' (which may have meant the pictures or the verses or both) to 'S.M.C.', this being Sarah Catherine Martin (1768–1826). According to tradition she made up the Mother Hubbard verses after being told by her country-house host, John Pollexfen Bastard, MP, to 'run away and write one of your stupid little rhymes'. Harris's *Mother Hubbard* was highly successful, perhaps partly because it was seen as a political satire. A sequel was brought out and the verses rapidly entered the *chapbook market.

The verses which follow the opening stanza, in which Mother Hubbard goes on a series of errands and returns to find the dog engaged in various antics, strongly resemble those of *Dame Trot and her 'Comical Cat', which were published in 1803 and known before that date. It seems possible that if Sarah Catherine Martin made up the greater part of the Mother Hubbard rhyme, she was following the model of the Dame Trot rhyme. Moreover the opening verse of *Mother Hubbard* is on a different metrical scheme from the rest, and it is possible that Miss Martin already knew it as a traditional rhyme. There is indeed evidence that some sort of Mother Hubbard rhyme was in circulation in the 18th cent., though it was not recorded. The title 'Mother' was given to elderly women of the lower classes, and Mother Hubbard seems to have been a known folktale character in the 16th cent., though any stories or characteristics attached to her have been lost. Edmund Spenser's *Satire called Prosopopoia; or Mother Hubberd's Tale* sets a scene of stories being told of 'Knights, Faeries, and Giaunts', in which 'a good old woman' tells a *fable of the fox and the ape. Another title, the *Tale of Mother Hubburd*, is mentioned in 1604 but not otherwise known. It cannot be proved that Mother Hubbard was then connected with a dog, though one theory derives her name from St Hubert, patron saint of hunting and of dogs.

The Mother Hubbard rhyme has continued to be printed as an individual book, and Mother Hubbard's name appears in the titles of numerous collections of nursery rhymes and other children's books. The words of the rhyme have varied from printing to printing, being sometimes expanded, sometimes cut, and sometimes modernized—the 'New Mother Hubbard', in March's Modern Juvenile Library (n.d.), goes by balloon, steam boat, and train.

Mother Hubbard's *Punch-like face, cloak, and pointed hat have been almost constant features of the rhyme's many illustrations, and a 'Mother Hubbard' became a name in general use for a large cloak in the 19th cent.

The success of Harris's *Mother Hubbard* led to a large number of books of the same type being produced, e.g. Harris's own illustrated *John Gilpin (1806) and *The *Butterfly's Ball* (1807), a version of *The *Queen of Hearts* probably written by Charles *Lamb and published by the *Godwins (1805), and, rather later, *Dame Wiggins of Lee* (1823). The Mother Hubbard book, in fact, inaugurated a period in children's literature which Harvey *Darton dubbed 'the dawn of levity'.

Mother's Offering to her Children, A,

'by a lady long resident in New South Wales' (1841) The first known children's book written and published in Australia. It takes the form of conversations between a mother and her four children. It conveys information about Australian flora and fauna, about the Aborigine population, and about disasters at sea, in *catechism style. The book was long believed to be the work of one Lady J. J. Gordon Bremer, on a visit to Government House in Sydney, but more recently it has been questioned whether she ever went to Australia at all, and no alternative author has been suggested.

Mouldiwarp, The In *The *House of Arden and *Harding's Luck* by E. *Nesbit.

Mouse and his Child, The (1967) A novel by Russell *Hoban, detailing the adventures of a clockwork mouse and his small clockwork son. The book is both an exotic quest story and a parable about human life (the wind-up toys passionately desire to become 'self-winding'), and it secured its author's reputation in America and Britain as an outstanding children's writer.

Mousehole Cat, The (1990) A picture book by *Carnegie Medal-shortlisted writer Antonia Barber (1932– ; real name Barbara Anthony), with illustrations by Nicola *Bayley. Inspired by the Cornish legend of a local fisherman, Tom Bawcock, Barber introduces Mowzer, Tom's cat, who accompanies Tom on his heroic voyage in the teeth of a storm to catch fish for the starving villagers. The storm, personified as the great Storm Cat, is won over by Mowzer's singing and finally soothed by her purring. The village is saved. Bayley's detailed illustrations capture both the timeless element of the story as well as the drama. It won the Illustrated Children's Book of the Year at the 1991 British Book Awards and the British Design Production Award (Children's Books), and was commended for the *Kate Greenaway Medal.

movable picture books Books in which flaps of paper or card can be raised or moved, or tabs can be pulled, to disclose new features of the picture. They first began to appear regularly in the mid-19th cent., though they had such precursors as the *harlequinades of the 18th cent., *Fuller's paper doll books of c.1810, and the *toilet books of William and Stacey Grimaldi, which were published in the 1820s. The first true movables were manufactured by *Dean of London; early titles include *Dean's Moveable Red Riding Hood* (c.1857), in which figures were moved by tabs, and *Dean's New Book of Dissolving Views*, a title given to three different volumes, published between 1860 and 1862, in which tabs were pulled to draw a second set of pictures down over the first. These and others of Dean's early experiments in movables were hand-coloured (*see* COLOUR).

In the 1870s Dean and other publishers began to issue cheaper and more garish movables printed by chromolithography (*see* LITHOGRAPHY). Among Dean publications from this period were a series of 'Flexible Faced Story Books' and a number of 'Pantomime Toy Books', e.g. *Cinderella with five set scenes and nine trick changes* (c.1880). Ward Lock issued a number of books with movable pictures, and two German companies, H. Grevel & Co. (representing Braun and Schneider of Munich) and Ernest *Nister & Son, published movables in England; Grevel specialized in the books devised and drawn by Lothar *Meggendorfer (e.g. *Comic Actors*, 1891), and Nister in 'dissolving views', e.g. *The Picture Show, a novel picture book for children* (1895).

Movables continued to be produced during the 20th cent., an outstandingly popular example being Robert Crowther's *Most Amazing*

Hide-and-Seek Alphabet Book (1977), in which an animal hides behind each letter. Since 1979 many of the most interesting movables published in England and the United States have been *pop-up books. (For these, and more varied contemporary examples, *see also* *NOVELTY BOOKS.)

MOWAT, Farley (McGill) (1921–2014) Canadian author, best known for *Owls in the Family* (1961), an autobiography about a boyhood spent largely in the company of two owls named Wol and Weeps. His other children's books include *The Dog Who Wouldn't Be* (1957), the bizarre story of an un-canine dog named Mutt, and *Lost in the Barrens* (1965).

Mowgli Hero of *The *Jungle Books* by *Kipling.

MOZLEY, Harriet (Elizabeth) (d. 1852) Sister of John Henry Newman and wife of his friend Thomas Mozley, Rector of Oriel College, Oxford. She wrote a number of books for children including *The Fairy Bower, or, The History of a Month* (1841), written in reaction to the *moral tale; it is one of the first English *family stories.

Mr Aladdin In *Rebecca of Sunnybrook Farm* by Kate Douglas *Wiggin.

Mr Benn Hero of a series of comic-fantastic adventures, in *picture books by David *McKee. The first was *Mr Benn, Red Knight* (1967). Mr Benn stories have appeared on British television.

Mr Fox See BLUEBEARD.

Mr Growser In the *Toytown* stories by S. G. Hulme Beaman.

Mr Gum A series of books by Andy *Stanton, illustrated by David Tazzyman, starting with *You're a Bad Man, Mr Gum!* (2006). The stories concern the inhabitants of the fictional town of Lamonic Bibber, and in particular Mr Gum, a fierce old man who is forced to keep his garden tidy by an angry fairy, who hits him on the head with a frying pan if he does not comply. The brilliantly surreal humour is somewhat in the style of Philip *Ardagh. Titles in the series have won a number of awards, including the inaugural *Roald Dahl Funny Prize, and a *Blue Peter Book Award for the Most Fun Story with Pictures.

Mr Gumpy's Outing (1970) A classic picture book by John *Burningham. Mr Gumpy owns a punt, which he takes out on the river by his house; one by one the animals ask him whether they can join him on the boat, and eventually the boat tips, and into the water they all go. *Mr Gumpy* and his friends have been deservedly popular for over forty years. *Mr Gumpy's Motor Car* (1973) is a sequel, which sees Mr Gumpy, plus two children and a lot of animals, piling into his car to go for a ride, but they soon get stuck in the mud and all have to get out and push.

Mr McGee (1988) A children's picture book by Pamela *Allen. Mr McGee lives under a tree, and when he eats an apple he blows up like a balloon and flies off into the sky. This book was the first in a series of seven books featuring the whimsical Mr McGee and his childlike response to the world. All the books are illustrated in Allen's lively pen-and-wash illustrations with strong composition and use of white space. The stories are witty and rhyming, fast-paced, and well suited to reading aloud.

Mr Majeika See CARPENTER, HUMPHREY.

Mr Men A series of small paperback *picture books for young children written and illustrated by Roger *Hargreaves. The first set—*Mr Tickle, Mr Bump, Mr Happy, Mr Greedy, Mr Nosy*, and *Mr Topsy-Turvy* were issued by the Thurman publishing company in September 1971. More titles followed in profusion, and by the early 1980s there were over fifty in print. Their huge popularity owes something to cartoon films based on them, shown on television (with Arthur Lowe as narrator), but even more to the production of innumerable types of Mr Men goods for children, ranging from first-aid bandages to yoghurt. The drawings are very simple—'I can't really draw,' Roger Hargreaves said, 'so I chose abstract subjects as no one can knock *my* ideas of what tickles look like.' A spin-off 'Little Miss' series was launched in 1981 (*Little Miss Helpful, Little Miss Shy*, etc.). Though Hargreaves himself died in 1988, new Mr Men and Little Misses continue to appear from time to time to this day, as well as occasional storybooks.

Mr Midshipman Easy (1836) A novel by *Marryat. Jack Easy is the son of a rich man with eccentric views. He goes to sea, has many adventures, and marries a Sicilian girl. The novel, which is filled with comic characters and sayings, was not written particularly for children. Nevertheless it soon became popular with them, and by the end of the 19th cent. was being issued specially for young readers.

Mr Popper's Penguins (1938) A comic children's novel written by Richard Atwater (1892-1938) and completed after his death by his wife Florence. Mr Popper is a dishevelled and dreamy housepainter who longs to be a polar explorer and to have a penguin as a pet. To his astonishment he acquires one (a gift from an explorer to whom he has written), and it is soon made comfortable in the Popper household—it sleeps in the refrigerator, to which Mr Popper considerately adds a handle on the inside. This first bird is soon joined by a female, and when they produce a family, the Poppers create a highly successful music-hall act. The book was illustrated by Robert *Lawson.

Mr Quelch Schoolmaster in the *Billy Bunter stories.

Mrs Coulter *See* HIS DARK MATERIALS.

Mrs Doasyouwouldbedoneby In *The *Water-Babies* by Charles *Kingsley.

Mrs Frisby and the Rats of NIMH (1971) A novel by Robert C. *O'Brien.

Mrs Leicester's School, *or, The History of Several Young Ladies, Related by themselves* By Charles and Mary *Lamb, first published by the *Godwins in 1809 with no author named. The book, which is modelled on Sarah Fielding's *The *Governess*, consists of a series of life histories told by each schoolgirl in turn. Charles Lamb wrote three of the stories: 'The Witch Aunt', 'First Going to Church', and 'The Sea Voyage', a description of a journey from India to England. Mary was responsible for the other seven stories, which, like Charles's, conform to the usual pattern of the *moral tale. The book shows little of the Lambs' talents, but it had reached eight editions by 1823 and has sometimes been reprinted in the 20th cent.

Mrs Overtheway's Remembrances (1869) The first children's book by Mrs *Ewing.

Mrs Pepperpot An old woman who frequently finds she has shrunk to the size of a pepperpot; in stories by Alf *Prøysen. In the Norwegian original she is 'Teskjekjerringa', the 'teaspoon-woman'.

Mrs Wiggs of the Cabbage Patch (1901) A novel by the American author Alice Hegan Rice (1870-1942), the most popular of a number of books she wrote for children. Mrs Wiggs lives in a tumbledown house called 'the Cabbage Patch' in a city tenement area. She and her children maintain a Micawber-like optimism throughout every kind of hardship. Mrs Wiggs's motto is 'every thing in the world comes right, if we jes' wait long enough.'

Mr Tumnus Faun in *The Lion, the Witch and the Wardrobe* (*see* NARNIA) by C. S. *Lewis.

MUCHAMORE, Robert (1972-) British writer. Teenagers around the world have to thank Robert Muchamore's nephew for complaining that he had nothing to read, as that was what started the idea for CHERUB—easy to read books for teens who want fast-paced stories about espionage, gangs, drugs, prison, and war. *The Recruit* (2004) starts the story of James and Lauren, kids who become spies. After all, who would expect a child to be bugging your house and searching your hard drive? The characters and story develop as the series progresses, as does the realism, since the later stories are definitely harder and darker than the early ones. The *Henderson's Boys* series (2009) sets up the origins of CHERUB in the Second World War, and a second CHERUB series starts with *People's Republic* (2012).

Muddle-Headed Wombat, The A character invented by the Australian author Ruth *Park, initially in a radio series and then in books (1962 onwards). He tends to add extra syllables to his words: 'That's a horribubble thing to do . . . You're a hidjus old pollywobble!'

Muffet, Little Miss *See* LITTLE MISS MUFFET.

Muffin the Mule A *puppet very popular on British children's television in the early 1950s, performing alongside Annette Mills (1894-1955), who narrated stories about him. She also wrote Muffin books and *annuals, illustrated by her daughter Molly Blake.

muggles In the *Harry Potter books, non-magical humans, most of whom live entirely unaware of the magical world. Harry himself has been raised among them in their world, in a world familiar to us (muggle) readers, and it is only at the start of his eponymous series, as he turns eleven, that he is first introduced to magic. The more unpleasant of the magical sort have contempt for muggles; and they use 'mudblood' as an insult against those who are half magical, half muggle.

MÜHLENWEG, Fritz (1898-1961) German author. His first book for children was *In geheimer Mission durch die Wüste Gobi* (1950),

reissued in 1963 as *Grosser Tiger und Christian* and translated into English in 1952 as *Big Tiger and Christian*. It is the story of two small boys in China who are accidentally carried off on a train, find themselves in Mongolia, and have to get home by their own initiative, making a journey across the Gobi Desert. It is one of the finest modern *adventure stories.

MUIR, Frank (1920–98) British humorist who wrote a series of children's books about an Afghan puppy called What-a-Mess. The first appeared in 1977.

MUIR, Marcie (1919–2007) Australian book collector and bibliographer who was born in Perth, Western Australia. Her bookseller husband encouraged her to collect Australian children's books. This became a lifelong pursuit, culminating in her *A Bibliography of Australian Children's Books* (1970), the standard work in the field. A second volume was published in 1976. Muir had identified over 6,000 Australian children's books, either locally written or with Australian themes. In the 1992 revision, *Australian Children's Books: a Bibliography*, a further 2,000 books were listed. In 1984 Marcie Muir was the inaugural recipient of the Nan Chauncy Award for her contribution to children's bibliography.

Muir's seminal work has since been revised, extended, and enlarged to 2000 by Dr Kerry White (1958–), formerly an academic before devoting her full energies to bibliography, including subject guides to Muir's bibliographies and *The Source*, a growing database guide to children's books, short stories, and poetry with an emphasis on Australian and New Zealand literature.

Muir's family placed 6,255 of her books dating from 1800 to 2001, as well as her papers, with the National Library of Australia in 2010. This was complemented by the acquisition of Dr White's collection, including 600 titles not already held.

MUIR, Percy (1894–1981) Antiquarian bookseller and historian of children's literature. His *English Children's Books, 1600–1900* (1954; reprinted with additions) was based partly on the work of Harvey *Darton but also on his own extensive collection of children's books.

MUKERJI, D. G. *See* GAY-NECK.

Mulch Diggums *See* ARTEMIS FOWL.

MULLINS, Patricia (1952–) Australian picture-book author-illustrator known for her collage illustrations using layered torn tissue paper. She also illustrates for other authors. She is fascinated by rocking horses and restores antique wooden horses, and several of her books feature rocking horses. Her most popular books are *Dinosaur Encore* (1992) and *Hattie and the Fox* (1986), both books showcasing lively animals with her trademark tissue-paper collage illustrations. Perhaps her most famous and most awarded book internationally is *V for Vanishing, an Alphabet of Endangered Animals* (1993), which was awarded the *CBCA Eve Pownall Award for Information Books. Her picture book, *Lightning Jack* (2012), with a text by Glenda *Millard was nominated for the 2014 *IBBY Honour list. She was awarded the *Dromkeen Medal 2012 for her significant contribution to children's books. Many of her books have been translated into other languages and are international bestsellers.

MULOCK, D. M. *See* CRAIK, DINAH MARIA.

MULREADY, William (1786–1863) Painter who has had attributed to him the illustrations of a number of children's books which appeared in the first decade of the 19th cent. They include *The *Butterfly's Ball* and *Tales from Shakespear*. Mulready's early life and struggles (he came from a poor Irish Catholic family in County Clare) were the subject of *The Looking-Glass* (1805) written and published by William *Godwin, with the author's name given as 'Theophilus Marcliffe'. In the 1840s he was among those artists who contributed to the 'Felix Summerly' *Home Treasury series.

multicultural children's literature

This has been loosely defined as books that reflect cultural and social diversity—and is often associated with discourses of race and ethnicity. It derives from particular socio-historic periods in children's literature that are implicitly linked to political movements to include marginalized or under-represented populations, and those groups which have been eliminated from or egregiously represented in children's books. In discussing multicultural children's literature, it is difficult to disregard the social and political historicity that underlies the term.

The story of representation and belonging reverberates and finds its echoes across continents, each with its own tale to tell, but it is possible to trace a movement comprising a number of authors, illustrators, and publishers who have worked to push against a monocultural tide of white, middle-class and

traditional family narratives. In the US, African-American pioneers such as Walter Dean *Myers, Jerry *Pinkney, Virginia *Hamilton, John *Steptoe, Tom *Feelings, and Langston Hughes sought to provide positive representations of an African-American experience which were severely lacking in children's books. Artists and illustrators Bryan Collier, Faith *Ringgold, Laurence *Yep, Lensey Namioka, bell hooks, Leo and Diane *Dillon, Simon Ortiz, and Pam Muñoz Ryan, among others, continue to push for and celebrate wider representations including Chinese-American, Latin American, and Native American children's literature (*see also* NATIVE AMERICAN LITERATURE). The Cooperative Children's Book Center (CCBC) began tracking the output of works by or about African Americans in 1985, and in 1994 included works by or about Native Americans, Asian/Pacific Americans, and Latinos. Over thirty years since its inauguration, despite the work of many, the equality of representation continues to be discouraging in the US.

In comparison with the US, the UK was relatively late in producing children's books by or about black, Asian, or minority ethnic communities. The 1970s–80s saw an increase in awareness of the importance of multicultural children's literature, perhaps in response to a political backdrop of racist hostility with the 1958 race riots, the Commonwealth Immigrants Act in 1962, and Enoch Powell's 'River of Blood' speech in 1968. In 1971, the Institute of Race Relations published *Books for Children: Homelands of Immigrants to Britain*, which recognized the lack of children's books reflecting a more ethnically diverse society. Legislation such as the Race Relations Act of 1976 and the inauguration of the Equal Opportunities Commission (1974) and the Commission for Racial Equality (1976) provided legal imperatives behind a new wave of multicultural publishing. However, despite a growing movement to represent the multicultural realities of British life, the actual output of literature was small. Key authors and illustrators of the 1970s and early 80s include Errol Lloyd, John *Agard, Grace *Nichols, Faustin Charles, Farrukh *Dhondy, and Shirley *Hughes. In 1987 Verna Wilkins set up Tamarind Press in response to the lack of multicultural content and to provide a space for more diverse voices. Authors and illustrators such as Jamila *Gavin, Beverley *Naidoo, Caroline Binch, Mary *Hoffman, Trish Cooke, Benjamin *Zephaniah, Elizabeth *Laird, Bali Rai, Catherine

Johnson, Sufiya Ahmed, and Malorie *Blackman continue to advocate for diversity in children's literature.

In Canada, a small number of feminist multicultural Canadian publishing houses like Tundra Books, Kids Can Press, Annick Press, and Groundwood Books began to materialize to counter a white Euro-Canadian perspective in children's books. Authors and illustrators such as Nicola Campbell, George Littlechild, Jan Bourdeau Waboose, Ann Blades, and Richard Van Camp have sought to represent Canada's First Nations, while new authors and illustrators such as Paul Yee, Rachna Gilmore, Rukhsana Khan, and Ange Zhang, write and illustrate to celebrate Canada's diversity.

In Australia, Magabala Books was established in 1990 as a non-profit organization to preserve, develop, and promote Australian Aboriginal and Torres Strait Islander cultures, but Aboriginal writers and illustrators such as Dick *Roughsey, Elaine Russell, Renee Fogorty, and Ambelin Kwaymullina are still few and far between. Other authors and illustrators such as Nadia *Wheatley, Randa Abdel-Fattah, Shaun *Tan, Armin *Greder, and Jeannie *Baker publish books that question, celebrate, and represent multicultural realities in present-day Australia, exploring themes of immigration, belonging, and transcultural relationships. Similarly, in New Zealand, *Māori books are far from mainstream and representations continue to be largely monocultural, with few authors such as Gavin *Bishop representing a more multicultural society.

Across continents, there is still a major concern that there is a lack of diversity in children's literature and that the reality of a predominantly white, middle-class workforce in the publishing industry results in a limited space for diverse voices.

Despite this growing awareness of a need for change, however, the very term 'multicultural' is regarded as problematic by many. If it is defined by ethnicity or cultures outside the dominant mainstream, it disregards language, class, *gender, geographical location, *sexuality, and the multiple hybrid identities that exist within the axis of culture, and it may assume a cultural separation from a white (working-class or other) culture of which any ethnicity is an inclusive part. Arguably, it is a term which should be rendered meaningless, since all children's literature is 'multicultural', and setting a body of literature apart creates problematic distinctions between what is 'normal' and what is 'other'. Rather than abandoning the

concept of multicultural literature, however many have used it alongside the term *diversity to advocate a holistic approach which also includes diverse representations of class, language, familial structure, ethnicity, religion, *disability, age, sexuality, culture, and gender.

Mumfie A toy elephant in stories by British author Katharine Tozer (1907-43), beginning with *The Wanderings of Mumfie* (1935).

mummers' play A traditional English folk drama, enacted at Christmas and sometimes at other winter festivals. It is thought to be a relic of a pagan ceremony performed to ensure the return of the new year and of fertility. The play has adopted different principal and subsidiary characters at different places and times, taking them from historical events, legends, and *romance literature: Saint, later sometimes King, *George, with his opponent the Turkish knight, is especially common; Oliver Cromwell, Bonaparte, *Robin Hood and Little John, *Father Christmas, Beelzebub, and a 'Bold Slasher' or 'Beau Slasher' are among others who appear.

Mummers' plays were published in *chapbook form, the first known being a Newcastle-upon-Tyne printing in 1771. These chapbooks continued to appear throughout the 19th cent., with children usually the intended readers. Chapbooks have been given some of the blame for changing the play from an adult ceremony into a children's entertainment.

A mummers' play forms part of *The Peace Egg* (1877) by Mrs *Ewing, and a complete text is printed as an appendix to that story. Several texts, edited by Alex Helm, were published in 1971 to encourage performance, chiefly in schools. Alan *Garner's *Holly from the Bongs* (1966) contains an adaptation of a Cheshire mummers' play.

In *The *Golden Age* (1895) by Kenneth *Grahame, there is a vivid description of mummers visiting a country house, and being observed by the children.

MUNARI, Bruno (1907-1998) Italian artist and illustrator, born in Milan, best known for his artistic and graphic design, which sprang out of (and distanced him from) the at times questionable Futurist movement. Munari was a firm believer in the didactic, but not pedantic, powers of art and reading, in both a cognitive and a material, multisensory approach. He famously created the 'Libro letto' (a readable written blanket), illustrated multiple covers for authors such as Gianni *Rodari,

was awarded the Lego Prize (1986) for his contributions to childhood creative development, the *Hans Christian Andersen Award (1974), and published over forty books for children, some of which have been exhibited in the New York Museum of Modern Art (MoMA). Munari was described by Pablo Picasso as 'the new Leonardo'.

Munchausen, Baron Hero of a series of *tall tales first published in England in 1785. The original book was the work of Rudolf Erich Raspe (1737-94), who distinguished himself in German intellectual circles, largely through his scientific work, but built up huge debts and had to decamp to England. In 1785 an Oxford printer named Smith printed a collection of anecdotes by Raspe, built round the figure of Hieronymus Münchhausen, a German nobleman and raconteur whom Raspe had known slightly in his youth and who was incensed at Raspe's treatment of him in print. *Baron Munchausen's narrative of his marvellous travels and campaigns in Russia* was soon being translated into German and other European languages. Various new English editions quickly appeared; in these, the original adventures were greatly enlarged by hackwriters. Among titles given to it in later printings were *Gulliver Revived* and *The Vice of Lying Properly Exposed*. The book's huge popularity meant that it was often read by children, especially in the 19th cent. A 1902 edition included illustrations by W. Heath *Robinson.

MUNROE, Kirk (1850-1930) American author of *adventure stories dealing with pioneer life. These include *The Fur-Seal's Tooth* (1894), set in Alaska, and a 'Mates' series— *Campmates, Canoemates, Raftmates*, etc.

MUNSCH, Robert (1945-) American-born Canadian children's author. In his early life he trained as a Jesuit priest but later gave it up to work with children. Munsch's bestselling picture book *Love You Forever* (1986), illustrated by Sheila McGraw, was written as a memorial for two stillborn babies Munsch had with his wife in 1979 and 1980. It became the bestselling children's book in Canada in 1986 and 1987. In 1994 the *New York Times* listed it as their bestselling children's book. Munsch also gained international recognition with the illustrator Michael Martchenko and their unconventional subversion of traditional stereotypes and gender roles including *The *Paper Bag Princess* (1980) and *Murmel, Murmel, Murmel*

(1982), which won a Juno Award in 1985. In 1986, *Thomas' Snowsuit*, also illustrated by Michael Martchenko, won the Ruth Schwartz Award. Munsch won the Canadian Booksellers Association's 'Author of the Year' in 1991 and received a star on Canada's Walk of Fame in 2009.

Muppets *See* SESAME STREET.

MURAIL, Marie-Aude (1954–) Immensely popular French author whose studies at the Sorbonne included a thesis devoted to adapting classic novels for children. Her work includes short stories in women's magazines and novels for adults, but it is her body of over eighty books for children that is most notable, particularly three series: *Émilien*, which starts with *Baby Sitter Blues* (1989) and charts a boy's adolescence; the adventure series *Nils Hazard*, starting with *Dinky Rouge Sang* (1991); and *L'Espionne*, a fantasy series involving elves, vampires, and other fantastical creatures, which starts with *Ma Vie a Changé* (1997). She has been translated widely, with English translations including *Golem* (5 vols., translated by Sarah *Ardizzone) and *My Brother Simple* (translated by Adriana Hunter).

MURPHY, Jill (1949–) English illustrator and author who wrote, illustrated, and bound (with a stapler!) her first books while still at primary school. Written with charm and illustrated in a style that is detailed and realistic, her books are warm-hearted and funny. Her dismal time at a convent school inspired the *Worst Witch* stories, and family life itself provided all she needed for stories about the Large family of elephants (as all she had to do was to look at the life of an overworked mum, for example)—the first in the series is *Five Minutes' Peace* (1986). There are also picture books that are not part of a series, including *The Last Noo Noo* (1995), a book designed specifically to encourage reading time.

MURPHY, Jim (1947–) American author of books for children and young adults which are predominantly about American history, acclaimed for his ability to make the past come alive for readers of all ages. He started his career as an editor and had his first book, *Weird and Wacky Inventions*, published in 1973. His well-researched, multilayered, and accessible books include *The Long Road to Gettysburg* (1992), *The Great Fire* (1995), about the Great Fire of Chicago in 1871, *A Young Patriot: The American Revolution as Experienced by One Boy* (1995), *Blizzard! The Storm That Changed America* (2000), and *An American Plague: The True and Terrifying Story of the Yellow Fever Epidemic of 1793* (2003).

MYERS, Walter Dean (1937–2014) Prolific African-American author of *young adultbooks, whose work never backed away from the grittiness of life. When he was about to drop out of high school to join the army, one of his teachers told him, whatever happened, to keep on writing—which he did. His own difficult childhood influenced his writing, as his books are often about boys who are struggling to survive, either on the streets, in gangs, in jail, or simply in a world set against them—books such as *Fallen Angels* (1988), which tells of a boy enlisting to fight in Vietnam; *Monster* (1999), about a Harlem shooting, which won the inaugural *Michael L. Printz Award; and *Lockdown* (2010), set in a jail for juveniles. Following his death, an award was set up in his name for books that celebrate *diversity. Myers's son Christopher (1974–) is a multi-award-winning illustrator.

My Friend Flicka (1941) By Mary O'Hara (really Mary O'Hara Alsop, 1885–1980), the first volume of a trilogy about American ranch life. Flicka is a half-wild horse belonging to ten-year-old Ken McLaughlin. The story is concerned with Ken's efforts to tame him, and the boy's difficult relationship with his strong-willed father. The sequels are *Thunderhead* (1943) and *Green Grass of Wyoming* (1946).

My Friend Mr Leakey (1937) A collection of *fantasy stories for children by the eminent British geneticist J. B. S. Haldane (the brother of Naomi *Mitchison). The book's purpose is explained in a note by the author to the *Puffin edition: 'Professor Haldane ... thinks a lot of magicians in the old days were only doing, or trying to do, what scientists and engineers do now, and that science can be more exciting than magic ever was.' The main part of the book is concerned with Mr Leakey, a magician who lives in a London flat in company with his animal servants; these include a small *dragon called Pompey who sits in the fire when he is not required, an octopus named Oliver, and a miniature cow, Phyllis. The narrator accompanies Mr Leakey on errands of kindness to the worthy and punishment for the unjust, and attends a 'fancy dress' party at which the guests may become any person, animal, or object of their choice.

The book is peppered with 'asides' on scientific topics. One of the best is the story of the physicist Mr Dobbs, who made a large income

out of the railways 'by travelling with excess luggage', having devised special suitcases which rose in the air when weighed: 'You see, if your bag weighs a hundred-weight more than it ought to you have to pay the railway company, but if it weighs a hundred-weight less than nothing, they have to pay you.'

My Mother A poem by Ann *Taylor which first appeared in *Original Poems, for Infant Minds* in 1804, and became for a time, according to E. V. *Lucas, 'the best known English poem'. It was printed on its own, and appeared at various times in the 19th cent. both as a short *chapbook and in a lavishly illustrated edition.

Some controversy was attached to the last of the poem's twelve verses:

> For God, who lives above the skies,
> Would look with vengeance in his eyes
> If I should ever dare despise
> My Mother.

Augustus de Morgan wrote in the *Athenaeum* in 1866 that 'one of the most beautiful lyrics ... is spoiled by the introduction of what was not uncommon in the little songs formerly written for children, a bit of religion, no matter what, thrust in.'

The poem suffered much parodying, a later example being a song popularized by the British comedian Terry Scott, 'My Brother'.

My Naughty Little Sister (1952) A series of stories by Dorothy Edwards, about a naughty little sister and narrated by her long-suffering older sibling, originally composed to amuse the author's daughter. Read on the radio programme *Listen with Mother*, they were published as a collection with illustrations by Henrietta Garland. Its success led to further collections. Though reflecting the cosy world of the period, *My Naughty Little Sister* retains its perennial appeal through the author's astute observation of its central character and the exasperated but affectionate voice of the storyteller. It was reprinted in 2007 illustrated by Shirley *Hughes.

My Side of the Mountain (1959) A novel by Jean Craighead *George.

Mysteries of Harris Burdick, The (1984) A picture book by American author and illustrator Chris *Van Allsburg, who explains in an introduction that the book's fourteen black-and-white illustrations, each accompanied by a title and single line of text, were the work of one Harris Burdick, who left them, promising to return with the complete stories, but instead disappeared. The mystery draws readers in, requiring them to provide their own stories in response to the words and images. The premise captured the imagination of writers including M. T. *Anderson, Louis *Sachar, and Lois *Lowry, who contributed to *The Chronicles of Harris Burdick* (2011), stories inspired by Van Allsburg's original book.

myths Collections of (often ancient) stories belonging to a given civilization, nation, or community, which sometimes serve to explain origins, the natural world, or cultural traditions; they are regularly retold in books for children. *See* NORSE MYTHS; HOMERIC LEGENDS (for Greek mythology); MĀORI STORIES; etc.

NAIDOO, Beverley (1943–) An award-winning South African author. Part of the underground resistance against the Apartheid regime, Naidoo was exiled to the UK in 1965. She became a teacher and wrote her first novel *Journey to Jo'burg* in 1984, depicting the harsh realities of Apartheid. The book was *banned in South Africa until 1991. *The Other Side of Truth* (2000), which won the *Carnegie Medal, is about two siblings who are smuggled to London from Nigeria after their father is targeted for his outspoken political journalism during the reign of General Sani Abacha in the mid-1990s. The story relays themes of political oppression, asylum, family, childhood, and the refugee experience in London. Its sequel, *Web of Lies* (2004), focuses on London gang culture. Naidoo is also the author of a number of picture books, including *S Is for South Africa,* a book of poetry with photographs by Prodeepta Das, and *Aesop's Fables,* illustrated by Piet *Grobler.

Nana Dog-nursemaid in *Peter Pan* by J. M. *Barrie.

Nancy Blackett In the *Swallows and Amazons* books by Arthur *Ransome.

Nancy Cock's Pretty Song Book for all Little Misses and Masters An early collection of *nursery rhymes, published *c.*1780 by John *Marshall.

Nancy Drew A teenage *detective in US novels written under the pen name Carolyn Keene for the *Stratemeyer Syndicate. Nancy Drew first appeared in 1930, outlined by Edward L. Stratemeyer (with his daughters) then handed to freelancers. Most of the first series of books were written by Mildred Wirt *Benson. Harriet Stratemeyer Adams continued to supervise and relaunch the Nancy Drew series after her father died and she took over the syndicate. The Nancy Drew books have been credited with supplying an important role model for girls and were adapted for film and television several times; the character still exists as the heroine of interactive games.

NAPOLI, Donna Jo (1948–) Prolific and versatile American author who writes for the whole age range and in a variety of genres. Her books for younger readers go from folk tales to stories about mathematics and science, while her middle-grade books include collections of myths and the sixteen-book *Angelwings* series (1999–2001). Standout works for older readers include her retelling of Hansel and Gretel in *The Magic Circle* (1993) and Rapunzel in *Zel* (1996), both of which feature complex mother-daughter relationships. *Stones in Water* (1997), about two Italian boys during the Second World War, won the Sydney Taylor Book Award; *The King of Mulberry Street* (2005) was a Sydney Taylor Honor book.

Nargun and the Stars, The (1973) A children's fantasy novel by Patricia *Wrightson, which won the *CBCA Book of the Year Award. Wrightson draws on *Australian Aboriginal legend to create the ancient creatures who dwell in the land. Simon, sent to live on a sheep station after the death of his family, suddenly discovers he has to protect the ancient creatures from the machines clearing the land. The book has as its central 'character' a huge creature which has been alive since the making of the earth, and is to all intents and appearances simply a rock—but it can move, cry out, and kill. The themes of life, death, and change pervade this book, with its beautiful language, poetic description, and strong characterization and plotting.

Narnia An imaginary country, setting of seven children's books by C. S. *Lewis: *The Lion, the Witch and the Wardrobe* (1950), *Prince Caspian: the return to Narnia* (1951), *The Voyage of the 'Dawn Treader'* (1952), *The Silver Chair* (1953), *The Horse and his Boy* (1954), *The Magician's Nephew* (1955), and *The Last Battle* (1956), which won the *Carnegie Medal. In the first volume published (though not the first in chronology), the four Pevensie siblings, Peter, Susan, Edmund, and Lucy, are evacuated to the country during the

Second World War. During a game of hide and seek Lucy discovers the entrance to Narnia through the back of a wardrobe. She and Edmund visit on separate occasions, but eventually all four children find themselves in Narnia, caught in a great war between the good, led by the lion Aslan, and the bad, led by the White Witch. The children must play an integral part and fulfil a prophecy. Despite becoming rulers of Narnia, the children are returned to their normal lives only minutes after they leave. They do not visit again until a year later (book two)—for them, although it is 1300 years later for Narnia; and during their absence the country has been taken over by the Telmarines. The children have been recalled to help Prince Caspian, the rightful heir, reclaim the throne.

The Magician's Nephew is the prequel to these books, where Digory and Polly use magic rings to arrive in Narnia at the moment of its creation by Aslan. Digory grows up to be the Professor Kirke who owns the house where the Pevensie children start their adventure, and the famous wardrobe is later crafted from wood grown in England from a Narnian apple. *The Horse and his Boy* is a separate, tangential story, in which the adult Pevensies appear as secondary characters. It is the only book that focuses on a child native to the Narnian world, Shasta, rather than the English children of the other books. Shasta and Aravis, two children on the run with their Narnian horses Bree and Hwin, find themselves caught up in a battle to save Susan from a forced marriage to the heir to the neighbouring throne.

In *The Voyage of the Dawn Treader*, Susan and Peter are too old to return to Narnia, so Edmund, Lucy, and their cousin Eustace are summoned instead, through a picture of a ship. They land in the ocean near the Dawn Treader, the ship of the now King Caspian. The three join him on his voyage, and at the end Aslan informs the children that like the older children, Edmund and Lucy can no longer return to Narnia. Eustace however returns in *The Silver Chair*, along with Jill, from his boarding school. King Caspian is now an old man, and requires help to find his missing son, Prince Rillian, who has gone to hunt for the serpent that killed his mother. When they meet and free a young man who must be tied nightly to a silver chair lest he turn into a serpent, they find Rillian, who had been cursed by the Lady of the Green Kirtle, also his mother's murderer.

In *The Last Battle*, all of the children return to Narnia except Susan, who has stopped believing in Narnia and is interested instead in trivial things. An ape has set up a donkey as a fake Aslan and is abusing the resulting power. At the end of the novel Aslan gives judgement and the children (except Susan) pass into Aslan's Country, widely perceived to be heaven, and the Pevensies are told that they have died in a train crash.

Lewis admitted that much of the Narnian world is allegorical, the most obvious example being Aslan as a Christ figure. Plato and his cave of shadows are mentioned in *The Last Battle* as the children progress to Aslan's Country. The series is still much beloved and regularly adapted for screen and occasionally stage, most recently with films of *The Lion, the Witch and the Wardrobe* (2005), *Prince Caspian* (2008), and *The Voyage of the Dawn Treader* (2010).

NASH, Ogden (1902–71) American comic poet who aimed one of his books of verse specifically at children: *Parents Keep Out* (1951).

National Ambassador for Young People's Literature *See* LAUREATE.

National Book Award A literary prize for an American citizen published by an American publisher. There have been prizes in a children's book category since 1969; the category is now called Young People's Literature and the prize is administered by the National Book Foundation.

National Velvet (1930) A sensationally successful story by the British novelist and playwright Enid Bagnold (1889–1981), the story of a fourteen-year-old girl, Velvet Brown, who acquires a horse. The book was filmed in 1944, starring Elizabeth Taylor as Velvet, and contributed to the establishment of the *pony story as a popular genre of fiction for girls.

Native American stories Following well over a century in which the portrayal of Native Americans in children's fiction was limited almost exclusively to stereotypes (*see* 'INDIANS' OF NORTH AMERICA), with rarely any distinction of tribe, and which was produced almost exclusively by writers who were not themselves Native American, in recent decades the balance has shifted, with the portrayals from the outside becoming more sophisticated and sympathetic, actively countering the stereotypes that came before; and while there is still an acute shortage of breadth

in what is published (*see also* MULTICULTURAL LITERATURE), books by Native Americans themselves are slowly becoming far less of a rarity than they were only a few decades ago, too, with new work spanning picture books, storybooks, poems, and *young adult fiction.

In the mid-20th cent., some significant work in this area came from non-Native American writers, with notable examples including Ann Nolan *Clark, a pioneer in writing books aimed at Native American children themselves; and later Paul Goble, whose *The Girl Who Loves Wild Horses* (1978) won the *Caldecott Medal. Susan *Cooper's *Ghost Hawk* (2013) is a more recent novel by a non-Native American writer to feature a Native American central protagonist.

Traditional stories, which have typically been passed on orally, have recently been collected and retold in print by writers such as the Abenaki author Joseph *Bruchac; and there are more and more writers—Louise *Erdrich and Cynthia Leitich Smith (1967–) among them—dealing with the Native American experience itself, whether historical or contemporary, often exploring those lives that straddle Native American and non-Native American cultures, and the friction that arises. Of the latter type, the work best known to a wider readership is probably Sherman *Alexie's award-winning young adult novel, *The Absolutely True Diary of a Part-Time Indian* (2007). Among the other significant figures working today are Virginia Driving Hawk Sneve (1933–), whose books include *The Christmas Coat: Memories of My Sioux Childhood* (2011) and *Dancing Teepees: Poems of American Indian Youth* (1989); and Cheryl Savageau (1950–), author of *Muskrat Will Be Swimming* (1996), about an isolated contemporary girl who draws strength from an ancient Native American story.

Natty Bumppo Hero of the *Leather-Stocking Tales* by James Fenimore *Cooper.

natural history A popular subject from the beginning of British juvenile publishing. A *Description of Three Hundred Animals* (1730), published (and probably written) by Thomas *Boreman, drew on the medieval *bestiaries and on Edward Topsell's *Histories of Four-Footed Beasts* (1608) for its description of fabulous as well as real creatures. John *Newbery's volume A *Pretty Book of Pictures for Little Masters and Misses* (published in 1752) was on the same lines. The first serious English *book of instruction devoted entirely to natural history seems to have been Mrs *Trimmer's *Easy Introduction to the Knowledge of Nature* (1780). This acknowledged the educational example of *Lessons for Children* (1778) by Mrs *Barbauld, whose own brother John Aikin wrote *The Calendar of Nature* (1784), a month-by-month description of the seasons and their effect on plant, animal, and bird life.

The considerable growth of children's bookselling in the first years of the 19th cent. led to many books on natural history being published, such as A *Concise Abridgement of Natural History*, a set of five volumes published in 1800 by John *Marshall, *Footsteps to the Natural History of Beasts and Birds* (*Darton and Harvey, 1806), and Alfred Mills's *Natural History of 48 Birds, with elegant engravings*, a set of *miniature books published jointly by Darton and John *Harris in 1816. The most substantial contribution to the subject in this period was made, however, not by an established author or a London publisher but by Thomas *Bewick, whose *History of British Birds* (2 vols, 1797 and 1804), illustrated with his own *wood engravings, was a *sine qua non* of the schooling of a 19th-cent. English gentleman's children.

From the 1820s natural history, like virtually every subject, began to be taught by the *catechism method, for example in A *Catechism of Botany* (1822) by William *Pinnock. Among notable contributions to the subject later in the 19th cent. was a book by Charles *Kingsley, *Glaucus; or the Wonders of the Shore* (1855). Mary *Howitt's *Sketches of Natural History* (1834) was in verse, and included her celebrated lines on 'The spider and the fly'. *See also* SCIENCE.

Naughtiest Girl in the School, The (1940) A book for young readers by Enid *Blyton. When spoilt little rich girl Elizabeth Allen is sent to progressive Whyteleafe School, she is determined to be so naughty she will be sent home. However, her plans do not quite go as expected. There are three sequels by Blyton herself, with more recent additions to the series by Anne Digby.

NAUGHTON, Bill (1910–92) British novelist and playwright, author of several books for children about working-class life, including *The Goalkeeper's Revenge* (1961).

Naughty Amelia Jane! (1939) By Enid *Blyton, a story about a doll (based on a real doll owned by Blyton's daughter Gillian). Amelia Jane is not a shop-bought toy and

this is seen as the excuse for her naughtiness. She indulges in all kinds of tricks and mischief—she pushes the toys into the goldfish bowl, pours milk down their necks, and runs wild with the scissors. Always contrite at the end, she promises to be good—hollow words. The stories originally appeared in the magazine *Sunny Stories* before being collected in a book illustrated by Sylvia I. Venus. It was republished with new illustrations in 2001.

NEEDHAM, Violet (1876–1967) English author, whose upbringing in a semi-aristocratic English-Dutch family led her to travelling through, and living in, many places in Europe—a background that gave many of her books a European flavour. Her father, a Life Guards officer, was a compulsive gambler—and many of her heroines have to battle to rescue their families from impecunious situations. Her love of stories was honed through telling bedtime tales to her nephews, though when in 1918 a manuscript was offered to a publisher it was turned down as being too difficult for children. It was not until 1939 that the first in the *Stormy Petrel* series, *The Black Riders*, was published (illustrated by Anne Bullen), when its Ruritanian story of good battling a military-style evil was immediately popular. Her other books are divided between contemporary adventure, such as *The Horn of Merlyns* (1943), and historical fiction, such as *The Woods of Windri* (1944). For many years her books were largely forgotten by all but collectors of classic children's books, but interest has revived in recent years.

NEEDLE, Jan (1943–) British writer, who produced as his first children's book *Albeson and the Germans* (1977), in which a London boy discovers that the portrayal of Germans in war *comics is not the whole truth. Needle is an unusually versatile writer: in *My Mate Shofiq* (1978) he writes about racial prejudice; *The Size Spies* (1979) is a farcical *fantasy; *A Fine Boy for Killing* (1979) is a grim *historical novel about naval press gangs; *The Bee Rustlers* (1981) is a thriller centring on the organized theft of swarms of bees; and *Wild Wood* (1981) is a novel about the events of *The *Wind in the Willows* as seen by the Wild Wooders. He has written adaptations for children of a number of classic novels, including *Moby Dick* (2006) and *Dracula* (2007).

Nelly's Silver Mine See JACKSON, HELEN HUNT.

NELSON, Kadir (1974) American artist and author specializing in books about the African-American experience. Nelson was a Caldecott Honor Award (*see* CALDECOTT MEDAL) winner in 2007 for *Moses: When Harriet Tubman Led Her People to Freedom* by Carole Boston Weatherford (2006), and again in 2008 for *Henry's Freedom Box* by Ellen Levine (2007). He won the *Coretta Scott King Award as author and was an Honor Award winner for illustration for *We Are the Ship: The Story of Negro League Baseball* (2008), his first book as both author and illustrator, and for *Heart and Soul: The Story of America and African Americans* (2011). His paintings have been exhibited widely.

Nelson Lee A *detective who turns schoolmaster. He first appeared in *Marvel* in 1894, and was created by the writer 'Maxwell Scott' (Dr John *Staniforth). Aquiline and *Sherlock Holmes-like in appearance, he had an assistant named Nipper, a street urchin of mysterious origins. In the *Nelson Lee Library* (1915 onwards) he goes to St Frank's School to escape from a gang who are pursuing him, and agrees to join the staff, Nipper receiving an education the while—this being what the editor of the stories called 'the detective element . . . intermixed with a school yarn'. His last appearance was in *Gem* in 1934; reprints of Lee stories were issued in the *Schoolboy's Own Library*.

Nemo, Captain In *Twenty Thousand Leagues under the Sea* by Jules *Verne.

NESBIT, E. (Edith) (1858–1924) Author of stories and novels for children, creator of the Bastable family, and, in a vein of comic *fantasy, of *Five Children and It, The *Phoenix and the Carpet, The *Story of the Amulet, and other books.

Edith Nesbit, known to the family as Daisy, was the youngest of the four surviving children of John Collis Nesbit, principal of an agricultural college in Kennington. He died in 1862 when Edith was only three. For several years his widow ran the college herself, but when Edith was about nine her mother decided to go abroad for the health of Edith's elder sister Mary. For a time the family led a nomadic existence around France.

After a happy time in one house in Brittany the family came back to England, and when Edith was about thirteen, settled at Halstead Hall, a large country house in Kent, which she loved, drawing on its setting for her later

works. During childhood Nesbit read vora-
ciously, and her own writings reflect a wide
knowledge of 19th-cent. children's books, to
which she and her heroes and heroines con-
stantly refer, either mockingly or with approval.

Mrs Nesbit's money ran out some three
years later, and the family had to make a dis-
piriting move to Barnsbury in North London.
Edith meanwhile wrote poetry and when she
was about fifteen, she began to have verse
accepted by a magazine, for a guinea payment.

Around 1877 Edith met Hubert Bland, a
handsome young bank employee, and appar-
ently fell in love with him at first sight, break-
ing off an engagement to another man. In
1880, when she was twenty-one and Bland
twenty-five, they were married in a registry
office. Edith was seven months pregnant.
Bland described himself at the time as a
'brush manufacturer', having left the bank
and invested all his money in a small brush
factory. Shortly after the marriage he became
critically ill with smallpox; during his absence
his partner absconded with his funds and the
family was left penniless. Edith supported
them by doing recitations at such places
as working-men's clubs, by mass-producing
hand-painted Christmas cards complete with
her own verses, and increasingly by selling
poems and stories to newspapers—much as
Mother does in The *Railway Children. Hubert
Bland collaborated in some of the stories, and
eventually himself became a distinguished
journalist.

Some two years after her marriage Edith
discovered that her husband had a child by
another woman, who believed herself to be
married to him. Edith befriended the woman—
the first instance of a remarkable response to
her husband's incurable philandering.

Edith became, like her husband, a socialist.
The Blands were founder members of the Fa-
bian Society and considered themselves to
belong to its practical, as opposed to its vision-
ary, wing. Edith was on the Pamphlet Com-
mittee, and worked with great energy for the
poor of Deptford, organizing Christmas
parties and *pantomimes for them. She fell in
love with another Fabian, George Bernard
Shaw (he seems to have been amused and
friendly, no more), and wrote verses to him.
She seems, with only a little of the usual
domestic help of her class, to have worked
immensely hard at writing poetry, a novel
(The Prophet's Mantle, 1885), and endless
short stories and other hack work, as well as
attending innumerable meetings and bearing

children. By 1885 she had Paul, Iris, and Fabi-
an; another was stillborn, and its burial was
marked by Edith's prolonged refusal to part
with the child's body.

She was effectively the centre of a salon, and
the Blands' entertaining of their socialist and
literary friends was well known; it was Bohe-
mian, often impromptu and impoverished,
but rich in talk. The household included
Alice Hoatson, formerly a manuscript reader
for a magazine that Edith wrote for; she had
answered an advertisement to be companion-
help to the Blands. Some years later she be-
came pregnant, not disclosing the father's
identity. Edith proposed the solution of adopt-
ing the baby and passing it off as her own, but
six months after the child's birth she discov-
ered that Hubert Bland was the father. How-
ever, the arrangement persisted, and in 1904
the daughter, Rosamund, was Edith's collabo-
rator in Cat Tales. Thirteen years later Miss
Hoatson gave birth to another child by Bland,
and he too was brought up to think that Edith
Nesbit was his mother. 'It was my own fault',
Edith once wrote to a friend. 'I might have
prevented the opportunity. I didn't, and I de-
served the consequences.'

Hubert's infidelities were well known, al-
though Edith's son-in-law remarked that the
marriage 'worked extraordinarily well in prac-
tice for 99/100ths of the time, allowing E. N. to
run about as she liked in her restless manner'.
And, perhaps mostly in retaliation, Edith her-
self had several affairs; she seems both to have
occasionally contemplated leaving Bland and
to have been exceedingly devoted to him, ad-
miring his abilities. After his death she edited
for publication a collection of his newspaper
essays—many of them about marriage.

The celebrated books for children by
'E. Nesbit' emerged almost without warning
when she was forty, out of a mass of more or
less hack writing in almost every genre. Stories
for children were among her magazine contri-
butions, and in 1892 the firm of Raphael
*Tuck, for whom she also designed Christmas
cards, brought out her first complete book for
children, The Voyage of Columbus, a verse
narrative. These she followed with such things
as a birthday book made up of her own poetry,
Pussy Tales and Doggy Tales, and *Shake-
speare retold for children, together with a se-
ries of twelve articles in The *Girl's Own Paper,
beginning in October 1896; these were called
'My Schooldays', but were in fact an account of
much else in her childhood. Then, apparently
unaware that she was engaged in anything

different from her usual breadwinning, she produced, in 1898, a series of stories for the *Pall Mall* and *Windsor* magazines concerning Oswald Bastable and his family. These were published as a book, *The *Story of the Treasure Seekers*, the following year. It was immediately successful, and introduced a period of prosperity in the Bland household.

They moved to Well Hall at Eltham, Kent, a moated house of 16th-cent. origin, which Edith loved and which became in her stories the 'Moat House' or the 'Red House'. The Blands' hospitality to famous and unknown alike became more bountiful during the ensuing four years; a friend wrote that 'the party never flagged once the Blands had appeared. A friendly atmosphere hung about them, an atmosphere of festivity. They were intensely *loveable.*' But the Well House period began tragically. In 1900 Edith's youngest son Fabian, whom she had always regarded as nearest to herself in personality, died under anaesthetic during an operation at home for the removal of his tonsils. In the midst of the family grief that followed, Rosamund discovered that she was Miss Hoatson's, not Edith's, child.

The second Bastable book, *The Wouldbegoods*, appeared in 1901, and a series of stories entitled 'The Psammead' began to be published in *The *Strand Magazine* the same year. They were illustrated by H. R. *Millar, who had produced drawings for an earlier series of Nesbit stories in the *Strand*, later published as *The Book of Dragons* (1901). Such was her satisfaction with Millar's interpretations that she credited him with telepathy. He thereafter became the most natural choice as illustrator of her children's books. The Psammead stories formed the basis of *Five Children and It* (1902); *The Phoenix and the Carpet* began to appear in the *Strand* in 1903, and *The New Treasure Seekers* (a collection of Bastable stories) in the *London Magazine* the same year; both were published as books in 1904. This was all at the same time as Edith was personally answering innumerable letters from child and adult admirers. Despite her success she felt that she had to write as prolifically as ever, for money.

Peter Pug, a dog story, and *Oswald Bastable and others*, a collection of assorted magazine stories, came out in 1905, the year in which she did the copious research for, and wrote, *The Story of the Amulet. The Railway Children* began as a serial in the *London Magazine* in 1904, and came out as a book in 1906, the year

that *The *Enchanted Castle* began to appear in the *Strand*. In 1907 she was occupied as joint editor of a new literary and art magazine, *Neolith*. Then in 1908 *The *House of Arden* came out as a book, after running in the *Strand*; its sequel, *Harding's Luck*, appeared in 1909. In 1908 was also published a collection of her retellings of *fairy stories entitled *The Old Nursery Tales*, this being the first volume of a series entitled 'The Children's Bookcase', which she was editing. Her books for adults at this time included a thriller, particularly gruesome for its time, called *Salome and the Head* (1909).

In 1910 *The *Magic City* appeared; but at the end of that year Hubert Bland became seriously ill and his eyesight, long poor, began to deteriorate; Edith wrote only two more new children's books, *The Wonderful Garden* (1911) and *Wet Magic* (1913). By now she was 'tired of work', but was still pressed by shortage of money. Hubert Bland, though he became quite blind, went on dictating articles for the *Sunday Chronicle* until the evening he died in 1914. Edith felt her life 'broken off short' by his death.

During the first years of the First World War she was lonely, often in poor health herself, and increasingly unable to keep up her large house. In 1915 she was awarded a small civil pension in recognition of services to literature. In 1917 she married T. T. Tucker, a widowed marine engineer nicknamed 'Skipper', an old friend who had at first simply made a habit of helping to sort out the chaos of her home. 'It is extraordinarily rum that I should have found someone who suits me like this', she wrote. 'It is like a consolation prize for all sorts of failures.' Eventually she enlisted the Skipper as a collaborator for short stories and sketches; 'Tammy Lee's Jack', one of the stories in her posthumously published *Five of Us and Madeline* (1925) was one of his seafaring anecdotes.

Well Hall was finally given up in 1921 for an economical double bungalow, nicknamed The Longboat and The Jolly Boat, at Jesson St Mary, near Dymchurch on the Kent coast. Nesbit died there at the age of sixty-five.

In *Wings and the Child, or the Building of Magic Cities* (1913), she identified herself as one of those who remain children in a grown-up world, who are 'trusting to the verge of what a real grown-up would call imbecility ... If these children, disguised by grown-up bodies, are ever recognised for what they are, it is when they happen to have the use of their pens—when they write for and about

children.' Certainly she attributed her success as a children's writer to the gift of memory—never forgetting what she had thought and suffered in childhood.

In Julia Briggs's detailed biography of the author, Briggs writes of Nesbit as 'the first modern writer for children'. Indeed in her books Nesbit drew away from the enclosed childhood worlds created by Golden Age writers such as Kenneth Grahame to engage with what Briggs calls the 'tough truths to be won from encounters with things-as-they-are'. It was an enduring formula and many of her books with their real-world settings combined with fantasy elements still remain popular with children. Equally, she has influenced a wide range of writers for children including C. S. *Lewis and J. K. *Rowling. Jacqueline *Wilson has written a modern reimagining of the Psammead trilogy entitled *Four Children and It*, and Kate Saunders a sequel (2014).

NESS, Evaline (1911–86) American illustrator-author who won the *Caldecott Medal with *Sam, Bangs, and Moonshine* (1966). Her other *picture books include two based on English folk tales collected by Joseph *Jacobs, *Tom Tit Tot* (1965) and *Mr Miacca* (1967).

NESS, Patrick (1971–) American-British novelist and screenwriter, born on Fort Belvoir army base in Virginia, now resident in the UK. Originally a novelist for adults (he now does both adult and *young adult fiction), he is also a reviewer and a former teacher of creative writing. Since 2008 he has published a young adult novel almost every year, starting with the first in the *Chaos Walking* trilogy, *The Knife of Never Letting Go*. The book was followed in the series by *The Ask and the Answer* (2009), *Monsters of Men* (2010), and three prequel short stories for each, included in the 2013 re-edition of the books. In 2012, he published, with illustrator Jim *Kay, the stunningly moving *A *Monster Calls*. Continuing his brave, ambitious questioning of pretty much all established conventions, Ness published *More Than This* in 2013, the same year he returned to 'adult' fiction with *The Crane Wife*. A recurring theme in his work appears to be the power that stories have on the mind of people, both his younger and older protagonists, be they stories of truth, lies, or things we are told or tell ourselves to shape our understanding of the world. He has won several prizes with both the *Chaos Walking* trilogy and *A Monster Calls*, including the *Booktrust Teenage Prize, the *Guardian Children's Fiction Prize, the Tiptree

Award, the *Costa Children's Book Award, and the *Carnegie Medal twice, becoming only the second author to be awarded it two years in a row.

Never-Ending Story, The See ENDE, MICHAEL.

Never Never Land The home of the Lost Boys in *Peter Pan*.

NEVILLE, Emily (Cheney) (1919–97) American author; she won the *Newbery Medal for her first book, *It's Like This, Cat* (1963), the story of teenager Dave Mitchell and his attempt to drop out of family life at his New York home, a book that appeared mildly revolutionary at the time, but now seems dated.

NEWBERY, Elizabeth and **Francis** See NEWBERY, JOHN.

NEWBERY, John (1713–67) London bookseller, acknowledged to be the first British publisher of children's books 'to make a permanent and profitable market for them, to make a class of book to be taken seriously' (S. Roscoe, *John Newbery and his Successors*, 1973).

Born the son of a small farmer at Waltham St Lawrence in Berkshire, and largely self-educated, Newbery became assistant to William Carnan, a Reading newspaper proprietor; on his employer's death he inherited part of the business and married Carnan's widow. Newbery specialized in books, newspapers, and periodicals, and in the patent medicines which probably always brought in the bulk of his income. He never hesitated to use his books to advertise his other wares: his foremost line in medicines makes an appearance in one of his most popular children's books, when *Goody Two-Shoes' father dies miserably, 'seized with a fever in a place where Dr James's powder was not to be had'.

Newbery published his first books in Reading in 1740, in partnership with other booksellers. In 1743 or 1744 he moved to London, and his first book specifically for the amusement of children, *A *Little Pretty Pocket Book*, was advertised and probably published in the summer of 1744, 'Price of the book 6d. alone, with a Ball or Pincushion 8d.' Shortly afterwards Newbery moved to the Bible and Sun, later no. 65 St Paul's Church Yard, which remained his and his successors' trading address for almost fifty years.

Most of Newbery's books were for adults; of the 2,400 or so new books and editions

published by him and by members of his family between 1740 and 1815, only some 400 were for the juvenile market, though it is almost entirely for these that the name Newbery is remembered. It may be argued also that John Newbery's heart was mostly in this portion of his business, and it is likely that he wrote several children's books himself. He and his successors did, however, publish for adults work by the poet Christopher *Smart (who was married to Newbery's stepdaughter) and by Oliver *Goldsmith, Smollett, and Dr Johnson. Johnson, in the *Idler*, dubbed Newbery 'Jack Whirler' who 'when he enters a house his first declaration is that he cannot sit down, and so short are his visits that he seldom appears to have come for any reason but to say he must go.'

One of John Newbery's earliest and most ambitious projects in children's publishing was the series *The *Circle of the Sciences* (1745-8). His other children's books include *A Museum for Young Gentlemen and Ladies: or, a Private Tutor for little Masters and Misses* (?1750), *The *Lilliputian Magazine* (1751-2), *A *Pretty Book of Pictures for Little Masters and Misses*, subtitled *Tommy Trip's History of Beasts and Birds* (by 1752), *Nurse Truelove's New-Year's Gift* (by 1753), *Be Merry and Wise: or, the Cream of the Jests, and the Marrow of Maxims, for the Conduct of Life . . . By Tommy Trapwit* (?1753), *A *Collection of Pretty Poems for the Amusement of Children Three Foot High* (?1756), *Food for the Mind, or a New Riddle Book . . . By John-the-Giant-Killer, Esq.* (?1757), *Fables in Verse by Abraham Aesop, Esq.* (1757), *The Newtonian System of Philosophy adapted to the Capacities of Young Gentlemen and Ladies . . . by Tom Telescope* (1761), *A *History of England, in a Series of Letters from a Nobleman to his Son* (1764, by Oliver Goldsmith), *Giles Gingerbread* (?1764), and *Goody Two-Shoes* (1765).

It is sometimes claimed that John Newbery was the first person to publish books of a purely entertaining nature for children, but in fact all his children's books were educational to some degree. Newbery believed in books as a means of influencing the rising generation for good, but as a disciple of John *Locke he was convinced that the pill must be sugared; books should represent to children 'their Duties and future Interests in a Manner that shall seem rather intended to amuse than instruct' (*Tom Telescope*). Thus many of his books are lighter in spirit than those published later in the century under the influence of Mrs

*Trimmer. Newbery's style of children's publishing was characterized mainly by energy in writing or commissioning new titles, by a fairly high standard of production and an almost invariable use of *Dutch paper covers, by constant advertising and uninhibited puffing of his own wares, and by mock sententious humour and generally avuncular tone. His good fortune was to catch the tide of increasingly leisured middle-class metropolitan life and to produce books suited both to the parents' aspirations and the children's taste. As to the latter, the rarity of surviving copies of Newbery's books indicates that they were 'read to pieces'.

During his lifetime John Newbery employed his stepson Thomas Carnan (*c*.1735–88), and after Newbery's death his son Francis and Thomas Carnan ran the business in uneasy partnership. Francis Newbery eventually retired from the publishing side and lived on the proceeds of patent medicines, setting himself up as a country gentleman. Carnan published Smart's *Hymns for the Amusement of Children* (?1771), Perrault's *Histories, or Tales of Past Times* had appeared under the Newbery and Carnan imprint by 1768, and *Mother Goose's Melody* is also first known as a Thomas Carnan production, though it may have been published earlier. But for the most part the firm's juvenile books were by this time simply editions of John Newbery's volumes.

John Newbery employed his nephew, also called Francis Newbery, and then set him up in his own book business. When John died, bitter rivalry and some confusion ensued between the two sets of heirs, Francis the son and Carnan at no. 65, and Francis the nephew at the corner of, St Paul's Churchyard. The nephew died in 1780; his business was taken over by his wife Elizabeth, who once again concentrated on children's books. Over 300 bore her imprint, either alone or in partnership, but rather more of them were of an obviously 'improving' nature than was the case with John Newbery's list. Whether Elizabeth Newbery was herself an active publisher, or whether her business was more or less managed for her, is not known. Certainly one of her employees, John *Harris, was a publisher and bookseller in his own right at the same time, and he finally took over the Newbery business in 1801. (*See* HARRIS, JOHN for the later history of the firm.) Elizabeth died in 1821. A few books, notably the earliest surviving edition of *Mother Goose's Melody* (1791), appeared under the imprint of Francis Power,

John Newbery's son-in-law, who operated briefly from no. 65 St Paul's Churchyard up to *c.*1793, when he abandoned books for the wine trade.

Many of Newbery's children's books were pirated and imitated in America, notably by Isaiah *Thomas of Worcester, Mass., who aimed to create a juvenile book-list equivalent to Newbery's. Newbery had in fact as great an influence on the development of children's literature in America as in Britain.

NEWBERY, Linda (1952–) Prolific British writer for all age groups, whose commercial popularity regrettably does not keep pace with her critical acclaim. Most recently, her *young adult novels, including the Victorian gothic novel, *Set in Stone* (2006, winner of the *Costa Children's Book Award), *The Shell House* (2002), and *Sisterland* (2003), have concerned themselves with adult relationships and experiences as much as those of younger people.

These three ambitious books reveal her to be at her most confident when writing about the past, particularly the First and Second World Wars. She examines the changes wrought by political instability on everyday lives and relationships, but is not afraid to examine the consequences of war and does so sympathetically. In both *The Shell House* and *Sisterland* contemporary teenagers use stories from earlier generations to make sense of their own lives and forge their own identities. *The Shell House* is noteworthy for its exploration of male homosexuality, still quite rare in British children's/young adult fiction—in this, and its structure, the influence of Aidan *Chambers is apparent.

Newbery has stepped into the realm of timelessness with her short novel, ostensibly for middle-grade readers, entitled *Lob* (2010). It is a charming retelling of the Green Man legend, rich and playfully reinterpreted, which also has a contemporary thread.

Newbery has also written wholly contemporary stories, and of them *Catcall* (2007), winner of the Silver Smarties Prize, is the best: a study of one brother's efforts to rescue his younger sibling, who is lost amidst the confusion of fractured family life.

NEWBERY, Thomas *See* DIVES PRAGMATICUS.

Newbery Medal The most coveted American award for children's books writing, given annually for 'the most distinguished contribution to American literature for children'

published during the previous calendar year. It is given by the Association for Library Service for Children, part of the *American Library Association. The first winner, in 1922, was *The Story of Mankind* by Hendrik *Van Loon. Each year a number of runners-up are 'Newbery Honor Books'. For a complete list of winners, *see* APPENDIX, D.

NEWELL, Peter Sheaf (1862–1924) American artist and creator of *picture books. His books include *A Shadow Show* (1896), *Peter Newell's Pictures and Rhymes* (1899), and *The *Hole Book* (1908).

New England Primer, The The most widely circulated school-book in America during the 17th and 18th cents. Known as the 'Little Bible' of New England, it was compiled by Benjamin *Harris, an English bookseller and writer of anti-Catholic verses who from 1686 to 1695 lived in Boston, Mass. The *Primer* was developed from Harris's *Protestant Tutor* (1683).

The precise date of the first edition of *The New England Primer* cannot be established, but it must have been between 1686 and 1690; a second impression, 'enlarged', was being advertised late in 1690. No copy of a 17th-cent. edition has been discovered, despite the fact that enormous numbers are known to have been printed; in 1700 a Boston bookseller recorded 44 dozen of them in his inventory.

The earliest surviving edition is that of 1727, of which there is a unique copy in the New York Public Library. This begins with the alphabet printed in various forms. Then comes an illustrated alphabet with rhymes; e.g. for the letter A: 'In *Adam's* fall | We Sinned all', which is accompanied by a crude *woodcut of Eve taking the apple. This rhyming alphabet, which appears some pages later in the text of most editions, was apparently of recent composition when the *Primer* was first published, since for the letter O it gives 'The *Royal Oak* | it was the Tree | That sav'd His | Royal Majestie.' Very likely the verses were the work of Harris himself, who was an admirer of Charles II.

Next in the *Primer* comes a set of sentences and prayers to be learnt by heart, then 'An Alphabet of Lessons for Youth', consisting of biblical sentences beginning with each letter of the alphabet. Only X has defeated the compiler, the sentence for that letter beginning 'EXhort one another . . .'. After this alphabet comes the Lord's Prayer, the Creed, and Commandments, and a section headed 'Duty of

Children Towards Their Parents', consisting of biblical sentences and short verses, one of which reminds the child that he may die an early death. After a table of the books of the Old and New Testaments and a chart of numerals is printed a poem supposedly written by a London dissenting minister, 'John Rogers', described as 'the first martyr in Q. Mary's Reign'. The poem is an 'Exhortation to his Children' before its author was burnt at the stake. The verses are in fact the work of one Robert Smith, who was burned in 1555; they were later attached to the name of Mathew Rogers, who was indeed the earliest martyr of Mary's reign; this in turn became 'John Rogers'. The original Rogers was, however, not burnt because of his Protestant views so much as because he was a priest who had married and at Mary's accession refused to give up his wife.

The New England Primer ends with a *catechism. In the edition of 1727 that used is the Shorter Catechism sanctioned by the Assembly of Divines at Westminster during the 1640s; in other editions John Cotton's catechism *Milk for Babes* was often printed in its stead or alongside it. Some versions of the *Primer* also included a poem entitled 'A Dialogue between Christ, Youth and the Devil', which was probably the work of Harris himself.

For a century after it was first issued *The New England Primer* was the principal school-book of the American Dissenters, and for another century after that it was still frequently reprinted. Throughout America it was, together with the *Bible, the most popular book on sale. Up to 1830 alone more than 360 editions were printed, and twenty years later it was reported that tens of thousands of copies were still in circulation. The *Primer* was also popular in Britain.

Each printer of the *Primer* regarded himself as being at liberty to change its contents, and sometimes its title, to suit his taste or the taste of his customers. There were many variations in the rhymed alphabet. The letter K had originally been accompanied by a verse praising Charles II, and later William III and Queen Anne. Eventually printers tired of changing the rhyme to fit every new monarch, and fixed on the form: 'Our King the good | No man of blood.' But soon Americans began to doubt the goodness of the English king, and this became: 'Kings should be good | Not men of blood'; later still, 'The British King | Lost States thirteen'. To the letter W was originally

attached a rhyme about the whale; after the American revolution this became: 'Great Washington brave | His country did save.' In about 1750 a new set of rhymes of markedly *evangelical character was substituted, each letter being represented by a biblical figure or event.

At various times other material was introduced into the *Primer*, including verses by Isaac *Watts and a set of questions to be answered from the Bible. About 1790 secular material began to intrude itself into some editions of the book, and the rewards promised to good children took on a distinctly worldly character ('Oranges, Apples, Cakes, or Nuts'). Parents, teachers, and printers soon found that material of this sort was more popular with children and more successful as a teaching aid than were the prayers and exhortations, and in consequence the religious parts of the *Primer* gradually disappeared. The last known trade edition of the book was printed in 1886.

New Mother, The See ANYHOW STORIES.

New Nursery Rhymes for Old (1952) A collection of rhymes rewritten by Geoffrey Hall, a textile manufacturer in Manchester, in order to exclude cruelty, deceit, stealing, and other undesirable qualities for which *nursery rhymes are from time to time censured. The alternative version of 'Goosey Goosey Gander', for instance, reads 'I took him by the left leg | And helped him downstairs.'

New Zealand Post Children's Book Awards These awards began as a government initiative in 1982. By 1997 the *New Zealand Post* was the sponsor. Since 2013 it has been known as the *New Zealand Post* Margaret Mahy Book of the Year Awards. Among the categories is the *New Zealand Post* Children's Choice Awards, sponsored by the newspaper and organized by Booksellers New Zealand with support from allied literary and trade bodies. Past category winners include Margaret *Mahy, Gavin *Bishop, David Elliot, Joy *Cowley, Jack Lasenby, Maurice *Gee, Tessa *Duder, and Kate *De Goldi.

NICHOLS, Beverley (1898–1983) British popular author who wrote four children's books, three of them about a magic wood and the animals that live there, beginning with *The Tree that Sat Down* (1945).

NICHOLS, Grace (1950–) A celebrated Guyanese poet and author who moved to the

UK in 1977 with her partner, poet John *Agard. Her first collection for adults *I Is a Long-Memoried Woman* tells the story of a young African woman transported into slavery and won the Commonwealth Poetry Prize in 1983. Her work for children also crosses a transatlantic triangle of Africa, the Caribbean, and the UK, but celebrates it through language with the rhythm and rhyme of her diasporic experience. Her poems play with words, using both Creole and Standard English in a linguistic hybridity that cries to be spoken aloud. Nichols and Agard have worked together professionally, producing anthologies of poetry including *No Hickory, No Dickory, No Dock* (1992), *A Caribbean Dozen* (1996), and *Under the Moon & Over the Sea* (2002). Nichols has also written picture books and novels for older children, including *Whole of a Morning Sky* (1986) set in Guyana. She won the Cholmondeley Award in 2001 and the CLPE Poetry Award in 2003.

NICHOLS, Ruth (1948–) Canadian writer of *fantasy. *A Walk out of the World* (1969), written when she was eighteen and published three years later, describes the journey of the children Judith and Tobit into another world, where they became adult participants in an epic struggle for a kingdom.

NICHOLSON, Georgia *See* ANGUS, THONGS AND FULL-FRONTAL SNOGGING.

NICHOLSON, William (1948–) Children's author and screenwriter. Nicholson was educated at Christ's College, Cambridge, and then joined the BBC, where he became a documentary film-maker. His best known children's series is the *Wind on Fire* trilogy (2000–2), consisting of *The Wind Singer, Slaves of the Mastery,* and *Firesong.* The Noble Warriors trilogy (2006–7) is about the quest of three heroes—Seeker, Morning Star, and the Wildman—to join the Nomana, otherwise known as the Noble Warriors, and the dangers and secrets they discover when they achieve their goal. The three books are *Seeker, Jango,* and *Noman.* Nicholson's novel for teenagers, *Rich and Mad,* is about young love and first sex. He is also a novelist for adults and an Oscar-nominated screenwriter. He wrote the screenplay for *Shadowlands* (1993) about C. S. *Lewis and was co-writer for *Gladiator* (2000), starring Russell Crowe.

NICHOLSON, Sir William (Newzam Prior) (1872–1949) Distinguished British artist and portrait painter who first became involved with children's books when in 1898 he produced *An Alphabet* for Heinemann. Nicholson illustrated *The Square Book of Animals* (1900), with rhymes by Arthur Waugh, father of Evelyn Waugh, and in 1904 he was the designer of costumes and scenery for *Peter Pan.* In 1922 he illustrated *The Velveteen Rabbit* by Margery *Williams, and soon afterwards produced two children's books of his own, *Clever Bill* (1926) and *The Pirate Twins* (1929). Marcus *Crouch puts them in 'the front rank among picture-books of this century'.

Nick Carter A *detective first featured in a story by John Russell Coryell in *Street and Smith's New York Weekly* for 18 September 1886. Subsequently Nick Carter *dime novels were written by Frederick van Rensselaer Dey, who produced them at the rate of about 30,000 words a week. In 1911 there appeared in Britain a *New Nick Carter Weekly.* Carter made something of a comeback (though he had never entirely disappeared) in 1933, with the issue in New York of a *Nick Carter Magazine,* containing stories supposedly written by Carter himself, though in the third person. In the 1970s he became 'Kill-master', a James Bond type of 'special agent', in which form he appeared again in paperback fiction.

NICOLAS *See* MORDVINOFF, NICOLAS.

NIERITZ, Gustav (1795–1876) German writer of sentimental stories for children. He produced over 200 books, some of which were translated into English. They include *Der blinde Knabe* (1837), translated into English in 1869 as *The Blind Boy.*

Night Before Christmas, The *See* VISIT FROM ST NICHOLAS, A.

Nightingale, The A story by Hans Christian *Andersen, published in 1845 and translated into English the next year. A nightingale with a superb song is brought to the palace of the Emperor of China, who rewards it for its fine music. However, it is eventually displaced by a mechanical nightingale which can sing just as well. The real bird flies away, but the mechanical one breaks down and cannot be mended. The Emperor is mortally ill when the real bird returns and by its song lures Death away from the bedside.

NILAND, Deborah and **Kilmeny** Australian illustrators. Together they produced *Birds on a Bough: a counting book* (1975). Deborah Niland's work includes illustrations to *Animal*

Tales (by various authors, 1974); her sister illustrated Jane Wilton-Smith's *Fairy-Tale Picture Dictionary* (1979). Their style is comic and somewhat resembles that of *Sendak.

Nils, The Wonderful Adventures of See WONDERFUL ADVENTURES OF NILS, THE.

NIMMO, Jenny (1944–) British author who, before turning to full-time writing, worked in theatre and on the children's television programme *Jackanory. She moved to Wales, where the landscape and mythology inspired her first major success, *The Snow Spider* (1986), the first in the *Magician Trilogy*. Its blend of well-realized characters, atmospheric mystery, magic, and adventure continued to be developed in her future work, particularly the much-loved *Children of the Red King* series, which starts with *Midnight for Charlie Bone* (2002), telling the story of a boy who is sent to a grim boarding school when his family find out he is one of the 'endowed' after he starts to hear voices coming out of photographs. *The Rinaldi Ring* (1999) showcases her lyrical style, encompassing death and heartbreak in a story about a boy in mourning for his mother and secrets festering since the First World War. Nimmo also produces books for younger readers, with illustrated chapter books, such as *The Owl Tree* (1997), and picture books.

Nipper Assistant to the detective *Nelson Lee.

Nipper A comic strip in the London *Daily Mail* from 1933 to 1947, afterwards revived in book form. It featured a mischievous toddler and a bald baby.

Nippers A series of books published from 1968 by Macmillan of London, edited by Leila *Berg. Intended as an improvement on the *Ladybird books, Nippers provide stories about working-class children and the kind of lives they really lead. Though the books were a great success with children, some teachers objected to their style and content.

NISTER, Ernest (*fl.* 1891–1900) Publisher of *movable picture books in Nuremberg and London. His *Panorama Pictures* was reissued in 1982 as part of the *pop-up craze.

NIX, Garth (1963–) Australian author who worked as a literary agent, marketing consultant, book editor, book publicist, book sales representative, bookseller, and as a part-time soldier in the Australian Army Reserve before becoming a full-time writer of books for older children in 2001. He is famous for his fantasy *Old Kingdom* trilogy which starts with *Sabriel (1996), and the *Keys to the Kingdom* series, starting with *Mister Monday* (2003). *A Confusion of Princes* (2012) is a dark, fast-paced science fiction novel about good and evil, set in a world where princes fight each other to become emperor.

Nkwala (1958) A novel by the Canadian author Edith Sharp (1917–74), about an '*Indian' boy of the Spokan tribe. *Nkwala* is among the very best Canadian books about Native Canadians.

Noddy A character created by Enid *Blyton in 1949. The idea of Noddy arose when David White of the London publishers Sampson Low was sent specimen drawings by a Dutch artist, Harmsen van der Beek, who specialized in pictures showing (in White's words) 'fantastically lively little people, beside tiny houses in the lee of bluebells as proportionately big as trees'. White had the idea of teaming van der Beek up with Blyton, and arranged for them to meet. Blyton was immediately excited by van der Beek's work and on the spot she thought up the character of Noddy, a toy figure of a small boy whose head is fixed in such a way that he has to nod when he speaks. Van der Beek sketched Noddy while they were discussing the idea and four days later the first two Noddy stories had been written. The first of them, *Little Noddy Goes to Toyland*, appeared later in 1949, and the second, *Hurrah for Little Noddy*, came out in 1950.

Soon Enid Blyton and van der Beek were producing Noddy books in large numbers, and the London *Evening Standard* began to run a Noddy strip. After van der Beek's death in 1953 other artists took over the illustrations, using a 'pictorial dictionary' compiled by Sampson Low so that the details were always consistent. Noddy also appeared on the television screen and on stage. Meanwhile the book sales reached unprecedented figures.

Noddy soon became the target of critical attacks. A lengthy article in *Encounter* for January 1958 condemned the books as facile and argued that the character of Noddy himself was deplorable, on the grounds that he seemed incapable of looking after himself and was always running to his friend Big-Ears for help; perhaps, the article suggested facetiously, the Noddy books were a satire on the British citizens' dependence on the Welfare State. Other writers detected 'murky undertones' in

Noddy's relationship with Big-Ears, quoting passages like this (from *Hurrah for Little Noddy*, 1950):

'"If you can squeeze into my tiny bed, you can sleep with me tonight" [said Big-Ears] . . . They squashed into Big-Ears' tiny, soft bed, put their arms round one another to stop themselves from rolling out, and fell fast asleep.'

Enid Blyton was also accused of *racism in her use, on occasion, of *golliwogs as villains. But such attacks could make no dent in the books' sales, and even though the final volume in the original series was published in 1963, the 'little nodding man' would survive as a children's favourite for decades afterwards, and hugely popular animations continue to appear.

Noggin the Nog Hero of a series of stories by the British writer-illustrators Oliver Postgate and Peter Firmin, published in the 1960s and 1970s. The Noggin tales are set in a Norse-like land, and are mock-sagas.

non-fiction for children A strong, if often undervalued, strand in writing for children. It may be argued that it has its origins in *books of instruction, though a clearer distinction is usually made today between books principally for educational function and books primarily for entertainment than at some times in the past. It tends to be written not by subject experts, but by writers of great adaptability to their material, often spanning sciences, humanities etc. Despite the growing amount of high-quality work (some of it designed to be sold to schools and libraries), often appealingly presented and entertaining and not merely didactic or crammed with undigested data, factual books remain in the English-speaking world a poor relative in terms of awareness (compared with the visibility of fiction). In recent years many initiatives have been set up to counter this lack of attention and celebrate fine non-fiction books for children. These include awards, such as the *American Library Association's Sibert Medal (Robert F. Sibert Informational Book Medal) and the NCTE's Orbis Pictus Award, and a non-fiction category for the *Blue Peter Book Awards; and a National Non-Fiction Day in the UK, established by the *Federation of Children's Book Groups, which subsequently expanded to fill a month, National Non-Fiction November.

For more information about different categories, *see* GEOGRAPHY AND TRAVEL BOOKS; HISTORY AND BIOGRAPHY; SCIENCE.

nonsense This genre made its appearance as a form of entertainment for children in certain folk tales current in England before the 19th cent. One such, printed by Joseph *Jacobs in *More English Fairy Tales* (1894), is entitled 'Sir Gammer Vans'; versions of it were found in *chapbooks. It begins:

Last Sunday morning at six o'clock in the evening as I was sailing over the tops of the mountains in my little boat, I met two men on horseback riding on one mare: so I asked them, 'Could they tell me whether the little old woman was dead yet who was hanged last Saturday week for drowning herself in a shower of feathers?'

Similar stories were found by collectors throughout England, and also recorded by the brothers *Grimm. A celebrated chapbook, *The *World Turned Upside Down*, featured various nonsensical incidents, and nonsense words and notions played a part in the *mummers' play. Many *nursery rhymes are nonsense, as is *The *Great Panjandrum*. But not until the era of Edward *Lear and Lewis *Carroll was nonsense brought under control and developed to its full potential.

Elizabeth Sewell in *The Field of Nonsense* (1952) and Francis Huxley in *The Raven and the Writing Desk* (1976) have shown that Lear's and Carroll's nonsense is a sequence of ideas which progresses logically once an initial premise has been accepted. This premise may involve the distortion, inversion, or exaggeration of some aspect of the real world: the size of human beings or animals may be greatly increased or decreased; time or events may be made to occur backwards or in some other strange fashion; food and other substances may take on outlandish characteristics, or unlikely objects may be chosen to serve as food ('Then fill up the glasses with treacle and ink, | Or anything else that is pleasant to drink'). Frequently the process is entirely linguistic: words are invented profusely, games are played with such devices as alliteration or rhyming words ('Did you say pig, or fig?'), and absurdity is achieved simply through the exercise of a literal-minded pedantry.

Lear exploited the nonsensical possibilities of the ABC (there are several nonsense alphabets in his books), while Carroll, in the words of Elizabeth Sewell, 'seems to spend much of his time investigating the language process itself'. Being a professional mathematician, he was also interested in the nonsensical possibilities inherent in many mathematical and logical concepts.

These processes were most effectively carried out in the two *Alice* books of Carroll, in

Lear's *limericks in his *Book of Nonsense, and in certain of his longer poems and nonsense stories. In these works the principles of nonsense are observed ruthlessly. The whole operation is conducted with the detachment of a player involved in a game, and the unpleasant consequences that must result from a methodical distortion of reality are not shirked.

Nonsense appeals to the adult mind just as much as, if not more than, to the child's, and after Lear and Carroll its best practitioners wrote largely for adults. Notable examples are W. S. Gilbert's *Bab Ballads* (1869), the comic verses of *Belloc, the novels of G. K. Chesterton, and *Finnegans Wake* (1939). A true descendant of Lear and Carroll was Spike *Milligan, whose radio scripts for *The Goon Show* during the 1950s and 1960s often reached the most brilliant heights of nonsense.

One of the few really satisfying 20th-cent. nonsense creations for children is the *Rootabaga Stories* (1922) of Carl Sandburg.

Nonsense Songs, Stories, Botany, and Alphabets Written and illustrated by Edward *Lear; published by Robert John Bush of London, probably in time for Christmas 1870 though dated 1871. It contained the first printed appearance of many of Lear's longer poems.

The first section, 'Nonsense Rhymes', consists of The *Owl and the Pussy-Cat, 'The Duck and the Kangaroo', 'The Daddy Longlegs and the Fly', 'The Jumblies', 'The Nutcrackers and the Sugar-tongs', 'Calico Pie', 'Mr and Mrs Spikky Sparrow', 'The Broom, the Shovel, the Poker, and the Tongs', and 'The Table and the Chair'. The section 'Nonsense Stories' contains 'The Story of the Four Little Children who Went Round the World' and 'The History of the Seven Families of the Lake Pipple-Popple'. Then comes 'Nonsense Cookery', 'Nonsense Botany', and three 'Nonsense Alphabets'. The book was first published in America by James R. Osgood of Boston in 1871.

NORDSTROM, Ursula (1910–1988) American editor, publisher, and author. At Harper & Row, where she eventually had her own imprint, Nordstrom edited novels and picture books that became classics: *Stuart Little* (1945) and *Charlotte's Web* (1952) by E. B. White, Margaret Wise Brown's *Goodnight Moon* (1947), *Harold and the Purple Crayon* (1955) by Crockatt Johnson, *Harriet the Spy* (1964) by Louise Fitzhugh, and more. An innovator who published books about realistic children—and sometimes their problems—

she was not afraid of controversy: she published Maurice Sendak's *Where the Wild Things Are* (1963) and the first gay-themed *young adult novel, *I'll Get There. It Better Be Worth the Trip* (1969) by John Donovan. Nordstrom herself wrote the acclaimed children's book *The Secret Language* (1960).

Norman and Henry Bones, the Boy Detectives Featured in a series of *Children's Hour radio plays by Anthony C. Wilson, and in *Norman Bones, Detective* (1949) and other books by him.

Norse myths These were first retold for English-speaking children by Annie and Eliza *Keary in *Heroes of Asgard* (1857). Later versions include Padraic *Colum's *The Children of Odin* (1920), illustrated by Willy *Pogány, and *Thunder of the Gods* (1952) by Dorothy Hosford, who also produced a prose version of the *Volsungasaga*, entitled *Sons of the Volsung* (1949). Arthur *Rackham's illustrations to a retelling of Wagner's *Ring of the Nibelungs* (1910, 1912), though printed in an edition intended for adults, first inspired C. S. *Lewis with a love of Norse mythology.

NORTHCLIFFE, Lord *See* HARMSWORTH, ALFRED.

Northern Lights The first book in the *His Dark Materials* trilogy.

NORTON, Andre (Alice Mary Norton) (1912–2005). American writer of *science fiction and *fantasy for children, best known for her 'Star' novels. The series began with *Star Man's Son, 2250 AD* (1952), and was followed by many others of the same sort (*Star Rangers, Star Born, Star Gate*, etc.). After establishing herself as a popular writer of 'galactic' fiction, she turned to the American West for such novels as *Fur Magic* (1968).

NORTON, Mary (1903–92) British children's author who spent much of her childhood in her family's Georgian manor house in Bedfordshire; this was to provide the setting for many of her books. During the Second World War, while her husband was in the Navy, she and her four children spent some time in America, and it was in New York that her first children's book, *The Magic Bed-Knob*, was published in 1943. *Bonfires and Broomsticks* appeared in 1947; it and its predecessor were eventually republished in one volume as *Bedknob and Broomstick*.

In 1952 came The *Borrowers, which established her as one of the leading British

children's writers of the post-war period. There were a number of sequels. She has also written *Are All The Giants Dead?* (1975), a dryly humorous story about the ageing heroes and heroines of the classic *fairy stories, who are living in languorous retirement.

NÖSTLINGER, Christine (1936–) Austrian writer, one of the most successful children's authors in the German language, who has written over one hundred books. Nöstlinger won the *Deutscher Jugendliteraturpreis in 1973, the *Hans Christian Andersen Award in 1984, and was honoured as one of the two recipients of the first *Astrid Lindgren Memorial Award in 2003, along with Maurice *Sendak. Nöstlinger's first book, *Die feuerrote Friederike*, which she also illustrated, was published in 1970, and translated into English as *Fiery Frederica* (1975). Nöstlinger writes for a range of age groups, and her books, whether based in fantasy or reality, always have a sense of social justice, dealing with issues such as discrimination and racism. The fantastic tale of *Konrad, das Kind aus der Konservenbüchse* (1975; translated as *Conrad, the Factory-Made Boy*, by Anthea *Bell, 1976; winner of the 1979 *Batchelder Award) is regarded as one of her masterpieces. One of Nöstlinger's most popular titles is *Maikäfer, Flieg!* (1973; translated as *Fly Away Home*, by Anthea Bell, 1975). *A Dog's Life*, Anthea Bell's translation of *Der Hund kommt!* won the inaugural *Marsh Award for Children's Literature in Translation in 1996 (1987; English translation, 1990). The Astrid Lindgren Memorial Award jury described Nöstlinger as a 'truly anti-authoritarian children's writer of the calibre of Astrid Lindgren'. She presents outsider figures with humour and warmth.

Not Now, Bernard (1980) A picture book by David *McKee. All Bernard wants is a bit of attention, but whenever he tries to talk to Dad or Mum, he gets the same reply—'Not now, Bernard'. Then a monster eats him. Dad and Mum don't even notice. With his distinctive line and bright palette, McKee manages to make what is, after all, a rather grim story of parental neglect into something very funny, which has been much loved by whole generations of children, and has made whole generations of parents just a little bit uncomfortable.

Noughts and Crosses (2001) This book and its sequels *An Eye for an Eye* (2003), *Knife Edge* (2004), *Checkmate* (2005), and *Double Cross* (2008) are set in an alternative *dystopian reality where 'real world' race relations are reversed. Malorie *Blackman's sensational pentalogy reflects, in photographic negative, the harsh truths of race and prejudice. The story of star-crossed lovers, Sephy and Callum, is told in the following four novels which expand into the alternate perspectives of three generations of light-skinned Noughts and dark-skinned Crosses in their fight for freedom and equality. Dealing with complex themes such as terrorism, gang culture, family loyalty, and love, the series has been massively popular. A short story, *Callum* (2012), published exclusively in digital format, returns to the same period as the first novel.

novels in verse *See* VERSE NOVELS.

novelty book Any book that contains a moving part or an element other than paper or card. Novelty books for children first became popular in the 18th cent. In 1770, London book publisher Robert Sayer started to produce 'Metamorphoses books' or 'Harlequinades', which had lift-up flaps with hidden pictures.

In the 19th cent., the peep-show format became popular. The reader looked through a small hole in the cover, to see an elaborately constructed scene. Then, in the latter half of the century, London company Dean & Son began to publish a large number of books with moving parts. In the 1880s, the McLoughlin Brothers of New York published the 'Little Showman's Series', which had three-dimensional scenes. A master of the technique at this time was the German illustrator Logan *Meggendorfer: he turned the movable book into an art form, using intricate hidden levers to great comic effect.

During the First World War, there was a dramatic slowdown in the production of novelty books. Then in 1929, British publisher S. Louis Giraud issued the first of a series of annuals, each containing a number of pop-ups. The series continued for twenty years.

In the latter half of the 20th cent., the concept of the novelty book began to have a much wider meaning. Eric Carle's much-loved *The *Very Hungry Caterpillar* (1969) used tiny die-cut holes to show what the caterpillar had eaten. His subsequent books have included acetate pages, sound chips, and flashing lights.

In the 1970s, Robert Crowther (1948–) and Jan *Pieńkowski came to the fore. Crowther's *The Most Amazing Hide-and-Seek Alphabet Book* (1977) contained twenty-six pop-ups— far more than was common at the time. Jan Pieńkowski scored a big hit with *Haunted

House (1979), which won the *Kate Greenaway Medal. In it, pop-ups and pull tabs are used to deliciously spooky effect. American pop-ups in the same year included Richard *Scarry's *Busytown Pop-Up Book,* a series of counting books and rhyming books based on *Sesame Street,* a pop-up version of *Superman, and several books from the *Disney organization.

By the early 1980s pop-ups had virtually become a major industry among children's book publishers. Examples from this period include a reworking of *Fungus the Bogeyman* by Raymond *Briggs as a 'Plop-Up Book' (1982) and *The Dwindling Party* (1982) by Edward *Gorey, in which a family, visiting a haunted mansion, are snatched away one by one by fearsome creatures.

Rod Campbell's *Dear Zoo* (1982) is conceptually extremely straightforward: lift-up flaps reveal a series of animals, all potential pets for the narrator. The book's very simplicity has made it incredibly appealing to toddlers, and it has become a classic.

Other notable novelty book creators during the last thirty years include, in the UK, Nick *Sharratt (*Moo Cow, Kung Fu Cow*), David Pelham (*Sam's Sandwich*), and Jo Lodge (*Mr Croc* series), and in the US, David Carter (*How Many Bugs in a Box?*), Bruce Foster (*Harry Potter: a Pop-Up Book*), Kees Moerbeek (*My Secret Scrapbook Diary* series), and Keith Moseley (*Victorian Dollhouse*).

Robert *Sabuda and Matthew Reinhart produce pop-up books of extraordinary complexity for older children. They have had great success with the *Encyclopedia Prehistorica* series, including *Dinosaurs, Sharks,* and *Mega-Beasts.*

The French illustrator Hervé *Tullet creates beautifully designed, playful books that encourage children to use their imagination. His *Game Of . . .* series uses a whole range of techniques, including split pages, glow-in-the-dark ink, and a book that you can turn into a 3D sculpture.

Fiona Watt started to produce a series of baby books in 1999 called *That's Not My . . .* Using a huge range of touchy-feely textures, and a formulaic, repetitive text, the series now comprises more than forty titles. At the opposite end of the age scale are the immensely popular *Dragonology* (2003) and its many sequels.

Today, novelty books contain every imaginable device. There are puppet books, books for babies with rattles, squeaks, and mirrors, jigsaw books, sound books, and more.

In 2007, Rufus Butler Seder published *Gallop!,* the first in a series called 'Scanimation'. It employed a technique that looked absolutely new, but in fact harked back to the days of the kinetoscope. A striped acetate layer is used to give an astonishing effect of movement when the page is turned, as though the reader were watching a film.

Now We Are Six (1927) The second of A. A. *Milne's books of verse for children, written in the three years following the appearance of *When We Were Very Young.* E. H. *Shepard was the illustrator and Christopher Robin, Milne's only son, now aged six, was again the ostensible subject of many of the poems. The dedicatee, Anne Darlington, was Christopher's best friend, who lived nearby in London and often spent holidays with the Milnes at Cotchford, their country home:

> Where is Anne?
> Head above the buttercups . . .
> What has she got in that firm little fist of hers?
> Somebody's thumb and it feels like Christopher's.

But Christopher Milne, in his autobiography *The Enchanted Places* (1974), vehemently disowns one of the verses, 'The Engineer', in which his toy train is supposed to have 'a good sort of brake | But it hasn't worked yet.' It was his father who was unmechanical, and at a very young age Christopher was the mender in the family: 'If I'd had a train (and I didn't have a train) any brake that I'd wanted to make for it . . . WOULD HAVE WORKED.'

Many of the poems are humorous verses unrelated to the childhood lives of either Christopher Robin or his father:

> King John was not a good man—
> He had his little ways.
> And sometimes no one spoke to him
> For days and days and days.

Nurse Matilda A nanny in stories by Christianna *Brand.

Nursery 'Alice', The A version of *Alice's Adventures in Wonderland* 'with the text adapted to nursery readers', made by Lewis *Carroll (C. L. Dodgson) himself, and published by Macmillan in 1889. The cover was by E. Gertrude Thomson, a friend of Dodgson's who specialized in nude sketches of children, and *Tenniel's original illustrations were enlarged and coloured.

The book opens with a poem by Dodgson, 'A Nursery Darling', and has a Preface explaining that the book is intended to be read by, or rather to, 'Children aged from Nought to Five'. The story begins: 'Once upon a time, there was a little girl called Alice: and she had a very curious dream.' Dodgson rewrote his original

text in a manner that removes almost all its virtues. He uses a fussy, condescending style and makes tiresome comments on the pictures; for instance, of the Pool of Tears illustration: 'Doesn't Alice look pretty?' Nevertheless the book proved popular and has often been reprinted.

nursery rhymes (Mother Goose rhymes)

Verses or chants spoken or sung by adults to small children. The practice of amusing or soothing children with *riddles, *lullabies, snatches of popular songs, and *nonsense seems to be universal. Classical Latin examples survive, and a collector in China at the end of the 19th cent. found 600 nursery rhymes in just two of the eighteen provinces.

The term 'nursery rhyme' seems to have been adopted in England in the first half of the 19th cent. 'Mother Goose's' or 'Tommy Thumb's songs' or 'ditties' were earlier terms, and 'Mother Goose Rhymes' has been retained as the term in America (*see* MOTHER GOOSE).

Over 500 rhymes in English, in a multitude of versions, are still traditional, that is, are primarily passed on to children by adults who remember hearing them in their childhood. Of these, a few are recorded in medieval texts and many more were almost certainly well known by 1650, while at least half the rhymes in circulation today are believed to have been current by the mid-18th cent. Yet very little of the present stock started life in the nursery.

Such *counting-out rhymes as 'Eeny, meeny, miney, mo' and its many variants are related to ancient shepherds' and fishermen's numeration. Some of the rhymes, such as 'Ladybird, ladybird', 'London Bridge', and 'We'll go to the wood', are relics of pagan rituals and charms. Some were proverbs or memorable lines from the annual *mummers' play, while others were rounds, catches, or drinking songs ('Nose, nose, jolly red nose'). A number, fewer than is sometimes thought (certainly many fewer than is argued in The *Real Personages of Mother Goose by K. E. Thomas, 1930), refer to historical figures. In some cases a nursery rhyme is the best-remembered verse or chorus of a popular *ballad ('Lavender's green, diddle diddle') or a successful stage song. Having a printed source does not prevent a rhyme from becoming part of an oral tradition; an example is *Mary had a little lamb, written by Mrs Sarah Josepha *Hale of Boston in 1830; another is 'Oh where, oh where has my little dog gone', composed as a comic ballad for adults by a Philadelphian, Septimus Winner, in

1864. The traditional repertoire of nursery rhymes is undoubtedly still growing in this way.

The first appearance of a British nursery rhyme in a book intended for children was in A *Little Book for Little Children, an early 18th-cent. *primer by 'T.W.' The first known collection of nursery rhymes, *Tommy Thumb's Song Book, was apparently published in 1744. By 1780 there had appeared the most influential of the early collections, *Mother Goose's Melody. Two later volumes, The *Nursery Rhymes of England (1842) and Popular Rhymes and Nursery Tales (1849), both edited by James Orchard *Halliwell, began the work of serious research into the sources of the rhymes, which culminated with Iona and Peter Opie's *Oxford Dictionary of Nursery Rhymes (1951).

The first nursery rhyme books were generally illustrated with *woodcuts, and many of the finest children's illustrators have made their own versions. Randolph *Caldecott produced, between 1878 and 1885, a celebrated series of *picture books largely based on nursery rhymes, and among modern illustrators Raymond *Briggs is perhaps the most notable, for his Mother Goose Treasury (1966).

Not infrequently objections have been raised to the coarse character of some of the rhymes; one such objector was S. G. *Goodrich, the original '*Peter Parley'. Attempts to censor them include Geoffrey Hall's *New Nursery Rhymes for Old (1952). The rhymes have often been used for satirical purposes; see, for example, the long list of parody versions of The *House that Jack Built in the Oxford Dictionary of Nursery Rhymes.

No other country has paid the same sort of attention as Britain to the collecting and studying of its nursery rhymes, though notable collections have appeared. These include Des Knaben Wunderhorn (1806-8), in which Clemens *Brentano and Achim von Arnim gathered many traditional German folk songs, including a number of 'Kinderlieder' (children's songs).

Stories have often been written around the characters of nursery rhymes, for example *Wanted: A King (1890) by 'Maggie Browne' and Compton Mackenzie's Santa Claus in Summer (1924).

Nursery Rhymes of England, The A collection edited by James Orchard *Halliwell, first published for the Percy Society in 1842, with the assertion that the rhymes were 'collected principally from Oral Tradition'. Halliwell divided the rhymes into classes—historical (i.e. those he ascribed to some historical

period or figure), jingles, *riddles, proverbs, *lullabies, etc.—and included notes on the supposed origins of many of them, and on lines that he thought needed annotation. The book was reissued several times, and in 1849 Halliwell published a 'sequel', *Popular Rhymes and Nursery Tales*, which contained nursery stories, *games-rhymes, and other pieces of nursery lore, with lengthy comments by Halliwell.

Despite the fact that some of his assertions about the sources of rhymes are highly dubious, Halliwell has been recognized as a collector of much importance, on whose books were based most other *nursery rhyme collections for the next hundred years. His was the first collection to produce evidence of the antiquity of the rhymes.

Nurse Truelove's New-Year's Gift: *or, the Book of Books for Children* A small illustrated miscellany published by John *Newbery not later than 1753. Among such items as the story of good Miss Polly who becomes Lady Mayoress, an ABC song, and an article on memory, it contains the first known appearance in print of the nursery rhyme *The *House that Jack Built*. 'Nurse Truelove' was used by the Newbery firm to sponsor a number of other 'gift' books of a similar kind.

Nutcracker, The A story first written by E. T. A. *Hoffmann, originally entitled *Nüssknacker und der Mäusekönig* (1816). It was adapted by *Dumas, as *Les Aventures d'un casse-noisette* (1845), in which form it was used as the basis of Tchaikovsky's ballet *The Nutcracker and the Mouse King* (1892); the *Nutcracker Suite* was extracted from this.

The story tells how a girl and boy are given as a Christmas present a nutcracker in the form of a little man. At night he leads the nursery toys in battle against a mouse army. He proves to be a young man (in Hoffmann's version, a prince), who has been enchanted into this shape by a mouse-sorceress. After killing the mouse king and regaining his human form, he takes the girl to a land made of sugar and other sweet delicacies and makes her his queen. Another version of the same story, *König Nüssknacker und der arme Reinhold* (1851), is by Heinrich Hoffmann, author of *Struwwelpeter.

NYE, Robert (1939–2016) British novelist and poet who wrote several children's books, including retellings of *Welsh traditional tales, *Taliesin* (1966) and *March Has Horse's Ears* (1966).

OAKLEY, Graham *See* CHURCH MICE, THE.

Obelix In the *Astérix books, he is the hero's 'inseparable friend'. Obelix is a very large (or, as he would say, 'well-covered') Gaulish men-hir-deliveryman, with superhuman strength gained from having been dropped as a baby into the magic potion brewed by the druid *Getafix. This does mean that when the other Gauls are being given doses of the potion, he isn't allowed any, which tends to make him grumpy. He can be cheered up, however, by the availability of copious wild boars to eat and copious Roman soldiers to thump.

O'BRIEN, Robert C. (Robert Leslie Conly) (1918–73) American author, best known for *Mrs Frisby and the Rats of NIMH* (1971), a story about a fieldmouse and a colony of laboratory rats, which is a parable about the choice between a destructive technological society and the 'natural' life. It won the *Newbery Medal, and has been filmed as *The Secret of NIMH*.

ODAGA, Asenath (?1938–2014) Kenyan author of many children's books, some in the Luo language, others in English, for example *Sweets and Sugar Cane* (1969).

Odd and Elsewhere Heroes of stories by James *Roose-Evans.

O'DELL, Scott (1898–1989) American novelist who won the *Newbery Medal for his first book for children, *Island of the Blue Dolphins* (1960), the true story of a Native American girl, Karana, left alone on a small island for eighteen years. His later books include *The King's Fifth* (1966), *The Dark Canoe* (1968), and *Sarah Bishop* (1980). His novels show a marked talent for assuming the identities of his narrators, female as well as male.

ogre A creature in *fairy stories, often a *giant, who devours human flesh. The word was first recorded by *Perrault, whose *Contes de ma mère l'Oye* (1697) include the appearance of several ogres, most notably that in *Hop o' my Thumb*.

It is widely assumed that Perrault invented the word, perhaps deriving it from a supposed Italian dialect form *ogro*, a hypothetical variant of *orco*, 'demon, monster'; cf. Latin *Orcus*, the god of the infernal regions. When Perrault used the word in a defence of fairy stories, in his *Parallèle des anciens et des modernes* (1688–97), he did so in a manner which suggests that it may have been unfamiliar to his readers.

The first English translator of Perrault's stories, Robert Samber, felt obliged to add an explanation (in *Histories, or Tales of Past Times*, 1729) that 'an Ogre is a giant that has long teeth and claws, with a raw head and bloody bones, that runs away with naughty little boys and girls, and eats them up.' In fact a form of the word had already appeared in English in 1713, in a translation of the *Arabian Nights*, which referred to 'one of those Savage Demons call'd *Hogres*, who stay in remote places, and make use of a thousand wiles to surprize and devour Passengers'.

O'HARA, Mary *See* MY FRIEND FLICKA.

O'KEEFE, Adelaide *See* ORIGINAL POEMS, FOR INFANT MINDS.

OKORO, Anezi (1929–) Nigerian children's author. His books include *The Village School* (1966), a picture of school life centring on a football match, and *One Week One Trouble* (1972), the story of a boy from a bush village who comes to St Mark's School and is soon tangled in the difficulties of school life.

Old King Cole Subject of a popular *nursery rhyme. One explanation of the rhyme's origin is that it refers to a Reading merchant named Colebrook, who featured in Thomas Deloney's *Historie of Thomas of Reading* (c.1598). Deloney refers to him as 'Old Cole' and states that he was vastly wealthy and maintained huge numbers of servants. Another explanation of the rhyme was given by Sir Walter *Scott, who

alleged that it referred to the father of the *giant, Fyn M'Coule.

Old Mother Hubbard See MOTHER HUBBARD.

Old Mother West Wind (1910) A series of whimsical tales by the American author Thornton W. Burgess (1874–1965), illustrated by Harrison Cady. The book is an undistinguished mishmash in imitation of The *Wind in the Willows, the stories of Beatrix *Potter, the *Just So Stories for Little Children, and *Uncle Remus, but was very popular in its time.

Old Possum's Book of Practical Cats A sequence of light verses by T. S. Eliot (1888–1965), first published by Faber and Faber in September 1939, then the following year with illustrations by Nicolas Bentley. The nickname 'Old Possum' was first given to Eliot by Ezra Pound. Eliot sometimes used it among his friends, signing letters to them with the initials 'T.P.' (Tom Possum). The poems were used as the basis for the musical *Cats*, with a score by Andrew Lloyd Webber, which received its first performance in London in 1981 and remained in the West End for twenty-one years; the same production opened on Broadway in 1982 and ran till 2000. A new edition of the poems, illustrated by Axel *Scheffler, was published in 2009. Individual poems have been made into children's books, too—for example *Macavity* (2014), illustrated by Arthur Robins.

Old Woman and Her Pig, The An English folk tale on the accumulative principle (the same as that of The *House that Jack Built), first recorded by J. O. *Halliwell and printed in *English Fairy Tales* (1890) by Joseph *Jacobs.

Oliver Optic See OPTIC, OLIVER.

Olivia (2000) The first in a picture-book series by illustrator and theatre designer Ian Falconer (1959–), about a strong-willed and arty young pig, utterly irrepressible and irresistibly funny. The stark illustrations in black, white, and red give the book its distinctively stylish look. It was chosen as a 2001 Caldecott Honor Book (see CALDECOTT MEDAL). There have been more than ten subsequent storybooks featuring the much-loved pig, and adaptations for various media. In 2006, she even appeared on a US stamp.

OLSEN, Ib Spang (1921–2012) Danish illustrator and creator of *picture books; his style is exuberant and his humour eccentric, as in

such books as *Lars Peters cykel* (1968; English translation as *Lars-Peter's Bicycle*, 1968).

OMAN, Carola (Mary Anima) (1897–1978) British historian who wrote several *historical novels for children, including *Alfred, King of the English* (1939).

ONADIPE, (Nathaniel) Kola (Kolawole) (1922–88) Nigerian children's author. His books include *The Adventures of Souza* (1963), a boy's account of his escapades in a Nigerian village; *The Magic Land of Shadows* (1971), a *fantasy (somewhat resembling *Diamonds and Toads*) in which a girl, ill-treated by her stepmother, acquires magical gifts; and two *historical novels, *The Boy Slave* (1966) and *The Return of Shettima* (1972).

Once, Then, Now, After (2006–12) A series of novels by Australian novelist Morris *Gleitzman. Set in occupied Poland during the Second World War, they feature a young Jewish boy called Felix. The series begins with *Once* (2006): Felix flees from his orphanage to try to find his parents (who he doesn't realize have been murdered by the Nazis). In *Then* (2009), Felix escapes from a train bound for Auschwitz with his friend Zelda, and they hide in the forest. *Now* (2010) is set in the present day, in which Felix recounts the horrors of his childhood to his granddaughter (named Zelda after Felix's now long-dead friend). *After* (2012) takes us back to 1945, to the final stages of the war.

The stories show the reader an experience of the Holocaust through a child's innocent eyes, without flinching from its horrors. Writing about *Then* in the *Sunday Times*, Nicolette Jones sums up the feel of the series: 'One of the reasons this humane and carefully crafted book is so readable is that the author celebrates ordinariness and childishness even as he chronicles terrible cruelty.'

Once and Future King, The A novel in four sections by T. H. *White, based on the King *Arthur legends as told by *Malory. The first three parts, The *Sword in the Stone, The Witch in the Wood (later retitled 'The Queen of Air and Darkness'), and The Ill-Made Knight, were originally published as separate books in 1938, 1939, and 1940; the fourth book, 'The Candle in the Wind', was added in 1958 when the entire text was issued in one volume, with revisions of the earlier parts, under its overall title. The Once and Future King was later made into a musical play, *Camelot*, which was also filmed.

A fifth section, *The Book of Merlyn* (1977), in which Arthur goes into an underground hide-out before his final battle, was not published until after White's death.

While *The Sword in the Stone* has much of the character of a children's book, and the entire cycle is sometimes read by children, the later sections of the story display a certain streak of cruelty, and they were not intended by White for a child readership.

Once upon a time... A formulation used (for over six centuries) for beginning many traditional stories in English. (Stories which will, for the most part, see the hero and/or heroine 'live happily ever after' at the other end.) Other languages around the world have equivalent formulations, some of them recurring in a number of languages, including 'A long, long time ago...' and 'There was, and there was not...'. Such phrases are used with particular regularity for *fairy tales. In 1917 A. A. *Milne wrote a sort of fairy tale which he called *Once on a Time*.

One Hundred and One Dalmatians, The (1956) A novel by Dodie *Smith. Pongo and Missis, a young pair of Dalmatian dogs, are stricken by the loss of their puppies. The crime is traced to Cruella de Vil, who has a passion for furs. The story was filmed by *Disney.

One Thousand and One Nights *See* ARABIAN NIGHTS ENTERTAINMENT.

O'NEILL, Rose *See* KEWPIES.

One, two, buckle my shoe A counting rhyme first printed in *Songs for the Nursery* (1805). It has sometimes been printed as a separate book with illustrations, e.g. *The Juvenile Numerator* (D. Carvalho, c.1825), and *One, Two, Buckle My Shoe* illustrated by Walter *Crane (1867).

Oojah Annual An *annual published from 1923 by Hulton Press of London, featuring 'Flip-Flap, the Great Oojah', an avuncular elephant.

OPIE, Peter (Mason) (1918–82) and **Iona (Margaret Balfour)** (1923–) Husband and wife collaborators on *The *Oxford Dictionary of Nursery Rhymes* and subsequent studies of children's folklore and literature.

Peter Opie, the only child of an army surgeon and his wife, was born in Cairo. At the age of seven he was put in an English preparatory school as a boarder while his parents were in India; he subsequently went to Eton,

where (he afterwards claimed) he was 'most ungifted' at both academic work and games. Just before the outbreak of war he joined the armed forces, and was soon commissioned in the Royal Sussex regiment, but in 1941 was invalided out and began to work for the BBC.

They married in 1943, and it was the birth of their first child the following year that suggested to them that they should study the folklore of childhood. The initial result of this was the appearance in 1947 of *I Saw Esau*, a small volume in which they collected many of the rhymes known to British schoolchildren but not usually printed. Meanwhile they laboured at what was now planned as a definitive study of the origin and meanings of British *nursery rhymes. *The Oxford Dictionary of Nursery Rhymes* finally appeared in 1951, and won universal praise for its deft combination of scholarship (unprecedented in this field) with cheerful humour.

The Opies' texts of the rhymes as given in the *Oxford Dictionary* are now generally regarded as the standard ones (though they were careful to give all significant variants), and have been used, with or without acknowledgement, in many subsequent collections. The Opies themselves compiled *The Oxford Nursery Rhyme Book* (1955), a collection for the use of children, which finely blends 18th- and early 19th-cent. engravings with modern illustrations in the same style by Joan Hassall, and *The Puffin Book of Nursery Rhymes* (1963). In the meantime they continued to do extensive original research, this time among present-day children, and this produced two outstanding books of child folklore, *The Lore and Language of Schoolchildren* (1959) and *Children's Games in Street and Playground* (1969).

While assembling *The Oxford Dictionary of Nursery Rhymes* the Opies had become collectors of early and rare children's books, and by 1973 their Collection of Child Life and Literature, housed at their Hampshire home, was unrivalled in this field. In that year appeared a catalogue of some items in it that had been put on exhibition, *Three Centuries of Nursery Rhymes and Poetry for Children*. This was reissued in enlarged form in 1977. The Opies' later work grew largely from their book collection. Their *Oxford Book of Children's Verse* (1973), which includes poems by many obscure and half-forgotten writers, was followed by *The Classic Fairy Tales* (1974), which contains the earliest published English texts of the tales selected, together with notes on the history and

analogues of the stories. In 1980 came *A Nursery Companion*, a volume containing nearly thirty facsimiles of early 19th-cent. children's illustrated books from their own collection, carefully reproduced with the original colouring.

The Opies generally divided their labour clearly. She did the fieldwork, which involved visiting schools all over Britain with a tape-recorder and processing facts collected from questionnaires, backed up by extensive correspondence and research in libraries. He undertook the writing, and the prefaces to their books strongly reflect his complex personality—both shy and ebullient, aware of a lack of formal academic training, but profoundly confident in the value of his and his wife's work. They received many awards in recognition of their achievements; he served as President of the Anthropology Section of the British Association (1962-3) and President of the Folklore Society (1963-4). What pleased him most was the granting in 1962, to himself and his wife, of honorary Masterships of Arts from Oxford University.

It was the Opies who first suggested an *Oxford Companion to Children's Literature*, a task which was finally assumed by Humphrey *Carpenter and Mari Prichard. At the time of Peter's death the Opies had almost completed a new *Oxford Book of Narrative Verse* (1983), and were already well advanced with other projects, at which Iona Opie continued to work.

OPPEL, Kenneth (1967-) Canadian author who by the age of twelve had decided he wanted to be a writer. Luck gave him a family friend who knew Roald *Dahl, and Dahl liked one of Oppel's manuscripts enough to send it to his own agent, and a new career was born with the publication of *Colin's Fantastic Video Adventure* (1985). Oppel's work is imaginative, featuring bats as heroes in the *Silverwing* quartet (1997-2002), or a world where airships are the main form of travel in the *Matt Cruse* series, starting with *Airborn* (2004). *Half-Brother* (2010) shows Oppel writing at a new level of sophistication; this is the thought-provoking, subtle, and humane story of a boy whose behavioural scientist father brings home an eight-day-old chimpanzee to be his brother. The *Apprenticeship of Victor Frankenstein* series delves deep into the mind of the troubled teenager who becomes a madman, starting with the excellent *This Dark Endeavour* (2011)—the story entwines the darkest of Gothic, alchemy, love, and the quest for eternal life.

OPTIC, Oliver (William Taylor Adams) (1822-97) American author who wrote a number of popular stories for boys. The first was *The Boat Club* (1854), a tale of intrigue and rivalry which was hugely successful. His total output was more than 125 books and about 1,000 short stories.

His best known tale was *Outward Bound; or, Young America Afloat* (1867), describing a group of reckless youths on board a school ship. The *magazines which he edited for juveniles included *The Student and Schoolmaster*, *Oliver Optic's Magazine*, and *Our Little Ones*. He also used the pseudonyms 'Irving Brown', 'Clinham Hunter, M.D.', and 'Old Stager'.

His stories were only slightly better than *dime novels. They were sometimes banned from *libraries because of their sensationalism, and Louisa *Alcott criticized them in her novel *Eight Cousins* (serialized in 1875).

Orange Pear Apple Bear (2006) A picture book by Emily *Gravett. It uses a vocabulary of just five words (four of them in the title), in rotating combinations (Apple-Pear, Orange-Bear), so cleverly that even within these constraints there is humour and even something resembling a narrative. With lovely water-colouring in beautiful pencil lines, this is a brilliantly simple book (it apparently took Gravett just eleven hours to draft out) but more effective and far more charming than most wordier fare.

Oranges and Lemons A *nursery rhyme which accompanies a children's game. It was recorded in one of the first collections of children's rhymes, *Tommy Thumb's Song Book* (1744). It is disputed whether 'the bells of St Clement's' are those of St Clement Danes or St Clement at Eastcheap, both of which are in the City of London.

Orbis Sensualium Pictus A *picture book illustrating Latin and vernacular vocabulary by *Comenius, printed in Germany in 1658, published in England in a translation by Charles *Hoole in 1659, and usually credited with being the first picture book designed exclusively for children. Hoole's translation was entitled *A World of Things Obvious to the Senses*. The book was for the use of children learning to read English and then, at the age of six or seven, Latin.

After an illustrated alphabet expressed in terms of animal and other noises, each picture shows a group of numbered objects in their

context, ranging from the solar system to a tailor's shop. Then come the names of objects, with descriptions. The introduction recommends that the book be freely given to children, even at home before they are put to school, 'to delight withal as they please, with the sight of the pictures'.

Hoole's translation of the *Orbis Pictus* was often reprinted up to the 19th cent. The first American edition was produced in 1810 by T. & J. Swords of New York, with illustrations by Alexander *Anderson.

ORCZY, Baroness (Emma Magdalena Rosalia Marie Josepha Barbara Orczy) (1865–1947) Author who was born in Hungary, the daughter of Baron Felix Orczy. In 1894 she married the illustrator Montague Barstow, and together they produced several children's books, before she turned to the writing of *historical novels with *The Emperor's Candlesticks* (1899).

Her most famous story, *The *Scarlet Pimpernel*, written in 1902, was turned down by every publisher to whom it was submitted. However, a play based on it was staged in London in 1905 and it was a huge success. As a result the novel was published, and Sir Percy Blakeney became one of the best known characters in English popular fiction. Baroness Orczy wrote sequels to the book and many other historical novels.

Original Poems, for Infant Minds, by *Several Young Persons* A collection of *poems for children by Ann and Jane *Taylor and others, published in two volumes in 1804 and 1805 by *Darton and Harvey. It was the first successful book of English verse for children since the *Divine Songs* (1715) of Isaac *Watts, and many of the poems in it became among the most widely known and loved of their day, pre-eminently Ann Taylor's *My Mother.

Ann and Jane Taylor were aged twenty-two and twenty-one respectively when the first volume was published. They had already contributed poems to a children's *annual, *The Minor's Pocket Book*, and as a result the publisher commissioned from them a collection of 'moral songs...or short tales turned into verse'. In the book individual authors are identified only by initials; the other contributors seem to have been the Taylors' younger brother Isaac, Bernard Barton, a Quaker and friend of *Lamb, and Adelaide O'Keeffe (1776–1855), who was the daughter of a penurious

Irish playwright; she wrote some of the best pieces in the book, but never again composed verse of the same interest. Ann Taylor regretted that she and her sister had had no control over the assembly of the book: 'We should have been better pleased if contributions from other hands had been omitted.'

The book's preface, addressed to parents 'and very affectionately to that interesting little race—the race of children', admitted to deficiencies in poetic style, with the excuse that imagery and even many-syllabled words had been curtailed for the benefit of children 'who have none but literal ideas'. Nevertheless the authors were usually masters of technique, and achieved a remarkably polished simplicity. The prevailing themes of the poems are all manner of everyday and domestic incidents, virtues and vices.

In the opening poem, 'little Ann' learns not to envy the rich ladies of Cavendish Square, pities the poor beggar girl, and becomes contented with her lot. Killing of animals in sport is condemned, except for fox hunting; Harry, in 'The Little Fisherman', gets his deserts by impaling himself accidentally on a hook: '"And oh," said he, "poor little fish, | What tortures they have borne."' He gives up fishing forever.

The book marks the beginning of the Awful Warning or *cautionary tale in verse. For example, Mary, who cries 'fire' too often in fun, is finally burnt in a real fire:

Her features all scarr'd leaving a lasting disgrace
For giving mamma false alarms.

The *animal story appears in Ann Taylor's 'The Notorious Glutton', where an overfed, sickly, and doomed duck consults Dr Drake, 'high in repute with his feathery friends'. But perhaps the book's vein of unsensational domestic verse, for example, Ann's 'Washing and Dressing' has survived best.

Original Poems was reprinted innumerable times during the 19th cent., and selections from it appeared as *chapbooks. As *Little Ann and other poems* it was illustrated by Kate *Greenaway in 1882, though by this time the poems' popularity had faded through over-use and parody. A centenary edition edited by E. V. *Lucas appeared in 1903, and in 1925 Edith Sitwell presented a selection entitled *Meddlesome Matty*. A facsimile of the original collection was published in New York in 1977.

The Taylors and their collaborators inspired a number of imitators: Elizabeth Turner, author

of *The *Daisy*; Sara *Coleridge; and Charles and Mary *Lamb, who published *Poetry for Children* in 1809. None of these, however, consistently equalled the standard of *Original Poems*.

Original Stories from Real Life; *with Conversations, calculated to Regulate the Affections, and Form the Mind to Truth and Goodness* (1788) By Mary *Wollstonecraft. After the death of their mother, Mary and Caroline are placed under the care of Mrs Mason, 'a woman of tenderness and discretion', who educates them according to principles of strict virtue. She is infallible and inflexible, and a modern reader will find her treatment of the children horrifically lacking in warmth; but, by the usual standard of the *moral tale, the book (which is on the pattern of *Sandford and Merton*) is exciting—Mrs Mason narrates vivid stories to the children to demonstrate the results of certain human actions.

A 1791 edition had engravings by *Blake. It was reprinted several times up to about 1835.

Orlando the Marmalade Cat Hero of a series of *picture books by Kathleen *Hale. The first to be published, in 1938, was *Orlando the Marmalade Cat: A Camping Holiday*. This introduced Orlando, his wife Grace, and their kittens 'Pansy the Tortoiseshell, the white Blanche, and coal-black Tinkle'. It was followed by *Orlando the Marmalade Cat: A Trip Abroad* (1939) and *Orlando's Evening Out* (1941), after which further stories followed thick and fast for more than a decade. By the early 1950s Orlando had become a household name in England, and a ballet featuring him was one of the events in the 1951 Festival of Britain. Only three Orlando titles were published during the 1960s, and the final book in the series, *Orlando the Marmalade Cat, and the Water Cats*, appeared in 1972.

The appeal of the series is almost entirely visual. Kathleen Hale seems to have been the first British picture-book artist to make full use of the possibilities of colour offset *lithography, producing pictures (which she drew directly on to the printer's plates) in which bright colours, such as Orlando's marmalade fur, were contrasted with softer pastel-like backgrounds, the whole having the appearance of a crayon drawing. The early books in the series, like the first *Babar stories, had an unusually large page-size (10 × 14in.), which allowed Hale to fill them with a profusion of detail that could hold a child's attention for many minutes. Unfortunately the later books

in the series had smaller pages, and some were partly in monochrome.

The stories themselves rely a good deal on puns, such as 'Catsule' for 'Capsule' in *Orlando the Marmalade Cat Goes to the Moon* (1968), but at their best they are wittily inventive, as in *Orlando's Invisible Pyjamas* (1949), in which Orlando, having lost a great deal of fur, has a pair of pyjamas made for him by Grace which look like real fur; then he meets a dog, and all his fur stands on end except the pyjamas. If there is a serious purpose in the series, it is, according to Kathleen Hale, to give children a taste of warm, happy family life—something she felt was lacking in her own rather cold upbringing.

Though the first book in the series was published simultaneously in London and New York, Orlando has consistently been more popular in the UK, where his arrival on the scene is considered a milestone in the development of the British picture book.

ORLEV, Uri (1931–) Israeli writer, winner of the 1996 *Hans Christian Andersen Award, best known for his child's-eye books on the Holocaust, influenced by his own childhood in wartime Poland. His work has been published in over three dozen languages, with a record four of his novels winning the *Batchelder Award, all in English translations by Hillel Halkin: *The Island on Bird Street* (1984), *The Man from the Other Side* (1991), *The Lady with the Hat* (1995), and *Run, Boy, Run* (2003). The first of these remains perhaps his most famous internationally; originally published in Hebrew in 1981, this semi-autobiographical story about a boy living in the Warsaw ghetto during the Second World War has been widely translated, and adapted into a critically acclaimed 1997 film.

ORMEROD, Jan (1946–2013) Australian picture-book illustrator and author who first came to prominence with her wordless picture book, *Sunshine* (1981), which won the 1982 Mother Goose Award as well as *CBCA Picture Book of the Year. *Moonshine* (1983) was shortlisted the following year for the Australian award. The approach is evocative, and small vignettes follow the child protagonist through daily life. The illustrations are warm, friendly, and moving, perhaps because of the quality of the child's expressions and the setting, with its small, acutely observed details of family life and love.

Many of Ormerod's later picture books, such as *IBBY Honour Book *Lizzie Nonsense*

(2004), reflect her interest in the Australian countryside and outback. *The Water Witcher* (2007), a poignant story of a boy in rural Australia during the Depression and drought who finds water in spite of his family's scepticism, was shortlisted for the Western Australian Premier's Award and the CBCA Picture Book of the Year in 2007. She collaborated with indigenous writer Boori Monty Pryor to create *Shake a Leg* (2010) from pictures of his family dancing. In *The Swap* (2013), illustrated by Andrew Joyner, Caroline Crocodile discovers why her dribbling baby brother is just right after all.

She won a Prime Minister's Literary Award in Australia. Although most famous for writing and illustrating her own books, Ormerod also wrote picture-book texts for other illustrators. Altogether she illustrated thirty-seven books over a thirty-year career.

Ornaments Discovered, The See HUGHES, MARY.

ORR, Wendy (1953–) Canadian-born, now Australian children's novelist who is known for writing junior fiction. *Ark in the Park* (1994) won the 1995 *CBCA Book of the Year: Younger Readers, but her most famous book has become *Nim's Island* (1999), which is also now a film starring Jodie Foster. A film sequel (after *Nim at Sea*, 2007) was released in 2013. A warmth and love of family, animals, and the environment pervade Orr's writing, which is gentle and lyrical, offering a deep insight into the characters. The settings are usually ordinary, yet realistic, keeping the writing and deep themes accessible.

OSBORN, Yotty (*fl.* 1878–82) British author of sentimental stories about children. Her first novel was *The Lyon's Den and its Eight Young Lions* (1882), a *family story about the children of a clergyman. Her other books include *Two Little Turks, or, Getting into Mischief* (1877) and *Pickles: a funny Little Couple* (1878), illustrated by T. *Pym. Yotty Osborn's books belong to a genre of child-stories current at this period, whose other exponents include Agnes *Giberne and Ismay *Thorn.

OSBORNE, Mary Pope See MAGIC TREE HOUSE, THE.

Osborne Collection A collection of notable British children's books which were published between the late 15th cent. and 1910. Its assembly was begun after the First World War by Edgar Osborne (1890–1978), County Librarian of Derbyshire from 1923 to 1954, who with his wife Mabel initially gathered together the books that they themselves had read in childhood. By 1949 the collection numbered about 2,000 volumes and, in memory of his wife who had died in 1947, Osborne decided to present it to the Boys and Girls House of the Toronto Public Library, because he admired its work. Sheila Egoff (1918–2005) was foremost in the bequest and became the first curator; she went on to be Canada's first professor of children's literature and an internationally renowned historian and critic in the field.

The collection has grown to over 80,000 books, including Canadian classics and modern books, related art and ephemera.

Ostrich Boys (2008) A *young adult novel by Keith *Gray, a roller coaster which takes its readers on a ride with friends Kenny, Sim, and Blake to pay their respects to their recently deceased friend Ross—along with his kidnapped ashes. As they travel halfway across the country from Cleethorpes to their friend's namesake town in Scotland, they discover more about themselves, as well as the fragility and strength of their friendships. The novel provides a strong visual and emotional landscape on the boys' journey, exploring their loss, the implications of Ross' potential suicide, and the complexities of youth.

Oswald Bastable In *The *Story of the Treasure Seekers* and *The *Wouldbegoods* by E. *Nesbit.

Other Awards A series of nominations made annually between 1975 and 1988 by the *Children's Rights Workshop in Britain, given in recognition of 'non-biased' books of literary merit.

OTIS, James (James Otis Kaler) (1848–1912) American author for boys. His best known book was *Toby Tyler, or Ten Weeks with a Circus* (1881), which was such a success that he gave up his job as a journalist and devoted himself to writing children's books full-time. He wrote three other circus stories, *Mr Stubbs' Brother* (*c.*1882), *The Wreck of the Circus* (*c.*1897), and *Found by the Circus* (*c.*1909).

Otterbury Incident, The (1948) A children's novel by C. Day *Lewis, illustrated by Edward *Ardizzone. Day Lewis's second (and final) novel for children, its plot, taken from the French film, *Nous les gosses* (1941), was

very different from the conventional *school story current at the time and part of a move to more realistic settings for children's novels. An exciting war game ends in disaster when a football goes through a classroom window. It must be paid for, but how? The two gangs join forces to raise the money by ingenious means. When it is stolen, Ted is suspected. His efforts to clear his name, helped by the narrator, George, find them facing real danger. In a dramatic climax a welcome intervention by adults saves the day.

OTTLEY, Reginald (Leslie) (1908–85) Children's author best known for his 'Yamboorha' novels, of which the first was *By the Sandhills of Yamboorah* (1965) about a boy on a large settler station in the South Australian desert. His other books include *The Bates Family* (1969), the saga of an itinerant cattle-droving family.

OUIDA (Marie Louise de la Ramée) (1839–1908) Born in England, the daughter of a Frenchwoman, she wrote romantic novels which were very popular with girls, despite the scandal attached to them. The American children's librarian Caroline M. *Hewins found in the 1870s that most of the girls of Hartford, Conn., were reading them, and she complained publicly about their influence on young minds.

Ouida wrote one book specifically for children, a collection of stories entitled *Bimbi* (1882). This includes *The Nürnberg Stove*, which has been reissued separately. Her *animal story *A Dog of Flanders* (1872) has also been popular with children.

Our Darlings *See* BARNARDO, DR THOMAS JOHN.

Our Exploits at West Poley A 'story for boys' by the celebrated English novelist and poet Thomas Hardy (1840–1928). Thirteen-year old Leonard, staying with his cousin Steve in the Mendip village of West Poley, is taken by him into the caves which, unknown to the village, contain the source of the stream which supplies the local mill and the rest of the population with water. Steve and Leonard divert the stream so as to get across its bed and explore the caves beyond; in doing so, they unintentionally cause the watercourse to dry up in West Poley and the mill to stop. Moreover the stream now begins to flow into the neighbouring village of East Poley, whose inhabitants begin to use it for their own profit. Steve and Leonard face a dilemma.

This short novel is Hardy's only book explicitly for children, yet it is one of the most subtle and genuinely exciting *adventure stories of the 19th cent., using the conventions of the boys' tale as a vehicle for what amounts to a philosophical debate; for, as Leonard himself remarks, the question faced by the boys when they find themselves controlling the future of two villages is a 'problem in utilitarian philosophy'. The story is also notable for the character of the Man who Failed, a person of great experience but no achievement who lives in the village, and whose advice Steve gradually learns to heed. However, the book made no impact in Hardy's lifetime because of the circumstances of its publication.

It was commissioned by the *Youth's Companion, one of the most celebrated American children's *magazines, in the spring of 1883, but never printed in its pages, for no known reason; Hardy himself assumed that the editors thought it 'too juvenile for your side of the sea'. The proprietor of the *Youth's Companion*, Daniel Sharp Ford, eventually passed it to one of his sons-in-law who ran a small story-paper for women called *The Household*, where it appeared as a serial in six monthly instalments between Nov. 1892 and April 1893, seemingly without Hardy's knowledge. Not surprisingly in this context it excited no reaction, and its existence was virtually forgotten until it was printed in book form in 1952, with illustrations by Lynton Lamb.

Our Island Story, *a child's history of England* (c.1910) By H. E. *Marshall, illustrated by A. S. Forrest. A collection of stories from history, told to two Australian children. The book includes 'stories which wise people say are only fairy-tales and not history', e.g. legends of King Arthur. It ends with the Boer War and the death of Queen Victoria. It was one of the most popular *history books during the first half of the 20th cent.

Our Young Folks A juvenile *magazine published monthly from January 1865 to October 1873 by Ticknor and Fields of Boston, Mass., under the editorship of John T. *Trowbridge, Lucy Larcom, and (at first) 'Gail Hamilton' (Mary Abigail Dodge). *The *Story of a Bad Boy* by Thomas Bailey Aldrich and *A *Holiday Romance* by Dickens first appeared in its pages.

OUTHWAITE, Ida Rentoul (*fl.* 1900–35) Australian illustrator and author, well known in her day for such lavish *picture books as *Elves and Fairies* (1916) and *The Enchanted*

Forest (1921). Her sister Annie Rentoul wrote the texts for several of her books, among them *Mollie's Bunyip* (1904).

Outlaws *See* WILLIAM.

Outside Over There (1981) A *picture book by Maurice *Sendak, regarded by its creator as the third in a trilogy of which the other two are *Where the Wild Things Are* (1963) and *In the Night Kitchen* (1970). Suggested by a tale in *Grimm ('The Goblins', also known as 'The Changeling'), it tells of the theft of a baby by *goblins, who substitute a changeling made of ice. Ida, the baby's sister, makes a journey to 'outside over there' to fetch her back—but first has to identify her among the baby-like goblins. The book's sources include Sendak's childhood memory of the kidnapping and death of the Lindbergh baby. He thought the book his best work, but also the most painful experience of his creative life.

Outsiders, The (1967) A novel by S. E. *Hinton, written when she was just sixteen. This story of gang culture is as powerful today as when it was written, and has sold over fourteen million copies. Taught in some schools, *banned in others, this book, with its authentic voices and gritty realism, changed the way books were written for teenagers. Ponyboy is a Greaser, one of a gang from the poor side of town and the Socs are the richer kids. What happens between them is as dark and violent as a Jacobean tragedy. Francis Ford Coppola directed a film of the book in 1983, with a cast of unknowns who went on to be famous.

Owl In *Winnie-the-Pooh* and *The *House at Pooh Corner* by A. A. *Milne.

Owl and the Pussy-Cat, The A poem by Edward *Lear, first published in *Nonsense Songs, Stories, Botany, and Alphabets* (1871). It was written for Janet, the daughter of John Addington Symonds. The poem, which tells the story of a cat and an owl sailing off to the land where the Bong-tree grows, where they eventually marry, has occasionally been set to music and is often published as a separate book. Among the many artists who have illustrated it is L. Leslie *Brooke, in *The Jumblies and Other Nonsense Verses* (*c.*1910). A sequel, *The Further Adventures of the Owl and the Pussycat*, by Julia *Donaldson and Charlotte *Voake, appeared in 2013.

Owl Babies (1992) A picture book by Martin *Waddell, illustrated by Patrick Benson (1956–). Owl babies Sarah, Percy, and Bill live in a tree

with their Owl Mother, but one night they awake and she has disappeared. They try to be brave and thoughtful (though Bill quite determinedly wants his mummy) and eventually she does come back to them. A beautiful, finely drawn book, touching and ultimately reassuring, this is a consistent favourite with parents and children.

Owl Service, The (1967) The fourth novel by Alan *Garner; it won the *Carnegie Medal and the *Guardian Children's Fiction Prize. It concerns three adolescents whose lives are overshadowed by a legend in *The *Mabinogion*—the story of a woman who is turned into an owl as a punishment for bringing about the killing of her husband. The legend begins to come alive when owl-like patterns on an old dinner service (the 'owl service' of the title) vanish from the plates and seem to be turning into real owls.

Owl Who Was Afraid of the Dark, The (1968) A children's book for young readers by Jill Tomlinson (1931–76). Plop is a barn owl chick. Unfortunately he is afraid of the dark. Encouraged by his parents, he embarks on a series on mini-adventures in which he encounters guides who each have a different view of the dark and what is special about it. Neatly arranged in chapters and with an attractive conversational style, it has proved an ideal book to read aloud and has become the most widely recommended title to help allay night-time fears. Still in print after nearly half a century, it has also been published in abridged form as a picture book (2001).

OXENBURY, Helen (1938–) British illustrator, winner of two *Kate Greenaway Medals, the first for both her *picture book of Edward *Lear's *The Quangle Wangle's Hat* and her illustrations to Margaret *Mahy's *Dragon of an Ordinary Family*, both published in 1969; her second, thirty years later, was for a generously illustrated edition of *Alice's Adventures in Wonderland*, in timelessly beautiful watercolours but with Alice herself an undoubtedly modern girl.

After art school and some years working in theatre design, Oxenbury turned to children's book illustration following her marriage to another illustrator, John *Burningham. She started out with books for babies (prompted by the arrival of her own first child). Other early books include a selection of children's rhymes made by Brian *Alderson, *Cakes and Custard* (1974). In 1989 she and Michael

*Rosen published what would go on to be one of the most successful picture books of all time, *We're Going on a Bear Hunt*. This was a Greenaway commended runner-up; she managed four such accolades in six years—the others were for Martin *Waddell's *Farmer Duck* (1991), Eugene *Trivizas's *The Three Little Wolves and the Big Bad Pig* (1993), and Trish Cooke's *So Much* (1994)—before achieving her second win, for *Alice*, in 1999.

Other acclaimed titles include *Big Momma Makes the World* (2002) by Phyllis Root, which won the *Boston Globe–Horn Book Award, and a welcome return to Wonderland with *Alice Through the Looking Glass* (2005).

In 2010, after forty-five years of marriage, Oxenbury and Burningham finally published a collaborative work, *There's Going to Be a Baby*.

OXENHAM, Elsie (Elsie Jeanette Dunkerley) (1880–1960) British writer of *girls' stories. She specialized in the *Camp Fire Movement, which was stronger in America than England. She wrote many novels about 'Abbey School' (e.g. *The Abbey Girls*, 1920).

Oxford Dictionary of Nursery Rhymes, The (1951; rev. edn 1997) Edited by Peter and Iona *Opie, the definitive study of extant British *nursery rhymes, their meaning (if ascertainable), their analogues, and the early history of their appearance in print.

Oxford Junior Encyclopaedia, The A twelve-volume reference work for children; it began to appear in 1949, under the editorship of Laura Salt, and was regularly revised.

OXLEY, James Macdonald (1855–1907) Canadian children's author. His first success was *Bert Lloyd's Boyhood, a story from Nova Scotia* (1889), the tale of 'a stout, sturdy, hearty boy, with nothing very remarkable about him', who in adolescence nearly dies of a fever; on his sickbed he converts a friend to Christianity. Oxley's other books include *The Boy Tramps; or, Across Canada* (1896), and *Fife and Drum at Louisbourg* (1899).

Oz *See* BAUM, L. FRANK.

Paddington Bear His first appearance was in *A Bear Called Paddington* (1958), which tells how the Brown family find an abandoned bear on Paddington Station; he has just arrived from Darkest Peru and has a label tied to him which reads 'Please look after this bear. Thank you.' They take him home, discover his fondness for marmalade, and allow him to become a much-loved member of their household.

Michael *Bond, author of the Paddington books, has explained that 'the original Paddington was a very tiny bear I found in a London store one Christmas . . . He'd been left on the shelf for Christmas all by himself. All the other bears had been sold, and I bought him as a present for my wife . . . We were living near Paddington Station. I'd always wanted to use the name Paddington.'

Though many Paddington stories have appeared in print (most recently *Paddington Here and Now*, published for the fiftieth anniversary in 2008) and on television, the bear has become largely known as a toy sold widely in Britain, distinguishable by his duffle-coat, hat, and red wellington boots; but an excellent 2014 film is now a good reminder of the appeal of the original stories.

PAGE, Thomas Nelson (1853–1922) Virginia-born writer, author of *Two Little Confederates* (1888), a memorable children's book about the Civil War as seen through Southern eyes. He went on to write many books for adults which paint a romantic and sympathetic picture of the antebellum South. His other children's books were *Among the Camps* (1891) and *Pastime Stories* (1894).

PAGET, Revd F. E. (Francis Edward) (1806–82) Rector of Elford in Staffordshire, he edited *The Juvenile Englishman's Library*, a series for children published in twenty-one volumes between 1844 and 1849. In its pages there appeared in 1844 Paget's *The *Hope of the Katzekopfs*, generally regarded as the first English children's *fantasy.

PAINE, Albert Bigelow (1861–1937) American author best known for his biography of Mark *Twain (1912). He also wrote a number of children's books including *Arkansaw Bear* (1898) and the 'Hollow Tree' series. In 1916 there appeared his much praised version for children of the life of Twain.

PALMER, C. (Cyril) Everard (1930–2013) West Indian author of stories set in a Jamaican village—his own birthplace of Kendal. The first, *The Cloud with the Silver Lining* (1966), is about two boys who keep a family small-holding going in a time of crisis.

Pamela, or Virtue Rewarded A novel by Samuel *Richardson, written in the form of a series of letters and first published in 1740. Though the book is regarded as the first English adult novel to be concerned chiefly with human character, the title page of the first edition declared that it was 'Published in order to cultivate the Principles of Virtue and Religion in the Minds of Youth of both Sexes'.

Pamela Andrews is a young maidservant whose 'good Lady' has just died. Amorous advances are made to her by 'Mr B.', the son of the household. She repels them and leaves his service, but she is kidnapped and taken prisoner by him. In 1769 Francis *Newbery (nephew) issued *The history of Pamela; or, virtue rewarded*, a one-volume abridgement for children (161 pages) which did not use the epistolary form, but narrated the story in the third person with occasional passages of dialogue. It was reprinted several times, and other abridgements were published in the late 18th and 19th cents.

Panchatantra An Indian story collection from which many *fables have passed into European literature and folklore. The *Panchatantra* was in existence by the 6th cent. AD. In it a learned brahmin instructs three princes in the ways of the world by means of stories, the majority of which are about animals. Like the fables of *Aesop, the *Panchatantra* counsels worldly wisdom and shrewdness.

The first English version was by Thomas North, and was entitled *The Morall Philosophie of Doni* (1570). Thereafter the book was usually known in England as 'The Fables of Pilpay' or 'The Fables of Bidpai'. Leonard *Clark published his retellings, *Tales from the Panchatantra*, in 1979.

Pandora Braithwaite *See* SECRET DIARY OF ADRIAN MOLE, AGED 13¾, THE.

'PANSY' (Isabella Macdonald Alden) (1841–1930) American writer known to millions of *Sunday school children for her sentimental religious fiction. One of her most popular books was *Esther Reid* (1870), the story of a girl who has 'a robe, and a crown, and a harp, and a place waiting for her, up before the throne of God'.

Pantheon, The, or *Ancient History of the Gods of Greece and Rome . . . by Edward Baldwin, Esq.* A book really written by William *Godwin and published by him and his wife in 1806. It was based on, and intended to correct the imperfections of, a 1729 English translation by Andrew Tooke of the *Pantheum Mythicum* of the Jesuit writer François Antoine Pomey, which had been widely used in English schools. In it Godwin emphasizes the beauties of the *Homeric legends, in the hope that his readers will one day read Homer and Virgil for themselves.

The book begins with introductory chapters on the nature of ancient religions, and then describes the principal gods one by one. Many of the most exciting myths appear in it, such as the stories of the Minotaur, the Gorgon's head, Cupid and Psyche, the labours of Hercules, and the Trojan Horse; Godwin retells them in clear plain prose. The book, which is illustrated with *copperplates, had reached five editions by 1821.

Panther *See* KI-YU.

pantomime A term now used for Christmas theatrical entertainments, it is derived from a Greek word for an actor using several different masks and meaning 'an imitator of all'. Early in the 18th cent. it came to be used in England for a type of dramatic performance in which a popular story was combined with the traditional Italian harlequinade.

Classical mythology was at first the chief source of plots, but by the beginning of the 19th cent. *chapbook tales and *fairy stories had taken its place, the latter eventually predominating. Though more and more emphasis

was placed on this 'speaking opening' of the performance, the harlequinade still featured, with a 'transformation scene' linking the two parts of the entertainment and providing a denouement. In the early 19th cent., most of the popular pantomimes were issued in the form of *toy theatres. A very detailed description of a pantomime in the middle of that century, at Drury Lane, is to be found in R. H. Home's *Memoirs of a London Doll* (1846).

The harlequinade eventually disappeared, and the new fashion was for burlesque scripts in verse, by such writers as H. J. Byron and J. R. *Planché. These treated the stories of *Perrault, Mme d'*Aulnoy, and others as the basis of comic plays with songs and topical and local references. In the 20th cent. the influence of music hall, and eventually of television, was responsible for a paring away of the plot to make way for 'speciality acts' by singers, comedians, and other performers. The result was often little more than a variety show which may be uninteresting or unsuitable for children. Christmas 'pantos' based on a handful of recurring traditional tales (*Dick Whittington, *Aladdin, *Jack and the Beanstalk*, etc.), remain popular today, often featuring celebrity performances, actors known from television soaps, audience participation, and knowingly bad jokes (some more risqué than others).

Pantouflia *See* PRINCE PRIGIO.

PAOLINI, Christopher (1983–) American children's fantasy writer who was home-schooled in his native Montana. *Eragon*, Paolini's first volume in the *Inheritance series about dragons, quests, and heroes, was published by his parents in 2001 with cover art by his sister, and he publicized it by touring schools and bookstores. Luckily for him one of his earliest readers was Carl *Hiaasen's stepson, and his enthusiasm led to the book's being taken up by Hiaasen's publishers and being republished, still as *Eragon* (2003), and to Paolini's becoming a *New York Times* bestselling author at the age of nineteen. Three sequels followed, all set in the mythic land of Alagaësia: *Eldest* (2005), *Brisingr* (2008), and *Inheritance* (2011).

Paper Bag Princess, The (1980) A bestselling picture book written by Robert *Munsch and illustrated by Michael Martchenko. Typically for Munsch, this picture book turns fairy tales on their head—it is Princess Elizabeth who outsmarts the dragon and

rescues Prince Ronald only to find out he is a 'bum' or 'toad' (depending on which edition you have) in the end. This little story made big waves in the early days of feminist books for children in the 1980s.

Parables from Nature A series of stories by Margaret *Gatty, published volume by volume between 1855 and 1871, and reprinted a number of times. The stories, illustrated by elegant *wood engravings, draw moral examples from the life of the animal and plant kingdoms. For example, a caterpillar who does not believe she will become a butterfly eventually learns that faith will be rewarded; a worker bee who resents not being a queen finally discovers the necessity of having one ruler over the masses. The parables are accompanied by detailed nature notes.

PARDOE, M. *See* BUNKLE.

Parent's Assistant, The (1796) The first collection of children's stories by Maria *Edgeworth; the result of her father R. L. Edgeworth's plan to provide reading-matter for young children along the lines set out by Mrs *Barbauld. A preface rejects Dr Johnson's assertion that children do not like to hear stories about other children, but want to have their imaginations excited by *fairy stories. 'Why should the mind be filled with fantastic visions, instead of useful knowledge?' ask the Edgeworths.

The first volume of the 1796 edition contains six stories including 'The Little Dog Trusty' and 'The Orange Man', simple tales for the youngest readers which demonstrate the ill rewards of lying and thieving; 'Lazy Lawrence', in which the results of industry and thrift are contrasted with those of idleness and keeping bad company; and 'The False Key', in which a servant boy is involved in a plot to burgle his mistress's house. 'Part II' consists of two volumes; the first of these, of which the sole known copy is now in the *Osborne Collection, contains 'The Purple Jar' (*see* EARLY LESSONS) and two other stories; the second includes a *play for children, 'Old Poz'.

These volumes were published in 1796 by J. Johnson of St Paul's Churchyard, who had issued Mrs Barbauld's books, and were described as the 'Second Edition', though no copies of a first edition are now known. A 'Third Edition' was published by the same bookseller in 1800. This was in six volumes, and included a number of new stories by Edgeworth. *The Parent's Assistant* was first printed in America in 1809, and was translated into French. It was reissued in various forms during the 19th cent., and stories from it sometimes appeared individually or in other collections. They have far more literary merit than do most stories in the *moral tale genre.

PARISH, Peggy (Margaret Cecile) (1927–88) American children's writer, author of *Amelia Bedelia* (1963) and its sequels, about a girl who causes havoc by taking all instructions literally (when asked to 'dust the furniture' she throws dust on it).

PARK, Linda Sue (1960–) American poet and author of books for children of all ages, whose background as the daughter of Korean immigrants strongly informs her work. With only a few exceptions (e.g. *A Long Walk to Water*, 2010, set in Sudan), most of her books involve Korean culture and history. Her first novel, *Seesaw Girl* (1999), is set in 17th-cent. Korea and is about a girl fighting against her traditional female role. *A Single Shard* (2001) is also set in the ritualized society of Korea and tells of an orphan, a potter, a contest, and a journey that is almost mythical in its scope. It won her the *Newbery Medal. *When My Name Was Keoko* (2002) is set during the Japanese occupation of Korea. Park has also authored the ninth volume in the *39 Clues* series, *Storm Warning* (2010).

PARK, Ruth (1917–2010) New Zealand author who lived most of her life in Australia. Her first novel, *The Harp in the South* (1948), was based on her own experiences of growing up in poverty and then living as an adult in the rough Surry Hills slums in Sydney. In 1942 she created *The *Muddle-Headed Wombat* for ABC radio, a show that continued until its cancellation in 1970 and was hugely popular, and between 1962 and 1982 Park wrote many books based on the series. Her most important novel is *Playing Beatie Bow* (1986), a time-slip story that takes a girl back to the Sydney of 1873. Her autobiographies, *A Fence Around the Cuckoo* (1992) and *Fishing in the Styx* (1993), deal with her life in New Zealand and Australia respectively.

PARKER, Kate Langloh *See* AUSTRALIAN LEGENDARY TALES.

PARKER, Richard (1915–90) British author of many books for children, including *Lion at Large* (1959), the story of an escaped lion;

a *science fiction story, *The Hendon Fungus* (1967); and several works of *fantasy.

PARKINSON, Siobhán (1954–) Irish author of books for young adults and children who worked as an editor on both *Inis*, the Children's Books Ireland magazine, and *Bookbird*, the *Ibby International magazine, and now also works as a publisher and teacher of creative writing. Her style is experimental and changes from book to book. *Sisters . . . No Way!* (1996) is about a pair of stepsisters, and the same story is told twice, once from each point of view; it won her the *CBI Book of the Year Award. *The Love Bean* (2002) is about two love triangles set thousands of years apart. Humane and empathic, her books often deal with difficult issues, such as abuse, in both *The Moon King* (1998) and *Bruised* (2011), and its companion, *Heart Shaped* (2013); and homelessness, in *Breaking the Wishbone* (1999). She also writes in her native Irish, with novels such as *Dialann-ár-Rúnda Amy Ní Chonchúir* (2008) and *Maitríóisce* (2011). Parkinson was Ireland's first Laureate na nÓg (*see* LAUREATE) from 2010–12.

PARLEY, Peter *See* PETER PARLEY.

Parley's Magazine was established in 1833 as a twice-monthly periodical, published in Boston, Mass., and edited at first by S. G. *Goodrich, who was already well known as '*Peter Parley'. It was a miscellany of *geography and travel, *Bible stories, *natural history, *moral tales, *fables, *poetry, correspondence, and scraps of information, as well as games and puzzles. In 1845 it was merged with its rival, *Merry's Museum*, which itself founded by Goodrich. It had no connection with the English *Peter Parley's Magazine*.

Parœmiologia Anglo-Latina A collection by John Clarke (?1596—1658) of proverbs for schoolchildren, in English and Latin, published in 1639. The book was based on the *Adages* of Erasmus, but included many native English sayings which were known to children at that time.

PARRISH, Maxfield (1870–1966) American artist and illustrator. A pupil of Howard *Pyle, he became known through his work for *Harper's Weekly* and other magazines. After illustrating L. Frank *Baum's *Mother Goose in Prose* (1897) he received other book commissions, including editions of the *Arabian Nights* and Kenneth *Grahame's *Dream Days*.

PARRY, Sir Edward Abbott (1863-1943) Author of *Katawampus* (1895), Parry was an English judge. His other children's books included two sequels to *Katawampus*, entitled *Butterscotia* (1896) and *The First Book of Krab* (1897), and *Gamble Gold* (1907), illustrated by Harry *Furniss.

PASCAL, Francine *See* SWEET VALLEY HIGH.

PATCHETT, Mary Elwyn (Osborne) (1897–1989) Prolific Australian writer of adventure novels and books about animals, published from the early 1950s; they include *Tiger in the Dark* (1964).

PATERSON, Katherine (Womeldorf) (1932–) Children's novelist who was born in China of German parents and came to the United States in 1940. She won the *Newbery Medal on two occasions, for *Bridge To Terabithia* (1978), a story about two children who invent a magic kingdom inspired by the *Narnia books, and *Jacob Have I Loved* (1981), an account of rivalry between twins on a lonely island during the Second World War. She was the second *National Ambassador for Young People's Literature.

Paths of Learning Strewed with Flowers, The, or *English Grammar Illustrated* A *book of instruction published by John *Harris in 1820. It consists entirely of elegant hand-coloured copperplates with the text engraved beneath the illustrations, and explains its purpose as 'to obviate the reluctance children evince to the irksome and insipid task of learning the names and meaning of the component parts of grammar'. The book describes and illustrates the various parts of speech. John *Marshall published a rival book, *The Path of Learning Strewed with Roses*, in 1821.

PATMORE, Coventry *See* CHILDREN'S GARLAND, THE.

PATON WALSH, Jill (Gillian) (1937–) British novelist who was born in London and educated at a convent day school before reading English at St Anne's College, Oxford. From 1959 until 1962 she taught at Enfield Girls' Grammar School. In 1961 she married Edmund Paton Walsh. She began to write to escape from 'the boredom of being trapped in a small house alone with a baby that could not yet talk'. Her first book, *Hengest's Tale* (1966), was a *historical novel set in barbarian northern Europe after the departure of the Romans. Paton Walsh's historical interests are reflected in several of her subsequent books: *Wordhoard* (1969), a collection of

stories based on Anglo-Saxon literature, written with Kevin *Crossley-Holland; *Farewell Great King* (1972), an adult novel (written as 'Gillian Paton Walsh') about Themistocles; and *The Emperor's Winding-Sheet* (1974), a story set during the fall of Constantinople, which won her the *Whitbread Children's Book Award. But the more characteristic, individual elements in her writing are to be found in the series of 'realistic' novels she has produced, aimed at the older child or teenager.

The first of these was *The Dolphin Crossing* (1967), set during the early months of the Second World War and concerning two boys, of different social classes, who take a small cruiser across the Channel to help with the Dunkirk evacuation. More successful was *Fireweed* (1969), again set during the war, a story of a teenage boy and girl fleeing from impossible family situations and managing to lead a secret life of their own in air raid shelters and bomb-damaged houses in the Blitz.

Jill Paton Walsh developed still further in *Goldengrove* (1972), the story of Madge and Paul, who believe themselves to be cousins (the relationship is actually much closer) and who meet each year for a holiday with their grandmother in her house on the Cornish coast. But this year is the final holiday before childhood's end, and Madge is drawn away from Paul to a blind professor living a miserable existence in a cottage to whom she shows kindness despite his warnings—and thereby hurts herself deeply. The sequel, *Unleaving* (1976), was an even more ambitious study of adolescent emotion, and won her the *Boston Globe–Horn Book Award. Madge's grandmother is now dead, and she herself has inherited the house, Goldengrove, which she makes available one summer to two Oxford dons, their families, and a reading party of undergraduates. One of the dons is entirely unable to cope with the fact that he has a disabled child, Molly. The elder brother of Molly, with whom Madge is falling in love, brings about Molly's death, though whether by accident or design remains uncertain.

Jill Paton Walsh's other full-length novel written during the 1970s, *A Chance Child* (1978), is part *fantasy, part historical documentary: the story of Creep, an unwanted and unnamed child who accidentally escapes from maltreatment in his present-day slum home and finds himself in the Victorian era, where he experiences the equally horrific maltreatment that children suffered then, in the coal

mines and the factory-dominated cities. His half-brother goes in search of him, and though he cannot himself travel back in time, he realizes what has happened to Creep, even managing to learn the remainder of Creep's life history—for Creep never returns.

Jill Paton Walsh's later books include two of her best: *A Parcel of Patterns* (1983), a powerful and engrossing historical novel about the village of Eyam threatened by the Plague; and *Gaffer Samson's Luck* (1984), in which James's elderly neighbour asks him to help find his lucky charm.

PATTEN, Brian (1946–) British poet who has published bestselling collections of comic (and other) verse for children, which include *Gargling with Jelly* (1985), *Thawing Frozen Frogs* (1990), and *Juggling with Gerbils* (2000). He has also written several books of children's stories and picture books, as well as *The *Story Giant* (2001, illustrated by Chris *Riddell).

Paul et Virginie (1787) A novel by Jacques-Henri Bernardin de Saint-Pierre (1737–1814). Two fatherless children are brought up to a simple life on Mauritius and come to love each other deeply. Virginie is sent back to France, but eventually returns to the island. As her ship arrives it is wrecked on the rocks, and Virginie, having for reasons of modesty refused to strip off her clothes and plunge into the waves, is drowned before the eyes of Paul, who soon afterwards dies of a broken heart. The book is strongly influenced by the ideas of *Rousseau; it was quickly translated into English and was read by many children.

PAUL, Korky (Hamish Vigne Christie Paul) (1951–) Zimbabwean-born illustrator whose distinctive energetically detailed style has graced dozens of books by an array of writers from Michael *Rosen to Tessa Dahl (1957–), Vivian *French to John *Agard. He is perhaps best known for the bestselling *Winnie the Witch* picture-book series (from 1987), with Australian writer Valerie Thomas (1938–), about a witch who has a black cat she is unable to see because everything else in her house is black, too. The award-winning series debut spawned more than a dozen sequels, as well as Winnie the Witch young fiction by Laura Owen, also illustrated by Paul.

PAULSEN, Gary (1939–) American author writing mainly for a *young adult audience. Prolific and versatile, he has written more than

175 books as well as articles and short stories. Born in Minneapolis, Paulsen ran away from home at fourteen, worked on farms, and joined a carnival (like the protagonist of his *The Beet Fields*, 2000). His first book was published in 1985. His real-life experiences inform his coming-of-age novels, in which survival is frequently a central theme. In *Hatchet* (1987), probably his best known novel, thirteen-year-old Brian fights to survive after a plane crash in the Canadian wilderness, armed only with a hatchet—Brian's story continues in several sequels. *Hatchet* is one of three of Paulsen's novels selected as Newbery Honor Books (*see* NEWBERY MEDAL); the others are *Dogsong* (1985), a novel inspired by the Iditarod dog race, and *The Winter Room* (1989), set on a farm in northern Minnesota.

PAUSEWANG, Gudrun (1928–) German writer whose books often tackle social issues and the environment. Pausewang's book *Die Wolke* (1987; translated as *Fall-Out* by Patricia *Crampton, 1995), which examined the threat of nuclear disaster, won the *Deutscher Jugendliteraturpreis in 1988. *The Final Journey*, Patricia Crampton's translation of Pausewang's holocaust novel *Reise im August*, won the *Marsh Award for Children's Literature in Translation in 1999. Other titles include the Second World War coming-of-age novel *Überleben!* (2005; translated as *Dark Hours*, by John Brownjohn, 2006).

PAVER, Michelle (1960–) A Malawi-born British novelist and children's author, best known for her historical fantasy series *Chronicles of Ancient Darkness* set in pre-agricultural Stone Age Europe. *Wolf Brother* (2004), the first in the series, introduces Torak, an adolescent boy, and his friends Wolf and Renn whose quest it is to defeat an evil clan of Soul Eaters. The sixth and last in the series, *Ghost Hunter* (2009), won the *Guardian Children's Fiction Prize. Hugely popular in the UK and beyond, the series has sold over six million copies and has been translated into nearly thirty languages. Michelle Paver's next series for children, *Gods and Warriors*, is set during the Bronze Age and tells the story of Hylas, a twelve-year-old goatherd whose adventures take him to Ancient Crete and Ancient Egypt.

Peace at Last (1980) A picture book by Jill *Murphy. It begins with the Bear family (Mr Bear, Mrs Bear, Baby Bear) tired and on their way to bed. But Mr Bear struggles to sleep—Mrs Bear is snoring, the clock is ticking,

the tap is dripping; he tries every room in the house, even tries sleeping in the garden or the car, but it's no use. Just when he's found peace at last, the alarm clock goes off. With a repeating text and onomatopoeic snoring, ringing, buzzing, and humming, it's much loved as a read-aloud bedtime book.

PEACH, L. (Lawrence) du Garde (1890–1974) British author, playwright, and screenwriter. He wrote regularly for *Children's Hour, contributing dramatized history and biography, and from 1956 wrote all the early titles of the *Ladybird *Adventures in History* series.

PEACOCK, Thomas Love *See* SIR HORNBOOK.

Peacock 'At Home', The A poem for children by Catherine Ann Dorset, published by John *Harris in September 1807 as a sequel to the immensely successful *Butterfly's Ball. It tells how 'the tenants of Air'—the birds—are envious of the splendours of the Butterfly's Ball and hold their own feast on St Valentine's Day, with the Peacock as host. The guests are described, as are the dancing and feasting. The first edition ascribed the poem to 'A Lady', but in 1809 Harris and others reissued it as *The Peacock At Home; and other poems by Mrs Dorset*, which included verses that had appeared in a book by Mrs Dorset's sister, the novelist and poet Charlotte *Smith. This version, in which the text of *The Peacock 'At Home'* was revised, contained ornithological notes on the rare birds mentioned in the poem. These appeared in subsequent editions.

The poem, which can be interpreted, as *The Gentleman's Magazine* (Nov 1807) suspected, as a 'Satire upon the manners of the times, and of the Great', was widely commended. According to Harris some 40,000 copies of Mrs Dorset's poem and *The Butterfly's Ball* were sold in the first twelve months after publication. In 1808 they began to be printed in America. Both continued to be reissued for many years and inspired very many imitations, of which one, *The Lion's Masquerade* (1807), was by Mrs Dorset herself. In 1979 there appeared *The Peacock Party*, a new poem faintly resembling Mrs Dorset's, with illustrations by Alan Aldridge.

Peacock Pie, A Book of Rhymes (1913) By Walter *de la Mare, an immensely popular collection of poems which finally established its author's reputation as a writer for children. Among the best known are

> Ann, Ann!
>> Come! quick as you can!
> There's a fish that *talks*
>> In the frying-pan

and

>> It's a very odd thing—
>> As odd as can be—
>> That whatever Miss T. eats
>> Turns into Miss T.

Many have the ring of traditional *nursery rhymes, such as the verse about 'Poor Jim Jay' who 'Got stuck fast | In Yesterday', and the poem beginning

>> Three jolly gentlemen,
>> In coats of red,
>> Rode their horses
>> Up to bed.

The book was put together by de la Mare from rhymes written over a number of years. Each rhyme was the product of much hard work; de la Mare wrote: 'I drudged and drudged even at the doggerel.' *Peacock Pie* was first printed without illustrations; an edition of 1916 had pictures by W. Heath *Robinson, who was ill-suited to the book; in 1924 another edition appeared with coloured embellishments by Claud Lovat Fraser, which were exactly to de la Mare's taste—they had been made under his eye before the book's first publication. Other illustrators of *Peacock Pie* have been Jocelyn Crowe (1936), F. R. Emett (1941), and Edward *Ardizzone (1946). In 2014, publishers Faber selected four poems from *Peacock Pie* to be used as picture-book texts, with accompanying illustrations from Carolina Rabei. Each one represents a different season, beginning with 'Snow'.

PEAKE, Mervyn (Laurence) (1911–68) British illustrator and author. His first children's book was an almost nonsensical comic story about *pirates entitled *Captain Slaughterboard Drops Anchor*; it was published in 1939, two years after his marriage.

The first of his three grotesquely fantastic novels about the huge, crumbling, ritual-bound castle of Gormenghast and its inmates, *Titus Groan*, was written during the war and published in 1946, with immediate success. *Gormenghast* followed in 1950 and *Titus Alone* in 1959. It is for these that Peake is now chiefly remembered (*see also* GORMENGHAST).

In the 1940s and early 50s he had a considerable vogue as an illustrator, producing pictures for, among others, *The *Hunting of the Snark* (1941), Coleridge's *Rime of the Ancient Mariner* (1943), an edition of *Grimm (1949),

*The *Swiss Family Robinson* (1950), and both *Alice* books by Lewis *Carroll (1954). His brilliant illustrations for *Treasure Island* (one of his childhood favourites, and a story which greatly influenced his own novels) appeared in an edition of 1949. He also illustrated a selection of *nursery rhymes, *Ride-a-Cock-Horse* (1940). His second storybook for children, *Letters from a Lost Uncle (from polar regions)* appeared in 1948.

Peanuts *See* SNOOPY.

PEARCE, A. (Ann) Philippa (1920–2006) One of the leading British 20th-cent. children's writers who was born in the village of Great Shelford in Cambridgeshire. She was brought up in the mill-house where her father had been born; she and her sister and two brothers swam and fished in the river and had an old canoe on it. This setting has featured in many of her stories, transmuted into the village of 'Great Barley' on the 'River Say'.

Philippa Pearce's first book, *Minnow on the Say* (1955), won widespread acclaim for its maturity and freshness, and was a runner-up for the *Carnegie Medal. She won that medal with her next book, *Tom's Midnight Garden* (1958), which is regarded as one of the outstanding children's novels of all time. (She has said that it is partly about the mill-house garden of her childhood as it must have been in her father's day.) *A *Dog So Small* (1962) consolidated her reputation.

During the 1960s and early 1970s she wrote the texts for several *picture books, including *The Strange Sunflower* (1966) and *The Squirrel Wife* (1971). In 1968 there appeared *The Children of the House*, her adaptation of a story by Major Sir Brian Fairfax-Lucy. But nothing substantial that was entirely her own work appeared again until 1969, when she produced *The Elm Street Lot*, a collection of short stories about a working-class street and the children in it. *What the Neighbours Did and other stories* appeared in 1972, after which there was a five-year gap until *The Shadow-Cage and other tales of the supernatural* (1977), a set of *ghost stories for children. *The Battle of Bubble and Squeak* (1978) describes a family's squabbles over a pair of gerbils.

Philippa Pearce's first three novels and several of her short stories touch on the same two themes: the relationship between childhood and old age, and the solitary child's creation of a *fantasy world which can be both enriching and destructive. The manner of

writing in these books is restrained, carefully avoiding melodrama, and in Philippa Pearce's later collections of short stories this restraint has become almost a mannerism. The *Times Literary Supplement* observed of *What the Neighbours Did* (which is a collection of stories about children's daily experiences) that its author had 'deliberately dispensed with all the usual props of children's fiction' and had 'limited herself to the severest realism'. In 1983 appeared her first long novel for many years, *The Way to Sattin Shore*, the story of a fatherless girl and a disappearing tombstone, and *The Little Gentleman* in 2004.

PEARSON, Kit (1947–) Canadian writer, three-time winner of the *CLA Book of the Year for Children award, beginning with *A Handful of Time* (1987), her second novel, a *time-slip story which sees Patricia sent off to spend a summer with her parents, only to find herself travelling back thirty-five years into the past. (Children being sent from home are a recurring theme in Pearson's work.) Her second CLA win was for *The Sky is Falling* (1989), the first volume in her 'Guests of War' trilogy, a well-researched story about an English sister and brother in 1940 who are sent to live in Toronto to escape the Blitz. (The trilogy is completed by *Looking at the Moon*, 1991, and *The Lights Go on Again*, 1993, which continue Norah and Gavin's story.) Her exceptional *Awake and Dreaming* (1996) won Pearson the *Governor General's Literary Award; it is a ghost story about a poor girl sent away from her abusive mother, who wishes for a perfect family. She has recently completed a duology set in the early 1930s about sisters sent to live with their grandmother on Kingfisher Island in the aftermath of some family crisis: *The Whole Truth* (2011), which won her a third CLA, and *Nothing but the Truth* (2012).

Peau d'asne **(Donkey Skin)** A *fairy story of the *Cinderella group. It was published as a poem by *Perrault in 1694. The poem is written in a more sophisticated manner than Perrault's later *Contes*, and sparked off a controversy at the time of writing amongst the author's fellow Academicians in Paris as to the relative merits of fairy tales.

A king's beautiful wife tells him on her deathbed that he must marry again, and must choose somebody even more beautiful than herself. Eventually he realizes that the only person who meets this requirement is his own daughter, and he proposes to her. She, distraught, consults her fairy godmother,

who tells her to refuse her father's proposal unless he can provide her with dresses of various impossible hues—the colour of the sky, of the moon, and of the sun. The dresses are duly made, so this time, on the fairy's advice, the princess refuses her father unless he will give her the skin of the donkey which daily excretes gold coins for the palace treasury. The donkey is killed and the skin given to her. In desperation the princess flees, disguised in the donkey skin, and goes to live at a farmhouse, where she acts as a scullion. Her beauty is, nonetheless, perceived by a passing prince, who eventually manages to discover who she is and marries her, her father having by this time lost all interest in his incestuous plan—he has married a neighbouring king's beautiful wife instead.

The story was traditional in France in the 17th cent., to the extent that 'Peau d'asne' became a synonym for fairy story. Among the many parallels which have been recorded is the tale of 'The She-Bear' in the *Pentamerone* (Day 2, tale 6). The story does not usually appear in English collections of Perrault's tales, though it is included in Angela Carter's *Fairy Tales of Charles Perrault* (1977).

PECK, George Wilbur (1840–1916) American humorist and journalist who became famous for his stories of a mischievous boy, published in the Wisconsin newspaper he had founded, the *Sun*. In 1883 they were collected in book form as *Peck's Bad Boy and his Pa*, which attained enormous popularity and provided material for a play. *The Grocery Man and Peck's Bad Boy* appeared in the same year.

PECK, Richard (1934–) Prolific and respected American author of *young adult and children's fiction that often deals with social issues. *Don't Look and It Won't Hurt* (1972), his first novel, deals with unmarried motherhood, and *Are You in the House Alone?* (1976) is about a girl who is raped by a 'respectable' boy. The Grandma Dowdel books, starting with the story sequence *A Long Way from Chicago* (1998), is set in rural, Depression-hit Illinois; the sequel, *A Year Down Yonder* (2000) won the *Newbery Medal.

PEDLEY, Ethel C. *See* DOT AND THE KANGAROO.

Peep Behind the Scenes, A (1877) A popular *evangelical story by Mrs O. F. *Walton; the tale of Rosalie, a fairground child who is helped by evangelical Christianity

to rise above her sordid background. As M. Nancy Cutt observes in her study of evangelical children's fiction (*Ministering Angels*, 1979), 'Writing with declared religious purpose, Mrs Walton had actually produced a most unlikely hybrid: an Evangelical fairy-tale.'

Peepo! (1981) A classic picture book for babies by Janet *Ahlberg and Allan *Ahlberg, in which the game of 'peepo' can be played through strategically placed holes in the page. It takes the reader through a day in the life of a baby, asking at each moment 'What does he see?', which is answered by peeping through the hole to the next page, which shows Janet's detailed illustrations of 1940s domestic life in wartime (Allan, born in 1938, has said that he is the baby depicted), full of beautiful period character.

Peep of Day A highly popular book of elementary *religious instruction first published in 1836. Its author was Mrs F. L. *Mortimer, who based the book on her experience teaching a class of infants in a parish school.

The book begins with several chapters explaining who and what is or are God, the angels, the soul, and so on. Then follows a retelling of the New Testament, with many comments. Mrs Mortimer embellished the text with her own verses and those of others. *Peep of Day* ends with a series of questions to test the child's comprehension and memory. The book was as popular in America as in England, and was translated into French and also into a number of 'barbarous tongues', that is, the languages of Africa, of Native Americans, etc., for the use of missionaries.

PEET, Bill (William) (Bartlett) (1915–2002) American author-illustrator of *picture books for young children, such as *Kermit the Hermit* (1965) and *The Whingdingdilly* (1970). He was on the staff of the *Disney studios from 1937 until 1974.

PEET, Mal (1947–2015) An award-winning English author, best known for his *young adult fiction. Mal Peet started his career in children's literature creating picture books with his wife Elspeth Graham (1954–). Together they wrote over a hundred books for children and teachers, including reading-scheme books, picture books, non-fiction, guides to the classics, and collections of poetry. Their most recent trilogy of picture books includes *Cloud Tea Monkeys* (2010), illustrated by Juan Wyngaard (shortlisted for the *Kate Greenaway Medal), *Mysterious Traveller* (2013), illustrated by P. J. *Lynch,

and *Night Sky Dragons* (2014), illustrated by Patrick *Benson. All three stories are brought together in one paperback, *Painting out the Stars* (2011), illustrated by Michael *Foreman.

Peet's first novel, *Keeper* (2003), set in an imaginary South American country, was born of an intention to break out of the stereotypical '*sports novel', which he did admirably, winning the *Branford Boase Award for the most outstanding debut novel for children. The protagonist Paul Faustino would appear in two further novels, *The Penalty* (2006) and *Exposure* (2008), this latter a modern retelling of Shakespeare's *Othello*, for which Peet won the *Guardian Children's Fiction Prize. This loosely connected trilogy comprises a heady mix of history, culture, the supernatural, crime, celebrity, and, of course, football. Peet's second novel, *Tamar* (2005), set across two different time periods during Nazi-occupied Holland in 1944–5 and London in 1995, also met with high acclaim, winning the *Carnegie Medal in 2006. *Life: An Exploded Diagram* (2011) is a sophisticated and exquisitely written coming-of-age story, set in 1962 against the backdrop of imminent Armageddon. In 2014 he published an adult novel, *The Murdstone Trilogy*, a brilliant, mischievous satire on the world of children's *fantasy writing. His final novel, *Beck*, was completed after his death by Meg *Rosoff, and published posthumously in 2016.

Peeta Mellark See HUNGER GAMES, THE.

Penderwicks, The: *A Summer Tale of Four Sisters, Two Rabbits, and a Very Interesting Boy* (2005) This debut novel by American author Jeanne Birdsall (1951–) won the *National Book Award for Young People's Literature. Responsible Rosalind, feisty Skye, artistic Jane, and shy Batty form a firm friendship with Jeffrey, the musical boy next door, despite his snobbish mother's disapproval of the girls. With its domestic setting and large family, *The Penderwicks* contains echoes of *Little Women* and the books of Elizabeth *Enright; its nostalgic quality adds to its appeal. Other books in the series are *The Penderwicks on Gardam Street* (2008) and *The Penderwicks at Point Mouette* (2011). At the time of writing, another two are planned.

Penguin (2007) A picture book by Polly *Dunbar. Ben tries everything he can to persuade Penguin to speak, including at one point tying him to a rocket and firing him into space, but Penguin refuses to say a word. It's only when Ben is swallowed by a lion that Penguin gives any indication of

being alive, and bites the lion on the nose. 'Ow!' says the lion, spitting Ben back out again, and Ben and Penguin are friends at last. It's simple enough, but it is also one of the most lovely picture books of recent years— a very popular one, and deservedly so.

PENNAC, Daniel (1944–) French writer of novels and non-fiction for adults and fiction for children, and a former schoolteacher, born (Daniel Pennacchioni) in Casablanca. His children's fiction includes *Cabot-Caboche* (1982, English translation *Dog*, 2002), *L'œil du loup* (1984; *Eye of the Wolf*, 2002, winner of the 2005 *Marsh Award for Children's Literature in Translation), and the Kamo series (from 1992) including *L'évasion de Kamo* (1997; *Kamo's Escape*, 2004). He is also the author of *Comme un roman* (1992; *The Rights of the Reader*, 2006, with illustrations by Quentin *Blake), a wise, personal, and sometimes subversive essay celebrating reading and incorporating a ten-point manifesto, 'The Rights of the Reader'; and *Chagrin d'école* (2007; *School Blues*, 2010), which takes his own teaching experience as a starting point for an impassioned plea for sympathy and creativity in education. His smart, playful prose is translated into English by Sarah *Ardizzone.

Pennington Hero of stories by K. M. *Peyton.

penny dreadful A familiar name for the penny-a-number serial story parts, *magazines, and novelettes, which purveyed cheap and sensational fiction for a mass readership in Britain from the 1830s onwards.

They were descendants both of *chapbooks and *broadsides and of Gothic novels such as Mrs Radcliffe's *The Mysteries of Udolpho*. Usually mass-produced by anonymous authors, they included everything that would sell, from *Varney the Vampire, or the Feast of Blood* to plagiarized *Dickens stories under such titles as *Oliver Twiss*. By the 1840s there were penny dreadfuls with every sort of setting: historical, buccaneering, domestic, ghoulish. The most notorious creation of the early penny dreadfuls was *Sweeney Todd, the Demon Barber of Fleet Street*, who first appeared in about 1840. (A history of this legend's emergence, as of other penny dreadful heroes, can be found in E. S. Turner's *Boys Will Be Boys*, revised edn, 1975.)

Penny dreadfuls were not at first explicitly aimed at the juvenile market, but they were consumed by the young from the beginning, and trying them out on the office boy was a recognized editorial technique. To a greater or lesser extent the legends of *Dick Turpin, *Jack Sheppard, *Rob Roy, and *Spring-Heeled Jack were brought to a wide audience by early penny dreadfuls; respectable persons bewailed the glamorizing of criminals and the presentation of the rich, the aristocratic, and the clergy as fair game. One Dick Turpin saga, Edward Viles's *Black Bess, or The Knight of the Road*, ran to 254 weekly parts; it was probably the longest serial by a single penny dreadful author, and it was published whole in 1868. Less lasting than Turpin's was the fame of *The Wild Boys of London* (1866) whose habitat was the London sewers, and whose adventures involved body-snatching doctors, a bare-breasted woman flogged by her uncle, ravishings, mutinous convict ships, and countless corpses. The rerun of the serial was stopped by the police.

When it became obvious that these publications were actually courting the juvenile market, a number of more high-minded boys' magazines were founded to provide healthy reading, such as Samuel Beeton's *Boy's Own Magazine* (1855), the Revd J. Erskine Clarke's *Chatterbox* (1866), and, later, *The *Boy's Own Paper* (1879). Meanwhile some of the publishers of the dreadfuls saw that there was much to be gained by occupying the middle ground; for example *Boys of England*, a weekly founded in 1866 by Edwin *Brett, one of those responsible for *The Wild Boys*, cultivated a certain air of respectability, yet proved very popular with its readers. The *Jack Harkaway stories first appeared in its pages.

Many more illustrated magazines in this style were started before the end of the century, published by Edwin Brett and by his competitors, with titles like *Young Men of Great Britain, Rovers of the Sea, Boys of the Empire*, and *The Boy's Comic Journal*. History furnished many of the settings for their stories, mythology others (with *Norse gods as heroes), and *school stories became a staple. Mixed in were all the standard ingredients of Victorian (and later) sensational fiction: hags and desperadoes, foreign villains, heirs cheated of their inheritance, sadistic drunken schoolmasters, torture, sex (up to a point), and cliché.

It was against these that Alfred *Harmsworth, later Lord Northcliffe, launched his crusade, with 'No more penny dreadfuls' as the slogan of his new *Halfpenny Marvel* (*see *MARVEL) in 1893. The penny dreadful, said an editorial, 'makes thieves of the coming

generation and so helps fill our jails. If we can rid the world of even one of these vile publications our efforts will not have been in vain.' The Harmsworth papers claimed never to cast rogues as heroes (a pledge they found impossible to keep to the letter). They used full-length paragraphs rather than the exclamation-peppered one-liners favoured by the 'dreadfuls', and their standards of production were much higher. Harmsworth *comics were advertised as 'funny but not vulgar'. But the main selling point was the price, a mere halfpenny, and A. A. *Milne wrote, a little cruelly, that 'It was Lord Northcliffe who killed the "penny dreadful" by the simple process of producing a ha'penny dreadfuller.'

See also BOYS' STORIES. For the history of the penny dreadful in America, *see* DIME NOVEL. British children today are more likely to know 'Penny Dreadful' as a character in books by Joanna Nadin.

Penrod (1914) A novel by the popular American writer Booth Tarkington (1869–1946), about 'The Worst Boy in Town', Penrod Schofield, brought up in a small Midwestern city. Penrod eats his way through his favourite menu (watermelon, chocolate creams, licorice sticks, lemon drops, peanuts, jawbreakers, sardines, raspberry lemonade, pickles, popcorn, ice cream, sausages, cinnamon drops, and waffles), writes a bloodcurdling *dime novel, and yearns for the curly-headed Marjorie Jones.

PENROSE, Elizabeth *See* MARKHAM, MRS.

Pentamerone A collection of popular tales published in Naples between 1634 and 1636 under the title *Lo cunto de li cunti* ('The Tale of Tales'). It contains versions of several of the best known *fairy stories.

The book was the work of Giambattista Basile (*c*.1575–1632), a court poet and holder of various military and administrative posts, who wrote in the Neapolitan dialect. *Lo cunto de li cunti* has a 'frame' story, in which a king's daughter, Zoza, learns that if she goes to a certain tomb and manages in three days to fill with her tears a jar that hangs there, she will awake an enchanted prince who will marry her. She has almost managed it when she falls asleep, and a Turkish slave-girl comes up and finishes the task, so obtaining the prince for herself. Zoza, however, manages to instil in the mind of the slave a longing to hear fairy stories, and for this purpose a group of old women are assembled nightly at the

palace to tell them to her. At the end Zoza relates her own history, and explains how she was cheated of her royal husband; the slave is put to death and the prince marries Zoza.

Into this frame are inserted forty-nine tales, ten for each night, the fiftieth being Zoza's own narrative. Basile presumably collected them from oral tradition. He wrote them down in a style that was both baroque and idiomatic; florid turns of phrase and descriptions jostle with popular expressions and slang terms.

The book was printed in sections after his death, and was often reprinted in its original Neapolitan language. By the late 17th cent. it had come to be known as the *Pentamerone*, a title modelled on the *Decameron* of Boccaccio. It was not translated into Italian until 1747.

*Perrault's *Contes de ma mère L'Oye* was published in France in 1697, and several stories resemble those of Basile, although there is no evidence to suggest that Perrault was familiar with the *Pentamerone* (*see* CONTES DE MA MÈRE L'OYE for a discussion of sources).

Other fairy stories which appear in the *Pentamerone* include versions of *Beauty and the Beast* and *Snow White*, but again there is no evidence that our modern 'standard' versions of these are derived from Basile's idiosyncratic book.

The *Pentamerone* was praised by the *Grimms in 1822 as 'for a long time the best and richest [collection of fairy stories] that had been found by any nation'. This accolade led to the publication of a German translation in 1846, and an abridged English edition appeared in 1848 under the title *The Pentamerone or the Story of Stories, Fun for the Little Ones*. The translator was J. E. Taylor and the book was illustrated by George *Cruikshank. The complete book was translated into English by Sir Richard Burton in 1893, and again by N. M. Penzer, in an edition with a full introduction and notes, in 1932.

Peppermint Pig, The (1975) By Nina *Bawden, for which she won the *Guardian Children's Fiction Prize. This is an outstanding 'realistic' novel about the experiences of childhood, and the story of an Edwardian family thrown suddenly into poverty and forced to leave their comfortable London home for a bleaker existence in a Norfolk market town. Father has gone to America and mother is struggling to make ends meet. But she buys Johnnie, the eponymous pig, for a shilling—he's the runt of the litter—and he quickly becomes the centre of the children's world.

Jill *Paton Walsh has called the book 'a perfect, small masterpiece'. It has a particularly brilliant opening paragraph, too.

Percy Jackson (from 2005) By Rick *Riordan. Percy Jackson has a temper, not to mention ADHD and dyslexia, and a feeling that things aren't quite normal, especially when one of his teachers turns into a monster and tries to kill him. Finding out that he is actually a demi-god and that his father is Poseidon explains some things, as does attending Camp Half Blood, where his adventures really begin. *Percy Jackson and the Lightning Thief* (2005) is the first in the *Percy Jackson and the Olympians* series. There are (to date) two accompanying movies (2010, 2013), and a follow-on series about the next generation of half-bloods, *Heroes of Olympus*, starts with *The Lost Hero* (2010).

Percy's Reliques of Ancient English Poetry (1765) A celebrated collection of *ballads and other poems, which was very influential in inspiring antiquarian interest in such folk heroes as *Robin Hood. In 1882 Sidney *Lanier produced a version of the *Reliques* for children, entitled *The Boy's Percy*.

Père Castor Supposed author of a French series of instructive and entertaining *picture books published in France since 1932. The series was initiated by Paul Faucher (1898–1967) and the original illustrator was Feodor Rojànkovsky ('Ròjan'), though many authors and artists have contributed. It began with *Albums du Père Castor* (1932 onwards). Many of the early titles were *animal stories, designed to instruct in the natural habits of creatures. Other subjects include the signs of the zodiac and books of *sports, and the series has also included the fables of *La Fontaine and the stories of Hans Christian *Andersen.

periodicals *See* MAGAZINES.

PERKINS, Lucy Fitch (1865–1937) American author-illustrator of the 'Twins' books, about children of different nationalities and historical periods, beginning with *The Dutch Twins* (1911).

PERRAULT, Charles (1628–1703) French writer responsible, possibly with the aid of his son **Pierre** (1678–1700), for setting down the collection of *fairy stories in which there first appeared *Bluebeard, *Cinderella, *Diamonds and Toads, *Hop O' My Thumb, *Little Red Riding Hood, *Puss In Boots, *Riquet à la houppe, and The *Sleeping Beauty.

Charles Perrault was born in Paris, the son of a barrister. He took a law degree, but tired of the legal profession and subsequently worked as Contrôleur Général in the Department of Buildings for the administration of Louis XIV.

In 1671 Perrault was elected a member of the Académie Française. Here he distinguished himself as a champion of those modern French writers with a 'progressive' outlook, supporting them against their opponents in the celebrated 'quarrel of ancients and moderns' who preferred to imitate classical authors. He published a number of writings on this topic. In 1672 he married, and he eventually became the father of three sons; but his wife died in 1678. He retired in 1683 and spent his time attending to the education of his children and writing devotional poetry, a set of biographical eulogies of remarkable men of his period, and his own memoirs.

In 1691 he published anonymously a poem in the style of *La Fontaine entitled *La Marquise de Salusses, ou la Patience de Griselidis*; its story was that of 'Patient Griselda', which is found in Boccaccio, though Perrault apparently derived his version from French *chapbook renderings. Two years later there appeared in a fashionable paper, *Le Mercure galant*, another verse-narrative by Perrault, *Les Souhaits ridicules*, a version of The *Three Wishes. In 1694 this poem and *Griselidis* were reprinted in a small volume, to which Perrault added a third poem, *Peau d'asne ('Donkey Skin'), a traditional story on the Cinderella theme. In a preface to the second edition of this book (1695) Perrault remarked upon the pleasure which such stories give to children.

In February 1696 another Perrault narrative, this time in prose, appeared in the *Mercure galant*. This was *La Belle au bois dormant* (*The Sleeping Beauty*). Then, in January 1697, the Paris publisher Claude Barbin reissued this story along with seven other prose tales, under the title *Histoires ou contes du temps passé, avec des Moralitez*. Before the end of the year the book had been reprinted several times. The tales it contained—*La Belle au bois dormant, Le Petit Chaperon rouge* (*Little Red Riding-Hood*), *La Barbe bleue* (*Bluebeard*), *Le Maistre Chat, ou le Chat botté* (*Puss In Boots*), *Les Fées* ('The Fairies', often known as *Diamonds and Toads*), *Cendrillon, ou la petite pantoufle de verre* (*Cinderella*), *Riquet à la houppe*, and *Le Petit Poucet* (*Hop O' My Thumb*)—quickly became the standard versions of stories on these themes. Perrault's narratives were translated into innumerable languages, were reprinted again and again, and soon re-entered the

oral tradition of most European countries, particularly England. The book quickly became known by the words which appeared in the frontispiece to first edition, 'Contes de ma mère l'Oye', which in English was rendered 'Mother Goose's Tales'.

No author's name was given on the titlepage of the first edition. However the dedicatory letter was signed 'P. Darmancour', and this was the name in which the book's copyright was registered. Charles Perrault's youngest son Pierre, who was eighteen at the time, had adopted an extra surname and was known as Pierre Perrault Darmancour. This would seem to indicate that it was he rather than his father who wrote down the stories. There is also other evidence to suggest a claim of authorship for Pierre Perrault, including the dedication to 'P. P' of a manuscript of *Contes de ma mère L'Oye* dated 1695, and a book published in 1695 or 1696 by Marie-Jeanne l'Héritier de Villandon, a relative of Perrault and herself a writer of fairy stories, which mentions a collection of 'Contes naïfs' 'mis depuis peu sur le papier' by one of Perrault's sons.

However, not all Perrault's contemporaries accepted that it was the boy who had written, or written down, the *Contes*. A dialogue on the subject of fairy stories published in 1699 talks of the book merely as 'attributed' to Perrault *fils*, and suggests that his father may have had a hand in it.

The manuscript of the *Contes* mentioned above, which is now in the Pierpont Morgan Library in New York and was published in a facsimile edition by Jacques Barchilon in 1956, gives another clue. The handwriting is a formal script, probably the work of a professional copyist, but a few corrections have been made in another hand, which appears to be that of Charles Perrault.

The question of the authorship cannot be answered conclusively. It is perfectly possible that Pierre Perrault heard the stories from his nurse or some such person and was encouraged by his father to write them down. On the other hand this seems a slightly unlikely pursuit for a youth of seventeen, while the father's interest in fairy stories is demonstrated by the poems that he published before the *Contes* were issued. Possibly, as some commentators have suggested, the tales were originally written out by the son, but the verse morals which conclude them were the work of the father. Yet the stories themselves display a certain sophistication, especially in their digressions on

love, manners, and feminine psychology, which would suggest that the father rather than the son was the author. It seems plausible therefore that Charles Perrault, having been attacked by his fellow Academicians for his verse tales, decided to publish the prose *Contes* under the alias of his son, who may indeed have originally passed on to his father his recollections of stories that he had heard at the nursery fireside.

For a discussion of the sources of the stories, *see* CONTES DE MA MÈRE L'OYE. For the history of their publication in English, *see* HISTORIES, OR TALES OF PAST TIMES.

Because we cannot be certain about the nature of Perrault's sources or the form in which he found the stories that he rewrote and published, we cannot be precise about his literary achievement. Nevertheless when his *Contes* are compared with the fairy stories of his French contemporaries, it becomes clear that he had a unique talent which combined simplicity and artifice. Without that talent, we would probably not possess *Cinderella*, *The Sleeping Beauty*, and the others in anything like the unforgettable form in which we know them today.

Persepolis *See* GRAPHIC NOVELS.

Peter and Wendy (1911) By J. M. *Barrie, a retelling of the story of *Peter Pan* in book form, originally published with illustrations by F. D. *Bedford. It contains much that is not in the play, including an opening chapter which relates how Wendy and her brothers knew of Peter Pan and the 'Neverland' (*sic*) before Peter ever came to their nursery; the last chapter, 'When Wendy Grew Up', describes how Wendy's daughter Jane takes Wendy's place in the Never Never Land in later years.

The book is long, and Barrie permitted reductions of the text, the first being *Peter Pan and Wendy* (1915), described as an 'authorized school edition' and published jointly by the Oxford University Press and Hodder and Stoughton, with the Bedford illustrations. The full text was used for *Peter Pan and Wendy* (1921), with illustrations by Mabel Lucie *Attwell, an artist quite unsuited to Barrie's story. The Attwell pictures, nevertheless, have been sometimes used since then to accompany a retelling of the story for small children by May Byron, which was first published in 1935. Other illustrators and authors have produced their own versions, the best to date being a 1962 retelling by Eleanor *Graham with illustrations by Edward *Ardizzone.

Peterkin Gay in *Coral Island* by R. M. *Ballantyne.

Peterkin Papers, The A collection of comic stories about the Peterkin family, written by Lucretia P. *Hale and first published in *St Nicholas*; it was issued as a book in 1880, and was later expanded.

The stories, told in deadpan fashion, record the extraordinary stupidities of Mrs Peterkin and her family. For example, a piano is delivered to the Peterkin house, and is set down with the keyboard facing the wrong way, up against a window. The Peterkins open the window and play the piano through it, from the outside of the house, before the lady from Philadelphia points out that there is a simpler solution. The stories are partly a satire on Boston society and its desire for self-improvement. There is a further volume, *The Last of the Peterkins* (1886).

Peter Pan, or *The Boy Who Wouldn't Grow Up* A *play by J. M. *Barrie, first performed in London in 1904, and since its initial appearance on the stage regarded as a permanent piece of children's mythology.

To the night nursery of the Darling children, Wendy, John, and Michael, comes Peter Pan, a motherless half-magical boy who teaches them how to fly and takes them through the skies to the Never Never Land, a country peopled with the most thrilling beings from children's stories: *Indians', *mermaids, wolves, and most of all *pirates, who are under the leadership of the dreadful Captain Hook, so named from the steel hook he wears instead of a right hand. This hand was bitten off by a crocodile, who, as Hook explains, 'liked my arm so much . . . that he has followed me ever since . . . licking his lips for the rest of me'. The crocodile eventually gets his man, but not before Hook has tried to poison Peter, has nearly killed Peter's *fairy Tinker Bell, and has made prisoners of Wendy, her brothers, and the Lost Boys who live with Peter. Hook having been despatched, the Darling children return home, and are reunited with their sorrowing parents and with Nana, the huge dog who is their nursemaid; but every spring Wendy is allowed to go back to the Never Never Land to do Peter's spring-cleaning for him, in the little house he and the Lost Boys once built for her, which now nestles in the treetops.

Barrie wrote the play at the height of his success as a novelist and playwright. It grew out of his preoccupation with himself as a 'boy who wouldn't grow up', already expressed in his novels *Sentimental Tommy* (1896) and *Tommy and Grizel* (1900). The incentive to handle this theme in a work for children came from his friendship with the young sons of Arthur and Sylvia Llewelyn Davies, George, Jack, Peter, Michael, and Nicholas; see BARRIE, SIR J. M. for an account of that friendship and its bearing upon the play.

The fullest account of the writing and staging of *Peter Pan* may be found in Roger Lancelyn *Green's *Fifty Years of Peter Pan* (1954), which points out that the male members of the Darling family all have Llewelyn Davies names: Mr Darling is George, the elder boy John is named after Jack, and the younger is 'Michael Nicholas Darling'. The name Wendy, an invention of Barrie's, was a recollection of Margaret, the small daughter of his friend the writer and editor W. E. Henley, who before her early death had called him 'my wendy', meaning 'my friend'. Mrs Darling's character was an amalgam of Sylvia Llewelyn Davies and Barrie's own mother, about whom he had written a book, *Margaret Ogilvy* (1896). Mr Darling's precarious financial position and his irascibility were both drawn from Arthur Llewelyn Davies, a struggling barrister who was understandably wary of Barrie's wholesale adoption of his family. Nana the dog-nursemaid was created from Barrie's own Newfoundland dog Luath.

The pirate names were largely taken from Charles Johnson's *General History . . . of the Most Notorious Pyrates* (1724), though Hook owes more to *Treasure Island* than to history; his origins may also be found in Hooky Crewe, a postman who features in Barrie's book of Scottish sketches *Auld Licht Idylls* (1888), 'so called because an iron hook was his substitute for a right arm'. The deeds of the pirates are based on Barrie's recollections of *penny dreadfuls read in childhood, while the name Never Never Land ('Never Never Land' in early versions of the play, but simply 'Never Land' in the published text) was that of a district of Australia; it was also the title of a play by Wilson Barrett, first performed in 1902.

Barrie wrote the first draft of *Peter Pan* between 23 November 1903 and 1 March 1904. It differs from the final version in some of its names (Michael is 'Alexander' and Tinker Bell is 'Tippy-Toe'), in the inclusion of certain episodes later discarded as impractical (among these being a stage direction for the pirate ship to sail on to the stage), and in the lengthy and rambling fashion in which Barrie concluded the play.

The text underwent many alterations before and during rehearsals for the first production. This was at the Duke of York's Theatre in London, which was to be the play's home for the first ten years of its life. Barrie's stage directions in early drafts of the play often called for the seemingly impossible—great birds to swoop down and carry off actors by the seats of their trousers, the crocodile to eat a wooden boat—but almost everything was attempted, this being the heyday of trickwork on the London stage.

It was assumed from the beginning that Peter would be played by a girl; until 1982 only twice in the play's history, in productions in France and Germany in the 1950s, was the part taken by a boy or young man. In fact in the first production and for some years afterwards, all the boys were played by girls or young women, with the exception of John Darling and Slightly, the Lost Boy who provides comic relief.

Preparations for the play were shrouded in secrecy, so that its impact should be all the greater; even the actors knew little about it before they began rehearsal, and Hilda Trevelyan, who played Wendy, was alarmed to receive a notice stating 'Flying, 10.30', and to be asked to insure her life.

The chief scenic and costume designer was Sir William *Nicholson, and Peter Pan's clothes were designed by H. J. *Ford, illustrator of the *Fairy Books of Andrew *Lang and a friend of Barrie. The appearances of Tinker Bell were achieved by catching the beam of a spotlight in a hand-held mirror and reflecting it on to the stage. Technical challenges proved so difficult to meet that the opening night was postponed for five days. The play was eventually seen for the first time on 27 December 1904, and even then it was necessary to omit the last part of the final scene, in which Peter and Wendy are seen at the doorway of the little house which raises itself to the treetops in the Never Never Land; the machinery to do this was not ready.

The cast and technicians were by no means certain of the play's success—Barrie alleged that a 'depressed man in overalls' used to flit about during rehearsals muttering 'The gallery boys won't stand it!'—but the reception at the first night was very enthusiastic, even though the audience consisted almost entirely of adults. The orchestra had been primed to lead the clapping that was to save Tinker Bell's life, after Peter's appeal 'Do you believe in fairies? . . . If you believe, clap your hands!',

but in fact the audience responded spontaneously. One of the few dissenting voices was that of 'Anthony *Hope', author of *The Prisoner of Zenda*, who allegedly remarked during the performance 'Oh, for an hour of Herod!'

Reviews of the play were generally favourable, if a little cautious and puzzled. The only really perceptive notice was by Max Beerbohm, writing in the *Saturday Review* for 7 January 1905. He said nothing of the production, but wrote of Barrie himself:

Undoubtedly, *Peter Pan* is the best thing he has done . . . for here he has stripped off from himself the last flimsy remnants of a pretence of maturity. . . . Mr Barrie is not that rare creature, a man of genius. He is something even more rare—a child who, by some divine grace, can express through an artistic medium the childishness that is in him.

The play ran at the Duke of York's until 1 April 1905, and by the time it closed an announcement had been made that it would reopen there the following December. Henceforth it was to be an annual London institution at Christmas, reappearing at the Duke of York's every December until 1914, and then at other London theatres without a break until 1939. There was no London production in 1940, but the tradition was resumed the next year, and in 1945 the play began what was to be more than twenty years' annual residence at the Scala Theatre. It has also been seen frequently in the provinces, usually in performances by the London company on tour.

For the 1905 revival Barrie wrote a new act to follow the first Never Never Land scene; this was 'The Mermaids' Lagoon', which called for the most elaborate stage effects, and concluded with Peter's remark 'To die will be an awfully big adventure'.

In 1924, Paramount made a silent film of the play. This was shown in England, where it was criticized for being no more than a photographing of the stage play; Barrie himself was inspired by it to write his own scenario for a silent film (printed in *Fifty Years of Peter Pan*), in the course of which he added many details to the Peter Pan myth. In 1953, Walt *Disney released an animated film of *Peter Pan*, which was among the best productions of his studio and included some excellent songs.

Barrie did not publish the play until 1928, when it appeared in a version that was at times almost a novelization, and which departed somewhat from the acting script. However in 1911 there was published *Peter and Wendy*, in which Barrie retold the story in book form, and which was closer in many respects to the

play as performed. Other retellings by different authors have been produced over the years (*see* PETER AND WENDY for details of some of these). In 1912 a statue of Peter Pan was placed, at Barrie's expense, in Kensington Gardens. Since 1929 royalties from the play and its various offshoots have gone to the Great Ormond Street children's hospital in London.

Revivals of the play were for many years notable for traditionalism rather than innovation or imaginative direction. Many actors appeared in the same minor roles for year after year, lured by the prospect of regular work at Christmas; one man, William Luff, was cast in the small part of the pirate Cecco in 1907, and, almost unbelievably, was still playing it when the play celebrated its jubilee in 1954. Then at Christmas 1982 came just such an entirely new production, by the Royal Shakespeare Company at the Barbican Theatre in London. A male actor (Miles Anderson) was cast as Peter, and material from *Peter and Wendy*, Barrie's film script, and other variant texts, was introduced, much of it spoken by an actor (Stephen Moore) dressed and made up to look like Barrie himself. Play versions are still occasionally performed, but the *Peter Pan* story is today more often seen in the seemingly endlessly proliferating screen adaptations and spin-offs.

Peter Pan and Wendy *See* PETER AND WENDY.

Peter Pan in Kensington Gardens *See* LITTLE WHITE BIRD, THE.

Peter Parley A pseudonym invented by the New England author and publisher S. G. *Goodrich for his immensely successful series of *books of instruction, beginning with *The *Tales of Peter Parley About America* (1827) and continuing until his death in 1860.

Goodrich's books, whose subjects included *history, natural science, *geography, biography, and mythology, with occasional excursions into pure fiction, were characterized by the homely, chatty style of the narrator, a generous use of illustrations, and (in many cases) the breaking up of each chapter into numbered paragraphs.

The books' popularity quickly led to their being pirated and imitated in Britain, first by the publisher Thomas Tegg (1776–1845), who was issuing Parley titles by 1832. Some of these were genuine Goodrich books; Goodrich made an agreement with Tegg that he should receive payment for these and subsequent publications, which Tegg failed to honour, though in 1842 he made a lump payment to Goodrich. Many other publishers went on to issue 'Peter Parley' books without authorization from Goodrich. The Parley name, in fact, became as much common property in Britain as that of, say, *Mother Goose, and even appeared in nursery *chapbooks which bore no resemblance to real Parley works, e.g. *Peter Parley's Tales about the Faithful Dog and the Little Prisoners* (Derby, Thomas Richardson, 1838).

Peter Parley's Annual *See* PETER PARLEY'S MAGAZINE.

Peter Parley's Magazine A British *magazine for children published monthly from 1839, using the pseudonym created by S. G. *Goodrich. The magazine was apparently first published by Simpkin, Marshall and Co., and not Goodrich, although it retained both the policy and the tone that he had made popular.

The magazine contained, often in serial form, *history, instructive stories, *poetry, articles about *sports and other factual topics, and a great deal of *natural history. The parts were also bound together and published as an *annual at Christmas, dated for the following year.

By Christmas 1845, in response to the use of colour in works by another writer ('Felix Summerly'/ Henry *Cole), *Peter Parley's Annual* pioneered an early use of 'Oil Colours, by Baxter's patent process' (*see* COLOUR). This made the *Annual* expensive, but a cheaper version, without the colour plates and keeping the title *Magazine*, continued to be published. The publication survived as an annual until 1892, long after the monthly magazine had ceased.

Peter Piper's Practical Principles of Plain and Perfect Pronunciation A book of *tonguetwisters first published by John *Harris in 1813. It contained a tonguetwister for each letter of the alphabet, on the model of 'Peter Piper picked a peck of pickled pepper', which first appeared in print in this book (without the word 'pickled'). The book was reprinted by Harris, was issued by other publishers, and appeared in America in about 1830. Though it was undoubtedly popular with children, a reviewer in the *London Magazine* in 1820 called it 'vile trash', apparently

on the assumption that it was meant to be taken seriously.

Peter Rabbit *See* TALE OF PETER RABBIT, THE.

PETERSHAM, Maud (1890–1971) and **Miska** (1888–1960) Author-illustrators of *picture books published between 1929 and 1958. Miska Petersham, born Mihaly Petrezselyen, emigrated to the United States from his native Hungary in 1912 and married Maud Fuller, a graduate of Vassar. Their first collaboration, *Miki* (1929), was written for their son and describes a child's experiences in Hungary. They produced other books based on Hungarian material, but in 1933 also began to turn their attention to modern Western life, with a series entitled 'Story Book', which was designed to instruct young children in the physical world and civilization. In addition, they illustrated books by other writers, including Carl Sandburg's *Rootabaga Stories* (1922). Miska Petersham worked as a commercial artist, and this had an influence on the style of the Petershams' books, which became more and more conventional as the years passed, even to the point of dullness.

Peter Simple (1834) A novel by Captain *Marryat which has often been enjoyed by children, though it was written for a general readership. Peter, regarded as the fool of the family, distinguishes himself while serving at sea and eventually inherits a title. The story is notable for portraits of such characters as Chucks the Bosun, who begins his sentences of reproach to other seamen with extreme courtesy, and ends them with the blackest of oaths.

Peter the Whaler, *his early life and adventures in the Arctic regions* (1851) A novel by W. H. G *Kingston. Fifteen-year-old Peter Lefroy, son of a Church of Ireland clergyman, is caught poaching; the offence is overlooked providing he goes to sea. He is bound to the villainous captain of a ship sailing to Quebec, is maltreated, and only just escapes with his life when the ship catches fire. Subsequently he becomes a *pirate against his will, is taken on board a whaling ship, and is marooned for some time on the Arctic ice, before he is rescued and enabled to return to his family and the captain's daughter whom he loves.

Petit Nicolas, Le (1959–64) By René *Goscinny, illustrated by Jean-Jacques *Sempé, humorous stories about a small boy and his experiences at school, published in a series of collections, originally in French but subsequently widely translated. Each title is narrated by Nicolas himself, who tells his stories with perfect seriousness, so the reader is left to divine their humour. Nicolas always describes his friends in the same way, and they invariably behave in character: Alceste, 'is fat and eats all the time'; Clotaire 'is bottom of the class'. The boys wreak chaos on the world without ever having any malicious intent. Nicolas's antics are brought to life by the incisively comic illustrations of cartoonist Sempé. Nicolas's first English incarnation appeared in a 1962 translation; there have been subsequent translations by Anthea *Bell, among others.

Petit Prince, Le *See* LITTLE PRINCE, THE.

PETRY, Ann (Lane) (1908–97) African-American author who wrote fiction and *history for children, including *Tituba of Salem Village* (1964), a novel set during the Salem witchcraft trials.

Petsetilla's Posy (1870) A novel for children by Tom *Hood, written in imitation of Thackeray's The *Rose and the Ring. Princess Petsetilla is the daughter of King Bungo and Queen Belinda; at her christening the place of honour is accidentally occupied by a *witch, who decrees that Petsetilla will marry a beggar. Petsetilla duly drops a posy from her window which is picked up by Remsky, penniless son of a rag-collector, though the story eventually produces the traditional happy ending.

The resemblance to Thackeray's book is emphasized by the illustrations by F. Barnard, which are very much in the style of those in *The Rose and the Ring*.

Pevensie family *See* NARNIA.

PEYTON, K. M. (Kathleen Wendy Peyton) (1929–) British writer of novels for older children. As a child she longed to own a pony, and wrote her own *pony stories as a substitute. When she was fifteen she completed a full-length children's novel, *Sabre, the Horse from the Sea*, which was published four years later in 1948 under her maiden name of Kathleen Herald. Two more books of this kind followed; meanwhile she studied at Manchester Art School, and eloped with a fellow student, Michael Peyton. The two of them began to produce potboiler *adventure stories for a *Boy Scout magazine; the stories appeared as

by 'K. and M. Peyton'. Three of these were published in book form, starting with *North to Adventure* (1958). The publisher, Collins, did not want two authors' names on the title page, so they were stated to be by 'K. M. Peyton'.

'When we were off the starvation line,' recalls Peyton, 'I then decided to write what I thought of as a "proper" book, and the collaboration ceased, as my husband had his own work anyway.' She continued to write as 'K. M. Peyton', explaining: 'I had never wanted to revert, as I reckon without my husband I would never have had such good material to draw on, he being of an adventurous nature and dragging me along after him, a few times to near extinction!'

Her first solo book was *Windfall* (1962), set, like virtually everything else she has written, in Essex, where she and her husband made their home. *Windfall* takes place in the 19th cent., and concerns a fisherman's son who gains a large reward for rescuing a man. This was followed by *The Maplin Bird* (1964), *The Plan for Birdsmarsh* (1965), and *Thunder in the Sky* (1966).

All these books were competently written, with ingenious plots; but as Frank *Eyre has observed they 'were not essentially different... from other books of their kind'. In 1967 Kathleen Peyton struck out in a new direction with *Flambards, the first volume in a series about a young girl's involvement with an Essex hunting family before and during the First World War. The second volume, *The Edge of the Cloud* (1969), won Peyton the *Carnegie Medal, and by the time that *Flambards in Summer* appeared in 1969, the series was recognized as one of the major achievements of modern British fiction for younger readers.

Peyton enjoyed almost as much success with a second series, about an unruly but talented schoolboy named Pennington; this began with *Pennington's Seventeenth Summer* (1970). The second volume, *The Beethoven Medal* (1971), brought into the story a girl named Ruth Hollis, who had already appeared as heroine of *Fly-by-Night* (1968), a pony novel. After the conclusion of the Pennington series with *Pennington's Heir* (1973), Peyton wrote two thrillers involving the schoolboy Jonathan Meredith, *Prove Yourself a Hero* (1977) and *A Midsummer Night's Death* (1978), and two *ghost stories, *A Pattern of Roses* (1973) and *Marion's Angels* (1979).

The novels of 'K. M. Peyton' have played a large part in establishing the genre of *young adult novels in Britain. The *Flambards* books in particular, while not her best writing, seem certain now to be the work for which she is most loved and remembered.

PFISTER, Marcus (1960–) Swiss writer and illustrator, best known for his *Rainbow Fish* series (in English from 1996), an international bestseller, which has been translated into over eighty languages and been made into an animated series. *Rainbow Fish* tells the story of a multicoloured fish with shiny silver scales (the book's distinctive look owes much to the foil used in representing these scales) who learns to share some of these shiny scales with the other fish and thereby win their friendship. Other titles by Pfister include *The Sleepy Owl* (1986), *Penguin Pete* (1987), and *The Yellow Cab* (2013).

Phantasmagoria (1869) A collection of poems by Lewis *Carroll.

Phantastes, *a Faerie Romance for Men and Women* (1858) The first work of *fantasy by George *MacDonald. The story, whose title is taken from Phineas Fletcher's poem *The Purple Island* in which 'Phantastes' is the personification of Fancy, owes much to German Romanticism and to Spenser (*see* FAERIE QUEENE, THE). It tells how Anodos, a young man whose name is from the Greek and means 'pathless', finds his way into fairyland, where he has a series of dream-like adventures. He encounters flower-fairies and tree-spirits, acquires a sinister shadow, and finally dies in the act of exposing a false religion. Coming to his senses again at his own home, he learns that he has been absent from it for twenty-one days.

Though not written for children, the book contains many of the elements that MacDonald was later to work into his children's novels and fairy stories, and it exercised a great influence over the young C. S. *Lewis.

Phantom Tollbooth, The (1961) A *fantasy by the American writer Norton *Juster. Milo is surprised when a mysterious package turns up in his family's apartment. It proves to contain a magic tollbooth; when he drives past it in his toy car he finds himself in a strange world containing such places and people as the Doldrums (embodiments of boredom and inactivity), Tock the Watchdog (whose body is a watch), Dictionopolis (the city that the words come from), and Faintly Macabre, the not-so-wicked Which. The book was described by

Naomi *Lewis as 'the best original *modern* book in the Carroll line'. It was illustrated by cartoonist Jules Feiffer (1929–).

PHELPS, Elizabeth Stuart *See* GYPSY BREYNTON.

PHILBRICK, Rodman (1951–) An American who worked as a docker and boatbuilder and who penned adult fiction under different pseudonyms before turning his hand to books for younger readers. With dystopian, historical, mystery, and contemporary novels to his name, his most successful book to date is the funny and sad *Freak the Mighty* (1993), the story of two young outsiders who form an unusual and life-affirming friendship. There is a sequel, *Max the Mighty* (1998). *Lobster Boy* (2004) is a companion to Hemingway's *The Old Man and the Sea*.

Philip Quarll One of the earliest stories to be written in imitation of *Robinson Crusoe*. The first edition, published in 1727, was entitled *The Hermit: or, The Unparallel'd Sufferings And Surprising Adventures of Philip Quarll, An Englishman: Who was lately discovered upon an uninhabited Island in the South Seas*. The dedication is signed 'Peter Longueville', to whom the book is nowadays usually ascribed, though other authors have been suggested.

The story tells how Quarll is discovered by a Bristol merchant, having lived on his island for more than 50 years; unlike Crusoe, he has no wish to come back to civilization and so remains there. His adventures, with his name sometimes spelt 'Quarle', were reprinted many times during the 18th and 19th cents. as children's *chapbooks, and were also included in miscellanies and anthologies, among them Charlotte M. *Yonge's *A Storehouse of Stories* (1870). Harvey *Darton wrote of Quarll that in his own childhood he 'liked him better than Defoe's own Robinson; he was not so wordy'.

PHILLIPS, Richard *See* TALBOT, BENJAMIN.

PHILLPOTTS, Eden *See* HUMAN BOY, THE.

PHIPSON, Joan (Margaret) (1912–2003) Australian children's author who began her career by writing *family stories. *The Family Conspiracy* (1962), in which children attempt to raise money to pay for their mother's operation, won the Australian Children's Book of the Year Award. Phipson's later books include *Peter and Butch* (1969) and *Fly Into Danger* (1977, later retitled *The Bird Smugglers*).

Phoenix and the Carpet, The (1904) The second *fantasy novel by E. *Nesbit, sequel to *Five Children and It*. Robert, Anthea, Jane, and Cyril acquire a nursery carpet in which is wrapped a mysterious egg; when the egg falls into the fire, there hatches out of it the Phoenix. He explains to the children that the carpet is a magic wishing-carpet. With the carpet to convey them wherever they want, and to carry out virtually anything they wish for, the children begin a series of adventures, the Phoenix accompanying them as a benevolent guide.

As in *Five Children and It*, they soon discover that almost every magic journey or wish has unforeseen consequences of the most alarming kind, and often the Phoenix's own ingenuity and powers are required to get them out of a tight spot.

Edith Nesbit's friend Laurence *Housman 'proposed the carpet and the phoenix as properties for a magic plot to be woven around'. The French castle with a ruined tower in which the carpet maroons the children was a memory from her childhood travels in France. The story was serialized in *The *Strand Magazine*, with illustrations by H. R. *Millar which were incorporated into the book.

Phronsie In *The *Five Little Peppers and How They Grew* by Harriet M. *Lothrop.

Piacevoli Notti, Le ('The Delightful Nights'), A collection of stories published in Venice in two parts in 1550 and 1553. It includes the tale of *Puss in Boots and a story resembling *Diamonds and Toads*. It was the work of Gianfrancesco Straparola (*c*.1480– 1557). The book was translated into French in 1560 (the second volume in 1573) and may have been known to *Perrault, who later published his own versions of the two stories mentioned above. Certainly other French writers of *fairy stories in the late 17th cent. borrowed from Straparola's collection.

PIAGET, Jean (1896–1980) Swiss developmental psychologist, the creator of influential theories of cognitive development. These theories, partly evolved through observation of his own three children, identified progressive stages of development, including the development of cognitive structures. Among his interests was the process of the development of knowledge, and in particular of conceptual and figurative thought. His outlines for the process of a child's and teenager's development (basic and improving sensorimotor

skills, curiosity, early speech and play, decreasing egocentrism, manipulating symbols, sophisticated questioning, ability to handle abstract thought, etc.) have been an important influence in many educational settings, especially early-years classrooms, and have inspired the shift towards a more 'child-centred' and interactive approach, but are also instructive for an understanding of what and how children and teenagers can read. Significant books by Piaget include *Le Langage et la pensée chez l'enfant* (1923; *The Language and Thought of the Child*, 1926); *La Représentation du monde chez l'enfant* (1926; *The Child's Conception of the World*, 1929)); *La Naissance de l'intelligence chez l'enfant* (1936; *The Origin of Intelligence in the Child*, 1953) and *La Construction du réel chez l'enfant* (1937; *The Child's Construction of Reality*, 1954).

PICARD, Barbara Leonie (1917–2011) British children's author who wrote a large number of retellings of traditional stories, from *The Odyssey of Homer* (1952) to *Tales of Ancient Persia* (1972), as well as *historical novels and original *fairy stories.

picture books Illustrated books, most often for younger children, usually in a large flat format with relatively few pages (32 is typical). Unlike, say, some illustrated fiction, the artwork is in no way seen as subservient to the text, but part of a balanced, integrated whole.

Among the earliest 'books' combining words and pictures which were looked at by the young were the Japanese illustrated scrolls of the 12th and 13th cents. Medieval *bestiaries, too, were often looked at by children.

In contrast, the earliest English printed books did not contain much in the way of illustration because of the technical limitations of *woodcuts at that time. *Caxton's edition of *Aesop's Fables* (1484) was one of the most generously illustrated books of the period. The first true picture book for children in England was Charles *Hoole's 1659 translation of the *Orbis Sensualium Pictus* of *Comenius.

During the early 18th cent., pictorial *ABC books for children began to appear. Newbery's *Pretty Book of Pictures for Little Masters and Misses* (published by 1752) was a small picture book resembling the bestiaries. The first English children's publisher to make a regular practice of issuing books for young children in which pictures predominated over text was John *Harris; his *Mother Hubbard* (1805) and *The *Butterfly's Ball* set a new fashion and spawned countless imitations. Harris was also among the first publishers to produce

children's books in which *colour played a considerable part.

Edward *Lear's drawings played such a large part in his *Book of Nonsense* (1846) that it may be considered as virtually a picture book; two years later came the first English edition of *Struwwelpeter* produced in Germany by *lithography. In the next decade, the firms of *Routledge and *Warne were among those who began to produce their own *toy books; from about 1865 Routledge's list included many by Walter *Crane, superbly engraved and printed in colour by Edmund *Evans. Evans also began to produce books for Warne, and towards the end of the 1870s he started to commission work from Randolph *Caldecott and Kate *Greenaway, who together with Crane raised the British picture book to a standard it had never before reached. (In the following century, these two illustrators would give their names to the most prestigious picture-book illustration awards in the US and UK, respectively.) Most other countries which now possess a highly developed literature for children produced their first picture books in the late 19th cent., for example, in Australia, *Cole's Funny Picture Book* (1879), and, in Norway, the *Norsk Billedbok for Barn* (1888).

By the early 20th cent. the focus of the picture book was becoming less on instruction and more on entertainment. The most notable examples of the period were those of Beatrix *Potter, whose *Tale of Peter Rabbit*, published in 1902, began a long and brilliant series.

In the 1930s auto-lithography, in which the artist draws directly on to the stone or plate, began to be used widely in the production of picture books, early examples being the French *Babar series, and, in Britain, Kathleen *Hale's *Orlando books. America's contribution to picture books between the World Wars included the introduction of a cartoon-like graphic style, particularly in stories by Dr *Seuss (1937 onwards). In Britain, Edward *Ardizzone began to write and draw his '*Little Tim' stories, with *Tim All Alone* (1955) winning the first *Kate Greenaway Medal. In America, Margaret Wise Brown and Clement Hurd produced *Goodnight Moon* (1947), in which a little rabbit slowly falls asleep in a room full of objects that grows slightly darker at each turn of the page.

In the years after the Second World War, improvements in the process of offset lithography greatly widened the scope of the picture book. By the 1960s it was possible for artists to work in full colour, using such widely differing

media as watercolour, gouache, collage, or pastel, and have their work produced comparatively cheaply. In consequence the picture book came into its first golden age in the hands of such notable artists as, in Britain, Raymond *Briggs, Charles *Keeping, and Brian *Wildsmith, and, in America, Ezra Jack *Keats, Richard *Scarry, Maurice *Sendak, and Eric *Carle. Sendak's subversive and many-layered *Where the Wild Things Are* (1963) is about as close to a perfect picture book as it is possible to be. Carle's painterly and interactive *The *Very Hungry Caterpillar* (1969) is still one of the most popular picture books today.

The concept of the picture book began to be more sophisticated, with the text and illustrations working in conversation, rather than one merely reflecting the other. Examples include *Rosie's Walk* (1968) by Pat *Hutchins, where the seemingly bland text appears to tell one story, while the illustrations reveal something much more exciting. John *Burningham's *Come Away from the Water, Shirley* (1977) demonstrates an even greater distance between words and pictures. The deliberately pedestrian text depicts Shirley's parents' mundane view of their family trip to the beach, while the pictures show Shirley's entirely different, highly imaginative experience of the day.

Throughout the latter decades of the 20th cent., picture books continued to grow in scope and inventiveness, in terms of their range of artistic styles (from traditional line-and wash to computer-generated), their interactivity (with pop-ups, flaps, and many other paper engineering devices), and their target audience (from babies to adults).

In the 1970s and 1980s, Shirley Hughes's beautifully realized books depicted the minutiae of a small child's daily life. These included *Dogger* (1977) and the *Alfie books (from 1981). Quentin *Blake is one of the foremost creators of the picture book in the modern age. His exuberant, deceptively simple illustrations and witty text can be seen in such classics as *Mister Magnolia* (1980) and *Fantastic Daisy Artichoke* (1999). Other illustrators prominent in the UK during this period included Helen *Oxenbury, David *McKee, Tony *Ross, Janet *Ahlberg, Michael *Foreman, Charlotte *Voake, Angela *Barrett, Patrick Benson, Max *Velthuijs, Judith *Kerr, Jan *Pieńkowski, Jan Fearnley, Debi *Gliori, Helen *Cooper, and Satoshi *Kitamura.

By the 21st cent. the range of outstanding picture books has become overwhelming, both in quality and diversity of approach. In the US, leading creators of picture books include Chris *Van Allsburg, David *Wiesner, Chris *Raschka, Lane *Smith, and Jerry *Pinkney; Ian Falconer has created the internationally beloved *Olivia, while Mo *Willems' books about a headstrong pigeon have a cartoon style with quirky humour. Australian picturebook authors and illustrators who have led the way in recent years include Shaun *Tan, Margaret *Wild, Ron *Brooks, Elaine Russell, Jackie *French, and Bruce *Whatley. From New Zealand, Lynley Dodd's *Hairy Maclary* has been hugely popular for three decades. Canadian Jon *Klassen's *This is Not My Hat* is notable for its slightly surreal, offbeat humour, while his compatriot Melanie Watt has created the highly popular *Scaredy Squirrel*.

Lauren *Child in the UK uses an eclectic mixture of painting, collage and photography, expressive typography, and a distinctively witty writing style. Nick *Sharratt employs computer technology to produce bold, graphic images. Emily *Gravett uses her remarkable drawing talent to produce picture books that are classic and beautiful in their appearance, but that subvert the whole picture-book genre in their content. Julia *Donaldson is one of the outstanding picture-book writers of recent times, using that most difficult of forms, the rhyming couplet, to stunning effect. *The *Gruffalo* (1999), created with her regular picture book partner Axel *Scheffler, is a modern classic. Other notable and critically acclaimed exponents from Britain and Ireland include Emma *Chichester Clark, Chris *Riddell, Lydia Monks, Mini *Grey, Adrian Reynolds, Rebecca Cobb, Ed Vere, Oliver *Jeffers, Chris *Haughton, and Catherine *Rayner.

Picture books are by no means con ned to the preschool age, with many complex and thought-provoking picture books existing for older readers, and indeed, for adults. The year 1998 was notable for such titles, all of them in the large format typically associated with books for the very young: Neil *Gaiman and Dave *McKean's *The Day I Swapped My Dad for Two Goldfish* is surreally humorous; *Voices in the Park* by Anthony *Browne is rich and multilayered; and Quentin Blake's *Zagazoo*, although entertaining to a four-year-old, can only be fully appreciated by an adult.

Pied Piper of Hamelin, The A celebrated narrative poem for children by Robert Browning (1812–89), first published in 1842 in *Dramatic Lyrics*, the third part of Browning's *Bells and Pomegranates*, where it was subtitled 'A Child's Story' and dedicated to 'W.M. the

Younger'—Willie Macready, son of the cele-brated actor.

Browning knew the story of the Pied Piper from childhood; his father wrote a verse nar-rative of it with illustrations. Browning also read versions of it in Nathaniel Wanley's *Won-ders of the Little World* (1678) and in the *Epis-tolae Ho-Elianae* of James Howell (1650). The tale appears in a number of other books, in-cluding Verstegan's *Restitution of Decayed In-telligence* (1634); the oldest written record of it dates from about 1450. This, apparently the work of the Dominican historian Heinrich von Herford, tells how in the town of Hamelin, which is near Hanover, in the year 1284, on the Feast of St John and St Paul (16 June), a strikingly handsome young man came over the bridge and in through the Weser Gate of the town, carrying a strange silvery pipe which he began to play. At once all the children who heard the pipe—almost 130—began to follow him. He led them out through the East Gate, whereupon they disappeared and no news could be discovered of them.

The same story is recorded in a 16th-cent. South German chronicle, where for the first time it is stated that the piper was a ratcatcher, hired to rid the town of a plague of rats but later defrauded of the agreed payment by the town councillors, whereupon he revenged himself by kidnapping the children. This, with the addition of the magically opening mountain, the lame boy, and the hint that the children finally reappear in Transylvania, is the outline of Browning's poem.

The story can in fact be related to a group of folk tales in which a magician, cheated of a promised reward, leads animals or children away. In one such tale, the town of Lorch (also in Germany) is cleared of a plague of ants by a hermit who, when denied his pay-ment, drives the inhabitants' pigs into the lake; and there is also a tale of an old man who clears away a town's rats, and, for his revenge on the defrauding councillors, leads the chil-dren into the mountain. Nevertheless there have been serious attempts to relate the story of *The Pied Piper* to some historical event.

A common interpretation is to connect the legend with the *Children's Crusade of 1212, when thousands of children in France and Germany left home, never to return. Others suggest that the story may have grown from a local feud in 1260 between Minden (in which diocese Hamelin stood) and Sede-münd, which caused the death of the greater part of the youth of Hamelin. It has also been observed that towards the end of the 13th cent. young people from Hamelin were enlisted by a representative of one Count von Shaumberg to colonize the territory of Moravia.

Browning was not at first very keen to publish his *Pied Piper*, having written it in May 1842 merely for the amusement of Willie Macready, who made some illustrations for it which Browning preserved. But once in print it was quickly recognized as a children's classic. Coventry Patmore included it in his pioneer anthology of children's verse, *The *Children's Garland From the Best Poets* (1862), and it has appeared in innumerable collections since that time. In 1888 Edmund *Evans printed an edition of the poem for which he engraved illustrations by Kate *Greenaway; Charles *Robinson illustrated an edition of 1907 and Arthur *Rackham one of 1934. Terry Pratchett used the Pied Piper story as the basis for his *Discworld fantasy *The *Amazing Maurice and His Educated Rodents* (2001).

Piemakers, The (1967) A novel by Helen *Cresswell, illustrated by V. H. *Drummond. The Roller family of Danby Dale, hereditary piemakers, are commissioned to make a gi-gantic pie for the King. The book established its author's reputation as a comic novelist for children.

PIEŃKOWSKI, Jan (1936–) Author, illustra-tor, and creator of pop-up books who was born in Warsaw and spent his childhood in Poland, Austria, Germany, Italy, and England. He read Classics and English at King's College, Cambridge, where he began to design posters and greetings cards. This led to the formation of Gallery Five, a card and book publishing firm, of which he became a director. He began to illustrate books by other writers, in-cluding Joan *Aiken's *The Kingdom Under the Sea* (1971), using the distinctive silhouette style for which he is now famous. In 1972 he collaborated with Helen Nicoll on the first of the *Meg and Mog* books, which would be-come picture-book classics. *Haunted House* (1979) is a humorously spooky pop-up book, which helped to lead the revival of that genre in Britain, and he followed that success with *Robot* (1980) and *Dinner Time* (1981), along with many others in the same style. He has used his silhouette technique for several re-tellings of traditional stories: *The Fairy Tales* (2005), *The Thousand Nights and One Night* (2007) (*see* ARABIAN NIGHTS), *The First Christ-mas* (2009), the first two of these retold by David Walser.

PIERCE, Tamora (1953-) American writer of *young adult fantasy whose books all have strong female heroes, as she felt that they were missing from most of the books she had loved. As a child she wrote *fan-fiction as well as stories of her own, but it was only after university and an eclectic career involving everything from being a housemother to teenage girls to being a radio producer that she began to write full-time. *The Song of the Lioness* quartet (1983) is her most influential and tells of a girl's training to become a knight, and other books set in Tortall followed. The *Circle Opens* series (1993) is the first in the Circle universe.

Piglet In *Winnie-the-Pooh* and *The *House at Pooh Corner* by A. A. *Milne.

Pigman, The (1968) A groundbreaking *young adult novel by Paul *Zindel which has been studied in schools both in the USA and in the UK. Disaffected teens Lorraine and John tell the story, alternating chapter by chapter, of how they accidentally make friends with an old man, Mr Pignati, who lives in their neighbourhood. He offers them a different view of life from their own miserable one but they cannot escape their own natures, with tragic results. There is a sequel, *The Pigman's Legacy* (1980), and the story of how Zindel used his own troubled childhood as inspiration, *The Pigman and Me* (1991).

Pilgrim's Progress, The, *From this World to that which is to come* A religious allegory by John *Bunyan, published in 1678, with later changes and additions. While not specifically for children, it has always been thought fit for them, though usually in abridged form.

The events are seen in a dream. Christian, with burden on back, flees from his home in the City of Destruction. He makes his way through the mire of the Slough of Despond, battles with the monster Apollyon, and comes to the Valley of the Shadow of Death, Vanity Fair, Doubting Castle (home of Giant Despair), and other hazards, finally reaching the Celestial City. First Faithful, then Hopeful, keep Christian company, and he meets other allegorical figures on the way, such as his neighbours Obstinate and Pliable, Mr Worldly Wiseman, Talkative, Lord Hategood, and Ignorance. In Part II, published in 1684, Christian's wife Christiana and her children follow him, meeting their own companions and obstacles but on the whole finding their pilgrimage less arduous.

The Pilgrim's Progress is simple, often colloquial in language, and humorous. The story is a quest, related to the secular *romances Bunyan read in his youth, such as *Bevis of Hampton*, and the characters have a life in them that far exceeds the demands of the allegory. The book enjoyed huge popularity in Bunyan's lifetime and has been continually republished ever since, making it one of the most lasting books in English. For its first century it was the property of ordinary people, and was scarcely thought of as 'literature' warranting critical attention from educated adults; but at the beginning of the 19th cent. the Romantic interest in such literature of the people as the *ballads encompassed Bunyan, too, and gave *The Pilgrim's Progress* a place among the 'classics'.

In the introduction to Part II, Bunyan himself acknowledged that the book appealed to 'the very children that do walk the streets', and it had the inestimable advantage of being one of the few books allowed for children's Sunday reading in many households. From the fifth edition onward there were illustrations, but it was not until the 19th cent. that there were editions specially for children. *The Pilgrim's Progress* has been translated into more than a hundred languages, and since 1920 over sixty editions have been published in English alone.

Imitations have sometimes been composed, such as *The Indian Pilgrim* and *The Infant's Progress*, both written in the early 19th cent. by Mrs *Sherwood. The oddest of these is perhaps *The Kitten Pilgrims* (1882) by R. M. *Ballantyne. Bunyan's story is alluded to in many 19th-cent. children's books, notably *Little Women*, where it provides a series of metaphors for the girls' tribulations. In 2011 it was the basis for a graphic novel by Stephen T. Moore, which is testament to its appeal, longevity, and adaptability.

Pilgrim Street: *a story of Manchester life* (1867) A novel by Hesba *Stretton.

PILKEY, Dav *See* CAPTAIN UNDERPANTS.

PILKINGTON, Mary (1766–1839) English writer of *moral tales and other books for children. She was the wife of a naval surgeon and had worked for some time as a *governess. Her first book was accepted by Elizabeth *Newbery in 1797. This was *Obedience Rewarded, and Prejudice Conquered; or, the History of Mortimer Lascells*, the story of a boy who becomes a sailor at the suggestion of his admiral uncle. He is rewarded by inheriting most of the admiral's fortune.

Mrs Pilkington followed this with some forty-five books, including *Tales of the Hermitage* (1798) and *Tales of the Cottage* (1799), imitations of Mme de *Genlis.

Pilpay, Fables of See PANCHATANTRA.

PINCHARD, Mrs Elizabeth (*fl.* 1790), A writer of *moral tales, best known for *The Blind Child, or Anecdotes of the Wyndham Family* (1791), the tale of Helen Wyndham, blind since infancy, who eventually regains her sight. The heroine, who submits bravely to an operation on her eyes, and her family, who are present, are commended by the author for their true sensibility and fortitude.

Pinkie and the Fairies (1908) A *play by W. Graham Robertson, with music by Frederic Norton; the first London production included Ellen Terry in the cast.

PINKNEY, Jerry (1939-) American illustrator, born in Philadelphia, known for his realistic watercolour paintings. His work often focuses on African-American themes. Pinkney illustrated *The Planet of Junior Brown* (1971) by Virginia *Hamilton and *Roll of Thunder, Hear My Cry* (1977) by Mildred Taylor and he has collaborated with Julius *Lester on folk tales and *fables. He won the 2010 *Caldecott Medal for his retelling of the *Aesop's fable *The Lion and the Mouse*, and has won five Caldecott Honor awards. His five *Coretta Scott King Awards include *Goin' Someplace Special* (2001) by Patricia C. *McKissak and *Minty: A Story of Young Harriet Tubman* (1996) by Alan Schroeder. Pinkney was the United States nominee for the 1998 *Hans Christian Andersen Award.

PINKWATER, Daniel (1941-) American author and illustrator. His surreal, humorous science fiction features misfit child protagonists and villains ranging from junk food-loving space pirates to an orchestra-conducting orang-utan. Standout young adult books include *Lizard Music* (1976), in which Victor goes in search of the jazz-playing lizards that appear on his TV, and *The Snarkout Boys and the Avocado of Death* (1982), in which aliens masquerade as estate agents. Work for younger readers includes a series starring badly behaved polar bears Irving and Muktuk (2001-7) and the trippy picture book *The Big Orange Splot* (1977).

Pinnock's Catechisms An extensive series of *books of instruction for children containing questions and answers on many fields of knowledge. William Pinnock (1782-1843) was a Hampshire schoolmaster who became a bookseller and established himself in London. He wrote several elementary textbooks for children and prepared a new edition of *Mangnall's Questions*. On the latter, he and his business partner Samuel Maunder modelled the *Catechisms*, of which eighty-three were eventually published, beginning in about 1817. Titles included *A Catechism of Modern History, A Catechism of Geography, A Catechism of Music*, and *A Catechism of Mineralogy*. They were priced at 9*d.* each, and were extraordinarily successful. Although his name appeared on the title page, he was not himself the author of most of the catechisms, which were the work of persons knowledgeable in the various subjects.

Pinocchio (1883) By 'Carlo *Collodi' (Carlo Lorenzini), one of the best known *fantasies, and the most popular children's book to come out of Italy.

Gepetto carves a *puppet. From the beginning the puppet, which he names Pinocchio, can walk and talk just like a real boy; he has 'an immense nose of ridiculous proportions' that grows even longer when he tells a lie. Pinocchio is a terrible scamp; a talking Cricket that lives in his 'father' Gepetto's house warns him that no good will come of his bad behaviour, but Pinocchio crushes the Cricket dead for his pains. However the Cricket's ghost soon appears, and takes up the same role of moral adviser.

Gepetto buys Pinocchio a spelling-book and Pinocchio promises to go to school, but instead he sells the book to buy a ticket for a puppet show. The puppets greet him as one of their own kind. The puppetmaster kidnaps him, but is persuaded to let him go and even gives him five gold pieces to take home to his 'father'. A fox and a cat meet up with Pinocchio and learn about the money; they try every method of stealing it from him, and eventually succeed. In the course of these adventures Pinocchio meets a 'beautiful Child with blue hair', who eventually turns out to be his guardian *fairy.

Pinocchio ignores all her good advice, and is persuaded by another boy to follow him to an earthly paradise; however, Pinocchio and his friend discover that in due course all boys in that land turn into donkeys. This happens to them both, and the Pinocchio-donkey is sold first to a circus, then to a man who wants to drown it to use the donkey-skin to make a

drum. But under the water Pinocchio turns back into a puppet, and goes in search of his father.

He eventually finds Gepetto in the belly of a giant dogfish; he rescues him and sets up home with him on dry land, taking proper care of his 'father' at last. He is rewarded by the fairy, who turns him into a real boy.

The story was written for a Rome children's *magazine, the *Giornale dei bambini*, where the first instalment appeared on 7 July 1881. It was published as a book in 1883 under the title *Le Avventure di Pinocchio: Storia di un burattino* ('History of a Puppet'), and quickly became a best-seller. It was translated into English in 1892 by M. A. Murray, whose version was published that year in Britain and America.

The story's composition as a serial partly explains its character. Even so, Lorenzini seems to have taken little care with the construction of the plot; apparently he wrote episodes only when the whim took him or when he was persuaded by enthusiastic readers. Almost nothing else in children's literature equals *Pinocchio* for wildness of invention. Nor is it for the most part concerned with Pinocchio's nature as a puppet. If there is any theme to the story it is that of the Prodigal Son, and Lorenzini is always stressing the moral that Pinocchio gets into trouble because he is disobedient.

The story's very wildness is, however, part of its charm. Unfortunately through the years it has been gradually emasculated, losing much of its character, a process that was accelerated by the release of Walt *Disney's film in 1940. In the Disney version (now far better known than the book), the plot was tidied up and a great deal of Hollywood sentimentality was injected.

Pip, Squeak, and Wilfred A famous British *comic strip, featuring the adventures of a dog, a penguin, and a baby rabbit; it ran in the *Daily Mirror* from 1919 to 1953. There were also *annuals, films, etc.

PIPER, Watty See LITTLE ENGINE THAT COULD, THE.

Pippi Longstocking (*Pippi Långstrump*) (1945) A celebrated Swedish children's book by Astrid *Lindgren. The original illustrator was Ingrid Vang. The book was first translated into English in 1950 (USA) and 1954 (UK), and has appeared in more than sixty other languages.

Pippi is a nine-year-old redhead living by herself in Villekula Cottage, 'at the end of a little Swedish town'. She has superhuman strength: she can lift a horse in her arms, and when two policemen try to take her off to a Children's Home she picks them up by their belts. But she is also ungainly and untidy, and she specializes in tall stories and nonsensical backchat. One of the best scenes in the book describes her one and only day at school, during which she ridicules the entire educational system. She is usually accompanied by Tommy and Annika, conventionally good little children, who are open-mouthed at her exploits and sayings.

The book was by no means universally praised in Sweden when it was first published (one reviewer criticized 'the inanities of the crazy style'), but soon established itself as an international classic. There are two sequels, *Pippi Goes on Board* (1946, English translation 1956), and *Pippi in the South Seas* (1948, English 1957). There are recent English-language editions with illustrations by Lauren *Child (2010) and Tony *Ross (2012).

pirates Pirates began to appear as stock figures of children's literature in the mid-19th cent. Two of the first books to include them were *Feats on the Fjord* (1841) by Harriet *Martineau and *Peter the Whaler* (1851) by W. H. G. Kingston. Ballantyne's *The *Coral Island* followed in 1858. One source of information about them was Charles Johnson's *General History of the Robberies and Murders of the most notorious Pyrates* (1724). R. L. *Stevenson created the all-time classic of pirate literature in *Treasure Island* (1881), and J. M. Barrie invented the immortal Captain Hook in *Peter Pan* (1904). *Howard Pyle's Book of Pirates* (1921) added to their romance. A hundred years on, pirates remain hugely popular characters in picture books and early readers, as well as in older fiction, from *The *Great Piratical Rumbustification* and *Captain Pugwash, to Sky Pirates in Kenneth *Oppel's *Airborn* and in Stewart and Riddell's *Edge Chronicles*, and pirate vampires in Justin Somper's *Vampirates* fusion fantasy series (2005-11), to Celia *Rees's *Pirates!*, Tanith Lee's *Piratica* series (2004-7), and *The *Princess Bride*. International Talk Like a Pirate Day is a parody holiday celebrated on September 19th.

PITZ, Henry C. (Clarence) (1895-1976) American illustrator, contributor to *St Nicholas*; he wrote on the life and work of Howard

*Pyle and on the technique of illustrating for children.

PLANCHÉ, James Robinson (1796–1880) Playwright who was the author of a large number of *pantomimes, burlesques, and extravaganzas performed in London from the 1830s to the 1870s. He made translations of the stories of Mme d'*Aulnoy and *Perrault, and adapted several of them for the stage. It is said that his work influenced the librettos of W. S. Gilbert. His daughter Matilda Anne, afterwards Mrs Mackarness, wrote *moral tales for children, most notably *A Trap to Catch a Sunbeam* (1849).

***Playbook for Children, A,** To Allure them to Read as soon as they can Speak Plain* By 'J.G.', one of the earliest books to attempt to teach reading by means of amusement. It was published in 1694 in London by one John Harris; no connection is known between him and the celebrated early 19th-cent. children's bookseller of the same name. The title-page explains that the book is 'Composed of small Pages, on Purpose not to tire Children, and Printed with a fair and Pleasant Letter. The Matter and Method plainer and easier than any yet Extant'.

The book, which is in well-spaced type, consists chiefly of sentences beginning with each letter of the alphabet, e.g. 'Tops are whipt when 'tis cold to get Boys a heat'. There are also lists of words arranged in one, two, and three syllables.

The *Playbook* anticipated by a few years a **Little Book For Little Children* by 'T.W.', and was the precursor of many 18th-cent. reading books of this type. It seems to have been the first attempt to break away from the dull, unchildlike *primers of the 16th-cent. and 17th-cent. schoolrooms, and was probably inspired by John *Locke, whose *Some Thoughts Concerning Education* appeared the year before it was published.

Playfellow, The (1841) Series title of stories by Harriet *Martineau.

Playing Beatie Bow (1980) A *time-slip story by Australian author Ruth *Park. Prickly Abigail Kirk travels back in time over a hundred years to 1873, where she meets Beatie Bow. Abigail is adopted by the working-class Bow family, who welcome 'the Stranger' into their family. Abigail will save the gift of prophecy for the family and learn how to love. Park has accurately rendered historical Sydney, the setting, the characters, the work, and the language. The book was made into a film in 1986.

plays For many years children's theatre in general fared better outside Britain than in it. In the USA, Charlotte *Chorpenning ran, and wrote plays for, the successful Goodman Children's Theater in Chicago from 1931 to 1952. Aurand *Harris was another prolific American children's playwright, who drew chiefly on classic children's stories and novels for his dramatizations. There was an active children's theatre in Australia, New Zealand, and Canada. In Europe, Scandinavia led the way, with Denmark having achieved much. Russia has had highly developed children's theatre companies since the 1920s.

In England and France plays written for children began to appear in the late 18th cent., when a number of writers of *moral tales cast some of their stories in dialogue or dramatic form. The *Theatre of Education* (1779–80) of Mme de *Genlis was a four-volume collection of comedies for performance by girls, intended for moral instruction. Other works in play form included *Berquin's *L'Ami des enfans* (1782–3), *Sacred Dramas* (1782) by Hannah *More, and *Dramas for Children: imitated from the French of L. F. Jauffret* (1809) by William *Godwin, or more probably his wife Mary Jane. The first English children's writer to compose plays intended chiefly for amusement seems to have been Maria *Edgeworth, whose *Parent's Assistant* (1796) included a one-act play, 'Old Poz'.

These early European writers of children's plays were not catering for the professional theatre, but simply for performance or reading at home or at school. The professional stage was long regarded as a danger to morals. However, from the end of the 18th cent. *pantomimes in British theatres provided children with a Christmas entertainment that was considered respectable by most parents. Meanwhile at home boys and girls could amuse themselves with *toy theatres. Many also saw *mummers' plays performed at Christmas, and themselves acted charades.

In 1854 the London firm of *Dean began to issue a series of 'Little Plays' by Julia *Corner, who argued that theatricals could be morally acceptable. The publication of *Alice's Adventures in Wonderland* (1865) and *Through the Looking-Glass* (1871) spawned a number of adaptations of both stories for acting, the first of each being made by Kate Freilgrath-Kroeker in 1880 and 1882 respectively.

Alice first appeared on the professional stage in an 'operetta' written by H. Savile Clark with music by Walter Slaughter, performed in 1886. Other celebrated children's books to be dramatized at this period include *Vice Versa* (first stage version 1883), *Little Lord Fauntleroy* (1888), *The *Rose and the Ring* (1890), *The *Water-Babies* (1902), *Struwwelpeter* (about 1903), and *Sara Crewe* (dramatized in 1902 by its author, Mrs Frances Hodgson *Burnett, as *A Little Princess*, under which title the book was subsequently reissued).

In 1904 J. M. *Barrie wrote *Peter Pan*, an outstanding piece of theatre which thereafter was revived annually in London. Five years later came the English translation of Maeterlinck's *The *Blue Bird*, a masterpiece of its kind, but very difficult to stage. The next original English children's play to make an impact was Clifford Mills and John Ramsey's fantasy *Where the Rainbow Ends* (1911).

A. A. *Milne was a successful playwright as well as a children's author, and among his works for the stage is *Make-Believe* (1918). Milne also adapted *The *Wind in the Willows* for the stage in 1929, as *Toad of Toad Hall*, thereby creating another Christmas 'regular' in the West End of London. Another British favourite in the post-war period was *The Windmill Man* (1921) by Frederick Bowyer (a writer of popular musical comedies), in which a selfish prince and his sister learn to do better through being punished by their toys.

In the years immediately following the Second World War a number of attempts were made to establish high-quality professional children's theatre in Britain. Caryl Jenner founded the touring company that would eventually become the Unicorn Theatre, for many years based at the Arts Theatre in London, but since 2005 at a purpose-built home on the South Bank of the Thames. Much work was also done by Brian Way, whose London Children's Theatre was founded in 1954. Plays were written by a number of authors, notably Nicholas Stuart *Gray, who made many stage adaptations of well known *fairy stories which received professional productions. However, economic considerations made it impossible to do much of this kind, and more was achieved by small touring companies (sometimes offshoots of provincial repertory theatres) visiting schools. Christmas pantomimes and such musicals as *Oliver!* (Lionel Bart's adaptation of Dickens's *Oliver Twist*) proved to be almost the only commercially successful stage shows for children, and

not until David *Wood began writing children's musical plays in the late 1960s did children's theatre find an author who could fill theatres and yet provide material of quality solely for children. The 1970s saw the foundation of the Children's Music Theatre, directed by Jeremy James Taylor, staging original musical plays performed by schoolchildren.

Much recent children's theatre in London and the UK has been based on existing books, whether adaptations for young children of picture books, such as those by Julia *Donaldson and Axel *Scheffler, Polly *Dunbar (several books brilliantly dramatized by Long Nose Puppets, a company Dunbar herself cofounded), or Judith Kerr's *The *Tiger Who Came To Tea*; Alan Bennett's much-loved *Wind in the Willows* (1990); or West End musical versions of Dahl's *Matilda* or *Charlie and the Chocolate Factory*. The Royal National Theatre has for some years developed major productions (often Christmas shows for families) out of existing children's or *young adult fiction—notable productions include *His Dark Materials* (2003), *Coram Boy* (2005), *War Horse* (2007), Terry *Pratchett's *Nation* (2009), and *The *Curious Incident of the Dog in the Night-Time* (2012).

Pleasant Work for Busy Fingers *See* WANTED: A KING.

PLOWMAN, Stephanie (1922–) British children's author of *historical novels, best known for her stories set in the last days of Imperial Russia: *Three Lives for the Czar* (1969) and *My Kingdom for a Grave* (1970). She has also written novels set in classical Greece.

Pluck One of *Harmsworth's adventure papers for boys, founded in 1894. At first it contained true stories (of Nelson, General Gordon, etc.), but soon it turned to fiction, printing *Nelson Lee adventures. In 1906 Charles *Hamilton ('Frank Richards') created *St Jim's, the first of his famous schools, in its pages, using his real name. The magazine ended in 1916, but its name was revived briefly in 1922 for 'A Great New Story Weekly', also published by Harmsworth's Amalgamated Press, which lasted for two years.

PLUMLY THOMPSON, Ruth *See* BAUM, L. FRANK.

Plutarch's Lives Translated into English by Sir Thomas North in 1579, *Plutarch's Lives* were first issued in an edition for children by John *Newbery in 1762–3. Other juvenile versions subsequently

appeared, among them F. J. Gould's *The Children's Plutarch* (1906), which had illustrations by Walter *Crane.

Pluto (the dog) A *Disney cartoon character.

Pobble Who Has No Toes, The A poem by Edward *Lear, first published in *Laughable Lyrics* (1876).

poetry for children (in the English language) Poetry has been used as a means of teaching and entertaining children for many centuries. Many *nursery rhymes have ancient origins, and traditional *ballads have played a large part in children's reading matter. Several 15th-cent. *books of courtesy laid out their precepts in verse. The *Puritans of the 17th cent. were the first English writers to use poetry methodically as a means of instructing children in religion, and *A *Book for Boys and Girls* (1686) by John *Bunyan may justly be called the first notable book of verse for children. Other Puritans who wrote poems for young readers include Abraham *Chear, Nathaniel *Crouch, and Benjamin *Keach. In 1715 there appeared the first edition of *Divine Songs* by Isaac *Watts, in which Puritan ideas found a milder form of expression; for the next century and a half it was one of the most widely distributed books for children in the English-speaking world.

The later 18th cent. saw the appearance of poems for children by, among others, John *Gay, Nathaniel *Cotton, and Christopher *Smart, but nothing of permanent importance appeared in England between Watts's book and the printing in 1789 of *Songs of Innocence* by William *Blake. Fifteen years later came *Original Poems, for Infant Minds*, chiefly by Ann and Jane *Taylor. Less remarkable as verse than the Taylors' efforts, but just as popular and even more widely imitated, was *The *Butterfly's Ball* (1806) by William Roscoe. The doggerel verses of the first *Mother Hubbard* book (1805) quickly became a staple of children's reading, along with the verse adventures of *Dame Trot and *Dame Wiggins of Lee.

America began to produce notable children's poetry in the first half of the 19th cent. Clement Clarke Moore's *A *Visit From St Nicholas* appeared in 1823 and Sara Josepha Hale's *Mary had a little lamb* in 1830. Moreover many children read and enjoyed the works of such major American poets as Longfellow (*see* Hiawatha) and John Greenleaf *Whittier. Minor but prolific children's poets of this century included, in America, Eliza *Follen and Eugene *Field, and, in England, Felicia *Hemans, Mary *Howitt, William *Allingham, and William Brighty *Rands.

Three children's verse classics appeared in England during the 1840s: *The *Pied Piper of Hamelin* (1842), Edward *Lear's first *Book of Nonsense* (1846), and the English translation of *Struwwelpeter* (1848). Notable collections published during the second half of the 19th cent. include *Goblin Market* (1862) by Christina *Rossetti; two pioneer anthologies, Coventry Patmore's *Children's Garland* (1862) and J. G. Whittier's *Child Life* (1871); and R. L. *Stevenson's outstanding *A *Child's Garden of Verses* (1885). Stevenson was a considerable influence on Walter *de la Mare, whose *Songs of Childhood* (1902) was followed by *Peacock Pie* (1913). De la Mare's *Come Hither* (1923) was an outstanding anthology.

English poets of the 20th cent. who have written notably for children include Roy *Fuller, Robert *Graves, Ted *Hughes, and James *Reeves. Hilaire *Belloc's various collections of satirical poems continue to be popular, as does T. S. Eliot's *Old Possum's Book of Practical Cats* (1939). Among many modern British anthologies is *The *Rattle-Bag* (1982), edited by Seamus Heaney and Ted Hughes. Memorable American collections of children's poems include Ogden *Nash's *Parents Keep Out* (1951), Lucille *Clifton's *Some of the Days of Everett Anderson* (1970), and Clyde *Watson's *Father Fox's Pennyrhymes* (1971).

The late 1970s saw the appearance of the exuberant and witty Kit Wright (1944–), and by the end of the century many poets were taking a playful attitude to children's poetry, with the emergence in the UK of 'urchin verse'. This involved collections such as Michael *Rosen's *Quick, Let's Get Out of Here* (1983), Allan *Ahlberg's *Please Mrs Butler* (1983), and Benjamin *Zephaniah's *Talking Turkeys* (1995). These collections were placed firmly in the modern-day child's experience—school, the playground, and around the house—and were written for a wider demographic. More traditional rhyming poetry was also presented in a mischievous light in the novels of Roald *Dahl and led to the collection *Revolting Rhymes* (1998). Much modern-day poetry for children in the 21st cent. is confined to the picture book and thus aimed at younger children, such as the work of Julia *Donaldson. In America, poets such as Shel *Silverstein, Jack *Prelutsky, and Theodor Geisel (Dr *Seuss) remain popular. *See also* VERSE NOVELS.

Poetry for Children (1809) By Charles and Mary *Lamb, published by the *Godwins as 'by the author of *Mrs Leicester's School'*. Mary wrote about two-thirds of the poems, many of which are tediously didactic. The book soon went out of print, though many verses from it were included in *The First Book of Poetry, for the use of schools*, edited by W. F. Mylius and published by the Godwins in 1811. An American edition was printed in Boston in 1812. *Poetry for Children* was reissued in 1872 and 1878, edited by Richard Herne Shepherd, and in 1892 Andrew *Tuer published a facsimile of the first edition.

Poetry for Children, *consisting of short pieces to be committed to memory* (1801) An anthology compiled by Lucy Aikin (1781–1864), niece of Anna Laetitia *Barbauld and daughter of John *Aikin. Unlike her aunt, whose *Hymns in Prose for Children* were written in the conviction that children could not appreciate poetry, Miss Aikin believed that 'the magic of rhyme is felt in the very cradle.' Her book included 'The Old Man's Comforts, And How He Gained Them', the poem by *Southey that *Carroll parodied in 'You are old, Father William', as well as pieces from Pope, Dryden, and Mrs Barbauld herself. The book was several times revised by Miss Aikin and others, continuing to appear in print until about 1845.

POGÁNY, Willy (Vilmos) (1882–1956) Hungarian-born illustrator who worked largely in America from about 1914, and was also known as a painter and designer. Children's books with illustrations by him include several by Padraic *Colum, an edition of *Gulliver's Travels* (1917), and *The Golden Cockerel* (1936).

POLACCO, Patricia (1944–) Prolific American author and illustrator. Her upbringing in multicultural neighbourhoods and on Midwestern farms and her close relationship with her grandparents are recurring influences on her work. *Chicken Sunday* (1992) is based on Polacco's childhood friendship with two African-American boys, a friendship that continues today. In *Mrs Katz and Tush* (1994), an elderly Jewish woman and an African-American boy become friends. Polacco's Russian-Ukrainian-Jewish grandmother appears in *Babushka's Doll* (1990) and *Babushka's Mother Goose* (2000). Polacco won the Sydney Taylor Book Award for *The Keeping Quilt* in 1988 and again in 2014 for its prequel, *The Blessing Cup*.

Polar Express, The (1985) A picture book by Chris *Van Allsburg that is now an American Christmas favourite. It tells the story of a boy on Christmas Eve who sees a train—the Polar Express—pull up outside his window. It carries him and hundreds of other children up to the North Pole, where he is selected by *Santa Claus to receive the first gift of Christmas—he chooses a bell from Santa's sleigh. When he gets home he discovers that his parents can't hear the bell's sound—only he and his sister can hear it, because they still believe. It won the 1986 *Caldecott Medal, and was adapted for the big screen in 2004.

Polar Scenes *See* CAMPE.

POLITI, Leo (1908–96) American author-illustrator, specializing in stories about Mexican children in California; he won the *Caldecott Medal for *Song of the Swallows* (1949), about the friendship between a small Mexican boy and an old bell-ringer at a mission.

Pollock's Toy Museum *See* TOY THEATRES.

Polly Character in the *Mr Gum books. (This is not her real name.)

Polly and Oliver Hero and heroine of stories by David Scott *Daniell.

Pollyanna (1913) A novel by the American writer Eleanor Hodgman Porter (1868–1920). Pollyanna Whittier comes to live with her spinster aunt in Vermont after the death of her father. She has a perpetually sunny disposition, and her favourite word is 'glad': 'Oh, Aunt Polly, Aunt Polly, I don't know how to be glad enough that you let me come to live with you.' She is knocked down by a motor-car and paralysed, but she recovers, and as a result of her good influence the previously sour-tempered aunt acquires a sunny disposition and marries the doctor who has treated Pollyanna.

Porter wrote a number of popular novels. *Pollyanna*, which became an international best-seller, has been dramatized and filmed several times. The first sequel, *Pollyanna Grows Up* (1915), was by the original author, but after her death a number of other writers produced further Pollyanna novels.

Pompey the Little *See* ANIMAL STORIES.

Pony for Jean, A (1936) By Joanna Cannan (1898–1961), one of the first *pony stories, virtually a prototype for its genre. Jean's family leave London to go to the country, where she is introduced to the delight of ponies by her

cousins. She is given The Toastrack, an animal regarded as a dud; she renames him Cavalier, spends hour after hour grooming and training him, and eventually wins a host of prizes in a gymkhana. Joanna Cannan was the mother of Christine, Diana, and Josephine *Pullein-Thompson.

pony stories for girls are descended from *Black Beauty* (1877). The first pony novel, *Moorland Mousie* (1929), closely resembles Beauty's story, but the next two notable examples, *Doney* (1934) by Primrose *Cumming and *A *Pony For Jean* (1936) by Joanna Cannan, pay as much attention to the girl riders as to the animals. Enid Bagnold's *National Velvet* (1930), though about a horse rather than a pony, belongs to the same genre.

From the start, one pony story was much the same as another. In the standard formula the heroine, usually a tomboy on the verge of adolescence who dresses in an Aertex shirt, shorts, and sandshoes, acquires a broken-down pony that is 'a perfect wreck', but which with loving care becomes not just 'a jolly pet' but the best jumper at the gymkhana. Parents give encouragement from the sidelines and provide funds, stables, and sometimes grooms.

Later practitioners in the genre include the three daughters of Joanna Cannan, Christine, Diana, and Josephine *Pullein-Thompson. Mary *Treadgold's *We Couldn't Leave Dinah* (1941) aimed to improve on the standard of pony books, and the stories by Monica *Edwards (1947 onwards) and Patricia Leitch (1960 onwards) continue to be read. *The *Far-Distant Oxus* (1937) by Katharine Hull and Pamela Whitlock, two schoolgirl authors, set a slightly different pattern—copied by later authors—in combining ponies with the type of adventure associated with Arthur *Ransome. *See also* HORSE STORIES.

Pooh *See* WINNIE-THE-POOH.

Poor Cecco (1925) A story about a wooden toy dog, by Margery *Williams.

Poor Little Rich Girl, The (1912) A novel by the American writer Eleanor Gates (1875–1951). Seven-year-old Gwendolyn, daughter of a rich society family, lives an isolated life, kept in the nursery and away from her mother and father. Taken ill, she has a dream in which all her misunderstandings of the adult world become realities: people are literally 'two-faced' or 'level-headed' or 'empty-headed'. The book was very popular in its day; it was made into a Broadway play (1916) and a film (1917) which starred Mary Pickford. Eleanor Gates was the author of nine other children's books.

Popeye the sailor-man American cartoon hero, created by E(lzie) C(risler) Segar (1894–1938) for *comic strips, and on film from 1933. Popeye has a pipe clenched between his teeth, he is passionately devoted to a lady named Olive Oyl, and, after consuming a strength-giving can of spinach, invariably conquers such opponents as his arch-enemy Bluto.

Popular Fairy Tales; or, *a Liliputian [sic] Library* A collection published in 1818 by Sir Richard Phillips & Co. It includes retellings of all the prose *fairy stories of *Perrault, several by Mme d'*Aulnoy, and a number of English *chapbook tales. The title-page claimed that the stories were 'now first collected and revised by Benjamin Tabart', but in fact the book was largely composed of texts that had already appeared from 1804 onwards in *Tabart's series *Popular Stories*.

Popular Rhymes and Nursery Tales (1849) A collection by J. O. *Halliwell, sequel to his *Nursery Rhymes of England*. It contained further rhymes and many traditional British prose tales that were here printed for the first time.

Popular Stories A series issued by the London bookseller *Tabart between 1804 and 1809. It consisted of newly-written versions of the most popular *fairy stories and *chapbook tales, illustrated with *copperplates.

The series began with the publication in 1804 of three volumes under the title *Tabart's Collection of Popular Stories for the Nursery: newly translated and revised, from the French, Italian, and old English writers*. These volumes contained stories such as: *Dick Whittington, *Fortunatus, *Robin Hood, *Jack the Giant-Killer, *Tom Thumb, *Goody Two-Shoes, The *Seven Champions of Christendom, *Valentine and Orson, and all the *Perrault stories. Between 1804 and 1809 further stories were published separately, under the series title *Popular Stories*; these included *Aladdin and *Ali Baba (1805), and the first printing of the now conventional form of *Jack and the Beanstalk (by 1807). In 1809 a fourth compendium volume was issued (it was advertised in 1804, but seems not to have been published that year) which contained these three stories, together with *Nourjahad; an Eastern Tale* and *Sindbad the Sailor*.

The series, whose texts subsequently became the standard nursery versions of many

of the stories, is sometimes said to have been edited by William *Godwin, though it seems more likely that his wife Mary Jane undertook the work.

Popular Tales from the Norse (1859) The first English translation of the Norwegian folk tales collected by *Asbjørnsen and Moe. It was the work of Sir George Webbe Dasent (1817–96). Dasent also translated the *Prose* or *Younger *Edda* in 1842, and *The Story of Burnt Njal* (1861). He wrote that his *Popular Tales* were meant for children and adults alike; in 1862 he brought out a selection especially for children, with illustrations. His translations have often been reprinted, and remain the standard English versions of the tales. To the second edition of *Popular Tales from the Norse* (also 1859) Dasent added a number of West Indian Ananzi stories (*see* ANANSE) told to him by his African nurse during his childhood on those islands.

pop-up books *See* MOVABLE PICTURE BOOKS; NOVELTY BOOKS.

PORTER, Eleanor H. *See* POLLYANNA.

PORTER, Gene Stratton (1863–1924) American novelist. A farmer's daughter, she grew up in Limberlost, Indiana. She wrote many magazine articles on *natural history, illustrated with her own expert photographs. Her most popular books were *Freckles* (1904), the story of a boy living in the Limberlost Swamp, and *A *Girl of the Limberlost* (1909).

PORTER, Sheena (1935–) British children's author. She won the *Carnegie Medal for one of her novels, *Nordy Bank* (1964), which starts out as an *adventure story set at the site of an Iron Age hill fort in Shropshire, until a character becomes strangely influenced by the place.

Possum Magic (1983) A children's picture book written by Mem *Fox and illustrated by Julie *Vivas. It is one of the most popular Australian books, having sold over 3 million copies by its thirtieth anniversary in 2013. The book is now available in several editions and has a plush toy and more. Grandma Poss makes Hush invisible—it's fun at first but Hush changes her mind. They search for the right Australian food for Hush to eat and become visible again. Hush began life as mouse, and over half the book was illustrated when it was decided to strengthen the Australian theme and make her a possum. The story celebrates Australian food, places, bravery, and the relationship between Hush and her Grandma. The book broke new ground with its strongly composed beautiful watercolours and innovative use of white space.

Postcards from No Man's Land (1999) *Carnegie Medal-winning *young adult novel by Aidan *Chambers. Love, betrayal, sex, and self-discovery are all here, wrapped in a beautifully constructed, compulsively readable story for young adults that is paced like an adventure story, but is thought-provoking long after you finish the last page. There are two linked stories, both set in Amsterdam, one in the modern day and one in 1944, when the Netherlands was occupied by Germany. Jacob is in the city to commemorate his grandfather who fought at Arnhem, but what he discovers about the past changes him, as do the people he meets. Though the fifth in Chambers's *Dance Sequence*, this stands well on its own.

POSTGATE, Oliver (1925–2008) British television writer and producer who wrote and directed pioneering children's story programmes, alongside artist Peter Firmin (1928–). The studio for Smallfilms, their joint company, was Firmin's unused cowshed, where they did stop-motion with improvised puppets and models. Their programmes included *Ivor the Engine*, *The Saga of Noggin the Nog*, *The Clangers*, and *Bagpuss*, which also become successful books.

Postman Pat Hero of a British television cartoon series for small children, created by John Cunliffe and Ivor Wood; he also appears in a series of *picture books (1981 onwards).

POTTER, (Helen) Beatrix (Mrs Heelis) (1866–1943) Author of the 'Peter Rabbit' series of books who was born in London, the elder child and only daughter of Rupert Potter and his wife Helen. Life in the childhood home was very quiet, indeed oppressive; in old age Beatrix spoke of the house as 'my unloved birthplace'. During her early childhood she passed most of her day upstairs in the third-floor nursery, to which her meals were taken on a tray, and where she was supervised by McKenzie, her nurse. Her childhood reading included stories by Maria *Edgeworth and the Waverley novels of *Scott. Until she was five she had no child companion; then her brother Bertram was born, and despite the discrepancy in their ages the two became close friends.

Every summer the Potters rented a furnished house in the country for three months,

for many years in Scotland, then (when Beatrix was in her teens) in the Lake District. These holidays were a revelation to Beatrix. When she was seventy she wrote: 'It sometimes happens that the town child is more alive to the fresh beauty of the country than a child who is country born.'

She was never sent to school, but was taught by *governesses until she was in her early teens. Thereafter her education was neglected. On holiday, Beatrix and her brother collected botanical specimens, and also dead animals which they dissected with skill, sometimes managing to reassemble and articulate the skeletons. They also made drawings of plants and creatures. Beatrix drew and painted from an early age; she was encouraged by her father and, for a time, was instructed by a lady who gave lessons in drawing. By her teens she had developed something of a critical eye for art; her father, who was a friend of Millais, began to take her to Royal Academy exhibitions.

Besides bringing dead animals back to London from the country, Beatrix also smuggled live creatures into Bolton Gardens. These included at various times a hare, several rabbits (including two named Peter and Benjamin), mice, a tortoise, a white rat named Sammy, and a hedgehog, Mrs Tiggy, whom she described as 'a charming little creature, quite tame and apparently happy as long as it has sufficient flies and raw meat'.

Her adolescent years passed as uneventfully as her childhood. Her brother was sent away to school at Charterhouse, but Beatrix remained at Bolton Gardens, only very rarely leaving home for any length of time without her parents, though she was allowed to pass many hours at the South Kensington Museum (now the Victoria and Albert) and the Natural History Museum, drawing embroidery and fossils. She began to consider making a book of watercolours of fungi, but could find no expert to write the text and was told that her drawings lacked scientific details. Disappointed, she turned instead to sketching her pet animals dressed in clothes and engaged in human activities, in order to amuse her young cousins or other children.

By 1890 the idea had occurred to her that she might use some of these drawings for greetings or Christmas cards and, chaperoned by an uncle, she approached the London card-publishing firm of Hildesheimer and Faulkner with some specimens of her work. The result was the publication of a little book entitled *A Happy Pair*, a set of pictures of elegantly-clothed rabbits (signed 'H.B.P.') accompanied

by doggerel verses by Frederic Weatherley, a barrister and possibly a friend of Beatrix's father, who was the author of the song 'Roses of Picardy'. Beatrix's drawings for this show the influence of Randolph *Caldecott.

A Happy Pair made no sort of public impact. But in 1892 Beatrix began to write picture letters to the children of one of her former governesses, a Mrs Annie Moore. On 4 September 1893 she sent to five-year-old Noël Moore a letter which contained the first version of *The *Tale of Peter Rabbit*; Peter was the name of one of her current rabbit pets. Further letters to the Moores (who lived in Wandsworth) and other children contained outlines or hints of other tales about her pet animals.

As the 1890s passed, Beatrix's brother Bertram managed to slip away from Bolton Gardens and became a farmer in Roxburghshire. But Beatrix herself remained in London, as (in her biographer Margaret Lane's words) the 'captive unmarried daughter'. The chief event in this period of her life, in her early thirties, was the discovery of the village of Sawrey in the Lake District, where her family first stayed in 1896 and to which she at once became deeply attached for the beauty of its small cottages and farmhouses.

In the Lakes she became friends with Canon H. D. Rawnsley, who lived near Keswick. It seems to have been partly on his advice that, about six years after it was written, Beatrix reworked her picture letter about Peter Rabbit into a little book, with the hope of publication. Canon Rawnsley gave her the names of six publishers, whom she approached, but none of them was entirely prepared to accept the book in the form in which she proposed it. After a time Rawnsley encouraged her to have it privately printed. This was done, and the book was finished by December 1901 in an edition of 250 copies. Both Beatrix and the Canon kept in touch with the London publisher who had shown the greatest interest in it, Frederick *Warne & Co., and Warne's soon decided to produce their own edition. This was issued during 1902 and quickly became a popular success, Peter Rabbit toys appearing in Harrods and other London shops. Meanwhile Beatrix had commissioned the private printing of another story, *The *Tailor of Gloucester*. This too was eventually accepted by Warne, who published it in 1903 at the same time as a third story, *The Tale of Squirrel Nutkin*. Beatrix now began to receive quite substantial royalties from Warne's. 'It is pleasant to feel I could earn my own living,' she wrote to them.

Frederick Warne & Co. was strictly a family business, and was at this time managed by the founder's three sons, of whom the youngest, Norman, was unmarried and lived with his mother in Bedford Square, Bloomsbury, where the firm had its offices. Beatrix was received very warmly by the Warnes, and began to correspond almost daily with Norman, who like her was in his middle thirties and was deeply shy, except with children. Mrs Potter made clear her disapproval of the friendship with a family who were not the Potters' social equals—being publishers, the Warnes were simply tradesmen—but Beatrix was quietly adamant, and in the summer of 1905 she accepted Norman's proposal of marriage, which was sent to her by letter. All seemed set fair: the success of her first three books had been equalled by *The Tale of Benjamin Bunny* and *The Tale of Two Bad Mice*, both published during 1904, and she had just finished *The Tale of Mrs Tiggy-Winkle*. But, almost at once, Norman Warne was taken ill, and he died of leukaemia in August 1905, less than a month after he and Beatrix had become engaged. In September Beatrix was in Bath; she wrote to Norman's sister Millie:

I find the names of the streets rather melancholy here. Do you remember Miss Austen's *Persuasion*, with all the scenes and streets in Bath? It was always my favourite, and I read the end part of it again last July. On the 26th, the day after I got Norman's letter [of proposal], I thought my story had come right, with patience and waiting, like Anne Eliott's did.

In her grief she turned back to Sawrey, where that summer she had managed to buy Hill Top Farm, a small property occupied by a local couple, John Cannon and his wife, with whom she was on friendly terms. They stayed on as her tenants and she paid visits to them whenever she could get to the Lake District. Her next book, *The Pie and the Patty-Pan* (1905), planned with Norman Warne before his death, was a celebration of Sawrey village and of Hill Top in particular, which can be seen in the frontispiece.

The years 1906–13 saw Beatrix Potter at the height of her powers. Margaret Lane has written: 'The little books in this period followed on one another's heels so fast... that one wonders in astonishment how so much good work could be accomplished as Miss Potter shuttled back and forth with her parents to the Lakes.' *The Tale of Mr Jeremy Fisher* (1906) was based on a picture letter to one of the Moore children, written in 1893, but most of the books that followed it were entirely new conceptions.

Many of them grew out of details of Sawrey life and scenery. *The Tale of Tom Kitten* (1907), for example, expressed Beatrix Potter's delight in Hill Top and its garden; and *The Tale of Jemima Puddle-Duck* (1908) portrayed the Cannon family as they went about their work on the farm; *The Roly-Poly Pudding* (1908), later known as *The Tale of Samuel Whiskers*, explored the rooms of Hill Top, and grew out of battles to evict rats from the house; *Ginger and Pickles* (1909) described the village shop; and *The Tale of Pigling Bland* (1913) roamed further afield in the Lakes—and was also something of an autobiography in its description of Pigling's escape from conventional society.

The Tale of the Flopsy Bunnies (1909) was a sequel to *Peter Rabbit* and *Benjamin Bunny*; *The Tale of Mrs Tittlemouse* (1910) grew out of Beatrix Potter's close observation and understanding of insects and smaller animals; and *The Tale of Timmy Tiptoes* (1911) reflected the growing American interest in her books, for its chief characters were a chipmunk and an American grey squirrel (as opposed to the red Squirrel Nutkin, a native of Britain).

This highly productive period came to an end in 1914 with 'Kitty-in-Boots'. The text was finished and set up in type, but only one picture was ever completed. No further Beatrix Potter books appeared until 1917. This was because her life underwent a radical change.

In 1909 she bought Castle Farm in Sawrey, a larger property than Hill Top and one which gave her vacant possession. The purchase was made through a local firm of solicitors, and the partner who looked after it was William Heelis, a quiet bachelor of about Beatrix's age. Before long they had become engaged. For a second time, and for the same reason as before, she faced her parents' disapproval, but she was supported by her brother Bertram, who now revealed that he himself had been married for some years to a farmer's daughter. In October 1913, Beatrix became Mrs William Heelis, a name she bore proudly, for it was proof that at last, as she was approaching her fiftieth year, she had broken free from her parents. Margaret Lane writes:

The change from Miss Potter to Mrs Heelis went far deeper than the name. It was as if, disliking so much about her earlier life that she could hardly bear to be reminded of it, she deliberately buried Miss Potter of Bolton Gardens, and became another person, Mrs Heelis of Sawrey, who for the next thirty years was to be known as a dominant, shrewd, good-humoured, and salty character of the Lake Country...

The surprise is that in these circumstances she ever wrote and illustrated another book. In fact the next, *Apply Dapply's Nursery Rhymes* (1917), had been put together in 1905. *The Tale of Johnny Town-Mouse* (1918), taken from *Aesop's fable 'The Town Mouse and the Country Mouse', was close in style and spirit to her pre-war work, but this was her last book in the old mould. It was followed by *Cecily Parsley's Nursery Rhymes* (1922), again based on earlier material, after which nothing appeared until 1929. In that year she was visited by her American publisher, Alexander McKay of the Philadelphia firm of David McKay, who asked her for a new book which would be printed only in the United States. She responded by writing a lengthy and rambling tale, built out of old material, *The *Fairy Caravan*.

Beatrix Potter's last years were as lively and independent as her childhood had been confined. Her father died not long after her marriage, and her brother Bertram did not survive beyond his late forties, so that Beatrix acquired a great deal of her family's substantial income. With it she was able to buy (in 1923) a 2,000-acre sheep farm at Troutbeck, about twelve miles from Sawrey. She soon became a successful breeder of, and expert on, the local Herdwick sheep, and was admired by other farmers for her shrewdness and wisdom. She also used her money to help the National Trust, buying up land in local places of beauty and then handing it over as a gift, on the condition that the donation remain anonymous.

In old age she came to resemble her own Mrs Tiggywinkle, round and twinkling-eyed, sometimes wearing a frilled white cap. She warmly welcomed admirers from America, but was profoundly suspicious and hostile towards those of her own nationality who wrote serious critical appraisals of her work or tried to approach her for assistance with any kind of study of her books. To Janet Adam Smith, who had written to her following an article in the *Listener* in which she compared the Beatrix Potter pictures to *Bewick and other distinguished artists, she replied: 'When a person has been nearly thirty years married it is not ingratiating to get an envelope addressed to "Miss".' Margaret Lane, attempting to meet her with a view to assistance with an article, was sent 'the rudest letter I have ever received in my life'. Moreover, happy as her marriage with William Heelis may have been, there is no doubt that she dominated him and kept

him firmly in the subservient role. To a friend she wrote candidly: 'I am the stronger half of the pair.' She died after a short illness in the winter of 1943, at the age of seventy-seven. Two more stories by her were published posthumously: *Wag-by-Wall* in 1944 and *The Faithful Dove* in 1955.

Her books were the first English classics for very young children, though their readership has always included many adults who return to them again and again to delight in their wit. Much has been written about her obvious talents, her faithful and loving pictorial evocation of the Lake District countryside, the charm of her watercolours, and the skill with which she drew animals (she always used live models). But she was also the first writer for the very young to bring to her task a sophisticated and ironic sense of comedy, much resembling that of Jane Austen in its use of dry understatement and in its drawing-out of large truths about character and behaviour from a small community of protagonists. (Her prose style resembles Jane Austen, too, and also owes much, as she herself admitted, to the Authorized Version of the Bible.) Caricature of social behaviour is frequent in her stories; for example, Mrs Tittlemouse's difficulties with her affable but unwanted toad-guest, Mr Jackson. It is not difficult to see how a child brought up in Victorian Kensington could develop such an eye for social nuance.

Even more dominant in her stories (many of which owe their origins to *nursery rhymes or folk tales) is the threat of physical danger; death is always lurking round the corner. This appears in its simplest form in *Peter Rabbit*, where the hero's father (we learn) was 'put in a pie by Mrs McGregor'. At the height of her powers Beatrix Potter achieves her greatest comic effects from direct confrontation with these menaces: for example, Samuel Whiskers and Anna Maria debating whether to coat Tom Kitten with butter and dough or breadcrumbs.

Beatrix Potter has sometimes been censured for her use of long words, but her deliberately over-elaborate vocabulary is a principal instrument of her comedy. 'I am persuaded', says Samuel Whiskers to his wife, when interrupted in their attempt to make a pudding out of Tom Kitten, 'that the knots would have proved indigestible, whatever you may urge to the contrary'; and no other words would do.

POTTER, F. (Frederick) Scarlet (b.1834) British author of nearly fifty books for children, beginning with *Melcomb Manor*,

a family chronicle (1875). Many of his stories were produced as *reward books, e.g. *Ned Dowdswell's Difficulties* (*c.*1877), the tale of a boy wrongly accused of breaking a church window.

Potter, Harry *See* HARRY POTTER.

POWER, Rhoda (1890–1957) British author of stories from history, among them *Boys and Girls of History* (1926), written with her sister Eileen.

Practical Education (1798) A pedagogical work by Richard and Maria *Edgeworth. Although advertised as co-authored when first published, it is now thought that Maria undertook the majority of the work. Its twenty-five chapters are each concerned with one aspect of a child's environment and education and drew widely on the work of educational philosophers such as John *Locke and Jean Jacques *Rousseau. This philosophical emphasis is, however, balanced with the practical experiences that the Edgeworths brought to bear on the publication: Maria was surrogate mother to many of her father's twenty-two children, most of whom were educated at home. Thus it is with authority that the introduction states that 'we have chosen the title of *Practical Education*, to point out that we rely entirely upon practice and experience'.

Indeed this experiential emphasis is also the basis for the pedagogy recommended for children. In line with Rousseauian philosophy, non-book-based learning is recommended, with 'observation, experiment and invention' foregrounded. Sports, games, and educational toys are vital to the Edgeworths' pedagogy, but fairy stories are dismissed, which led many critics to connect *Practical Education* with a more generally perceived dismissal of imaginative literature by Rational Moralist writers. However, in the Edgeworths' work, creativity and imagination sit alongside reason as vital to the child's upbringing. Parents are advised, for example that children need to be given toys or practical experiences which 'exercise their senses or their imagination, their imitative, and inventive powers'.

Practical Education quickly became popular and influential, feeding the contemporary education debate and sparking discussion in magazines and newspapers, as well as in society circles. *The Gentleman's Magazine* for May 1800 emphasizes the 'fashionable' nature of its content, calling it 'education à la mode', but speaks rather disapprovingly that there is 'not a word on God, Religion, Christianity, or a hint that such topics are ever to be mentioned'. Indeed *Practical Education* continues to generate debate in current academic circles (as, for example, in the work of Susan Manly and Julia Douthwaite), particularly in relation to the question of innovation and/or conservatism in its pedagogic agenda. The new edition of the text edited by Manly and published in 2003 calls it a 'pioneering classic of modern pedagogy'.

PRATCHETT, Terry (1948–2015) British fantasy writer born in Beaconsfield, north-west of London. He debuted at the age of twenty-three with *The Carpet People* (1971), also producing his own illustrations for the book. It was then revisited and re-released in 1992, after he had published the first book in the globally extremely popular *Discworld series, *The Colour of Magic* (1983), and co-authored the book that launched international superstar Neil *Gaiman, *Good Omens* (1990). He published over fifty novels, forty of them set in the Discworld universe (including *The *Amazing Maurice and His Educated Rodents*), with multiple multimedia adaptations of his work, from comics to TV films, theatre, videogames, music, and role-play games.

Pratchett wrote several novels that are not part of the Discworld series, and are aimed at younger readers: *The Nome Trilogy*: *Truckers* (1989), *Diggers* and *Wings* (1990), published as *The Bromeliad* in the US; the *Johnny Maxwell* trilogy: *Only You Can Save Mankind* (1992), *Johnny and the Dead* (1993), and *Johnny and the Bomb* (1996); the critically acclaimed Michael L. Printz Honor Book (*see* MICHAEL L. PRINTZ AWARD) *Nation* (2008), one of his best, set in an alternative semi-fantasy 19th cent. on an island in the Great Southern Pelagic Ocean; and most recently the Victorian-style, Dickensesque *Dodger* (2013). He is on a par with Charles *Dickens for number of books (five) listed in the BBC's *The Big Read* of 2003. Pratchett was awarded the Locus Award for Best Young Adult Book, a *Carnegie Medal, an Andre Norton Award, a Margaret A. Edwards Award, as well as the Skylark, British Science Fiction, World Fantasy Award for Life Achievement, nine honorary doctorates from UK universities, and was made a Knight Bachelor in 2009 for services to literature—his coat of arms, established in 2010, bears the motto 'Don't Fear The Reaper', in Latin, a reference to his popular Discworld character Death. In 2007, Pratchett announced he had been diagnosed with a rare

form of Alzheimer's disease, but that he would keep on writing for as long as possible.

PRELUTSKY, Jack (1940–) American poet, singer, and songwriter who has written over seventy books of playful, sometimes frightening, and often funny verse about everyday events, and has set some of his poems to music. Nonsense verse in *Scranimals* (2002) and *Behold the Bold Umbrellaphant and Other Poems* (2006) features Edward *Lear-esque hybrid creations. Among his best-known titles are *Nightmares: Poems to Trouble Your Sleep* (1976), *The New Kid on the Block* (1984), and *The Dragons Are Singing Tonight* (1993). In *Hooray for Diffendoofer Day!* (1998), he completed unfinished material by Dr *Seuss. In 2006, he was named the Poetry Foundation's first Children's Poet Laureate.

PRENTISS, Elizabeth (1818–78) Popular American writer widely read in England who was the author of *Little Susy's Six Birthdays, by her Aunt Susan* (1854) and *Stepping Heavenward: a tale of home life* (1872).

Pretty Book of Pictures For Little Masters and Misses, A, or, *Tommy Trip's History of Beasts and Birds, To which is prefix'd, The History of little Tom Trip himself, of his Dog Jouler, and of Woglog the great Giant* A children's book published by John *Newbery in 1752, consisting of a collection of *woodcuts, mostly of animals and birds, with short verses and prose descriptions.

It is related to the *bestiaries. Some of the woodcuts derive from Topsell's *Historie of Four-Footed Beastes* (1608). An assortment of other scenes fills up the book. Tommy Trip, a *Tom Thumb-like character with bookish tastes who rides on his dog, features only in the opening tale of his prowess against the *giant Woglog, told in the characteristically jolly, conversational style of Newbery's books and possibly the work of John Newbery himself.

The book continued to be published by the Newbery family for some thirty-five years, and also appeared in America from 1791. An edition issued by a Newcastle publisher, Thomas Saint, in 1779 had woodcuts by the young Thomas *Bewick.

PREUSSLER, Otfried (1923–2013) Popular German author for younger children whose simply told, engaging tales of fantasy have a timeless quality. They include *Der kleine Wassermann* (1957) (English, *The Little Water-Sprite*, 1960), *Die kleine Hexe* (1958) (*The Little Witch*, 1961), and *Der Räuber Hotzenplotz*

(*The Robber Hotzenplotz*, 1961), a comic tale about an uncatchable thief. He has been translated into English by Anthea *Bell.

PRICE, Evadne *See* JANE.

PRICE, Susan (1955–) Brought up in the English Black Country, Price always knew she wanted to be a writer, despite coming from a family of factory workers who had never been to university, let alone written a book. This determination led to her first novel, *The Devil's Piper* (1973), being published when she was still just a teenager. Though she has written for children of all ages and in many genres, it is her *young adult books that remain most influential, especially *The *Sterkarm Handshake* (1998) and its sequel, *A Sterkarm Kiss* (2003), an extraordinary mixture of fantasy and science fiction set in the Scottish border country. Her icy, magical, myth-like novel *The Ghost Drum* won the 1987 *Carnegie Medal.

PRICE, Willard *See* ADVENTURE SERIES.

PRIESTLEY, Chris (1958–) English author and illustrator of books that keep you fearfully awake at night. Starting his career as an illustrator, he began to write his own stories, coming up with the award-winning *Death and the Arrow* (2003), about a boy in 18th-cent. London and a gruesome murder. His love of psychological horror led him to move further towards that genre with *Uncle Montague's Tales of Terror* (2007), a collection of dark and frightening linked short stories, a model repeated in *Tales of Terror from the Black Ship* (2008) and *Tales of Terror from the Tunnel's Mouth* (2009). These were followed by a series of consistently good—and truly unsettling— standalone novels: *The Dead of Winter* (2010); *Mister Creecher* (2011), which looks afresh at Frankenstein's monster; *Through Dead Eyes* (2013); *The Dead Men Stood Together* (2013), which spins on Coleridge's poem *The Rime of the Ancient Mariner*; and *The Last of the Spirits* (2014), in which a boy is led by ghosts through the past, present, and future of the life of Ebenezer Scrooge.

primer Originally the name for a prayer book, but eventually used to describe elementary *books of instruction by which children were taught their letters and prayers.

The medieval primer was a prayer book for the laity, in Latin or in English, or in both languages. It contained Offices of the Church and other prayers, and its name may have been derived from the first Office of the day,

Prime. It was used in England up to, and for some time after, the Reformation.

Primers were given to children in school. Many primers began with a table of the alphabet, so that the book could be used for first exercises in reading. One such was *The Primer in English for children, after the use of Sarum* (1537). Shorter books containing the alphabet, a syllabary to teach spelling, and a few prayers began to be printed for the use of children *c.*1538; *see* ABC BOOKS. During the 17th cent. it became customary to print the *catechism in an ABC book. The meaning of 'primer' given in Johnson's Dictionary (1755) is 'A small prayer-book in which children are taught to read'. By the early 19th cent. the word was in use in the sense of a small introductory book to any subject. This meaning gradually displaced the older one entirely.

For an anti-Catholic primer produced by Benjamin *Harris, *see* PROTESTANT TUTOR, THE. Harris also produced the most celebrated early American *schoolbook, the *New England Primer. One of the most popular primers in England during the 17th cent. was Coote's *English Schoolmaster. Daniel Fennin's *Universal Spelling Book*, an illustrated primer containing *fables and an early *moral tale ('the natural History of Tommy and Harry') was first published in 1756 and was still in print in 1847. Another very popular primer during the 19th cent. was William Mavor's *English Spelling Book* of 1801.

Primrose Prettyface, *The Renowned History of* An early *moral tale of unknown authorship, published by John *Marshall *c.*1783. Primrose Thompson, the daughter of an agricultural labourer, earns her nickname because of good looks but also through 'sweetness of temper and pretty behaviour'. She pleases Lady Worthy by being able to recite her lessons, and, like *Goody Two-Shoes, becomes unofficial teacher to the local children. When she goes into service at Lady Worthy's house, her mistress's son Sir William falls in love with her and marries her, so that, in the words of the title-page, she is 'raised . . . to great Riches, and the Dignity of Lady of the Manor'.

Prince and the Pauper, The A novel by 'Mark *Twain' (S. L. Clemens) published in 1882. Prince Edward, the future Edward VI of England, finds he has a double in the pauper boy Tom Canty. He and Tom exchange clothes for fun, but each is mistaken for the other and the prince is driven from the court, Tom being obliged to impersonate him. Edward sees how monstrously unfair are the social conditions prevalent in the country he is to rule. By the time he comes to be crowned king he has learnt a true sense of justice. Among those whom he rewards is Tom, who becomes King's Ward.

The book was more specifically intended for children than Twain's other writings; it is dedicated to his daughters, 'those good-mannered and agreeable children Susie and Clara Clemens'—phraseology which enthusiasts for *The *Adventures of Tom Sawyer* and *The *Adventures of Huckleberry Finn* may suspect to be slightly sarcastic.

Prince Caspian (1951) The second published *Narnia novel by C. S. *Lewis.

Prince Dolor In *The *Little Lame Prince* by Mrs *Craik.

Prince Dorus, *or, Flattery put out of Countenance, A poetical version of an Ancient Tale* A comic *fairy story in verse, written by Charles *Lamb and published by the *Godwins in 1811. Dorus is born with a huge nose, but he and his mother are deluded by flattering courtiers into believing it normal. Because of a spell he can only marry the princess Christabel, whom he loves, when he learns at last that his nose is absurdly long. *Prince Dorus* is based on a story in the *Magasin des enfans* of Mme de *Beaumont. A retelling of this, under the title 'Prince Hyacinth and the Dear Little Princess', appears in the *Blue Fairy Book* (1889) of Andrew *Lang (*see* FAIRY BOOKS).

Prince Prigio (1889) A *fantasy by Andrew *Lang. After a very long wait, the King and Queen of Pantouflia have a son. The queen fails to invite the fairies to the christening; but they come just the same. The gifts they bring— all the magic properties of the classic fairy tales—are thrown into the lumber room, and the baby, Prince Prigio, is brought up to be so clever and rational that he is hated by everyone except the queen. When a Firedrake ravages the country the king encourages Prigio to do battle with it, but he refuses, for he does not believe in the monster and in any case knows that in these matters it is youngest sons who always succeed. When Prigio's popular two younger brothers fail to return from the quest, the court abandons the obnoxious Prigio and, alone, he accidentally discovers and uses the magic gifts and falls in love with Rosalind, the English ambassador's daughter—whereupon 'in one instant *he knew all*

about it. He believed in fairies and fairy gifts, and understood that his cap was the cap of darkness, and his shoes the seven league boots, and his purse the purse of Fortunatus' (*see* FORTUNATUS). Prigio effectively vanquishes the volcanic Firedrake, brings his brothers back to life, marries Rosalind, and finally achieves popularity by dint of a wish to *seem* no cleverer than other people.

The book discloses its ancestry by stating that Prigio is descended from *Cinderella*, the Marquis de Carabas (*see* PUSS IN BOOTS), and Giglio I (*see* ROSE AND THE RING, THE by Thackeray), and it is full of witty uses of traditional material.

Lang's *Prince Ricardo of Pantouflia* (1893) is a sequel. Prigio's son, more familiarly known as Dick, by contrast loves reading *fairy stories but not much else. Moreover Ricardo never takes any further interest in the maidens he rescues and he depends heavily on his magic gifts. When his father substitutes imitations for them, Ricardo fails in his next adventure. Abashed, Ricardo then sets out to kill, without fairy help, The *Yellow Dwarf, 'the greatest villain in history'. After a further adventure, with a giant, Ricardo does marry a rescued maiden and discovers 'There's something in the books after all.'

Both books were illustrated by Gordon *Browne. Both were reprinted, as *Chronicles of Pantouflia*, in Lang's *My Own Fairy Book* (1896), and they have been periodically reissued since then. Lang's attempt to write further Pantouflian stories in *Tales of a Fairy Court* (1907) did not, however, measure up to his earlier successes.

Princess and Curdie, The By George *MacDonald, serialized in the magazine *Good Things* from January to June 1877 and published as a book by Chatto and Windus in 1882 (dated 1883), with illustrations by James Allen.

The story, which is a sequel to *The *Princess and the Goblin*, tells how Curdie the miner's son is sent, by the more than half-magical great-great-grandmother of the little Princess Irene, to the city of Gwyntystorm, where stands the palace of Irene and her father the king. Evil councillors have taken control of the city, and indeed virtually the entire population of Gwyntystorm is corrupt. Thanks to the help of his companion, a grotesque but loving animal named Lina, Curdie gets into the king's private chamber and discovers that the old man is being kept in a stupor of nightmares by means of poison. Soon dispatching the

poisoner, the villainous Dr Kelman, Curdie rouses the king to his senses, much to the gratitude of Irene. With the aid of a whole troop of beasts who are as grotesque as Lina—'the Uglies', Irene calls them—the evil courtiers and the dishonest servants are chased from the palace, and when war is made on Gwyntystorm by a neighbouring power (in league with the villains) the king's small force is victorious. Gwyntystorm is set to rights, and Irene and Curdie marry and in due time become queen and king. But they have no children, and after their day the city goes to the bad again, eventually crashing in ruins in a destruction brought about by its own occupants.

The end of the book is often cited as an example of MacDonald's misanthropy, which became a marked characteristic as he grew older. In fact the entire book is coloured by this; humanity is shown as almost entirely rotten, and Curdie, who has the magical gift of being able to perceive men's true natures simply by touching their hands, constantly finds treachery and mean-heartedness in those he encounters. This bitter attitude to MacDonald's fellow human beings means that the story has little of the charm of *The Princess and The Goblin* or *At the Back of the North Wind*; nevertheless the excitement is considerable, and the book has remained popular with children since it was first published.

Princess and the Goblin, The The second children's novel by George *MacDonald, first published as a serial in *Good Words For The Young* between November 1870 and June 1871, and issued as a book by Strahan & Co. late in 1871 (dated 1872). Both the magazine serialization and the book were illustrated by Arthur *Hughes.

The Princess Irene lives 'in a large house halfway up a mountainside, where she is looked after by her nurse Lootie; her father the king sometimes visits her. Also living in a tower in the house is Irene's great-great-grandmother, an intriguing, magical character stumbled upon by Irene one day, who can only be found by those whom she wishes to see her, who believe in her, and who need her help. Beneath the mountain in a series of caves lives a race of goblin-like beings that once dwelt above ground and were much like other people, but were driven underground, since when they have become grotesquely ugly and have come to despise humans.

Adjacent to the goblin caves are mines, worked for precious metal by the humans.

One of the miners is a fearless lad named Curdie Peterson. One evening Irene and her nurse are caught out on a mountainside by the approach of darkness, and are surrounded by goblins as they try to make their way home. Curdie appears and rescues them and is rewarded by the promise of a kiss from the princess. Soon afterwards Curdie discovers that the goblins are plotting some great outrage against the royal house; he is captured and imprisoned in the goblin caves. Irene rescues him and Curdie warns the royal guards of imminent disaster, but he is accidentally wounded by a guard and falls ill with a fever. The goblins break into the royal house; Curdie recovers and, with the help of Irene's great-great-grandmother, helps to rout them, while Irene finds safety in Curdie's parents' cottage. The goblins are drowned in an underground flood caused by themselves, and, with the approval of her father the king, Irene rewards Curdie with the promised kiss.

MacDonald himself said that the story was 'as good work of the kind as I can do', and the book, beside being his own best tale for children, is one of the most accomplished 19th-cent. *fantasies by a British author. Hughes's illustrations, admirably supplemented in a 1911 *Blackie edition with coloured plates by 'H. S.', exactly complement the text. Admirers of *The Princess and the Goblin* have included G. K. Chesterton and C. S. *Lewis, while the goblin mines beneath the Misty Mountains in *The *Hobbit* owe much to it—the book was among the childhood favourites of J. R. R. *Tolkien.

In 1877 MacDonald published a sequel, *The *Princess and Curdie*.

Princess Bride, The (1973) Tongue-in-cheek fairy-tale adventure by American author William Goldman (1931–). In the imaginary land of Florin, farmhand Westley sets out to prove that he is a worthy husband for beautiful Buttercup and embarks on a series of adventures featuring pirates, giants, and an evil prince. The novel is presented as an abridged version of a work by S. Morgenstern and is peppered with 'facts' about both Goldman's life and that of the non-existent Morgenstern. Goldman maintained the elaborate hoax by enlisting his publishers to respond to requests for a section of the book that he had supposedly omitted in the abridgement. It was made into a successful film by Rob Reiner in 1987.

Princess Diaries, The (2000–9) A popular series by Meg *Cabot. An ordinary girl in New York finds out one day that she is not so ordinary after all and is in fact heir to the throne of a far-off country called Genovia. How do you cope with this new life? With princess lessons? A bodyguard? And what happens to your friends? This is a ten-book series that ends when Mia turns eighteen. Fast-paced, peppered with pop-culture references, lightweight (but very funny), it manages to answer some difficult questions about growing up, in amongst the froth. A film was made of the books in 2001.

Princess on the Pea, The A story by Hans Christian *Andersen, included in his first collection of tales (1836). A prince who wishes to find a true princess for his bride cannot discover one. There comes to the town gates a girl drenched with rain, who claims to be a real princess. The Queen Dowager tests her by having a bed made up with twenty mattresses and twenty feather beds, all piled on top of each other; beneath them all is one pea. The next morning the girl complains of having spent a wretchedly uncomfortable night because there was something hard in the bed. By this they know her to be truly a princess, and she marries the prince.

Andersen claimed to have heard the tale in childhood; in fact it does not seem to have been traditional in Denmark, but to have been developed by him out of Swedish folk tales of the same sort; in Swedish versions she is subjected to a number of tests and is told of the presence of objects in the bed by her dog and cat.

Printz Award *See* MICHAEL L. PRINTZ AWARD.

Prisoner of Zenda, The (1894) A novel by Anthony *Hope.

Private Peaceful (2003) A *young adult novel by Michael *Morpurgo. Taking his knowledge of the 'Shot at Dawn' scandal—the story of the men who were executed for cowardice, but who were rarely anything more than confused or suffering from shell shock—Morpurgo, without sentimentality, but with real passion, crafts the story of the Peaceful brothers. Over the course of eight hours, through 'Tommo', he tells of their childhood in the countryside, the outbreak of the First World War, their enrolment into the army and all that came after. *Private Peaceful* was made into a film in 2012.

Professor Branestawm A character created by Norman *Hunter. Stories about him were read on BBC *Children's Hour, and then appeared in *The Incredible Adventures of Professor Branestawm* (1933), illustrated by W. Heath *Robinson, a perfect match. In this first book the professor makes a time machine ('which looked something like a cross between a typewriter, an egg timer, and a conjuring trick'), causes all the waste paper in his house to come to life by means of a patent elixir, and builds a burglar-catching mechanism which accidentally trusses up its inventor. The second book appeared in 1937, the next not till 1970, just after the first two had been televised, and further new titles followed until 1983.

Professor Calculus See TINTIN.

Protestant Tutor, The By Benjamin *Harris (1683), a *Puritan reading book (*see* PRIMER). Vehemently anti-Catholic, besides an ABC, it includes a lengthy prayer to God to spare 'these Protestant Kingdoms from Popery and Slavery' and an account of the Gunpowder Plot. Shortly after publishing *The Protestant Tutor* Harris went to America, where he produced *The *New England Primer*.

PROVENSEN, Alice (1917–) and **Martin** (1916–87) Chicago-born illustrators who collaborated on more than forty books, including *The Glorious Flight* (1983), which they also co-wrote. This story of Louis Blériot's 1909 cross-Channel flight won them the *Caldecott Medal. (Two years earlier a book they illustrated, Nancy *Willard's *A Visit to William Blake's Inn* (1981), had won its author the *Newbery Medal.) Other books include Louis Untermeyer's *Tales from the Ballet* (1968) and *The Provensen Book of Fairy Tales* (1971), typically beautiful pieces of work now sadly long out of print. Following Martin's death in 1987, Alice would continue to produce children's books alone for another two decades.

PROVOOST, Anne (1964–) Belgian essayist and author of *young adult books who started to write while living in America. Her debut novel, *My Aunt is a Pilot Whale* (1991), was first published in Dutch, and was the first novel from the Low Countries aimed specifically at a teen audience to deal with child abuse. Her second book, *Falling* (1994), addressed the possible allure of extreme right-wing rhetoric and went on to be translated into many languages and made into a 2001 film. *The Rose and the Swine* (1997) retells the fairy tale *Beauty and the Beast*, while *In the Shadow of the Ark* (2001) tells the story of the Great Flood from the perspective of a girl who is not one of those chosen to board Noah's ark. Both books take a critical look at rigid religious thinking. *Looking into the Sun* (2007) is set in Australia and is about a girl trying to save her family's farm after the death of her father.

PRØYSEN, Alf (1914–70) Norwegian author-illustrator, creator of 'Mrs Pepperpot', a little old woman who frequently shrinks to the size of a pepperpot and in consequence has some very odd adventures, often befriending animals (to whom she can talk) along the way.

Prydain cycle A series of five novels by Lloyd *Alexander. The hero is Taran, who in the first volume, *The Book of Three* (1964), is Assistant Pig-Keeper in the kingdom of Prydain and is searching for the missing oracular pig Hen Wen. His further adventures are told in *The Black Cauldron* (1965), *The Castle of Llyr* (1966), *Taran Wanderer* (1968), and *The High King* (1968), which won the *Newbery Medal.

Alexander began work on the cycle as a result of reading The *Mabinogion. His stories are, however, entirely his own invention and bear no real resemblance to traditional Welsh legends. They have been very popular in the United States, but less successful in Britain.

Psammead, The A bad-tempered magical being in *Five Children and It* and The *Story of the Amulet* by E. *Nesbit. He returns in Kate Saunders's *Five Children on the Western Front* (2014).

Puck of Pook's Hill (1906) By Rudyard *Kipling, a collection of tales based freely on English history, linked by a frame narrative and punctuated with poems.

Two children, Dan and Una, are acting a scene from *A Midsummer Night's Dream* within an old Fairy Ring in a meadow near their Sussex home. It is Midsummer's Eve, and quite by accident they summon Puck himself from the nearby Pook's Hill (i.e. 'Puck's Hill'). He explains that the fairies, or People of the Hills, are now all gone from England, except himself; and: 'I'm Puck, the oldest Old Thing in England, very much at your service if—if you care to have anything to do with me.' He tells them that the Old Things began as gods, but then came down in the world. For example, Weland, the blacksmith of the gods, was once a deity himself, worshipped in a temple, but was eventually obliged to ply his trade

shoeing horses by the wayside. Weland is eventually freed from this thraldom when a good-natured novice from a monastery forces an ungrateful farmer to say thank-you for having his horse shod. Weland vanishes from England, but makes a great sword in gratitude to the novice, whose name is Hugh.

In the next story, 'Young Men at the Manor', the children meet a Norman knight riding in their meadow, Sir Richard Dalyngridge. He came over with the Conqueror, fought at Hastings, and—despite the fact that they were theoretically enemies—took up with Hugh, the former novice and possessor of the sword. He spares Hugh's family and is granted their manor if he can hold it peacefully.

Sir Richard is again the narrator of the next two stories. 'The Joyous Venture' tells of his captivity, with Hugh, on a Danish ship which takes them on a search for gold. 'Old Men at Pevensey' tells of the disposal of the treasure and of attempted treachery against de Aquila, Hugh, and Richard in the days of Henry I.

'A Centurion of the Thirtieth' introduces a new narrator, Parnesius, a Roman centurion. 'On the Great Wall' is Parnesius's account of his service on Hadrian's Wall alongside his friend the centurion Pertinax. It is followed by one of Kipling's finest poems, 'A Song to Mithras'. 'The Winged Hats' takes its title from the name Parnesius and his fellow Romans give to the Vikings, who try to make an alliance with the soldiers on the Wall when Rome is falling. (It was these two stories, read in childhood, which gave Rosemary *Sutcliff her 'first feeling for Roman Britain'.)

'Hal o' the Draft' introduces Sir Harry Dawe, Tudor church-builder, craftsman, and artist. It is followed by the celebrated 'Smugglers' Song' ('Watch the wall, my darling, while the Gentlemen go by!'). 'Dymchurch Flit' tells of the *fairies leaving England by boat during the Tudor religious persecutions. The final story, 'The Treasure and the Law', has as its narrator Kadmiel, a Jew from the time of King John, whose dealings at Pevensey Castle with the treasure left there by Hugh and Richard in an earlier story is a cause of the signing of the Magna Carta. Puck, commenting on this, emphasizes the view of history which is the basis of all the stories:

'Well,' said Puck calmly, 'what do you think of it? Weland gave the Sword! The Sword gave the Treasure, and the Treasure gave the Law. It's as natural as an oak growing.'

Puck of Pook's Hill owes much of its inspiration to Kipling's purchase of a country house

in Sussex in 1902, 'Bateman's', near Burwash. The house had an old mill which plays a not inconsiderable part in the stories. During the summer of 1904 his children John and Elsie, together with their father, acted parts of *A Midsummer Night's Dream* in an old quarry near the house, and by September Kipling had begun to write *Puck*.

Much of the book was based on fact. 'Pook' is a Sussex place name found in at least two parts of the county, though it apparently comes not from 'Puck' but from a family named Pooke. (The hill near Kipling's house at Burwash is now known as Pook's Hill, but this is a tribute to the book's popularity; in Kipling's day it was Perch Hill.) Kipling studied Domesday Book and other historical records in search of ideas for the book. It has been suggested that one of his few major departures from truth was to imply that the worship of Mithras was a principal cult of Roman Britain, at a time when in fact Christianity was the official religion of the Empire. However in 1954 the remains of a Roman temple dedicated to Mithras were found in the City of London (thereby reviving a certain amount of interest in *Puck of Pook's Hill*), and it appears that Kipling may in fact have been near the mark.

Stories from the book appeared in a number of magazines, and it was serialized in its entirety in *The *Strand Magazine* beginning in January 1906. The book was published the following September, with illustrations by H. R. *Millar. The American edition, published the same year, also had four coloured plates by Arthur *Rackham. Both *Puck* and its sequel *Rewards and Fairies* (1910) had a slow start, thanks to Kipling's increasing unpopularity because of his role as 'missionary of empire', but they were often reprinted and soon gained a permanent place in children's reading. Quite apart from their narrative excitement, they have also come to be admired as reconstructions of history.

PUDNEY, John (Sleigh) (1909–77) British poet and author who wrote a number of children's books, including *Saturday Adventure* (1950), and sequels for other days of the week, and *Spring Adventure* (1961), which has sequels for the other seasons. These are action-packed and highly improbable *adventure stories.

Pueriles Confabulatiunculae: *or Children's Dialogues* A popular schoolbook translated from Latin into English (1617) by John *Brinsley. Although intended as a series

of exercises in the Latin language and the translating of it into English, the book is also of interest for the pictures it gives of the life of a 17th-cent. schoolboy.

It begins with a series of phrases in which, for example, the pupil asks permission of the master to leave the room to go to the privy. Then follows a set of dialogues, in which, for example, a mother tries to rouse her lazy son from his bed, a boy is reproved for coming late to school, the master restores order between two boys fighting over a quill pen, and another boy is in trouble for speaking English in class rather than Latin. The dialogues are vigorous and lifelike. The work was again translated (1659) by Charles Hoole.

Puffin books A division of the publishing house Penguin Books (now Penguin Random House); for many decades after its foundation in 1941 one of the leading publishers of original paperback children's fiction in Britain. It was created by Allen Lane, founder of Penguin, who chose as the first Puffin editor Eleanor *Graham. She and he determined that Puffins should contain 'definitely not a series of out-of-copyright classics . . . [but] the best of the *new* classics of the new generation'. The imprint was launched despite wartime paper shortages, the reluctance of many publishers to sublease their best recent titles, and a lack of enthusiasm from many librarians, who disliked paper-bound books.

The first five fiction titles, all published during 1941, were *Worzel Gummidge* by Barbara Euphan Todd, *Cornish Adventure* by Derek *Mcculloch ('Uncle Mac' of *Children's Hour), *The *Cuckoo Clock* by Mrs *Molesworth, *Garram the Hunter* by Herbert Best (an African *adventure story), and *Smoky* by Will James. These first Puffins had red and white jackets, resembling the orange and white of the adult Penguins, with small drawings on the covers; they were fully illustrated. By 1945 full colour covers were being used. In 1948 the Puffin edition of *A *Child's Garden of Verses* carried an introduction by Eleanor Graham entitled 'How the Book Came to be Written', a feature that was repeated with many other classics. Later, new books were commissioned, such as Roger Lancelyn *Green's retelling of the King *Arthur stories (1953). Eleanor Graham's place as editor was taken in 1961 by Kaye *Webb. Initiatives such as the Puffin Club and *Puffin Post* magazine made the house for years the only publishing brand widely known to children.

In 1941 Allen Lane also launched a series of Puffin Picture Books, edited by Noel Carrington; the first titles were non-fiction. The first fiction title to be printed as a Puffin Picture Book was *Orlando's Evening Out* by Kathleen *Hale which appeared during 1941.

Pugwash *See* CAPTAIN PUGWASH.

PULLEIN-THOMPSON, Christine (1925–2005), **Diana** (1925–2015) and **Josephine** (1924–2014) Prolific British authors of *pony stories, daughters of Joanna Cannan (*see* PONY FOR JEAN, A). Working at first together, on *It Began with Picotee* (1946), and then separately, the Pullein-Thompson sisters, of whom Christine and Diana are twins, dominated the market in this corner of girls' fiction for many years.

PULLMAN, Philip (1946–) A celebrated English author for adults and children, best known for *His Dark Materials*, an award-winning trilogy featuring the indomitable Lyra Belacqua. Pullman began his career as a teacher, later becoming a lecturer in English at Westminster College, Oxford. He maintains a passionate interest in the teaching of English in the UK and is an outspoken advocate of reading for pleasure and of *libraries.

Pullman's first book *Count Karlstein* (1982), a Gothic melodrama, was first written as a play for schoolchildren when he was an English teacher. This was followed by *The *Ruby in the Smoke* (1986), the first in a popular series of historical books featuring Sally Lockhart, which later was adapted for the TV screen. Pullman has also written a number of short stories and fairy tales including *The Firework-Maker's Daughter* (1995), *I Was a Rat! . . . or The Scarlet Slippers* (1999), *Clockwork, or All Wound Up* (1995), and a 2012 collection of *Grimm retellings.

He came to prominence with *His Dark Materials*, starting with *Northern Lights* (*The Golden Compass* in the US) in 1995, which won numerous awards including the *Carnegie Medal and which later went on to win the Carnegie of Carnegies in 2007; *The Subtle Knife* followed in 1997, and finally *The Amber Spyglass* in 2000, which won the Whitbread Book of the Year (*see* WHITBREAD CHILDREN'S BOOK AWARD), the first time it was awarded to a book for children. *Lyra's Oxford* (2003) and *Once Upon a Time in the North* (2008) provide a sequel and a prequel respectively to the popular series, both beautifully illustrated by artist John *Lawrence. A film adaptation of *Northern Lights*, using the book's US title, was

released in 2007. Pullman's forthcoming *The Book of Dust*, a companion novel to the trilogy, promises an exciting addition to the series. *Daemon Voices: Essays on Storytelling* (2017) is a collection of non-fiction.

In 2002, Pullman received the *Eleanor Farjeon Award and in 2005 he was the joint winner of the *Astrid Lindgren Memorial Award, sharing it with the Japanese illustrator Ryoji *Arai.

Punch and Judy Performances were first recorded in the form which persists today in the 18th cent. The figure of Punch was originally derived from Pulcinella in the Commedia dell'arte, apparently first imported into English *puppet plays in 1662 and soon renamed 'Punchinello' by the public and the puppeteers. Punch adopted many of the characteristics of the English court jester and clown. First as a marionette, then as a glove puppet, he became a regular feature of fairgrounds, where he took part in crude and bawdy comedies, and engaged in backchat with a human performer who stood in front of the booth. By 1742 Punch had reached America.

In England by 1800 Punch performers had started to take to the streets, setting up their booths wherever they could draw a crowd. In 1828 John Payne Collier published the text of a Punch and Judy play with illustrations by George *Cruikshank; Collier took this text orally from one of the Italians who gave Punch and Judy performances in the London streets, though he seems to have embellished it a good deal before publishing it. Other texts have since been printed.

The play, which has resemblances to the *mummers' plays, varies greatly from performer to performer, but its outlines may be summarized as follows. Punch introduces himself, is bitten on the nose by the dog Toby (sometimes played by a real dog), is given the Baby to nurse by his wife Judy and, when it cries, throws it into the audience. Judy hits him, so he kills her. He is arrested by the Constable and is about to be hanged by Jack Ketch when he tricks Ketch into stringing himself up on his own noose. The Devil then appears (or, in modern performances, more usually a Crocodile) and after a battle Punch kills him.

Many other characters may be introduced, and there is generally comic business, often with a string of sausages. Punch is usually on stage the whole time, being manipulated by the puppeteer's right hand; the left hand works all the other characters, who appear one by one. Punch's high, squeaky voice is traditionally produced by means of a 'squeaker'

or 'swazzle' which is placed in the back of the mouth; this device, consisting of two pieces of metal holding a vibrating strip of tissue paper, was for many years a closely guarded secret among puppeteers, many of whom have swallowed it by accident, usually without ill-effect.

George Speaight's critical history *Punch and Judy* (1970) provides first-hand accounts of performers and other historical details.

Punchbowl Farm (1947) With almost no formal education, Monica Edwards (1912–98) drew on her own life to create this much-loved series set on a farm and its companion, the *Romney Marsh* series, which was set around Rye, where she had grown up. Punch Bowl farm was real, as in 1947 Edwards and her husband moved into the near derelict collection of buildings and land on the edge of the Devil's Punchbowl in Surrey and set about turning into a profitable dairy concern—just like the Thornton's in the books. The first story about the family, *No Mistaking Corker* (1947), predates the farm's purchase, but it is *Black Hunting Whip* (1950) that really begins the farm's story.

Punctuation Personified, *or Pointing Made Easy, by Mr Stops* A *book of instruction published by John *Harris in 1824. Its elegant and witty illustrations depict punctuation marks in human form; for example, the question mark appears as a 'little crooked man' who is 'always asking this and that'. It was one of the most ingenious and successful attempts from that period at combining instruction with amusement. It is reprinted in the *Opies' *Nursery Companion* (1980).

puppets Puppets were used for entertainment in classical Greece and Rome; Apuleius, writing in AD 200, recorded that Roman marionettes could even roll their eyes. Both marionettes and glove puppets were employed throughout the Middle Ages, and became especially ingenious in Italy, where during the mid-16th cent. a writer described marionettes as able to 'fight, hunt, dance, play at dice, blow the trumpet, and perform most artistically the part of cook'. In France, 'Polichinelle' (i.e. Pulcinella) was the chief hero of puppet plays, taking the role of compère, hero, and clown.

In England, glove puppets were known in the 14th cent. At Witney in Oxfordshire there was a pre-Reformation resurrection miracle play in which puppets represented the persons of Christ, Mary Magdalene, a Watchman, and others. Puppets became an increasingly popular means of entertainment from the mid-

16th cent. Subjects for puppet performances at this period included the Gunpowder Plot, biblical stories, and plays by *Shakespeare and Marlowe. Glove puppets probably predominated; there was often an 'interpreter', a live actor who narrated the action and engaged in backchat with the puppets.

The *Puritans tried to suppress puppet shows along with other forms of entertainment, but they were revived at the Restoration, when Pepys recorded seeing 'an Italian puppet play' in Covent Garden in May 1662; this was a performance by 'Signor Bologna, alias Pollicinella', who seems to have been the first puppeteer to introduce Punch to England. A notable 18th-cent. performer was Martin Powell, who established Punch's Theatre in Covent Garden in 1711 and also performed regularly at Bath. He had twenty plays in repertoire, many of them based on such *chapbook tales as *Dick Whittington and *Friar Bacon. Meanwhile the cruder popular puppet shows continued at fairs all over England; Joseph Strutt (see GAMES-RHYMES), writing at the end of the 18th cent., recalled from his own youth shows consisting of

a wretched display of wooden figures, barbarously formed and decorated, without the least degree of taste or propriety... The dialogues were mere jumbles of absurdity and nonsense, intermixed with low immoral discourses.

English puppetry received a new impetus when *Punch and Judy shows took to the streets in the late 18th cent. Much is recorded about this and the history of puppetry in George Speaight, *Punch and Judy* (1970).

English puppets had reached America by 1742, when 'a merry dialogue between Punch and Joan his wife' was advertised in Philadelphia. In the 1780s Chinese-style shadow puppets, operated with rods, began to give performances in various American cities. During the first half of the 19th cent. the fashion in America was for variety shows done with marionettes, which were known as 'Fantoccini' or 'Artificial Comedians'. In New York these could be found in such places as P. T. Barnum's American Museum on Broadway. Meanwhile Punch and Judy shows were held in pleasure gardens and on beaches, though not generally in the streets. Punch also played in American music halls and at children's parties.

Paul McPharlin, in *The Puppet Theatre in America* (1949), records that by the late 19th cent. American puppetry had become very sophisticated. There were a number of 'Vaudeville Manikin' companies, some using as many as twenty-five puppeteers, musicians, and speakers. During the 1880s and 1890s the Deaves family gave performances with a proscenium stage which was flanked by boxes in which sat applauding puppets; there were also puppet musicians in the orchestra pit. Among the Deaves productions was a version of Jules *Verne's *Twenty Thousand Leagues Under the Sea*. In 1916 the Chicago Little Theatre began to perform puppet plays for children, including an adaptation of The *Little Mermaid, and a few years later Tony *Sarg began to be celebrated for his New York puppet productions, among them versions of *Alice's Adventures In Wonderland and The *Rose and the Ring. Sarg was also one of the first puppeteers to explore the possibilities of the cinema; he made a series of short puppet films for cigarette commercials, and also experimented with stop-motion filming techniques. At this period a number of American entertainers gave floor-show cabaret performances with marionettes; they themselves were fully visible, but were clothed in black so as to concentrate attention on the puppets. Some operators began to use rod puppets, worked from below.

A later 20th-cent. innovation was the use of fluorescent puppets (again with black-clothed operators) in *pantomimes. Many television programmes for children from the 1950s onwards made much use of puppets and a new standard of excellence was reached in the 1970s by Jim Henson's Muppets (see SESAME STREET). Though puppets remain most commonly found in entertainment for younger audiences, some recent theatrical productions based on books for older children have depended on puppetry, which can be great in scale and sophistication—for instance, London's National Theatre adaptations of *War Horse and *His Dark Materials (see also PLAYS).

Puritans English Protestants who regarded the established church under Elizabeth I as insufficiently 'purified' from its former unbiblical and corrupt Roman Catholic practices. Later, more generally, any who separated from the established English church in the belief that its doctrines, organization, or ritual were not authorized by Scripture. The term apparently originated as a jibe, then came to be a convenient name for religious reformers of the 16th and 17th cents. and their followers, who were conspicuous for moral seriousness,

simplicity of life and dress, stress on the Bible, and awareness of sin and damnation.

Two interpretations of the moral nature of children coexisted in the 17th cent. Writers such as Vaughan and Traherne, foreshadowing the *Romantic movement, idealized childhood as a state of innocence and nearness to God. On the other hand the Christian doctrine of original sin suggested, especially to Puritans, that each child was doomed to hell unless some action prevented it. The Puritans' emphasis on Bible-reading as a tool of salvation made them particularly active in teaching reading (*see* PROTESTANT TUTOR, THE), and most children's play they considered a sinful waste of time that should be spent studying godly books. The popular *romances that would naturally have attracted a literate child were thought too frivolous, and so, to extend the range of suitable reading, writers such as *Janeway, *Keach, *Chear, and others wrote in the second half of the 17th cent. books and verses that now seem unacceptably didactic, full of fear of early death and hell, but which were widely bought in their time. Bunyan's *A *Book for Boys and Girls* (1686) stands out among the books written specially for children by choosing to entice, rather than terrify, its readers into godliness.

The Puritans who fled persecution in England to found or join colonies in America eventually formed a large part of the audience for children's books with a religious purpose, and quickly generated their own writers. In 1641 John Cotton, a Nonconformist minister in Boston, composed a children's catechism, *Milk for Babes, and during the 1680s a dissenting London bookseller resident in Boston, Benjamin *Harris, published the first edition of *The *New England Primer, a Puritan schoolbook which became the most popular work of instruction for children in America during the next hundred years.

Purple Jar, The A story by Maria *Edgeworth, first published in *The *Parent's Assistant* (1796) and reissued as part of *Early Lessons* (1801).

PUSHKIN, Alexander Sergeyevich (1799–1837) Celebrated Russian poet who made narrative poems of a number of his country's folk tales or *Skazki*, all of them written during the 1830s. *The Golden Cockerel*, for example, is the story of a magic bird given to a fat and lazy king by a wicked sorcerer; it was made into an opera by Rimsky-Korsakov

(1909), was used as the basis of a *picture book by Willy *Pogány (1936), and has been translated by James *Reeves (1969). *The Fisherman and the Fish*, also known as *The Golden Fish*, tells how a fisherman is granted unlimited wishes by a magic fish, but they are abused by his wife, who determines to make herself rich and powerful.

Pushmi-pullyu Two-headed animal in the *Doctor Dolittle books by Hugh *Lofting.

Puss in Boots A story recorded by *Perrault in his *Contes de ma mère L'Oye* (1697) under the title *Le Maistre Chat, ou le chat botti*.

A miller dies, leaving his three sons nothing but his mill, his ass, and his cat. The brother who inherits the cat bemoans his luck, but the cat asks him to provide him with a bag and a pair of boots and then he 'will see that you haven't had such a bad share as you think'. The miller's son does what the cat asks and the cat uses the bag to catch a rabbit, which he takes to the king, telling him that it is a present from his master, the Marquis of Carabas. The king thanks him, and the cat subsequently brings other presents from the supposed Marquis. One day, when he knows that the king and his beautiful daughter will be taking the air by the riverside, he tells his master to go and bathe in the river. When the king passes by, the cat pretends his master the Marquis of Carabas is drowning and explains that the Marquis has lost all his fine clothes, which were stolen while he was in the river. The king arranges for the miller's son to be clothed from his own wardrobe, the king's daughter falls in love with him, and he is invited into the royal coach to drive on with them. The cat runs ahead and threateningly tells all the farm labourers he meets that they must say that their meadows belong to the Marquis of Carabas. The trick duly works, and the king is astonished at the vast estates belonging to the Marquis. Finally the cat tricks an *ogre who owns a nearby castle into changing himself into a mouse, which the cat then kills. When the king arrives at the castle he is welcomed by the cat 'to this castle of Monsieur the Marquis of Carabas', and a lavish meal which had been prepared for the ogre's friends is served to the royal party. The king is so charmed that he gives the 'Marquis' his daughter's hand in marriage and the cat becomes a lord.

A story very like Perrault's appears in the *Piacevoli Notti*, which was printed in a French translation in 1560 and could well have been known to Perrault. In another

version, found in the 17th-cent. *Pentamerone* (Day 2, tale 4), there is no castle, but the cat manages to make his master so rich through his subterfuges that he can eventually buy himself land and other property. This story continues beyond the end of Perrault's, with the cat's master finally betraying the cat. Though variants on the story have been found in India, there is no evidence to support the theory of some 19th-cent. commentators that it originated in a Buddhist *fable showing how animals are kinder than humans.

Perrault's story was first published in English in 1729, in *Histories, or Tales of Past Times*. Later in that century it began to appear in *chapbooks under the title given to it in the 1729 translation, *The Master Cat, or Puss in Boots*.

The lack of moral content in the story meant that Perrault's original *'moralité'* simply remarks that industry and *savoir faire* pay off better nowadays than inherited wealth, and, as such, the tale was often attacked by 19th-cent. opponents of *fairy stories. George *Cruikshank, in his *Fairy Library* (1870), denounced it as 'a succession of successful falsehoods—a *clever* lesson in lying'. Cruikshank rewrote the story for his book to enable an ending where no deception has actually occurred. *Puss in Boots* has often been made into a *pantomime; it was adapted for the stage by J. R. *Planché and Charles Dance in 1838, as a one-act 'original, comical, magical, mew-sical fairy burletta'.

PYLE, Howard (1853–1911) Popular American author-illustrator who was born in Wilmington, Delaware, to Quaker parents. After the foundation of *St Nicholas in his twenty-first year he began to contribute *Fables with pictures to that magazine for a few dollars each. He was married in 1881 and two years later published The *Merry Adventures of Robin Hood, which established him as one of America's leading children's authors and artists.

He followed it with a collection of original short fairy stories, *Pepper & Salt, or Seasoning for Young Folk* (1886), which showed his skill at reworking European folk motifs into new tales. This was followed by another volume of the same sort, *The Wonder Clock, or Four and Twenty Marvellous Tales* (1888). In 1888 he also produced his first *historical novel, *Otto of the Silver Hand*, which is set in medieval Germany. Another historical romance, *Men of Iron*, appeared in 1892. For his third and final historical novel, *Jack Ballister's Fortunes* (1895), Pyle turned to 18th-cent. America for a story, somewhat resembling *Kidnapped, in which a British youth is taken to America against his will and encounters a celebrated *pirate, Blackbeard (Pyle was obsessed with pirates).

The Garden Behind the Moon (1895), Pyle's only novel-length *fantasy, is an allegory inspired by the death of his son. After this came *Twilight Land* (1895), a third and final collection of original short fairy stories. In 1902 he began the huge task of writing and illustrating his own version of the Arthurian legends; *King Arthur and His Knights* came out in 1903, and was followed by three further volumes completing the series.

Besides creating his own children's books, Pyle illustrated the works of many other writers, including James *Baldwin and James Branch Cabell. After his death several collections of his writing and illustrations were published, among them *Howard Pyle's Book of Pirates* (1921).

His illustrations are outstanding among the work of late 19th-cent. American children's artists. Like Walter *Crane in England, to whom he had many similarities, he was concerned with the total appearance of a book and page. His style may be compared to the Pre-Raphaelites (William *Morris was among his admirers), but the influence of Dürer may also be perceived. He had the advantage of working at the time when the photomechanical reproduction of artists' drawings was replacing the old method of *wood engraving, and this gave him a great deal of freedom. His influence as an illustrator was considerable, the most notable example being his pupil N. C. *Wyeth.

As a writer, he was much praised in America; stories from *Pepper & Salt* and *The Wonder Clock* were used for *storytelling in American *libraries. However, he never had much literary following in Britain, where most readers were irritated by the archaic prose style of his Robin Hood and Arthurian volumes.

PYM, T. (Clara Creed) British late Victorian illustrator who specialized in sentimental line drawings of young children. She illustrated stories by Ismay *Thorn and Yotty *Osborn.

Q

Quangle-Wangle's Hat, The A poem by Edward *Lear, first published in *Laughable Lyrics* (1876). There are picture book versions illustrated by Helen *Oxenbury (1969) and Louise Voce (2005).

QUAY, Emma (1968–) British-born Australian picture-book illustrator and writer. Her name appears frequently on the *CBCA Notable Books list and occasionally as a shortlisted title. *Bear and Chook* (2002), shortlisted for CBCA Book of the Year: Early Childhood, is one of her most popular books, and she won that award with its sequel, *Bear and Chook by the Sea* (2009). *Baby Bedtime* (2013), written by Mem *Fox, is a celebration of the bedtime ritual. Quay's illustration style is very loose and lively, with a lot of pace and movement. She employs colour to create the mood for each book and to extend the emotion in the text, and uses different media for each book. Her work is always fresh and appealing.

Queechy (1852) A sentimental novel by 'Elizabeth Wetherell', that is, Susan Bogert *Warner, author of *The *Wide, Wide World*. Its plot closely resembles that of her more famous novel.

Queen of Hearts, The A *nursery rhyme first printed in 1782 as one of four twelve-line stanzas dealing with kings, queens, and knaves of all four suits of cards. The other stanzas do not have the same character as the first, which is almost certainly traditional. In 1805 it was used as the basis of a comic *picture book by Charles *Lamb, *The King and Queen of Hearts*. The text of this, in rhyming couplets, described the theft, the knave's punishment, and his eventual pardon. A more conventional version was produced by Randolph *Caldecott in 1881.

Quelch, Mr *See* MR QUELCH.

Quidditch A team game played on flying broomsticks that was invented by J. K. Rowling as part of her *Harry Potter series. It is played over an oval-shaped pitch using four balls, the Quaffle, two Bludgers, and the Golden Snitch, and each team is made up of seven players, consisting of three Chasers, two Beaters, one Keeper, and one Seeker. Rowling published a slim volume about the game, using the name Kennilworthy Whisp—*Quidditch Through the Ages* (2001).

QUILLER-COUCH, Sir **Arthur (Thomas)** (1863–1944) English man of letters who wrote several books for children, including two *historical novels, *The Splendid Spur* (1889) and *Fort Amity* (1904). His *The World of Adventure: a collection of stirring scenes and moving incidents* was published in three volumes in 1889–91, and in 1895 there appeared his collection of retellings of *Fairy Tales, Far and Near* with illustrations by H. R. *Millar.

Rabbit In *Winnie-the-Pooh* and *The *House at Pooh Corner* by A. A. *Milne.

Rabbit Hill (1944) Written and illustrated by Robert *Lawson, a popular American animal *fantasy which won the *Newbery Medal. The rabbits and other animal occupants of a hill in Connecticut eagerly anticipate the arrival of New Folks at the Big House. The story is lightweight, but is enlivened by Lawson's pictures. Though the book was first published in Britain in 1947 it made little impression there until its appearance as a *Puffin book in 1977.

racism During the 1970s the charge of racism began to be levelled against a number of well-known children's books, chiefly (in Britain) by members of such radical groups as the *Children's Rights Workshop and the Writers and Readers Publishing Cooperative. The latter group published *Racism and Sexism in Children's Books,* edited by Judith Stinton (1976, revised and enlarged, 1979), which contained attacks on the portrayal of black characters in such books as *Uncle Tom's Cabin, The *Adventures of Huckleberry Finn, *Little Black Sambo,* the *Doctor Dolittle books (in which the character of Prince Bumpo was objected to), *Mary Poppins,* and *Charlie and the Chocolate Factory.* (The texts of the two last-named had already been altered to remove supposedly racist passages, but criticism was still levelled at them.) Even such modern 'liberal' portrayals of black people as were found in Theodore Taylor's *The *Cay* and Paula *Fox's *The Slave Dancer* were criticized as embodying, if subtly, a white writer's views and prejudices. Further attacks were made by a British teacher and lecturer in education, Bob Dixon, in *Catching Them Young: Sex, Race, and Class in Children's Fiction* (1977), and the World Council of Churches in Geneva published *The Slant of the Pen: racism in children's books* (ed. Roy Preiswerk, 1980). In America, where the debate has been equally heated, much was published on the subject, including Donnarae MacCann and Gloria Woodard's *The Black American in Books for Children* (1972), and the periodical *Interracial Books for Children.* Contemporary debates more often focus on the lack of representation of non-white characters (*see* MULTICULTURAL CHILDREN'S LITERATURE) than on whether existing portrayals are stereotypical or offensive, though the fact that certain 'classic' books remain on sale unaltered can be controversial—*Tintin in the Congo* (1931), challenged for the apparently racist attitudes it embodies towards the colonized Congolese, is a case in point. (*See also* BANNED BOOKS.)

RACKHAM, Arthur (1867–1939) British illustrator who was born in south London and called himself a 'Transpontine Cockney'. After showing an early talent for caricatures and fantastic drawings, Rackham went at the age of twelve to the City of London School, where his skill was generally encouraged and appreciated—one of the masters carefully collected drawings confiscated from him in class. After leaving school, he enrolled at Lambeth School of Art and by day, for the next seven years, earned his living as a clerk in an insurance office.

Gradually his pictures began to be published, occasional illustrations appearing in light journals. He finally gave up his clerkship, and at first made a living mainly from work as a kind of roving reporter for the *Westminster Budget,* producing drawings from life of such subjects as Queen Victoria watching a play and Gladstone convalescing from illness. The pictures that resulted from this were quite matter-of-fact, except for such fantasies as his drawing, in the winter of 1893, of *goblin-like influenza fiends lassooing assorted victims with their tails. Realizing that photography would soon almost entirely replace the work of artists in journals, he turned more and more to imaginative illustration. Editions of *The *Ingoldsby Legends* (1898) and *Tales from Shakespeare* (1899) began this phase of his career.

In 1900 *Fairy Tales of the Brothers Grimm* was published by Freemantle & Co., with ninety-nine illustrations by Rackham in black and white and a frontispiece in colour. It was immediately successful and established his reputation. Gradually over the next ten years he reworked it, so that by 1909 it had achieved its best known form, in which almost half the illustrations were in colour.

J. M. *Barrie's *Peter Pan had been the theatrical sensation of Christmas 1904, and the Leicester Galleries arranged for Rackham to meet Barrie. The outcome was *Peter Pan in Kensington Gardens* (1906), not an illustrated version of the play but a reprint of parts of *The *Little White Bird*, an earlier book by Barrie in which Peter had first appeared. Barrie wrote that Rackham had 'shed glory' on his work, and certainly the popularity of Rackham's work now amounted to a craze.

In 1907 the copyright of *Alice's Adventures in Wonderland* expired and a number of new illustrated editions of the book came out. Rackham's version, though predictably criticized at the time for daring to supplant *Tenniel, has survived as the original illustrations' only real competitor. In fact it was meant to complement rather than compete with them, and it has deliberate echoes and quotations from Tenniel's ideas.

Next Rackham illustrated *A Midsummer Night's Dream* (1908); Kenneth *Grahame wanted him to illustrate *The *Wind in the Willows* (1908), but Rackham said he was too busy. In 1912 came an edition of *Aesop, and the following year *Mother Goose*, which had first appeared in the magazine *St Nicholas. During the First World War, Rackham illustrated *Dickens's *A Christmas Carol* (1915) and more Grimm (*Little Brother and Little Sister*, 1917). Then after the war came the outstanding silhouette work of *Cinderella* (1919) and *The *Sleeping Beauty* (1920).

During the war Rackham's wife Edyth had pneumonia followed by a heart attack, which left her permanently weakened, and in 1920, Rackham moved his family to an old farmhouse near Arundel in Sussex, keeping just a studio in London. He walked and cycled a great deal, played tennis energetically, and worked with undiminished enthusiasm. During his middle and late fifties there appeared, among other books, his illustrations to Milton's *Comus* (1921), *A *Wonder Book* by Nathaniel *Hawthorne (1922), and *The Tempest* (1926). In 1927 he sailed for New York to supervise a large exhibition of his work. He

was pleased at being so familiar a name to 'so many others than artists: the bookish people—librarians, book-lovers and so on'. His two 1928 books were both American: Abbie Farwell Brown's *The Lonesomest Doll* and Washinghton *Irving's *The Legend of Sleepy Hollow*.

In 1929 the Rackhams moved to a new house, convenient but not pleasing, at Limpsfield in Surrey. Rackham's wife was increasingly an invalid, but his work kept up its pace: *Goldsmith's *The Vicar of Wakefield* in 1929, Walton's *Compleat Angler*, Clement C. Moore's *The Night Before Christmas* (*see* VISIT FROM ST NICHOLAS, A), and, in a limited edition, Dickens's *The Chimes* in 1931; and in 1932 Ruskin's *The *King of the Golden River* and Hans Christian *Andersen's fairy tales—a book he had long wanted to do. He went to Denmark with his daughter to sketch for it, and get 'that nearer view of the author's country that I needed—a view that helped me to realise again the sensation I felt as a child when I first read Andersen'. In 1933 he made his one excursion into theatre design, for a production of Humperdinck's opera of *Hansel and Gretel*, and he also illustrated *Goblin Market* by Christina *Rossetti and *The Arthur Rackham Fairy Book*.

The year after *The *Pied Piper* (1934) he illustrated, not entirely happily, Poe's *Tales of Mystery and Imagination*, with pictures that he himself thought (according to a friend) 'so horrible that he was beginning to frighten himself'. His *Peer Gynt* came out in 1936. In that year, too, when Rackham was sixty-eight, an American named George Macy called on him, representing the Limited Editions Club of New York. Macy chanced to suggest to Rackham an edition of *The Wind in the Willows* for the Club: 'Immediately a wave of emotion crossed [Rackham's] face; he gulped, started to say something, turned his back on me and went to the door for a few minutes.' When he returned, Rackham explained that he had long regretted his decision not to illustrate the book, which had become one of his own favourites, and said how for many years he dearly hoped for another chance. He now revelled in the task, visiting Kenneth Grahame's widow in order to be shown the right features of the Thames to draw. But he was ill; during 1938 he was operated on for cancer, but grew weaker, became bedridden, and knew he was dying as he started to finish the *Wind in the Willows* drawings. The picture of Rat and Mole loading the boat for their picnic was his last, its final detail being the oars, which he had at first

forgotten. He died in September 1939 at the age of seventy-one. The Limited Editions Club *Wind in the Willows* was published the next year, and Rackham's illustrations to the book first appeared in England in an edition of 1950.

Rackham's nephew by marriage, Walter Starkie, remembered as a child his 'first impression of the painter, coloured by the fairy stories my aunt Edyth told me at bedtime... His face was wizened and wrinkled like a ripe walnut, and as he peered short-sightedly at me out of his goggle spectacles I thought he was one of the goblins out of Grimm's Fairy Tales. Dressed in his shabby blue suit and hopping about his studio in his carpet slippers he reminded me of Rumpelstiltskin, but when armed with palette and paint brushes he became for me a wizard, who with one brush of his magic wand could people my universe with elves and leprechauns.' Rackham's resemblance to a character from a fairy tale struck other visitors, and he was often his own model, with self-portraits dotted throughout his work; in *Mother Goose*, for instance, he appears, complete with spotted bow tie, as the Man With Seven Wives. He believed in founding his fantasy as much as possible on known models, having 'no use for flimsy representation of spiritual realities', so that, whether the artist believed in a fairy or not, he 'must make it as real as if he did'.

Rackham had, in his heyday, a huge adult following. It is true that volumes such as *Peter Pan in Kensington Gardens*, priced at 15 shillings, were unsuited to becoming the property of children. But much of Rackham's best work is to be found in such smaller-format books as his *Aesop* and *Mother Goose*, published at six shillings; and even the books clearly aimed at adults found child devotees. C. S. *Lewis remembered encountering Rackham's *Siegfried and the Twilight of the Gods* as a schoolboy:

His pictures, which seemed to me then to be the very music made visible, plunged me a few fathoms deeper into my delight. I have seldom coveted anything as I coveted that book: and when I heard that there was a cheaper edition at fifteen shillings (though the sum was to me almost mythological) I knew I could never rest till it was mine. I got it in the end, largely because my brother went shares with me.

Rackham made his name in a heyday of fairy literature and other fantasy which the First World War brought to an end. In the words of his biographer Derek Hudson, he has consequently 'suffered from the diminishing acceptance of fairies in a disillusioned world'. Hudson also writes:

It would be idle to deny that Rackham has detractors, who fail to distinguish between the master and his imitators and competitors, who mock at 'Fairies at the bottom of the garden', and who associate him, most unfairly, with terracotta gnomes outside seaside bungalows. This prejudice cannot, it is submitted, survive an acquaintance with the width and range of his accomplishment.

In all Rackham illustrated some ninety books, with immense versatility. A detailed analysis of Rackham's work may be found in Fred Gettings, *Arthur Rackham* (1975). For all the virtuosity of his work in colour, Rackham remained an artist in line, his mastery having its roots in his early work for periodicals, then breaking free to create the swirling intricate pictures of his prime, and finally reaching the economy and impressionism of his last work.

RAE, Gwynedd (1892–1977) British children's author of the 'Mary Plain' stories, about a bear-cub—'an unusual first-class bear from the bear-pits at Berne'. The first book in the series was *Mostly Mary* (1930).

Raffles, the Amateur Cracksman Hero of stories by E. W. *Hornung.

Ragged Dick (1868) A novel by Horatio *Alger.

Raggedy Ann Rag doll in books by American author-illustrator Johnny Gruelle (1880–1938), beginning with *Raggedy Ann Stories* (1918).

RAIKES, Robert (1735–1811) English philanthropist, generally taken to have founded the *Sunday school movement. He was the prosperous proprietor of the *Gloucester Journal*, a newspaper founded by his father. He became involved first in local prison reform then, after making forays into the Gloucester slums that he termed 'botanising in human nature', he took steps to relieve the destitution of the city poor and prevent the dangerous boredom of their children, on their one day of freedom from factory work and other labour.

There is some controversy as to whether Raikes himself or his friend the Revd Thomas Stock, a local curate, actually initiated the first Gloucester school; it seems possible that they collaborated in devising a scheme for Stock's parish but that Raikes started another school in his own area in July 1780. The idea of Sunday schooling was not in itself innovatory, but Raikes's action effectively started the Sunday school movement, partly because it was well publicized, first in his own journal, then in the

Gentleman's Magazine and elsewhere, and because he had hit on a scheme which was comparatively cheap, unambitious, and simple to emulate.

Railway Children, The (1906) A novel by E. *Nesbit. The contented life that Roberta (Bobbie), Peter, and Phyllis live in London is shattered when their father is suddenly taken away. They and their mother have to move to a simple country cottage and live carefully on a reduced income; the children spend much of their time watching the railway line which emerges from a tunnel a short distance from their cottage. The children make a habit of waving every day to an Old Gentleman who rides in a corner seat on the 'Green Dragon'. When Mother falls ill with fever the children (much to her horror) beg a hamper of food for her from the Old Gentleman. Not long after this, the children witness a landslip which entirely blocks the railway cutting and are able, by their prompt action, to prevent an accident, thus earning themselves the commendation of the railway company.

The story was serialized in the *London Magazine* in 1904 and is dedicated to the author's eldest son, Paul Bland. The original illustrator was C. E. *Brock. It has been adapted many times for television, film (most famously the 1970 version, adapted and directed by Lionel Jeffries), and stage. The book is written with E. Nesbit's usual confident portrayal of children, though it is possible to discern a slight falling-off from her previous high level of achievement. John Rowe *Townsend writes of it: 'It is none too tidily organized. It is too sentimental for the present-day taste and the long arm of coincidence reaches all over the place. But . . . it is a much-loved book among British children and a favourite choice for film and television versions.'

Railway Series *See* THOMAS, THE TANK ENGINE.

Rainbow A British *comic, the first to be aimed exclusively at children, published from 1914 until 1956. It featured *Tiger Tim and the Bruin Boys.

Rainbow Fish *See* PFISTER, MARCUS.

Ralph Rover In *Coral Island* by R. M. *Ballantyne.

Ramona An inventive small girl whose plans usually misfire, in stories by Beverly *Cleary. She first appeared in the *Henry Huggins books, and later had her own series (*Ramona*

the Pest, 1968, *Ramona the Brave*, 1975, and others). *Beezus and Ramona* (1955) is told from the point of view of Ramona's sister Beatrice ('Beezus').

Ranald Bannerman's Boyhood (1871) An autobiographical novel about a Scottish childhood by George *MacDonald.

RANDS, William Brighty (1823–82) One of the better British children's poets of the 19th cent.; he was the son of a shopkeeper and became a parliamentary reporter. His *Lilliput Levee* (1864, enlarged 1867), first published anonymously, has a title poem describing a revolution in which children take control from adults. Rands contributed to *Good Words for the Young* and other *magazines, and used various pseudonyms, including 'Henry Holbeach' and 'Matthew Browne'; under this second name he published *Chaucer's England* (1869). He was the author of several books of moral talks for children, including *Lilliput Lectures* (1871).

RANSOME, Arthur (Michell) (1884–1967) Author of the *Swallows and Amazons* series, who was born in Leeds. His father, who was a good shot and a fanatical fisherman, used to take his family to the Lake District each summer holiday, where they stayed at a farm on Coniston Water. Arthur, who was the eldest of four children, described in his autobiography (1967) the annual return there:

I used first of all to race down to the lake... The harbour was a rough stone-built dock, with an old shed or two, and beside it was a shallow cut... where the Swainsons' [the farm family] boat, *our* boat, was pulled half way out of the shallow, clear water...I had a private rite to perform. Without letting the others know what I was doing, I had to dip my hand in the water, as a greeting to the beloved lake or as a proof to myself that I had indeed come home. In later years, even as an old man, I have laughed at myself, resolved not to do it, and every time I have done it again.

He experienced a sense of desolation each time the holiday came to an end and he had to return to 'smoky old Leeds'. Yet, happy though these holidays were, Arthur realized that he was a disappointment to his father.

At the age of seventeen, Ransome became an office boy in the publishing firm of Grant Richards.The next few years of his life are a remarkable story of success through sheer effort. He worked hard at his job, found a better one, and spent all his spare time 'trying to write something'; soon he was earning small sums by placing stories and articles in

newspapers. Whenever he could afford a holiday he would hurry north to Coniston, his boyhood summer haunt, where he made the acquaintance of W. G. Collingwood, friend and biographer of *Ruskin. The Collingwood family adopted him. With the Collingwood daughters Barbara and Dora, who were slightly younger, he 'lived in a golden haze', making picnics on the lake shore or Peel Island (the original of Wild Cat Island in *Swallows and Amazons*) and learning to sail in their boat *Swallow*. Sometimes he and the girls were joined by their schoolboy brother Robin—the future philosopher and ancient historian R. D. Collingwood.

In 1903, though he was not yet twenty, Ransome decided to give up his job and try to make a living as a freelance writer. He was 'sometimes put to strange shifts to keep afloat', producing articles on every kind of subject for anyone who would pay him and on one occasion 'ghosting' for famous sportsmen who were supposedly the authors of manuals of sporting instruction. He turned out a few children's books that have long since been forgotten, with titles such as *Highways and Byways in Fairyland* (1906) and edited a twelve-volume series of *The World's Story-Tellers* (1908–9).

In 1909 he married Ivy Walker, a Bournemouth girl who proved to be self-dramatizing and neurotic. The marriage was unhappy from the beginning—he called it 'a bad, incredible dream'—but for a long time she refused to divorce him.

He escaped to Russia, for little reason other than that it was far away, and was soon living happily there and getting to know *Russian folk tales. This eventually resulted in a children's book, *Old Peter's Russian Tales* (1916), and more of them appeared after his death, as *The War of the Birds and the Beasts and other Russian Tales* (1984). During 1915 he was appointed Russian correspondent for the London *Daily News* and in the following years he had many encounters with Lenin and Trotsky. He fell in love with Trotsky's secretary, Evgenia Shelepina, and after living together for some years they were able to marry in 1924.

Journalism had always seemed to him a temporary distraction from authorship and in 1928 he asked himself 'Was I or was I not to give up any idea of returning to the writing of books?' In the spring of 1929 he began to write *Swallows and Amazons*. The book was published the following year and proved to be the first of a series of twelve. When he was not writing, sailing took up much of his energies. He and his second wife bought a seven-ton cutter which they renamed *Nancy Blackett* after one of the heroines of *Swallows and Amazons*; in 1936 he sailed to Flushing and back as 'research' for *We Didn't Mean to Go to Sea* (1937).

Ransome's first marriage produced one daughter; his second was childless. In old age he denied that he had modelled the Walker children in *Swallows and Amazons* on any particular family. However, a biography of him by Hugh Brogan (1984) reveals that they were drawn closely from the Altounyans, children of his old friend Dora Collingwood and Ernest Altounyan; they supplied not only the Walkers' characters but three of their names, Susan, Titty, and Roger. *Swallows and Amazons* was dedicated to these four and their parents in return for a birthday present ('To the six . . . in exchange for a pair of slippers'), but Ransome later became resentful of the Altounyans' claim that they had inspired him.

Ransome's books had an immense influence on English children's literature in the years immediately following their publication. Obvious imitations began to appear, such as M. E. *Atkinson's series about the Lockett family (1936 onwards) and Katharine Hull and Pamela Whitlock's *The *Far-Distant Oxus* (1937). More subtly, it became the accepted notion for the next thirty years or so that children enjoyed reading stories about other children on holiday, who had plausible but exciting adventures involving such 'props' as boats and horses.

Rapunzel A *fairy story collected by the *Grimms.

A pregnant woman persuades her husband to take some rapunzel plants, which she desperately desires to eat, from a *neighbour's garden. The neighbour is a *witch, and will only agree to the plants being taken provided that the baby, when born, is handed over to her. This duly happens, and the witch brings up the girl, who is given the name Rapunzel, in a high tower. When the witch wants to get into the tower Rapunzel lets down her hair for the witch to climb. A prince sees this and climbs up to Rapunzel in the same way. When the witch discovers what is going on, she cuts off Rapunzel's hair and causes the prince to fall from the tower as he is climbing. He is blinded in his fall, but eventually he and Rapunzel find each other again and by her tears his eyes are restored to sight.

RASCHKA, Chris (1959–) American author and illustrator. An artistic and musical child, Raschka planned a career in zoology, but settled on medicine instead. Following a period working abroad he returned to the US for medical school, but realized on the first day that he would rather be an artist. He became a political cartoonist before moving to New York, where he wrote and illustrated his first book, *Charlie Parker Played Be Bop* (1992). He returned to the theme of jazz in *Mysterious Thelonius* (1997) and *John Coltrane's Giant Steps* (2002). His book *Yo! Yes?* (1993) was a Caldecott Honor Book and he has twice won the medal itself (*see* CALDECOTT MEDAL), in 2006 for *The Hello, Goodbye Window*, written by Norton *Juster, and 2012, with the wordless picture book *A Ball for Daisy*. *Arlene Sardine* (1998) met with controversy for its story of a small fish who wants to become a sardine, finally achieving her dream and ending up in a tin. Working primarily in watercolours, ink, and textured materials, his flowing lines bring energy and movement to his work. With over fifty books to his name, Raschka was the 2012 US nominee for the *Hans Christian Andersen Medal.

RASKIN, Ellen (1928–84) American author-illustrator who produced *picture books for small children and eccentric *detective stories, one of which, *The Westing Game* (1978), won the *Newbery Medal.

Rat In *The *Wind In The Willows* by Kenneth *Grahame.

Rattle-Bag, The (1982) An anthology of poetry, intended for children, edited by Seamus Heaney and Ted *Hughes. The poems are arranged in alphabetical order by title, and there is no thematic or chronological organization, so that the reader may respond freshly to each poem. A follow-up, *The School-Bag*, was published in 1997.

RAWLINGS, Marjorie Kinnan *See* YEARLING, THE.

RAY, Jane (1960–) A British illustrator and picture-book creator. Ray is well known for her richly illustrated work, which often celebrates stories from around the world, as well as fairy tales, myths, and legends. Ray is a supporter of a number of organizations that promote inclusion, *diversity, equality, and accessibility in children's literature, and her own work is often multicultural in content (*see* MULTICULTURAL CHILDREN'S LITERATURE),

featuring children from diverse ethnic backgrounds. She has illustrated for many esteemed poets and authors, such as Carol Ann *Duffy, Berlie *Doherty (the exquisite *Fairy Tales*, 2000; *Jinnie Ghost*, 2005), Jeanette Winterson (*The King of Capri*, 2004) and Joyce *Dunbar. She also writes and illustrates her own picture books, including *Can You Catch a Mermaid?* (2003); and *The Story of Creation*, which won the Smarties Award in 1992.

RAY, Mary (Eva Pedder) (1932–) British *historical novelist for children, best known for her series of books about the beginning of the Christian church. The first of these is *A Tent for the Sun* (1971).

RAYNER, Catherine (1982–) An award-winning English picture-book author and illustrator whose first book, *Augustus and his Smile* (2006), was originally created as part of her final degree exhibition at the Edinburgh College of Art in 2004.

Rayner was awarded the Best New Illustrator Award at the *Booktrust Early Years Awards in 2006 and was named one of Booktrust's ten Best New Illustrators in 2008. Her second book, *Harris Finds His Feet* (2008), won the 2009 *Kate Greenaway Medal. Rayner is known for her imaginative use of composition, scale, and evocative line drawings. Her books mainly feature anthropomorphic animals brought to life by her subtle, yet vivacious use of mixed media, often employing watercolour, crayon, and silkscreen printing. In 2012, Rayner won the UKLA Children's Book Award for *Iris and Isaac* (2010), a beautiful tale of two bears who realize it's better to be together than apart.

reading books *See* ABC BOOKS; PRIMER.

Reading Made Easy A type of ABC and simple lesson book, published from the mid-18th to the mid-19th cents. The title was usually pronounced as one word, 'Readingmadeasy'.

One of the earlier and most widely distributed examples, *Reading Made Most Easy*, issued by William Rusher of *Banbury in 1786, sets out the alphabet and then prints words of two, three, four, and five letters. At the end are extracts from the Psalms in words of two divided syllables. This *Reading Made Most Easy* was reprinted again and again; an issue of 1840 is described as the 'four hundred and fifth edition'.

'Readingmadeasies' were published in America and Canada as well as England; for example, *Reading Made Easy, in some*

Scriptural Instructions for Children (Philadelphia, 1785), and *Reading Made Easy . . . for the use of schools in Upper Canada* (Toronto, 1839).

Reading Without Tears See MORTIMER, MRS F. L.

Real Personages of Mother Goose, The (1930) A book by an American writer, Katherine Elwes Thomas, devoted to relating all the well known *nursery rhymes to historical figures and events. Little Bo Peep is identified with Mary Queen of Scots, the three blind mice with Latimer, Ridley, and Cranmer, and so on.

While it is undoubtedly true that a few rhymes originated as political squibs, the book is largely a flight of fancy, and cannot be taken much more seriously than can the 'research' into nursery rhymes conducted a century earlier by John Bellenden *Ker.

Rebecca of Sunnybrook Farm (1903) A novel by Kate Douglas *Wiggin. The high-spirited Rebecca Rowena Randall, one of seven fatherless children brought up at Sunnybrook Farm, is sent across the State of Maine to stay with her two elderly unmarried aunts. There she goes to school for the first time and is soon very happy among her school-friends and teacher; but her Aunt Miranda's severity is a sore trial to her. She and her friends try to sell soap from door to door so as to acquire for a poor family a 'banquet lamp', which is being given away by the soap company as a 'premium' or reward for sales. In the process she meets 'Mr Aladdin', this being her name for Adam Ladd, a rich young businessman. He buys 300 bars of soap simply because he is charmed by Rebecca's eyes.

The book, one of the best known American *girls' stories, has considerable charm and rarely lacks interest, despite the consistently good nature of Rebecca; Thomas Bailey Aldrich called her 'the nicest child in American literature'. The story was filmed in 1917, with Mary Pickford in the title role, and again in 1938, with Shirley *Temple.

Rectory Umbrella, The A comic magazine written for the amusement of his family by the young 'Lewis *Carroll' (C. L. Dodgson). It dates from 1850, when he was eighteen, and takes its title from his home at Croft Rectory in Yorkshire. It was published in facsimile on the centenary of his birth in 1932. The illustrations, by Dodgson himself, include a frontispiece showing a jolly bearded figure sheltering beneath a big umbrella which bears the words 'Tales—Poetry—Fun—Riddles—Jokes'. The contents include a burlesque Gothic novel entitled 'The Walking-Stick of Destiny', a mock-medieval poem not unlike *Jabberwocky, a gallery of absurd pictures, two mathematical paradoxes, and several nonsensical 'Zoological Papers'. The magazine is peppered with mock-learned footnotes.

Red Fox, *The Story of His Adventurous Career in the Ringwaak Wilds and of His Final Triumph over the Enemies of His Kind* (1905) A novel by Charles G. D. *Roberts, one of the most notable *animal stories. Red Fox is one of a litter of five whose father has been killed by the farmer Jabe Smith. The book recounts his numerous adventures as he grows up in the Canadian wilds, mates with a vixen and rears a family of his own, fights off every kind of predator (including a lynx, a great white owl, and even a red deer), and establishes a reputation as the most cunning fox in the district.

Red House Children's Book Awards See FEDERATION OF CHILDREN'S BOOK GROUPS.

Red Indians See 'INDIANS' OF NORTH AMERICA.

Red Planet (1949) A novel by Robert *Heinlein.

Red Queen In *Through the Looking-Glass* by Lewis *Carroll.

Red Riding-Hood See LITTLE RED RIDING-HOOD.

Red Shift (1973) The fifth novel by Alan *Garner. Tom and Jan, two adolescent lovers living in present-day Cheshire, reach a crisis in their relationship. Alongside their story are told two others, both set in Barthomley, a village discovered by Tom and Jan in their wanderings. The first takes place during the Roman occupation, the second during the Civil War; both concern massacres, and both contain characters (Macey and Thomas) whose predicament relates to Tom's. But Garner leaves the reader to make the connection between the three narratives, and to understand their significance. A full exposition of *Red Shift* may be found in Neil Philip's study of Garner's writings, *A Fine Anger* (1981).

Redwall See JACQUES, BRIAN.

REED, Talbot Baines (1852–93) English writer of *School Stories, the son of Sir Charles Reed, a Member of Parliament and Chairman

of the London School Board. He was educated at the City of London School on Victoria Embankment, a day school, and he had no first-hand experience of the public schools he was to write about so prolifically. He worked all his life in his father's London type-foundry, of which he eventually became managing director, and he was an expert on the history of typography.

His family was closely involved with the *Religious Tract Society, which in 1879 established *The *Boy's Own Paper. Reed, who was already writing for journals and newspapers, contributed the piece which opened the first number, 'My First Football Match, by an Old Boy'. Thereafter he wrote similar pieces on other sports, sketches of types of schoolboys ('the sneak', 'the sulk', and so on), and stories about 'Parkhurst', the first of a series of fictitious schools that he invented. He eventually began to supply serials to the magazine, such as *The Adventures of a Three Guinea Watch*. His first full-length story purely about school life, *The *Fifth Form at St Dominic's*, serialized in the *B. O. P.* in 1881–2 and published as a book in 1887, was immensely influential, inspiring school novels by many other authors over the following half-century.

Reed himself wrote more than a dozen books, all of which began life as serials in the *Boy's Own Paper* and most of which had school settings. Though Reed was not an ex-public schoolboy, his books were praised for their accuracy by those who had attended such schools. Reed more than any other writer was responsible for establishing the school story as a genre popular enough to rival the *adventure story in sales and readership.

Reepicheep Mouse in the *Narnia stories by C. S. *Lewis.

REES, Celia (1949–) English author for children and young adults who came to writing after a career teaching English—a career which made her think about what teens actually want to read and which led her to writing adventure stories, often with historical backgrounds, that are beautifully characterized and deepened by dark undercurrents. Fear and magic feature in *Witch Child* (2000), an enthralling book, set in 17th-cent. England and America, about being an outsider in a world where that can mean being accused of witchcraft. The sequel is *Sorceress* (2002). There's more historical fiction in *Sovay* (2008), about a female highwayman, and *Pirates!* (2003), in which a rebellious English girl and

an escaped slave become pirates. *This is Not Forgiveness* (2011) takes Rees into new territory with its hard-hitting look at modern teen life.

REES, David (Bartlett) (1936–93) British children's author who began his writing career with *Storm Surge* (1975). His many later books include *The Exeter Blitz* (1978), a wartime story set in the West Country, which won the *Carnegie Medal. He wrote a volume of essays on contemporary children's authors, *The Marble in the Water* (1980).

Rees's writing is thoughtful and versatile. The real hero of *The Exeter Blitz* is not the boy who watches the German air-raids and the terrible damage they inflict, but the city of Exeter itself.

REES, (George) Leslie (Clarke) (1905–2000) Australian author who wrote a 'Digit Dick' series about an Australian *Tom Thumb, and a number of *animal stories, beginning with *The Story of Shy the Platypus* (1944).

REEVE, Philip (1966–) An English author and illustrator best known for his brilliantly inventive fantasy and science fiction series. Reeve started out as a freelance illustrator for well-known titles such as *Murderous Maths* and *Horrible Histories* amongst many others. His first book for older readers *Mortal Engines* won the Nestlé Children's Book Prize Gold Award in 2002 and was also shortlisted for the *Whitbread Children's Book Award. *Mortal Engines* is the first in the series known as the *Hungry Cities* quartet or *Predator Cities*, which includes *Predator's Gold* (2003), *Infernal Devices* (2005), and *A Darkling Plain* (2006), the last winning the 2006 *Guardian Children's Fiction Prize and the Los Angeles Times Book Award. Reeves wrote a prequel series to the *Hungry Cities* quartet: *Fever Crumb* (2009), which was shortlisted for the 2010 *Carnegie Medal and followed by two more in the series, *A Web of Air* (2010) and *Scrivener's Moon* (2011). His *Larklight* trilogy for younger readers is set in outer space, where a desperate battle to save the universe ensues. His latest comic fantasy novel *Goblins* (2012) and its sequel *Goblins vs Dwarves* (2013) are due to be continued on in a series. *Here Lies Arthur* (2007), a stand-alone retelling of Arthurian legend, won the Carnegie Medal in 2008. Reeve has recently found a kindred talent in fellow illustrator Sarah *McIntyre; their first co-authored book was *Oliver*

und the Seawigs (2013), an adventure with a lot of sea-monkeys, the first of many successful collaborations.

REEVES, James (1909-78) British poet who made a substantial contribution to children's literature. From 1956 he began to write children's books in prose, some of which were collections of short stories, some original, others based on traditional tales. They include *Pigeons and Princesses* (1956) and *Sailor Rumbelow and Britannia* (1962), both illustrated by Edward *Ardizzone.

His real achievement for children, however, lies in his poetry, which is generally regarded as the best British 'serious' children's verse since that of Walter *de la Mare—though the poems are usually far from serious in subject matter. Magical happenings are treated quite matter-of-factly, and sometimes Reeves indulges in *nonsense:

> A scandalous man
> Was Mr Tom Narrow,
> He pushed his grandmother
> Round in a barrow.
> And he called out loud
> As he rang his bell,
> 'Grannies to sell!
> Old grannies to sell!'

(But the neighbours take a look at her, remark that 'She'd be very small use', and refuse to buy her.)

Reeves's first book of children's poems, *The Wandering Moon*, appeared in 1950; his *Complete Poems for Children*, illustrated by Ardizzone, was published in 1973.

REID, Captain (Thomas) Mayne (1818-83) Prolific writer of *adventure stories the son of a Northern Ireland Presbyterian minister. In his early twenties he emigrated to America, where, after doing various jobs, he became a journalist. In 1847 he volunteered to serve in the war against Mexico, in which he was severely wounded. His experiences gave him material for many novels, of which the first, *The *Rifle Rangers*, was begun in 1848 and published two years later. It was followed by *The *Scalp Hunters* (1851). Reid settled in England and the publisher David Bogue suggested that he should produce books specifically for boys—the first two having been for a general readership. The first result of this, *The *Desert Home*, appeared in time for Christmas 1851 and *The *Boy Hunters* a year later, after which Reid produced at least one new title virtually every Christmas until the end of his life.

Besides the novels, Reid wrote works of *natural history, and his stories contain frequent digressions about flora and fauna. The imparting of such information, indeed, takes the place that piety and moralizing have in the works of his contemporaries R. M. *Ballantyne and W. H. G. *Kingston. Many of the heroes of Reid's novels have a distinctly Byronic character, and indeed Byron was one of the author's idols, and he sometimes gave lectures on him. Reid's novels were translated into many languages, including Russian. Vladamir Nabokov cites *The Headless Horseman* as one of his favourite childhood adventure stories.

REID BANKS, Lynne (1929-) British novelist who was born in London and worked as an actress and journalist before coming to fame with *The L-Shaped Room* (1960). In 1961 she went to live for eight years in Israel, which led to the writing of *One More River* (1973), a novel set during the Six Day War of 1967, and its sequel *Broken Bridge* (1994). Her many and varied works for children include *The Adventures of King Midas* (1976), *I, Houdini: the Autobiography of a Self-Educated Hamster* (1979), the fairy-tale-like *The Farthest-Away Mountain* (1976), the amusing *Harry the Poisonous Centipede* (1996—illustrated, like its sequels, by Tony *Ross) and the frankly disturbing *Angela and Diabola* (1997). Her greatest success for children, however, remains the hugely popular series that starts with *The *Indian in The Cupboard* (1980), telling the story of Omri and the plastic toy Iroquois man he inadvertently brings to life, which was made into a film in 1995.

REINIGER, Lotte (1899-1981) German creator of shadow plays and silhouette animated films, many of them based on children's classics.

religious instruction This was the purpose behind the majority of children's books before the mid-18th cent. English children were taught to read by means of *hornbooks and *primers that included prayers. The English and American *Puritans produced innumerable pious books for young people, of which the most widely distributed was *A *Token for Children* (?1671-2) by James *Janeway. Bunyan's *The *Pilgrim's Progress* was the work of fiction best known to most children in this period. The *Bible was often made available in forms thought suitable for children.

The *moral tales that dominated children's fiction from about 1780 to 1830 were largely

concerned to inculcate 'rational' virtues, but often incorporated Christian teaching. In 1794 Hannah *More inaugurated her scheme of *Cheap Repository Tracts, through which much improving literature was distributed to *Sunday schools, and her example led to the founding of the *Religious Tract Society, which played a large part in religious education during the Victorian period. Much influence was exerted by The *Fairchild Family (1818), in which Mrs *Sherwood helped to found the genre of the *evangelical novel for children; this reached its zenith in the mid-19th cent. with such books as (in England) *Ministering Children and (in America) The *Wide, Wide World.

In the second half of the 19th cent. two profoundly Christian writers, Charles *Kingsley and George *MacDonald, began to show that the *fairy story could be imbued with religious feeling—an example that was followed in the next century by C. S. *Lewis with his *Narnia stories and Madeleine *L'Engle with Meet the Austins (1960). Lewis, indeed, is almost the only 20th-cent. English-language children's writer of note who used fiction as a vehicle for the Christian message, and even he did so with a lightness of touch that makes it possible for readers of his Narnia stories to be unaware that this was his purpose. In contrast the religious element in Madeleine L'Engle's Meet the Austins (1960) is obtrusive.

Religious Tract Society Publisher of many 19th-cent. children's books. It was founded in 1799 at a breakfast in St Paul's Coffee House by a number of evangelicals who wished 'to promote the dispersion of religious tracts', intending that their publications should give more emphasis to *evangelical doctrine than Hannah *More had done in her *Cheap Repository Tracts. The Society began to publish specifically for children in about 1812. Its list included, over the years, many sentimentally pious books which were printed again and again, such as The *Dairyman's Daughter (1810). The Society also founded many *magazines, including The *Boy's Own Paper. During the 20th cent. the Society's publications have appeared under the imprint of the Lutterworth Press.

A similar organization began in America in 1814 as the New England Tract Society; as a result of a merger with the New York Tract Society (founded in 1812) it was renamed the American Tract Society in 1825. It published innumerable pamphlets and books, among

them The Young Christian (1832), the first successful work by Jacob *Abbott. Handsomely illustrated, attractively packaged, its children's books had a decided effect on the American juvenile market.

Reluctant Dragon, The A short story by Kenneth *Grahame; see GOLDEN AGE, THE.

RENNISON, Louise (1951–2016) English comedian and author of books for teenage girls, including *Angus, Thongs and Full-Frontal Snogging (1999) and It's OK, I'm Wearing Really Big Knickers (2001), part of the hugely successful, ten-volume Confessions of Georgia Nicholson. The huge success of that series was followed by another, also focusing on how girls struggle through the maze of teen friendships, boys, and growing up, beginning with Withering Tights: The Misadventures of Tallulah Casey (2010). The books have been a global success and yet are often *banned or challenged because of their honesty about certain aspects of life for teenage girls.

reviewing The first serious reviewing of children's books was undertaken in Britain by Mrs *Trimmer in The *Guardian of Education (1802–6). Some of the children's *magazines which began to be published in the mid-19th cent. reviewed children's books, notably *Aunt Judy's Magazine, in which reviews were a regular feature. In 1887 Charlotte M. *Yonge published What Books to Lend and What to Give, a survey of children's books with an eye to their suitability for parish and *Sunday school use, and the next year came Edward Salmon's *Juvenile Literature As It Is, notable for its opinion-polls of children's favourite books and authors.

The outstanding children's reviewer in England in the late 19th cent. was Andrew *Lang, whose enthusiastic notices in many journals helped to promote a number of authors who are now household names.

In America reviews played a prominent part in the short-lived but influential *Riverside Magazine, a children's periodical which appeared between 1867 and 1870. The principal literary journals, such as the Nation and Scribner's Monthly, reviewed many children's books during the second half of the 19th cent. Among those who spoke out in favour of better children's books was the Revd George S. Bacon, in a series of articles in Hours at Home during 1870, who complained that there were far too many Sunday school books that were simply 'virtuous twaddle'. In

1882 Caroline M. *Hewins published her *Books for the Young*.

America continued to lead the way after the First World War. In 1924 Anne Carroll *Moore began to edit a weekly page of reviews of children's books in the *New York Herald Tribune*, and in the same year the *Horn Book Magazine* was founded in Boston. Britain lagged behind for some years, and when in 1930 the Library Association published *Books to Read . . . a guide for young readers*, the result was reminiscent of Charlotte Yonge's 1887 guide, with books of Christian instruction predominating over fiction. Not until 1936 did Britain gain a regular mouthpiece for reviews of children's literature, in the form of the periodical *Junior Bookshelf*. This, together with Margery *Fisher's journal *Growing Point* (founded 1962), would play a leading part in British children's book reviewing for several decades. From the 1970s a number of British radical critics, such as Bob Dixon and Rosemary *Stones, began to concern themselves with the detection and (where possible) the expurgation of *racism and sexism in children's books; the same trend may be observed in the United States. The British periodical *Signal*, edited by Nancy and Aidan *Chambers, was founded in 1970 to encourage a more detailed study of children's books than could be achieved in normal review space. Some specialist publications still thrive, but by the start of the 21st cent., even those regular newspapers that had in previous decades been giving space to reviews of children's books were reducing their coverage (in the context of a general shrinking of book review space), and online criticism began to fill the gap, with a profusion of specialist blogs, discussion groups, recommendation sites, etc. Notably, in 2011 British newspaper *The Guardian* launched a dedicated book review site aimed at a child readership; it met deservedly with considerable success, but was discontinued in 2016.

Revolting Rhymes (1982) A collection of retellings in rhyming verse of six popular fairy tales, by Roald *Dahl and with illustrations by Quentin *Blake. They are often grotesque, bloody, and sometimes surreal, and distort the familiar versions in ways that are very funny. When Little Red Riding Hood realizes that she's not talking to her grandmother, but the wolf dressed in her grandmother's nightie, she 'whips a pistol from her knickers' and shoots him dead. When the three little pigs are under siege in the brick house, and the wolf, having failed to blow it down, threatens to blow it

up instead, whom do they call for help? Little Red Riding Hood, of course—she's dealt with wolves before, after all. The other stories to get the *Revolting Rhymes* treatment are 'Cinderella', 'Jack and the Beanstalk', 'Snow White', and 'Goldilocks'.

Revolver (2008) A *young adult novel by Marcus *Sedgwick, set in the Arctic circle in 1910, where fifteen-year-old Sig sits beside his father's corpse—but how did he die? The arrival of a stranger forces Sig to investigate his parents' past and reveals questions to answer about his own future. Sedgwick's sparely written narrative flips between the past and recent present, but the tension is never dissipated. Sedgwick is one of the most consistently ambitious and accomplished writers of young adult prose, and *Revolver* sees his craft used to its best effect yet.

reward books Originally a name for books or tracts given to *Sunday school children or distributed among poor households by parish workers. They were designed to teach virtuous conduct and to warn against such evils as intemperance, swearing, and the nurturing of ambitions above their readers' social station.

The *Religious Tract Society was advertising 'reward books to the children of Sunday-schools' in about 1812, and its list of such books in the following years included such works as Burder's *Early Piety*, the *Divine Songs* of Isaac *Watts, and *Doddridge's *Principles of the Christian Religion*. Soon, the *Society for Promoting Christian Knowledge (SPCK), a more 'broad church' organization than the evangelical Religious Tract Society, began to publish books of this kind.

The output steadily increased; Gillian *Avery has written (in *Childhood's Pattern*, 1975):

The 1850s and 60s were the golden years for the amateur writer. Torrents of little books cascaded down upon the Sunday schools, advising, exhorting, and laying down the law for the cottage child. Only modest talent was needed to tell young Sally to avoid light conduct and vanity in dress, and many a clergyman's wife or daughter seems to have made pin-money in doing so. Though there was the occasional flash of professional talent, such as the stories that Charlotte Yonge wrote for her parish school-girls, most are monotonously drab.

By this time, fiction was the dominant element in reward books, a typical (and highly popular) title being *The *Dairyman's Daughter*. A number of *magazines were also produced for distribution to the same readership, most notably *The *Child's Companion*, published by the Religious Tract Society from 1824 to 1889.

By the 1870s reward books were being made more durable and attractive to look at: they were now often bound in boards and stamped with gold, and were advertised more for their appearance than for the piety of their contents. Favourites from this period were the American *Wide, Wide World* and two sentimental novels by English evangelicals, *Christie's Old Organ* and *Jessica's First Prayer*. Charlotte *Yonge tried to improve the general standard by compiling *What Books to Lend and What to Give* (1887) and herself wrote many reward books. However, by this time some of the religious societies were issuing fiction that the early Victorians would have considered quite inappropriate. In 1889 the SPCK's 'Library of Fiction' consisted chiefly of *adventure stories and other melodramatic secular tales, while the Religious Tract Society's most popular publication was *The *Boy's Own Paper*; *historical novels, too, featured prominently in 'Reward' lists. Nevertheless the old-style 'Rewards' continued to be printed again and again; *The Dairyman's Daughter* was listed in 1928 in *Recommended Gift Books for Children* by Mrs Clement Pearson.

In the United States the American Tract Society published innumerable reward books, some of which were reprints of British titles, while others made use of American settings, such as *Eliza, the Indian Sorceress* (c. 1830). The *American Sunday-School Union also produced many religious books especially for children.

In Britain the term 'Reward' eventually came to be used to describe cheap mass-produced juvenile books of every kind, designed for school prizes and Christmas and birthday presents as well as to meet the continuing Sunday school market. Popular 'Reward' authors of this era included such boys' writers as *Brereton, *Westerman, and *Strang; the *girls' story authors Angela *Brazil and Evelyn Everett *Green; and the *school story writer Harold *Avery.

Rewards and Fairies (1910) By Rudyard *Kipling, a sequel to *Puck of Pook's Hill*. The book takes its title from the poem 'Farewell, Rewards and Fairies' by Richard Corbet (1582–1635), which Kipling first read in F. E. Paget's *The *Hope of the Katzekopfs* (1844).

The two children Dan and Una meet, through the agency of Puck, a further series of people from past times, who appear to them in the woods and meadows around their Sussex home and on the Downs near the sea. As with the first book, Kipling drew much from historical fact, for example portraying (in 'Marklake Witches') René Laennec, the inventor of the stethoscope. Dudeney, the shepherd in 'The Knife and the Naked Chalk', was a real Sussex countryman. *Rewards and Fairies* contains two of Kipling's best poems, 'The Way through the Woods' and 'If—'. On the other hand the construction of its stories is even more complex than in *Puck of Pook's Hill*, and they require more than one reading to make Kipling's purpose fully clear.

REY, H. A. (Hans Augusto) (1898–1977) American illustrator and author who was born in Hamburg and came to the USA in 1940. His children's books, written with his wife Margret Rey (1906–96), include a series about a monkey named '*Curious George', originally published from the 1940s till the 1960s. In the first British editions the monkey was renamed Zozo (apparently to avoid giving the monkey the same name as the then reigning monarch).

Reynard The Fox A *beast-epic current in medieval Europe and found in many different versions. The fox is known in French as *Renart*, in German as *Reineke*, and in Dutch as *Reinaert*. The first English book of this title was published by *Caxton in 1481, with a narrative derived from a Dutch text based on the 12th- to 13th-cent. French *Roman de Renart* and the medieval Latin poem *Ysengrimus*, which tells of the enmity between the fox and the wolf.

The lion summons the animals to court and hears accusations against the fox. Reynard is put on trial and condemned to death, but by a trick he obtains a pardon. After he has escaped the court his treachery is discovered, and he commits further misdeeds which lead to him being put on trial once more; but again he eludes justice, and the tale ends with him leaving the court in triumph.

Editions for children have occasionally been printed, for example that by Sir Henry *Cole in his *Home Treasury* (1843), a version (based on Caxton) by Joseph *Jacobs (1895), and a retelling by Roy *Brown (1961).

REYNOLDS, Peter H. (Hamilton) (1961–) American author and illustrator. His picture books include *The North Star*, about following one's dreams; a 'Creatrilogy' extolling the virtues of creativity, consisting of *The Dot* (2003), *Ish* (2004), and *Sky Color* (2012); and *I'm Here* (2011), which encourages empathy with

difference. Reynolds's watercolour and ink cartoons are integral to Megan McDonald's *Judy Moody* and Stink series, and he has illustrated new editions of Judy *Blume's books for younger readers, including *Superfudge* and *Tales of a Fourth Grade Nothing*. With his twin brother, he is co-director of an educational publishing company dedicated to creative learning.

REYNOLDS NAYLOR, Phyllis (1933-) American author of over 130 books for children. Naylor published her first children's book, *The Galloping Goat and Other Stories*, in 1965. Her *young adult novel *Shiloh*, the first book in a trilogy about a young boy who befriends an abused dog, received the *Newbery Medal in 1991 and brought her widespread acclaim. In 1992 she published *Alice in Rapture, Sort Of*, a sequel to her 1985 novel *The Agony of Alice*, which was about an eleven-year-old girl growing up without a mother. She went on to write twenty sequels and a trilogy of prequels in the Alice series. Naylor has written numerous other series and picture books.

Rhyme? and Reason? (1883) A collection of poems by Lewis *Carroll, illustrated by A. B. *Frost and Henry *Holiday.

Rhymes for The Nursery, *by the Authors of Original Poems* A collection of verses for children largely by Ann and Jane *Taylor, published by *Darton and Harvey in 1806. It much resembles its predecessor *Original Poems for Infant Minds* in style and in choice of subjects, such as domestic scenes, the virtues of the worthy poor, kindness to animals, and piety.

The best known poem in the collection is Jane Taylor's 'The Star', better known as *Twinkle, twinkle, little star*.

Another poem, 'The Little Negro', speaks against the slave trade, abolished in the British dominions a year later.

About half the eighty-one poems were reprinted in a shorter volume in 1808 under the title *Select Rhymes for the Nursery*. *Rhymes for the Nursery* was also the title of an American compilation of similar verses published by Munroe and Francis of Boston in 1837, but this contained only a few of the rhymes appearing in the English version.

RICE, Alice Hegan *See* MRS WIGGS OF THE CABBAGE PATCH.

RICHARDS, Frank A pseudonym used by Charles *Hamilton for his *Billy Bunter stories,

beginning in *The *Magnet* in 1908. Hamilton preferred it to all his other pen-names and came to identify so closely with it that he published his life story as *The Autobiography of Frank Richards* (1952).

RICHARDS (Howe), Laura E. (Elizabeth) (1850–1943) American children's poet and prolific author who was born in Boston, Mass., one of six children of Julia Ward Howe, author of 'The Battle Hymn of the Republic'.

Following the birth of the first of her seven children, she began to write down verse jingles 'which seemed to bubble up as if from some spring of nonsense'; she used the baby's back to prop up her writing pad as the child lay prone on her knees.

Her best known poem is probably 'Eletelephony', which begins:

> Once there was an elephant,
> Who tried to use the telephant—
> No! No! I mean an elephone
> Who tried to use the telephone—
> (Dear me! I am not certain quite
> That even now I've got it right).

As her own children started to grow up Mrs Richards began to write stories; her early successes include *The Joyous Story of Toto* (1885) and the immensely popular *Captain January* (1890), a sentimental tale of a girl waif brought up by a lighthouse keeper; it was twice filmed, the second time with Shirley *Temple. In 1889 she began a series of *girls' stories about fifteen-year-old Hildegarde Graham with *Queen Hildegarde*. Altogether she published about seventy children's books.

When the family paper-mill had to close down, Mrs Richards and her husband made their living by setting up and running the first summer camp for boys in the State of Maine. She remained active until the end of her long life; when she was over ninety she wrote a poem about the evacuation at Dunkirk.

RICHARDSON, Samuel (1689-1761) English writer and printer, the author of the first English 'novel of character', which was written partly with young adults in mind. *Pamela*, published in 1740, was a novel in epistolary form. The book's title page declared that it was intended for 'the Youth of Both Sexes'.

In 1740 Richardson also published an illustrated edition of *Aesop, intended for children; this proved very popular, and abridged versions of his novels were brought out by publishers such as the *Newbery family.

RICHLER, Mordecai (1931–2001) Canadian novelist, born in Montreal, the author of the Jacob Two-Two series of children's novels, about a boy called Jacob (named after Richler's own son), known as 'Two-Two' because he's the youngest of five and so has to say everything twice in order to be heard. In the first, and most famous, book, *Jacob Two-Two Meets the Hooded Fang* (1975), Jacob is sentenced to two years, two months, and two weeks in the Children's Prison, where he meets the horrible Hooded Fang. This hilariously told, finely plotted story, has been adapted for television and cinema. Richler also wrote *Jacob Two-Two and the Dinosaur* (1987) and *Jacob Two-Two's First Spy Case* (1995), and the series was continued by other writers after his death.

RICHTER, Hans Peter (1925–93) German author of novels for young people about the Nazi regime and the Second World War. *Wir waren dabei* (1962) (*I Was There*, 1973) is a first-person narrative by the son of a Nazi who joins the Hitler Youth and eventually becomes a soldier in the front line. Richter's message is that he and his contemporaries followed Hitler's leadership because no one spoke out against what was happening.

RICHTER, Jutta (1955–) German writer. As a fifteen-year-old, Richter spent a year in Detroit, where she wrote her first book, which was subsequently published. She won the *Deutscher Jugendliteraturpreis in 2001 for Der Tag, als ich lernte die Spinnen zu zähmen*. Her book *Die Katze oder Wie ich die Ewigkeit verloren habe* (2006; translated as *The Cat: Or, How I Lost Eternity*, by Anna Brailovsky, 2007) was a Batchelder Honor Book (*see* BATCHELDER AWARD) in 2008. Other titles include *Hechtsommer* (2004; translated as *The Summer of the Pike*, by Anna Brailovsky, 2006) and *Hinter dem Bahnhof liegt das Meer* (2001; translated as *Beyond the Station Lies the Sea*, by Anna Brailovsky, 2009).

RIDDELL, Chris (1962–) A political cartoonist and an author and illustrator, and highly renowned for both. His detailed pen-and-ink line drawings are reminiscent of the work of earlier children's book illustrators, such as Ronald *Searle and John *Tenniel (*Alice's Adventures in Wonderland* was an influence). Riddell published picture books in the mid-1980s and subsequently focused on black-and-white line drawings for fiction. A breakthrough came when he teamed up with fellow Brighton resident, Paul *Stewart, which led first to a series of picture books known as the 'Rabbit and Hedgehog' series (beginning with *The Birthday Presents* in 1998). Their next collaboration was a full-length novel, *Beyond the Deepwoods* (1998), which saw Riddell become immersed in the generation of plot. Ten more *Edge Chronicles* titles have followed, to huge critical and commercial acclaim.

Stewart and Riddell also collaborated on the 'Far Flung Adventures' chapter books (the first, *Fergus Crane* (2004), won the Smarties Gold Prize), the 'Blobheads' sequence, the 'Barnaby Grimes' novels, and the novel *Muddle Earth* (2003) and, more recently, the 'Wyrmeworld' sequence. Riddell's other collaborations include the extravagant picture book, *Pirate Diary* (written by Richard Platt) for which he won the first of his three *Kate Greenaway Medals.

More recently, Riddell has both written and illustrated his own chapter books, notably the 'Ottoline' trilogy, beginning with *Ottoline and the Yellow Cat* (2008). The book has been favourably compared in terms of style and tone with *Pippi Longstocking*. And in 2014 he won the *Costa Children's Book Award for *Goth Girl and the Ghost of a Mouse*. This gothic tale focuses on Ada, who wants for nothing, but lacks friends, and whose life is changed by the arrival of a small phantom mouse. This excellent book indulges Riddell's fascination with language by involving puns and parodies, but is entirely accessible, in part thanks to its enticing, lavish design. In 2015 he was named the UK's ninth Children's *Laureate.

Riddle of the Sands, The (1903) One of the first British spy novels, written by Erskine Childers (1870–1922). Two Englishmen, Carruthers and Davies, are on a yachting holiday in the Baltic when they discover a plan to launch a German naval attack on England from the sandy shores of the Frisian Islands. Childers, who was executed in Ireland in 1922 for his part as a Republican fighting against the Free State, wrote the book as a warning to Britain about German naval power.

riddles A form of guessing game in which one person challenges another to identify something that is described in enigmatic terms. The most celebrated early riddle is that set in Greek legend by the Sphinx, the monster that plagued Thebes. It asked passers-by: 'What has one voice, and walks on four legs in the morning, two at noon, and three in the evening?' All who could not answer were destroyed. Eventually the

solution was provided by Oedipus: 'A man, who crawls on all fours as an infant, walks on two feet when grown, and leans on a stick when he is old.'

From the time of classical Greece until the Middle Ages riddle contests were popular, and accounts of them formed a minor branch of literature.

A celebrated collection of early English riddles, in the form of poems of some length, is found in the Anglo-Saxon manuscript (*c*.975) known as the Exeter Book. No solution to these riddles is provided in the manuscript and scholars have not managed to solve them all. By the time riddles began to appear in print in England in the 16th and early 17th cents. they were simpler in character, and solutions were provided. For example: 'Two legs sat upon three legs, and had one leg in her hand, then in came four legs and bare away one leg.' Solution: a woman sitting on a stool eating a leg of mutton, which is stolen from her by a dog; from *The Booke of Meery Riddles* (1629).

Riddle books of the 18th cent. often contained verses, some of which were well known as *nursery rhymes. For example: 'Nancy with the white petticoat, and the red nose, | The longer she stands, the shorter she grows.' Solution: a candle; from *The Royal Riddle Book* (1788).

Many 18th-cent. riddles were bawdy, as they had been since the time of the Exeter Book. By contrast the taste of 19th-cent. riddlers was innocuous and was largely for puns, for example: 'Why is St Paul's Cathedral like a bird's nest? Because it was built by a Wren.' (From *Do You Give It Up?*, 1861.) Riddles of this sort were popular on both sides of the Atlantic. They were parodied in *Alice's Adventures in Wonderland*, when the Mad Hatter asked Alice: 'Why is a raven like a writing-desk?' and, when challenged to produce the solution, answered: 'I haven't the slightest idea.'

During the 19th cent. collections of riddles often consisted of various different types of guessing game: 'Enigmas', a term used for riddle poems of some length and also for puzzles resembling a modern crossword clue; 'Conundrums', a word that came to be used for short punning riddles; 'Rebuses', word puzzles of various kinds; and charades, for both recitation and acting.

Among 20th-cent. children's writers who have used riddles in their stories are Beatrix *Potter, in *The Tale of Squirrel Nutkin* (1903),

and J. R. R. *Tolkien in *The *Hobbit* (1937). Modern collections of riddles include Kevin *Crossley-Holland's *The Riddle Book* (1982); and riddles play a part in, for example, the plot of Salman Rushdie's *Luka and the Fire of Life* (2010).

RIDGE, Antonia (1895–1981) British writer who produced collections of short stories for children, of which the first was *The Handy Elephant* (1946). She also wrote children's radio *plays and translated stories from the Netherlands (where she was born) and France.

RIDLEY, Philip (1964–) London-based artist, performance artist, photographer, filmmaker, playwright, and author of novels for adults and children whose prodigious output began with his own theatre group (aged six) and his first solo exhibition (aged fourteen). His quirky fiction is influenced by all his interests, including pop lyrics, art, and computer games: *Krindlekrax* (1991), which features a monster and the unlikeliest boy hero, *Scribbleboy* (1997), about a boy who tries to emulate the local hero and his amazing scribbles that had brightened up the grim neighborhood, and *Mighty Fizz Chilla* (2002) which once again mixes extraordinary characters, a handful of voices, and, this time, the shadow of *Moby Dick*.

Rifle Rangers, The, *or, the Adventures of an Officer in Southern Mexico (1850)* The first novel by Mayne *Reid. The narrator, Captain Henry Haller, joins a band of volunteers to go to the war with Mexico and is elected an officer. His subsequent adventures, based on the author's own experiences in that war, include a romance with a Mexican girl, capture by guerrillas, and a struggle to the death on a precipice.

Rifles for Watie (1957) A novel by Harold *Keith.

Rikki-Tikki-Tavi *See* Jungle Books, The.

RILEY, James Whitcomb (1849–1916) Indiana poet who wrote several poems which became popular with children. These include 'Little Orphant Annie' (first published in 1885), which, like many of his poems, is written in the 'Hoosier' dialect of Indiana. Its refrain warns that

> the Gobble-uns'll git you
> Ef you
> Don't
> Watch
> Out!

RINALDI, Ann (1934–) American author who started her career as a journalist before becoming a writer. Best known for her *young adult historical fiction, her books are often set in America's troubled past and deal particularly with slavery. *The Last Silk Dress* is set during the Civil War (1988), *Wolf by the Ears* (1991) is about a girl rumoured to be the daughter of Thomas Jefferson and a slave, and *Hang a Thousand Trees with Ribbons* (1996) tells the story of Phillis Wheatley, who was taken into slavery in 1761 but who became America's second published black poet.

Ring a ring o' roses A children's singing game in which the players dance round and tumble to the floor, to the line 'A-tishoo! A-tishoo! We all fall down.' The belief has grown up that the rhyme refers to the Great Plague. There is in fact no evidence to support this theory of the rhyme's origin. It was not printed before the 19th cent., and the forms in which it first appeared (both in England and overseas) suggest that it originated simply as a tumbling or curtseying game with no sinister connotations.

RINGGOLD, Faith (1930–) An African-American artist, author and activist best known for her richly detailed quilted artworks. Her first children's book, *Tar Beach* (1991), won over thirty awards including a Caldecott Honor (*see* CALDECOTT MEDAL), the *Coretta Scott King Award and the Ezra Jack Keats New Writer Award. *Tar Beach* is based on the first of five quilts from Ringgold's 'Woman On a Bridge' series in 1988. It tells the story of Cassie who flies above George Washington Bridge, taking in her landscape and making it her own, while also alluding to the practice of excluding Native Americans and African Americans from unions in the United States. Other notable works include *Aunt Harriet's Underground Railroad in the Sky* (1992), *My Dream of Martin Luther King* (1995), *The Invisible Princess* (1998), an original African-American fairy tale, and *If a Bus Could Talk: The Story of Ms. Rosa Parks* (1999). Ringgold was highly active in forming several feminist, anti-racist organizations, and her work is represented in many of the US's major permanent collections.

Rin-Tin-Tin An Alsatian (or German shepherd) dog, star of a long series of Hollywood films made from 1927 onwards. After the original dog's death in 1932 the role was taken over by a number of successors, and Rin-Tin-Tin remained popular until the arrival of *Lassie in 1943.

RIORDAN, Rick (1964–) American author who started writing when he was young, and even got into trouble for publishing an underground newspaper that made fun of his school. After college he became a teacher and wrote mystery stories for adults, and it was while he was teaching Greek mythology that he had the idea for his most famous creation, *Percy Jackson. His lifelong fascination with myths and legends also led to his writing stories that draw on Greek and Roman mythology in *The Heroes of Olympus* (2010), Egyptian myth in *The Kane Chronicles* (2010), and Norse myth in a forthcoming series. He helped develop *The 39 Clues* series and wrote its first book, *The Maze of Bones* (2008).

Rip Van Winkle A story by Washington *Irving, based on a traditional German tale.

Rip Van Winkle lives in a village at the foot of the Catskill Mountains in the days when the North American states are still British colonies. Wandering up the mountains one day with his gun and his dog, he meets an old man in quaint costume who asks his aid in carrying a barrel of liquor. Rip accompanies him and meets a group of strange old men who give him great quantities of Hollands gin to drink, whereupon he falls into a deep sleep. Waking (as he thinks) next morning, he is stiff in the joints, his clothes are ragged, and he has a long grey beard. He descends to his village which is greatly changed; the villagers are talking of the great War of Independence, Rip's house is derelict, and his wife dead. He has in fact been asleep for twenty years. Rip Van Winkle gradually gets his bearings in the new world in which he has awakened, and finds himself a role as the oldest inhabitant of the village, forever telling stories of his strange experience.

Rip Van Winkle first appeared in print in the first number of Irving's miscellany *The Sketch Book of Geoffrey Crayon, Gent.* (1819). Illustrated editions include those by Gordon *Browne (1887) and Arthur *Rackham (1905).

Riquet à la houppe (Ricky with the Tuft) One of the *Contes de ma mère l'Oye* of *Perrault.

A queen gives birth to a dreadfully ugly son, who gains his nickname from the tuft of hair on top of his head. He falls in love with a beautiful but exceedingly stupid princess who has an ugly but highly intelligent sister. The beauty, by accepting his proposal of marriage,

gains the gift of intelligence. Armed with this, she regrets her promise to marry Riquet and is about to choose another husband when she sees Riquet's preparations for the wedding. She learns from him that if she can love him, he will become as beautiful as herself—which duly happens, though Perrault suggests that the transformation may not have been magical but simply a case of the princess finding Riquet handsome in her eyes because of his good qualities.

Riquet was first translated into English in *Histories, or Tales of Past Times.* (1729) and appeared in several 19th-cent. English collections of fairy tales, for example *Popular Fairy Tales* (1818) and Mrs Craik's *Fairy Book* (1863). The story is the least popular of all Perrault's fairy tales, not least because it says nothing of the fate of the ugly but brilliant sister. Moreover, in his concluding comment about Riquet's transformation being 'subjective', Perrault virtually removes the fairy element from the story and makes it a *moral tale. It is not often printed nowadays, but it appears in Angela Carter's *Fairy Tales of Charles Perrault* (1977).

RITSON, Joseph (1752–1803) Antiquary and collector of *nursery rhymes and *ballads. Inspired by a reading of *Mother Goose's Melody*, he set his nephew to gather nursery rhymes, and in 1783 or 1784 published, in his native Stockton, the collection *Gammer Gurton's Garland*. In 1795 he published the first collection of *Robin Hood ballads, which had much influence on 19th-cent. writings about the outlaw. In 1825 there was published posthumously Ritson's 'Life' of King *Arthur, which dismissed Geoffrey of Monmouth's Arthurian stories as beyond belief, but offered an account of Arthur that was equally fanciful.

The parcel of juvenile books bought by the bibliophile Francis Douce at the sale of Ritson's effects after his death forms the nucleus of the Douce Collection in the Bodleian Library at Oxford, an important gathering of early children's books.

Riverside Magazine for Young People

A juvenile monthly *magazine published in Boston, Mass., from 1867 to 1870, under the editorship of Horace E. *Scudder. It was notable for its column 'Books for Young People' (featuring Scudder's reviews), and for its frequent inclusion of stories by Hans Christian *Andersen. When the magazine was founded, Scudder managed to obtain ten new Andersen tales for it, some of which had not yet appeared in print in Denmark.

Roald Dahl Funny Prize Established in 2008 by *Booktrust and the then Children's *Laureate Michael *Rosen to recognize funny novels and picture books for children, based on a contention that funny books tended to be overlooked by existing awards. The first three winners in the fiction category were Andy Stanton's *You're a Bad Man, Mr Gum* (*see* Mr Gum), Philip *Ardagh's first *Grubtown Tales* book, and Louise *Rennison's *Withering Tights*. The prize was discontinued in 2014.

Roald Dahl Museum and Story Centre

Opened in 2005 in the village of Great Missenden in Buckinghamshire, the home of children's author Roald *Dahl. The museum and story centre house and care for Dahl's archive, which includes his manuscripts and correspondence. There are two main interactive galleries: *Boy*, which explores Dahl's childhood, and *Solo*, which features Dahl's original writing hut. The Story Centre offers regular workshops for schools and events to encourage children and adults to engage with reading and enhance their creative writing skills.

ROBERTS, Sir Charles G. D. (George Douglas) (1860–1943) Canadian writer of *animal stories. After an education at the University of New Brunswick he became a headmaster in Fredericton; in 1885 he was appointed a professor at King's College in Windsor, Nova Scotia. Ten years later he turned to full-time writing and became known as a poet and novelist. The publication of *Wild Animals I Have Known* (1898) by Ernest Thompson *Seton inspired him to write his own realistic stories about animals, of which the best known volumes are *The Kindred of the Wild* (1902), a collection of short stories, and *Red Fox* (1905).

He was the author of nearly seventy books, many of them for children, and has been called 'Canada's first man of letters'. In 1911 he moved to England, where he served as an army officer during the First World War despite the fact that he was in his mid-50s. He was knighted by George V in 1935.

ROBERTS, David (1970–) English illustrator with a gloriously quirky and individual pen-and-ink style, who has worked with some of the biggest names in children's books—both picture books and fiction—including Julia *Donaldson, for whom he illustrated *Tyrannosaurus Drip* (2007), *The Troll*

(2009), and *Jack and the Flum Flum Tree* (2011). He has collaborated with his sister, Lynn Roberts, on an art deco version of *Cinderella* (2001) and a 1970s *Rapunzel* (2003) who lived in a tower block. He has illustrated—and originally also wrote—the *Dirty Bertie books, as well as illustrating Philip Ardagh's *Eddie Dickens* series (*see* AWFUL END), and indulged his darker side with elegant and detailed period work in Chris *Priestley's *Tales of Terror*. 2012 saw the publication of Roberts' newly illustrated edition of *The *Wind in the Willows* from which the cover illustration to this volume is taken.

ROBERTS, Elizabeth Madox *See* UNDER THE TREE.

ROBERTS, Margaret (1833–1919) British author, prolific writer of *historical novels. She generally published anonymously, describing herself as 'the author of *The Atelier du Lys*', this being her best known book. Others included *Banning and Blessing* (1890), a story of Devon witchcraft in the late 18th cent., and *Stéphanie's Children* (1896), set in France at the same period.

ROBERTSON, Keith *See* HENRY REED.

Robin Hood Legendary outlaw, hero of numerous *ballads and stories. Many attempts have been made to prove that he was a real person and antiquaries over several centuries wrote 'historical' accounts of him.

According to some of these, he was born at a place called Locksley or Loxley about 1160, was really named Robert Fitzooth, and was created Earl of Huntingdon. Others have attempted to show that he was one Roger Godberd, an adherent of Simon de Montfort who did indeed become an outlaw at the scene of Robin Hood's activities, Sherwood Forest, in the 1260s and who was notorious for robbery and the murder of travellers. Godberd's activities may have influenced the development of the legends, but there is no evidence that he ever called himself 'Robin Hood'. In fact the frequency with which 'Robin Hood' is used in place-names all over England (Robin Hood's Stone, Robin Hood's Well, etc.) suggests that the character may have evolved from some primitive mythological figure.

Robin Hood seems to have become established as a hero of popular poems by the late 14th cent., for the character of Sloth in *Piers Plowman* admits that he is better acquainted with 'rymes of Robyn hood' than with the Lord's Prayer. Later in the 15th cent. a Derbyshire criminal was recorded as having established himself in the woods with a gang of associates 'like it hadde be Robyn Hode and his meynee'.

The legend that Robin Hood robbed the rich to pay the poor had originated by about 1500, when a Scottish chronicler called him 'the gentellest thief that ever was'. A century later Michael Drayton wrote in *Polyolbion*: 'What often times he tooke, he shar'd amongst the poore.'

Though verse-narratives about the outlaw were undoubtedly common before 1500, only a few of those which have survived can be said with certainty to have originated earlier than that date. The most notable of these, the *Gest of Robyn Hode*, a long poem apparently based on shorter ballads or tales from an earlier period, was printed by Wynkyn de *Worde at some time between 1492 and 1534 and reprinted a number of times before 1600. Many other Robin Hood tales are recorded in 16th-, 17th-, and 18th-cent. ballads printed on *broadsides.

The figure of Maid Marian first appears in conjunction with Robin Hood in May festivities, folk plays, and morris dances from the late 15th cent. onwards, both Robin and Marian being familiar figures in these performances, in which Friar Tuck also sometimes appeared. Several Elizabethan and Jacobean dramatists wrote full-length Robin Hood plays. Among these is the anonymous *George a Green, the Pinner of Wakefield*.

Throughout the 18th cent. there was a ready market for books known as 'Robin Hood Garlands', collections in one *chapbook (larger than the usual size) of a number of ballads about the outlaw. The first scholarly collection of the Robin Hood material was published in 1795 by Joseph *Ritson.

Ritson's *Robin Hood* was used as a source-book by many 19th-cent. writers, who further elaborated the legends. Thomas Love Peacock wrote the comic novel *Maid Marian* (1822), and Sir Walter *Scott introduced Robin Hood and Friar Tuck into *Ivanhoe* (1819). Lord *Tennyson composed a Robin Hood play, *The Foresters* (1892).

The 19th cent. also saw the first appearance of Robin Hood books for children. In 1840 there was published Pierce Egan the younger's *Robin Hood and Little John*, the first Robin Hood 'novel' for children, in which Robin makes his first appearance as an abandoned baby in a forester's cottage. Egan's book was

used by Alexandre *Dumas as the basis of two Robin Hood novels, *Le Prince des voleurs* (1872) and *Robin Hood le proscrit* (1873), building on the French interest in 'Robin des bois', started by *Ivanhoe*. Robin Hood novels became very popular in late 19th-cent. America, the best known example being Howard *Pyle's lengthy *The *Merry Adventures of Robin Hood* (1883).

In the early 20th cent. there were many Robin Hood books for children, including one by Henry Gilbert with illustrations by Walter *Crane (1912) and another that was extremely popular by E. C. Vivian (1927). Even Enid *Blyton wrote a version, *Tales of Robin Hood* (1930). In general little originality was shown and there were only rare efforts to recast the legends into some new form, such as Geoffrey *Trease's *Bows Against the Barons* (1934).

The best 20th-cent. versions have been those closely based on the old ballad-stories, for example, Roger Lancelyn *Green's *Adventures of Robin Hood* (1956). Ian *Serraillier wrote two verse narratives, *Robin in the Greenwood* (1967) and *Robin and his Merry Men* (1969), a rendering of the *Gest* into modern English. Rosemary *Sutcliff's first published book was *The Chronicles of Robin Hood* (1950).

There have been many Robin Hood films, most notably those starring Douglas Fairbanks (1922), Errol Flynn (1938), Kevin Costner (1991), and Russell Crowe (2010), and the stories have often been adapted for television. The *Disney studios have made two Robin Hood cartoon films, the second (1973) portraying the outlaws as animals.

Tom Sawyer and Joe Harper, in Mark Twain's *The *Adventures of Tom Sawyer* (1876), agree that they 'would rather be outlaws a year in Sherwood Forest than President of the United States forever.'

Robins, The *See* FABULOUS HISTORIES.

ROBINSON, Charles (1870–1937) British illustrator who was born in London the elder brother of W. Heath *Robinson and the son of a wood engraver and illustrator. He began to have drawings published when he was twenty-five and was almost immediately chosen by the publisher John Lane to illustrate a new edition of R. L. Stevenson's *A *Child's Garden of Verses*. This, published in 1896, established his reputation, and he was thereafter commissioned to provide drawings for well over 100 books, many of them for children. They

include editions of *Alice's Adventures in Wonderland* (1907), *The *Secret Garden* (1911), and *Once On A Time* by A. A. *Milne (1925).

Robinson was influenced by the late 19th-cent. 'aesthetic' movement—his drawings somewhat resemble those of Beardsley—and, when allowed by the publisher, he liked to design the entire book, paying as much attention to binding and endpapers as to the actual illustrations. He was one of the first illustrators to have all his work reproduced photo-mechanically by line and half-tone blocks, and his experience as an apprentice to the printers Waterlow in his youth contributed to his expertise in working to the requirements of the blockmakers.

ROBINSON, Joan (Mary) G. (Gale) (1910–88) British children's author best known for *Teddy Robinson* (1953) and its sequels, about a *teddy bear, and *When Marnie Was There* (1967), a ghost story.

ROBINSON, W. (William) Heath (1872–1944) British cartoonist, illustrator, and author, the younger brother of Charles *Robinson. Born in London, he trained at Islington School of Art and the Royal Academy Schools. His first important work was for editions of *Don Quixote* and the stories of Hans Christian *Andersen (both 1897); his early drawings resembled those of his brothers Charles and Thomas (all three of whom collaborated on an 1899 Andersen for J. M. Dent) and his style was close to that of *Crane and Beardsley. But he soon began to develop his own flat, comic style, and he broke free from all restraints with *Uncle Lubin* (1902), a comic tale for children (reminiscent of Baron *Munchausen) which he wrote himself. It tells of an uncle's search for his baby nephew, who has been carried off by a Bag-Bird; the uncle constructs a ramshackle airship, sailing-boat, and submarine before achieving his objective. It was the first book to include the kind of drawings that gave rise to 'Heath Robinson' as a term to describe eccentric machinery.

Uncle Lubin led to commissions for Heath Robinson to illustrate a number of other books, including editions of Baron Munchausen (1902) and the verse of *Kipling (1910). His next original children's book was *Bill the Minder* (1912).

In 1915 Heath Robinson illustrated a reissue of Kingsley's *The *Water-Babies* and the next year provided pictures for a new edition of Walter de la Mare's *Peacock Pie*. By this time he had become known as a humorous

cartoonist in the *Strand* and other magazines, chiefly notable for his drawings of weird contraptions. He wrote one further children's book, *Peter Quilp in Search of a Friend* (1921), which is like *Uncle Lubin*; he also illustrated the stories of *Perrault (1921) and *The Incredible Adventures of Professor Branestawm* (*see* PROFESSOR BRANESTAWM) (1933) by Norman Hunter.

Robinson Crusoe A romance by *Defoe, which, though not written for children, has since its publication in 1719 been widely popular (usually in abridged versions) as a children's book and has been the model of numerous other narratives of the same sort.

The story is based on the experiences of Alexander Selkirk, a Scottish shoemaker's son who ran away to sea, quarrelled with his captain, and was at his own request put ashore on an uninhabited island where he remained from 1704 to 1709, when he was rescued. Captain Woodes Rogers, his rescuer, published an account of what had happened and Steele interviewed Selkirk for his journal *The Guardian* on Selkirk's arrival in England in 1711. Eight years later Defoe, then aged nearly 60, published his first work of fiction, *The Life and Strange Surprizing Adventures of Robinson Crusoe, of York, Mariner . . . Written by Himself.*

The book, which gave no indication of its real authorship and was presented as a true narrative, is an embellishment of Selkirk's experiences. Defoe vividly describes Crusoe's gradual establishment of a tolerable way of life for himself on the island; the most dramatic moment is Crusoe's discovery of a human footprint in the sand, a prelude to his meeting with the savage whom he names Friday, 'which was the Day I sav'd his Life'. The book continues with Crusoe's efforts to educate Friday and teach him the Christian religion and concludes with his rescue by sailors from an English ship.

The first edition, published by W. Taylor, was issued on 25 April 1719 and was an immediate success. Taylor reprinted the book three times in that year and in August he published a sequel by Defoe, *The Farther Adventures of Robinson Crusoe*. Defoe also wrote a third volume, *Serious Reflections . . . Of Robinson Crusoe: With His Vision Of The Angelick World*, which Taylor issued in 1720.

Abridgements of the story began to appear almost as soon as it was printed. A volume 'Printed for the Book-Sellers of London and Westminster' and giving the hero's name on the title-page as *Robeson Cruso* and an edition printed for T. Cox at the Amsterdam Coffee-House were both issued in 1719. These were abridgements of Defoe's first volume; in 1722 was issued an abbreviated form, in one volume, of all three Defoe volumes, under the title *The Life And most Surprizing Adventures of Robinson Crusoe, of York, Mariner*. The text was probably the work of Thomas Gent. This text was reissued again and again during the 18th cent. and was still in print in the 1840s, even though it was apparently never authorized by the persons to whom Defoe had sold his copyright. Many other abridgements also appeared.

Gent's version reduced the text of the first volume of Defoe's story to 192 pages from an original of 364. In about 1750 *chapbook versions began to appear in which Crusoe's adventures were often compressed into as little as 24, 16, or even 8 pages, including *woodcuts. Though Defoe was by then known to have been the author, his name was not given on the chapbook title-pages and Crusoe's date of birth (1632) was sometimes brought forward into the 18th cent. to enhance the impression that the narrative was a true story of recent events.

The first abridgement intended especially for children seems to have been that advertised by F. *Newbery and T. Carnan, 1768, price sixpence. Another children's version was published by *Tabart in 1805. Many other children's editions appeared. The story was illustrated by, among others, *Cruikshank (1831) and 'Phiz', Dickens's illustrator H. K. Browne (1860). It has remained hugely popular with children; a poll published in 1888, in *Juvenile Literature As It Is* recorded that it was easily the top favourite boys' book, while a century later there were more than a dozen children's editions in print in Britain and some twenty-five in America. Books based on Defoe's story have been printed in virtually every modern language.

The book has inspired a whole genre of literature, known as *Robinsonnades. The earliest example to achieve lasting success was *The *Swiss Family Robinson* (1812–13). Defoe's story was much admired by *Rousseau, and was recommended by him in *Émile* (1762), a book that might almost be described as a philosophizing of Defoe's narrative.

Robinsonnades Stories on the model of *Robinson Crusoe*. One of the earliest was *Philip Quarll, first published in 1727. Another

popular imitation was J. H. *Campe's *Robin son der jüngere* (1779-80), translated as *Robinson the Younger*.

In 1812-13 there first appeared the German original of *The *Swiss Family Robinson*. From this time Robinsonnades were plentiful, and indeed became for a time the dominant form in fiction for children and young people. Examples include Agnes *Strickland's *The Rival Crusoes* (1826), Ann Fraser Tytler's *Leila, or the Island* (1833), *Masterman Ready* by *Marryat (1841-2), *Canadian Crusoes* by Catharine Parr *Traill (1852), *The *Coral Island* by *Ballantyne (1858), and Jules *Verne's *L'Île mystérieuse* (1874-5), to mention only a very few.

Elements of the Robinsonnade turn up again and again in the typical children's *adventure story from the mid-19th cent. onwards and feature also in such novels of outdoor life as *Bevis* (1882) and *Swallows and Amazons* (1930). Less conventional examples of the genre include *Floating Island* (1930) by the American writer Anne Parish, in which a dolls' house family are shipwrecked on a tropical island. The last word on the subject might be thought to have been said in William Golding's *Lord of the Flies* (1954). Nevertheless the Robinsonnade has continued to flourish, later examples being Jean *George's *My Side of the Mountain* (1959) and Scott *O'Dell's *Island of the Blue Dolphins* (1961). Yann Martel's 2001 Novel *Life of Pi* is a contemporary take on the Robinsonnade, though not for child readers.

Rob Roy (1671-1734) Scottish freebooter and outlaw whose real name was Robert MacGregor; his self-adopted nickname derived from his red ('roy') hair. His physical strength was legendary. He acquired the reputation of being a Highland *Robin Hood and was made the subject of a poem by Wordsworth and of a novel by Sir Walter *Scott (*Rob Roy*, 1817). Rob Roy later became a hero of *penny dreadfuls and other popular literature.

RODARI, Gianni (1920-80) Italian pedagogue, journalist, literary theorist, and celebrated children's author whose writings are distinguished by surreal, heart-warming humour and a sprinkle of political satire. One of his most celebrated works, *Favole al telefono* (English translation, *Telephone Tales*, 1965, by Patrick Creagh), is a collection of very short stories told by a commercial traveller on the telephone to his daughter, including all the quirks of a phone conversation. A master of the medium himself, Rodari also published a theoretical volume on the art of storytelling,

Grammatica della fantasia (1973). A very prolific writer, Rodari received multiple literary awards, including the Hans Christian *Andersen Award (1970), and innumerable Italian libraries, primary schools, parks, and buildings for children and education now bear his name.

RODDA, Emily (Jennifer Rowe) (1948-) Australian author who worked for many years for the Sydney publisher Angus and Robertson and submitted her first manuscript under her grandmother's maiden name. This book was immediately successful and won the *CBCA Junior Book of the Year Award in 1985. Rodda has since won that award (now called CBCA Book of the Year Award: Younger Readers) a further four times. She worked full-time as editor of *The Australian Women's Weekly* while bringing up four children and writing prize-winning children's books and crime novels.

Rodda's children's book work is highly regarded, and she specializes in writing for younger readers. She is an extraordinary stylist, with careful world-building for both her contemporary and fantasy novels. Her works are meticulously planned, with clever plotting, mysteries, and frequent riddles, and are always fast-paced, compelling literature.

Rodda has achieved success in the children's choice awards for *Deltora Quest*, a series of eight high-fantasy novels for younger readers which received the Aurealis Awards: Peter McNamara Convenors' Award in 2002. The *Deltora Quest* series has achieved sales of over 15 million. In 2008 she won the Aurealis Awards Best Children's Novel for *The Wizard of Rondo* (2008). She received the *Dromkeen Medal in 1995.

ROGERS, John *See* New England Primer, The.

Roller Skates (1936) A novel by Ruth *Sawyer, set in New York City in the 1890s. Ten-year-old Lucinda Wyman is left to board with two spinsters while her parents visit Europe. Roller-skating around the city, she makes friends with Mr Gilligan, the 'best hansom cab driver in New York City', Tony, the son of an Italian fruit-stall keeper, and Rags-an'Bottles, a rubbish collector.

The book was a *Newbery Medal winner and has been much admired, but there is an element of condescension in Lucinda's attitude to her friends of the street—they are portrayed somewhat in the manner of the Ruggles

family in a British book written at the same period, Eve Garnett's The *Family from One End Street (1937)—and the death of little Trinket, the daughter of a poor Polish couple, is as sentimental as anything in 19th-cent. children's fiction.

Rollo A character invented by Jacob *Abbott for a series of instructive books. Rollo is a small boy learning the ways of the world; he first appeared in The Little Scholar Learning to Talk; a picture book for Rollo, by his father and Rollo Learning to Read; or easy stories for young children, both published by J. Allen & Co. of Boston, Mass., in 1835.

Abbott explained his aim as chiefly to entertain, but also to make children think, to help them with their reading, and to cultivate 'the amiable and gentle qualities of the heart'. The stories, which bear some resemblance to Maria *Edgeworth's writings for young children, are very simple and placid in character. They are not swamped by piety—they bear more resemblance to *Sandford and Merton than to the work of the severer writers of *moral tales—but they lack any real originality or distinction, and are now chiefly of interest for their picture of New England life at the time that they were written.

Roll of Thunder, Hear My Cry (1976) A sequence loosely based on author Mildred D. *Taylor's own family history, telling, through the Logan family, the African-American story. Cassie Logan is a young black girl living in Mississippi at the height of the Depression. Her family are landowners, which not only makes them comparatively rich but the target for the powerful whites in the area. It is beautifully realized, and the twists and turns of life show Cassie maturing to understand the importance of the land, the need for pride in who you are, and how racism is wrong, simply because everyone is the same deep down.

romances Lengthy narratives of adventure that first appeared in English in the 14th cent. or earlier and became very popular with children, though they were not written specifically for them. They were usually derived from French or other European sources and were presented as stories from the distant past, 'of eldirs, that byfore us were' (Sir Ysumbras). Though concerned to illustrate moral truths with an exemplary story, they also contained many marvels, especially fights with *dragons and *giants. The knight's love for his lady and his rejection of all other women was a frequent theme.

Many were produced in *chapbook form, with a prose narrative consisting of little more than a bald summary of the hero's adventures and *woodcuts illustrating the dragon-killings and other exploits. Some also appeared as *ballads printed on *broadsides. In the 19th cent. the romances faded from popularity, though since 1800 there have been occasional retellings of some of them for children, including those by W. J. *Thoms which appeared in the 1840s.

Among the most notable romances are *Bevis of Hampton and *Guy of Warwick, both of which were great favourites with children. Others which were read by young people from the 16th to the 19th cents. are *Don Bellianis of Greece, *Valentine and Orson, and *Fortunatus.

Ronia, the Robber's Daughter (1981) A novel by Astrid *Lindgren, about two feuding robber clans, who live in two halves of the same castle (split in half by a lightning-bolt), and a girl called Ronia who by befriending a boy from the rival gang manages through great adventures to bring them together. The English translation (1983) is by Patricia *Crampton.

RONKSLEY, William (fl. c. 1680–1700) Author of The Child's Weeks-Work: or, a little book...that...will infallibly allure and lead him on into a way of reading (1712). It contained a series of simple rhymes, combining piety with amusement, arranged to form a four-week course. The verse has a freshness about it uncharacteristic of the *Puritan writers of the period.

Ron Weasley one of Harry's best friends in the *Harry Potter books.

Rookwood A fictional school created by Charles *Hamilton, using the pseudonym 'Owen Conquest'. It first appeared in the pages of the *Harmsworth weekly Boys' Friend in 1915. Rookwood stories were shorter than Hamilton's tales of *Greyfriars and *St Jim's, and did not contain so much of his characteristic repetition and use of catch-phrases. The principal hero was Jimmy Silver of Study no. 8, whose motto is 'Keep smiling'. Rookwood also included its equivalent to *Billy Bunter, named Tubby Muffin. Between the Second World War and Hamilton's death in 1961 Rookwood stories also appeared in book form.

Room on the Broom (2002) A picture book by Julia *Donaldson and Axel *Scheffler, about a witch who agrees to let a series of animals join her on the broom—first a dog, then a bird, then a frog—until finally there are too many of them and the broom snaps in two! But when the witch finds herself threatened by

a hungry dragon, it's the quick thinking of her erstwhile passengers that saves the day. *Room on the Broom* was adapted as an animated short, which was nominated at the 2014 Academy Awards.

ROOSE-EVANS, James (1927-) British theatre director who has written a series of children's books about 'Odd and Elsewhere', a *teddy bear and a toy clown, of which the first was published in 1971.

Roosevelt Grady (1963) A novel by Louisa R. *Shotwell.

Rootabaga Stories (1922) A collection of *nonsense tales by the American poet Carl Sandburg (1878-1967), about the 'big, big, Rootabaga country'. Its capital is the Village of Liver and Onions and its inhabitants include the Potato Face Blind Man, a small girl named Wing Tip the Spick, and Jason Squiff, the Cistern Cleaner, who dresses in popcorn. Tales in the book include 'How They Bring Back the Village of Cream Puff When the Wind Blows It Away', and 'The Two Skyscrapers Who Decided to Have a Child'.

The influence of Edward *Lear and Lewis *Carroll is discernible, but the stories are distinctively American and reflect Sandburg's fascination with United States folk songs and *Ballads. There are two further collections of Rootabaga tales, *Rootabaga Pigeons* (1923) and *Potato Face* (1930).

Rosamond A volume in the series *Early Lessons* (1801) by Maria *Edgeworth.

ROSCOE, William Author of *The *Butterfly's Ball*.

Rose and the Ring, The (1855) The last and most successful of the series of Christmas books written between 1846 and 1855 by William Makepeace Thackeray (1811-63).

In 1853, Thackeray took his daughters Anny, aged sixteen, and Minny, thirteen, with him on a visit to Italy. The girls wanted to give a Twelfth Night party for their friends among the English living in Rome, but could not procure the 'characters', pictures of such figures as King, Queen, Lover, Dandy, and Captain, which traditionally accompanied a Twelfth Night cake. Thackeray proceeded to draw them. One child, Edith Story, the daughter of an American friend, was too ill with malaria to be at the party, so after it Thackeray worked a story round the pictures and read it aloud on visits to her.

Later she wrote that Thackeray 'used to sit on the edge of the bed or draw his chair close up to it, and, and, joy of joys, he brought, chapter by chapter, to read to me "The Rose and the Ring". After he had done reading we talked of the people in the story—they were real people to me and to him.'

Thackeray continued to write the story later in the year—he read it aloud to his daughter Anny when she had scarlet fever in Naples—and he put eighty-two sketches in all into the manuscript. Having then decided to rework it into a Christmas book, he followed his usual practice by himself transferring the drawings to be used on to the wood blocks for publication. But, much as he loved and excelled at drawing, he was never happy in the techniques required for *wood engraving or etching, and his original drawings, eventually published in 1947 by their owners the Pierpont Morgan Library, are far livelier than their published form.

The Rose and the Ring was subtitled 'A Fireside Pantomime for Great or Small Children', and it follows the *pantomimes of the time closely in its arrangement of characters and scenes. A reviewer suggested that adults could find in the book a 'quiet quizzing of the fairy tales that charmed our youth', and Thackeray incorporated plenty of his usual satire and social comedy.

His equivalent of the pantomime fairy queen is the Fairy Blackstick, who once gave to two godchildren presents of a magic rose and a ring, each intended to make them seem charming to whoever beheld them and make any faults ignored. But the effect was only to make the wearers impossibly vain and so now, after two or three thousand years of fairy activity, Blackstick has given up conjuring—'I might as well shut my incantations up, and allow things to take their natural course'—and so when the hero, Prince Giglio of Paflagonia, is born she gives no present, saying, 'My poor child, the best thing I can send you is a little *misfortune*'; and she does the same for the heroine, the Princess Rosalba of Crim Tartary.

Giglio is deprived of his throne by his wicked uncle, King Valoroso XXIV. The principals suffer appropriate fairy-tale vicissitudes before coming into their rightful inheritances and marrying each other. Subsidiary characters include Prince Bulbo and Princess Angelica, who need the magic rose and ring to seem amiable while the principals obviously do not; Doctor Pildrafto the court physician; the French cook Marmitonio; Count Kutasoff Hedsoff the captain and fencing master; and Countess Gruffanuff, who bears the role of

pantomime dame, ugly except for a brief spell of charm as the accidental possessor of the magic ring.

The Rose and the Ring led to a number of imitations by other authors, of which the best was *Petsetilla's Posy* (1870) by the humorist Tom Hood.

ROSEN, Michael (1946–) British children's poet, and vocal advocate for the importance of books, reading, and libraries. His first book, *Mind Your Own Business* (1974), caused a stir with its childlike, sometimes crude, and often very funny verses. Like many other collections by Rosen, such as *Wouldn't You Like to Know* (1977), *You Can't Catch Me* (1981), and *Mustard, Custard and Grumble Belly and Gravy* (2006), it was illustrated by Quentin *Blake. The collaboration between the two men continued, culminating in an extraordinarily original and powerful picture book about grief, *Michael Rosen's Sad Book* (2004), about the death of Rosen's son from meningitis. Of all his varied and prolific output, from anthologies of his own and others' poems, retellings of *Aesop and *fairy tales to first readers and dyslexia-friendly books such as *Wolfman* (2014), Rosen's most loved book to date probably remains the superb picture book *We're Going on A Bear Hunt*, illustrated by Helen *Oxenbury. Rosen was the UK's fifth Children's *Laureate, using his tenure especially to promote poetry, as well as launching the *Roald Dahl Funny Prize.

ROSENBACH, A. S. W. (Abraham Simon Wolf) (1876–1952) Philadelphia dealer in rare books and manuscripts. In 1928 he bought Lewis *Carroll's original manuscript of *Alice's Adventures under Ground*. After assembling an outstanding collection of American juvenile literature he published a catalogue, *Early American Children's Books* (1933). Following Rosenbach's death in 1952, and his brother's the following year, the Rosenbach Museum and Library was founded in 1954 in Philadelphia, with their collection at its heart. Subsequent additions include the illustrations and manuscripts of Maurice *Sendak.

Rosie's Walk (1968) A picture book by Pat *Hutchins. Hutchins's text describes the walk taken by Rosie, a hen, around the farmyard. Past the mill, over the haycock, around the pond . . . There's an additional story, however, and a much more interesting one, in the timeless, stylized autumn-coloured pictures in which we see the attempts of a fox to get to

her repeatedly thwarted. As Rosie crosses the yard, the fox steps on a rake; as she passes the mill, a bag of flour drops on his head; Rosie, unaware of it all, calmly finishes her walk, returning home in time for dinner. *Rosie's Walk* remains one of the finest examples of a picture book where the disconnect between words and pictures is deliberate and absolutely delightful to a child being read to. There is a sequel, *Where, Oh Where, Is Rosie's Chick?* (2015).

ROSOFF, Meg (1956–) An American-born novelist based in the UK best known for her award-winning *young adult debut *How I Live Now* (2004), which was made into a film by Kevin MacDonald in 2013. Her next, *Just In Case* (2006), a thrilling and thought-provoking coming-of-age story, won the *Carnegie Medal and the *Deutscher Jugendliteraturpreis. *What I Was* (2007) is narrated by Hilary, an elderly man, who looks back to his early days at boarding school and the love he once found there. It was shortlisted for the Carnegie Medal and the *Costa Children's Book Award. The ever eclectic Rosoff's next book, *The Bride's Farewell* (2009), is a historical novel set in the 19th cent., while the more comic *There Is No Dog* (2011) features God as a teenage boy. *Picture Me Gone* (2013) is her latest novel, in which a girl and her father take a life-changing roadtrip across America. Whilst Rosoff's work is predominantly *crossover fiction or young adult fiction, she has also collaborated with illustrator Sophie Blackall on picture books *Meet Wild Boars* (2006), *Wild Boars Cook* (2010), and *Jumpy Jack and Googily* (2009). She was the 2016 winner of the *Astrid Lindgren Memorial Award.

ROSS, Diana (1910–2000) British author of The *Little Red Engine series. Other books include *Whoo, Whoo, the Wind Blew* (1946), about washing blowing round a town.

ROSS, Tony (1938–) Author/illustrator of over 800 titles and best known for the *Little Princess books and for illustrating the *Horrid Henry books by Francesca *Simon. Ross was the UK nominee for the international *Hans Christian Andersen Award in 1994.

Born in London, Ross dreamed of working with horses, and when he was seventeen he wrote to John Wayne asking whether he could have a part in a western. Sadly, there was no reply, and Ross ended up at the Liverpool School of Art and Design instead. He started work as an art director in an advertising agency and as a cartoonist for *Punch*. In 1976, Ross brought his portfolio to the new publishing

company Andersen Press, owned by Klaus Flugge. This led to the publication of *Goldilocks and the Three Bears* (1976), one of Andersen's very first titles. The collaboration has continued ever since.

In 1986 Ross published the first Little Princess book, *I Want My Potty*. It was to be the beginning of a successful series about a strong-willed small girl who just happens to be a princess, each title dealing with a developmental or behavioural issue, such as good manners or going to bed, always with high humour and an extreme lightness of touch.

Ross has an anarchic, comedic style and does not gloss over the darker parts of the stories he illustrates. In *My Favourite Nursery Rhymes*, for example, some of the characters in 'Ring o' Roses' are looking decidedly dead.

In addition to his collaboration with Francesca Simon on the enormously popular Horrid Henry series, he has had an enduring partnership with author Jeanne *Willis, with whom he has produced a number of (mostly comic) titles, including the Dr Xargle books (from 1988), *Don't Let Go* (2002), *Misery Moo* (2003), and the award-winning *Tadpole's Promise* (2005), with what is surely one of the most surprising endings in all of picture books.

ROSSETTI, Christina Georgina (1830–94) Poet who was born in London, the daughter of Gabriele Rossetti, an Italian exile who taught at King's College; she was the sister of Dante Gabriel Rossetti. Brought up on the *Arabian Nights*, the English poets of the Romantic movement, and Italian literature, she began to write verses as a child, and in 1847 the best of her juvenile poems were privately printed by her maternal grandfather. She then began to contribute poems to the short-lived Pre-Raphaelite periodical *The Germ*. Eventually Dante Gabriel persuaded her to publish a book of poems, and *Goblin Market* came out in 1862. It was followed in 1866 by another book of verses, *The Prince's Progress*.

These works made Rossetti's name as a poet. She followed this success in 1872 with her first book of verses specifically for children, *Sing-Song*, and two years later came *Speaking Likenesses*, a rambling story partly in imitation of *Alice's Adventures in Wonderland*. Both *Sing-Song* and *Speaking Likenesses* were illustrated by Arthur *Hughes. Christina Rossetti's later years were clouded by the decline and death of Dante Gabriel and of her mother.

The verses in *Sing-Song* were highly praised when first published and compared to Blake's *Songs of Innocence*. However, Rossetti is still best known for her poem 'Goblin Market' (*see* GOBLIN MARKET), which, although not written specifically for children, has long held considerable appeal for them.

Rossetti was also the author of the celebrated Christmas hymn 'In the bleak mid winter'. Her poetry shows a passionate Pre-Raphaelite romanticism which has been disciplined into what her biographer Georgina Battiscombe has called 'a correct Church of England mould'. Indeed Rossetti's strict Evangelism was a hallmark of her life and biographers have speculated that her religion was a key factor in her rejection of proposals of marriage from the Pre-Raphaelite painter James Collinson and the classical scholar Charles Bagot Cayley. All the same, few other poets of her period laid their emotions so bare to the world, and delighted so obviously in beauty.

After her death, her brother William Michael Rossetti published *Maude* (1897), a short story with verses about the moral and religious character of a teenage girl, which Christina had written at the age of 19.

ROUGHSEY, Dick (1924–85) Australian aboriginal author. *The Giant Devil Dingo* (1973) is one of a series of *picture books by him based on aboriginal myths.

Round and Round the Garden (1983) The first book for children by the illustrator Ian *Beck, whose previous work had been in the field of advertising and album covers. This slim collection of play rhymes compiled by Sarah Williams was an immediate success. It established the artist as a new talent for creating illustrations that appeal to the very youngest audience and their parents. It was followed by further titles adopting a similar format: *Oranges and Lemons* (1985), *Ride a Cock Horse* (1988), and *Pudding and Pie* (1989).

ROUNDS, Glen (Harold) (1906–2002) American author-illustrator, best known for a 'Whitey' series about a *cowboy (*Whitey's First Round-Up*, 1942, and many others), based on his own experience as a ranch hand.

Round Table *See* ARTHUR, KING.

Round the World in Eighty Days *See* AROUND THE WORLD IN EIGHTY DAYS.

ROUSSEAU, Jean-Jacques (1712–78) French writer and philosopher who expounded a new approach to education which had a widespread effect on attitudes to children.

Rousseau was born in Geneva, the son of a watchmaker. During a rebellious adolescence he fled to Savoy, spent some time in a Catholic seminary, worked as a music teacher, and became the lover of his patron, Mme de Warens. In 1740 he served as tutor to a family in Lyons; during this period he wrote a dissertation on 'modern music', composed an opera, and completed a comedy and several works on chemistry. In 1745 he took up with a chambermaid at the Paris hotel where he was staying and subsequently had several children by her. These were dispatched by him to a foundlings' hospital almost as soon as they were born, despite opposition from their mother.

For some years Rousseau worked as secretary to a wealthy Paris family. His *Émile*, a treatise on upbringing and education, was published in 1762. In the same year his *Du Contrat social* expounded his theory that the individual's rights should be surrendered to the 'general will' of society. Both books were condemned by the French parliament as contrary to government and religion, and Rousseau fled first to Switzerland and then to England, where he found a patron in the philosopher David Hume, but the two eventually quarrelled and Rousseau returned to France under an assumed name. He was eventually allowed to live there unmolested until his death. Towards the end of his life he married the woman who had given birth to his children.

Émile was translated into English as soon as it appeared in France and attracted much attention. His work influenced a number of English children's writers and educationalists, most notably Thomas *Day, author of *Sandford and Merton*, and his friend R. L. Edgeworth, father of Maria *Edgeworth. The hallmarks of Rousseau's educational philosophy can be seen in many children's books of the period.

ROUTLEDGE, George (1812–88) London publisher of children's books. He opened his own shop in 1833 and from 1851 to 1865 was in partnership with his brother-in-law Frederick *Warne. His sons continued the business after his death. Routledge published many of the *toy books of Randolph *Caldecott and Walter *Crane.

Rover One of D. C. *Thomson & Co.'s 'Big Five' *adventure story papers for boys, founded in 1922 and published until the early 1980s. Its heroes have included Hawkeye the Redskin *detective, who wears Native American costume while doing battle in mid-

Manhattan with Black Bat, the King of the Underworld; and Blue Blaze, Demon of the Air, who pilots a 'phantom plane'.

ROWE, Jennifer See RODDA, EMILY.

ROWE, Richard (1828–79) British journalist and author of children's books, among them one of the earliest to be set in Australia by an author who knew the country. He emigrated there as a young man, but later returned to Britain to work in Edinburgh and London.

The Boy in the Bush (1869), published under the pseudonym 'Edward Howe', consists of a number of episodes in the life of a fourteen-year-old settler, Sydney, and his family and companions. There are encounters with bushrangers, snakes, a drought, a flood, a gold rush, and marauding Aboriginals. These are savage enemies, but 'you can't blame the beggars. I can't see what right we whites have to their country'. The whites' response is also perceived as savage: 'Whenever they saw a black, they tried to kill him, as "naturally" as one tries to kill a snake or a wasp or any vermin. It is not pleasant to have to write about such things, but I must if I am to tell the whole truth about Australia. . . . When blood has once been tasted, so to speak, in savage earnest, "civilisation" peels off like nose-skin in the tropics.'

Rowe's other Australian book for boys, *Roughing it in Van Diemen's Land* (1880), is similarly thoughtful about the indigenous population, and unusually outspoken in its criticism of government policy.

ROWLING, J. K. (Joanne) See HARRY POTTER.

RUBINSTEIN, Gillian (1942–) Australian children's novelist who now writes as Lian Hearn, the name she adopted for her *young adult fantasies, the Otori trilogy, with which she has achieved international success. Beginning with *Across the Nightingale Floor* (2002), this series, a fantasy set in a world reminiscent of feudal Japan, was her first work to reach an adult audience.

Born in Britain, Rubinstein emigrated to Australia in 1973. She broke new ground with her first book *Space Demons* (1985), a story in which teenagers battle a sinister artificial intelligence. Her work is often science fiction or fantasy and features strong plotting, characterization, and world-building. Rubinstein has also written several picture books, and has now published over thirty titles and won a number of major awards, including the *CBCA Book of the Year twice, for *Beyond the Labyrinth* (1988) and *Foxspell* (1994).

Ruby in the Smoke (1985) The first in a quartet of novels by Philip *Pullman featuring the young heroine, Sally Lockhart. Sally, alone and orphaned, is determined to discover the truth behind her father's death. It is a quest that draws her into the dangerous underworld of Victorian London, bringing her into contact with the evil Mrs Holland and the mystery of the Ruby of Agrapur. Her adventures bring her enemies, but also friends, especially Frederick Garland, the young photographer, and his sister Rosa. *The Shadow of the North* (1986—original title *Shadow in the Plate*) and *The Tiger in the Well* (1990) follow Sally as she pursues an independent life. She also appears in *The Tin Princess* (1994).

Rufty Tufty A *golliwog in stories by Ruth Ainsworth.

Ruggles family In *The *Family from One End Street* by Eve *Garnett.

Rumble Fish *See* HINTON, S. E.

Rumpelstiltskin A *fairy story collected by the brothers *Grimm.

A boastful miller declares that his clever and beautiful daughter can spin gold out of straw. The king decides to test this boast and locks the girl up in a roomful of straw with a spinning wheel. She is lamenting her fate when a little man appears and offers to do it for her in return for her necklace. He completes the task, takes the necklace, and vanishes. The king greedily repeats the experiment and this time the little man takes the girl's ring as payment. On a third night, when the girl has been promised the king's hand in marriage if she can spin yet another roomful of straw into gold, she has no payment to give the little man, so he demands that her first child be handed over to him when it is born. Unthinkingly she agrees, the task is completed, and she becomes queen.

When the child is born, the little man arrives to remind her of her promise, but says he will give her three days in which to discover his name. If she can do this, she may keep the child. Messengers are sent out to find all the odd names they can collect, but nothing is achieved until one of them accidentally comes across the little man dancing round a fire outside his hilltop hut and chanting a rhyme which gives away the answer: 'Rumpelstiltskin is my name!' The queen duly confronts the little man with this name, and he is so enraged that he stamps his foot so hard that his leg goes into the earth, 'and then in rage he pulled at his left leg so hard with both hands that he tore himself in two'. (Many later

editors modified this, so that Rumpelstiltskin merely has to make some effort to pull his foot free, after which he stomps off, to the mockery of the court.)

The Grimms' text was assembled from four slightly different versions of the story found in Hesse. The tale has been collected in most European countries and a number of British versions have been recorded, in which the little man is given such names as 'Terrytop', 'Whuppity Stoorie', and 'Tom Tit Tot'. Kevin *Crossley-Holland's book for young children *Stars of Mine* (2013) is an engaging retelling of the Rumpelstiltskin story.

Runaway, The (1872) A novel by E. A. *Hart.

RUNDELL, Katherine (1987–) British author of novels for children, and fellow of All Souls College, Oxford. Though a relative newcomer to children's books, Rundell is already, in the words of Philip *Pullman, 'a writer with an utterly distinctive voice and a wild imagination'. Her striking debut, *Girl Savage* (2011), is the story of Will (Wilhelmina), who lives with her father in Two Tree Hill farm in Zimbabwe, but is forced to swap the bright colours and heat for the grey of an English boarding school. *Rooftoppers* (2013) is about a girl who was rescued from a shipwreck as a baby. Although she is told her mother died in the wreck, she is convinced that she is still alive, and sets off across the roofs of Paris in search of her. *Rooftoppers* won a *Blue Peter Book Award and was shortlisted for the *Carnegie Medal. Rundell has continued her book-on-book improvement with *The Wolf Wilder* (2015), her third and so far her best novel. Set in Russia a century ago, it is a story of a girl and her friends (some of whom are wolves) forced to be brave, to right some great wrongs—a ferociously paced, brilliantly imagined piece of gorgeous immersive storytelling.

Rupert Bear A bear cub who features in British *comic strips for children. He was created for the *Daily Express* in 1920 by Mary Tourtel, wife of the paper's night editor. Rupert wears checked trousers, a jumper, and a scarf. He lives in Nutwood with his parents and goes on adventures with his pals Algy Pug, Bill Badger, and Edward Trunk the elephant.

By 1930 a Rupert League was in existence and Rupert stories had begun to appear in book form. Five years later, when Mary Tourtel's eyesight failed, the strip was taken over by Alfred *Bestall, in whose hands it remained until 1965 and who greatly enlivened it,

injecting colourful characters and eccentric narrative into what had previously been a rather colourless strip. In consequence Rupert maintained his popularity for decade after decade; Rupert *annuals sold in millions, and the stories were adapted for television.

RUSHER family *See* BANBURY.

RUSKIN, John (1819–1900) Celebrated English writer on art and architecture. His story *The *King of the Golden River* (1851) was one of the earliest English *fantasies for children. He wrote one other children's book, *The Ethics of the Dust* (1866), a set of ten lectures to 'little housewives' on the elements of crystallization (the lectures were originally delivered to a girls' school).

In his monthly publication *Fors Clavigera* he attacked the *reward books which were distributed to *Sunday school pupils. Similarly in an introduction to an 1868 edition of *Grimm he lamented that juvenile literature was addressed to 'children bred in schoolrooms and drawing-rooms, instead of fields and woods', and inveighed against parents who tried vainly to substitute *moral tales for good example and 'wholesome discipline'.

During the 1880s he struck up a friendship with Kate *Greenaway and exercised a powerful influence over her work and life.

Russian fairy and folk tales The poet *Pushkin had turned a number of Russian tales into poems in the 1830s, before they were systematically collected by Aleksandr Nikolaevich Afanasyev (or Afanas'ev) (1826–1871) whose *Russian Fairy Tales* appeared in eight volumes from 1855 onwards. Afanasyev was inspired by the Brothers *Grimm; he worked in the Archives of Moscow and his almost six hundred folk stories, including *fairy stories and legends, came from those and other archives as well as from colleagues and contributors. Since publications in Russian were then censored, stories demonstrating Russian peasants' pagan beliefs, or deemed anticlerical or obscene, were forbidden, and some of his tales were then published anonymously in Switzerland. A little later Ivan Aleksandrovich Khudiakov (1842–1876) published his *Great Russian Tales* (1860–62) which he had collected from oral sources during his student vacations; he continued to study local folklore when he was exiled to Siberia for his revolutionary activities. Russian folklorists in the early Soviet Union collected and studied folk tales freely,

but censorship again set in under Stalin until strong support for folk story, and reinterpretation of its significance, made the genre again politically acceptable.

Russian tales were first introduced into English by W. R. S. Ralston (1828–89) with his *Russian Folk Tales* (1873), which was primarily a folklore treatise. In 1893 there appeared *Russian Fairy Tales* by R. Nisbet Bain (1854–1909), based on an 1874 *fairy story collection made from traditional sources by Peter Nikolaevich Polevoi; this had illustrations. Bain's *Cossack Fairy Tales and Folk Tales* (1894), also illustrated, was based on tales in the Cossack dialect. Many of the *Fairy Books* of Andrew *Lang (1889 onwards) included Russian tales. Arthur *Ransome's first substantial book for children was *Old Peter's Russian Tales* (1917).

The best known Russian folk stories include *The *Firebird, tales about *Baba Yaga the *witch, and anecdotes about 'Ivanushko, the Little Fool', who finally outwits his two 'clever' elder brothers.

RUTGERS, An (Anna Rutgers van Der Loeff-Basenau) (1910–90) Prolific Dutch children's novelist. Her books include *Avalanche!* (1954, Great Britain, 1957), about a village buried under snow, and *De Kinderkaravaan* (1954) (*Children on the Oregon Trail*, 1961), the true story of a Dutch family journeying through north-western America in 1844.

Ruthless Rhymes for Heartless Homes (1899) A collection of poems by Harry *Graham.

RYAN, John *See* CAPTAIN PUGWASH.

RYLANT, Cynthia (1954–) American author of more than one hundred books for children. After studying English literature at university, Rylant taught English and worked as a librarian. Her first picture book, *When I Was Young in the Mountains*, inspired by her childhood in the Appalachians of West Virginia, was published in 1982. Five years later, her *young adult novel *A Fine White Dust* was named a Newbery Honor book (*see* NEWBERY MEDAL), and she received a Newbery Medal for *Missing May* in 1993. Rylant has written numerous series, including the much-loved Henry and Mudge books, which feature a young boy and a large English mastiff. She has also written poetry and non-fiction, and has illustrated several of her own books.

S

S., Svend Otto (Svend Otto Sørensen) (1916–96) Danish illustrator and creator of *picture books. He illustrated stories by *Andersen, *Grimm, and *Asbjørnsen and Moe.

Sabriel (1995) By Garth *Nix, the first title in a powerful fantasy trilogy of the Old Kingdom. The series tells of two neighbouring states, one very similar to 20th-cent. Earth, complete with technology, and the other a place full of magic and necromancers. Sabriel's father is lost in Death, so she takes up his role as Abhorsen, whose task is to keep the living safe from the dead, and sets off across the Old Kingdom to find out what has happened to him. She is armed with her knowledge, her father's sword, and the bells, the Abhorsen's tools. The situation is desperate, the enemy powerful. Sabriel, with companions she is not sure she can trust, must risk all to save him—and the Kingdom. With a strong and intrepid female hero, this is a thoughtful take on modern fantasy. *Lirael* (2001) and *Abhorsen* (2003) continued the story.

SABUDA, Robert (1965–) Paper engineer who produces *pop-up books which are highly intricate and technically sophisticated (yet also surprisingly robust, for all their apparent delicacy), some of the most accomplished being based on classic works (such as his superb take on *Alice's Adventures in Wonderland* in 2003). His titles include *The 12 Days of Christmas* (1996), the Encyclopedia Prehistorica series, including *Dinosaurs* and *Sharks and Other Sea Monsters, The Wonderful Wizard of Oz* by L. Frank Baum (2000), and *The Little Mermaid* (2013). Sabuda says that he learned the ability to create with his hands from his father, who was a carpenter, and the art of visual storytelling from his mother, who ran a dance school. He has three times been awarded the Meggendorfer Prize by the Movable Book Society of America.

SACHAR, Louis (1954–) American writer who was born in New York. Sachar's father worked on the seventy-eighth floor of the Empire State Building, something that may have inspired Louis Sachar's much loved *Wayside School* series (1978), though all the children in that series are based on kids he knew at a school where he worked as a teaching assistant. With jobs as diverse as selling brushes door-to-door and working in a sweater warehouse, he ended up as a lawyer, something he only finally gave up in order to write full-time. He is best known for *Holes* (1997), though has written many other excellent novels for young readers, including *There's a Boy in the Girls' Bathroom* (1987), *Dogs Don't Tell Jokes* (1991), and *The Boy Who Lost His Face* (1997).

SACHS, Marilyn (1927–2016) American novelist whose books are about real lives, high school, and surviving being a teenager, such as *The Fat Girl* (1984), which is an ironic take on *Pygmalion*, in which loving someone and the thrill of controlling them are confused; and *First Impressions* (2006), in which a modern bookish girl becomes involved with the life of the middle sister in Jane Austen's *Pride and Prejudice*. Bullying is one of the subjects that looms large in Sachs's work, most notably in *Veronica Ganz* (1968), somewhat dated now but still an effective and uncomfortable read.

Saffy's Angel The first book in the *Casson Family series.

St Clare's (1941–) A light, amusing, and engaging series of boarding-school novels begun by Enid *Blyton in 1941 with *The Twins at St Clare's*, which tells of Pat and Isabel's arrival at a new school and their struggle to settle in and make friends. The following books each focus on a different term or a new girl, such as *Summer Term at St Clare's* (1943) and *Claudine at St Clare's* (1947). The series has been continued by Pamela Cox, starting with *Third Form at St Clare's* (2000). (*See also* MALORY TOWERS.)

SAINT-EXUPÉRY, Antoine de See LITTLE PRINCE, THE.

St Jim's A school created by Charles *Hamilton, at first under his own name in *Pluck* during 1906. Its earliest boy heroes were Jack Blake and his pals Herries and Digby, of School House, and Figgins & Co. of New House. Soon, at the editor's suggestion, Hamilton added the monocled Arthur Augustus d'Arcy—'Bai Jove!...Fancy wunnin' into you, deah boy!' In 1907 the St Jim's stories were transferred to the new *Gem*. Among early pupils were Fatty Wynn, a precursor of *Billy Bunter; later came Bagley ('Baggy') Trimble, consciously modelled on Bunter.

ST JOHN, Judith (1914–2007) Canadian children's librarian and historian of children's literature. For many years curator of the *Osborne Collection, she also wrote the children's book *Where the Saints Have Trod* (1974), an account of her childhood in a Methodist parsonage.

St Nicholas An American *magazine for children, published between November 1873 and March 1940, with further issues appearing during 1943. It was the brainchild of Rowell Smith, one of the founders of *Scribner's Monthly* in 1870. He selected as editor Mary Mapes *Dodge, who was then juvenile editor of *Hearth and Home*. Rowell Smith was the publisher, acting for Scribner & Co. of New York. An English edition was issued by *Warne.

Mrs Dodge, writing anonymously in *Scribner's Monthly* for July 1873, stated that a successful children's magazine 'must not be a milk-and-water variety of the periodical for adults. In fact, it needs to be stronger, truer, bolder, more uncompromising than the other; its cheer must be the cheer of the bird-song; it must mean freshness and heartiness, life and joy.' The publisher's initial announcements took the same line, emphasizing that in the new magazine there would be 'no sermonizing, no wearisome spinning out of facts'.

St Nicholas was handsomely produced, first with forty-eight pages, eventually with ninety-six. Its circulation is said to have been around 70,000. Louisa M. *Alcott was soon contributing serials (*Eight Cousins* and *Jack and Jill*), as was 'Susan *Coolidge'. *Little Lord Fauntleroy* made its first appearance in print in *St Nicholas* from November 1885 to October 1886, and *Two Little Confederates* during 1888. The 1890s saw the serialization of *Tom Sawyer Abroad* by 'Mark *Twain', and works by G. A.

*Henty and R. L. *Stevenson ('Letters to Young Friends'). The most outstanding contribution came from Rudyard *Kipling, who, having 'scrambled' to get his copy of *St Nicholas* in childhood, accepted Mrs Dodge's invitation to write for it, and let her have the first American printing of stories from the first *Jungle Book* during 1893 and 1894.

Mrs Dodge died in 1905 and thereafter the magazine began to decline a little in quality and circulation. Contributions were solicited from readers and in consequence the magazine printed early work by F. Scott Fitzgerald, Edmund Wilson, and others who were to become celebrated. By this time the owners were the Century Co., proprietors of the *Century Magazine*, Scribner's having sold it in 1881. In May 1930 *St Nicholas* was sold again, this time to a publisher in Columbus, Ohio, though it returned to New York in 1934. Its last years were undistinguished; but for more than three decades following its foundation it was, in the words of Alice M. Jordan (*From Rollo to Tom Sawyer*, 1948), 'a treasure house of riches... the very kernel of American books for children'.

St Trinian's An outrageous girls' school in cartoons by Ronald *Searle, first collected in *Hurrah for St Trinian's!* (1948). A number of St Trinian's films were also produced.

St Winifred's, or, the World of School (1862) A novel by F. W. *Farrar, first published anonymously. Walter Evson is sent as a pupil to St Winifred's, a seaside public school, where he starts out well but soon goes to the bad. Matters come to a crisis when, in an act of vengeance on a master who has punished him without complete justice, Walter burns the manuscript of a scholarly book which the master has been writing for fifteen years. But the master shows Christian charity and forgiveness to Walter, who is allowed to remain at the school and gradually comes to be regarded as one of its finest pupils, distinguishing himself in several acts of heroism.

St Winifred's was never as popular as Farrar's *Eric, or, Little by Little*, but it was reprinted a number of times.

Sajo and her Beaver People See GREY OWL.

SALGARI, Emilio (1862–1911) Starting out his career as a navy-bent student with a journalistic streak, Verona-born Salgari published his first work at the age of twenty, as a four-part novella through a Milàn magazine. His first critical, but not economic, success was the serialized *Le tigri di Mompracem*

('The Mompracem Tigers' 1883), which introduced one of his best-known characters from the Indo-Malaysian set adventure cycle: Sandokan. Salgari produced over 200 pieces, with stories, novels, and series, spanning adventure, Wild West, science fiction, and historical settings, but was never a happy writer, working on multiple projects at once in extremely unhealthy conditions, and he eventually committed suicide. Nonetheless, he is remembered as one of the 'classic' writers in Italian genre literature, and Alitalia planes, an asteroid, and multiple Italian pop songs all bear his name—which is still regularly mispronounced to this day (the stress is on the second, not the first syllable).

SALINGER, J. D. *See* CATCHER IN THE RYE, THE.

SALKEY, (Felix) Andrew (Alexander) (1928–95) Jamaican author living in London, who wrote children's novels set in the West Indies.

SALMON, Edward *See* JUVENILE LITERATURE AS IT IS.

SALTEN, Felix (Siegmund Salzmann) (1869–1947) Author of *Bambi*. He was born in Budapest and worked as drama critic of the *Neue freie Presse* in Vienna before spending the Second World War in America. He wrote adult novels and plays as well as several other *animal stories for children. These include a sequel to *Bambi*, published in 1939 and entitled *Bambis Kinder* (Bambi's Children).

SALZMANN, C. G. (Christian Gotthilf) (1744–1811) German Protestant educational writer and author of *moral tales. His *Moralisches Elementarbuch* (1785) formed the basis of Mary *Wollstonecraft's *Elements of Morality* (1790).

SAMBER, Robert (1682–c.1745), *see* HISTORIES, OR TALES OF PAST TIMES.

Sam Pig In stories by Alison *Uttley.

Samuel Whiskers In *The Tale of Samuel Whiskers* by Beatrix *Potter.

SÁNCHEZ-SILVA, José María (1911–2002) Spanish writer, winner of the 1968 *Hans Christian Andersen Medal. His best-known work, *Marcelino Pan y Vino* (1953; 'Marcelino Bread and Wine'), is a religious fantasy about a boy who grows up in a monastery (having been abandoned at the door as a baby) and discovers Jesus there; it was made into a successful film (1955; English title: *The Miracle of Marcelino*), spawned a number of further books about the same character, and has been widely translated.

SANDBERG, Inger (1930–) and **Lasse** (1924–2008) Prolific Swedish husband-and-wife team of author-illustrators. Their *Lille Spöket* ('Little Spook') series of comic *picture books, published since 1965, about a small ghost and his baby sister, has been popular in Sweden and abroad.

SANDBURG, Carl *See* ROOTABAGA STORIES.

Sandford and Merton (in full *The History of Sandford and Merton, A Work Intended for the Use of Children*) A collection of stories with a linking narrative by Thomas *Day, published in three parts in 1783, 1786, and 1789. Day was a friend of Maria *Edgeworth's father, and *Sandford and Merton* was at first intended as a contribution to one of Edgeworth's educational works. In his preface Day claims that the lack of suitable books for children learning to read first prompted him to collect and adapt stories for this purpose, but he 'resolved to proceed a step further... to connect them by a continued narration', and all were 'intended to form and interest the minds of children'. The stories come from a variety of sources and from Day's imagination; for the most part they have some moral value. It was, however, the linking narrative that gave the book its fame and then its notoriety.

Tommy Merton, the spoilt child of a rich merchant, comes back to be educated in England after spending his first six years being indulged by his mother and by black servants in Jamaica. While he is out one day a snake fastens upon him, and Harry Sandford, a local farmer's son, appears and rescues him. Harry is little older than Tommy, but is an entirely good-natured boy who has become the voluntary pupil of Mr Barlow the local clergyman and already reads well and knows much. Tommy's father recognizes that 'this little peasant has within his mind the seeds of true gentility,' and desires that Mr Barlow shall take on his son as well as Harry. The conversation that follows, which Day confessed was for adults, sets out the book's educational theories, derived from *Rousseau, and the rest of the narrative illustrates them.

Gradually, and with several backslidings, Tommy is educated, morally improved, and made more amiable, though the vices of his genteel station in life frequently war against the virtues of the natural and industrious

Harry Sandford. One of the most successful scenes in the book is a fight between Harry and Tommy's snobbish and bullying acquaintance Master Mash.

Through Barlow, Day introduces political theory as well as useful fact; one Socratic conversation concludes that 'The rich do nothing and produce nothing, and the poor everything that is really useful.' Slavery is condemned, and the words of a courageous Negro who joins the Sandford household make Tommy blush 'at the remembrance of the prejudices he had formerly entertained, concerning blacks and his own superiority'.

For all its seriousness of purpose and lack of humour, *Sandford and Merton* was, and is, readable. It was reprinted many times during the century following its first publication, and (drastically reduced) entered the *chapbook market. But its optimism about human educability and its cardboard and priggish characters were easily mocked. A parody by F. C. Burnand, *The New History of Sandford and Merton*, appeared in 1872, and the book came to be rejected in terms such as those of Percy *Muir (in *English Children's Books*, 1954), who called it a 'masterpiece of sentimentality and bathos'.

SANDHAM, Elizabeth (*fl.* 1810) The author of a number of *moral tales, such as *The Twin Sisters: or, The Advantages of Religion* (1805), of which 12,000 copies had been sold by 1819. One of her best known books was *The Adventures of Poor Puss* (1809), in which two cats, old Tabby and young Tib, recount their experiences of the world to each other; Tib is often ill-treated by humans, but when Tabby dies she becomes the favourite of the boy who had looked after the old cat. Miss Sandham was one of the most widely read juvenile authors of her period.

Sans Famille (1878) A novel for children by the French author Hector Malot (1830–1907). A foundling is brought up by a kindly woman, but poverty strikes the household and he is sold to Signor Vitalis, the manager of a troupe of performing animals. The book appeared in English under various titles, including *The Adventures of Remi* and *Nobody's Boy*. Malot also wrote *En Famille*, which appeared in English as *Nobody's Girl*.

SANSOM, Clive (Henry) (1910–81) British-born poet living in Australia from 1950; his volumes of verse for children include *The Golden Unicorn* (1965) and he has collected

speech rhymes, counting rhymes, and acting rhymes. *Return to Magic* (1969) is a set of poems commenting on the events of well known *fairy stories.

Santa Claus *See* FATHER CHRISTMAS.

Sapper *See* BULLDOG DRUMMOND.

Sara Crewe, *or what happened at Miss Minchin's* A short novel by Frances Hodgson *Burnett, first published in 1887, with illustrations by Reginald *Birch. Sara Crewe, a pupil at 'Miss Minchin's Select Seminary for Young Ladies', is badly treated because her father has died, leaving no money to pay the school fees, and consoles herself by pretending to be a princess. When she performs an act of kindness to a beggar-girl her own luck changes; she discovers that she is wealthy, and is given a home by a friend of her father's—the very man responsible for her father's apparent loss of fortune.

The book, though slight compared with the same author's *The *Secret Garden*, is memorable for the character of Sara, 'a queer little child, with old-fashioned ways and strong feelings'. In 1888 it was reissued by *Warne in a volume also containing Mrs Burnett's *Editha's Burglar*.

In 1902 *Sara Crewe* was dramatized by Mrs Burnett as *A Little Princess*, and three years later the book was reissued under this title, in an expanded version adopting many incidents and characters that had been devised by its author to fill out the play. In 1939 it was filmed with Shirley *Temple as Sara, and it has also been televised.

Sarah, Plain and Tall (1985) A short novel by Patricia *MacLachlan. In the late 19th-cent. Midwest, widower Jacob advertises for a mail-order bride to help look after his children Caleb and Anna, the book's narrator. Straight-talking Sarah from Maine replies, agreeing to come for a month's trial, but her homesickness for the ocean competes with her growing affection for the family. *Sarah, Plain and Tall* is the first in a series of five books, three of which have been made into television films. It won the *Newbery Medal and the Scott O'Dell Award for Historical Fiction.

SARG, Tony (1882–1942) American illustrator and puppeteer, born in Guatemala. He organized a *puppet workshop, made animated films, and illustrated children's books,

contributing to many *magazines of the 1920s and 1930s.

SASEK, M. (Miroslav) (1916–80) Author, artist, and illustrator. He was born in Prague, but after the 1948 coup spent most of his life in Germany or France. He trained as an architect before noticing that most travel books were aimed at adults. This led to his famous 'This Is...' series of books about different places and countries for children, which started with *This Is Paris* (1958) and eventually grew to eighteen titles including Rome, Hong Kong, and the Moon! His funny, beautifully observed books are recognizable from their distinctive illustrations—a style very much of its time, which led to his books being lately reissued when the taste for the art and design of the 50s and 60s came back into vogue.

Saturdays, The (1955) The first in Elizabeth Enright's four-book series about the four Melendy children: Mona, Rush, Miranda, and Oliver. The Melendy children are bored; their pocket money is not enough for each alone. Then Miranda—Randy—has the idea of pooling their resources, allowing each to do something exciting in turns. So the Saturday Club is born. Though very much of its time, the series remains enjoyable and very readable. It exemplifies the continuing tradition of the *family story established by writers like Louisa May *Alcott in America and Catherine *Sinclair in the UK.

SAUNDERS, Marshall (Margaret Marshall Saunders) (1861–1947) Canadian author of many *animal stories, most notably *Beautiful Joe* (1894). She was born in Milton, Nova Scotia, the daughter of a Baptist clergyman. Her books are sentimental and poorly written.

SAVILLE, (Leonard) Malcolm (1901–82) British author of children's thrillers and *adventure stories. His first children's novel, *Mystery at Witchend* (1943), introduced the group of young people subsequently known as 'The Lone Piners', who featured in many of his stories.

SAWYER, Ruth (1880–1970) American storyteller and author of more than twenty children's books, Sawyer was born in Boston and trained to be a *kindergarten teacher. At the age of twenty she went to Cuba and helped to organize kindergartens and train teachers in *storytelling. She was then given a scholarship to Columbia University, and worked as a volunteer storyteller in institutions in New York City slums.

In 1905 she went to Ireland to report for the *New York Sun* and while there she met and listened to Irish traditional storytellers, which stirred memories of tales told by her own Irish nurse in childhood. She later travelled to Spain to collect folk tales, which led to the publication of her *Picture Tales from Spain* (1936). Her first great success came in the same year with the novel *Roller Skates*, which was based on a year in her own childhood when her parents were abroad and she was sent to live with two New York spinsters.

She specialized in books of Christmas stories, including *This Way To Christmas* (1916) and *The Long Christmas* (1941). She continued to work as a storyteller in (among other places) a women's prison in West Virginia; she also lectured on the art of storytelling and wrote *The Way of the Storyteller* (1942).

SAXBY, (Henry) Maurice (1924–2014) Sydney-born teacher, academic, library consultant, reviewer, and author of children's literature. A world authority on children's literature (especially Australian), he has written several definitive books, beginning with *A History of Australian Children's Literature 1841–1941* (1969) and a companion volume covering 1941 to 1970 (1971). *The Proof of the Puddin': Australian Children's Literature 1970–1990* (1993) extended the history to recent times.

Saxby trained as a teacher and was soon lecturing in teachers' colleges. He remained in this field, inspiring and mentoring several generations of teachers and librarians. He was the first president of the Australian Children's Book Council, beginning with a NSW branch in 1945. The next year a children's book week was organized to encourage reading, with an accompanying Book of the Year to promote the efforts of writers and illustrators. The awards and the book week continue to be annual events, and Saxby himself continues in his lifelong work of promoting reading as a vital element in the complete development of children and the place of children's literature in the world with his well-researched, practical, enthusiastic, and inspirational approach.

Saxby is a recipient of the *Dromkeen Medal (1983) and the Lady Cutler Award (1989) for his outstanding work in children's literature, the Rotary Award for Vocational Excellence, and the Nan Chauncy Award (2002). He is a life member of the *Children's Book Council of

Australia (1990) and a member of the Order of Australia (1995). In 2012 both the Maurice Saxby Award, to honour those displaying excellence and passion in the field, and the annual 'Maurice Saxby Lecture' were inaugurated.

SAY, Allen (1937–) Japanese-born American author and illustrator. His first children's book illustrations, for Dianne Snyder's retelling of a Japanese folk tale, *The Boy of the Three-Year Nap* (1988), won a Caldecott Honor Award (*see* CALDECOTT MEDAL). Several of his books are autobiographical, including *Tree of Cranes* (1991), *Tea with Milk* (1999), and *The Sign Painter* (2000). *Grandfather's Journey* won the 1994 *Caldecott Medal.

Scalp Hunters, The, or, *Romantic Adventures in Northern Mexico* (1851) By Mayne *Reid. Henry Haller goes on an expedition to 'the trackless prairies of the "Far West"'. He encounters Seguin the Scalp-Hunter, who has a reputation as a committer of atrocities against '*Indians' but is in fact a tragic and heroic figure.

Scarecrows, The (1981) A terrifying novel by Robert *Westall. Simon hates everything. His mother has a new man in her life and everyone, including his sister, seems more than willing to forget his dead father. Simon particularly hates his flashy new stepfather, the man who embarrassed him at parents' day. Having had to move to a new home, Simon rebels by spending as much time as he can in an old water mill, but the mill has a murderous secret and though in his misery Simon calls on his dead father to help him, it is three scarecrows that appear in the field by their house, scarecrows that are moving inexorably closer. Dealing with adult sexuality and schoolboy 'smut', the book reveals that Simon's Hamlet-like feelings about his stepfather and his mother are the result of his emotional immaturity. Atmospheric, thought-provoking, deeply unsettling, this is a genuinely 'leave the light on' horror story.

Scarlet Pimpernel, The (1905) An immensely popular *historical novel by Baroness *Orczy. It is the year 1792, and scores of French aristocrats have escaped the guillotine thanks to an organization with an anonymous head, 'The Scarlet Pimpernel'. This is none other than Sir Percy Blakeney, an English fop with a languid manner ('Demmed uncomfortable things, duels, ain't they?' he remarks when challenged). Blakeney makes up a rhyme

which expresses the French government's predicament:

> We seek him here, we seek him there,
> Those Frenchies seek him everywhere.
> Is he in heaven?—Is he in hell?
> That demmed, elusive Pimpernel?

The book became a huge success after a play based on it was staged in London, and, some thirty years later, it was filmed with Leslie Howard in the title role.

SCARRY, Richard (McClure) (1919–94) Popular American illustrator and author who was born in Boston, and began to contribute pictures to children's books after war service in North Africa and the Mediterranean. His more than 300 *picture books include a 'Tinker and Tanker' series (1960 onwards) and collections of *nursery rhymes. His most enduring works are those about 'Busytown', featuring recurring characters such as Lowly Worm, Huckle Cat, etc. Titles include *Cars and Trucks and Things that Go* (1974) and *Busiest People Ever* (1976). He draws in a simple, popular style, and fills the page with detail.

SCBWI (The Society for Children's Book Writers and Illustrators) An international professional society with over eighty regional chapters in the US and around the world. Founded in California in 1971, the Society has a membership of over 20,000, and its portfolio of activities has grown similarly—it now hosts conferences, presents awards, publishes a journal, etc.

SCHART HYMAN, Trina (1939–2004) Prolific American illustrator known primarily for her work on folk and fairy tales and retellings of classic stories. Inspired by illustrators such as Arthur *Rackham, Edmund *Dulac, and N. C. Wyeth, she displays in many of her finely detailed paintings a classic Romantic quality in keeping with their subject matter, but she was also an early advocate of including culturally diverse images in children's books illustration. Schart Hyman won the *Caldecott Medal in 1985 for *Saint George and the Dragon* by Margaret Hodges and was a three-time Caldecott Honor Award winner for titles such as her own retelling of *Little Red Riding Hood* (1984).

SCHEFFLER, Axel (1957–) German illustrator, born in Hamburg and resident in the UK since 1982. He is best known for his partnership (since 1993) with Julia *Donaldson,

which has made his distinctive and appealing round-eyed cartoony style recognizable to millions of children around the world. Particular successes of the partnership include The *Gruffalo and *Room on the Broom, but there are more than a dozen to choose from (see DONALDSON, JULIA for titles).

Scheffler has also collaborated with Philip *Ardagh on a series of funny chapter books about the Grunts (beginning in 2012 with The Grunts in Trouble); and in 2011 launched a new series of his own for younger children, about a rabbit and a mouse, Pip and Posy. He has also illustrated—among much else—a retelling of *Mother Goose nursery rhymes (2006), several picture books by Ian *Whybrow, and an edition of *Old Possum's Book of Practical Cats (2009, for the book's seventieth anniversary).

SCHMID, Christoph Von (1768–1854) Author of a number of sentimental and moral stories for young German readers, of which the best known were Die Ostereier ('Easter Eggs') (1816) and Das Blumenkörbchen (1823). The latter became very popular in England as The *Basket of Flowers.

SCHMIDT, Annie M. G. (1911–1995) Dutch writer best known for her children's books, including the eternally popular series Jip en Janneke, with its familiar silhouette illustrations by Fiep Westendorp (written in the 1950s; translated into English as Jip and Janneke by David Colmer, 2008), and Minoes (1970; translated into English as The Cat Who Came in off the Roof by David Colmer, 2014), and for her poems for children (a selection has been published as A Pond Full of Ink in a translation by David Colmer, 2014). Schmidt won the *Hans Christian Andersen Medal in 1988.

schoolbooks See BOOKS OF INSTRUCTION.

School Friend A *magazine for girls published weekly by *Harmsworth's Amalgamated Press from 1919 to 1929, after which it was superseded by Schoolgirl. Its principal feature was a series of stories about *Bessie Bunter and Cliff House School. These were written for the opening issues by Charles *Hamilton, under the pseudonym 'Hilda Richards', but Hamilton was soon replaced by other writers using the same pen-name.

school stories These had precursors in such books of school dialogues as *Pueriles Confabulatiunculae (1617). Sarah Fielding's The *Governess (1749) used a school setting

as a framework for a series of tales, and a school played a large part in *Goody Two-Shoes (1765), but the first stories to be written purely about school life were by Dorothy *Kilner. Her *Village School (c.1795) is merely the typical *moral tale of the period, but in *First Going to School (1804) she showed some interest in schoolboy pranks. Maria *Edgeworth in 'The Barring-Out', a story printed in The *Parent's Assistant (1796), provides a rare instance of a late 18th-cent. account of public school life. Two stories by Elizabeth *Sandham, The Boys' School; or, Traits of Character in Early Life (1800) and The Schoolfellows (1818), are didactic narratives set in boarding establishments, the latter in a girls' school. Charles and Mary *Lamb's book *Mrs Leicester's School (1809) is on the model of The Governess. Harriet *Martineau's The Crofton Boys (1841) began to show what could be done in a school narrative, with its tale of goings-on, including a tragic accident, in a small boarding school for boys. In The *Cherry-Stones (1851) by the Revd William Adams a boarding school is the setting for a tale about a moral dilemma. But the full potential of the school story was not realized until 1857, when *Tom Brown's Schooldays by Thomas *Hughes appeared, with immediate and huge success.

By contrast with Tom Brown, *Eric, or, Little by Little, which appeared the next year (1858), was almost a step backwards with its excessive concentration on the morals of its hero; but the same author, F. W. *Farrar, wrote a livelier account of public school life in *St Winifred's, or, the World of School (1862). Though other school novels were published during the 1860s and 1870s, such as Schoolboy Honour (1861) by the Revd H. C. *Adams and *Oudendale (1865) by Ascott R. *Hope, nothing further of note appeared until the 1880s.

'F. Anstey's' *Vice Versa (1882) was an outstanding comic *fantasy about the tribulations of school. The year before it appeared, Talbot Baines *Reed wrote his first full-length school story for The *Boy's Own Paper. This was The *Fifth Form at St Dominic's; Reed went on to write a number of other novels on the same model, and he soon had many imitators. Isabel Quigly, in The Heirs of Tom Brown: the English school story (1982), dismisses as 'hack and humdrum' what she calls 'the many minor writers of school stories in the tradition of Reed'. From this mass of mediocre fiction, *Kipling's remarkable *Stalky & Co. (1899) stands sharply out; despite its brutality, it has a claim to be regarded as the only entirely

successful 'serious' school story in existence—
though it is not one story, for Kipling eschews a
continuous plot and presents a set of tales.

Desmond Coke's *The *Bending of a Twig*
(1906) attempted to parody the conventional
school story and show what school was 'really'
like. Many early 20th-cent. school novels set
out to give a documentary account of real
schools; of these, the only one to achieve last-
ing fame was Alec Waugh's *The Loom of Youth*
(1916), which contained 'revelations' about
public school life that at the time were a cause
of scandal. Meanwhile P. G. *Wodehouse, be-
fore developing his own brand of fiction, pro-
duced a number of school stories of which
Mike (1909) is the most accomplished. Prolific
British writers in the genre during the 1920s
included Hylton *Cleaver and Gunby *Hadath.

The school story in England had come of
age with the burgeoning, in the era of Dr
Thomas *Arnold, of the boys' public school.
The absence of similar institutions from Amer-
ica left that country without such rich material
at hand. Edward Eggleston's *The *Hoosier
School-Boy* (1883) was one of the first notable
American school stories, a striking attempt to
describe (and largely to condemn) conditions
in rural day schools. About twenty years later,
Ralph Henry *Barbour wrote a number of
novels set in private academies for boys.

The girls' school story made its first success-
ful appearance in Britain with *A *World of Girls*
(1886) by L. T. *Meade, which was the precur-
sor of many novels set in girls' boarding
schools by the same author and by the highly
popular Angela *Brazil. A whole host more of
such books were produced in the 1920s and
1930s by Dorita Fairlie *Bruce, creator of
'*Dimsie', and Elinor *Brent-Dyer. (Enid *Bly-
ton's popular if unoriginal *St Clare's and
Malory Towers would follow.) Of a far higher
quality were the girls' school novels by the
Australian author Louise *Mack, beginning
with *Teens* (1897).

In Britain, school stories aimed at an unso-
phisticated readership featured widely in the
boys' and girls' weekly papers produced from
the 1890s onwards by *Harmsworth's Amal-
gamated Press; it was in the pages of these
that 'Frank *Richards', creator of *Billy Bunter
and *Greyfriars, first made his name. The chief
rival to Amalgamated Press, D. C. *Thomson &
Co. of Dundee, also made much use of school
stories in their 'tuppenny blood' papers, of
which the best known were *Rover, *Wizard,
and *Hotspur, all first published between the
two World Wars.

Many 'serious' British novelists in the 1920s
and 1930s produced fiction set in schools,
which is discussed at length in Isabel Quigly's
study. By 1945 it seemed that the school story
was beginning to burn itself out as a genre.
Little was being written in the popular, main-
stream vein—though the *Jennings stories of
Anthony *Buckeridge (1948 onwards) showed
that there was still some life left in old material.
A number of British writers, such as Geoffrey
*Trease and Laurence *Meynell ('A. Stephen
Tring'), began to produce novels set in state-
run day schools. Early attempts to do this were
rather self-conscious, but in the mid-1950s
there began to appear writers, such as E. W.
*Hildick, who had first-hand experience of such
schools and could produce convincing fiction
set in them. Published in 1953, *Down with
Skool* by Geoffrey *Willans introduced Nigel
Molesworth, one of the great comic schoolboy
heroes—an accolade he would later share with
his near namesake *Adrian Mole.

The day-school story established itself con-
fidently thanks to writers such as Gene *Kemp,
herself a teacher like several other modern
school story authors. On British television
from the late 1970s the series *Grange Hill*
showed what could be done with the big com-
prehensive school as a setting. Meanwhile the
traditional boarding school did not entirely
vanish from modern children's fiction. Wil-
liam *Mayne gave it new life in *A *Swarm in
May* (1955), and a number of late 20th cent.
writers treated it with chilling accuracy—for
example, Robert *Westall in the opening chap-
ters of *The Scarecrows* (1981). Dahl's *Matilda*
is a school story which does not aim at realism,
but is an effective portrait of the gruesomeness
of some school experiences, nonetheless. The
novel *The *Chocolate War* (1974) by the Amer-
ican author Robert *Cormier, meanwhile, did
for the school story what Golding's *Lord of the
Flies* did for the *Robinsonnade.

Many of the today's most accomplished
writers for children regularly use school set-
tings for their stories—whether Louis *Sachar
in the US or Anne *Fine in the UK. Meanwhile,
as the twentieth century drew to a close, the
classic boarding-school story was rescued
from any risk of outdatedness and obscurity
by *Harry Potter, a series that also continues
a healthy tradition of school-based *fantasy
writing (such as *The *Demon Headmaster*)
and specifically echoes those books about
schools of magic, which include *The *Worst
Witch, *Le Guin's *A Wizard of *Earthsea, and
many others.

SCHULZ, Charles M. (1922–2000) It's hard to imagine a world without the characters that American artist Charles M. Shultz created in his *Peanuts* cartoons, characters such as Snoopy, Charlie Brown, and Woodstock. Over the course of his life he drew almost 18,000 newspaper strips (1950–2000), which were syndicated around the world. He was hugely influential on other cartoonists, and his warm, ironic, funny, poignant, and unique take on life was inspirational for his readers. The strips have been collected into many books and made into animated television specials, such as *A Charlie Brown Christmas* (1965) and *It's the Great Pumpkin, Charlie Brown* (1966). There is a museum dedicated to his work in Santa Rosa, California.

SCHWARTZ, Viviane (1977–) A German-born illustrator and author. She writes in English and received her Master's degree in illustration at Falmouth College of Arts in Cornwall. Schwartz has collaborated with Alexis *Deacon, illustrating his stories in *A Place Called Home* (2012) and *Cheese Belongs to You* (2013), and has written a number of picture books illustrated by Joel *Stewart, including the quirky *The Adventures of a Nose* (2002). Her picture book *There Are Cats in this Book* (2009) was shortlisted for the 2010 *Kate Greenaway Award. Its sequel *There are No Cats in this Book* (2011) was shortlisted in 2012. Both titles are wonderfully metafictive and engage the child reader in a particularly interactive experience. Schwartz won the *Booktrust Best New Illustrators Award in 2011. *The Sleepwalkers*, her first graphic novel, was shortlisted for the British Comics Award in 2013.

science The first children's book to teach 'natural philosophy' was *The Newtonian System of Philosophy* (1761), supposedly written by 'Tom Telescope' and published by John *Newbery. The *Scientific Dialogues* (1800 onwards) of Jeremiah Joyce became a standard work and were followed by a number of imitations, most notably the various *Conversations* of Mrs *Marcet. Her *Conversations on Chemistry* (1806) are said to have inspired the young Michael *Faraday to take an interest in the subject; Faraday would in turn lecture and publish his own books for young people. Many of the *Catechisms* of William *Pinnock, which were published from about 1817, were on scientific subjects. (*See also* NATURAL HISTORY.)

In America the original '*Peter Parley' (S. G. *Goodrich) dealt with many scientific topics in his instructive books for the young, and the equally prolific Jacob *Abbott wrote a *Science for the Young* series (1871–2), as well as including *Rollo's Experiments* (1839) among his *Rollo stories. One of the most imaginative British 19th-cent. scientific books for children was Charles *Kingsley's *Madam How and Lady Why* (1870). Arabella *Buckley was another British author of this period who tried to make science palatable.

*The *Children's Encyclopaedia* (1908 onwards), edited by Arthur *Mee, included a good deal of scientific information, but there was little in the way of imaginative British 20th-cent. scientific writing for children until 1928, when Amabel Williams-Ellis produced *How You Began: a child's introduction to biology*; though highly imaginative in its treatment of the development of the human fetus, this book managed to cover the subject without mentioning sex. (Compare this with Babette *Cole's unashamedly straightforwardly honest and direct *Mummy Laid an Egg!*, published in 1994.) During the 1930s two eminent British scientists wrote works of fantasy for children in which science played some part, J. B. S. Haldane (*My Friend Mr Leakey*, 1937) and J. W. *Dunne (*The Jumping Lions of Borneo*, 1937, and *An Experiment with St George*, 1939). Scientific subjects were included in *An Outline for Boys and Girls and their Parents* (1932), edited by Naomi *Mitchison, with articles on physics, astronomy, and mathematics by Richard *Hughes. In 1934 and 1935 Julian Huxley, with E. N. da C. Andrade, produced two volumes of *Simple Science*. By this time a good many books were appearing that explained new scientific discoveries to children.

While illustrated non-fiction remains even today the primary means for informing children about science (from lavishly photo-illustrated large picture books to the comic-strip art of Nick Arnold and Tony de Saulles's *Horrible Science* series), the subject is often effectively explored through fiction, too, with Joanna Cole's *Magic School Bus* series a particular success (*see* DEGEN, BRUCE). Among many versatile British science writers, author and zoologist Nicola Davies has written extensively for children about the natural world, in both fiction and non-fiction (*see also* ANIMAL STORIES).

science fiction (sci-fi) This genre was pioneered by Mary Shelley, daughter of William *Godwin, whose *Frankenstein* appeared in 1818, and by Edgar Allan Poe. It became an established

genre in the hands of Jules *Verne, whose first books were published in the 1860s.

Verne-like *adventure stories became a regular feature of the *Harmsworth boys' weeklies which began publication in the 1890s, a typical subject in their pages being flying machines with extraordinary powers. 'Frank Reade', who featured in the *Aldine 'Invention, Travel and Adventure Library' in the early 20th cent., was an inventor whose greatest creation was the Steam Man, a giant steam-powered robot. Meanwhile H. G. *Wells, whose first scientific romance *The Time Machine* was published in 1895, exerted an influence that could be seen in many stories in boys' magazines in the early 1900s; these described the invasion of England at some future date by Germany and other foreign powers, with the aid of such machines as 'aeroplanic battleships'.

By 1923 the *Boys' Magazine* was running a serial about a war which would destroy civilization and at about the same time it also published 'The Raiding Planet', the story of a war between Earth and the planet Thor in 1987. Interplanetary travel was a stock subject of boys' magazines from at least the beginning of the 20th cent. (for example 'In Trackless Space', a 1902 serial in *Union Jack*), while equally popular were 'lost civilization' stories about Atlantis and El Dorado.

In the second half of the 20th cent. science fiction began to find some able practitioners for children. Chief among these in the United States were Robert *Heinlein, Andre *Norton, and Madeleine *L'Engle; in Britain, Donald *Suddaby and John *Christopher; and in Canada, Monica *Hughes. Many writers of 'realistic' children's novels turned to science fiction after a time, examples being William *Mayne (*Earthfasts*, 1966, and other books), John Rowe *Townsend (*The Xanadu Manuscript*, 1977), and Virginia *Hamilton (*Justice and her Brothers*, 1978, and its sequels).

Much modern *fantasy writing for children may be classed as science fiction, and the overlapping of the genres has led to the emergence of the umbrella term of 'speculative fiction' to include both, with the notable inclusion of the ever-more-popular *dystopian fiction. Found in work such as Lois Lowry's *The *Giver* (1993), Malorie Blackman's *Noughts and Crosses* (2001-8), Suzanne Collins' *The *Hunger Games* (2008-10) and Patrick Ness's *Chaos Walking* trilogy (2008-10), dystopian fiction continues the science fiction genre's tradition of social commentary, dealing with themes of racism, genocide, war, gender, and sexuality, usually in speculative/futuristic settings.

Scientific Dialogues, *intended for the instruction and entertainment of Young People* By the Revd Jeremiah Joyce (1763-1816), one of the most popular books of *science for children in the 19th cent. The main part of the work is divided into six volumes, first published between 1800 and 1805, dealing with Astronomy, Hydrostatics (the behaviour of fluids, including a passage on sea-diving), Pneumatics (which includes sound waves and the steam engine), Optics and Magnetism, and Electricity. In 1809 there was added a companion volume containing examination questions. The *Dialogues*, which are illustrated with simple diagrams, were reprinted a number of times up to 1868.

SCIESZKA, Jon (1954–) American author, born in Michigan. Scieszka grew up in a family of six brothers, moved to New York to study at Columbia University for a Master of Fine Arts in fiction writing, and then worked as a teacher for ten years before becoming a full-time writer. His childhood and his teaching experience showed him that the way to get attention was by being funny and the way to make learning fun was to tell a good story. The sixteen-book historical time-travel series, *The Time Warp Trio* (1991-2005), was made into an animated television series and the picture book *Math Curse* (1995), in which a boy finds that everyday situations are turned into maths problems, was adapted for the stage. In *Science Verse* (2004), famous songs and rhymes are transformed into poetry about science. His latest series is the multimedia *Spaceheadz* (2010–), about aliens who disguise themselves as ten-year-old boys.

Many of Scieszka's books are illustrated by Lane *Smith; the two met when their wives, both designers, worked together. Their picture books include *The True Story of the Three Little Pigs* (1989), the Caldecott Honor Book (*see* CALDECOTT MEDAL) *The *Stinky Cheese Man and Other Fairly Stupid Tales* (1992), *Squids will be Squids* (1998), and *Seen Art?* (2005).

Scieszka was America's first National Ambassador for Young People's Literature (2008-10; *see* LAUREATE). During his tenure he focused on broadening schools' definition of reading to include non-fiction and graphic novels and on providing reading role models for boys. These themes came together in a charity he founded called Guys Read.

SCOTT, Michael (1789-1835) British author of two *sea stories which, though not written for children, were popular with them: *Tom Cringle's Log* (serialized in *Blackwood's Magazine* starting in 1829 and published as a book in 1836) and *The Cruise of the Midge* (1836).

SCOTT, Sir **Walter** (1771-1832) One of the most popular and esteemed British novelists of the 19th cent. He wrote only one book specifically for children: *Tales of a Grandfather* (1827-30), the history of Scotland and of France; but many of his novels were read as avidly by young people as by adults, and his fictional treatment of history was one of the most important precedents for the popularity of the *historical novel in children's literature. In 1888 he was nominated third in a poll (in *Juvenile Literature As It Is*) of boys' favourite authors.

The first of Scott's novels, *Waverley*, appeared anonymously in 1814. Many more followed, including *Guy Mannering* (1815), *Rob Roy* (1817), *The Heart of Midlothian* (1818), *Ivanhoe* (1819), and *Redgauntlet* (1824). He acknowledged his authorship of them in 1827. While Scott's reputation rested mainly in his treatment of Scottish history, he made excursions into other settings. *Ivanhoe* takes place at the time of Richard the Lionheart and his brother John, during the Crusades. *Robin Hood appears as a character, and the book helped form the modern image of the outlaw. *Ivanhoe* was sold out in a week, and has remained the most popular of Scott's books despite its inaccuracies as history. Of all his stories it slipped most easily into the genre of *adventure stories for boys; hence the many editions and retellings specifically for children from the late 19th cent. onwards.

In their time most of his novels counted children among their audience: John *Ruskin remembered his father reading them aloud to his family, and he recommended Scott for schools. In the early 19th cent., indeed, Scott was one of the few authors of fiction thought to be respectable by serious-minded households, at a time when the novel was suspect. One effect of this wide appeal was that Scott came in time to be regarded often only as 'a glorified writer of children's books' (E. M. Forster) with no place in serious adult literature, a judgement that his first readers would have found astonishing.

Scott's tastes for folklore and for vivid history were hugely influential. Because of his poor health and lameness in childhood he was allowed to read what he liked, and avoided the standard diet of the Classics, so that 'I think of the fairies oftener than the Dryads and of Bannockburn and Flodden than Marathon and Pharsala.' He brought up his own children on *fairy stories (but also on the verses of Ann and Jane *Taylor), and wrote to Edgar Taylor, the first English translator of the *Grimms' stories, that there was 'a sort of wild fairy interest' in the German tales 'which makes me think them fully better adapted to awaken the inspiration and soften the heart of childhood than the good-boy stories which have been in late years composed for them'.

Scott firmly advocated that children should read entertaining history. His *Tales of a Grandfather* was written, in imitation of J. W. Croker's *Stories from the History of England*, for his six-year-old grandson, John Hugh Lockhart. He said that he had begun by simplifying drastically for the child's benefit, but soon concluded that 'there is no harm, but on the contrary there is benefit in presenting a child with ideas somewhat beyond his easy and immediate comprehension.' The first four volumes of *Tales of a Grandfather* were reprinted in 2001 with an introduction by George Grant and the incomplete fifth series has been published in manuscript form by Illinois University Press (1996) with a preface by Baker and Alexander. The Corson Collection at the University of Edinburgh has an important digital and physical archive relating to Scott.

Scottish folk material This is divided between the Lowland and Border stories and *ballads, which are in English, and the Gaelic of the Highlands. J. F. Campbell of Islay collected huge numbers of the Highland tales, and a proportion of them were translated and published in his *Popular Tales of the West Highlands* (1860-2); Joseph *Jacobs drew on these and on subsequent collections for his *Celtic Fairy Tales* (1892).

Scout, The See DIMMOCK.

Scouting for Boys (1908) By 'B.-P.', Lord *Baden-Powell, the book which helped to initiate the *Boy Scout movement. It was first published in fortnightly parts. Besides containing advice about tracking and camping in the wild, it has many 'Camp Fire Yarns'.

SCUDDER, Horace E. (Elisha) (1837-1902) American editor and author. He worked as reader and editorial assistant for the publishers Hurd and Houghton (later Houghton Mifflin Co.) and in 1867 he began to edit their

new **Riverside Magazine for Young People*. His **Bodley series of books began in 1875 and in 1881 he compiled *The Children's Book; a collection of the best and most famous stories and poems in the English language*. In 1890 he became editor of the *Atlantic Monthly* and four years later published *Childhood in Literature and Art*.

Sea Egg, The (1967) By L. M. **Boston: the story of two boys who acquire a strange green egg-shaped stone which they place in a rockpool; from it there hatches a Triton in whose company they explore the sea.

SEARLE, Ronald (1920–2011) British cartoonist, creator of **St Trinian's and illustrator of the **Molesworth books.

sea stories The sea, navigation, and shipwreck have played a large part in children's reading since the first appearance of **Robinson Crusoe* (1719) and **Gulliver's Travels* (1726). Captain **Marryat was the first British 19th-cent. **adventure story writer to make a speciality of sea tales. His contemporaries E. G. G. **Howard and Michael **Scott produced sea stories which were read by young people, and R. H. Dana's **Two Years Before the Mast* (1840) was very popular in America. Among 20th-cent. boys' writers about the sea are Norman **Duncan and Richard **Armstrong.

Second Jungle Book, The See JUNGLE BOOKS, THE.

Secret Diary of Adrian Mole, aged 13¾, The (1982) The first in a long-running series by Sue Townsend (1946–2014). The first book introduces us to Adrian, a neurotic teenager, who in his diary writes of his desperation to be discovered as an intellectual and escape his school, his family, the bullies, his whole wretched life. The first book and its immediate sequel, *The Growing Pains of Adrian Mole* (1984), are an exquisitely funny portrait of the precipitous highs and lows of the teen emotional experience. He writes execrable poetry, anxiously measures his 'thing', and accidentally glues an Airfix Spitfire to his nose. As the books progress, we watch Adrian fall in love (with the beautiful new girl in class, Pandora Braithwaite) as his parents' marriage disintegrates, with many other things that are calamitous for him but side-splitting for his many grateful readers. The series would follow Adrian into adulthood, with the final volume being the eighth, *Adrian Mole: The Prostrate Years* (2009).

Secret Garden, The A novel by Frances Hodgson **Burnett, generally held to be her most accomplished and lasting work. It was published in October 1911, with illustrations by Charles **Robinson.

Mary Lennox, the sickly and spoilt orphaned daughter of a British official in India, is sent to Misselthwaite Manor in Yorkshire to live under the care of an uncle she has never met, a hunchback recluse who spends most of his time abroad. Now begins the gradual and almost magical transformation of Mary into a healthy and agreeable child. Mary discovers the way into a secret garden, an enclosure that has been shut up since the death of her guardian's wife ten years earlier. Without telling anyone she begins gardening there, and her own character warms with the effect of spring on her handiwork. Then she meets and enlists the help of Dickon, young brother of Martha, the housemaid, and a boy with almost supernatural powers of charming nature. The final secret of Misselthwaite that Mary uncovers is Colin, her guardian's son, kept hidden in the house. Bedridden, the boy is convinced he is an invalid who will develop his father's deformity and is scarcely likely to live. Mary succeeds where no one else has dared to try, persuading him to lead a normal life, though she does this by almost brutal methods. (It is almost a revolution in children's literature when an unattractive child, acting reprehensibly, can achieve such a moral victory.) From now on Colin and Mary share the secret garden, and Colin's strength grows as he watches it coming into bloom. He learns to walk and to know that he is well.

The idea for the book came to Mrs Burnett partly from the Rose Garden at Maytham Hall, Kent, her home from 1898, where she made friends, like Mary in the story, with a robin that would come to take crumbs from her hand. By 1907 her lease on Maytham Hall had run out and she left it; her son Vivian believed that the book 'grew out of regretful feeling' when she heard (mistakenly) that the new occupants were planting the Rose Garden with vegetables. Her belief in the power of the mind for healing, partly influenced by religious and psychological movements of the time, also drives the story.

The book did not at first make much impression, and was not even mentioned in *The Times* obituary of Mrs Burnett thirteen years after its publication, but it gradually acquired devoted readers.

Secret Seven, The A series by Enid *Blyton, sparked off by one of her publishers, Ewart Wharmby of Brockhampton Press, mentioning that his children had formed a secret society in a shed at the bottom of the garden. The result was *The Secret Seven* (1949), a story about seven children and their dog, Scamper. Eventually fifteen titles in the series were published, ending with *Fun for the Secret Seven* (1963). The series was similar to the same author's *Famous Five, but was for younger readers.

SEDGWICK, Marcus (1968–) British writer, widely praised as a writer of 'goth-froth'— ambitious novels which play with genre and pay homage to admired writers such as Arthur *Ransome and Edgar Allan Poe. He regular appears on the major shortlists, and won the *Booktrust Teenage Prize for his brilliant, original *vampire story, *My Swordhand Is Singing* (2006).

Rarely do Sedgwick's narratives unfold in a conventional way. *The Foreshadowing* (2005), set during the First World War, tells of one girl's horrifying discovery that she can foresee imminent death, and the sense of inevitability is partly conveyed by the way the chapters run in reverse order. *Blood Red, Snow White* (2007), a Russian-set love story, fairy tale, and spy thriller, consists of three discrete long stories. With this book, style triumphs over substance, so it lacks some of the overall coherence of Sedgwick's best work.

Sedgwick's best is achieved when he is at his simplest and most sparse: *Revolver is almost unbearably tense. But his 2013 novel *She Is Not Invisible* is in some ways an even more impressive work, as it brings a new compassion and sensitivity to his writing. It's the story of a resilient blind girl's desperate efforts to locate her missing father while protecting her younger, socially inept brother in New York. Sedgwick fills the book with clever in-jokes but they never detract from the story, which is a true page-turner.

Sedgwick has also taken goth-froth down an age level with the Raven Mysteries (six books— 2009–11) and Elf Girl and Raven Boy (four books—2012–14), which are more playful in tone and densely illustrated by Pete Williamson.

SÉGUR, Sophie Rostopchine, Comtesse de (1799–1874) Author of *Les *Malheurs De Sophie*, who was was born and brought up in Russia. Her family fled after the Napoleonic invasion of 1812 and eventually settled in France. She was an invalid from about 1835,

and when confined to the sofa she made up stories to amuse her children and grandchildren. Hachette eventually began to publish these, beginning with *Nouveaux Contes de fées* (1857). She wrote many children's novels, among them *L'Auberge de l'Ange Gardien*, which has been translated into English by Joan *Aiken as *The Angel Inn* (1976).

SELDEN, George (George Selden Thompson) (1929–89) American children's writer, who made his name with *The Cricket in Times Square* (1960), the story of a cricket named Chester who comes to New York from rural Connecticut. Selden's other books include a sequel, *Tucker's Countryside* (1969).

Selfish Giant, The A story by Oscar Wilde (*see* HAPPY PRINCE, THE). An illustrated (and abridged) version by Alexis *Deacon was published in 2013.

SELLAR, W. C. (Walter Carruthers) and **YEATMAN, R. J. (Robert Julian)** *See* 1066 AND ALL THAT.

SELZNICK, Brian (1966–) Author and artist, best known for *The *Invention of Hugo Cabret*. His first picture book, *The Houdini Box* (1991), is about a boy who meets Harry Houdini. He has illustrated many books, including *Frindle* (1996) by Andrew Clement, and *The Dinosaurs of Waterhouse Hawkins* (2001) by Barbara Kerley, which won a Caldecott Honor (*see* CALDECOTT MEDAL).

It was *The Invention of Hugo Cabret*, however, that brought him international recognition. Told sometimes with intricately detailed pencil drawings, sometimes with words, it is the tale of an orphan living in the walls of a Paris train station. The story is incredibly rich and multilayered, both in its plot and presentation. *Wonderstruck* (2011) plays with a similar form, this time taking two characters living fifty years apart, and telling the story of one in words, and of the other in pictures; while the words and pictures of *The Marvels* (2015) tell two distinct stories, seemingly quite unconnected.

SEMPÉ (Jean-Jacques Sempé) (1932–) A world-renowned French cartoonist and illustrator best known for his series *Le *Petit Nicolas* written by René *Goscinny, originally published in *Le Moustique* in 1954. Sempé's illustrations of Nicolas and his friends embody Goscinny's schoolboy adventures and epitomize the French 1950s while adding depth, humour, and charm to the series. Written between 1959 and 1965, these classic books are

continually reprinted and are available in over twenty-six languages. Alongside *Le petit Nicolas*, Sempé had a full-page cartoon in *Paris Match* for many years and achieved international reputation through his covers for the *New Yorker* magazine. *Monsieur Lambert*, his 1962 graphic novel for adults, brings a small Parisian bistro to life. Like all the best cartoonists, Sempé is adept at telling a whole story or making a political comment through one single image.

SENDAK, Maurice (Bernard) (1928–2012) Outstanding American illustrator and creator of several classic *picture books who was born in Brooklyn, New York. His parents were Jewish immigrants from Poland—the name Sendak means 'godfather' or 'sponsor' in Hebrew—and he was brought up on tales from the Old Testament and Jewish folklore told to him by his father. He was also enthralled by *Mickey Mouse (who was created in the year of his birth), by American *comics, and by the bright lights of Manhattan where his father worked as a dressmaker. The family was not well-off; Maurice's childhood fell during the years of the Depression and the Sendaks moved from house to house in Brooklyn as their resources dictated.

For his first six years Sendak was a sickly child, and spent much of his time in bed. His favourite reading included *Pinocchio* and *Toby Tyler*. He attended Lafayette High School, but hated formal education—though his talent for drawing was encouraged there and he drew a comic strip for the school magazine. On leaving school he worked in a number of jobs in New York City, chiefly window-dressing; in the meanwhile he painted and sketched. While working on window-displays at the Fifth Avenue toy store F. A. O. Schwarz, he browsed in their children's book department and encountered the work of great illustrators. Of these it was Randolph *Caldecott whom he most admired, and his own picture books, though they have little in common with Caldecott's style, emulate Caldecott's use of just a few words to inspire a wealth of pictorial detail.

The book buyer at Schwarz, noticing Sendak's interest in illustration, introduced him to the children's book editor at Harper and Brothers, Ursula Nordstrom. She commissioned him to illustrate *The *Wonderful Farm* (1951) by Marcel Aymé. This was the beginning of a fruitful professional relationship between Nordstrom and Sendak; over

the next decade she gave him a steady stream of work, taking care to find texts that especially suited him, and virtually shaping his career.

His first major success was *A Hole Is to Dig* (1952), a book in which Ruth *Krauss collected children's definitions of words ('Dogs are to kiss people', 'The world is so you have something to stand on', and so on). For this he produced a series of pictures of small children which were both humorous and unsentimental. *Charlotte and the White Horse* (1955), again by Krauss, was Sendak's first book in full colour, and shows something of his fondness for the drawings of *Blake. Much of his best work during this early, busy period—he illustrated more than forty books between 1951 and 1962—is to be found in the *Little Bear* readers by Else *Minarik.

In these apprentice years, while American illustrators in general were beginning to favour abstract and other non-realist styles, Sendak's work became more and more firmly tied to European 18th- and 19th-cent. traditions, with careful line work and cross-hatching (suggesting *wood engraving) and restrained wash colours. The results recall, at different times, the work of such diverse artists as Dürer, *Bewick, Hogarth, Rowlandson, and *Cruikshank.

At the same time he began to develop a special talent as a portrayer of child faces. Early critics of his work sometimes objected that his children looked too European; later observers have remarked that they generally resemble the artist himself. Sendak says of this: 'Yes, they're all a kind of caricature of me. They look as if they've been hit on the head and hit so hard they weren't ever going to grow any more.' He also explains that an obsession with childhood lies at the heart of his work:

You see, I don't really believe that the kid I was has grown up into me. He still exists somewhere, in the most graphic, plastic, physical way for me. I have a tremendous concern for, and interest in, him. I try to communicate with him all the time. One of my worst fears is losing contact.

The theme of his mature work, the child's mixture of fear and exhilaration as it explores its own fantasy world and relates it to reality, is clearly stated, but developed in muddled fashion, in the first picture book for which Sendak wrote his own text, *Kenny's Window* (1956), the story of a boy trying to achieve a number of impossible tasks he has been set in a dream. In *Very Far Away* (1957), a boy retreats from his

jealousy of a new baby by going to a place 'very far away' (in fact just around the block) where he can live a fantasy life before returning home. *The Sign on Rosie's Door* (1958) came closer to realizing Sendak's private vision of the world, in a tale about a Brooklyn girl (whom Sendak had observed from his window) entertaining her friends on a long, dull summer's day by putting on a show. (Sendak later adapted this for television, as *Really Rosie*, 1975.) Then in 1962 came *The Nutshell Library* (four small books for the youngest readers), *Alligators All Around* (an *ABC Book), *One Was Johnny* (a counting book), *Pierre* (a *cautionary tale), and *Chicken Soup with Rice* (a story based on the months of the year). These show Sendak at the height of his powers as a comic illustrator.

The next year, 1963, appeared the book that made Sendak's name internationally, *Where The Wild Things Are*. It is generally regarded as unequalled in its exploration of a child's fantasy world and its relation to his real life. The book had huge sales, giving Sendak financial security.

His subsequent work included illustrations to work by Randall *Jarrell, George *MacDonald, and a selection of tales from *Grimm (*The Juniper Tree*, 1973) for which Sendak travelled through Europe to visit landscapes associated with the stories. Meanwhile he continued to produce his own picture books. *Hector Protector and As I Went Over the Water* (1965) is a visual interpretation of two nonsensical *nursery rhymes—Sendak makes a strikingly comic story out of the first—which was intended as a homage to Caldecott. *Higglety Pigglety Pop! or There Must Be More to Life* (1967), suggested by a rhyme by S. G. *Goodrich, is the story of a dog named Jennie (in fact Sendak's own beloved Sealyham terrier) who leaves home in search of excitement and becomes a performer in the World Mother Goose Theatre. Next came *In The Night Kitchen* (1970), a further exploration of a boy's fantasy world, this time closely based on Sendak's childhood memories of New York life. After two slight pieces, *Seven Little Monsters* (based on drawings done by Sendak for *Sesame Street*) and *Some Swell Pup*, both published in 1976, appeared *Outside Over There* (1981), the third book in what Sendak now regarded as a trilogy on the subject of make-believe. Darker in subject matter than *Where the Wild Things Are* and *In the Night Kitchen*, it was published on both adult and children's book lists, and showed a marked change in illustrative style, entirely away from the comic-strip manner that was always partly evident in the other two.

Sendak's life and work are fully recorded in two volumes of *The Art of Maurice Sendak*, the first (1980) by Selma G. Lanes, the second (2003) with text by Tony Kushner.

Sendak was one of only a handful of writers or illustrators to win both the *Astrid Lindgren Memorial Award (2003) and the *Hans Christian Andersen Award (1970). Quite apart from his outstanding draughtsmanship and mastery of styles, Sendak's exploration of the realms of the unconscious in *Where the Wild Things Are* and its successors lifts his work beyond the confines of the typical children's picture book, and places it among major art of the 20th cent.

Separate Peace, A (1959) A novel by John Knowles (1926–2001) based on his short story, 'Phineas'. It is a tale of friendship and betrayal set against a backdrop of the Second World War. Charismatic athlete Finny and brainy introvert Gene form a close friendship at their New England boarding school, but gradually Gene's insecurity causes him to view Finny as a rival. Gene's complex mix of emotions leads to a spontaneous act of aggression, with tragic consequences. The same school is revisited in Knowles' otherwise unconnected 1981 novel *Peace Breaks Out*.

Sephy Hadley *See* NOUGHTS AND CROSSES.

SEREDY, Kate (1899–1975) Born in Budapest, Seredy emigrated to the USA in 1922 and wrote and illustrated a number of children's books set in her native Hungary. *The Good Master* (1935), a *family story set on a farm in the Hungarian plains, is her most famous book, together with its sequel *The Singing Tree* (1939). *The White Stag* (1937), a collection of Hungarian legends, won the *Newbery Medal.

Series of Unfortunate Events, A (1999–2006) A thirteen-book series by Lemony *Snicket. After their parents are killed in a fire, Violet, Klaus, and Sunny Baudelaire are sent to live with Count Olaf, who has designs on Violet's future inheritance. When they are removed from his care, Olaf spends the rest of the series hatching dastardly plots to get his hands on the fortune, which result in the demise of subsequent guardians by such means as poisoning, drowning, and leeches. Snicket's sardonic humour and frequent interjections of teacherly direct address are central to the appeal of this Gothic series, which shows influences of the work of Edward *Gorey.

SERRAILLIER, Ian (Lucien) (1912–94) British writer for children, best known as the author of The *Silver Sword (1956). He was a Quaker and for many years a schoolmaster. His first published work was poetry and many volumes of his verse for children have appeared, among them The Windmill Book of Ballads (1962), which contains his verse retelling of Beowulf, and The Tale of Three Landlubbers (1970), a comic poem illustrated by Raymond *Briggs. He wrote several conventional *adventure stories, including They Raced for Treasure (1946) and The Cave of Death (1965). The Silver Sword stands apart from these, being one of the most remarkable of all post-war children's books; it was researched with great care and took five years to write. From 1948 he edited, later with his wife Anne, the New Windmill series for Heinemann, created to bring good modern books cheaply into schools.

Sesame Street An outstandingly popular American television programme for preschool children, broadcast since 1969.

It was the creation of the Children's Television Workshop, a New York group set up by a number of people who were concerned that young children in certain communities were watching television for hour after hour without getting any benefit from it. They aimed to create a programme that would 'stimulate the intellectual and cultural growth of young children—particularly those from disadvantaged backgrounds'.

Though the programme sometimes included 'guest' appearances by celebrities, emphasis was less on human performers than on puppets (Jim Henson's 'Muppets'). Five programmes of one hour were shown each week.

Sesame Street attracted huge audiences—by the 1990s it was estimated that most American preschool children had watched it—and early surveys indicated that it was having a remarkable effect on cognitive skills. It has continued to be televised worldwide, and Muppet lookalikes now also star in the (adult) musical Avenue Q.

SETON, Ernest Thompson (1860–1946) Naturalist and author, who was born Ernest Thompson, in South Shields, County Durham. His family emigrated to Canada when he was six, living briefly in the small town of Lindsay, Ontario, which is the setting of *Two Little Savages (1903). Thompson adopted the surname Seton and from 1896 lived in the United States. He founded a youth movement called the 'Woodcraft Indians' and was one of the founders of the *Boy Scouts of America. He began to write *animal stories in the 1880s and collected these in *Wild Animals I Have Known (1898). His many other animal books include The Biography of a Grizzly (1900). His admirers have included Richard *Adams, who acknowledges the influence of his books upon *Watership Down (1972).

Settlers in Canada, The (1844) A children's novel by Captain *Marryat. The Campbell family find that they have no legal right to their country house in Cumberland, so they emigrate to Canada, buy land cheaply, and make a good life for themselves until they finally reacquire their English home. The book is chiefly notable for its description of life in the wilds: one of the boys is taught hunting by the weather-beaten settler Malachi Bone and another is captured by '*Indians' (Native Americans).

SEUSS, Dr (Theodor Seuss Geisel) (1904–91) Author-illustrator of a large series of popular American *picture books. He was born in Springfield, Mass., and educated at Dartmouth College and Lincoln College, Oxford, after which he worked as a freelance cartoonist for American magazines and advertising agencies and as a writer and animator in Hollywood.

His first children's book was *And To Think That I Saw It On Mulberry Street (1937), in which a small boy makes up a *tall tale about what he sees on the way home from school. The 500 Hats of Bartholomew Cubbins (1938) is a comic *fantasy with a prose text about a lad who, every time he takes his hat off to the king, finds that another has appeared on his head. It was followed by many more comic storybooks in verse; then in 1957 Seuss began to write and draw a series of 'Beginner Books' for Random House, starting with The *Cat in the Hat. The series used a simple vocabulary and was designed to help teach reading. Besides including many Dr Seuss titles, the 'Beginner Books' had contributions from Helen Palmer (Seuss's wife), P. D. Eastman (1909–86; the art director of the series), and the humorist Bennett Cerf. By 1970 some 30 million copies had been sold in America; the series (and other books by Seuss) has also had much success in Britain. Other particularly popular and enduring Seuss titles include *How the Grinch Stole Christmas! (1957), *Green Eggs and Ham (1960), *Fox in Socks (1965), The *Lorax (1971), and collections such as The *Sneetches and other stories

(1961). Several deal in a playful way with political or social issues—consumerism, the environment, racism, etc.

Seuss's style, both pictorial and verbal, owes much to *comic strips and cartoons. Figures and objects are elasticated to convey an impression of violent movement or emotion. The verse texts are skilfully written and at his best Seuss is richly inventive of curious creatures, situations, characters, and landscapes.

In 1955 his self-conferred 'doctorate' was made real by his old college, Dartmouth.

Seven Champions of Christendom, The

A lengthy *romance by Richard *Johnson, published in two parts in 1596 and 1597. The champions are St *George of England, St Denis of France, St James of Spain, St Anthony of Italy, St Andrew of Scotland, St Patrick of Ireland, and St David of Wales. Johnson seems to have based some of his story of St George on medieval legends, but the rest is his own invention.

St George is born in Coventry, the son of the Lord High Steward of England. His mother dies at his birth, and a few days later he is stolen by the enchantress Kalyb. She cares for him till he reaches manhood but then, enamoured of him, is tricked into giving him her powers of enchantment. St George then releases the other champions from Kalyb's power and destroys her. The champions set out together, but at a place where seven roads meet they each choose different ways.

St George goes to Egypt, where a *dragon has been terrorizing the country for twenty-four years, devouring a virgin every day. Only the king's daughter, Sabra, remains, due for sacrifice the following day. St George destroys the dragon and the hand of Sabra is to be his reward, but a rival, the Moorish prince Almidor, devises a series of treacheries, culminating in George's imprisonment by the Soldan of Persia.

After their individual adventures have been described at great length, the brotherhood of champions is reunited at the King of Greece's tournament, and a huge battle ensues between Christian and heathen armies. Further exploits follow, and the champions manage to convert Persia, Egypt, and Morocco to Christianity and return safely together to England. Part II of the book contains the death of Sabra, more deeds of the champions and of George's three sons, and finally the deaths of the seven champions.

The Seven Champions of Christendom went into at least ten editions in the century following its publication. A number of *broadside ballads were quickly based on it, a spurious Part III was added to it, and *chapbook versions drastically abridged it. It was among John *Bunyan's preferred reading in his youth, and *The *Pilgrim's Progress* is indebted to it. The story was thought appropriate for children for two centuries more, although it was often altered, as in an 1823 version by John Harris, to project courtly knighthood as a model of good behaviour for young gentlemen. Harvey *Darton published a finely produced and illustrated edition in 1913.

Seven Little Australians

(1894) The first and most successful of the children's novels written and set in Australia by Ethel S. *Turner. It begins with a manifesto: 'If you imagine you are going to read of model children, with perhaps a naughtily-inclined one to point a moral, you had better lay down the book immediately...Not one of the seven is really good, for the very excellent reason that Australian children never are.'

The seven are the sons and daughters of Captain Woolcot of Sydney, a proud, irritable, and almost entirely unsympathetic character who 'did not understand children at all, and was always grumbling at the noise they made and the money they cost'. His first wife, mother of six of the seven, is dead, and the second wife, Esther, is 'only twenty—just a lovely, laughing-faced girl, whom they all adored'. The first escapade described is a rebellion against bread-and-butter nursery tea, which takes place while the Captain and Esther are dining separately on chicken with a military guest. The children take turns to visit the dining room and beg for slices of fowl; the Captain, shamed, cancels their visit to the *pantomime in punishment. The children's attempts to 'assume virtues they had not' in order to win back favour are variously disastrous, and Judy is sent to boarding school for the ruse of depositing her infant half-brother the General in her father's barracks while she and Pip visit Bondi aquarium.

Seven Little Australians was immediately successful in Australia and England; it was also published in America, and was quickly translated into several other languages; it had reached twenty-seven editions by 1934. It was dramatized on the Sydney stage a year after publication and has been adapted for Australian television.

Seven Stories

The UK's national centre dedicated to children's literature, in Newcastle

upon Tyne. It houses the original manuscripts and illustrations of many writers and artists from the 1930s to the present day, including Judith *Kerr, Enid *Blyton, Philip *Pullman, and David *Almond. Drawing upon this exceptional archive, which reveals the creative imagination of some of the UK's best authors and illustrators, Seven Stories also curates special exhibitions and events as well as offering a unique resource for researchers.

Seventeenth Summer (1942) By Maureen Daly (1921–2006), an Irish-born American author. Written when Daly herself was seventeen years old and published while she was a college student, the novel details the romance between prep-school girl Angie Morrow and local boy Jack Duluth during the summer between high-school graduation and Angie's departure for college. It is considered by some to be the first *young adult novel. With its frequent references to smoking, emphasis on etiquette and class, and absence of explicit sexual content, the book is very much a product of its time; despite this, it has remained continuously in print since its first publication.

SEVERN, David (David Storr Unwin) (1918–2010) British children's writer. The elder son of the publisher Sir Stanley Unwin, he worked briefly in the family firm of Allen and Unwin. But he had a difficult relationship with his father, and during the 1940s he began to make an independent career as a children's novelist. His reputation was made by *Dream Gold* (1949), about two boys who have the same dream which transports them to a desert island, and *Drumbeats!* (1953), a *fantasy about schoolchildren and a magical African drum.

SEWELL, Anna (1820–78) author of *Black Beauty*. She was born at Great Yarmouth in Norfolk, the daughter of Quaker parents, but when she was two years old her family had to move to London for financial reasons. Anna probably suffered from some chronic and undiagnosed disease of the bones or muscles, for when she was young she sprained an ankle, and thenceforward could never walk easily again. By her mid-thirties she was severely lame.

In 1871 she was told that she had only eighteen months to live; by the end of that year she had begun *Black Beauty*, her only book, and five years later she was still alive and at work on it. A note on a scrap of paper says that her 'special aim' for this 'little book' was to 'induce

kindness, sympathy, and an understanding treatment of horses'.

She lived to see the book published, but died a few months later, before she could know of its huge success. Sewell's use of the autobiographical genre to tell the story through the eyes of an animal broke new literary ground and the novel itself resulted in a heightened awareness in Victorian England of the mistreatment of animals.

SEWELL, Elizabeth Missing (1815–1906) English author of novels for young people in which *religious instruction played a large part. She wrote somewhat in the manner of Charlotte M. *Yonge. One of her best known books was *Laneton Parsonage: a tale for children, on the practical use of a portion of the Church catechism* (1846), which was 'edited' by her brother the Revd William Sewell, author and Warden of Radley College.

Sexton Blake Hero of *detective stories, who made his first appearance in the pages of *Marvel* in 1893. Blake was later labelled 'the office-boy's Sherlock Holmes', and is sometimes supposed to have been deliberately modelled on Conan *Doyle's detective, created six years before.

The first author of Blake stories was 'Hal Meredith', pseudonym of Harry *Blyth; many others were named over the years and altogether more than 100 people have written about the detective.

Very soon Sexton Blake began to appear in the *Union Jack* and other *Harmsworth papers and gradually acquired his hawk-like and incisive manner and appearance (now certainly copied from Holmes), his home in Holmes's own Baker Street, and his assistants. The first of these is said to have been a Chinese boy named We-Wee, soon dropped for obvious reasons. In the years that followed Blake was employed by the Lord Chancellor, strapped to a moon rocket, locked in an Iron Maiden, pronounced dead (and revived with adrenalin), and worked energetically for his country during the First World War. After the demise of the *Union Jack* in 1933 he made his home in the *Detective Weekly*; then from 1940 in the Sexton Blake Library. In 1963 the Library came to an end, but Blake's survival was assured by paperbacks produced by the Howard Baker organization.

Blake's qualities have never included intellectual brilliance; in E. S. Turner's words, 'His successes are due less to pure deduction than to calculated coincidence, an ability to recover

almost instantly from concussion, and such special attainments as the power to out-stare cobras.'

sexuality It has only been fairly recently in the history of children's literature that sexuality has become an accepted topic in books for younger readers. In the 1960s, authors of books for young adults began writing in a mode of realism, depicting topics that previously would have been considered unacceptable, such as drugs, violence, difficult home lives, or sex. This was due to a combination of factors, such as the change in the way that young people were viewed, a greater acceptance of sexuality in society more generally, and a developing perspective on what children's literature was and what it could do. For example, premarital sex is in general not considered as much of an issue as it was before the 1960s, and young people are no longer thought to need as much protection from the facts of life. At the same time, adults have started to think that young people need information about sex and sexuality, and that literature might be a key way of giving them this information.

Despite this, however, sexual interactions in literature in the 1960s and 1970s were frequently portrayed as having negative consequences, such as pregnancy, sexually transmitted illnesses, or emotional anguish. Also, only a very few books, such as John *Donovan's *I'll Get There. It Better Be Worth the Trip* (1969), featured non-heterosexuality, but these too generally had unhappy endings.

In the 1970s, a couple of groundbreaking authors wrote the first books for teenage readers that showed sexuality to be a healthy part of life, and in these works, sex was often depicted in a more positive light; an important example is Judy *Blume's *Forever* (1975). In the 1980s, Nancy *Garden and other authors followed suit in regard to homosexual relationships; Garden's lesbian novel *Annie on My Mind* (1982) proved controversial and was challenged and even burned by adults in the United States who did not want their children to have access to works on homosexuality.

Later that decade and in the 1990s, picture books featuring two-mother or two-father families started being produced; examples include Lesléa Newman's *Heather Has Two Mommies* (1989) and Michael Willhoite's *Daddy's Roommate* (1991), and both these works are among the most challenged and *banned

in English-speaking countries, as is *And Tango Makes Three* by Peter Parnell and Justin Richardson (2005), a true story about two male penguins who bring up a chick together.

In the past couple of decades, depictions of sex and sexuality in works for younger readers have become both more commonplace and more nuanced. Characters are shown having explicit sex, as in Melvin *Burgess's novel *Doing It* (2003), but often this is safe sex, as though to remind readers, too, to use protection, and the emotional consequences of sex are explored in more detail, beyond the previous simplistic notion that sex naturally leads to suffering.

Many of the early books with non-heterosexual characters suggested that being gay was a problem or focused solely on the issue of sexuality, implying that the characters had nothing more to their personalities besides their homosexuality. Now more authors, including David Levithan (*Boy Meets Boy, 2003), Ellen *Wittlinger (*Hard Love*, 1999), Aidan *Chambers (*Dance on My Grave*, 1982), and Maureen *Johnson (*The Bermudez Triangle*, 2006), are writing about gay and lesbian characters who have complex lives that do not revolve solely around their sexuality. Furthermore, some books are now referring to bisexuality, such as Lili Wilkinson's *Pink* (2009), while others, such as the *Rainbow* trilogy by Alex Sanchez (2001–5), feature polyamorous or asexual characters, although these latter aspects of sexuality are still as yet not fully explored.

Shadow of a Bull (1964) A novel by Maia *Wojciechowska.

Shakespeare The plays of Shakespeare were first recast into stories for children by Charles and Mary *Lamb, whose *Tales From Shakespear* was published in 1807. Before that time, children could read excerpts from the plays in *The Beauties of Shakespear* (1752), a collection made by William Dodd, and in Enfield's *The *Speaker* (1774, often reprinted). The influential late 18th-cent. *nursery rhyme collection *Mother Goose's Melody* included songs from Shakespeare's plays.

In 1818 appeared Thomas *Bowdler's *Family Shakespeare*, in which the plays were censored for the benefit of family audiences. *The Girlhood of Shakespeare's Heroines* (1850–2), by Mary Cowden Clarke, author of a Shakespeare concordance, invented lengthy narratives (intended chiefly for children) about the

early years of Portia, Lady Macbeth, Desdemona, and others.

For many years, the Lambs were not imitated, but in 1883 there appeared *Shakespeare's Stories Simply Told* by Mary Seymour. E. *Nesbit's *The Children's Shakespeare* (1897) was an attempt to produce a narrative even simpler than the Lambs'; its most notable feature was that the illustrator depicted all the characters—with the sole exception of King Lear—as children. Arthur *Quillercouch's *Historical Tales from Shakespeare* (1899) contained retellings of several history plays omitted by the Lambs, while Mary Macleod's *The Shakespeare Story-Book* (1902) aimed to make good some of the Lambs' defects, especially their omission of such characters as Malvolio and Jaques. Arthur *Mee summarized scenes and excised 'coarse and gross' passages in *The Children's Shakespeare* (1926). Later retellings include Marchette Chute's *Stories from Shakespeare* (1956), Ian *Serraillier's *The Enchanted Island* (1964), and Bernard Miles's *Favourite Tales from Shakespeare* (1976), which has illustrations by Victor *Ambrus. Of the large—and growing—number of adaptations still available today, the *Shakespeare Stories* of Leon *Garfield (two vols., 1985 and 1994), illustrated by Michael *Foreman, remain outstanding.

SHAN, Darren (Darren O'Shaughnessy) (1972–) Irish writer whose blood-curdling horror for young adults has become a huge international success with over fifteen million copies in print. He bought his first typewriter when he was fourteen and by the age of twenty-four had become a full-time writer. Vampires, monsters, zombies, demons, and buckets of gore have filled his eagerly anticipated books since *Cirque du Freak* was published in 1999. That was the first of *The Saga of Darren Shan*, which was made into a film in 2009 and a bestselling manga series (2008), and launched a prequel series, *The Saga of Larten Crepsley* (2010). *The Demonata* series (2005) continued to cause sleepless nights, as Shan's writing has turned progressively darker as his core readership has grown up. The *Zom-B* series (2011) has a high body count, and is a fast-paced, grisly, gritty look at a zombie apocalypse.

SHARKEY, Niamh (Niamh Ní Shearcaigh) (1972–) Irish author and illustrator who was Ireland's second Laureate na nÓg (*see* LAUREATE) from 2012–14. Her painstaking oil-on-gesso technique produces vibrant illustrations

that perfectly complement mythical stories such as Malachy *Doyle's *Tales from Old Ireland* (2000), Hugh Lupton's *Tales of Wisdom and Wonder* (1998, winning her the *CBI Book of the Year Award), and Aleksei Tolstoy's *The Giant Turnip* (2006). The stories she also writes herself are mostly illustrated in a less formal style, such as *On the Road with Mavis and Marge* (2011), about two farmyard friends who like to go wandering, and *I'm a Happy Hugglewug* (2009), which has been made into a preschool TV series, *The Happy Hugglemonsters* (2013), that she also co-produced.

SHARP, Edith *See* NKWALA.

SHARP, Margery (1905–91) British children's author, best known for a series of 'Miss Bianca' stories about a white mouse and her hair-raising adventures. The first book in the series was *The Rescuers* (1959).

SHARRATT, Nick (1962–) An award-winning British author-illustrator known for his bold style, with black outlines and flat, bright colours. Sharratt was born in Bexleyheath in Greater London, and showed a great interest in art from an early age. At school, he was allowed to go and draw in the art supplies cupboard instead of doing games, by which means he managed to get his art O and A Levels. He then studied graphic design at St Martins' School of Art (now Central St Martins). At first, Sharratt combined the creation of children's books with illustrating for magazines, and he didn't specialize exclusively in children's books until the mid-1990s.

Sharratt's books are always humorous, sometimes have elements such as lift-up flaps, and have a tendency to subvert the everyday, turning it into something fantastical. He has illustrated over forty of Jacqueline *Wilson's books, and his distinctive style has become inseparable from her stories in the minds of her many fans. Other popular pairings have been with Julia Donaldson (e.g. *Chocolate Mousse for Greedy Goose*, 2005), Jeremy Strong, Kes Gray (the Daisy books, including *Eat Your Peas*), and Giles Andreae (*Pants*, 2002; and *More Pants*, 2007).

The books he has written himself are often in rhyme, and the deceptively simple texts conceal a lot of careful craftsmanship. These include *Ketchup on Your Cornflakes* (1994), which has split pages, which allows you to make all sorts of surprising and revolting combinations of objects, and *Shark in the Park* (2000), in which Timothy Pope is constantly

convinced that he has seen a shark through his telescope.

One of his most popular books is *You Choose* (2003), written by Pippa Goodhart, in which each large double page covers a different theme. On the food page, for example, are vignette illustrations of every conceivable type of food, which allow readers to use their imagination to interact with what they see.

SHAW, Flora *See* CASTLE BLAIR.

Sheep-Pig, The (1983) A popular animal story by Dick *King-Smith. When Farmer Hodge wins the piglet at the village fete it is a surprise. Even more surprising is what follows. Babe, the orphaned piglet, proves to be such an apt pupil under the tutelage of the collie Fly he is soon herding the sheep by himself. From there it is a short step to the sheepdog trials. Winning these is Farmer Hodge's dream. How Babe succeeds makes a warm-hearted story full of humour and devoid of sentimentality. After the success of the film adaptation, *Babe* (1995), this became one of King-Smith's best known titles.

SHELDON, Ann Author of the *Linda Craig series of mystery novels.

SHELDON, Dyan New York-born, London-based author. Sheldon is best known for her *young adult novels, in particular the *New York Times*-bestselling *Confessions of a Teenage Drama Queen* (1999), which was made into a film in 2004. The sequel, *My Perfect Life* (2002), is told from the perspective of the drama queen's best friend. In *Sophie Pitt-Turnbull Discovers America* (2003), a British girl is forced to spend the summer in Brooklyn, while a New Yorker crosses the pond in the other direction in *I Conquer Britain* (2006). Sheldon's picture book *The Whales' Song* (1991) won illustrator Gary Blythe the *Kate Greenaway Medal.

SHELLEY, Noreen (1920–85) Australian author who wrote a 'Piggy Grunt' series for young children (1944 onwards), and a number of *family stories, beginning with *Family at the Lookout* (1972).

SHEPARD, E. H. (Ernest Howard) (1879–1976) British illustrator, best known for his drawings accompanying the work of A. A. *Milne and his illustrations to The *Wind in the Willows.

He drew precociously as a boy and his father quickly decided that he should become a professional artist, though he himself 'considered

an artist's life to be a dull one and looked for something more adventurous'. In 1897 he won a scholarship to the Royal Academy Schools and began to have work accepted by minor periodicals. At the Academy he met a fellow student, Florence Chaplin, to whom he was married in 1904. They had very little money at first, and lived for five years in a spartan cottage in Surrey, where their children Graham and Mary were born. (Mary herself eventually became an artist, and illustrated the *Mary Poppins books. She married E. V. Knox of *Punch.)

Shepard often said (though without bitterness) that he and his friends set out to earn their living as painters and finished as illustrators. He loved working in oils and had paintings exhibited—and sold—at the Academy, but he knew his strength lay in line rather than colour. He did a series of comic impressions of an art student's life for the *Graphic* (in 1906) and undertook book jackets and illustrations for such things as editions of *David Copperfield*, *Tom Brown's Schooldays*, and *Aesop.

At the outbreak of war he applied for a commission in the Royal Artillery, fulfilling a long-held ambition to be a soldier (many of his schoolboy drawings were of battle scenes). He manned a siege battery at the Somme, where his brother was killed, and won the MC at Arras, reaching the rank of Major. On his return home in 1919 he illustrated Hugh Walpole's novel about a small boy, *Jeremy, drawings of children already being a salient part of his reputation. In 1921 he was invited to join the 'table' at *Punch, the equivalent of a staff appointment, with at least a regular income.

The suggestion that Shepard should illustrate A. A. Milne's children's poems, when they were printed in *Punch* before being issued as *When We were Very Young* (1924), came from a fellow member of the *Punch* table, E. V. *Lucas. Milne was initially reluctant to accept Shepard as illustrator, and the editor of *Punch* was at first dismayed at the unconventional appearance of the pages, with the illustrations airy, unframed, and running informally all round the verses. But the partnership was a huge success with the public, so that there was no doubt about Shepard as illustrator for Milne's *Winnie-the-Pooh* (1926), *Now We Are Six* (1927), The *House at Pooh Corner* (1928), and their associated song books.

Shepard visited the Milnes at their home at Cotchford Farm to sketch, taking endless

trouble to get details of countryside correct; he also worked from photographs of Christopher Milne and his toys. His own son Graham played with the delighted Christopher and relieved the boy's obvious loneliness. But Milne and Shepard never became close. Shepard wrote: 'I always had to start at the beginning with Milne, every time I met him.' And there are hints that Milne was uneasy about the manner in which the toys and animals in the stories took on an additional life and character, not of his own making, in Shepard's drawings of them.

Shepard received only a small fee for *When We Were Very Young*; he learnt to ask for a royalty from the subsequent books and gradually became more prosperous, starting to have a fine house built for his family near Guildford. Then, entirely unexpectedly, his wife Florence died during a small exploratory operation in 1927. Shepard buried himself in his work, which, besides the Milne books, included a new edition of The **Golden Age* by Kenneth **Grahame (1928). His illustrations for *The Wind in the Willows* followed in 1931 (Shepard believed that this was a book that should not be illustrated, but felt he could improve on the editions already in existence).

He was political cartoonist for *Punch* (not entirely happily) from 1935 to 1949. His son was killed in action in 1943. Late the same year Shepard was married again, to a London nurse. In 1953, dismissal from *punch* made him doubly active, and he illustrated such books as editions of The **Cuckoo Clock* and **At The Back of the North Wind*, reillustrated the Christopher Robin books in colour, and wrote his memoirs. Shepard was asked to illustrate **Peter Pan*, but refused, though he took on an edition of Hans Christian **Andersen (1961) and wrote and illustrated two children's books of his own: *Ben and Brock* (1965), a somewhat wild **fantasy about a boy and a badger, and *Betsy and Joe* (1966), full of reminiscences of the First World War. The Pooh industry rolled on and Shepard dutifully served it. In the last years of his life he produced more coloured drawings for new editions of the Pooh stories.

Everyone spoke of Shepard as a serene man, amiable, unpompous, and approachable. But parts of him were remote; he gave no outward sign of grief at the loss of his wife or son and believed unquestioningly in strenuous work. He ran his life (according to Rawle Knox, in *The Work of E. H. Shepard*, 1979), 'both in and out of the house, to suit his work, and would

have been genuinely surprised to hear that any arrangements of his had inconvenienced anyone else. I doubt he ever did so hear; they were all too fond of him.'

As an artist, he has been called the last of the great Victorian fine black-and-white illustrators. Though his Pooh drawings made him famous, he finally grew weary in private of what he called 'that silly bear'. But he escaped from Milne with outstanding illustrations to *The Wind in the Willows* and other classics.

Shepherd of Salisbury Plain, The (1795) One of the first of Hannah **More's series of **Cheap Repository Tracts, and the best known; it was written by Miss More herself under the pseudonym 'Z'. It is an account of how 'a very worthy, charitable Gentleman' riding across the Plain, meets a poor but pious shepherd who tells of his love of the Bible and his contentment with his lot, despite the fact that his invalid wife is bringing up eight children on almost no money. Because he and his children are able to earn a little money he thinks himself 'not so badly off as many are'.

When the shepherd's wife is given half a crown and two blankets, she cries out: 'It is too much, we are too rich.' The gentleman, Mr Johnson, decides that he is 'more disposed to envy than to pity the Shepherd'.

Shere Khan Tiger in the **Jungle Books* by **Kipling.

Sherlock Holmes Fictional **detective, the creation of Sir Arthur Conan **Doyle. The first Holmes story, *A Study in Scarlet*, made its bow in print in *Beeton's Christmas Annual* (see BEETON, SAMUEL ORCHART) and its author received £25 for it. Conan Doyle then began to write Holmes stories for The **Strand Magazine* and these swiftly brought fame to him and to Holmes. There are many spin-offs written specifically for child readers.

SHERWOOD (Butt), Mary Martha (1775–1851) An English author of numerous stories for children and the most fiercely didactic of all writers of the **moral tale. She imbued it with a religious fervour and an emphasis on human sinfulness which had not been seen in juvenile books since the writings of the 17th-cent. **Puritans.

Mrs Sherwood, the daughter of a Church of England clergyman, was brought up in a Worcestershire village. It was an upbringing of the strictest kind with the child eating the 'plainest possible food; dry bread and cold milk' and being made to wear 'iron collars round the

neck, with back-boards strapped over the shoulders' during school lessons. Yet she writes that her father 'was very, very kind to me'.

Her childhood reading consisted of *Robinson Crusoe*, The *Governess*, *Aesop, and 'two sets of Fairy Tales'; and she and her brother were encouraged by their father to write their own stories.

At the age of fifteen she was sent to the Abbey School in Reading, where she acted in *plays and continued to write. In her holiday time she visited Bath, attended balls, and was admired as a beauty. But this gaiety was brought to a close in 1795 when her father, who was in his fifties, died of a stroke. Mary's mother settled with the children at Bridgnorth and here Mary lived a retired life. She began to teach in a local Low Church *Sunday school and for it wrote *Susan Gray*, the story of a pious servant-girl who rejects the advances of her employer and dies a happy death, secure in her Christian faith. Pious deaths were to become a regular feature of her stories, occurring as frequently as in the writings of *Janeway more than a century earlier.

In 1803 Mary married her cousin, Captain Henry Sherwood of the 53rd foot regiment, and the next year she accompanied him to India, leaving their first child, a daughter, with her family in England. In India she gave birth to a son and another daughter, but the boy, Henry, died of whooping cough. Mrs Sherwood taught in the regimental school and devoted herself to the care of soldiers' orphans. In Cawnpore she became friends with the missionary Henry Martyn, and was soon under the influence of his *evangelical zeal. In 1808 her beloved Lucy died of dysentery; Mrs Sherwood felt that this blow was a rebuke from God for her excessive love of the child.

About two years later she made an adaptation of The *Pilgrim's Progress* for Indian readers under the title The Indian Pilgrim. She also wrote another reworking of Bunyan's allegory, this time especially for children, which she called The Infant's Progress from the Valley of Destruction to Everlasting Glory. These and a third book, *Little Henry and His Bearer* (1814), became extremely popular both in India and in England.

In 1812 she began work on what she called 'The Child's Manual'; this became The *Fairchild Family*. In 1816 she and her husband returned to England and set up home in Worcestershire. She began to take in pupils, and also to write prolifically. Some 350 books, essays, tracts, and pamphlets by her can be traced. The majority of these books have her distinctive fervour and vitality. Her later writings include The History of Henry Milner (1822-37), a three-volume account of a boy's religious education, and The Lady of the Manor (1825-9). She also kept a diary of voluminous size and wrote an autobiography.

Though her books are chiefly characterized by religious zeal, she was also a shrewd observer of human (especially child) behaviour and her vigorous prose style makes her stories far more readable than those of most other practitioners of the moral tale. Her eventful early years gave her a mass of experience to draw on and she always constructed narratives that were exciting as well as pious. The Calvinism of her earlier writing was modified after she came back to England, and by the end of her life she had reached the belief that 'salvation was wholly unconditional, a free gift of Divine love, that every creature was safe in the hands of his Creator and his Redeemer'.

Ship That Flew, The (1939) A novel by Hilda Lewis (1896-1974). A model Viking ship, bought by a boy in a seaside antique shop, grows in size at its owner's wishes and transports him and his brothers and sisters through time and space to Ancient Egypt and to Asgard, home of the *Norse gods. The story, which was one of the most admired *fantasies of its period, closely resembles (but does not match up to) E. *Nesbit's tales about magic. Lewis was a prolific British historical novelist for adults who also wrote four children's books, all concerned with historical events or characters.

Shock-Headed Peter See Struwwelpeter.

SHOTWELL, Louisa R. (Rossiter) (1902-93) American author, best known for *Roosevelt Grady* (1963), the story of a black boy brought up in an itinerant fruit-picking family in the South.

Shrek! (1990) A picture book written and illustrated by William *Steig, perhaps more famous today for having inspired (albeit rather loosely) the 2001 DreamWorks film and the resulting spin-off stage show. Shrek the ogre of Steig's book is a lot uglier, meaner, and more violent than his cuddly round counterpart of screen and stage. The original Shrek is an anti-hero, knocking dragons unconscious with his breath, triumphantly despatching knights with a blast of fire, and even frightening himself in a hall of mirrors until he recognizes himself and is 'happier than ever'. *Shrek!*

is more subversive than many a fractured fairy tale, with a message of being true to yourself even if you're an ogre inside as well as out.

SHULEVITZ, Uri (1935–) Author and illustrator whose life has taken him from childhood in Poland, fleeing from the Warsaw blitz, ending up in Paris in 1947, Israel in 1949, and eventually making a home in New York. Often using classic stories for inspiration, his gentle and evocative work includes *The Twelve Dancing Princesses* (1966) and *The Fool of the World and the Flying Ship* (1968), Arthur *Ransome's retelling of a Russian fairy tale, though his most successful work is often all his own: *Snow* (1998) magically tells of one boy, his dog and a snowy day; *How I Learned Geography* (2008) is based on his own memories of fleeing war to find poverty in a strange country but finding hope in the power of imagination; and *Dusk* (2013) delicately describes a boy, his dog, and his grandfather walking through a city just as night falls and seeing the city's lights come on, revealing the Hanukkah, Kwanza, and Christmas displays in the streets.

SHUSTERMAN, Neal (1962–) American *young adult author, film director, and screen- and television-writer best known for his *science fiction and *fantasy adventures. In the 'Unwind Dystology' series (2007–14, beginning with *Unwind*), adults have the power to get unwanted teenagers' body parts harvested. The Skinjacker Trilogy (*Everlost*, 2006, *Everwild*, 2009, and *Everfound*, 2011) is about teenagers caught in a world between life and death. Shusterman won the *Boston Globe– Horn Book Award for the realist novel *The Schwa Was Here* (2004), in which Antsy and his friend Calvin test the latter's ability to go through life seemingly unnoticed. Its sequels are *Antsy Does Time* (2008) and *Ship Out of Luck* (2013).

SIDNEY, Margaret *See* LOTHROP, HARRIET M.

SIERRA i FABRA, Jordi (1947–) Immensely prolific Spanish author, who writes for children and young adults in both Spanish and Catalan. Sierra i Fabra's roster of books has already surpassed 400 titles (selling more than ten million copies in Spain alone), which span realism, science fiction, fantasy, and crime fiction, usually in a readable, snappy prose style. The Fundació Jordi Sierra i Fabra is a non-profit foundation he established to support young writers.

Signal A British critical review of children's literature published from 1970 to 2003 (a total of one hundred issues) by Nancy and Aidan *Chambers, aimed at encouraging a deeper study of the subject than can be achieved in brief articles or reviews.

Silmarillion, The (1977) By J. R. R. *Tolkien, a collection of narratives related to *The *Lord of the Rings*, published posthumously.

Silver Brumby, The (1958) The first of a series of *horse stories by Australian author Elyne Mitchell (1913–2002), about Thowra, a silver 'brumby' (wild horse) of the Snowy Mountain region of Australia.

Silver Chair, The (1953) The fourth of the *Narnia novels by C. S. *Lewis.

Silver Skates, The *See* HANS BRINKER.

Silver Sword, The (1956) A novel by Ian *Serraillier. A Polish family is broken up by the Nazis during the German occupation, and the three children, Ruth, Edek, and Bronia, determine to reunite themselves with their parents, whom they know to be in Switzerland thanks to a message left by their father with another child, Jan. The father has given Jan a silver penknife in the shape of a sword which he knows his children will recognize, and this becomes their mascot on the seemingly impossible journey.

Ian Serraillier says that the book 'has a basis in fact'; before writing it, he 'studied the general background and the case histories of many refugees', though all the characters are fictitious. *The Silver Sword* has been published in many translations and was twice dramatized on BBC television.

SILVERSTEIN, Shel (Sheldon) (1930–99) American author, poet, cartoonist, and songwriter, much loved and widely translated. While producing work for an adult readership, Silverstein was introduced to editor Ursula *Nordstrom by his friend Tomi *Ungerer; Nordstrom persuaded him to write and illustrate for children. His whimsical wordplay has drawn comparisons with Dr *Seuss and Edward *Lear. His illustrations are simple black-and-white line drawings. His first children's book was *Uncle Shelby's Story of Lafcadio, the Lion Who Shot Back* (1963); an earlier work featuring Uncle Shelby, *Uncle Shelby's ABZ Book* (1960), is a satire for adults. *The *Giving Tree* (1964) has sold over ten million copies. Silverstein's recording of *Where the Sidewalk Ends* (1974), his first and most

acclaimed self-illustrated poetry collection, won a Grammy Award in 1984. *A Light in the Attic* (1981) was the first children's book to appear on the *New York Times* bestseller list. Despite their enduring popularity, his books have been widely challenged and *banned in the United States for a wide variety of reasons. The poetry collection *Every Thing On It* was published posthumously in 2011.

SIMON, Francesca (1955-) A British-American author best known for her popular and enduring *Horrid Henry series. Simon originally worked as a journalist before turning her hand to children's books after her son was born in 1989, publishing her first book *Papa Forgot* in 1993. Simon's first novel for older readers *The Sleeping Army* (2011) draws upon her interest in Medieval Studies, which she read at both Yale and Oxford Universities, and is a humorous tale of an alternate modern Britain in which the official state religion remains that of the pagan Saxons and Vikings. There is a sequel, *The Lost Gods* (2013).

Simon and the Witch (1976) A *fantasy by Margaret Stuart *Barry.

Simple Simon A *nursery rhyme character. It seems likely that the name was applied to simpletons for some centuries before the appearance of the rhyme, which was first printed as a *chapbook verse tale in the second half of the 18th cent. Certainly the name was current in the late 17th cent., when a *ballad was in circulation describing a henpecked husband and his scold of a wife, under the title *Simple Simon's Misfortunes and his Wife Margery's Cruelty*; the same story also appeared in prose.

SINCLAIR, Catherine (1800-64) Author of *Holiday House* (1839), which is entirely original in its flouting of the conventions of the *moral tale and is one of the first books that accepts children as they really are. She was the daughter of Sir John Sinclair, a Scottish philanthropist and man of public affairs. Catherine acted as her father's secretary and in his lifetime wrote one conventional children's book, *Charlie Seymour; or the good aunt and the bad aunt* (1832), the story of a boy who is left in the care of two relatives and has to choose which one is to be his guardian.

After her father's death in 1835 she began to publish novels for adults. *Modern Accomplishments* (1836) and its sequel *Modern Society* (1837). *Holiday House* appeared in 1839, and

was followed by further adult novels. Not until the end of her life did Miss Sinclair turn her attention to children again, beginning to produce a series of *Picture Letters* (1861-4), hieroglyphic letters to a child reader, possibly modelled on the *hieroglyphic bibles produced during the 18th and 19th cents. These were immensely successful, selling up to 100,000 copies each.

Sindbad the Sailor A story included by Antoine *Galland in his French version of the Arabic *Thousand and One Nights* (*see* ARABIAN NIGHTS) though it came from a different group of tales. Sindbad, a wealthy man, gives an account to Hindbad, a poor porter (in some versions also called Sinbad), of how he gained his riches. He has made seven remarkable voyages, during each of which he has encountered great marvels; for instance, a sea-monster mistaken for an island, a gigantic bird which carries him through the air, a cyclops, a tribe of cannibals, and a race of people who bury widows and widowers alive with their dead spouses. And the tale of the Old Man of the Sea, who clings onto Sindbad's neck all day until finally Sindbad gets the man drunk and kills him when he falls off in a stupor, only then discovering that this was the Old Man of the Sea, who had treated many other sailors the same way, not letting go of them until they were dead.

The *Sindbad* voyage stories resemble the *Odyssey* in many incidents and are probably linked to Persian, Indian and Arabic folk tales or early written stories, but now set firmly in Baghdad in the time of the Caliph Harun al-Rashid, during the 8th cent. Sir Richard Burton, the Victorian translator of the *Nights*, quotes from a commentary on the *Koran* which explains how evil becomes personified as a figure who rides on the back of an Infidel. Perhaps it is because of this allegorical element in the story that many English versions of the tale spell the hero's name 'Sinbad'.

'The Story of Sindbad the Sailor' was first printed in English in the third volume of *The Arabian Nights Entertainments*, published in 1712. The first separate printing of the story seems to have been that issued by Elizabeth *Newbery in 1794 under the title *The History of Sinbad the Sailor*. Many other editions for children subsequently appeared, and the story was often adapted into a *pantomime during the late 19th cent.

SINGER, Isaac Bashevis (1904-1991) Distinguished Jewish author, born in Poland and

resident in the United States from 1935. He wrote a number of books of stories for children, many of them based on folk tales from his childhood; the first was *Zlateh the Goat and other stories* (1966), illustrated by Maurice *Sendak. Singer wrote in Yiddish, his first language, and then supervised the translation of his books into English. Many of his children's stories are about the follies of the inhabitants of Chelm, a 'silly village' not unlike the English *Gotham.

SINGER, Nicky (1956–) English author of *young adult and adult books who always knew she wanted to tell stories. At first she wrote those stories for adults, but a chance conversation with her son—and a wander into a deserted house—inspired *Feather Boy* (2002), an intense, gripping, emotional thriller about a bullied boy, self-empowerment, and death. Death and the power of objects also feature in *The Flask* (2012), about a girl, grieving for her aunt and worried about her newborn brothers, who finds an old glass flask she believes has magical properties. Other titles include *Doll* (2003), *The Innocent's Story* (2005), *Gem X* (2006), and *Knight Crew* (2009). Despite the serious nature of the themes, these are lightly written, character-driven, uplifting stories.

SINGLETON, Sarah (1966–) English journalist who was inspired to write books for teenagers after reading David Almond's *Skellig*. With a style steeped in Gothic suspense and poetic luminosity, Singleton's books are beautifully written stories that set our real world against the unseen one of the paranormal. In the award-winning *Century* (2004) two sisters live with their rarely seen widowed father in a house perpetually shrouded by winter. They sleep during the day and question nothing, until a snowdrop appears on Mercy's pillow. There's religion and the fairy world in *Heretic* (2006), perfume, poison, and murder in *The Poison Garden* (2009), and *Dark Storm* (2012) gives us a love story that spans this world and the next.

Sing-Song, *a nursery rhyme book* (1872) A collection of short original poems by Christina *Rossetti, with illustrations by Arthur *Hughes. The verses in *Sing-Song* appear outwardly as appealing, yet simple poems, but the simplicity of the exterior in fact hides a carefully constructed balance that, as work by Virginia Sicklebert and others has shown, provides a challenge to orthodox Victorian values. In celebrating an equality of the mother-child relationship, and eschewing much of the moral and religious didacticism and sentimentality of many of her forebears and contemporaries, Rossetti produced a touching collection of nursery verses that still holds much resonance for the 21st-cent. reader. Work by Lorraine Janzen Kooistra (*Victorian Poetry* 37:4, 1999) has also shown that the careful interaction between Hughes' skilful illustrations and Rossetti's text produces a work where 'social and spiritual meanings [are] available at the simplest level for even the "innocent" child audience but [which] deepe[n] in implications for the "experienced" adult [reader]'.

Sintram See LA MOTTE FOUQUÉ, FRIEDRICH HEINRICH KARL, BARON DE.

Sir Charles Grandison A novel by Samuel *Richardson published in 1754 and sometimes abridged for children. The beautiful and talented Harriet Byron is carried off by the unscrupulous Sir Hargrave Pollexfen, but she is rescued by Sir Charles Grandison, who, after disentangling himself from a betrothal to an Italian lady, eventually marries her. Like Richardson's *Pamela* and *Clarissa Harlowe*, the book is written in the form of letters. R. Baldwin published a summary for children in 1756, and in about 1769 an abridged *Sir Charles Grandison* was published by Francis *Newbery.

Sir Hornbook; *or, Childe Launcelot's Expedition, a Grammatical-Allegorical Ballad* A mock *ballad in which Childe Launcelot enlists Sir Hornbook, his twenty-six merrymen A–Z, and other grammatical officers, to help him reach the goal of the Muses' bower. In turn they conquer and press into service all the parts of speech.

Published anonymously, probably in late 1813, by Sharpe and Hailes of Piccadilly, it is the early work of the poet and satirist Thomas Love Peacock (1785–1866). It was illustrated and was popular enough as a piece of grammar-without-tears to go through several editions in the next five years. In 1843 it surfaced again, as part of Sir Henry *Cole's series *The *Home Treasury*. Its last appearance was in another publisher's edition twelve years later.

Sir Toady Lion A novel by S. R. *Crockett.

SÍS, Peter (1949–) Czech-born American author and illustrator. Sís began his career as a children's book illustrator after seeking

asylum in the United States while making a film for the Czech government for the 1984 Olympics. A frequent collaborator of Sid *Fleischman, Jack *Prelutsky, and George Shannon, he is a three-time Caldecott Honor Award winner (*see* CALDECOTT MEDAL) for books that he also wrote: *Starry Messenger: Galileo Galilei* (1996), *Tibet through the Red Box* (1998), and the autobiographical *The Wall: Growing Up Behind the Iron Curtain* (2007). Sís was a 2003 MacArthur Fellow and the 2012 winner of the *Hans Christian Andersen Medal for illustration.

Sixteen-String Jack *See* DICK TURPIN.

Skellig (1998) Stunning first children's novel by David *Almond. The story is about Michael, whose family has just moved into a new house, where Michael is left largely to his own devices, as his parents are focused on his baby sister, who is very ill. In the falling-down garage he finds someone he thinks is a tramp, but the man is strange and not quite human, with a body crooked with arthritis and an obsession with Chinese takeaways numbers 27 and 53. The plot adds in Mina, a home-schooled girl with an interest in William *Blake, and around the reality of the children's lives weaves an ambiguous story that encompasses mysticism, evolution, and the value of friendship. The book has been made into an opera, a film, and a play. A prequel about Mina, *My Name is Mina*, was published in 2011.

Skulduggery Pleasant (2007) A series of books that read as if author Derek Landy (1974–) had decided to create a genre that mixed together all the most popular ones in order to find one all of his own, so here we have humour, horror, romance, mystery, action, and fantasy, all spun around a hero who is dead. Well, undead, really, as Skulduggery Pleasant is a once dead mage whose skeleton is animated by magic and who, in order to appear 'normal', wears a tan overcoat, wig, hat, sunglasses, and scarf. His meeting with twelve-year-old Stephanie Edgley (who later calls herself Valkyrie Cain) at her uncle's funeral starts an epic magical adventure. Though this book stands alone, there are many sequels, including a spin-off, *The Maleficent Seven* (2013), featuring Tanith Low.

Slave Dancer, The (1973) A novel by Paula *Fox.

Sleeping Beauty, The A *fairy story best known in the version by *Perrault, first published in 1696 under the title *La Belle au bois dormant.*

A daughter is born to a king and queen after they have been childless for some time. At the christening feast for the child, an old fairy who has not been invited arrives. Instead of bestowing wonderful gifts such as beauty, wit, and gracefulness on the child as do the other fairies present, she curses the girl, stating that one day the princess will pierce her hand with a spindle and die. A young fairy manages to modify the curse so that she will not die but instead 'fall into a deep sleep which will last a hundred years, at the end of which a king's son shall come and wake her up'. Despite a ban on spindles by the King, the princess does prick her finger when she is sixteen years old and as per the prophecy falls into a deep sleep along with the rest of the court. A thick forest grows up around the palace which remains in place for a century until a prince arrives and cuts through it to find the sleeping princess. He wakes her, and they fall in love and are married. The prince then returns to his own court, keeping Sleeping Beauty a secret even from his own father. However, he visits the princess almost every day and at the end of two years the princess has given birth to two children.

Eventually the prince's father dies and he becomes king, declaring his marriage openly. However, his mother the queen, who is an ogress, conceives a desire to eat her two grandchildren and Sleeping Beauty. However the ogress is tricked into eating other animals instead of the children and the queen. The ogre queen soon afterwards discovers that she has been duped and that her victims are still alive and in hiding; she is about to cast them into a tub filled with 'toads, vipers, snakes, and serpents' when her son arrives home and sees what is happening. The ogress throws herself into the tub and is devoured in an instant; the young king 'could not help being sorry, for she was his mother, but he soon consoled himself with his beautiful wife and his children'.

The earliest recorded form of the story is in the 14th-cent. French prose *romance *Perceforest*, a rambling narrative which includes a story of 'Troylus and Zellandine'. The princess Zellandine, cursed at birth by a slighted goddess, falls into a deep sleep when she begins to spin with a distaff. Her sleeping form is duly discovered by the prince Troylus, who rapes her while she is sleeping, with the result that when she does wake she finds herself to be pregnant.

A similar story is found in the 17th-cent. Neapolitan *Pentamerone* (Day 5, tale 5), This time Talia, the daughter of a great lord, falls asleep after accidentally driving a splinter of hemp into her finger. Her body is discovered by a king who is out hunting, and he, like Troylus, rapes her. Nine months later and still unconscious, she gives birth to a boy and a girl, who are looked after by two fairies. One day one of the babies sucks at Talia's finger and draws out the splinter, so that Talia awakes. The story then continues as in Perrault, with the difference that the ogress is not the king's mother but his jealous wife. The story concludes with the king rewarding the cook who has saved the two royal children from being eaten, a detail that was incorporated into English *chapbook versions of Perrault's tale, either by coincidence or because of direct copying from the *Pentamerone*. The *Grimms recorded a similar story, *Little Briar-Rose*, which is clearly derived from Perrault. It omits the episode of the ogre queen, but adds a number of small embellishments to the narrative. There is also a resemblance between the motif of the sleeping maiden in a castle surrounded by an enchanted wood and the passage in the *Volsungasaga* in which Odin places Brynhild in a castle surrounded by a barrier of flame and sends her into an enchanted sleep to preserve her youth and beauty until there should arrive a man brave enough to penetrate the barrier and win her.

The story was first published in English in 1729 in *Histories, or Tales of Past Times. La Belle au bois dormant* was rendered (inaccurately) as *The Sleeping Beauty in the Wood*. In 1764 the tale was printed separately in a chapbook issued by Cluer *Dicey and Richard Marshall. Later chapbook versions include those printed by J. Drewry of Derby in 1787, and by Fordyce of Newcastle *c.*1820–30. These versions were loosely based on Samber's translation, departing a little from his text, perhaps to avoid obvious plagiarism. Many retellings, such as those in *Tabart's early 19th-cent. series *Popular Stories*, and in The *Fairy Book* (1863) by Mrs *Craik, omit the ogress and her attempts to eat the children and conclude the story with the marriage of the prince and princess.

The abbreviated title *The Sleeping Beauty* became common in the later part of the 19th cent. A versification of the story was illustrated by Walter *Crane in 1904. Most 20th-cent. versions add to Perrault by making the old woman with the spindle in the tower room the wicked fairy herself.

The story has often been made into a *pantomime. *The Sleeping Beauty, a Grand Legendary Melo-Drama* was presented at Drury Lane in 1806, and among other stage versions was an 1840 Covent Garden extravaganza, by J. R. *Planché, *The Sleeping Beauty in the Wood*. Tchaikovsky's ballet *The Sleeping Beauty* was first performed in 1890. In 1958 the tale was filmed by the *Disney studios.

SLEIGH, Barbara (1906–82) British children's writer who had much success with her stories about Carbonel, King of the Cats (*Carbonel*, 1955, and other titles).

SLOBODKIN, Louis (1903–75) American illustrator and author who won the *Caldecott Medal for his illustrations to James *Thurber's *Many Moons* (1943). He was the illustrator of (among much else) the *Moffat stories by Eleanor *Estes.

SMART, Christopher (1722–71) English poet who was closely associated with John *Newbery. After an education at Cambridge, Smart established himself in London by 1750 as a professional writer and was engaged by Newbery to contribute to, and probably edit, his new humorous magazine *The Midwife*. Newbery also published Smart's poems. By 1753 Smart had married Newbery's stepdaughter, Anna Maria Carnan.

He began to suffer from physical and mental illness, but Newbery seems to have driven him as hard as ever. In 1757 he was put into an asylum, where he wrote his brilliant and deranged *Jubilate Agno* ('Rejoice in the Lamb'). After his release in 1763 he published *A Song to David*, arguably his masterpiece, but his reputation as a madman prevented it from gaining the recognition it deserved. Smart's wife had now left him. Newbery specified several times in his will (he died in 1767) that Smart was to receive no part of his estate.

Smart began to be ill again, and was eventually imprisoned for debt. While in confinement he completed his last book, *Hymns for the Amusement of Children*. It was printed by Thomas Carnan, Newbery's stepson and successor, who had determined to do something to help him. Smart died a few months after it appeared in 1771.

Smaug A *dragon in The *Hobbit* by J. R. R. *Tolkien.

Smee A *pirate in *Peter Pan* by J. M. *Barrie.

Smith (1967) A novel by Leon *Garfield. Smith is a thief, but when he picks the pocket

of an elderly gentleman who is then murdered before his eyes, is then found in real trouble. Is it worth it? All Smith has for his effort is a document he cannot read. Smith's attempts to solve the mystery of the document and the murder lead him into danger in which he faces implacable enemies. However, he does make new friends and he learns to read before his adventure reaches a dramatic climax. One of Garfield's earliest novels, it is also one of his best. It was the recipient of the 1987 Phoenix Award (for the best book not to receive any other major award).

SMITH, Andrew (1959–) American author of *young adult books. He started as a journalist but spent many years travelling the world, taking on whatever jobs were available as he went. After settling in California he became a teacher and then a writer, when challenged by a friend to try. He achieved immediate success, producing books that are complex, intriguing, and challenging. His first, *Ghost Medicine* (2008), is a coming-of-age story about friendship, growing up, and grief that is woven through with imagery and philosophy. There's more graphic violence and a hero teetering on the edge on insanity in *The Marbury Lens* (2010) and, just to prove that his books cannot be easily categorized, *Winger* (2013) is a hilarious, painful, boarding-school romp. Meanwhile *Grasshopper Jungle* (2014, winner of the *Boston Globe–Horn Book Award) has giant praying mantises taking over the world and *100 Miles Sideways* (2014) is about an epileptic boy searching for meaning.

SMITH, Charlotte, (Turner) (1749–1806) English poet and novelist who wrote several books of moral and instructive conversations for children. The most notable, written with her sister Mrs Dorset, author of *The *Peacock 'At Home'*, was *Conversations introducing Poetry* (1804). In her essay 'Benevolent Brothers and Supervising Mothers', Donelle Ruwe discusses the value of *Conversations* to a radical pedagogy that promotes 'women's literary aspirations' (*Children's Literature* 25, 1997), and work by scholars such as Jaqueline Labbe has highlighted the importance of Smith's entire canon to Romantic era writing and the work of Wordsworth and Austen in particular.

SMITH, Dodie (1896–1990) Popular British playwright who wrote three children's books: *The *One Hundred and One Dalmatians* (1956), *The Star-light Barking* (1967), and *The Midnight Kittens* (1978), and other fiction including *I Capture the Castle*.

SMITH, Mrs E. T. *See* MEADE, L. T.

SMITH, Jessie Wilcox (1863–1935) American illustrator, pupil of Howard *Pyle, who was especially known for her drawings of children at work and play.

SMITH, Lane (1959–) American author and illustrator. With influences ranging from Paul Klee to Monty Python, Smith's art is stylized, funny, and offbeat. His works as author and illustrator include the historical picture books *John, Paul, George, and Ben* (2006) and *Abe Lincoln's Dream* (2012). Other titles include *It's a Book* (2010), which is about a monkey whose reading is interrupted by a jackass with a laptop who has never seen a book before. *It's a Book* has been translated into twenty languages. *Grandpa Green* (2011) was a Caldecott Honor Book (*see* CALDECOTT MEDAL). Smith collaborated with Jon *Scieszka on the bestselling *The True Story of the Three Little Pigs* (1998), the Caldecott Honor Book *The *Stinky Cheese Man and Other Fairly Stupid Tales* (1992), *Math Curse* (1995), and *Science Verse* (2004). Other titles include Dr *Seuss's last book, *Hooray for Diffendoofer Day!* (1999), completed by Jack Prelutsky, and the Lulu books by Judith *Viorst. Smith was conceptual designer for the 1996 Disney film of *James and the Giant Peach*. He was named a Carle Honor Artist in 2012 for lifelong innovation in the field of children's books.

SMITH, Lillian H. (1887–1983) Pioneer Canadian children's librarian. She joined the Toronto Public Libraries in 1912 and her work there was widely recognized as outstanding. She was the author of *The Unreluctant Years: a critical approach to children's literature* (1953). A collection of children's books, intended as a continuation of the *Osborne Collection, has been established at Toronto and named in her honour.

SMITH, Sarah *See* STRETTON, HESBA.

Smoky, the Cowhorse (1926) By Will James, the story of a horse's experiences, narrated in idiomatic *cowboy language. 'Will James' was the pseudonym of Joseph E. N. Dufault (1892–1942), who worked as a cowhand, rodeo rider, and Hollywood stunt man, as well as writing cowboy fiction for children and adults. *Smoky* was his best known book, and like his other stories for children was illustrated by the author. It won the *Newbery Medal.

Snape, Professor Severus A more than usually sinister member of staff at *Hogwarts in the *Harry Potter books.

Sneetches and Other Stories, The (1961) A collection of four stories in rhyming verse by Dr *Seuss, of which the title story is the most famous. It describes two tribes of Sneetches, one who have stars on their bellies and one without. In Seuss's witty allegory of the silly irrationality of prejudice and discrimination, each group has contempt for the other, but eventually, after some travails, they learn their lesson. The other stories in the collection are 'The Zax', 'Too Many Daves', and 'What Was I Scared of?'

SNICKET, Lemony (Daniel Handler) (1970–) American author. Themes of death and misfortune, along with the number 13, frequently appear in his darkly funny literary novels and picture books. 'Snicket' wrote the thirteen-volume *A *Series of Unfortunate Events* in memory of Beatrice Baudelaire after her death in a suspicious fire. Baudelaire was the mother of Violet, Klaus, and Sunny Baudelaire and at one time Snicket's fiancée. Snicket has written a number of picture books, such as *13 Words* (2010), ('despondent', 'panache' and 'dog' among them); the Hanukkah story *The Latke Who Couldn't Stop Screaming: a Christmas Story* (2007); *The Lump of Coal* (2008), a Christmas story; *The Composer is Dead* (2009), a murder mystery with a musical score and accompanying CD narrated by Snicket; *The Dark* (2013), illustrated by Jon *Klassen and shortlisted for the *Kate Greenaway Medal; and *29 Myths on the Swinster Pharmacy* (2014). Snicket has published three books in *The Wrong Questions* series for middle-grade readers: *Who Could That Be at This Hour?* (2012), *When Did You See Her Last?* (2013), and *File Under: 13 Suspicious Incidents* (2014). In 2014 he set up 'The Lemony Snicket Prize for Noble Librarians Faced with Adversity' in honour of school librarians who have been active in fighting attempts to ban books.

Snoopy A dog featured in the 'Peanuts' comic strip by the American artist and writer Charles M. *Schulz, which first appeared in October 1950. In the strip Snoopy is notable for his daydreams about himself as a great writer, athlete, and lover, and as an ace fighter pilot of the First World War ('Some day I'll get you, Red Baron').

Snork Maiden In the *Moomin stories by Tove *Jansson.

Snow Goose, The (1941) By Paul *Gallico. First published in 1940 as a short story in a newspaper, Gallico revised the text for publication as a novella in 1941. Though originally written for adults, its subject—Dunkirk—and the timeless quality of the storytelling, despite the inherent sentimentality, have seen it become a classic for younger readers. Set on the marshes of Essex, it tells of the friendship between the solitary artist Rhayader and the girl Fritha, who brings a wounded snow goose to him for healing. When the call for boats to rescue the troops trapped on the beaches of Dunkirk goes out, Rhayader answers. Accompanied by the snow goose, his efforts become part of a legend, while Fritha is left to mourn.

Snowman, The (1978) A wordless picture book by Raymond *Briggs, which won the *Boston Globe–Horn Book Award. A boy makes a snowman; at night the snowman comes to life and he and the boy become friends, just for the night. In the best-remembered episode they take a flight across the night sky over a snowy landscape. By the time the boy wakes the next morning, the snowman has melted. The magical story, illustrated entirely in coloured pencil, has become a Christmas classic, especially since the production of an animated version broadcast regularly since 1982 (famously featuring the song 'Walking in the Air', sung by Peter Auty). An animated sequel, *The Snowman and the Snowdog*, appeared in 2012.

Snow Queen, The A *fairy story by Hans Christian *Andersen. The devil makes a mirror which causes everything good to appear unpleasant and vice versa. The mirror shatters and splinters of its glass fly around the world. Two enter the eyes and heart of Kai, a little boy, who becomes cynical and hard in character, beginning to turn against his former playfellow, the little girl Gerda. Soon he is carried off by the icily beautiful but cruel Snow Queen. Gerda goes in search of him and has many strange adventures before she finds him and melts the splinters and his frozen heart with her tears. The story, one of Andersen's longest and most crowded with imaginative incident, was first published in 1846. Among other influences, the Snow Queen features significantly in David Almond's *Kit's Wilderness.

Snow-white and Rose-red A *fairy story collected by the brothers *Grimm, sometimes printed as a separate book.

Two young sisters, Snow-white and Rose-red, live with their widowed mother. They give shelter for the winter to a bear. In the spring he goes away, explaining that he must guard his treasure from wicked *dwarfs. Soon the children meet an old dwarf whom they help out of various predicaments, but he treats them with surliness and ingratitude. Finally the bear appears and kills the dwarf, after which the bearskin drops off and he is revealed as a handsome prince; he tells them: 'I was bewitched by that wicked dwarf, who had stolen my treasures; I have had to run about the forest as a savage bear until I was freed by his death.'

Snow White and the Seven Dwarfs A
*fairy story collected by the brothers *Grimm.

The Grimms' story tells how Snow White, the daughter of a king, is envied by her beautiful but cruel stepmother, whose magic mirror tells her that Snow White is even fairer than herself. In a rage, the queen orders that Snow White be abandoned in a wood (in the original German, she intends that Snow White be killed and her heart cut out). Snow White, lost in the forest, comes to a cottage where the table is laid for seven and helps herself to food and drink from each of the places. She then tries each of the seven beds that she discovers upstairs before settling into one of them. The owners of the cottage, seven *dwarfs who mine for gold in the hills, come home and discover her and marvel at her beauty. Waking, she offers to keep house for them, and they accept; she intends by this to hide from the queen.

The queen learns Snow White's whereabouts, which are betrayed to her by the magic mirror, and she tries to kill her three times, first by disguising herself as a pedlar and selling Snow White a lace which is then used to pull her stays so tight that the girl falls down, apparently dead, secondly by means of a poisoned comb, and finally with a poisoned apple. Having failed to save her on the third occasion, the dwarfs place her in a coffin of glass. She is eventually discovered by a prince, who lifts her up, so that the piece of poisoned apple falls from her lips and she comes to her senses and marries the prince. Her wicked stepmother dies of envy—or, in the original Grimm text, is put to death with red-hot slippers.

The story became popular in England in the 1820s, as soon as the Grimms' tales had been translated. However, its present status as one of the best known of all fairies stories seems to derive largely from the 1937 Walt *Disney animation, in which the dwarfs are given names (Happy, Sleepy, Doc, Bashful, Sneezy, Grumpy, and Dopey) and the wicked queen changes into a hideous *witch before she visits Snow White at the cottage.

Snowy The hero's dog in the *Tintin books.

Snowy Day, The A picture book by Ezra Jack *Keats.

Snuffy A small dog in stories by Dick *Bruna.

Snugglepot and Cuddlepie A pair of
'gumnut babies' (small children who supposedly grow on gum trees), the creation of Australian author-illustrator May *Gibbs. *Snugglepot and Cuddlepie: Their Adventures Wonderful* was published in 1918; further books followed and *The Complete Adventures of Snugglepot and Cuddlepie* appeared in 1948.

The babes' adventures are of the simplest kind, but are memorable for the wicked Banksia Men and the curious prose style:

'Where's the Banksia man?' asked Snugglepot.
'Deadibones,' said Cuddlepie.
'Good root,' said Snugglepot.

SNYDER, Zilpha Keatley (1927–2014) American author of books for children and young adults. Best known for her fantasy and adventure novels, she also wrote books for younger readers. Snyder received the Newbery Honor (see NEWBERY MEDAL) for *The Egypt Game* (1967), *The Headless Cupid* (1971), and *The Witches of Worm* (1972). She decided at the age of eight that she wanted to become a writer, but it wasn't until her own children were in school, and after several years as an elementary-school teacher, that she wrote her first novel, *Season of Ponies* (1964), in which a girl visits a gypsy boy and a herd of ponies similar to the glass figures on her bookshelf. She wrote more than forty books for young people, and her works have been published in thirteen languages.

Society for Promoting Christian Knowledge (SPCK) A Church of England society founded in 1698 to promote the establishment of charity schools, and to distribute religious books and tracts. During the second half of the 19th cent. it published a good deal of popular fiction as *reward books.

SOMMERFELT, Aimée (1892–1975) Norwegian children's author. Her books include

Miriam (1950), a novel set during the German occupation and dealing with a girl whose family takes over a house belonging to Jews, and *Vien til Agra* (1959) (*The Road to Agra*, 1961), about a boy in India who takes his sister on an immense journey to a hospital which can cure her failing eyesight.

Songs for the Nursery, *Collected from the Works of the Most Renowned Poets* First published in 1805 by *Tabart and reprinted a number of times, notably in a finely illustrated edition by William *Darton (1818). It was a source of the American *nursery rhyme collection *Mother Goose's Quarto* (*c.* 1825), and of James Orchard *Halliwell's influential collection of rhymes (1842).

Songs of Childhood (1902) The first published collection of poems by Walter *de la Mare, issued under the pseudonym 'Walter Ramal', the surname being 'Lamar[e]' spelt backwards. The publisher, Longman, felt that they were over the heads of children, and so printed them without illustrations (de la Mare did not, in any case, approve of the illustration of imaginative works), though Longman did include a frontispiece by Richard *Doyle of fairies dancing. Andrew *Lang, literary adviser to Longman, was probably responsible for the book being accepted for publication.

Songs of Childhood includes several poems which have become nursery classics, such as 'John Mouldy' ('I spied John Mouldy in his cellar') and 'Bunches of Grapes' ('Bunches of grapes,' says Timothy; | 'Pomegranates pink,' says Elaine). The book was reprinted in 1916, 1923, and 1942, on the last two occasions with illustrations.

Songs of Innocence (1789) An 'illuminated book' by William *Blake. Its twenty-three poems and their integral illustrations and decorations were engraved on *copperplate by Blake himself, using an unconventional process by which the lettering and drawings were left as raised parts of the plate, the rest being etched away. The plates were printed—again by Blake himself—in a chosen colour, and other colours were then added by hand. No more than twenty-three copies are known to exist, and Blake never intended the book for mass production. Each copy was apparently executed at a different time, when a customer had commissioned it. No two copies are identical, there being many differences in the colouring.

The introductory poem, 'Piping down the valleys wild', describes a child seated on a cloud, who tells the piper to 'Pipe a song about a Lamb' and to 'Sing thy songs of happy chear'.

The poems which follow include 'The Lamb' ('Little Lamb, who made thee?'), 'The Chimney Sweeper' ('My mother died when I was very young'), and 'The Little Black Boy' ('My mother bore me in the southern wild, | And I am black, but O! my soul is white'). Geoffrey Keynes, editor and bibliographer of Blake's work, has written: 'The poems are happy lyrics, children's songs, written intuitively by one who understood that the imagination of a child is unfettered, capable of comprehending without the impediments of sophisticated reason and experience. They are the expression of joy in this world, and yet . . . they are not mere nursery rhymes. Already Blake had begun to use symbols, which when understood add overtones of philosophic meaning to songs intrinsically beautiful.'

In 1794, Blake reconstructed the book and added new poems, this time giving the work the title *Songs of Innocence and of Experience Showing the Two Contrary States of the Human Soul*. His purpose now was also to portray the period of inevitable disappointment which results from a more mature acquaintance with the world. In the 1794 book, some poems from the first volume now appeared in the 'Experience' section. Of the new poems, the best known is 'The Tyger' ('Tyger Tyger, burning bright, | In the forests of the night').

The poems were reprinted in 1839 and again in 1863, but on both occasions were partly rewritten by editors—in the latter case by Dante Gabriel Rossetti, who prepared them for inclusion in a Life of Blake. In 1868 an edition was printed that was based on the original texts, though with 'modernized' spelling and punctuation and without illustrations. Subsequently editions appeared with illustrations by various artists, and in the 20th cent. a number of facsimiles of Blake's original books have appeared. Several of the poems are still better known in anthologies than in the form in which Blake originally presented them.

Sooty A glove *puppet in the form of a *teddy bear with black ears, who featured in British television programmes during the 1950s and 1960s, with his creator Harry Corbett. A number of Sooty books for small children were published.

Sophie The heroine of *The *BFG*.

Sorcerer's Apprentice, The The story of a boy who, in his magician master's absence, tries out one of the spells he has overheard, but then cannot countermand it. The story is now best known in the form made by *Disney in his film *Fantasia* (1940), in which *Mickey Mouse is the apprentice. This was devised as a visual accompaniment to the music of the symphonic poem *L'Apprenti sorcier* (1897) by Dukas, which was based on a poem by Goethe; this in turn is based on a dialogue by the 2nd-cent. AD Latin poet Lucian. The story has sometimes been issued as a *picture book.

SØRENSEN, Svend Otto *See* S., Svend Otto.

SORENSEN, Virginia (1912–91) American novelist who won the *Newbery Medal with her fourth children's book, *Miracles on Maple Hill* (1956), about a father returning home from a prisoner-of-war camp. Her other books for children include *Plain Girl* (1955), set among the Amish.

SOTO, Gary (1952–) American author and poet whose work often draws on his experience growing up as a Mexican-American in central California. His *young adult short story collection *Baseball in April* (1990) was an *American Library Association Best Book for Young Adults, and its 'The No-Guitar Blues' was adapted for film. Two of his picture books illustrated by Susan Guevara have won awards: *Chato Goes Cruisin'* (2005) was a *New York Times* best illustrated book, while *Chato and the Party Animals* (2000) won the Pura Belpré Medal for best illustration. *Marisol* (2005), part of the 'American Girl' series, unleashed a storm of protest because the protagonist's mother described the family's Chicago neighbourhood as 'dangerous'.

Sounder (1969) A novel by William H. Armstrong, the story of an African-American family living in the South sometime between the American Civil War and 1900. *Sounder* won the *Newbery Medal, but was subsequently attacked for its supposed dehumanization of the black characters; several critics objected to the fact that the boy who is the book's central figure is never named. The author, born in Lexington, Virginia, in 1914, was for many years a high-school teacher in Kent, Connecticut.

SOUTHALL, Ivan (Francis) (1921–2008) The best known Australian children's author of the 1960s and 1970s who was born in Canterbury, Victoria. During the Second World War he was a pilot in the Royal Australian Air Force, and won the Distinguished Flying Cross. He then became a freelance writer, producing novels about Squadron Leader Simon Black of the RAAF (9 volumes, 1950–62). A decade of this work was enough for him, and he decided to reject the conventional *adventure story for novels of character featuring 'real' children like his own four. Nevertheless his new-style books had at first something of 'adventure' in their make-up.

The first of them, *Hills End* (1962), presents a group of young people faced with the dangers of storm and flood, and the same formula governed the writing of *Ash Road* (1965), in which three boys start a terrible forest fire. These novels, and others, are full of excitement yet always plausible. At the same period Southall wrote several shorter books, including *The Fox Hole* (1967), about a boy trapped in a mine shaft, and *Let the Balloon Go* (1968), about a spastic boy climbing a tree.

Bread and Honey (1970) (US title, *Walk a Mile and Get Nowhere*) showed a change of direction to a more reflective type of novel, in this case about a teenage boy's strange relationship with a younger girl. *Josh* (1971) won the *Carnegie Medal; set in a small, remote Australian town, it describes a boy's visit to a domineering aunt (who runs the local *Sunday school) and the pain caused by the increasing difficulties of his relationship with the local children.

Southall wrote with great energy, usually adopting a stream-of-consciousness narrative technique. His books are rich in characterization and lovingly evoke earlier times in Australia's history, particularly the 1930s.

SOUTHEY, Robert (1774–1843) English poet. His verses were generally approved by parents as being safe for their children. The two favourites in children's anthologies were 'The Old Man's Comforts and how he Gained Them', which Lewis *Carroll parodied in 'You are old, Father William', and 'The Cataract of Lodore'.

Southey also wrote the first printed version of *The *Three Bears*, which appeared in his book *The Doctor* (1837). His edition of the *Morte Darthur* (1817) played a part in the revival of the King *Arthur stories as children's reading matter.

space stories *See* SCIENCE FICTION.

SPCK *See* SOCIETY FOR PROMOTING CHRISTIAN KNOWLEDGE.

Speaker, The, *or, miscellaneous pieces selected from the best English writers, and disposed under proper heads, with a view to facilitate the improvement of youth, in reading and speaking* (1774) An anthology designed for the teaching of elocution, compiled by William Enfield (1741–97) and intended for use at the dissenting Warrington Academy, where he taught. It contained pieces of verse and prose by authors ranging from *Shakespeare to Mrs *Barbauld, whose father was a tutor at the Academy; it was very popular, passing through many editions in the decades that followed its first publication.

SPEARE, Elizabeth George (1908–94) American author of *historical novels for children. She won the *Newbery Medal with *The Witch of Blackbird Pond* (1958), which concerns witch-hunting in 17th-cent. Connecticut, and was awarded it again for *The Bronze Bow* (1961), the story of an Israelite confronted by Jesus. She was awarded the *Laura Ingalls Wilder Medal in 1989.

SPECKTER, Otto (1807–71) German illustrator. One of his best known books was a collection of *fables by Wilhelm Hey, published as *Fünfzig Fabeln* (1833) and *Noch fünfzig Fabeln* (1837). An English version, translated by Mary *Howitt, was published in 1844, and a later translation (1858) had coloured wood-engravings by the *Dalziel Brothers.

spelling books See ABC BOOKS; BATTLEDORE; HORNBOOK; PRIMER.

SPENCE, Eleanor (1928–2008) Australian author of *family stories and *historical novels, including *The Green Laurel* (1963), about a girl from a fairground family, and *The Switherby Pilgrims* (1967) and *Jamberoo Road* (1969), a pair of stories set in the 1840s, in which a determined Yorkshirewoman emigrates to Australia with a group of destitute children, to whom she adds an aboriginal orphan and a convict who acts as servant.

SPENSER, Edmund See FAERIE QUEENE, THE.

SPERRY, Armstrong (1897–1976) American children's author and illustrator who won the *Newbery Medal in 1941 with *Call It Courage*, a short novel about a Polynesian boy who has a dread of the sea and finds himself adrift on it.

Spiderwick Chronicles, The See BLACK, HOLLY.

SPIEGELMAN, Art See MAUS.

SPIER, Peter (1927–) American illustrator born (to an illustrator father) and brought up in the Netherlands, but resident in the US since the 1950s. Spier's intricately detailed illustrations have won him many awards, including a *Caldecott Medal for *Noah's Ark* (1977) and the *Boston Globe–Horn Book Award for *London Bridge Is Falling Down* (1967). Since his 1953 debut, *Cocoa* (by Margaret G. Otto), Spier has illustrated over 150 books, mostly to texts by other writers but also to some of his own. Other notable titles include the *picture book *The Fox Went Out on a Chilly Night* (1961), *People* (1980), an irresistible celebration of difference and tolerance, and an edition of *Hans Brinker* (1958), a book whose eponymous protagonist grew up very close to Spier's own childhood home.

SPINELLI, Jerry (1941–) American author whose career was kick-started when his father had a poem he'd written published in the local paper—seeing it in print was enough to determine his future career. Luckily he had the talent to go along with the enthusiasm, as his books are successful, accessible stories of American life, full of emotions and situations that young adults identify with. The *Newbery-winning *Maniac Magee* (1990) is about a runaway orphan boy's encounter with racism; *Stargirl* (2000) is the least slushy of love stories (and the most touching); *Milkweed* (2003) tells of a child who does not fully comprehend what is happening around him in the Warsaw ghetto; and *Wringer* (1997) is about a boy who must learn to stop being afraid in order to stand up for what he believes in.

Spiritual Milk for Boston Babes See MILK FOR BABES.

Sponge and Spiker See JAMES AND THE GIANT PEACH.

sports, books of A popular genre for children, especially in the early 19th cent. One of the first examples of a book recording games commonly played by children is *Les Jeux et plaisirs de l'enfance* (1657), a set of elegant *copperplates engraved by Claudine Bouzonnet Stella which depict naked and cherubic children blowing bubbles, playing leapfrog, and so on. In 1780 Thomas Carnan, one of the successors to John *Newbery, published *Juvenile Sports and Pastimes* by 'Master Michael Angelo' (probably Richard *Johnson).

One of the most attractive works of this sort is *The Book of Games; or, a History of the Juvenile Sports practised at the Kingston*

Academy, which was published by *Tabart in 1804. This is the story of Tom White, who is sent to school and learns how to play hockey, trap ball (a form of cricket), fives, football, and less formal games such as kite-flying, leap-frog, and hunt the slipper.

sports fiction featured in many British boys' magazines and *comics from the late 19th cent. The opening story in the first issue of the *Boys' Own Paper* (1879) was 'My First Football Match' by Talbot Baines *Reed, and innumerable others in the same vein appeared. More sensational material was to be found in the *Harmsworth story-papers and their rivals, which first appeared at the very end of the 19th cent., and continued in print until the Second World War. E. S. Turner has written of such stories (*Boys Will Be Boys*, rev. edn, 1975):

Fictional sport . . . was vastly dirtier than in real life. No one is likely to forget the long and unflagging sequence of stories about football matches in which the lemons were poisoned at half-time, in which rascally backs hacked the home forwards with boots containing poisoned nails, and bogus referees blew poison darts at the star players . . . The one honest player in the team spent the week shaking off kidnappers and trying to clear his own or his father's name.

In the early 20th cent, the *Aldine company produced many 'libraries' of sporting stories. From the 1920s onwards, sport played a large part in the adventure-thrillers which filled the D.C. *Thomson boys' weeklies; these featured such heroes as *Wilson the Wonder Athlete.

Sports continue to feature regularly in contemporary children's and *young adult fiction in the twenty-first century, both collected into multi-author anthologies (collections of football stories, say) or as full-length novels. Sometimes the sporting activity itself is the main purpose of the narrative, such as the many children's and young adult novels by sports columnist Mike Lupica (1952–) on baseball, basketball and American football. (This is also usually the way with series written by successful sportspeople themselves, such as US baseball player Cal Ripken Jr. or British footballer Frank Lampard.) In other cases, the sports are merely a context or background for a story with another important subject and driving-force. Neil Arksey's *MacB* (1999), a *Macbeth* reworking, Walter Dean *Myers's basketball titles or Mal *Peet's Paul Faustino novels are high-quality examples of these. Sports books continue to be marketed principally at boys—and seen as a way of encouraging reluctant readers to engage with books through this theme—though there are exceptions, such as Helena Pielichaty's *Girls FC* series (from 2009).

Spot *See* WHERE'S SPOT?

SPRING, Howard (1889–1965) Best selling British adult novelist (his most famous book was *Fame Is The Spur*, 1940), Spring also wrote three children's books in which boys narrate their childhood experiences: *Darkie & Co.* (1932), *Sampson's Circus* (1936), and *Tumbledown Dick* (1939). Each of these books reflects Spring's own childhood in a comparatively impoverished family.

Spring-heeled Jack A legendary figure whose superhuman leaps and feats of running are made possible by springs in the heels of his boots. Various attempts have been made to found him in actual personages, ranging from an eccentric marquess to a Warwickshire coal-merchant's son. The legend was developed in the Victorian *penny dreadfuls, Spring-heeled Jack there becoming a 'weird being' in a skin-tight crimson suit, with bat-wings, diabolic horns, and sulphurous breath, who could leap over houses and would terrify all spectators when he arrived to rescue various victims of tyranny, or just to make mischief. Underneath this disguise, according to one account, he was a respectable human being who had been cheated of his rightful inheritance. Spring-heeled Jack was probably the most celebrated of the superhuman and freak heroes of 19th-cent. popular fiction, whose film and *comic paper successors include *Batman and *Superman.

SPYRI (Heusser), Johanna (1827–1901) Celebrated Swiss children's author, who was born in a village near Zurich, the child of a doctor. She began to write to earn money for refugees from the Franco-Prussian war; *Heidi* (1881) was her first full-length story and her greatest success, though she wrote many other children's books, some of which were translated into English.

Squash and a Squeeze, A *See* DONALDSON, JULIA; SCHEFFLER, AXEL.

Squirrel Nutkin *See* TALE OF SQUIRREL NUTKIN, THE.

STABLES, (William) Gordon (1840–1910) Regular contributor to *The *Boy's Own Paper*

and author of many children's books. He was born in Scotland, became a naval surgeon, and served on a whaler in polar regions. After he was invalided out of the service in the 1870s he began to write for boys, and was soon closely associated with the *BOP*, to which he contributed *adventure stories, articles on animals and other subjects, and an 'Advice' column.

In his later years he became known to Fleet Street for his wearing of full Highland dress. Typical titles of his stories are *Born to Wander: a boy's book of nomadic adventures* (1887), *The Cruise of the Snowbird: a story of Arctic adventure* (1890), and *Hearts of Oak: a story of Nelson and the navy* (1893).

Stalky & Co. (1899) A book of linked stories by Rudyard *Kipling, about Beetle, M'Turk, and Corkran, friends and allies who share Number Five study at 'the College', a boys' boarding school on the north coast of Devon which specializes in preparing pupils for training in the armed forces. Corkran is nicknamed 'Stalky', which is a school slang-word meaning 'clever, well-considered and wily, as applied to plans of action'.

Many of the stories in the book harp on the moral and intellectual short-sightedness of many (though by no means all) of the masters, the cunning and wit of Stalky and his friends, and the shrewd and humane judgement of the Head. The final story in the book presents Stalky as a grown man, commanding Indian troops on the North-West Frontier, and bringing off a tactical coup against hostile locals by means of much the same trick that he played on a schoolmaster in an earlier tale.

The book is based very closely on Kipling's own schooldays at the United Services College at Westward Ho! in Devon, and is dedicated to his headmaster there, Cormell Price, a talented and unconventional man who was a friend of *Morris, Swinburne, and Rossetti. Kipling himself is portrayed as 'Beetle', bespectacled, literary-minded, and editor of the school magazine. The original for 'M'Turk' was G. C. Beresford, the son of an Anglo-Irish major, who shared a study with Kipling together with L. C. Dunsterville, later to become a distinguished Major-General, who was the original of 'Stalky'. The portraits of the masters, too, were taken almost entirely from life.

While Kipling was living near Torquay in 1896 there came to him 'the idea of beginning some tracts or parables on the education of the young'. He had kept in touch with his old

school, and towards the end of that year had a visit from Cormell Price. The stories began to appear in December 1898 in the *Windsor Magazine* in Britain and in *McClure's* in America, with illustrations by L. Raven Hill, which for some reason were not included when the book was published in October 1899.

A correspondent to the *Kipling Journal* for July 1953, who was eleven when *Stalky & Co.* was first serialized, remembered how his parents and elder sisters 'fought for the monthly *Windsor* and read the latest "Stalky" story with joy'. Andrew *Lang, reviewing the book in *Longman's Magazine* for May 1899, remarked: 'I am only in sympathy with Mr Kipling's boys when they bully the bullies . . . I do trust that his heroes will be converted from clandestine tobacco.' Twenty years later H. G. *Wells was objecting to the book on rather different grounds; in his *Outline of History* he called it 'the key to the ugliest . . . idea of modern imperialism', and particularly complained of the torturing of the bullies, which is undertaken at the instigation of the school chaplain. Many other critics have judged the book equally harshly, though nobody has denied its status as one of the most accomplished *school stories of all time.

Stalky & Co. was not quite as revolutionary as might be supposed. Its sympathetic portrayal of schoolboy sins and pranks was to some extent anticipated in F. Anstey's *Vice Versa* (1882) and Kipling's contemporary Eden Phillpotts wrote of them in much the same way in *The *Human Boy*, which appeared in the same year as *Stalky*. Certainly Kipling rejected the moral tone of F. W. *Farrar's two school novels, *Eric, or, Little By Little* and *St Winifred's*, both of which are referred to mockingly several times by Stalky and his friends. Yet Kipling's book is not entirely unlike that other mid-Victorian school classic, *Tom Brown's Schooldays*, in its portrayal of an almost godlike headmaster.

Kipling wrote four more Stalky stories in later years, one of which, 'The United Idolators', is about the school's craze for *Uncle Remus stories. They appeared in various volumes of Kipling's tales, and were all collected in *The Collected Stalky & Co.* (1929).

STANIFORTH, Dr **John William** (1863–1927) Boys' writer. He was a Yorkshire physician who took to authorship to pass the time during his isolation from the world while in charge of a fever hospital during a smallpox epidemic. He subsequently became a general

practitioner in a moorland district. He wrote the first *Nelson Lee stories, created other *detectives, and turned out various types of popular fiction.

Stanley Yelnats See HOLES.

Stans Puer ad Mensam See BOOKS OF COURTESY.

STANTON, Andy (1973–) Author of the *Mr Gum series. He studied English Literature at Oxford University, but was unhappy there and was asked to leave for not working hard enough (although when children ask, he tells them that it was because he killed a man). After drifting through a series of jobs, he wrote the first of the silly and surreal *Mr Gum* series from start to finish one Christmas Eve. It was published in 2006 and developed into an immensely popular series.

Starkey A *pirate in *Peter Pan*.

STEAD, Rebecca (1968–) New York based author of children's and *young adult books whose ambition to be a writer was sidetracked by a career in law. She continued to write in her spare time, but it was only when her entire body of work was accidentally destroyed by her young son that she really found her voice, as then, instead of attempting 'serious' work, she wrote for fun, using stories she remembered loving in her childhood as inspiration. Her finely detailed books include *First Light* (2007), which mixes science fiction with mystery to explore global warming; *When You Reach Me* (2009), which transports its readers to 1970s Manhattan and brings it—and the narrator, sixth-grader Miranda—vividly to life (with a bit of A *Wrinkle in Time* thrown in), and which won her the *Newbery Medal; and the *Guardian Children's Fiction Prize-winning *Liar and Spy* (2012), in which Georges moves into a new apartment and befriends upstairs neighbour Safer, who has a spy club and a secret.

Steadfast Tin Soldier, The A story by Hans Christian *Andersen, published in 1838 and translated into English in 1846 by Mary *Howitt. A toy tin soldier has only one leg, but stands steadily on it. He falls in love with a paper-doll ballerina who perches delicately on one leg. One day, thanks to the malicious influence of a jack-in-the-box imp, he tumbles out of the window into the street, lands in the gutter, is washed into the canal, and is swallowed by a fish. The fish is then caught and cut open, and the soldier finds himself back in the

house where he started; but—again thanks to the malign imp—he is thrown into the fire, and the ballerina is blown into it too, by the wind. Both perish in the flames.

STEELE, William O. (Owen) (1917–79) American author of boys' fiction, chiefly about pioneering, fighting the '*Indians', and wilderness travelling. His first novel was *The Golden Root* (1951). From the mid-1960s he began to portray events from the Indian (i.e. Native American) point of view, for example in *Wayah of the Real People* (1964)

STEIG, William (1907–2003) Prolific American cartoonist, author, and illustrator who worked for many years for the *New Yorker* magazine. In his sixties he turned to writing for children, going on to write over thirty books. His best-known work, the picture book *Shrek!* (1990), formed the basis for the DreamWorks Animation film *Shrek*. His other works include *Sylvester and the Magic Pebble* (1969), in which a donkey's life is saved from a lion by his thoughtless wish that a pebble turn him into a rock; *Abel's Island*, a survival story about a mouse stranded on an island; and *Doctor De Soto* (1982), about a mouse-dentist who must help a fox with toothache—without being eaten.

STEIN, Gertrude (1874–1946) Celebrated American-born avant-garde author who wrote one children's book, *The World is Round* (1939), applying her highly idiosyncratic narrative technique to the experiences of a child named Rose.

STEPHENS, Charles Asbury (1844–1931), American writer of boys' stories who was engaged in 1870 to contribute to the *Youth's Companion*, and maintained his connection with it for more than sixty years. He once estimated that he had written more than 3,000 short stories and over 100 serials. He travelled widely, and wrote a Knockabout Club series of *travelogue story books.

STEPTOE, John (1950–89) African-American author-illustrator whose first book, *Stevie* (1969), about a boy living in a ghetto, was started when he was sixteen and published to acclaim three years later when the entire book was printed in *Life* magazine. His fiction deals mainly with the urban African-American experience, but his most important book, *Mufaro's Beautiful Daughters* (1989), is a retelling of an African folk tale. In 1995 the

*American Library Association awarded the inaugural John Steptoe New Talent Award.

Sterkarm Handshake, The (1998) A powerful *time-slip story by Susan *Price, which won the 1999 *Guardian Children's Fiction Prize. It tells a story of romance and revenge that juxtaposes a stark historical background with the values of the present. Aiming to exploit mineral resources, the corporation FUP has built a Tube that allows travel to the past, specifically, the 16th-cent. Scottish Borders. It is the home of the Sterkarm clan, whose handshake is not to be trusted, though, as the young scientist Andrea knows, they can be fiercely loyal. When Per Sterkarm is wounded, the two centuries are brought into violent collision with devastating consequences. A sequel, *The Sterkarm Kiss*, appeared in 2003.

STEVENSON, James (1929–) American illustrator and writer. As well as providing illustrations for books by many other distinguished writers (Charlotte *Zolotow, Jack *Prelutsky, Judy *Blume, etc.), Stevenson has written nearly a hundred of his own books, from young series fiction to witty *poetry, *picture books to dark *young adult novels. The free and amusing cartoony style of his illustrations gives a clue to Stevenson's other line of work, as a long-term regular cartoonist for the *New Yorker*.

STEVENSON, Robert Louis (1850–94) Novelist, essayist, and poet, the son of Thomas Stevenson, an Edinburgh civil engineer, and Margaret Balfour, a minister's daughter. He was baptized Robert Lewis Balfour, but changed his second name to 'Louis' when a young man and was always called that by his family and friends. He was an only child; his mother suffered from poor health and he was largely brought up by his nurse, Alison Cunningham ('Cummy'). Louis was ill for much of his childhood, suffering especially from a bad chest, and his wakeful feverish nights were often soothed by his father telling him stories from the bedroom door. He did not learn to read until he was seven, but entertained himself with tales of his own devising and (a little later) with *toy theatres.

He was sent to school at Edinburgh Academy, and when he was seventeen he became a student at Edinburgh University. He paid little attention to academic work, but spent much of his time exploring the low life of the Old Town of Edinburgh.

Louis was intended by his father for the family engineering firm, but though he studied engineering while at university and was far from uninterested in the work—the Stevensons were the builders of the great Scottish lighthouses, including Bell Rock—he decided by the time he was twenty-one that he wanted to be a writer. His father responded sympathetically, and it was arranged that Louis should study law so as to give him a profession to fall back upon. He was eventually called to the Edinburgh bar, though he never practised as a barrister.

Instead, while depending on his father's financial support, he began to make the acquaintance of literary men, including Andrew *Lang, and to have essays published. His poor health encouraged him to spend a good deal of time on the continent, and a journey he made in France in 1878 led to his first notable book, *Travels with a Donkey*, which appeared the next year with illustrations by Walter *Crane. Through the colony of English artists at Fontainebleau he met Fanny Osbourne, an American ten years his senior, who was married with children but virtually estranged from her husband. She and Louis became lovers, and in 1879 he followed her to California—a journey that did serious damage to his health. After her divorce they were married in 1880, and he brought her home to Edinburgh where she was warmly received by his parents.

It was now believed that Louis had tuberculosis, and in the years that followed his marriage he and Fanny travelled in Europe and Scotland in search of a climate which might benefit him. They were accompanied by Fanny's young son Lloyd. Louis and Lloyd began to write comic verses—some of them parodies of *moral tales—and they printed these, embellished with *woodcuts by Stevenson, on a small hand-press. In the summer of 1881, when they were all staying with the Stevenson parents at Braemar, they drew a map which led to the writing of *Treasure Island*.

It was immediately accepted for serialization in the magazine *Young Folks*. The next summer there appeared his *New Arabian Nights*, a collection of short stories first published in the *Cornhill* and elsewhere. Meanwhile, in France, he also worked at the sequence of poems that eventually became A *Child's Garden of Verses* (1885).

He also wrote *The Black Arrow*, serialized during 1883 and published as a book in 1888; this was a *historical novel for boys, a frank attempt to make money. Stevenson himself

called it 'tushery', a verdict that modern readers are inclined to agree with. Set in the time of the Wars of the Roses, with dialogue in mock-archaic English, it has none of the distinction of Stevenson's best books, though it has often been reprinted and as a serial was reputedly more popular than *Treasure Island*. However when *Treasure Island* itself appeared as a book in 1883 it attracted much admiration from the critics and brought Stevenson the fame that he had been denied up to that time. He next wrote **Kidnapped* and *The Strange Case of Dr Jekyll and Mr Hyde*, both published during 1886.

In 1887 he returned to America with his wife and stepson, and while there he wrote another novel based on the Jacobite uprising in 18th-cent. Scotland, *The Master of Ballantrae* (1889). He also collaborated with his stepson Lloyd Osbourne, who was now in his early twenties, on the comic novel *The Wrong Box* (1889). In June 1889 he, Fanny, and Lloyd set off on a trip to the South Pacific, financed initially by an advance from an American publisher. The climate greatly benefited Stevenson's health, and he decided to settle there, building a home on Samoa which he and the family began to occupy in 1891. His books from this period include *Catriona* (1893), a sequel to *Kidnapped*, and *Weir of Hermiston*, which was never completed (a fragment was published in 1896) but which has been regarded as a potential masterpiece. He died suddenly and quite unexpectedly shortly before his 44th birthday, of a brain haemorrhage.

Stevenson never intended to be a writer of **adventure stories, but with *Treasure Island* and *Kidnapped* he brought that genre to the peak of its achievement in the 19th cent. and inspired many later writers; his influence can be seen in such diverse works as **Peter Pan* and the thrillers of John Buchan. His gift as a children's author and poet was partly the result of his complete lack of condescension towards a child-audience. *The Journal of Stevenson Studies* published by the University of Stirling contains contemporary articles on the author and his work by Stevenson scholars from around the world.

STEWART, Alan Breck *See* ALAN BRECK STEWART.

STEWART, Joel (1977–) English illustrator, animator, director, and musician. His first picture book, *The Adventures of a Nose* (2002), created with author-illustrator Viviane **Schwarz, is a wonderfully surreal tale of finding your place in

the world—a place where you can both fit in and stick out. He is perhaps best known for his picture book *Dexter Bexley and the Big Blue Beastie* (2007). Stewart's illustrations are varied in style from his original interpretation of *Tales of Hans Christian Andersen* (2004) and Lewis **Carroll's *Jabberwocky* (2003), which is somewhat reminiscent of Edward **Gorey, to the soft lines of *Addis Berner Bear Forgets* (2008). In 2011, Stewart turned his hand to creating and directing *The Adventures of Abney & Teal*, an animated series featuring two rag dolls for BBC television.

STEWART, (Lady) **Mary (Florence Elinor)** (1916–2014) Popular British novelist. Besides her 'Merlin' fantasy series (beginning with *The Crystal Cave*, 1970), she wrote three children's books, *The Little Broomstick* (1971), *Ludo and the Star Horse* (1975), and *A Walk in Wolf Wood* (1980).

STEWART, Paul (1955–) English author, best known for his collaborations with illustrator Chris **Riddell. His books are some of the most loved fantasy stories in contemporary UK children's fiction. He studied English and was taught by Angela Carter and Malcolm Bradbury before teaching English in the UK and overseas. He has written for young children (*Blobheads*, 1999, and *Dogbird*, 1998, are both good) but he is most famous for the epic ten-volume **Edge Chronicles*, co-written and illustrated by Riddell, starting with *Beyond the Deepwoods* (1998). The two men also conjured up the hilarious **Tolkien parody *Muddle Earth* (2003) and are currently working on another epic fantasy, *Wyrmeweald*, which began with *Returner's Wealth* (2011).

STIEFVATER, Maggie (1981–) American author and artist whose career, after homeschooling, included being a calligraphy instructor, wedding musician, technical editor, portraitist, and equestrienne. Her books in many ways have set the bar for **young adult supernatural romance, as they are poetically written, exquisitely romantic, yet peopled with fully developed characters. *Shiver* (2009) is about Grace, who is fascinated by a wolf who once saved her life, until she finds he is human too. *The Raven Boys* (2012) blends an ancient Welsh prince, psychics, beautiful boys, and a doom-laden kiss, whilst *The Scorpio Races* (2011) is about a yearly race astride savage water horses that brings together two of the riders.

Stig of the Dump (1963) A novel by Clive **King, illustrated by Edward **Ardizzone;

the story of a boy, Barney, who finds a Stone-Age cave-dweller living in a rubbish dump and befriends him. It has been immensely popular and reprinted countless times, as well as being adapted for television in 1981 and 2002.

STINE, R. L. (Robert Lawrence) (1943–) With over 350 million books in print, American writer R. L. Stine is one of the world's bestselling children's authors. He started writing at the age of nine, when he would spend hours locked away with a typewriter thinking up jokes. When he left university he started writing jokes and humorous books, and set up *Bananas* magazine, which ran for ten years. But in 1986 it all changed with the publication of his first teen *horror, Blind Date* (1986). With that book's huge success he launched into writing more and more horror. Two massive series, *Fear Street* (from 1989) and *Goosebumps* (from 1992), followed, and each now has over a hundred titles, with spin-offs such as *Fear Street Nights* (2005) and *Goosebumps Most Wanted* (2012) keeping the series up to date.

Stinky Cheese Man and other Fairly Stupid Tales, The (1992) A picture book written by Jon *Scieszka and illustrated by Lane *Smith, containing hilariously imaginative versions of fairy tales, with titles including 'The Really Ugly Duckling' and 'Little Red Running Shorts'. A much-cited example of postmodernism in picture books, it contains metafictive features, such as the narrator, Jack (of *Jack and the Beanstalk), informing readers that he has turned the dedication upside down and the Little Red Hen becoming irritated that her story has not received adequate attention from the author and illustrator.

STOBBS, William (1914–2000) British illustrator who was Head of the Design Department at the London School of Printing from 1950 until 1958, then Principal of Maidstone College of Art. He illustrated many children's novels and produced *picture books based on traditional tales, with drawings in a variety of styles.

STOCKTON, Frank R. (Richard) (1834–1902) Philadelphia writer who was the author of original short *fantasies and whimsical tales for children, many of which were published in the *Riverside Magazine* and later in *St Nicholas, of which he was associate editor for five years from its foundation in 1873. These stories were collected under the titles *Ting-a-Ling* (1870), *The Floating Prince and other fairy tales* (1881), and *The Bee-Man of Orn*

and other fanciful tales (1887) (*see* BEE-MAN OF ORN). Maurice *Sendak illustrated editions of *The Bee-Man of Orn* (1964) and another Stockton tale, *The Griffin and the Minor Canon* (1963).

STODDARD, William O. (Osborn) (1835–1925) American author, inventor, and secretary to President Lincoln. He wrote more than seventy books of boys' *adventure stories, of which the most popular was *Little Smoke* (1891), a story of the Sioux. His *Lives of the Presidents* were published in ten volumes in 1886–9.

STOLZ, Mary (Slattery) (1920–2006) Prolific American children's author. She wrote many realistic stories for younger readers, including *A Dog on Barkham Street* (1960) and *The Bully of Barkham Street* (1963), two complementary stories in which the same events are described from different viewpoints, and *A Wonderful, Terrible Time* (1967), about two black girls from impoverished homes who go to summer camp. She also produced books for *young adult readers, such as *By the Highway Home* (1971).

Stone Book Quartet, The A sequence of four short novels by Alan *Garner, illustrated by Michael *Foreman. In order of narrative (though not of publication) they are: *The Stone Book* (1976), *Granny Reardun* (1977), *The Aimer Gate* (1978), and *Tom Fobble's Day* (1977). They tell the story of a family of Cheshire craftsmen (in fact Garner's own ancestors) at four points in history: 1864, 1886, 1916, and 1941.

The Stone Book describes the ambition of Mary, daughter of the stonemason Robert, to read and write. In *Granny Reardun*, Mary's illegitimate son Joseph apprentices himself to a blacksmith to become 'a generous, ingenious hammerman'. *The Aimer Gate* is about the failure of the old crafts to survive in the modern world; its central character, Joseph's son Robert, has no apprenticeship to serve or craft to learn. *Tom Fobble's Day*, set during the Second World War, describes how Joseph the smith makes for his grandson William a sledge finer and swifter than those owned by the other village boys, his last piece of work.

The four books, Garner's finest achievement, use their author's native Cheshire dialect to construct prose-poems of a unique character and quality. Neil Philip, in his study of Garner's work (*A Fine Anger*, 1981), observes that each one of the stories presents a 'sacramental' moment in the family's history, and that the four

books achieve 'that perfect equilibrium between public and private concerns which is the hallmark of mature art'.

STONES, Rosemary (1947–) Radical British critic of children's literature, associated with the *Children's Rights Workshop, and the longtime editor of *Books for Keeps. Together with Andrew Mann she compiled *Mother Goose Comes to Cable Street* (1970), a collection of *nursery rhymes with illustrations (by Dan Jones) set in multiracial working-class London.

STONG, Phil See HONK: THE STORY OF A MOOSE.

STORR, Catherine (1913–2001) British writer and psychiatrist who wrote many children's books, some of them in a mode that has been described as 'psycho-fantasy'. They include *Marianne Dreams* (1958), in which a convalescent girl constructs a dream-house which acquires reality, and *Rufus* (1969), about a boy in a children's home. Her stories for younger children include *Clever Polly and the Stupid Wolf* (1955), a comic inversion of the *Little Red Riding-Hood motif.

Story of a Bad Boy, The (1869) An autobiographical novel by the American writer and editor Thomas Bailey Aldrich (1836–1907), based on his own childhood.

Tom Bailey is brought to Rivermouth by sea from New Orleans to the care of his grandfather (Captain Nutter) and his maiden great-aunt. Tom joins a secret society at school and takes part in such exploits as the burning of an old stagecoach and the firing of cannon left over from the Civil War.

The book has had a considerable reputation in America; in some respects it anticipates *The *Adventures of Tom Sawyer* (1876), but it lacks some of the vitality of Twain's story and it has never been popular outside the United States. Its success there, and that of Twain's stories, helped to establish a 'bad boy' genre in America, of which other examples include *Peck's Bad Boy and his Pa* (1883) by George Wilbur *Peck and Booth Tarkington's *Penrod* (1914). These in turn begat such English books as the *William series by Richmal Crompton (1922 onwards).

Story of a Red-Deer, The (1897) An *animal story set on Exmoor, by Sir John Fortescue (1859–1933), who was chiefly known for his works of military history.

Story of a Short Life, The (1885) By Mrs *Ewing.

Story of Ferdinand, The (1936) A celebrated American *picture book by Munro *Leaf, illustrated by Robert *Lawson. Ferdinand is a young Spanish bull who 'liked to sit just quietly and smell the flowers'. Stung by a bumblebee, he leaps about in pain and rage, and so is chosen for a bullfight on account of his supposed fierceness. But when he is put in the ring he sits down and smells the flowers in the ladies' hats—so he is taken home again to his favourite tree.

Story of the Amulet, The (1906) The third *fantasy novel by E. *Nesbit, sequel to *Five Children and It* and The *Phoenix and the Carpet*. Cyril, Robert, Anthea, and Jane are sent to stay with their family's old Nurse, who keeps lodgings near the British Museum. They find the Psammead (the grumpy sand-fairy of *Five Children and It*) caged and on sale in a pet shop as a monkey. They rescue it, and it leads them to an amulet—a shaped stone with magical properties—telling them that it can give them their heart's desire. However, when they buy it they find that it is only one half of the complete amulet, the other half having been lost. Nevertheless this half-amulet has magic powers: it grows into an arch the size of a doorway, through which the children can step into whatever place or time they choose.

The Psammead advises them that they should make journeys back into time past in order to discover and gain for themselves the missing piece of the amulet. They begin their time-travelling, visiting ancient Egypt, Babylon, and *Atlantis before its inundation. At last it is found, and the children immediately have their 'heart's desire'—the return from foreign parts of their mother and father and 'the Lamb', their baby brother.

Edith Nesbit's biographer (Doris Langley Moore) tells how in 1905 Nesbit approached Dr Wallis Budge, one of the keepers at the British Museum, for suggestions for a new story: 'She found the ordinary materials for children's tales rather hackneyed and exhausted, and wanted to explore some different avenue.' He suggested ancient Egypt as a source of ideas and described the use of amulets and Words of Power. As the story got under way she brought each chapter to him, and took care to make her descriptions of Egypt and Babylon as accurate as possible. The finished book was dedicated to Dr Budge, and he is also portrayed in it as 'the nicest gentleman' in the group who witness alarming goings-on when the Queen of Babylon, brought from ancient times by the amulet

and the Psammead, turns up at the Museum and demands the return of her 'property', the Babylonian treasures that are housed there.

C. S. *Lewis wrote of the book: 'It first opened my eyes to antiquity, the "dark backward and abysm of time".' Its influence may be seen on his *Narnia stories.

Story of the Little Mole Who Knew It Was None of His Business, The (1989)

A highly original children's book by the German author and illustrator pairing of Werner Holzwarth (1947–) and Wolf *Erlbruch about a mole who finds himself with a turd on his head and his adventures trying to discover who it belongs to. It is not a book for the easily offended, but children have made it an international bestseller.

Story of the Treasure Seekers, The,

Being the adventures of the Bastable children in search of a fortune A novel by E. *Nesbit. Some chapters appeared in the *Pall Mall Magazine*, the *Windsor Magazine*, the *Illustrated London News*, and *Nister's Holiday Annual* during 1898, and the complete book was published by T. Fisher Unwin in 1899, with illustrations by Gordon *Browne and Lewis Baumer. The first of the 'Bastable' books, it made E. Nesbit's name as a children's writer.

The six Bastable children are Dora, Oswald, Dicky, the twins Alice and Noël, and Horace Octavius, known as H.O. Their mother is dead, 'and if you think we don't care because I don't tell you much about her you only show that you do not understand people at all.' Their father being in financial straits, they have made it their mission to restore the fallen fortunes of 'the ancient House of Bastable'. Each episode describes a different child's ploy for making money, and each ends in disaster, embarrassment, and comedy. Their triumph comes when they invite their rich but apparently unhelpful uncle to nursery dinner, believing him to be poor and in need of their charity; thus they charm him into taking the whole family under his wing, a happy ending which, says the narrator, 'is like what happens in Dickens's books . . . I can't help it if it is like Dickens, because it happened this way. Real life is often something like books.'

Charles *Dickens's children's book *A *Holiday Romance* (1868) may in fact have been one of E. Nesbit's inspirations for the device of a child as narrator, which she uses ingeniously and wittily. The narrator of *The Treasure Seekers* admits he is 'one of us', but says 'I shall not tell you which'—whereupon the narrative is peppered with remarks like 'Oswald is a boy of firm and unswerving character.' *The Treasure Seekers'* more striking correspondence to E. Nesbit's own life was not to her childhood but to the impoverished but high-spirited early years of her marriage.

storytelling The term preferred by its practitioners for the art and practice of the oral narration of stories. Universal to cultures of every era, it has come under threat in modern life. Since the early 1980s, however, major revivals have taken place in countries from Denmark to New Zealand, Ireland to Australia. One factor in the UK was the practice, inherited from the US and Canada, of holding children's storytelling sessions in public libraries. Eileen *Colwell insisted on it in the library she founded in Hendon in 1929. Her influence proved long-lasting, for example, on librarians in Japan, and when the UK's Society for Storytelling was formed in 1993, she was made its first patron.

During the 1960s, another pioneering British librarian, Janet Hill, created the Lambeth Libraries Storytelling Scheme to bring told stories to children in parks and community groups. A further boost came in the 1980s when growing multicultural awareness brought storytellers such as Beulah Candappa, Grace Hallworth, and Godfrey Tuup, respectively from Burmese, Trinidadian and Guyanese backgrounds, fresh opportunities to share traditional stories. The National Oracy Project also exerted significant influence by encouraging speaking and listening as curriculum themes. By today, storytelling for children has grown to include storytelling clubs and competitions as well as festival performances and work in schools.

Classic texts on children's storytelling include two from American storytellers: Marie L. Shedlock's *The Art of Story-Telling* (1915) and Ruth Sawyer's *The Way of the Storyteller* (1942). Like Margaret Read McDonald in America today, both provided encouragement to adult beginners. In the UK, Elizabeth Cook's *The Ordinary & the Fabulous* (1969) emphasized the role of the storytelling teacher in developing imagination. Eileen Colwell's *Storytelling* (1980) emphasized the pleasure a told story can give. Michael *Morpurgo and Philip *Pullman, who both told stories when they worked as teachers, are among many contemporary writers who speak of its impact.

STOWE, Harriet Beecher (1811–96) Author of *Uncle Tom's Cabin*, who was born in

Litchfield, Connecticut, the daughter of Lyman Beecher, a celebrated Congregationalist minister. Harriet taught in her sister's school and began to write short tales and sketches, some of which were published. She married Calvin Ellis Stowe, who taught biblical literature in her father's theological seminary. This seminary was committed to the abolition of slavery.

Harriet, though not at first a confirmed abolitionist, crossed the Ohio River to visit a Kentucky plantation and see conditions for herself. *Uncle Tom's Cabin* first appeared as a serial in an anti-slavery paper published in Washington, DC, during 1851 and 1852, being issued in book form in March 1852. Mrs Stowe's name immediately became anathema in the South; in England, on the other hand, she was idolized during a visit she paid there in 1853. However, when in 1869 she published an article alleging that Byron had had an incestuous relationship with his sister, she was virtually pilloried by the English.

After *Uncle Tom* Mrs Stowe settled down to a literary life; her later work included several collections of stories for children. But it was her first book, which has been cited among the causes of the American Civil War, that made by far the biggest impression on child readers, even though it was not intended for them.

Strand Magazine, The (1891 until 1950) An illustrated British monthly *magazine, edited initially by George Newnes, with the object of supplying 'cheap, healthful literature' by 'the best British writers, and special translations from the first foreign authors'. It was a family magazine and as such generally included a story specifically for children, although most of the rest of the magazine would not have been unsuitable for them; Conan *Doyle's *Adventures of Sherlock Holmes*, for instance, was among its early serials.

The magazine was large: 112 pages of text and illustrations in its first issue, and over 30 of advertisements, for a price of sixpence. The first children's story it printed was a translation of Voltaire's *The Two Genies*. E. Nesbit's *Five Children and It* and other stories by the same author first appeared serialized in its pages, and Gordon *Browne and H. R. *Millar were among its regular illustrators.

Struggling against post-war conditions and publishing costs, it came to an end in March 1950, announcing that the title would be protected by incorporation into *Men Only*.

STRANG, Herbert Pseudonym of the collaborators **George Herbert Ely** (1866–1958)

and **James L'Estrange** (1867–1947), two staff members of the Oxford University Press, who wrote *adventure stories and *historical novels during the first thirty years of the 20th cent. Typical examples of their work are *Boys of the Light Brigade* (1905), *Lion-Heart, a story of the reign of Richard the First* (1910), and *With Our Brave Allies* (1917). They also wrote for girls under the name of 'Mrs Herbert Strang'.

STRANGER, Joyce (Joyce Muriel Wilson) (1921–2007) British author of *animal stories, many of them for children. They include *Paddy Joe* (1973), the first of a series of books about an Alsatian dog.

STRAPAROLA, Gianfrancesco *See* PIA-CEVOLI NOTTI, LE.

Stratemeyer Syndicate Created by Edward L. Stratemeyer (1862–1930) and continued by his daughter Harriet Stratemeyer Adams (1892–1982). Edward L. Stratemeyer was a hugely prolific American writer and publisher of juvenile literature. He often started a series by outlining and writing books himself, and then used teams of freelancers working under Stratemeyer Syndicate pen names, and sometimes had other publishers bring out his books. He is credited with being the first book packager for children, and becoming, by the 1920s, the publisher of most of the titles read by American children. His first series was *The Rover Boys* (1899); later ones included *The *Bobbsey Twins, Tom Swift, The *Hardy Boys*, and *Nancy Drew*. His two daughters, Harriet and Edna, already involved in the business, inherited on his death; Harriet bought out her sister not long afterwards and ran the syndicate, writing, revising and relaunching many of its series, until her death.

STREATFEILD, Noel (1895–1986) British children's author. She was one of five children of a Sussex clergyman, and found vicarage life very restricting, not least because her father conducted his household in a Victorian manner with family prayers and a strictly observed Sunday. She became a rebel and on the day of her confirmation threw a bottle of ink at her *governess. At her first day school, which she hated, she formed a society whose members began the term with a hundred marks and lost one each time they were polite to a teacher. The headmistress discovered this and asked Noel's father to remove her. He, however, was a governor of the school, and she remained there.

She began to show a talent for acting in parish plays and concerts and was eventually sent to the Academy of Dramatic Art in London, after which she acted professionally for several years. In 1936, Mabel Carey, the newly appointed children's editor at J. M. Dent, suggested she write a children's book about theatrical life. The result was *Ballet Shoes* (1936), a huge success and the real initiator of the *career novel for British children. In 1937 came *Tennis Shoes*, followed by *The Circus is Coming* (1938—also published as *Circus Shoes*), in which two children running away from an orphanage discover that their uncle is a circus clown. The book won the *Carnegie Medal; Noel Streatfeild had toured for some months with Bertram Mills Circus to gather material for it.

During the Second World War she wrote *The House in Cornwall* (1940), which was her only thriller, *The Children of Primrose Lane* (1941), about a group of evacuees and a German spy, *Curtain Up* (1944), and *Party Frock* (1945). *The Painted Garden* (1949) centres on a child who is playing the part of Mary in a Hollywood film of *The *Secret Garden*.

Noel Streatfeild's other post-war books are generally either career novels (such as *White Boots*, 1951, about a skater), or *family stories, which include *The Bell Family* (1954), and a 'Gemma' series about a child film star, beginning with *Gemma* (1968). Her popularity has been, and continues to be, considerable, but relatively little critical attention has been paid to her, possibly because despite the excellence of much of her writing she never improved on the achievement of her first books. Mary Cadogan and Patricia Craig, in *You're A Brick, Angela!* (1976), remark on 'a slight but perceptible falling-off' after *The Painted Garden*, observing: 'In the four Gemma books there is hardly a memorable incident.'

street Arab stories A genre of homeless urchin stories particularly popular with *evangelical writers in Britain and America during the 19th cent. British authors who produced examples include 'Hesba *Stretton' (*Jessica's First Prayer*, 1867, and *Little Meg's Children*, 1868), Mrs O. F. *Walton (*Christie's Old Organ*, 1874), '*Brenda' (*Froggy's Little Brother*, 1875), and Silas *Hocking. America produced *The *Lamplighter* (1854), but more characteristically American were the rags-to-riches stories of Horatio *Alger. Accounts of real street-orphans were written by Dr *Barnado.

street cries *See* CRIES OF LONDON.

STRETTON, Hesba (Sarah Smith) (1832–1911), *Evangelical writer of about sixty stories, many of which were about *street Arabs. Her most popular books were *Jessica's First Prayer* (1867) and *Little Meg's Children* (1868). She was a founder of the London Society for the Prevention of Cruelty to Children. Her pseudonym was taken from the initial letters of the names of her brothers and sisters, which made up 'HESBA', and from Stretton, a village in her home county of Shropshire.

Hesba Stretton has been described as the typical lady *Sunday school writer. Brought up in a dissenting family and unmarried, she took to writing to improve her position and income. She began to turn out children's books at the rate of several a year; her literary aspirations were originally high (her adult fiction was compared favourably with *Jane Eyre*), but after the publication of *Jessica's First Prayer* she followed the formula which had brought her success. She eventually became comparatively wealthy.

She wrote with real seriousness and anger about conditions of child poverty and was privately contemptuous of the parading of piety by many members of the *Religious Tract Society and similar organizations. She herself did much to fight the maltreatment of children.

STRICKLAND, Agnes (1796–1874) Victorian author who was the sister of Catharine Parr *Traill, writer of the first notable Canadian children's book. Her own books for children include *The Rival Crusoes, or, the Shipwreck* (1826) and *The Moss-House, in which many of the works of nature are rendered a source of amusement to children* (1822).

STRONG, Jeremy (1949–) Fabulously prolific English author of some of the funniest contemporary books for children. An eventful childhood (at three he fell out of a window and landed on his head, ending up, he says, with a broken arm and a headache) led eventually to a teaching career, which in turn led him to putting some of his stories into book form. He now writes full-time and is a much-applauded visitor to schools across the country. His current books boast 'laugh your socks off with Jeremy Strong', and readers do, with books such as *The Karate Princess* (1986), *There's a Pharaoh in Our Bath!* (1995), *The Hundred-mile-an-hour Dog* (1996—and sequels), *Pirate School: Just a Bit of Wind* (2002), and *My Brother's Famous Bottom* (2007).

STROUD, Jonathan (1970–) English author of *fantasy books for children and young adults. After he completed his studies in English literature at the University of York, he worked in London as an editor for Walker Books. Among his most prominent works is the bestselling Bartimaeus trilogy featuring teenage magician Nathanial and Bartimaeus, a 5,000-year old djinni. The series is made up of *The Amulet of Samarkand* (2003), *The Golem's Eye* (2004), and *Ptolemy's Gate* (2005). *The Ring of Solomon* was published as a prequel in 2010. *The Screaming Staircase* (2012) is the first in his new series, *Lockwood & Co.*

Struwwelpeter A collection of *cautionary tales in verse by Heinrich Hoffmann (1809–94), published in German with the author's own illustrations in 1845, and in an anonymous and immensely successful English translation first printed in Leipzig in 1848. Some of its characters have become almost proverbial for the generations brought up on the verses, notably foolish Harriet, who plays with matches, and, most graphically gruesome of all, 'The great, long, red-legg'd scissorman', who visits little thumb-suckers 'And cuts their thumbs clean off,—and then, | You know, they never grow again.' Harvey *Darton described the collection as 'the Awful Warning carried to the point where Awe topples over into helpless laughter'; nevertheless the book has long oscillated between being accepted as harmless hilarity and being condemned as excessively horrifying, morbid, and even a source of trauma to the sensitive child.

Hoffmann was a Frankfurt doctor who also superintended a local lunatic asylum, where he made something of a reputation for humane innovations. In later editions of the book there appeared an introduction, 'How I came to write Struwwelpeter'. In this, he recounted how one Christmas he went out to try to buy a present for his three-year-old son, but could find only 'long tales, stupid collections of pictures, moralizing stories, beginning and ending with admonitions like "The good child must be truthful"'. The child, he wrote, 'does not reason abstractedly', and one tale or fable would 'impress him more than hundreds of general warnings'. So he bought a blank notebook and proceeded to write and draw his own Christmas present.

Friends then persuaded him to publish it, at first anonymously, and the book achieved 100 editions in its first thirty years and countless more since. Its original title was *Lustige Gesichten und drollige Bilder*, or 'Merry stories and funny pictures'; from the third German edition onwards this was prefaced by *Der Struwwelpeter*, 'Shock-headed Peter', the name of the first character to appear in the book and its usual cover illustration. The original title-page also suggested that it was suited for readers of between three and six years of age.

Struwwelpeter had the distinction of being 'one of the earliest and most successful author-artist books for the very young' (M. F. Thwaite, *From Primer to Pleasure*), and the book was also one of the first to popularize the comparatively new process of chromolithography (*see* LITHOGRAPHY) for children's publishing. In 1868, however, the illustrations were redrawn for the more traditional *wood engraving process and, apart from the generally more stylized and perhaps more menacing effect this produced, it was only at this time that the scissor-man acquired his characteristic stiffly pointed right leg, outstretched like the blade of the scissors itself. Later editions often reverted to Hoffmann's originals; attempts to furnish other, more modern, illustrations have not generally succeeded.

Struwwelpeter spawned several offspring in such forms as *ABC books and painting books. It was also adapted for the stage; in E. *Nesbit's *The New Treasure Seekers* (1904) Oswald Bastable refers to a production at the Garrick Theatre entitled *Shock-Headed Peter*.

'Mark *Twain' (S. L. Clemens), while staying in Berlin with his three children, made his own highly colloquial translation of *Struwwelpeter* as a Christmas present for them. It was eventually published in 1935 with an introduction by Twain's daughter, Clara Clemens.

Heinrich Hoffmann wrote other *picture books for children, but none with the same success. His *König Nüssknacker und der arme Reinhold* (1851) was adapted by J. R. *Planché as *King Nutcracker; or, The Dream of Poor Reinhold* (1855).

Verses in imitation of *Struwwelpeter* appear in *Charlie and the Chocolate Factory* (1964) by Roald *Dahl. A notable British 'junk opera' adaptation, *Shockheaded Peter*, had its debut in 1998.

Stuart Little (1945) A novel by E. B. *White.

STUCLEY, Elizabeth *See* MAGNOLIA BUILDINGS.

STUDDY, G. E. *See* BONZO.

Stumps *See* AUSTIN, STELLA.

Subtle Knife, The The second book in the *His Dark Materials* trilogy.

SUDDABY, Donald (1900–64) British author of children's *science fiction and *fantasy. His books include *Lost Men in the Grass* (1940, first published under the name 'Alan Griff'), the story of three men reduced to the size of insects; *The Death of Metal* (1952), in which all metals disintegrate; and several novels about *Robin Hood.

Sue Barton Nurse in stories by Helen Dore *Boylston.

SUMMERLY, Felix *See* COLE, SIR HENRY.

Summer of My German Soldier (1973) A novel by Bette *Greene.

Sunday schools Classes associated with Protestant churches, originally for poor children to learn religious principles and if necessary literacy. They are generally held to have begun in earnest in England with Robert *Raikes's experiments in Gloucester from 1780.

Raikes's first motive seems to have been that of keeping the labouring slum children of Gloucester from spending their one free day roaming the streets, open to all the temptations of swearing, gambling, frequenting alehouses, and generally embarking on a life of crime. Some may have had a couple of years at dame, charity, or other schools before they started such work as chimney-sweeping or pin-factory hands at the age of seven or eight, but Raikes assumed that one function of the Sunday school was to teach reading. He also assumed that the main content of reading and all other lessons would be religious and moral. *The Sunday Scholar's Companion*, which he probably had privately printed by 1786 (it was formally published in 1794), contains his choice of lesson: the usual material of *primers, with graded Scripture words and sentences for teaching reading; a form of *catechism apparently of his own composition; and hymns.

At first Raikes paid a small sum to an experienced woman teacher, who taught the children in her own home; the whole school, including obligatory attendance at church services, lasted (according to one account) from nine o'clock till twelve-thirty and again from three till six. But Raikes was convinced that Sunday schooling alone was inadequate, and he made classes available during the children's weekday meal breaks. Sunday schools were approved and promoted on the one

hand by Queen Charlotte and on the other by Wesley and their spread was rapid. Mrs *Trimmer was among the first to copy Raikes: the schools she had organized in Brentford by 1786, with the cooperation of both Anglicans and Nonconformists, were unusually large and soon also involved training workshops to teach industrial skills. Later in 1786 her meeting with Queen Charlotte led to her publishing her manual on Sunday school organization, *The Œconomy of Charity*.

In 1789 William Wilberforce visited Hannah *More and her sisters at their Somerset cottage and pointed out the pressing need for schools for the poor in the Cheddar district of the Mendips. He, Hannah, and the sisters sketched out a plan for Sunday schools in the area, a scheme even larger than Mrs Trimmer's. Hannah More's motives were explicitly religious; she did not at all wish to educate the poor above their social station, believing that religious teaching should emphasize doing one's duty in whatever walk of life God called one to, even the lowest.

Schools were established by the More sisters in about fifteen places between Cheddar and the Bristol Channel. By 1791, more than 500 children were involved in the project. Schoolhouses were built, a search was continually made for suitable teachers (one was a dairymaid), and the More sisters themselves visited one of their schools each Sunday.

*Cheap Repository Tracts were devised, and largely written, by Hannah More herself in order to supply more edifying reading for Sunday school pupils than the *chapbooks which were the chief popular literature of the time.

Whereas in the early days the schools tended to be organized to serve a whole area, increasingly they became attached to single churches. However, the Sunday School Union, formed in 1803, was interdenominational, and the early cooperation between Protestant sects to promote the schools continued. The paid teachers of the pioneer schools soon gave way to volunteers, often from the leisured classes; and whereas Raikes's scheme had served only the poorest city slum-dwellers, attendance at Sunday school eventually came to be a part of childhood routine for a wide social spectrum.

The impact of Sunday schooling on the literacy of working-class children, and on the literature available to them, was enormous. A new market opened both for existing books and for new titles. The *Society for Promoting Christian Knowledge (SPCK) and the British and Foreign Bible Society helped to provide

free *Bibles to Sunday scholars, and classics of *religious instruction such as Janeway's *Token for Children and *Watts's hymns were printed and read in huge numbers. The Cheap Repository Tracts organization and the *Religious Tract Society produced original books for children, and commercial publishers also took advantage of the new readers; *reward books became established as a new category of children's reading. Charlotte M. *Yonge, herself first a pupil then a teacher in a Sunday school, wrote for this market and eventually tried to influence the literature that the movement sponsored with her pamphlet What Books to Lend and What to Give (1887). For a time, however, in the first half of the 19th cent., publishing directed at Sunday scholars could be charged with accentuating the divide between books fit for working-class children and those for the privileged.

The Sunday school movement spread quickly into other Protestant countries. In America the different denominations quickly developed their own Sunday school policies, the movement being particularly welcomed because of the absence of religious instruction in schools established by the public authorities. However, again there was interdenominational cooperation, and the first Sunday School Union in the United States was set up in Philadelphia in 1791. In 1817 the *American Sunday-School Union was formed, and proved very influential in establishing standards for juvenile books. One of the most popular American Sunday school authors was '*Pansy' (Isabella M. Alden).

Sunny Stories A *magazine containing fiction by Enid *Blyton.

superhero A genre of fiction understandably popular with young readers, which found its modern rebirth in, and still mostly belongs to, the *comics medium, but can be traced back to any heroic epic and exploit in world mythologies, folklore characters such as *Robin Hood, and pulp heroes like Zorro or Conan the Barbarian. The first US comic book superhero is usually recognized as being *Superman, an alien from the dying planet Krypton who gains powers including speed, flight, and strength by absorbing the radiation of the Earth's Sun, debuting in Action Comics #1 (1939; by Jerry Siegel and Joe Shuster). The character prompted innumerable imitations, copies, and parodies, including the equally successful Batman (created by Bill Finger and Bob Kane in Detective Comics #27), who

is in fact just a really rich, ninja-trained, gadget-laden human, Bruce Wayne. Other types of superpowered beings include humans who have been infected with or affected by chemicals/science, such as Stan Lee and Steve Ditko's Spider-Man or Lee and Jack Kirby's Hulk; mutants like the various members of the X-Men teams and franchise; and magical and mythological beings such as Elizabeth and William Moulton Marston's Wonder Woman. Multiple homages and parodies have appeared in different publications, from overt spoofs to plain comedic twists, such as Bananaman, the yellow-fruit-fuelled, superpowered (but not too bright) alter ego of Little Eric in D. C. *Thomson's *Dandy. While usually confined to comics, the genre has also spilled into narrative prose, with instances such as Dav Pilkey's successful *Captain Underpants series.

Superman American *comic strip hero who was first developed in 1933–4 by two teenagers from Cleveland, Ohio, American writer Jerry Siegel and Canadian-born artist Joe Shuster, for their science fiction fanzine. They worked over the following few years to break into comics and to sell the Superman story, until it was taken up by National Allied Publications, in 1938 and in the following year syndicated as the Superman comic strip. Since then, Superman has featured in radio and television serials, on the Broadway stage, and on the cinema screen. He was born on the dying planet Krypton, was sent to Earth as a baby, and was brought up under the name 'Clark Kent'. He works as a reporter for the Daily Planet in the city of Metropolis and is an unassuming bespectacled young man, but when trouble strikes he turns into Superman and has superhuman powers, most notably superhuman strength and the ability to fly. Superman's context was the authors' teenage reading, detective and science fiction, together with swashbuckling films, but the character may also recall such Victorian heroes as *Spring-Heeled Jack, and the American *tall tale.

Surya trilogy See GAVIN, JAMILA.

Susannah of the Mounties: a Canadian story of the nineties (1936) A novel by Muriel Denison about a child who wants to become a Mountie and, after an act of bravery, is allowed to wear their uniform. There were several sequels, including Susannah at Boarding School (1938), and the original story was filmed with Shirley *Temple.

SUTCLIFF, Rosemary (1920–92) Author of *The *Eagle of the Ninth* (1954), *The *Lantern Bearers* (1950), and over thirty other novels and retellings; one of the foremost figures in the development of the modern *historical novel.

Rosemary Sutcliff was born in Surrey, the daughter of a British naval officer, and until the age of ten she travelled with her parents to various naval postings around the world. When she was two she contracted Still's Disease, a polyarthritic condition which severely restricted her mobility, eventually confining her to a wheelchair. This led her to write again and again about disability and adjustment to scars, both physical and mental. She has remarked that 'there's a great loneliness about having any kind of handicap in a world which in general doesn't, however much you get to the stage where neither you nor anybody else notices. You tend to create somebody on your side of the barrier who will talk your own language.'

Her father's naval background had an influence on her imagination: she listened entranced as he and his cronies swapped yarns of their experiences, 'proceeding perhaps from a tale of a snotty [midshipman] on the Andromeda, to good advice about catching gun-runners in the Persian Gulf'. This gave her an understanding of 'the working of the service mind, its special loyalties and the manner of young men who roam'. Understandably in view of this, *Kipling was the author to whose whole body of work she took most enthusiastically. It was the character of Parnesius in *Puck* who aroused in her the 'first feeling for Roman Britain, filling my small opening mind with a splendour of distant trumpets, long before I had the least idea what the Roman Empire was all about'.

At the age of 14 she was sent to an art school to train as a painter, having shown artistic talent since she was a small girl. During the Second World War, while in her early twenties, she began to make some money from painting miniatures of young men serving in the armed forces. But she was told that large canvases would be impossible because of her disability, so, wanting to spread herself, she turned to writing. Her school reports had always made her out to be 'virtually illiterate', but she set about retelling a series of British legends. Without her knowledge, a friend showed the manuscript to the Oxford University Press. They rejected it, but suggested that she tackle *Robin Hood, offering her an advance of £50,

which was 'the greatest thrill of her life'. *The Chronicles of Robin Hood* appeared in 1950.

In the same year she had her second book published: *The Queen Elizabeth Story*, about a small girl in Devon (where her family had now settled) to whom the fairies grant a sight of the great Queen. One character in the story, the lame orphan Adam Hilyarde, hints at themes to come, but like Rosemary Sutcliff's next two books, *The Armourer's House* (1951) and *Brother Dusty-Feet* (1952), it is for younger children; Margaret *Meek, in her 1962 Bodley Head monograph on Sutcliff, judges the style of dialogue in these books to be uncertain and the atmosphere sheltered, the effect being of a 'domestication of the past for the younger reader'. Then, out of this apprenticeship, there sprang quite suddenly *Simon* (1953), the first of Sutcliff's mature and complex stories, dealing with idealism, conflicting loyalties, the test set for the developing adolescent, and the cruelty of historical events—in this case the final West Country campaigns of the English Civil War.

The Eagle of the Ninth (1954) was the first of a sequence about the Roman occupation of Britain and its aftermath. One family and its dolphin-ring straddle that book and the next two in the cycle (though not the next to be published), *The Silver Branch* (1957) and *The Lantern Bearers* (1959). Two further Sutcliff novels, *Outcast* (1955) and *Dawn Wind* (1961), deal with the same broad historical period.

Interspersed with these books Sutcliff produced others set outside the Dark Ages. *The Shield Ring* (1956) tells of the Norsemen's resistance to William the Conqueror at the time of the Domesday Book. *Warrior Scarlet* (1958) comes closest to Kipling, with its setting of the Sussex Downs during the Bronze Age. The central theme is the ritual of achieving adulthood, in this case by slaying a wolf in single combat. The boy hero Drem has a withered right arm; but with immense determination, fuelled by anger at his disability, he qualifies himself for the fight—and fails.

After *The Bridge Builders* (1959), a short novel about Hadrian's Wall, came *Knight's Fee* (1960), whose hero Randal is also almost an outcast, a dog-boy in Arundel Castle near the beginning of the Norman period. *The Mark of the Horse Lord* (1965) concerns Phaedrus, a freed Roman gladiator who agrees to impersonate the Lord of the Horse People of Northern Britain; it has been called her finest novel, though it has not achieved the popularity of the earlier books.

In the ten years that followed its appearance she published no full-length children's novels. A number of her radio scripts about Roman Britain were collected as *The Capricorn Bracelet* (1973) and three stories for younger readers appeared, first published separately and then collected as *Heather, Oak and Olive* (1972).

Blood Feud (1977) broke her comparative silence. Its narrator, Jestyn, is a half-Celtic, half-Saxon boy taken into slavery by a Viking; he becomes a blood-brother to his master in the heat of a feud. *Shifting Sands* and *Sun Horse, Moon Horse*, both also published in 1977, deal respectively with a moving sand-dune which threatens a prehistoric Orkney village and with the making of the White Horse on the Berkshire Downs. *The Light Beyond the Forest* (1979) is the beginning of a cycle about King *Arthur. *Frontier Wolf* (1980) returned to Roman Britain and the family of Aquila. In 1983 Rosemary Sutcliff published an account of the early years of her own life, *Blue Remembered Hills*.

She made no claim to be a historian, but said she had 'never knowingly falsified history'. The few unfavourable criticisms of her books have generally been directed at the style of dialogue, which often verges on the poetic but is sometimes rather awkwardly colloquial.

Many critics have commented on Sutcliff's preoccupation with darkness and light as symbols of the great changes which took place in the period about which she generally writes, the late Roman Empire. She said that she believed that 'the disintegration of the Roman Empire and the onset of the Dark Ages contain truths for our own time . . . We have the same uncertainty the Romans must have had whether the light would show up again at the end of the tunnel.'

SUTTON, Eve (Evelyn Mary) (1906–92) New Zealand author who wrote a *picture book, *My Cat Likes to Hide in Boxes* (1973), illustrated by Lynley Dodd, and three *historical novels for younger children about pioneer life in New Zealand: *Green Gold* (1976), *Tuppenny Brown* (1977), and *Johnny Sweep* (1977).

Swallows and Amazons The first of twelve novels by Arthur *Ransome, published between 1930 and 1947, concerning the adventures of several groups of children on holiday. Intended to impart the author's love of sailing and other outdoor activities, they are mainly set in the Lake District and East Anglia, the chief exception being two books of 'imaginary' happenings.

Swallows and Amazons (1930) introduces the Walker children, John, Susan, Titty, and Roger, who are on holiday with their mother and baby Vicky at Holly Howe, a farm in the Lakes, while their father is overseas with the Navy. The tone of the series is set when the father telegraphs his permission for the children to go sailing on the lake upon whose shore stands the farm; the telegram reads 'BETTER DROWNED THAN DUFFERS IF NOT DUFFERS WONT DROWN'. Thereafter the children spend the holiday as the crew of the sailing dinghy *Swallow*. They set up camp on an island in the lake, but find that it has rival claimants. These are the crew of another small sailing craft, *Amazon*: 'Nancy' Blackett (whose real name is Ruth) and her sister Peggy. The Swallows and the Amazons begin a friendly rivalry—a 'treaty of offence and defence'—and unite against a common enemy. This is 'Captain Flint' (a name taken from *Treasure Island*), in reality the Blackett sisters' Uncle Jim, who is living on a houseboat and trying to write a book.

Ransome wrote *Swallows and Amazons* with the objective of restarting the literary career which he had abandoned because of work as a foreign correspondent in Russia and elsewhere. In his autobiography he has this to say of the book's birth:

I had for some time been growing intimate with a family of imaginary children . . . I had only to write it, but dreaded the discovery that after all these years of writing discursively I was unable to write narrative. I well remember the pleasure I had in the first chapter, and my fear that it would also be the last. I could think of nothing else.

The book was in effect a reliving of two very happy periods in his life, both of them at Coniston Water: childhood holidays with his family at a farm on the lake shore and later visits to his friends the Collingwoods, who lived there and owned a sailing dinghy named *Swallow*. The Walker children were based on the offspring of one of the Collingwood daughters, Taqui, Susan, Titty, and Roger Altounyan, and *Swallows and Amazons* was dedicated to this family. There is no obvious model in Ransome's life for Nancy Blackett, though his second wife Evgenia seems to have had an Amazonian streak; she certainly participated eagerly in her husband's sailing trips. 'Captain Flint', desperately trying to write a book despite interruptions, is of course Ransome himself.

When about fifty pages of *Swallows and Amazons* were written, Ransome mentioned

the book to the publisher Jonathan Cape, who agreed to publish it simply on the strength of Ransome's description of the plot. (Ransome always planned his stories in detail before beginning them, and did not necessarily write chapters in the order in which they would appear.)

In England it sold very slowly at first, but in the United States, where it was published by Lippincott of Philadelphia, a book club took a large number of copies, and both Cape and Lippincott pressed Ransome for a sequel. He had already begun to write a rather different kind of novel about the same set of children, *Peter Duck*, but put that on one side to write *Swallowdale* (1931), as a 'follow-up' to the first book. *Swallowdale* takes place in the same setting during the next summer holiday; the sinking of *Swallow* makes boating temporarily impossible for the Walkers, so they and the Amazons take to their feet and climb 'Kanchenjunga', really the Old Man of Coniston.

Peter Duck appeared in England in 1932, and described an imaginary adventure invented during a Christmas holiday on the Norfolk Broads. Set in the Caribbean, it involves a race for buried treasure. The book had strikingly favourable reviews, with the result that, in Ransome's words, 'sales of the first two books began to catch up...and I knew I could afford to write another.'

Peter Duck was the first book in the series to have illustrations, supposedly drawn 'with help from Miss Nancy Blackett'. Ransome made a virtue of the fact that he was no artist (he had never received any training) and he provided simple line-drawings that could well have been the work of a child on the verge of adolescence. This undoubtedly increased the feeling among child readers that the stories were true.

Winter Holiday (1933), set once more in the Lakes, introduces Dick and Dorothea Callum, a scientifically-minded boy and his literary younger sister, both of whom are anxious to win the approval of the Walkers and Blacketts. Their characters are close to that of Ransome himself as a child; at school he was mocked for being bookish and unsporting. *Coot Club* (1934) features neither Swallows nor Amazons but just the D's, who are spending a Christmas holiday on the Norfolk Broads, where they meet the Coot Club, a secret bird-protection group. *Pigeon Post* (1936), which won the *Carnegie Medal for its year, has the Swallows and Amazons establishing a camp some way from their base in the Lakes, and releasing

pigeons as a reassurance to adults that they are all right.

We Didn't Mean to Go to Sea (1937), generally judged to be the most exciting book in the series, describes how the Walkers drift out to sea and find themselves navigating the boat to the coast of Holland. Ransome himself made this journey in his own boat before writing the novel. *Secret Water* (1939) has the Walkers' father playing a greater role for the first time as he gives the children a lesson in surveying in an East Anglian creek. *The Big Six* (1940) is set on the Broads and has the same cast as *Coot Club*, with boat-stealing as its theme. *Missee Lee* (1941) is a fantasy on the lines of *Peter Duck*, set on the China Sea, with a suave female *pirate captain. *The Picts and the Martyrs* (1943) returns to the Lakes, and describes the conflict of the Amazons and the two D's against the Blackett girls' fearsome Great Aunt. *Great Northern?* (1947) concludes the series with an adventure in the Hebrides.

Ransome's stories are distinguished by a very plain narrative style which is almost childlike in its simplicity. The series attracts children who want to read about adventures which are remote from ordinary experience and yet within the bounds of possibility. The books have received much praise from parents and teachers and little criticism. Yet there are those who are irritated by his portrayal of a world where no real worries ever intervene. As John Rowe *Townsend has written, 'Faced with a million words about the Walker children and their friends, we may wonder if they could really be so consistently right-minded; we may wish we could see them in a living relationship with their parents, instead of having the parents mainly as understanding figures in the background; we may even wish they were not always on holiday... The older children, though well into their teens before the series ends, maintain a sexless comradeship which does not quite accord with the facts of adolescence. And on the whole there are rather few insights; rather few of those moments when the reader is pulled up in sudden awareness that life is richer or stranger than he had realised.'

Swarm in May, A (1955) The novel which established the reputation of its author, William *Mayne. John Owen is a choirboy at an English cathedral choir school (recognizably Canterbury, where Mayne was himself a chorister). The book is superficially a *school story, but presents a very unconventional

picture of the relationship between the boys and their masters – Mr Ardent the headmaster, Dr Sunderland the organist (whose idiosyncracies of speech Mayne brilliantly represents), and the irascible Mr Sutton the Latin master. The book perfectly evokes the tensions and delights of a small, closed community, while the plot is at once simple and very complex. Frank *Eyre echoed the judgment of most critics when he called *A Swarm in May* 'a minor masterpiece . . . one of the twentieth century's best children's books'. The sequels, *Choristers' Cake* (1956), *Cathedral Wednesday* (1960), and *Words and Music* (1963) have much less striking plots, but are equally accomplished evocations of choir-school life.

Sweeney Todd *See* PENNY DREADFULS.

Sweet Valley High (1983–) A popular teen-romance series created by US author Francine Pascal (1938–) along with a team of ghostwriters. The books chronicle the lives of identical twins Elizabeth and Jessica Wakefield. With the strapline 'One twin is good, one is bad—both are California blonde', it is deemed somewhat controversial in its unrealistic portrayal of the all-American 'good life' spiked with a dash of downright mean girls. However, the series was hugely successful—the twins were introduced in 1983 and their melodramas continued over 150 books in the series. Numerous spin-offs follow the twins from second graders in *Sweet Valley Kids* to graduation in *Sweet Valley University*. Pascal herself saw the twins into adulthood with *Sweet Valley Confidential* (2011) and *The Sweet Life* (2012), a series of e-book novellas about the twins in their thirties.

SWIFT, Jonathan *See* GULLIVER'S TRAVELS.

Swift Pure Cry, A (2006) A debut novel by Siobhan *Dowd, which won the 2007 *Branford Boase Award and the Eilís Dillon Award. Dowd eloquently captures the small-town community of Coolbar in Ireland in the mid-1980s, and the lives of Shell and her siblings, Jimmy and Trix. Shell is an immensely sympathetic character, and the reader is drawn along with her, wondering where life might take her. Subtleness and flair keep you reading in this sad and moving tale of loss and innocence.

SWINDELLS, Robert (1939–) A highly regarded English author who left school at fifteen, embarking on a variety of jobs before he discovered his talent for writing stories.

Deeply political, his books often deal with modern issues, though the issues never swamp the characters or the plots. Constantly surprising, they are never less than page-turning, engaging the reader at a visceral level. Homelessness, abuse, and a serial killer come together in his thought-provoking classic *Stone Cold* (1993), while *Brother in the Land* (1984) is set in the misery of a post-nuclear future. *Abomination* (1998) shows the narrow-mindedness of religious extremism and the star-crossed lovers in *Daz4Zoe* (1990) live in an all too possible dystopian future.

Swineherd, The A *fairy story by Hans Christian *Andersen. A prince, having failed to win an emperor's daughter by presenting her with two truly marvellous gifts (a superb rose and a fine nightingale), disguises himself and obtains a job in her father's palace as a swineherd. Here he attracts her attention by making toys which, though magical, are really mere trifles. Nevertheless, the princess covets them, and she eventually agrees to pay the swineherd for them with kisses. Her father discovers her kissing him and throws them both out of his empire, whereupon the swineherd reveals his true identity, tells the princess he now despises her for wanting the toys but spurning the truly precious gifts, and returns to his own kingdom, leaving her desolate.

Andersen's story is a reworking of a Danish folk tale; it has an analogue in a story in the *Pentamerone, as well as resembling *King Thrush-beard* in the *Grimm collection and *Hacon Grizzle-beard* in the stories of *Asbjørnsen and Moe. Andersen dispenses with the granting of sexual favours by the princess, which features in some traditional versions, and also departs from tradition in making the prince reject the princess at the end. He published the story in his third collection (1842), and it appeared in English four years later.

Swish of the Curtain, The (1941) The first in a series of four books by actress and BBC TV producer Pamela *Brown. Filled with the love and excitement of making theatre, this book tells the story of seven kids who build a theatre in a disused hall and perform their own plays. It is charming, old-fashioned, and inspiring by turns. The subsequent books follow the characters' adventures at RADA, in weekly rep, and, in Maddy's case, starring in a film.

Swiss Family Robinson, The An adventure story on the model of *Robinson Crusoe*,

originally written by a Swiss pastor, Johann David *Wyss, and subsequently much enlarged by translators and editors.

A Swiss family—a pastor, his wife, and four boys—are shipwrecked on an uninhabited island. They gradually establish an attractive way of life for themselves, and their many adventures are used by their father to form the basis of lessons in *natural history and the physical sciences. His attitude to education, which resembles *Rousseau's, is 'to awaken the curiosity of my sons by interesting observations, to leave time for the activity of their imagination, and then to correct any error they might fall into'.

Wyss, an army chaplain, told the story episode by episode for the entertainment of his four sons. He left the manuscript incomplete and disorganized, and it was prepared for publication at Zurich in 1812–13 as *Der schweizerische Robinson*. The editor was his son Johann Rudolf Wyss (1781–1830). A French translation by Mme la Baronne Isabelle de Montolieu, *Le Robinson suisse*, was issued in 1814, with some new material added by the translator. The first English version was probably the work of William *Godwin; it was published by his wife M. J. Godwin in 1814 as *The Family Robinson Crusoe*, and was described as a translation 'from the German of M. Wiss', though it also incorporated some of Mme de Montolieu's additions. The Godwin edition was reissued in a longer version in 1816, and the book's more familiar title was first used in an edition of 1818. In 1824–6 Mme de Montolieu published a much enlarged French text—the enlargements were her own work—and it was in this that many of the most exciting adventures of Fritz, Franz, Ernest, and Jack appeared for the first time. Other writers added further incidents at later dates, most notably the episode of the boa constrictor which kills the family's beloved donkey.

The story as originally published lacked a clear ending, and concluded with the boys' father wondering (after two years on the island) whether the family would ever see another human face again. An editor's postscript followed, explaining that three or four years later they were discovered by an English vessel whose Captain was given their journal, but the ship was driven away again before they could be rescued. Later texts introduced the character of an English girl who is shipwrecked on a neighbouring rock and discovered by one of the boys. He returns to England with her while

the rest of the family remain; other settlers join them, and the island eventually becomes a flourishing colony, 'New Switzerland'.

English editions by W. H. Davenport Adams (1869–70) and by Mrs H. B. Paull (1879) claimed to include the complete Wyss-Montolieu narrative, but most other printings of the story consist of much shorter versions, such as that edited by W. H. G. *Kingston (1889). With all the expansions and contractions, Wyss's original narrative has long since been obscured, and the book is chiefly characterized by its improbable profusion of animals—penguins, kangaroos, monkeys, and even a whale—conveniently gathered together on a tropical island.

The book directly inspired *Masterman Ready, and was a model for the other children's novels of *Marryat.

Sword in the Stone, The A novel by T. H. *White, first published in 1938 with line drawings by the author. Taking as its starting-point a few sentences in *Malory's *Morte Darthur*, the book describes the life of the boy Wart in the castle of Sir Ector, in medieval England. Wart is brought up alongside Kay, Sir Ector's son. The two boys acquire a tutor, Merlyn, who arranges many adventures for them. He often turns Wart into an animal or fish so that he may be educated by the experience of other ways of life than the human. Eventually Kay is knighted, but Wart, being only Sir Ector's fosterson, must remain a squire. Greatly saddened by this, Wart scarcely notices what is happening when, in London, he draws out a sword that has been fixed magically in a stone, and so reveals his true identity as King *Arthur.

The original text of the book was revised by White for republication in 1958 as part of his Arthurian tetralogy, *The *Once and Future King*. White said of *The Sword in the Stone*: 'It seems impossible to determine whether it is for grown-ups or children. It is more or less a kind of wish-fulfilment of the things I should like to have happened when I was a boy.' It is, in fact, one of the finest children's books of its period, especially in its first version. White gets good value out of anachronisms, picturing Merlyn's study as including among its books a set of the *Encyclopaedia Britannica*, and describing Sir Ector and his friend Sir Grummore drinking port while they discuss whether it would be possible to send the boys to Eton. White's characterization of Merlyn, who lives backwards in time and can foresee the future but scarcely remembers what

has just happened, is a masterpiece, rivalling *Tolkien's Gandalf. The book was made into a cartoon film by the *Disney studios, but this failed to bring out any of its charm.

Sylvie and Bruno A long children's story by Lewis *Carroll (C. L. Dodgson), published in 1889, with a continuation appearing in 1893.

The germ of the tale was 'Bruno's Revenge', a short story about a fairy boy who is coaxed out of bad temper towards his sister Sylvie and sets to work to improve her garden; this appeared in *Aunt Judy's Magazine in 1867. Some six or seven years later Dodgson conceived the idea of making it the nucleus of a longer story which, as well as being comic, would contain elements (as he put it) 'not wholly out of harmony with the graver cadences of life'. After jotting down odd ideas and fragments of dialogue, Dodgson organized these concepts into a connected tale and in 1885 approached Harry *Furniss for illustrations. During 1888 Dodgson decided to split the book into two volumes. The first of these, Sylvie and Bruno, was published by Macmillan in December 1889.

Sylvie and Bruno are the fairy children of the Warden of Outland, whose title is usurped by the unpleasant Sub-Warden, assisted by his stupid wife and his horrid son Uggug. Sylvie and Bruno's adventures are observed by the narrator, a man of about Dodgson's age, who is sometimes visible to them and sometimes not; he slips in and out of their world by dreaming, or by experiencing what he calls an 'eerie' state. Meanwhile in the real, mortal world he is caught up in the hopes of his friend Arthur Forester, a doctor, of marrying the beautiful Lady Muriel, daughter of an earl.

There is little plot; much of the story is taken up with the chatter of the two children and with discursions on religion, morality, and similar topics. There are *nonsense inventions equal to those in the *Alice* books—examples include a pair of umbrellas to be worn on the knees in case of horizontal rain—but these are buried in page after page of sentimentality, moralizing, or mere dullness. Only the Mad Gardener's song ('He thought he saw...') has become a popular part of the Lewis Carroll canon, and in fact Harry Furniss's illustrations, which owe a good deal to Thackeray (see ROSE AND THE RING, THE) and *Doyle as well as to *Tenniel, are the most consistently entertaining thing in the book.

Dodgson continued the story in *Sylvie and Bruno Concluded* (1893), which tells of the supposed death of Arthur Forester in a cholera epidemic (he is actually found to be alive at the end of the book), the return of Sylvie and Bruno's father, and the transformation of Uggug into a huge porcupine.

The two books never remotely rivalled the popularity of the *Alice* stories, but the first volume did reach its 13th thousand by 1898. In 1904 Macmillan published an abridgement of the two books, *The Story of Sylvie and Bruno*, made by Dodgson's younger brother Edwin, which omitted all the discursive passages; it was reprinted several times.

SYMONS, (Dorothy) Geraldine (1909–97), British author of five children's novels about two girls growing up in the years immediately before the First World War. They include *Miss Rivers and Miss Bridges* (1971), in which the two become suffragettes.

TABART, Benjamin (*fl.* 1801–18) London bookseller who issued many notable children's books of the early 19th cent.

'Tabart & Co.' were in business at the 'Juvenile and School Library' in New Bond Street, London, by 1801. In 1804 there began to appear a series entitled 'Tabart's Popular Stories' (*see* POPULAR STORIES), in which many of best known *fairy stories and tales from *chapbooks were printed as separate illustrated books for children, often for the first time; this was in spite of the strong disapproval of such stories being expressed at the time by Mrs *Trimmer and many writers of *moral tales. The editor of the 'Popular Stories' seems to have been William *Godwin's wife, Mary Jane. In 1805 Tabart issued a book of *nursery rhymes, entitled *Songs for the Nursery; it included several rhymes that were mildly indecorous, and was again in marked contrast to the moral severity of many contemporary children's publications. In about 1812 the firm moved to Clifford Street, and continued in business for about two years more. In 1818 the 'Popular Stories' were collected in one volume under the title *Popular Fairy Tales. This time the publisher was Sir Richard Phillips; the editor's name was given as 'Benjamin Tabart'.

Little is known about Tabart himself and it is possible that his name was used as a cover for the real proprietor of the firm, who could have been Sir Richard Phillips himself. Phillips (1767–1840), the son of a Leicestershire farmer, was an energetic hack-writer, bookseller, and publisher. He was sent to prison for selling Paine's *Rights of Man* and afterwards established a magazine which attacked the government. He published innumerable cheap *books of instruction, many of them written by himself under various pseudonyms such as 'Dr Blair', 'the Rev. J. Goldsmith', etc. Phillips became a sheriff of London and was knighted when he presented an address from the corporation to George III. Several of the early Tabart books had Phillips's name on the joint imprint. George Borrow's *Lavengro* (1851) portrays Phillips, whom it describes as having a partner or assistant, 'a pale, shrivelled-looking person' who nevertheless had 'a dull twinkle in his eye', and whom Borrow names as 'Taggart'. This may well have been Tabart, and it is possible that Phillips used his name for the juvenile side of the business because his own was too 'hot' politically to be associated with nursery literature.

Tabitha Twitchett Cat in stories by Beatrix *Potter.

Tailor of Gloucester, The A story written and illustrated by Beatrix *Potter, printed privately in 1902 and published by *Warne in 1903.

It originated during a visit that Beatrix Potter paid in 1894 to Harescombe Grange near Stroud in Gloucestershire, where she heard from her cousin Caroline Hutton the true account of a Gloucester tailor named John Samuel Prichard who had left a waistcoat half-made in his shop one Saturday and had returned on Monday to find it finished except for one button-hole, on which was pinned a scrap of paper with the message 'No more twist'. It later transpired that Mr Prichard's grateful apprentices had done the work out of kindness, but the tailor put in his shop window the sign 'Come to Prichard where the waistcoats are made at night by the fairies.' Beatrix Potter decided to make a story out of this and she visited Gloucester to sketch streets and buildings; she also made drawings of their coachman's son sitting cross-legged like a tailor. Back in London she found a promising-looking tailor's shop in Chelsea, pulled a button off her coat, went inside to ask to have it mended, and struck up a friendship with the tailor, so that she could learn something of his craft. The story was eventually finished by December 1901, when she gave an illustrated manuscript of it to Freda Moore, daughter of her former governess and

brother of the boy to whom the original **Tale of Peter Rabbit* had been sent.

This first version of *The Tailor of Gloucester* had only twelve watercolours (Beatrix Potter apologized to Freda Moore for being 'lazy' and not painting more).

In 1902 she decided to have an edition of the book printed privately, just as she had originally done with *Peter Rabbit*. The private edition, now with sixteen pictures and a somewhat shortened text, was issued by the author in December 1902 in an edition of 500 copies, some being given to family and friends, others being sold, and one copy given to the Chelsea tailor.

Warne's now decided to publish it, and at their request the author greatly reduced the number of rhymes in the Christmas Eve passage. She drew eighteen new illustrations, but cut out one from the private edition which depicted rats carousing in a cellar, with one of them drinking from a bottle; it was apparently thought that *Sunday schools and *temperance societies might object. The book was ready for Christmas 1903.

Some years later Beatrix Potter described it as 'my own favourite amongst my little books', though she preferred the private edition. The book is indeed a small masterpiece, both of illustration and text, though it lacks her distinctive sardonic wit and love of black comedy. Mr Prichard the tailor died in 1934 and his grave near Cheltenham bears the inscription 'The Tailor of Gloucester'; a house in Gloucester thought to have been one of the models for the pictures is now a Beatrix Potter museum.

TALBOT, Ethel (1880–1944) British author of *girl guide novels, *school stories, and *adventure stories published during the 1920s and 1930s. They include *Peggy's Last Term* (1920) and *Patricia Prefect* (1925).

Tale of Despereaux, The (2003) By Kate *DiCamillo, with illustrations by Timothy B. Ering. Told through the voice of an omniscient narrator and adopting the conventions of the fairy tale, this fantasy follows the mouse, Despereaux, in his quest to rescue the Princess Pea from the evil rat, Roscuro. It is also the story of Miggery Sow, the unprepossessing serving girl, who nevertheless has an impossible wish. The book won the *Newbery Medal, has been adapted as a film (2005), and included in the *School Library Journal*'s list of Top 100 Chapter Books (2012).

Tale of Peter Rabbit, The First book to be written and illustrated by Beatrix *Potter, printed privately in 1901 and published by *Warne in 1902.

The story was first told in a picture-letter to Noël Moore, son of Beatrix Potter's former *governess, written in 1893. It was based on the author's own pet rabbit Peter, bought the previous year; she recorded that 'he really is good at tricks when hungry, in private, jumping (stick, hands, hoop, back and forward), ringing a little bell and drumming on a tambourine.' Some years later, she decided to make a book out of the story and rewrote it in an exercise book, with forty-two black-and-white drawings and a coloured frontispiece, entitling it 'The Tale of Peter Rabbit and Mr McGregor's Garden, by H. B. Potter'. The real Peter had recently died, so she used another rabbit as model for the drawings.

This manuscript was shown to at least six publishers without immediate success; it seems to have been rejected partly because Beatrix Potter wanted it to be printed in small format. She wrote to Noël Moore's sister that she 'would rather make two or three little books costing 1/− each than one big book costing 6/−'. She decided to have it printed privately and this was done by the London firm of Strangeways, who produced 250 copies, entitled *The Tale of Peter Rabbit*, in time for Christmas 1901. Beatrix Potter gave some to her relatives and friends, and sold others for a halfpenny each. The demand was sufficient for a further 200 copies to be printed, with slight alterations in the text.

Meanwhile the author's friend Canon H. D. Rawnsley kept in touch with one of the publishers who had seen the manuscript, Frederick Warne & Co., and they reconsidered their decision. (At one point Rawnsley offered them a forty-one-page versification of the story, which he had made himself, but they preferred Beatrix Potter's text.) Warne's decided to produce an edition themselves, with all the illustrations in colour; these were to be restricted to thirty in number, plus the frontispiece. Beatrix Potter made new watercolours, and the blocks were engraved, on the recently-introduced three-*colour process, by Hentschel of Fleet Street, who had produced the frontispiece for the private edition. The printers were Edmund *Evans & Co.

The book was ready by October 1902 and went on sale in two forms, in an art-paper binding at one shilling and in boards at one and sixpence. It was reprinted several times in the following months. After the first four printings coloured endpapers were added, and four

pictures were removed to make room for them. These included a drawing of Mrs McGregor serving the rabbit pie that contained Peter's father. Beatrix Potter always had difficulty drawing human figures and had made several attempts at this picture, eventually using a caricature of herself as Mrs McGregor.

Warne's did not copyright *Peter Rabbit* in America when it first came out and in 1904 pirate editions began to appear there. It remains the best known, though not the best, of her books, and has been translated into thirty-five languages, selling over 150 million copies. It has also been adapted for the stage and screen, sometimes (notably the 1971 ballet film) to considerable success, while the CGI series that launched in 2012, though a travesty of Potter's art, gained great popularity; Peter Rabbit images have been used for merchandise and spin-offs of every imaginable kind, from children's plates to a Japanese rollercoaster.

Tales from Shakespear. *Designed for the use of young persons* (1807). By Charles and Mary *Lamb. The preface to the first edition explains that the *Tales* are meant as 'an introduction to the study of Shakespear'. The book was commissioned by the *Godwins. Mary undertook the greater part of the work, with Charles concentrating on the tragedies. The *Tales* were published in January 1807 under the imprint 'Thomas Hodgkins', a pseudonym then being used by the Godwins. The book contained *copperplate illustrations (of which Charles did not approve, because they related to the plays rather than the Lambs' own narratives) which are believed to have been drawn by William *Mulready and engraved by *Blake. The title page bore Charles's name alone; Mary's reputation was overshadowed by the fact that ten years earlier, while out of her mind, she had stabbed her mother to death.

The *Tales* were the first version of *Shakespeare to be published specifically for children. They are written in a clear, vigorous style, not often encumbered by the attempt to make the language resemble that of the original. A lot is left out: the version of *A Midsummer Night's Dream* omits all the 'mechanicals' except Bottom, and the full horror of Lear's tragedy is somewhat toned down. Sometimes, too, there is obvious 'writing down' for children. But the literary quality of the *Tales* makes them outshine almost every other English children's book of this period, and they proved an immediate and lasting success.

A second edition, with slight alterations, was issued by the Godwins in 1809 and they also printed some of the tales as separate books, with different plates (apparently also by Blake), plain or hand-coloured. Further Godwin editions followed in 1816 and 1822 and the book then began to appear under other imprints. From the sixth edition (1838) Mary's name began to appear on the title-page. Later illustrators include Arthur *Rackham (1899) and Heath *Robinson (1902). The book has continued to be reprinted again and again.

Tales from Shakespear inspired Charles Cowden Clarke (*see* BOWDLER, THOMAS), who was a friend of the Lambs, to write *Tales from Chaucer* (1833).

Tales of passed times by Mother Goose *See* HISTORIES, OR TALES OF PAST TIMES.

Tales of Peter Parley about America, The The first *Peter Parley book, written by the originator of the pseudonym, S. G. *Goodrich, and published by Carter, Hendee & Co. of Boston in 1827. In response to great enthusiasm, it was reissued in a revised form the next year, with the text divided into chapters and questions added at the foot of the page. Both the first and second editions were generously illustrated with *woodcuts.

The book begins:

Here I am! My name is Peter Parley! I am an old man. I am very gray and lame. But I have seen a great many things, and had a great many adventures, and I love to talk about them.

There follows an account of how, in his youth, Parley met an *'Indian' named Wampum, visited his wigwam, and learned his history. In the following chapters there are recounted the history of New England and New York, the discoveries of Columbus and Cortés, the settlement of North America, the War of American Independence, and other features of American history. The book includes 'The Story of America in Verse', which begins:

> Columbus was a sailor brave,
> The first that crossed th' Atlantic wave.
> In fourteen hundred ninety-two,
> He came far o'er the ocean blue.

The *Tales* proved to be the first of more than 100 Peter Parley titles written or edited by Goodrich himself, not to mention a large number of imitations by other hands.

Tales of the Castle (1785) A collection of *moral tales by Mme de *Genlis, first published as *Les Veillées du château* (1784). The

setting is a chateau reminiscent of St-Aubin-sur-Loire, where the author had spent her childhood; the narrator, Mme de Clémire, entertains her children with evening readings—not *fairy stories, of which Mme de Genlis profoundly disapproved, but accounts of real, fact-based marvels.

Tales Uniting Instruction with Amusement: *consisting of The Dangers of the Streets; and Throwing Squibs* Two prose *cautionary tales published by John *Harris *c.* 1810. In 'The Dangers of the Streets' George Manly, a careless child, loses a leg as a result of falling in front of a wagon. He is given a wooden leg, and 'at every step' reproaches himself for his folly. The other story, 'Throwing Squibs', tells how Tom Tindall blinds his father and loses the sight of one of his own eyes through behaving foolishly with fireworks.

tall tale A narrative composed chiefly of impossible events. An early classic of the genre is the Baron *Munchausen collection, first published in England in 1785. Tall tales about such supposed superheroes as John Smith and Daniel Boone (*see* WESTERNS) and *Davy Crockett were common among settlers in America and left their mark on the literature of the United States. For example, such widely differing books as *Uncle Remus* by Joel Chandler Harris and *Moby Dick* by Herman Melville have affinities to the 'tall tale'. Examples of tall tales written specially for children in the 20th cent. include *The *Twenty-One Balloons* (1947) by William Pène *Du Bois and the 'McBroom' stories by Sid *Fleischman.

TAN, Shaun (1974-) Internationally renowned Australian picture-book creator and illustrator, Tan was honoured for his contribution to children's and young adult literature, receiving the *Astrid Lindgren Memorial Award in 2011. His collaboration with Gary Crew resulted in his first picture book, *The Viewer* (1997), a dark, cyclical representation of human history which sets a precedent for Tan's work in exploring human nature through disturbing expository narratives which are often political, surreal, and deeply moving. *The Rabbits* (1998), with John *Marsden, is a visually stunning allegorical fable about colonization which won numerous awards in Australia, the US, and UK. Tan's *The Lost Thing* (2000), a warm-hearted and humorous tale about a young boy and a rather overlooked bizarre creature received an Academy Award for its animated film adaptation in 2011. *Tales from Outer Suburbia* (2008) is a collection of illustrated short stories which reveals something of Tan's suburban upbringing but with his hallmark fantastical twists. *The *Arrival* (2006) is a multi-award-winning wordless graphic novel about immigration, while *Rules of Summer* (2013) is a unique, atmospheric exploration of the rules that might bind any relationship between close friends or siblings. Tan writes widely about his work and the role of picture books in both adults' and children's lives.

Tanglewood Tales for girls and boys; *being a second Wonder-Book* By Nathaniel *Hawthorne, published by Ticknor, Reed and Fields of Boston in 1853, with a first British edition issued the same year by Chapman and Hall. As in *A *Wonder-Book for Girls and Boys*, we meet Eustace Bright, who in the first book told versions of Greek myths to a party of children at Tanglewood Manor. Now he presents the 'editor' (Hawthorne) with a pile of manuscript containing more retellings of Greek stories. Hawthorne remarks that the originals are 'so brimming over with every thing that is most abhorrent to our Christianised moral sense' that they have had to be severely rewritten, 'at the expense of such liberties with their structure as must be left to plead their own excuse'. The myths are then narrated with no further reference to Eustace or Tanglewood.

Hawthorne's introductory remarks are a key to the character of the book. The *Wonder-Book* was written in a cheerful, sunny manner throughout, but here the material is much more sombrely presented, and Hawthorne is visibly preoccupied with what he regards as the impurity of much of the original material. For example, in the story of the Minotaur he substitutes for Theseus' seduction and desertion of Ariadne a passage in which she renounces him out of love and duty to her father.

Tanglewood Tales was illustrated in 1919 by Edmund *Dulac, and continued to be reprinted at intervals. Noel *Streatfeild observed in an introduction to a 1957 edition that in childhood she knew the book better than the classic *fairy stories.

Tapestry Room, The (1879) A novel by Mrs *Molesworth. Jeanne, who lives in a French chateau, is joined by her English cousin Hugh, who is given a bedroom in which hangs a tapestry of a castle. Dudu, the gruff old raven who is among Jeanne's animal

companions, takes Hugh into the tapestry castle and Hugh finds that Jeanne is already there. Together they visit wonderful lands before returning to real life. The first edition of the book was illustrated by Walter *Crane.

The Tapestry Room is, of Mrs Molesworth's works, second in popularity only to *The *Cuckoo Clock*, and is indeed much the same sort of story. Like the earlier book, its charm lies chiefly in the portrayal of domestic life—in this case the chateau in winter.

Tar-baby In the *Uncle Remus* stories by Joel Chandler *Harris.

Tarka the Otter (1927) An *animal story by Henry *Williamson. Originally written for adults, this hugely influential book has become a children's classic. Set in North Devon around the Taw and Torridge rivers, it tells in exquisite prose the story of the first and final years in the life of an otter. The book helped change public attitudes to otters, which were considered vermin, and influenced authors as diverse as Ted *Hughes and Rachel Carson (1907–64), who claimed it as the book she would take to a desert island. It was adapted as a film in 1979.

TARKINGTON, Booth *See* PENROD.

Tarzan The son of a British peer, supposedly abandoned in the African jungle in childhood, reared by apes, and eventually discovered by the beautiful blonde girl Jane. Tarzan was the creation of Edgar Rice *Burroughs in a series of novels beginning with *Tarzan of the Apes* (1914); the first of many Tarzan films was made in that year and in 1929 he began to feature in American *comic strips and books. He continues to inspire spin-off fiction a century on, such as Andy Briggs's 'rebooted' series beginning with *The Greystoke Legacy* (2011).

TATE, Joan (1922–2000) British author specializing in books for reluctant readers, such as *Wild Boy* (1972), about a boy found living wild on the Yorkshire moors. She was also a distinguished translator from Swedish.

TAYLOR, Ann (1782–1866) and **Jane** (1783–1824) Authors, in collaboration, of *Original Poems for Infant Minds*, *Rhymes for the Nursery*, and *Hymns for Infant Minds*, collections of verse which contained some of the most celebrated English children's poetry of the 19th cent., including Ann's *My Mother* and Jane's 'The Star' (*Twinkle, twinkle, little star*).

Ann and Jane Taylor were born in London, twenty months apart, the children of Isaac *Taylor, a successful engraver and devout Nonconformist, whose own father had been an innovator in engraving and worked with *Bewick. To ease the expense of bringing up a large family the Taylors moved to Lavenham in Suffolk, and from there Isaac Taylor was called to be minister of a Nonconformist congregation, first in Colchester, then at Ongar in Essex from 1810. When the whole family became celebrated in print, they were known as 'The Taylors of Ongar' to distinguish them from another literary family of the same name.

Ann's autobiography draws a picture of a gently *Puritan, carefully regulated, and immensely hardworking family, yet one in which humour, imagination, play, music and writing, and love of garden and countryside, all received full encouragement in the time left after work, devotion, and study. The Taylors educated their own children: Isaac Taylor supervised their lessons in the room where he engraved; later he taught them engraving and eventually Ann and Jane worked almost full time as his assistants. Their mother always read aloud at breakfast and tea. On the strength of public interest in the whole family after the children's success, Isaac Taylor and his wife had their own educational works published.

The Taylor sisters romped and play-acted together; Jane was remembered as living much of her time in a world of her own, composing verses and plays while spinning a top. Ann writes in her autobiography that she began writing verses at the age of about seven or eight and from then on 'it became my perpetual amusement to scribble'.

In 1799 Ann had a verse published in an *annual, *The Minor's Pocket Book*; thereafter she contributed to it regularly. In 1804 a poem by Jane beginning 'I'm a poor little beggar, my mammy is dead', printed in the *Pocket Book*, inspired *Darton and Harvey the publishers to commission more of this kind of *moral tale in verse, preferably short and easy for younger children. Darton's letter, addressed to Isaac Taylor and offering 'a suitable return in cash or in books', brought from him the response 'I do not want my girls to be authors'; but Ann remembered thinking 'Books good, but cash better.' The project was allowed as spare-time occupation for Ann, Jane, and their younger brother Isaac, and they received cash (£15 for the second volume of *Original Poems*) as well

as 'occasional presents of fish, fruit, and other acceptable "oddments"'.

Rhymes for the Nursery, to be even simpler in style, followed in 1806 and earned them £20, 'so that we felt our purses comfortably filling, and from this time for several years were never without commissions of some sort'. *Hymns for Infant Minds*, the Taylor sisters' first book with no additional contributors, came out in 1810, and became the most frequently printed of all their works.

A later edition quoted Dr *Arnold of Rugby's belief that 'The knowledge and love of Christ can nowhere be more readily gained by young children than from the hymns of this most admirable woman.' (The sisters' full individual names were not attached to their poems until long after first publication, and in some cases it has never been possible to say who wrote which.)

Ann and Jane were also commissioned to revise and improve on what they called 'a queer book', *The *World Turned Upside Down*, for *Tabart (1810). Ann was moved by the flood of inferior imitations of William Roscoe's *The *Butterfly's Ball* to write her own poem in the genre, *The Wedding among the Flowers* (1808), and Jane wrote *Display* (1815), a brisk 'tale for young people' about the conquest of a young lady's vanity.

Each of the sisters went on publishing intermittently, Jane beginning to sign her work and becoming the better known, but collaboration ended for the most part with Ann's marriage in 1813. She lived most of her married and widowed life in Nottingham, where she died at the age of eighty-five. Jane, whose health had never been strong, never married, and died aged forty. Their brother Isaac, who had contributed to *Original Poems* as a seventeen-year-old, eventually made a career of writing books, including *The Natural History of Enthusiasm* and a memoir of his sister Jane. A younger brother, Jefferys *Taylor, wrote books for children.

It has been suggested that Ann and Jane Taylor were the first authors to write a juvenile classic who were *only* writers for children; they were certainly among the first to combine high literary ability with a precise notion of the child they were writing for. Ann remembered Jane saying, when she sat down in the evenings to write children's verse for their publisher, 'I try to conjure some child into my presence, address her suitably, as well as I am able, and when I begin to flag I say to her "There love, now you may go".'

TAYLOR, Isaac (1759–1829) Father of Ann and Jane *Taylor; he wrote a number of instructional works for children. He was best known for his series of *geography books, *Scenes . . . for the amusement and instruction of little tarry-at-home travellers*, which were published between 1818 and 1830 by John *Harris. His other books include *Bunyan Explained to a Child* (1824), a set of verses and illustrations based on *The *Pilgrim's Progress*, and *Beginnings of Biography, being the lives of one hundred persons eminent in British story* (1824).

TAYLOR, Jefferys (1792–1853) Younger brother of Ann and Jane *Taylor. He wrote a number of children's books, including *Harry's Holiday; or, The doings of one who had nothing to do* (1818), *Aesop in Rhyme* (1820), *Parlour Commentaries on the Constitution and Laws of England* (1825), *The Forest; or, Rambles in the woodland* (1831), and *The Farm; a new account of rural toils and produce* (1832).

TAYLOR, Mildred D. (1943–) African-American author famous for the groundbreaking *Logan Family Saga* (including *Roll of Thunder, Hear My Cry*) which, based on the author's own family history, tells of one family's struggle to maintain their integrity, pride, and independence in the face of racism and social injustice over nearly one hundred years of American history. Chronologically the series begins with *The Land* (2001), about Paul-Edward, the son of a plantation owner and a slave, and the farm he owns. His granddaughter, Cassie Logan, will be the much-loved heroine of *Roll of Thunder, Hear My Cry*, which is set during the Depression.

TAYLOR, Theodore (1921–2006) American author, best known for *The *Cay* (1969). He worked in the film industry before beginning to write children's fiction. Besides producing several other novels, he is the author of *People Who Make Movies* (1967).

teddy bears These have featured in countless picture books (often animate, as active characters), and appear to owe their name to a cartoon by Clifford Berryman in the *Washington Evening Star* on 18 November 1902, showing President Theodore ('Teddy') Roosevelt refusing to shoot a small bear; it bore the caption 'Drawing the Line in Mississippi', and referred to a boundary dispute between that state and Louisiana. The bear became popularly associated with Roosevelt, and a Brooklyn toy manufacturer, Morris Michtom, displayed a toy bear in the window of his shop

bearing the notice 'Teddy's Bear'. He started to manufacture such bears in large quantities and eventually founded the Ideal Toy Corporation to market them.

However the true inventor of the teddy bear, if not of its name, may have been Margarete Steiff, a toymaker from Giengen in Germany, who was supplying bears to the New York store FAO Schwarz by 1904. These bears were apparently at first known as 'Friend Petz', but soon acquired the name 'Teddy' too. Millions of Steiff bears had been sold by 1908, and the company is still producing them today; their bears and those of their imitators remain as popular as ever. 'The Teddy Bears' Picnic' by John Walter Bratton was published in New York in 1907, as instrumental dance music only; the lyrics were added by the Irish songwriter Jimmy Kennedy in 1932, and first recorded by Henry Hall in England.

Further information may be found in Peter Bull, *Bear With Me* (1969) and *Peter Bull's Book of Teddy Bears* (1977).

Teddy Robinson A *teddy bear in stories by Joan G. *Robinson.

Teddy Tail A mouse in a *comic strip in the London *Daily Mail* from 1915 to 1960 (with the exception of the years of the Second World War). It was created by illustrator Charles Folkard. *Teddy Tail* books were published.

teenage fiction See YOUNG ADULT.

Teens, *a story of Australian schoolgirls* (1897) By Louise *Mack, this book describes the experiences of Lennie Leighton, the daughter of a doctor. The story centres on her relationship with Mabel, a girl two years older than herself, whose mother has died and who delights in being virtually adopted by the Leighton family—Lennie's three sisters, her brother Bert, and 'the Mother'.

When Bert tricks Mabel into going home two hours early by putting the clocks forward, Mabel and Lennie get their revenge by breaking up his football club meeting through a trick of their own. At school the two girls found a magazine, for which they write stories and poems energetically; their paper survives a crisis when the top class launches a rival periodical. The story ends sadly with Mabel's departure for Paris with an aunt and uncle, and the narrator states bleakly that Lennie would never again find such a friend. (Mabel does in fact return in the sequel, *Girls Together*, 1898, though at the end of that book she

nearly breaks Lennie's heart by becoming engaged to Bert.)

Teens is one of the first notable Australian children's books, a vivid story of home and school life which makes no pretence of being British; the Sydney setting is described with relish, and the girls behave with a charming and very un-English abandon.

Teeny-tiny An English folk tale first collected by J. O. *Halliwell, and included by Joseph *Jacobs in *English Fairy Tales* (1890). A 'teeny-tiny woman' who 'lived in a teeny-tiny house in a teeny-tiny village' finds a bone in a churchyard, and takes it home to make soup. She puts it in a cupboard and goes to bed, whereupon a 'teeny-tiny voice' cries 'Give me my bone!', again and again, until the old woman 'said in her loudest teeny-tiny voice, "TAKE IT!"'

Tell, William See WILLIAM TELL.

temperance stories for children began to appear in Britain in the late 18th cent.; one of the earliest is Hannah *More's verse tale *The Carpenter; or, The Danger of Evil Company*, published as one of her *Cheap Repository Tracts in 1795. The inauguration of the Band of Hope in 1847 led to the production of a number of temperance periodicals for children, such as *The Band of Hope Review and Sunday Scholar's Friend* (1851 onwards), while at the same period the publishers Simpkin, Marshall & Co. were advertising 'Ipswich Juvenile Temperance Tracts, assorted packets'.

A typical story teaching children about the evils of drink was *Alice Leigh's Mission* (n.d.), published by the *Religious Tract Society; the heroine goes to a public house to fetch her father, whereupon the landlord declares that 'the sight of that child was enough to make any man sober.' In 1853 George *Cruikshank began to issue his own versions of *fairy stories with teetotal morals added, and by the 1870s warnings about the dangers of alcohol had become a commonplace of children's stories which featured scenes of urban poverty, such as George MacDonald's *At the Back of the North Wind* and Anna Sewell's *Black Beauty*. Drink is one of the vices which undoes the hero of F. W. Farrar's *Eric, or, Little by Little*, though by the end of the 19th cent. attitudes had softened sufficiently for *Kipling to make light of schoolboy drinking in *Stalky & Co.*

In the United States, the National Temperance Society produced literature similar to

that issued by the Band of Hope. Its most prolific authors included Julia P. Ballard and Mary Dwinell Chellis, whose books appeared in the late 19th cent.

TEMPLE, Shirley (1928–2014) American child film star who appeared in many film adaptations of children's classics, including *The *Little Colonel* (1935), **Heidi* (1937), **Rebecca of Sunnybrook Farm* (1938), *A Little Princess* (*see* SARA CREWE) (1939), and *The *Blue Bird* (1939).

TENNIEL, Sir John (1820–1914) British artist who first made his name as illustrator of an 1848 edition of **Aesop*. This led Mark *Lemon to invite him to join *Punch* as a replacement for Richard *Doyle. In 1864 he succeeded Leech as principal cartoonist to the magazine. Tom Taylor of *Punch* introduced him to 'Lewis *Carroll' (C. L. Dodgson) and **Alice's Adventures in Wonderland*, with his illustrations, appeared in 1865.

Despite the often fraught relationship between author and illustrator, Dodgson brought out the best in Tenniel. His illustrations for the two *Alice* books have a lightness of touch and a wit that is almost totally lacking from his *Punch* drawings.

The *Alice* drawings owe something to Thackeray's illustrations for his *The *Rose and the Ring* (1855), as well as to the work of Doyle, and it seems that Tenniel was also influenced by the work of the French artist J.-J. *Grandville, whose *Un Autre Monde* (1844) is a brilliant collection of *nonsense drawings.

Tenniel also illustrated editions of Thomas Moore's *Lalla Rookh* (1861) and R. H. Barham's *The *Ingoldsby Legends* (1864), and contributed pictures to the *Dalziels' edition of the **Arabian Nights* (1863–5), but after illustrating *Alice* he undertook almost no further book work.

Tenniel was blind in one eye, the result of an accident when, at the age of twenty, he was fencing with his father. He married in 1852, but there were no children, and his wife died two years later. He was knighted in 1893. Tenniel was extremely retiring by nature; he would not use live models or draw from nature, saying that he had 'a wonderful memory of *observation*'. The excellence of his published drawings owes much to the work of the *wood engravers who interpreted them, especially Joseph Swain, resident engraver at *Punch*, and the Dalziel brothers, who cut the blocks for *Alice*. In appearance Tenniel somewhat resembled his own drawing of the White Knight.

1066 and All That (1930) A hilarious mock-history book, subtitled *A Memorable History of England, comprising all the parts you can remember, including 103 Good Things, 5 Bad Kings and 2 Genuine Dates,* written by W. C. Sellar (1898–1951) and R. J. Yeatman (1897–1968). It was published more than eighty years ago and has been a joy to schoolchildren and adults ever since. A parody of the stolid style of history teaching at the time, it was first published as a series in *Punch* magazine, where its iconoclastic humour fitted perfectly, with its mix of half-remembered dates, skewed facts, and terrible puns. It inspired a handful of sequels and a play, and many authors have used the '...and All That' tag in their own titles.

TERHUNE, Albert Payson (1872–1942) American writer of *animal stories about collie dogs, chief among them *Lad: a Dog* (1919).

TERLOUW, Jan (1931–) Dutch author; his books include *Koning van Katoren* (1971) (*How to Become King*, 1976), a *fantasy about a teenage boy who claims a throne and is set many impossible tasks before he gains it. *Oorlogswinter* (1972) (*Winter in Wartime*, 1975) concerns a fifteen-year-old boy hiding a wounded English paratrooper under the eyes of German soldiers. Both of these have recently been made into feature films.

textbooks *See* BOOKS OF INSTRUCTION.

TEZUKA, Osamu *See* MANGA.

THACKERAY, W. M. *See* ROSE AND THE RING, THE.

theatre for children *See* PLAYS; PUPPETS.

Theatre of Education (1781) An English translation of *Le Théâtre d'éducation* (1779), a set of twenty-four *plays for children by Mme de *Genlis, giving expression in dramatic form to the ideas of *Rousseau. The plays were often performed in English girls' schools.

There are fairies at the bottom of our garden *See* FYLEMAN, ROSE.

There was a little girl | *Who had a little curl* Opening lines of a famous verse about a child who 'When she was good...was very, very good, | But when she was bad she was horrid.' The poem is usually ascribed to H. W. Longfellow (*see* HIAWATHA) but the evidence is very uncertain.

There was a little man | *And he wooed a little maid* The opening lines of a comic

*ballad first printed as a *broadside in 1764 by Horace Walpole, who credited authorship to Sir Charles Sedley or Sidley. The poem was included the next year in *The Fairing*, published by John *Newbery. It reappeared in print several times in the late 18th cent., and in 1807 an extended version was issued by *Tabart as a separate children's book, with sophisticated comic illustrations in the manner shortly afterwards to be associated with *Cruikshank. The Tabart edition was entitled *Memoirs of the Little Man and the Little Maid*.

There Was an Old Lady Who Swallowed a Fly A popular nursery rhyme with cumulative verses—the old lady swallows a fly, then swallows a spider to catch the fly, and then a bird to catch the spider to catch the fly; by the end she has swallowed seven animals, of which the largest is a horse. ('She's dead, of course.') An illustrated version by Pam Adams, with holes cut into the pages showing the growing collection of animals, was published in 1973, and probably remains the most ubiquitous edition.

Thief Lord, The (2000) A fantasy novel by Cornelia *Funke, published in 2002 in an English translation by Funke's agent, Oliver Latsch. Desperate to avoid being separated after the death of their parents, Prosper and Bo run away to Venice, the city of their imagination. It is all rather different until they meet the little band of displaced children living in the abandoned cinema under the protection of the Thief Lord. But who is he really? And what is the mystery hidden on Secret Island. Solving this will change everything. This was the first of Funke's novels to appear in English. Against the atmospheric setting of Venice, it combines the realism of an exciting adventure, a mystery to solve, and a villain to outwit with an intriguing fantasy, all hallmarks of this increasingly accomplished author.

THIELE, Colin Milton (1920–2006) Australian writer who combined writing with a long career in academia until his retirement in 1980. He was a native of South Australia, and most of his books celebrated his home state—from the Adelaide Hills, threatened by bushfire in the exciting *Jodie's Journey* (1988), to the opal fields of Coober Pedy in *The Fire in the Stone* (1973), to the Coorong River, setting of his best-known book, *Storm Boy* (1964), about a white boy, his Aboriginal friend, and the pelican they save. An environmental theme runs through much of Thiele's work

and his desire to inform children about the need to protect the natural world often led to claims of didacticism. He could also be very funny, as in *Uncle Gustav's Ghosts* (1974), set in the town of Eudunda, where he grew up, and where *Emma Keppler* (1994), a late and particularly accomplished historical novel, is also set.

13 Clocks, The (1951) Children's novel by James *Thurber. The evil Duke of Coffin Castle has slain time and is keeping his niece, Saralinda, the only warm thing in his life, a prisoner. She can only be freed by the completion of an Impossible Task. Who will succeed? It will require a prince whose name begins with X but doesn't, and the help of the one and only Golux. It is particularly notable for its complex wordplay and prose rhythms reminiscent of blank verse, with traditional motifs emphasizing the fairy-tale character of the story. Originally illustrated by Marc Simont, the illustrations for the 1961 *Puffin edition were by Ronald *Searle.

THOMAS, Isaiah (1750–1831) American printer and publisher of a large number of books for children. Born in Boston, Massachusetts, he was apprenticed to a printer of *ballads and *chapbooks at the age of six, and by his early teens he was managing a shop for his master. Later he established a celebrated newspaper, the *Massachusetts Spy*, which supported the liberties of the people. When the British occupied Boston in 1775, he escaped, and re-established his business in Worcester, Mass., where he became a leading publisher of the day, employing 150 people and running his own paper mill and bindery; he had eight branch offices in New England. His books were noted for their fine typography.

Among more than 100 titles for children were editions of *Mother Goose's Melody, The *New England Primer*, *Goody Two-Shoes, A *Little Pretty Pocket Book*, the *Divine Songs of *Watts, and *Tommy Thumb's Song Book*. His practice was to reprint English children's books with a minimum of alteration. By 1802 he had become rich enough to retire and devote himself to scholarship. He wrote *The History of Printing in America* (two volumes, 1810), which remained authoritative for a century.

Thomas, the Tank Engine (1946) One of the first, and the most famous, in the series of small *picture books by the Revd W. *Awdry. The 'Railway Series' began in 1945 with *The Three Railway Engines*; in 1947 came *James,*

the Red Engine, then *Tank Engine Thomas Again* (1948), after which fresh volumes appeared almost every year until Awdry's twenty-sixth and last, *Tramway Engines* (1972). Further books were written by Awdry's son, Christopher.

Thomas, 'a fussy little engine', lives at the Big Station and is bossed by the Fat Controller. At first he is just a shunting engine, and irritates Gordon, the Big Engine, and other dignified locomotives; but eventually he is rewarded with his own Branch Line. The books have no high literary or artistic aims, but have been immensely popular with British children. The first illustrator was C. Reginald Dalby; many of the later books have been illustrated by Gunvor and Peter Edwards. The stories take place on the non-existent Isle of Sodor, which takes its name from the fact that the real Isle of Man is under the ecclesiastical jurisdiction of the Bishop of Sodor and Man.

Thomas remains an enormously popular character, seventy years on, both for the consistently bestselling books, and for other incarnations, including a highly successful animated TV series, *Thomas & Friends* (1984–).

THOMPSON, Colin (1942–) Australian children's book author-illustrator who was born in Ealing (UK) and moved to Australia in 1995. Although he did not begin writing and illustrating until 1990, he has now published over sixty-five books and has been granted several awards as well as being nominated for the *Astrid Lindgren Memorial Award. Thompson works in a number of genres, including science fiction, but is best known for writing series children's fiction and picture books. His books always leave the reader thinking about the world they live in. *Fearless* (2009), shortlisted for the *CBCA Book of the Year Awards: Early Childhood, is a funny, yet profound, book which can be interpreted in many different ways and shows us how appearances can be deceptive. He received an Aurealis Award for his novelization of his highly original picture book *How to Live Forever* (2004) and the CBCA Picture Book of the Year for *The Short and Incredibly Happy Life of Riley* (2005), a juxtaposition of a human's life and that of a rat. Best known of his fiction series is *The Floods* (from 2005), an outrageous, funny series which shows us a scary family of wizards and witches—to date there are thirteen novels in the series, plus a picture book and a 2012 'Floodsopedia'. Thompson's work is typified by quirky humour and a fresh look at life, sometimes in a magical setting.

THOMPSON, Daniel Pierce (1795–1868) New England author of a number of *historical novels which were read by children in America, most notably *The Green Mountain Boys* (1839), which is set in Vermont during the Revolutionary War.

THOMPSON, Kate (1956–) English poet and author of children's and *young adult books who has lived in Ireland for many years, and whose stories weave together history, myth, and modern-day life. Growing up around racing stables, she worked with racehorses before spending time living in India and then Ireland, where she worked a smallholding. Joining a writers' workshop led to her first book, *Switchers* (1994), about a shapeshifter, though, as its original Irish publisher folded, it took republication in the UK in 1997 to make it a success. Thompson is a fiddle player, and her interest in Irish music and myth led to the award-winning *The New Policeman* trilogy (2005), and the eerie and compelling *Creature of the Night* (2008) cemented her place as an original and essential author for teenagers.

THOMPSON, Kay *See* ELOISE.

Thompson and Thomson In *Tintin. See* THOMSON AND THOMPSON.

THOMS, William John (1803–85) British antiquary who wrote versions of many old *chapbook stories which were published for children in the mid-19th cent. by Joseph *Cundall. Many of them appeared under the title *Gammer Gurton's Story Books. Thoms, who was clerk and deputy librarian to the House of Lords, founded the journal *Notes and Queries*, and is credited with having invented the term 'folklore', which he used in an article in the Athenaeum on 22 August, 1846.

THOMSON, D. C., & Co. of Dundee Publishers of British *comics and adventure magazines. During the 1920s and 1930s they began to produce their 'big five' adventure papers, *Adventure* (1921), *Rover* and *Wizard* (both 1922), *Skipper* (1930), and *Hotspur* (1933). All five were known as 'tuppenny bloods', and contained adventures, sporting stories, historical tales, *school stories, *science fiction, and *westerns. They were nearer to comics in style than were the equivalent papers produced by *Harmsworth (*Marvel, etc.). *Skipper* ceased publication during the Second World War and *Adventure* not very long afterwards, but the other three continued

until the end of the 1970s. Thomson's are also the publishers of *Dandy* and *Beano*, and their companion paper *Beezer*. One of their leading artists, Leo *Baxendale, gave a description of their working methods in his autobiography, *A Very Funny Business* (1978).

Benny Green, in an article on their comics and papers (*Spectator*, 26 December 1970), wrote that Thomson's 'stumbled ... on the fact that working-class children need a mythology they can understand.' Certainly in such figures as *Wilson the Wonder Athlete, Desperate Dan, Minnie the Minx, Beryl the Peril, Pansy Potter, and *Dennis the Menace, Thomson's added a whole gallery of archetypes to British juvenile reading.

Thomson and Thompson In *Tintin. See THOMPSON AND THOMSON.

THORN, Ismay (Edith Caroline Pollock) (*fl.* 1890) Prolific British author of stories about young children. Her first book was *Pinafore Days: the Adventures of Fred and Dolly by Wood and Wave* (1879), which like many others written by her was illustrated by T. *Pym. It was followed by about thirty more, with titles such as *Only Five* (1880), *Spin and Podgie* (1886), and *Happy-Go-Lucky* (1894). They are written in an arch style clearly aimed at adult readers as well as children.

Thorntons of Punchbowl Farm In stories by Monica *Edwards.

Thousand and One Nights See ARABIAN NIGHTS' ENTERTAINMENTS.

Three Bears, The A story first printed in 1837 in *The Doctor*, a miscellany by Robert *Southey. The book consists of essays, linked by the history of Dr Daniel Dove of Doncaster. The narrator introduces the tale as one that was told to the doctor by his uncle William, and says that it 'never fails of effect with that fit audience for which it is designed, if it be told with dramatic spirit'. Southey tells of a 'little old Woman' who comes across a house in a wood. Being not a 'good, honest old Woman', she goes into the house and helps herself to the porridge which is set out on the table: the big bear's is too hot, 'and she said a bad word about that', and the middle bear's is too cold, 'and she said a bad word about that, too', but the little bear's is just right and she eats it all up. Then she tests out the chairs in the house; one is too hard, one too soft, but the little bear's chair is just right, 'and there she sate till the bottom of the chair came out, and

down came hers, plump upon the ground'. Finally, she tries the beds upstairs; the little bear's bed is just right, 'so she covered herself up comfortably, and lay there till she fell fast asleep'. The bears return home and finding that someone has eaten the porridge and broken the chair, they go upstairs and each observes that 'Somebody has been lying in my bed!' To which the little bear adds: 'Somebody has been lying in my bed,—and here she is!' The old woman wakes up, tumbles out of the bed, and runs to the window, jumping out; 'and whether she broke her neck in the fall; or ran into the wood and was lost there; or found her way out of the wood, and was taken up by the constable and sent to the House of Correction for a vagrant as she was, I cannot tell. But the Three Bears never saw anything more of her.'

In the same year that Southey's 'Three Bears' appeared in print, the story was retold in verse by 'G.N.' (George Nicol), who fully acknowledged the debt to *The Doctor*; Southey was very pleased with this retelling, having wished that the story should become more widely known.

Joseph *Jacobs, in *English Fairy Tales* (1890), stated that 'the story was invented by Southey'; but his illustrator, John D. Batten, subsequently told him that he had heard a similar tale from a 'Mrs H.' who had been told it by her mother more than forty years earlier. This version, printed in Jacobs' *More English Fairy Tales* (1894), differed from Southey's chiefly in that the intruder was not an old woman but a fox. Jacobs suggested that Southey might have heard it in this form, and could have supposed that the 'vixen' really meant a harridan rather than an animal.

In fact there is a manuscript in possession of the *Osborne Collection which not only confirms that the tale is traditional but shows that it was not Southey who introduced the old woman into it. This manuscript, entitled *The Story of the Three Bears metrically related*, was written and illustrated by Eleanor Mure, aunt of a child named Horace Broke, to whom she addressed it. It was dated 1831; it set the story at Cecil Lodge, Miss Mure's father's house in Hertfordshire, and its heroine, if such she can be called, was 'an angry old woman'.

The old woman was, however, soon judged to be an unsatisfactory element in the tale. In the version printed in Joseph *Cundall's *Treasury of Pleasure Books for Young Children* (1850) the intruder is a little girl named Silver-Hair.

Though 'Silver Hair' remained the name of the girl in many texts for some time after this, *Aunt Mavor's Nursery Tales* (1858) calls her 'Silver-Locks' and *Aunt Friendly's Nursery Book* (*c.*1868) (*see* AUNT FRIENDLY) has 'Golden Hair'. The first use of the name 'Goldilocks', which is now universally attached to the story, seems to have been in *Old Nursery Stories and Rhymes*, illustrated by John Hassall (*c.*1904). The name may have been taken from Miss Annie Macdonell's translation of Mme d'*Aulnoy's *La Belle aux cheveux d'or* (1892), where it was used for the heroine.

No one, not even Southey, seems to have been quite certain how to end the tale. Some modern versions conclude with Goldilocks running off into the wood, while others finish with her coming home, telling her mother what happened, and promising to be a good girl in future. Perhaps the best ending, however, is that supplied by Eleanor Mure, whose bears are determined to punish the old woman for her impertinence:

On the fire they throw her, but burn her they couldn't,
In the water they put her, but drown there she wouldn't.
They seize her before all the wondering people
And chuck her aloft on St Paul's church-yard steeple.

And there, says Miss Mure, she remains to this day.

Three Billy-Goats Gruff A Norwegian folk tale collected by *Asbjørnsen and Moe. Three goats set off for a pasture. They have to cross a bridge, beneath which lives a *troll. Their feet go 'Trip, trap! trip, trap!' and the troll calls out: 'Who's that tripping over my bridge?' The youngest goat tells the troll not to eat him, but to wait for the next goat, who is fatter. The second goat says the same, and when the third goat crosses the bridge it announces: 'It is I! The Big Billy-Goat Gruff!' It kills the troll.

Sir George Dasent, who translated the story into English in his *Popular Tales from the Norse (1859), pointed out that the goat was sacred to the Norse god Thor and drew his chariot; Thor was a great foe of all trolls.

Three blind mice A *nursery rhyme which, though it is descended from a round recorded several times in the 17th cent., was not printed in the form known today until the mid-19th cent. The earliest recorded version, in Thomas Ravenscroft's *Deuteromelia* (1609), mentions

'the Miller and his merry olde Wife', but makes no mention of tails being cut off.

Three Heads in the Well, The A *fairy story first printed in an 18th-cent. English *chapbook. The King of Colchester's wife dies, and for a second wife he takes a rich but ugly woman who has an ill-natured daughter. The unpleasantness of these two causes the king's own daughter to leave court with only a small bag of provisions. She meets an old man, offers him food and drink, and is rewarded with good advice. Following his instructions, she passes through a magic hedge and comes to a well from which three heads arise. Each of them asks her to comb its hair, which she does, and the heads reward her with three gifts: an increase of beauty, a sweet perfume, and a promise that she will become the greatest queen that reigns. As a result of these gifts she is married to a king. When her stepmother learns of this good fortune she sends her own daughter in search of similar rewards, but the girl is rude to the old man and hits each of the three heads with the bottle that she is carrying. She is rewarded with three gifts: a leprous face, stinking breath, and a cobbler for a husband.

The chapbook in which the story first appeared, *The History of Four Kings . . . Being the Merry Tales of Tom Hodge*, was issued by a number of printers in the second half of the 18th cent. The tale, which resembles *Perrault's story *Diamonds and Toads, seems to have been traditional in England for some time before this, for a version of it appears in George Peele's play *The Old Wives Tale* (1595).

Three Little Kittens, The A *nursery rhyme beginning 'Three little kittens they lost their mittens', often attributed to the New England children's writer Eliza *Follen but in fact recorded by her as 'traditional'. In 1856 was published a *picture book based on the rhyme, the work of R. M. *Ballantyne.

Three Little Pigs, The A folk tale collected by J. O. *Halliwell in 1853 and printed in Jacobs's *English Fairy Tales (1890). Three pigs build houses; one is of straw, one of furze (or twigs), and one of bricks. A wolf comes to the straw house and asks to be let in, to which the pig replies: 'Not by the hair of my chinny chin chin.' The wolf answers: 'Then I'll huff, and I'll puff, and I'll blow the house in'—which he does, and eats up the pig. The same fate befalls the second house and its owner. But the wolf cannot blow down the brick house. He tries various methods of

getting at the third pig and eventually declares that he will go down the chimney after him. The pig lights a fire and boils a cauldron on it; the wolf falls into the cauldron and the pig cooks and eats him.

The story has some resemblance to *The Wolf and the Seven Little Kids* in *Grimm. *The History of the Celebrated Nanny Goose*, printed by S. Hood of London in 1813, appears to be the earliest recorded English variant of the tale: in it, the wisest of three goslings foils the fox by building a strong house of bricks. The same tale was retold more ornately in *The History of the Prince Renardo and the Lady Goosiana* (London, H. Fores, 1833).

In 1933 *The Three Little Pigs* was made into a highly successful 'Silly Symphony' cartoon by *Disney, featuring the song (written for the film by Frank Churchill) 'Who's Afraid of the Big Bad Wolf?' Filmgoers saw the wolf as a symbol of the Depression, and the song became something of a national rallying cry in America.

Three Midshipmen, The (1873) An *adventure story by W. H. G. *Kingston. Three schoolfellows, Jack Rogers, Alick Murray, and Terence 'Paddy' Adair decide to go to sea together. They have many adventures in different parts of the world, including China and Africa, and at the end of the book are commissioned as lieutenants. Their further experiences are recounted in *The Three Lieutenants* (1875), *The Three Commanders* (1876), and *The Three Admirals* (1878).

Three Mulla-Mulgars, The (1910) A novel for children by Walter *de la Mare. 'Mulgar' means 'monkey'; the three 'mulgars' of the title, Thumb, Thimble, and Nod, are the sons of Seelem, an old wanderer of royal blood who sets off to revisit the royal palace in the Valleys of Tishnar. He does not return home and the three decide to follow him, taking the magical Wonderstone with them. Before they reach their journey's end they encounter such strange creatures as Gunga the Fish-catcher, the flesh-eating Minimuls, and an Oomgar (man)—a sailor named Andy Battle, who teaches Nod to speak English and for a time detains him from the quest. Many details in the story were taken from 'The Strange Adventures of Andrew Battell' in *Purchas his Pilgrim* (1619) by Samuel Purchas, the 17th-cent. redactor of *Hakluyt.

The story was written for de la Mare's children, to whom it is dedicated. Though not easy to read, it is virtually unique as a children's book—a quest story with allegorical overtones. It was reissued in 1921 and 1924, and in 1936 Faber republished it as *The Three Royal Monkeys*.

Three Musketeers, The (1844) Romance, action, courage, humour, and friendship—all you could want from a story is here in Alexandre *Dumas' great classic tale. Set in 1625, the story (with hardly a pause for breath) takes an impoverished young nobleman, d'Artagnan, to Paris to join the King's musketeers—and on to an epic adventure that starts with him attempting to duel with three musketeers, Athos, Porthos, and Aramis, and ends with the four men friends for life, living by their saying 'one for all and all for one'. There are two sequels, *Twenty Years After* (1845) and *The Vicomte of Bragelonne: Ten Years Later* (1850). First published in serial form (French: *Les Trois Mousquetaires*), Dumas' story inspired countless other writers and has been adapted for plays, games, comics, musicals, TV series, and films.

Three Sillies, The A folk tale common in many countries. In an English version, collected in the 19th cent. and published by Joseph *Jacobs in *English Fairy Tales* (1890), a gentleman courting a farmer's daughter is so astonished by the silliness of his fiancée and her parents that he says he will only marry her if he can find 'three bigger sillies than you three'. Setting out on his travels, he does indeed find extreme examples of silliness, such as an old woman who is trying to make her cow climb up a ladder, so that it can eat some grass growing on her roof. Thus, he returns home and marries the girl, 'and if they didn't live happy for ever after, that's nothing to do with you or me'. *The Three Sillies* is sometimes printed as a separate children's book.

Three Wise Men of Gotham *See* GOTHAM.

Three Wishes, The A *fairy story first printed in English in 1757, in *The Young Misses Magazine* by Madame de *Beaumont.

A man and his wife are granted three wishes by a fairy, but they waste them on absentminded wishing for, amongst other things, some black pudding. After realizing their stupidity, the couple console themselves by saying: 'Let us wish for nothing, and take things as it please God to send them; in the mean time, let us sup upon our pudding, since that's all that remains to us of our wishes.'

The story had been in circulation for many hundreds of years by the time that Madame de

Beaumont wrote it down in this form. There is a version in the *Book of Sindibad*, which probably originated in Persia during the 9th cent. AD, but the version of the story closest to Madame de Beaumont's is *Perrault's *Les Souhaits ridicules* ('The Ridiculous Wishes'), a poem published in 1693, which differs from her narrative chiefly in that the granter of the wishes is Jupiter, who descends from the sky in response to the husband's complaint that the gods never listen to his requests.

Catherine Anne Dorset published a version entitled *Think Before You Speak* in 1809 and W. W. Jacobs (1863–1943), in *The Monkey's Paw*, rewrote the story in macabre fashion. The *Opies have recorded an alternative ending, remembered from their own schooldays, in which the final wish is that all the wishes ever wished should come true.

Through the Looking-Glass and *What Alice Found There* By Lewis *Carroll (C. L. Dodgson), published in 1871 (dated 1872). A sequel to *Alice's Adventures in Wonderland* (1865), it equals its predecessor in the brilliance of its *nonsense, and features many characters who quickly became immortals of children's literature, among them the Red Queen, the White Queen, *Tweedledum and Tweedledee, *Humpty Dumpty, and the White Knight.

Dodgson began to consider writing a sequel to the first *Alice* book about eighteen months after its publication, but he did not manage to finish the text until early in 1871.

The notion of basing the story on a chess game grew out of impromptu tales about chessmen, told to Alice Liddell and her sisters in the days when (in her own words) 'we were excitedly learning chess'. The device of going through the looking-glass, upon which many of the story's nonsensical inventions and jokes are based, is supposed to have been suggested to Dodgson by a remark made to him by a young cousin, Alice Raikes, probably in 1868. Standing her in front of a mirror, and giving her an orange, he asked her 'which hand the little girl you see there has got it in'. She remarked that, though *her* orange was in the right hand, that of the mirror-girl was held in the left. He pressed her for an explanation, and she answered: 'If I was on the *other* side of the glass, wouldn't the orange still be in my right hand?'

As with the previous book, Dodgson made frequent criticisms of Tenniel's drawings while the artist was at work; Tenniel for his part

suggested that Dodgson omit an entire episode from the story. This was an encounter with an elderly, bad-tempered wasp in a yellow wig. 'A wasp in a *wig*', wrote Tenniel, 'is altogether beyond the appliances of art.' Dodgson duly omitted this passage, but the galley proofs survived, and the text was eventually published in 1977 as *The Wasp in a Wig*.

Sentimentality plays a larger part in *Through the Looking Glass* than in *Alice's Adventures in Wonderland*, for example, in Alice's encounter with the Fawn in the wood where things have no name and in the description of her picking scented rushes while in the Sheep's boat. Her farewell to the White Knight, often thought to represent Dodgson's sundering from the child Alice, also has emotional overtones.

On the other hand the nonsense in the book is even more ruthless than in the first *Alice* story. Dodgson exploits all the possibilities of looking-glass reversal; *Jabberwocky* (a poem that was in existence before the book was written) introduces a note of real horror; and there is a frequent threat of death or dissolution. The oysters in *The *Walrus and The Carpenter* are gobbled up despite (or perhaps because of) their childlike innocence; Alice cuts a slice of pudding (at the banquet in her honour) even though it can speak and she has been introduced to it; and she herself is under threat of extinction if the Red King's dream, of which she is allegedly a part, should end with his waking up.

The book was first published by Macmillan in an edition of 9,000 copies in December 1871, with the date 1872 on the title page, and 15,000 copies were sold in two months. The first American edition was issued by Lee and Sheppard of Boston and New York in 1872. A second British edition, commencing with the 45th thousand, was issued in 1878. As the book's copyright did not expire until 1948, fewer publishers issued their own editions of *Through the Looking-Glass* than of *Alice's Adventures in Wonderland* during the first half of the 20th cent. and few artists apart from Tenniel have drawn pictures for it. Incidents from it often appear in dramatizations of the first *Alice* book.

Thumb, Tom See Tom Thumb.

Thumbelina A *fairy story by Hans Christian *Andersen, published in 1836 and first translated into English ten years later. A woman desires to have a child; she consults a *witch and is given a grain of barley which opens to reveal a flower, in which sits a tiny

girl. The woman in the Danish original names her 'Tommelise', which is usually translated as 'Thumbelina'. The story narrates Thumbelina's adventures as she is carried off first by a toad, and then by an insect. She takes refuge with a field mouse, who cajoles her into agreeing to marry a mole, but before the wedding Thumbelina is rescued by a swallow whose life she has saved. She is taken to a warm southern land, where she becomes the bride of a tiny man, the king of the flower-angels. Though the story was Andersen's own composition, it has obvious resemblances to *Tom Thumb, which has analogues all over Europe.

Thunder and Lightnings (1976) A novel by Jan *Mark. Andrew's family move to Norfolk, near RAF Coltishall, just when the Royal Air Force is phasing out its Lightning fighter planes and bringing in Jaguars. He makes friends with another boy interested in aeroplanes, and the story is their friendship. Simply told, this is a realistic look at moving house, making friends, and growing up. Mark lived near the same air-base, and the vivid descriptions of planes in flight were drawn from her everyday experiences. This was her first novel.

THURBER, James (Grover) (1894–1961) Celebrated American humorist who wrote five children's books, of which four are modern *fairy stories: *Many Moons* (1943), *The Great Quillow* (1944), *The White Deer* (1945), *The *13 Clocks* (1950). A fifth, *The Wonderful O* (1955), is about a gang of *pirates who set about removing the letter O from all words that contain it. Failing eyesight forced Thurber to stop drawing in 1951, so this last book was illustrated by his friend Marc Simont.

Thursday's Child (2000) A novel for older readers by Sonya *Hartnett, shortlisted in 2001 for the *CBCA Book of the Year Award: Older Readers award. Harper Flute's family struggle to survive in drought-ridden Depression Australia. Court Flute served in the trenches in the Second World War and now lives on a soldier settlement, but lacks farming skills. The family struggles with the father's alcoholism and poverty, and eventually Tin—Harper's Thursday-born little brother—begins to escape to a life of living and tunnelling underground. It seems inevitable that Tin should undermine the shanty and it subsides. The family are left without a home, and their situation worsens until neighbours rally round to rebuild. Audrey is forced to work for a local farmer,

and she is abused. Tin watches over his family and avenges her. The dark, almost gothic, themes are lightened by magical realism and carried by beautiful prose, vivid imagery, strong characters, a powerful narrative voice, and convincing dialogue and setting.

THWAITE, Ann (1932–) British author and biographer who edited the children's *annual *Allsorts* (1968–75) and has written a number of children's stories. She has also written acclaimed biographies of Frances Hodgson *Burnett (1974) and A. A. *Milne (1990) and the scrapbook-like *Brilliant Career of Winnie-the-Pooh* (1992).

Tiger Tim The longest-lived hero of British *comics first appeared in 1904 in the *Daily Mirror* and then in other publications, including the monthly reissue of the *Children's Encyclopaedia* (1910 onwards), before settling in *Rainbow* (1914–56). He later featured in the nursery comic *Jack and Jill* and in various *annuals. Tiger Tim is the ringleader of a group of naughty animals, the Bruin Boys, who in *Rainbow* were pupils at Mrs Bruin's Boarding School.

Tiger Who Came to Tea, The (1968) A classic picture book by Judith *Kerr. The story is simple and pleasingly surreal (a tiger shows up and eats all the food in the house, and drinks 'all the water in the tap', and then leaves, so the family have to go off to a cafe for their dinner), and Kerr's words and pictures manage a perfect balance between the oddity of the events and the unphased way this normal family accepts the slight inconvenience of a tiger coming to tea. The book has been read as an allegory for many things, including visits by the Gestapo, rationing, etc., none of them ever confirmed by the author. Kerr herself has since commented that she can't in fact draw tigers. ('It's not really a tiger at all. Quentin Blake would have made it much funnier and Michael Foreman would have drawn it better.') The book was successfully adapted for the stage by David *Wood (2008).

Tigger In *The *House at Pooh Corner* by A. A. *Milne.

Tim In stories by Edward *Ardizzone; *see* LITTLE TIM.

time-slip story A book that moves between settings in the present and past, often featuring one or more main characters actually travelling between these time periods, though not

necessarily by design. (Stories featuring the more general 'time travel' include those where the travel is deliberate—the building of time machines, and so on.) Both time periods are often kept running as parallel strands throughout the book. The device is common in children's fiction as a way of placing a modern (and easily relatable) character in a setting more typical of *historical fiction.

Early examples of the time-slip story include Kipling's *Puck of Pook's Hill* and E. *Nesbit's *Story of the Amulet* (both of which appeared in 1906). The form was taken up with particular success by Alison Uttley (*A *Traveller in Time*), Lucy Boston (the *Green Knowe* series), Philippa Pearce (*Tom's Midnight Garden*), Penelope *Lively (*A Stitch in Time* and others), Joan G. *Robinson (*When Marnie Was There*) and Penelope Farmer (*Charlotte Sometimes*). More recent time-slips that have been popular with children and teenagers include (though in some cases disputably, as the boundaries of the category can be blurry): The *Sterkarm Handshake*, *Playing Beattie Bow*, Helen *Cresswell's *Moondial*, Robert *Westall's *The Devil in the Road*, Melvin *Burgess's *An Angel for May*, Terry *Pratchett's *Johnny and the Bomb*, Susan Cooper's *King of Shadows*, the *Stravaganza* series by Mary *Hoffman, and Marcus *Sedgwick's *Midwinterblood*.

Tinder Box, The A *fairy story by Hans Christian *Andersen. A soldier is persuaded by a *witch to climb down a hollow tree into a series of underground halls where there are three sets of treasure, each guarded by a dog with huge eyes. While there he fills his pockets with money and also fetches an old tinderbox that the witch desires him to bring her. When she will not tell him why she wants it, he cuts off her head and keeps the tinderbox for himself. For a time he lives like a lord, but soon spends all the money he has gathered. He strikes a light with the tinderbox, wanting to have a smoke, and is astonished when one of the dogs appears. At the soldier's request it fetches him more wealth from the underground caverns. Next he orders another of the dogs to fetch to his room the Princess from a neighbouring palace, who is kept from common sight. The same thing happens on subsequent nights, and eventually the soldier is identified as her abductor and put in prison. He is about to be hanged when he strikes a light with the tinderbox for a last smoke and summons the dogs, who quickly despatch the king and his councillors.

The soldier becomes king and marries the princess.

The story, which appeared in Andersen's first collection of fairy tales (1836) and was translated into English in 1846, is based on a Scandinavian folk tale in which the magic instrument is a candle and the supernatural servant an iron man. There is also a resemblance to *The Blue Light* in *Grimms' tales and to *Aladdin*, which Andersen knew from childhood readings of the *Arabian Nights*. The story was one of the inspirations for Sally *Gardner's novel, *Tinder* (2013).

Ting-a-Ling (1870) A volume of stories by Frank R. *Stockton.

Tinker Bell Fairy in *Peter Pan* by J. M. *Barrie.

Tintin The hero of a series of *comic strips, first printed in the Belgian newspaper *Le Vingtième Siècle* in 1929 and from 1930 reissued in book form, beginning with *Tintin au pays des Soviets*. He is the creation of the Belgian author-artist 'Hergé' (Georges Remi, 1907–83), whose pseudonym was derived from reversing his initials, 'R.G.' The Tintin books began to appear in England in 1958 (in translations by Leslie Lonsdale-Cooper and Michael Turner) and have also been published in America and around the world in more than seventy languages to date. In Germany, the hero is renamed 'Tim'

Tintin, who has been described as 'a Belgian boy scout', is a teenage reporter-cum-amateur-*detective who gets embroiled in every kind of thriller-adventure, along with his dog Snowy ('Milou' in the original French), the confusingly (but coincidentally) named plain-clothes and dim-witted policemen Thomson and Thompson (originally 'Dupont et Dupond'), the stormy Captain Haddock ('Thundering typhoons! Billions of blistering barnacles!'), and the deaf and absent-minded Professor Cuthbert Calculus. The stories are notable for their absurd characters, grotesquely farcical humour, and unusual freshness of plot and dialogue. Tintin, has, at various times, visited the moon, gone in search of *pirate treasure, crossed the desert, and in *King Ottakar's Sceptre* (originally published in 1939), become involved in a political imbroglio which bears a resemblance to European events during the 1930s. Tintin stories have been adapted for a number of film cartoons and live-action feature films, most recently the computer-animated *Adventures of Tintin: The Secret of the Unicorn* (2011), the

first in a planned trilogy from Steven Spielberg and Peter Jackson.

Tir na n-Og Awards Given annually since 1976 by the Welsh Book Council to children's books in both Welsh- and English-language categories (the latter limited to books with an authentic Welsh background). Winners of the English-language category have included Catherine *Fisher, Susan *Cooper, Daniel Morden, (1964–) Kevin *Crossley-Holland, and Jackie *Morris; Welsh-language winners include Gareth F. Williams (1955–2016; he won on a record five occasions) and T. Llew *Jones. The awards take their name from Tír na nÓg, the 'Land of Youth' in Irish folklore.

Tituba of Salem Village (1964) A novel by Ann *Petry.

TITUS, Eve *See* ANATOLE.

Toad In *The *Wind in the Willows* by Kenneth *Grahame.

Toad of Toad Hall *See* WIND IN THE WILLOWS, THE.

Toby Tyler, *or Ten Weeks with a Circus* (1881) Novel by the American author James *Otis. Toby Tyler, a waif who lives with 'Uncle Dan'l' in the little town of Guilford, runs away with a circus. He is treated roughly by the man who employs him, among other things being beaten with an India-rubber cane, but finds solace in his friendship with a monkey named Mr Stubbs. He is also treated kindly by two circus inmates, the Living Skeleton and his wife the Fat Woman. Toby eventually appears in a circus act himself, as an acrobatic rider under the name 'Monsieur Ajax'. He and Mr Stubbs escape from the circus and become lost; Mr Stubbs is accidentally shot dead by a hunter and Toby returns home, where he is granted Uncle Dan'l's forgiveness.

The book was a favourite for many generations. Maurice *Sendak was devoted to it in childhood.

TODD, Barbara Euphan (1890–1976) Creator of *Worzel Gummidge, born in Yorkshire; she became a regular contributor of verses to *Punch* during the 1920s, using the pseudonym 'Euphan'. She wrote a number of other children's books besides her Gummidge stories.

TODD, H. E. (Herbert Eatton) (1908–88) Creator of *Bobby Brewster. He was born in London and educated at Christ's Hospital before beginning a long career as a businessman.

His first Brewster book was *Bobby Brewster and the Winkers' Club* (1949).

toe-rhymes *See* INFANT AMUSEMENTS.

toilet books A type of book with *movable flaps, devised in the 1820s and published in London. The first, *The Toilet* (1821), consisted of a series of hand-coloured engravings of toilet articles from a lady's dressing-table; when the flaps were raised the names of the appropriate virtues were disclosed. For example, rouge revealed 'modesty', eye water 'benevolence', and white paint 'innocence'. The pictures were by the miniaturist William Grimaldi and the captions, with accompanying moralizing verses, by his son Stacey. *The Toilet* was so successful that the Grimaldis followed it with a similar book for boys, *A Suit of Armour for Youth* (1824), and it was imitated by other artists and publishers. One version, *My Lady's Casket*, was printed in Boston, Mass., as late as 1885.

Token for Children, A, *being an Exact Account of the Conversion, Holy and Exemplary Lives, and Joyful Deaths of several young Children* (probably 1672) By James *Janeway; one of the two most popular *Puritan books for children, only less widely circulated than *The Pilgrim's Progress*. It opens with a letter to parents and anyone having a hand in the education of children, entreating them to use their 'utmost endeavour to deliver them from the wrath to come', though 'a corrupt nature is a knotty thing to hew.' The preface for children is specific about the behaviour that leads to hell: wasting time in play and idleness, swearing, lying, disobeying parents, profaning the sabbath day by 'running up and down', and not reading and learning. Then follow the accounts of godly children, most dying young but joyful, 'several passages taken *verbatim* from their dying lips'.

Janeway's preface recommends his readers to get their fathers to buy them Thomas White's *Little Book for Little Children* (1660), a work which probably provided Janeway with the model for his own book. *A Token for Children* is recorded by the Stationers' Company as being published in October 1671, but the earliest surviving copy is an edition of 1672 which would seem to be the first.

The book had a huge success in England and America and remained in use for more than 200 years. The original Janeway text describes thirteen joyful deaths; in 1799 James Mathews of London published an edition in

which he enlarged it with the addition of fifteen further death-bed scenes, including that of his own ten-year-old daughter who had died in 1790. In 1828 there appeared a new version by Lucy *Cameron which contained thirty-six deaths. The *Token* was still being used in 1875 when the *Religious Tract Society printed an edition. It was imitated in a number of 18th- and 19th-cent. books for children, such as *Early Piety* by George Burder.

To Kill a Mockingbird (1960) By Harper Lee (1926–2016), this is a Pulitzer Prize-winning Southern Gothic novel set in the Great Depression. Narrator Scout Finch, her older brother Jem, and their friend Dill try to catch a glimpse of their reclusive neighbour, Boo Radley, while Scout and Jem's lawyer father, Atticus, defends an African-American man falsely accused of raping a white woman. *Mockingbird*, Lee's only novel, is rooted in characters and incidents from her childhood; the character of Dill is based on Lee's childhood friend, the writer Truman Capote. The novel was made into an Oscar-winning film. Shortly before Lee's death, an early draft of Mockingbird was 'discovered' and controversially published, as *Go Set a Watchman* (2015).

TOLKIEN, J. R. R. (John Ronald Reuel) (1892–1973) Author of *the *Hobbit* and *The *Lord of the Rings*. He was descended from two English midland families (the Tolkiens had a German surname, but arrived in England many generations before his birth), though he was born in Bloemfontein, South Africa, where his father was working as a bank manager. At the age of three he was brought back to England by his mother for the sake of his own and his younger brother's health, and while they were away from Bloemfontein the father, who had remained there, died of rheumatic fever. Tolkien's mother was left poorly off, but she managed to make an attractive home for the boys at Sarehole Mill, a rural hamlet then on the southern edge of Birmingham. Tolkien's childhood there, until the age of eight, left him with a love of the English countryside which permeates his writings. His mother, who gave him his early education, introduced him to the *Fairy Books* of Andrew *Lang which were then appearing at the rate of one a year. In the *Red Fairy Book* (1890) he read an abridgement of the *Volsungasaga* and fell under the spell of *dragons. He also enjoyed the 'Curdie' stories of George *Mac-Donald, but had certain marked dislikes, which included *Treasure Island, the stories

of Hans Christian *Andersen, and The *Pied Piper.

In 1900 the Tolkiens left Sarehole and moved into Birmingham so that the boys could go to school. In this year Tolkien's mother became a Roman Catholic and when she died of diabetes four years later it was to a Catholic priest at Birmingham Oratory that she bequeathed the guardianship of her boys. This guardian, Father Francis Morgan, was responsible for separating Tolkien from Edith Bratt, the girl with whom he fell in love during his teens—with the result that the two became engaged to be married as soon as Tolkien was twenty-one—but Tolkien remained deeply grateful to Father Morgan for his affection and for an upbringing in the Catholic faith. Religion, in fact, became one of the dominating forces in Tolkien's imagination as well as in his daily life.

At school and as an undergraduate at Exeter College, Oxford, where he began to read Classics but changed to English Language and Literature, Tolkien saw himself largely as a poet in the making and produced much verse (most of which remained unpublished) that was influenced by the 'fairy' fashion of the Edwardian period, a fashion that manifested itself most strikingly in *Peter Pan* and the drawings of Arthur *Rackham. A stronger and much less conventional streak in his imagination was the desire to make up languages, a desire that had begun in childhood and which was fuelled by his study from schooldays of such historical languages as Anglo-Saxon, Old Norse, and Gothic. By the time he graduated from Oxford with a First Class in 1915, he was not only an extraordinarily promising philologist but also the possessor of at least two complete languages of his own, supposedly spoken by *elves. Meanwhile his fairy poetry gradually transmuted itself into the writing, at first in verse but then in prose, of a mythological epic about the Elves of 'Middle-Earth' (supposedly the planet Earth at an earlier age), which provided what he called 'a history and a habitation' for his invented languages.

This process was disrupted by the First World War, in which Tolkien served as a signalling officer in the Lancashire Fusiliers, but the experience of the trenches of Flanders, rather than making Tolkien turn his attention to 'real life', drove him even further into his imaginative creation; and it was apparently the death of two school friends during the Battle of the Somme that directly inspired him to begin work in earnest on *The Silmarillion*, as he eventually came to call his epic.

Most of it was written in first draft by 1925 when, after working at the University of Leeds, he returned to Oxford as its Professor of Anglo-Saxon (at the age of thirty-three he was one of Oxford's youngest ever appointees to a professorial chair). But he made no attempt to publish it and instead turned his attention largely to the telling and writing of bedtime stories for his children, of whom by 1929 there were four. Several children's stories were completed by him during this period; they include *Mr Bliss*, a comic *picture book about an eccentric car-driver (Tolkien himself had unconventional habits when at the wheel), which was eventually published in 1982. At the same time he also wrote an illustrated letter each Christmas to his children, supposedly from *Father Christmas; these *Father Christmas Letters* became another posthumous publication, in 1976. But the outstanding product of Tolkien's pen during this period was *The Hobbit*, begun around 1930 but not completed and published until 1937.

Its British publishers Allen and Unwin pressed him for a sequel, and with some reluctance he began the book which eventually became *The Lord of the Rings*. The process of composition was long and difficult and was only sustained because of the encouragement of C. S. *Lewis, one of Tolkien's colleagues in the English Faculty at Oxford and a close friend; Tolkien read chapters from the new book to Lewis and to the weekly gathering of Lewis's friends known as 'The Inklings'. Even with this support, Tolkien frequently abandoned work on the book or turned aside to write such other stories as 'Leaf By Niggle', a short allegory about his despair at failing to finish the larger work (first published in the *Dublin Review* in 1945), and *Farmer Giles of Ham*, a burlesque for children which, like *The Hobbit*, is largely concerned to show the absurdity of conventional heroism. *Farmer Giles* was published in 1949, with superb illustrations by Pauline *Baynes, but (rather oddly, in view of Tolkien's later fame) it has never received the attention it deserves as a piece of comic writing. (Pauline Baynes also illustrated Tolkien's 1962 collection of verse, *The Adventures of Tom Bombadil*.)

The Lord of the Rings was eventually finished in 1949, but for a number of reasons was not published until 1954–5, by which time Tolkien had passed his sixtieth birthday. He retired from university teaching four years later, intending to devote himself to the completion of *The Silmarillion*, which he now

wished to publish; but once again the work proceeded only by fits and starts. Once more he turned aside to write an allegory about his own plight, *Smith of Wootton Major* (1967), originally an attempt to provide an introduction to George MacDonald's *The *Golden Key* for an American publisher (the task was eventually taken over by W. H. Auden), but which quickly became a children's story in its own right, an eloquent statement about old age and the necessity of bidding farewell to the lands of the imagination. When Tolkien died in 1973 the task of finishing *The Silmarillion* was taken over by his third son, Christopher, and the book was eventually published in 1977.

The spectacular popularity of *The Lord of the Rings*, which began in the mid-1960s and kept it on the best-seller lists in Britain, America, and many other countries, has somewhat overshadowed Tolkien's achievement as a writer for children, especially in *The Hobbit*. Historians of children's literature, however, agree in placing that book among the very highest achievements of children's authors during the 20th cent. Tolkien himself came to believe that no author could write especially 'for' children—the first edition of *The Hobbit* contains a number of patronizing 'asides' to the child-audience, but many of these were removed later, when its author's views on the subject changed—and he argued in a 1939 lecture *On Fairy-Stories* that the fairy tale has a real and explicable appeal to the imaginations of readers of all ages, if they are prepared to surrender themselves to it and to enter willingly the 'secondary world' that it creates. The popularity of *The Lord of the Rings* with millions of adult readers is proof that he was right.

His life is recorded in a biography by Humphrey *Carpenter (1977), while T. A. Shippey's *The Road to Middle-Earth* (1982) is an authoritative account of the relationship between his scholarly work and his imaginative writings. Christopher Tolkien has published further volumes of the 'history' of Middle-Earth, edited from his father's papers.

TOLSTOY, Count **Leo (Lev) (Nikolaye-vich)** (1828–1910) Russian novelist who tried at several stages of his life to establish an experimental school for children of serfs on his country estate. He wrote a series of graded readers for use in such schools, and these include some very simple stories for children which were afterwards collected and reprinted. A longer story, *How Varinka Grew Up*

in a Single Night, written for Tolstoy's nephews and nieces, has been made into a *picture book in English (Canada, 1966; illustrations by Hilary Abrahams).

Tom In *The *Water Babies* by Charles *Kingsley.

Tom and Jerry A perpetually battling cat and mouse, the creation of William Hannah and Joseph Barbera. They first appeared in the 1939 cartoon *Puss Gets the Boot*, and subsequently featured in over 100 films released by Metro-Goldwyn-Mayer, as well as in *comic books.

Though humorous, the *Tom and Jerry* cartoons are invariably violent. The names Tom and Jerry are traditionally associated with roistering young men-about-town, apparently from Pierce Egan's *Life in London; or, The Day and Night Scenes of Jerry Hawthorn, Esq., and his Elegant Friend Corinthian Tom* (1821).

Tom Brown's Schooldays, *by an Old Boy* A novel by Thomas *Hughes, first published in 1857.

The story is set in the 1830s and begins with a description of Tom's childhood (he is the son of a country squire) in the Vale of the White Horse. After a brief period at a small private school, Tom is sent by his father to Rugby during the early period of the headmastership of Dr Thomas *Arnold, 'the Doctor'. Tom quickly makes friends with another Rugby boy, Harry ('Scud') East, and distinguishes himself in one of the huge and impromptu games of Rugby Football.

A few days after arriving at Rugby, Tom hears his first sermon from Dr Arnold in the chapel. The author writes of this experience:

What was it, after all, which seized and held these three hundred boys, dragging them out of themselves, willing or unwilling, for twenty minutes, on Sunday afternoons?... We couldn't enter into half that we heard; we hadn't the knowledge of our own hearts or the knowledge of one another, and little enough of the faith, hope, and love needed to that end. But we listened, as all boys in their better moods will listen (ay, and men too for the matter of that), to a man whom we felt to be, with all his heart and soul and strength, striving against whatever was mean and unmanly and unrighteous in our little world.

In the early part of their schooldays together, Tom and East are certainly not notable for righteousness; the author calls them 'fair specimens... [of] the most mischievous and reckless age of British youth'. When 'old Brooke'

leaves School House and his influence for the good has been removed, a bully named Harry Flashman takes advantage of the situation to tyrannize the younger boys. East and Tom, who has already been half roasted in front of the fire by Flashman, resist the bully and eventually come to blows with him—with the result that Flashman 'never laid a finger on either of them again'; indeed he is soon expelled for drunkenness. (In 1969 the author George MacDonald Fraser continued the account of Flashman's career in *Flashman*, the first of a series of picaresque novels for adults, featuring the bully as hero.)

East and Tom are soon marked out by Dr Arnold for constantly getting into minor trouble. In order to aid Tom's moral and religious development Arnold secretly engineers that he should share a study with a new pupil, George Arthur, who is effete, intellectual, and highly religious. The strategy works and during the following years Tom still gets into scrapes, but Arthur's influence over him is strong. When Arthur falls dangerously ill with fever, Tom acknowledges that he 'owes everything to him'; and after Arthur's recovery his example leads even the apparently irreligious East to ask to be prepared for Confirmation and Communion. Tom only discovers as he leaves Rugby that Dr Arnold has instigated his relationship with Arthur, which prompts him to praise the headmaster for the care he took over the moral as well as pedagogic education of himself and countless others.

The final chapter takes place in the year 1842, when Tom suddenly learns of Arnold's death and decides to travel at once to Rugby and stand at his grave. In the last paragraph Hughes declares that Tom's hero-worship of his old headmaster was a stage on the way to 'the worship of Him who is the King and Lord of heroes'.

Hughes began the book—his first piece of fiction, and indeed of any kind of serious writing—in the summer of 1856, intending it for his eight-year-old son: 'Thinking over what I should like to say to him before he went to school, I took to writing a story, as the easiest way of bringing out what I wanted.' A few weeks later he showed the manuscript to his friend J. M. Ludlow, who thought it 'a work of absorbing interest' and encouraged Hughes to send it to the publisher Alexander Macmillan, who was active in the Christian Socialist movement, of which Hughes and Ludlow were both members. Macmillan greatly liked the book and quickly got on with having proofs

prepared, even before Hughes had finished writing it. Then in December 1856 Hughes's eldest daughter Evie died of scarlet fever and his wife nearly perished of the same infection. Hughes could not bring himself to finish the book for some months, and when he did he produced concluding chapters whose seriousness of tone and subject-matter (Arthur's illness) reflected his own recent experiences, though they were also the natural development of the story.

Charles *Kingsley, who was also closely involved with the Christian Socialists, saw the finished book in mid-February 1857, and declared: 'It will be a very great hit.' This was an accurate forecast; when *Tom Brown's Schooldays* was published by Macmillan on 24 April it was an instant success with both critics and public; a reprint had been put in hand even before publication day and by November a fifth edition had appeared. The first illustrated edition, with pictures by Arthur *Hughes (no relation to Thomas Hughes) and S. P. Hall, appeared in 1869. The first American edition was issued in 1857 by Ticknor and Fields under two different titles: *Schooldays at Rugby* and *Tom Brown's Schooldays at Rugby*. By 1890 the book had gone through nearly fifty editions or reprints in England alone, and it is still finding new readers today.

It has been widely assumed that Tom Brown is a self-portrait of the author, but, though Tom's character certainly resembles that of Hughes in schooldays, Hughes did not intend to portray himself in the hero but simply to draw a picture of the typical English schoolboy. He did on the other hand base the characters of 'old Brooke' and 'young Brooke' on his elder brother George and himself. The name 'Tom Brown' was, said Hughes, simply meant to indicate 'everyman', though it is possible that the choice was also influenced by a memory of a story by Dorothy *Kilner, entitled *First Going to School; or the story of Tom Brown and his Sisters* (1804).

The book's achievement was to portray English public school life realistically, with all its unpleasantness, and at the same time to drive the narrative along with moral fervour and Christian idealism. Hughes excelled particularly in the description of 'set pieces', such as Tom's coach ride to school in the early morning, his first football game, and Arnold preaching in the chapel. It should be appreciated, on the other hand, that the book is far from being a complete portrait of Arnold, to whom Hughes was never close; Arnold did not subscribe to the 'Muscular Christianity' of the Christian Socialists, which finds its most vivid expression in this novel, notably in the passage in which Hughes defends fist fighting, which begins, 'As to fighting, keep out of it if you can, by all means,' but ends 'if you do fight, fight it out; and don't give in while you can stand and see'. Hughes made no apologies for the didactic tone which has often been criticized in the novel, stating in a preface to the sixth edition, 'My whole object in writing at all was to get the chance of preaching!'

Tom Cringle's Log *See* SCOTT, MICHAEL.

Tom Hickathrift Legendary English folk hero. Supposed to have been born in the Isle of Ely in the time of William the Conqueror, he was brought up by his poor widowed mother, reached some six foot in height by the time he was ten, and then began to show phenomenal strength. He performed many herculean exploits, such as carrying home a tree singlehanded and throwing a hammer, wrestling, and labouring more successfully than any of his fellows. He vanquished a *giant and became a rich man, dignified by the title *Mr* Hickathrift. Together with a brave tinker, the only man his equal in fighting, he put down a local rebellion and was knighted by the grateful king. He married, dealing bloody but just retribution to his rival, then dispatched another giant, a *dragon, and several bears and lions, before settling down to enjoy his bettered status.

The History of Thomas Hickathrift was a popular *chapbook title: the first surviving copy dates from the late 17th cent. The tale was among the 'fireside stories' published by J. O. *Halliwell in *Popular Rhymes and Nursery Tales* (1849), and it appears in Joseph *Jacobs's *More English Fairy Tales* (1894).

Tom Kitten In *The Tale of Tom Kitten* and *The Tale of Samuel Whiskers* by Beatrix *Potter.

TOMLINSON, Jill *See* OWL WHO WAS AFRAID OF THE DARK, THE.

Tom Merry A schoolboy hero, created by 'Martin Clifford' (Charles *Hamilton). He first appeared in the *Gem* in March 1907, in the story 'Tom Merry's Schooldays'. In this he is an orphan in the charge of Miss Priscilla Fawcett, his nurse and guardian, who dresses him in a *Little Lord Fauntleroy suit. But he is 'Merry by name and Merry by Nature . . . his high spirits could not be damped for long.' He

is sent to Clavering College, but this is soon closed (a seam of coal is found beneath it) and Tom and his schoolmates are sent to *St Jim's—a school imported from the magazine *Pluck*. Here he is one of the Terrible Three of the Shell. New Tom Merry stories by Hamilton and substitute writers continued to appear in the *Gem* every week until 1931, when a series of reprints began. Tom Merry stories were also published in book form after the Second World War.

Tommy Tagg *See* COLLECTION OF PRETTY POEMS FOR THE AMUSEMENT OF CHILDREN THREE FEET HIGH, A.

Tommy Thumb's Pretty Song Book, Voll. [*sic*] **II** A successor to *Tommy Thumb's Song Book*, published by Mary *Cooper of London in 1744 only a few weeks after the first volume. The only surviving copy is in the British Library. It is a *miniature book (7.5 × 4 cm) with its pages printed alternately in red and black. It contains forty rhymes. These include 'Bah, bah, a [*sic*] black sheep', 'Who did kill Cock Robin?', and an unbowdlerized version of 'Little Robin Redbreast': 'Little Robin red breast'.

Brian *Alderson has pointed out that the book, the earliest surviving copy of an English *nursery rhyme collection, was apparently printed entirely from *copperplates, with the lettering stamped on the same plates as the illustrations.

Tommy Thumb's Song Book *for all little Masters and Misses; to be sung to them by their Nurses 'till they can sing themselves. By Nurse Lovechild. To which is added, a Letter from a Lady on Nursing* The earliest known collection of British *nursery rhymes, apparently published by Mary *Cooper of London in 1744. The book was advertised in the *London Evening Post* for 17–22 March of that year, but no copy has survived. However a book of precisely the same title was published in 1788 by Isaiah *Thomas of Worcester, Massachusetts. As it was Thomas's practice to reprint English books much as he found them, this volume is very likely to be identical in contents with the original edition. There is also in existence an abridged edition, under the same title, published by J. *Lumsden of Glasgow in 1815.

The 'Letter on Nursing' with which the small volume begins commends Nurse Lovechild's 'laudable Design, of compiling a Collection of Songs, so fit for the Capacities of Infants, both in Words and Tunes, by which

they are often lull'd to Rest, when cross, and in great Pain'. The letter also asks the nurse not to frighten the child by singing too loud, nor by mentioning the names of various nursery *bogies; nor is the nurse to risk injuring the child by swinging it by the arms.

The book proper begins with pictures of animals accompanied by representations of the sounds they make; the reader is asked to show the child the pictures and make the sounds, 'by which Means the Child in a short Time, will be able to do the same itself'. Then comes the face-rhyme 'Brow Bender | Eye peeper', etc., followed by a number of nursery rhymes (thirty-three in the Thomas edition), each illustrated with a *woodcut. These include 'Lulliby [*sic*] Baby Bunting', 'Hush a by [*sic*] baby', 'Patty cake, patty cake', 'Oranges and lemons', 'London bridge | Is broken down', and others. A few weeks after the book was published, Mrs Cooper issued a second volume of rhymes, *Tommy Thumb's Pretty Song Book, Voll.* [*sic*] *II*.

Tommy Trip *See* PRETTY BOOK OF PICTURES FOR LITTLE MASTERS AND MISSES, A.

Tommy Tucker A character of *nursery rhyme. The verse 'Little Tommy Tucker | Sings for his supper' is not recorded before 1744, but the phrase 'to sing for one's supper' is much older. During the 19th cent. several printers of juvenile *chapbooks issued *The History of Little Tom Tucker* (or a similar title), in which the nursery rhyme was padded out with a very simple story about a naughty boy who eventually reforms. Tommy Tucker has also occasionally been made the subject a *pantomime.

Tomorrow When the War Began (1993–9) A series (or sometimes 'sequence') of seven young adult books by John *Marsden. It is set in Australia in the near future, when the country has been invaded by a nation never named. The action is given entirely from Ellie's point of view—she was camping in a remote area when the country was invaded, and with a small group of teenagers, resists the invaders. Ellie and her friends fight and have both successes and failures in this believable, compelling series. A sequel series, *The Ellie Chronicles*, was published from 2003–7. A film was made in 2010.

Tom Sawyer *See* ADVENTURES OF TOM SAWYER, THE.

Tom's Midnight Garden (1958) A novel for children by Philippa *Pearce. When his brother develops measles, Tom is sent away to stay with a childless uncle and aunt who live in a flat that is part of what was once a fine country house. Tom is bored and lonely and cannot sleep because of the rich food his doting aunt gives him. Then he hears the grandfather clock in the hall downstairs strike thirteen; going to investigate, he discovers a door that leads into a splendid garden. In the morning the garden is not there; Tom learns that it used to exist but was built over years ago. Each night he finds that he can return to it, and he soon becomes deeply involved in the lives of the people he meets there, the Victorian family who once inhabited the house. Most of all he becomes companion and playmate to Hatty, an orphan girl. His friendship with her becomes very close, but he soon realizes that time does not stand still in the garden: Hatty's life is changing and his changes with it.

Tom's Midnight Garden is one of the most accomplished and mature works of modern English children's fiction, brilliantly combining narrative excitement with seriousness of purpose. Its meaning is hinted at in the words of Hatty at the end of the book: 'Nothing stands still, except in our memory.'

Tom Telescope Supposed author of *The Newtonian System of Philosophy*, a *book of instruction published in 1761 by John *Newbery.

Tom, the Piper's Son Character who appears in two *nursery rhymes. The first, in which he 'stole a pig', refers to sweetmeat pigs which were sold in the streets during the 18th cent. The second describes his piping: 'And all the tune that he could play | Was, "Over the hills and far away."' This last phrase occurs in many poems and songs, but there may be a particular reference here to a *ballad (c. 1670) entitled 'The Wind hath blown my Plaid away', in which the words 'Ore the hill and far awa' appear.

Tom was a name familiarly given to pipers in poetry and elsewhere. At the end of the 18th cent. there first appeared a juvenile *chapbook entitled *Tom, The Piper's Son*, in which the two nursery rhymes were combined into a narrative. According to this, Tom's pipe made everyone dance who heard it—a motif presumably derived from *The *Friar and the Boy*. Some versions conclude with Tom going to France to 'teach Boney a dance'.

Beatrix *Potter developed *The Tale of Pigling Bland* (1913) out of the two rhymes.

Tom Thumb Traditional folk-tale character, a being no larger than a thumb. The adventures of a 'thumbling' appear to be international; the brothers *Grimm in their notes on two German versions cite many other European instances, and there are correspondences with Indian and Japanese tales. The first known allusion in print to the English Tom Thumb was in 1579, and Reginald Scot's *Discoverie of Witchcraft* (1584) includes Tom Thumb in his list of such objects of popular superstition as hobgoblins, elves, hags, and imps, with which servants frightened children.

The History of Tom Thumbe retold 'for the delight of merry time-spenders' by 'R.J.' (probably Richard *Johnson, author of *The *Seven Champions of Christendom*) was in print by 1621, the date of the sole surviving copy, and metrical versions of the story were popular during the 17th and 18th cents. That the verses were common knowledge is implied by their appearance in a satire in 1712; a burlesque *Tom Thumb* by Henry Fielding was produced on the London stage in 1730.

By 1630, the date of the earliest surviving copy of the metrical version, Tom Thumb seems to have been established in the written tale as 'a little knight . . . in King Arthur's time'. He is born in answer to the wish of a childless poor couple, who desire a son even if he should be no bigger than his father's thumb. This beginning resembles the German versions, but in the English tale *Merlin answers the wish, Tom is born, and then named and clothed by the Fairy Queen.

Tom then encounters many adventures appropriate to his size and to his mischievous, clever, and magical nature. He climbs into schoolchildren's cherrybags, hangs cooking pots on a sunbeam, and gets by accident into his mother's pudding-mix. He is eaten in turn by a cow, a *giant and a fish, and thereby achieves his entry to court when the fish is caught for King *Arthur's table. He becomes a knight famous for chivalry and finally dies, mourned by the court.

Later versions include many more incidents, and indelicacies were also removed.

By the mid-18th cent. Tom Thumb was established as the most suitable nursery character to sponsor children's books, especially the tiny 2×4 in. productions favoured at the time. Examples are *Tommy Thumb's Song Book, Tom Thumb's Royal Riddle Book*, and

*Newbery and Carnan's *Tom Thumb's Folio*; the latter, published in 1768, contains a facetious, mock-learned version of the story (typical of John Newbery) in which Tom Thumb's stay at the court of the giant Grumbo becomes an opportunity for him to teach printing, grammar, and religious and moral lessons to the giant and his readers. Another notable retelling of the story was the lengthy and annotated version by Charlotte M. *Yonge. Her *History of Sir Thomas Thumb* (1855) uses much additional material, some Arthurian and some from Grimm, and she introduces a Goblin Tempter.

The term 'Tom Thumb' was employed generally for the small-statured; at the beginning of the 19th cent. it was used as a jibe against Napoleon. It became the standard name for a midget in a show when P. T. Barnum presented the American Charles Stratton (1838–83), known as General Tom Thumb.

A modern successor to Tom Thumb is 'Digit Dick', hero of a series of adventures by the Australian writer Leslie *Rees (1942 onwards).

Tom Tit's Song Book, The An early collection of *nursery rhymes, published *c.*1790 by C. D. Piguenit of Aldgate, London, and subtitled *Being a Collection of Old Songs, with which most Young Wits have been delighted*. It included a full version of 'Who killed *Cock Robin?', and also a coarse version of one of the *Jack Sprat rhymes. A similar rhyme is found in *The Delightful Adventures of Honest John Cole* (1732).

tongue-twister A phrase, sentence, or set of sentences designed to trip the tongue of the person saying it. The most famous, 'Peter Piper picked a peck of pickled pepper', was known in the late 18th cent. and engendered an entire book on the same lines, *Peter Piper's Practical Principles of Plain and Perfect Pronunciation* (1813). The term 'tongue-twister', was not, however, recorded before the late 19th cent. 'Peter Piper' itself is not the most testing of tongue-twisters; tougher examples include lines beginning 'She sells seashells on the seashore' and 'Miss Smith's fish-sauce shop'.

Top Book of All, The, for *Little Masters and Misses* Published *c.*1760 by R. Baldwin, S. Crowder, and Benjamin Collins, this was one of the earliest English books to contain *nursery rhymes. Among those that made their first appearance in it were 'Jacky Nory' and 'There were three jovial Welshmen'. The book also

included A *gaping wide-mouthed waddling frog* and the story of *Little Red Riding-Hood.

TOPELIUS, Zachris (Sakari) (1818–98) Finnish poet and author writing in Swedish who founded the tradition of the Finnish *historical novel and also wrote *fairy stories and plays for children. His *Läsning for barn* ('Stories for Children') appeared between 1865 and 1896. Some of his tales were translated into English and several appeared in *Aunt Judy's Magazine*.

Topsy In *Uncle Tom's Cabin* by Harriet Beecher *Stowe.

Topsy and Tim In a series of well over a hundred British *picture books for very small children, by Jean (1928–) and Gareth Adamson (1925–82), published since 1960, with a relaunched series appearing from 2003. To date the books have sold over 21 million copies.

TOURTEL, Mary *See* RUPERT BEAR.

TOWNSEND, John Rowe (1922–2014) British children's writer and critic, born in Leeds. After war service in the RAF he became a reporter on the *Yorkshire Post* in Leeds, and then a subeditor with the *Manchester Guardian*. In 1955 he was appointed Editor of the *Guardian Weekly*, a post he held until 1969.

His first children's book, *Gumble's Yard*, arose in his mind after he had been reporting on the activities of the National Society for the Prevention of Cruelty to Children in Manchester (the 'Cobchester' of his story), and perceived the gap between the experiences of working-class children and the subject matter of most of the children's books being reviewed by his newspaper. *Gumble's Yard* was welcomed for its attempt to write about life in a deprived inner-city area, and he was commended for not giving the book the usual expected 'happy ending'. *Gumble's Yard* (published in America as *Trouble in the Jungle*) has two sequels: *Widdershins Crescent* (1965) takes the same family to a new housing estate and deals with their difficulties in accommodating themselves to a different way of life; *Pirate's Island* (1968) returns to 'The Jungle', the slum area of Cobchester where *Gumble's Yard* was set, and goes back in time to 1946.

Gumble's Yard, *Widdershins Crescent*, and *Pirate's Island* can be classed fairly confidently as 'children's books'. His next seemed to be aiming more at the *young adult reader: *Hell's Edge* (1963) is set in the North Country town of

Hallersage and deals chiefly with the relationship between a local boy and a girl from the South; and *The Hallersage Sound* (1966) involves rivalry between towns, and a local pop group. Townsend went on to write *Good-night, Prof, Love* (1970), a tragicomic story of a middle-class boy's infatuation with an easy-going waitress. This was one of the best teenage novels of its period, frank in its treatment of sex (which is described, like most of the events in the novel, by means of dialogue) and with no element of condescension or 'outside-looking-in'. It bears a close resemblance to such adult novels of the 1960s as Keith Waterhouse's *Billy Liar* and David Storey's *This Sporting Life*. Townsend followed it with *The Summer People* (1971), another novel about teenage love, this time set in 1939 in a seaside resort.

He then began to experiment with a number of forms, from short books for younger readers (*A Wish for Wings*, 1972, and *Top of the World*, 1976), to explorations of adolescent love (*Forest of the Night*, 1974, told in somewhat baffling terms taken from *Blake's poem 'Tyger! Tyger!'; followed by *The Xanadu Manuscript*, 1977, and *King Creature, Come*, 1980, both with a *science fiction plot); meanwhile *Noah's Castle* (1975) is set in the near future, when economic collapse and mass starvation prompt a father to barricade his family inside their house. *A Foreign Affair* (1982) is a comic-romantic novel about an English girl's involvement with a Ruritanian prince. *Dan Alone* (1983) is another story in the *Gumble's Yard* setting, this time about a child who runs away from his family.

After writing reviews of children's books for the *Guardian* for many years, John Rowe Townsend compiled a history of children's literature in the English language, *Written for Children* (1965, revised several times over the next thirty years), which remains one of the most useful books on the subject. *A Sense of Story* (1971), a collection of his critical essays on contemporary writers for children, was revised and reissued in 1979 as *A Sounding of Storytellers*.

TOWNSEND, Sue *See* Secret Diary of Adrian Mole, aged 13¾, The.

toy book A term used particularly for a type of *picture book which became popular in Britain in the mid-19th cent. The format was eventually fairly standard, a large, almost square page (often 26 × 22 cm.) with six or eight *colour pages sometimes interspersed with pages of text (though usually there was very little reading matter). The covers were of paper and the original pricing was generally sixpence, or a shilling for an 'indestructible' version printed on linen.

The pioneers of these toy books were apparently *Dean & Son, who were among the earliest users of chromolithography (*see* lithography) as a colour process for children's books (alongside hand-colouring); colour was a main selling point of the toy books. The subject matter was usually traditional tales and rhymes, with some original stories. By 1858 Dean's catalogue boasted more than 200 of these books. Several other publishers, notably *Warne and *Routledge, began to compete with them to take advantage of the fashion. Walter *Crane and Randolph *Caldecott designed numerous high-quality books in this format for them; these were printed from *wood engravings by Edmund *Evans.

Toy books needed huge print orders to keep their price low; George Routledge alleged that he would only begin to make a profit on a title if he sold more than 50,000, and a first print order of 10,000 was common. Collections of toy books were often bound up and sold in one volume.

toy-making books Popular in Britain during the 19th cent. One of the first and most widely read was *Philosophy in Sport* (1827), ascribed to J. A. Paris. The book uses toys and other curious objects to demonstrate the principles of such things as gravity, weight, motion, elasticity, etc. Toys described include a jack-in-the-box, a figure that dances on a fountain, a whip and peg top, and a peashooter. The book is dedicated to Maria *Edgeworth.

In 1858 appeared *The Boy's Own Toy-Maker* by Ebenezer Landells, a notable artist in *wood engraving and a pupil of *Bewick, and the original projector of *Punch*. This book gives instruction in the making of model boats, equipment for archery and angling, and certain types of puzzle; it also includes a section on the manufacture of paper and cardboard toys. It was reprinted many times. Landells also wrote *The Girl's Own Toy-maker* (1860) and *The Illustrated Paper Model Maker* (1860).

toy theatres ('Juvenile Dramas') Sheets printed with characters and scenes from well known *pantomimes, melodramas, and other plays, which could be cut out, mounted on cardboard, and used for miniature

performances. They began to appear in the early 19th cent.

By 1811 several London shops were producing and selling them; most notable among their publishers was William West of Exeter Street, Strand, who in that year issued versions of *Bluebeard*, *Tom Thumb*, and *Aladdin*, as well as other titles. In 1822 Hodgson & Co. established a toy theatre business in the City of London; between that year and 1830 they published sheets of some 70 plays, which were sold along with books of the words, including stage directions, often elaborate, for moving the cardboard characters about and operating 'trick effects'. Melodramas began to predominate—*The Miller and his Men*, which included a spectacular explosion, was the best known toy theatre drama—but the plays of *Shakespeare and the novels of *Scott were also used as fodder.

Toy theatres at their best show excellent examples of *copperplate engraving and late Georgian scenic design; the artists often worked direct from the life, sitting with pencil and paper in the stalls of a real theatre where the play was being performed and, at least in the early days, depicting the features of the particular actors who were playing the roles. As the decades passed, however, quality degenerated, and plates were passed from one publisher to another, were re-engraved, pirated, and clumsily copied.

The first Juvenile Dramas were generally sold at a penny plain or twopence hand-coloured (*see* COLOUR IN CHILDREN'S BOOKS), which was very cheap at contemporary prices, though some of the more elaborate Hodgson plays cost much more. From 1835 the family of Skelt, trading in the Minories district of London, reissued many of the favourite titles at one penny or even a halfpenny a sheet. Skelt's were notable for the geographical spread of their distribution; George Speaight, in his *History of the English Toy Theatre* (rev. edn 1969) observes that their sheets were on sale throughout Britain, so that 'a generation of boys grew up to whom the toy theatre meant Skelt, and the words became almost synonymous'.

Besides the Skelts, who remained in business until 1872, other prolific publishers of toy theatres in the mid-19th cent. were J. K. Green of Walworth, John Redington of Hoxton, and the Webb family of Smithfield and Bermondsey. For several years from about 1866 one of the *penny dreadful magazines, *Boys of England*, issued toy theatre plays.

After 1850 the toy theatre ceased to acquire new plays, continuing merely to reproduce the repertoire of the early 19th-cent. London stage with increasing crudity, rather as *chapbooks had copied earlier works of literature. The Juvenile Drama was kept alive largely by an article by R. L. Stevenson's entitled 'Penny Plain and Twopence Coloured' (1884).

Webb's company remained in business until 1933, and in 1946 Redington's Hoxton's business, which had been taken over by Benjamin Pollock in 1856, was bought by Alan Keen, a rare-book dealer, who moved the business to central London, where it was managed by George Speaight. A new play, *The High Toby*, was commissioned from J. B. Priestley, with designs by Doris Zinkeisen. The enterprise was not successful financially and in 1952 the firm went into the hands of a receiver. However it was bought up by Marguerite Fawdry, a regular customer whose son was an enthusiastic toy theatre performer. 'Pollock's Toy Museum' was established first in Monmouth Street, and then Scala Street (where Pollock's Toy Museum is still located), and during the 1960s the prevalent taste for Victoriana made it fashionable and successful. In 1980 Pollock's opened a toy theatre shop in the refurbished Covent Garden Market.

Although the modern Pollock publications include cardboard sheets which can be cut out to make the actual theatre (proscenium, stage floor, and wings), most 19th-cent. enthusiasts bought or made wooden theatres which included footlights and sometimes even trapdoors.

Toytown A series of stories created by S. G. Hulme Beaman (1886–1932), at first in books, then as radio plays on *Children's Hour.

Sydney George Hulme Beaman was born in London and trained as an artist; after the First World War he set up as a toymaker in Golders Green. He produced wooden figures about four inches tall, with jointed limbs, and these soon became fashionable. Beaman then began to write and draw a *comic strip featuring some of them, which appeared from 1923 in the *Golders Green Gazette*. The first Toytown story to be published was *The Road to Toytown* (1925), and other books followed. When *Tales of Toytown* appeared in 1928 it came to the notice of May Jenkin of Children's Hour, who launched the first radio adaptation in 1929. Up to this time the character of Larry the Lamb had not featured prominently in the stories, but on the radio Larry was played by

Derek *McCulloch (who also narrated), with such comic effect that Larry and his friend Dennis the Dachshund were given central roles in subsequent episodes.

In all Beaman wrote about three dozen Toytown stories before his sudden death from pneumonia in 1932. Children's Hour continued to broadcast them regularly until its demise in 1964, and they were usually top of the list of listeners' favourites. They were published in book form, at first with Beaman's own illustrations; Beaman set up the actual toys in a model theatre before drawing them, so that the pictures emphasize their woodenness.

Beaman's stories are pure farce, most of them being developed from some simple misunderstanding or mistake. His vein of comedy resembles A. A. *Milne's and has affinities with P. G. *Wodehouse. Characters include the Magician and the Inventor, who rival each other in the incompetence of their spells and inventions; Ernest the Policeman ('Be more careful what you say, Larry my lad'); the perpetual complainer Mr Growser ('It's disgrraceful! It ought not to be allowed!'); and the pompous Mayor ('Take your time, my good animal, take your time'). Central to all but the earliest tales is the inept, too knowingly innocent Larry, whose baa-ing exactly expresses his character ('Mister Maaaa-yor, Sir, I'm only a liiii-ttle lamb!'), and his companion Dennis the Dachshund, whose upside-down syntax is that of a German immigrant confronted by the English language.

TOZER, Katharine *See* MUMFIE.

Tracy Beaker The troublesome, yet lovable character first introduced in *The Story of Tracy Beaker* (1991) by Jacqueline *Wilson, superbly illustrated by Nick *Sharratt, whose wild and curly depictions bring Tracy to life. Tracy, like many of Wilson's characters, comes from a difficult background. She lives in a residential care home nicknamed 'the Dumping Ground' where she causes general trouble in her desire to be reunited with her mother. Tracy's character later reappears in *The Dare Game* (2000), *Starring Tracy Beaker* (2006), and *Thumping Heart* (2009), as well as in novelty books *The Tracy Beaker Quiz Book* (2009) and *Ask Tracy Beaker* (2010). In 2002, the BBC made a popular children's series based on the books which ran for five series on CBBC and included a one-off feature-length film, *Tracy Beaker's Movie of Me* (2004). An additional three series of *Tracy Beaker Returns* were broadcast, in which an adult Tracy Beaker returns to 'the Dumping Ground'. The character has also appeared in a stage adaptation of the book, *Tracy Beaker Gets Real,* which toured the UK in 2006. In 2009, Tracy Beaker became a video-game character in *Tracy Beaker: The Game.*

trades, books of *See* BOOKS OF TRADES.

TRAILL, Catharine Parr (Strickland) (1802–99) Author of the first notable Canadian children's book, *Canadian Crusoes*; she was one of the six daughters of Thomas Strickland, a Suffolk landowner and educational theorist. In childhood she and her younger sister Susanna discovered reams of paper and dozens of goose quills in an old chest and began to write stories which they read aloud. One of Catharine's collections of stories was submitted without her knowledge to John *Harris, who paid five guineas for it and published it as *The Blind Highland Piper, and other tales* (1818). (It was afterwards reissued as *The Tell-Tale.*) Catharine went on to make a reputation for herself as a children's author, producing such books as *Little Downy; or, The history of a fieldmouse* (1822) and *The Keepsake Guineas or, The best use of money* (1828). Meanwhile her brother Samuel (himself an author) accepted a family friend's offer of a new home in Canada. Catharine wrote *The Young Emigrants; or, Pictures of Canada* (1826), and then in 1832 she and her sister followed him across the Atlantic.

In Canada she and Susanna experienced the hardships of pioneer living and, meanwhile, both continued to pursue literary careers. (Susanna wrote children's books as Susanna Moodie.) *Canadian Crusoes* appeared in 1852; Traill's subsequent works include *Lady Mary and her Nurse; or, A peep into the Canadian Forests* (1856), which was based on her extensive knowledge of Canadian wild flowers; it provided Beatrix *Potter with the initial idea for *The Tale of Squirrel Nutkin* (1903), with its mention of squirrels journeying to an island on rafts.

Two of Traill's sisters who remained in England became known as authors and produced a number of children's books: Agnes *Strickland and Jane Margaret Strickland, whose works include *National Prejudice; or, The French prisoner of war* (1828) and *The Village Flower* (1838), a story designed to encourage the better treatment of gypsies.

translation is essential to the history of children's literature. International classics such as

*Pinocchio, The *Swiss Family Robinson, *Heidi, *Alice in Wonderland, the set of stories known as the *Arabian Nights and, above all, Little Red Riding-Hood, *Cinderella, The *Emperor's New Clothes, and other tales from the collections of Charles *Perrault, the *Grimm Brothers and Hans Christian *Andersen have all inspired new directions and genres in children's literature across the world. In the 21st cent., the global success of the *Harry Potter series and the widespread translation of Japanese *manga are fresh manifestations of the literary travels of children's culture.

Arguments for the publication of translations range from the politically worthy—the potential for increased international understanding—to the literary aspiration of facilitating access to the very best writing for children. In the English-speaking world, the *Batchelder Award in the US and the *Marsh Award in the UK promote the publication of contemporary literature in translation. Judges seek that fine balance of affective content, creativity, simplicity of expression, and linguistic playfulness that characterizes successful writing, and therefore successful translation, for younger readers. At the upper end of the age range, translators have found particular challenges, where novels addressing the fragility of the adolescent's self-image demand up-to-date information on rapidly changing youth cultures.

Translators have in the past exercised censorship (the omission of the mutilation of the heels and toes of Cinderella's sisters in translations of the Grimms' version of the tale is a frequently cited example), and still face a fundamental dilemma concerning the localization of coinage, foodstuffs, and other cultural markers in order not to alienate inexperienced young readers. Yet children relish difference, provided, as Astrid *Lindgren famously commented, that a good translator assists them to re-experience the most distant circumstances. Translation enhances children's literature through cultural exchange and by acting as a catalyst to a child's imagination, which will 'continue to build where the translator can go no further' (Astrid Lindgren, Babel, 1969: 98). Gillian Lathey's The Role of Translators in Children's Literature: Invisible Storytellers (2010) includes profiles of translators Sarah *Ardizzone, Anthea *Bell, and Patricia *Crampton.

travel books See GEOGRAPHY AND TRAVEL BOOKS.

Traveller in Time, A (1939) A novel in which Alison *Uttley combined two of her passions, the countryside where she lived and Elizabethan history. It starts with Penelope, a young, slightly fey girl, travelling to Derbyshire to visit her aunt and uncle. Almost immediately she finds she can pass from her present (late Victorian times) to the time when Mary, Queen of Scots, was held captive in the nearby Wingfield manor. In the past she meets the Babington family, and becomes deeply involved in their plot to free the captive queen. There are many *time-slip stories, but this one, with its light touch, understated writing and heartfelt emotions, is one of the very best.

travelogue storybook A narrative in which *geography (together with the history, customs, and folklore of nations) was taught by means of an account of the fictional adventures of a child, a family, or some other group.

The origins of the genre may be found in such books as The Young Northern Traveller, being a series of letters from Frederick to Charles, during a tour through the north of Europe (1813 or earlier), which was by the English writer Mrs *Hofland. Other English authors to produce books of this kind in the first half of the 19th cent. included Maria *Hack, whose Winter Evenings; or, Tales of travellers appeared in four volumes in 1818–20; Mary Ann Hedge, author of such books as The Orphan Sailor-Boy; or, Young Arctic voyager (1824); and Mrs Favell Lee *Mortimer, whose Near Home (1849) described Europe, with a sequel, Far Off (1852–4) giving an account of Africa and America.

The first celebrated American travelogue storybooks were the *Rollo tales by Jacob *Abbott, which described their young hero's experiences touring Europe with his uncle; they were in print by 1840. In the next decade William *Howitt's travelogue A *Boy's Adventures in the Wilds of Australia (1854) ushered in what has been called 'the guidebook period of Australian literature'.

During the 1870s travelogue storybooks by American writers began to appear in large numbers. The most popular and enduring from this decade were the *Bodley Books of Horace E. *Scudder; others from this period include the 'Young Yachters' series by Charles Asbury *Stephens and the 'Boy Travellers' stories of Thomas W. *Knox (1879 onwards). The 1880s saw Stephens producing his 'Knockabout Club' stories, a series continued from 1887 by Frederick Albion Ober; and 1881 saw the beginning of the *Zigzag Journeys by

Hezekiah *Butterworth and the 'Family Flight' series by Edward Everett *Hale and his sister Susan. In 1883 Elizabeth Williams *Champney began to take her 'Vassar Girls' abroad, and in 1891 opened her 'Witch Winnie' series, which was largely set in France.

Many travelogue storybooks were based on real experience and first-hand knowledge of the countries described. Knox was one of the most widely travelled Americans of his generation; his 'Boy Travellers' book on Siam was rewarded for its accuracy when the king of that country conferred the Order of the White Elephant on him, and the whole series was praised by Henry Stanley, discoverer of Dr Livingstone. Stephens was paid to go abroad to research his stories by his magazine, *The Youth's Companion*. But Butterworth does not seem to have travelled much before beginning his 'Zigzag' series, which was largely plagiarized from *Voyages en Zigzag* by Rodolphe Toepffer. He and others were also obliged to construct their narratives largely around such *wood engravings as their publishers happened to have in stock.

TRAVERS, P. L. (Pamela Lyndon) (1899–96) Creator of *Mary Poppins, who was born on the Queensland coast of Australia, into a family of Irish descent. She was educated privately and came to England when she was seventeen, working as a dancer and actress; she continued on the professional stage until 1936. She was encouraged to write poetry by the Irish man of letters 'Æ', who published some of her work in the *Irish Statesman*. The first Mary Poppins stories were written when she was recovering from an illness, and were told to two children of her acquaintance. *Mary Poppins* appeared in 1934 and was an immediate success, as was *Mary Poppins Comes Back* (1935). There have been further sequels.

Travers's other books for children include *I Go By Sea, I Go By Land* (1941), about two children's evacuation to America during the Second World War, *The Fox at the Manger* (1962), in which a fox is among the animals at Bethlehem, and *Friend Monkey* (1971), the story of an English family who adopt a wild monkey.

TREADGOLD, Mary (1910–2005) British children's author who worked as children's books editor with the London publisher Heinemann until 1940, when she decided that she could improve on the many *pony stories which were submitted to her office. The result was her first novel, *We Couldn't Leave Dinah*

(1941), set in the Channel Islands after the German invasion; it concerns a family of children stranded there who use their Pony Club to help the resistance movement. The book won the *Carnegie Medal, and was followed by another pony-cum-war story, *No Ponies* (1946). Treadgold's many subsequent novels repeated the themes and preoccupations of her first work.

TREASE, (Robert) Geoffrey (1909–98) British children's novelist and writer on children's literature. As a boy at Nottingham High School his best subject was history, but he was drafted unwillingly into Classics, and won a scholarship to The Queen's College, Oxford, in 1928. However, he left University at the beginning of his second year, disliking the style of teaching. He then worked with slum children in a settlement in the East End of London, was employed at hack journalism, became a pacifist, and was involved with a 'Promethean Society' whose 'major prophets' were Freud, Marx, Wells, Shaw, Lenin, Trotsky, Gandhi, and D. H. Lawrence ('We did not worry unduly', he wrote, 'about reconciling the contradictions'). He next became a teacher in a seaside private school and married a fellow member of the staff, Marian Boyer. After marriage he lived precariously for a time on freelance journalism. It was then that the idea occurred to him of writing 'children's stories, but children's stories as there had never been before'. He was inspired by the Soviet children's book *Moscow Has a Plan* and by the consciousness that English children's books were 'still rooted in the pre-1914 assumptions which serious adult literature had abandoned … [that] the lower orders, like the lesser breeds, figured only in one or two possible roles, as howling mobs or faithful retainers.'

He wrote to a left-wing publisher to suggest a retelling of *Robin Hood in which Robin would be presented as a proletarian hero fighting the rich oppressors. *Bows Against the Barons* came out in 1934. In it Robin speaks like a member of the British Communist Party during the 1930s: 'Don't call me "sir". We're all equals in Sherwood—comrades.' Trease revised the book in 1966 and removed some of its political preaching. But *Bows Against the Barons*, besides being polemic, is also a well-crafted *adventure story, showing the narrative skill which is characteristic of all Trease's fiction.

Bows Against the Barons was followed later the same year by *Comrades for the Charter*,

which again used historical events (the Chartist movement) as a mirror of 1930s politics. Trease also tried various forms of hack-work in juvenile fiction, including a *school story for *The *Boy's Own Paper* and several thrillers, such as *The Christmas Holiday Mystery* (1937) and *Detectives of the Dales* (1938).

Cue for Treason (1940) was the first of a group of children's novels with the background of the English Civil War of the 17th cent. and its preceding years. Trease was now less of a propagandist and put both sides' cases, while still committing himself to historical judgement. His experience as a teacher of history in a preparatory school in Cumbria while waiting for his army call-up developed in him 'a new reverence for objective truth' and a suspicion of dogma. In 1942 he became an infantry private and he was later transferred to the Army Educational Corps. Off duty he began to lecture at the new *Children's Book Weeks in public *libraries, giving an exposition for children on how 'A book is born', a performance which he repeated on hundreds of occasions in following years. At one such talk to schoolchildren two girls asked him to write what was at that time almost unthinkable, 'true-to-life stories, about real boys and girls, going to day-schools as nearly everybody did'—a request which eventually led to *No Boats on Bannermere* (1949) and its four sequels. This series about a group of modern teenagers at a grammar school begins with the schoolboy narrator saying: 'People don't often put day-schools into stories. I don't know why. Life there is just as interesting as it is at boarding-schools.'

In 1947, at the request of a progressive educational book club, Trease wrote *Tales Out of School* (1949), a survey of children's literature which was a milestone in the formation of new attitudes to the subject. He argued in it that the moral and political stance of children's literature was of great importance, and advocated stringent criticism and selection (but not censorship). When a new edition of the book was called for in 1964, Trease had to rewrite much of it to take account of the massive improvement in British children's books during the intervening fifteen years. He said of this: 'I like to think that this need for wholesale revision was, at least in part, my own fault. I had asked for [improvement], and, whether by coincidence or not, I had certainly got it.'

Besides further children's books, Trease also wrote radio and television plays, adult novels, and non-fiction for both adults and children, including a children's biography of

D. H. Lawrence (1973) and *The Young Writer: a Practical Handbook* (1961).

Treasure Island The first *adventure story for young readers by Robert Louis *Stevenson, published as a serial in 1881 and as a book in 1883.

The story is set in the mid-18th cent. and owes a little in style to *Robinson Crusoe*, but the prefatory poem makes it clear that the principal models are the tales of W. H. G. *Kingston, R. M. *Ballantyne, and James Fenimore *Cooper. In the summer of 1881 Stevenson was staying at Braemar in Scotland with a family party that included his twelve-year-old stepson Lloyd Osbourne, the child of his American wife Fanny. Lloyd and Stevenson amused themselves by making a map that showed the location of buried treasure on an island, and this prompted Stevenson to begin writing the tale. He read it aloud to the family group, which included his parents, every evening as it was being written. Stevenson's father, an engineer and lighthouse builder, was delighted by it, and spent the best part of a day making an inventory of the things that would be found in Billy Bones's sea-chest when it was opened; Stevenson adopted this into the story.

The character and appearance of the pirate and ship's cook Long John Silver were based by Stevenson on his close friend the writer W. E. Henley, who had lost a foot but did not allow his disability to damp his huge energy or the exuberance of his manner. The episode—seemingly improbable—of Jim Hawkins overhearing the mutineers' conspiratorial conversation while being by chance inside an apple-barrel on deck actually happened to Stevenson's father as a lad; he had overheard the captain of the Lighthouse Board's vessel conspiring against his own father while he was himself concealed in a barrel of apples.

The melodramatic character of the story probably owes something to the influence of *toy theatre plays, with which Stevenson was fascinated during his childhood. Discussing the book some years after its publication, he was quite open about its debt to other writers. 'No doubt', he said, 'the parrot once belonged to Robinson Crusoe ... The stockade, I am told, is from *Masterman Ready*.' He said he had taken the character of Billy Bones and the opening scene at the inn (unconsciously at the time) from Washington *Irving's *Tales of a Traveller*. Nevertheless Stevenson himself

was the first to bring together in one book what became the stereotyped details of *pirate stories—such things as the parrot which sits on Silver's shoulder and cries 'Pieces of eight!', and the shanty 'Fifteen men on the dead man's chest'.

Stevenson found the early chapters easy enough to write, but later his inspiration dried up for a time and he might have abandoned the book had not he been visited at Braemar by one Dr Alexander Japp, an expert on Thoreau, with whose writings Stevenson was concerned at the time. Dr Japp heard some of the chapters of *The Sea Cook*, as the story was then entitled, being read aloud, and he asked Stevenson to let him show the tale to James Henderson, the editor of the magazine *Young Folks*. Henderson bought it for serialization (for some £30) and it began to appear in that periodical in October 1881, with the subtitle 'The Mutiny of the Hispaniola' and with the author named as 'Captain George North'.

The serial was not, on the whole, a success; but in 1883 the publishers Cassell bought the book rights for £100. The first edition of *Treasure Island*, which named Stevenson as author and appeared during that year, had no illustrations except the map (which Stevenson had to redraw painfully, having lost the original), but it was immediately hailed by the critics as one of the best adventure stories then in print. The book was dedicated to Lloyd Osbourne, identified as 'S.L.O., an American gentleman, in accordance with whose classic taste the following narrative has been designed'.

In 1885 Cassell brought out an illustrated edition, with rather undistinguished pictures by various artists and engravers. A second illustrated edition (1899) had drawings by W. Paget; N. C. *Wyeth (1911) and Edmund *Dulac (1927) were among later illustrators, but the story had to wait until 1949 to find an artist exactly fitted to it, Mervyn *Peake.

Stevenson said that *Treasure Island* was intended merely 'to be a story for boys; no need of psychology or fine writing'. There is in fact plenty of both in the book. Silver, the book's real hero, possesses a degree of courage and ingenuity not shown by the 'good' characters; Jim Hawkins comments almost approvingly on the 'remarkable game' that he plays to get his own ends. Jim himself is ill-defined by comparison, being often a mere observer of human nature. One of Stevenson's biographers, Jenni Calder, remarks that, perhaps because of this, *Treasure Island* 'has always been a story that adults have relished

perhaps more than children; in fact it may be adult favour that has kept it so very much alive.' The book also owes much of its continued life to the frequent dramatizations for children.

Treasure Island inspired many imitations; one of the best adventure stories written under its influence was *Moonfleet* (1898) by J. Meade *Falkner. Several sequels to the story have been written; examples include *Flint's Island* (1972) by Leonard *Wibberley and *Silver's Revenge* (1979) by Robert *Leeson.

Treasure Seekers, The *See* STORY OF THE TREASURE SEEKERS, THE.

TREECE, Henry (1911–66) British novelist who was from 1946 until 1959 Senior English Master at Barton on Humber Grammar School, Lincolnshire. His reputation as a writer was first made through poetry, and then as a writer of adult fiction. He began his career as a children's writer in 1954 with *Legions of the Eagle*, about the conflict between Romans and Celts. In this and in Treece's other early *historical novels for children there is distinct evidence of 'writing down'; he employs the conventional, and not always plausible, device of the boy hero as observer of the historical events. *The Eagles Have Flown*, also published in 1954, deals with Britain after the Romans and with the supposed historical figure behind the legends of *Arthur. In the same year Treece produced his first thriller for children, *Desperate Journey*, which was full of stereotyped villains and incidents. There were to be five more books in this genre, including *Hunter Hunted* (1957) and *Don't Expect Any Mercy* (1958). All were artificial in plot but not without entertainment-value.

Treece's development as a historical novelist for children happened swiftly, in such books as *Viking's Dawn* (1955), *The Road to Miklagard* (1957), and *Viking's Sunset* (1960), a trilogy about the adventures of the Viking Harald Sigurdson from adolescence to middle age. A second Viking trilogy, for younger readers, is formed by *Hounds of the King* (1955), *Man With a Sword* (1962), and *The Last of the Vikings* (1964), which follow the fortunes of Harald Hardrada. In all Treece wrote twenty-five historical novels for young readers in twelve years. The last was *The Dream-Time* (1967), the story of a Stone Age boy who does not want to be a warrior—a book which showed an enormous advance upon his early work.

His books show a preoccupation with what he called 'the cross-roads of history' (periods of extreme change); another recurring motif is that of a son in search of a father-figure, which is said to have grown from Treece's reaction to the early death of his own elder son. Besides his novels he wrote several non-fiction *history books for children, and a retelling of *Njal's Saga* (1964).

TRIMMER, Mrs Sarah (1741–1810) Reviewer and author of children's books and writer on education, who was born in Ipswich. She was the daughter of John Kirby, an architect who later became Clerk of Works to the royal palace at Kew. She was well educated at a local school. Her family moved in circles that included Dr Johnson and the artists Gainsborough, Hogarth, and Reynolds. In 1762 she married James Trimmer of Brentford and spent the rest of her life there, bringing up twelve children of whom nine survived her.

She became seriously interested in education as soon as she started teaching her own children (the only part of the curriculum she delegated was the boys' Classics) and her authorship grew out of these lessons. To make time for writing she rose at four or five in the morning, until her older children were able to take over teaching the youngest. Encouraged by the example of Mrs *Barbauld she published an *Easy Introduction to the Knowledge of Nature* in 1780, followed by selections from Scripture for children. She originated a series of *copperplate prints of biblical and secular *history, with the idea that these could be displayed on nursery walls, and wrote the accompanying volumes of notes.

She became involved with the *Sunday school movement soon after its foundation in 1780 and by 1786 she had organized schools for over 150 poor children in Brentford. The Queen sent for her to discuss setting up a Sunday school at Windsor, and Mrs Trimmer then wrote *The Œconomy of Charity* to promote Sunday schools and advise on their organization. A number of her later books, both educational and leisure reading, were written for the needs of Sunday schools and the literate poor. Some of these were published by the *Society for Promoting Christian Knowledge and had an immense circulation for many years.

Mrs Trimmer's best known and most enduring children's book was her *Fabulous Histories* (1786), later known as *The History of the Robins*, an early *animal story. The human beings in *The Robins* are middle-class, and the book's success encouraged her to write another, 'a short tract for the poor, that might answer the purpose of my *Fabulous Histories*'. This, *The Two Farmers*, appeared in 1786 and was advertised as 'an agreeable vehicle for conveying to Sunday Scholars, under the idea of amusement for their leisure hours, such lessons, which, if imprinted on their minds, may be beneficial to them in the future part of their lives'.

From 1788 to 1789 Mrs Trimmer edited, and wrote much of, a monthly periodical for 'cottagers and servants', called *The Family Magazine*. It included such weighty items as abridged sermons, discourses on the Sabbath and on contentment, hymns, and meditations; but there was leavening in the form of *moral tales, general knowledge, housekeeping and gardening tips.

From 1802 to 1806 Mrs Trimmer produced another periodical, *The *Guardian of Education*, this time addressed to parents and *governesses. It was remarkable for being the first attempt to chart the history of children's literature so far and systematically to *review the products of its age. It also made Mrs Trimmer notorious for her opinions, notably her strict censure of tales which fell below the very highest moral standard and her condemnation of *fairy stories. Pressure of other work and the impossibility of reviewing single-handed all the children's books that were being published eventually forced Mrs Trimmer to issue the *Guardian* less frequently and finally to give it up altogether.

Mrs Trimmer kept a diary of her domestic and working life, interspersed with her own prayers, as a spiritual exercise; it was published after her death and reveals a woman of great moral certainty, energy, and piety, and also of great charm and intelligence.

TRING, A. Stephen Pseudonym of Laurence *Meynell.

Tripods, The (1967–68) A science fiction series for young adults by John *Christopher, which also served as the basis for a television series of the same name. The Tripods, enormous three-legged machines piloted by unseen alien invaders known as the Masters, stride through the trilogy that took their name. Here a post-apocalyptic world is imagined in which the human race is kept under control by a system of Capping; resistance seems futile. The Tripods are all-powerful. In the first book, *The White Mountains* (1967),

Will Parker flees Capping, journeying across France to find a rebel group based in the White Mountains. *The City of Gold and Lead* (1968) sees Will with a companion Fritz infiltrating one of the great Cities established by the Masters. The final volume, *Pool of Fire* (1968), charts the final battle against the Masters and their monstrous machines, the Tripods. (There is also a prequel, *When the Tripods Came* (1988), written two decades later, which sets the scene for the invasion.)

Owing not a little to H. G. *Wells's vision of alien invasion, the books derive their power from the image of these machines rather than from the actual alien species; it is the Tripods who are memorable rather than their Masters.

Tristan (Tristram) A knight of King *Arthur's court who features in many of the Arthurian romances and in retellings of the Arthurian legends for children.

The full Tristan story was first recorded in the *Tristan* of Thomas, a poet writing in French at the court of Henry II of England, *c.* 1170. (Most of the poem is lost, but its contents can be reconstructed from its derivatives.) Tristan is the nephew of King Mark of Cornwall, whose favour he wins by slaying the Irish champion Morholt, who had threatened Cornwall. A fragment of Tristan's sword which had lodged in Morholt's skull is removed and preserved by Morholt's niece, the Irish princess Isolt, who vows to find her uncle's slayer. Later Tristan is sent in search of a bride for King Mark. He reaches Ireland and is wounded in a fight with a *dragon, which he kills. Isolt tends his wounds and recognizes him as Morholt's slayer by the piece missing from his sword. She spares him, and Tristan wins her as his uncle King Mark's bride.

He takes her back to Cornwall and on their voyage a love potion intended for Isolt and Mark's wedding night is accidentally given to Tristan and Isolt, who fall passionately in love. Isolt becomes Tristan's mistress. On the night of her marriage, to conceal the loss of her virginity, she persuades her servant Brangain to take her place in the marriage bed. Subsequent episodes of the story deal with King Mark's suspicions and the lovers' subterfuges. Eventually Tristan is sent in exile to Brittany, where he marries Isolt of the White Hand because she bears the same name as his beloved. After further adventures Tristan is seriously wounded and sends to Cornwall for the other Isolt to come and heal him. Isolt takes ship with the messenger, but Tristan's jealous

wife falsely reports that she is not on board and Tristan dies of despair. When Isolt finds that she has arrived too late she dies of grief beside him.

The story of Tristan and Isolt (also spelt Isolde or Iseult) was first joined to the Arthurian matter by the 12th-cent. poet Chrétien de Troyes. 'Tristram of Lyonesse' featured largely in the *Morte Darthur* of *Malory, which eventually became the basis of most 19th- and 20th-cent. children's books about Arthur and his knights, though these have usually censored the erotic parts of the Tristan story.

TRIVIZAS, Eugene (1946–) Award-winning Greek writer, probably the most popular, and prolific, children's author in Greece, having written over 100 books—mainly picture books, but also comic books, plays for children, opera librettos, and a novel. He is known for his imagination and humour, his amusing rhymes, puns, wordplay, neologisms, and use of onomatopoeia, and his books often feature the work of some of Greece's best illustrators, while his best-known book, the wittily subversive *The Three Little Wolves and the Big Bad Pig* (1993), was illustrated by Helen *Oxenbury. Other books and comics include *The Last Black Cat* (tr. Sandy Zervas, 2005), *Fruitopia* (from 1983), *Little Bear in Trouble* (tr. Hilary Kyriazis, 2005), and *The Village of Joy* (tr. Hilary Kyriazis, 2007). Trivizas has won many awards, including the 2003 Athens Academy Award (Kostas and Eleni Ouranis) for Children's Literature.

trolls Among the most recognizable supernatural beings from Old Norse stories, trolls are creatures described as dwelling in isolated caves or mountains in small family units and as unfriendly to humans. From Scandinavian myth they have travelled into popular culture, featuring in many fantasy novels including *The *Hobbit* (1937), in which Tolkien used the idea that trolls caught in sunlight turn to stone. They feature commonly in retellings of Norse fairy tales and novels that use Norse mythology, and have now been adopted and adapted for all kinds of *fantasy writing.

TROWBRIDGE, J. T. (John Townsend) (1827–1916) American novelist and poet who wrote a large number of children's books. One of the best known was *Jack Hazard and His Fortunes* (1871), the story of a boy who runs away from his rough stepfather, a boatman on the Erie Canal. It was serialized in *Our Young Folks*, of which Trowbridge was

joint editor, and there were several sequels. Trowbridge was on the staff of *St Nicholas* for some years.

Trumpeter of Krakow, The (1928) A novel by Eric *Kelly.

TUCK, Raphael (1821–1900) Publisher; a German who became a British subject in 1875. He was a London furniture dealer who turned to fine-art publishing and began to mass-produce Christmas and greetings cards and to print *annuals under the name 'Father Tuck'. The firm brought out E. *Nesbit's first children's book, *The Voyage of Columbus* (1892).

TUCKER, Charlotte Maria *See* A.L.O.E.

Tuck Everlasting (1975) A novel by Natalie *Babbitt. The Tuck family have drunk from water that has made them immortal. When they think that Winnie, a young girl who is growing up and testing boundaries, has guessed their secret, they kidnap her to try and persuade her of the realities of living forever. Influential and popular, Babbitt's slender book deals with massive issues such as happiness, where human lives fit in the greater scheme of things, and the possibilities, both good and bad, inherent in living forever.

TUDOR, Tasha (1915–2008) American author-illustrator who created many books about the delights of country life, one of the best known being her first, *Pumpkin Moonshine* (1938). Her *Mother Goose* and *1 Is One* were chosen as Caldecott Honor Books (*see* CALDECOTT MEDAL) in 1945 and 1957, respectively. Many of her books (of which there were nearly a hundred in total) celebrated domestic skills, such as cooking, craft work, and gardening.

TUER, A. W. (Andrew White) (1838–1900) British antiquary and historian of children's books who wrote a definitive history of the *hornbook (1896), compiled *Pages and Pictures from Forgotten Children's Books* (1898) and *Stories from Old-Fashioned Children's Books* (1899), and, with his firm Field and Tuer (the Leadenhall Press) republished several early 19th-cent. children's picture books in facsimile. He was the first publisher to accept work by the young Jerome K. Jerome.

Tulip Touch, The (1996) A *young adult novel by Anne *Fine. The friendship between lonely little girls, Natalie, with her stable family background, and Tulip, alone, neglected, abused, starts well. However, as they grow older, it changes, becoming darker and more dangerous. Natalie has to break away from Tulip, but there is a cost—one that will affect her and her whole family. A winner of numerous awards including the Whitbread Children's Book of the Year (*see* COSTA CHILDREN'S BOOK AWARD), the novel explores the idea of evil—its existence and its effect. The author's subtle handling of the friendship between the two girls introduces ideas of accountability in a way that is both sympathetic and challenging.

Tulku (1979) A historical novel by Peter *Dickinson, set during the Boxer Rising in China. An American missionary's son flees from his ruined home, journeys in company with an outspoken Cockney woman who is a plant collector, reaches Tibet, and discovers that life is more complicated (especially in terms of religion) than his father had taught him. Marcus *Crouch described the book as 'a miraculous blend of oriental philosophy, high drama and melodramatics'. It won Dickinson both the Whitbread Award (*see* COSTA CHILDREN'S BOOK AWARD) and the *Carnegie Medal.

TULLET, Hervé (1958–) An internationally renowned French picture-book creator whose dynamic and innovative books delight children both young and old. Tullet worked as an art director in the advertising industry for over ten years before producing his first book *Comment Papa a rencontré Maman* in 1994. His work has since been widely celebrated, winning numerous awards including the Sorcières Prize in 2011 for *Un livre* (2010; published in the UK as *Press Here* in 2011), a wonderfully imaginative book that creates a whole new degree of interaction with the physical page. *The Game of Light* (2011) brings another dimension to bedtime, and children will delight in creating their own characters in *The Finger Game Circus* (2013). His work is highly conceptual and imaginative, and his 'out-of-the-box' thinking makes him one of the most interesting visual artists and picture-book creators for children in recent times.

TUNIS, John R. (Roberts) (1889–1975) American author of children's novels about sports who was a sports writer and radio commentator in New York. His books include *All-American* (1942), *Young Razzle* (1949), and *His Enemy, His Friend* (1967).

Turbulent Term of Tyke Tiler, The (1977) By Gene *Kemp, a lively story set in a contemporary primary school which received

both the *Carnegie Medal and the Other Award. Considered innovative in its realistic portrayal of both characters and setting, it is particularly noteworthy for the way it challenges assumptions of both gender and ability.

It is Tyke's last term at Cricklepit Combined. It should be memorable, and it is. But it is not a smooth journey. As the headmaster is only too aware, the friendship between Tyke Tiler and Danny Price is a recipe for trouble. It is not malicious; Danny needs protection and that is Tyke's job. The results can be painful, but there is always something to laugh about. Kemp's other titles based on Cricklepit School include *Gowie Corbie Plays Chicken* (1979), *Charlie Lewis Plays for Time* (1984), and *Just Ferret* (1990).

Turf-Cutter's Donkey, The (1934) A novel by Patricia *Lynch.

TURKLE, Brinton (1915–2003) American illustrator and author who wrote a series of books for young children about 'Obadiah', a Quaker boy in Nantucket in the early 19th cent. The first was *Obadiah the Bold* (1965). *Thy Friend, Obadiah*, was chosen as a *Caldecott Honor Book in 1970 (*see* CALDECOTT MEDAL). Turkle also illustrated many books by other writers.

TURNER, Elizabeth *See* DAISY, THE.

TURNER, Ethel S. (**Sibyl**) (1872–1958) Australian writer of novels and short stories for children and young people, who was hailed, after the publication of *Seven Little Australians* (1894), her first and best known *family story, as the Australian Louisa M. *Alcott.

Born in Doncaster in England, she went to Australia with her parents when she was eight and began writing while still at the Girls' High School in Sydney, where she was a contemporary of Louise *Mack. She and her sister Lilian, who also went on to publish fiction, together edited schoolgirl magazines. Ethel became a contributor to Sydney newspapers, with a children's page of her own under the name of 'Dame Durden'.

Over the next thirty-five years or so she published some twenty-seven novels. These include *The Family at Misrule* (1895), a sequel to *Seven Little Australians*, and *The Little Larrikin* (1896), about a *street Arab. A collection of stories, *The Camp at Wandinong*, followed in 1898; one of these was 'The Child of the Children', whose first English publication was in the *Windsor Magazine* during the previous year. In it a committee of rich and well-meaning children adopt a slum girl called Flip

Huggins. They rename her Eliza, teach her French, dancing, and some proper English. Convinced that she is now a real 'lyedy', Eliza is introduced to society at a 'swell party', with disastrous results. Flip Huggins has been put forward as the inspiration for Eliza Doolittle in George Bernard Shaw's *Pygmalion* (1912). Of the many more stories that Ethel Turner wrote, two were about the Woolcot family whose adventures first made her international reputation: *Little Mother Meg* (1902) and *Judy and Punch* (1902).

Ethel Turner married in 1896 Herbert Raine Curlewis, a Sydney lawyer who became a notable judge with a reputation for rebuking counsel for any misuse of English. They had two children, with whom they toured Europe just before the First World War; Ethel Turner's impressions of the tour were published as *Ports and Happy Havens* in 1912. Her daughter Jean also wrote books about childhood, set against the Sydney seascape, and mother and daughter together published *The Sunshine Family, A Book of Nonsense for Girls and Boys*.

Like E. *Nesbit a little after her (and it is possible that Nesbit may have read her stories), Ethel Turner deals with uncommonly independent children, usually middle-class and often hard up, whose parents are dead, absent, or emotionally distant and whose confidence and spirit depends on their solidarity as a family. Her children are never simply good or naughty; they quarrel, are alternately heroic and foolish, and find their baby (a fairly active character in the stories) both a pest and a delight. But ultimately they share common and for the most part admirable values, including devotion to each other.

TURNER, Philip (William) (1925–2006) Canadian-born British author who won the *Carnegie Medal in 1965 for *The Grange at High Force*, an *adventure story set on the fells, the second in a series which had begun the previous year with *Colonel Sheperton's Clock*. Besides writing other children's novels under his own name, Turner produced a series of 'Septimus' *detective stories for older children (1971–79) as 'Stephen Chance'. He was also a priest in the Church of England and a former Head of Religious Broadcasting for the BBC Midland Region.

Turpin, Dick *See* DICK TURPIN.

TWAIN, Mark (Samuel Langhorne Clemens) (1835–1910) American writer who was born in Missouri and spent most of his childhood in the town of Hannibal, on the

Mississippi. His father died impecunious when Samuel was twelve, and the boy had to leave school to earn money. He became a printer and worked his way to New York and Philadelphia, also writing articles for newspapers. In 1857, having abandoned a plan to seek his fortune in South America, he apprenticed himself to a Mississippi river pilot and spent the next four years in this occupation. After the beginning of the Civil War he became a reporter, starting to use the pseudonym 'Mark Twain'. It is said that he stole this from another river pilot who sometimes published articles; the name is supposed to have been a river navigation term meaning 'two fathoms deep'.

Soon becoming a very successful journalist, he travelled to the Mediterranean and the Holy Land and afterwards published a richly comic account of his journey and his American fellow-travellers, *The Innocents Abroad* (1869). In 1870 he was married, a step which some critics believe was responsible for making his outlook more bitterly satirical, in reaction to the conservative social milieu of his wife. *Roughing It* (1872) satirized his earlier Bohemian experiences, but in *The *Adventures of Tom Sawyer* (1876) he changed his approach and wrote a comic but more nostalgic account of boyhood, based closely on his childhood days in Hannibal. After publishing *A Tramp Abroad* (1880) and *Life on the Mississippi* (1883) he completed a sequel to *Tom Sawyer*, the brilliant *Adventures of Huckleberry Finn* (1884).

His later books include *A Connecticut Yankee in King Arthur's Court* (1889) and *Pudd'nhead Wilson* (1894). In 1894 he became bankrupt owing to the failure of publishing ventures and of a typesetting machine in which he had invested. *Tom Sawyer Abroad* (1894) and *Tom Sawyer, Detective* (1896) are mere potboilers. He spent his last years dictating his autobiography—which had, of course, in fictionalized form, been the subject of many of his books.

Another book by Mark Twain, *The *Prince and the Pauper* (1882), is a perennial favourite with children.

Tweedledum and Tweedledee Charac-
ters who feature in a *nursery rhyme which appeared in *Original Ditties for the Nursery*, published by John *Harris *c.*1805. The names are included in a satirical verse dating from 1725, and the nursery rhyme may well have existed by that time. Lewis *Carroll made use of the rhyme

to provide a chapter in *Through the Looking Glass* (1871), and his illustrator *Tenniel gave the characters their definitive appearance as two morose, ageing schoolboys.

Twelve and the Genii, The (1962) A novel
by Pauline *Clarke, awarded the 1962 *Carnegie Medal. This unusual fantasy deftly blurs the boundaries between the real world and that of the imagination. When Max discovers twelve wooden soldiers in the attic, he little knows what adventures are in store. The soldiers are the toy soldiers that inspired the Brontë children, and they come alive. Now there are collectors anxious to profit from their discovery. The Twelve, under the leadership of Butter Crashey, and with the help of Max and his siblings, must make the epic journey back to Haworth.

Twelve Dancing Princesses, The One of
the best known of the *Grimms' fairy tales.

A king's twelve daughters wear out their shoes every night, but no one knows how and their father offers a reward to anyone who can discover the cause; anyone who tries and fails will be put to death. After a number of failures by kings' sons, who are duly executed, an old soldier takes on the task, having been warned by an old woman not to drink the wine that is given him by the princesses; she also gives him a cloak of invisibility. When night comes he is given the drugged draught, but only pretends to drink it, and when the princesses leave their apartment by a hidden trapdoor he follows them, having made himself invisible. They journey to a fine castle where they dance all night, wearing out their shoes as usual, and the soldier follows them back, plucking a branch from a tree as a token that he has been there. The same thing happens on a second and a third night, during which the soldier acquires other mementoes of the princesses' errand, and at last he tells everything to their father. Confronted with this, the princesses confess all, and the soldier chooses one of them—the eldest—for his bride; he also becomes the king's heir.

The story, also known as *The Shoes that were Danced to Pieces*, *The Dancing Shoes*, and *The Worn Shoes*, was found by the Grimms in several German versions. It seems to be Central European in origin, and is probably not older than the 17th cent.

A British parallel is the tale of *Kate Crackernuts*, collected in the Orkneys and published by Andrew *Lang in his column in *Longman's*

Magazine in 1889. In this a king's son is sickening away to death and no one can find the cause. Kate, herself a king's daughter, offers to sit up and watch. At midnight he gets out of bed and goes dancing with the fairies beneath a hill. Kate follows him and gathers nuts along the way, and it is largely by means of these that she eventually cures him of his dancing sickness. This story was printed in Joseph Jacobs's *English Fairy Tales* (1890).

Twenty-One Balloons, The (1947) A *tall tale written and illustrated by William Pène *Du Bois. One of the outstanding American humorous books for children of its period, it won the *Newbery Medal.

Professor William Waterman Sherman has taught arithmetic to small boys for forty years, and now proposes to 'get away from it all' by crossing the Pacific in a giant balloon. But not many days after his departure he is picked up in the Atlantic—the wrong ocean—clinging to the wreckage of not one but twenty balloons. The Professor's explanation of what has occurred, which he will not give to anyone (even the President) until he is in front of his chosen audience, the Western American Explorer's Club, is reminiscent of Baron *Munchausen. It also has touches of Heath *Robinson in such details as the Professor's method of washing up during his balloon journey: letting his cups and plates down into the sea, some 1,400 feet below, by means of an extra long fishing line.

Twilight (2005–8) Hugely successful *vampire fantasy series by US novelist Stephenie Meyer (1973–) which tells the story of Bella Swan, mostly in her own voice. Seventeen-year-old Bella moves to the town of Forks, Washington, where she falls in love with classmate Edward Cullen, who twice saves her life, but (less helpfully) is a vampire, struggling to resist his desire for her blood. Meanwhile another vampire appears in town with much less self-restraint than Edward—James is a 'tracker' vampire with a special tracking ability who hunts humans for sport, and it falls to Edward and his family to rescue Bella after an attack, and destroy James once and for all. Edward refuses to change Bella into a vampire even though she wishes it, because he sees his immortality as a curse (he is 104); she is not convinced. Other characters in the first book include Bella's friend Jacob. He had been intended as only a minor character, but Meyer decided to write him up to a more

prominent role in *New Moon* (2006), in which he becomes closer to Bella in Edward's absence, the Cullens having left Forks for Bella's own safety. It transpires that Jacob and his friends are werewolves, or shapeshifters. Besides Jacob's tribe, this book also introduces the Volturi, a corrupt coven of vampire royalty who enforce the rule that humans must not know of vampires' existence. On discovering Bella, they insist that she either be killed or transformed into a vampire herself.

In book three, *Eclipse* (2007), Jacob reveals that he is in love with Bella—she eventually admits that she loves him, too, but that she loves Edward more. Victoria, once James's lover, is out for revenge, seeking to kill Bella. There is a great battle between Victoria and her newborn vampires on the one side, and the Cullens and the werewolves on the other. Following success in battle, Bella and Edward marry at the beginning of *Breaking Dawn* (2008), and the rest of this concluding volume of the saga describes her troubled pregnancy and final transformation into a vampire. When their child Renesmee is threatened by the Volturi, the Cullens gather allies from around the world to defend her. A central section of the book is narrated not by Bella herself but by Jacob, who has learned of Bella's pregnancy and is forced to protect her from his old pack.

In addition to the principal tetralogy, Meyer has published a novella, *The Short Second Life of Bree Tanner* (2010), the first-person story of one of the newborn vampires who appeared in *Eclipse*.

With its massive sales the *Twilight* series has been credited with spawning a new interest in vampire fiction and a flood of mostly very poor imitations. The saga has little to do with its vampire predecessors in tone or effect, and is closer to swooning romance than to *horror. The passionate romance, coloured with great unresolved sexual tension (the series has been criticized for its attitude to teenage sexuality, largely believed to be influenced by Meyer's Mormon beliefs), may explain the series's huge popularity, primarily (but not exclusively) with teenagers, mostly girls, though it does also have an active older female readership. The series's large and enthusiastic fan base comes despite, rather than because of, its prose style, which is unremarkable at best. However, sales of over 100 million copies to date suggest that Meyer's readers are untroubled by this.

The series has been filmed, again with great commercial success, with Kristen Stewart and

Robert Pattinson as the young lovers; the *Twilight* film was released in 2008, and the concluding instalment, *Breaking Dawn*, in 2011–12 (the final volume was split into two films).

Midnight Sun is a companion piece to *Twilight*, telling the story from Edward's point of view, but despite the fervent enthusiasm of Meyer's fans, this remains as yet unpublished (as a result of the initial chapters being leaked online and Meyer's consequent disinclination to share the project). Meyer has also written *Forever Dawn*, which was to have been the sequel to *Twilight*, but which she abandoned when she learned the first book was to be published for young adults, and wrote *New Moon* instead. (Meyer claimed to have written the first book without any expectation that it would see publication.) *Forever Dawn* is also unpublished, and Meyer claims it too will remain so.

Twinkle, twinkle, little star A poem by Jane *Taylor, originally published as 'The Star' in *Rhymes for the Nursery* (1806). It became so popular that the first verse at least (there are five in all) entered oral tradition as a *nursery rhyme. It had been set to music (by J. Green) by about 1860, and a *pantomime, *Twinkle, Twinkle, Little Star; or, Harlequin Jack Frost*, was performed about ten years later. It has often been parodied, the best known example being the Mad Hatter's song in *Alice's Adventures in Wonderland*, 'Twinkle, twinkle, little bat!'

Twits, The (1980) A novel for younger readers by Roald *Dahl. It is the story of the grotesquely ugly and grotesquely mean Mr and Mrs Twit, who delight in playing nasty tricks on each other—he gradually adds length to her walking stick so she believes she's got the shrinks, she feeds him spaghetti made with worms, and so on. Finally the four monkeys they keep in a cage, together with the Roly-Poly Bird, play a trick on the horrible couple and all ends well. Exceptionally bad things often happen to adults in Dahl books, but they usually deserve it.

Two Little Confederates (1888) By Thomas Nelson *Page, the story of Frank and Willy who live on a Virginia plantation during the Civil War. Their elder brother joins the Confederate army, and he and his General have to hide on the plantation when the Yankees come. The boys help to shelter them, while the maid Lucy Ann outwits the Yankees, pretending that she wants to help them and so get her freedom. Frank and Willy show kindness to a dying Yankee soldier and afterwards become close friends with his mother and young son.

The book, written early in Page's literary career, was serialized in *St Nicholas* before publication. As in his other works of fiction, he wished to depict the Civil War from a Confederate point of view and to demonstrate that Southern slavery was not cruelty but good-natured paternalism.

Two Little Savages (1903) A novel written and illustrated by the naturalist Ernest Thompson *Seton, designed to teach 'woodcraft' to boys. Yan, a boy, living in a Canadian town, is obsessed by '*Indians' and wildlife. At weekends he builds himself a shanty, but it is pulled down by tramps. After suffering from tuberculosis he is sent to convalesce on a farm in the backwoods, where he teams up with his host's son, Sam Raften. Yan and Sam visit Caleb Clark, an old trapper who has been turned off his own farm; he teaches them how to build a 'teepee', how to make rubbing sticks that produce fire, how to make a bow and arrows, and many other things; the author supplies detailed diagrams of all these. Eventually Caleb Clark gets his farm back and the son-in-law who dispossessed him is thrown out.

Two Years Before the Mast (1840) A celebrated autobiographical account of life as a common sailor, written by the New England author Richard Henry Dana Jr. (1815–82) and first published anonymously. Though not intended for children, it was read by many of them, especially in America.

TYTLER, Ann Fraser *See* LEILA.

UDERZO, Albert (1927–) With René *Goscinny, one half of the empire that created the *Astérix series. A French comic-book artist and scriptwriter, Uderzo began a successful career as an artist in Paris after the Second World War in 1945, where he created several comics including 'Arys Buck', 'Le Prince Rollin' and 'Belloy l'invulnérable'. Uderzo met Goscinny in 1951 and they collaborated until Goscinny's death in 1977. Together they created the character 'Oumpah-pah le Peau-Rouge'—a controversial comic strip about a Native American '*Indian'. Uderzo also collaborated with Jean-Michel Charlier on a more realistic comic series featuring pilots Michel Tanguy and Ernest Laverdure and their adventures in the French Air Force. In 2007, Uderzo was made a Knight of the Order of the Netherlands Lion.

Ugli-Wuglies In *The *Enchanted Castle* by E. *Nesbit.

Ugly Duckling, The A story by Hans Christian *Andersen. A duck's brood includes one duckling that is big and ugly. At first his mother is proud of him and defends him against attacks from other ducks, but soon even she turns against him and he runs away. After many hardships he meets three swans, and finds that they greet him as one of their own kind. Andersen published the story in 1845 and it was translated into English the next year. According to his biographer, Signe Toksvig, it is 'the most poignant of [Andersen's] many veiled autobiographies'.

UMPHELBY, Fanny *See* CHILD'S GUIDE TO KNOWLEDGE, THE.

Una and Dan In *Puck of Pook's Hill* and *Rewards and Fairies* by *Kipling.

Uncle An immensely wealthy elephant in a series of books by J. P. Martin (1879–1966), a British Methodist minister and missionary. Uncle lives in a gigantic house called Homeward, rides around in a traction engine, and is surrounded by enemies who try to prove that he is a pompous imposter and that he once stole a bicycle (which he did). These enemies include Beaver Hateman, Hitmouse, Jellytussle, and the Wooden-Legged Donkey. The Uncle books (of which there are six; the first, *Uncle*, appeared in 1964) are full of the wildest schoolboy-style inventions and implausibilities, narrated with dead-pan humour. They are illustrated by Quentin *Blake. All six books were reissued in a single-volume 'omnibus' edition in 2013.

Uncle Lubin (1902) A story by W. Heath *Robinson.

Uncle Oojah *See* OOJAH ANNUAL.

Uncle Remus, *his songs and his sayings; the folklore of the old plantation* Title of the first collection of American 'Negro' *fables to be made by Joel Chandler *Harris. It was published in November 1880 (the title page reads '1881') by D. Appleton of New York, with illustrations by Frederick Church and James Moser.

In his introduction Harris wrote of the book:

However humorous it may be in effect, its intention is perfectly serious . . . My purpose has been to preserve the legends themselves in their original simplicity, and to wed them permanently to the quaint dialect . . . through the medium of which they have become part of the domestic history of every Southern family.

The first section of the book, 'Legends of the Old Plantation', consists of tales told by Uncle Remus, an old black man, to the small son of the plantation owner. The hero of most of them is Brer Rabbit, and a constant theme is the attempts of Brer Fox to catch him. These always fail: 'Brer Fox ain't never kotch 'im yet,' Uncle Remus tells the boy, 'en w'at's mo', honey, he ain't gwineter.' In one of the most memorable tales Brer Fox makes a counterfeit black human baby out of tar; Brer Rabbit comes down the road, can get no answer to the remarks he addresses to the Tar-Baby ('Tar-Baby, she ain't sayin' nuthin''), and hits

out at it—whereupon he sticks fast. The boy asks Uncle Remus if this means that Brer Fox caught and ate Brer Rabbit. 'Dat's all de fur de tale goes,' replies the old man. 'He mout, en den agin he moutent.'

In another story, Brer Rabbit's friend Brer Tarrypin (terrapin) falls off a shelf and stuns Brer Fox, an episode which, as Harris observed in his introduction, has a parallel in Amazonian Indian folklore.

The other two sections of the book are 'His Songs', a collection of African-American hymns and work-songs, and 'His Sayings', a series of anecdotes displaying African-American humour, which Harris attaches to the character of Uncle Remus.

The book was hailed by the critics on its American publication and English editions began to appear at once. *Uncle Remus and his Legends of the Old Plantation* was issued by David Bogue of London and *Uncle Remus or Mr Fox, Mr Rabbit, and Mr Terrapin* appeared under the *Routledge imprint, both in 1881. The former consisted merely of the animal tales, but the latter included the 'Songs and Sayings' as well.

Harris produced a sequel, *Nights with Uncle Remus* (1883), partly compiled from folk tales sent to him by readers of the first collection; it included other narrators: African Jack, who speaks in the Gullah dialect of African Americans from the coastal rice plantations, Aunt Tempy, who tells *witch tales, and 'Tildy, the house girl, who contributes *ghost stories. This book was more obviously aimed at folklorists than was the first volume, but in further volumes in the series Harris wrote explicitly for children. These include *Uncle Remus and His Friends* (1892) and *The Tar-Baby and Other Rhymes of Uncle Remus* (1904).

The 'Uncle Remus' stories include such titles as 'Why Mr Possum has no Hair on his Tail' and 'Why the Negro is Black'. They were read during his teens by *Kipling, and their influence may be seen in his *Just So Stories*.

The best known illustrations are those by A. B. *Frost, originally published in an edition of 1895.

Uncle Tom's Cabin, *or, Life Among the Lowly* A novel by Harriet Beecher *Stowe, first published in serial form between June 1851 and April 1852, in the *National Era* (Washington, DC).

The plantation-owning Shelby family, though kindly by nature, are obliged from financial pressure to put their slaves up for sale. Eliza, one of the slaves, runs away before she can be sold, taking her little boy; but Uncle Tom is bought by a slave trader and separated from his wife, Aunt Chloe. Travelling on a boat up the Mississippi, he saves the life of Eva St Clair, the small daughter of a kindly gentleman, who at her request buys Tom himself. Tom is kindly treated by the St Clairs. While he is with them the household is joined by Topsy, a little black girl who has been rescued from drunken owners. Little Eva St Clair dies and her father loses his life after intervening in a fight. Tom is sold again and is bought by a drunken and degenerate plantation owner, Simon Legree. When two slaves escape Tom is blamed, and is given a flogging which causes his death. The book ends with George Shelby, who has learnt of Tom's end and is now a confirmed abolitionist, giving his slaves their freedom.

Uncle Tom's Cabin appeared in book form in March 1852. A copy was sent by an enterprising young man in a New York publishing house to a London publisher, with the suggestion that it might sell well in England. It appeared during May under the imprint of Clark & Co., the young man receiving £5 for his trouble but the author getting no royalties, this being a conspicuous case of piracy. Within a year some eighteen British editions were available, including one illustrated by *Cruikshank. Children's retellings soon began to appear on both sides of the Atlantic, and in shortened form the book quickly became a nursery classic.

Under the Tree (1922) A book of verses by the American poet and novelist Elizabeth Madox Roberts (1886–1941). They are an attempt—unusually successful, in the opinion of some critics—to record a view of the world exactly as children see it, with language that is simple almost to the point of banality.

Under the Window (1879) Kate *Greenaway's first *picture book for children, consisting of her own verses and illustrations. It was accepted for publication, and engraved and printed, by Edmund *Evans, at a time when the artist was relatively unknown, and it made her reputation. The verses are generally simple but many of them display her gentle sense of humour.

Like her contemporary Walter *Crane, Kate Greenaway was concerned with the appearance of the whole book (the contents pages of *Under the Window* are among its prettiest) and with the arrangement of the complete page. Each is framed with subtle variation,

sometimes with decorative borders of flowers or, in one case, teacups, and the figures are set carefully around the text. But, unlike Crane, Kate Greenaway enjoyed pale tints and spacious areas of white paper, producing a delicate and airy effect. *Under the Window* also amply displays the characteristic repertoire of quaint clothes and accessories which made her work an influence on children's dress as well as on their books:

Five little sisters walking in a row;
Now isn't that the best way for little girls to go?
Each had a round hat, each had a muff,
And each had a new pelisse of soft green stuff.

Undine A story by *La Motte Fouqué, published in German in 1811 and first translated into English in 1818. The water-sprite Undine, whose name the author took from Goethe, has been adopted and brought up by an old fisherman and his wife who have lost their own child. She meets the knight Huldbrand, who comes to the fisherman's cottage; the two fall in love and Undine marries him, only then revealing that she is not human. By the marriage she gains a soul. Huldbrand subsequently falls in love with Bertalda, who proves to be the fisherman's long-lost daughter. Undine returns to her watery element, but when Huldbrand marries Bertalda the water-sprite reappears and kills the knight with a kiss.

The story, which has resemblances to *The *Little Mermaid* by *Andersen, is descended from *Mélusine*, the French folk tale of a water-sprite who marries a knight on condition that he shall never see her on Saturdays, when she resumes her mermaid shape. *Undine* has been made into a ballet and an opera, and it was the basis of the 1938 play, *Ondine*, by Jean Giraudoux. An abridged English edition of the story published in 1909 has fine illustrations by *Rackham. George *MacDonald thought *Undine* 'the most beautiful' of all *fairy stories, and the references to it in such works as Charlotte Yonge's *The *Daisy Chain* and Louisa Alcott's *Little Women* show that it was one of the best loved of all books for many 19th-cent. children.

Ungava, *A Tale of Esquimaux-Land* (1858) A novel by R. M. *Ballantyne. Twenty-two-year-old Frank Morton and his older friend George Stanley are among the volunteers on a Hudson's Bay Company expedition to establish a trading station in Canada, at Ungava Bay. Stanley's ten-year-old daughter Edith accompanies the party and rescues Frank when he nearly dies after a fall in the mountains. In an epilogue, set seven years later, she marries Frank.

UNGERER, Tomi (Jean Thomas Ungerer) (1931–) Cartoonist and author who was born in Strasbourg and moved to the USA in 1957. He is probably best known today for *The Three Robbers*, in which the three ruthless eponymous characters kidnap a little girl, who causes them to have a change of heart. (There is also a 2007 feature film adaptation.) His other children's books include stories about 'The Mellops' (1957 onwards); *Moon Man* (1966), with admirers including Maurice *Sendak; *Zeralda's Ogre* (1967), about an *ogre cured of eating children by the superb cooking of a farmer's daughter; *The Hat* (1970), the story of a magic hat blown onto the head of an old soldier; and *Otto: The Autobiography of a Teddy Bear* (1999), an original and moving Holocaust story. He was also the original illustrator for Jeff Brown's *Flat Stanley. He won the 1998 *Hans Christian Andersen Medal.

Union Jack A name first used for a British *adventure story journal published from 1880 to 1883, at first edited by W. H. G. *Kingston and then after a few months by G. A. *Henty. The magazine failed to obtain a big enough readership to keep in print, but its title was revived in 1894 for an adventure magazine launched by *Harmsworth. Like *Marvel, his *Union Jack* claimed to publish 'pure, healthy tales only'. At first it specialized in open-air stories of *'Indians' (Native Americans), explorers, and the like, and in Henty-like tales of daring British heroes, but *Sexton Blake also appeared in it from early numbers and soon took over as the magazine's sole hero. In this form *Union Jack* ran till 1933, when it was merged with *Detective Weekly*.

UNSTEAD, R. J. (Robert John) (1915–88) British author of innumerable *history books for children, Unstead was a schoolmaster from 1936 until 1957, finally at Grange School, Letchworth. His earliest and best known work is *Looking at History* (1953). He co-edited *Black's Children's Encyclopaedia* (1961).

UNWIN, David *See* SEVERN, DAVID.

UNWIN, Nora S. (Spicer) (1907–82) British author and illustrator. The first children's book she illustrated was E. *Nesbit's posthumously published *Five of Us—and Madeline* (1925). She herself wrote the text for ten children's books, of which the first was *Round the Year: Verses and Pictures* (1939).

UPDALE, Eleanor (1953–) A versatile British author who became a writer after a successful career as a BBC producer. She is most acclaimed for her award-winning series beginning with *Montmorency: Thief, Liar, Gentleman?* (2003), about a youth in Victorian times who leads a double life—above ground he is a gentleman, in the tunnels under London he is a thief. A fifth in the series, *Montmorency Returns*, appeared in 2014. *Johnny Swanson* (2010) is a historical novel set in 1929. *The Last Minute* (2013) is a structurally highly original book, describing the final minute in the lives of each of the people in a small town just before a great tragedy; it is told in sixty fragmentary chapters, each advancing the action by a single second, and was also supported by an imaginative online campaign.

UPTON, Florence K. (1873–1922) The artist who invented the *golliwog in a series of *picture books which began to appear in the 1890s. Born in the United States of English parents, Upton went to England when she was twenty and remained there for the rest of her life. Her mother Bertha Upton (1849–1912) wrote the verse texts for the picture books; the first of these, *The Adventures of two Dutch Dolls and a 'Golliwogg'* (1895), tells how two wooden dolls on the loose in a toyshop suddenly see 'a horrid sight! The blackest gnome'. This is the 'Golliwogg', an invention (both in name and appearance) of the artist. The first book was followed by *The Golliwogg's Bicycle Club* (1896) and other titles, up to 1909. Miss Upton's drawings, which were printed by *lithography, are not innovative in style but make a bold use of colour. The series became a great favourite with many children. Upton and her mother did not copyright their invention, however. They missed the opportunity of making a fortune, for a 'golliwogg' craze soon began; every kind of novelty was produced

(paperknives, greetings cards, wallpaper, games, etc.), and the composer Claude Debussy's suite *Children's Corner* (1906–8) included a 'Golliwogg's Cake-Walk'.

URE, Jean (1943–) A prolific English author of books for children whose first book, *Dance for Two*, was published in 1960, when she was just sixteen. With stories that are about real lives told with humour, her books are perfect for children who want recognizable characters and a reassurance that there are other kids out there just like them. The funny, insightful nine-volume Diary series starts with *Skinny Melon and Me* (1996), the most recent title to date being *Jelly Baby* (2014). The much darker *Plague 99* (1989), in which three teens are left alive after a plague hits England, and *Bad Alice* (2003), about abuse, are for older readers.

UTTLEY, Alison (1884–1976) Creator of the *Little Grey Rabbit books. She was born on a farm in rural Derbyshire, studied physics at Manchester and Cambridge, and became a science teacher in London until her marriage in 1911. She began to write for magazines in the 1920s and produced the first Little Grey Rabbit book in 1929. Her husband died the following year, whereupon Alison (who was actually christened 'Alice Jane') began to write more prolifically—her output for children totals some eighty titles, as well as twenty books for adults about country life. Other than Little Grey Rabbit, her most popular series was about 'Sam Pig' (1940 onwards). She also wrote a *play for children based on the life and stories of Hans Christian *Andersen. *The Country Child* (1931) is an account of her own upbringing. *A Traveller in Time* (1939) is a *fantasy in which a modern girl becomes involved in the attempt by a 16th-cent. family to rescue Mary, Queen of Scots.

VACHELL, H. A. *See* HILL, THE.

VAIZEY, Mrs George de Horne (1860–1916) English *girls' story writer who created the heroine Pixie O'Shaugnessy, 'the joy and terror of the school'. She also wrote 'Peggy Savile' novels. Besides producing about forty books she contributed to *The *Girls' Own Paper*.

VALENTINE, Jenny (1970–) British author whose English degree led her to writing via a varied career including jewellery-making and working in a health food shop. Deeply empathic, subtle, literary but funny, her books explore the complexities of growing up in the here and now and often deal with fragile people, the search for individuality in a homogenized world, and the workings of chance and fate. Her first novel, *Finding Violet Park*, with the story of Lucas and the ashes he finds, was an immediate success. Other books include *Broken Soup* (2008), about how one girl and her family deal with grief, *The Ant Colony* (2009), which brings together all the strangers inhabiting a boarding house, *The Double Life of Cassiel Roadnight* (2010), about a boy, in desperation, taking on the identity of a missing person, and *Fire Colour One* (2015), her best to date, about inadequate parents, secrets, friends, and the surprising redemptive power of art.

VALENTINE, Mrs L. B. *See* AUNT LOUISA.

Valentine and Orson A medieval *romance which became a popular *chapbook, and was among the favourite adventure stories of many English children from the 16th to the 18th cent.

The wife of Alexander, Emperor of Constantinople, gives birth to twin sons, but she and the children are cast out of the court because of her supposed unfaithfulness and she subsequently loses the children. One is brought up by the King of France and the other is nurtured by a bear. The first is named Valentine, the second Orson (bear's-son). The two eventually meet, neither knowing who the other is, and fight; Orson is then tamed by Valentine's kindness and is taken back by him to court. They have many subsequent adventures together. Valentine and Orson are eventually crowned as joint Emperors of Greece, but after a time Valentine withdraws from court and becomes a hermit, ending his days in solitude.

The plot is rambling and complicated even by the standard of medieval romances. Nevertheless it achieved great popularity in England. The first English version, by Henry Watson, was printed c.1505 by Wynkyn de *Worde and again several times in the 16th cent. In 1637 an abbreviated chapbook version made its first appearance, and many other shortened versions followed.

Valentine and Orson seems to have provided Spenser with a number of incidents in *The *Faerie Queene*, and the talking head and the flying wooden horse in *Don Quixote* may perhaps have been derived from one of the European versions of the romance. In the 19th cent. it was occasionally used as the basis of a *pantomime. Various versions specially for children were printed, including those published by John *Harris (1804) and *Tabart (1813) and a *toy book illustrated by Walter *Crane (1870).

Valiant Little Tailor, The A story collected by the brothers *Grimm, sometimes published as a separate book.

A tailor kills seven flies and is so pleased with himself that he sets out to show the world how brave he is, donning a girdle embroidered with the words 'Seven at one stroke'. He tricks a *giant into believing him to be immensely strong and is then commissioned by a king to kill two more giants who are troubling the land. The tailor throws stones at them from a tree, making each believe that the other is the aggressor, and goads them into killing each other. Finally, by further tricks, he catches a unicorn and a wild boar, and is rewarded with the king's daughter and half the kingdom. Similar stories are found all over Europe, an English equivalent being *Jack the Giant Killer*.

vampires A staple of children's and especially *young adult fiction, as well as *horror fiction for adults. Since Bram Stoker's *Dracula* (1897)—by no means the originator of the figure, but the earliest incarnation whose popularity really endures—there have been two strands to the cultural obsession: one sees the vampire as the supremely romantic figure—tormented, agonized by the curse to need human blood, immortal, and perpetually beautiful; the other sees beneath the exquisite skin to the killer below; though there is fascination in both. Stephenie Meyer's *Twilight*—in the former category, with the vampires shimmeringly beautiful—takes the anti-hero well-known to popular culture and transforms it into a 21st-cent. phenomenon. Hugely influential, it inspired many other writers, especially in the US. A school for vampires puts the genre into the world of boarding schools in Richelle Mead's (1976-) *Vampire Academy* (2007) as does the *House of Night* series by P. C. Cast (1960-) and Kristen Cast (1986-), starting with *Marked* (2007). A town controlled by vampires is the setting for Rachel Caine's (1962-) *Morganville Vampires* series, the first being *Glass Houses* (2006). *The Vampire Diaries* series (1991) by L. J. Smith (1965-) is the story of vampire brothers and the girl caught between them, and *Blue Bloods* (2006) by Melissa de la Cruz (1971-) starts a series set in New York. *Cirque Du Freak* (1999) by Darren *Shan is high on gore. Vampire fiction in the UK today spans the age ranges, from Ann Jungman's amusing *Vlad the Drac* books (1982-), to Justin Somper's swashbuckling *Vampirates* series (a vampire-pirate combination, 2005-) right up to the sophistications of books like Marcus *Sedgwick's *My Swordhand Is Singing*.

VAN ALLSBURG, Chris (1949-) American illustrator, artist, and writer who became an artist almost by accident, signing up for art at college because it looked like fun. When he was already an acclaimed sculptor, his wife recognized the illustrative potential in his hyper-realistic drawings, and his first book, *The Garden of Abdul Gasazi* was published in 1979. Surreal, dark-edged, and clearly realized, it led to *Jumanji* (1981) and its companion book, *Zathura* (2002), both about a magical board game. *The *Polar Express* (1985) is a Christmas story about the joys and innocence of childhood and *The *Mysteries of Harris Burdick* (1984) contains a series of pictures with a single line of text on the opposite page.

VAN LOON, Hendrik (Willem) (1882-1944) Born in the Netherlands, Van Loon came to the United States in 1903, and wrote a number of *books of instruction for children, of which the best known is *The Story of Mankind* (1921), a world *history from prehistoric times to the present century. The book won the first *Newbery Medal and was much admired in its day for bringing a fresh energy to its subject, but it has a degree of naïve optimism that now seems dated; for example, Van Loon writes of the First World War that it 'brought about the coming of a new day'.

VAN STOCKUM, Hilda (1908-2006) Dutch-born author, living in the United States, who is best known for *The Winged Watchman* (1962), a story of resistance and betrayal during the Nazi occupation of Holland.

VELTHUIJS, Max (1923-2005) An award-winning, internationally renowned illustrator and picture-book creator from the Netherlands. Velthuijs began his career as a commercial illustrator and artist but began illustrating children's books in the 1960s with a special tenth edition of *Versjes die wij nooit vergeten* (1962; *Rhymes we will never forget*). His second book *A is een aapje* (1964; *A is for Monkey*) demonstrates his strong sense of graphic design and bold colour palette. The first picture book he created, *Der Junge und der Fisch* (1969; *The Boy and the Fish*) won the Golden Apple award at the Biennial of Illustrations Bratislava in 1971. However, it is the picture-book series featuring the philosophical and somewhat distempered Frog (whose favourite colour is green) that he is best known for. Frog first appears in *Little Man Has No House* (1983), but the first in the series, *Frog in Love*, was published in the UK in 1989. The series brings profound existential thought into picture books, introducing children to complex themes in a safe and sensitive way. *Frog and the Birdsong* (1991) is a beautifully simple account of death which won the Gouden Griffel Award, while *Frog Is Sad* (2003) is a touching depiction of depression. Velthuijs was awarded the biennial *Hans Christian Andersen Award in 2004.

Velveteen Rabbit, The (1922) A picture book by Margery *Williams illustrated by Sir William *Nicholson (1872-1949). When a stuffed rabbit yearns to be alive, a wise toy horse explains to him that the love of a child can make a toy become real. The rabbit becomes the boy's favourite toy, but the boy

gets scarlet fever and the doctor recommends that his playthings be destroyed. At the last minute a fairy appears and transforms the stuffed animal into a living rabbit.

Frequently republished in its long life, the book has acquired the status of a modern fairy tale. Themes of love, faithfulness, and the desire to belong combine with subtler ideas about loss and growing up to add depth and give it a timeless appeal that balances an inherent whimsicality. The theme of toys coming to life is not infrequent in children's books: *Pinocchio is an earlier example; later ones include the *Toy Story* animation series and *The Journey of Edward Tulane* by Kate *DiCamillo.

VERNE, Jules (1828–1905) Pioneer writer of *science fiction who was born in Nantes, the son of a lawyer. He studied for the legal profession himself, but, as a young man living in Paris, began to have some small success as a playwright. He became a stockbroker and meanwhile wrote *Cinq Semaines en ballon* (*Five Weeks in a Balloon*, 1863), which was suggested by the project of his friend 'Nadar' (Feliz Tournachon) to ascend in a huge gas balloon. Verne wrote the story at his club, because the crying of his baby son annoyed him. The novel was accepted by the publisher Hetzel, who wanted serials for a new journal, the *Magasin d'éducation et de récréation*.

Voyage au centre de la terre (*Journey to the Centre of the Earth*), appeared in 1864, followed by *De la terre à la lune* (1865), first published in English in 1873 as *From Earth to the Moon Direct* and *Les Enfants du Capitaine Grant* (*The Children of Captain Grant*, 1868). Verne continued the story of his moon travellers in *Autour de la lune* (*Around the Moon*, 1870).

The book which is generally regarded as his most remarkable work, *Vingt mille lieues sous les mers* (1870, first translated into English in 1873 as *Twenty Thousand Leagues under the Seas*), owed much to the exploits of the huge experimental French submarine *Le Plongeur* and to the work of Verne's friend Jacques-François Conseil, who developed a steam-driven submarine and whose surname Verne gave to Professor Arronax's servant in the story. Verne continued to write prolifically while serving as a coastguard in the Franco-Prussian War. His most popular novel, *Le Tour du monde en quatre-vingts jours* appeared in 1873. English translations came out shortly afterwards, entitled *Around the World in Eighty Days* or *Round the World in Eighty Days*.

In 1874–5 there appeared in three volumes *L'Île mystérieuse* (*The Mysterious Island*), the last of Verne's novels that is an enduring classic. By this time Verne was a celebrated public figure and a wealthy man. His later books in the series *Les Voyages extraordinaires*, of which there was at least one a year up to his death, are mostly unremarkable, and his sales gradually dwindled. In 1886 he was shot in the foot by a nephew, who was thereafter shut up in a psychiatric hospital; the injury left Verne with a limp for the rest of his life.

Though Verne did not write his books with a child audience in mind, they immediately became popular with young readers and many of his stories first appeared in English in the pages of juvenile *magazines. W. H. G. *Kingston translated a number of them for *The *Boy's Own Paper*.

Verne was by no means the first writer of science fiction; in 1865, the year in which his novel describing a moon-shot was published, at least four other books describing interplanetary travel appeared in French alone. Nor was Verne a true scientist: he invented scientific 'facts' or adapted them to his needs with a complete disregard for reality. But he had a remarkable understanding of the possibilities of science; for example, his description of the details of space travel is very close to what actually happened in the 1960s—the design of the capsule, the use of rockets to alter its orbit, and the final 'splashdown' in the sea. Moreover his admiration in childhood for *Defoe, *The *Swiss Family Robinson*, and (rather later) the novels of *Scott, James Fenimore *Cooper, and Edgar Allen Poe, rooted his work in the best kinds of *adventure story and gave it a life which has carried it into the 20th cent.

VERNEY, (Sir) John 2nd Baronet (1913–93) British artist and children's author. He illustrated books by Gillian *Avery, drew the cover pictures for *Young Elizabethan* magazine, and wrote children's and adult novels and works of autobiography.

Verse novels, pieces of long-form fiction told through series of poems, most usually free verse. In recent years most successful verse novels for children and teenagers have come out of the US; good examples of the form include: Sharon *Creech's *Love that Dog*, Virginia *Euwer Wolff's *Make Lemonade* and its sequels, Karen *Hesse's *Out of the Dust*, Jacqueline *Woodson's *Locomotion* and *Brown Girl Dreaming*, Ron *Koertge's *The Brimstone Journals*, Kwame Alexander's *Newbery Award-winning *The Crossover* (2014), and various books by Ellen Hopkins (1955–) and Sonya

Sones (eg. *What My Mother Doesn't Know*, 2001; *One of Those Hideous Books where the Mother Dies*, 2004). Significant examples from the rest of the English-speaking world include books both by prose writers making only brief occasional forays into the medium (eg. Malorie *Blackman's *Cloud Busting* or Margaret *Wild's *One Night*) and by those with a speciality in this way of telling a story: see, for example, the work of Irish writer Sarah *Crossan, and Australian Steven Herrick (1958- , author of *The Simple Gift* and others).

Very Hungry Caterpillar, The (1969) A counting-book by Eric *Carle, one of the most enduringly popular children's books of all time, with sales to date topping thirty million copies. With bright collage artwork, Carle tells the story of a caterpillar who pops out of an egg one Sunday morning, hungry, and starts to eat: one apple on Monday, two pears on Tuesday, three plums on Wednesday, and so on. By the end of the week he is ready to build himself a cocoon, and soon he is a beautiful butterfly. Carle's original plan had been to make his story about a bookworm; it was his editor who suggested the caterpillar as potentially more sympathetic. (Apparently the possibility of concluding with a butterfly transformation sealed the deal.)

Vicarage Family, The (1963) By Noel *Streatfeild. 'Oh the poor Vicar. How dreadful for him having such a tomboy for a daughter.' It is the early 20th cent., when children's lives are governed by rules and teenagers do not exist. In this thinly disguised autobiography (it is subtitled 'a biography of myself'), Streatfeild paints a portrait of a world that is very different from that experienced by most young people today, a world that ended as the book ends, with the First World War. This is not an idyllic portrait. Like Anne Frank's *Diary of a Young Girl*, it gives young readers the chance to meet a real girl with whom they can empathize, and to experience an everyday life many children would have known. The story continues in *Away from the Vicarage* (1965) and *Beyond the Vicarage* (1971).

Vice Versa, *or, a Lesson to Fathers* (1882) A novel by 'F. *Anstey' (T. A. Guthrie). Through the power of an oriental talisman Mr Paul Bultitude, a middle-aged and pompous City businessman, takes on the appearance of his son Dick and finds himself suffering all the rigours of Crichton House, Dick's boarding school, while Dick, who has taken on his father's shape, leads the comfortable life of a City gentleman.

Guthrie began to write the story when he was an undergraduate at Cambridge. After being rejected by several magazine editors it was accepted by Smith and Elder in return for a payment of £25 per edition printed. It had very enthusiastic reviews (including two by Andrew *Lang) and instantly became a best-seller. It was dramatized in 1883 by Edward Rose and again by Guthrie himself in 1910. Among those who read it when it first appeared was Guthrie's old headmaster, the original of 'Dr Grimstone', who observed to Guthrie's father: 'I recognized myself in that book.' To which Guthrie *père* replied that he 'recognized *himself* too'.

C. S. *Lewis, who was educated at a preparatory school closely resembling Crichton House, called *Vice Versa* 'the only truthful school story in existence'.

VILDRAC, Charles (1882-1971) French children's author, best known for *Les Lunettes du lion* (1951) (*The Lion's Eyeglasses*, 1969), a comic story about the King of the Beasts losing his glasses.

Village School, The, *or a Collection of Entertaining Histories* By Dorothy *Kilner, first published *c.* 1795. Mrs Bell keeps a school at Rose Green; the book describes the misdemeanours of her pupils and the consequences of them, and provides further examples of the rewards of virtue and vice from the storybooks that the children read at school. Miss Kilner does not hesitate to show the awful fates that can result from carelessness: one child falls down a well and is drowned, and Mrs Bell herself burns to death.

Violet Elizabeth Bott In the *William stories by Richmal *Crompton.

VIORST, Judith (1931-) American author of prose and poetry for children and adults, writer for television, and newspaper columnist. Her debut picture book, *I'll Fix Anthony* (1969), illustrated by Arnold *Lobel, introduces what would become her main subject matter: the less enjoyable aspects of childhood, a topic which she often handles with humour. Viorst is best known for *Alexander and the Terrible, Horrible, No Good, Very Bad Day* (1972), the success of which led to two sequels: *Alexander, Who Used to be Rich Last Sunday* (1978) and *Alexander, Who's Not (Do You Hear Me? I Mean It!) Going to Move* (1995). She adapted the first and third Alexander books as musicals and *Alexander and the Terrible, Horrible, No Good, Very Bad Day* is being made into a feature film for release in

late 2014. *The *Tenth Good Thing about Barney* (1987) deals sensitively with a boy's grief after the death of his pet. Viorst's other works for children include *The Good-bye Book* (1988), *Super-Completely and Totally the Messiest* (2001), two volumes of poetry, and, most recently, *Lulu and the Brontosaurus* (2010) and *Lulu Walks the Dogs* (2012), both illustrated by Lane *Smith.

VIPONT, Elfrida (1902–92) British author of nearly two dozen children's novels, of which the best known are *The Lark in the Morn* (1948) and *The Lark on the Wing* (1950), both about a Quaker schoolgirl, Kit Haverard, who becomes a brilliant singer. The second volume won the *Carnegie Medal. In 1969 she and Raymond *Briggs produced a classic *picture book for small children, *The *Elephant and the Bad Baby*.

Visit from St Nicholas, A A poem by Clement Clarke *Moore which played a large part in developing the modern myth of *Father Christmas, or Santa Claus. It begins:

'Twas the night before Christmas, when all
 through the house
Not a creature was stirring, not even a mouse;
The stockings were hung by the chimney with
 care,
In hopes that St Nicholas soon would be there.

The narrator hears a 'clatter' on the lawn, and looks out of his bedroom window to see a sleigh carrying 'St Nick', who calls to his reindeer:

'Now, *Dasher!* now *Dancer!* now, *Prancer* and
 Vixen!
On, *Comet!* on, *Cupid!* on, *Donder* and *Blitzen!*'
He leaps down the chimney:
He was dressed all in fur, from his head to
 his foot,
And his clothes were all tarnished with ashes
 and soot;
A bundle of Toys he had flung on his back,
And he looked like a pedlar, just opening his
 pack . . .
He had a broad face and a little round belly,
That shook when he laughed, like a bowlfull
 of jelly.
Nicholas fills the stockings, ascends the chimney
 again, and exclaims
'Happy Christmas to all, and to all a good night.'

The poem is said to have been written by Moore to amuse his children (he had nine in all) in 1822 and to have been transcribed by a guest who passed it to a newspaper published near New York, the *Troy Sentinel*. Certainly it first appeared there anonymously in 1823. It was soon being reprinted in school readers

and eventually Moore himself included it in his *Poems* (1844), thus resolving disputes about its authorship. It was also published separately, the first such edition apparently being that printed by Henry M. Onderdonk of New York in 1848. Subsequently it has been widely translated; its illustrators have included F. O. C. *Darley (*c.* 1862), W. W. Denslow (1902), and Arthur *Rackham (1931). It has generally been published under the title *The Night Before Christmas*.

Whether or not Moore was responsible for attaching the St Nicholas tradition to Christmas, he was certainly the first person to describe in print the flying sleigh, the reindeer, and Nicholas's method of entering houses by the chimney. (The Dutch St Nicholas comes into houses by a variety of means, and on his own feast day, 6 December) According to one of Moore's granddaughters, he based his description of Nicholas's appearance on a rotund and jolly Dutchman who did odd jobs for him on his family estate. The detail of the sleigh is supposed to have come from Moore's own journeys to his estate from the city by sleigh in winter weather. It is notable that the *wood engravings which illustrate Onderdonk's 1848 edition of the poem show a Nicholas who looks something like a Dutch artisan and who has certainly not yet acquired the hooded cloak which popular tradition nowadays invariably dresses him in.

Vitalstatistix Chief of the Gaulish tribe in the *Astérix books.

VIVAS, Julie (1947–) Australian picture-book illustrator whose reputation was established with the bestseller, *Possum Magic*, written by Mem *Fox. This well-loved book had sold three million copies worldwide in various formats by 2011, and won a number of children's choice awards. Her use of white space and the strong composition of the illustrations did much to establish standards of excellence for the picture-book format worldwide.

Vivas's work is sometimes regarded as controversial. She was shortlisted in 1987 for *The Nativity* (1986), the text being the King James Version of the Bible story of the birth of Jesus. Vivas's portrayal of the characters was realistic, first showing Mary as heavily pregnant and later exhausted, although joy pervades this book, with gesture contributing to vitality of the story. *Let the Celebrations Begin!* (1991) by Margaret *Wild was shortlisted for *CBCA Picture Book of the Year in 1992. Although set in

Belsen concentration camp, this book is not morose: Vivas's evocative illustrations show the happiness women find in creating toys and a special party for the children.

Vivas remains one of Australia's most popular and in-demand illustrators, with over twenty-five books to date. She sets high standards, making complete dummies and several roughs of illustrations, and her work, whether watercolour or pastel, is always empathetic, poignant, and sometimes humorous. Vivas has a delicacy of touch and an eloquent use of colour, and creates outstanding characters.

VOAKE, Charlotte (1957–) British author and illustrator of charming, whimsical picture books about families, cats, and nature. She works in ink and watercolour; her style has been said to contain echoes of Edward *Ardizzone's. She was shortlisted for the *Kate Greenaway Medal and won the Nestlé Smarties Gold Award for *Ginger* (1997). (The cat also features in two other titles.) *Hello Twins* (2007) won the British Book Design and Production Award. Voake was chosen by the family of Eleanor *Farjeon for the first illustrated version of Farjeon's 1937 story *Elsie Piddock Skips in Her Sleep* (1997).

VOIGT, Cynthia (1942–) American author of books for children and young adults who started writing when she was a teacher. Her first books were the *Tillerman Cycle*, starting with *Homecoming, about four children abandoned in a shopping mall and their search for a home. The hero of the books is Dicey, a strong female character who fights against all odds for her family's, and her own, happiness. Dicey is the first of many independent female heroes in Voigt's books, including those in *Jackaroo* (1985) and *Bad Girls* (1996).

Voldemort (Tom Riddle; 'He-Who-Must-Not-Be-Named'; 'You-Know-Who') The arch-villain of the *Harry Potter books.

Voyage of the 'Dawn Treader', The (1952) The third of the *Narnia novels by C. S. *Lewis.

WADDELL, Martin (1941–) A Belfast-born writer who started his career writing for adults but has since become famous for writing picture books. The *Big Bear, Little Bear* series, illustrated by Barbara *Firth, started with *You and Me, Little Bear* (1980) and instantly endeared itself to innumerable families. *Farmer Duck* (1991), illustrated by Helen *Oxenbury, *Owl Babies* (1992), illustrated by Patrick Benson, and *Sailor Bear* (1992), illustrated by Virginia Austin, along with many others, further cemented his reputation as one of the best storytellers for the young. Using the pseudonym Catherine Sefton he writes for older children, and in *In A Blue Velvet Dress* (1972) he tells the delightful story of a bookish girl stranded without books who is helped by a ghost. In 2004 he was awarded the prestigious *Hans Christian Andersen Award.

WAGNER, Jenny (1939–) Australian author. With illustrator Ron *Brooks she has produced such *picture books as *The Bunyip of Berkeley's Creek* (1973) (*see* BUNYIP) and *John Brown, Rose, and the Midnight Cat* (1977) and she has written *The Nimbin* (1978), a *fantasy about a strange creature which lives in a girl's beach-bag.

WAKEFIELD (Bell), Priscilla (1751–1832) English Quaker, philanthropist, and pioneer of the savings bank movement, Wakefield was a prolific writer of children's books which conveyed useful knowledge combined with moral instruction. Her works include *Juvenile Anecdotes, founded on fact* (1795) and *Instinct Displayed, in a collection of well-authenticated facts, exemplifying the extraordinary sagacity of various species of the animal creation* (1811).

WAKEFIELD, S. A. *See* BOTTERSNIKES AND GUMBLES.

WALKER, David Harry (1911–92) Canadian writer of John Buchan-like *adventure stories, including *Sandy was a Soldier's Boy* (1957), *Pirate Rock* (1969), and *Big Ben* (1970).

Walk Two Moons (1994) Novel by Sharon *Creech, which won the *Newbery Medal and the Children's Book Award among others. It explores a number of themes involving grief, death, and identity. Sala (Salamanca) is on a journey, travelling with her grandparents from Euclid, Ohio, to Idaho. Sala really misses her Kentucky home, where she lived until the day her mother left—and did not return. On the journey, Sala tells her grandparents about Phoebe Winterbottom, the girl next door, who has also lost her mother. Through the stories she is able to explore her feelings, which leads to understanding and a new beginning.

WALL, Dorothy (1894–1942) Australian author-illustrator who wrote a series of stories about Blinky Bill the Koala, beginning with *Blinky Bill the Quaint Little Australian* (1933). Her other books include *Brownie, the Story of a Naughty Little Rabbit* (1935). She illustrated books by other writers.

WALLIAMS, David (1971–) English author, actor, comedian, and TV personality whose first foray into the world of humorous books for children, *The Boy in the Dress* (2008, illustrated by Quentin *Blake) was an immediate success with readers, particularly boys. It has been noted that his books are influenced by other writers, particularly Anne *Fine and Roald *Dahl, but Walliams's sense of humour and modern spin on families make his work his own. His other joke-filled books include *Mr Stink* (2009, also illustrated by Blake), in which a girl befriends a tramp, and the award-winning *Ratburger* (2012, illustrated by Tony *Ross), which adds a fresh dimension to the Wicked Stepmother trope (Ross has also illustrated Walliams's *Billionaire Boy* (2010) and *Gangsta Granny* (2011) in a similar vein).

Wallypug of Why, The (1895) An imitation of *Alice's Adventures in Wonderland*, written by G. E. *Farrow and illustrated by Harry *Furniss. The heroine, Girlie, drowsing in her armchair, is addressed by her doll,

Dumpsey Deazil, who says she will take her 'to the land of Why, where all the questions and answers come from'. On her way Girlie meets such characters as the Doctor-in-law, who gives 'professional advice' without being asked for it and then demands a large fee, and a Fish who is 'fishing for compliments'. Eventually she encounters the Wallypug, 'a kind of king, governed by the people instead of governing them'. Lewis *Carroll's nonsense is imitated in such remarks as 'I don't want a watch that will *go*, I want one that will stay.'

WALPOLE, Hugh *See* JEREMY.

Walrus and the Carpenter, The A poem by Lewis *Carroll which appears in *Through the Looking-Glass* (1871). Unlike the majority of Carroll's *nonsense-poems, it is not a parody, though it takes its style from Thomas Hood's 'Dream of Eugene Aram'. Carroll left the choice of the Walrus's companion to his illustrator, *Tenniel, presenting him with three alternatives, a butterfly, a baronet, or a carpenter, all of which fitted the metre.

WALSH, Jill Paton *See* PATON WALSH, JILL.

WALTON, Mrs O. F. (Amy Catherine) (1849–1939) Popular British *evangelical writer, author of *Christie's Old Organ* (1874), *A *Peep Behind the Scenes* (1877), and other stories published by the *Religious Tract Society.

Wanted: a King; *or How Merle Set the Nursery Rhymes to Right* (1890) A *fantasy by 'Maggie Browne', with illustrations by Harry *Furniss. Merle is lying ill in bed after a fall; she dreams of a visit to the land of Endom, where such *nursery rhyme characters as *Jack Horner, the Old Woman who Lived in a Shoe, and *Jack and Jill plan to overthrow the tyrant Grunter Grim and find their true king. With Merle's help this is achieved; Baby Bunting becomes king and the unhappy nursery rhymes are made to end happily.

The author's real name was Margaret Andrewes, *née* Hamer; her other children's books included *The Surprising Adventures of Tuppy and Tue* (1904), which was illustrated by Arthur *Rackham, and *Pleasant Work for Busy Fingers, or, Kindergarten at Home* (1896).

WARD, Elizabeth Stuart Phelps *See* GYPSY BREYNTON.

Warden's Niece, The (1957) The first children's novel by Gillian *Avery, set in the 1870s. Maria runs away from her boarding school to Oxford, where her uncle, the Warden of Canterbury College, gives her a home and allows her to study Latin and Greek with the three sons of Professor Smith. With the encouragement of the eccentric clergyman Mr Copplestone, she discovers the excitement of 'original research', and even gatecrashes the hallowed Bodleian Library to pursue her inquiries into the history of the family who once lived in Jerusalem House, a great mansion near Oxford.

The book established Gillian Avery as one of the leading British children's writers of her generation, and proved to be the first in a cycle about Victorian Oxford, which continued with *The Elephant War* (1960) and *The Italian Spring* (1964).

War Horse (1982) A novel by Michael *Morpurgo. Without apparent deliberation, in this slim tale, based on the memories of three men who fought in the First World War, Morpurgo somehow encapsulated all the destructive wastefulness and the heroism of that conflict. The truthfulness of this story is what shines out—truthfulness of the horror of war for both humans and animals, but also of what life was like in rural Devon and what love can exist between man and beast. The story was made into a hugely successful stage show (2007–) with innovative puppetry bringing the horses to life, as well as a live-action film directed by Steven Spielberg (2011).

WARNE, Frederick (1825–1901) A London publisher of children's books, originally in partnership with his brother-in-law George *Routledge. He established his own business in 1865, at first specializing in *toy books, many of them engraved and printed by Edmund *Evans. In 1895 he retired and was succeeded by his three sons, one of whom, Norman, was briefly engaged before his early death (in 1905) to the firm's most famous author, Beatrix *Potter.

WARNER, Susan Bogert (1819–85) Author, under the pseudonym 'Elizabeth Wetherell', of *The *Wide, Wide World* and *Queechy*; she was born in New York City and had childhood experiences much like those of her heroines. Like them, too, she was (according to the *Dictionary of American Biography*) 'given to frequent and copious weeping'. She produced several other novels, some of them in collaboration with her sister Anna, who wrote books independently as 'Amy Lothrop'.

Watch House, The (1977) Some writers can make your skin crawl with little more than a description of dust skittering across an old wooden floor. Robert *Westall is one such writer, and this book—in which dust skitters alarmingly—is one of his scariest. Anne is sent away for the summer, and alone and lonely in the seaside town she finds herself intrigued by the old watch house that overlooks the sea. But there are ancient enmities at work, and before the summer ends Anne will have fought for her life and her sanity, a fight that involves religion, hatred, and a confrontation with not just one ghost, but two.

Water-Babies, The, *A Fairy Tale for a Land-Baby* (1863) By Charles *Kingsley, appearing in print two years before *Alice's Adventures in Wonderland*, this book was one of the first classic *Fantasies by an English author.

Tom, a small boy with neither father nor mother, is employed by Grimes, a villainous chimney-sweep, to climb up flues and brush down the soot. His master beats him, but Tom is cheerful enough, knowing no better life. Early one morning they go to Harthover, a grand mansion, to sweep the chimneys. Tom loses his way in the dark flues and comes down into the bedroom of Ellie, the squire's little daughter, who screams in alarm at the sight of him. Losing his nerve, he jumps out of the window, and is soon being pursued across the park by Sir John Harthover's household, who believe that he has been caught in the act of stealing. Tom gives them the slip, descends a steep limestone cliff, and comes to Vendale. Tom is exhausted and feverish after his ten-mile run and wanders in a daze down to the river, thinking he hears church bells. Longing to cool himself, he strips off his clothes and gets into the water, where he falls asleep. His physical body, in fact, is drowned, but he is given a new form—that of a water-baby, tiny, amphibious, and immortal.

For a long time he stays in the shallow stream at Vendale, learning the ways of the river-creatures, and behaving towards them with the same kind of selfishness that he had displayed when a human child. At last, longing to find the company of other water-babies like himself, he sets off downstream. Through an act of kindness to a lobster he acquires the ability to see the other water-babies, who were there all the time but were invisible to him because of his selfish character. With them, he swims to the magical St Brandan's Isle, out in the sea, where he meets the fierce

Mrs Bedonebyasyoudid, who rewards and punishes the water-babies for their good and bad behaviour, and the tender and motherly Mrs Doasyouwouldbedoneby, who is pure love.

On dry land, Tom's death through drowning has caused great sorrow. Ellie, the squire's daughter, is at the seaside one day when she catches a glimpse of Tom the water-baby beneath the sea and, struggling to see him again, loses her footing and hits her head on a rock. The injury proves fatal, and Ellie herself soon comes to Tom's undersea world as a water-baby. Her pure character has earned her a special reward: on Sundays she leaves the water-babies and goes to a special place, where Tom may not accompany her. He longs to go with her, but can only gain this privilege if he sets off on a quest to the Other-end-of-Nowhere, to rescue his old master Grimes from the particular hell in which he is immured. After seeing many strange lands and peoples, he accomplishes his quest, and is rewarded by going 'home' with Ellie on Sundays—in other words, to Heaven.

After the death of her husband, Fanny Kingsley published this account of the book's inception:

Sitting at breakfast one spring morning this year [1862], the father was reminded of an old promise, 'Rose, Maurice, and Mary have got their book, and baby must have his.' He made no answer, but got up at once and went into his study, locking the door. In half an hour he returned with the story of little Tom. This was the first chapter of 'The Waterbabies', written off without a correction. The rest of the book, which appeared monthly in 'Macmillan's Magazine', was composed with the same quickness and ease as the first chapter.

Rose, Maurice, and Mary, the three elder children, had been the dedicatees of Kingsley's *The *Heroes* (1856). The new story, when it was printed in book form, bore the dedication: 'To my youngest son, Grenville Arthur, and all other good little boys.'

Kingsley created the character of Tom and described his experiences partly through reading a government report on child labour, but also (it seems) from the life of a local chimney-sweep's boy, James Seaward of Wokingham, who helped to sweep the chimneys at Eversley Rectory, Kingsley's home. The detailed description of underwater and undersea life showed Kingsley's great skill as a marine naturalist, already displayed in his *Glaucus; or the Wonders of the Shore* (1855).

The serialization in *Macmillan's Magazine* was from August 1862 to March 1863. The first

edition of the book, with Macmillan as publisher, had two illustrations by J. Noel Paton: a frontispiece depicting Mrs Doasyouwouldbedoneby surrounded by babies and a plate entitled 'Water Babies'. An edition of 1869 retained these plates and added decorations by Percival Skelton. Macmillan's commissioned Linley Sambourne to provide new pictures in 1886. The most successful illustrations are those by Heath *Robinson for a Constable edition of 1915; in that year, Mabel Lucie *Attwell illustrated an abridged version. From the beginning illustrators have been uncertain about the nakedness of the water-babies. Although Paton's original illustrations allowed the babies to be naked, Skelton's 1869 additions mostly clothed them, as have subsequent artists—Heath Robinson often shows Tom in a stout pair of swimming pants.

The story achieved huge popularity as soon as it was published. Edward *Lear wrote to Kingsley that he 'firmly believed it all to be true'. The Water-Babies has often been dramatized—the children in E. *Nesbit's novel The *Phoenix and the Carpet (1904) are taken to a performance of a musical play based on it—and several times filmed. It also appears to have helped to abolish the use of child chimney-sweeps, for a law prohibiting them was passed within a year of its publication.

The book's success was largely due to the crusading spirit in which it was written. Kingsley was attacking not only the obvious evil of the child sweeps—as one of F. D. Maurice's Christian Socialists he had long been involved in such issues—but also what he considered to be the deplorable fashion in children's books for rejecting *fairy stories in favour of factual *books of instruction. The whole of The Water-Babies is, in fact, an argument in favour of the imagination and against the cramming of facts. Tom's journey to save Grimes takes him through a land where a notice declares 'Playthings not allowed here'. Kingsley also attacks *evangelical children's fiction, which he exemplifies scornfully in such burlesque titles as 'the Pump-lighter' and 'the Narrow Narrow World', references to The *Lamplighter and The *Wide, Wide World. The Water-Babies is also in part a satire supporting Charles Darwin's Origin of the Species (published four years earlier) against the narrow-mindedness of its detractors. Tom himself undergoes a process of evolution in becoming a water-baby and Kinsley's reference in the text to the 'Hippopotamus' in the brains of the 'Doasyoulikes' echoes contemporary debate on the 'Hippocampus question' in scientific circles.

Most 20th-cent. critics of children's fiction deplored the didacticism of The Water-Babies, regarding it as a flawed masterpiece because Kingsley could not resist the urge to preach. Certainly its didactic nature has meant that the book has dated far more than the writings of Lewis *Carroll. But Kingsley's message, that 'people's souls make their bodies', is worked out in symbolism which is almost always ingenious and entertaining. Most of the passages of open moralizing (such as the attack on bad children's books) are fired with an infectious energy and written with great humour.

Watership Down (1972) An outstandingly popular *animal story by Richard *Adams. A group of rabbits flee from their Berkshire warren when it is destroyed to make way for a building site and begin a quest for a new, safe home on the Downs. The book is notable for its intricate descriptions of rabbit society (much detail was taken by the author from R. M. Lockley's The Private Life of the Rabbit), and for its characterization of Hazel, Fiver, Bigwig, and the other rabbits.

The book was turned down by all the major publishing houses to which it was offered; it was finally issued by the small firm of Rex Collings. In the first year 100,000 copies were sold in Britain, and the book was awarded both the *Carnegie Medal and the *Guardian Children's Fiction Prize. Sales in the United States were even more spectacular, and for a time the book's popularity in English-speaking countries had come to rival that of The *Lord of the Rings. It was eventually filmed.

The story originated as a tale told by Adams to his two daughters to while away a long car journey. He acknowledges the influence upon it of the nature writings of Ernest Thompson *Seton ('he didn't dodge danger, fear, bloodshed and death,' says Adams), and points out that the character of Bigwig owes something to that of Elzevir Block in J. Meade Falkner's *Moonfleet (1898). Watership Down, like the writings of *Tolkien, has attracted adverse criticism for its supposed sexism and its conservative view of society.

WATKINS-PITCHFORD, D. J. See 'B. B.'.

WATSON, Clyde (1947–) American writer of verses for children; her first collection was Father Fox's Pennyrhymes (1971). Her poems have the nonsensical character of true *nursery rhymes.

WATTS, Isaac (1674–1748) Author of *Divine Songs*, Watts was born in Southampton, the son of a Nonconformist clothier; he had a classical education at grammar school and in a dissenting academy. He earned his living first as a tutor, then became a minister of a Congregationalist meeting on the outskirts of London. He was frequently ill and spent the last thirty-six years of his life leading a sheltered existence at the home of Sir Thomas Abney, a wealthy member of his congregation, having gone there originally for a week's convalescence. Watts never married. However, he enjoyed family life with the Abneys and tutored their three daughters, to whom he dedicated *Divine Songs*. His writing on education shows some moderation of the *Puritan attitude to children.

Watts's adult hymns gave hymn singing a security and importance in Nonconformist worship that it had never had before; some of them, such as 'O God our help in ages past', are among the best-known English hymns. *Divine Songs* enjoyed huge popularity and influence during his lifetime and for more than a hundred years afterwards. Watts's imitators in the mid-18th cent. include Nathaniel *Cotton and Philip *Doddridge; his achievement was not rivalled until Ann and Jane *Taylor began to write verse early in the 19th cent.

WEBB, Kaye (1914–96) Editor of the British children's magazine *Young Elizabethan* from 1955 to 1958 and from 1961 to 1979 in charge of *Puffin Books, founding the Puffin Club in 1967 and editing *Puffin Post*. She bought paperback rights to many established books, as well as acquiring new titles, beginning with *Stig of the Dump* (the first Puffin Original). During her time at Puffin, Webb would publish Roald *Dahl, Joan *Aiken, Philippa *Pearce, and countless other stars of the children's book world of the sixties and seventies. From 1948 to 1967 she was married to the illustrator Ronald *Searle. There is a good and sympathetic life of Webb by Valerie Grove (2010).

WEBB, Marion St John *See* LITTLEST ONE.

WEBSTER, Jean *See* DADDY LONG-LEGS.

WEBSTER, Noah *See* AMERICAN SPELLING BOOK, THE.

Wee Willie Winkie A *nursery rhyme in which sleep is personified. It was written by the Scottish children's poet William Miller (1810–72) and was first published in 1841 in a version of five verses. The first stanza quickly became part of oral nursery rhyme tradition, and shortly afterwards appeared, adjusted to English pronunciation and without acknowledgement to its author, in an undated *chapbook printed by Rusher of *Banbury and in *Nursery Rhymes, Tales and Jingles* (J. Burns, 1844). If the story of its authorship were not well authenticated (in Robert Ford, *Willie Winkie*, 1902) there would be grounds for suspecting that this first verse was in fact traditional.

WEGNER, Fritz (1924–2015) An Austrian-born British illustrator, well-known for his collaboration with author Allan *Ahlberg on such classics as *Please Mrs Butler* (1984) and *Heard It in the Playground* (1991). Wegner emigrated to London as a Jewish refugee at age thirteen in 1938 after having drawn an image of Hitler for which he was beaten and expelled. At just fourteen, Wegner was offered a scholarship to St Martin's School of Art and has worked since as an illustrator, contributing to books, magazines, and stamp designs throughout his long career. His first published work for children was in 1950 with *Enid Blyton's Christmas Story*. He would later illustrate the enduring 1968 edition of *Fattypuffs and Thinifers*, as well as work by Leon *Garfield, Michael *Rosen, and others. Wegner taught at St Martin's School of Art, inspiring the next generation of picture-book artists such as Nick *Sharratt and Patrick Benson. Wegner's playful and energetic illustrations are drawn in ink with a fine nib and dashes of watercolour adding a vitality to the texts he illustrates. While his name is not instantly recognizable, his work is familiar and much loved, and widely admired by his fellow illustrators.

WEIR, Harrison (1824–1906) English illustrator specializing in animal drawings. His interpretation of *Aesop was published in 1867, and he illustrated large numbers of children's books about animals by a variety of authors.

Weirdstone of Brisingamen, The (1960) The first novel by Alan *Garner. Subtitled *A Tale of Alderley*, it is set in the Cheshire village of Alderley Edge, the author's home, and is based on a local legend of a king and his knights sleeping beneath the hill. Two children, Colin and Susan, become involved in a fight for the possession of a magic jewel which has power over the sleepers; the protagonists include the wizard Cadellin and the Morrigan, an evil enchantress who can summon *goblin-like 'svarts'.

The Weirdstone of Brisingamen and its sequel *The Moon of Gomrath* (1963), in which

the children are drawn again into the Old Magic, were widely praised at their appearance as evidence of an energetic new talent. Compared with Garner's later work they now seem jejune and crude, as Garner himself became the first to admit. Yet both books have a force and conviction which lift them above the majority of *fantasy novels. Moreover Garner was the first writer to exploit the new possibilities opened up five years earlier by Tolkien's *The *Lord of the Rings*, and in doing so he set an example to a number of other British and American authors, as well as clearing the ground for his own more mature writing.

WELCH, D'Alté (Aldridge) (1907–70) American bibliophile, compiler of *A Bibliography of American Children's Books printed prior to 1821* (1963–7).

WELCH, Ronald (Ronald Felton) (1909–82) British author of *historical novels for children, best known for his books about the Carey family, soldiers through several centuries. The first of these, *Knight Crusader* (1954), won the *Carnegie Medal. His pseudonym comes from his wartime regiment, the Welch.

Well of the World's End, The See FROG PRINCE, THE.

WELLS, H. G. (Herbert George) (1866–1946) Novelist and social commentator who wrote several works of *science fiction which have often been enjoyed by young readers; they include *The Time Machine* (1895), *The Invisible Man* (1897), *The War of the Worlds* (1898), and *The First Men in the Moon* (1901). These novels are, to use Wells's own term, 'social fables' rather than true scientific romances, for their scientific invention (which is more cursory and less imaginative than that of Jules *Verne) chiefly exists to provide the setting or mechanism for a devastating analysis of human behaviour.

The influence of Wells's stories seems to have been exercised not only over later science fiction writers, but over his friend E. *Nesbit, who uses time-travel in several of her fantasies, most notably *The *Story of the Amulet* (1906) and *Harding's Luck* (1909).

Wells wrote one book exclusively for children, *The Adventures of Tommy*, composed in 1898 for the daughter of a doctor friend and published in 1929.

WELLS, Rosemary (1943–) A versatile American author and illustrator whose work covers a wide range of age groups and genres.

Wells' succinct humour is apparent in picture books that are sometimes about serious subjects. Many of them have animal protagonists. Among the best known are *Noisy Nora* (1973), a brilliant picture of sibling jealousy; two *Mother Goose collections (1996 and 1999); and a series about rabbit siblings Max and Ruby, which was made into a television series, as well as books featuring Yoko, a Japanese kitten, and McDuff, a West Highland Terrier. Her middle-grade titles include the historical novels *Red Moon at Sharpsburg* (2008), *On the Blue Comet* (2012), and *Ivy Takes Care* (2013).

Welsh traditional tales available for retelling to children include both those in *The *Mabinogion* and other medieval bardic texts and *fairy stories and other folk tales found both in written sources and in oral tradition. One of the earliest references to a British fairy story is in the work of Giraldus Cambrensis, describing his journey through Wales in 1188. This is the story of a boy called Elidyr or Elidor, who is invited by fairies (simply small but perfectly proportioned and fair-haired people) to go with them through an underground passage to their country 'full of delights and sports ...most beautiful...but obscure, and not illuminated with the full light of the sun'. He goes freely between the fairies and his own country until his mother asks him to bring her some of the fairies' plentiful gold. On his next visit he steals a golden ball while playing with the king's son and runs home with it. Chased by the fairies, he trips and loses his prize, and thereafter by no amount of searching can he recover the way to fairyland; when asked about his experience he can 'never relate the particulars without shedding tears'.

Of the many retellings of Welsh tales, one of the earliest for children was William Jenkyn Thomas's *The Welsh Fairy Book* (1908); later notable versions include Robert *Nye's *March Has Horse's Ears* (1967). Gwyn Jones's *Welsh Legends and Folk-Tales* (1955) was reissued in 2009 and remains one of the better English-language introductions to these stories for children. In addition to straight retellings, these stories have influenced the work of many writers of richly imagined children's fiction (Welsh and not Welsh), from Alan *Garner to Catherine *Fisher.

Wendy Heroine of *Peter Pan* by J. M. *Barrie.

We're Going on a Bear Hunt (1989) A classic picture book by Michael *Rosen and Helen *Oxenbury. With Rosen's rhythmic, onomatopoeic text and pictures by Oxenbury that alternate black-and-white drawing and warm watercolours, it describes a family's expedition through the long grasses, the thick mud, a swirling snowstorm...only to come across a real bear in a cave and race back home the way they'd come and pull the covers over their heads. *Bear Hunt* has remained one of the most consistently popular read-aloud books for the youngest children for more than a generation.

WERSBA, Barbara (1932–) American author for young people whose books include *Tunes for a Small Harmonica* (1976), a *young adult novel about a rebellious teenage girl who dresses in boys' clothes and falls in love with her poetry teacher. Barbara Wersba was for many years a professional actress.

WEST, Joyce (1908–85) New Zealand novelist; her best known children's book is *Drovers Road* (1953), a set of linked short stories in which Gabrielle (Gay) Allan describes her life with her Aunt Belle, her Uncle Dunsany, and her cousins on a sheep station.

WESTALL, Robert (1929–93) British author who was born in Newcastle upon Tyne, the setting of many of his stories. His catalogue of work is staggering, offering brilliantly told, compassionate, emotionally intense stories that are timeless. His first children's book, *The *Machine-Gunners* (1975), concerns Newcastle gang rivalry during the Second World War, and the theft by boys of a machine gun taken from a crashed aircraft. He wrote a sequel, *Fathom Five* (1975). Acutely realistic in terms of place and character, his stories often use supernatural elements: *The Wind Eye* (1976) deals with the effect a saint from ancient times has upon a modern family; *The *Watch House* (1977) is a ghost story; *The Devil in the Road* (1979) a *time-slip story; and *The *Scarecrows* (1981) is a complex, scary and brilliant book about a boy's resentment of his mother's second marriage. He returned to the Second World War, using it brilliantly as background to *Blitzcat* (1989) and *The Kingdom by the Sea* (1990).

WESTERFELD, Scott (1963–) American author who, after working in software design and as a composer for modern dance, turned to writing hugely successful *young adult novels. His series, set in the future, starting with *Uglies* (2005), imagines a society in which everyone has to be beautiful and cosmetic surgery is compulsory at sixteen—and what happens to those who want to keep their own faces. *Leviathan* (2009) starts another series, which is a steampunk reimagining of the First World War, complete with walking machines and living airships. *The Manual of Aeronautics: An Illustrated Guide to the Leviathan Series* (2009) is an in-depth companion, illustrated—as are the books themselves—by Keith Thompson.

WESTERMAN, Percy F. (1876–59) Writer of over 170 *adventure stories for boys, many of them set in the battlegrounds of the First and Second World Wars, beginning with *A Lad of Grit* (1908). He was voted 'most popular boys' author' during the 1930s.

westerns Popular stories and films about the 'Wild West' of America which have their origins in *tall tales about the early settlers of the North American continent. John Smith (1580–1631), an English-born adventurer who wrote a first-hand account of events during colonization (including the story of Pocahontas) was one of those who became renowned even during his lifetime as a superhuman hero: *A Generall Historie of Virginia* (1624) describes epic fights in which he vanquishes six or eight '*Indians' (Native Americans) in hand-to-hand skirmishes. Other heroes rose out of the Indian wars of the Colonial period, most notably Daniel Boone (1734–1820), whose supposed exploits and grandiloquent speeches during his exploration and settlement of Kentucky were written up by John Filson and published in 1784. Boone soon became the subject of a series of tall stories in which he fights wild animals, makes breathtaking escapes, and kills two Indians with one bullet. The Boone legend influenced the *Leather-Stocking Tales* of James Fenimore *Cooper. Another writer from the East Coast who was drawn to legends of the frontier was Washington *Irving, whose *Adventures of Captain Bonneville* (1837) describes a trapping expedition in the Rockies.

The 1830s saw the emergence of *Davy Crockett as a folk hero, while in the next decade *Kit Carson began to be featured in magazine stories and cheap 'yellowback' novels. The first outlaw to be celebrated in such writings was *Billy the Kid, one of the earliest figures to have the word *cowboy attached to his name (though he was scarcely a true cowboy), for example in *The Cowboy's Career; or,*

the *Dare Devil Deeds of 'Billy, the Kid' by 'One of the Kids'* (1881). Other historical persons who became legends during the late 19th cent. included *Wild Bill Hickok, *Wyatt Earp, and *Jesse James; a different type of hero appeared after 1876 in the person of George Armstrong *Custer. Much of the popularity of westerns was due to the celebrated Wild West Show of *Buffalo Bill (W. F. Cody), which toured America and Europe from 1883.

The real-life originals of most western heroes were men with chequered careers and flawed characters. In the hands of writers they underwent a transformation into the pure and noble. They neither drink, nor smoke, nor swear; they treat women chivalrously, serve good causes, and are prone to uttering terse philosophical observations. Any lapse from this standard is excused as a temporary aberration, or is justified as the accepted habit of the time.

In Britain, westerns for juvenile readers were produced in large numbers by the *Aldine Publishing Company and played a large part in the D. C. *Thomson adventure papers. The writing of westerns was not confined to the English language, however. The German author Karl *May wrote, during the late 19th and early 20th cents., a number of popular novels about such fictitious western characters as 'Old Shatterhand' and 'Winnetou', a Native American.

Westward Ho! (1855) A novel by Charles *Kingsley.

WETHERELL, Elizabeth *See* WARNER, SUSAN BOGERT.

Wet Magic (1913) A novel by E. *Nesbit about children who rescue a *mermaid they find captive in a fairground.

WEYMAN, Stanley J. (John) (1855–1928) A popular British *historical novelist, mentioned by Graham *Greene as among his favourite authors in childhood. His books included *A Gentleman of France* (1893), *The Man in Black* (1894), and *Under the Red Robe* (1896).

What Katy Did (1872) A celebrated novel by 'Susan *Coolidge' (Sarah Chauncy Woolsey).

Katy Carr lives in a small American town with her brothers and sisters—three girls and two boys—of whom she is the eldest, and with her kind and tolerant father, Dr Carr, and her prim Aunt Izzie, who has looked after the house since the children's mother's death. The children are usually joined in their exploits by Katy's friend Cecy Hall. Katy, tall,

gangling, and untidy, is constantly planning 'how, by and by, she would be beautiful and beloved, and amiable as an angel.' She and the other children get into trouble at home and school for their unruly behaviour; they also compile a magazine for Sunday reading (which includes an absurd *moral tale). They are visited by their invalid Cousin Helen, who cannot walk. After that visit Katy disobeys Aunt Izzie's orders and plays on a swing that has just been erected—and which (though she does not know it) is not properly fixed. She falls from it, severely injuring her back, and for a long time it seems that she will be permanently paralysed. At first she despairs, but Cousin Helen tells her that she may learn something to her own good in 'The School of Pain', and shows her how to be a cheerful and kindly member of the household despite her disability. When Aunt Izzie dies Katy takes over the supervision of the housekeeping, and after two years she is able to begin to walk again.

The book has been popular since its first appearance, and has plenty of vitality, but it seems tame in comparison with *Little Women* (published four years earlier) and both the sudden disabling of the heroine and her eventual recovery are rather transparent devices for the achievement of her moral and spiritual education. *What Katy Did At School* (1873) is concerned with the minor intrigues and crises of life in a New England girls' boarding school, and *What Katy Did Next* (1886) takes its heroine on a visit to England, France, and Italy, and concludes with her attachment to a young American naval officer. Jacqueline *Wilson retold the story in *Katy* (2015), though she replaces the moralising ending with something rather more palatable to modern readers.

WHATLEY, Bruce (1954–) Australian picture-book creator, who was born in Wales and trained in Manchester, where one of his tutors was Tony *Ross. He and his family moved to Australia, where he worked in advertising before moving into children's book illustration. The books Whatley writes and illustrates are mostly whimsical stories of everyday family life, and he often works with his wife, Rosie Smith. His texts have a natural flowing rhythm and he uses different styles to illustrate different kinds of books. He has won many awards, both from the *CBCA and internationally. *Diary of a Wombat* (2002) and its sequels may be his most famous books, and he illustrates them with a pen-and-acrylic style. Although he has illustrated sixty books to date, his favourite

book is *Whatley's Quest* (1994), an alphabet book with complex highly rendered illustrations. Whatley uses both hands to illustrate, each producing a quite a different mood. In 2008 he completed a PhD titled *Left Hand Right Hand: Implications of Ambidextrous Image Making. Flood* (2012) and *Fire* (2014), both illustrated with his left hand, use texts by Jackie *French.

WHELAN, Gerard (1957-) Irish writer, born in Enniscorthy, the winner of four *CBI Book Awards—two Merit Awards, a Book of the Year, and an Eilís Dillon award. In *The Guns of Easter* (1996) a twelve-year-old boy from the Dublin slums is caught up in the drama of the Easter Rising. His other *historical novels (set in Ireland in a similar period) include *A Winter of Spies* (1998—a sequel to *The Guns of Easter*) and *War Children* (2002), but Whelan has also written *fantasy, most notably *Dream Invader* (1997), a thrilling good-and-evil story about Saskia and her cousin, Simon, who has started having terrifying nightmares—it will take the wisdom of old Birdie Murray to save him from the ancient forces that are taking hold.

When Hitler Stole Pink Rabbit (1971) The first in Judith *Kerr's autobiographical trilogy *Out of the Hitler Time*. The first book in the trilogy sees the protagonist Anna escape Berlin and documents her journey to Switzerland, and then to Paris and London, through the eyes of a curious, nine-year-old child. *Bombs on Aunt Dainty* (1975) and *A Small Person Far Away* (1978) depict Judith Kerr's later life with acuity, bringing to life a war-ravaged, bombed-out London as well as the personal difficulties faced by a young woman dealing with her family's new-found identity in a war-torn Europe.

When We Were Very Young (1924) The collection of verses which was the first of A. A. *Milne's four classic books for children. It was dedicated to, and was mostly apparently about, his only child Christopher Robin, who was four years old when the book came out.

Milne brought to the book a genius for light verse already highly developed for his contributions to *Punch*. He was at pains to point out that writing for children involved no relaxing of effort or of concentration on technique.

The name 'Christopher Robin', though it was never used by the Milnes at home (their son was known as 'Billy' or 'Moon'), had the quality of being metrical, of crying out to be put into verses. Sometimes these were

composed around incidents specific to the boy's life: he and his nanny did go to Buckingham Palace and watch the changing of the guard, and they did give buns to the elephant at the zoo. But Christopher Milne avers, in his book *The Enchanted Places* (1974), that it would have been entirely out of character for his nanny (whose name was not 'Alice' but Olive Brockwell) to say 'Sure to dear, but it's time for tea.' Many of the poems were based, A. A. Milne makes clear in his autobiography, on his recollections of his own childhood; others derived from observation and understanding of the fancies common to all children. Milne did not, however, claim any special fondness for children. The best known of the poems in *When We Were Very Young* is 'Vespers', which was also published separately. But Milne disliked the misty-eyed sentimentality which generally characterized appreciation of 'Vespers' and pointed out that it in fact depicted a child's natural and extreme egotism: 'Not "God bless Mummy, because I love her", but "God bless Mummy, I know that's right."'

Because he so successfully illustrated those of the verses that appeared in *Punch* in advance of the book, E. H. *Shepard earned the work of making the drawings for all four Christopher Robin books, as well as the song-books derived from them. Fourteen of the verses were published with musical settings by H. Fraser-Simson only a few weeks after the original book, and more appeared in subsequent song books by the same composer: *The King's Breakfast* (1925), *Teddy Bear and Other Songs* (1926), and *More Very Young Songs* (1928). Walford Davies set *Bad Sir Brian Botany and Other Rhymes* to music in 1939.

When We Were Very Young was reprinted six times between its first appearance at the beginning of November and Christmas 1924, and by 1965 it had been reprinted sixty-five times, making it probably the most popular book of children's verse by a 20th-cent. author.

Where's Spot? The first in Eric *Hill's much-loved and hugely successful *Spot the Dog* series. Published in 1980, its charming 'lift-the-flap' device paved the way for many more interactive books (*see* POP-UP BOOKS) and its distinctive font and clever design have made this book a modern classic. In this first book, Sally the dog looks for Spot alongside the child reader in a variety of places only to find different animals under the flaps—triumphantly finding Spot at the end. Wonderful to

share, this book has delighted adult and child readers for over thirty years. Spot 'the franchise' appears in numerous books, CDs, *apps and toys as well as several animated television programmes.

Where's Wally? (in America, **Where's Waldo?**) (1987–) These phenomenally successful books by English artist Martin Handford (1956–) have over the years been made into notebooks, pillows, posters, video games, a syndicated comic strip, and an animated TV series. The premise is brilliant in its simplicity—a double-page spread of finely drawn activity hides the Wally character, and all you have to do is find him. Children can spend hours poring over the pages, and never seem to tire of returning to the books again and again.

Where the Rainbow Ends A *play for children by Clifford Mills and 'John Ramsey' (Reginald Owen), first produced in London in 1911; a book based on it was published in 1912. Rosamund Carey and her brother Crispian, a naval cadet, are sorrowing for the loss of their parents in a shipwreck. Rosamund reads in a mysterious book that 'all lost loved ones are found . . . [in] the land where the rainbow ends.' With the aid of a magic carpet, she and Crispian escape from their wicked aunt and uncle and set off in search of that land; the aunt and uncle pursue them, with the Dragon King as their evil ally. The children obtain the protection of St *George, who finally kills the Dragon King, and are reunited with their parents in the Land Where the Rainbow Ends.

The book is dedicated 'To the children of the Empire', and the story is imbued with patriotic fervour, as well as being tinged with a sentimentalism borrowed from *Peter Pan. The play, which had music by Roger Quilter, was for some time an annual institution in London at Christmas.

Where the Sidewalk Ends A collection of poems by Shel *Silverstein.

Where the Wild Things Are (1963) A *picture book by Maurice *Sendak, a world bestseller and winner of the *Caldecott Medal. Max, banished to his bedroom without supper for causing havoc while wearing his wolf suit, imagines himself away to the country of the Wild Things, who make him their king; but he tires of their company, wants to be 'where someone loved him best of all', and goes home to his bedroom, where supper is (after all) waiting for him, 'and it was still hot'.

The book was greeted warily on its first appearance; reviewers spoke of the story as 'pointless and confusing', and feared that the grotesque Wild Things, with their claws and beaks and staring eyes, would frighten children (as Sendak admitted they indeed did). In fact, however, Max is firmly in control of events throughout, and the Wild Things are docile and obedient to him, so that the book gratifies the wish for power over the unknown and horrific. Its supremacy among modern picture books was soon established, and it has been translated into many languages and sold close to twenty million copies. The British composer Oliver Knussen has made it into an opera, with a libretto by Sendak. It has also been adapted as an animated short (1974), and inspired a live-action feature film (2009); this film in turn became the novel, *The Wild Things*, by Dave Eggers (2009).

Sendak has remarked that, among the story's other origins, the Wild Things owe something to the Jewish adult relatives who used to visit the Sendak home in Brooklyn when he was a child: 'They'd lean way over with their bad teeth and hairy noses, and say something threatening like "You're so cute I could eat you up."' The story took many years to reach its final form. An early version, entitled 'Where the Wild Horses Are', drawn in 1955, has little resemblance to the published book.

Whispers in the Graveyard (1994) A novel by Theresa *Breslin. While working as a librarian, Breslin noticed that a frequent request was for books about dyslexia. After attending meetings of her local Dyslexia Association, she determined to write a story in which the hero suffered from acute dyslexia—and which would help non-sufferers to understand the condition. That she also wrote a cracking story of supernatural suspense is down to her skill as a writer. Solomon is twelve and angry: his father is an alcoholic, his mother's a no-show, and everyone at school thinks he's thick. Then workmen dig up a rowan tree in the graveyard, unleashing dark forces . . . The book won the 1994 *Carnegie Medal.

Whitbread Children's Book Award *See* Costa Children's Book Award.

WHITE, E. B. (Elwyn Brooks) (1899–1985) American writer, contributor to the *New Yorker* and co-reviser of the guide to American English, *The Elements of Style*, who wrote three

children's books. *Charlotte's Web* (1952), is regarded as a classic; *Stuart Little* (1945) is equally brilliant in its way: the story of a *Tom Thumb-like child born to a New York couple, who is to all intents and purposes a mouse.

The first part of the book explores, with dead-pan humour, the advantages and disadvantages of having a mouse in one's family circle. Then Stuart sets out on a quest in search of a bird named Margalo, and the story ends in mid-air. The book is outstandingly funny and sometimes touching, but was too eccentric for the doyenne of American children's librarians, Anne Carroll *Moore, who tried to persuade White not to publish it. (She also disliked *Charlotte's Web*.)

White's third children's book is *The Trumpet of the Swan* (1970), in which a Trumpeter Swan overcomes the fact that he has no voice by—quite literally—learning to play the trumpet. He goes to Boston, where his musicianship soon makes him a celebrity.

WHITE, T. H. (Terence Hanbury) (1906–64) Author of a series of retellings of Malory's King *Arthur narratives. The son of an Englishman serving as a District Superintendent of Police in India, White had a deeply unhappy childhood as a result of his parents' disagreements. He was educated at Cheltenham College and Cambridge, where he took a First Class in English Literature. He became a schoolmaster and in 1932 was appointed Head of English at Stowe School. By 1936 he had published a number of novels, but he did not achieve wide popularity until, after leaving Stowe and devoting himself full time to writing, he produced (in 1938) *The *Sword in the Stone*, the first of his Arthurian books. Two other volumes in the series followed in 1939 and 1940, but a disagreement with his publishers delayed the appearance of the fourth book. It was finally issued in 1958 as part of a one-volume edition of the entire tetralogy, under the overall title *The *Once and Future King*.

White did not write specifically for children in his Arthurian books, but among his other novels are a story for young readers, *Mistress Masham's Repose* (1947) and *The Master* (1957) a *science fiction story.

He took an intense interest in many kinds of human skill, and learned (among other things) how to fly planes, deep-sea diving, and hawking, about which he wrote passionately in *The Goshawk* (1951).

WHITE, Thomas *See* LITTLE BOOK FOR LITTLE CHILDREN, A.

White Cat, The (La Chatte blanche) One of the better known *fairy stories of Mme d'*Aulnoy. An ageing king, afraid that his three sons want to usurp him, sets a task to keep them occupied: the son who after a year's travel brings him back the handsomest dog will inherit the kingdom. The youngest son's travels lead him to a magnificent castle, where every act of hospitality is performed for him. But he sees only the hands of servants; their bodies are invisible. The visible inhabitants of the castle are cats, their queen a particularly beautiful white cat. After a year of ease she sends the king's son back to his father with a dog that appears from an acorn and outshines every other. But the king then sets a second task: the finding of a length of cloth fine enough to pass through the eye of a needle. Again with the help of the white cat the youngest son wins the contest. Still refusing to give up his throne, the king sets the last task of finding the most beautiful woman. The youngest son returns to the white cat. After the year has passed as usual she tells him to break her enchantment by cutting off her head and tail and throwing them in the fire. Reluctantly, he obeys, whereupon the white cat is transformed into the fairest of women, and her whole court becomes human.

She tells the prince the whole story of her enchantment, the result of her mother's giving her to the fairies in return for herself being allowed to eat her fill of their irresistible fruits. They then go to the king together, and the youngest son is undoubtedly the winner of the contest. But to spare the feelings of all, the queen who was the white cat, heiress to six kingdoms, divides her lands between the king and his sons. All three sons then marry their ladies and much happiness ensues. A moral verse follows, on gratitude fanning love and the sad conduct of the white cat's mother.

The White Cat appeared in *Contes nouveaux ou Les Fées à la mode* (1698). English translations, among them *The Renowned History of the White Cat, and other interesting stories* (Elizabeth *Newbery, apparently 1795), inspired many *pantomime versions, and J. R. *Planché used the story in 1842 for the first of his series of stage extravaganzas based on Mme d'Aulnoy's tales. A number of adaptations of the story, sometimes printed as *picture books, have been published.

White Fang *See* LONDON, JACK.

White Knight In *Through the Looking Glass* by Lewis *Carroll.

White Queen In *Through the Looking Glass* by Lewis *Carroll.

White Rabbit In *Alice's Adventures in Wonderland* by Lewis *Carroll.

White Witch *See* NARNIA.

WHITLOCK, Pamela (1920–82) British children's writer and editor who was co-author of *The *Far-Distant Oxus* (1937) while in her teens. In 1948 she became editor of *Collins' Magazine for Boys and Girls* (*see* YOUNG ELIZABETHAN). She was also the author of *The Open Book* (1957), an attempt to explain religious belief to children, and the editor of *All Day Long*, a children's verse anthology.

WHITNEY (Train), Adeline Dutton (1824–1906) Massachusetts author who wrote a number of *girls' stories, beginning with the very popular *Faith Gartney's Girlhood* (1862). Some of her stories were serialized in *Our Young Folks*.

WHITTIER, John Greenleaf (1807–92) Massachusetts poet who wrote many *ballads and narrative poems which were favourites with American children. These include *Skipper Ireson's Ride* (1828, revised 1857), in which a skipper is tarred and feathered for abandoning his wrecked ship; it is frequently referred to in *Captains Courageous* (1897). Whittier edited *Child Life* (1871), a notable children's poetry anthology.

Whittington, Richard *See* DICK WHITTINGTON.

Who Killed Cock Robin? *See* COCK ROBIN.

Who's Afraid of the Big Bad Wolf? *See* THREE LITTLE PIGS, THE.

Who Sank the Boat? (1982) A picture book by Pamela *Allen in which a cow, a donkey, a sheep, a pig, and a tiny little mouse go for a row. In this poetic text, the question 'Who sank the boat?' is repeated, and . . . surprise . . . it was the 'little mouse, the last one to get in'. Children instantly respond to the humour in the text and illustrations, and seem to understand the physics of the situation, because the pen-and-wash illustrations communicate so well. Illustrations from this book were reproduced as one of a set of four postage stamps for Australia Post to acknowledge the fiftieth anniversary of the *CBCA awards.

WHYBROW, Ian (1941–) Prolific British author whose work as a teacher led him into writing books for children. *Little Wolf's Book of Badness* (1995) begins the series about Little Wolf, who is just too nice to ever be a beast, so is sent off to school to learn the rules of badness. The classic picture-book series that begins with *Harry and the Bucketful of Dinosaurs* tells the delightful story of a boy, his toy dinosaurs, and their adventures. Whybrow's successful *Books for Boys* series stemmed from a belief that more reading books were needed with boy-friendly content, and started with *Robin Hood's Best Shot* (2006). The most recent to date is *Rory's Piratical Leg* (2014).

Why the Sea Is Salt A Norwegian folk tale collected by *Asbjørnsen and Moe. A poor man acquires from the Devil a magic mill which can grind out anything that is asked for. His envious brother buys it from him and tells it to produce herrings and broth. This it does in such quantity that the man's home is flooded with fish and soup, for he does not know how to tell it to stop. Subsequently the mill is sold to a sea-captain who wishes for a cargo of salt to bring him wealth. The mill begins to grind away on board ship; soon the vessel is full of salt, but the mill will not stop. The ship sinks and the mill falls to the bottom of the sea, where it grinds away at this very day—'and that's why the sea is salt.' The story appears in the *Blue Fairy Book* (1889) of Andrew *Lang.

Why the Whales Came (1985) A novel by Michael *Morpurgo. Grace and Daniel live an idyllic life on the island of Bryher, one of the Scilly Isles. Ignoring the warning never to speak to the strange old man who lives in a remote cottage, they end up befriending him, finding out that he is deaf and communicating through a form of sign language. With a story that encompasses all the fear people felt in 1914, local legend, the power of guilt, and the strength of friendship, this is one of Morpurgo's most powerful and emotional books.

WIBBERLEY, Leonard (Patrick O'Connor) (1915–83) Irish author, resident in the USA. He wrote many books for children, including *Flint's Island* (1972), which is a sequel to *Treasure Island*; a series of stories about motor racing (under the pseudonym 'Patrick O'Connor'); and a four-volume life of Thomas Jefferson.

Wide Awake An American children's *magazine published monthly from 1875 until 1893 by the Daniel Lothrop Company of Boston. It resembled *St Nicholas*, though its style was rather old-fashioned by comparison; it

included contributions from such writers of *girls'* stories as Elizabeth Stuart Phelps (author of *Gypsy Breynton*), Mrs A. D. T. *Whitney, and 'Sophie *May'.

Wide, Wide World, The (1950) A novel by 'Elizabeth Wetherell', pseudonym of Susan Bogert *Warner. Ellen Montgomery, whose parents are leaving America for Europe, is sent to the home of her grumpy Aunt Fortune in the backwoods of New York State. She is befriended by Alice Humphreys and her brother John. Alice dies, and after the death of her own parents Ellen is obliged to make a journey to Scotland where she is to live for a time with relatives, but she remains on close terms with John Humphreys, and by the end of the book she has learnt true Christian fortitude.

The story has become notorious for its sentimentality and lachrymosity: tears of regret and self-reproach flow on almost every page. But the picture of American rural life is attractive, and there are several entertaining character-sketches.

The book was rejected by nearly every leading American publisher. It was eventually shown to G. P. Putnam, who passed the manuscript to his mother; she insisted that it be published, and reluctantly Putnam complied. It quickly proved a huge success, passing through some thirteen American editions in two years and also finding immediate popularity in England. Abridged editions soon appeared, some retaining the pious passages but others concentrating on the more exciting aspects of the story.

WIESE, Kurt (1887–1974) Illustrator who was born in Germany and emigrated to the USA in 1928. He illustrated more than 300 books, among them *Honk, The Story of a Moose* (1935).

WIESNER, David (1956–) American illustrator and writer who started off illustrating other people's work, but soon changed to focusing solely on his own books. With a unique style that marries realistic images with dreamlike stories, he uses few words, leaving his pictures to tell each tale eloquently. *Tuesday* (1997) describes the day that the lily pads become magic carpets so that the frogs could cause gentle mischief while travelling around the town. *The Three Pigs* (2001) is a delightful reimagining of the classic fairy tale that plays metanarrative games, allowing the pigs to escape from their story (they get away in the

gaps between the frames of the illustration, and fold up the wolf picture to be quite sure they're safe), and journey into other quite different tales; and *Flotsam* (2006) shows a boy spending a day at the beach, where he uncovers many fantastic mysteries about the seas.

WIGGIN (Smith), Kate Douglas (1856–1923) American author who was born in Philadelphia, the daughter of a lawyer; she spent her childhood in a village in Maine after the death of her father and her mother's remarriage. When her family moved to California for the benefit of her stepfather's health she established the first kindergarten west of the Rockies, in the slums of San Francisco.

Her first children's book, *The Story of Patsy* (1883), was written to raise money for the kindergarten movement; it was about a crippled waif, and sold in huge numbers. In 1881 she married a lawyer and went to live in New York City; she had no intention of taking up writing seriously, but after a few years she began *The Birds' Christmas Carol*, the story of Carol Bird, an invalid girl so named because she was born at Christmas; it was a success on its publication in 1887. *Polly Oliver's Problem* (1893) was the story of a teenager whose mother keeps a boarding house in Santa Barbara, California, and proved very popular, but her greatest success was *Rebecca of Sunnybrook Farm* (1903).

WILBERFORCE, Samuel *See* AGATHOS.

WILD, Margaret (1948–) Born in South Africa, now living in Sydney, this Australian author of over seventy books was a journalist and then, for sixteen years, an editor in children's book publishing. The most unlikely subject for a picture book is perfectly handled in her *Let the Celebrations Begin* (1991, illustrated by Julie *Vivas), which is set in a concentration camp; it is a child's view that focuses on the creation of toys—the horrors are delicately handled and the result is a true celebration of courage and humanity. Latterly Wild has turned her hand to books for young adults, though her focus on love and loss has continued in both of her verse-form novels, *Jinx* (2001) and *One Night* (2003).

Wild Animals I Have Known (1898) A collection of *animal stories by Ernest Thompson *Seton, said by the author to be taken entirely from true life. Among the tales are 'Lobo, the King of Currumpaw', an account of the leader of a wolf pack who

constantly evades destruction by the hunters, and 'Raggylug, the story of a Cottontail Rabbit', in which a young buck rabbit is taught the ways of the wild by his mother, Molly Cottontail, gets his ear torn during an encounter with a snake (hence his name), and survives to see a rival for his territory killed by a fox.

Though Seton sometimes puts words into the animals' mouths, he otherwise scrupulously observes and describes their real ways and habits. The book is illustrated with line drawings and half-tone plates by the author.

Wild Bill Hickok A *western folk hero, in reality James Butler Hickok (1837–76), who came to fame in 1861 when he was acquitted of a multiple murder. He subsequently became a scout in the Civil War, then a professional gambler, then a Sheriff, and was finally shot at Deadwood, Colorado, during a poker game. Following his death he was made into a national hero, thanks initially to J. W. Buel's *Life and Marvellous Adventures of Wild Bill* (1880), and was the subject of a number of *dime novels, including some supposedly written by *Buffalo Bill.

WILDE, Oscar See Happy Prince and Other Tales, The.

WILDER, Laura Ingalls (1867–1957) American author of the 'Little House' series of children's novels, describing her own childhood, adolescence, and marriage.

Little House in the Big Woods (1932) tells the story of her earliest days 'in the Big Woods of Wisconsin, in a little grey house made of logs'. The style of narrative is simple, almost naïve, but the pioneer life is described unsqueamishly, with attention to such details as the butchering of the family hog. As in the later books, the author refers to herself in the third person as 'Laura'. The record of daily life far from any town is punctuated with stories told in the evenings by Pa, who is also a great singer of folk songs.

At the start of *Little House on the Prairie* (1935) he decides that 'there were too many people in the Big Woods now', and takes his family West in a covered wagon. They experience dramatic river crossings and other hardships before building themselves a new log house in '*Indian' (Native American) territory; but the government orders all settlers to withdraw from the area and the Ingalls family have to move on again. *On the Banks of Plum Creek* (1937) follows them back East to Minnesota, where Pa becomes a wheat farmer and experiences the devastation of his crop by an invasion of grasshoppers.

By the Shores of Silver Lake (1939) has the family moving West again, to Dakota Territory. Laura's sister Mary is now blind as a result of scarlet fever and Pa has to earn his living at a railway camp. *The Long Winter* (1940), generally regarded as the best book in the series, begins with a snowstorm that cuts off the little town where the Ingalls family now lives, for seven months, without supplies, and gives a gripping account of how they survive by burning twists of hay to keep warm and by eating grains of wheat ground in a coffee mill.

Little Town on the Prairie (1941) describes Laura's training as a schoolteacher and her courtship with Almanzo Wilder, whose own childhood had been described in the second book to be published in the series, *Farmer Boy* (1933). *These Happy Golden Years* (1943) concludes the series proper with an account of Laura's experiences as a teacher in a prairie school and the beginning of her marriage, though there also exists an unfinished sequel, *The First Four Years* (found among Wilder's papers after her death and not published until 1971), the story of the start of the Wilders' married life and their experiences of the same kind of crises that punctuated their parents' life before them.

Laura Ingalls married Almanzo Wilder in 1885; they farmed in De Smet, Dakota (the scene of the final books in the series), until 1894, when they moved to Mansfield, Missouri. Wilder was in her sixties when her daughter suggested she write down her childhood memories. The Little House series quickly achieved classic status in the United States, but did not begin to appear in Britain until the 1950s, where, thanks to being used as the basis of a television series, it would come to have almost as strong a following as in America.

The books are unusual in that they 'grow up' as Laura does—that is, their style becomes gradually less childlike, and they are successively suited to the progress of a child reader.

Wilderness Champion (1944) A novel by Joseph Wharton *Lippincott.

WILDSMITH, Brian (Lawrence) (1930–2016) British illustrator who was born at Penistone in Yorkshire, the son of a miner. He specialized in chemistry at school, and then at the age of seventeen he decided he wanted to be an artist and went to Barnsley School of Art.

His potential as a children's illustrator was realized by Mabel George of the Oxford University Press, who commissioned him to illustrate *The Oxford Book of Poetry for Children* (1960) and a 1961 edition of tales from the *Arabian Nights*. He won the *Kate Greenaway Medal for *Brian Wildsmith's ABC* (1962), and went on to produce a series of *picture books based on *fables by *La Fontaine (1963 onwards). In 1967 came *Brian Wildsmith's Birds*, which was followed by *Brian Wildsmith's Wild Animals, Fishes, Puzzles*, and *Circus* (1968–70). He wrote and illustrated over eighty books; these include *The Owl and the Woodpecker* (1971), *The Twelve Days of Christmas* (1972), *Squirrels* (1975), a version of Maeterlinck's *The *Blue Bird* (1977) (based on his designs for a musical film of it), *Hunter and his Dog* (1979), *Animal Games, Animal Homes, Animal Shapes*, and *Animal Tricks* (all 1980), and *A Christmas Story* (1989). In 1994 the Brian Wildsmith Art Museum was opened in Izukogen, Japan.

Wild Swans, The A *fairy story by Hans Christian *Andersen, loosely based on a Germanic folk tale. A king has eleven sons and one daughter, Elisa. Their wicked stepmother casts out the girl and changes the sons into swans. Elisa learns that, to transform her brothers back into their proper shapes, she must make shirts for them out of stinging nettles and must remain silent until she has clothed them all. Her silence leads to her being condemned to death as a *witch, and she is about to be burnt at the stake when the swans fly to her and she clothes them in the shirts. They are duly transformed—all but the youngest, who retains a swan's wing instead of one arm because his shirt was unfinished. Elisa's innocence is proved, and she lives in happiness with a king she has married.

Wild West Show *See* BUFFALO BILL.

Wilfred Gordon McDonald Partridge *See* FOX, MEM.

Will *See* HIS DARK MATERIALS.

WILL and NICOLAS *See* MORDVINOFF, NICOLAS.

WILLANS, (Herbert) Geoffrey (1911–58) British writer, author of the *Molesworth books. He was educated in English private schools and spent some time teaching at one, a prep school for boys up to thirteen, before becoming a journalist. He also wrote

humorous novels and, during the war, became a temporary naval officer. Having returned to journalism, Willans wanted to expand into a book some wartime comic articles based on his schoolteaching. He consulted the cartoonist Ronald *Searle who was looking for something to follow his *St Trinian's*. The outcome was Searle illustrating *Down with Skool!* (1953). Two more books and a 'compleet' compilation followed, and the text for the fourth was finished, when Willans died suddenly, aged forty-seven, of a heart attack. Willans's name remained relatively little known, while the name of his schoolboy narrator quickly entered the language as shorthand for a style of humour, and, in the decades that followed, the books came to be recognized as classics of English satire.

WILLARD, Barbara (1909–94) British novelist best known for her *Mantlemass series of *historical novels (1970–88). She began to write children's books in the mid-1950s after having produced adult fiction for some years, and was the author of more than forty children's novels.

WILLARD, Nancy (1936–) American author for both children and adults, equally expert in both poetry and prose, who has even occasionally illustrated her own titles or those of other authors. *A Visit to William Blake's Inn: Poems for Innocent and Experienced Travelers* (1981), illustrated by Alice and Martin *Provensen, won the *Newbery Medal and was a Caldecott Honor Book (*see* CALDECOTT MEDAL). Other original children's titles include the Anatole Trilogy (1974, 1979, 1982), illustrated by David McPhail; *Firebrat* (1988), illustrated by David *Weisner; and *Pish, Posh Said Hieronymus Bosch* (1991), illustrated by Leo and Diane *Dillon. She has also written many notable retellings, such as *East of the Sun and West of the Moon* (1989) and *Beauty and the Beast* (1992), both illustrated by Barry *Moser, and *The Sorcerer's Apprentice* (1993), illustrated by Leo and Diane Dillon.

WILLEMS, Mo (1968–) American author-illustrator. Born in New Orleans, he studied at NYU's Tisch School for the Arts, and then continued to live and work in New York until he relocated with his family to Massachusetts in 2008. As a writer and animator for children's television, Willems won six Emmy Awards for his work on *Sesame Street*. He also wrote for other series, including the

popular *Codename: Kids Next Door*, before turning to originating picture books so that he could work from home while his daughter was a baby. His 2003 debut **Don't Let the Pigeon Drive the Bus!* introduced his trademark child-like cartoons, zany humour, and endearing characters. (The Pigeon's habit of directly addressing child readers was not common at the time and children were sometimes uncertain as to how they should respond to the bird's entreaties.) Willems's simplicity of line and the frustrations that his characters experience contain emotional echoes of the *Peanuts* cartoons of Charles M. *Schulz, whose work has most inspired Willems's along with that of Saul *Steinberg. *Don't Let the Pigeon Drive the Bus!* was a Caldecott Honor Book (*see* CALDECOTT MEDAL). Other *Pigeon* titles include *The Pigeon Finds a Hot Dog* (2004), *Don't Let the Pigeon Stay Up Late!* (2006), and most recently *The Pigeon Needs a Bath!* (2014).

Willems has created over forty books for children since 2003. Other memorable characters include *Knuffle Bunny: A Cautionary Tale* (2005), which immortalized Willems's daughter Trixie and their Brooklyn neighbourhood. Both *Knuffle Bunny* and its sequel, *Knuffle Bunny Too: A Case of Mistaken Identity* (2007), were Caldecott Honor Books. The third and final book in the series is *Knuffle Bunny Free: An Unexpected Diversion* (2010). Willems went on to create a series for early readers about friends Elephant and Piggie, winning the Theodor Seuss Geisel Award for the most distinguished American book for beginning readers for *There Is a Bird on Your Head* (2007) and *Are You Ready to Play Outside?* (2008). The *Elephant and Piggie* titles *We Are in a Book!* (2011) and *A Big Guy Took My Ball* (2013) were Theodor Seuss Geisel Honor Books. Willems has written stage plays based on the *Knuffle Bunny* and *Elephant and Piggie* books. His stand-alone titles include *Leonardo the Terrible Monster* (2005), *Naked Mole Rat Gets Dressed* (2009), and *Goldilocks and the Three Dinosaurs* (2012).

William (William Brown) An unruly English schoolboy, hero of some forty books by Richmal *Crompton, published between 1922 and 1970. Her first published story about him, 'Rice Mould Pudding', was not written for children but was printed in a women's magazine in 1919. However, soon after the William books began to appear (the first was *Just—William*, 1922) they were accepted as belonging in children's lists. In fact they are in a tradition of books about the 'ordinary boy' which may be traced back to the American novel *The *Story of a Bad Boy* (1869); among their English predecessors is Eden Phillpotts's *The *Human Boy* (1899).

William Brown lives in a typical English village. His family consists of an irritable father, a comparatively long-suffering mother, an elder brother Robert (who has 'the crushing superiority of eighteen'), and an elder sister Ethel, pursued by endless young men whose raptures never cease to puzzle William. The household also includes William's mongrel dog Jumble, and—until the Second World War—several servants. William himself remained at the age of eleven throughout all the years that the books were appearing. As John Rowe *Townsend has written: 'Born at the age of eleven, he remained eleven for all the forty-seven years of his life. Never did a boy's twelfth year hold so many birthdays, so many Christmases, so many unwilling visits to aunts, so many tangles with beery tramps or eccentric spinsters, so many ingenious schemes gone so far awry, so many reluctant washings of so dirty a face.'

Whenever possible, William escapes from the constraints of family life (usually with a bottle of liquorice water tucked under his arm) and joins up with the Outlaws, of whom he is leader. The other members are his friends Henry, Douglas, and Ginger, though there is also a self-appointed Outlaw who attaches herself to them, despite frequent attempts to blackball her. This is the unforgettable Violet Elizabeth Bott, member of a nouveau riche household recently arrived in the village. William and his friends have no respect for the sauce that made the Bott family's fortune, but there is no getting away from her wealth, or her lisp: 'Violet Elizabeth's eyes brimmed with tears. Her lip quivered ... "My fatherth rich," she said. "I oughter be firtht becauth my fatherth rich."'

The first William short stories (included in *Just—William*), such as 'The Outlaws', present his character fully-fledged; like its 350 or so sequels, it depends largely on the narrative style (reminiscent of P. G. *Wodehouse) for its humour. William is asked by his mother to take a neighbour's baby out in its pram:

'Now, William, I'm sure you'd like to help, and I'm sure you wouldn't like your father to hear that you wouldn't even do a little thing like that for poor Mrs Butler. And she's got such a headache.'

'*A little thing like that!*' repeated William out of the bitterness of his soul.

From *Just—William* to *William and the Witch* (1964) the books were illustrated, with great humour and vigour, by 'Thomas Henry' (Thomas Henry Fisher, 1879–1962, who never actually met Richmal Crompton until 1954), after which Henry Ford took over. Later volumes have the superficial appearance of modernity, for example *William and the Moon Rocket* (1954), *William's Television Show* (1958), and *William and the Pop Singers* (1965). (Some of the stories have themselves been televised and filmed.) But William's world remains fundamentally the same, and the lifestyle is always recognizably that of the 1920s. After the author's death her niece Richmal Ashbee modernized some of the details in the earlier books, so that the stories should not seem 'period pieces' to modern children—for example, she took William out of shorts and put him into jeans.

William is chiefly notable for his aggressive style of conversation: '"Oh yes!" went on William in triumph. "Go on! Write a note. Write a note without paper and pencil, and we'll all watch. Huh!"'

Just William Through the Ages by Mary Cadogan (1994) chronicles the character and his world. The books' popularity has been enhanced by an excellent series of audiobook recordings from the 1990s voiced by the actor Martin Jarvis.

WILLIAMS, Garth (1912–96) American illustrator known for his work on classic children's books by Margaret Wise *Brown, Russell *Hoban, Randall *Jarrell, George *Selden, Charlotte *Zolotow, and more. He was given his first job as a children's illustrator by the editor Ursula *Nordstrom, who sent him the manuscript with a note pinned to it by the author: 'Try Garth Williams'. The book was E. B. White's *Stuart Little* (1945). The two also collaborated on White's *Charlotte's Web* (1952). Before working on Laura Ingalls Wilder's *Little House on the Prairie* books, Williams visited the Wilders, and then travelled around the Midwest getting to know the landscape. As well as working as an illustrator, Williams also wrote seven books.

WILLIAMS, Marcia (1945–) English author and illustrator of cartoon-strip books, most of them retelling well-loved stories, featuring her distinctive take on mythology, legend, Shakespeare, and Homer, which have entertained and educated—though the high level of entertainment should mean that readers don't notice the education—since her first book, *The First*

Christmas, in 1987. The light-hearted images are immediately engaging, whether they are of Macbeth in *Mr William Shakespeare's Plays* (2009), Troy in *The Iliad and the Odyssey* (1996), India in *The Elephant's Friend* (2013), or England in *The Adventures of Robin Hood* (2007).

WILLIAMS, Margery (1881–1944) British children's writer who was the daughter of a barrister and classical scholar; she eventually made her home in America, after marrying Francisco Bianco. She wrote several adult novels, but produced nothing remarkable until she was in her forties. *The *Velveteen Rabbit* (1922), her first children's book, was illustrated by Sir William *Nicholson (1872–1949). It was followed by another book about a toy, *The Little Wooden Doll* (1925), for which the illustrator was her own daughter Pamela, who at the age of twelve had produced drawings which inspired Walter *de la Mare to write a verse text for them (*Flora*, 1919). Margery Williams's third children's book, the much admired *Poor Cecco* (1925), is the story of a wooden toy, a 'loose-jointed thing like a dog', who gets out of the toy cupboard and has a lengthy series of adventures with his friend Bulka the rag puppy. The first edition was illustrated by Arthur *Rackham; a 1973 reissue has pictures by Anthony *Maitland. Margery Williams wrote fifteen other books for children, but none of them has had a lasting reputation.

WILLIAMS, Ursula Moray (1911–2006) British author of more than fifty books for children, including *Adventures of the Little Wooden Horse* (1938); *Gobbolino, the Witch's Cat* (1942), about a magical witch's cat, with one white paw, who just wants to be a normal kitchen cat; *The Three Toymakers* (1945); and *Grandpapa's Folly and the Woodworm-Bookworm* (1974).

WILLIAMSON, Henry (1895–1977) British novelist, best known for *Tarka the Otter* (1927), possibly the most accomplished 20th-cent. *animal story, not written for children, but often read by them. Williamson wrote many other books in the same genre.

William Tell Swiss folk hero best known for his supposed exploit of shooting with an arrow an apple placed on his son's head, and for stirring up a rebellion against his country's Austrian oppressors. There does not seem to have been a real William Tell, but stories about him were current from the 15th cent. and versions for children began to appear in the mid-19th cent.

WILLIS, Jeanne (1959–) A picture-book writer and novelist, best known for her collaborations with Tony *Ross. Sometimes writing in rhyming couplets, she plays with language to highly witty effect. Her picture books with Ross include *Misery Moo* (2003), about a friendship between a lamb and a depressed cow; *Susan Laughs* (1999), a book much praised for its enlightened depiction of a child with special needs; and the tear-jerking *Don't Let Go* (2002), about a father teaching his daughter to ride a bike. She has collaborated with many other illustrators including Adrian Reynolds (*Who's in the Loo?*, 2006), Garry Parsons (*There's an Ouch in my Pouch!*, 2008), and Gwen Millward (*The Bog Baby*, 2008).

Her *young adult novel *Naked Without a Hat* (2004) was shortlisted for the Whitbread Award (*see* COSTA CHILDREN'S BOOK AWARD).

Willy Wonka *See* CHARLIE AND THE CHOCOLATE FACTORY.

WILSON, Jacqueline (1945–) An English author and one of the best-known and most popular figures in British children's literature. She has sold over thirty-five million books, which have been translated into over thirty languages. In 2007 she was awarded the title of Dame Commander of the Most Excellent Order of the British Empire (DBE) for her services to children's literature. Wilson is known for her sensitive portrayals of feisty heroines with difficult and troubled family lives, her books often featuring children in care, bullying, depression, divorce, and domestic violence. However Wilson's popularity stems from her ability to cover these difficult and emotive subjects with a humorous, light touch and in a way that is manageable for a relatively young readership.

One of Wilson's most successful character creations is *Tracy Beaker, who first appears in *The Story of Tracy Beaker* (1991), illustrated by Nick *Sharratt. Since Tracy Beaker, Wilson has gone on to win numerous awards including the Smarties Medal and the Children's Book Award for *Double Act* (1995), which was also highly commended for the *Carnegie Medal. Wilson wrote her own screen adaptation of the novel for Channel 4, which won the Royal TV Society Best Children's Fiction Award. *The Illustrated Mum* (1999), again illustrated by Sharratt, is a brilliant novel about dealing with a parent's alcoholism and depression, and won the *Guardian Children's Fiction Prize and the Children's Book of the Year at

the British Book Awards in 1999. Her series of books for older readers includes *Girls in Love* (1997), *Girls Under Pressure* (1998), *Girls Out Late* (1999), and *Girls in Tears* (2002). Wilson has written two autobiographical books, *Jacky Daydream* (2007) and *My Secret Diary* (2009). *Hetty Feather* (2009), set in 1876, is Wilson's first historical novel, about a child left in London's infamous Foundling Hospital. Her latest book *Queenie* (2013) features little Elsie Kettle and her Nan in the year of the Queen's Coronation in 1953.

WILSON, the Revd **William Carus** (1792–1859) Founder of a Clergy Daughters' School at Cowan Bridge in Lancashire, which was attended by Charlotte Brontë. Afterwards in *Jane Eyre* she portrayed the school as 'Lowood' and Carus Wilson as 'the Revd Mr Brocklehurst'. Carus Wilson was the author of a number of homiletic writings for children and he published the periodical *The *Children's Friend* (founded 1824). There is evidence that Charlotte Brontë somewhat maligned Wilson, who appears to have been unaware of conditions at his school.

Wilson the Wonder Athlete Hero of stories in the boys' magazine *Wizard (and later in *Hornet* and *Hotspur), and then revived briefly in *Spike* in the 1980s. Wilson lives such a healthy life that he has reached the age of 128 without even looking middle-aged. His home is a cave in 'the remote wilderness of Axmoor'; he sleeps on the bare ground beneath the stars and eats a diet of 'gruel, nuts and berries'. Now and then he emerges to perform amazing athletic feats. His achievements are summed up by Benny Green in an article in the *Spectator* (26 December 1970):

In one episode he takes a giant leap and breaks the world long jump record while in the act of running a *three*-minute mile... His most tangible legacy is a parlour game still played occasionally by grown men of my own vintage who ought to know better. The game is called 'Wilsonisms' and its aim is to arrive at the ultimate absurdity in physical achievement.

1st Player: Wilson climbed Mount Everest.
2nd Player: At night.
3rd Player: Barefoot.
4th Player: Without oxygen.
1st Player: With a twelve-stone man on his back.
2nd Player: In fifteen minutes.
3rd Player: Backwards.
4th Player: With a tray of drinks in each hand.

Wind in the Willows, The (1908) By Kenneth *Grahame, one of the central classics of children's fiction; it was his fourth book.

It began life as a series of bedtime stories told to his son Alastair, known as Mouse, who was the Grahames' only child; the first of these was told on Mouse's fourth birthday, 12 May 1904, and concerned 'moles, giraffes & water-rats', these being the animals the boy had selected for subjects. Grahame's wife Elspeth has recorded that later the same month their Wiltshire housemaid told her that Mr Grahame was telling Mouse 'some ditty [story] or other about a Toad'. Probably the stories continued at intervals over the next three years; certainly a lengthy narrative in which Toad played the principal part (and in which there were no giraffes) had been begun by May 1907.

It began as a series of letters from Grahame to Mouse (who was on holiday with his governess). The first is dated 10 May 1907, and after wishing the boy a happy birthday it continues as follows:

Have you heard about the Toad? He was never taken prisoner by brigands at all. It was all a horrid low trick of his. He wrote that letter himself—the letter saying that a hundred pounds must be put in the hollow tree. And he got out of the window early one morning, & went off to a town called Buggleton, & went to the Red Lion Hotel & there he found a party that had just motored down from London, & while they were having breakfast he went into the stable-yard & found their motor-car & went off in it without even saying Poop-poop! And now he has vanished & everyone is looking for him, including the police. I fear he is a bad low animal.

The letters, some of which were addressed to 'Michael Robinson', Mouse's pet name for himself, continued every few days until September (there are 15 in all, with one apparently missing from the series); they describe Toad's adventures much as in the published book, but pay no more than cursory attention to Rat, Mole, and Badger. The early ones tell the tale abruptly in the manner of a synopsis, but by the end Grahame is writing the story at its proper pace, with dialogue and detailed, carefully-written narrative.

It seems that his decision to try to get it published was the result of meetings with Constance Smedley, an American lady who among other things was European representative of the magazine *Everybody's*. Its editor asked her to try to persuade Grahame to produce a new book; she was living at Bray in Berkshire, not far from his current home at Cookham Dean, and she went to see him, somehow discovered about the story being told to Alastair, and encouraged him to work it up for publication. He told her that he found

writing extremely hard work, and the amount of effort that he put into *The Wind in the Willows* is indicated by the number of drafts which survive (most of them are in the Bodleian Library, Oxford). There are fragments of a rough first version, then a neatly-written draft in pen; this has the title 'The Mole and the Water-Rat'. Next comes a typescript which contains the book much as published, though major alterations went on right up to proof. Until a late stage the book's title was to be 'The Wind in the Reeds'.

The book was not accepted by *Everybody's*, Miss Smedley's magazine, and indeed Grahame's agent Curtis Brown had great difficulty in placing it at all. But it was finally taken in England by Methuen, who published it in October 1908, and in America by Scribner, whose decision was allegedly influenced by a letter from Theodore Roosevelt, who was an enthusiast for Grahame's earlier works, *The *Golden Age* and *Dream Days*.

Grahame himself wished to discourage readers from the belief that the book has secondary layers of meaning. He wrote to Theodore Roosevelt: 'Its qualities, if any, are mostly negative—i.e.—no problems, no sex, no second meaning—it is only an expression of the very simplest joys of life as lived by the simplest beings of a class that you are specifically familiar with and will understand.' But this was ingenuous, and indeed betrays the fact that the book is not really about animals.

Grahame takes far less trouble than, say, Beatrix *Potter to present his animals realistically; in many episodes they are, for example, far larger than real life, so that Toad can drive a motor-car and Mole lead a horse by the reins. They are, perhaps more than in any other *animal story, simply human beings given the shape of various animals as an expression of their personalities and as a disguise for the author's real purpose, which is to observe and comment on the behaviour of the English gentry of the upper middle class. C. S. *Lewis has observed that the character of Badger is an 'amalgam of high rank, coarse manners, gruffness, shyness and goodness', and continues: 'The child who has once met Mr Badger has got ever afterwards, in its bones, a knowledge of humanity and English social history which it certainly couldn't get from any abstraction.' Peter Green, in the course of a lengthy analysis of *The Wind in the Willows* in his 1959 biography of Grahame, observes that Rat, Mole, and Badger are in effect 'static rural traditionalism' under attack

from Socialism, in the form of the worker-like Wild Wooders.

Green also points out that while the principal characters owe something to members of Grahame's circle, they are also expressions of the conflicting side of Grahame's own personality. Certainly the chapter 'Wayfarers All', in which Rat is nearly drawn away to 'go South, with the rest of them', is beyond doubt an expression of Grahame's own longing to give up the life of a City businessman and become a wanderer in Mediterranean countries.

This chapter and 'The Piper at the Gates of Dawn' did not form part of the original plan for the book, and they puzzle and even irritate many readers, seeming to be out of character with the rest of the story; but for Grahame they were probably the most important parts of *The Wind in the Willows*. 'The Piper at the Gates of Dawn' closely resembles the style of his many 1890s lyrical essays about the English countryside, in which he espoused a so-called 'paganism' which seeks rural pleasures as an antidote to the deadness of urban life.

The Wind in the Willows was not at first a success with the public. Many readers who were devoted to *The Golden Age* and *Dream Days* were disconcerted to find that the new book was not about children but animals. Almost no reviewer perceived anything of its purpose; *The Times* remarked that 'as a contribution to natural history the work is negligible', and the young Arthur *Ransome, writing in the *Bookman*, thought it largely a failure. Only two critics came near understanding what Grahame was about. Arnold Bennett, in *Punch*, wrote that 'the book is an urbane exercise in irony at the expense of the English character and of mankind', and Richard Middleton remarked in *Vanity Fair*: 'If I may venture to describe as an allegory a work which critics, who ought to have known better, have dismissed as a fairy story, it is certain that *The Wind in the Willows* is a wise book.'

Despite the disappointing reception, sales were high enough for Methuen to reprint the book before the end of 1908, and further reprints were issued in 1909, 1910, 1911, and 1913. By 1926 it was in its twenty-first printing, and when Grahame died six years later his name had become associated far more with *The Wind in the Willows* than with his earlier successes. In 1930 its popularity was further increased by the first London production of *Toad of Toad Hall*, a children's musical play adapted from it by A. A. *Milne, who was one of the book's most devoted admirers and

championed it several times in print. Milne omitted 'The Piper at the Gates of Dawn' and 'Wayfarers All', and—more seriously—replaced Grahame's lyricism with somewhat shallow sentimentality. But the play was a great success, and for many years was performed every Christmas in the West End, the part of Mole being taken regularly by the actor Richard Goolden, who was still performing it when in his 90s. The many other stage versions include one by Alan Bennett, which had its premiere at London's National Theatre in 1990 and has since been revived.

The first edition of the book had an embossed binding and a frontispiece by Grahame's friend Graham Robertson, but these made no attempt to depict the animals and there were no other illustrations. Grahame himself is said not to have wanted illustrations because of the difficulties they posed. Peter Green writes: 'When asked specifically (apropos the escape on the railway train) whether Toad was life-size or train-size, he answered that he was both and neither: the Toad was train-sized, the train was Toad-sized, and therefore there could be no illustrations.'

In fact Grahame's publishers did approach Arthur *Rackham to ask him to illustrate the first edition, but he was 'too busy illustrating the *Midsummer Night's Dream*', and had to refuse. Rackham came to regret this decision a great deal and was delighted when, at the very end of his life, he was asked to illustrate an edition of the book for the Limited Editions Club of New York; this appeared in 1940. Another well known illustrated edition has pictures by E. H. *Shepard (1931); other artists to tackle the book include Paul Bransom (1913), Nancy Barnhart (1922), Wyndham Payne (1927), Paul Henning (1947), Michael Hague (1982), John *Burningham (1983), Patrick Benson (1994), Robert *Ingpen (2007), and David *Roberts (2012).

In *Wild Wood* (1981) the modern children's author Jan *Needle examines the events of the story from the point of view of the Wild Wooders. There are several sequels by William Horwood, beginning with *The Willows in Winter* (1993).

Windmill Man, The See PLAYS.

Wind on Fire, The (2000–2) A fantasy trilogy by William *Nicholson. In *The Wind Singer* (2000), we meet the Manth people of Aramanth, a city whose social structure is determined by exam results. Every citizen has to take exams—even toddlers—and the results

decide where the families are allowed to live and what privileges they receive. Kestrel Hath despises the regime, and she and her twin brother Bowman set off on a dangerous journey to save Aramanth from the evil that grips it. In *Slaves of the Mastery* (2001), the entire population of Aramanth is captured and brought into slavery by the cruel Mastery. Kestrel has not been captured, and she is determined to find her beloved brother and to free her people. In *Firesong* (2002), the Manth people flee from the Mastery and embark on a perilous journey to find their homeland, led by the prophetess Ira Hath, who is Kestrel and Bowman's mother. Meanwhile, Bowman prepares to make a great sacrifice for his people. *The Wind Singer* won the Nestlé Smarties Best Book Award in 2000, and the *Blue Peter Book Award for the 'Book I Couldn't Put Down'.

Wind on the Moon, The (1944) A *fantasy for children by Eric *Linklater. Dorinda and Dinah are warned by their father, who is going abroad, that there is 'a wind on the moon' and they may find themselves behaving very badly. And so they do: enlisting the services of a *witch, they turn themselves into kangaroos and join a zoo. However, later in the story they rescue their father from imprisonment by a Hitlerian dictator, Count Hulagy Boot.

The book's wild inventiveness and arbitrary turns of plot reflect the fact that it originated as an impromptu tale told in a desperate attempt to entertain the author's daughters on a rainy walk in Scotland. It won the *Carnegie Medal.

Winnie-the-Pooh (1926) The first of the Christopher Robin storybooks by A. A. *Milne, illustrated by E. H. *Shepard. Together with its companion *The *House at Pooh Corner*, it is one of the best loved of all children's books.

Milne's only son Christopher was six when the book was published, and for a year the family had owned Cotchford Farm on the edge of Ashdown Forest in Sussex. This became the setting for stories about the boy (always 'Christopher Robin' in books, but never to his family) and a group of toys and animals. The bear and the other toys were Christopher's in real life; in his autobiography *The Enchanted Places* (1974) he wrote: 'Pooh was the oldest, only a year younger than I was, and my inseparable companion.' 'Pooh' was in fact a name transferred from a swan, encountered on an early holiday; 'Winnie' was the name of an American black bear cub,

mascot of Princess Pat's Canadian Regiment, who came to the London Zoo in 1914 while the regiment went on to fight in France; she was much loved by child visitors to the Zoo, among them Christopher Milne.

The other original inhabitants of the boy's nursery (and of the books' setting, the Hundred Acre Wood), were Piglet, a present from a neighbour, and Eeyore, the gloomy droopy-necked donkey ('After all, one can't complain... Somebody spoke to me only yesterday'). Rabbit and Owl were entirely imaginary, invented by A. A. Milne when the stories needed them, while Kanga and Roo, and Tigger (who only appears in the second book) were later presents from Christopher's parents, 'carefully chosen, not just for the delight that they might give to their new owner, but also for their literary possibilities'. A host of smaller creatures were all Rabbit's friends-and-relations. Among these creatures the boy's status in the stories is somewhat that of a favourite grown-up or friendly, reassuring, and useful elder brother; he is sometimes called on to be *deus ex machina*, always to be understanding.

Both A. A. Milne and his son have acknowledged the role of Milne's wife Daphne in helping Christopher to bring his toys to life and give them voices, until they reached the point where Milne could begin writing. The process was circular, for Christopher remembers also some of the effect the finished stories had on his life: 'The Pooh in my arms... was a Pooh who had climbed trees in search of honey, who had got stuck in a rabbit hole, who was "a bear of no brain at all"...'

Of the stories enacted by these characters, Christopher wrote: 'It is difficult to be sure which came first. Did I do something and did my father write a story around it? Or was it the other way about, and did the story come first. Certainly my father was on the look-out for ideas; but so was I. He wanted ideas for his stories, I wanted them for my games, and each looked towards the other for inspiration. But in the end it was the same: the stories became part of our lives, we lived them, thought them, spoke them. And so, possibly before, but certainly after that particular story, we used to stand on Poohsticks Bridge throwing sticks into the water.'

Some incidents and places Christopher remembered deriving clearly from his life at Cotchford: the great rain and the flood that stopped just short of their house; the tree that was so obviously a house for Owl; the

heffalump trap which got him into trouble when the gardener's wife caught her foot in it; and his own tree house which he shared with his toy bear. Other incidents were more freely invented.

The original toys, after their owner had grown out of them, were at first kept in a glass case on the nursery wall in London. During the Second World War they were removed to America and housed in the offices of Milne's New York publisher, E. P. Dutton. A facsimile of the original manuscript of *Winnie-the-Pooh* was published in 1971, and shows how relatively few corrections or afterthoughts interrupted Milne's composition.

Frederick C. Crews, Professor of English at Berkeley, California, chose the Christopher Robin books as the text for his devastating satire of literary criticism, *The Pooh Perplex, a freshman casebook* (1963), since when any commentator on Milne's creations has risked sounding like one of Crews' parodies—and has also risked saying rather less, for Crews' witticisms are often as obliquely pertinent as they are funny. But, *pace* Crews, it remains to be said that Milne's characters are archetypal and the books' incidents endlessly useful as metaphors for daily life. In 1982 there appeared Benjamin Hoff's *The Tao of Pooh*, which argues that 'Pooh's way is amazingly consistent with the principles of living envisaged long ago by the Chinese founders of Taoism.'

Winnie-the-Pooh has been translated into Latin and Esperanto (among countless other languages) and has been published in many different versions, some of them deriving from the 1965 Walt *Disney film and its spin-offs. The composer H. Fraser-Simson, a friend of Milne's, set *The Hums of Pooh* (1929). In the manner of all the foremost nursery story characters, Pooh has become, too, a sponsor for innumerable spin-off books and countless lines of merchandise, sadly often based on the Disney rather than the Shepard illustrations. 2009 saw the publication of the first sequel to the original books to be authorised by the Milne estate, David Benedictus's *Return to the Hundred Acre Wood*; and a new collection of stories, *The Best Bear in All the World*, by a quartet of authors, appeared in 2016. Both were beautifully illustrated in the Shepard style by Mark Burgess.

Winnie the Witch *See* PAUL, KORKY.

Wishing-Chair series A childhood favourite for generations, *Adventures of the Wishing-Chair* (1937) was the prolific Enid *Blyton's first full-length book, and told in short episodes the story of Mollie and Peter, who, when searching for a birthday present for their mother, find a chair in an antique shop that can grow wings and fly. Their adventures lead them to befriending a pixie called Chinky who comes to live with them in their playroom. A sequel, *The Wishing-Chair Again* (1950), sees the chair being stolen by giants and the children's efforts to save it. In 2000 a compilation was issued in *More Wishing-Chair Stories* and included stories taken from the Enid Blyton annuals.

witch A word derived from Anglo-Saxon *wicce*, the feminine of *wicca*, 'wizard, soothsayer, magician'. Witchcraft was condemned in the Middle Ages (e.g. by the Bull of Pope Innocent VIII in 1484), and in 1487 was published the *Malleus Maleficarum* ('Hammer of Witches'), a manual for inquisitors tracking witches. Reginald Scot's *Discoverie of Witchcraft* (1584) regarded most witches as 'poor doting women' and James I's own *Daemonologie* warned against unfair persecution. But in America in 1692 the Salem witchcraft trials were notoriously cruel; Cotton *Mather and his father were active in them.

Witches feature in the folklore of all countries; notable witches of folk literature include *Baba Yaga of Russia, who travels about on a hut that walks on chicken's legs, *Morgan Le Fay of the King *Arthur legends, and the *ogre-witch of *Hansel and Gretel. T. H. White's *The *Sword in the Stone* (1938) included in its first version a magical battle between *Merlin and the witch Madame Mim, with Hecate as umpire. In *The *Wonderful Wizard of Oz* (1900), L. Frank *Baum introduced the figures of two 'good witches' as counterparts to the 'wicked witches'. Other witches in modern children's literature include the Hag Dowsabel, the creation of Lorna *Wood; Meg in the *Meg and Mog* picture books illustrated by Jan *Pieńkowski; *Dorrie, the creation of Patricia *Coombs; *The *Worst Witch* in stories by Jill Murphy; Roald Dahl's eponymous *The *Witches*; and the *Winnie the Witch* series by Valerie Thomas and Korky *Paul. Witches play a significant part in Philip Pullman's *His Dark Materials*; Pullman's creations have the skill to be invisible—they are not *truly* invisible (which is impossible), but rather are able to remain entirely unnoticed through a 'fiercely held modesty'. Norton Juster's *The *Phantom Tollbooth* features 'Faintly Macabre, the not-so-wicked Which' [*sic*].

Witches, The (1983) A novel by Roald *Dahl. A nameless (unusually for Dahl) seven-year-old narrator is warned by his fantastic cigar-smoking granny that there are witches about, that the English ones are particularly nasty, and that they like nothing more than squelching children. But when boy and grandmother are holidaying at Bournemouth's Hotel Magnificent, he finds himself right in the middle of the English witches' Annual Meeting. The witches are planning to turn all English children into mice, and our hero himself suffers that transformation; but soon he and his granny manage to turn the tables and the witches drink their own potion and are themselves transformed. As the book concludes, the boy remains a mouse, but he doesn't mind, as it means he won't have to outlive his grandmother, and the two of them prepare for more witch-hunting adventure.

WITTLINGER, Ellen (1948–) American author, primarily of *young adult fiction. Her books focus on questions of identity and relationships. She is best known for *Hard Love* (1999), a Michael L. Printz Honor book (*see* MICHAEL L. PRINTZ AWARD) about John (Gio), an intellectual loner struggling after his parents' divorce, and his friendship with Marisol, a lesbian zine writer. *Love & Lies* (2008) continues the story after high school and is told from Marisol's perspective. Among Wittlinger's other books are *Lombardo's Law* (1993), *Razzle* (2001), *Zig Zag* (2003), *Heart on My Sleeve* (2004), *Parrotfish* (2007), about a transgendered teenager, and *Gracie's Girl* (2000) and *This Means War* (2010), both with pre-teen protagonists.

Wizard One of D. C. *Thomson & Co.'s adventure magazines for boys, founded in 1922. It contained the usual Thomson mixture of high adventure, *school stories, *science fiction, and improbable tales of every kind. It ceased publication in the early 1980s.

Wizard of Earthsea, A (1967) The first of the *Earthsea novels by Ursula *Le Guin.

Wizard of Oz, The *See* WONDERFUL WIZARD OF OZ, THE.

WODEHOUSE, Sir P. G. (Pelham Grenville) (1881–1975) The outstanding British comic novelist of his generation who began his literary career by contributing a series of *school stories to the magazine *Captain*. Books resulting from this were *A Prefect's Uncle* (1903), *Tales of St Austin's* (1903), *The Gold Bat* (1904), *The Head of Kay's* (1905), and, most notably, *Mike* (1909), which describes the experiences of Mike Jackson, skilled cricketer, at Wrykyn School. Though it has many elements of the conventional school story, *Mike* is full of shafts of the inimitable P. G. Wodehouse wit and the schoolboy dandy Psmith proved to be such a character that Wodehouse used him in stories for adult readers.

WOJCIECHOWSKA, Maia (Teresa) (1927–2002) Polish-born author who emigrated to the USA in 1942. Her children's books include *Shadow of a Bull* (1964), about the son of a great bullfighter, for which she won the 1965 *Newbery Medal.

Wolf Brother (2004) The first book in Michelle *Paver's *Chronicles of Ancient Darkness*, a sequence of six novels that follow twelve-year-old Stone Age boy Torak in his quest to defeat the Soul Eaters. In this book, the opening chapter of the adventure, Torak, alone and orphaned, is befriended by a young wolf cub who will become his companion over the series. Tracking the demon bear who killed his father, he is captured by the Raven Clan, and meets Renn, who becomes his friend. With her, he sets off to find the Mountain of the World Spirit. This is the beginning of a journey that takes him from childhood to manhood and reaches its climax in the final volume, *Ghost Hunter* (2009), recipient of the *Guardian Children's Fiction Prize.

WOLLSTONECRAFT, Mary (1759–97) Author, campaigner for women's rights, and first wife of William *Godwin. She wrote a children's book, *Original Stories from Real Life* (1788), and translated C. G. Salzmann's *Das moralische Elementarbuch* into English as *Elements of Morality, for the use of children* (1790).

Wolves (2005) The debut picture book by Emily *Gravett, for which she was awarded the *Kate Greenaway Medal and the Boston Globe–Horn Book Honor (*see* BOSTON GLOBE–HORN BOOK AWARDS). Gravett wrote the book as part of her BA course in illustration. A rabbit borrows a book about wolves from the library and is so engrossed in reading it that he doesn't notice a real threatening wolf looming ever larger. There is a postscript to reassure nervous readers that this wolf was a vegetarian and the rabbit came to no harm. The soft pencil line, the use of the space on the page, and the witty interplay between text and image contributed to a remarkable book by a significant new author.

Wolves of Willoughby Chase, The
(1962) A novel by Joan *Aiken which established its author's reputation as a leading children's writer. Set in an imaginary period of English history, the reign of James III in the 1830s, it describes how the countryside is overrun with wolves that have strayed into Britain via the newly opened Channel Tunnel. Sir Willoughby, master of a great country house, goes abroad with his sick wife, leaving his daughter Bonnie and her cousin Sylvia in the hands of a villainous *governess, Miss Slighcarp, who with her accomplice Josiah Grimshaw is determined to make the Willoughby inheritance her own. The book is an outstanding mixture of wild humour and gothic imagination. The next book set in this alternative historical England (though not quite a sequel) is *Black Hearts in Battersea.

Wombles A race of creatures invented by British author Elizabeth *Beresford; they first appeared in her book *The Wombles* (1968) and were subsequently featured on television and in a pop song, with huge success. Wombles are semi-human in appearance; they are furry and have long snouts and are distinguished from one another chiefly by their eccentric clothes. They include Great Uncle Bulgaria, Tobermory, Bungo, Orinoco, Tomsk, and Wellington. Their habitat is underground (originally beneath Wimbledon Common in London), and their occupation is collecting, at night time, rubbish left by humans, which they make 'into all kinds of useful things'.

Wonder One of the *Harmsworth juvenile papers, founded in 1892. A mixture of *comic and *adventure paper, it ran under different titles for nearly half a century, ending as the *Jolly Jester* in 1940.

wonder book A term which came to be used for children's books containing collections of information or stories. It seems to have originated with *A *Wonder-Book for Girls and Boys* (1851) by *Hawthorne, and in the 1860s there appeared *The Wonder-Book of Nature's Transformations* (1863) and *The Wonder Book of Perils and Adventures all over the World* (1868), both anonymous.

Forty years later F. J. Harvey *Darton revived the 'Wonder Book' title with his *Wonder Book of Old Romance* (1907) and *Wonder Book of Beasts* (1909). 'Wonder' was used as one of the subject headings in Arthur *Mee's immensely popular *Children's Encyclopaedia* (1908 onwards), and this may have been responsible

for the inauguration in 1911, by the publishers Ward Lock, of a Wonder Book series about aspects of the physical world. The series, edited by Harry Golding, began with *The Wonder Book of Railways* (1911). Subsequent titles covered every kind of subject and most letters of the alphabet, from *The Wonder Book of Aircraft* (1919) to *The Wonder Book of Would You Believe It?* (1938). The series, which was ahead of its time in its use of photographs and imaginative layout, was hugely successful, and updated versions of its books are still in print.

Wonder-Book for Girls and Boys, A By Nathaniel *Hawthorne, first published in America by Ticknor, Reed and Fields of Boston late in 1851 (it is dated 1852). The book was undertaken at the suggestion of the American publishers, who wished to build on Hawthorne's success with *The Scarlet Letter* (1850). Hawthorne wrote the *Wonder-Book* in six weeks, using an idea he had long had of making 'one or two mythological story-books'.

The narrative is set at Tanglewood Manor, a New England country house. A group of children, under the leadership of an eighteen-year-old college student, Eustace Bright, are going nutting. Before they set out he entertains them with an extempore version of the story of Perseus and the Gorgon's head. On the expedition they hear the story of Midas and the Golden Touch; later, as the seasons pass at Tanglewood, Eustace relates the myths of Pandora's Box, the Golden Apples of the Hesperides, Philemon and Baucis, and the Chimaera. The book ends with Eustace declaring that he will have the stories published 'through the eminent house of Ticknor & Co.', and that he expects as a result to be 'reckoned among the lights of the age!'

The presentation of the myths is deliberately gothic and romantic, Hawthorne preferring this to what he called 'classic coldness'. Scenic descriptions are lush (Tanglewood itself gets plenty of descriptive prose), the style is expansive and even chatty, and the myths are made immensely readable and vivid. The original stories are, however, treated in cavalier fashion, which greatly irritated Charles *Kingsley and spurred him into writing his own version of them.

Editions of the *Wonder-Book* quickly proliferated on both sides of the Atlantic. In 1892 there appeared a version illustrated by Walter *Crane, and Arthur *Rackham illustrated it in 1922.

Two years after it appeared Hawthorne produced a sequel, *Tanglewood Tales.

Wonderful Adventures of Nils, The
(1906-7) A celebrated story by the Swedish
novelist Selma *Lagerlöf.

Nils Holgersson, a lazy boy of fourteen, fails
to keep a promise he has made to an *elf and
is changed by it into a tiny *Tom Thumb-like
being. He discovers that he can understand the
speech of animals and birds, and when a gander
on his father's farm is lured away by a flock of
wild geese who are flying north to Lapland, Nils
goes with it, flying on the creature's back. At first
he is treated with disdain by the geese's leader,
an old grey bird named Akka of Kebnekaise, but
after he has performed several valorous deeds,
he is accepted by Akka and is allowed to go with
the geese all the way to Lapland.

On his journey over Sweden he has great
adventures, which continue in *The Further
Adventures of Nils*. Finally he returns home,
where he discovers that news of his exploits
has reached his parents, who are proud of
their once good-for-nothing son. He is re-
leased from his enchantment and resumes
his normal size, though he half wishes he
were back with the geese.

The book was written at the request of the
National Teachers' Association of Sweden,
who wanted a work that would teach children
the geography and folklore of their country.
Selma Lagerlöf spent some time researching
into regional traditions and folk stories before
writing it. It was published in Swedish as *Nils
Holgerssons undebara resa genom Sverige*. The
story at once became a bestseller and was
quickly translated into English, German, and
Danish. Comparisons were soon being made
with the stories of Hans Christian *Andersen
and with *The *Jungle Books*, and it has some-
thing of the character of both, though it is a
strikingly original work and remains one of
Sweden's outstanding contributions to chil-
dren's literature.

Wonderful Farm, The The English title of
Les Contes du chat perché (1939) by the French
author Marcel Aymé (1902-67); a collection of
*fable-like stories about two girls, Delphine
and Marinette, who live on a farm where the
animals can speak. *Autres Contes du chat
perché* (1950) was translated as *Return to the
Wonderful Farm* (1954).

The 1951 American edition of *The Wonder-
ful Farm* was the first children's book to be
illustrated by Maurice *Sendak.

Wonderful Wizard of Oz, The (1900)
A novel by L. Frank *Baum, the story of the

orphan Dorothy who is carried by a cyclone
from her aunt and uncle's Kansas farm to the
land of Oz. There she begins a quest with the
Scarecrow, the Tin Woodman, and the Cow-
ardly Lion: all are in search of the wizard of Oz
himself, who can give each of them what he or
she wants—Dorothy's desire being that she
get back home to Kansas. The book was first
published in 1900 by the Geo. M. Hill Co. of
Chicago and New York, with illustrations by
W. W. Denslow.

The introduction by Baum states that tradi-
tional *fairy stories such as those collected
and written by the *Grimms and *Andersen
have now become matters of chiefly 'histori-
cal' interest; this book 'aspires to being a
modernized fairy tale, in which the wonder-
ment and joy are retained and the heart-ache
and nightmares are left out'.

The first draft of the book was entitled 'The
Emerald City'; this was altered allegedly be-
cause of a superstition that it is unlucky to
publish a book with a jewel in the title. The
book appeared in May, and the first printing of
10,000 copies sold out in a few weeks; by the
following January nearly 100,000 had been
sold.

The book's success was largely due to Den-
slow's illustrations. These were strongly rem-
iniscent of Walter *Crane as well as being
influenced by Art Nouveau and Japanese
prints. There were over 100 text illustrations,
in black and one additional colour (sepia,
green, mustard yellow, brown, or red), many
of them spreading into and around the text
itself; twenty-four three-colour plates were also
included. Baum himself seems not to have
cared particularly for the pictures, but Den-
slow's representation of the Tin Man and the
Scarecrow have been faithfully copied by later
illustrators, film-makers, and stage-designers.

Many of the first critcs of Baum's story com-
pared it to Lewis *Carroll, and as with *Alice's
Adventures in Wonderland* there was also a
tendency to praise illustrator rather than au-
thor. The *New York Times* (8 September 1900)
was one of the few journals to give due praise
to Baum, describing the story as 'a book that
rises far above the average children's book of
today, high as is the present standard'.

The Wonderful Wizard of Oz is unquestion-
ably the best original American *fantasy to be
written up to 1900. Baum was not, however,
altogether faithful to his declaration that hor-
rific elements would be excluded: the death of
the two wicked *witches and the Tin Man's
account of his self-wounding with the axe are

notably gruesome. Moreover, though he claimed to be superseding 'historical' fairy tales, he makes use of motifs that can be found in European folk literature.

The question remains whether the book is an allegorical comment on American society. Henry M. Littlefield claimed in *American Quarterly*, in spring 1964, that many incidents in the story are satirical references to contemporary political issues. Other readers have perceived in this queststory, in which a journey is made down a gold-paved road in search of a Wizard who finally proves to be a charlatan, a parable of the American Dream.

In 1903 the book was reissued by the Bobbs-Merrill Company of Indianapolis (Hill, the original publisher, having gone bankrupt) under the title *The New Wizard of Oz*. This was to avoid confusion with *The Wizard of Oz*, a musical play by Baum only loosely based on the story, which opened in Chicago in June 1902. The play included gag lines and all the inconsequential paraphernalia of a musical revue; it proved a great success, ran on Broadway, and continued to tour for some years. Nowadays the book is usually published as *The Wizard of Oz*.

Baum was an experimenter in cinematography and he filmed scenes from the book himself. In 1925 Chadwick Pictures made a silent movie of it with Oliver Hardy as the Tin Man; but *The Wizard of Oz* is today known very largely through the outstanding 1939 MGM film, with Judy Garland as Dorothy and music by Harold Arlen. There are a number of highly popular (if loose) stage adaptations, including *The Wiz*, a 'Super Soul Musical', which premiered in 1974 (and was also filmed, with Diana Ross and Michael Jackson, in 1978); and *Wicked*, the 2003 stage musical telling the Oz story from the witches' perspective, based on Gregory *Maguire's 1995 novel of the same name.

Baum wrote a series of sequels to the book and further Oz stories were produced by other writers after his death. In addition Denslow, Baum's illustrator, produced *Pictures from the Wonderful Wizard of Oz* (1903), with a new story to fit the pictures by Thomas H. Russell, and also created a series of 'Scarecrow and Tin Man' *comic pages for the McClure magazine syndicate in December 1904 and January 1905. Full information about the book, its author and illustrator, and its 'spin-offs', can be found in *The Annotated Wizard of Oz* (1973), with introductory text and notes by Michael Patrick Hearn.

Two new editions of the book appeared in 1982, one with pictures by Michael Hague, the other illustrated by David *McKee. There is a superb *pop-up version by Robert *Sabuda (2000).

Wonka, Willy *See* CHARLIE AND THE CHOCOLATE FACTORY.

WOOD, Anne (1937–) Teacher who in 1965 founded *Books for Your Children* (*see* CAROUSEL), which she would edit for thirty years; and in 1968 she established the *Federation of Children's Book Groups. She won the *Eleanor Farjeon Award in 1969, an award the Federation itself would win in 2011. For much of her career Wood worked as a highly successful producer of children's television.

WOOD, David (1944–) British children's playwright and actor. His musical *plays for children include *The Owl and the Pussycat Went to See* (1968), based on Edward *Lear's poem, *Flibberty and the Penguin* (1971), and—the most successful and enduring of all—*The Gingerbread Man* (1976), based on a fairy tale first published in 19th-cent. America. Nearly half a century into his career he remains preeminent in his field, having particular success with adaptations of tried and tested children's fiction, including *Meg and Mog* (1981, and much revived), Dahl's *The *Witches* (1992, among many other Dahl titles), *Tom's Midnight Garden* (2000), an opera version of Philip Pullman's *Clockwork* (2004) and an acclaimed *The *Tiger Who Came to Tea* (2008).

WOOD, Kerry (Edgar Allardyce Wood) (1907–98) Canadian author of stories set in Red Deer, Alberta, his own home all his life. They include *Wild Winter* (1954), based on his experiences as a teenager alone in the wilds.

WOOD, Lorna (1913–2010) British author who wrote a popular series of stories about a *witch, the Hag Dowsabel. These include *The Hag Calls for Help* (1957).

woodcut The oldest method of reproducing an illustration. It was known in China by the 7th cent. and its use in Europe antedated the invention of metal movable type by Gutenberg in 1445. The term 'woodcut' is often used loosely to cover both woodcuts and *wood engravings, but 'woodcut' is also used more specifically for the 'black-line' manner of using woodblocks, which was almost universal for illustration from the beginning of printing until *copperplate engraving superseded it for more expensive books from the 16th cent. onwards.

Woodcuts were generally made on the side or plank surface of a soft wood, planed flat along the grain. The design was occasionally cut out, so that it printed white on a black background, but the fact that the printers's metal type and a woodcut illustration could be printed on the same page at the same time argued that their appearance should harmonize, and their lines be of similar thickness. Thus the area around a line of illustration was cut away with chisels, gouges, and knives, and the line remained in relief to print black (or whatever other colour was chosen). *Caxton's 1484 edition of *Aesop has comparatively crude woodcut illustrations; later English books show that a more sophisticated and delicate style, and sometimes actual blocks, had been imported from the continent.

From the end of the 16th cent. woodcuts were increasingly regarded as the cheaper, and inferior, alternative to copper engraving, but they remained appropriate for the popular market, and for children's books such as the *Orbis Sensualium Pictus of *Comenius (1659). Stocks of woodcuts were a staple of early printers, and *chapbooks and *broadsides abound in very crude (though often engaging) cuts, sometimes selected with scant regard for their relevance to the story. This style of illustration was ingeniously parodied by Robert Louis *Stevenson in *Moral Emblems* (1882), a privately printed pamphlet with ridiculously crude cuts by Stevenson himself.

Woodcuts continued to have the advantage over copperplates (especially for children's books) of being printed by a relief process, like type, so that pictures could appear on the same page as text, and many of John *Newbery's mid-18th-cent. books, 'adorned with cuts', are well-designed examples of this, with specially-commissioned and appropriate, though anonymous, illustrations.

wood engraving The advanced form of *woodcut process for illustration. It shares with the earlier technique the advantage of being a relief method, easily integrated with text, the type and illustration commonly sharing the same page. This was the main process in use for children's book illustration for much of the 19th cent.

By the mid-18th cent. *copperplate engraving was the favoured medium for reproducing illustrations in books of quality, but at the same time some attempt was made to allow wood to compete, by developing blocks made of harder wood and using the end grain rather

than the planed plank surface. This produced a block more able to hold the fine lines and reproductions of tone characteristic of copperplate. Thomas *Bewick is often credited with this innovation and with first using the copper engraver's tools on wood. Whether or not this is true, he was the first to perfect these techniques, and to gain a reputation as an artist in his medium.

Bewick's main rival, using a similar technique, was Robert Branston in London. He did not design his own blocks, but he and his pupils developed a mastery of translating artists' sketches into wood engravings that further helped raise the craft to its surprising position in the mid-19th cent. as the most popular way of reproducing book and periodical illustrations. In America the most notable engraver to emulate Bewick's technique was Alexander *Anderson.

During this period the artist would either draw a sketch to be copied, or would draw or trace directly on to a block for the engraver to interpret his lines and tones according to the possibilities of the craft. The separation of functions naturally produced disagreements, especially in the case of artists who were not familiar with the technicalities of the method. For instance, though the *Dalziel Brothers were virtuosi engravers whose abilities significantly prolonged the commercial life of the medium, Dante Gabriel Rossetti believed that their work ruined his designs. Nor did Thackeray's drawings always transfer comfortably on to wood (see ROSE AND THE RING, THE). Artists could leave much to an engraver's discretion, in many cases giving him comparatively unfinished sketches; *Tenniel seems to have been one such. The advantages of photographing a drawing and developing it directly on to a block with a specially treated surface were seen as early as the 1830s, and by the 1860s this had become regular practice.

Notable 19th-cent. children's book illustrators whose work was reproduced by wood engraving also included George *Cruikshank (when he was not making his own etchings), Richard *Doyle, and Arthur *Hughes. Besides the Dalziels, notable engravers included Joseph Swain, who supplied blocks for the cartoons in *Punch*.

By the end of the 19th cent. photomechanically engraved blocks had finally ousted wood engraving from most commercial use, but the method was revived by Eric Gill and his followers in the 1920s, and there were occasional examples of its appearance in 20th- and 21st-

cent. children's books, such as the work of John *Lawrence.

The possibilities of wood-blocks for *colour printing were slow to be taken up for books, but it was this method of colour reproduction that eventually revolutionized *picture books for children; see EVANS, EDMUND.

Wood Magic (1881) A novel by Richard Jefferies (*see* BEVIS: THE STORY OF A BOY). The book is part realistic description of the surroundings of Jefferies's childhood home by Coate Water, near Swindon, and part fantasy. The small boy Bevis ('little "Sir" Bevis . . . was his pet name') becomes involved in the feuds and intrigues of the animals of farmyard and woodland, who tell him of their troubles and concerns. Much of the story is taken up with their attempt to dethrone their king, Kapchack the magpie. Jefferies's writings about the English countryside were probably an influence on the early essays of Kenneth *Grahame.

WOODSON, Jacqueline (1963–) African-American author whose books for young adults address complex issues of growing up in the 21st cent. Gritty, honest, and not shy of spelling out the complexities of race, abuse, teenage pregnancy, and homosexuality, her books are not always approved of by some adults but her teen readership is passionate about them, loving that they can see themselves in the pages and find answers there too—answers that are always full of hope, and about leaving the world a better place. *After Tupac and D Foster* (2008), the verseform *Locomotion* (2003), and *Feathers* (2007) are all excellent examples of her work.

Wool-Pack, The (1951) Classic English coming-of-age story by Cynthia *Harnett, set in the Cotswolds in 1493. In a beautifully told, slow-burning tale packed with detail about early Tudor life, we learn of twelve-year-old Nicholas, who finds out that he is engaged, but whose life is subsequently complicated by treachery within his father's trade guild. There are illustrations by the author.

WOOLSEY, Sarah Chauncy *See* COOLIDGE, SUSAN.

WORDE, Wynkyn de (d. 1534/5) Early printer and bookseller in London, assistant and successor to *Caxton. His real name was Jan van Wynkyn. Books printed by him include the *Gesta Romanorum, *Bevis of Hampton, *Guy of Warwick, and the Gest of Robyn Hode (*see* ROBIN HOOD).

World of Girls, A (1886) By L. T. *Meade, the first successful *school story for girls. Hester Thornton is sent to Lavender House boarding school after the death of her mother. She expects it to be a 'a dreadful place', but is soon reassured by the character of the headmistress, Mrs Willis. The school's views are narrow: one of the mistresses discovers that a pupil possesses a copy of *Jane Eyre*, and reminds the girls that this book 'is not allowed to be read at any time in Lavender House'. A prank played on another girl, Annie Forest, nearly results in Annie's death, but all ends happily. The book is mawkish and banal, but remained popular until the 1920s.

World Turned Upside Down, The A *chapbook for children and adults, consisting of *woodcuts depicting people and animals engaged in unlikely pursuits, for example, an ass singing a ballad, or a man trying to jump down his own throat. Each cut is accompanied by a descriptive verse. A recurrent theme is animals turning on men who usually hunt or slaughter them: a bird is seen shooting a man in a tree, a fish catches a man with a hook, and a goose roasts a cook on a spit. The idea and some of the actual illustrations are found elsewhere in European popular literature.

A version of *The World Turned Upside Down* was published by *Kendrew of York, c. 1830. In 1810 Ann and Jane *Taylor adapted it for *Tabart as *Signor Topsy-Turvey's Wonderful Magic Lantern*.

WORMELL, Chris (1955–) English picture-book creator, illustrator, and printmaker. Entirely self-taught, Wormell works flawlessly in a range of mediums with a print specialism of wood engraving and linocut. His first children's book, *An Alphabet of Animals* (1990), won the *Bologna Ragazzi Award for graphic and editorial design at the Bologna International Children's Book Fair. In 2004 he received the *New York Times Book Review* Best Illustrated Children's Book Award for *Teeth, Tails, and Tentacles. Two Frogs* (2003), a hilarious tale of self-protection, was shortlisted for the *Kate Greenaway Medal and was awarded the Nestlé Smarties Book Bronze Medal Prize. His narratives provide a perfect complement to his illustrations, resulting in books that are often quirky and amusing.

Worst Witch, The (1974) The first book in a series by British author-illustrator Jill *Murphy. Mildred Hubble is a pupil at Miss Cackle's Academy for Witches, which despite

its curriculum is in many respects a conventional boarding school (the girls all wear black gym-slips). She makes an enemy for life when she turns Ethel, an unpleasant fellow-pupil, into a pig—and Ethel's revenge gets Mildred into even deeper trouble. Other memorable characters include Mildred's loyal best friend, Maud, and their terrifying form teacher, Miss Hardbroom. There have been six sequels (*The Worst Witch Strikes Again*, 1980; *A Bad Spell for the Worst Witch*, 1982; *The Worst Witch All at Sea*, 1993; *The Worst Witch Saves the Day*, 2005; *The Worst Witch to the Rescue*, 2007; and *The Worst Witch and the Wishing Star*, 2013), as well as TV adaptations and spin-off book series.

Worzel Gummidge A scarecrow who can walk and talk, the creation of the British author Barbara Euphan *Todd. He first appeared in *Worzel Gummidge, or the Scarecrow of Scatterbrook Farm* (1936), which tells how John and Susan, staying at Scatterbrook Farm with the Braithwaite family, encounter Worzel Gummidge, whose favourite phrases are 'Ooh aye!' and 'Stands to reason!' His adventures involve the pompous Mrs Bloomsbury-Barton, and a scarecrow tribe that includes Worzel's Aunt Sally (who scolds him just as a real aunt might scold a nephew), Hannah Harrow the invalid scarecrow, Upsidaisy (who, being made of a three-legged stool, keeps falling over), and Worzel's wife-to-be, Earthy Mangold. There were ten sequels.

Worzel Gummidge became known nationally when his exploits were dramatized on *Children's Hour, and the first book about him was chosen as the first *Puffin fiction title in 1941. In the late 1970s the stories were used as the basis of a television series by Keith Waterhouse and Willis Hall, with Jon Pertwee as Worzel. For the television series, Earthy Mangold was discarded and her place as Worzel's sweetheart was taken by Aunt Sally (played by Una Stubbs), while the scriptwriters also introduced the Crowman, a kind of *deus ex machina* who is Worzel's maker and repairer. Books based on the television series have been published.

Wouldbegoods, The (1901) By E. *Nesbit, sequel to *The *Story of the Treasure Seekers*.

WRIGHTSON, (Alice) Patricia (1921–2010) One of the leading Australian children's writers of her generation. She was born in Lismore, New South Wales, and was educated largely by means of the State Correspondence School.

She was the editor of *School Magazine* in Sydney.

Her first book, *The Crooked Snake* (1955), was a conventional adventure novel about a school secret society. *The Bunyip Hole* (1958) (*see* BUNYIP) has the same kind of plot, but showed more concern with character. Wrightson's first outstanding book, *The Rocks of Honey* (1960), begins with the arrival on a white family's farm of an Aboriginal family. A boy from this family makes friends with the farmer's son; they learn about a mysterious stone axe of Aboriginal legend, and go in search of it. *The Rocks of Honey* was one of the first Australian children's books to make a successful blend of realism and the supernatural and to draw with real imagination on the country's indigenous legends.

After *The Feather Star* (1962), a realistic novel about a girl growing up, Wrightson wrote *Down to Earth* (1965), a gently comic *fantasy about a Martian boy who observes modern Australian city life. She then hit a high level of popularity with *I Own the Racecourse!* (1968) (US title *A Racecourse for Andy*), in which a boy is 'sold' a racecourse by an old tramp, for three dollars—and believes that he really owns it.

In the 1970s Wrightson began to produce books chiefly concerned to exploit Aboriginal folk myths. In *An Older Kind of Magic* (1972) a Sydney property speculator plans to 'develop' part of the Botanical Gardens into a car park, but comes up against a host of indigenous spirits and tricksters from Aboriginal tales, who eventually turn him to stone. Arguably Wrightson's finest achievement was *The *Nargun and the Stars* (1973). *The Ice is Coming* (1977), *The Dark Bright Water* (1978), and *Journey Behind the Wind* (1981) form a trilogy in which the Aboriginal hero Wirrun has to combat all kinds of disturbances of nature by the spirit world.

She won the *Hans Christian Andersen Award in 1986.

Wrinkle in Time, A (1962) A novel by Madeleine *L'Engle. Meg Murry's scientist father has disappeared; together with her brother Charles Wallace and his friend Calvin, both of whom have some kind of extra-sensory perception, she goes searching for him. Aided by three strange beings, Mrs Whatsit, Mrs Who, and Mrs Which, the children travel across 'a wrinkle in time' to the planet Camazotz, which is under the control of the ultimate power of evil; Meg and the others must show

themselves stronger than it before her father can return home.

A Wrinkle in Time won the *Newbery Medal, and rises above most children's *science fiction in its portrayal of the children and their odd helpers, though the chapters set on Camazotz fall into many of the clichés of the genre. There are four sequels: *A Wind in the Door* (1973), *Many Waters* (1986), *A Swiftly Tilting Planet* (1978), and *An Acceptable Time* (1989), as well as a number of further books featuring the next generation of the family.

writing sheets *See* COPYBOOKS.

Wyatt Earp (1848–1929) Hero of *westerns. He was an armed guard for the Wells Fargo company at Tombstone, Arizona, where he became involved in the celebrated 'Gunfight at the OK Corral', from which he was the only man to emerge unhurt. Earp has featured in many children's books and films.

WYETH, N. C. (Newell Convers) (1882–1945) American artist, pupil of Howard *Pyle, who illustrated editions of such classics as *Treasure Island* (1911), *Kidnapped* (1913), and Jules *Verne's The Mysterious Island* (1918). He was the father of the painter Andrew Wyeth.

WYNDHAM, John (1903–1969) Hugely influential British author of *science fiction, though he called it 'logical fantasy', as his books are set in what is recognizably our world, but with something strange added in. *The *Day of the Triffids* (1951) is his most famous work and has a world turned blind and overrun by sentient plants. In *The Kraken Wakes* (1953) the threat to humanity rises out of the oceans and in *The Midwich Cuckoos* (1957) all the women in a village become pregnant on a single night—and suddenly humans are as evolutionally redundant as the dinosaurs.

WYNNE-JONES, Tim (1948–) British-born Canadian author of picture books and novels. In 2000, he won the Mystery Writers of America's Edgar Award for the best *young adult novel for *The Boy in the Burning House*. His 2012 novel *Blink & Caution* won Canada's Arthur Ellis Award for the best crime novel for young people. Wynne-Jones is a double winner of the *Governor General's Literary Award for Children's Literature, for the short story collection *Some of the Kinder* Planets (1993), and *The Maestro* (1995), and was again shortlisted for *The Uninvited* (2009). He was Canada's nominee for the *Hans Christian Andersen Award in 2012.

WYSS, J. D. *See* Swiss Family Robinson, The.

YA *See* YOUNG ADULT.

Yankee Doodle A *nursery rhyme which is an unofficial national song of the United States. It seems to have originated in America some time around the mid-18th cent. and was adopted by the British troops in the War of Independence as a jibe against their opponents. After the battle of Bunker Hill, however, it was used by the Americans to taunt the British. A version of it first appeared as a nursery rhyme in the 1810 edition of *Gammer Gurton's Garland*.

YATES, Elizabeth (1905–2001) American author. She won the *Newbery Medal for her best-known book, *Amos Fortune, Free Man* (1950), based on a true story she researched after finding, in a New Hampshire cemetery, the grave of a man who came from Africa as a young slave, bought his freedom, and then built a successful business. Her obituary in the *New York Times* credited it with having 'taught young readers about black history in New England for half a century'.

Yearling, The (1938) By the American novelist Marjorie Kinnan Rawlings (1896–1953), this book is set in the Florida scrub country during the 1870s. Twelve-year-old Jody Baxter tames a fawn, Flag, which provokes a crisis in his relationship with his father. The book won a Pulitzer Prize for its author. Rawlings wrote one other children's book, the posthumous *The Secret River* (1955), the story of a magic fish-filled stream.

Yellow Dwarf, The (*Le Naine jaune*) A *fairy story by Mme *D'Aulnoy.

When the princess All-Fair is fifteen, her mother wants her to marry, but the girl disdains all suitors. The queen resolves to visit the Desart Fairy for advice, but the lions guarding the fairy must be placated with a cake of millet, sugar candy, and crocodiles' eggs. The queen sets out, but falls asleep under an orange tree, wakes, and finds her

cake gone and the lions roaring. In return for her safety she is forced to promise her daughter in marriage to the yellow dwarf who lives in the orange tree. She does not tell her daughter of the promise, but is so melancholy that All-Fair herself decides to ask the Desart Fairy's advice.

On her way All-Fair dallies to pick the fruit of the orange tree and again the cake is lost. The yellow dwarf appears and tells All-Fair that he is to marry her. She is horrified, but the lions roar and she agrees. All-Fair does not divulge her promise, and agrees to marry the powerful and handsome King of the Golden Mines. The wedding-day celebrations are magnificent, but in the midst of them a ragged old woman appears and accuses the princess of breaking her word. The dwarf now appears, and makes off with All-Fair. The Desart Fairy herself abducts the king in hopes of marrying him. She appears to him as a beautiful nymph, but the king escapes with the help of a *mermaid who then gives him an invincible diamond sword. Fighting his way to rescue All-Fair, his worst trial is the need to kill twenty-four nymphs guarding her, which runs counter to all his gallant instincts. He wins through, but at the moment of his reunion with All-Fair he lets fall his sword. The yellow dwarf seizes it, traps the king, and stabs him. All-Fair then dies too, and the mermaid does all that is left in her power by transforming them into two palm trees growing side by side.

The Yellow Dwarf first appeared as one of the tales set into the story of Don Fernand de Tolède in the fourth volume of *Contes noveaux ou Les Fées à la mode* (1698), and had been translated into English by 1721. Many of the motifs of the story have parallels in French and other folklore, but the tale as a whole is clearly a literary composition, exceptional in its genre for its unhappy ending. Retellings and stage versions have often altered it, with the king finally vanquishing the yellow dwarf and marrying All-Fair. *Mother Bunch and the Yellow*

Dwarf was the title of an 1807 *pantomime*, and some sixteen other adaptations of the story, including J. R. *Planché's in 1854, were performed before the end of the century.

The Yellow Dwarf reappears as a character in Andrew *Lang's *Prince Ricardo of Pantouflia* (1893) (*see* PRINCE PRIGIO), where he finally meets his just deserts.

YEP, Laurence (1948–) Prolific Chinese-American author. As a child, Yep felt that he didn't fit into either American or Chinese culture, and the experience of being an outsider is a recurring theme in his books. His most acclaimed work is the ten-volume 'Golden Mountain Chronicles', which tell the stories of several generations of a Chinese immigrant family, beginning in the 19th cent. Two books in the series, *Dragonwings* (1975) and *Dragon's Gate* (1993), were Newbery Honor Books (*see* NEWBERY MEDAL), and *Dragonwings* also won the Children's Literature Association's Phoenix Award in 1995. Yep won the 2005 *Laura Ingalls Wilder Award for his contribution to children's literature.

YOLEN, Jane (1939–) American author of over three hundred books of folklore, fantasy, poetry, and science fiction for children and young adults. Her first book was published on her twenty-second birthday. She is past-president of the Science-Fiction Writers of America and has won awards as diverse as the Nebula Award, the World Fantasy Association's Lifetime Achievement Award, and the Association of Jewish Libraries Award. Perhaps her most influential book is *The Devil's Arithmetic* (1988), a Holocaust story in which a modern girl finds herself back in the Poland of 1942. For younger children her series which starts with *How Do Dinosaurs Say Good Night?* (2000) leads the reader reassuringly through all the tricky things in life, such as doctors, counting, and friendship.

YONGE, Charlotte M. (Mary) (1823–1901) Novelist who was the daughter of a country squire living in Otterbourne, Hampshire. She was for a long time an only child, until the birth of a brother in 1831, and she made up for this by creating a 'family' out of her dolls. She was brought up according to the Edgeworths' principles of education (*see* EDGEWORTH, MARIA; EDGEWORTH, R. L.), and was given *Sandford and Merton* and the books of Mrs *Trimmer and Mrs *Sherwood; at the age of ten she discovered *Scott. Her own books reflect the influence of all these writers. Her

father undertook much of her education himself, and at the age of only seven she began to teach simple lessons in the village *Sunday school. When she was twelve John Keble was appointed vicar of the Yonges' parish church, Hursley. Keble prepared Charlotte for Confirmation when she was fifteen and, in the words of her biographer Georgina Battiscombe, she 'fell headlong in love with religion'.

In the same year, 1838, she published her first book, *Le Château de Melville*, a story in French which was sold in aid of a church school. From the time that she was twenty-one she was encouraged by Keble to write Sunday-school stories; the first of these, *Abbeychurch, or, Self Control and Self Conceit*, appeared in 1844. Two years later she began to write a series of tales about schoolchildren; these were published in the *Magazine for the Young*, and in 1850 a collection was issued as *Langley School*. (Other 'Langley' books would follow.)

The success of this encouraged her to found a Church of England *magazine for girls, *The Monthly Packet*, and at about the same time she began to write her most celebrated book, *The *Heir of Redclyffe* (1853). Most of the income from this she donated to help provide a missionary ship for the South Seas. In 1854 appeared her first of many *historical novels for children, *The *Little Duke*. Its successors included *The Lances of Lynwood* (1855), set in the reign of Edward III, *Pigeon Pie, a tale of Roundhead times* (1860), *The Prince and the Page, a story of the last Crusade* (1866), *The Chaplet of Pearls* (1868), set in 16th-cent. France during the persecution of the Huguenots, and *Unknown to History, a story of the captivity of Mary of Scotland* (1882). She also produced several volumes of stories from history, such as *Aunt Charlotte's Stories of English History for the little ones* (1873), and wrote a version of *Tom Thumb* (1855).

The success of *The Heir of Redclyffe* led her to write another dramatic-romantic novel, *Heartsease* (1854). At the same time she began to work on a chronicle of family life intended largely for young readers; this was *The *Daisy Chain*, which appeared as a book in 1856 after serialization in *The Monthly Packet*. It helped to establish a new genre, the *family story. Miss Yonge's later children's novels include *The Stokesley Secret* (1861), the story of an unruly brood of children left in the charge of a *governess, and *Countess Kate* (1862). *The Pillars of the House* (1873) is another family story, set in the household of a poor but well-bred clergyman.

Charlotte M. Yonge did not allow her name to appear on title pages even after her books had become famous and was identified only as 'the author of *The Heir of Redclyffe*'. She remained in Otterbourne until the end of her life, continuing to edit *The Monthly Packet* until 1890 and depending chiefly on a small circle of Anglican friends. She never experienced religious doubts and carefully avoided sceptical books or persons.

Her books show great insight into the character of children, whose rough-and-tumble ways she cheerfully accepted. A reader may feel that inside the careful Church of England Sunday school teacher there was a novelist of real distinction trying to get out. Many of her novels are rewarding to read, especially her family chronicles, which give a vivid picture of mid-19th-cent. middle-class life. In her hands, the religious severity of Mrs Trimmer and Mrs Sherwood was modified by the gentler piety of Oxford Movement Anglicanism, and the moral development of children, though still a principal theme, was presented in realistic and credible terms.

Yonghy-Bonghy-Bò, *The Courtship of the* A poem by Edward *Lear, first published in *Laughable Lyrics* (1877). Lear first mentioned its hero in a nonsense alphabet printed in *More Nonsense* (1872), where 'Y' stands for 'The Yonghy-Bonghy-Bò, whose Head was ever so much bigger than his Body, and whose Hat was rather small'. On 31 December 1871 Lear told his friend Chichester Fortescue: 'I have written a ballad lately on the "Yonghy Bonghy Bò."'

You are old, Father William A poem by Lewis *Carroll, included in *Alice's Adventures in Wonderland*. It parodies *Southey's 'The Old Man's Comforts and how he Gained Them'.

YOUNG, Ed (Tse-chun) (1931–) American illustrator and author who was born in China but moved to America in 1951 in order to study architecture, though he soon switched to studying art before becoming a commercial artist. His first book, *The Mean Mouse and Other Mean Stories* (1962), was meant to be a one-off, but its success led to a career that has so far produced over eighty picture books. His technique shows the influence of Chinese art, but is uniquely his own: he uses pencil, pastel, cut paper, collage, ink, and found materials as the subject requires. His thoughtful books often retell folk tales, for example, *Lon Po Po*

(1989), a Chinese version of *Little Red Riding Hood*, and *Seven Blind Mice* (1992). He illustrates for others too, including Jane *Yolen, for *The Emperor and the Kite* (1968), in which a young princess tries to rescue her imprisoned father; and Mark Reibstein, for *Wabi Sabi* (2008), about a cat who travels across Japan to discover the meaning of her name.

YOUNG, Egerton Ryerson (1840–1904) Canadian children's writer who was born in Ontario, the son of a Methodist minister. He served as a missionary in the north of Canada. This led to the writing of *Three Boys in the Wild North Land* (1896), which tells how three British boys (one English, one Scottish, one Irish) come to Canada, stay with a retired official of the Hudson Bay Company, and experience the excitement of life in the wilds. Young also wrote *Children of the Forest; a story of Indian love* (1904). His son, Egerton Ryerson Young, Junior, wrote *Duck Lake; stories of the Canadian backwoods* (1905).

young adult (YA) Refers to a type of fiction, sometimes described as 'teen' fiction, that is, generally speaking, a relatively modern phenomenon. Until the middle of the 20th cent., children who grew out of juvenile books were expected to read popular classics, such as the works of *Dickens and *Scott, before graduating to more demanding adult novels. Although a distinction was drawn surprisingly early— *The Guardian of Education* back at the very start of the 19th cent. had defined a category of 'Books for young persons' as relating to readers aged fourteen to twenty-one—dedicated production for this readership barely existed till well over a century later. Louise *Mack's *Teens* (1897) is an almost isolated example of a pre-20th-cent. teen novel.

The present-day teenage novel has its origins in America between the two World Wars, when authors such as Stephen W. *Meader, Florence Crannell *Means, and John R. *Tunis began to write with older children in mind. In the 1950s the novels of Mary *Stolz (*To Tell Your Love*, 1950, and others), showed what could be done with 'love interest', though she and Beverly *Cleary (in *Fifteen*, 1956) worked chiefly within the tradition of romantic pulp fiction. The new wave of teenage fiction which came into print in the 1960s had a very different approach to adolescence. It was heavily influenced by J. D. Salinger's *The *Catcher in the Rye* (1951)—though Salinger's book, like *Lord of the Flies* in the UK, was not written deliberately

for a young audience, however much both may be read primarily by teenagers today.

Many writers who had read Salinger in their own adolescence began to create Holden Caulfields of their own, with comic self-regarding attitudes and complicated feelings about the adult world. Novels by John *Donovan, Barbara *Wersba, and Paul *Zindel were typical of the post-Salinger generation in portraying parents as, almost without exception, neurotics of one kind or another. For example, the mothers in Dono-van's *I'll Get There, It Better Be Worth the Trip* (1969) and Zindel's *Pardon Me, You're Stepping on My Eyeball!* (1976) are both heavy drinkers; Zindel's hero 'Marsh' Mellow calls his parents Schizo Suzy and Paranoid Pete. The mother of the heroine 'J. F.' in Wersba's *Tunes for a Small Harmonica* (1976) passes her day shopping in Fifth Avenue stores and having her hair done; the father spends all his time at his office, 'was staunchly Republican, drank only the best scotch, played squash on Saturdays and was charming to women without really liking them'.

As well as attacking parents, the typical American teenage novel of this period was largely concerned with sex. Homosexuality gradually began to be mentionable (*see* SEXUALITY), one of the first teenage books in which it appeared being Isabelle *Holland's *The Man Without a Face* (1972). By 1975 it was permissible for Judy *Blume to give a detailed description of adolescent heterosexual love-making in *Forever*. The next year came Richard *Peck's *Are You in the House Alone?*, which dealt with rape. Divorce and remarriage featured in Blume's *It's Not the End of the World* (1972), E. L. *Konigsburg's *(george)* (1970), and in many other novels of this period. Death (a subject, as John Rowe *Townsend has said, 'which for long was no more mentionable in modern children's books than was sex in those of the Victorians') played an important part in, for example, Betsy *Byars's *Goodbye, Chicken Little* (1979) and John Donovan's *Wild in the World* (1971).

Sometimes the heroes and heroines of these books have a precocious view of the world around them. 'J. F.', in Wersba's *Tunes for a Small Harmonica*, decides that 'We lived . . . in an age of ugliness . . . in which people went drinking and smoking themselves to death, in which love meant sex and sex was ridiculous.' More often they are as confused as the adults and regard themselves as losers; the typical American teenage novel opens with its central character in this predicament, and

describes how he or she gradually comes to terms with the world. Chris, in Zindel's *Confessions of a Teenage Baboon* (1977), starts out as a 'demented' (his own word) fifteen-year-old, 'ashamed and mixed up', who doesn't 'know how to handle the problems of being alive that people don't warn you about'. By the end of the book, a year later in his life, 'the cloud that had been hanging over me . . . was suddenly lifting . . . I felt an understanding and a compassion for the entire human race.'

For a time, novels in this genre rarely had much to distinguish them from each other; there was an almost uniform shrillness of tone and predictability of character development. But more subtle studies of adolescence were produced by certain other American writers, such as Paula *Fox, in *Blowfish Live in the Sea* (1970), Vera and Bill *Cleaver, in such books as *Where the Lilies Bloom* (1969), and Robert *Cormier, who presented a view of teenage life which is harsher, more luridly dramatic, but at the same time more convincing than that of the Salinger imitators.

For a time the American teenage novel was something of an isolated phenomenon. In Australia H. F. *Brinsmead was an early specialist in writing books about and for teenagers, but others were few and far between. Though in Britain from the mid-1950s many books were written with older children or teenagers in mind, there was not the same concentration on adolescence itself as subject matter, nor the same shrill tone of voice in writing about it, and *Red Shift* (1973) by Alan *Garner was one of the few early British books to approach the American genre in its harsh portrayal of Tom's mental isolation from his mother and father. But in this and Garner's *The *Owl Service* (1967), which also contains unsympathetic portraits of parents, the author is more concerned with the effect of history and myth on present-day adolescents than with their psychological problems in isolation. K. M. *Peyton has produced much popular fiction for and about teenagers, but her books are related to established genres and attitudes (the romantic novel in her *Flambards* series, and the *school story in her 'Pennington' novels) rather than striking out in any new and radical line. John Rowe Townsend and Jill *Paton Walsh were typical of their generation of British authors in producing 'adolescent' books (such as Townsend's *The Intruder*, 1969, and Paton Walsh's *Unleaving*, 1976) which deal with their heroes' quests for personal identity, but do so in a reflective

'interior' manner derived from the mainstream of the English novel rather than from Salinger.

It was not until the 1980s and the decades since, however, that young adult fiction truly came of age in the English-speaking world. Mainstream publishers began to commission work specifically for this demographic category, and marketed it accordingly, as youth culture itself became a heavily marketed commodity in other areas; libraries and bookshops followed suit, beginning to arrange their stock to reflect this new delineation; and—as important as any of these—a small number of standout writers came into the market at around the same time, driving the momentum of these new developments with works that were popular, high-profile, and critically acclaimed. Dedicated prizes for young adult literature were launched in several countries (such as the *Michael L. Printz Award in the US and the *Booktrust Teenage Prize in the UK), and many of the more general prizes (the *Newbery Medal and the *Carnegie Medal, say) began to be won by—indeed, in some cases, some would say dominated by—exceptional and sophisticated young adult books.

Young adult fiction in English now spans every genre, though there are certainly some types of book—*dystopian fiction, for example, and certain kinds of *graphic novel—that seem to lend themselves particularly to work for this readership. And the readership itself is a group with porous boundaries, too; while typically young adult fiction tends to be seen as—very roughly—corresponding to readers aged twelve to sixteen or eighteen, the recent rise of the *crossover book has made such a sharp delineation less meaningful than once it was.

The diversity in young adult fiction is not only generic, but thematic, too. The range of subjects tackled grows every year, and while some publishers remain risk-averse and anxious about adult reactions, there are plenty of others who allow their writers to break each new boundary. Because much young adult fiction focuses on the experience and perspective of teenagers themselves as protagonists, it is unsurprising that these readers' concerns, and the sense of boundary-testing, self-determination, and experimentation that defines so much teen experience, are reflected in the books. Recent years have seen increasingly explicit writing on drug use, sex and sexuality, violence and abuse, suicide, incest, and almost any other subject imaginable.

Conventions about what teenagers can read about, but also about how those stories ought to be told (e.g. any subject can be broached so long as the book's resolution is ultimately hopeful), are no sooner defined than they are broken. Naturally each developmental stage is met with its share of concern and criticism, as well as general enthusiasm.

Isolated early examples of the teenage novel can be found in the world outside the Anglosphere, for example, in Russia, Vadim Frolov's *What It's All About* (1968), about a boy coming to terms with the break-up of his parents' marriage and his own emotional development, but such examples that predate the English-language boom are rare. And while there is now at last a substantial body of work in certain places—Scandinavia and elsewhere in northern Europe in particular—the production of young adult fiction even today remains sparse in most places; English-language young adult fiction is translated widely, but this is on the whole not supplemented with domestic production to any significant degree, though there are already signs in many countries that this is beginning to change.

Young Elizabethan A British children's monthly *magazine, founded in 1948 by the publishers Collins under the editorship of Pamela *Whitlock. At first named *Collins' Magazine for Boys and Girls*, it took on its new title at the beginning of the reign of Elizabeth II. Among later editors was Kaye *Webb. It contained stories and features by leading children's authors and illustrators of the day. It latterly became a 'teenage magazine', surviving in this form until 1973.

Young Fur-Traders, The, *A Tale of the Far North* (1856) The first *adventure story by R. M. *Ballantyne. The first edition, published by Nelson of Edinburgh, bore a title page beginning *Snowflakes and Sunbeams; or, The Young Fur Traders*, but after three editions the first part of the title was dropped. The story is based on the author's experiences in North America working for the Hudson's Bay Company. Fifteen-year-old Charley Kennedy adamantly refuses to take a desk job with that Company, and embarks on the life of a *voyageur* or hunter at a remote outpost. The book also describes the adventures of Harry Somerville, another young employee of the Company, and concludes with his marriage to Charley's sister Kate.

Youngsters of Murray Home, The

(1896) An Australian *family story by M. Ella Chaffey. The children of the Olsen family live on a well-developed bush station on the Murray River, with their parents and a German *governess called Miss Kowshorn, and are 'so constantly out of doors that to be confined to the house for even a single hour was irksome to them'. The author's account of station life and the children's adventures is unsensational, convincing, and engaging. She is both gently pious and realistic about children's ideas of fun; the death of a baby on the station is followed by the younger children's play funeral for a broken doll. In another episode Katrina, absurdly terrified of black people, finds her brother and sister playing happily, and being generously entertained, in an Aboriginal camp, and learns from the experience.

Young Visiters, The, or Mr Salteena's Plan

(1919) A story by Daisy Ashford (1881–1972), written in 1890 when she was nine. She was the daughter of W. H. R. Ashford, a retired War Office official, who encouraged her to make up stories while still in the nursery. Mrs Ashford had been married before, having abandoned an engagement to a peer and eloped with a penniless Hussar who later died—events which may have contributed to Daisy's liking for fast-moving narratives of romance and high society, which she emulated in *The Young Visiters*.

She rediscovered the manuscript of her story among her mother's papers in 1917 and showed it to a friend, who brought it to the attention of Chatto and Windus. They published it in May 1919 with an introduction by J. M. *Barrie, who was popularly (but erroneously) thought to be its real author. It proved immensely successful—there were eleven reprints in less than three months—and has been regarded as a classic ever since.

The Young Visiters, which is crudely spelt and lacks a good deal of punctuation, is the story of Mr Salteena, 'an elderly man of 42', and his seventeen-year-old friend Ethel, who are invited to the country house of Bernard Clark. Mr Salteena asks his host's advice about improving himself socially, and is sent off to London. He visits the Crystal Palace and meets the Earl of Clincham, who lives in one of the 'Private Compartments' there. (This is a memory of the author's visit to Hampton Court.) The Earl, in return for payment in cash, undertakes to make Mr Salteena a gentleman.

Bernard Clark, meanwhile, takes Ethel off for a jaunt to London ('Chaperone seems to be one of the very few good words of which our authoress had never heard,' remarked Barrie), engages rooms in the 'Gaierty Hotel', and proposes to her. The wedding is in Westminster Abbey; Mr Salteena, who had hoped to win Ethel for himself, cries into his handkerchief, and has to content himself with marrying a Maid-in-Waiting at Buckingham Palace, where he has obtained a job 'galloping madly after the Royal Carrage'. Ethel and Bernard return from their honeymoon 'with a son and hair'; Mr Salteena pines for Ethel, 'still he was a pius man in his way and found relief in prayer.'

The success of *The Young Visiters* led Chatto to publish more of Daisy Ashford's childhood writings, under the title *Daisy Ashford: Her Book* (1920). All the stories in this have since been reprinted: three (including one by Daisy's sister Angela) as *Love and Marriage* (1965, repr. 1982) and the remaining two in *The Hangman's Daughter and other stories* (1983), which also contains a previously unpublished story by Daisy about 'Father McSwiney' (her family's parish priest) and the Pope.

Youth's Companion, The

The longest-lived American children's *magazine, published weekly from Boston from 1827 until 1927, when it became a monthly; the last issue was dated September 1929.

The Youth's Companion was founded and edited until 1856 by Nathaniel Willis. The contents of the paper in the early days were miscellaneous, with religious and edifying matter much in evidence. For a time the paper had the subtitle *Sabbath School Recorder*. In the 1840s it became somewhat livelier and included such 'departments' as biography and *natural history as well as *moral tales. In 1857 it was bought by Daniel Sharp Ford, a Baptist newspaper proprietor who published it under the name 'Perry Mason & Co.' and broadened its outlook further, making fiction more important and reducing the *Sunday school element.

Contributors from the late 1860s included Harriet Beecher *Stowe and Louisa M. *Alcott. A regular feature from the beginning was the inclusion of 'moral anecdotes'; it is said that the anecdotes were read avidly and the morals ignored. From after the Civil War the *Youth's Companion* also offered 'premiums', rewards for new subscriptions sold by readers, in the

form of magic lanterns, printing presses, chemistry sets, and the like.

Circulation reached half a million before Ford's death in 1899, largely due to the popularity of the stories by Charles Asbury *Stephens, who wrote for the magazine for sixty years, beginning in 1870; he is now remembered chiefly for his 'Young Yachters' and 'Knockabout Club' series of *travelogue storybooks. But despite this large circulation, the paper's style remained rather cautious; crime, improper language, and love-making were strictly banned from its stories, and in the early 20th cent. it began to seem dated. Sales figures diminished, and in October 1929 it merged with the *American Boy* of Detroit.

In 1883 the *Youth's Companion* commissioned a story from Thomas Hardy, though it never published the result, *Our Exploits at West Poley.*

Youth's Magazine, The A British *evangelical periodical published monthly from 1805 to 1865.

Zagazoo (1998) A witty cycle-of-life picture book by Quentin *Blake, which begins with a young couple, George and Bella, who have many hobbies in common, including making model planes and eating strawberry and vanilla ice cream. The postman delivers a parcel containing a baby—'Its name is Zagazoo'—and the book shows this funny little creature growing by characterful stages into a young man himself (having first been through a vulture phase, a warthog phase, an elephant phase, etc.). Both simple and subtle, this is the funny, wise Quentin Blake at his very best.

ZEI, Alki (1925–) Greek children's writer, mainly of historical novels, the first to write for children about politics, the war, and Greece's recent history. Her books include the great favourite, *Wildcat Under Glass* (tr. Edward Fenton, 1968), *Petros' War* (tr. Edward Fenton, 1973), *Alice in Marbleland* (tr. Amy Mims, 1997), and *Tina's Web* (tr. John Thornley, 2007). Her work has been included in the school curriculum and translated into over twenty languages. She has won, among other awards, the 2003 *IBBY-Greece best teenage book prize. In 2010 she received the Athens Academy Award (Kostas and Eleni Ouranis) for Children's Literature.

ZELINSKY, Paul O. (1953–) American author and illustrator. Known for his diverse range of styles, he has illustrated novels by *Avi, Beverly *Cleary, E. *Nesbit, Jack *Prelutsky, and others, as well as picture books including the exceptional *Z Is for Moose* (2012, by Kelly Bingham). He was awarded the 1998 *Caldecott Medal for his retelling of *Rapunzel and has won three Caldecott Honor Awards, for his retelling of *Rumpelstiltskin* (1986), and for *Hansel and Gretel* (1984), retold by Rika Lesser, and *Swamp Angel* (1994) by Anne Isaacs. His bestselling movable book *The Wheels on the Bus* (2002) was made into an animated film.

ZEMACH, Margot (1931–89) American illustrator and writer of *picture books. She won the *Caldecott Medal for *Duffy and the Devil* (1973), which was, like many of her books, a collaboration with her husband Harvey Fischtrom, who wrote texts under the name Harve Zemach until his death in 1974.

ZEPHANIAH, Benjamin (1958–) English writer and poet. His self-imposed mission to save poetry from academia was in part sparked by his own troubled childhood and how poetry was a lifeline for him. Severely dyslexic, and having given up early on the school system, by the time he was fifteen he was already known for his poetry in the Jamaican community in his local part of Birmingham. Politically aware, he realized that he needed to reach into the wider community, so he moved to London and started to perform his poetry as if it were theatre or music. *Talking Turkeys* (1994) was his first book of verse for children, and it was an immediate success. He has written five *young adult novels, including *Face* (1999), *Refugee Boy* (2001), and *Terror Kid* (2014). In 2003 he turned down an OBE and in 2008 was included in *The Times* list of Britain's top fifty post-war writers.

Zigzag Journeys A series of *travelogue storybooks by the American writer Hezekiah *Butterworth. They recount the adventures of the Zigzag Club, a group of boys whose aim is 'to study and gain information about certain countries during the spare hours of the school year, and to visit those countries under the guidance of the principal of the school during the summer vacation'. The series eventually numbered seventeen volumes, beginning with *Zigzag Journeys in Europe* (1879).

ZIMNIK, Reiner (1930–) German author-illustrator of *picture books, many of them about man's struggle to survive in a technological world. One of his best-known is *Der Bär auf dem Motorrad* (1962) (*The Bear on the Motorcycle*, 1963).

ZINDEL, Paul (1936–2003) American writer of *young adult fiction, born and educated in

New York City. He began his literary career as a playwright, achieving considerable success with *The Effect of Gamma Rays on Man-in-the-Moon Marigolds* (1965). His first novel for teenagers was *The *Pigman* (1968). The citation for the Margaret A. Edwards Award from the *American Library Association called it 'one of the first authentic young adult novels'. Many of his books draw on the loss and neglect he experienced in his own childhood. His later books include *My Darling, My Hamburger* (1969), *I Never Loved Your Mind* (1970), *Pardon Me, You're Stepping on My Eyeball!* (1976), *Confessions of a Teenage Baboon* (1977), *The Undertaker's Gone Bananas* (1978), and *A Star for the Latecomer* (1980), written with his wife Bonnie Zindel.

ZION, Gene (1913–75) American author for children, creator with illustrator Margaret Bloy Graham of *Harry, the Dirty Dog*.

ZIPES, Jack (1937–) A world-renowned American author, editor, scholar, activist, and translator. Specializing in *fairy tales, Zipes is keenly concerned with the social and political role of storytelling and its impact on children's lives. A Professor Emeritus of German and Comparative Literature at the University of Minnesota, Zipes has taught widely in Europe and the United States. He has written and edited over twenty-five books, including *Don't Bet on the Prince: Contemporary Feminist Fairy Tales in North America and England* (1987), *Spells of Enchantment: The Wondrous Fairy Tales of Western Culture* (1991), *The Trials and Tribulations of Little Red Riding Hood* (1993), and *The Irresistible Fairy Tale: The Cultural and Social History of a Genre* (2012). In addition to his scholarly work, Zipes has translated numerous works, including *The Complete Fairy Tales of the Brothers Grimm* (1987), *Beauties, Beasts, and Enchantment: Classic French Fairy Tales* (1989), *The Fairy Tales of Hermann Hesse* (1995), and a new complete *Grimm translation in 2014. In 1997, Zipes co-founded the internationally recognized literacy programme, Neighbourhood Bridges, in collaboration with the Children's Theatre Company of Minneapolis, to promote storytelling and critical literacy, by using theatre, dance, puppetry, and creative writing to empower and engage young people as active and creative tellers of their own stories. He has edited both *The Oxford Companion to Fairy Tales* (2002) and the monumental four-volume *Oxford Encyclopedia of Children's Literature* (2006).

ZOLOTOW, Charlotte (1915–2013) American author of more than fifty books for young children. She was also a successful and influential editor of many other children's books. Her own books include *Mr Rabbit and the Lovely Present* (1962), illustrated by Maurice *Sendak, in which a rabbit helps a little girl choose a gift for her mother, and *William's Doll* (1972), illustrated by William Pène *Du Bois, the story of a boy who longs for a doll. This book was much praised by opponents of sexism in children's literature.

ZUSAK, Markus (1975–) Australian novelist, born in Sydney, who writes for both children and adults. Zusak has achieved international acclaim for his children's books. *The Messenger* (2002), which won the *CBCA Book of the Year Award for Older Readers in 2003, has a dark theme in which the underdog and underage taxi driver is challenged to solve the clues and help improve the lives of people around him. Zusak's most famous book, *The *Book Thief* (2005), was made into a film in 2013. It has been translated into over thirty languages and has won numerous awards. Zusak, who claims he writes 'story first, subject second', is a master of literary devices such as foreshadowing, imagery, rhythm, characterization, structure, language, and plot, and presenting challenging ideas in a fresh way.

ZWERGER, Lisbeth (1954–) Austrian illustrator specializing in fairy tales, who has illustrated a number of stories by classic authors including E. T. A. *Hoffmann, Theodor Storm, Rudyard *Kipling, Hans Christian *Andersen, Lewis *Carroll, and the brothers *Grimm. Zwerger received the *Hans Christian Andersen Award for illustrators in 1990.

Appendix – Award Winners

A. Astrid Lindgren Memorial Award
B. Hans Christian Andersen Awards
C. Caldecott Medal
D. Newbery Medal
E. Kate Greenaway Medal
F. Carnegie Medal
G. Costa Children's Book Award (formerly Whitbread)
H. Guardian Children's Fiction Prize

(For more information about each of these awards, see the relevant entries.)

A. Astrid Lindgren Memorial Award

2003 Maurice *Sendak
2003 Christine *Nöstlinger
2004 Lygia *Bojunga
2005 Philip *Pullman
2005 Ryoji *Arai
2006 Katherine *Paterson
2007 Banco del Libro
2008 Sonya *Hartnett
2009 Tamer Institute
2010 Kitty *Crowther
2011 Shaun *Tan
2012 Guus *Kuijer
2013 Isol (Marisol Misenta)
2014 Barbro Lindgren
2015 PRAESA (Project for the Study of Alternative Education in South Africa)
2016 Meg *Rosoff

B. Hans Christian Andersen Awards

i. Writing

1956 Eleanor *Farjeon
1958 Astrid *Lindgren
1960 Erich *Kästner
1962 Meindert *De Jong
1964 René *Guillot
1966 Tove *Jansson
1968 James *Krüss
 José María *Sánchez-Silva
1970 Gianni *Rodari
1972 Scott *O'Dell
1974 Maria *Gripe
1976 Cecil Bødker

1978 Paula *Fox
1980 Bohumil Riha
1982 Lygia *Bojunga
1984 Christine *Nöstlinger
1986 Patricia *Wrightson
1988 Annie M. G. *Schmidt
1990 Tormod Haugen
1991 Virginia *Hamilton
1994 Michio Mado
1996 Uri *Orlev
1998 Katherine *Paterson
2000 Ana Maria *Machado
2002 Aidan *Chambers
2004 Martin *Waddell
2006 Margaret *Mahy
2008 Jürg Schubiger
2010 David *Almond
2012 Maria Teresa Andruetto
2014 Nahoko Uehashi
2016 Cao Wenxuan

ii. Illustration

1966 Alois Carigiet
1968 Jiří Trnka
1970 Maurice *Sendak
1972 Ib Spang *Olsen
1974 Farshid Mesghali
1976 Tatjana Mawrina
1978 Svend Otto *S.
1980 Suekichi Akaba
1982 Zbigniew Rychlicki
1984 Mitsumasa *Anno
1986 Robert *Ingpen
1988 Dusan Kállay
1990 Lisbeth *Zwerger
1992 Kveta Pacovská
1994 Jörg Müller
1996 Klaus Ensikat
1998 Tomi *Ungerer
2000 Anthony *Browne
2002 Quentin *Blake
2004 Max *Velthuijs
2006 Wolf *Erlbruch
2008 Roberto Innocenti
2010 Jutta *Bauer
2012 Peter *Sís
2014 Roger Mello
2016 Rotraut Susanne Berner

C. Caldecott Medal (illustrator)

1938 *Animals of the Bible* – Dorothy P. Lathrop
1939 *Mei Li* – Thomas Handforth
1940 *Abraham Lincoln* – Ingri and Edgar Parin *d'Aulaire
1941 *They Were Strong and Good* – Robert *Lawson
1942 *Make Way for Ducklings* – Robert *McCloskey
1943 *The Little House* – Virginia Lee *Burton
1944 *Many Moons* – Louis *Slobodkin
1945 *Prayer for a Child* – Elizabeth Orton Jones
1946 *The Rooster Crows* – Maud and Miska *Petersham
1947 *The Little Island* – Leonard Weisgard
1948 *White Snow, Bright Snow* – Roger *Duvoisin
1949 *The Big Snow* – Berta and Elmer *Hader
1950 *Song of the Swallows* – Leo *Politi
1951 *The Egg Tree* – Katherine Milhous
1952 *Finders Keepers* – Nicolas [Nicholas *Mordvinoff]
1953 *The Biggest Bear* – Lynd Ward
1954 *Madeline's Rescue* – Ludwig *Bemelmans
1955 *Cinderella, or the Little Glass Slipper* – Marcia *Brown
1956 *Frog Went A-Courtin'* – Feodor Rojankovsky
1957 *A Tree Is Nice* – Marc Simont
1958 *Time of Wonder* – Robert *McCloskey
1959 *Chanticleer and the Fox* – Barbara *Cooney
1960 *Nine Days to Christmas* – Marie Hall *Ets
1961 *Baboushka and the Three Kings* – Nicolas Sidjakov
1962 *Once a Mouse* – Marcia *Brown
1963 *The Snowy Day* – Ezra Jack *Keats
1964 *Where the Wild Things Are* – Maurice *Sendak
1965 *May I Bring a Friend?* – Beni Montresor
1966 *Always Room for One More* – Nonny *Hogrogian
1967 *Sam, Bangs and Moonshine* – Evaline *Ness
1968 *Drummer Hoff* – Ed Emberley
1969 *The Fool of the World and the Flying Ship* – Uri *Shulevitz
1970 *Sylvester and the Magic Pebble* – William *Steig
1971 *A Story a Story* – Gail E. Haley
1972 *One Fine Day* – Nonny *Hogrogian
1973 *The Funny Little Woman* – Blair Lent
1974 *Duffy and the Devil* – Margot *Zemach
1975 *Arrow to the Sun* – Gerald McDermott
1976 *Why Mosquitoes Buzz in People's Ears* – Leo and Diane *Dillon
1977 *Ashanti to Zulu: African Traditions* – Leo and Diane *Dillon
1978 *Noah's Ark* – Peter *Spier
1979 *The Girl Who Loved Wild Horses* – Paul Goble
1980 *Ox-Cart Man* – Barbara *Cooney
1981 *Fables* – Arnold *Lobel
1982 *Jumanji* – Chris *van Allsburg
1983 *Shadow* – Marcia *Brown
1984 *The Glorious Flight* – Alice and Martin *Provensen
1985 *Saint George and the Dragon* – Trina *Schart Hyman
1986 *The Polar Express* – Chris *van Allsburg
1987 *Hey, Al* – Richard Egielski

1988 *Owl Moon* – John Schoenherr
1989 *Song and Dance Man* – Stephen Gammell
1990 *Lon Po Po: A Red Riding-Hood Story from China* – Ed *Young
1991 *Black and White* – David *Macaulay
1992 *Tuesday* – David *Wiesner
1993 *Mirette on the High Wire* – Emily Arnold McCully
1994 *Grandfather's Journey* – Allen *Say
1995 *Smoky Night* – David Diaz
1996 *Officer Buckle and Gloria* – Peggy Rathman
1997 *Golem* – David Wisniewski
1998 *Rapunzel* – Paul O. *Zelinsky
1999 *Snowflake Bentley* – Mary Azarian
2000 *Joseph Had a Little Overcoat* – Simms Taback
2001 *So You Want to Be President?* – David Small
2002 *The Three Pigs* – David *Wiesner
2003 *My Friend Rabbit* – Eric Rohmann
2004 *The Man Who Walked Between the Towers* – Mordicai *Gerstein
2005 *Kitten's First Full Moon* – Kevin *Henkes
2006 *The Hello, Goodbye Window* – Chris *Raschka
2007 *Flotsam* – David *Wiesner
2008 *The Invention of Hugo Cabret* – Brian *Selznick
2009 *The House in the Night* – Beth Krommes
2010 *The Lion and the Mouse* – Jerry *Pinkney
2011 *A Sick Day for Amos McGee* – Erin E. Stead
2012 *A Ball for Daisy* – Chris *Raschka
2013 *This Is Not My Hat* – Jon *Klassen
2014 *Locomotive* – Brian Floca
2015 *The Adventures of Beekle: The Unimaginary Friend* – Dan Santat
2016 *Finding Winnie* – Sophie Blackall

D. Newbery Medal (writer)

1922 *The Story of Mankind* – Hendrik *van Loon
1923 *The Voyages of Dr Dolittle* – Hugh *Lofting
1924 *The Dark Frigate* – Charles Hawes
1925 *Tales from Silver Lands* – Charles Finger
1926 *Shen of the Sea* – Arthur Bowie *Chrisman
1927 *Smoky, the Cowhorse* – Will *James
1928 *Gay Neck, the Story of a Pigeon* – Dhan Gopal Mukerji
1929 *The Trumpeter of Krakow* – Eric P. *Kelly
1930 *Hitty, Her First Hundred Years* – Rachel *Field
1931 *The Cat Who Went to Heaven* – Elizabeth *Coatsworth
1932 *Waterless Mountain* – Laura Adams Armer
1933 *Young Fu of the Upper Yangtze* – Elizabeth Lewis
1934 *Invincible Louise: The Story of the Author of* Little Women – Cornelia *Meigs
1935 *Dobry* – Monica Shannon
1936 *Caddie Woodlawn* – Carol Ryrie *Brink
1937 *Roller Skates* – Ruth *Sawyer
1938 *The White Stag* – Kate *Seredy
1939 *Thimble Summer* – Elizabeth *Enright
1940 *Daniel Boone* – James *Daugherty
1941 *Call It Courage* – Armstrong *Sperry
1942 *The Matchlock Gun* – Walter *Edmonds

1943 *Adam of the Road* – Elizabeth Janet *Gray
1944 *Johnny Tremain* – Esther *Forbes
1945 *Rabbit Hill* – Robert *Lawson
1946 *Girl* – Lois *Lenski
1947 *Miss Hickory* – Carolyn *Sherwin Bailey
1948 *The Twenty-One Balloons* – William Pène *du Bois
1949 *King of the Wind* – Marguerite *Henry
1950 *The Door in the Wall* – Marguerite *de Angeli
1951 *Amos Fortune, Free Man* – Elizabeth *Yates
1952 *Ginger Pye* – Eleanor *Estes
1953 *Secret of the Andes* – Ann Nolan *Clark
1954 *...and Now Miguel* – Joseph *Krumgold
1955 *The Wheel on the School* – Meindert *De Jong
1956 *Carry On, Mr Bowditch* – Jean Lee *Latham
1957 *Miracles on Maple Hill* – Virginia *Sorensen
1958 *Rifles for Watie* – Harold *Keith
1959 *The Witch of Blackbird Pond* – Elizabeth George *Speare
1960 *Onion John* – Joseph *Krumgold
1961 *Island of the Blue Dolphins* – Scott *O'Dell
1962 *The Bronze Bow* – Elizabeth George *Speare
1963 *A Wrinkle in Time* – Madeleine *L'Engle
1964 *It's Like This, Cat* – Emily *Neville
1965 *Shadow of a Bull* – Maia *Wojciechowska
1966 *I, Juan de Pareja* – Elizabeth Burton *de Trevino
1967 *Up a Road Slowly* – Irene *Hunt
1968 *From the Mixed-Up Files of Mrs Basil E. Frankweiler* – E. L. *Konigsburg
1969 *The High King* – Lloyd *Alexander
1970 *Sounder* – William H. *Armstrong
1971 *Summer of the Swans* – Betsy *Byars
1972 *Mrs Frisby and the Rats of NIMH* – Robert C. *O'Brien
1973 *Julie of the Wolves* – Jean Craighead *George
1974 *The Slave Dancer* – Paula *Fox
1975 *M.C. Higgins, the Great* – Virginia *Hamilton
1976 *The Grey King* – Susan *Cooper
1977 *Roll of Thunder, Hear My Cry* – Mildred D. *Taylor
1978 *Bridge to Terabithia* – Katherine *Paterson
1979 *The Westing Game* – Ellen *Raskin
1980 *A Gathering of Days: A New England Girl's Journal, 1830–1832* – Joan W. *Blos
1981 *Jacob Have I Loved* – Katherine *Paterson
1982 A *Visit to William Blake's Inn: Poems for Innocent and Experienced
 Travelers* – Nancy *Willard
1983 *Dicey's Song* – Cynthia *Voigt
1984 *Dear Mr Henshaw* – Beverly *Cleary
1985 *The Hero and the Crown* – Robin *McKinley
1986 *Sarah, Plain and Tall* – Patricia *MacLachlan
1987 *The Whipping Boy* – Sid *Fleischman
1988 *Lincoln: A Photobiography* – Russell *Freedman
1989 *Joyful Noise: Poems for Two Voices* – Paul Fleischman
1990 *Number the Stars* – Lois *Lowry
1991 *Maniac Magee* – Jerry *Spinelli
1992 *Shiloh* – Phyllis *Reynolds Naylor
1993 *Missing May* – Cynthia *Rylant

1994 *The Giver* – Lois *Lowry
1995 *Walk Two Moons* – Sharon *Creech
1996 *The Midwife's Apprentice* – Karen Cushman
1997 *The View from Saturday* – E. L. *Konigsburg
1998 *Out of the Dust* – Karen *Hesse
1999 *Holes* – Louis *Sachar
2000 *Bud, Not Buddy* – Christopher Paul *Curtis
2001 *A Year Down Yonder* – Richard *Peck
2002 *A Single Shard* – Linda Sue *Park
2003 *Crispin: The Cross of Lead* – *Avi
2004 *The Tale of Despereaux* – Kate *DiCamillo
2005 *Kira-Kira* – Cynthia Kadohata
2006 *Criss Cross* – Lynne Rae Perkins
2007 *The Higher Power of Lucky* – Susan Patron
2008 *Good Masters! Sweet Ladies! Voices from a Medieval Village* – Laura Amy Schlitz
2009 *The Graveyard Book* – Neil *Gaiman
2010 *When You Reach Me* – Rebecca *Stead
2011 *Moon over Manifest* – Clare Vanderpool
2012 *Dead End in Norvelt* – Jack *Gantos
2013 *The One and Only* – Katherine *Applegate
2014 *Flora & Ulysses: The Illuminated Adventures* – Kate *DiCamillo
2015 *The Crossover* – Kwame Alexander
2016 *Last Stop on Market Street* – Matt de la Peña

E. Kate Greenaway Medal (illustrator)

1955 no prize awarded
1956 *Tim All Alone* – Edward *Ardizzone
1957 *Mrs Easter and the Storks* – V. H. *Drummond
1958 no prize awarded
1959 *Kashtanka / A Bundle of Ballads* – William *Stobbs
1960 *Old Winkle and the Seagulls* – Gerald Rose
1961 *Mrs Cockle's Cat* – Antony *Maitland
1962 *A.B.C.* – Brian *Wildsmith
1963 *Borka: The Adventures of a Goose with No Feathers* – John *Burningham
1964 *Shakespeare's Theatre* – C. W. *Hodges
1965 *The Three Poor Tailors* – Victor *Ambrus
1966 *Mother Goose Treasury* – Raymond *Briggs
1967 *Charlotte and the Golden Canary* – Charles *Keeping
1968 *Dictionary of Chivalry* – Pauline *Baynes
1969 *The Quangle Wangle's Hat / The Dragon of an Ordinary Family* – Helen *Oxenbury
1970 *Mr Gumpy's Outing* – John *Burningham
1971 *The Kingdom under the Sea* – Jan *Pieńkowski
1972 *The Woodcutter's Duck* – Krystyna Turska
1973 *Father Christmas* – Raymond *Briggs
1974 *The Wind Blew* – Pat *Hutchins
1975 *Horses in Battle / Mishka* – Victor *Ambrus
1976 *The Post Office Cat* – Gail E. Haley
1977 *Dogger* – Shirley *Hughes
1978 *Each Peach Pear Plum* – Janet *Ahlberg
1979 *Haunted House* – Jan *Pieńkowski
1980 *Mr Magnolia* – Quentin *Blake
1981 *The Highwayman* – Charles *Keeping

1982 *Long Neck and Thunder Foot / Sleeping Beauty and Other Favourite Fairy Tales* – Michael *Foreman
1983 *Gorilla* – Anthony *Browne
1984 *Hiawatha's Childhood* – Errol *Le Cain
1985 *Sir Gawain and the Loathly Lady* – Juan Wijngaard
1986 *Snow White in New York* – Fiona French
1987 *Crafty Chameleon* – Adrienne Kennaway
1988 *Can't You Sleep, Little Bear?* – Barbara *Firth
1989 *War Boy: A Country Childhood* – Michael *Foreman
1990 *The Whales' Song* – Gary Blythe
1991 *The Jolly Christmas Postman* – Janet *Ahlberg
1992 *Zoo* – Anthony *Browne
1993 *Black Ships Before Troy* – Alan Lee
1994 *Way Home* – Gregory Rogers
1995 *The Christmas Miracle of Jonathan Toomey* – P. J. *Lynch
1996 *The Baby Who Wouldn't Go to Bed* – Helen *Cooper
1997 *When Jessie Came Across the Sea* – P. J. *Lynch
1998 *Pumpkin Soup* – Helen *Cooper
1999 *Alice's Adventures in Wonderland* – Helen *Oxenbury
2000 *I Will Not Ever Never Eat a Tomato* – Lauren *Child
2001 *Pirate Diary* – Chris *Riddell
2002 *Jethro Byrde, Fairy Child* – Bob *Graham
2003 *Ella's Big Chance* – Shirley *Hughes
2004 *Jonathan Swift's Gulliver* – Chris *Riddell
2005† *Wolves* – Emily *Gravett
2007† *The Adventures of the Dish and the Spoon* – Mini *Grey
2008 *Little Mouse's Big Book of Fears* – Emily *Gravett
2009 *Harris Finds His Feet* – Catherine *Rayner
2010 *Harry & Hopper* – Freya *Blackwood
2011 *FArTHER* – Grahame Baker-Smith
2012 *A Monster Calls* – Jim *Kay
2013 *Black Dog* – Levi Pinfold
2014 *This Is Not My Hat* – Jon *Klassen
2015 *Shackleton's Journey* – William Grill
2016 *The Sleeper and the Spindle* – Chris *Riddell

[† Until 2005/6, the medal was dated for the publication year; from 2007, for the year the award was made.]

F. Carnegie Medal (writer)

1936 *Pigeon Post* – Arthur *Ransome
1937 *The Family from One End Street* – Eve *Garnett
1938 *The Circus Is Coming* – Noel *Streatfeild
1939 *Radium Woman* – Eleanor Doorly
1940 *Visitors from London* – Kitty *Barne
1941 *We Couldn't Leave Dinah* – Mary *Treadgold
1942 *The Little Grey Men* – '*B. B.'
1943 no prize awarded
1944 *The Wind on the Moon* – Eric *Linklater
1945 no prize awarded
1946 *The Little White Horse* – Elizabeth *Goudge
1947 *Collected Stories for Children* – Walter *de la Mare

1948 *Sea Change* – Richard *Armitage
1949 *The Story of Your Home* – Agnes Allen
1950 *The Lark on the Wing* – Elfrida *Vipont
1951 *The Woolpack* – Cynthia *Harnett
1952 *The Borrowers* – Mary *Norton
1953 *A Valley Grows Up* – Edward Osmond
1954 *Knight Crusader* – Ronald *Welch
1955 *The Little Bookroom* – Eleanor *Farjeon
1956 *The Last Battle* – C. S. *Lewis
1957 *A Grass Rope* – William *Mayne
1958 *Tom's Midnight Garden* – Philippa *Pearce
1959 *The Lantern Bearers* – Rosemary *Sutcliff
1960 *The Making of Man* – I. W. Cornwall
1961 *A Stranger at Green Knowe* – Lucy M. *Boston
1962 *The Twelve and the Genii* – Pauline *Clarke
1963 *Time of Trial* – Hester *Burton
1964 *Nordy Bank* – Sheena *Porter
1965 *The Grange at High Force* – Philip *Turner
1966 no prize awarded
1967 *The Owl Service* – Alan *Garner
1968 *The Moon in the Cloud* – Rosemary *Harris
1969 *The Edge of the Cloud* – Kathleen *Peyton
1970 *The God Beneath the Sea* – Leon *Garfield and Edward *Blishen
1971 *Josh* – Ivan *Southall
1972 *Watership Down* – Richard *Adams
1973 *The Ghost of Thomas Kempe* – Penelope *Lively
1974 *The Stronghold* – Mollie *Hunter
1975 *The Machine Gunners* – Robert *Westall
1976 *Thunder and Lightnings* – Jan *Mark
1977 *The Turbulent Term of Tyke Tiler* – Gene *Kemp
1978 *The Exeter Blitz* – David *Rees
1979 *Tulku* – Peter *Dickinson
1980 *City of Gold* – Peter *Dickinson
1981 *The Scarecrows* – Robert *Westall
1982 *The Haunting* – Margaret *Mahy
1983 *Handles* – Jan *Mark
1984 *The Changeover* – Margaret *Mahy
1985 *Storm* – Kevin *Crossley-Holland
1986 *Granny Was a Buffer Girl* – Berlie *Doherty
1987 *The Ghost Drum* – Susan *Price
1988 *A Pack of Lies* – Geraldine *McCaughrean
1989 *Goggle-Eyes* – Anne *Fine
1990 *Wolf* – Gillian *Cross
1991 *Dear Nobody* – Berlie *Doherty
1992 *Flour Babies* – Anne *Fine
1993 *Stone Cold* – Robert *Swindells
1994 *Whispers in the Graveyard* – Theresa *Breslin
1995 *Northern Lights* – Philip *Pullman
1996 *Junk* – Melvin *Burgess
1997 *River Boy* – Tim *Bowler
1998 *Skellig* – David *Almond
1999 *Postcards from No Man's Land* – Aidan *Chambers

2000 *The Other Side of Truth* – Beverley *Naidoo
2001 *The Amazing Maurice and His Educated Rodents* – Terry *Pratchett
2002 *Ruby Holler* – Sharon *Creech
2003 *A Gathering Light* – Jennifer *Donnelly
2004 *Millions* – Frank *Cottrell Boyce
2005† *Tamar* – Mal *Peet
2007† *Just in Case* – Meg *Rosoff
2008 *Here Lies Arthur* – Philip *Reeve
2009 *Bog Child* – Siobhan *Dowd
2010 *The Graveyard Book* – Neil *Gaiman
2011 *Monsters of Men* – Patrick *Ness
2012 *A Monster Calls* – Patrick *Ness
2013 *Maggot Moon* – Sally *Gardner
2014 *The Bunker Diary* – Kevin *Brooks
2015 *Buffalo Soldier* – Tanya *Landman
2016 *One* – Sarah *Crossan

[† Until 2005/6, the medal was dated for the publication year; from 2007, for the year the award was made.]

G. Costa Children's Book Award (formerly Whitbread Children's Book Award)

1973 *The Butterfly Ball, and the Grasshopper's Feast* – Alan Aldridge and William Plomer
1974† *How Tom Beat Captain Najork and His Hired Sportsmen* – Russell *Hoban and Quentin *Blake
 The Emperor's Winding Sheet – Jill *Paton Walsh
1975 no Children's Prize awarded
1976 *A Stitch in Time* – Penelope *Lively
1977 *No End to Yesterday* – Shelagh Macdonald
1978 *The Battle of Bubble and Squeak* – Philippa *Pearce
1979 *Tulku* – Peter *Dickinson
1980 *John Diamond* – Leon *Garfield
1981 *The Hollow Land* – Jane *Gardam
1982 *The Song of Pentecost* – W. J. Corbett
1983 *The Witches* – Roald *Dahl
1984 *The Queen of the Pharisees' Children* – Barbara *Willard
1985 *The Nature of the Beast* – Janni Howker
1986 *The Coal House* – Andrew Taylor
1987 *A Little Lower than the Angels* – Geraldine *McCaughrean
1988 *Awaiting Developments* – Judy Allen
1989 *Why Weeps the Brogan?* – Hugh Scott
1990 *AK* – Peter *Dickinson
1991 *Harvey Angell* – Diana Hendry
1992 *The Great Elephant Chase* – Gillian *Cross
1993 *Flour Babies* – Anne *Fine
1994 *Gold Dust* – Geraldine *McCaughrean
1995 *The Wreck of the Zanzibar* – Michael *Morpurgo
1996 *The Tulip Touch* – Anne *Fine
1997 *Aquila* – Andrew Norriss
1998 *Skellig* – David *Almond
1999 *Harry Potter and the Prisoner of Azkaban* – J. K. *Rowling
2000 *Coram Boy* – Jamila *Gavin
2001 *The Amber Spyglass* – Philip *Pullman [also Whitbread Book of the Year]

2002 *Saffy's Angel* – Hilary *McKay
2003 *The Fire-Eaters* – David *Almond
2004 *Not the End of the World* – Geraldine *McCaughrean
2005 *The New Policeman* – Kate *Thompson
2006 *Set in Stone* – Linda *Newbery
2007 *The Bower Bird* – Ann Kelley
2008 *Just Henry* – Michelle *Magorian
2009 *The Ask and the Answer* – Patrick *Ness
2010 *Out of Shadows* – Jason Wallace
2011 *Blood Red Road* – Moira Young
2012 *Maggot Moon* – Sally *Gardner
2013 *Goth Girl and the Ghost of a Mouse* – Chris *Riddell
2014 *Five Children on the Western Front* – Kate Saunders
2015 *The Lie Tree* – Frances *Hardinge [also Costa Book of the Year]
2016 *The Bombs that Brought Us Together* – Brian Conaghan

[† joint winners in 1974]

H. Guardian Children's Fiction Prize

1967 *Devil in the Fog* – Leon *Garfield
1968 *The Owl Service* – Alan *Garner
1969 *The Whispering Mountain* – Joan *Aiken
1970 Flambards trilogy – K. M. *Peyton
1971 *The Guardians* – John *Christopher
1972 *A Likely Lad* – Gillian *Avery
1973 *Watership Down* – Richard *Adams
1974 *The Iron Lily* – Barbara *Willard
1975 *Gran at Coalgate* – Winifred Cawley
1976 *The Peppermint Pig* – Nina *Bawden
1977 *The Blue Hawk* – Peter *Dickinson
1978 *Charmed Life* – Diana Wynne *Jones
1979 *Conrad's War* – Andrew *Davies
1980 *The Vandal* – Ann Schlee
1981 *The Sentinels* – Peter *Carter
1982 *Goodnight Mr Tom* – Michelle *Magorian
1983 *The Village by the Sea* – Anita Desai
1984 *The Sheep-Pig* – Dick *King-Smith
1985 *What Is the Truth?* – Ted *Hughes
1986 *Henry's Leg* – Ann Pilling
1987 *The Story of Spit MacPhee* – James Aldridge
1988 *The Runaways* – Ruth Thomas
1989 *A Pack of Lies* – Geraldine *McCaughrean
1990 *Goggle-Eyes* – Anne *Fine
1991 *The Kingdom by the Sea* – Robert *Westall
1992 *The Exiles* – Hilary *McKay
 Paper Faces – Rachel Anderson
1993 *Low Tide* – William *Mayne
1994 *The Mennyms* – Sylvia Waugh
1995 *MapHead* – Lesley Howarth
1996 *The Sherwood Hero* – Alison Prince
 Northern Lights – Philip *Pullman
1997 *Junk* – Melvin *Burgess
1998 *Fire, Bed and Bone* – Henrietta *Branford

1999 *The Sterkarm Handshake* – Susan *Price
2000 *The Illustrated Mum* – Jacqueline *Wilson
2001 *The Seeing Stone* – Kevin *Crossley-Holland
2002 *Thursday's Child* – Sonya *Hartnett
2003 *The Curious Incident of the Dog in the Night-Time* – Mark *Haddon
2004 *How I Live Now* – Meg *Rosoff
2005 *The New Policeman* – Kate *Thompson
2006 *A Darkling Plain* – Philip *Reeve
2007 *Finding Violet Park* – Jenny *Valentine
2008 *The Knife of Never Letting Go* – Patrick *Ness
2009 *Exposure* – Mal *Peet
2010 *Ghost Hunter* – Michelle *Paver
2011 *Return to Ribblestrop* – Andy Mulligan
2012 *The Unforgotten Coat* – Frank *Cottrell Boyce
2013 *Liar & Spy* – Rebecca *Stead
2014 *The Dark Wild* – Piers Torday
2015 *A Song for Ella Gray* – David *Almond
2016 *Crongton Knights* – Alex Wheatle

More Literature titles from OUP

The Oxford Companion to Charles Dickens
edited by Paul Schlicke

Reissued to celebrate the bicentenary of Charles Dickens's birth, this companion draws together an unparalleled diversity of information on one of Britain's greatest writers; covering his life, his works, his reputation, and his cultural context.

Reviews from previous edition:
'comes about as close to perfection as humanly possible'

Dickens Quarterly

'will prove invaluable to scholars, readers and admirers of Dickens'

Peter Ackroyd, *The Times*

The Oxford Companion to the Brontës
Christine Alexander and Margaret Smith

This Companion brings together a wealth of information about the fascinating lives and writings of the Brontë sisters.

'This book is a must ... a treasure trove of a book'

Irish Times

The Oxford Companion to Classical Literature
edited by M. C. Howatson

A broad-ranging and authoritative guide to the classical world and its literary heritage.

Reviews from previous edition:
'a volume for all seasons ... indispensable'

Times Educational Supplement

'A necessity for any seriously literary household.'

History Today

Oxford Companions

'Opening such books is like sitting down with a knowledgeable friend. Not a bore or a know-all, but a genuinely well-informed chum ... So far so splendid.'

Sunday Times [of *The Oxford Companion to Shakespeare*]

For well over 60 years Oxford University Press has been publishing Companions that are of lasting value and interest, each one not only a comprehensive source of reference, but also a stimulating guide, mentor, and friend. There is a wide range of Oxford Companions available at any one time, covering topics such as music, art, and literature, as well as history, warfare, religion, and wine.

Titles include:

The Oxford Companion to English Literature
Edited by Dinah Birch
'No guide could come more classic.'

Malcolm Bradbury, *The Times*

The Oxford Companion to Music
Edited by Alison Latham
'probably the best one-volume music reference book going'

Times Educational Supplement

The Oxford Companion to Theatre and Performance
Edited by Dennis Kennedy
'A work that everyone who is serious about the theatre should have at hand'

British Theatre Guide

The Oxford Companion to Food
Alan Davidson
'the best food reference work ever to appear in the English language'

New Statesman

The Oxford Companion to Wine
Edited by Jancis Robinson
'the greatest wine book ever published'

Washington Post

Oxford Quick Reference

The Concise Oxford Companion to English Literature
Dinah Birch and Katy Hooper

Based on the best-selling *Oxford Companion to English Literature*, this is
an indispensable guide to all aspects of English literature.

Review of the parent volume:
'the foremost work of reference in its field'

Literary Review

A Dictionary of Shakespeare
Stanley Wells

Compiled by one of the best-known international authorities on the
playwright's works, this dictionary offers up-to-date information on all
aspects of Shakespeare, both in his own time and in later ages.

The Oxford Dictionary of Literary Terms
Chris Baldick

A best-selling dictionary, covering all aspects of literature, this is an
essential reference work for students of literature in any language.

A Dictionary of Critical Theory
Ian Buchanan

The invaluable multidisciplinary guide to theory, covering movements,
theories, and events.

'an excellent gateway into critical theory'

Literature and Theology

Oxford Quick Reference

The Concise Oxford Dictionary of English Etymology
T. F. Hoad

A wealth of information about our language and its history, this
reference source provides over 17,000 entries on word origins.

'A model of its kind'

Daily Telegraph

New Oxford Rhyming Dictionary

From writing poems to writing birthday cards, and from composing
advertising slogans to music lyrics, this dictionary has what every writer
(or budding writer) needs. It contains rhymes for over 45,000 words,
including proper names, place names, and foreign terms used in English.

'All wordsmiths are bound to enjoy feeling indebted (fetid, minareted,
rosetted . . .)'

Julia Donaldson (author of *The Gruffalo*)

The Oxford Dictionary of Slang
John Ayto

Containing over 10,000 words and phrases, this is the ideal reference for
those interested in the more quirky and unofficial words used in the
English language.

'hours of happy browsing for language lovers'

Observer

Oxford Quick Reference

A Dictionary of Marketing
Charles Doyle

Covers traditional marketing techniques and theories alongside the latest concepts in over 2,000 clear and authoritative entries.

'Flick to any page [for] a lecture's worth of well thought through information'

Dan Germain, Head of Creative, innocent ltd

A Dictionary of Media and Communication
Daniel Chandler and Rod Munday

Provides over 2,200 authoritative entries on terms used in media and communication, from concepts and theories to technical terms, across subject areas that include advertising, digital culture, journalism, new media, radio studies, and telecommunications.

'a wonderful volume that is much more than a simple dictionary'
Professor Joshua Meyrowitz, University of New Hampshire

A Dictionary of Film Studies
Annette Kuhn and Guy Westwell

Features terms covering all aspects of film studies in 500 detailed entries, from theory and history to technical terms and practices.

A Dictionary of Journalism
Tony Harcup

Covers terminology relating to the practice, business, and technology of journalism, as well as its concepts and theories, organizations and institutions, publications, and key events.

Oxford Quick Reference

The Oxford Dictionary of Dance
Debra Craine and Judith Mackrell

Over 2,600 entries on everything from hip-hop to classical ballet, covering dancers, dance styles, choreographers and composers, techniques, companies, and productions.

'A must-have volume ... impressively thorough'

Margaret Reynolds, *The Times*

The Oxford Guide to Plays
Michael Patterson

Covers 1,000 of the most important, best-known, and most popular plays of world theatre.

'Superb synopses ... Superbly formatted ... Fascinating and accessible style'

THES

The Oxford Dictionary of Music
Michael & Joyce Kennedy & Tim Rutherford-Johnson

The most comprehensive, authoritative, and up-to-date dictionary of music available in paperback.

'clearly the best around ... the dictionary that everyone should have'

Literary Review

Oxford Quick Reference

The Concise Oxford Dictionary of Quotations
SIXTH EDITION
Edited by Susan Ratcliffe

Based on the highly acclaimed seventh edition of *The Oxford Dictionary of Quotations*, this dictionary provides extensive coverage of literary and historical quotations, and contains completely up-to-date material. A fascinating read and an essential reference tool.

Oxford Dictionary of Quotations by Subject
Edited by Susan Ratcliffe

The ideal place to discover what's been said about what, the dictionary presents quotations on nearly 600 areas of special interest and concern in today's world.

The Oxford Dictionary of Humorous Quotations
Edited by Ned Sherrin

From the sharply witty to the downright hilarious, this sparkling collection will appeal to all senses of humour.

The Oxford Dictionary of Political Quotations
Edited by Antony Jay

This lively and illuminating dictionary from the writer of 'Yes Minister' presents a vintage crop of over 4,000 political quotations. Ranging from the pivotal and momentous to the rhetorical, the sincere, the bemused, the tongue-in-cheek, and the downright rude, examples include memorable words from the old hands as well as from contemporary politicians.

'funny, striking, thought-provoking and incisive ... will appeal to those browsing through it at least as much as to those who wish to use it as a work of reference'
Observer